The New Professional Chef™

SIXTH

EDITION

SIXTH

The New Professional Chef™

THE CULINARY INSTITUTE OF AMERICA®

EDITION

WITH FOREWORDS BY

Paul Bocuse

AND

Ferdinand Metz, C.M.C.

President, The Culinary Institute of America

Mary Deirdre Donovan

Editor

VAN NOSTRAND REINHOLD

I⟨T⟩P™ A Division of International Thomson Publishing Inc.

New York • Albany • Bonn • Boston • Detroit • London • Madrid • Melbourne
Mexico City • Paris • San Francisco • Singapore • Tokyo • Toronto

The Culinary Institute of America Staff:

Project Director: Tim Ryan

Editor: Mary Deirdre Donovan

Assistant Editor: Terry Finlayson

Director of Photography: Henry Woods

Photographers: Elizabeth C. Johnson, Lorna Smith

Consultants: Richard Czack, Fritz Sonnenschmidt

Van Nostrand Reinhold Staff:

President: Marianne Russell

Vice President, EDP: Renee Guilmette

Vice President, Marketing Communications: Marie Terry

Senior Editor: Melissa A. Rosati

Editorial Assistant: Amy Beth Shipper

Production Director: Jacqueline A. Martin

Art Director: Mike Suh

Production Manager: Louise Kurtz

Marketing Consultant: Ralph Petrillo

Support Staff: Sharon Cornell, Liz Curione, Ilene Elagroudy, Stan Hatzakis, Lori Jacobs, Sharon Kaufman, Margaret Madigan, Laura Morelli, Andrea Olshevsky, Joan Petrokofsky

Line Illustrations: TCA Graphics, Inc., Tom Cardamone, Ann Cardamone

Copyright © 1996 by The Culinary Institute of America

Published by Van Nostrand Reinhold

I(T)P™ A division of International Thomson Publishing, Inc. The ITP logo is a trademark under license

Printed in the United States of America

For more information, contact:

Van Nostrand Reinhold
115 Fifth Avenue
New York, NY 10003

Chapman & Hall GmbH
Pappelallee 3
69469 Weinheim
Germany

Chapman & Hall
2-6 Boundary Row
London
SE1 8HN
United Kingdom

International Thomson Publishing Asia
221 Henderson Road #05-10
Henderson Building
Singapore 0315

Thomas Nelson Australia
102 Dodds Street
South Melbourne, 3205
Victoria, Australia

International Thomson Publishing Japan
Hirakawacho Kyowa Building, 3F
2-2-1 Hirakawacho
Chiyoda-ku, 102 Tokyo
Japan

Nelson Canada
1120 Birchmount Road
Scarborough, Ontario
Canada M1K 5G4

International Thomson Editores
Campos Eliseos 385, Piso 7
Col. Polanco
11560 Mexico D.F. Mexico

2 3 4 5 6 7 8 9 10   RRD-WL   01 00 99 98 97 96

Library of Congress Cataloging-in-Publication Data

The new professional chef / with forewords by Paul Bocuse and Ferdinand Metz.—6th ed.
    p.   cm.
    At head of title: The Culinary Institute of America.
    Includes bibliographical references and index.
    ISBN 0-442-01961-0 (hard cover)
    1. Quantity cookery.   I. Culinary Institute of America.
TX820.N49   1996   95-35590
641.5'7—dc20   CIP

Contents

Recipe Contents   *ix*

Foreword by P. Bocuse   *xvii*

Foreword by F. Metz   *xix*

Preface   *xxi*

Acknowledgments   *xxiii*

Part **I**
Introduction to the Profession   *1*

Part **II**
The Foodservice Professional   *9*

Chapter **1**

The Professional Chef   *11*

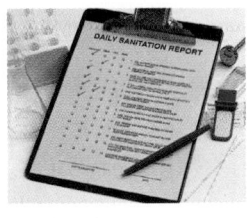

Chapter **2**

Food and Kitchen Safety   *31*

Chapter **3**

Nutrition and Healthy Cooking   *47*

Chapter **4**

Equipment Identification   *65*

Chapter **5**

The Raw Ingredients   *83*

Part *III*
Cooking in the Professional Kitchen   181

Chapter **6**
Mise en Place   183

Chapter **7**
Soups   259

Chapter **8**
Sauces   275

Chapter **9**
Dry-Heat Cooking Methods   301

Chapter **10**
Moist-Heat and Combination Cooking Techniques   329

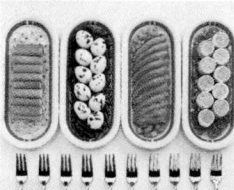

Chapter **11**
Charcuterie and Garde-Manger   353

Chapter **12**
Baking and Pastry   375

Part *IV*
The Recipes   417

Chapter **13**
Mise en Place and Stock Recipes   419

Chapter **14**
Soup Recipes   449

Chapter **15**
Sauce Recipes   521

Chapter **16**
Meat Entrées   555

Chapter **17**
Poultry Entrées   621

Chapter **18**
Fish Entrées   657

Chapter **19**
Vegetarian Entrées   709

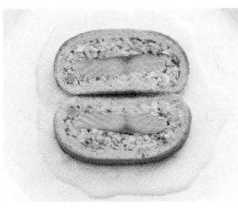

Chapter **20**

International Entrées   *733*

Chapter **21**

Vegetable Side Dishes   *791*

Chapter **22**

Potato, Grain, and Pasta Dishes   *817*

Chapter **23**

Breakfast Recipes   *857*

Chapter **24**

Salads and Salad Dressings   *881*

Chapter **25**

Sandwiches and Pizzas   *917*

Chapter **26**

Hors d'Oeuvres and Appetizers   *935*

Chapter **27**

Sausages, Pâtés, and Terrines   *993*

Chapter **28**

Breads   *1025*

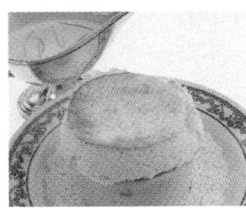

Chapter **29**

Kitchen Desserts   *1045*

Chapter **30**

Cakes and Pastries   *1079*

Appendix **1**
Seasonal Availability of Produce   *1129*

Appendix **2**
Tables   *1133*

Appendix **3**
Weights and Measures Conversions   *1139*

Glossary   *1141*

Recommended Reading List   *1161*

Food Associations   *1169*

Index   *1171*

Recipe Contents

Chapter 13
Mise en Place and Stock Recipes *419*

Vegetable Combinations

Mirepoix *420*
White Mirepoix *420*
Matignon *420*
Sofrito *421*
Dry Duxelles *421*
Pesto *422*
Persillade *422*

Thickeners

Basic Roux *423*
Beurre Manié *423*
Liaison *423*

Aromatics and Spice Blends

Standard Bouquet Garni *424*
Standard Sachet d'Épices *424*
Barbecue Spice Mix *425*
Chili Powder *425*
Chinese Five Spice *426*
Curry Powder *426*
Dry Cure for Smoked Fish *427*
Fines Herbes *427*
Garam Masala *428*
Seasoning Mix for Spit Roasting Meats
    and Poultry *428*
Quatre Épices *428*
Red Curry Paste *429*
Standard Reduction *429*

Marinades

Asian-Style Marinade *430*
Barbecue Marinade *430*
Basic Meat Marinade *430*
Cumin-Lime Marinade (Adobo) *431*
Fish Marinade *431*
Lamb and Game Marinade *432*
Latin Citrus Marinade *432*
Red Wine Game Marinade *433*
Red Wine Marinade *433*
Rosemary and Gin Marinade for Game
    Meats *434*
Teriyaki Marinade for Game Meats *434*
Teriyaki Marinade *434*

Croutons

Croutons *435*
Bean and Cheese Croutons *435*
Cheddar Cheese Rusks *436*
Goat Cheese Croutons *436*
Rye Bread Croutons *436*

Basic Meat Stocks

Brown Veal Stock (Jus de Veau) *437*
Estouffade *438*
Glace de Viande *438*
Veal Stock *439*
White Beef Stock *439*
Pork Stock *440*
White Lamb Stock *440*
Remouillage *441*

Poultry Stocks

Chicken Stock *442*
Game Bird Stock *442*

Fish Stocks

Fish Fumet *443*
Fish Stock *444*
Shellfish Stock *444*

Vegetable Stocks/Court Bouillon

Vegetable Stock *445*
White Wine Court Bouillon *446*
Vinegar Court Bouillon *446*
Wild Mushroom Essence *447*
Blanc *448*

Chapter 14
Soup Recipes *449*

Broths and Consommés

Double Chicken Broth *450*
Beef Broth *451*
Lamb Broth *452*
Smoked Turkey Broth *453*
Beef Consommé *454*
Fish Consommé *455*
Chicken Consommé *456*
Mushroom Consommé *457*
Game Hen Consommé with Roasted
    Garlic Custard *458*
Smoked Turkey Consommé with Fennel
    Ravioli *459*
Clear Oxtail Soup *460*

Vegetable Soups

American Bounty Vegetable Soup *461*
Amish-Style Chicken Corn Soup *462*
Minestrone *463*
Onion Soup Gratiné *464*
Potage au Pistou *464*
Potage Garbure *465*

Cream Soups

Cream of Broccoli Soup *466*
Cream of Cauliflower Soup *467*
Cream of Chicken Soup *468*
Cream of Tomato Soup *469*
Cheddar Cheese Soup *470*
Wild Mushroom Soup *471*
Cream of Mushroom Soup *472*
Watercress Soup *473*
Butternut Squash Soup *474*
Wild Rice Soup *475*

Purée Soups

Purée of Split Pea *476*
Purée of Black Bean *477*
White Bean Soup *478*
Senate Bean Soup *479*
Purée of Lentils *480*
French Lentil Soup *481*
Potage Purée Crecy *482*
Sweet Potato Soup *483*
Autumn Squash Apple Cider Soup *484*

Bisques

Shrimp Bisque *485*
Pumpkin Bisque *486*
Oyster Bisque *486*

Cold Soups

Chilled Red Plum Soup *487*
Chilled Apple Soup *488*
Beet Fennel Ginger Soup *489*
Chilled Gazpacho *490*

American Regional Soups

New England-Style Clam Chowder *491*
Manhattan-Style Clam Chowder *492*
Corn Chowder *493*
Fish Chowder *494*
Chicken and Shrimp Gumbo *495*
Ham Bone and Collard Greens Soup
    496
Maryland Crab Soup *497*
Peanut Soup *498*
Philadelphia Pepper Pot Soup *498*
Santa Fe Chili Soup *499*
Seafood Gumbo *500*

International Soups

Bergen Fish Soup *501*
Billi Bi Soup *502*
Borscht *503*
Budnersuppe—Barley Soup with Air-
    Dried Beef *504*

Cock-A-Leekie Soup   *504*
Corned Beef and Barley Soup   *505*
Finnish Salmon Soup   *506*
Goulash Soup   *506*
Erwtensoep (Green Split Pea Soup)
   507
Menudo—Tripe Soup   *508*
Minestrone Genovese   *509*
Mansahari Mirchi Soup (Mulligatawny
   Soup)   *510*
Oxtail Soup à l'Anglaise   *511*
Potato Kale Soup (Caldo Verde)   *512*
Scotch Broth   *513*
Seafood Minestrone   *514*
Velouté Dieppoise   *515*
Waterzooi de Poulet (Chicken Soup)
   516

Asian Soups

Chicken Egg Drop Soup   *517*
Hot and Sour Soup   *518*
Wonton Soup   *519*

Chapter 15
Sauce Recipes   *521*

Basic Brown Sauces

Demi-Glace   *522*
Brown Sauce (Sauce Espagnole)   *522*
Jus de Veau Lié   *523*
Wild Mushroom Jus   *524*

Small Brown Sauces

Marsala Sauce   *525*
Sauce Madeira   *525*
Sauce Perigeaux   *526*
Fines Herbes Sauce   *526*
Sauce Marchand de Vin   *527*
Mushroom Sauce   *527*
Piquant Sauce   *528*
Robert Sauce   *528*
Sauce Bordelaise   *529*
Sauce Chasseur   *530*
Sauce Châteaubriand   *531*

Velouté Sauces and Derivatives

Velouté   *531*
Dill Sauce   *532*
Horseradish Sauce   *532*
Sauce Albuféra   *533*
Nantua Sauce   *533*
Suprême Sauce   *534*
Shrimp Sauce   *534*

Béchamel Sauce and Derivatives

Béchamel   *535*
Cheddar Cheese Sauce   *536*
Cream Sauce   *536*

Tomato Sauces

Fresh Tomato Sauce   *537*
Marinara Sauce   *538*
Tomato Sauce   *538*
Meat Sauce   *539*

Warm Butter Sauces

Hollandaise Sauce   *540*

Béarnaise   *541*
Béarnaise Reduction   *541*
Choron Sauce   *542*
Creole Mustard Sauce   *542*
Sauce Mousseline   *543*
Royal Glaçage   *544*
Sauce Palois   *544*

Beurre Blancs

Lemon Beurre Blanc   *545*
Mustard Tarragon Sauce with Green
   Peppercorns   *545*
Tarragon Beurre Blanc   *546*

Compound Butters

Chili Butter   *546*
Maître d'Hotel Butter   *547*
Pimiento Butter   *548*
Scallion Butter   *548*
Shellfish Butter   *549*

Coulis and Vegetable Sauces

Red Chili Sauce   *549*
Green Chili Sauce   *550*
Red Pepper Coulis   *550*
Tomato Coulis   *551*

Barbecue Sauces

Barbecue Sauce   *552*
Mango/Bourbon Barbecue Sauce   *553*

Chapter 16
Meat Entrées   *555*

Beef: Sautéed

Beef Tournedos Sauté à la Niçoise   *556*
Beef Stroganoff   *556*
Tenderloin of Beef with Red Chili Sauce
   and Jalapeño Cheese   *557*

Beef: Roasted

Roast Prime Rib au Jus   *557*
Roast Top Round of Beef au Jus   *558*
Standing Rib Roast au Jus   *558*
Roast Strip Loin au Jus   *559*
Tenderloin of Beef with Blue Cheese
   Herb Crust   *560*
Beef Wellington   *560*

Beef: Grilled and Broiled

Broiled Sirloin Steak with Chile Butter
   561
Beef Tenderloin with Scallion Butter
   561
Broiled Sirloin Strip Steak with Sauce
   Marchand de Vin   *562*
Barbecued Sirloin Steak "Star of Texas"
   562
Strip Steak "Provençale"   *563*
Beef Tenderloin with Garlic Glaze   *564*
Blackened Beef with Corn-and-Pepper
   Sauce   *564*
London Broil   *565*

Beef: Braised and Stewed

Braised Beef Bourgignonne   *566*

Yankee Pot Roast   *567*
Shaker Stuffed Flank Steak   *568*
Braised Short Ribs   *569*
Savory Swiss Steak   *570*
Beef Rouladen in Burgundy Sauce   *571*
Estouffade of Beef (Beef Stew)   *572*
Chili Con Carne   *573*
Big Jim's Chili   *574*

Beef: Poached and Simmered

Corned Beef with Cabbage and Boiled
   Vegetables   *574*
Poached Tenderloin with Green
   Peppercorn Sabayon   *575*
New England Boiled Dinner   *576*

Veal: Sautéed and Pan-Fried

Veal Scalopine Marsala   *577*
Sautéed Veal with Lump Crabmeat and
   Asparagus   *578*
Swiss-Style Shredded Veal   *579*
Sautéed Veal with Wild Mushrooms and
   Marsala Sauce   *580*
Veal Cordon Bleu   *581*
Veal Medallions with Red Pepper Sauce
   582
Sautéed Veal Scalopine with Tomato
   Sauce   *583*
Veal Scalopine Shaker Village   *583*
Sautéed Veal Scalopine with Sauce
   Zingara   *584*
Breaded Veal Cutlet Gruyère   *585*

Veal: Roasted and Poêléd

Veal Shoulder Poêlé   *585*

Veal: Braised and Stewed

Fricassée de Veau   *586*
Veal Blanquette   *587*
Braised Veal Breast with Mushroom
   Sausage   *588*

Lamb: Sautéed

Emincé of Lamb with Green Peppercorns
   589
Noisettes of Lamb Judic   *590*

Lamb: Roasted

Roast Leg of Lamb Boulangère   *590*
Roast Rack of Lamb Persillé   *591*
Roast Leg of Lamb with Mint Sauce   *592*

Lamb: Grilled and Broiled

Grilled Lamb Chops with Mint Sauce
   592
Lamb Chops with Arizona Chili Butter
   593
Grilled Lamb Chops with Whole Cloves of
   Garlic   *594*
Lamb Chops with Artichokes   *595*

Lamb: Stewed and Braised

Lamb Stew   *596*
Braised Lamb Shanks   *597*

Pork: Sautéed and Pan-Fried

Pork Cutlet Sauce Charcutière *598*
Pork Scalopine with Herb Sauce *599*
Pork Medallions with Red Onion Confit *599*
Tenderloin of Pork with Apples and Caraway *600*
Sautéed Medallions of Pork with Warm Fruits *601*
Pork Cutlets with Wild Mushrooms and Crabmeat *602*
Pan-Fried Breaded Pork Cutlets *602*
Pan-Fried Pork Chop Forestiére *603*
Baked Stuffed Pork Chops *604*

Pork: Roasted

Pork Roast with Jus Lié *605*
Pork Loin Stuffed with Apples and Prunes *606*
Roast Tenderloin of Pork with Honey and Thyme *606*

Pork: Grilled and Broiled

Broiled Pork Chop *607*
Broiled Pork Chops with Sesame Ginger Butter *608*

Pork: Braised and Stewed

Pork Goulash *609*
North Carolina-Style Barbecued Pork *610*

Game Recipes

Stewed Rabbit with Prunes *611*
Rabbit and Oyster Étouffé *612*
Rabbit, Sausage, and Prosciutto on Skewer *614*
Roast Venison with Mustard Sauce *614*
Coniglio in Umido (Liquarian Rabbit Stew) *613*
Indian Grilled Buffalo *615*

Variety Meats

Calf's Liver with Bacon Cream Sauce *616*
Braised Oxtails *616*
Smoked Beef Tongue Madeira Sauce *617*

Ground Meats

Italian Meat Balls *618*
Meat Loaf *618*
Roast Beef Hash *619*

Chapter 17
Poultry Entrées *621*

Chicken: Sautéed and Pan-Fried

Chicken Provençal *622*
Chicken Suprêmes with Fines Herbes Sauce *623*
Breast of Chicken Chardonnay *624*
Sautéed Chicken Breast with Tarragon Sauce *625*

Breast of Chicken with Mushroom and Ham Stuffing *626*
Chicken Suprême Maréchal *627*
Southern Fried Chicken with Country-Style Gravy *628*

Chicken: Roasted

Roast Chicken with Pan Gravy *629*
Poêlé of Capon with Tomatoes and Artichokes *630*
Pan-Smoked Chicken with Apples and Green Peppercorns *631*
Smoked Chicken Breast with Barbecue Sauce *632*
Chicken Legs with Duxelles *633*
Breast of Cornish Game Hen *634*
Breast of Chicken with Oyster Stuffing and Roasted Garlic Sauce *635*

Chicken: Grilled and Broiled

Grilled Paillards of Chicken with Tarragon Butter *636*
Grilled Chicken Breast with Fennel *637*
Grilled Chicken with Black Bean Sauce *638*
Asian-Style Broiled Chicken Breast *638*
Broiled Chicken Tex Mex *639*

Chicken: Braised and Stewed

Chicken Fricassée *640*
Chicken Legs Hunter-Style *641*
Chicken Pot Pie *642*

Chicken: Poached and Simmered

Poule au Pot (Chicken with Vegetables) *642*
Poached Chicken Florentine *643*
Poached Chicken Breast with Tarragon Sauce *644*
Poached Cornish Game Hen with Star Anise *645*
Chicken Eugene *646*

Game Bird

Roast Duckling with Sauce Bigarade *647*
Roast Duckling with Red Pears, Ginger, and Green Peppercorns *648*
Roast Duckling with Plum Sauce *649*
Marinated Grilled Duck Breast *650*
Roast Pheasant with Cranberry-Peppercorn Sauce *651*

Turkey

Roast Turkey with Chestnut Stuffing *652*
Roast Turkey Supréme with Pan Gravy *653*
Pan-Smoked Turkey with Port Wine Sauce *654*
Turkey Cutlet California *655*

Chapter 18
Fish Entrées *657*

Fish: Sautéed and Pan-Fried

Sauté Trout Meunière *658*
Trout Amandine *658*

Sautéed Sole with Mango Chutney and Grilled Bananas *659*
Seared Sea Scallops with Saffron Rice, Asparagus, and a Light Tomato Sauce *659*
Stir-Fried Scallops, San Francisco-Style *660*
Pan-Fried Halibut with Puttanesca Sauce *661*
Fisherman's Platter *662*
Flounder Stuffed with Crabmeat with Lemon Beurre Blanc *662*
Pan-Fried Trout with Bacon *663*
Pan-Seared Black Sea Bass with Ratatouille *664*

Fish: Deep-Fried

Deep-Fried Flounder with Rémoulade Sauce *665*
Deep-Fried Squid (Calamari) *665*
Flounder à la Orly *666*
Deep-Fried Breaded Shrimp *667*
Deep-Fried Sole Anglaise *667*

Fish: Grilled and Broiled

Broiled Salmon Steaks *668*
Bluefish with Creole Mustard Sauce *668*
Broiled Stuffed Lobster *669*
Broiled Mackerel with a Pimiento Butter *669*
Broiled Mako Shark with Grilled Scallions and Tomato-Basil Coulis *670*
Broiled Lemon Sole on a Bed of Leeks *671*
Broiled Tuna with Salsa Cruda *671*
Grilled Tuna with Roasted Peppers and Balsamic Vinegar Sauce *672*
Grilled Tuna with Pecan-Lime Butter *673*
Grilled Swordfish with Pepper Cream Sauce *674*
Grilled Salmon with Roasted Pepper Salad *675*
Grilled Spanish Mackerel with Tomato Fondue *676*
Fillet of Mahi-Mahi with Pineapple Chutney *676*
Scallion-Studded Swordfish with a Red Pepper Coulis *677*
Broiled Seafood Platter *678*

Fish: Roasted and Baked

Salmon Baked in Phyllo with Saffron Sauce *678*
Potato-Roasted Cod *679*
Baked Lemon-Stuffed Trout *680*
Roasted Monkfish with Niçoise Olives and Pernod Sauce *681*
Salmon Fillet with Smoked-Salmon-and-Horseradish Crust *682*
Noisettes of Salmon with Cucumber-Dill Sauce *683*
Hot Smoked Salmon Fillet with Sun-Dried Tomato Coulis *683*
Smoked-Roasted Bluefish with Leek Compote and Horseradish Sauce *684*

Fish: Braised and Stewed

Cioppino *685*

Seafood Newburg   *686*
Shrimp Jambalaya   *687*
Shrimp Creole   *688*

Fish: Poached and Simmered

Fillet of Snapper en Papillote   *689*
Orange Roughy en Papillote with Shrimp and Scallions   *690*
Salmon Fillet and Cucumbers en Papillote   *691*
Poached Turbot with Lemon Beurre Blanc   *691*
Mussels Mariner-Style (Moules à la Marinère)   *692*
Cold Poached Salmon Steak with Green Mayonnaise   *693*
Poached Salmon with Bearnaise Sauce   *693*
Coquilles St. Jacques au Gratin   *694*
Poached Salmon and Asparagus with Basil Sauce   *695*
Poached Sole Vin Blanc   *696*
Poached Halibut with Saffron Sauce   *697*
Paupiettes of Sole Véronique   *698*
Tilapia with Capers and Tomatoes   *699*
Perch Bordelaise-Style   *700*
Poached Sea Bass with Clams, Bacon, and Peppers   *701*
Poached Red Snapper Veracruz   *702*
Poached Striped Bass with Watercress Sauce   *703*
Paupiettes of Trout with Saffron Filling   *704*
Catfish Topped with Crabmeat and Cornbread Crumbs   *705*
Boiled Lobster with Drawn Butter   *706*
New England Shore Dinner   *706*
Seafood Poached in a Tomato Broth with Fennel   *707*

Chapter 19
Vegetarian Entrées   709

Egg and Crêpe Dishes

Artichoke Soufflé   *710*
Artichoke Spinach Ricotta Pie   *711*
Stuffed Spinach Rolls   *712*
Spinach Crêpe with Wild Mushrooms and Roasted Red Pepper Coulis   *713*

Beans and Tofu Dishes

Falafel   *714*
Grilled Marinated Tofu with Black Bean Salsa   *714*

Loaves and Burgers

Pecan-Herb Loaf with Tomato-Tahini Sauté   *715*
Vegetable Burger   *716*

Roulades and Strudels

Spinach Roulades with Mushrooms and Sour Cream   *716*
Vegetable Strudel   *717*
Escarole-Feta Turnovers   *718*

Pasta and Rice

Wild Mushroom Mille Feuille   *719*

Cannelloni with Swiss Chard and Walnuts, Piedmont Style   *720*
Vegetable Lasagna   *721*
Roasted Eggplant Ravioli   *722*
Vegetable Curry with Brown Rice Pilaf   *723*
Eggplant Parmesan   *724*
Cheese-Filled Risotto Croquettes with Tomato Sauce   *724*
Whole Wheat Pasta Primavera with Basil Cream Sauce   *725*
Pasta Pomodoro   *726*
Macaroni and Cheese   *726*
Stuffed Cabbage Roll on a Lentil Ragout   *727*

Vegetable Stews

Casablanca Stew over Couscous   *728*
Rice and Beans, Mexican Style   *729*

Tex-Mex Specialties

Black Bean and Cornmeal Loaf with Fresh Salsa   *730*
Vegetarian Chili   *731*
Vegetarian Tamales   *732*

Chapter 20
International Entrées   733

Europe: Beef

Beef Tenderloin with Spicy Tomato Sauce (Medaglione di Bue alla Pizzaiola)   *734*
Beef Goulash   *735*
Sauerbraten   *735*
Zwiebel Rostbraten   *736*

Europe: Veal

Veal Saltimbocca   *737*
Veal Piccata, Milanese-Style   *738*
Wiener Schnitzel   *739*
Scalloppine of Veal with Stuffing (Scalloppine di Vitello Porta Foglia)   *740*
Ossobucco alla Milanese   *741*

Europe: Pork

Grilled Pork Chop with Spicy Sauce (Lombata di Maiale Grigliata con Piccante)   *742*
Pork Chops with Fennel (Costatine al Finnocchio)   *743*
Pork Medallions with Eggplant (Nodini di Maiale con Melanzane)   *744*
Roasted Stuffed Pork Loin Genoa-Style with Garlic-Flavored Jus   *745*

Europe: Lamb

Portuguese Stuffed Leg of Lamb (Pierna de Cordero)   *746*
Irish Stew   *747*

Europe: Poultry

Chicken Breast with Ham and Sherry   *748*

Roast Chicken with Walnut Sauce (Kotmis Satsivi)   *749*
Roast Stuffed Spring Cornish Hens with Garlic Sauce (Pollastrino Farcito Arrosto al Sugo d'Aglio)   *750*
Chicken Cacciatore   *751*

Europe: Fish

Salmon in Brioche   *752*
Stuffed Squid (Calamares Rellenos)   *753*
Shellfish Soup Flavored with Fennel and Saffron (Zuppa di Pesce alla Modenese)   *754*
Sea Bass with Vegetables (Branzine all Verdure)   *755*
Stuffed Swordfish (Bracilolo di Pescespada)   *756*

Europe: Mixed

Paella   *757*
Cassoulet   *758*
Choucroute Garni   *760*
Polish Stuffed Cabbage   *761*

Latin: Beef

Beef and Pork Tamales   *762*
Braised Stuffed Flank Steak (Matambre)   *763*

Latin: Pork

Pork in Orange and Lemon Sauce with Sweet Potatoes   *764*

Latin: Poultry

Chicken Mole (Mole Poblano de Pollo)   *765*
Chicken Enchiladas   *766*

Latin: Fish

Vatapa   *767*

Asia: Beef

Beef Teriyaki (Yakiniku)   *768*
Beef with Red Onions and Peanuts   *768*
Skewered Beef and Scallions   *769*
Sateh of Beef with Spicy Peanut Sauce   *770*

Asia: Pork

Chinese-Style Barbecued Spareribs   *771*
Braised Pork Stew with Chestnuts   *772*
Stir-Fried Pork   *773*

Asia: Lamb

Indian Grilled Lamb with Fresh Mango Chutney   *774*
Pakistani-Style Lamb Patties   *775*
Spicy Hunan Lamb   *776*
Couscous with Lamb Stew   *776*

Asia: Poultry

Tandoori-Style Chicken   *778*

Aromatic Chicken   *778*
Chicken in Curry Sauce   *779*
Chicken Teriyaki (Yakitori)   *780*
Chicken with Cashews   *781*
Hot Sesame Chicken   *782*
Miso Chicken   *783*
Roast Chicken with Lemongrass   *784*

Asia: Fish

Hot and Sour Fish   *784*
Indian Prawn Curry (Jheenga
    Shorwedder)   *785*
Scallops with Crispy Noodles   *786*
Shrimp in Chili Sauce   *787*
Shrimp Tempura   *788*
Squid and Peppers   *789*

Chapter 21
Vegetable Side Dishes   *791*

Green Vegetables

Steamed Broccoli   *792*
Pan-Steamed Peas   *792*
French-Style Peas (Petits Pois à la
    Française)   *793*
Viennese-Style Green Peas   *793*
Gingered Snow Peas and Yellow Squash
    794
Asparagus with Roasted Pepper and
    Shallot Chips   *794*
Italian-Style Spinach   *795*
Spinach Pancakes   *795*
Pan-Fried Zucchini   *796*
Zucchini with Chorizo and Tomatoes
    796
Green Beans with Walnuts   *797*
Green Beans with Bacon, Shallots, and
    Mushrooms   *797*

White Vegetables

Cauliflower Polonaise   *798*
Glazed Turnips   *798*
Parsnip and Pear Purée   *799*
Belgian Endive à la Meunière   *799*
Summer Squash "Noodles"   *800*

Red and Yellow Vegetables

Boiled Carrots   *800*
Glazed Carrots   *801*
Pecan Carrots   *801*
Carrots and Salsify with Cream   *802*
Glazed Beets   *802*
Corn Fritters   *803*
Creamed Corn   *803*
Mexican Corn   *804*
Baked Acorn Squash with Cranberry-
    Orange Compote   *804*

Braises and Stews

Braised Red Cabbage   *805*
Braised Lettuce   *805*
Ratatouille   *806*
Stewed Tomatoes Creole   *807*

Grilled Vegetables

Grilled Ratatouille Provençale   *808*

Grilled Vegetables   *809*
Grilled Shiitake Mushrooms with Soy-
    Sesame Glaze   *810*

Mixed Vegetable Dishes

Vegetables "Jardinière"   *810*
Macédoine of Vegetables   *811*

Asian Vegetable Dishes

Broccoli in Garlic Sauce   *812*
Garden Treasures   *812*
Gingered Green Beans and Cabbage
    813
Hot and Spicy Eggplant   *814*
Hot and Spicy Mixed Vegetables   *815*
Rainbow Garden   *815*
Vegetable Tempura   *816*

Chapter 22
Potato, Grain, and Pasta Dishes   *817*

Boiled Potatoes

Steamed New Potatoes with Fines Herbes
    818
Boiled Parslied Potatoes   *818*

Baked Potatoes

Baked Idaho Potatoes with Fried Onions
    819
Baked Stuffed Potatoes   *819*
Roasted Potatoes with Garlic and
    Rosemary   *820*

Potato Casseroles

Potatoes au Gratin   *820*
Dauphinoise Potatoes   *821*
Savoyarde Potatoes   *821*
Sweet Potatoes Baked in Cider with
    Currants and Cinnamon   *822*

Pan-Fried and Sautéed Potatoes

Hash Brown Potatoes   *822*
Potatoes Hashed in Cream   *823*
Châteaubriand Potatoes   *823*
Potato Pancakes   *824*
Roësti Potatoes   *824*
Potatoes Anna   *825*
Swedish-Style Candied Potatoes   *825*
Glazed Sweet Potatoes   *826*

Potato Purées

Potato Purée   *826*
Duchesse Potatoes   *827*
Croquette Potatoes   *827*
Lorette Potatoes   *828*
Berny Potatoes   *828*
Macaire Potatoes   *829*

Deep-Fried Potatoes

French-Fried Potatoes   *829*
Potato Nest   *830*
Souffléed Potatoes   *830*
Sweet Potato Chips   *830*

Rice: Boiled and Pilafs

Basic Boiled Rice   *831*
Rice Pilaf   *831*
Wild Rice Pilaf   *832*
Cilantro Lime Rice   *832*
Brown Rice with Pecans and Scallions
    833

Risotto

Basic Risotto   *833*
Risotto with Escarole and Parmesan   *834*
Risotto with Asparagus Tips   *834*
Saffron Risotto with Shrimp   *835*

Cornmeal Dishes

Basic Polenta   *835*
Polenta with Parmesan Cheese   *836*
Hush Puppies   *836*
Garlic Cheese Grits   *837*

Other Grains

Couscous   *838*
Bulgur with Dried Cherries and Apples
    838
Quinoa Pilaf with Red and Yellow Peppers
    839
Kasha with Spicy Maple Pecans   *840*

Beans

Black Beans   *840*
Black Beans with Peppers and Chorizo
    841
Refried Beans   *842*
Southwest White Bean Stew   *842*
Braised Lentils with Eggplant and
    Mushrooms   *843*
Lentil Ragout   *843*
Stewed Garbanzo Beans with Tomato,
    Zucchini, and Cilantro   *844*
Hoppin' John   *845*

Pasta

Basic Pasta Dough   *846*
Black Pepper Pasta   *846*
Basic Boiled Pasta   *847*

Pasta Dishes

Spaghetti alla Carbonara   *847*
Wild Mushroom and Artichokes over
    Black Pepper Pasta   *848*
Shrimp with Curried Pasta   *848*
Lasagne di Carnevale Napolitana   *849*
Lobster Tortellini with Ginger-Lime Sauce
    850
Chorizo-Filled Pasta with Tomato-Basil
    Coulis and Fresh Tomato Salsa   *851*

Dumplings

Spaetzle Dough   *852*
Spinach and Cheese Spaetzle   *853*
Gnocchi Piedmontese   *853*
Semolina Gnocchi   *854*
Chinese Dumplings (Fried or Boiled)
    854
Bread Dumplings   *855*
Biscuit Dumplings   *856*

Chapter 23
Breakfast Recipes   *857*

Eggs: Boiled and Poached

Soft-Cooked Eggs   *858*
Hard-Boiled Eggs   *858*
Poached Eggs   *858*
Eggs Benedict   *859*

Fried Eggs and Omelets

Fried Eggs   *859*
Scrambled Eggs   *860*
Plain Rolled Omelet   *860*
Frittata (Farmer-Style Omelet)   *862*
Souffléed Omelet   *862*

Baked Eggs and Quiche

Baked Eggs   *863*
Shirred Eggs   *863*
Corn and Pepper Pudding   *864*
Leek and Tomato Quiche   *865*
Quiche Lorraine   *866*
Seafood Quiche   *866*

Soufflés

Savory Cheese Soufflé   *866*

Breakfast Cereals

Cream of Wheat   *868*
Oatmeal with Cinnamon and Dried Fruits   *868*
Granola   *869*
"Muesli" Parfait   *869*

Pancakes

Basic Pancakes   *870*
Pumpkin or Banana Pancakes   *871*
Crêpes   *872*
Waffles   *873*
French Toast   *873*

Breakfast Meats

Red Flannel Hash   *874*
Pan-Fried Ham Steak with Red-Eye Gravy   *875*
Creamed Chipped Beef   *875*
Creamed Sherried Chicken on Toast Points   *876*

Fruits and Beverages

Cinnamon Apples   *876*
Fresh-Fruit Compote   *877*
Dried-Fruit Compote   *877*
Strawberry Compound Butter   *878*
Orange-Mango Compound Butter   *878*
Maple Syrup-Pecan Butter   *878*
Hot Chocolate   *879*
Breakfast Shake   *879*

Chapter 24
Salads and Salad Dressings   *881*

Green Salads

Mixed Green Salad   *882*

Sherried Watercress and Apple Salad   *882*
Spinach-Arugula Salad with Blood Oranges and Goat Cheese   *883*
Mesclun Salad with Apples and Goat Cheese   *883*
Caesar Salad   *884*
Spinach, Avocado, and Grapefruit Salad   *884*
Wilted Spinach Salad with Warm Bacon Vinaigrette   *885*

Composed Salads

Buffalo-Style Chicken Salad   *886*
Chef Salad   *886*
Cobb Salad   *887*
Taco Salad   *888*
Taco Sauce   *888*
Lobster Salad with Avocado and Apples   *889*
Goat Cheese in Filo with Roasted Pepper Salad   *890*

Vegetable Salads

Coleslaw   *891*
Citrus Slaw with Avocado and Red Onion   *891*
Corn and Jicama Salad   *892*
Carrot and Raisin Salad   *892*
Celeriac and Tart Apple Salad   *893*
Jícama and Cucumber Salad   *893*
Waldorf Salad   *894*

Mediterranean Salads

Tomato and Mozzarella Salad   *894*
Panzanella   *894*
Niçoise Salad with Tuna   *895*
Greek Salad   *895*
Cucumber Yogurt Salad   *896*
Moroccan Carrot Salad   *896*
Mediterranean Peppers with Lemon Thyme Vinaigrette   *897*
Tabbouleh Salad   *898*

Meat and Fish Salads

Chicken Salad   *898*
Ham Salad   *898*
Crab or Lobster Salad   *899*
Tuna Salad   *899*
Shrimp Salad   *899*
Seafood Ravigote   *900*
Egg Salad   *901*

Potato Salads

Potato Salad   *901*
European-Style Potato Salad   *902*
German Potato Salad   *902*

Grain, Pasta, and Bean Salads

Curried Rice Salad   *903*
Macaroni Salad   *903*
Pasta Salad with Pesto Vinaigrette   *904*
Lentil Salad   *904*
Mixed Bean Salad   *904*
Warm Black-Eyed Pea Salad   *905*

Vinaigrette

Basic Vinaigrette   *906*

Vinaigrette Gourmand   *906*
Mustard-Herb Vinaigrette   *907*
Peanut Oil and Malt Vinegar Salad Dressing   *907*
Roasted Garlic and Mustard Vinaigrette   *908*
Lemon Garlic Vinaigrette   *908*
Lime and Olive Oil Vinaigrette   *909*
Georgia Peanut Salad Dressing   *909*
Curry Vinaigrette   *910*
Catalina Dressing   *910*

Mayonnaise and Creamy Dressings

Basic Mayonnaise   *911*
Aïoli (Garlic Mayonnaise)   *911*
Anchovy Caper Mayonnaise   *912*
Caesar-Style Dressing   *912*
Green Goddess Dressing   *913*
Ranch-Style Dressing   *913*
Creamy Black Pepper Dressing   *914*
Blue Cheese Dressing   *914*
Cucumber Dressing   *915*
Rémoulade Sauce   *915*
Tartar Sauce   *916*

Chapter 25
Sandwiches and Pizzas   *917*

Hot Sandwiches: Coffee Shop and Deli Standards

Chicken Burgers   *918*
Sloppy Joes   *918*
Barbecued Beef Sandwich   *919*
Hot Turkey Suprême with Caramelized Onions   *919*
Meat Loaf Sandwich with Mushroom Gravy   *920*
Western Sandwich   *920*

Hot Sandwiches: Grilled

Reuben Sandwich   *921*
Three-Cheese Melt   *921*
Tuna Melt   *922*
Grilled Vegetable and Cheese Sandwich   *922*
Croque Monsieur   *923*

Hot Sandwiches: Tex-Mex and Caribbean

Chicken and Green Chili Tacos   *923*
Roasted Vegetable Quesadilla with Red Chili Sauce   *924*
Chicken and Walnut Quesadilla   *925*
Beef Tacos   *925*
Media Noche (El Cubano)   *926*

Pizzas and Savory Breads

Bruschetta with Tapenade, Tomato, and Gorgonzola   *926*
Tapenade   *927*
Grilled Duck Sausage, Roasted Garlic and Peppers on Focaccia   *927*
Apple Cheddar Pizza   *928*
Grilled Vegetable Pizza   *929*

Cold Sandwiches

CIA Club   *930*

"Philly" Hoagie (Italian Combo) *930*
Roasted Vegetables in Pita with Roasted
    Garlic Tahini Dressing *931*
Roasted Garlic Tahini Dressing 931
Oven-Dried Tomato, Cream Cheese, and
    Arugula Sandwich *932*

Tea Sandwiches

Cucumber with Herb Cream Cheese Tea
    Sandwich *932*
Apples with Curry Mayonnaise Tea
    Sandwich *933*
Elena Ruz Tea Sandwich *933*
Gorgonzola with Pears Tea Sandwich
    933
Tomato with Oregano Sour Cream Tea
    Sandwich *934*
Watercress with Herb Mayonnaise Tea
    Sandwich *934*

Chapter 26
Hors d'Oeuvres and Appetizers *935*

Dips and Spreads

Fresh Tomato Salsa *936*
Black Bean Salsa *936*
Guacamole *937*
Baba Ghannouj (Eggplant and Tahini
    Dip) *937*
Moutabel with Belgian Endive *938*
Hummus B'Tahini *939*
Yogurt Tahini Sauce *939*

Marinated Salads and Ceviche

Caponata-Eggplant-Vegetable Salad *940*
Celery Root and Roasted Red Pepper
    Rémoulade *941*
"Ceviche" of Artichoke Hearts *942*
Charred Tuna and Scallop Ceviche *942*
Ceviche of Snapper *943*

Meat Dishes

Beef Carpaccio *944*
Charred Beef with Garlic Herb
    Mayonnaise *945*
Chicken Croustade *946*
Chicken Stir Fry with Peanuts *947*
Paper-Wrapped Chicken *948*
Vitello Tonnato *948*

Eggs and Cheese

Pickled Eggs *949*
Deviled Eggs *950*
Mozzarella Roulade *951*
Mozzarella Roulades Canapés with
    Prosciutto and Basil *952*
Gorgonzola Custard *952*
Warm Iowa Blue Cheese Mousse *953*

Strudels, Fritters, and Crêpes

Wild Mushroom Strudel with Goat
    Cheese and Madeira Sauce *954*
Fennel and Chorizo Strudel *955*
Broccoli and Cheddar Fritters *956*
Rissoles *956*
Samosa *957*

Corn Crêpes with Asparagus Tips and
    Smoked Salmon *958*
Spinach Crêpes with Seafood *959*

Asian

Sushi *960*
Shrimp Spring Roll *961*
Vietnamese Fried Spring Rolls *962*
Gyoza *963*
Thai Fish Cakes *964*
Cucumber Relish *964*
Oriental Pearl Balls *965*

Fish and Seafood

Raw Tuna Marinated in Sake with Shiitake
    Salad *966*
Carpaccio of Salmon *967*
Gravad Lox *968*
Smoked Salmon Set-Up *968*
Smoked Salmon Mousse Barquettes *969*
Salmon with a Yogurt Gratin *969*
Poached Scallops Mornay *970*
Cold Poached Scallops with Tarragon
    Vinaigrette *970*
Scallop Mousseline Timbales *971*
Scallop Timbale Sampler with Saffron-
    Cream Sauce *972*
Broiled Shrimp with Garlic and Aromatics
    972
Cajun-Style Barbecued Shrimp *973*
Coconut Macadamia Shrimp with Ginger
    Soy Sauce *974*
Fish Tempura with Dipping Sauce *975*
Stuffed Shrimp *976*
Moules Marinière *977*
Mussels and Clams with Saffron and
    Tomatoes *978*
Oysters Diamond Jim Brandy *979*
Oysters Gratinée *980*
Fresh Artichoke Bottoms with Oysters in
    Warm Champagne Vinaigrette *980*
Clams Casino *981*
Clam Fritters *982*
Deviled Crab Cakes *983*
Marinated Mackerel in White Wine *984*

Fruit and Vegetable

Melon and Prosciutto *984*
Dates Stuffed with Boursin Cheese *985*
New Potatoes with Snails and Brie *985*
Caviar in New Potatoes with Dilled Crème
    Fraîche *986*
Black Bean Cakes *987*
Santa Fe-Style Black Bean Cakes with
    Sautéed Crab and Corn *988*
Stuffed Mushrooms with a Gratin
    Forcemeat *989*
Stuffed Grape Leaves *990*
Broccoli Flan *991*
Red Pepper Mousse *991*

Chapter 27
Sausages, Pâtés, and Terrines *993*

Basic Forcemeats

Pâté de Campagne *994*
German-Style Bratwurst (Forcemeat)
    994

Chicken Liver Gratin-Style Forcemeat
    995
Chicken Mousseline Forcemeat *996*

Basic Preparations

Pâté Dough *996*
Pâté Spice *997*
Aspic Gelée *997*

Sausages

Andouille Sausage *998*
Breakfast-Style Sausage *998*
Italian Festival Sausage *999*
Chicken and Herb Sausage *1000*
Duck Sausage *1001*
Spicy French-Style Apple Sausage *1002*
Greek Sausage-Loukanika *1002*
Italian-Style Sausage *1003*
Fresh Chorizo *1004*
Seafood Sausage *1004*
Smoked Venison Sausage *1005*

Pâtés

Pheasant Pâté *1006*
Duck Pâté en Croute *1006*
Quail Pâté en Croute *1008*
Salmon Pâté en Croute *1009*
Turkey Pâté en Croute *1010*
Tuscany-Style Pâté en Croute *1011*

Terrines, Galantines, and Roulades

Country Terrine *1012*
Country-Style Duck Terrine *1013*
Roasted Eggplant and Pepper Terrine
    1014
Potato, Trout, and Leek Terrine *1015*
Chicken Galantine *1016*
Roulade of Foie Gras *1017*
Chicken Roulade *1018*
Terrine of Foie Gras *1019*

Specialty Items

Fish Quenelles on a Bed of Spinach
    1020
Cold Beef Daube *1021*
Duck Rillettes *1022*
Trout Savarin *1023*

Chapter 28
Breads *1025*

Quick Breads

Basic Muffins *1026*
Blueberry Muffins *1026*
Corn Muffins *1027*
Bran Muffins *1028*
Date Nut Bread *1028*
Pumpkin Bread *1029*
Zucchini Bread *1030*
Banana Nut Bread *1030*
Irish Soda Bread *1031*
Biscuits *1032*
Popovers *1032*

Yeast-Raised Breads

Pain de Campagne *1033*

Sourdough Starter   *1034*
Pumpernickel Bread and Rolls   *1034*
Multigrain Bread   *1035*
Peasant Pecan Loaf   *1036*
Cottage Dill Bread   *1036*
Raisin Bread   *1037*
Sunflower Seed Bread   *1037*
Bagels   *1038*
Challah Bread   *1039*
Cinnamon Buns   *1039*
Sweet Dough   *1040*
Stöllen   *1041*
Danish   *1042*
Croissants   *1042*

Fillings and Toppings

Pan Filling for Sticky Buns   *1043*
Holland Dutch Topping   *1044*

Chapter 29
Kitchen Desserts   *1045*

Puddings

Rice Pudding with Fresh Raspberries
   1046
Warm Chocolate Pudding   *1046*
Chocolate Pudding   *1047*
Petits Pots du Crème   *1048*
Chocolate Mousse in Tuiles   *1048*
Lemon Mousse   *1049*
Bread and Butter Pudding   *1050*
Savarin Syrup   *1050*
Savarin with Fresh Fruit   *1051*

Creams and Custards

Zabaglione   *1052*
Crème Caramel   *1052*
Crème Brûlée   *1053*
Tiramisù   *1054*
English Trifle   *1055*

Soufflés and Other Egg Desserts

Hot Dessert Soufflé   *1055*
Salzburger Nockerl   *1056*
Oeufs à la Neige   *1056*

Crêpes

Basic Dessert Crêpes   *1057*
Crêpes Suzette   *1057*
Crêpes Normandy   *1058*

Frozen Desserts

Basic Parfait   *1059*
Soufflé Glacé   *1060*
French Ice Cream   *1061*
Gélato   *1061*
Vanilla Ice Cream   *1062*
Lemon Sorbet   *1062*
Raspberry Granità   *1063*
Sour Cherry Granità   *1063*
Green Tea Granità   *1064*
Rum Mango Granità   *1064*

Watermelon Granità   *1064*
Fresh Ginger Granità   *1065*

Fruits

Poached Apples   *1065*
Poached Pears   *1066*
Basic Poaching Liquid for Fruit   *1066*
Glazed Pineapple Madagascar   *1067*
Strawberries with Green Peppercorns
   1067
Gratin of Fresh Fruits   *1068*
Individual Warm Fruit Tartlettes   *1068*
Fruit Fritter Batter   *1069*

Dessert Sauces

Vanilla Sauce   *1070*
Wild Turkey Sauce   *1070*
Lemon Curd   *1071*
Strawberry Sauce   *1072*
Raspberry Sauce   *1072*
Raisin Sauce   *1072*
Melba Sauce   *1073*
Fruit Coulis   *1073*
Sabayon Sauce   *1073*
Nuss Sauce   *1074*
Hard Sauce   *1074*
Cinnamon Sauce   *1074*
Chocolate Sauce   *1075*
Chocolate Ganache   *1075*
Chocolate Fudge Sauce   *1076*
Caramel Sauce   *1076*
Cinnamon Rum Syrup   *1077*
Simple Syrup   *1077*

Chapter 30
Cakes and Pastries   *1079*

Pastry Doughs

Pie Crust Dough   *1080*
Pâte Brisée   *1080*
Pâte à Choux   *1081*
Short Dough for Crust   *1082*
Almond Dough   *1082*
Linzer Dough   *1083*
Butter Puff Pastry Dough   *1083*
Blitz Puff Pastry   *1084*

Cookies

Regular Cookie Dough   *1085*
Special Cookie Dough   *1085*
Shortbread   *1086*
Spritz Cookies   *1087*
Chocolate Chip   *1088*
Pfeffernusse   *1088*
Coconut Macaroons   *1089*
Lemon Cookies   *1090*
Dixie Butterscotch Icebox Cookies   *1090*
Crumiri Cookies   *1091*
Hermit Cookies   *1091*
Cake Brownie   *1092*
Fudge Brownie   *1092*
Tuiles   *1093*
Florentines   *1094*
Hazelnut Florentine   *1094*
Ladyfingers   *1095*

Biscotti al'Anice   *1095*

Fillings and Pies

Pastry Cream   *1096*
Vanilla Bavarian Cream   *1096*
Wine Cream   *1097*
Apple Pie   *1097*
Pumpkin Pie   *1098*
Pecan Pie   *1099*
Lemon Meringue Pie   *1099*
Cherry Pie   *1100*
Pithiviers   *1101*
Frangipan   *1102*
Hazelnut Filling   *1102*
Apple Filling for Strudel   *1103*
Baker's Cheese Filling   *1103*
Cream Cheese Filling   *1104*

Meringues

Meringue Topping for Pies   *1104*
Regular Meringue   *1104*
Italian Meringue   *1105*
Swiss Meringue   *1105*
Meringue Shells   *1105*

Frostings and Buttercreams

Devil's Fudge Icing   *1106*
Cream Cheese Icing   *1106*
French Buttercream   *1106*
German Buttercream   *1107*
Italian Buttercream   *1107*
Swiss Buttercream   *1108*

Basic Cakes

Sponge Roulade   *1108*
Vanilla Sponge   *1109*
Chocolate Sponge   *1110*
Pound Cake   *1110*
High-Ratio Cake, White   *1111*
Fudge Cake   *1112*
Angel Food Cake   *1112*
Devil's Fudge Cake   *1113*
Carrot Cake   *1114*
Roman Apple Cake   *1115*
Gugelhopf (Yeast-Raised)   *1116*
Kugelhopf   *1117*
CIA Christmas Fruitcake   *1118*

Cheesecakes

Cheesecake   *1119*
Sicilian Cheesecake   *1120*
Chiffon Cheesecake   *1121*

Layer Cakes, Tortes, and Candies

Sacher Torte Layers   *1122*
Rum Torte Cake   *1122*
Joconde Cake Layer   *1123*
Hazelnut Torte Cake Layers   *1124*
Havana Torte Cake   *1124*
Dobos Torte Cake Batter   *1125*
Apple Cream Cheese Torte   *1126*
Pecan Diamonds   *1127*
Chocolate-Coated Almonds, Dragee
   Method   *1128*

PAUL BOCUSE

Foreword

Lors de ma visite au Culinary Institute of America de Hyde Park, New York, en 1989, j'ai eu l'occasion de voir et d'apprécier les méthodes d'enseignement appliquées dans cette école qui en font l'une des meilleures du monde.

Une éducation structurée donne d'excellents résultats, conduisant les élèves au titre honorable de "Chef Professionnel".

Restant convaincu que le respect des traditions pour les générations actuelles et à venir, sera beaucoup plus profitable en matière d'enseignememt culinaire, permettant aux jeunes de maîtriser parfaitement les différentes techniques de base. Cette formation donnant enfin sur le marché des chefs qui savent rôtir, griller, faire une mise en place, prêts à répondre aux besoins spécifiques de leur métier.

Encore toutes mes félicitations à cet Institut.

· · ·

During my visit to The Culinary Institute of America in Hyde Park, New York in 1989, I had the opportunity to see and appreciate the training methods applied at the school, which make it one of the best in the world.

A structured education yields excellent results, leading the students to the honorable title of "Professional Chef."

I remain convinced that respect for tradition in the teaching of culinary arts will be made most effective by enabling students to perfectly master the fundamental techniques. This approach to teaching, as featured in *The New Professional Chef*, finally provides the marketplace with chefs who know how to roast, grill, and prepare proper mise en place, and are ready to address all of the specific needs of their profession.

Once more, all my congratulations to the Institute.

Paul Bocuse

Foreword

There is a widespread misconception about how one becomes a chef. It is not simply the rote memorization of hundreds or thousands of recipes. Neither is it the case that a chef has access to tools and ingredients not available to those outside the profession. There is no special magic in the knives, spices, and recipes found in a professional kitchen. Anyone who is serious about cooking must learn lessons of greater value and wider application than a single recipe could provide.

The process of mastering the basic kitchen skills is not all that is involved in becoming a chef. The drive to achieve technical excellence, paired with the motivation to learn the importance of flavor, and about its subtleties, harmonies, and contrasts, moves us along the journey from apprentice to chef. As students of cooking, we must all continue to grow through our experiences so that we can distinguish the nuances that differentiate the true professional: the ability to judge, assess, and appreciate true quality.

The guiding principle in preparing this book has been to explain the techniques and preparations that any student of cooking must fully comprehend and assimilate in order to be truly proficient at his or her craft. These skills must then be carefully practiced and refined over the course of a lifetime.

This book should function as far more than a reference tool. If we have accomplished our purpose, you will be inspired to use this book as a springboard to continually learn more, for there is always more to learn. The youngest apprentice and the most experienced master chef alike are at their best only if they aspire toward greater perfection of technique and the most ideal combinations of flavors. As we continue to learn, we are brought at last to the realization that it is simplicity, in cooking as in all arts, that demands the greatest artistry and offers the greatest rewards.

Ferdinand E. Metz, Certified Master Chef
President
The Culinary Institute of America

Preface

People often find cooking mysterious. They assume that all gifted chefs have a bag full of special tricks and closely guarded recipes that enable them to prepare the dishes that seem so amazing to the uninitiated. Really, it is the chef's reliance on basic cooking principles and fundamental preparation techniques that provides the canvas for the artwork.

Creativity takes on a substance only when it is paired with the primary lessons of cooking. Mastery of these lessons eliminates the mystery and makes it easier to differentiate the merely trendy from the valid and valuable.

It is not enough to know how to prepare a particular dish, or to reproduce a complicated recipe. As professionals, we all need to move our orientation away from a specific combination of ingredients to reach a prescribed, predetermined finished dish. It is even more important to delve behind the "formulas" so that we can grasp the basics of cooking, such as roasting, poaching, grilling, baking, and charcuterie.

As students of cooking, we must all continue to gain confidence through experience, so that we can answer the questions of: "How much?" "How long?" "And when?" When we learn where the benchmarks of quality are found, we can begin to answer those questions. In order to prepare food with a sense of passion, the chef must learn the harmonies of flavor. It is important that the true flavors of foods—earthy, comfortable, honest, identifiable —be allowed to speak for themselves. At the same time, the intriguing interplay of contrasting colors, textures, shapes, and cooking techniques on the plate can provide depth, excitement, and interest.

What we have tried to accomplish in this book is to provide professionals and students with a text that can function as a reference point. By reading and learning the lessons set down in this book, a student can begin a lifelong process of education, first learning the fundamentals of identifying and working with a variety of foods, then actually cooking the food. The next part of the process is to examine closely what is contained in the book and hold its lessons up against the experience that he or she has had in the kitchen. Learning is the most effective when you are engaged in critically evaluating, investigating, and challenging the written word through practical application. If we have accomplished our purpose in developing this text, you will be inspired to go beyond the lessons explained here.

This book's aim is to act as an inspiration to always learn more, for there is always more to learn. The youngest apprentice and the experienced master chef alike are only truly at their best when they continue to search for the greatest perfection of technique, the most ideal harmonies of flavors and foods. It is simplicity, in cooking as in all arts, that demands the greatest artistry and offers the greatest rewards.

The Professional Chef, now in its sixth edition, is far more than a simple updating of material. The motivation for this new book was our desire to incorporate as many contemporary cooking concepts as possible, while remaining true to the principles that govern all good cooking. Increased interest in nutritional cooking, working profitably with a dwindling supply of high-quality fish and shellfish, the excitement of learning about cuisines from our own and other countries—all of these elements have combined to change the way we view a culinary education. In addition, we know that issues regarding management of resources, time, and people are perhaps the greatest single challenge facing chefs and restaurant owners today.

By reorganizing the book, we have brought the important lessons more clearly into focus. The book is arranged in a progressive, logical sequence, separated into four parts. We begin with a brief historical overview of the chef's role in society. Then, we move on to an in-depth discussion of the specific areas of concern for the professional including food safety and sanitation, nutrition, the ability to purchase and fabricate foods, and to use equipment efficiently and safely.

In the third part of the book, Cooking in the Professional Kitchen, the emphasis is on providing a clear picture of the basic cooking techniques using both words and pictures. Cooking is not always a perfectly precise art, but a good grasp of the basics gives the chef or student the ability not only to apply the technique, but also to learn the standards of quality so that one begins to develop a sense of how cooking works. The arrangement of cooking techniques moves in a progression, beginning with mise en place, on into soups and sauces, then the basic cooking methods, pantry cooking and garde manger, and concluding with baking and pastry.

The surest way to "de-mystify" cooking is to understand that it is not recipes or an arsenal of secret ingredients that make the chef. Rather, it is the chef's knowledge and expertise in three key areas: selecting ingredients with an eye to quality and seasonality; handling foods and equipment carefully to get the best results with the least waste; and applying fundamental cooking techniques with due respect for the food and the intended effect of the finished dish. These are the supports that hold the recipe up.

The recipes themselves, found in Part IV of the book, are grouped according to the way that professionals will use them. Five separate chapters include entree recipes. Chapters devoted to international and vegetarian entrées, sandwiches, and kitchen desserts have been newly created.

New recipes can be found for marinades, spice blends, relishes, grains, and legumes throughout the book. In fact, over 500 new recipes have been included in this edition of the book, ranging from such classics as Chicken Pot Pie to less traditional offerings such as Roast Chicken with Lemongrass. These recipes have been developed, reviewed, and prepared by our chef instructors and students. Yields have been regulated and standardized. Additional information, or "trucs," have also been incorporated, so that you can read the following information: ways to make nutritional modifications, variations, substitutions, historical and anecdotal information, step-by-step photographs, and serving suggestions.

The recipes given here have been written with metric equivalents; it should be noted the conversions have usually been rounded to the nearest even measurement. Whenever teaspoons and tablespoons are the most accurate means of measurement we have left them the same for both U.S. and metric measures.

Photographs throughout the book were prepared using equipment that allowed us to show the technique clearly. This has meant that in some cases we have prepared a much smaller batch, in a smaller pan, than you might select.

Ours is a dynamic profession, one that provides some of the greatest challenges and some of the greatest rewards. There is always another level of perfection to achieve and another skill to master. It is our hope that this book will function both as a springboard into further growth and as a reference point to give ballast to the lessons still to be learned.

Tim Ryan
Senior Vice President

Acknowledgments

The common wisdom says "Leave well enough alone." It is because the following people knew that "well enough" isn't the same thing as "good as we can make it" that this newly revised edition of the book came into being:

Tim Ryan
Mary Donovan
Terry Finlayson
Richard Czack
Fritz Sonnenschmidt
Henry Woods

The heart of this book is the detailed explanation of cooking methods in words and images, as well as the amazingly diverse collection of recipes, running a gamut from simple broths to multi-layered dishes composed of sauces, stuffings, garnishes, and side dishes. For their dedication to excellence in several areas (reading and critiquing the text; testing and reviewing recipes; and being the hands you see in the photographs throughout the book), the following individuals are to be congratulated and thanked:

Mark Ainsworth
Wayne Almquist
Liz Briggs
Robert Briggs
Shuliang Cheng
Corky Clark
Phil Delaplane
Ron DeSantis
Dieter Doppelfeld
Joseba Encabo
Mark Erickson
Dieter Faulkner
Anton Flory
Uwe Hestnar
Morey Kanner
Tom Kief
Jean-Luc Kieffer
Frank Lopez
Jim Maraldo
Peter Michael
Al Natale
John O'Haire
Claudio Papini
Bill Phillips
Tim Rodgers
Eric Saucy
Kathy Shepard
Rudy Smith
David St. John-Grubb
Claude Swartvagher
Dan Turgeon
Jonathan Zearfoss

There are many subjects that a chef must master. To those who assisted in the development and review of chapters dedicated to such topics as management, food safety issues, nutrition, food purchasing, and the selection of equipment, a special thank you:

Pat Bottiglieri
John Canner
Amy Coleman
Bob DelGrosso
George Engel
Craig Goldstein
Audrey Hynes
Fred Mayo
Cathy Powers
Jay Stein
Marianne Turow
Rich Vergili
Mark Westfield

Breakfast and Pantry Cooking, Garde-Manger and Charcuterie text and recipes:

Anthony Ligouri
Norman Peduzzi
Frank Rinaudo

Baking and Pastry text and recipes:

Gunther Behrendt
Ed Bradley
Richard J. Coppedge, Jr.
Peter Greweling
Markus Färbinger
George Higgins
Noble Masi
Joseph McKenna
Paul Prosperi
Walter Schreyer

The images in this book were created in the new photography studio. Many thanks to the photographers: John Grubell, Liz Johnson, and Lorna Smith.

The foods you see in the photographs were selected from among those in our school's storeroom; Brad Matthews and Todd Perkins went beyond the call of duty.

We also thank the following for their contributions: Gary Allen, Maryanne Monachelli, and the A-Copy and mailroom staff.

We particularly wish to recognize all of the students and graduates of The Culinary Institute of America, to whom this book is dedicated. They use these recipes, each and every day. It is in the crucible of the classroom that this book came into being. We thank all the students and alumni who have helped to make this book what it is, but especially wish to mention: Jewel Bishop, Tim Champness, Thomas Schroeder, and Julio Vega.

Van Nostrand Reinhold, our partners in this grand effort, showed great dedication, patience, and an extraordinary degree of flexibility in bringing this book home:

Marianne Russell	Amy Shipper
Renee Guillmette	Jackie Martin
Marie Terry	Mike Suh
Melissa Rosati	Louise Kurtz

And Van Nostrand Reinhold's support staff: Sharon Cornell, Liz Curione, Ilene Elagroudy, Stan Hatzakis, Lori Jacobs, Sharon Kaufman, Margaret Madigan, Laura Morelli, Andrea Olshevsky, and Joan Petrokofsky.

We would like to thank the following corporations and groups for the equipment, software, china, and foods used in the recipe editing, testing, and photography portions of this book:

AllClad	J. B. Peel
Cuisinart	Susan Shaffer, creator of ExecuChef
F. Dick	Villeroy and Boch

This book has had an enormous impact on many lives. It is with great joy that we extend our heartfelt thanks to our families, and a welcome to the newest members of The Culinary Institute of America's "New Professional" family: Jackson Ryan and Molly Schroeder.

SIXTH

The New Professional Chef™

EDITION

PART I

Introduction
to the Profession

Humans are distinct from other species in that we, for the most part, prefer to make eating a social act. We have created elaborate systems of manners, rituals, and taboos to govern how we eat, what, where, and with whom. The role of the chef in such a complex system is a fascinating story. This overview of the history of cooking, dining, and hospitality as a whole will touch on many aspects of human endeavor—agriculture, communal living, social structure, war and conquest, and much more. In particular, we will concentrate on the way that a special institution—the restaurant—has come into being. All of this is, of course, a way of understanding the background and significance of a very special career path—that of being a professional chef.

An Historical Perspective

Humans tend to seek out and prefer the familiar, reassuring foods of their native countries. Brillat-Savarin knew this well when he said, "Tell me what you eat and I will tell you who you are." The foods that grow in a particular region, the cooking methods typically used, the seasonings, and the style of eating are all part of a community's shared behavior.

There is an equally strong tendency in humans to explore new regions, to learn about other groups, and to acquire as our own whatever we come across that fits into our ideas of what is "right." Travel has a broadening influence, not only on the kinds of foods that are deemed suitable, but also on the ways in which familiar and unfamiliar foods are prepared. Although some peoples have tended to stay in one area for generations upon generations, others have roamed from one end of a continent to the other, ventured out onto the high seas and discovered new lands.

The quest to conquer other lands has been another potent spur to the growth and evolution of cooking. The Greeks and Romans were, perhaps, the most effective at bringing about changes that altered completely the eating habits of most Western hemisphere inhabitants. The delicacies and choicest goods of each conquered country became their "property." Leavened breads, sweet wines, forcemeats, sauces, and "composed dishes" all became part of the Greek repertoire after they gained control of Egypt, Persia, Babylon, and India.

This exchange was never completely one-sided. When the Romans marched through what would one day become Europe, they brought along their own way of seasoning dishes, as well as recipes for pickles, cheeses, and special cakes and breads. Several of these influences can still be seen today; examples include the sweet-sour sauces of modern Italy and the sauerkraut or sauerbraten of modern Germany.

Another example of culinary influence through conquest is that of the Moors over the Spaniards. The use in Spain and Portugal of typically Moorish ingredients, such as sweet syrups, pastries, and almonds, is evidence today of their centuries-long dominion.

As the world moved into the Dark Ages, travel began to diminish, although crusaders in the eleventh to the thirteenth centuries still were making journeys to the Holy Land, and the devout continued to make pilgrimages to various shrines and holy places. Most of the books that discussed food and cookery and the formulas for rich exotic dishes were safe-guarded in monastaries' libraries, while outside their walls the people continued to prepare the rough, simple dishes that had sustained them for generations.

Exploration of new worlds was slow, and it took many decades before any real influence on the established European cuisines was felt. Eventually European explorers traveled to the Americas and the West Indies. They returned with such "new world" foods as chocolate, chilies, beans, corn, tomatoes, and potatoes.

Many of these items were at first regarded as poisonous. Potatoes, a member of the deadly nightshade family, met with especially strong resistance. A famous French agronomist, Antoine-August Parmentier (1737–1813), finally broke through the deep-seated fear of potatoes with a campaign begun in 1774. By the time the French Revolution began in 1789, they were as familiar on the French table as bread. Other new foods that seemed more familiar, or at least bore a surface resemblance to foods already available in Europe, such as the turkey, were taken up immediately and enthusiastically.

With the end of the Dark Ages came a resurgence of travel by the wealthy. At first, this was a time-consuming and hazardous undertaking. However, new modes of travel, such as improved ships able to make long sea journeys, made it possible for the noble classes to move with greater freedom. They carried their own approach to foods and cookery with them, but also were influenced by the foods that they found. The number of French chefs in Russia in the eighteenth and nineteenth centuries is a testimony to the way in which cuisines tended to travel from one part of the world to another. Thomas Jefferson's repeated trips to Europe introduced macaroni, ice cream, and a host of new fruits and vegetables to the United States.

Immigrants traveling from one country to another, whether to escape religious persecution or to try to find a better life, brought with them their traditional dishes and ways of cooking. Each new group's special drinks, breads, cakes, and other foods eventually were intermingled with the foods brought by previous arrivals and with indigenous foods.

The soldiers from the United States who fought in the World Wars returned to this country with a newly acquired taste for the traditional foods of France, Italy, Germany, and Japan. As the twentieth century wore on, the middle class was able to afford foreign travel for pleasure. Today, travel influences the type of cuisines featured in contemporary restaurants. Foods from the Caribbean, the Middle East, and previously lesser-known French and Italian regions have become more familiar as the world continues to "shrink." Chefs and patrons alike are discovering the pleasures of foods from countries as diverse as Portugal, Thailand, and New Zealand. Just as travel has made it easier for the guest to get to the food, it is also a far simpler, faster, and cheaper matter to get food from all over the world to the chef's kitchen.

Royalty and the Rise of the Middle Class

European royal families often intermarried for reasons of state and to form political alliances. With the union of these families came a blending of the customs of different countries. This mingling resulted not only in the exchange of cooking styles and special dishes, but also of social etiquette as well. For example, Caterina de Medici, a sixteenth-century Italian princess who came to France as the result of a royal alliance, brought her chefs from Florence. The number of "Florentine" dishes in the classic French repertoire attests to their influence.

Once the monarchies and the feudal system began to decline, a change occurred in the social structure. The chefs who had once worked in royal households took positions in the wealthy homes of a newly rich and "non-noble" class. The result was an expansion of the cuisine of the nobility, first to the upper class, and eventually to the large and growing middle class.

The gradual dissolution of strict class lines, and the ability of people to move from the lower class to the middle or upper classes, allowed the cookery of the upper class or nobility, known as *haute cuisine,* to blend with the cooking of hearth and home, *cuisine bourgeoisie.* This exchange between domestic cooks and classically trained chefs in all countries produced a number of innovations and refinements. The effect was to spur growth and change, and to keep classic cooking from becoming dull and stale.

Science and Technology

From the time that man first learned to control fire, advances in science and technology have had a direct relationship to food production and preparation. Many of these changes have been heralded as great advances for humankind. Others have been met with resistance.

Advances in farm technology have increased yields and improved quality and overall availability of many foods. One of the less desirable changes is an increased reliance on single-crop farming on a more "industrial" scale. This style of farming encourages a strong reliance on chemical fertilizers, pesticides, and other man-made substances in order to enhance crop yields. Some of this has been done at the expense of soil quality. It certainly has changed the face of farming across the world, as small family farms are less and less part of the overall picture.

Hybridization of crops has cut down on the variety of foodstuffs that are grown. This means that, unless a crop has been preserved in a privately owned seed bank, an entire strain can be lost. We are only now beginning to understand the consequences of allowing cultivated and wild species to become extinct.

Animal husbandry, through the ability to breed desirable characteristics in and undesirable ones out, allows us to raise animals that provide better yield and flavor, as well as less fat. It also has led to ever-increasing problems with diseases that need to be treated with antibiotics. These drugs and others, such as growth hormones used to stimulate milk production in cattle, are being looked at with some alarm.

Equipment and tools have undergone an evolution, from the rudimentary cutting tools and cooking vessels that first allowed foods to be boiled in liquids to the gas and electric stoves, microwave ovens, and computerized equipment of today. Refrigeration allows foods to be held longer and shipped farther, without significant loss of quality.

Scientific developments have allowed us to improve on techniques for food storage, increasing both the shelf life and wholesomeness of foods and reducing the incidence of food spoilage, contamination, and poisoning. Examples of these technical advances include pasteurization, freeze-drying, vacuum packing, and irradiation.

Improved methods of transportation make possible the availability of food from other geographic areas and the ability to use foods once considered "out of season." High-quality produce is now available year-round, and special items once usable only in the area where they were produced are now available worldwide. This has had a negative impact, too. We have become increasingly less aware of what foods are native to a given region, when and for how long they are in season, and how they taste when they ripen on the vine instead of in transit.

Nutrition

Nutrition has become so much a part of everyday life that we can easily forget just how young a science it actually is. The study of how foods help the body grow, rejuvenate, fight disease, and prevent the onset of certain conditions is constantly uncovering clues to how we can eat "smarter". The chef's role is challenging in this regard.

The first task is to learn the rudiments of nutrition. In Chapter 3 you will learn the basic components of foods as they relate to nutrition. You will also see the dietary recommendations currently suggested. This type of information is important for your overall menu plan, production techniques, and recipe development.

Your guests have as much access to this information as you do. Remember that much of the data released by the popular press is seen as contradictory. People remain perplexed by such topics as cholesterol in the diet versus cholesterol in the blood. They find it hard to separate the hard facts about alcohol as a beverage from the reports about the

French Paradox. They are no longer certain if it is butter that is evil, margarine that must be avoided, or coconut and palm kernel oil that is responsible for cardio-vascular disease, or if they should immediately start pouring extra-virgin olive oil over everything they eat.

It is no easier for a professional chef to glean the most pertinent facts and put them to practical use. Reading current books and magazines is a starting point. Work with professional nutritionists or use some of the excellent software available. There are courses available to you and your staff through various continuing education programs that can help you to apply new information to classic techniques and recipes, or to develop new approaches to creating a whole new menu or individual menu items.

Restaurant History and Evolution

The first restaurant (as we know restaurants today) opened in Paris in 1765. Monsieur Boulanger, a tavern-keeper, served a dish of sheep's feet, or *trotters,* in a white sauce as a restorative or *restorante.* Although he was brought to court for infringing on a separate guild's monopoly on the sale of cooked foods, he won the case and was allowed to continue. Once the ice was broken, other restaurants followed in fairly rapid succession.

The French Revolution (1789-99) had a particularly significant effect on restaurant proliferation, because many chefs who previously had worked for the monarchy or nobility fled the country to escape the guillotine's specter. Although some sought employment with the noble classes in other countries, others began to open their own establishments.

Restaurants became increasingly refined operations. Although they were at first frequented only by men, this would change as customs in society and in the foodservice industry as a whole changed.

The *grand cuisine,* a careful code established by Antonin Carême detailing numerous dishes and their sauces in *La Cuisine Classique* and other volumes, came to restaurants much more slowly than it did to nobility's kitchens. The menus of most hotels and restaurants offered a simple *table d'hôte,* which provided little if any choice. The *grande cuisine* offered a *carte* (or list) of suggestions available from the kitchen. The *à la carte* restaurant had begun to make inroads on the traditional "men's club" atmosphere of most restaurants and cafes.

When the Savoy Hotel opened in London in 1898 (under the direction of Cesar Ritz and Auguste Escoffier), *grande cuisine* was still the exception. These two gentlemen waged a successful campaign to assure that their *à la carte* offerings were of the finest, that their service was the best, and that it was all delivered to the guest on the finest china and crystal. As a result, ladies and gentlemen of good standing finally could be found in the dining rooms of restaurants in England, France, and elsewhere.

Today, the variety of dining establishments reflects the interests, lifestyles, and needs of a modern society: brasseries, bistros, "white tablecloth" or fine dining, ethnic restaurants, fast-food spots, takeout companies, hotel dining rooms, banquet halls, and the list goes on.

Major Historical Figures

The following list of major influential figures is by no means complete. Further reading about notable figures throughout the history of cooking is recommended. Refer to the Recommended Readings at the end of this book for other sources.

Caterina de Medici (1519–89), an Italian princess from the famous Florentine family, married the Duc d'Orleans, later Henri II of France. She introduced a more refined style of dining, including the use of the fork and the napkin. Her Florentine chefs influenced French chefs as well, most particularly in the use of spinach.

Anne of Austria (1601–66), wife of Louis XIII, was a member of the Spanish Hapsburg family. Her retinue included Spanish chefs who introduced sauce Espagnol and the use of roux as a thickener for sauces.

Pierre François de la Varenne (1615–78) was the author of the first cookbook to summarize the cooking practices of the French nobility. His *Le Vrai Cuisinier François* was published in 1651.

Jean-Anthelme Brillat-Savarin (1755–1826) was a French politician and gourmet and a renowned writer. His work, *Le Physiologie de Gout (The Physiology of Taste),* is highly regarded to this day.

Marie-Antoine Carême (1784–1833) became known as the founder of the *grande cuisine* and was responsible for systematizing culinary techniques. He had a profound influence on the later writing of Escoffier, and was known as the "chef of kings, king of chefs."

Charles Ranhofer (1836–99) was the first internationally renowned chef of an American restaurant, Delmonico's, and the author of *The Epicurean.*

Georges Auguste Escoffier (1847–1935) was a renowned chef and teacher. He was the author of *Le Guide Culinaire,* a major work codifying classic cuisines that is still widely used by professional chefs. His other significant contributions include simplifying the classic menu in accordance with the principles advocated by Carême, and initiating the brigade system. Escoffier's influence on the food-service industry cannot be overemphasized.

Fernand Point (1897–1955) was the chef/owner of La Pyramide restaurant in Vienne, France. He went even further than Escoffier in bringing about a change in cooking styles and laid the foundations for *nouvelle cuisine.*

Contemporary Chefs

From the time of Fernand Point to the present day, there has been a virtual explosion in the kitchen. New or rediscovered cooking styles have changed the landscape of restaurants throughout the world. Nouvelle cuisine, first made popular by such famed chefs as *Paul Bocuse, Jean Troisgros, Roger Vergé,* and *Michel Guerard,* swept onto the scene with enormous force.

An emerging sense of national cuisine gave rise to American cuisine. *Larry Forgione* (The River Cafe, An American Place), *Jeremiah Tower* (Stars), *Alice Waters* (Chez Panisse), and *Dean Fearing* (Mansion on Turtle Creek) were among those in the vanguard of this new cooking style. For the first time, chefs trained in the United States were achieving worldwide recognition.

Keeping track of the latest "hot" chef in the restaurant world has become a nearly impossible task. Media attention on new restaurants, "rising star" chefs, and the latest dining trends has continued to grow in importance. As we enter the twenty-first century, the face of this industry is changing just as surely as other industries are changing.

Throughout the world, individual chefs are raising the standards of this profession. They are well-trained and highly motivated. Today, the profession has attained a level of respect that was not always forthcoming in this nation. The considerable amount of interaction between cultures, the more widespread availability of special foods, and an increasingly sophisticated clientele have been the driving forces behind the growth, diversity, and excitement found in the restaurant world today.

Chefs are not the only people to attain status and high regard in the foodservice industry. Writers, critics, and reviewers have made a mark on the evolution of the field. While there is a great tradition of food writing from time immemorial, today's food writers have become versed in such specialized areas as nutrition, history and culture, ecology as it relates to the foodservice industry, and health issues. Teachers, photographers, and food stylists help to shape what appears on menus and plates throughout the country.

The list of names of those who have had a measurable impact on the public's perception of all manner of food-related issues is long and grows longer each day.

Today's Currents and Trends

The restaurant business as a whole is subject to the same changes that affect our entire culture. Today's family is not what is was 20 or 30 years ago. There are whole new ways to go to work, study, and be entertained now. The future is bristling both with possibilities and uncertainties.

Family Structure Changes

The extended family—grandparents, parents, children, and assorted aunts, uncles, and cousins all living together—is now a rarity. The traditional "nuclear" family—working father, mother at home, two children in school—also is getting harder to find. It is far more likely that both the father and mother are working, or that the family has only a single parent.

"Baby boomers" who waited until much later in life to start their families are often unwilling to give up their careers. For any family in which the major caregivers are also the major wage earners, finding ways to minimize demands on time is essential. More and more often, meals are either eaten in a restaurant or they are takeout foods.

The double-income family and increasing numbers of single professional people have brought about significant growth in the foodservice industry. These people have more disposable income but less time to cook at home, so they tend to eat out more often. This circumstance also has spurred the growth of "carryout cuisine" or "takeout," which is offered by gourmet shops, delicatessans, and supermarkets, as well as by restaurants filling orders for home consumption.

Single professionals and the growing numbers of retired persons have shifted the demographics of this country dramatically. Though the requirements of these two groups may not be identical, they are both looking to the foodservice industry to meet their special needs, whether it be gourmet shops or "early bird" specials.

Media and the Information Superhighway

There are many ways to get information. Print media, including books, magazines, periodicals, and newsletters, crowd the shelves of the local newsstand and bookstore. Special interest publications are among the most often used resources for any professional. Videos, video-conferencing, and multi media forums such as CD-Rom and interactive software are moving rapidly into center stage as a source for information, inspiration, and networking.

Information overload is a very real concern. It has become a more difficult task to sort out what is truly reliable. Fads grow (and die) quickly. In fact, it is becoming increasingly difficult to distinguish a passing fad from a newly emerging trend. "Stars" and "hot spots" come and go rapidly as well. The pressure of being the latest, hottest, and best can be overwhelming. It is no longer uncommon to hear a talented chef bemoan the fact that he or she is away from the kitchen too much, is being pulled in too many directions, and feels burned out. Media attention can be a mixed blessing.

Accurate and timely reporting has and will always be a valued commodity. Journalists have assumed a larger importance in the food world as well as in the total news and media picture.

Concerns about food safety, health, nutrition, and matters of cultural interest are important to a wider audience than chefs.

Summary

The social act of dining is one of the ways that humans are distinct from other species. We eat, not just to nourish our bodies, but also to strengthen our ties as a group. Foods are prepared before they are eaten. They are grown, hunted, or gathered; cut, cleaned, and trimmed; cooked and presented to the assembled group. This collection of activities has become a central focus of daily life and one of the unifying factors of all human society and culture. Chefs have played a critical role in the spread of these civilizing behaviors. Understanding how this profession first began, how it has changed, and what its potential can be is the first step on a life-long path toward becoming a professional chef.

PART II

The Foodservice Professional

There are many pieces in the makeup of a professional chef. Just like any other craftsman, you must begin with a thorough knowledge of how to work as a professional, including a code of behavior, knowledge of the tools of the trade, and the raw materials you will use in plying your craft.

The first chapter in this part of the book discusses what it means to be a chef. Education, (whether in a professional cooking school or as an apprentice), networking, and a brief survey of the current status of society and how that impacts the definition of "chef" are topics of great significance to the working chef.

Next, you must be able to work in a safe manner. This means not only handling foods carefully to avoid transmitting a foodborne disease to a guest, but also to prevent the numerous accidents that seem to be part and parcel of a job that puts you in nearly constant contact with hot, sharp, and heavy objects.

Nutrition has become a topic of no small significance to this profession. Chefs and patrons alike are wondering how they can eat better to ensure greater energy. Weight control, health concerns, and an upsurge of interest in vegetarianism have made inroads on the types of foods featured on menus and the ways in which they are being prepared. As a chef, you need to have the rudiments of nutrition well in hand.

Chapter 4 introduces the large and small equipment that you will work with on a daily basis. Some items, such as knives and sieves, haven't changed design or function in centuries. Others (microwave ovens, convection steamers, and induction cooktops) represent the con-tinued march of technology. Many kitchens have reverted to equipment patterned on old-style items, such as wood-fired grills and ovens, to provide foods with a special appeal.

The basic ingredients you will use to create the items offered on your menu are illustrated and explained in Chapter 5. The quality of the foods you purchase will determine the quality of the finished dish.

Working efficiently, carefully, and creatively with the foods, staff, and equipment at your disposal in the kitchen is one of the greatest challenges facing you as a professional.

CHAPTER *1* : *The Professional Chef*

The term "chef,"
although frequently
used to describe anyone
who cooks, is considered
a mark of respect by
those within the
profession. The title is
one that can only be
earned through diligent
practice and dedication. Those chefs who have made, or will make, the
most lasting impression on this industry know that their success
depends on their ability to fulfill many different roles. A true chef is,
among other things, a lifelong student, a teacher, a craftsman, a
leader, and a manager. An open and inquiring mind, an appreciation
of and dedication to quality and excellence, and a sense of responsi-
bility to self and the community are among the professional chef's
cardinal virtues.

Today's chefs are often looked upon as a new breed—respected,
even admired, for their skill, craftsmanship, and artistry. Some chefs
have received so much press that their names are household words.
Books, magazines, entire sections of the newspaper, even a television
network are devoted to food and cooking, commanding an impressive
share of the consumer's disposable income. The elevation of the chef to
a legitimate profession has helped to attract bright and talented people
to the industry.

It has been estimated that at the turn of the century, there will be one million more foodservice industry jobs available than there will be trained people to fill them. This industry's evolution has been one of steady growth, increased diversification, and expanding opportunities. The interaction of new trends in foods and dining, combined with the traditions and customs of other eras and other social groups, creates new styles of cooking, new dishes, and new types of eating establishments. The increasing communication between chefs and professionals in other areas (production, farming, computers, for example) has stimulated growth and opened up new potentials.

At the same time, it has increased the number of businesses offering a vast array of services and goods. Competition between restaurants for clients is growing each day. Learning more than just how to sauté and make a good sauce is more important than ever before.

Becoming a Craftsman

There is something fascinating about watching a chef who wields a knife with the dexterity of Jacques Pépin or Martin Yan. They can reduce an onion to a pile of exquisitely even dice within seconds. Acquiring the skills that enable you to handle a knife with authority, to flip an omelet with finesse, or to poach a piece of salmon in a court bouillon that appears to barely quiver is all part of a chef's education.

Getting an Education

There are many chefs today who learned the basics of their craft by attending an accredited school. Under the tutelage of experienced chefs, they begin a journey that starts with simple skills, such as

FIGURE 1-1   Chefs Selecting Produce for the *Bocuse d'Or* Competition

dicing onions and peeling carrots, and progresses through the intricacies of preparing French pastries and such elaborate composed dishes as *Veal à l'Orloff.* Formal training in a school supplies a solid grounding in basic and advanced culinary techniques. It also is a good laboratory where you can become "fluent" in the language of the trade. There is no substitute for experience, however. It is only with a great deal of hands-on practice that class-learned theory becomes fully assimilated.

Others may begin their training as an apprentice *(stagiare),* either in a special apprenticeship program or a self-directed course of study, advancing from kitchen to kitchen, learning at the side of those chefs who are involved in the day-to-day business of running a professional kitchen.

For most individuals, training is an on-going matter. Whether you learn your trade in school, through an apprenticeship program, or on-the-job, the responsibility for acquiring that training is yours. It is never fully complete at any point in time. Instead, it is achieved in a variety of guises, all of which are important to your education at various stages throughout one's career.

Continuing Education

Continuing education, once initial training has been completed, is equally important, because the foodservice industry is constantly evolving. Attending classes, workshops, and seminars helps keep practicing cooks and chefs in step with new methods and new styles of cooking, or serves to hone skills in specialized areas.

The more you keep abreast of changes and new developments in the restaurant industry, the more clear the need for continuing education becomes. As a case in point, consider the enormous impact the following areas have had over the last several years:

Nutrition Chefs no longer can afford to ignore nutrition. It is as much a part of the dining experience for many individuals as whether or not a restaurant has a wine list or serves a wonderful hot soufflé. The ability to make nutritional adaptations to dishes, to identify to your waitstaff or guests those items that are good choices for those with concerns about eating a low-fat or low-cholesterol diet, or to simply enhance the overall nutritional value of any meal are critical points.

There are many excellent books available that address nutrition. But you may find that enrolling in a class, or even meeting with a registered dietitian or nutritionist is valuable.

Food safety issues One of the areas of great concern to customers and people who work in this industry is that of food safety. Regulations and standards are under constant review. Changes to existing standards occur quickly, often in almost immediate response to a specific foodborne illness outbreak. The glove law, requiring food handlers to wear gloves whenever handling a food that will not be cooked again before it is served to the guest, is a case in point. The recommended safe handling procedures for eggs, beef, chicken, and other potentially hazardous foods are also under scrutiny and revision.

Organic foods Organic farming has become an increasingly important issue for virtually all sectors of our society. Farmers, restaurateurs, and consumers are all looking at organic foods more carefully than ever before. The concept behind organic farming is simple. Farmers use organic matter to enrich the soil, control pests, and enhance the yield they can generate.

At this point in time, farmers who use organic methods are at a slight disadvantage in relation to large-scale "industrial" farms. First, there are relatively few farms producing organic foods, so the supply does not yet meet the demand. Second, the costs of organic farming is still greater than it would be to grow foods using chemicals. There may be several reasons to account for this, but the net result is that until there are more farms using organic farming methods, costs will remain slightly higher for organic meats, poultry, wines, fruits, vegetables, and herbs.

How do you know if foods labeled as organic are actually any different than nonorganic products? There are several organizations on the national and state level that monitor organic farming. Regulations may vary from organization to organization, but in essence, the farmer must have used no chemicals on the fields for a specified number of years before any foods grown there can be labeled organic. So, if you are purchasing foods that are supposedly organic, ask the farmer or purveyor who has done the inspection of the farm.

The other big question regarding organic foods is: Are they better for you? The jury is still out. Some reports seem to indicate that any nutritional edge that they have is wishful thinking. Others swing to the other end of the scale, claiming greatly improved nutritional levels. While there is no clear-cut answer to this question, you will certainly find that there is a particular clientele who will prefer organic foods, and will actively seek them out on the menus of restaurants they frequent.

Environmental concerns Probably the main point of moving toward organic farming has to do with its impact on the environment. The farmer works to improve the quality of the soil by introducing organic matter such as compost. Enriching the soil is seen as the best way to ensure a good harvest.

Other environmental concerns for this industry include concerns about solid waste disposal. Composting, recycling, and overall reduction in the materials used in each phase of your operation are all ways to contribute to the solution. In some communities, you may be able to find farmers willing to take your compost for example.

Each community has its own standards about recycling. It is important that you and your staff know what can be recycled and how it should be prepared for recycling. Set-up the appropriate containers in the kitchen to encourage everyone to recycle and periodically retrain your staff.

Conservation of water, electricity, and oil is another way that restaurants can contribute to the health of our environment. A major benefit to you is a reduction in operating costs for your restaurant. As you review your daily operation, think long and hard about how you can cut down on your energy and water consumption. This means reviewing when certain tasks are done; for example, if you can cluster a number of roasting tasks into a specific time slot, you won't need to have the stoves turned on when they aren't actually in use. If you need assistance in finding ways to conserve resources, contact your local utility company for an energy audit.

Vegetarianism   Many more individuals than ever before have adopted a vegetarian diet. To capture this share of the market, you need to learn what types of vegetarians there are. Then you need to develop a set of menu options to reach those people. Even those who are not strict vegetarians may look for meatless options on the menu. As interest in traditional diets from cultures around the world continues to be a strong influence, you should find it relatively easy to incorporate appetizers, entrees, and soups that meet the needs of all types of vegetarians. For more information, read about vegetarians in Chapter 3.

The list of concerns that you and your guests bring with them to your restaurant will depend upon what type of service you offer and the general makeup of your audience. Evaluate your market, and then take the appropriate steps to keep on top of the latest information in the areas they are most concerned about. Magazines, newsletters, electronic bulletin boards, government publications, and books are all excellent sources. Whenever possible, you should try to attend seminars, workshops, and lectures. To find out more in any given area, consider joining professional organizations in order to network with other professionals in the field.

Networking with Other Chefs

Creating a professional network is a task that should be taken seriously. Working with other professionals to share information and knowledge is an

FIGURE 1-2   Research in the Library

important avenue of growth—both professional and personal. Networks can be formal or informal. The way to begin is simply to introduce yourself to others in your field. Have business cards with you when you go out to other restaurants or to trade shows.

When you make a good contact, follow up with a phone call or a note. Keep the names and cards that you acquire organized in some sort of filing system. An established network makes it much easier for you to find a new job or an employee. It also makes any travel that you do more pleasurable and effective, since you will already know colleagues in other cities and countries before you arrive. The communication that you develop with your peers will keep your own work fresh and contemporary.

A Chef's Professional and Personal Attributes

Every member of a profession is responsible for upholding the profession's image, whether he or she is a teacher, lawyer, doctor, or chef. As our profession continues to become accessible to individuals who might formerly have been denied a spot in the professional kitchen, a consistent code of conduct is even more important.

A Commitment to Service

The foodservice industry is predicated on service. Therefore, you, as a chef, should never lose sight of what that word implies. Good service includes (but is not limited to) providing good food, properly and safely cooked, appropriately seasoned, and attractively presented in a pleasant environment—in short, your job is making the customer happy. The degree to which an operation maintains a standard of excellence in these areas is the degree to which it will succeed. The customer must always come first.

A Sense of Responsibility

When you are truly responsible, it means that you have considered what effect your actions will have not just on yourself, but on those directly around you, and beyond, out into the community. As we learn more about how things work in the world at large, it becomes abundantly clear that "community" means far more than a few surrounding blocks. As long as you are able to see and accept the fact that what you do does make a difference, even to people you may never meet, you are acting as a responsible member of the world community.

When employees and guests feel that their needs are given due consideration, your entire operation will benefit. Employees' self-esteem will increase and their attitudes toward the establishment will improve. Making each staff member a part of the team will help to increase their productivity and reduce pilferage and absenteeism. Guests will enjoy their dining experience, certain that they are getting good value for their money. They will come back, and they will tell friends and colleagues about your restaurant.

Foods, equipment, staff, and the facility are all valuable assets that must be treated with care and respect. This will become the norm when you make it clear by your own actions that this is the only acceptable way to behave. Waste, recklessness, disregard for others, and misuse and abuse of any commodity are clearly unprofessional and unacceptable. Abusive language, harassment, ethnic slurs, and profanity do not have a place in the professional kitchen. No operation, in any business, can afford to act as if there were people, assets, or time to waste.

Judgment

Although it is not easy to learn, a sense of what is right—whether you are seasoning a dish, develop-

ing new menu items, making out a weekly schedule, or disciplining an employee—is a litmus test for evaluating professional behavior. This sense of what is appropriate is acquired throughout a lifetime of experience. Good judgment is never completely mastered; rather, it is a goal toward which one should continually strive.

Looking the Part

A chef's uniform is an outward symbol of the profession. Looking like a professional helps you to act like one. The uniform's history is intriguing, reflecting both a practical, utilitarian side as well as some of the "romance" associated with being a chef.

The most recognizable part of the uniform is the *toque blanche,* or hat. There are many explanations for the shape of the hat. Some believe, for example, that the tall white hat may have originated at the time the Byzantine empire was under siege by the barbarians. Men from all walks of life (including philosophers, and artists, as well as chefs to royalty) fled to Greek Orthodox monasteries for protection. They adopted the same dress as the priests so that they would not be recognized. After the threat of persecution lessened, the chefs wore white hats, to differentiate themselves from the ordained priests.

The pleats on a chef's hat also have a story. According to some, the hundred pleats are said to represent the one hundred different ways a chef can prepare eggs.

Career Paths for Professionals in Foodservice

Types of Restaurants and Other Foodservice Establishments

Chefs are needed not just in hotel dining rooms and traditional restaurants but in a variety of settings—public and private, consumer-oriented, and institutional. An increased emphasis on nutrition, sophistication, and financial and quality control means that all settings, from the "white tablecloth" restaurant to the fast-food outlet, can offer you interesting challenges.

Hotels often have a number of different dining facilities, including fine dining restaurants, room service, coffee shops, and banquet rooms. The kitchen staffs are large, and there will often be separate butchering, catering, and pastry kitchens on the premises.

Full-service restaurants such as *bistros, "white tablecloth,"* or *family-style restaurants* feature a full menu, and the patrons are served by trained waitstaff.

Private clubs generally provide some sort of foodservice to their members. It may be as simple as a small grill featuring sandwiches, or it may be a complete dining room and banquet hall. The difference is that the guests are paying members, and the food costs generally are figured differently than they would be for a public restaurant.

Executive dining rooms are operated by many corporations. The degree of simplicity or elegance demanded in a particular corporation will determine what types of food are prepared, how they are prepared, and what style of service is appropriate.

Institutional catering (schools, hospitals, employee cafeterias, colleges, airlines, correctional institutions) often requires a cycle menu. In a cafeteria, the guests serve themselves, choosing from the offered foods. The range of menu selections depends a great deal on the institution's needs, available moneys, and the desires of those operating the cafeteria.

Caterers provide a particular service, specifically tailored to meet the wishes of a special client for a special event, whether it be a wedding, a cocktail reception, or a gallery opening. Caterers may provide either on-site services (the client comes to the caterer), off-site services (caterer comes to the client), or both.

"Carryout" foodservices are growing in importance as more couples, single professionals, and families try to enjoy meals at home without having to spend time preparing them. These shops prepare entrées, salads, side dishes, and desserts.

Alternative Careers in Foodservice

As long as the foodservice industry grows, a continual need will exist for well-trained personnel to fill the traditional careers of chef, sous chef,

saucier, and other "back-of-the-house" positions. Of great importance, as well, are other opportunities available to a well-trained and motivated *cuisinier.* A growing number of less traditional opportunities exist, many of which do not involve the actual production or service of foods.

Consultants and design specialists will work with restaurant owners, often before the restaurant is open, to assist in developing a menu, designing the overall layout and ambiance of the dining room, and establishing work patterns for the kitchen. Joe Baum, restaurant consultant, made an indelible mark on the design of restaurant interiors, setting new standards in such renowned establishments as The Four Seasons. Barbara Lazaroff has made an equally strong impact through her design work at Spago and Chinois on Main.

Well-informed *salespeople* help chefs determine how to best meet their needs for food and equipment, introduce them to new products, and demonstrate how to properly use the new equipment that is essential to the well-run, modern kitchen.

The number of cooking schools in this country has swelled from one to nearly 300 over the course of the last five decades. *Teachers* with solid experience in addition to teaching skills are what set the good schools apart. Chefs who turn to the classroom bring with them the experience that gives students a more thorough understanding of what restaurant cooking is like. Culinary historians, writers, and table service instructors are all playing an increasing role as the education of a chef becomes more fully rounded.

For those who read about food as voraciously as some people devour mystery novels, good food writing is a cherished commodity. There are several different types of *food writers:* cookbook authors, historians, reviewers, critics, and journalists. Individual writers have, over time, played crucial roles in setting the tone for this profession. M.F.K. Fisher, Elizabeth David, James Beard, Jane Brody, Craig Claiborne, Bryan Miller, Paula Wolfert, and Florence Fabricant have all had an impact, directly or indirectly, on the restaurant industry.

Food photography and styling has become a significant factor in the promotion of new products, as well as in magazines and books. This has become an increasingly specialized field. As food continues to have a starring role on television programs, videos, and movies, this area will remain an important avenue for professional growth.

Research and development kitchens employ a great many chefs. These may be run by food manufacturers who are developing new products or food lines. Advisory boards, such as the American Dairy Association or the California Prune Board, may also operate research, development, and testing facilities. Magazines for both the industry and consumers also maintain test and development kitchens. *Eating Well* and *Saveur,* for example, have a great deal of prestige and pride invested in their test kitchens.

The Chef as Executive, Administrator, and Manager

As you continue your career, you will move from positions where your technical prowess is your greatest contribution into those where your skills as an executive, an administrator, and a manager are more clearly in demand. This does not mean that your ability to grill, sauté or roast foods to the exact point of doneness is less important than it was before. It does mean that you will be called on to learn and to assume tasks and responsibilities that are more managerial, marking a shift in the evolution of your career.

Becoming a Good Executive

What do executives do? They are the individuals who develop a mission or a plan for a company or organization. They are also the ones responsible for developing a system that allows that plan to come into fruition. As an executive, then, you must shoulder a large portion of responsibility for the success or failure of your restaurant.

Executives can't operate in a vacuum, however. Nor do they emerge full-blown one day out of the blue. Even before you wear a jacket embroidered with "Executive Chef," you will have begun to exercise your abilities as an executive already.

Becoming a Good Administrator

Once a restaurauteur has laid down an overall goal and game plan, the next task is to establish systems to implement and track those plans. Now your hat becomes that of an administrator. Some administrative duties may not sound at all glamorous—preparing schedules, tracking deliveries, computing costs, and so forth. If a restaurant is small, the "executive" and "administrator" will be the same person. That same person also might be the one who dons a uniform and works the line.

The best administrators are those who can create a feeling throughout the entire staff that they have a stake in getting things done correctly. When you give people the opportunity to help make decisions, and the tools needed to perform as well as they can, you will see that it is easier to achieve the goals you have established on an executive level.

There are tools that you can and should learn to use. Computers, accounting systems, and careful record keeping all play a role. Many organizations, from large chains and hotels down to the smallest one-person catering company are relying more and more on software systems that enable them to track purchases, losses, sales, profits, food cost, recipes, and customer comments. If you (or the professionals that you employ to do this for you) are not already using a system capable of incorporating all of this information and more, you cannot be as effective as you need to be.

FIGURE 1-3 Using a Computer as a Management Tool

Becoming a Good Manager

Management issues have received a good deal of attention in this industry, as well as in others. All businesses must operate more effectively and efficiently, with fewer resources. Managing a restaurant, or any other business, is a job that requires the ability to manage four areas effectively:

- Physical assets

- Information

- People (human resources)

- Time

The greater your skills in managing any of these areas, the greater your potential for success will be. Many management systems today stress the use of quality as a yardstick. Every aspect of your operation needs to be seen as a way to improve the quality of service you provide your customers. As we look at what you might be expected to do in order to manage resources, information, people, and time effectively, the fundamental question you need to ask, over and over, is this:

How does a change (or lack of change) affect the quality of service or goods that I am offering my customer?

Unless you are different, better, faster, or unique in some way, there is every chance that, as competition continues to increase, you may not survive, let alone prosper.

Managing Physical Assets

The primary purpose of being in business is to make money. If you squander your assets, then you cannot make a profit. The increasingly complex problems of budgeting, taxes, wages, and many other business considerations make it a good idea to hire professionals trained specifically to handle these areas. In order to be sure that these professionals are able to do what a specific operation requires, you need to be aware of how a business operates—and you must be realistic about what can be expected.

When we talk about managing physical assets, we are considering how anything that you must purchase or pay for affects your ability to do business well. This includes, but is certainly not limited to, the items listed below:

- Food and beverage

- Operating costs such as utilities, waste removal, taxes, and insurance

- Rent, mortgage, or lease payments

- Tables, chairs, linens, china, flatware, glassware

- Computers, cash registers

- Pots, pans, and other large and small kitchen equipment

- Cleaning supplies and/or services, ware washing machines

The first step to bringing the expenses associated with your physical assets under control is to know what your expenses actually are. Then, you can begin the process of making the adjustments and instituting the control systems that will keep your organization operating at maximum efficiency.

Each restaurant has different needs, and only you, along with your management team, can decide how best to purchase, lease, or rent various commodities that you need. For instance, you may find that buying linens and washing them on the premises represents a slight increase over the cost of renting. Still, you might decide not to rent, since owning your own linens allows you to have a specific quality, style, or color not available through the companies in your area. Or, you might compromise on linens and opt to apply the money saved by using a linen service toward purchasing better quality flatware. There are no hard and fast rules, just principles that you will apply to your own situation.

One of the biggest expenses for any restaurant will always be food and beverage costs. You or your purchasing agent will have to work hard to develop and sustain a good purchasing system. The principles outlined below offer a way to analyze and improve what you are already doing or to act as a guide in establishing a new system. You should constantly re-evaluate your purchasing practices to accommodate changes in your operation and in the marketplace.

Purchasing

Purchasing has a direct impact on cost control. An adequate store of supplies is needed so that the restaurant can operate efficiently. This includes not only food but nonfood items, such as cleaning supplies, small tools, and equipment. Having too little of any given item is a clear sign of poor planning. On the other hand, it is wasteful to have more supplies than can be used in a reasonable amount of time, or to own unnecessary equipment and tools. An excess of anything is simply tying up money, space, and time.

When you apply the nine steps outlined here, foods, supplies, and equipment can be purchased wisely and efficiently.

1. Develop a list of your needs.

All food and equipment purchased for the kitchen should have a direct relation to the menu. Review your menu carefully. Create master lists for foods, small and large equipment needs, and any special service items.

2. Develop quality and purchasing specifications.

This is a precise description of the product, including trade or common names, type of container, brand names or federal grades, container size, and the unit (pound, case, bunch, can, and so on) on which the item's price is quoted. Any other pertinent specifications, such as whether meats should be aged, should also be included. These specifications should take the form of a written communication between you and the purveyor.

You may wish to make use of local farmer's markets to get some or all of your food. If so, use the same standards you would in purchasing food from a purveyor. There are often bargains to be had, especially if you can time your trip to coincide with the very opening of the market. An alternate strategy might be to wait until the market is about to

close. Restaurants can often make use of the very large tomatoes or other "odd"-sized produce that the home cook is less likely to want.

3. Select purveyors.

It is best to have a minimum of two purveyors for any item purchased. Well-chosen purveyors can provide an operation with products of consistent quality. They will also work with an operation to help set up delivery schedules. To find a good purveyor, check with the Better Business Bureau and with other restaurant owners. There are many ways you can determine if your purveyor is giving you the best possible service:

- The price quoted by the salesperson should be the same as the price paid upon receipt of the goods
- Foods should be of the quality and quantity requested
- Delivery trucks should be clean, and refrigerated if necessary
- Invoices should be clearly written
- Returns of unacceptable products should be handled quickly
- Foods should arrive in appropriate containers

4. Organize a delivery schedule.

A consistent and reliable delivery schedule is one way that you even out the workload. If you cannot be certain when a delivery will arrive, it may force you into unwise purchasing patterns. You may find it necessary to overpurchase some items in order to be prepared in case a delivery is delayed. Or, you may be in the position of removing a dish from the menu in the middle of service if the fish that normally arrives at 4 o'clock on Thursday afternoon is not on hand until 10 o'clock in the evening.

5. Develop a parstock.

Parstock is the amount of stock you should have consistently available to cover operating needs between deliveries. Being overstocked can be as bad as having too little stock. If there is too much stock, valuable space and money are tied up. If there is not enough, it may be impossible to produce a given menu item. It is one thing to run out of a "special" but it is bad business to have to apologize that a regular menu item is unavailable.

6. Take purchase inventory.

This is a physical count of what is available. You and your staff should take a quick inventory of the food items, linens, and equipment for each station at the end of every shift. A more detailed and accurate count should be taken weekly, monthly, quarterly, and yearly. The amount you have on hand should then be "brought to par" by ordering enough of an item to replace the depleted stores.

7. Forecast contingency needs.

Keeping full and complete business records can help predict what times of the year, month, or week may be busier than others. If your restaurant is located in a tourist area, there may be a predictably busy season. Other factors to consider are parties, banquets, and special events, such as festivals in the area. Additional stock may then be ordered to cover especially high-volume times. If your restaurant is a new operation, you can learn some of this information by talking with other owners or chefs in the area.

8. Take market quotes.

Many factors can affect what you pay for food and beverage items. A strike, a flood or hurricane, poor growing conditions, a drought, or an unexpected shortage of certain goods due to seasonal swings can send the cost of certain goods soaring. When you find, for instance, that broccoli or red pepper are no longer within your operating budget, you may need to make adjustments.

9. Maintain a purchase log.

Keeping good records of all orders, invoices, and price lists helps to make ordering, receiving, and storing procedures efficient. An up-to-date purchase log eliminates costly guesswork when you must decide what foods and beverages to purchase from which vendors. You may be required by local ordinance, state, or federal law to produce certificates or receipts for specific foods, such as shellfish.

Storage Areas

If all storage areas, no matter how small, are well-maintained and well-monitored, then the amount of money lost through waste and spoilage will automatically be lowered. Keep all refrigerators and freezers cleaned and properly maintained. Check their temperatures consistently, and whenever a unit appears to be functioning at less-than-optimal temperatures, have it repaired or serviced quickly.

Storage areas for dry goods, cleaning supplies, linens, and paper goods should also be carefully maintained. Shelving, storage bins, and other storage systems must be sturdy enough to hold supplies. Doors and windows should be rodent- and pest- proof. Dry storage areas must be properly ventilated. The lighting in these areas should be adequate to permit you and your staff to easily and safely store and retrieve the items you need.

Food Cost

The food and drink that are ultimately served to the guest are the raw materials of our industry. It is impossible to overemphasize how important it is for you to be aware of what food and drink actually cost, and to take steps to maximize the use of these raw materials. You must make a great effort to squeeze the most out of every product that passes through the door into your kitchen, all the while keeping your quality standards intact.

Controlling spoilage and waste is one of the first lines of defense. Many of the materials you work with are perishable. Having adequate space to store foods properly is imperative. Refrigerators, walk-ins, reach-ins, freezers, and dry storage should be carefully maintained and monitored. Insist that foods be labeled, dated, and used in sequence (first in, first out).

Another area that deserves attention is trim loss. Whenever foods are cut, trimmed, and cleaned, there is a possibility that you can lose money through carelessness or mishandling. The cost of the food when it is received is referred to as the *as purchased* or AP cost. Once it is properly processed, prior to cooking, you can determine its *edible portion* or EP cost. Once all of the trim has been removed, the food is measured again, and the resulting EP weight is divided by the AP cost in order to determine how much the food you serve your guests is actually costing you.

To cut down on trim loss, be sure that your kitchen staff is trained properly. If you can use the ends of the red pepper to make a coulis, then let the person who does the advance preparation of peppers know how to process every bit of the pepper, including where to store the usable trim so that it can be retrieved and used in a timely fashion.

Portion control is another area that deserves special vigilance. When hamburgers are made up into patties, check to see that portion scales are used consistently. Spot-check portion sizes periodically, and let the line cooks see what the correct portion of sauce, salad, and other side dishes and entrees should look like on your plates. Having portioning tools available during preparation as well as on the line helps reduce waste by a significant amount.

Keeping food costs in line is your responsibility. You can only be effective at this job if you are constantly aware of what food and beverage costs are, and how to maximize each dollar you spend. You should know what yield you can expect from particular foods, from fish to foie gras. Then, you will be able to tell quickly if you are experiencing undue losses, and where that loss is occurring.

Recipes as Tools

We often think of recipes as performing one function—telling someone the steps in preparing a dish. That is one of the prime purposes of a recipe of course. For a restaurant, recipes have an equally important role in helping to control costs, ensure consistency, and maintain quality standards.

Recipes need to be carefully written so that everyone can prepare the dish correctly from start to finish. They should be revised whenever you make a modification. The measurements need to be very accurate, so that there is as little loss as possible during production. Check the yields and measurements periodically to be sure that you are getting what you expect from a recipe. Check, too, that both you and any other line cooks involved in food preparation haven't strayed too far from the recipe.

In many establishments, proper procedures for maintaining wholesomeness and safety are also identified, along with methods for monitoring proper food handling. Recipes written in a HACCP model (see Chapter 2 for more information) clearly identify "critical control points" and correct

cooking, holding, and service temperatures. Careful handling at all phases of production is important, not only to insure that your customers don't suffer from foodborne illness at your hands. It also increases the life of foods that might otherwise become part of the "loss" column when you do the books at the end of the day.

Portion Control

Cutting down on losses by monitoring waste during advance preparation and cooking is important. Equally important is establishing the appropriate portion size of all the items you serve your guests. This includes large and small items alike. An ounce or two extra on the steak, a spoonful of extra sauce, even the three or four too many croutons on a salad, can, by the end of the year, add up to a significant drain on your profits.

Once standard portion sizes for foods have been established, it is important that this information be passed along to anyone who plates the food. So, if soups are handled by the waitstaff, your salads are prepared and plated in one part of the kitchen, and desserts in another, all of these stations need to be informed about what is considered an acceptable portion. This important point needs to be constantly monitored and reinforced. It has a bearing on more than just the bottom line. It also can have a very direct influence on how customers perceive the dining experience. If a steak or ice cream sundae is consistently the same in both quality and quantity, that speaks volumes about the care and concern that is promoted in all aspects of the operation.

Menu Pricing

Once you have calculated the true food cost and determined the correct serving or portion size for a menu item, your next task is establishing a menu price. A variety of methods may be used. You will need to assess your market, the cost of food you serve, and the type of establishment you operate.

All three of these factors will play an important part in deciding the final menu price. For instance, some restaurants will keep their menu prices relatively low and rely upon volume to make a profit. Others will use a higher markup, making their menu prices relatively higher, but requiring a lower sales volume to make a profit.

There are several different methods used for menu pricing. Three of them will be discussed here. Remember that no matter which method you actually use, the price you charge for a menu item should cover not only the cost of food and the labor of those preparing and serving the food, but also any and all additional operating expenses, such as rent, utilities, and advertising.

1. *Factor method.* The factor method reflects the idea that the cost of the food sold should fall within a range that is equal to a specified percentage of the sales in dollars.

To use this method, you must first determine the raw cost of food using your standardized recipes. Then, you need to decide what an acceptable food-cost percentage is for your operation. If you select, for example, a food-cost percentage of 25 percent of the total sales, you can calculate your factor as follows:

Divide the desired percentage, 25 percent, into 100. The resulting number, 4, is the "factor" you would use to multiply the food cost in order to arrive at the selling price.

So, if the raw food cost for a serving prepared according to a standardized recipe is $2.50, you multiply by 4 to arrive at a menu price of $10.

There are some advantages to this method, such as its relative simplicity. But, there are also some serious disadvantages as well. Your calculated profit may not match your actual profit, since many operating costs won't be deducted from the profit until the end of the month, when costs other than food, can be calculated.

2. *Prime cost.* This pricing method is more complex than the factor method and, if done exactly as specified according to its definition, might be an extremely complex and time-consuming process. Most managers that use this particular strategy will modify the method slightly. They make a few initial assumptions, based on a good understanding of the total operating costs for their restaurant. Percentages of the prime cost are assigned to cover raw-food, direct-labor, and operating costs.

Once these percentages are established as standards, you need only use raw-food cost and cost of labor for food preparation to determine a menu price.

3. *Actual cost.* If you have accurate records on hand, this method can be used to determine menu prices as follows: First, you need to determine as accurately as possible the actual cost of the raw ingredients, using your standardized recipes. You would also use payroll records or other sources to determine the actual cost of labor involved in food preparation. Finally, you will determine the cost of all of the other fixed and variable expenses involved in operating the restaurant. All of these costs are assigned a percentage of the actual sales. Use the percentages to determine what the dollars-and-cents value for these items ought to be, so that you will have actual figures to work with.

Then you determine your menu price by adding together actual food cost, actual labor cost, other variable costs, other fixed costs, and an amount for your profit. The sum is the menu price.

Menu pricing is a complex process and there are a number of books that can assist in determining which method is appropriate to an operation and how to use the chosen method. Such books include *The Restaurant Operator's Manual* by Allen Z. Reich (1990, Van Nostrand Reinhold), *Foodservice Organizations* by Marion C. Spears (1994, Macmillan), and *The Business Chef* by Tom Miner (1989, Van Nostrand Reinhold). Also refer to the resources listed in the Recommended Readings.

Cost of Errors

One area that many chefs tend to overlook is the cost of mistakes. This can have a great impact on your profit. Say, for example, that a steak is overcooked and returned by the guest. Not only are you losing the cost of the food that must be discarded, you are also losing the time spent in preparing the food, including any advance work done during the day as well as the time lost by the chef and waiter during service. If you "comp" a dessert or after-dinner drink, you are also losing that food and labor cost. You may also be losing return business, and cutting into potential new customers who won't come on the basis of a negative review.

In a similar vein, overportioning should be considered an error. If you are giving away an extra

FIGURE 1-4 A Management Training Session

ounce or two of salmon on each plate, at the end of the month, the loss will tally up to quite an impressive figure. Inaccurate or inconsistent portioning will have the same effect, compounded by the fact that repeat customers will notice the swings in portion sizes, and may decide to take their business elsewhere.

If this happens only once in a great while, the damage to your overall business is not going to be too substantial. If it happens consistently, however, the actual cost can be staggering.

Managing Information

It often seems that there is so much information available that you can never keep current in all the important areas of your work. And, at our current rate of growth in the sheer volume of information being generated each day, you are probably right. The ability to tap into the information resources you need, as well as the ability to use information gathering tools, has never been more important.

Restaurants, menus, and trends in dining room design have all been dramatically impacted by such societal trends as an interest in nutrition, Mediterranean, and other traditional diets. There are also a number of influences that may not seem, at first glance, to have much to do with restaurants and food. Yet, the prevailing tastes in politics, art, fashion, movies, and music also have no small effect.

Gathering all of the information you need to successfully operate your business is a full-time task. You need to learn ways to manage both gathering and processing tasks so that information becomes a useful tool, rather than a staggering burden.

Computers as Kitchen Tools

Unlike other labor-saving devices, such as food processors, one of the most useful tools to show up in the kitchen in recent years has no direct interaction with the food itself. The computer, however, is almost as essential today as a stove to allow a chef to operate successfully. Chefs are using them for everything from tracking inventory to submitting purchase orders to purveyors. Given a computer's many advantages to a foodservice operation, computer literacy is now a vital part of every chef's education.

Selecting the appropriate computer system and software is extremely important. You should spend some time doing research and trying out a variety of systems to find one that is most suited to your needs. Systems are available that can act as a database for recipes, create menus for special events, track salaries, or be a watchdog to help avoid loss through spoilage, pilferage, or inaccuracy in writing checks.

Computers are one of the best ways to gather, store, process, and retrieve all sorts of information about virtually every phase of your operation. One of the most basic computer functions is to assist in maintaining accurate business records: bookkeeping, inventory, costing, reservations, customer lists, staff schedules, and budget information.

Recipes are one of the ways that you can keep your kitchen operating in a smooth, cost-efficient manner. If you create standardized recipes using the appropriate software, you can manipulate your recipe database as often as you need to with ease. You can, of course, store and retrieve recipes easily. Most programs will also allow you to scale them to the correct yield. Nutritional analysis can also be performed with some programs. You may even be able to link recipe information to be used in calculating costs or maintaining purchase orders and a current inventory.

Interactive software, CD-ROM, and other computer applications are being used throughout the country, permitting chefs wider and easier access to information of all sorts. Networking and information gathering are the two other important ways in which computers can help you to work more efficiently. Updates to FDA regulations regarding safe food handling practices, information about product availability on a local, national, and worldwide scale, and answers to questions are available to you 24 hours a day through on-line services, forums, bulletin boards, and databases. You can give yourself a perceptible edge in your business when you exploit the potential of your computer.

The Media

Newspapers, magazines, newsletters, journals, and books about food have become a major part of the newsstands and bookstores throughout the world. Even those publications that are not directly aimed at you as a professional may offer some special insight, recipe, tip, or news item that you can turn to your use. For more information, review the recommended Reading List at the end of this book.

Professional Organizations

There are professional organizations in this industry that you will want to join. An affiliation with a national or international group, such as the American Culinary Federation (AFC) or National Restaurant Association (NRA), or with more special-interest and locally-run groups (National Association of Catering Executives (NACE) or Culinary Historians of New York, for example) is one way to reap the benefits that only such a group can offer. Not only do they have various memberships services, they are also one of the best sources of job opportunities, pending legislation that might affect you, and other types of "insider" information.

Managing Human Resources

Restaurant operations rely directly on the work and dedication of a number of people, from executives and administrators to line cooks to waitstaff and maintenance and cleaning staff. No matter how large or small your staff may be, the ability to engage all your workers in a team effort is one of the major factors in determining whether you will succeed or not.

Your goal should be creating an environment in which everyone feels that they have a distinct and measurable contribution to make within the organization. Knowing how they can work within the team and how their efforts will be part of the bottom line makes it much easier to understand and accept organizational policies that might otherwise seem to have little to do with an individual's needs or wants.

The first task for a good manager is to establish clear criteria, otherwise known as a job description. Having created that description, it is a far easier task to recruit employees and get them oriented and trained.

Training is another key component. If you want someone to do a job well, you have to first show them exactly what the quality standards are that you expect to see. You need to continually reinforce those standards with clear, objective evaluation of an employee's work through feedback, constructive criticism and, when necessary, additional training or disciplinary measures.

The classic brigade systems, used in both the kitchen and dining room have clearly defined jobs. These systems provide a good place to begin the work of writing job descriptions.

The Kitchen Brigade System

The "brigade system" was instituted by Escoffier to streamline and simplify work in hotel kitchens. It served to eliminate the chaos and duplication of effort that could result when workers did not have clearcut responsibilities. Under this system, each position has a station and defined tasks, as outlined below. In smaller operations, the classic system is generally abbreviated and responsibilities are organized so as to make the best use of work space and talents. A shortage of skilled personnel also has made modifications in the brigade system necessary. The introduction of new equipment has helped to alleviate some of the problems of smaller kitchen staffs.

The *chef* (chief) is responsible for all kitchen operations, including ordering, supervision of all stations, and development of menu items. He or she may be known also as *"chef de cuisine"* or executive chef.

The *sous* ("under") *chef* is second in command, answers to the chef, may be responsible for scheduling, fills in for the chef, and assists the station chefs (or line cooks) as necessary. Small operations may not have a sous chef.

Station chefs *(chefs de partie)* are considered "line cooks" and include the following:

The sauté station *(saucier)* is responsible for all sautéed items and their sauces. This position is often considered the most demanding, responsible, and glamorous on the line.

The fish station *(poissonier)* is responsible for fish items, often including fish butchering, and their sauces; this position is sometimes combined with the *saucier* position.

The roast station *(rôtisseur)* is responsible for all roasted foods and related jus or other sauces.

The grill station *(grillardin)* is responsible for all grilled foods; this position may be combined with *rôtisseur.*

The fry station *(friturier)* is responsible for all fried foods; this position may also be combined with *rôtisseur.*

The vegetable station *(entremetier)* is responsible for hot appetizers, and frequently has responsibility for soups and vegetables, starches and pastas. (In a full, traditional brigade system, soups are prepared by the soup station or *potager,* vegetables by the *legumier.)* This station may also be responsible for egg dishes.

The roundsman *(tournant)* is also known as the swing cook. This individual works as needed throughout the kitchen.

The pantry chef *(garde-manger)* is responsible for cold food preparations, including salads, cold appetizers, and pâtés. This is considered a separate category of kitchen work.

The butcher *(boucher)* is responsible for butchering meats, poultry, and (occasionally) fish. The butcher may also be responsible for breading meat and fish items, and is often considered part of *garde-manger.*

The pastry chef *(pâtissier)* is responsible for baked items, pastries, and desserts. The pastry chef frequently supervises a separate kitchen area or a separate shop in larger operations. This position may be further broken down into the following areas of specialization: *confiseur* (prepares candies, petits fours), *boulanger* (prepares nonsweetened doughs as for breads and rolls), *glacier* (prepares frozen and cold desserts), and *decorateur* (prepares show pieces and special cakes).

There are other brigade positions: The expediter or announcer *(aboyeur)* accepts orders from the dining room and relays them to the various station chefs. This individual is the last person to see the plate before it leaves the kitchen. In some operations, this may be either the sous chef or kitchen steward. The *communard* cooks for the staff; the *commis,* or assistant, works under a *chef de partie* to learn the station and its responsibilities.

The Dining Room Brigade System

The other "traditional" type of foodservice industry positions are classified under the term "front of the house." The traditional line of authority in a dining room is as follows:

The *maître d'hôtel,* known in American service as the dining room manager, host, or hostess, is the person who holds the most responsibility for the front-of-the-house operation. The *maître d'hôtel* trains all service personnel, oversees wine selection, works with the chef to determine the menu, and organizes seating throughout service.

The wine steward *(chef de vin,* or *sommelier)* is responsible for all aspects of restaurant wine service, including purchasing wines, preparing a wine list, assisting guests in wine selection, and serving wine properly. If there is no wine steward, these responsibilities are generally assumed by the *maître d'hôtel.*

The head waiter *(chef de salle)* is generally in charge of the service for an entire dining room. Very often this position is subsumed into the positions of either the captain or the *maître d'hôtel.*

The captain *(chef d'étage)* deals most directly with the guests once they are seated. The captain explains the menu, answers any questions, and takes the order. Any tableside food preparation is generally done by the captain. If there is no captain, these responsibilities fall to the front waiter.

The front waiter *(chef de rang)* assures that the table is properly set for each course, that the food is properly delivered to the table, and that the needs of the guests are promptly and courteously met.

The back waiter or busboy *(demi-chef de rang* or *commis de rang)* is normally the first position assigned to new dining room workers. This person clears plates between courses, fills water glasses and bread baskets, replaces ashtrays, and assists the front waiter and/or captain as needed.

Legal Responsibilities for Managers

Everyone has the right to work in an environment that is free from physical hazards. This means that as an employer you must provide a work space that is well lit, properly ventilated, and free from obvious dangers, such as improperly maintained equipment. Employees must have access to potable water and bathroom facilities. Beyond these bare minimum requirements, you may offer a locker room, a laundry facility that provides clean uniforms, aprons, and side towels or other such amenities.

Workers compensation, unemployment and disability insurance is also your responsibility. You are required to make all legal deductions from an employee's paycheck and to report all earnings properly to state and federal agencies. Liability insurance (to cover any harm to your facility, employees, or guests) must be kept up-to-date and at adequate levels.

Your workers may require additional forms of assistance, which you may be able to offer as part of an employee benefits package. Life insurance, medical and dental insurance, assistance with such things as dependent care, family leave, adult literacy training, enrollment in and support for those enrolled in substance abuse programs are all items of which you need to be aware. You may have a legal responsibility in some cases. The responsibility may be ethical but not legal in others.

This industry is notorious for its problems with illegal aliens. You need to be familiar with the regulations that could affect you or those you employ.

Managing Time

It seems that, no matter how hard you work or how much planning you do, the days aren't long enough. Learning new skills to be as efficient and competitive as possible ought to be an ongoing part of your education. The more time you can save using any of the following strategies, the greater your potential for profit can be.

If you look over your restaurant, you will most likely see that there are some key areas where time is wasted. The top five time wasters, in most operations, can be categorized as:

- no clear priorities for tasks

- poor, inadequate, or nonexistent training standards for staff

- poor communication

- poor organization

- missing or inadequate tools to accomplish tasks

To combat these time wasters, use the following strategies:

Invest Time in Reviewing Daily Operations   Consider the way you, your coworkers, and staff spend the day. Does everyone have a basic understanding of which tasks are most important? Do they know when to begin a particular task in order to bring it to completion on time?

It can be an eye-opening experience to take a hard look at where the work day goes. Once you see that you and your staff need to walk too far to gather basic items, or that the dishwasher is sitting idle for the first two hours of the shift, you can take steps to rectify this.

You can try to reorganize storage space (see below for more about organization). You may decide to train the dishwasher to do some prep work or you can rewrite the schedule so the shift begins two hours later. Until you are objective about what needs to be done, in what order, you can't begin the process of saving time.

Invest Time in Training Others   Assigning work to others is one area where managers often tend to waste time, both theirs and their staffs. If you expect someone to do a job properly, take enough time to explain the task carefully. Let the person who will be receiving orders know what you expect: where items should be stored, how to handle and process invoice slips, and where packing boxes go for recycling, for example. Walk yourself and your staff through the jobs that must be done, and make sure that everyone understands how to do the work, where the tools they need can be found, how far their responsibility extends, and what to do in case a question or emergency crops up. Give them the yardsticks they need to evaluate the job and determine if they have done what was requested, in the appropriate fashion, and on time. If you don't invest this time up front, you may find yourself squandering precious time following your workers around, picking up the slack, and handling work that shouldn't be taking up your day.

Learn to Communicate Clearly Whether you are training a new employee, introducing a new menu item, or ordering a piece of equipment, clear communication is important. Be specific, use the most concise language you can, and be as brief as possible, without leaving out necessary information.

If some tasks are handled by a number of different people, be sure to write that task out, from the first step to the last. Encourage people to ask you questions if they don't seem to understand you. You may find that your terminology isn't the same as theirs, or that a phrase you find succinct someone else finds baffling.

Spoken, written, and nonverbal communication is fundamental to all you do throughout the day. If you need help learning communication skills, consider taking a workshop or seminar to strengthen any weak areas.

Take Steps to Create an Orderly Work Environment If you have to dig through five shelves to find the lid to the storage container you just put the stock in, you haven't been using your time wisely. Planning work areas carefully, thinking about all the tools, ingredients, and equipment you need for preparation and throughout service, and grouping like activities together are all techniques that can help you better organize your work.

Schedules are another effective and time-honored means of achieving organization. If this is Thursday, you must plan your meat order to be phoned in on Friday. If this is January, you know that you need to get your fryolater serviced and the fire extinguishers inspected.

Purchase, Replace, and Maintain All Necessary Tools A well-equipped kitchen will have enough of all the tools necessary to prepare every item on the menu. If you are missing something as basic as a sieve, your cream soups won't have the right consistency. If you put pizza on the menu and don't have enough oven space, will pizza orders start to crowd out other baked and roasted items on your menu? If you have a menu with several sautéed appetizers, entrees, and side dishes, are you and your line cooks cooling your heels while the pot washer scrambles to get you restocked with sauté pans? If you can't purchase new equipment, then think about restructuring your menu to even out the workload. If you can't remove a menu item, then invest in the tools you need to prevent a slow-up during service.

Poor placement of large and small tools is a great time waster. Use adequate, easy-to-access storage space for common items like whips, spoons, ladles, and tongs. Electrical outlets for small equipment such as food processors ought to be within reach of everyone who works in your kitchen. While you may be forced to work within the limits of your existing equipment and floor plan, be on the lookout for products or techniques that can turn a bad arrangement into one that works smoothly and evenly.

Marketing

There may have been a time when restaurants were not actively concerned with courting and cultivating a market. In today's climate, however, a restaurant chef who is ignorant of the problems of marketing is willfully ignoring an area that can make or break a business.

When you develop your organization's mission statement, you need to make it clear who you think is likely to come to your restaurant. To a large extent, your answer may lie in your geographic location. If you are in a busy downtown area where business and government offices are located, then you are talking about one subset of the city's population. If you are in a resort location, it is another group altogether. Your mission and your market need to line up. If they don't, you need to go back to the drawing board.

Just as menu development is not a single-stage operation, or one can be done only once at a very particular point in an operation's life, a marketing plan is also something that should be part of the review and analysis of virtually every day's business. It should be looked at carefully, so that elements that are working well get reinforced, and those that are less successful are modified. It is an ongoing challenge—one that you need to stay fully aware of, even if it is not your primary charge.

Defining the Customer Base

If you haven't opened your doors yet, then you should at least know who you would like to come through the door. If you are in business already, then it is clear who is coming to your restaurant. But, there may be other, wider markets you think you could tap. How do you find out what will appeal to your intended market? Having gotten that far, how do you determine what will sway someone to choose you over the other restaurants within reach of your potential guest?

There are numerous marketing strategies, and, as with virtually every area we have touched on throughout this chapter, it is a good idea to arm yourself with additional information. Beyond the broad definitions and overviews we can offer here, you will be ahead of the game if you keep up with current journals, publications, books, and on-line services that can keep you and your business out in front.

Today's clientele is a more sophisticated and widely traveled group than ever before. These consumers' "food savvy" has had a direct impact on the types of food served in restaurants, as well as what they are able to purchase in supermarkets and specialty shops. Small farms and bakeries producing specialty produce, cheeses, and breads are becoming more widely known and appreciated. The continuing demand for such foods will provide a great avenue for growth. Already it is opening doors for those who wish to participate in less "mainstream" operations, as entrepreneurs supplying restaurants and retail outlets.

The public's growing interest in grains, legumes, fish, vegetables, and fruits, along with a desire to decrease overconsumption of animal fat, protein, and sodium, have helped popularize "nutritional cooking." This has spurred fundamental changes in the preparation and presentation of traditional foods. Classic dishes from both the classical and peasant traditions are being reevaluated to reduce or eliminate fats, sodium, and cholesterol.

Going out for dinner has become a form of entertainment and the restaurant has become a "destination," not just a place to have a quick meal before moving on to another activity. Rather than spending an evening at the theater followed by supper, or a night of dancing preceded by a light dinner, lingering over dinner at a restaurant has become "the evening."

The way in which a foodservice establishment presents itself to its customers has a definite influence on whether or not the business will succeed.

The Menu as a Marketing Tool

A menu is a powerful tool. It can be a marketing and merchandising vehicle. It can establish and reinforce the total restaurant concept, from the style of china and flatware selected to the training needs for the service staff. It can assist the chef in reducing waste and increasing profits.

The way a menu is developed or adapted is a reflection of how well the total concept has been designed. Sometimes, the two evolve hand in hand. In other scenarios, the concept comes first and the menu comes later. In still others, the menu may be the guiding principle that gives a particular stamp to the way the restaurant concept evolves.

You may engage in menu development, redesign, or overhaul at any time. It is fairly certain that, whenever you turn your attention to the menu, you will need to address a number of issues. The following list of questions is not meant to be exhaustive. Each operation has special needs, and as you look over this list, you will see that this is just the jumping-off point.

- Do you have a particular cuisine or cuisines in mind? Or, do you have a different set of standards to guide you in making selections? What are they?

- What meal period is the menu geared toward?

- Is your menu seasonally driven, cycle driven, or set?

- Do you expect to have, or do you already have, signature dishes?

- Do you have both the staff and the equipment

necessary to properly serve your guests from the menu you have established?

• How large is your menu, and how does that translate into stations and staff in the kitchen, equipment needs, service needs?

• How is your menu pricing structured? Is it an *á la carte* (all items priced individually), *prix fixe* (one single price for a meal, that is all inclusive), *table d'hôte* (a single price for an entrée that includes a set number of accompanying dishes, which may or may not allow the guest some choice), or a combination of pricing strategies?

• Do you have a wine list? Does it complement your menu, both in terms of wine and food pairings as well as in pricing? Can your waitstaff use it to promote wines with foods, especially with special menu items?

• What are your portion sizes? Can you assure that they are consistently adhered to?

• Can your menu incorporate some profit-engineering techniques such as cross-utilization of foods, promotion and merchandising efforts, use of in-season items to take advantage of their low cost?

• Is your menu varied enough that regular customers will have enough selections to keep them from being bored? At the same time, are your signature dishes available consistently so that the regular customer doesn't feel cheated when his or her favorite dish is not on the menu?

• Will you have supplemental or special menus: grazing menus, light fare menus, pub menus?

• Do you have a set of menus established for special events, banquets, or catered events (Mother's Day brunch, Thanksgiving, New Year's Eve, weddings, for instance)?

• Is the descriptive language on the menu appropriate to your concept? For instance, a family-style restaurant might not be the best place to use unfamiliar Italian or French names for dishes, while a bistro could more easily incorporate a foreign language.

• Do you have a system that allows you to analyze your sales?

• How easy is it for you to cost out and price a new item?

After you have developed or refined your menu, you can clearly see that it is far more than a simple list of dishes offered to the customer. It sets the tone and style for your restaurant in a way no other single element of your business can, and it impacts directly and indirectly on virtually everything you do, from ordering linen to choosing a computer system to selecting new kitchen equipment.

This brief look at menus is meant only as an introduction to the topic and its potential value to the chef. For further information on menu development and use, refer to the resources noted in the Recommended Reading List, found at the end of the book.

Restaurant Design and Ambiance

First and foremost, a foodservice establishment should be appealing to the eye and the nose. This means keeping all visible areas clean, well lit, and well maintained. Lighting should be appropriate and adequate to allow the menu to be read easily. It should be flattering to the food and to the guest, in order to promote a pleasant feeling. Chairs should be comfortable. Tables should be sturdy and appropriately appointed with flatware and china that are suitable to both the food and to the atmosphere of the restaurant. Music may be good for some styles of operations. It should be at a level that makes it easy to hear but not so loud that it intrudes on the meal or conversation.

Other areas in the restaurant where customers are welcomed, including bathrooms, bars, or "open kitchens," need to be given the same degree of thought and care as the dining room and the tabletop.

Service

In an industry based on service, the type and quality of service offered to the guest is of ultimate importance. You should realize, however, that the definition of "quality service" can and does change from one establishment to another. In a fast-food restaurant, courtesy is important but speed is paramount. In a white tablecloth restaurant, other skills are more valuable: the ability to help a guest select an appropriate wine, to "intuit" how to pace the meal to avoid rushing the guest, and to provide as much or as little interaction as the customer appears to want.

Proper training for service staff at all levels is the only way to be sure that the caliber of service you provide is appropriate to the menu you are offering, the prices you charge, the style of the dining room, and the clientele you hope to serve. Schedule sessions to bring the kitchen and dining room staff together. Airing concerns about communication and finding solutions before tempers flare on a busy Saturday night is good for everyone.

Summary

As the chef, you must deal with a great many people every day: salespeople, waitstaff, kitchen staff, customers. In order to be successful in these dealings, you must constantly work at upholding the standards of the profession.

It is not always easy to define what makes someone a true professional. It is actually much simpler to describe it in terms of what it is not. Anyone can recognize behavior that is below the industry's acceptable standards.

Education, work experience, more education, more experience, and still more education are the cornerstones of true professionalism. Learning through daily contact with other professionals what professionalism means, and how it shows itself to coworkers and guests, will do much to elevate the chef's image both within the profession and to our guests. Carrying professionalism into all areas is your responsibility.

CHAPTER 2 : *Food and Kitchen Safety*

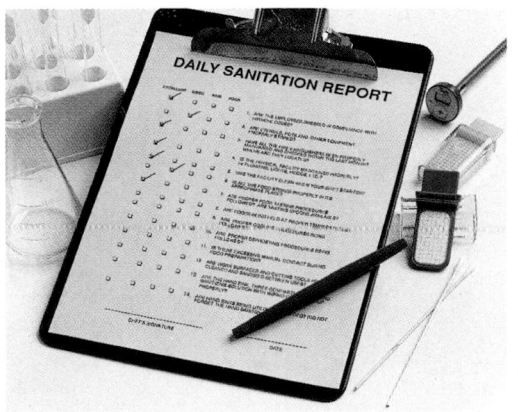

There is a belief that in the good old days, all foods were pure, unadulterated, and wholesome. With each newly reported food poisoning outbreak, fears about food safety escalate. This is of enormous concern to the entire foodservice industry. Over three-quarters of all foodborne diseases reported to the Centers for Disease Control in Atlanta can be traced to improper food handling in restaurants. This number overshadows all other sources of foodborne disease. Around 20 percent of foodborne diseases are due to improper cooking and handling of foods in the home, and the other cases, less than 5 percent of the total, can be attributed to food processing and handling plants.

Improved methods of food processing and handling procedures, as well as enhanced inspection practices have helped to reduce the total number of officially reported outbreaks of foodborne illnesses. At the same time, it should be noted that the new processing technologies (aseptic packaging, vacuum-packed foods, and foods prepared by a cook/chill process) may have created a number of new problem areas.

Chefs working together with health officials have developed their own standards, aimed at improving the quality and safety of the foods prepared and served to the public. Additional information to help chefs set and meet high standards for health, sanitation, and safety in the kitchen can be found in Appendix 2.

This chapter will look at three important facets of maintaining a working environment that helps promote food and worker safety in a commercial kitchen: food safety, running a clean kitchen and dining room to reduce the risk of foodborne illnesses, and worker safety. All three areas are so firmly intertwined that, as you will see, keeping standards high in one area will automatically upgrade the others.

Safe Foods

A brief survey of food writers from ancient times to the most contemporary food writer will quickly assure you that the problem of adulterated or otherwise "unclean" foods is as old as recorded history. As T. Braun writes in "Ancient Mediterranean Food" (*The Mediterranean Diets in Health and Disease*): "It is not a modern failing to adulterate food with chemicals. What is modern is adequate consumer protection." A big part of that adequate consumer protection is a news reporting system that transmits stories of food poisoning outbreaks rapidly and widely.

Yesterday's worries about alar on apples has become today's concern about genetically engineered foods and irradiation. Stories in magazines, newspapers, and television stress the fact that more and more foods are likely to be contaminated with *E. coli* bacteria, the same bacteria responsible for the 1993 deaths of three toddlers in the Northwest, all of whom had eaten contaminated ground beef.

Still other stories detail parasites or viruses found in fish harvested from polluted waters. Herbicides and pesticides banned from use in the United States are found in high concentrations in the produce we import from countries that do not have the same standards.

There is enough information given to frighten and even anger consumers, but often not enough to really understand the issue or the ways in which it can be addressed. It is your responsibility, then, to learn what you can about these questions, and to take the appropriate action. That is the only way you can make sure that your guests will feel confident dining in your restaurant. As anyone involved with the disastrous Jack-in-the-Box incident can tell you, recovery from an official outbreak of foodborne poisoning that originated in your restaurant is painfully slow, if it comes at all.

A Safe Food Supply

One of the major concerns today regarding foods is that they have become tainted with life-threatening substances. Current agricultural practices do tend to rely heavily on fertilizers, feeds, pesticides, and herbicides made from a variety of chemicals, antibiotics, and hormone supplements. The argument is made that, without the aid of these technological advances, our world food supply would fall dramatically short of current needs. Since alternatives to the current growing methods are not yet widely practiced, organically grown foods or those with minimal amounts of chemicals remain hard to find and expensive.

Once foods are ready to be harvested or butchered, the potential for contamination is certainly not lessened. Food-processing plants are inspected by agents of the Food and Drug Administration. The foods themselves may undergo testing to determine wholesomeness—meats, dairy products, and all processed/prepared foods are supposed to be tested regularly.

Whether or not these tests are adequate is a subject of debate. The sheer volume of food produced in this country and imported into the country is overwhelming. Logic would indicate that there is a limit to the number of trained inspectors available, as well as to the quantity of food they can physically inspect. In addition, inspection standards first established near the turn of the century were not designed to cope with modern issues. Revisions to food safety codes have begun to address these issues. Updated codes from federal, state, and local agencies are being issued in response to current needs.

We are still unsure what, if any, long-term effects there might be with regard to such techniques as irradiation and biologically or genetically engineered foods. Other foods do not yet have established safety standards or inspection procedures. However, most food processors are using Hazard Analysis Critical Control Point (HACCP) systems to identify when foods are most at risk, and what can be done to eliminate food hazards throughout the processing operation.

While there is a sense of urgency about maintaining safe foods and offering adequate protection to the consumer, the process of making changes or establishing new systems is slow. It remains to be seen how consumers will react to a tomato that has had a gene spliced into it to promote longer vine ripening combined with sufficient firmness to withstand the rigors of shipping.

It is clear, then, that simply trying to buy foods from reputable purveyors is not always going to be enough. You may even begin to wonder if it is possible to find foods that are "safe." As a chef, you need to make a choice about food purchasing practices based on an understanding of the quality of the food purchased, the reliability of the purveyors used, and the degree of commitment to sustainable and organic agriculture the business can afford.

Types of Foodborne Diseases

Nearly everyone has had a brush with food poisoning. The culprit might be a bacteria, a virus, a yeast or mold, or a parasite. The symptoms vary, but typically include that unholy quartet: vomiting or nausea, diarrhea, fever, and cramps. Not a pretty picture, and certainly not something you would like to be responsible for inflicting on one of your most valuable commodities: the guest.

Each pathogen will produce a particular set of symptoms, with the actual onset of the disease occurring anywhere from within an hour or two up to several days after eating contaminated foods. This may mean that you are being unfairly blamed for someone else's poor kitchen safety. It may also mean that a guest that contracted the illness at your restaurant will not necessarily be able to identify the ultimate culprit. They may even write it off to a "bug" that they picked up from some other source.

Some of the more common diseases include the following:

Salmonellosis is caused by eating foods contaminated with the salmonella bacteria. Common culprits include undercooked poultry, eggs, mayonnaise, milk, soft cheese, even unrefrigerated sliced fruits such as melons. Laboratory studies have shown that chickens and eggs may harbor salmonella on their skin or shells. Even "free-range" and "organically grown" birds appear to have as good a chance of being contaminated as those raised in large factory-style operations. Scrupulous attention to personal hygiene, the religious use of sanitizing solutions to swab work surfaces and cutting equipment, and proper cooking are the best ways to combat this most common of all foodborne diseases.

Trichinosis is the disease brought on by eating infected pork products. Proper cooking to an internal temperature of at least 155°F (68°C) according to the latest Food and Drug Administration (FDA) standards is the only way to be sure that any existing parasites have been killed.

Botulism is another foodborne disease that is

FIGURE 2-1 Flat of Eggs

FIGURE 2-2 Stuffings are Thoroughly Chilled Before Adding to Meats

well fixed in the public mind. Typically caused by consuming improperly canned or jarred foods, it is of great concern to the foodservice industry. Discard any bulging or otherwise "mysterious" cans or jars. Avoid storing foods in their original jars or cans. There are also advisories against leaving oils infused with garlic and shallots at room temperature for long periods of time.

Toxic poisoning from eating mushrooms is an issue of concern as well. Learn to identify the wild mushrooms that you typically use, and purchase them from reputable purveyors. No matter what, don't accept a basket of mushrooms that were harvested by an amateur forager. While some mushrooms only cause minor discomfort, others can kill the unlucky guest who has one bite too many.

There are other diseases that are contracted by eating infected foods. For a more complete list, along with a description of their likely sources, symptoms, and appropriate preventative measures, refer to the table in Appendix 2.

The majority of foodborne illnesses can be traced to biological sources, particularly specific bacteria. As we look at the types of foodborne illnesses, remember that, usually, this danger can be

eliminated by making sure that bacteria are not introduced to foods through careless handling or cross-contamination. In addition, those foods, such as eggs in the shell or raw chicken, which may arrive at your establishment carrying a particular bacteria, should be properly handled so that bacteria is not able to become so well established that it can cause illness. This is accomplished primarily through temperature control and strict adherence to safe food-handling guidelines.

Reducing the Risk of Foodborne Illness

A professional chef needs to have a thorough understanding of how to operate a kitchen safely. Certification programs are available throughout the country, and it is strongly recommended that at least one member of the kitchen staff have certification.

The United States Food and Drug Administration (USFDA) has prepared a Food Code that is intended to act as a model for the prevention of foodborne disease. Local and state health departments may have other regulations and requirements intended to meet the particular needs of a given location. Be sure to check with local health authorities about any permits, inspections, or certifications that might be necessary for your restaurant.

A certificate, by itself, is no guarantee that a commercial kitchen is preparing foods that are safe and wholesome. The real issue is consistent, day-to-day application of the standards and guidelines for keeping foods as safe and clean as possible. A good knowledge of how it is that foods can be the carriers of disease offers the chef the battle plan for preventing such outbreaks.

Chemical Contamination in the Kitchen

We have already looked at one source of contamination, the *chemical contamination* that occurs when foods are treated with such things as man-made fertilizers, pesticides, herbicides, antibiotics, steroids, and hormones. Chemical contamination can also occur in the kitchen. Accidental or inten-

FIGURE 2-3 Potentially Hazardous Foods—Poultry, Eggs, Custard, Rice, Potatoes, and Melon

tional contact with other substances, such as cleaning compounds or copper in a scratched saucepan may be the culprit at fault when there is chemical contamination. If these compounds are present in foods in significant amount, they will cause chemical poisoning. The onset of symptoms may take from minutes to hours. Be sure that all copper pans are well lined, that storage containers are made of approved materials (e.g., food-grade plastics, glass, or stainless steel), that all cleaning compounds that might contain toxic materials are stored well away from foods, and that foods are not allowed to come in contact with pesticides or disinfectants at any time.

Physical Contamination in the Kitchen

Physical contaminants include any of the wide array of items that might be accidentally left in foods. Sometimes this occurs during harvesting or butchering. It is equally likely to occur in the kitchen. Bits of plastic wrap, dirt, hairs, bandages, fingernails, glass or wood splinters, even whole insects are all examples. While these contaminants can cause disease (if nothing more, revulsion could cause someone to feel nauseated), the most obvious danger is causing injury. If someone unwittingly eats a bit of shell or a shard of crockery, the gastrointestinal tract could be lacerated, or

worse. Swallowing a bit of broken glass or biting down on a piece of metal might cause a wound, a lost filling, or a broken tooth.

The government has established standards known as GRAS ("generally recognized as safe"). These guidelines, while they might elicit some unhappy reactions from consumers, are a concession to the way in which foods are handled. A certain level of physical contamination is consider reasonable and accepted. The restaurant's staff should be aware, however, that even if the government considers several parts per million of rodent hair to be an acceptable quantity of contamination, the guest who finds even one eyelash sprinkled on the soup will be hard to mollify.

Biological Contamination

The majority of foodborne illnesses are caused by *biological contamination*. Sometimes molds are responsible. A classic example is ergot, which attacks rye and can cause hallucinations and convulsions. Viruses, such as hepatitis, can also be transmitted through foods. Parasites, such as the one responsible for trichinosis, are also found in foods. However, far more foodborne illnesses are caused by a wide range of bacteria.

Throughout the next section, we will look at the types of foods likely to carry a foodborne disease, the way in which they can become contaminate, and steps that can be taken to prevent contamination from taking hold. Many of the same procedures that help to keep bacterial contamination at bay are those required to inactivate viruses and parasites as well.

Potentially Hazardous Foods

The first line of defense is knowledge about why it is that some foods are likely to be culprits in a case of food poisoning and others are not.

When we think about the types of illnesses a customer might contract in a restaurant, terms like salmonella, trichinosis, botulism, and hepatitis come to mind. Some foods are more likely to act as good carriers for these types of disease. These foods are referred to as *potentially* hazardous *foods.*

All foods are teeming with a variety of microorganisms. Some are harmless to humans, others are beneficial, and some, known as pathogens, can cause humans to become ill when they are found in sufficient quantity in foods, or are ingested by someone whose natural defenses are unable to combat them even in much smaller quantities. Unless pathogens find an environment that will encourage them to grow and reproduce, however, they cannot make anyone sick.

The Three Requirements of Pathogens

Pathogens thrive when three basic living conditions are readily available: protein, water, and appropriate pH. A large percentage of foods typically contain these three elements in ratios favorable to the rapid growth of pathogens. The greater the abundance of protein and water and the more favorable the pH, the higher the likelihood that foods will become contaminated. In addition, some bacteria do best with a good supply of oxygen, others when oxygen is absent. Some can get along either way. The handling procedures noted in sections on cooling, reheating, and thawing help to prevent any single condition from becoming so predominant that it will favor the pathogen's growth and reproduction.

Protein

Most foods contain some protein. Meats, fish, poultry, and eggs are among the foods with the greatest percentage of protein, making them, and prepared foods containing them, highly susceptible to food poisoning and intoxication. But, grains and legumes also contain protein in significant quantities. They become especially vulnerable once cooked. Rice and potatoes are among the most likely carriers of disease. Vegetables contain very small amounts of protein, and fruits contain very little if any protein at all.

Water

Foods that are moist enough to be soft and easy to chew are also moist enough to support the growth of many types of pathogens. There are some foods that are naturally "dry" and have a lesser chance of becoming infected: certain root vegetables have a relatively low moisture content. Other foods, once processed, lose much of their moisture; very hard cheeses such as Romano or Parmesan cheeses; dried, salted, or preserved foods such as olives and hams; nuts and seeds, and uncooked grains, cereals, and meals. These are the foods that we treat as "nonperishables," a recognition of the fact that they can be stored at room temperature without fear of immediate loss of quality or wholesomeness.

Moderate pH

The pH of most foods falls within a range considered "moderate"; a state that makes foods attractive for the growth and reproduction of many different types of microorganisms. A substance that is extremely acid (e.g., lemon juice) will be closer to a value of zero. Those that are extremely alkaline (e.g., baking soda) will measure closer to 14.

Most foods tend to fall within a range of about 4 to 10. Foods that are either more acidic or more alkaline than that will generally no longer be susceptible to microorganisms. Vinegar, lemon or lime juice, and other very tart and sour-tasting foods are acid; baking soda, alum, cream of tartar are bitter-tasting and cause the mouth to pucker, these items are alkaline. We use this general principle to preserve foods when we pickle, salt, or brine them in order to change their pH level to above 10 or below 4, increasing the shelf life of the food.

The Danger Zone

There are two other variables that can affect the overall freedom from harmful levels of pathogens: time and temperature. The disease-causing microorganisms found in food need to be present in significant quantities in order to make someone ill. Once pathogens have established themselves in a food source, they will either thrive or be destroyed, depending upon how time and temperature are manipulated.

Temperature

There are pathogens that can live at all temperature ranges. For most of those capable of causing foodborne illness, however, the most friendly environment provides temperatures within a range of 40 to 140°F (4 to 60°C). They are usually destroyed at temperatures above 140°F. Storage at temperatures below 40°F will destroy some pathogens; the cycle of growth and reproduction will be slowed or interrupted in others.

Time

When conditions are favorable, pathogens can grow and reproduce at an astonishing rate. There are four distinct stages of bacterial growth. The first is the *lag phase,* during which newly introduced bacteria become adjusted to their environment.

During the *accelerated growth phase,* the bacteria reproduce rapidly. Bacteria reproduce asexually; as each bacterium grows, it will split into two bacteria of equal size. Under ideal circumstances, each bacterium can reproduce every 20 minutes. One bacterium could produce 72 million bacteria in just 12 hours.

The growth phase leads to the *stationary phase.* This is a plateau, during which the rate of growth and reproduction is matched by the rate of death. At this point, there is no increase in the number of bacteria. Finally, there is the *decline phase.* Now, the essential elements for life are exhausted. The death rate exceeds the growth rate.

The time during which foods remain in the danger zone is one of the most critical to the prevention of contamination through foodborne illness. The techniques outlined below are intended to shorten the total amount of time that they spend in the danger zone.

Handling Foods Safely

From the time that foods arrive at your restaurant until they are placed in front of the guest, it is important that they be carefully handled, during storage, cooking, cooling, and reheating.

Storing Foods

As soon as a shipment of food is delivered and has been properly checked in, it should be placed into storage. Three types of storage are used in most establishments: refrigerated units, freezers, and dry storage. A storage principle that effectively rotates stock of both perishable and nonperishable items helps to prevent foods from spoiling or rotting. This system is known as "First In, First Out," or FIFO. It means that any food or preparation that is newly delivered or freshly prepared goes to the back of the shelf.

Refrigeration and freezing units should be regularly maintained and equipped with thermometers to make sure that the temperature remains within a safe range. Although we have seen that chilling foods doesn't actually destroy pathogens, cold temperatures do drastically slow down reproduction. In general, refrigerators should be kept between 36 and 40°F (2 and 4°C), but food quality is better maintained if certain foods can be stored at specific temperatures:

Meat and poultry—32 to 36°F (0 to 2°C)

Fish and shellfish—30 to 34°F (–1 to 1°C)

Eggs—38 to 40°F (3 to 4°C)

Dairy products—36 to 40°F (2 to 4°C)

Produce—40 to 45°F (4 to 7°C)

Separate refrigerators for each of the above categories is ideal, but if necessary, a single unit can be divided into sections. The front of the box will be the warmest area, the back the coldest.

Reach-in or walk-in refrigerators should be wiped out and put in order at the end of every shift. Before being put in the refrigerator, food should be properly cooled, stored in clean containers, wrapped, and labeled clearly with the contents and date. Store raw products below and away from cooked foods to prevent cross-contamination by dripping. Make sure the fan is not blocked and that the doors close properly.

Freezers should be at 32°F (0°C) or below. They also should be cleaned and put in order regularly. Foods need to be very clearly labeled and a system for checking and rotating frozen goods should be maintained. Freezer burn makes foods unfit for any use. The primary cause of freezer burn is inadequate wrapping.

Dry storage is used for foods such as canned goods, spices, condiments, cereals, staples such as

FIGURE 2-4   Cooling a Hot Liquid Properly

2. Place the container in a cold water bath.

It may be difficult to find enough space to cool things properly, but even so, it must be done. Special cooling tables may be available in some larger kitchens, but failing that, a setup such as that shown in the accompanying photos should be used. An overflow pipe is ideal, allowing a constant stream of cold water to run into the sink. Or, add more ice and/or drain out the water as it warms and replace it with cold water.

3. Remember to stir the liquid as it cools.

This prevents anaerobic bacteria from gaining a foothold, and speeds the overall cooling process by equalizing the temperature.

4. Once the entire batch has been cooled to a temperature of 40°F(4°C) it may be covered and labeled with the name of the contents and the date. Should you prefer, the liquid can be transferred to plastic containers for storage purposes.

flour and sugar, as well as for some fruits and vegetables that do not require refrigeration and have low perishability. Keep this area clean and be sure that there is proper ventilation. Moisture, direct light, and heat are likely to reduce shelf life for many foods.

Foods should not be stored directly on the floor or near the walls. Provide adequate shelving to prevent crowding. All containers (including boxes and cans) should be labeled with a date. Use a separate area for cleaning supplies.

Cooling Foods Safely

Be sure that the containers you use for cooling and storing foods are properly cleaned and sanitized.

To cool liquids such as stocks, soups, and sauces:

1. Transfer to a clean container such as a stainless steel bain-marie or other container that conducts heat readily.

Metals are most effective at dispersing heat, glass is next best, and plastic is least appropriate for cooling.

The larger the quantity of liquid, the more time it will take to cool completely. If you can, try to split large batches into two or more smaller batches.

To cool very small batches of items such as custard sauce, lemon curd, or leftover stew, place the container in a large bowl or tub filled with equal quantities of ice and cold water as shown in Figure 2-5. Remember to stir the contents of the container as it cools. Stabilize the container, so that water does not splash inside and so the container will not tip over.

The greater the amount of surface exposed to the cold water bath (through the medium of a bain-marie or other container), the more quickly the liquid will cool.

To cool semi-solid or solid foods, a different approach may be required. For example, a stuffing mixture added to a chicken or used to fill a pork chop should be well chilled before it is introduced to the bird or chop. Sautéed onions, carrots, celery, and peppers should be removed from the pan, spread in a thin layer on a clean baking sheet and, placed in a refrigerator to cool quickly before combining the stuffing with other ingredients.

This same principle is used to cool cooked pasta, rice, or other items that cannot easily be stirred as

FIGURE 2-5 Cooling Custard

they cool, or would be damaged by being piled up in a large pot or bain-marie.

Large cuts of meat or other solid foods should be cut into slices or chunks, whenever possible. The idea is to reduce the diameter of the food, enabling it to cool within a safe time period (less than two hours). Place the sliced or chunked food into clean containers, and cool, uncovered, until the item is thoroughly chilled. Then, cover, label, and date properly.

Reheating Foods

Foods should be kept chilled at 40°F (4°C) or less until you are ready to reheat them. At that point, they should be heated as quickly as possible to a safe service temperature—at least 140 to 145°F (60 to 63°C). Use an instant-reading thermometer to check the food's temperature after it has been stirred.

Liquid or semi-liquid foods should be placed in clean pots and reheated over direct heat. Simply placing soups and sauces into steam table inserts is not a good method. The food will take far too long to come up to a safe serving temperature, if it ever does.

Individual portions, or small batches, can be reheated successfully in the microwave. Use the high-

est power setting you can without harming the food. If the microwave does not have a turntable, turn the food manually as it reheats. Stir soups and stews as they reheat so that the food becomes evenly hot.

Solid foods, such as roasted foods, are more difficult to reheat, especially meats that need to be at a particular doneness. Reheating them in an oven or convection oven may be the best method.

To cut back on the amount of food you must discard at the end of service, reheat batches that are only large enough to last through a meal period, or part of a meal period. This approach may seem a little more time-consuming, if you have been accustomed to filling a pot with more soup than you think you need so you are only heating it once. However, the overall savings and increased quality of your food will more than repay any nuisance you may experience.

Holding Cooked Foods at Service Temperature

Keeping foods such as sauces, soups, stews, grains, and potatoes hot during a meal period is an important concern. Not only do you want foods to be at the best possible temperature to assure your guests enjoyment, you also want them to stay safe and wholesome. Check to be sure that heat lamps, steam tables, or other holding devices are maintained properly. This includes a thorough cleaning at the end of each meal period.

Use an instant-reading thermometer to be sure that foods that have been properly heated or cooked are staying above 140°F (60°C). This needs to be done consistently throughout service. Any foods that are not at a safe temperature should be immediately brought back to within the desired range. If you cannot be certain how long they have been in the danger zone, your best option is to get rid of the food item and start over, reheating or preparing a fresh batch.

Thawing Foods

There are a number of foods purchased in a frozen state for most restaurants, including vegetables, fruits, meats, processed foods, prepared items, and more. Handling these foods properly as they thaw is of great importance in order to retain the quality of the food, as well as to avoid possible contamination.

The best way to thaw a frozen item is to remove it from the freezer to a refrigerator. It should be left in its wrapping, placed in a shallow container, and allowed to thaw, taking as much time as necessary. However, the reality is that many times you will need to speed up the process in order to meet the demands of the evening's service. When this is the case, there are two alternatives that can be employed, depending upon both the nature of the item being thawed and the amount of time available to thaw it.

First, you can place the well-wrapped item in a container and set it in a sink. Turn the cold water on and allow it to flow over the food constantly, until it is thawed. Very large items will still take a long time to thaw, but it is crucial to keep the temperature of the item below 40°F (4°C) as much as possible, both to avoid creating an environment that would favor the growth of pathogens and to prevent the loss of quality often associated with improperly thawed foods.

Or, you can place it in a microwave, using the defrost setting or lower power. This is most effective for foods that are small, thin, and relatively uniform in composition. It is not the best way to thaw meats, since the uneven thawing could destroy the tissue of the meat, causing a significant loss of flavor and moisture in the meat, once it is cooked. Foods defrosted in the microwave should be cooked immediately after they are thawed.

It is not ever a good idea to simply remove an item from the freezer and place it on a counter or anywhere else at room temperature in order to thaw it more quickly. It is also rarely advisable to cook foods from a frozen state, unless directions from the manufacturer specifically state that it is acceptable to do so (for instance, some prepared items such as frozen pastries or pizza dough can be prepared directly from a frozen state).

Hazard Analysis Critical Control Point (HACCP)

The HACCP system has been adopted both by food processors and restaurants, as well as by the FDA in

FIGURE 2-6   Fried Eggs May Be Potential Carriers of Foodbourne Illness

its latest code (1993). At this time, there are no particular mandates that HACCP inspection forms must be used by all foodservice establishments. However, instituting such a plan may prove advantageous on a variety of levels.

If you decide to begin instituting HACCP procedures in your restaurant, you should know that it does require some initial investment of time and human resources. It is becoming obvious, however, that this system can save money and time, and improve the quality of service you are able to provide your customers.

Computer systems help make many of the parts of a HACCP system easier to institute: flowcharts, standards and measures to control hazards, and tracking how and when control measures are used by you and your staff.

The heart of HACCP is the following seven principles:

1.   Assessment of hazards and risks.

2.   Determining the critical control points (CCPs).

3.   Establishing critical limits (CLs).

4. Establishing procedures for monitoring CCPs.

5. Establishing corrective action plans.

6. Establishing a system for maintaining records.

7. Developing a system to verify and record actions.

The way in which an individual operation may apply these principles will vary. Not only is it permissible to make the system fit your establishment's style, it is imperative. Chain restaurants receive and process foods differently than an à la carte restaurant.

In order to make full use of a HACCP system, you need to clearly identify where foods are most likely to be in danger of contamination, and when and where you can do something to eliminate the risk or reverse the danger.

Foods can become contaminated at many points as they travel from their point of origin to your guests. Those particular points at which food is in immediate danger of becoming a source of a food-borne disease are referred to as critical control points.

Examples of these points include any of the following situations:

• Raw foods come in contact with pathogens through exposure to contaminated cutting boards, an employee's hands, or through cross-contamination. For instance, a knife is used to cut a chicken, and then used to cut cabbage for cole slaw without cleaning and sanitizing the knife.

• Egg yolks or hamburgers are not cooked to a safe temperature, thus allowing pathogens that might have been killed at proper temperatures to survive and establish themselves in the food.

• Foods, especially those considered as potentially hazardous foods, are allowed to remain at a temperature within the danger zone for more than 3 hours.

• Foods are not cooled to below 40°F (4°C) before storing.

• Foods are stored in containers that are not properly cleaned.

As you look over the path that foods take, from the time that you receive them until they are served, you will be able to establish acceptable procedures for handling them safely. This may include a set of standards for receiving, storing, and reheating that outlines acceptable temperatures, containers, procedures for thawing, cooling and reheating, and other food-handling issues addressed in this chapter.

Maintaining High Standards of Cleanliness

Customers today want to be sure their meals are prepared in a clean kitchen, free of grease, rats, cockroaches, and flies. They want the people who handle their food to be clean, and to take enough pride and care in their work to do things the right way. The glasses, silverware, plates, and linens that are on the table also come in for careful scrutiny. The image of a fussy diner automatically wiping down his knife and fork, and sending back glasses that are spotty may get a few laughs on a situation comedy. It is not so funny if it is your restaurant.

Should word spread that your staff in the kitchen and dining room are well groomed and careful, your bathrooms are spotless, and your napery faultless, you are ahead of the game. On the contrary, charges of hair in the soup, flies in the sauce, and fingerprints all over the plate can spell failure, no matter how brilliant the menu. Somehow, this kind of informal review spreads more rapidly and means more to the potential guest than any three- or four-star critique in a newspaper or guidebook might.

Keeping the kitchen and dining room clean is important on many other levels as well. It is clear that it plays a key role in keeping foods safe. It also helps prevent many of the common accidents that can occur in the workplace, as well as the transmission of diseases that might happen from person-to-person contact.

One additional benefit of keeping standards of cleanliness high is that it sends a clear message to your guests and employees. You take pride in the restaurant and all that goes on there. You want everyone to have a safe, pleasant experience, whether they have come to dine or to work.

The Role of the Uniform

There is a standard of dress for professionals working in a kitchen that has come to be accepted by both the profession and the public. The white jacket, tall hat (known as a *toque blanche*), apron, side towel, are all part of the image. Pants (typically a houndstooth check in this country, solid black in European countries), hard shoes, and a neckerchief all are considered important elements as well. More than simply completing the "look" of the chef, these parts of the typical uniform have important roles to play in keeping workers safe as they work in what is a potentially dangerous (some might say hostile) environment.

The Hat

Escoffier wore a black beret, and Gordon Sinclair wears a baseball cap. Most chefs in this country and throughout the world have adopted a tall, chimney-like hat. The idea is to help contain the chef's hair, preventing it from falling into the food. There may be some absorption of sweat from overheated brows as well.

The Jacket and Pants

A sparkling clean jacket does more than give the chef a crisp professional look. The fact that the jacket is double-breasted means that there are two layers of cloth to protect the chest area from steam burns, splashes, and spills. Interestingly, the jacket is one item of apparel that knows no gender, since it can be buttoned on either side. In fact, you can easily rebutton your jacket to cover up any stains, should you need to appear in all your glory in the dining room or for an interview with the press.

Sleeves on chefs' jackets are long, and should be worn long, so that as much of the arm as possible is covered, again to protect against burns and splashes. The same is true of pants. Shorts, while they may seem like a good idea for such a hot environment, are inappropriate, offering no protection from hot stoves, accidental encounters with steam kettles, and splashes from sloshing pots of stock or pasta water.

The jacket and pants should be clean at the start of each shift, and kept as white as possible by proper laundering. If you do not have a linen/laundry service, be sure that you use the correct technique for washing them. Use hot water, a good detergent, and a sanitizer, such as Borax or chlorine bleach, to remove bacteria and grime.

As unlikely as it may seem, jackets can harbor bacteria, molds, parasites, even viruses that can be transferred to the food, rendering it unsafe for human consumption.

Apron and Side Towels

The apron is worn to protect the jacket and pants from excessive staining. It should be clean at the start of the shift and, if necessary, should be changed during the course of a working shift. The same is true of side towels. Most chefs use side towels to protect their hands when working with hot pans, dishes, or other equipment. They are not meant to be used as wiping cloths. If you do use a side towel to clean up a spill or wipe off a cutting board, replace it with a clean one.

Side towels used to lift hot items must be dry in order to provide protection. Once they become even slightly wet, they can no longer insulate your hands; the heat passes through the wet cloth quickly. If, like most people, you react by dropping the pan or pot, it is likely that you will wind up with even more burns, from the hot food that splashes on your legs and feet.

Shoes

While athletic shoes are very comfortable, they are not ideal for working in a kitchen. If a knife or other sharp object should fall from a work surface onto your feet, most athletic shoes would offer very little resistance, and you would wind up with a puncture wound. Hard leather shoes with slip-resistant soles are recommended, both because of the protection they offer from knives and because of the support they can give to your feet. A job that involves standing for several hours in a row, without moving around a great deal (chefs typically spend most of their day standing in a single spot at their work station or on the line) puts a premium on good-quality, supportive, protective foot gear. There are several brands available, and it is worth the time and trouble to try on several different types of shoes to determine which are most suitable for you. Neglecting your feet is a bad business, one that will pay you back with foot trouble, back pain, and discomfort throughout your life. If you develop trouble with your feet, seek professional help, consider orthotics, and carefully heed advice about what shoes and other devices are best for your particular needs.

Neckerchief

Some chefs feel that, without a neckerchief, the uniform has an unfinished look. Others find it bulky, fussy, and prefer to go without, except possibly for a press photo! If the neckerchief is worn, it should be impeccably clean, and replaced as necessary throughout a shift to keep the neck cool and clean. Neckerchiefs do absorb perspiration.

Pest Control

Rodents, flies, and other pests are a real problem. Take the necessary steps to prevent them from gaining a foothold in the kitchen. Keep screens on all doors and windows that might allow them entrance. By covering garbage cans and dumpsters, getting rid of trash promptly, and closing up any holes around the foundation of the building, infestation will be kept to a minimum. Cleaning the kitchen, storing foods carefully, and checking incoming deliveries is also part of a first line of defense. When necessary, you may need to rely on insecticides, traps, or other pest-control measures. If you do, be sure that you or the service you hire handles all such items with extreme care to avoid contaminating the food, air, and water in your restaurant.

Cleaning and Sanitizing

Cleaning something means that you have removed all visible traces of soil, food particles, or grease. Sanitizing something means that moist heat or chemical agents have been used to destroy disease-causing pathogens.

Cleaning is not enough for some things, such as pots, pans, cutting boards, knives, plates, glassware, and silverware. Sanitizing food-contact surfaces is an extremely important part of preventing foodborne illnesses.

At your work station, you should have a cloth in a double-strength sanitizing solution handy to wipe down your knives, steel, and cutting board between each use. This is not done in place of careful cleaning. It is done to assure that you won't inadvertently transmit pathogens through cross-contamination. Iodine, chlorine, or quaternary ammonium compounds are all common sanitizing agents. Be sure to learn how to use these compounds properly and safely.

Ware Washing

Ware washing must be handled properly as well. Both three-compartment sinks and ware-washing machines can be used to properly clean and sanitize utensils, pans, and service ware.

Hand washing of dishes is performed as follows:

Fill the first sink with water and an approved detergent. The water should be at least 120°F (49°C). Wash the dishes well. Remember to drain and replace the water and detergent as necessary, so that all grease and food particles are being completely removed.

The second sink should hold water at about 130°F (54°C). This is used to rinse the dishes, removing any traces of detergent.

The third sink is used to sanitize dishes. This can be accomplished by filling the sink with water that is 170°F (77°C). Dishes are submerged in this water

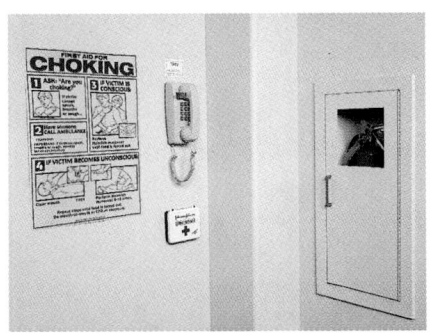

FIGURE 2-7
Safety Measures

for at least 30 seconds, then transferred to a clean area where they can drain and air dry. Or, you may use a chemical sanitizer. Dilute it properly and follow the manufacturer's instructions. Generally a water temperature of 75°F (24°C) and a one-minute submersion is adequate.

Allow pots, pans, and all tableware to dry completely before storing them.

If you have an automatic ware washing machine, be sure to check that the water reaches the correct temperature for each stage of washing and sanitizing. Keep the equipment properly serviced and use only approved cleaning and sanitizing compounds.

If your water is "hard," it will contain high levels of iron, calcium, or magnesium. These minerals can interfere with detergents and sanitizers. If necessary, use water-softening additives or install a water-softening system.

Safety Issues

Making your restaurant safe for everyone who walks through the door means many things. Foods need to be kept safe and wholesome, of course. Making the surrounding environment as hazard free as possible also means keeping equipment functioning and having established procedures in case of fires or choking incidents. It means having safe drinking water, adequate ventilation, and keeping the workplace free from such obvious hazards as asbestos, lead in the water or paint, and unnecessary distractions and noises.

Kitchens and dining rooms are filled with potential dangers. Sharp knives, hot coffee, broken glassware, frayed electrical wires, wet floors, and heavy crates or pots and pans are just part of the day-to-day life in a restaurant. Train new employees and remind everyone periodically that working safely means working "smart." Several guidelines for handling knives and large equipment can be found in Chapter 4. In addition, make sure that everyone is aware that keeping the kitchen and dining room safe is part of their official job description. You should:

• Wipe up spills immediately. Throwing a handful of salt or cornmeal over the spill isn't enough. Take the time to clean away all traces of grease or oil.

• Let coworkers know that you are coming up behind them with something hot or sharp.

• Alert the pot washer if pots, pans, and handles are especially hot.

• Respect knives and handle them carefully.

• Know what to do in case of fires.

• Learn about first aid, including how to deal with cuts, and burns.

• Pick up anything on the floor that might trip the unwary.

• Get help before lifting anything heavy, and use your legs, not your back.

• Learn how to administer the Heimlich maneuver, CPR, and mouth-to-mouth resusitation.

Occupational Health and Safety (OSHA)

The Occupational Health and Safety Administration (OSHA) is a federal act that was instituted during the Nixon presidency, in 1970. This federal organization falls within the Health and Human Services branch of the federal government. It's goal is helping employers and workers to establish and maintain a safe, healthy work environment. Among its regulations are stipulations that all places of employment must have an adequate and easily accessible first-aid kit on the premises.

In addition, if an organization has more than ten employees, records must be kept of all accidents and injuries to employees requiring medical treatment. Any requests for improvements to the safety of the workplace, including repair or maintenance of the physical plant and equipment necessary to perform one's job, must be attended to by the organization.

As money for many health and human service organizations has dwindled, OSHA's ability to make on-site inspections has also been reduced. It now concentrates its efforts on providing services where the danger of risk to the worker's safety is greatest. This does not mean that small businesses can operate with impunity. Employees can call OSHA offices and report violations.

Fire Safety

It only takes a few seconds for a simple flare-up on the grill or in a pan to turn into a full-scale fire. Grease fires, electrical fires, even a waste container full of paper going up when a match is carelessly tossed into the garbage can are all easy to imagine happening in any busy kitchen. Burns and blisters are almost certainties for people who work over open flames, serve hot coffee, or deep-fry potatoes. Just because they are common injuries and accidents does not mean that they should be thought of as "part of the territory." A comprehensive safety plan to reduce burns and open fires should be in place and a standard part of all employee training.

The first step to take in avoiding fires is to make sure that the entire staff for both the kitchen and dining room are fully aware of the potential dangers of fire everywhere in a restaurant. If you see someone handling a situation improperly, get the situation under control, and then take the time to explain what your concern is, and how to avoid the situation in the future.

Second, be sure that all equipment is up to code. Frayed or exposed wires and faulty plugs can all too easily be the cause of a fire. Overburdened outlets are another common culprit. Any equipment that has a heating element or coil must also be maintained carefully, both to be sure that workers are not likely to be burned as well as to prevent fires.

The third key element in any good fire safety program is thorough training about what to do in case of a fire. Have fire drills often. Instruct your kitchen staff in the correct way to handle a grill fire or a grease fire.

There should be fire extinguishers in easily accessible areas. Check the extinguisher to see what type of fire they are meant to control, and make sure that everyone understands when and how to operate them.

Proper maintenance of extinguishers and timely inspections by your local fire department are vital. Fire control systems such as an Ansel system need to be serviced and monitored so that, if you need them, they will perform correctly. Above all make sure that employees know that they should never try to put out a grease, chemical, or electrical fire by throwing water on the flames.

Everyone should know where the fire department number is posted and who is responsible for calling the department in case of need. The exits from all areas of the building should be easy to find, clear of any obstructions, and fully operational. Your guests will have to rely on your staff to get them safely through any crisis that requires them to quickly exit the building. Have a plan established so that all employees will assemble at one spot outside the building at a safe distance. Then, you will know immediately who may still be inside the building and might need to be rescued by firefighters.

The main rule for fires is to be prepared for all possibilities. You cannot assume it will not happen to you.

Americans with Disabilities Act (ADA)

This act is intended to make public places accessible and safe for those with a varieties of disabilities. Any new construction or remodeling done to the restaurant must meet ADA standards. This includes being sure that telephones are located so that they are can be reached by a person in a wheelchair, and providing toilets with handrails. Whenever you build or remodel, you must make sure that all work is done with respect to the ADA standards. Most contractors will have the necessary information, but if you are unsure, contact a local agency.

A Special Note about Smokers

Many restaurants today have already opted to ban smoking completely. Those that have not yet done so may find that public pressure or even legislative mandates will force their hands in the future. While this may increase the air quality within the restaurant itself and provide a pleasanter dining experience for non-smoking guests, there is one thing that should be kept in mind: Simply banning smoking from the dining room and the bar may not ban smoking from the entire premises. Common sense will tell you that smokers will very likely smoke cigarettes up to the moment they walk in the door, and light-up as soon as they step back outside. One carelessly flung match, a single smoldering cigarette butt can spell ruin.

Place sand-filled buckets or urns near the areas you expect or prefer to have smokers take their cigarette breaks. If you do allow smoking in your restaurant, make sure that bartenders, bus people, and waitstaff have a safe way to dispose of the contents of ashtrays.

Drugs and Alcohol in the Workplace

One final topic that is of great importance in the workplace is the right of all workers to be free from the hazards imposed by a coworker who comes to work under the influence of drugs or alcohol. The abuse of any substance that can alter or impair one's ability to perform their job is a serious concern. Reaction times are slowed. The ability to concentrate and to comprehend instructions is reduced. Inhibitions are often lowered, and judgment is generally impaired.

People's lives may be at stake: A poorly judged attempt at emptying the hot oil from the fryolater could result in permanent disability. A playful attempt at passing a knife could literally put out an eye. Forgetting to take the time to properly store and reheat foods could lead to an outbreak of food-borne illness that could kill someone. The responsibilities of a professional working in any kitchen are too great to allow someone suffering from a substance abuse problem to diminish the respect and trust you have built with your customers and staff.

Summary

Safe foods, safe dining rooms, and safe kitchens ought to be the underlying goal of everyone who works in a restaurant. Changes to safe-food handling regulations should be implemented quickly. Being sensitive to the safety of your guests and employees is your responsibility as a professional.

CHAPTER 3 *Nutrition and Healthy Cooking*

Nutrition is the study of the way humans make use of the foods they eat in order to fulfill the body's needs for growth, repair, and maintenance. Our knowledge of nutrition has increased tremendously over the past several years. Your guests probably are asking for menu options that are lower in fats and cholesterol, prepared with sauces on the side. When you stop to think about the changes in the way people select food, both to prepare at home and when they dine out, it is clear that things are quite different now from even a few short years ago.

Healthy cooking refers to the ways that you as a chef or restaurant owner can meet your guests' needs for dishes that fit some specific nutritional guidelines. The level of sophistication that a typical restaurant consumer has in the field of nutrition makes it more important than ever that you continue to learn more about the guidelines and recommendations. You need to not only respond to your guests' requests, but also be sure that you have not crossed the line on your menu between informative copy into an area that might be looked upon as making health claims.

You will undoubtedly find that, despite a growing consciousness that eating more grains and vegetables is a way to promote better health, most people are interested primarily in weight control. Unless you are creating a entire menu devoted to nutritional cooking, however, it is not necessary to exclude such items as foie gras and Camembert from your selections. The responsibility for making selections from your menu, and throughout the entire day, belongs to the individual. You should not be seen as a dictator of what people can or ought to eat.

The dietary guidelines and recommendations from the United States Department of Agriculture (USDA), the World Health Organization (WHO), the American Heart Association (AHA), and the American Diabetes Association (ADA) have undergone some dramatic changes over the last two decades. This has resulted in a whole new clientele interested in different foods, different menu options, and a broader sense of what "eating healthy" means. For the chef, this might translate into some simple modifications—using olive oil to replace butter on the table, including whole grain breads in the bread basket, offering skim milk and nonfat yogurt. It also can give a whole new look to appetizers, soups, and entrées. Grains that were not familiar a few years ago are now finding greater acceptance. Vegetables, dried beans, and fruits are taking a more dominant spot on the plate. A greater variety of foods are being combined on individual plates. This means that not only are dishes more interesting in terms of colors, textures, flavors, and aromas, changed slightly, they are also a better source of varied nutrients.

News stories about the USDA Food Guide Pyramid, the Mediterranean diet, studies about the role of antioxidants and phytochemicals in maintaining health and preventing disease, the role olive oil and other monounsaturated fats in the diet, and the French Paradox have made their mark on our collective consciousness. Sometimes that mark is clearly a question mark.

The personal health and diet concerns your guests have today may not be the same ones they will have tomorrow. It is likely, however, that one of the greatest motivators for selecting a menu item that fits particular nutrition guidelines is a concern with weight loss.

We will look at some of the current issues in nutrition that your guests may hope to find reflected on your menu: The lessons of traditional diets from around the world, an upswing in the number of individuals who consider themselves vegetarians, the USDA Food Guide Pyramid and other dietary guidelines, the impact of continuing studies in the relationship of food choices and the prevention or reversal of certain diseases.

Dietary Goals and Recommendations

The USDA's Food Guide Pyramid is a set of dietary recommendations that translates the suggested number of servings of various sorts of foods into a graphic image. The broad base of the pyramid includes pasta, rice, cereals, breads, and other foods made from grains. The majority of the foods eaten throughout the day should come from this group. Fruits and vegetables make up the next layer. Dairy products such as milk, yogurt, and cheeses are included on the same tier as meats, poultry, fish, eggs, beans, and nuts. The top of the pyramid, to be consumed sparingly, includes fats, oils, and sweets. Refer to Figure 3-1.

The Mediterranean Food Pyramid gives a strikingly similar message (see Figure 3-2). There are some differences to be noted. Olive oil is considered important enough in the diet to deserve its own tier. Red meats occupy the top tier of the pyramid; it is suggested that they be consumed only a few times per month. Poultry and fish can be eaten a few times per week. Wine in moderation can be seen near the top of the pyramid, and is an optional

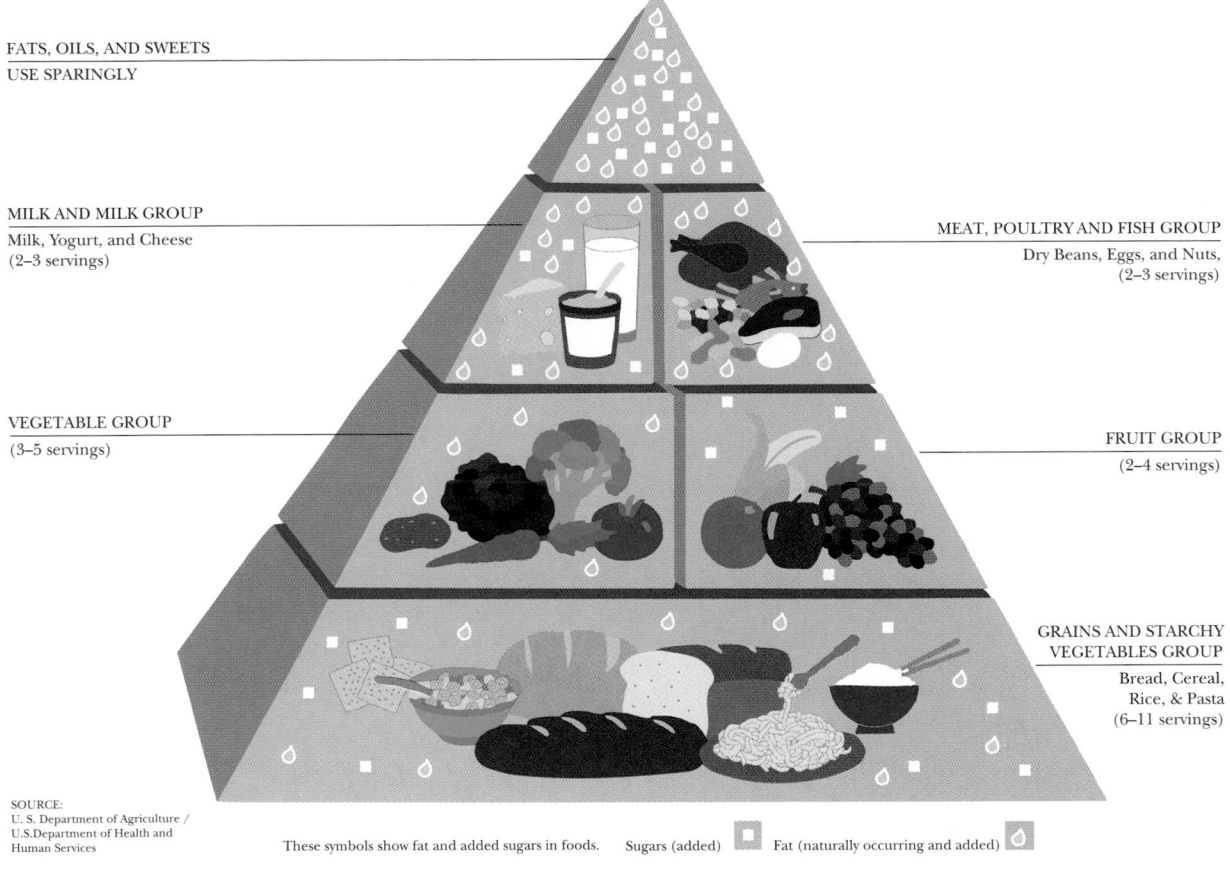

FATS, OILS, AND SWEETS
USE SPARINGLY

MILK AND MILK GROUP
Milk, Yogurt, and Cheese
(2–3 servings)

MEAT, POULTRY AND FISH GROUP
Dry Beans, Eggs, and Nuts,
(2–3 servings)

VEGETABLE GROUP
(3–5 servings)

FRUIT GROUP
(2–4 servings)

GRAINS AND STARCHY
VEGETABLES GROUP
Bread, Cereal,
Rice, & Pasta
(6–11 servings)

SOURCE:
U. S. Department of Agriculture /
U.S.Department of Health and
Human Services

These symbols show fat and added sugars in foods.   Sugars (added)   Fat (naturally occurring and added)

FIGURE 3-1   The USDA Food Guide Pyramid

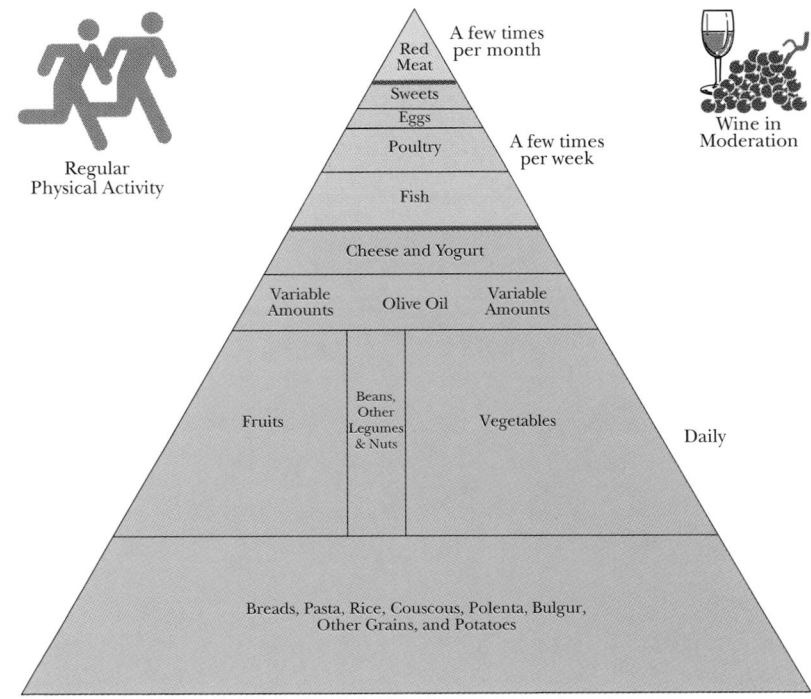

Red Meat — A few times per month

Sweets

Eggs

Poultry — A few times per week

Fish

Cheese and Yogurt

Variable Amounts | Olive Oil | Variable Amounts

Fruits | Beans, Other Legumes & Nuts | Vegetables — Daily

Breads, Pasta, Rice, Couscous, Polenta, Bulgur,
Other Grains, and Potatoes

Regular
Physical Activity

Wine in
Moderation

FIGURE 3-2   Mediterranean Food Pyramid

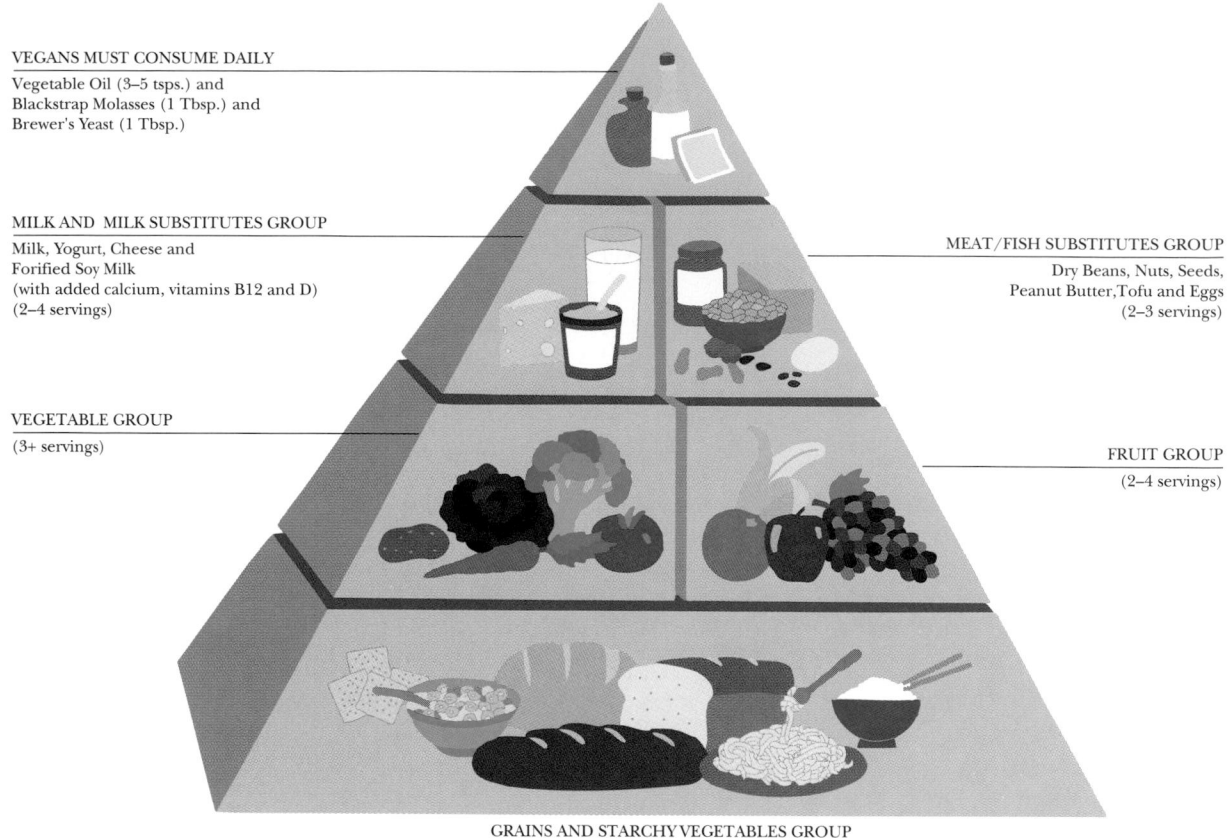

VEGANS MUST CONSUME DAILY
Vegetable Oil (3–5 tsps.) and
Blackstrap Molasses (1 Tbsp.) and
Brewer's Yeast (1 Tbsp.)

MILK AND MILK SUBSTITUTES GROUP
Milk, Yogurt, Cheese and
Forified Soy Milk
(with added calcium, vitamins B12 and D)
(2–4 servings)

MEAT/FISH SUBSTITUTES GROUP
Dry Beans, Nuts, Seeds,
Peanut Butter, Tofu and Eggs
(2–3 servings)

VEGETABLE GROUP
(3+ servings)

FRUIT GROUP
(2–4 servings)

GRAINS AND STARCHY VEGETABLES GROUP
Bread, Cereal, Rice, Pasta, Potatoes, Corn, and Green Peas (6–11 servings)

FIGURE 3-3   The Vegetarian Pyramid

component of the diet. Regular physical exercise is also made part of this traditional healthy diet.

The Vegetarian Pyramid (see Figure 3-3) gives the option of replacing dairy products with milk substitutes, such as soy or nut milks and cheese, and suggests that they be fortified with calcium and vitamins B_{12} and D. If a vegan diet is followed, the meats, poultry, and fish suggested for those following a nonvegetarian diet can be replaced with dry beans, nuts, seeds, tofu, nut butters, and eggs. The top tier of the pyramid includes some foods that vegans must consume daily to maintain optimal levels of specific nutrients: vegetable oil, blackstrap molasses, and brewer's yeast.

The USDA's Department of Health and Human Services has targeted the end of this century to turn around some of the less desirable dietary habits found in this highly industrialized Western culture. This program, known as Healthy People 2000, is aimed at making it easier for people to understand what constitutes a healthful diet, and to make informed choices about what they eat.

This will continue to have enormous impact on what restaurants, from fast-food restaurants to chain restaurants to upscale restaurants, are offering to their guests. As more Americans start to adopt the USDA Food Guide Pyramid (see Figure 3-1), a broader range of grains, legumes, vegetables, and fruits are being featured in virtually every course of the menu. Couscous, bulgur, barley, quinoa, kasha and other grains are no longer seen as unusual. Cooking greens (including collards, turnip greens, and escarole), squashes, sweet potatoes, and broccoli rabe are featured not only as side dishes, but also as the main element on the plate.

There are many different sets of dietary recommendations, including those shown here (USDA, Vegetarian, and Mediterranean). The American Heart Association, and the American Cancer Society, as well as other organizations whose aim is to help those with specific health concerns to eat well and live better through controlling their diets, also have standards and recommendations that they offer to their members.

When you look at these recommendations as a group, one thing is clear. Every set of these goals recommends the following:

• Maintaining a healthy body weight through a combination of a healthful diet and exercise

• Thinking of a balanced diet as something to be achieved over the course of a day or week, rather than in each dish, recipe, or meal

• Reducing total calories

• Keeping total fat intake at or below about 30% of the day's total calories

• Replacing saturated fats with monounsaturated fats

• Drinking sufficient water throughout the day (see Figure 3-4)

• Eating more fruits, vegetables, and starchy foods, as well as selecting a good variety, to assure adequate levels of vitamins, minerals, and fiber

• Reducing portion sizes and the frequency with which meats, poultry, fish, eggs, and whole milk cheeses are included in the diet

• Reducing the amount of refined sugars consumed

• Avoiding highly processed or refined foods

• Keeping sodium consumption below approximately 2,400 milligrams per day

• Reducing the amount of dietary cholesterol in the diet

• Keeping alcohol consumption at moderate levels (for instance, 1 to 2 glasses of wine a day for men, 1 per day for women)*

Some individuals or programs recommend completely eliminating meat from the diet or keeping total fat intake below 20, 15, or even 10 percent of the day's total calories. These eating programs may be important for individuals with specific dietary needs—for instance, heart disease patients, diabetics, or those with severe hypertension. If you are preparing menus to meet these needs, be sure to get assistance either from medical professionals and nutritionists, or from books, software, and journals that specialize in these areas.

*Not all dietary recommendations condone or suggest that alcohol is important or beneficial. This is an optional part of any diet.

FIGURE 3-4 Water: The Forgotten Nutrient

The Lessons of Traditional Diets

Traditional Mediterranean cultures, as well as those of the Pacific Rim and South America, have relied for centuries upon a combination of foods and eating habits that appear to result in a more healthful, disease-free life. There are many lessons that we can learn from these traditional food habits.

Snack foods, small meals, and street foods play an important role. Unlike our fat- and sugar-laden junk foods, the traditional choices in the Mediterranean, Asian, and South American countries are predominantly those based on grains, pastas and noodles, breads, fruits, and vegetables. Grazing has many benefits. It is often easier to control your appetite, since you never really become ravenous waiting for dinner to arrive. Blood sugar levels are even throughout the day. It is more likely that you will eat a wider variety of foods by eating little dishes throughout the day.

Cooking oils tend to be monounsaturated and are derived from nuts, olives, and vegetables. Saturated fats, such as those found in butter, lard, and cheeses, play a far less significant role. When they are used, they play the part of a condiment or seasoning. Meats, fish, and poultry similarly are viewed as flavoring ingredients, not the main event.

FIGURE 3-5   Regular and "Tasting" Portions of Wine

In those cultures where alcohol is part of the diet, wine is the basic alcoholic beverage (see Figure 3-5). It is consumed moderately, with food, and in a social setting.

Which brings us to what may well be the most elusive but important component of these traditional cultures: Coming together at the table to dine is an important part of the day. It is becoming harder and harder for Americans to carve out time each day to devote to relaxing at the table, enjoying a meal and each other's company.

Vegetarianism

Many people today prefer to reduce or completely eliminate animal foods from their diets. Nearly 12.5 million people refer to themselves as vegetarians, a number that has nearly doubled over the last ten years.

The reasons for becoming a vegetarian can range from a concern with health to ethical or moral concerns. From a health standpoint, diets that cut out meats are likely to have lower levels of fats, especially saturated fats. They may also, depending upon the type of vegetarian diet adopted,

greatly reduce or even eliminate a dietary source of cholesterol.

Just as there may be many reasons for becoming a vegetarian, there is more than one type of vegetarian. The following list provides some definitions and standards for a range of vegetarian options:

Vegans: This diet is based purely on vegetable foods, and excludes all forms of animal-based foods, including eggs, honey, fish, dairy foods, poultry, and red meat. There are some special concerns vegans need to be aware of so that they can balance their nutritional needs adequately.

Fruitarian: Similar to a vegan diet, eating predominantly fruits, nuts, and seeds.

Ovo-vegetarians: This diet adds eggs but no animal flesh or dairy to the vegan's diet.

Lacto/ovo-vegetarian: This indicates an individual who eats dairy products (milk, yogurt, cheese) in addition to the ovo-vegetarian diet. All animal flesh is excluded.

Pesco-vegetarian: fish is included, but no other type of animal flesh.

Semi-vegetarian: all foods, excluding only beef, veal, pork, lamb, and game, are eaten. Fish and chicken are occasionally part of a meal.

One phenomenon today's chef needs to keep in mind is the growing number of individuals who consider themselves situational vegetarians, or *alternivores.* An alternivore is any person who might, given an attractive choice, opt to order a vegetarian or a meatless meal.

Many restaurant operators have found that introducing such selections on a menu has numerous benefits. It offers guests an agreeable new choice, and may increase their inclination to return. Such offerings may have a reduced food cost, and provide a real chance to make a better margin of profit on that menu selection. They are a viable way to introduce new flavors, ingredients, or preparations to an audience that is already disposed to be more adventurous in their food choices.

Dietary Supplements and "Nutraceuticals"

Dietary supplements are looked upon by many as an alternative to medical care. When antioxidants, lecithin, or beta-carotene hits the headlines or the nightly news, people are anxious to learn if taking a pill is likely to cure or reverse a medical condition.

In addition to vitamin and mineral supplements, we are beginning to see the possibility of engineering foods to increase levels of certain nutrients. This might mean that a "super food" could be developed that your doctor would prescribe as part of the treatment for cancer, hypertension, or heart disease.

The FDA has become increasingly concerned about the blurring of lines between foods and medicines. Making health claims about a food is no longer an acceptable practice. What this means in terms of the menu is that you should stay away from any indication, whether it is an obvious or implied claim, that eating a single food or menu item will guarantee health, provide a cure for, or prevent a disease. You can still tell your clients that a dish is low in fats, calories, cholesterol, and sodium, however.

The Language of Nutrition

Nutrition is the study of the way humans make use of the foods they eat in order to fulfill the body's needs for growth, repair, and maintenance. Nutrients are not foods all by themselves. They are, instead, the elements found in foods. We do not eat pure nutrients, we eat the foods that offer them in good supply. You should still be seeing a beautiful, ripe, glossy, juicy, delicious piece of fruit when you look at an apple—not a carbohydrate/fiber/vitamin/mineral/water delivery system!

A well-nourished body requires adequate supplies of all of the nutrients known to be important in maintaining health. While it is likely that there are some essential nutrients not yet identified, we do know that eating a wide variety of foods should provide enough of those we have identified as essential—protein, carbohydrates, fats, vitamins, and minerals—as well as those that we know less about.

The following discussion of the various nutrients our bodies use in the day-to-day process of maintaining, growing, and repairing is meant as a brief introduction to the terms that are frequently used to discuss foods and the ways that they are used in a cooking style that has included nutrition as a basic

concern, along with flavor, texture, color, and overall appeal.

Calories

A calorie is a unit of measure used to indicate the energy value of a particular food or beverage. Counting calories is a time-honored method of weight control. It is a simple formula: When the energy you consume equals the energy you expend, your weight remains the same. If you take in more calories than you use up through your metabolism, daily activities, and exercise, you will gain weight. If you take in fewer calories than you body needs, you will lose weight.

Of course, it is not all that simple to lose or gain weight, as the number of weight loss books and programs available attests. It appears that the calories from certain foods, especially fats and oils, are handled differently by the body. An individual's metabolism has a big part to play as well. If your metabolism has slowed because of repeated sessions of dieting, or if it has been boosted by a program of physical activity, your ability to gain or lose weight is similarly confounded or enhanced.

We need to maintain a concern about the amount of calories we put on a plate, since overconsumption of calories, in combination with a lack of exercise, is the major cause of overweight—one of this country's leading health problems. Americans, on average, are still well over their ideal weights. This health hazard can become manifest in a number of secondary diseases. High blood pressure, eating disorders, heart disease, stroke, certain types of cancer, and diabetes have all been linked to overweight and obesity. Arthritis is aggravated by carrying around extra pounds. Sleeping problems, back problems, foot problems, and a variety of emotional disorders have all been shown to have a direct correlation to overweight and obesity.

Empty Calories

All nutrients provide calories. Carbohydrates and proteins contain 4 calories in each gram. Fats contain more than double the number of calories with 9 per gram. Alcohol has 7 calories per gram.

FIGURE 3-6   Foods Rich in Carbohydrates

(1) Complex carbohydrates are found in foods made from whole grains and cereals.

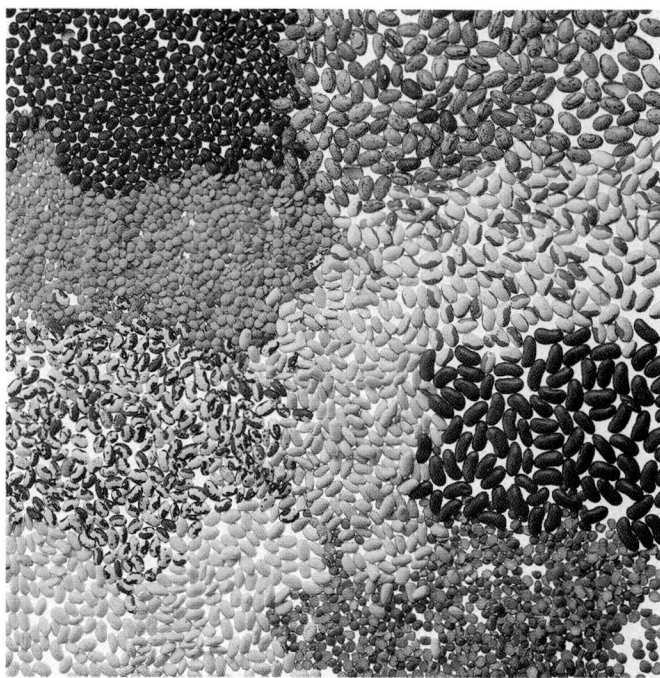

(2) Legumes are another source of complex carbohydrates.

Foods that have been significantly refined sometimes offer nothing beyond calories. Processing and refining often strips away those elements from the food that your body needs, including vitamins, minerals, and fiber. Alcohol also offers no nutritive elements for your body. These calories from highly refined foods and alcohol are known as empty calories.

Carbohydrates

When the USDA Food Guide Pyramid was released, the broad base of the pyramid showed clearly that a healthful diet should be selected primarily from foods that provide good-quality carbohydrates. Carbohydrates are your body's preferred source of energy.

Carbohydrate-rich foods include a wider selection of items than you might at first imagine. Figure 3-6 illustrates just how broad the possibilities are. These foods contribute to a healthful diet by providing an energy source that is released in an even, gradual manner. When your body breaks down the

(3) Fruits and vegetables provide both simple and complex carbohydrates.

starches in these foods into glucose, it actually expends some energy. Your body's organs and muscles can use protein and fats to provide energy, but these nutrients must first be altered into a form that your body is able to use. This taxes the body, and also generates toxins that must be cleared out of your system

Complex Carbohydrates

When complex carbohydrates are made part of the meal in the form of whole grains, cereals and meals, starchy vegetables, and dried legumes, they provide additional elements your body requires, including fiber, proteins, vitamins, and minerals.

Many whole foods are refined or processed in some way. In some instances, this can be beneficial. Cracking grains makes it easier to both cook and eat them. However, some foods can be refined to the point that they offer little more than starch, without the nutritional benefits you can derive from the unprocessed version. Steel-cut oats, cooked into a rich porridge, are a better value than cookies made with quick-cooking instant oats. This is true not only because the cookies have added fats and refined sugar, but also because the process of refining the oats has removed much of the vitamins, minerals, and fiber of the oat groats.

Simple Carbohydrates

Often referred to as "simple sugars," simple carbohydrates are found in great concentration in fruits, as well as in vegetables and milk. The naturally occurring sugar found in fruit is referred to as fructose. Milk contains lactose, and grapes contain a simple sugar known as maltose.

When you eat whole fresh fruits, you get the added benefit of a whole host of additional nutrients, including vitamins, minerals, fiber, and water.

Refined Sugars

Clever food-label writers realize that the term fructose or "fruit sugar" will often give the consumer a false sense that they are getting something

"healthful" when in fact, the type of fructose they are using is no better than any other type of refined sugar.

Honey, maple syrup, molasses, white and brown sugar, corn syrups, and other sweeteners are all refined, and offer very little beyond a few traces of minerals and calories. These calories provide nothing beyond "empty calories" to distinguish them from other sugars. Even blackstrap molasses provides very little in terms of vitamins or minerals.

Refined sugars do play an important part in many recipes. They moisten, preserve, and flavor foods. However, they can boost the calorie level of foods without offering any other benefit. Too many calories in your diet will result ultimately in weight gain.

Fiber

Your body cannot digest fiber; it is not really a source of nutrition. Still, it has an important role in regulating the body properly. In some studies, soluble fiber has been shown to aid in reducing the overall levels of cholesterol in the blood. Insoluble fiber helps to move foods through the gut quickly, preventing various gastrointestinal upsets such as constipation, diarrhea, and diverticulitis.

Meeting Carbohydrate and Fiber Requirements

Most dietary guidelines recommend that at least 50 percent of your day's total calories come from carbohydrates, with as few of those calories as possible derived from refined sugars found in sweeteners, jams, jellies, and confections.

Fiber is another important part of a healthful diet. Most Americans do not include enough fiber-rich foods in their diets at the correct level.

The suggested number of servings of carbohydrate-rich foods ranges from 8 to 12, depending upon how many calories a person needs each day.

Proteins

Most Americans remember learning in grade school that protein was one of the most important of all nutrients. It is certainly one of the essential

FIGURE 3-7   Protein-Rich Foods

nutrients, but Americans and most Western people rarely suffer from a protein deficiency. Instead, our diets tend to be skewed heavily toward protein, especially in the form of meats. This also has the effect of increasing the quantity of dietary fats in our diets, resulting in an unbalanced diet that shortcuts carbohydrates, includes more than adequate quantities of protein, and has us consuming far more saturated fat than is necessary or beneficial.

Shifting toward leaner cuts of meat, and away from those with high levels of saturated fats (and cholesterol), and using more poultry, fish, and foods such as dried beans and tofu are good ways to offer high-quality foods that provide good sources of protein without overdoing fats in the diet (see Figure 3-7).

Essential Amino Acids

Proteins are composed of smaller groups known as amino acids. There are 20 amino acids, and our bodies are capable of creating over half of them. The remaining amino acids are referred to as the "essential" amino acids. This indicates that in order

to produce proteins, we need to find a dietary source for that particular acid. According to age and other conditions there may be eight or nine essential amino acids.

Mutual Supplementation or Complementary Proteins

Animal foods, including meat, milk, cheese, and eggs, will provide "complete" protein. This means that a single food can supply all of the essential amino acids. Plant-based foods also supply a good source of protein, even though some foods may have low levels of particular amino acids.

This was once considered an issue of some concern for vegetarians. If they were eating a food low in tryptophan, for instance, they were cautioned to be sure to eat a food that was a good source of that amino acid at the same meal.

It is no longer thought to be critical to get all of the essential amino acids combined in a single meal, as long as you do get them over the course of the day. Most well-balanced vegetarian meals rely on time-honored food combinations, such as rice and beans, that provide all of the essential amino acids.

Meeting Protein Requirements in a Typical Diet

Getting an adequate supply of protein in our diets is not a mysterious process. The recommended amounts of protein for most adults of average size ranges from 56 to 65 grams each day. In general, a single 6-ounce portion of meat, coupled with a few servings of low- or nonfat dairy foods throughout the day will meet an individual's needs quite well.

What this means to the chef is that the "standard" portion of 6 to 8 ounces of meat, fish, or chicken is really fine. The trick is in making it appear bountiful, attractive, and filling to patrons who are accustomed to thick center-cut chops, platter-size steaks, chicken halves, and whole pan-ready fish. Certainly you will not be in the position of dictating whether or not an individual can or ought to have more meat at another meal. But, even if this were the only meal that person ate all day, a larger portion offers no nutritional advantage.

Fats and Oils

Fats and oils are essential elements in any healthful diet. For most chefs, they are an equally critical staple in the restaurant larder. Fats do more than supply some important nutrients. They also make foods feel and taste rich and satisfying. They signal the stomach that enough food has been eaten, giving people the feeling of satiety that encourages them to stop eating before they overeat.

Fats are found in some foods, notably meats, poultry, fish, cheeses, eggs, and nuts. The type of fats a food contains may be monounsaturated, polyunsaturated, or saturated. Each appears to have a different effect on the body (see Figure 3-8).

Monounsaturated Fats

When findings about the Mediterranean diet were released, it seemed clear that the use of olive oil in those diets played a role in a generally lower incidence of cardiovascular disease.

Monounsaturated fats have a tendency to lower the levels of certain types of cholesterol in the blood and raise others. The net result of this is that diets that rely upon monounsaturated fats, rather than saturated fats, are likely to encourage low levels of serum cholesterol. This means that the chances of developing atherosclerosis are reduced.

Nuts and olives, as well as oils made from those foods, contain primarily monounsaturated oils.

Polyunsaturated Fats

Oils made from corn, safflower, and rapeseed (canola), and other vegetable sources are referred to as polyunsaturated. While these oils are still preferred over saturated fats in a healthful diet, they do not appear to have precisely the same benefits as monounsaturated fats.

Vegetable oils are frequently used to prepare shortening and margarine. This process, known as hydrogenation, changes the overall structure of the fat. Instead of pouring at room temperature, these hydrogenated oils become "plastic," or solid, at room temperature.

Saturated Fats

Saturated fats are found typically in animal foods including butter, marbling in meats, lard, chicken skin, bacon, sausages, and eggs. The so-called "tropical oils" are also saturated fats: coconut and palm oils, for example.

Saturated fats have been linked to increase levels of serum cholesterol and an increased risk of developing cardio-vascular diseases.

Cholesterol

This is a type of fatty acid found in animal foods. There is a distinction between dietary cholesterol and serum cholesterol. Dietary cholesterol is that which is found in the foods themselves. Serum cholesterol is found in your bloodstream.

When you have a blood test done to determine your personal cholesterol levels, the doctor will review specific components found in the blood, known as lipoproteins. Low-density lipoproteins (LDL) are associated with an increased risk of developing arteriosclerosis. High-density lipoproteins (HDL) appear to reduce the risk, since HDL actually removes LDL from your blood.

Certain individuals are more sensitive to dietary cholesterol than others. Learning how to reduce the amount of foods containing cholesterol in your diet is critical if you are one of those individuals. But, it may not always be enough. Your body produces cholesterol on its own, whether or not you eat foods containing it.

Plant-based foods, even those high in fats and oils, do not contain cholesterol. This means that peanut butter, almonds, olives, beans, and sesame seeds are all "cholesterol free." They always have been.

Maintaining Proper Levels of Fat and Cholesterol in the Diet

Another dietary problem facing most Westerners, and Americans in particular, is that we consume far more fat, both the fats that occur in foods naturally and those that are added to foods during cooking or other processing, than we actually require. There is a great correlation between increased fat intake and the increased risk of developing certain diseases.

FIGURE 3-8　Fats and Oils

(1) *Corn oil, sesame seeds and sesame seed oil, and walnut oil are all sources of polyunsaturated fats.*

(2) *Olive oil, avocados, most nuts and nut oils are monounsaturated.*

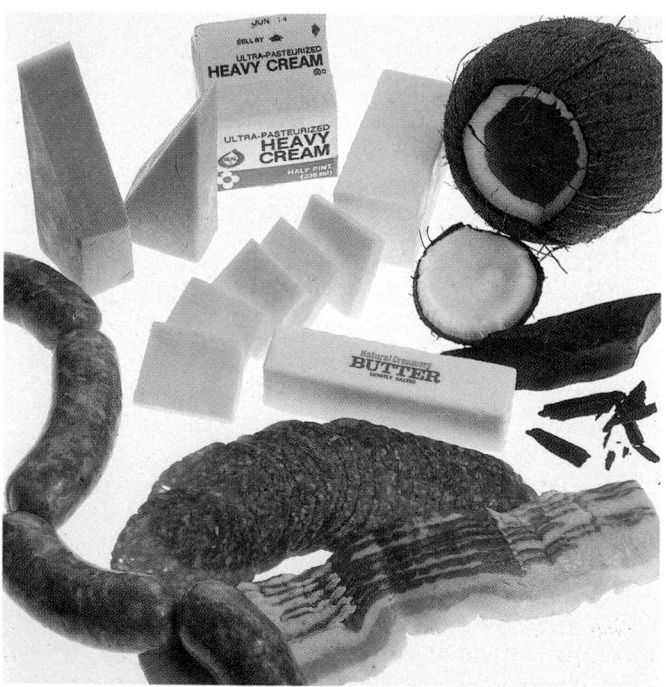

(3) *Saturated fats are found in meats, butter, cheese, cream, and coconuts.*

(4) *Foods high in cholesterol include egg yolks and organ meats such as liver, sweetbreads, and kidneys.*

FIGURE 3-9 Vegetables are Good Sources of Vitamins and Minerals

The stance taken by most nutritionists and expounded in various eating plans and pyramids states that current levels of fat intake should be reduced to at or below 30 percent of the day's total calories.

Vitamins and Minerals

Vitamins and minerals are crucial to your health. Even though they do not provide you with energy per se, they are important to various functions in the body (see Figure 3-9). A deficiency of a particular vitamin or mineral can cause disease. Many folk cures are based on the fact that a specific food could replenish the missing nutrient. Around the turn of the century, chemists were able to isolate these compounds. They were given letter names, and later on, more specific names. Deficiency diseases were also identified. The United States Recommended Daily Allowance (USRDA) recommendations for vitamins and minerals were established based on the levels required to prevent those diseases.

Water Soluble Vitamins

Vitamin C (ascorbic acid) and the B vitamins can be dissolved in water. This means that you need to replenish stores of these vitamins daily, since they are readily lost from the body in waste fluids. They are also sensitive to prolonged exposure to heat, air, and light. Cooking foods to retain maximum levels of the water soluble vitamins is a challenge for the chef.

Since the body can excrete water soluble vitamins with ease, you normally need not worry about building up toxic levels of these vitamins. It is possible to take too much of these vitamins, however.

Phytochemicals

Phytochemicals are those compounds found in plant-based foods. They have been linked with a variety of health benefits.

Beta-Carotene

This vitamin is found in red and orange vegetables, leafy greens, and members of the cabbage family. Beta-carotene is a precursor for vitamin A, and has been shown to have a variety of health benefits.

Anti-Oxidants

The antioxidants include vitamins C and E. These compounds help to prevent other substances, such as the membranes of red blood cells and vitamin A from being destroyed. They do this by bonding with the oxygen that would otherwise destroy white and red blood cells, as well as cell membranes in the lungs. This means that the mechanisms required to keep the immune system strong and functioning are preserved.

Fat-Soluble Vitamins

Vitamins A, D, E, and K are fat soluble. This means that they are stored in fat, which is far less simple to remove from the body than water. Megadoses of vitamin supplements can easily cause toxic levels to build up, leading to serious disease, even death.

Unlike water-soluble vitamins, these vitamins are much more stable during cooking.

Figure 3-10   Sodium and Salt

(1) Salt is one of the most common sources of sodium in the diet.

(2) Use other flavorings to reduce or replace some salt in recipes.

Major Minerals

Calcium, potassium, and sodium are required by your body in significant quantities. They are essential to maintaining a proper balance of fluids in your body, as well as the proper acid/base balance. Calcium is associated with bone strength and density. Potassium has been linked to maintaining the heart's rhythm, while sodium has a great deal to do with blood pressure. These minerals need to be part of your daily diet.

Trace Minerals

Other minerals known to be important to maintaining health are required in very small amounts. Iron, zinc, manganese, and fluoride are all trace minerals.

Dietary Requirements for Vitamins and Minerals

Today, as we continue to learn more about the role of vitamins and minerals in maintaining health, questions about the value of supplementa-

tion are cropping up. Many people are attempting to use vitamin and mineral supplements to bolster their immune systems, fight diseases, and prevent the development of everything from osteoporosis to cancer. Self-medicating can have serious consequences if an individual takes megadoses, especially of the fat-soluble vitamins and some minerals.

For most people, supplementation is unnecessary if a varied diet rich in whole grains, fruits, and vegetables is followed (see Figure 3-10). For those who do not get a good dietary source of some vitamins or minerals, supplementation may be suggested.

Water: "The Forgotten Nutrient"

Like vitamins and minerals, water is a noncaloric essential nutrient, which means that you need it to keep your body running properly, but it does not provide you with energy or with building materials for growth or repair of tissues. Our bodies are mainly water. Drinking the recommended eight glasses of water per day keeps joints properly cushioned, and increases the body's ability to get the necessary nutrients to the spot where you need them, and to clean out toxins from your system.

The Seven Guidelines for Nutritional Cooking

Bringing nutrition out of the textbook and into the kitchen requires far less in terms of actual change than many people fear. If you are already doing your best to select foods that are fresh, fully flavored, ripe, and wholesome, you are well on the way. Cook these foods as quickly as possible in as little water as possible to maximize nutrient retention. Serve a variety of foods, including as many whole grains, unprocessed fruits and vegetables, and legumes as possible.

The guidelines below for introducing healthful cooking practices into any kitchen capitalize on this approach to selecting, preparing, and serving foods. You will undoubtedly begin to see a change for the better in all aspects of your foodservice establishment as healthful practices become the norm.

1. Cook all foods with care to preserve their nutritional value, flavor, texture, and appeal.

Match the cooking method you select to the food you are preparing. Whenever possible, opt for methods that do not introduce additional fats and oils. Grilling, roasting, and steaming are good examples.

Whenever possible, cook foods close to the time that they are to be served. This will minimize nutrient loss, and ensure that the food is at its best when you serve it to your guests. For those foods or in those situations where it is not reasonable to do an à la carte preparation, use batch cooking.

2. Shift the emphasis on plates toward grains, legumes, vegetables and fruits as the "center of the plate."

Traditional diets from around the world place a strong emphasis on grains, vegetables, fruits, and legumes. These foods, rich in carbohydrates, and in an array of vitamins, minerals, and fiber, and play an important part in a balanced diet.

3. Serve appropriate portions of foods; know what a standard serving for all foods is.

Setting standards for portion sizes and teaching your staff to adhere to them will benefit you and your guest.

4. Select foods that help to achieve the nutritional goals and guidelines your guests are striving to meet.

In general, the closer a food is to its natural state, the higher its nutritional value. Locally picked fruits and vegetables, for example, do not travel as far or as long to get to the market. This means that they will retain more of their nutrients. Whole grains, with the germ and bran intact, are a better source of a wider variety of nutrients than polished, refined, or quick-cooking varieties.

There are instances when processed foods may be necessary, but you can exert some control over what effect these foods have on the overall value of the foods you prepare for your guests. Be sure to read the label on any processed, packaged, canned, or frozen food. Make comparisons to be sure that you are getting the most flavor, the best quality, and the least unwanted additives possible.

5. Opt for monounsaturated cooking fats and oils whenever possible and reduce the use of saturated fats.

The average American consumes nearly 38 percent of a day's calories in the form of fats. This is well above the current recommendations from any of a number of sources. Limiting the use of foods that contain too much fat and cholesterol need not be the punishment many fear. Chefs know a great deal about how to get the flavor value from foods that patrons demand without falling back on classic "disguises."

6. Use calorie dense foods (eggs, cream, butter, cheeses, and refined sugars) moderately.

This one simple step often presents a great challenge to anyone who is accustomed to relying on rich foods as the major carriers of flavor on a plate. Cutting calories nearly always includes cutting fats. Cream, cheese, butter, and oils add more calories, gram for gram, than other foods. When you do add them to a dish, use them sparingly.

7. Learn a variety of seasoning and flavoring techniques to help reduce reliance on salt.

FIGURE 3-11   Flavor is the Key

(1) A selection of seasonings used in Asian cooking: gingerroot, tamarind, wasabi powder, lemongrass, and mustard.

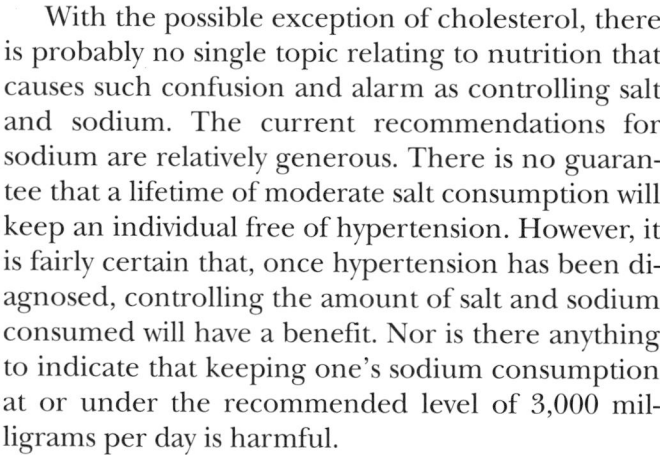

(2) Herbs, spices, and seeds used to flavor foods.

With the possible exception of cholesterol, there is probably no single topic relating to nutrition that causes such confusion and alarm as controlling salt and sodium. The current recommendations for sodium are relatively generous. There is no guarantee that a lifetime of moderate salt consumption will keep an individual free of hypertension. However, it is fairly certain that, once hypertension has been diagnosed, controlling the amount of salt and sodium consumed will have a benefit. Nor is there anything to indicate that keeping one's sodium consumption at or under the recommended level of 3,000 milligrams per day is harmful.

Salt is relied upon as a seasoning and flavor enhancer in many dishes. Learning to add only enough to get the taste benefit may be enough. If your palate is less likely to detect salt in foods before a significant quantity is added, you may need to take the time to measure at first, until your own palate adjusts. Remember, there are many other ways to add flavor to foods that will not add salt. Wines, vinegar, citrus juices, fresh herbs, and low-sodium soy sauces can all be used [see Figure 3-10(2) and 3-11].

If you add an ingredient to a dish, such as capers, olives, or hard grating cheeses, that is high in sodium, you should make an even further reduction in the amount of salt you add. Processed, canned, or frozen foods also may be high in salt or sodium. Read the labels carefully and opt for reduced sodium versions.

Putting Nutrition Guidelines into Practice

These are the ways that a chef can make solid, practical use of the suggestions to modify a typical "American" diet in favor of one that relies more on whole grains, meals, cereals, fresh fruits and vegetables, leaner meats, fish, poultry, and a more judicious use of ingredients that are typically high in fats, sodium, and cholesterol.

Developing Menu Items and Recipes

Recipe development and modification is one of the chef's main tools for introducing nutrition into the menu. If you want to begin slowly, you can make some simple adaptations of existing recipes. You might grill a piece of chicken rather than sautéing it. Or you might replace a fattier cut of meat with a leaner one. For some operations, it will be helpful to use nutrition software to evaluate where existing recipes fall with respect to suggested guidelines.

Current interest in dishes from cuisines around the Mediterranean, the Southwest, and the Pacific Rim offer new flavors, textures, and ingredients to feature on menus. Books, magazines, and newspapers can offer inspiration and recipes to help.

Portion control is an important point. Even if you remove the skin from chicken breasts, trim all of the visible fat from steaks, and omit the heavy cream sauces from fish entrées, you can still exceed optimal amounts of fat, sodium, cholesterol, and calories if your entrée is too large. If you are worried about customer acceptance of small portions of meats, fish, and poultry, make changes slowly. Be sure that as the size of the steak becomes more in line with current recommendations, you are keeping the plate full and appetizing by serving generous and varied portions of grains, vegetables, and legumes.

Identifying Healthful Cooking Techniques

Grilling, roasting, steaming, poaching, and baking are all excellent ways to prepare foods without adding fats during the cooking process. When possible, opt to use these techniques instead of pan-frying, broiling in butter, or deep-frying.

Sauces made from vegetables and herbs, salsas, and chutneys are popular alternatives to heavier toppings and side dishes.

Purchasing for Nutrition

Identify those foods that naturally fit this style of cooking. They have been noted throughout this discussion. Many of them are those already found in your kitchen. When an ingredient you might typically use in a recipe falls into the category of foods too high in fat, total calories, or sodium, consider using substitutes. For instance, you might replace regular sour cream with a reduced-fat version, a traditional soy sauce with a low-sodium tamari sauce. Remember that no one expects to sacrifice flavor when they attempt to make their diets more healthful, so be sure to sample different brands to get the best quality.

In some cases, there is no really good substitute. In that case, it is better to simply reduce the ingredient, or change the way in which these foods are used in a menu item. Instead of blending a large amount of heavy cream into a soup, for instance, try floating a rosette or dollop on top of the soup. It will still add richness and flavor, without as many calories.

Summary

Nutrition may have been viewed askance by classically trained chefs even as recently as a few years ago. In today's climate, however, there is no excuse for failing to meet your guests' needs for highly nutritious and delicious foods. The two needs are intertwined in the best of health-conscious cooking.

CHAPTER 4 *Equipment Identification*

Using the right tool for the job is one of the hallmarks of a professional. Equally important is the ability to handle and care for all tools, whether it is a cutting board, a knife, a mandoline, or a stockpot. Tools, large and small, are what make it possible for a chef to do the job well. This does not mean that you cannot perform well without the newest, most advanced, or most expensive. Many of the pieces described in this chapter are simple items—including pots, pans, and other utensils whose design and construction have not changed in decades, even centuries.

Assembling a personal collection of knives is one of the first elements in becoming a professional. Just as an artist or craftsman gathers together the pieces necessary for painting, sculpting, or drawing, you will need to begin a lifetime of selecting the knives that fit your hand the best. They will become as important to you as your own fingers—quite literally an extension of your own hands.

In addition to knives, well-equipped kitchens need a variety of other pieces: bowls, pots, pans, stoves, refrigerators, storage and service pieces, mixers, blenders, food processors, slicers, and smokers. Learning to handle all types of equipment with care and respect is a crucial part of your training. As technology continues to refine old tools and introduce new ones, you will need to learn constantly about what is being used elsewhere. Trade shows, journals, and your own network of contacts will expose you to various tricks and tools, from a food-grade piece of PVC pipe used as a mold to a software program that tracks sales, inventory, prep lists, staffing, and payroll.

Knives

The importance of knives to a professional chef or cook cannot be overstated. The only piece of equipment more basic to cooking is the human hand. All knives should be treated with great respect and care. The following rules concerning knife care, use, and storage are automatic behavior for professionals:

1. *Handle knives with respect.* Professionals have their own collection of knives, which they care for, maintain, and use daily. You should never use someone else's personal knife without first obtaining permission. Handle it with the same care that you would your own, and be sure to return it promptly.

Many people will engrave their name on the blade of the knife, so that they can identify which knives belong to them. If you work in a large kitchen, this is generally a good idea.

2. *Keep knives sharp.* Learn the proper techniques for both sharpening and honing knives. (See Figures 4-1 and 4-2.) A sharp knife not only performs better but is safer to use, because less pressure is required to cut through the food. When too much pressure is exerted, there is a good possibility the knife will slip and cause injury to the user.

Various tools are used to sharpen knives. A steel should be within reach at all times. Use a stone periodically to sharpen knives, or use a sharpening machine, such as the one shown here. Severely

FIGURE 4-1   Sharpening a Knife on a Stone

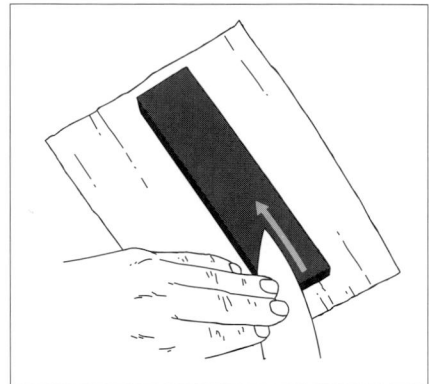

(1) Place the stone on a towel to prevent slipping. Hold the knife at a 20-degree angle and push it over the stone's surface, using your guiding hand to keep even pressure on the blade.

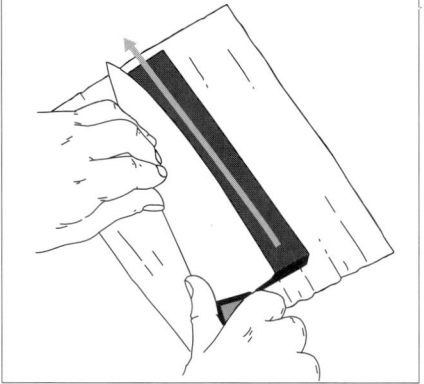

(2) Continue to push the knife over the surface, so that the entire length of the blade is sharpened.

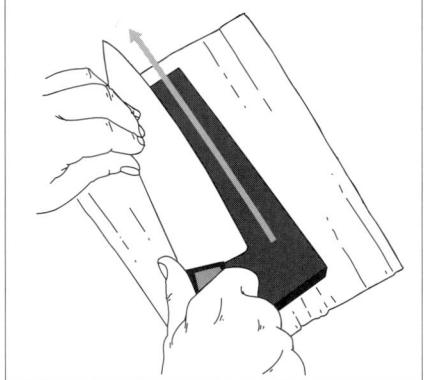

(3) Pull the knife off the stone smoothly, making sure that the total length of the blade has been sharpened, from the tip to the heel.

(4) Turn the knife over and repeat the process on the second side. Notice that the position of the guiding hand changes.

FIGURE 4-2   Honing a Knife with a Steel

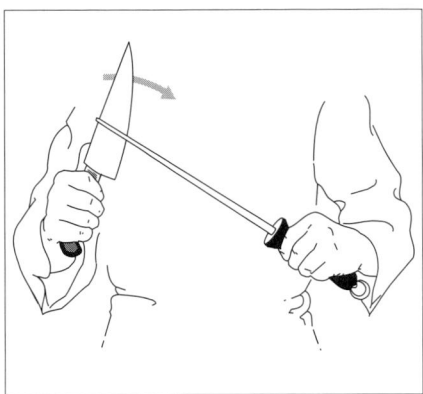

(1) Hold the steel away from the body in one hand and hold the knife in the other. Start with the knife nearly vertical, with the blade resting on the inner side of the steel at a 20-degree angle.

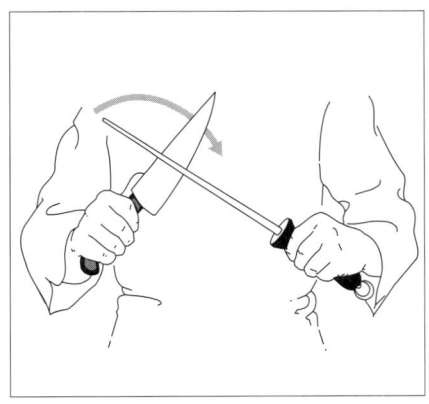

(2) Pass the blade along the entire length of the steel, rotating the wrist as the blade moves. Keep the pressure even and light.

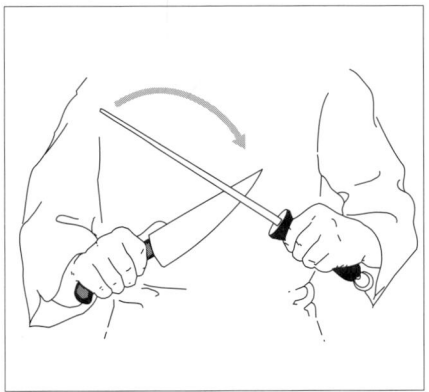

(3) Keep the blade in contact with the steel for the last few inches, so as to be properly honed.

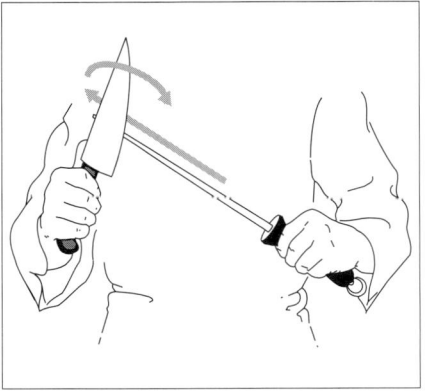

(4) Return the blade to a nearly vertical position, this time on the outer side of the steel, to hone the second side of the knife.

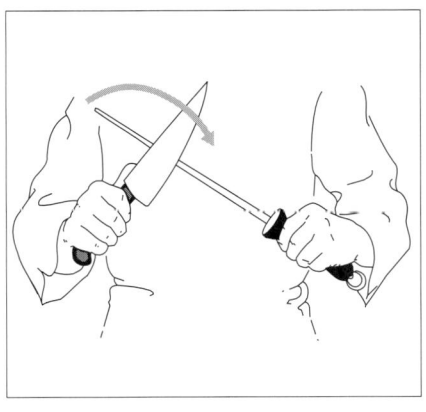

(5) Use the thumb to maintain even, light pressure.

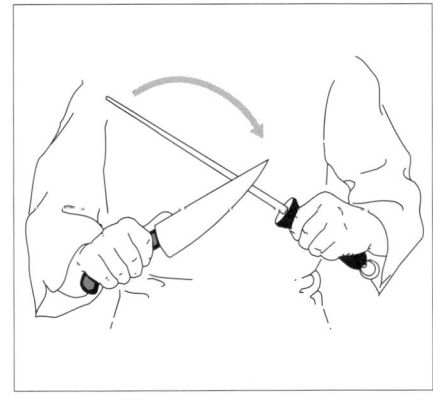

(6) Finish the second pass, making sure the entire length of the blade, including the tip, is properly honed.

dulled or damaged blades may need to be reground in order to restore the edge. This usually is done on sharpening wheels, by professionals who specialize in the maintenance of knives.

3. *Keep knives clean.* Clean knives thoroughly immediately after using them. Do not leave them lying in or near the sink. Work carefully, and pay attention to what you are doing, so that you do not cut yourself as you wipe down the blade. Sanitize the entire knife, including the handle, bolster, and blade, as necessary, so that the tool will not become a site for food cross-contamination. Keeping knives clean helps to extend their lives.

Never drop a knife into a full pot sink. The knife might be dented or nicked by heavy pots; also, someone who reaches into the sink could be seriously injured by grabbing the blade. Do not clean knives in a dishwasher, because the handles are likely to warp and split.

4. *Use safe handling procedures for knives.* In addition to the etiquette involved in borrowing a knife, there are other standards of behavior that should be remembered. When you are passing a knife, lay it down on a work surface so that the handle is extended to the person who will pick it up. Whenever you must carry a knife from one area of the kitchen

to another, hold the blade down and let people know you are passing by with something sharp. Ideally, you should sheathe or wrap the knife before walking anywhere with it, or transport it in a carrier.

When you lay a knife down on a work surface, be sure that no part of it extends over the cutting board or worktable. That will prevent people walking by from brushing against it or knocking it onto the floor. Be sure that the blade is positioned so that it extends away from any edges.

Knives are intended for specific cutting tasks. They are not built for opening bottles and cans, prying lids loose, or other such tasks. Using them inappropriately can, at best, nick or mar the blade. At worst, the blade can break, and pieces may fly off into the surrounding area.

5. *Use an appropriate cutting surface.* Cutting directly on metal, glass, or marble surfaces will dull and eventually damage the blade of a knife. Wooden or composition cutting boards should always be used to prevent dulling the knife edge. For information about caring for cutting boards, see Chapter 2.

6. *Keep knives properly stored.* There are a number of safe, practical ways to store knives. They may be kept in knife kits or rolls for one's personal collection, and in slots, racks, and magnetized holders in the kitchen. Storage systems should be kept just as clean as the knives stored in them. Cloth rolls should be washed and sanitized periodically. Proper storage will prevent damage to the blade or harm to an unwary individual. Knives should be carefully dried after cleaning, then stored in sheaths to help retain their edge.

A wide array of knives is available to suit specific functions. Over time a chef's knife kit will grow to encompass not only the basics—chef's or French knife, boning knife, paring knife, and slicer—but also a number of special knives, such as a tourné knife, serrated knife, utility knife, flexible-blade knives, and clam and oysters knives.

The Parts of a Knife

Selecting a knife of good quality that fits the hand and is suitable for the intended tasks depends on a

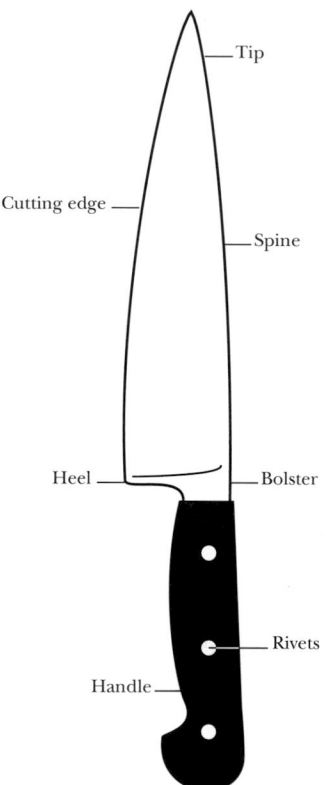

FIGURE 4-3   Parts of the Knife

basic knowledge of the various parts of the knife (see Figure 4-3).

Blades

The most frequently used material for good-quality blades is high-carbon stainless steel. Other materials, such as stainless steel and carbon steel, are also available.

For many years, carbon steel was used to make most knife blades. Although carbon steel blades take a better edge than either regular or high-carbon stainless steel, they tend to lose their sharpness quickly. Also, carbon steel blades will discolor in contact with high-acid foods, such as tomatoes or onions.

Carbon steel blades must be treated carefully to avoid discoloration, rusting, and pitting; they should be washed and thoroughly dried between uses and before storage. The metal is brittle and can break easily under stress.

Stainless steel is much stronger than carbon steel and will not discolor or rust. It is very difficult to get a good edge on a stainless steel blade, although once an edge is established, it tends to last longer than that on a carbon steel blade.

High-carbon stainless steel is a relatively recent development that combines the advantages of carbon and stainless steel. The higher percentage of carbon allows the blade to take and keep a keener edge; the fact that it is stainless steel means that it will not discolor or rust readily.

The most desirable type of blade is "taper-ground." This means that the blade has been forged out of a single metal sheet and has been ground so that it tapers smoothly from the spine to the cutting edge, with no apparent beveling. Frequently used knives should be made with taper-ground blades.

Hollow-ground blades are made by combining two sheets of metal; the edges are then beveled or fluted. Although hollow-ground blades often have very sharp edges, the blade itself lacks the balance and longevity of a taper-ground blade. This type is often found on knives, such as slicers, that are used less frequently in the kitchen.

Tangs

The tang is a continuation of the blade and extends into the knife's handle. Knives used for heavy work, such as chef's knives or cleavers, should have a full tang; that is, the tang is as long as the entire handle. A partial tang does not run the length of the handle. Although blades with partial tangs are not as durable as those with full tangs, they are acceptable for less-used knives. Rat-tail tangs are much thinner than the spine of the blade and are encased in the handle (not visible at the top or bottom edges); these tangs tend not to hold up under extended use.

Handles

A preferred material for knife handles is rosewood, because it is extremely hard and has no grain, which helps to prevent splitting and cracking. Impregnating wood with plastic protects the

handle from damage caused by continued exposure to water and detergents. Some state codes require that plastic handles be used in butcher shops, because they are considered more sanitary than wood. Care must be taken to thoroughly remove grease, however, because it adheres more closely to plastic than it does to wood.

The handle should fit your hand comfortably. Manufacturers typically produce handles that fit a variety of hands. Spend some time holding the knife. A comfortable fit will improve the ease and speed with which you work. A poor fit can result in fatigue, or cramping. People with very small or very large hands should be sure that they are not straining their grip to hold the handle. Some knives are especially constructed to meet the needs of left-handed chefs.

Rivets

Metal fasteners called rivets are used to secure the tang to the handle. The rivets should be completely smooth and lie flush with the surface of the handle to prevent irritation to the hand and to avoid causing pockets where microorganisms can gather.

Bolsters

In some knives there is a collar or shank, known as a bolster, at the point where the blade meets the handle. This is a sign of a well-made knife, one that will hold up for a long time. Some knives may have a collar that looks like a bolster but is actually a separate piece attached to the handle. These knives tend to come apart easily and should be avoided.

Types of Knives

The number of knives that a chef will accumulate over the course of a career will undoubtedly include a number of special knives that are not discussed below. There are, for example, several special knives and cutting tools found exclusively in

FIGURE 4-4   Knives

(from left to right) Chef's knives of various sizes, paring knife, clam knife, oyster knife.

FIGURE 4-5   Knives

(clockwise from top left) Tourné knives, scimitar, slicers (two sizes), utility knife, boning knife, filleting knife, meat cleavers, Asian cleaver.

the bakeshop; still others are required for butchering meats and fabricating fish. This list is intended as a guide to the knives that may be found in nearly any well-outfitted knife kit. See Figures 4-4 and 4-5 for examples of several types of knives.

Chef's Knife, or French Knife   This all-purpose knife is used for a variety of chopping, slicing, and mincing chores. The blade is normally 8 to 14 inches long.

Utility Knife   This smaller, lighter chef's knife is used for light cutting chores. The blade is generally 5 to 7 inches long.

Paring Knife   This short knife, used for paring and trimming vegetables and fruits, has a 2- to 4-inch blade.

Boning Knife   A boning knife is used to separate raw meat from the bone. The blade, which is thinner and shorter than the blade of a chef's knife, is about 6 inches long, and is usually rigid.

Filleting Knife   Used for filleting fish, this knife is similar in shape and size to a boning knife, but has a flexible blade.

Slicer   This knife is used for slicing cooked meat. It has a long blade with a round or pointed tip. The blade may be flexible or rigid and may be taper-ground or have a fluted edge that consists of hollow ground ovals.

Cleaver   Used for chopping, the cleaver is often heavy enough to cut through bones. It has a rectangular blade and varies in size according to its use.

Tourné Knife   This small knife, similar to a paring knife, has a curved blade to make cutting the curved surfaces of tournéed vegetables easier.

Sharpening and Honing Tools

The key to the proper and efficient use of any knife is making sure that it is sharp. A knife with a sharp blade always works better and more safely because it cuts easily, without requiring the chef to exert pressure, which may cause the knife to slip and an injury to result. Knife blades are given an edge on a sharpening stone and maintained between sharpenings by honing with a steel (see Figure 4-6).

FIGURE 4-6 Sharpening and Honing Tools

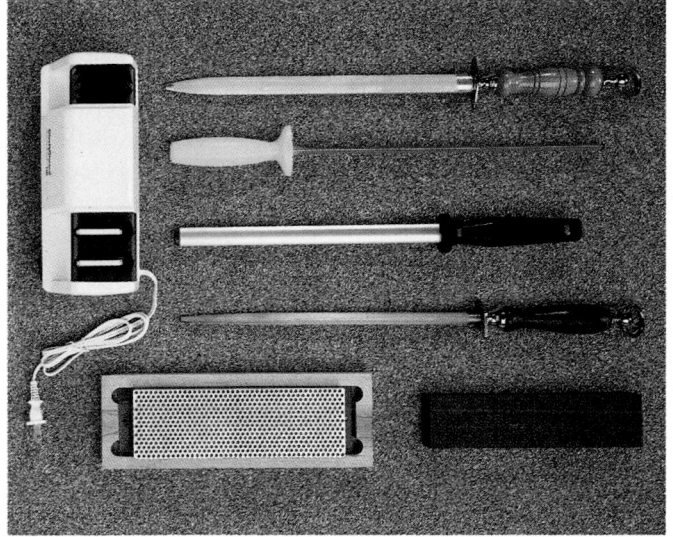

(from top left) Electric knife sharpener, variety of steels, carborundum stone, diamond-impregnated stone in case.

Sharpening Stones

Sharpening stones are essential to the proper maintenance of knives, and are used to sharpen the blade by passing its edge over the stone at the correct angle. The grit—the degree of coarseness or fineness of the stone's surface—abrades the blade's edge, creating a sharp cutting edge. When sharpening a knife, always begin by using the coarsest surface of the stone and then move on to the finer surfaces. A stone with a fine grade should be used for boning knives and other tools in which an especially sharp edge is required. Most stones may be used either dry or moistened with water or mineral oil. Once oil has been used on a stone's surface, that practice should be continued. Three basic types of stones are commonly available:

• *Carborundum stones* have a fine side and a medium side.

• *Arkansas stones* are available in several grades of fineness and some consist of three stones of varying degrees of fineness mounted on a wheel.

• *Diamond-impregnated stones* are also available. Although they are expensive, some chefs prefer them because they feel these stones give a sharper

edge. The standard size for sharpening stones is 8-by-2-by-$\frac{13}{16}$ by inches.

Before using a stone, the chef should be sure that it is properly stabilized. Place carborundum or diamond stones on a dampened cloth to stabilize them. Make sure you have enough room to work. A triple-faced stone is mounted on a rotating framework that can be locked into position so that it will not move. The blade should be held at a 20-degree angle to the stone's surface and the entire length of the blade should be drawn across the stone.

Grinding wheels, electric sharpeners, leather strops (such as those used to sharpen barbers' blades), and other grinding tools may be necessary to replace or restore the edge of a badly dulled knife.

Steels

A steel should be used both immediately after sharpening the blade with a stone and also between sharpenings to keep the edges in alignment. The length of the steel's working surface can range from 3 inches for a pocket version to over 14 inches. Hard steel is the traditional material for steels. Other materials, such as glass, ceramic, and diamond-impregnated surfaces, are also available.

Steels come with coarse, medium, and fine grains. Some are magnetic, which helps the blade retain proper alignment and also collects metal shavings. A guard or hilt between the steel and the handle protects the user, and a ring on the bottom of the handle can be used to hang the steel.

When using a steel, the knife is held almost vertically, with the blade at a 20-degree angle, resting on the inner side of the steel. The blade should be drawn along the entire length of the steel.

Hand Tools

A number of small tools other than knives belong in a knife kit (see Figure 4-7). It should be noted that, in addition to the hand tools listed here, many others such as cherry pitters, strawberry hullers,

FIGURE 4-7   Small Tools

(from top left) spider, skimmer, tongs, offset spatula, flexible spatulas, fish spatula (peltex), kitchen forks, wooden spoon (slotted and solid), pasta fork/spoon, slotted and solid kitchen spoons, swivel-bladed peeler, zest, channel knife, parisienne scoops/melon ballers, ladels, whips, box grater, and in center, scoops.

and tomato knives (also known as tomato witches) are used in the professional kitchen for various specific functions. Tools designed to scale fish, open clams and oysters, or even cut eggs can be found in some knife kits.

Rotary or Swivel-Bladed Peeler   This is used to peel the skin from various vegetables and fruits. The swivel action accommodates the contours of various products. Because the blade is sharpened on both sides, it will peel in both an upward and downward motion. Using it correctly will greatly increase the speed with which you can "prep" vegetables.

Parisienne Scoop (Melon Baller)   This is specifically designed for scooping out balls or ovals (depending upon the shape of the scoop) of vegetables and fruits.

Kitchen Fork   The fork is used to test the doneness of braised meats and vegetables, for lifting finished items to the carving board or plate, and to steady the item being carved. A kitchen fork should not be used to turn foods being sautéed, grilled, or

broiled, because the tines will pierce the food and let the juices emerge.

Palette Knife (Metal Spatula)   This is a flexible, round-tipped tool used in the kitchen and bakeshop for turning pancakes or grilled foods, spreading fillings and glazes, and a variety of other functions. A palette knife with a serrated edge is useful for preparing and slicing sandwiches.

Whips   Whips are used to beat, blend, and whip foods. Balloon whips are sphere shaped and have thin wires to incorporate air for making foams. Sauce whips are narrower and frequently have thicker wires. The chef should have a number of whips in various sizes.

Offset Spatula   This spatula is used to turn or lift foods on grills, broilers, and griddles. It has a wide, chisel-edged blade set in a short handle.

Pastry Bag   This plastic, canvas, or nylon bag is used to pipe out puréed foods, whipped cream, and various toppings. Pastry bags have uses in both the kitchen and the bakeshop.

   Other kitchen hand tools include (but are not limited to) items such as rubber scrapers; ladles of various sizes; skimmers for skimming the surface of stocks, soups, etc.; "spiders" for lifting foods out of liquids or fats; spoons of various sorts, wooden and metal serving spoons, tasting spoons, and slotted or solid spoons; scoops of various sizes; hardwood rolling pins; and plastic or wooden cutting boards.

Small Equipment

The tools outlined in this section are available in any well-equipped kitchen. For the sake of clarity, they have been categorized here according to their general function.

Measuring Equipment

   Measurements are determined in many different ways in a professional kitchen, depending upon the ingredient to be measured and the system employed by a specific recipe. This makes it important to have equipment for liquid and dry volume measures for both U.S. and metric, as well as a variety of scales for accurate measurement by weight. Thermometers should display both Fahrenheit and Centigrade temperatures.

Graduated Measuring Pitchers These are used for measuring liquids and are generally available in pint, quart, and gallon sizes.

Scales These are used to weigh ingredients for preparation and portion control. Ounce/gram and pound/kilo scales both should be available. Scales may be spring-type, balance beam, or electronic.

Thermometers An instant-reading thermometer is used to measure the internal temperature of food. The stem, inserted in the food, gives an instant reading. Candy and deep-fat thermometers are also helpful.

Measuring Spoons Measuring spoons typically come in the following sizes: tablespoon, teaspoon, ½ teaspoon, and ¼ teaspoon. Some sets also have ½ tablespoon and ⅛ teaspoon measures.

Bowls for Mixing

Most kitchens are equipped with a variety of bowls, usually a nonreactive material, such as stainless steel. Copper bowls are often included in the kitchen's stock of mixing bowls, since they are considered best for whipping egg whites.

Bowls should be reserved for mixing, rather than using them for storage containers, unless there is no other option.

Storage Containers

Foods in the kitchen are stored as raw products, partially prepared items, or as cooked items that are to be held for the next day's service. It is crucial to have an adequate store of containers to hold foods safely in the refrigerator or freezer. In addition to plastic or stainless steel containers (which

FIGURE 4-8 Sieves, Strainers, and Chinois

(from top left) salad spinner, cheesecloth, pasta machine, colander, ricer, food mill with interchangeable disks, parchment, cone sieve/chinois (regular and fine), and food-handlers gloves, in center.

may or may not have fitted lids), you will also require butcher's paper, plastic wrap, foil, and freezer wrap. Tools for securing and marking stored foods include tape and waterproof markers.

Sieves, Strainers, and Chinois

Sieves and strainers (see Figure 4-8) are mainly used to sift, aerate, and help to remove any large impurities from dry ingredients. They are also used to drain or purée cooked or raw foods.

Food Mill This is a type of strainer used to purée soft foods. A flat, curving blade is rotated over a disk by a hand-operated crank. Most professional models have interchangeable disks with holes of varying fineness. An exception is the Foley food mill, which has a mesh disk that is fixed in place.

Note: Many mixing machines may be used like a food mill through the addition of attachments that allow them to strain and purée foods.

Drum Sieve (Tamis) This sieve consists of a tinned-steel, nylon, or stainless-steel screen stretched in an aluminum or wood frame. A drum sieve is used for sifting or puréeing. A *champignon* (mushroom-shaped pusher) or a rigid plastic scraper is used to push the food through the screen.

Chinois   This conical sieve is used for straining and/or puréeing food. The openings in the cone can be of varying sizes, from very large to a fine mesh. A fine chinois (also known as a bouillon strainer) is a valuable piece of equipment and should be treated with great respect. It should be cleaned immediately after each use and stored properly; never drop it into a pot sink where it could be crushed or torn.

Colander   This stainless-steel sieve, with or without a base, is used for straining foods. Colanders are available in a variety of sizes.

Ricer   This is a device in which cooked food, often potatoes, is placed in a hopper, which is pierced with holes. A plate on the end of a lever pushes the food through the hopper walls. Garlic presses and french-fry cutters operate on the same principle.

Cheesecloth   This light, fine mesh gauze is frequently used in place of a fine chinois and is essential for straining some sauces. It is also used for making sachets. Before use, cheesecloth should be rinsed thoroughly in hot water and then cold water to remove any loose fibers. Cheesecloth also clings better to the sides of bowls, chinois, and so forth when it is wet.

Pots, Pans, and Molds

Various materials and combinations of materials are used in the construction of pots, pans, and molds. Because form and function are closely related, it is important to choose the proper equipment for the task at hand.

Pots made of copper transfer heat rapidly and evenly; because direct contact with copper will affect the color and consistency of many foods, copper pots are generally lined. (An exception is the copper pan used to cook jams, jellies, and other high-sugar items, often known as preserving pans.) Great care must be taken not to scratch the lining, which is usually a soft metal, such as tin. Copper also tends to discolor quickly, and so it requires significant time and labor for proper upkeep.

Cast iron has the capacity to hold heat well and transmit it very evenly. The metal is somewhat brittle, however, and must be treated carefully to prevent pitting, scarring, and rusting. Cast iron is sometimes coated with enamel during manufacture to simplify care and increase its useful life.

Stainless steel is a moderately good conductor of heat, but is often preferred because it has other advantages, including easy maintenance. Other metals, such as aluminum or copper, are often sandwiched within stainless steel to improve heat conduction. Stainless steel will not react with foods; this means, for example, that white sauces will retain a pure white or ivory color.

Blue-steel, black-steel, pressed-steel, or rolled-steel pans are all prone to discoloration but transmit heat very rapidly. These pans are generally thin, and are often preferred for sautéing foods because of their quick response to changes in temperature.

Aluminum is also an excellent conductor of heat; however, it is a soft metal that wears down quickly. When a metal spoon or whip is used to stir a white or light-colored sauce, soup, or stock in an aluminum pot, it could take on a gray color. Anodized or treated aluminum tends not to react with foods, and it is one of the most popular metals for pots used in contemporary kitchens. The surfaces of treated aluminum pans tend to be easier to clean and care for than most other metals, with the exception of stainless steel.

Nonstick coatings on pans have some use in professional kitchens, especially for those that try to offer foods that are cooked with less fats and oils. These surfaces are not as sturdy as metal or enamel linings, so care must be taken to avoid scratching during cooking and cleaning. New methods of adding nonstick coatings as well as new materials used to create these coatings have produced more durable nonstick pans, suitable in many cooking situations.

The following guidelines should be observed for the choice of a pan or mold:

• *Choose a size appropriate to the food being cooked.*

The chef should be familiar with the capacity of various pots, pans, and molds. If too many pieces of meat are crowded into a sauteuse, for instance, the food will not brown properly. If the sauteuse is too large, however, the *fond* (caramelized drippings from the meat) could scorch. If a small fish is poached in a large pot, the *cuisson* (cooking liquid) will not have the proper flavor intensity. It is also easier to overcook the fish in a too-large pot. If the pot is too small, there may not be enough cuisson available for the sauce.

- *Choose material appropriate to the cooking technique.*

Experience has shown, and science has verified, that certain cooking techniques are more successful when used with certain materials. For instance, sautéed foods require pans that transmit heat quickly and are sensitive to temperature changes. Braises, on the other hand, require long, fairly gentle cooking, and it is more important that the particular pot transmit heat evenly and hold heat well than that it respond rapidly to changes in heat.

- *Use proper handling, cleaning, and storing techniques.*

Avoid subjecting pots to heat extremes (for example, placing a smoking-hot pot into a sinkful of water) because some materials are prone to warping. Other materials may chip or even crack if allowed to sit over heat when they are empty or if they are handled roughly. Casseroles or molds made of enameled cast iron or steel are especially vulnerable. In order to protect the "seasoning" of rolled steel pans, do not clean the surface with detergents or abrasives such as steel wool or cleansing powders.

- *Be sure to dry pans before storing.*

Air drying is best to prevent the pitting and rusting of some surfaces, as well as to keep them clean and sanitary. Proper and organized storage prevents dents, chips, and breakage, and expedites the work load, because staff can more readily find what they need.

Pots and Pans for Stove Top Cooking

Pots and pans are not only available in a variety of materials but are also produced in a number of different sizes. (See Figure 4-9.) All must be able to withstand direct heat from a flame. A poorly produced pot will have weak spots that will eventually warp. Different manufacturers, however, may use different styles of handles, loops, or lids.

Stockpot (Marmite) This large pot, of medium-gauge metal, is taller than it is wide, and has straight sides. Some stockpots have a spigot at the base so that the liquid can be drained off without lifting the heavy pot. Anodized aluminum and stainless steel are the preferred materials.

Saucepot This pot is similar in shape to a stockpot, although not as large, with straight sides and two loop handles for lifting.

Saucepan This pan has straight or slightly flared sides (a pan with flared sides may be known as a *fait-tout*) and has a single long handle.

Rondeau This is a wide, fairly shallow pot with two loop handles. When made from cast iron, these pots are frequently known as "griswolds," and they may have a single short handle rather than the two loop handles. A brazier is similar to a rondeau and may be square instead of round.

Sauteuse This shallow skillet with sloping sides and a single long handle is often referred to as a sauté pan.

Sautoir This shallow skillet has straight sides and a single long handle. It is also often referred to as a sauté pan.

Omelet Pan/Crêpe Pan This shallow skillet has very short, slightly sloping sides, and is most often made of rolled or "blue" steel.

Bain-Marie (Double-Boiler) These are nesting pots with single long handles. The bottom pot is filled with water that is heated to gently cook or warm the food in the upper pot. The term also refers to the stainless-steel containers used to hold food in a steam table.

Griddle This is a heavy round or rectangular surface for griddling. A griddle is flat with no sides or handles and may be built directly into the stove.

FIGURE 4-9   Pot Rack

(top row) stock pot, steamer insert, colander; (second row) various sauteuse, saucepans, and small sauce/stock pot; (third row) in foreground, various sizes of sauteuse; stainless steel, bimetals/copper, anodized aluminum; in background; lids, couscousière, fish poacher, small copper roasting pan/baking dish; hanging: paella pan; (fourth row) foreground, crepe pan; background, nested saucepots with loops handles, copper saucepan with handle, saucepot with loop handles, and copper roasting pan, rondeau and nested sauce pots; hanging, wok; (bottom row) marmite/stockpot, half-size sheet pans, chinois, perforated insert for hotel pan and hotel pan, roasting pan (with various lids) on full-size sheet pans.

There may be a groove or indentation around the edge to allow grease to drain away.

Fish Poacher This is a long, narrow pot with straight sides and may include a perforated rack for holding the fish.

Steamer This consists of a set of stacked pots. The upper pot has a perforated bottom and is placed over a larger pot, which is filled with boiling or simmering water. The perforations allow the steam to rise from the pot below to cook the food above. Tiered steamers are also available.

Specialty Pots and Pans Woks, couscoussières, paella pans, and grill pans (the latter is essentially a skillet with ridges that can simulate grilling) are among the stove-top pots and pans used to prepare special, usually ethnic, dishes.

Pots and Pans for Oven Cooking

Pans used in ovens are produced from the same basic materials as those used to make stove-top pots and pans. Glazed and unglazed earthenware, glass, and ceramics are also used. The heat of the oven, less intense than that of a burner, prevents these more delicate materials from cracking and shattering because of extreme temperature. It is important to remember not to submerge these materials into water immediately after removing them from the oven.

Roasting Pan This rectangular pan with medium-high sides is used for roasting or baking and comes in various sizes.

Sheet Pan This shallow, rectangular pan is used for baking and may be full or half size.

Hotel Pans These are rectangular pans, used occasionally for preparing foods, but more often as containers to hold foods that are already cooked in steamtables, hot boxes, or for use in electric or gas steamers. They are also frequently used to marinate meats or for food storage under refrigeration. They may be shallow, deep, divided, or half-size. Chafing dishes usually are of standard sizes, so that most hotel pans will fit them properly.

Pâté Mold A deep rectangular metal mold, the pâté mold usually has hinged sides to facilitate removal of the pâté. Special shapes (oval, triangular, and others) may be available.

Terrine Mold The terrine mold may be rectangular or oval, with a lid. Traditionally an earthenware mold, it may also be made of enameled cast iron.

Gratin Dish A shallow oval baking dish, this may be ceramic, enameled cast iron, or enameled steel.

Soufflé Dish This is a round, straight-edged ceramic dish of various sizes.

Timbale Mold This small metal or ceramic mold is used for individual portions of various molded, cooked vegetables, usually made with a custard base.

Specialty Molds These include dariole, savarin, ring, and other molds that are used to achieve varying shapes.

Large Equipment

Safety precautions must be observed and proper maintenance and cleaning consistently applied in order to keep this equipment functioning properly and to prevent injury or accident. Observe the following guidelines when working with large equipment:

1. *Obtain proper instruction in the machine's safe operation. Do not be afraid to ask for extra help.*

2. *First turn off and then unplug electrical equipment before assembling or breaking down the equipment.*

3. *Use all safety features: Be sure that lids are secure, hand guards are used, and the machine is stable.*

4. *Clean and sanitize the equipment thoroughly after each use.*

5. *Be sure that all pieces of equipment are properly reassembled and left unplugged after each use.*

6. *Report any problems or malfunctions promptly and alert coworkers to the problem.*

FIGURE 4-10   Blenders

(clockwise from top left) bar blender with stainless jar, glass jar, and immersion (burr/stick) blender.

Grinding, Slicing, and Puréeing Equipment

Grinders, slicers, and cutting equipment (see Figures 4-10 and 4-11) all have the potential to be extremely dangerous. The importance of observing all the necessary safety precautions cannot be overemphasized. As these tools are essential for a number of different operations, all chefs should be able to use them with confidence.

Meat Grinder   This is a free-standing machine or an attachment for a standing mixer. A meat grinder should have dies of varying sizes and in general will have a feed tray and a pusher. All food contact areas should be kept scrupulously clean. To make sure all the food has been pushed through the worm, feed a twisted coil of plastic wrap through the feed tube.

Vertical Chopping Machine (VCM)   This machine operates on the same principle as a blender. A motor at the base is permanently attached to a bowl with integral blades. As a safety precaution, the

FIGURE 4-11   Mandoline with Guard

hinged lid must be locked in place before the unit will operate. The VCM is used to grind, whip, emulsify, blend, or crush foods.

Food Chopper (Buffalo Chopper)   The food is placed in a rotating bowl that passes under a hood, where blades chop the food. Some units have hoppers or feed tubes and interchangeable disks for slicing and grating. Food choppers are available in floor and tabletop models and are generally made of aluminum with a stainless-steel bowl.

Food Processor   This is a processing machine that houses the motor separately from the bowl, blades, and lid. Food processors can grind, purée, blend, emulsify, crush, knead, and, with special disks, slice, julienne, and shred foods.

Food/Meat Slicer   This machine is used to slice foods in even thicknesses. A carrier moves the food back and forth against a circular blade, which is generally carbon steel. There may be separate motors to operate the carrier and the blade. To avoid injury, all the safety features incorporated in a food slicer, especially the hand guard, should be used.

Mandoline   This slicing device is made of nickel-plated stainless steel with blades of high-carbon steel. Levers adjust the blades to achieve the cut and thickness desired. As with food slicers, be sure to use the guard—the carriage device that holds the food—to prevent injury. The mandoline can be used to make such cuts as slices, juliennes, gaufrettes, and batonnet.

Kettles and Steamers

Kettles and steamers enable a chef to prepare large amounts of food efficiently, since the heat is applied over a much larger area than is possible when a single burner is used. Cooking times for dishes prepared in steamers and large kettles are often shorter than for those prepared on a range top.

Steam-Jacketed Kettle This free-standing or tabletop kettle circulates steam through the walls, providing even heat. Units vary; they may tilt, may be insulated, and may have spigots or lids. Available in a range of sizes, these kettles are excellent for producing stocks, soups, and sauces. They are generally made of stainless steel and sometimes have a specially treated nonstick surface. Gas or electric models are available.

Tilting Kettle This large, relatively shallow free-standing unit is used for braising and stewing. Most tilting kettles have lids, allowing for steaming as well. They are usually made of stainless steel and are available in gas or electric models.

Pressure Steamer Water is heated under pressure in a sealed compartment, allowing it to reach higher than boiling temperature (212°F/100°C at sea level). The cooking time is controlled by automatic timers, which open the exhaust valves at the end. The doors cannot be opened until the pressure has been released.

Convection Steamer The steam is generated in a boiler and then piped to the cooking chamber, where it is vented over the food. Pressure does not build up in the unit; it is continuously exhausted, which means the door may be opened at any time without danger of scalding or burning.

Stoves, Ranges, and Ovens

It is difficult to imagine a kitchen without a stove. The stove top is known as the range; the oven is usually below the range. There are a number of different variations on this standard arrangement, however, just as there a number of different range tops and ovens available today.

Ranges

Gas or electric ranges are available in many sizes with various combinations of open burners, flat-tops (not to be confused with griddle units), and ring-tops. Open burners and ring-tops supply direct heat, which is easy to change and control. Small units known as candy stoves or stockpot ranges have rings of gas jets that allow for excellent heat control. Flat-tops provide indirect heat, which is more even and less intense than direct heat. Foods that require long, slow cooking, such as stocks, are more effectively cooked on a flat-top.

Open-Burner Range This is an individual grate-style burner that allows for easy adjustment of heat.

Flat-Top Range This consists of a thick plate of cast-iron or steel set over the heat source. Flat-tops give relatively even and consistent heat but do not allow for quick adjustments of temperature.

Ring-Top Range This is a flat-top with concentric rings or plates that can be removed to widen or close the opening, supplying more or less direct heat.

Ovens

Ovens cook foods by surrounding them with hot air, a gentler and more even source of heat than the direct heat of a burner. Many types of roasted and baked food are prepared in ovens. Delicate foods such as custards are also cooked in an oven usually in a hot water bath (bain-marie). Different ovens are available to suit a variety of needs, and both the establishment's menu and its available space should be evaluated before determining what type and size oven to install.

Convection Oven Hot air is forced through fans to circulate around the food, cooking it evenly and quickly. Some convection ovens have the capacity to introduce moisture. They are available in gas or electric models, in a range of sizes, with stainless steel interiors and exteriors, and glass doors. Special features may include infrared and a convection-microwave combination.

Conventional/Deck Ovens   The heat source is located on the bottom, underneath the deck, or floor, of the oven. Heat is conducted through the deck to the cavity. Conventional ovens can be located below a range top or as individual shelves arranged one above another. The latter are known as deck ovens, and the food is placed directly on the deck, instead of on a wire rack. Deck ovens normally consist of two to four decks, though single-deck models are available. Some deck ovens have a ceramic or firebrick base. Deck ovens usually are gas or electric, although charcoal and wood-burning units are also available. The basic deck oven is most often used only for roasting, but several variations are available for other purposes.

Additional styles of ovens include pizza ovens, rotary ovens for spit roasting, conveyor ovens, and rotating deck ovens.

Slow Cookers/Combi Stoves

These stoves have been used extensively in Europe and are becoming more common in this country. The stove cooks at low temperatures, and may also steam foods. It can be used for both cooking foods and holding them at the correct service temperature, making them desirable in a number of different instances (catering, banquets, large scale operations, and so forth.) Some versions of these stoves are capable of smoking foods as well.

Smokers

A true smoker will treat foods with smoke (after they have been properly brined and cured, if necessary) and can be operated at either cool smoking or hot smoking temperatures. Racks or hooks are generally installed, allowing foods to hang so that the smoke circulates evenly around the item.

Small home-style smokers can be used in some operations if you will only be preparing a small volume of specialty items, such as smoked trout or cheese.

Griddles and Grills

Two other oven/range features, the griddle and the grill, are part of the traditional commercial foodservice setup.

Griddle   Similar to a flat-top range top, a griddle has a heat source located beneath a thick plate of metal, generally cast-iron or steel. The food is cooked directly on this surface. A griddle may be gas or electric.

Grill/Broiler/Salamander   In a grill, the heat source is located below the rack; in a broiler or salamander, the heat source is above. Some units have adjustable racks, which allow the food to be raised or lowered to control cooking speed. Most units are gas, although electric units with ceramic "rocks" create a bed of coals, producing the effect of a charcoal grill. Salamanders are small broilers, used primarily to finish or glaze foods.

Refrigeration Equipment

Maintaining adequate refrigeration storage is crucial to any foodservice operation; therefore, the menu and the available refrigeration storage must be evaluated and coordinated. All units should be maintained properly, which means regular and thorough cleaning, including the insulating strips. Such precautions will help reduce spoilage and thus reduce food costs. Placing the units so that unnecessary steps are eliminated will save time and labor. Both of these factors will save money for the operation.

Walk-In

This is the largest style of refrigeration unit and usually has shelves that are arranged around the walls. It is possible to zone a walk-in to maintain appropriate temperature and humidity levels for storing various foods. Some walk-ins are large enough to accommodate rolling carts for additional storage. The carts can then be rolled to the appropriate area of the kitchen when needed. Some units have pass-through or reach-in doors to facilitate access to frequently required items.

Walk-ins may be situated in the kitchen or outside the facility. If space allows, walk-ins located outside the kitchen can prove advantageous, because deliveries may be made at any time without disrupting service.

Reach-In

A reach-in may be a single unit or part of a bank of units, available in many sizes. Units with pass-through doors are especially helpful for the pantry area, where salads, desserts, and other cold items can be retrieved by the waitstaff as needed.

On-Site Refrigeration

These are refrigerated drawers or undercounter reach-ins, which allow foods on the line to be held at the proper temperature during service. This eliminates unnecessary walking, which can create a hazard during peak periods.

Portable Refrigeration

This is basically a refrigerated cart that can be placed as needed in the kitchen.

Display Refrigeration

These are display cases that are generally used in the dining room for desserts, salads, or salad bars.

Summary

Learning to use all the tools in a professional kitchen properly, efficiently, and skillfully is one of the initial hurdles on the road to becoming a chef. The care you expend in using and maintaining your personal knives, as well as the large and small equipment that are common property throughout the kitchen, is a mark of your level of professionalism and commitment to excellence.

CHAPTER 5

The Raw Ingredients

The successful operation of any foodservice establishment will demand careful attention in many areas. One of the most critical is the purchase of the foods that will be served to your guests.

This chapter offers a look at the factors you should take into account when deciding which foods to buy.

There is a great deal more to purchasing foods than could be covered here. You will find a number of other books listed in the Recommended Reading List—found at the end of this book—that can provide more information.

Whether the purchasing is handled directly by the chef or by a separate purchasing agent, it is the chef's responsibility to assure that any foods received and accepted are of excellent quality. They must be handled properly from the time they are received, throughout each phase of handling and service. You will find a good deal of information in Chapters 1 through 4 to help you make the most of one of the most precious commodities in a restaurant—the raw ingredients.

Meat Identification and Purchasing

For most restaurants, the purchase, preparation, and service of meats is one of the most expensive, as well as one of the most potentially profitable, areas of the business. In order to get the most value out of the meats purchased, it is important to understand how to select the right cut for a particular menu item.

Meat Basics

The meat, poultry, and game cuts that a restaurant should buy will depend upon the nature of the particular operation. A restaurant featuring predominantly *à la minute* preparations—especially those with a preponderance of grilled or sautéed items—will need to purchase extremely tender (and more expensive) cuts. A restaurant that uses a variety of techniques may be able to use some less tender cuts, for example, the veal shank in a braise such as osso bucco.

Meats can be purchased in a number of forms, and at varying degrees of readiness to cook. The chef should consider several factors when deciding what type of meat to buy. Storage capacity, equipment required to prepare a menu item, the kitchen staff's capability to butcher, or "fabricate" larger cuts, and the volume of meat required must all be taken into consideration. Once this information is evaluated, you can determine whether it is more economical to purchase large pieces, such as whole legs of veal, or prefabricated meats, such as veal already cut into a top round, or perhaps even precut scallopini, which have been trimmed and cut into portions (known as "pc").

Storage

Meats, poultry, and game should be loosely wrapped and stored under refrigeration. When possible, they should be held in a separate unit, or at least in a separate part of the cooler. They should always be placed on trays to prevent them from dripping on other foods or onto the floor.

FIGURE 5-1 Meats in Cryovac

The chef should separate different kinds of meats; for example, poultry should not come in contact with beef, or pork products in contact with any other meats. This will prevent cross-contamination.

Meats packed in Cryovac® (a special type of plastic wrapping shown in Figure 5-1) can be stored directly in the Cryovac®, as long as it has not been punctured or ripped. Once unwrapped, meats should be rewrapped in air-permeable paper, such as butcher's paper, because air-tight containers promote bacterial growth that could result in spoilage or contamination. Variety meats, poultry, and uncured pork products, all have short shelf lives, and should be cooked as soon as possible after they are received. Meat stored at the proper temperature and under optimal conditions can be held for several days without a noticeable quality loss, although there may be some loss of volume and weight.

Inspection and Grading

Government inspection of all meats is mandatory. Inspections are required at various times—on the farm or ranch and at the slaughterhouse (*ante-mortem*), and, again, after butchering (*post-mortem*). This is done to assure that the animal is free from disease, and that the meat is wholesome and fit for

FIGURE 5-2   Inspection Stamp

FIGURE 5-3   USDA Grade Shield

FIGURE 5-4   USDA Yield Grade

TABLE 5-1			
Beef	*Veal*	*Pork*	*Lamb*
Quality grades			
Prime*	Prime*	Acceptable*	Prime*
Choice*	Choice*	Utility	
Choice*			
Select	Good		Good
Standard	Standard		Utility
Commercial	Utility		Cull
Utility	Cull		
Cutter			
Canner			
Beef	*Veal*	*Pork*	*Lamb*
Yield Grades			
1	None	U.S. No. 1	1
2		U.S. No. 2	2
3		U.S. No. 3	3
4		U.S. No. 4	4
5			5

*These grades are used widely in foodservice and retail operations. Others are used for commercial operations, processing, and canning.
**Pork must have Acceptable grade in order to qualify for yield grades 1 to 4

human consumption. Inspection is a service paid for by tax dollars. (See Figure 5-2.)

Most states have relinquished the responsibility for inspecting meats to federal inspectors. Those states that still administer their own inspections of meat must at least meet, if not exceed, federal standards.

Grading, however, is not mandatory. The United States Department of Agriculture (USDA) has developed the specific standards used to assign grades to meats, and also trains graders. The costs involved in grading meats are absorbed by the individual meatpacker, not the taxpayer, since it is voluntary. The packer may, however, choose not to hire a USDA grader and may assign his or her own grade instead.

Depending upon the particular animal, the grader will consider the overall carcass shape, the ratio of fat to lean, ratio of meat to bones, color, and marbling of lean flesh. The grade placed on a particular carcass is then applied to all the cuts from that animal. (See Figure 5-3.) The eight USDA beef grades are: Prime, Choice, Select, Standard, Commercial, Utility, Cutter, Canner. Only a small percentage of meats produced will receive the "Prime" grade. Choice and select are more often available. Grades lower than Select are generally used for processed meat products. They are of no practical importance to the restaurant (or retail) industry.

Some meats may also receive yield grades (see Figure 5-4). This grade is of the greatest significance to wholesalers. It indicates the amount of salable meat in relation to the total weight of the carcass. Butchers refer to this as "cutability." In other words, it is a measure of the yield of edible meat from each pound of the carcass.

Table 5-1 indicates the range of quality and yield grade designations possible for beef, veal, pork, and lamb.

FIGURE 5-5   Kosher Stamp

Kosher Meats

Kosher meats are specially slaughtered, bled, and fabricated in order to comply with religious dietary laws. In this country, only beef and veal forequarters, poultry, and some game are customarily used for kosher preparations. The stamp for kosher meats is shown in Figure 5-5. Kosher meats are butchered from animals that have been slaughtered by a scholet. The animal must be killed with a single stroke of a knife, and then fully bled. All the veins and arteries must be removed from the meat. This process would essentially mutilate the flesh of loins and legs of beef and veal; therefore, they are generally not sold as "kosher" meat.

Market Forms of Meat

The obvious step after slaughtering, inspection, and grading the animal is to cut the carcass into manageable pieces. These divisions break the animal into what are referred to as "sides," "quarters," and "saddles." Sides are prepared by making a cut down the length of the backbone. Quarters are made by cutting sides into two pieces, dividing them between specifically determined vertebrae. Saddles are made by cutting the animal across the belly, again at a specified point or vertebrae. The exact standards for individual animal types govern where the carcass is to be divided.

The next step is cutting the animal into what are referred to as "primal cuts." There are also uniform standards for beef, veal, pork, and lamb primals. These large cuts are then further broken down into "subprimals." These cuts are generally trimmed and packed. There may be even more fabrication (butchering) done in order to prepare steaks, chops, roasts, stew, or ground meat. These cuts are referred to as retail cuts.

As the illustrations of the cuts of beef, pork, veal, and lamb shown in Figure 5-6 indicate, the divisions

FIGURE 5-6   Carcass Division

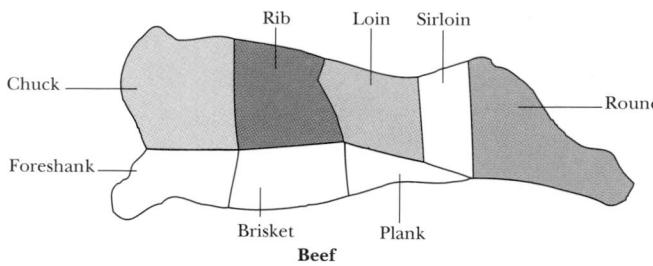

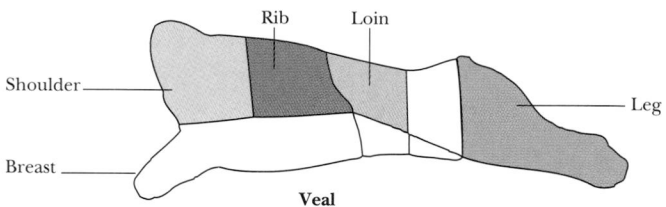

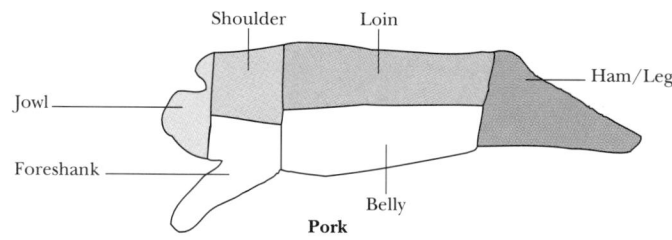

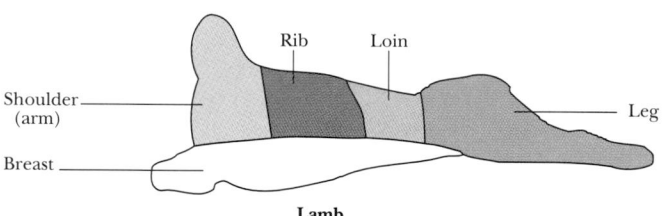

follow a similar pattern, whichever animal is being butchered, with only minor variations by type.

The amount of butchering done in packing plants has increased over the past several years. While it is still possible to purchase "hanging meat," as shown in Figure 5-7, most operations will buy what is referred to as "boxed meats." This indicates that the meat has been fabricated to a specific point (primal, subprimal, or retail cut), then packed in Cryovac®, boxed, and shipped for sale to purveyors, butchers, chain retail outlets, and so forth.

Beef

The beef industry is of great importance to the United States. We devote nearly 600 million acres of

FIGURE 5-7 Hanging Meat

land to pasture land in order to raise livestock. We produce more beef (and veal) than any other nation or group in the world. We also consume more on a per-capita basis than any other country in the world with the exception of Argentina. Special types of beef, including the Japanese "Kobe," French "Limousine," and, in this country, "Brae," "Certified Angus," "natural," "organic," and "aged" beef may be reputed to have specific benefits. If you purchase special meats for use on your menu, be sure that you identify them as such to derive the best value from them.

Organic and natural beef have not yet been clearly defined by the USDA. The terms are currently used in accordance with standards set by individual groups. Organic and natural may not necessarily mean that meats are free of antibiotics, steroids, or growth hormones although nationwide standards are being more clearly defined.

Aged beef was once more readily available, and had greater consumer acceptance than it enjoys today. Aging is traditionally done to a number of meats, including beef, venison, and game birds. The meat is allowed to hang, uncovered, in a controlled environment such as a meat locker. The temperature and humidity are carefully monitored.

Enzymes present in the meat begin to break down the meat fibers. This gives the meat a more pronounced, "higher" flavor and increases tenderness, but at the same time, reduces the overall yield. Some butchers still age meats, and will work with individuals to custom age meats to exact specifications.

Restaurants that feature beef, such as steak or chop houses, are an institution. Even if your restaurant only features one or two entrées based on beef, you cannot take shortcuts with this all-American commodity. Take the time to do your homework: Learn which cuts react best to which cooking methods. Get a good working knowledge of average yields from the cuts you feature on your menu. Consider the ways to maximize yield and profit without cutting into the customer's perception of dollar value. For more information refer to Table 5-2.

The Beef Primals

Primal and market cuts of beef are shown in Figures 5-8 to 5-14.

Chuck This large portion of the animal contains some of its most exercised muscles. This means that, as a general rule, cuts from the shoulder will be best when prepared by one of the moist or combination cooking methods. Long, slow cooking brings out the flavor of these cuts, while ameliorating any toughness.

In addition to cuts and steaks for braising, stewing meat and ground beef are often prepared from the chuck.

Rib The rib contains many of the most prized roasts and steaks. These cuts are tender, and well-suited to dry-heat cooking methods such as sautéing, roasting, grilling, and broiling.

"Prime" rib really has no specific meaning, and should be avoided in menu copy. It is often a confusing term, leading the customer to assume that the beef is graded "Prime." Rib roasts may be bone-in, or boneless. There are many specific menu terms used throughout the country to describe the size of the cut, including King cut, Queen's cut, English cut, or double cut. Doneness is generally of great concern.

Steaks cuts from the rib may be bone-in or boneless.

TABLE 5-2 BEEF CHART

Item Number	Product/Cut	Weight Range (Pounds)	Suggested Cooking Method
103	Rib	28–38	roast, sauté, panfry, broil, grill
104	Rib, oven-prepared, regular	22–30	roast, sauté, panfry, broil
107	Rib, oven-prepared	19–26	roast, sauté, panfry, broil
107A	Rib, oven-prepared, blade bone in	19–26	roast, sauté, panfry, broil
109	Rib, roast ready	16–22	roast
109A	Rib, roast ready, special, tied	16–22	roast
109B	Rib, blade meat	over 3	stew, braise
109C	Rib, roast ready, cover off	15–21	roast
109D	Rib, roast ready, cover off, short cut	14–20	roast
110	Rib, roast ready, boneless, tied	13–19	roast
112	Rib, ribeye roll	6–10	roast, sauté, panfry, broil
112A	Rib, ribeye roll, lip-on	7–11	roast, sauté, panfry, broil
113	Chuck, square-cut	79–106	roast, braise, simmer
114	Chuck, shoulder clod	15–21	roast, braise, simmer
114A	Chuck, shoulder clod, roast	15–21	roast
114B	Chuck, shoulder clod, roast, tied	15–21	roast, braise
115	Chuck, square-cut, boneless	65–88	roast, braise
116B	Chuck, chuck roll, tied	15–21	roast, braise
117	Foreshank	8–12	braise, simmer
118	Brisket	14–20	braise
120	Brisket, boneless, deckle-off	8–12	braise
121	Plate, short plate	27–35	braise, cook in liquid
121C	Plate, skirt steak (diaphram), outer	2–up	sauté, braise, grill, broil
121D	Plate, skirt steak, inner	3–up	sauté, braise, grill, broil
121E	Plate, skirt steak, skinned, outer	2–up	sauté, braise, grill, broil
123	Short ribs	3–5	braise
123A	Short plate, short ribs, trimmed	amount as specified	braise, broil, grill
123B	Rib, short ribs, trimmed	amount as specified	braise, broil, grill
123C	Rib, short ribs	amount as specified	braise, broil, grill
124	Rib, back ribs	amount as specified	braise, broil, grill
125	Chuck, armbone	88–118	braise, roast
126	Chuck, armbone, boneless (3-way)	70–90	braise, roast
126A	Chuck, armbone, boneless, clod-out	57–77	braise, roast
158	Round	71–95	roast, braise, simmer, broil, sauté, grill
158A	Round, diamond-cut	76–102	roast, braise, simmer, broil, panfry, sauté
159	Round, boneless	53–71	roast, braise, simmer, broil, panfry, sauté
160	Round, shank off, partially boneless	57–76	roast, braise, simmer, broil, panfry, sauté
161	Round, shank off, boneless	51–71	roast, braise, simmer, broil, panfry, sauté
163	Round, shank off, 3-way, boneless	50–66	roast, braise, simmer, broil, panfry, sauté
164	Round, rump and shank off	48–64	roast, braise, simmer, broil, panfry, sauté
165	Round, rump and shank off, boneless	43–57	roast, braise, simmer, broil, panfry, sauté
165A	Round, rump and shank off, boneless, special	46–60	roast, braise, simmer, broil, panfry, sauté
165B	Round, rump and shank off, boneless, special, tied	46–60	roast, braise
166	Round, rump and shank off, boneless, tied	43–57	roast, braise
166A	Round, rump partially removed, shank off, boneless, tied	52–70	roast, braise

BEEF CHART *(continued)*

Item Number	Product/Cut	Weight Range (Pounds)	Suggested Cooking Method
166B	Round, rump and shank partially removed, handle on	52–70	roast, braise, simmer, broil, panbroil, panfry, sauté
167	Round, knuckle	9–13	braise
167A	Round, knuckle, peeled	8–12	braise
167B	Round, knuckle, full	12–16	braise
169	Round, top (inside)	17–23	braise, roast
170	Round, bottom (gooseneck)	23–31	stew, braise, roast
170A	Round, bottom (gooseneck), heel out	20–28	roast, braise, simmer, broil, panbroil, panfry, sauté
171	Round, bottom (gooseneck), untrimmed	21–29	roast, braise, simmer, broil, panbroil, panfry, sauté
171A	Round, bottom (gooseneck) untrimmed, heel out	20–28	roast, braise, simmer, broil, panbroil, panfry, sauté
171B	Round, outside round	10–16	roast, braise, simmer, broil, panbroil, panfry, sauté
171C	Round, eye of round	3–up	roast, braise, simmer, broil, panbroil, panfry, sauté
172	Loin, full loin, trimmed	37–52	sauté, panfry, broil, grill
172A	Loin, full loin, diamond cut	42–57	sauté, panfry, broil, panbroil, grill
173	Loin, short loin	24–35	sauté, panfry, broil, panbroil, grill
174	Loin, short loin, short-cut	20–30	sauté, panfry, broil, panbroil, grill
175	Loin, strip loin	14–22	sauté, panfry, broil, panbroil, grill
176	Loin, strip loin, boneless	10–14	sauté, panfry, broil, panbroil, grill
179	Loin, strip loin, short-cut	10–14	sauté, panfry, broil, panbroil, grill
180	Loin, strip loin, short-cut, boneless	7–11	sauté, panfry, broil, panbroil, grill
181	Loin, sirloin	19–28	sauté, panfry, broil, panbroil, grill
182	Loin, sirloin butt, boneless	14–19	sauté, panfry, broil, panbroil, grill
183	Loin, sirloin butt, boneless, trimmed	10–15	sauté, panfry, broil, panbroil, grill
184	Loin, top sirloin butt	10–14	sauté, panfry, broil, panbroil, grill
185	Loin, bottom sirloin butt	6–8	sauté, panfry, broil, panbroil, grill
185A	Loin, bottom sirloin butt, flap	3–up	sauté, panfry, broil, panbroil, grill
185B	Loin, bottom sirloin butt, ball tip	3–up	sauté, panfry, broil, panbroil, grill
185C	Loin, bottom sirloin butt, tri-tip	3–up	sauté, panfry, broil, panbroil, grill
185D	Loin, bottom sirloin butt, tri-tip, defatted	3–up	sauté, panfry, broil, panbroil, grill
186	Loin, bottom sirloin butt, trimmed	3–5	sauté, panfry, broil, panbroil, grill
189	Loin, full tenderloin	5–7	sauté, panfry, broil, panbroil, grill
189A	Loin, full tenderloin, side muscle on, defatted	4–6	sauté, panfry, broil, panbroil, grill
189B	Loin, full tnederloin, side muscle on, partially defatted	4–6	sauté, panfry, broil, panbroil, grill
190	Loin, full tenderloin, side muscle off, defatted	3–up	sauté, panfry, broil, panbroil, grill
190A	Loin, full tenderloin, side muscle off, skinned	3–up	sauté, panfry, broil, panbroil, grill
191	Loin, butt tenderloin	2–4	sauté, panfry, broil, panbroil, grill
192	Loin, short tenderloin	3–up	sauté, panfry, broil, panbroil, grill
193	Flank steak	1–up	braise, sauté, panfry, grill
134	Beef bones	amount as specified	simmer
135	Diced beef	amount as specified	braise, stew, simmer, sauté
135A	Beef for Stewing	amount as specified	braise, stew, simmer, sauté
136	Ground beef	amount as specified	bake, broil, panbroil, panfry, braise, sauté
136A	Ground beef and vegetable protein product	amount as specified	roast, panfry, sauté
136B	Beef pattie mix	amount as specified	roast, panfry, sauté

FIGURE 5-8   Beef Rib

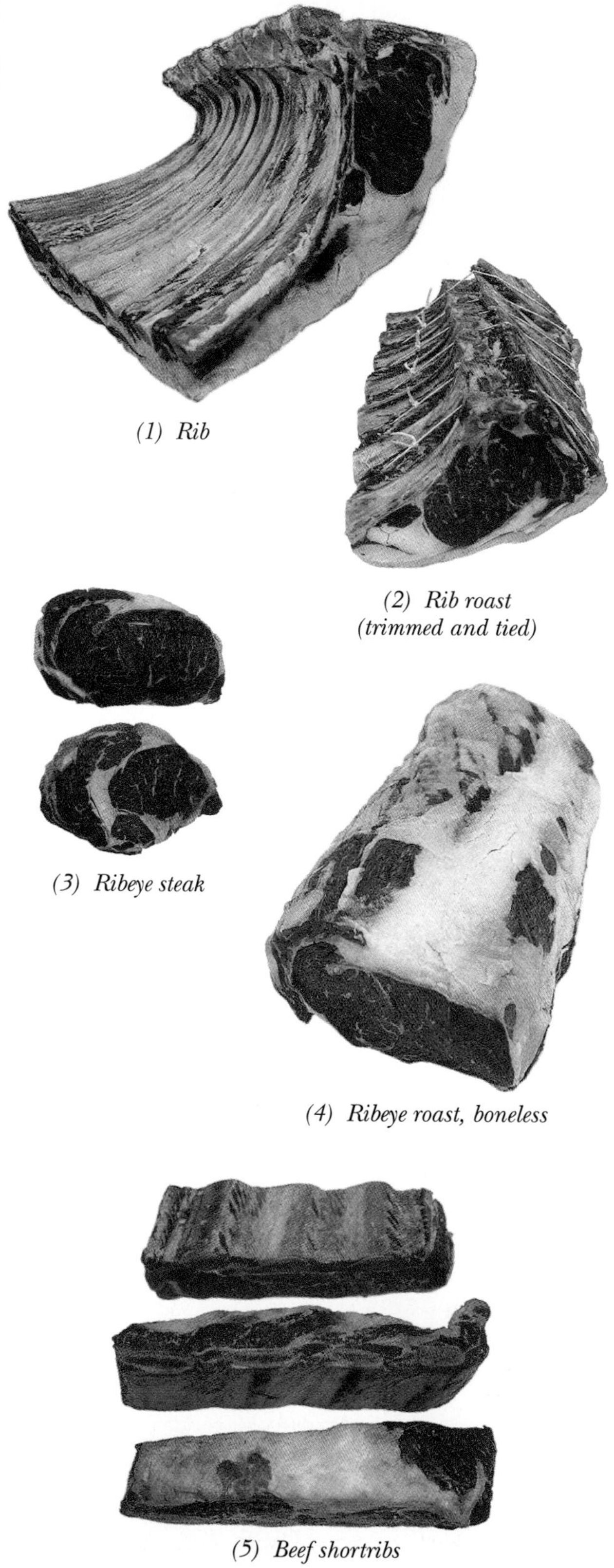

(1) Rib

*(2) Rib roast
(trimmed and tied)*

(3) Ribeye steak

(4) Ribeye roast, boneless

(5) Beef shortribs

FIGURE 5-9   Beef Loin

(1) Strip loin (top view)

(2) Strip loin (bottom view)

(3) Tenderloin (top view)

(4) Tenderloin (bottom view)

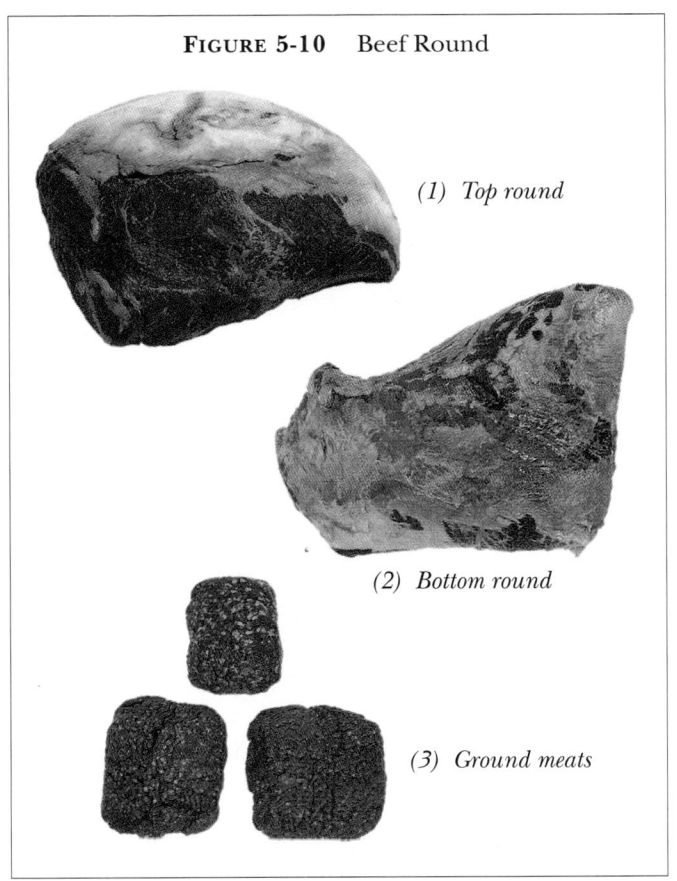

FIGURE 5-10   Beef Round

(1) Top round

(2) Bottom round

(3) Ground meats

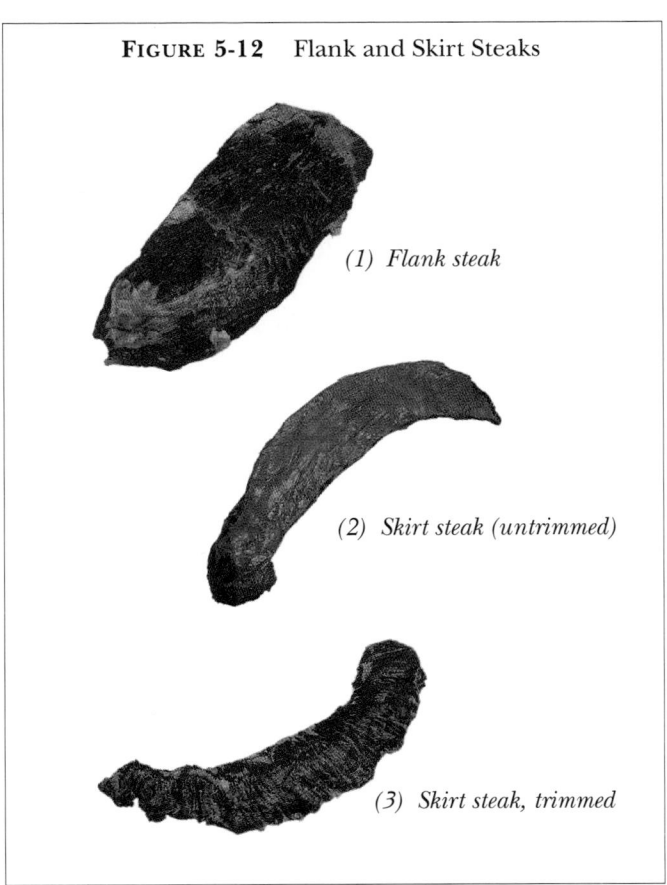

FIGURE 5-12   Flank and Skirt Steaks

(1) Flank steak

(2) Skirt steak (untrimmed)

(3) Skirt steak, trimmed

FIGURE 5-11
Beef Shank

Loin   The loin also yields a variety of cuts prized by those who value tenderness in beef. The tenderloin is one very important subprimal fabricated from the loin. Some terms often used in conjunction with cuts from the tenderloin include *châteaubriand*, *tournedos*, medallions, *filet mignon*, and tenderloin tips.

Roasts from the loin may be referred to as strip loins or New York strips. A variety of steaks are also available by fabricating the loin, or may be purchased by specification from your purveyor, allowing you to indicate weight and fat trim.

Round   This section of the animal produces a range of meats. Some cuts are best when braised, stewed, or simmered, while others, if handled properly, can be roasted with great success. These cuts are generally less tender than those from the rib and the loin, but there are instances when a top round or even a carefully roasted bottom round may make more sense than an expensive cut from the rib or loin. Roast beef sandwiches can be prepared from any well-cooked cut of meat, and since economics dictate that the lower your food cost the greater your margin of profit, you may want to make some tests before deciding that bottom rounds are only for pot roast.

Good-quality, lean ground meats are made from the round as well.

Shank   The foreshank is occasionally available, and may be used for braising or stews. One additional use made of this meat in many kitchens is as an ingredient in the clarification of consommés.

Flank and Skirt Steak   These cuts have become increasingly popular as more restaurants serve grilled and broiled flank and skirt steak, and as the American love affair with "barbecued" meats shows no signs of fading.

Both steaks are found along the very edge of the rib and loin portion of the animal. The fibers, though long and relatively coarse, are even. There is enough intramuscular fat to assure that the meat stays tender, as long as it is carefully sliced and not overcooked.

Brisket   Brisket may be found fresh or corned. Fresh brisket is often favored for pot roasts and other braises. It responds well to slow cooking in a sauce. Corned beef has been brined and cured with

spices. It is traditionally prepared by simmering, with or without its root vegetable accompaniments. Sliced corned beef is a favorite sandwich meat.

Miscellaneous Cuts of Beef

Oxtail. This intensely flavored cut is excellent in stews, soups, and braises. It may be purchased whole or as cross cuts.

Heart. Fresh heart can be prepared in the same way that any well-exercised cut is handled—by braising or stewing. Though not a common cut of meat in many U.S. restaurants, it does have a high level of respect accorded it in many ethnic cuisines.

Liver. Beef liver is darker and more deeply flavored than other livers. It, like heart, is not a commonly found meat in many restaurants or homes. However, aficionados of liver and onions, liver pies and puddings, and other dishes can be found in this country and in others where variety meats are accorded a more welcome place on the table.

Tongue. Tongue is available fresh, smoked, or cured. Japan and other Asian countries esteem tongue highly, making it more difficult to obtain in this country than it used to be. This cut is best prepared by simmering in a flavored court bouillon or broth, and is often served "pickled" or with sharply flavored sauces. Sliced tongue sandwiches are a deli specialty, where its leanness and unique texture shine.

FIGURE 5-13
Brisket

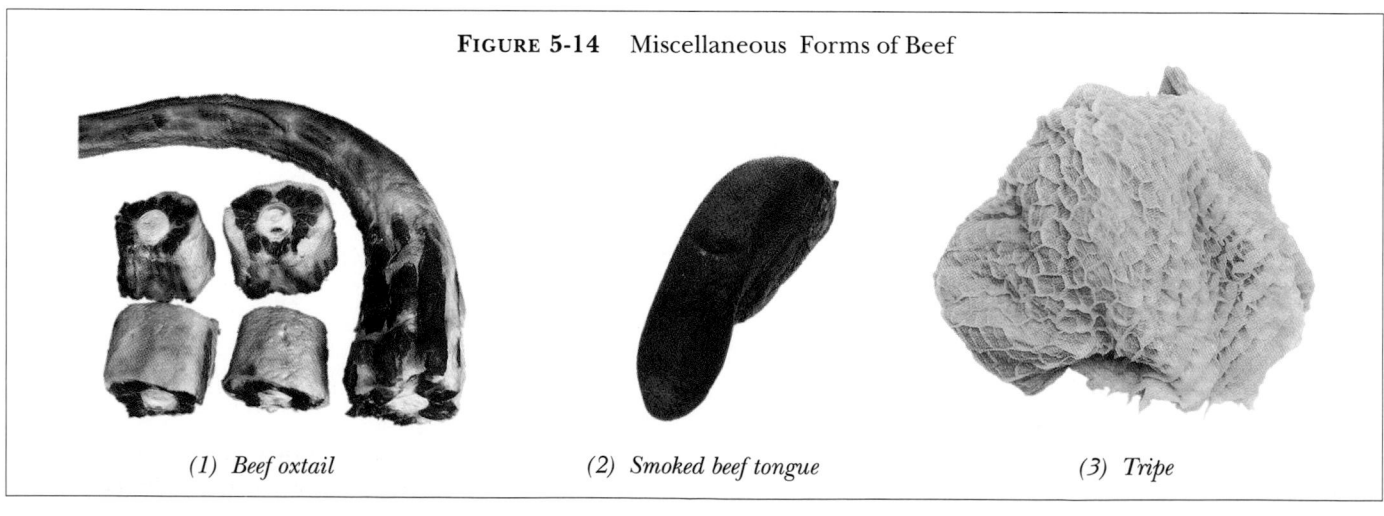

FIGURE 5-14   Miscellaneous Forms of Beef

(1) Beef oxtail   *(2) Smoked beef tongue*   *(3) Tripe*

TABLE 5-3 VEAL CHART			

Item Number	Product/Cut	Weight Range (Pounds)	Suggested Cooking Method
304	Foresaddle, 11 ribs	44–86	roast, panfry
306	Hotel rack, 7 ribs	9–14	roast, panfry
307	Rack, ribeye	3–5	roast, panfry
308	Chucks, 4 ribs	40–70	braise, roast
309	Chucks, square-cut	20–36	braise, roast
309B	Chuck, square cut, boneless	19–33	braise, roast
309D	Chuck, square-cut, neck off, boneless, tied	18–32	braise, roast, panfry
310	Chuck, shoulder clod	4–7	braise, roast, panfry
310A	Chuck, shoulder clod, special	4–7	braise, roast
310B	Chuck, shoulder clod roast	4–7	braise, roast, panfry
310C	Chuck, scotch tender	½–1	braise
311	Chuck, square-cut, clod out, boneless, tied	18–32	braise, roast
312	Foreshank	2–4	braise, simmer
313	Breast	6–10	braise, roast
314	Breast with pocket	6–10	braise, roast
330	Hindsaddle, 2 ribs	50–88	braise, roast, panfry, broil, grill
331	Loin	10–18	braise, roast
332	Loin, trimmed	8–14	braise, roast, panfry, broil, grill
344	Loin, strip loin, boneless	3–6	braise, roast, panfry, broil, grill
344A	Loin, strip loin, boneless, special	2–5	braise, roast, panfry, broil, grill
346	Loin, butt tenderloin	1–1 ½	roast, panfry, broil, grill
346A	Loin, butt tenderloin, skinned	½–1	roast, panfry, broil, grill
347	Loin, short tenderloin	½–1	roast, panfry, broil, grill
334	Leg	40–70	roast, braise, panfry, broil
335	Leg, boneless, roast ready, tied	15–26	roast, braise
336	Leg, shank off, boneless, roast ready, tied	11–19	roast, braise
337	Hindshank	2–4	braise, simmer
338	Shank, Osso buco	1–3	braise, simmer
341	Back, 9 ribs, trimmed	15–25	braise, roast, panfry
348	Leg, TBS, 4 parts	24–32	panfry, sauté, broil, grill
348A	Leg, TBS, 3 parts	16–24	panfry, sauté, broil, grill
349	Leg, top round, cap on	8–12	roast, braise, panfry, sauté, broil
349A	Leg, top round, cap off	6–8	roast, braise, panfry, sauté, broil
395	Veal for stewing	amount as specified	stew, simmer
396	Ground veal	amount as specified	roast, panfry, sauté

Tripe. Tripe is the edible lining of the first and second stomachs of a cow. The type of tripe most often found is referred to as "honeycomb" tripe. One of the most famous recipes for this meat is *tripes à la mode de Caen,* which is a long-cooked, braise, finished with Calvados.

Veal

Considered by some to be the finest meat available, veal is more an offshoot of the dairy industry than a commodity raised specifically as veal. Dairy cows must be bred in order to produce milk. Once the calves are born, they are generally separated from their mothers and raised to a specific age. The practices used in raising veal for slaughter have been cause for concern among many individuals. This issue is outside the scope of this book, and is more a matter for individual conscience—yours and your guests.

Fine veal is known as "milk-fed" or "nature-fed." Calves who never receive grain, grass, or more adult feed have finely textured meat with a pale pink color. Because the overall ratio of meat to bone is necessarily less than it would be in a full-grown heifer or steer, there are proportionately fewer cuts of veal.

Veal, like beef, may be split in two parts, known as the fore and hind quarters. Alternatively, it may

FIGURE 5-15   Veal Shoulder Roast

FIGURE 5-16   Veal Shank

FIGURE 5-17   Veal Rib

FIGURE 5-18   Veal Loin

be cut into a foresaddle and a hindsaddle, which is accomplished by splitting the carcass at a point between the eleventh and twelfth ribs.

Veal Primals and Market Forms

The primal cuts for veal are the shoulder (chuck), shank, rack (rib), loin, and leg. Organ meats (offal) from veal are highly prized, especially the sweetbreads, liver, calf's head, and brains. A number of primal and market cuts are shown in Figures 5-15 to 5-21. Refer also to Table 5-3 for additional information.

Shoulder (Chuck)   Cuts from this primal may be handled in the same way that beef chuck cuts are used. Stew meat and ground meat are commonly fabricated from less desirable cuts, or the trim from roasts used for braises.

Veal Shank   The veal hindshank is most commonly available, though it may be possible to procure the foreshank as well. The hindshank is generally meatier, and typically braised. Osso bucco is one of the most famous dishes made from the shank. There are many regional variations on this dish.

Rib   The rib may be roasted whole (bone-in or as a boneless rolled roast). Portion-size cuts from the rib are referred to as "chops." The rib bones may be left attached and are generally "frenched." This indicates that the bone has been scraped free of all meat, cartilage, and sinew.

Loin   The loin of veal is one of the most expensive and prized portions of the veal. Chops, medallions, and roasts are all easily prepared from the loin. Tenderloins of veal may also be fabricated from this cut.

Leg   The leg yields numerous cuts, perhaps the most familiar of which is the cutlet. Veal cutlets fabricated from the top round have the best texture and cook the most evenly. It is possible to make cutlets from other areas of the leg, including the bottom round. Some butchers may even make them from cuts fabricated from the chuck, but they are not suitable for sautéing or panfrying.

Veal legs may be purchased whole and then broken down into their various components in-house. This offers the chef a good bit of flexibility, but re-

FIGURE 5-19   Veal Leg

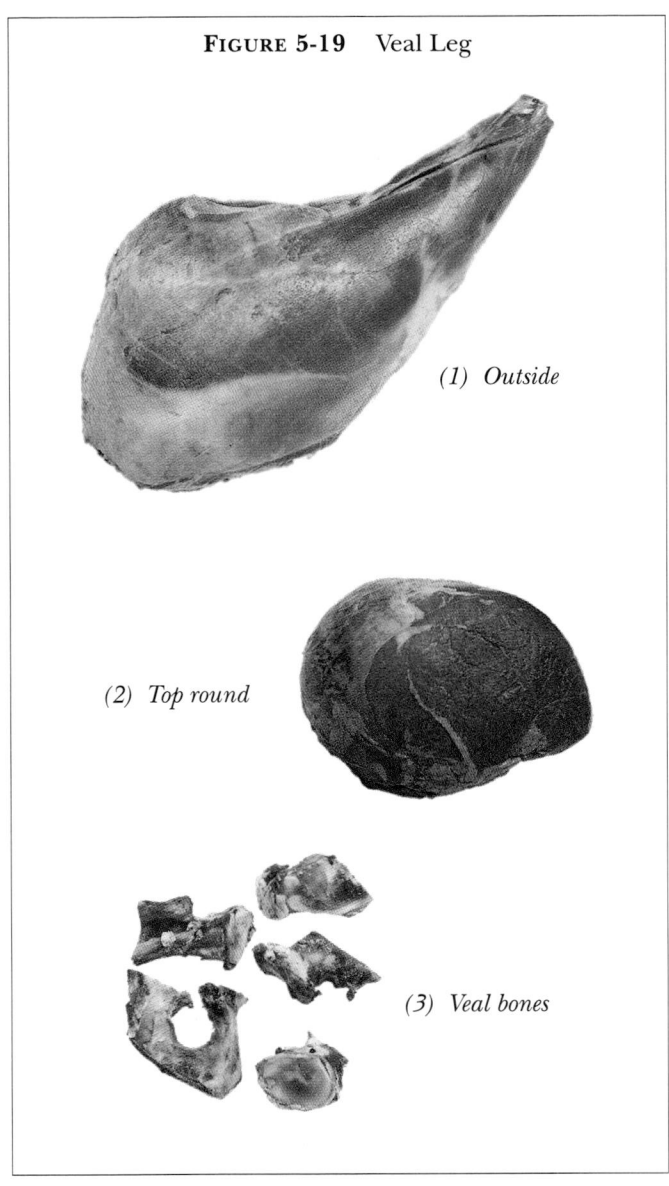

(1) Outside

(2) Top round

(3) Veal bones

FIGURE 5-20
Veal Breast

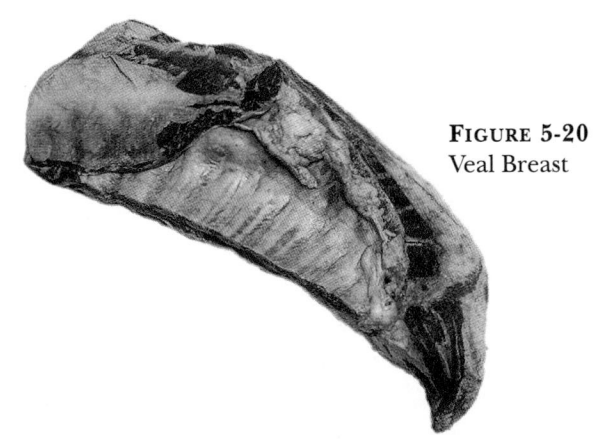

FIGURE 5-21   Miscellaneous Forms of Veal

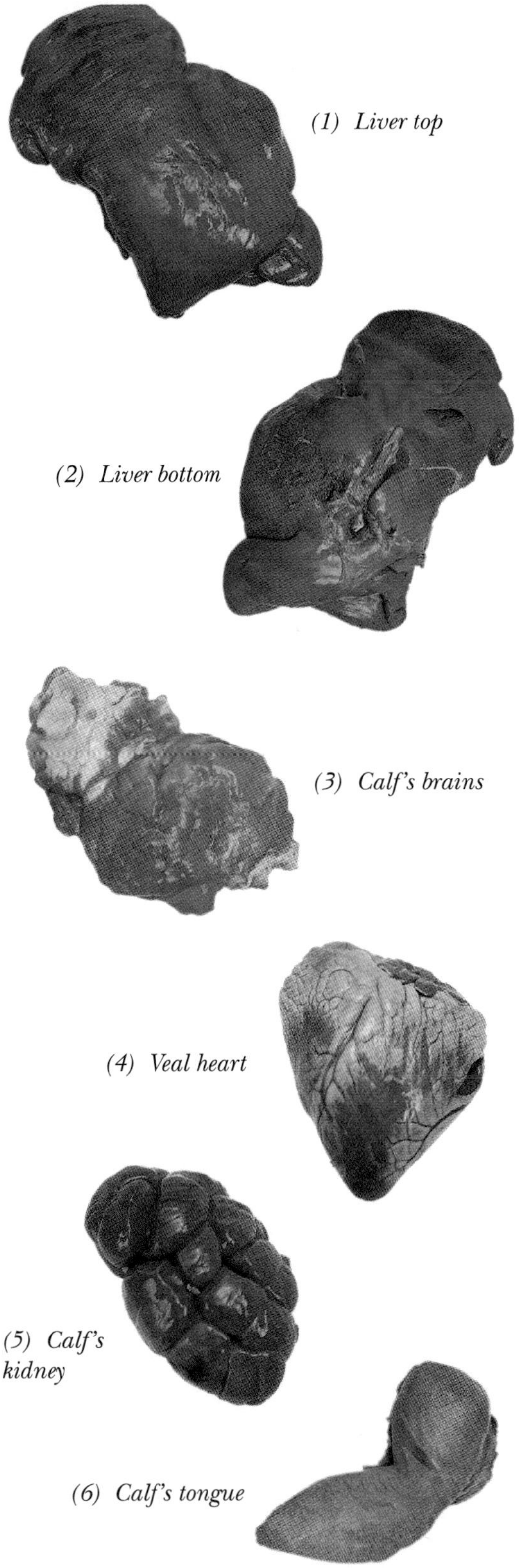

(1) Liver top

(2) Liver bottom

(3) Calf's brains

(4) Veal heart

(5) Calf's kidney

(6) Calf's tongue

quires some knowledge of meat-cutting techniques. The general instruction given is to follow the natural seams in the meat, which separate one large muscle group from another. The meat is cut and scraped from the bone. If an operation is capable of butchering a leg of veal, the initial cost per pound is less than when smaller roasts or portion-size cuts are purchased. There is also a greater opportunity to control costs through the use of lean trim and bones in other preparations.

There are many names for cutlets, and they vary from one cuisine to another: scallops (English term), *scallopine* (Italian term), *escalope* (French term) are some of the more familiar. A cutlet that has been pounded and then cooked is sometimes referred to on the menu as a *paillard*.

Breast   Veal breast is often prepared as a bone-in roast or as a rolled and tied boneless roast. It is also boned, butterflied, stuffed, and rolled. Long cooking methods, such as braising, are best for this cut.

Organ Meats/Variety Meats and "By-Products"
Veal or calf's liver, tongue, and bones are among those most familiar and frequently used in American kitchens. Sweetbreads (the thymus gland), brains, and heart can also be found. There is a relatively small proportion of the public interested in these specialty items. However, menus that draw from regions of the world where such cuts have greater acceptance than in this country, may find that the clientele they serve will order them.

Many of these items are so popular in other countries that it has become increasingly difficult to find them in the United States. Tongue, for example, is quite popular in Japan, and the majority of the tongue produced here is exported.

Cooking methods for these cuts vary: Sweetbreads are generally poached and then prepared in a sauce or used as a garnish in forcemeats. Brains may be cooked *á la meunière* or prepared, as in a classic French dish, with scrambled eggs. Tongue is generally simmered until tender, then sliced; it may also be pickled or smoked. Heart is braised. Veal bones and feet are excellent for preparing stocks and foundation sauces.

Pork

Pigs were once raised by city dwellers and farmers alike. These animals tended not to require pen-

ning or extensive acreage. They would forage for feed. Those days are gone, at least in this society. We have rules and codes regarding how livestock is raised, slaughtered, and butchered. These regulations have as their primary goal the protection of the public health.

Today, pork is among the most popular meats sold in the United States, despite growing concerns over health issues related to meats perceived as high in fat and cholesterol. Pigs have been specifically bred over many generations in order to produce leaner meat cuts. They are slaughtered and butchered in facilities that handle no other type of meat, to prevent the spread of disease and infection, such as trichinosis.

Chefs and consumers alike are more conscious of how to handle pork to avoid foodborne illnesses. While beef remains the number one favorite in restaurants across the country, pork continues to grow in popularity as dishes that showcase its special qualities take their place on menus. Barbecued spareribs, tender chops and cutlets, and a range of smoked and cured meats are all to be found.

Pigs were once commonly slaughtered in the late fall. The meat was used to make a number of items that were specially handled to assure that they would last through the winter, providing some meat during the colder months. Processed, cured, and brined pork cuts are traditionally popular.

Today, we continue to enjoy such items, primarily because we enjoy the taste. This change in emphasis, from food storage needs to simple enjoyment, has encouraged some modification in processing methods, resulting in hams, sausage, bacon, and other items that contain fewer additives and preservatives.

Purchasing agents, chefs, and consumers alike will seldom see the inspection stamps or grading

FIGURE 5-22
Boston Butt

TABLE 5-4 PORK CHART

Item Number	Product/Cut	Weight Range (Pounds)	Suggested Cooking Method
401	Fresh ham	17–26	roast, braise, simmer, broil, panfry
401A	Fresh ham, short shank	17–26	roast, braise, simmer, broil, panfry
402	Fresh ham, skinned	17–26	roast, braise, simmer, broil, panfry
402A	Fresh ham, skinned, short shank	17–26	roast, braise, simmer, broil, panfry
402B	Fresh ham, boneless, tied	8–12	roast, braise
402C	Fresh ham, boneless, trimmed, tied	8–12	roast, braise
402D	Fresh ham, outside, tied	6–12	roast, braise
402E	Fresh ham, outside, trimmed, tied	6–up	roast, braise
403	Shoulder	12–20	roast, braise, simmer, broil, panbroil, panfry
404	Shoulder, skinned	12–20	roast, braise, simmer, broil, panbroil, panfry
405A	Shoulder, picnic, boneless	4–8	roast, braise, simmer
405B	Shoulder, picnic, cushion, boneless	amount as specified	roast, braise, simmer
406	Shoulder, Boston butt	4–up	roast, braise, simmer, broil, panfry
406A	Shoulder, Boston butt, boneless	4–up	roast, braise, simmer, broil, panfry
407	Shoulder butt, cellar-trimmed, boneless	3–7	roast, braise, simmer, broil, panfry
408	Belly	12–18	sauté, panfry, simmer
409	Belly, skinless	9–13	sauté, panfry, simmer
410	Loin	14–22	roast, braise, panfry
411	Loin, bladeless	14–22	sauté, panfry, simmer
412	Loin, center cut, 8 ribs	6–10	roast, braise, panfry
412A	Loin, center cut, 8 ribs, chine bone off	5–9	roast, braise, panfry, sauté, braise, grill
412B	Loin, center cut, 8 ribs, boneless	4–6	roast, braise, panfry, sauté, braise, grill
412C	Loin, center cut, 11 ribs	7–11	roast, braise, panfry, sauté, braise, grill
412D	Loin, center cut, 11 ribs, chine bone off	6–10	roast, braise, panfry, sauté, braise, grill
412E	Loin, center cut, 11 ribs, boneless	5–7	roast, braise, panfry, sauté, braise, grill
413	Loin, boneless	8–12	roast, braise, panfry, sauté, braise, grill
413A	Loin, boneless, tied	8–12	roast, braise
413B	Loin, boneless, tied, special	8–12	roast, braise
414	Loin, Canadian back	4–6	roast, braise, panfry
415	Tenderloin	1–up	roast, braise, grill, panfry, sauté
415A	Tenderloin, side muscle off	1–up	roast, braise, grill, panfry, sauté
416	Spareribs	2 ½–5 ½	braise, smoke, broil, grill
416A	Spareribs, St. Louis style	2–3	braise, smoke, broil, grill
416B	Spareribs, breast bones	½–¾	braise, smoke, broil, grill
417	Shoulder hocks	¾–up	braise, simmer
418	Trimmings	amount as specified	braise, simmer
420	Pig's feet, front		simmer
421	Neck bones	amount as specified	simmer
422	Loin, back ribs	1 ½–2 ¼	braise, broil, grill
423	Loin, country-style ribs	3–up	braise, broil, grill
435	Diced pork	amount as specified	braise, simmer, saute
496	Ground pork	amount as specified	roast, sauté, panfry

shields often found on beef, veal, or lamb. This is due to several factors. The inspection stamp is applied to the carcass before it is cut into wholesale and retail cuts. Trimming and cutting will generally remove the stamp. Quality grades are less frequently assigned to pork than other meats. Packers will often use their own grading system, instead of paying for federal graders to be on hand. This does not necessarily mean that you cannot be certain that various cuts of pork will have good quality. The grading systems used by major packers are clearly defined and generally reliable guides.

Pork Primals and Market Forms

The pork carcass, once split into two halves along the backbone, is divided in a slightly different manner from most other meats. Instead of a primal rib, the loin is cut long. This is done to maximize the number of cuts possible from the prized loin.

FIGURE 5-23   Pork Loin

(1)   Trimmed pork loin

(2)   Center cut pork chops

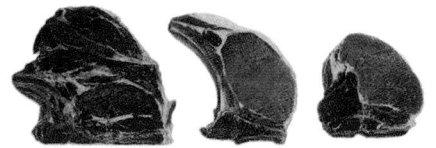

(3)   Pork chops from arm, center, and leg section

(4)   Pork tenderloin (bottom view)

However, chops cut from the "rib" end are generally indicated as rib chops. Those from the leg end may be referred to a "sirloin" chops. Various primals and market cuts are shown in Figures 5-22 to 5-26. Refer also to Table 5-4 for additional information.

The Shoulder or Butt   Roasts, stew meat and ground pork are often made from this primal and the subprimals it produces. The ratio of fat to lean is somewhat higher than in other portions of the animal. This makes it highly desirable for use in sausages and other items prepared by the charcutière. For more information, refer to Chapter 11 and recipes that can be found in Part IV, Chapter 27 of this book.

There are many regional names given to cuts from the shoulder, including daisy ham, Boston butt, picnic ham (or butt). Because of the greater abundance of fat in these cuts, it is possible to roast

them with some success. However, they are generally best for stewing and braising.

The Loin   This is the largest single primal cut from the pig. It is intentionally cut longer than the loins for beef, veal, or lamb. The loin is often roasted, bone-in or boneless. One rather impressive cut produced from the rib portion of the loin is a crown roast of pork. This is occasionally prepared for banquet service. The roast may be stuffed before it is roasted.

Cuts from the loin include chops of various thickness. The composition of the chop varies greatly from one end of the loin to the other. Boneless cutlets are also prepared from the loin. They are generally sautéed, grilled, or broiled. Thick chops are often stuffed and baked. Chops from the shoulder end of the loin may be braised.

The tenderloin, a prized subprimal of the loin, is widely available. Noisettes and medallions are often fashioned from the tenderloin. These cuts are sautéed, grilled, or broiled.

A boneless smoked loin (sometimes referred to in the United States as Canadian bacon) is also popular. One of its classic uses is as a component of Eggs Benedict. (See below for more information about bacon, salt pork, and other cured pork products.)

FIGURE 5-24   The Ham

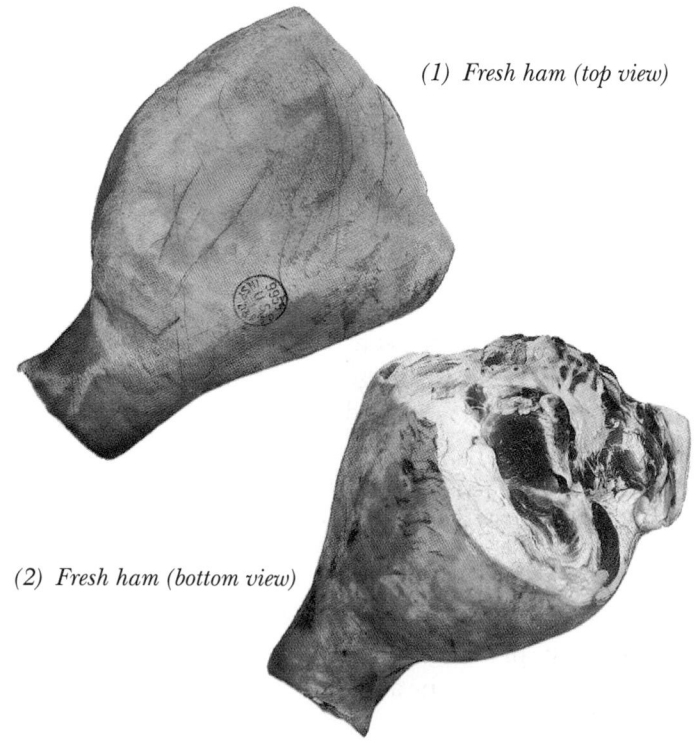

(1)   Fresh ham (top view)

(2)   Fresh ham (bottom view)

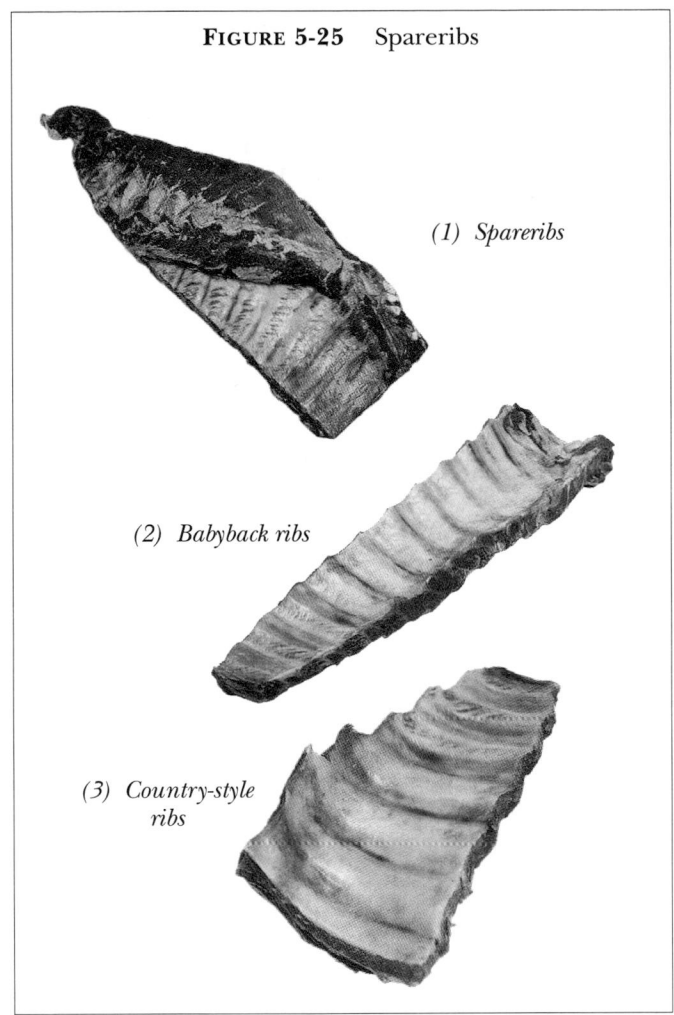

FIGURE 5-25   Spareribs

(1) Spareribs

(2) Babyback ribs

(3) Country-style ribs

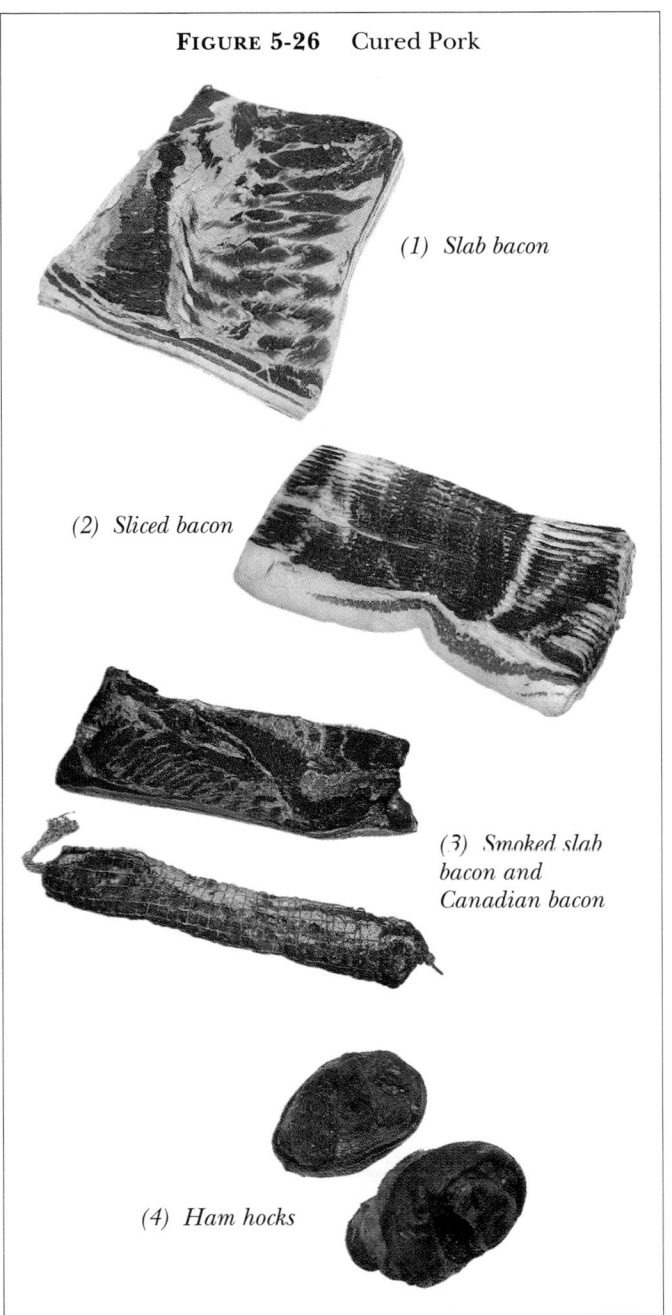

FIGURE 5-26   Cured Pork

(1) Slab bacon

(2) Sliced bacon

(3) Smoked slab bacon and Canadian bacon

(4) Ham hocks

The Ham (Leg)   This primal cut is often referred to as the ham, regardless of whether of not it has been cured. Fresh pork roasts or hams are quite different in flavor and texture from cured hams.

Ham steaks (available fresh, cured, or smoked) are also available, and are popular breakfast items as well as having a place on lunch and dinner menus.

Cured or smoked hams occasionally are fully cooked and ready-to-eat. These items may often benefit from simmering, or they may be roasted to enhance tenderness and flavor. Others, including such hams as prosciutto and Smithfield, need not be cooked after curing. They are often simply sliced thinly and used "as is." Or they may be used as a special flavoring ingredient in pasta dishes, appetizers, or other preparations.

Stew meat and ground pork are also cut from lean trim produced when smaller cuts are fabricated from this primal.

Spareribs   Spareribs are similar to short ribs, breast of veal, and breast of lamb. This cut has more bone than meat, but it is immensely popular throughout the country. Other cuisines have also developed trademark preparations that feature this particular cut. Spareribs are sold whole or cut into portions. Baby back ribs and country-style ribs are also available.

Cured Pork and Pork "By-Products"   It has often been said that you can use everything on the pig except the oink. Even in our society, where we tend to prefer recognizable cuts such as roasts, chops, and steaks, we enjoy a number of specialty items produced from the pig.

Bacon is made by curing and/or smoking the belly. This classic breakfast item may be sold as slab bacon, with or without the rind, or sliced. Special types of bacon are produced by different cuisines, including *pancetta* among others.

Fatback, used for larding, barding, and lining pâté and terrine molds, comes from the "clear fat" along the animal's back. It is referred to as clear fat to distinguish it from the belly, sometimes known as "streak of lean," an apt description of bacon's composition. Jowl bacon is not well-suited for cooking as strips, but is excellent for use as a cooking or flavoring ingredient.

Ham hocks, pig's feet and knuckles, and even snouts are used to produce a variety of regional and ethnic dishes. These items are available fresh, cured, and smoked. They are often simmered, and are traditionally paired with "peasant" foods including beans and greens, and in soups and stews.

Liver, heart, and kidneys are sometimes available, but their use is limited both by availability and consumer acceptance.

Lamb and Mutton

Lamb has grown in popularity over the last several years, and the impression that it will have a "sheepy" flavor is fading fast because of improved methods for breeding, raising, and feeding sheep. Improved breeding techniques mean that lamb is

TABLE 5-5 LAMB CHART

Item Number	Product/Cut	Weight Range (Pounds)	Suggested Cooking Method
204	Rack	5–9	roast, grill, broil, panfry
204A	Rack, roast-ready, single	2–4	roast, grill, broil, panfry
204B	Rack, roast-ready, single, Frenched	2–4	roast, grill, broil, panfry
204C	Rack, roast-ready, single, Frenched, special	1 1/2–3 1/2	roast, grill, broil, panfry
206	Shoulders	19–27	roast, grill, broil, panfry
207	Shoulders, square-cut	13–19	roast, grill, broil, braise, panfry
208	Shoulder, square-cut, boneless, tied		roast, braise
209	Breast	7–11	braise, simmer, broil, grill
209A	Ribs, Denver-style	5–9	braise, simmer, broil, grill
210	Foreshank	2–3	braise, simmer
230	Hindsaddle	27–38	roast, braise, grill, sauté
231	Loins	8–12	roast, grill, broil, panfry, sauté
232	Loins, trimmed	5–9	roast, grill, broil, panfry, sauté
232A	Loins, short-cut, trimmed	3–7	roast, grill, broil, panfry, sauté
232B	Loins, double, boneless, tied	2–5	roast
233	Legs	19–27	roast, braise, grill, broil, panbroil, panfry, sauté
233A	Leg, lower shank off, single	9–14	roast, grill, broil, panfry
233B	Leg, boneless, tied	8–13	roast
233C	Leg, shank off, single	4–7	roast
233E	Leg, hind shank	1–up	roast, braise
233F	Leg, hind shank, heel on	1–up	roast, braise
234	Leg, lower shank off, partially boneless	6–9	roast, braise
234A	Leg, shank off, single, partially boneless	8–11	roast, braise
234B	Leg, shank off, boneless, tied	8–11	roast, braise
236	Back, trimmed	11–15	braise, panfry
238	Hindsaddle, long-cut, trimmed	29–41	roast, grill, broil, panfry, sauté
295	Lamb for stewing	amount as specified	stew, braise, simmer
295A	Lamb for kebobs	amount as specified	roast, broil, grill
296	Ground lamb	amount as specified	roast, panfry
240	Leg, ¾, single	7–11	roast
241	Leg, steamship	6–10	roast
245	Sirloin, boneless	2–4	panfry, sauté

FIGURE 5-27   Shoulder of Lamb

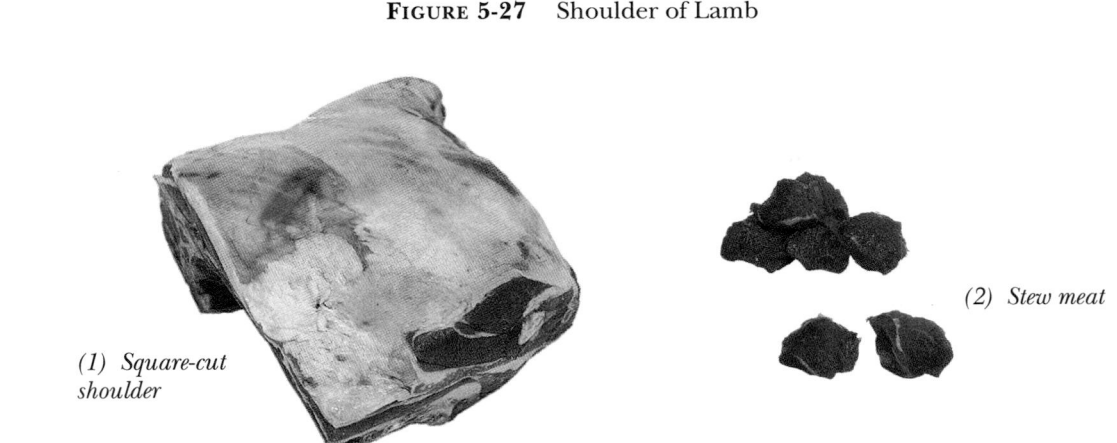

*(1) Square-cut
shoulder*

(2) Stew meat

FIGURE 5-28   Rib of Lamb

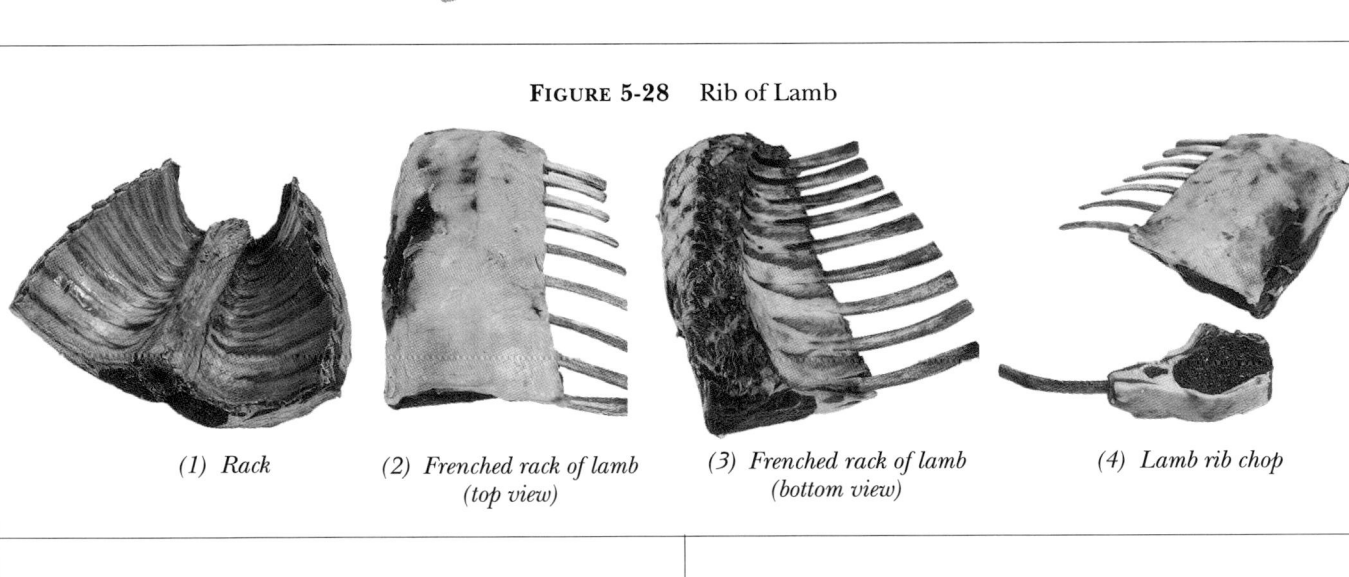

(1) Rack

*(2) Frenched rack of lamb
(top view)*

*(3) Frenched rack of lamb
(bottom view)*

(4) Lamb rib chop

FIGURE 5-29   Lamb Loin

FIGURE 5-30   Leg of Lamb

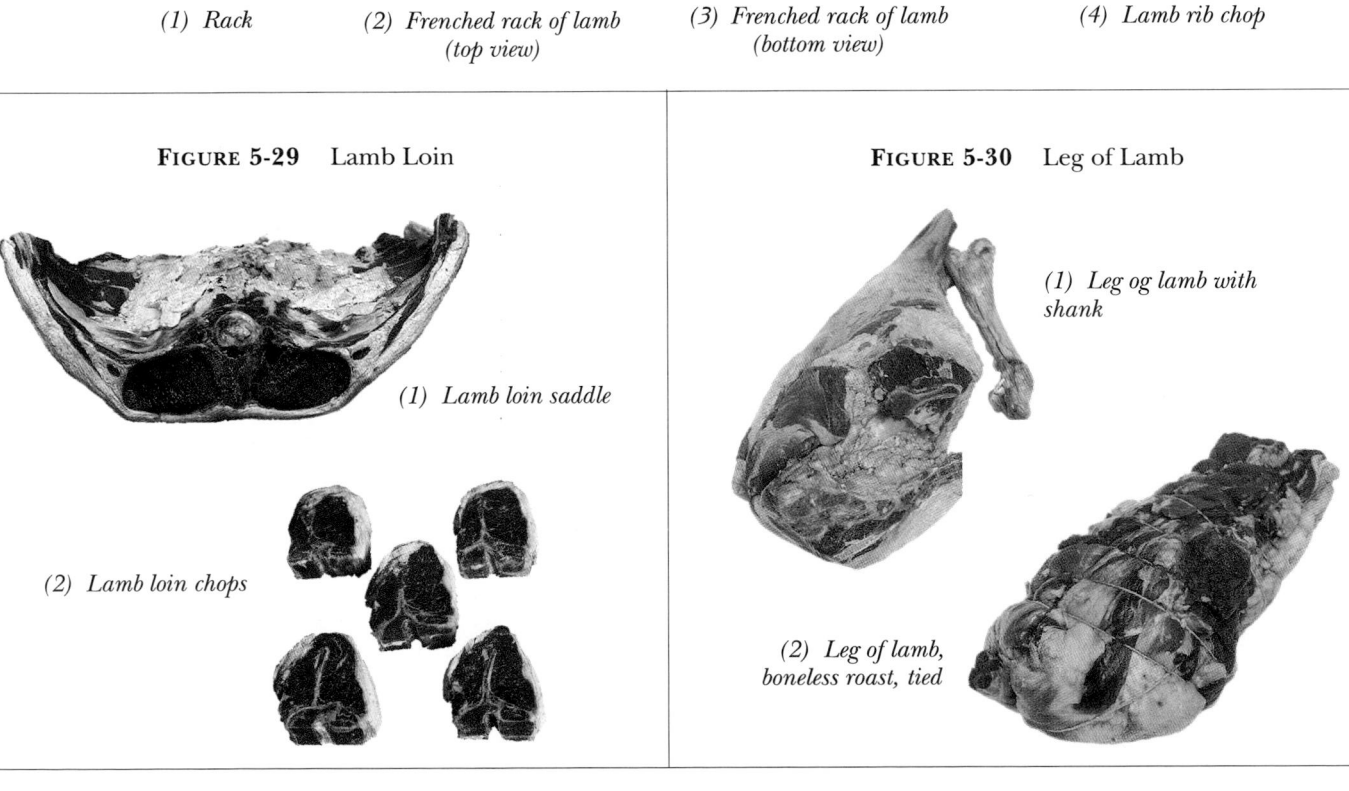

(1) Lamb loin saddle

(2) Lamb loin chops

*(1) Leg og lamb with
shank*

*(2) Leg of lamb,
boneless roast, tied*

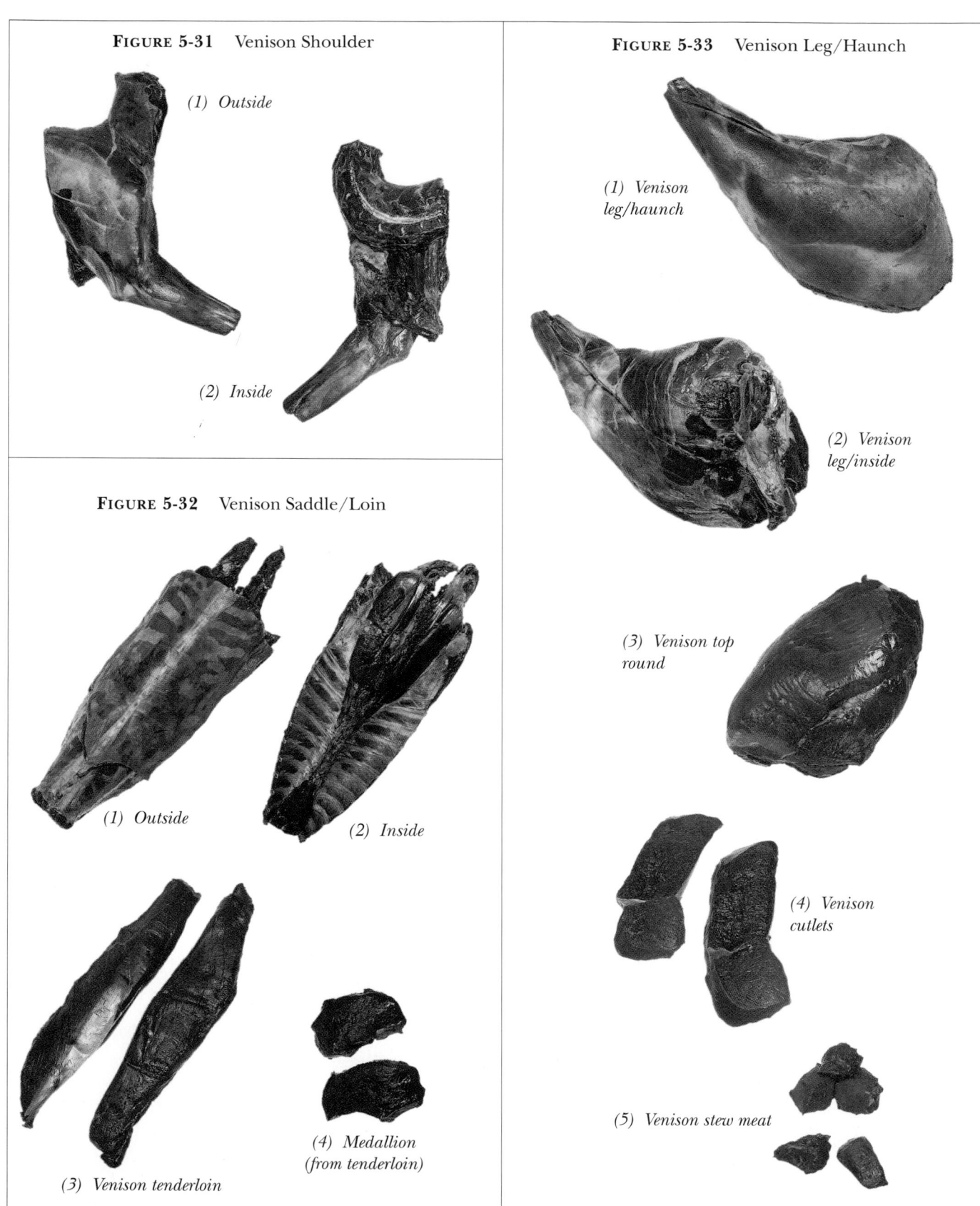

FIGURE 5-31   Venison Shoulder

(1) Outside

(2) Inside

FIGURE 5-32   Venison Saddle/Loin

(1) Outside

(2) Inside

(4) Medallion (from tenderloin)

(3) Venison tenderloin

FIGURE 5-33   Venison Leg/Haunch

(1) Venison leg/haunch

(2) Venison leg/inside

(3) Venison top round

(4) Venison cutlets

(5) Venison stew meat

no longer available only in the spring (the traditional time for "lambing" or "dropping young").

Because the lamb is slaughtered when still quite young, it is almost completely tender, and most cuts can be cooked by any method. Spring lamb and hot-house lamb are not fed grass or grain because once the lamb begins to eat grass, the flesh loses some of its delicacy. As the animal ages, the flesh will darken in color, take on a slightly coarser texture, and have a much more pronounced flavor. Sheep slaughtered under the age of a year may still be labeled lamb; if slaughtered after that, however, they must be labeled mutton.

Like veal, lamb is also cut into a foresaddle and hindsaddle and may also be cut into sides. The major lamb cuts are: rib (known also as rack), square-cut shoulder, breast, shank, loin, and leg. Various lamb cuts are shown in Figures 5-27 to 5-30 and described in Table 5-5.

Venison and Large, Furred Game

Fallow deer (a farm-raised deer) produces a lean, tasty meat with less fat and cholesterol than beef. The loin and the rib are quite tender and can be suitable for most cooking techniques, especially roasting, grilling, and sautéing. The haunch and legs are more exercised, and are best when prepared by moist-heat or combination techniques. (See Figures 5-31 to 5-33.)

Depending upon the area of the country, other types of game—including wild boar, elk, and bear—may also be available. The same general rules that determine how to cook a red meat cut will work for these meats:

1. Cuts from less-exercised portions of the animal may be prepared by any technique and are frequently paired with dry-heat methods such as grilling or roasting.

2. Well-exercised areas of the animal, such as the leg (or haunch), shank, and shoulder are best when cooked by moist-heat or combination methods. These cuts are also used for preparing pâtés and other charcuterie items.

Rabbit

Rabbit, raised domestically, is available throughout the year. The loin meat is delicate in flavor and

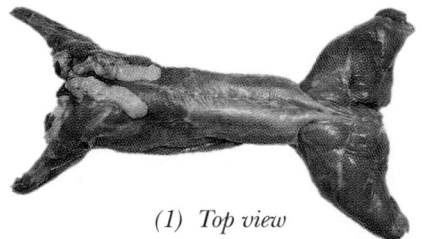

FIGURE 5-34 Rabbit

(1) Top view

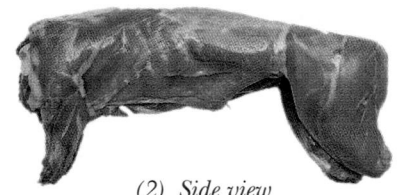

(2) Side view

color, and has a tendency to dry out if not handled carefully. Traditional preparation methods include roasting, braising, and "jugging," which preserves the meat by cooking and storing it in fat. The loin and legs are often prepared by two separate techniques—the loin is roasted or sautéed and the legs, which are more exercised, are cooked by stewing or braising. (See Figure 5-34.)

Poultry and Game Birds

As better rearing methods have been perfected, chicken, once reserved for special occasions, and other poultry have become commonplace in restaurants and homes. Poultry production is now a big business, with breeding, care, and feeding all scientifically controlled.

Today, chicken, turkey, and game birds can be found sold as "free-range," and/or "organic." Just as these terms may not have a precise meaning when applied to beef, they are equally unclear in relation to the methods used to raise poultry. Some chefs are inclined to prefer birds raised in a free-range environment. There is a greater likelihood that these birds have been allowed at least some exercise in a lot, rather than spending their entire lives in a cage. They may be allowed to forage for some of their feed but, most likely, a commercial operation of any size will need to more carefully regulate the care and feeding of birds intended for

TABLE 5-6 POULTRY CLASSIFICATION

Name	Description	Weight
Rock Cornish Game Hen	Very tender, suitable for all cooking techniques	3/4–2 pounds (.34–.9 kilograms)
Broiler	Very tender, suitable for all cooking techniques	1 1/2–2 pounds (.7–.9 kilograms)
Fryer	Very tender, suitable for all cooking techniques	2 1/2–3 1/2 pounds (1.2–1.6 kilograms)
Roaster	Very tender, suitable for all cooking techniques	3 1/2–5 pounds (1.6–2.3 kilograms)
Stewing Hen*	Mature female bird, requires slow, moist cooking	3 1/2–6 pounds (1.6–2.7 kilograms)
Capon (castrated male)	Very tender, usually roasted or poeléed	5–8 pounds (2.3–3.6 kilograms)
Young Hen or Tom Turkey	Very tender, suitable for all cooking techniques	8–22 pounds (3.6–10 kilograms)
Yearling Turkey	Fully mature but still tender, usually roasted	10–30 pounds (4.5–14 kilograms)
Broiler or Fryer Duckling	Very tender, usually roasted, but suitable for most techniques	2–4 pounds (.9–1.8 pounds)
Roaster Duckling	Tender, usually roasted	4–6 pounds (1.8–2.7 kilograms)
Young Goose or Gosling	Tender, usually roasted	6–10 pounds (2.7–4.5 kilograms)
Guinea Hen or Fowl	Related to pheasant; tender, suitable for most techniques	3/4–1 1/2 kilograms (.34–.7 kilograms)
Squab (domestic pigeon that has not begun to fly)	Light, tender meat, suitable for sauté, roast, grill; as bird ages, the meat darkens and toughens	under 1 pound (under .45 kilograms)

*Note: Very mature turkeys, ducks, and geese are also available, though not listed here; they are tough, with hardened cartilage and windpipes.

sale to the public. This means that feed formulas will be prepared, and certain health precautions including immunizations and treatment with antibiotics are necessary. Organically raised birds may be free of chemically produced growth enhancers or steroids, but it is important to ask questions about any product you buy that is sold to you as either natural or organic.

Poultry, like other meats, must undergo a mandatory inspection for wholesomeness. It may be graded as USDA A, B, or C. The following factors determine the grade: shape of the carcass; ratio of meat to bone; freedom from pinfeathers, hair, and down; and number (if any) of tears, cuts, or broken bones.

After post-mortem inspection, the birds are plucked, cleaned, chilled, and packaged. (See Figures 5-35 and 5-36.) They can be purchased whole or in parts. The younger the bird, the more tender its flesh. As birds age, their flesh toughens, and the cartilage in the breast hardens. The windpipe and bill of ducks and geese will also harden.

Poultry is classified by size and age (maturity). (See Table 5-6.)

Chicken

Chicken is usually available as broilers, fryers, or roasters. Very small chicken, or baby chicken, is sometimes available, and may be referred to as *"poussin."* These birds are sold whole or as parts. They may be roasted, grilled, broiled, baked in pieces, sautéed, pan-fried, or deep-fried.

Stewing hens or fowls are more mature and are best simmered, stewed, or braised. They are excellent for soups.

Chicken feet and cock's combs, though difficult to obtain, are traditional elements in stocks and soups, providing excellent flavor and body.

Chicken livers, gizzards, hearts, backs, and necks are also sold and have various applications in the kitchen. *Schmaltz*, or rendered chicken fat, is also available, and is an important component in kosher cooking.

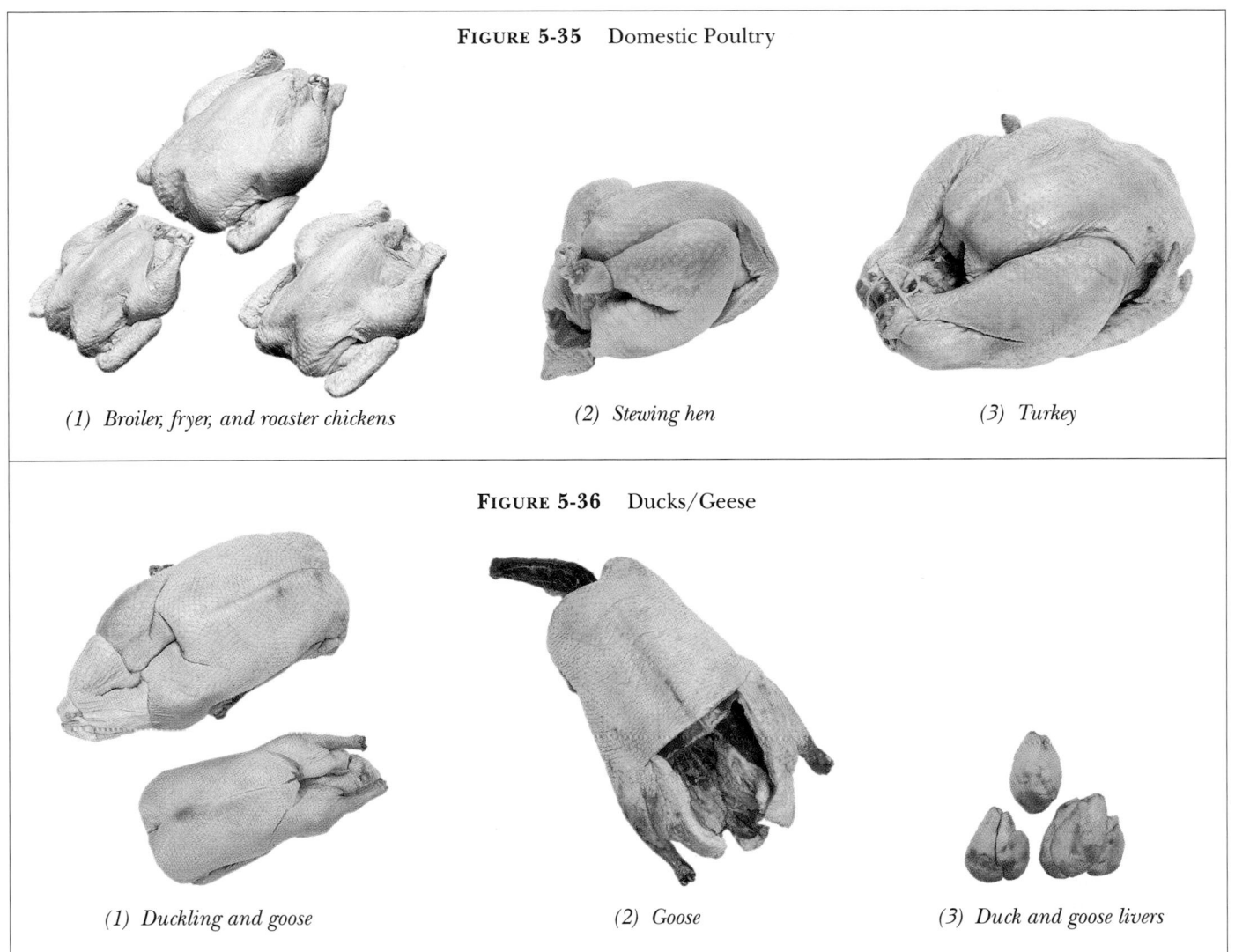

FIGURE 5-35   Domestic Poultry

(1) *Broiler, fryer, and roaster chickens*   (2) *Stewing hen*   (3) *Turkey*

FIGURE 5-36   Ducks/Geese

(1) *Duckling and goose*   (2) *Goose*   (3) *Duck and goose livers*

Cornish Game Hen/Rock Cornish Game Hen

These birds are the result of careful breeding. They are small, relatively plump birds. There is more breast meat, in relation to its overall size and composition, than dark or leg meat.

Turkey

Benjamin Franklin made a strong case for endorsing the turkey as the national bird for the United States. This large bird has gained in popularity over the years, and turkey products are finding their way onto the menu year-round, instead of only at Thanksgiving.

Turkeys are classified as either young hen or tom, or mature hen or tom birds. In general, the meat-to-bone ratio is best at weights over 12 pounds.

Turkey is increasingly available as parts: breast with neck and back attached, boneless breast meat, legs only, even portion-cut scallops or cutlets. Turkey has a more distinct flavor than chicken and as such may be preferred by some consumers. The traditional turkey club or sandwich remains popular on all menus.

Wild turkey is infrequently available through special purveyors. It must meet certain health and safety standards in order to be sold legally in restaurants. If you are unsure, contact your local health department for more information.

Ducks and Geese Ducklings (ducks under one year of age) are generally roasted. Full-grown ducks may be roasted, but are also braised, stewed, or made into confit. Peking duck, Long Island duck, moularde duck, and muscovy duck constitute the breeds of duck commonly found in this country.

It is possible to purchase duck parts, including breasts, legs, and liver. The breast is often sautéed, grilled, or pan-seared. Legs are typically slow roasted or braised. The fattened liver of the moularde duck, known as *foie gras*, is produced commercially in this country, making it more readily available as a fresh product. Foie gras shrinks when cooked, so great care should be taken to sauté it correctly. It is also used in a variety of sausages, gratins, and other charcuterie preparations.

Geese are referred to a goslings when young. These birds are generally suited to roasting. Geese over one year old may be better stewed or braised.

Wild Game Birds

Traditionally, chefs could obtain most game birds only during the hunting season, usually late fall and early winter. Today many game birds are raised on farms year-round. However, many game birds, especially those allowed "free range," will still be at their best from October through December or January. Game birds are "wild" species. This means that while they may be farm-raised, their characteristics are usually not reproductively controlled. (See Figure 5–37.)

FIGURE 5-37 Game Birds (Pheasant, Squab, and Quails)

Young fowl should have soft, smooth, pliable skin. The breastbone cartilage should be flexible, as it is for domestic fowl. The flesh should be tender, with a slight "gamy" taste. The types of game birds most often used today in cooking are the following:

Quail The smallest of the game birds, these are traditionally spit-roasted, poêléed, or poached.

Snipe/Woodcock The snipe is available in three sizes: large, common, and small, and traditionally has been considered by gourmets to be one of the finest of all game birds.

Wild Duck Teal, a small duck, is considered a delicacy. As wild duck ages, the flesh may take on a fishy or oily taste.

Pheasant One of the meatiest of all game birds, the pheasant may be roasted or braised. Domestically raised pheasant will not have a pronounced gamy flavor.

Fish and Shellfish

Fish were once plentiful and inexpensive, but due to various factors, including nutritional concerns, pollution of fishing beds, and the search for variety, demand has begun to outstrip supply. At this time, regulations have been passed by a number of countries, restricting commercial fishing concerns to an ever smaller percentage of such renowned fishing waters as the Grand Banks and St. George's Bay. No one can be certain how long it will take for the great fishing banks to replenish themselves, if in fact they ever do.

What this means to most chefs and consumers is that longtime menu favorites, including cod, tuna, bluefish, true striped bass, and red snapper, are increasingly unavailable. Aquaculture, or fish farming, is growing in importance as they become reliable sources of fresh fish. Today, hybrid striped bass, trout, salmon, halibut, snails, tilapia, catfish, oysters, mussels, and clams are more easily found because they are farm raised.

Fish's dietary importance has gained a great deal of credibility. Americans, who traditionally have favored red meats both at home and when they eat out, are ordering fish entrées more often. The chef should be familiar with many fish, includ-

FIGURE 5-38 Checking Fish

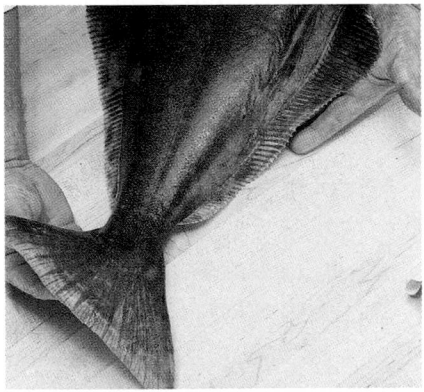

(1) Looking at the fins and tail.

(2) Feeling the skin.

(3) Checking the gills.

(4) Checking the belly.

ing underutilized varieties that until quite recently were grouped together as "trash fish" or "junk fish." Although not well-known, these fish can be excellent alternatives to species that are no longer available either because of overfishing or because their habitats have become polluted.

Fish Basics

The chef should select absolutely fresh fish of the best quality. The first step in this process is assessing the purveyor or market. The fishmonger should properly handle, ice, and transport the fish and should be able to answer any questions regarding the fish's origin and its qualities: lean or oily, firm-textured or delicate, appropriate for moist-heat methods or able to withstand a grill's heat.

Purchasing

Fish can be transported rapidly from the source to the consumer, but to ensure that fish are of the best quality, the chef should apply as many as possible of the following tests: If a fish smells fresh and looks fresh, but has a slight browning of the gills, it may still be acceptable. If a fish smells bad, no matter how clear the eyes or firm the flesh, reject it. (See Figure 5-38.)

1. *Smell the fish.* It should have a fresh, clean "sea" aroma, appropriate to the fish. Very strong odors are a clear indication that the fish is aging or was improperly handled or stored.

2. *Feel the skin.* The skin should feel slick and moist. The scales, if any, should be firmly attached.

3. *Look at the fins and tail.* They should be moist, fresh, flexible, and full, and should not appear ragged or dry.

4. *Press the flesh.* It should feel firm and elastic. There should be no visible fingerprint as soon as your finger lifts away.

5. *Check the eyes.* Eyes should be clear and full. As the fish ages, the eyes will begin to lose moisture and sink back into the head. (Note: The wall-eyed pike's eyes *should* appear milky.) This test should be used in conjunction with as many others as possible.

6. *Check the gills.* They should have a good red to maroon color, with no traces of gray or brown, and should be moist and fresh looking. The exact shade of red will depend on the fish type.

7. *Check the belly.* There should be no sign of "belly burn," which occurs when the guts are not removed promptly; the stomach enzymes begin to eat the flesh, causing it to come away from the bones. There should also be no breaks or tears in the flesh.

8. *Check live shellfish for signs of movement.* Lobster and crab should move about. Clams, mussels, and oysters should be tightly closed. As they age, they will start to open. Any shells that do not snap shut when tapped should be discarded; the shellfish are dead. If a bag contains many open shells the delivery should be rejected.

Storage

Ideally, the chef should purchase only the amount of fish needed for a day or two at most, and should store it properly as described below. When the purveyor is only able to make deliveries once or twice a week, then proper storage becomes a critical concern. (See Figure 5-39.)

Under proper storage conditions, fish and shellfish can be held for several days without losing any appreciable quality. When the fish arrives, the following things should be done:

1. *Check the fish carefully for freshness and quality.* The fish may be rinsed at this point; scaling and fabricating should be delayed until close to service time.

2. *Place the fish on a bed of shaved or flaked ice in a perforated container;* stainless steel is preferred. Round fish should be belly down, flat fish on its side. The belly cavity should be filled with shaved ice as well.

3. *Cover with additional shaved or flaked ice;* the fish may be layered, if necessary. Cubed ice can bruise the fish's flesh. It also will not conform as closely to the fish. Shaved or flaked ice makes a

FIGURE 5-39   Storing/Icing

(1) Pans for storing.

(2) Icing fish. They should be positioned in the ice as if they were swimming.

FIGURE 5-40   Dressed or Pan-dressed Fish

(1) Pan-dressed trout.

(2) Pan-dressed flounder.

tighter seal around the entire fish. This prevents undue contact with the air, slowing the loss of quality and helping to extend safe storage life.

4. *Set the perforated container inside a second container.* In this way, as the ice melts, the water will drain away. If fish is allowed to sit in a pool of water, some flavor and texture loss will occur. The longer it sits, the greater the loss of quality.

5. *Re-ice fish daily.* Even when properly iced, the fish will gradually lose some quality. To slow this loss down, remove the fish from its storage containers. Replace the fish in its ice in clean pans or containers. Whenever possible, perform this task in a refrigerated area.

Clams, mussels, and oysters should be stored in the bag in which they were delivered, but should not be iced. They last better at a temperature range from 35° to 40°F (2° to 4°C). The bag should be closed tightly and lightly weighted to keep the shellfish from opening up.

Figure 5-41 Market Forms of Fish

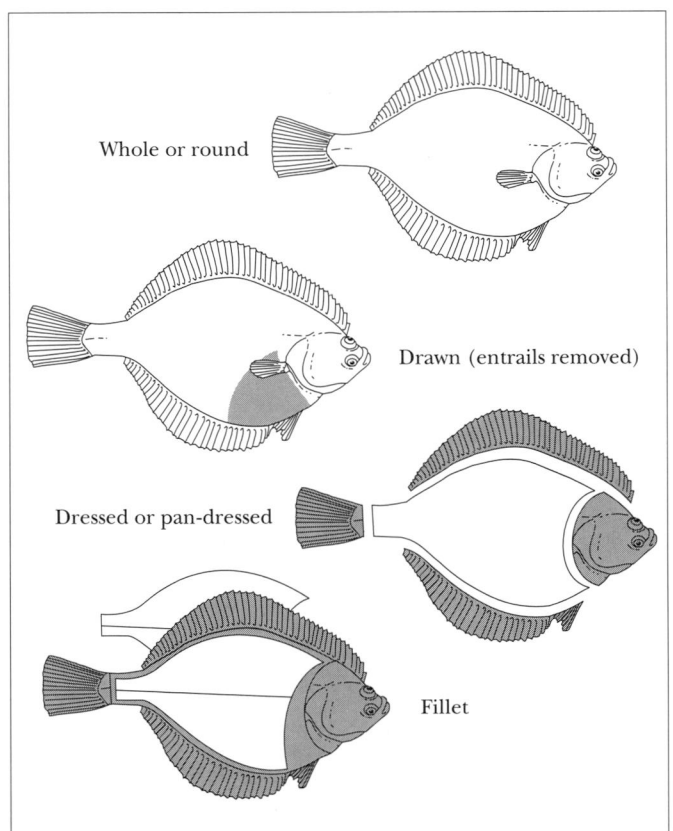

Whole or round

Drawn (entrails removed)

Dressed or pan-dressed

Fillet

Scallops out of the shell and fish purchased as fillets should be stored in metal or plastic containers set on or in the ice. They should not be in direct contact with the ice, however, because as it melts much of the flavor and texture of the scallop or fish would be lost.

Crabs, lobsters, and other live shellfish should be packed in seaweed or damp paper upon delivery. They can be stored directly in their shipping containers at 39° to 45°F (4° to 7°C) until they are to be prepared, if a lobster tank is not available. Do not allow fresh water to come in direct contact with lobster or crab during storage, as it will kill them.

Frozen fish, including glazed, whole fish (fish repeatedly coated with water and frozen so that the ice builds up in layers, coating the entire fish) and frozen shrimp, should be stored at -20 to 0°F (-29° to -18°C) until they are ready to be thawed and cooked. (Storage at -10°F/-2°C is ideal and will greatly extend shelf life.)

Do not accept any frozen fish with white frost on its edges. This indicates freezer burn, the result of improper packaging or thawing and refreezing of the product.

Market Forms Butchering fresh fish is relatively simple, and many restaurant chefs probably will prefer to do this, retaining the bones and head for stocks or fumet. As with meats, the available working space and the staff's level of skill in butchering should be evaluated. Fish are too expensive to be cut up carelessly, and the extra money spent on buying fish fillets may balance out the money lost through waste. Fish may be purchased frozen, smoked, pickled, or salted in addition to the market forms shown in Figures 5-40 and 5-41. Table 5-7 also includes helpful purchasing information.

A description of basic cuts and butchering techniques, as well as instructions for shucking clams and oysters can be found in Chapter 6.

Categories

There are many different fish species and even greater numbers of names for these fish, not all of which may be of culinary importance. The name a fish will go by depends upon the region in which it is sold. However, basic groupings can be used to sort fish and shellfish. Once these groupings are ex-

FIGURE 5-42   Skeletal Structure of Fish

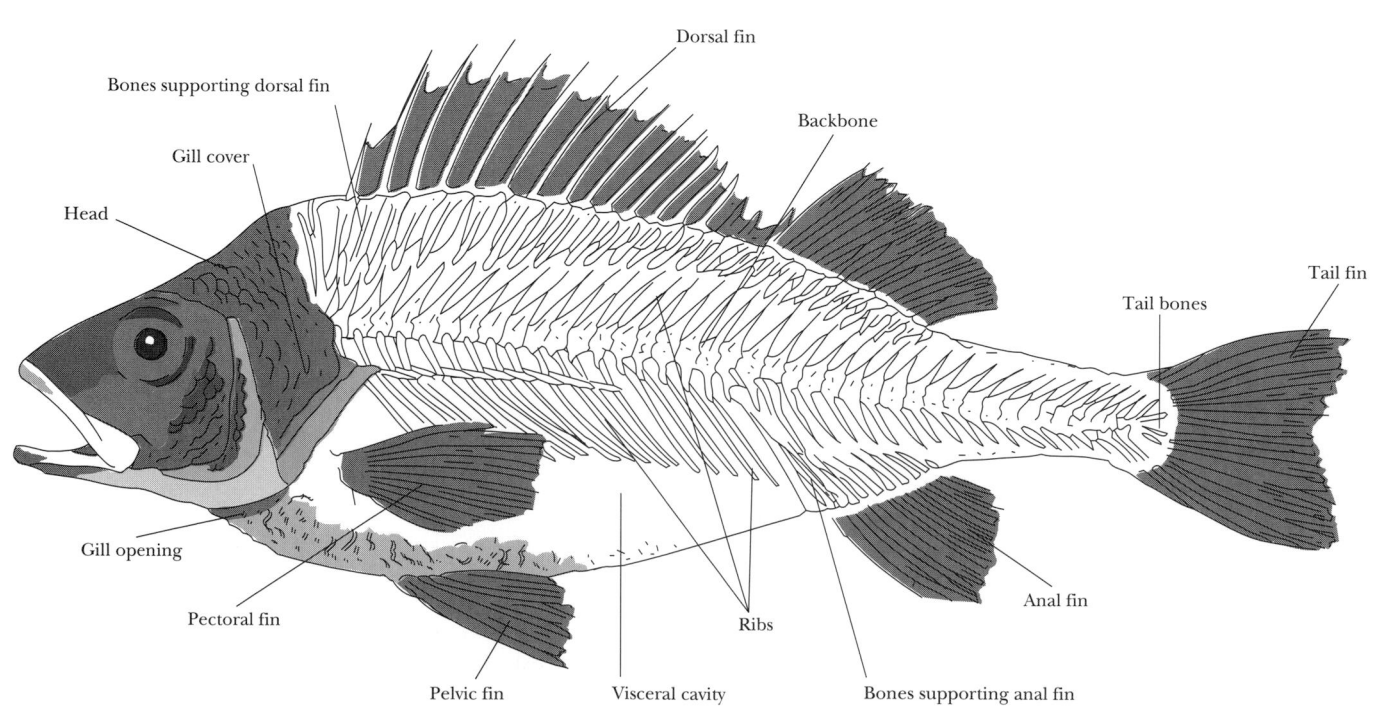

(1) The basic skeletal structure of a flat fish.

(2) The basic skeletal structure of a round fish.

TABLE 5-7 MARKET FORMS OF COMMON FISH

Commom Name	Commom Market Forms	Characteristics	Location
Fin Fish			
Barracuda	round, dressed, steaks, fillet	moderate fat, firm textured	salt water, Pacific
Bluefish	round, drawn, fillet	fat soft, strong tasting	salt water, Atlantic and Gulf
Bass	all	moderately fatty, fairly firm, smooth-textured	salt water, Atlantic and Pacific
Butterfish	round, drawn, fillet	fatty, soft, mild	salt water, Atlantic and Pacific
Catfish	round, dressed	moderately fatty, firm, sweet	primarily fresh water or farmed except hogfish which is saltwater
Chub	dressed, smoked	fat, smooth, firm texture, strong taste	fresh water, northern lakes
Cod	all, salted, smoked, dried	lean, firm white flesh, mild-flavored	salt water, Atlantic (New England)
Croaker	round, dressed, fillet, steaks	fine, sweet flesh	see Drum
Cusk	drawn, dressed, whole, fillet	lean white, mild taste	salt water, Atlantic
Drum	round, drawn, fillet, steaks	lean, fine, sweet tasting (except white sea bass—stronger flavor, coarse texture)	salt water
Flounder	dressed, fillet	lean, delicate, mild taste	salt water, Atlantic
Grouper	all	lean, firm white flesh, mild taste	salt water, Atlantic and Gulf
Haddock	fillet, sticks	lean, firm white flesh, mild taste	salt water, Atlantic
Hake	fillet	lean, firm white flesh mild flavor	salt water, Atlantic, and northern Pacific
Halibut	all	lean, fine-textured, delicate flavor	salt water, Atlantic, and northern Pacific
Herring, sea	round	fairly fat, soft-textured	salt water, Atlantic and Pacific
Herring, lake	round, dressed, smoked	fatty, smooth, firm texture, salty and oily taste	fresh water, northern lakes
Mackerel, Spanish	round, dressed	high fat, soft flesh, oily	salt water, Florida coast and Gulf of Mexico
Mackerel, king	all	high fat, firm flesh	salt water
Lingcod	dressed, fillet	lean, firm, mild, sweet flavor	salt water, Pacific
Mullet	round, dressed, fillet	moderate fat, firm flesh, nutty flavor	salt water, South Atlantic and Gulf
Perch, white or yellow	dressed, fillet	lean, firm, sweet flavor	fresh water, northern lakes and rivers
Perch, ocean	fillet	fat, firm, well-flavored flesh	salt water, Atlantic
Pickerel	dressed, fillet	lean, firm, bony flesh	fresh water, northern lakes and rivers
Pike, blue	round, fillet		
Pike, wall-eye	dressed, fillet	lean, firm, sweet	fresh water, northern lakes and rivers
Pollock	fillet	lean, firm, mildly sweet-flavored	salt water, Atlantic
Pompano	dressed, round	moderate fat, firm texture, full flavor	salt water, south Atlantic and Gulf
Sablefish, black cod	dressed, steaks, smoked	high fat, finely grained, buttery flavor	salt water, north Pacific
Salmon, Atlantic	dressed, steaks	moderately fat, firm flesh distinctive rich flavor	salt water, only salmon from the Atlantic
Salmon, chum	drawn, dressed, steaks, fillet	lowest fat content of all salmon	salt water, Pacific

(Table continued on following page)

TABLE 5-7   MARKET FORMS OF COMMON FISH *(CONTINUED)*

Commom Name	Commom Market Forms	Characteristics	Location
Salmon, king	drawn, dressed, steaks, fillet	high fat, soft texture, rich flavor	salt water, Pacific, Alaska
Scrod	all	white, lean, and firm	salt water, Pacific and Atlantic
Shellfish			
Abalone	meat in shell	lean, rubbery, sweet flavor	coast of California, Mexico, and Japan
Clams, butter	shell—100# sack, shucked—100–250/gal	small, sweet, hard shell	Puget sound
Clams, quahog	Bushel—11# EP, 80# sack, shucked—100–250/gal	large, hard shell	East coast
Clams, littleneck	60# bushel	small, usually eaten "on the half shell"	East and West coast
Clams, razor	80# box, 16 EP /bushel	soft shelled	West coast
Clams, soft	45# bushel, shucked—200–700/gal, 16# EP/bushel	soft shelled	East and West coast
Conch	15# EP/bushel	tough, should be pounded to be tenderized	southern, Florida, Gulf and Carribean
Crabs, blue, hardshell	5# EP/bushel	sweet, succulent meat	Atlantic and Gulf coast
Crabs, blue, soft shell	3# EP/doz	sweet, succulent meat, blue crabs that have shed their shells	Atlantic and Gulf coast
Crabs, rock	5# EP/bushel	firm, sweet, succulent, claw meat	Atlantic, North Carolina to Texas
Crabs, Dungeness	all	sweet, succulent meat	Pacific coast
Crabs, king	legs only		north Pacific
Lobsters	whole	firm, sweet meat	Atlantic
Lobsters, spiny (crayfish)	tails only	firm, stringy meat, not as sweet as Main lobster	Tropics, Austrailia, South Africa
Mussels	45–55#/bushel, 10# EP/bushel	slightly tough, sweet flavor	Atlantic, Pacific, and Mediterranean
Oysters, Eastern	80#/bushel, shucked—150–200/gal (bluepoint)	range from bland to salty, from tender to firm; superior to Pacific oyster	Atlantic
Oysters, Pacific	80#/sack, 64–240/gal shucked	range from bland to salty, from tender to firm	Pacific coast
Oysters, Olympia	120# sack, 1600–1700/gal	range from bland to salty, from tender to firm	Puget Sound
Scallops, bay	shucked—500/gal	sweet, succulent meat, sweeter than sea scallops	East coast
Scallops, sea	shucked—150/gal	sweet and moist, but less tender, more chewy than bay	
Sea urchins	5# EP/bushel	edible roe, served briefly cooked or raw	salt water, moderate climate throughout the world
Shrimp, see Table 5-8			
Squid	5–6/#	light, extremely firm flesh	salt water, moderate climate throughout the world
Snails	imported as tinned; live from CA farms	dense, chewy	California (farm raised)

plained, appropriate selection becomes a much easier matter.

The skeletal structure of finfish can also be used as the initial way to separate fish types into more readily understandable subjects. There are three basic skeletal types. (See Figure 5-42, for two types.)

1. *Round fish,* such as trout, bass, perch, salmon; these have a backbone along the upper edge with two fillets on either side. A round fish has one eye on each side of its head.

2. *Flat fish,* such as the various flounders and Dover sole; these have a backbone that runs through the center of the fish to create four quarter fillets, two upper and two lower or two full fillets (one from top, one from bottom). Both eyes are on the same side of the head.

3. *Nonbony fish,* such as ray, skate, sharks, and monkfish, which have cartilage rather than bones. For simplicity, these fish have been grouped with other round fish in the following section.

Shellfish can also be broken into distinct categories, also based on their skeletal structure:

1. *Univalves* (single-shelled), such as abalone, snails, conch, whelle, and sea urchins.

2. *Bivalve* (two shells joined by a hinge), such as clams, mussels, oysters, and scallops.

3. *Crustaceans* (jointed exterior skeletons or shells), such as lobster, shrimp, and crayfish.

4. *Cephalopods,* such as squid and octopus. The name translates as "head-footed," and is a reflection of the fact that the tentacles and arms are attached directly to the head.

FIGURE 5-43
Herring, Smelt, and Anchovies

FIGURE 5-44
Bass

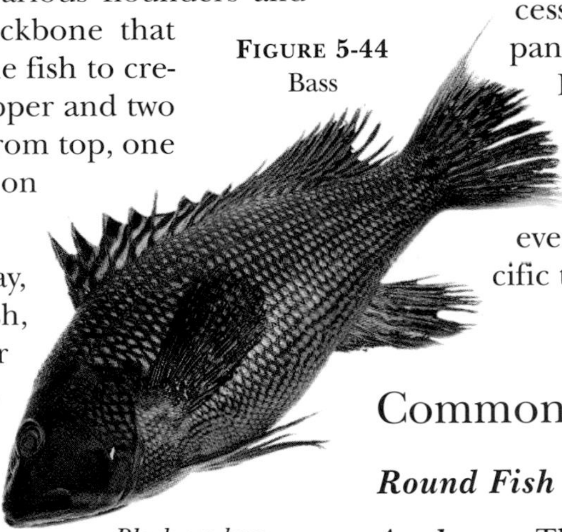

Black sea bass

Within these fairly broad categories are a wide range of flavors and textures. Some fish are naturally lean; others are more oily; some have extremely delicate and subtle flavors; others are robust and meaty.

The best way to pair a fish with a cooking technique is to consider the flesh. For example, oily fish—bluefish and mackerel, for example—are often prepared by dry-heat techniques such as grilling or broiling. Fish with moderate amounts of fat (salmon and trout) work well with any technique, with the possible exception of deep-frying. Very lean fish, such as sole or flounder, are most successfully prepared by poaching, sautéing, pan-frying, or deep-frying.

Knowing how to work with fish and shellfish is a skill that takes time and experience to truly master. There are some classic preparations, however, that combine certain fish with specific techniques.

Commonly Available Fish

Round Fish

Anchovy The most common form for the anchovy is the canned fillet packed in oil, with or without a caper. In addition, they are sold as anchovy paste or smoked fillets and may be available fresh. The salted and oil-packed fillet is a classic component in Caesar salad.

Bass Black sea bass feed primarily on shrimp, crabs, and molluscs. It has firm, well-flavored flesh that can be prepared by all cooking techniques. Considered to hold a close resemblance to a Mediterranean fish called the sea bream, black sea bass generally weigh from 1 to 3 pounds, but may be larger in the fall. Other so-called bass—striped bass,

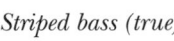
Striped bass (true)

Striped bass (hybrid)

sea bass, pike, and red snapper, for example—are not necessarily related by family, but share culinary similarities.

The flesh of striped bass is sweet and relatively firm. Some freshwater species are landlocked in the United States, but those fished from clean saltwater tend to have the best texture and flavor.

FIGURE 5-45
Catfish

FIGURE 5-46
Cod/Haddock

Striped bass can tolerate polluted waters, and its sale has been severely restricted until recently. A hybrid striped bass is farm raised and has a firm white flesh and is growing in popularity.

Bluefish A fish with a relatively strong flavor and oily flesh, it should be drawn as soon as possible after it is caught and should be very fresh. Young bluefish generally have an excellent flavor, as they feed on molluscs and shrimp. The flesh has a loose, flaky texture and is excellent broiled or grilled. The strip of dark-colored flesh in the fillet has a more pronounced flavor and tends to hold any pollutants or contaminants. Bluefish has become more difficult to find as its habitat becomes increasingly polluted. There may be restrictions regarding availability in some areas.

Catfish Catfish are farmed and marketed under carefully controlled conditions. Catfish should be skinned before cooking and are commonly sold as skinless fillets. The flesh is delicately flavored, lean, and very firm in texture. This fish can be prepared by any cooking technique; a traditional preparation is dipped in cornmeal and pan-fried. (See Figure 5-45.)

Cod Cod has a lean, white flesh. The cod family has a number of distinct species, each with different identifying

FIGURE 5-49
John Dory

marks. (See Figure 5-46.) Cod may be poached, used in chowder, or steamed, and is also available salted (known as *baccala*). *Finnan haddie* is split, smoked haddock, a species of cod. Atlantic cod, haddock, cusk, whiting, hake, and pollock are all members of the cod family. Severe restrictions have been imposed throughout the Grand Banks and St. George's Bay making shortages likely.

FIGURE 5-47
Eel

Dolphin Fish (Mahi Mahi) This fish, harvested from the Pacific and Atlantic Oceans, has firm flesh with a sweet, delicate flavor. It can be prepared by all cooking techniques and is excellent in ceviche. The skin should be removed before cooking.

Eel Eel has a rich, oily flesh. Eels spawn in the Sargasso Sea, which is part of the North Atlantic, and then begin the journey back to either Europe or America. They are available live, whole, skinned, in fillets, smoked, and jellied. (See Figure 5-47.) One of the most famous eel dishes is a French stew known as *matelote*.

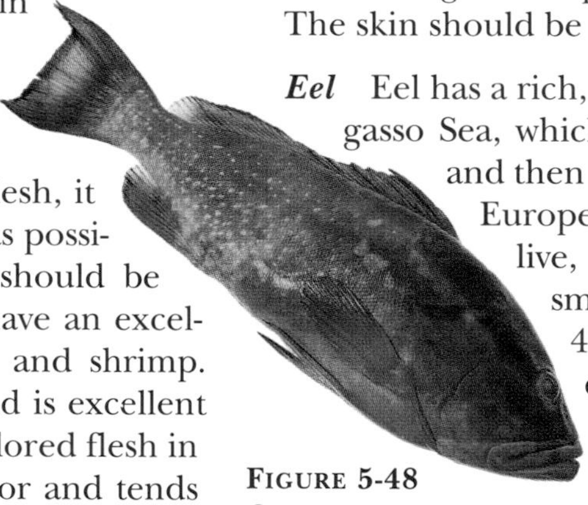

FIGURE 5-48
Grouper

Groupers There are several kinds of grouper, all members of the sea bass family. (See Figure 5-48.) One of the most commonly available is red grouper. Grouper has lean, firm, white flesh that is best when sautéed, pan-fried, steamed, or shallow-poached. The skin should be removed before cooking.

Haddock (see Cod)

John Dory John Dory, also known as *San Pedro*, is identified by the large "thumbprint of Saint Peter" on either side of its body. This fish is well known in the Mediterranean and the Bay of Biscay, although it can be found as far north as Norway. The white flesh is very delicate and may be poached, and grilled whole or filleted. The proportion of fillet to whole fish is

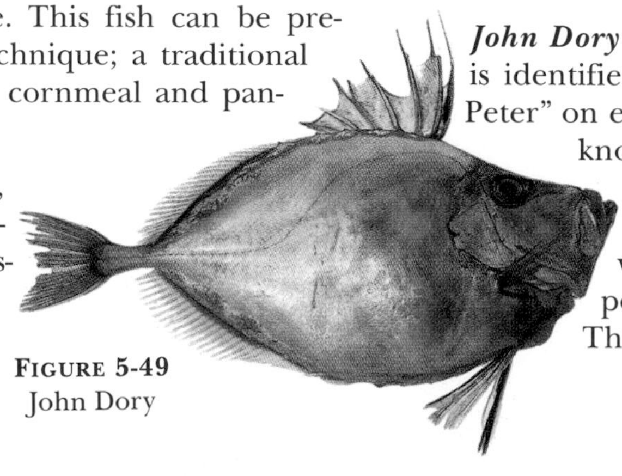

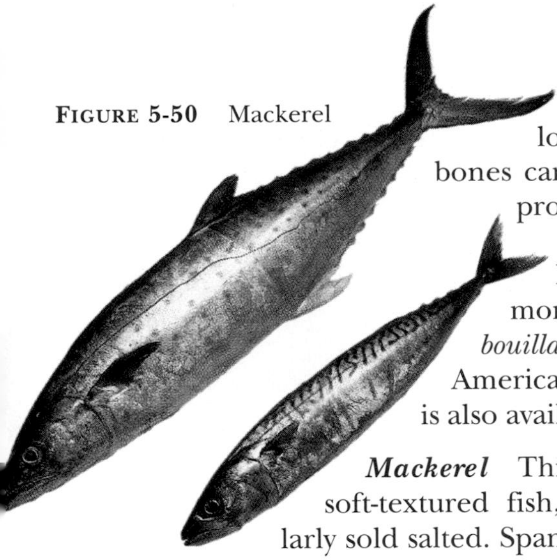

FIGURE 5-50   Mackerel

low, but the bones can be used to produce a good fumet. John Dory is commonly used in *bouillabaisse*. The American John Dory is also available.

Mackerel This is an oily, soft-textured fish, once regularly sold salted. Spanish and king mackerel both are considered fish of eating quality, but the Spanish mackerel is conceded to be the best. The flesh flakes easily when cooked. Mackerel is best when prepared by dry-heat cooking techniques and is commonly broiled.

Monkfish This fish has been known by a number of names, including angler fish, goosefish, lawyer fish, and belly fish. The French name is *lotte*. It is available as the fillet from the tail. Monkfish has a firm, dense texture and sweet taste. Suitable for any cooking technique, it is commonly used in fish stews such as *cioppino* and bouillabaisse.

FIGURE 5-52
Permit

Perch Perch and its close relative the wall-eyed pike, has a lean and delicate flesh. The best perch are harvested from the fresh waters of lakes and reservoirs. Small perch may be deep-fried and served whole; large fish are cut into fillets and then either pan-fried, steamed, or shallow-poached. The wall-eyed pike (not truly a pike) is used for forcemeats and *gefilte* fish.

Permit This warm-water fish is found from North Carolina to the Gulf of

FIGURE 5-51
Monkfish

FIGURE 5-53
Pike

FIGURE 5-55
Puffer

Mexico. It is a larger relative (averaging 9 pounds) of the more popular pompano. (See Figure 5-52.) When purchasing, select the smaller permits, which have better flavor. It can be poached, baked, or broiled.

Pike Most famous for its use in *quenelles de brochet,* wall-eyed pike has sweet, white, firmly textured flesh that is relatively lean but stands up well to dry-heat techniques. It is also commonly poached or used to prepare mousses or terrines. It should not be confused with pickerel, a fish of virtually no culinary importance. (See Figure 5-53.)

Pompano Considered by some as one of the finest-eating saltwater fish, pompano is becoming increasingly expensive. Pompano has firm, well-flavored flesh and is often broiled or prepared *en papillote*. Most pompano comes from the Gulf of Mexico. (See Figure 5-54.)

FIGURE 5-54
Pompano

Puffer This fish (see Figure 5-55) is named for its ability to inflate to a size that makes it impossible for the puffer's predator to devour it. It is a warm-water fish, but is found as far north as New York and southern Newfoundland. Also known as blower or northern swellfish, the American variety of this fish is considered less dangerous than the Japanese species. To prepare, cut off the head and peel back the skin. The meat with the backbone, can be fried whole or filleted and pan-fried. Because of the prickly scales, wear gloves when skinning the fish.

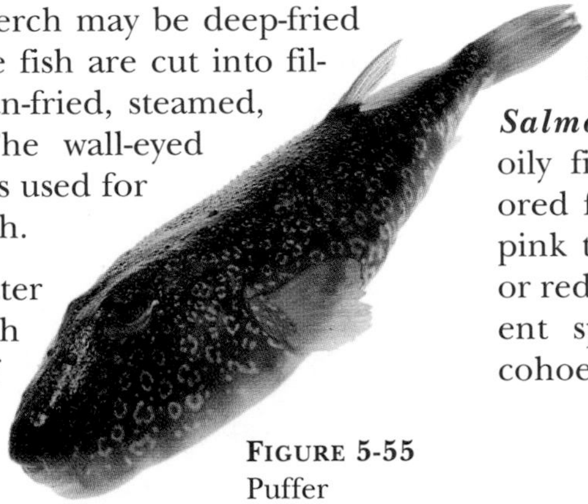

Salmon This firm, moderately oily fish has a distinctively colored flesh, ranging from light pink to a deep orange-pink or red. A number of different species, including cohoe, king, and At-

FIGURE 5-56
Salmon

lantic, are available. The Atlantic species is commonly farm-raised.

Salmon may be prepared using any technique and among the more popular presentations are poached, baked in pastry *(coulibiac),* and grilled. Salmon is available fresh, smoked, or cured as *gravad lox.* Salmon shares flavors, textures, and culinary treatments with trout.

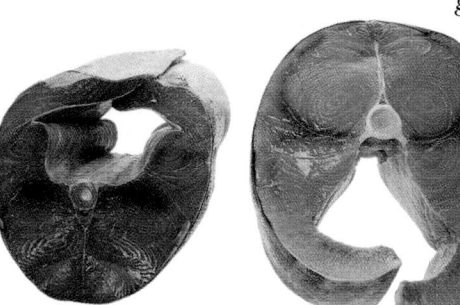

FIGURE 5-57   Shark/Swordfish Steaks

Shad   Shad usually enter the rivers of the Atlantic coast from the Gulf of St. Lawrence to northern Florida from May to December. The flesh of both sexes, which is sweet and white but extremely bony, and the roe of the female are highly regarded. A traditional preparation method for shad and shad roe is to sauté or pan-fry them with bacon. The American Indians used to smoke-roast the fish, a technique referred to as "planking."

Shark   Mako and blue shark are very popular, and other types of shark, including yellow-tip and black-tip, are becoming important in the marketplace, especially as overfishing of the mako depletes supplies. Shark sometimes may be sold to the unwary as swordfish. Be sure to check the pattern of the strip of the dark-colored flesh to be sure you are receiving what was ordered. (See Figure 5-57.) The flesh of shark is sweet and relatively firm and moist, but the skin is extremely tough. Shark is commonly made into steaks and grilled, broiled, or sautéed.

Skate/Ray   The flesh of the skate or ray is sweet and firm and has been compared to scallops. It is sold as wings, which should be skinned prior to sautéing, although they may be

FIGURE 5-59   Tautog

poached with the skin on. Skate wings are easier to skin after poaching. One famous presentation method is to sauté the skate and serve it with *beurre noir.*

Snappers   There are a number of different snappers. One of the most popular is red snapper (see Figure 5-58), which has become greatly reduced in overall supply. True red snapper comes from the Gulf of Mexico and adjacent Atlantic waters. Among other desirable snapper species are vermillion, silk, mutton, mangrove, gray, beeliner, pink, and yellowtail. The flesh is firm, moist, and finely textured. Almost any preparation technique can be used; snapper is often prepared *en papillote* or baked.

(2) Vermillion snapper

Swordfish   Swordfish has an extremely firm texture with a unique flavor. Commonly cut into steaks and grilled, swordfish has a lot of characteristics similar to shark. Swordfish's darker strip of flesh has a Y-shaped pattern, which is one way to distinguish it from shark, which has a round pattern. The distinction between swordfish and mako shark steaks is clearly illustrated in Figure 5-57. Tuna has the same kind of meaty flavor and firm texture as swordfish and shark.

Tautog   This fish (see Figure 5-59) is found from Nova Scotia to South Carolina, but predominately from Cape Cod to the Delaware Bay. Its white flesh is dry and delicate and suitable for grilling and baking. It is firm enough to to be used in fish chowder.

FIGURE 5-58
Snapper

(1) Red snapper

FIGURE 5-60
Tilapia

(1) Hybrid

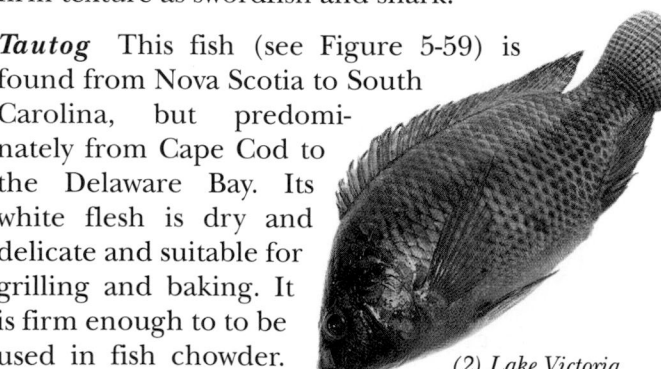

(2) Lake Victoria

Tilapia A popular freshwater fish in Asian cuisine, tilapia is now being farm raised extensively in the United States. (See Figure 5-60.) Any undesirable muddy taste once associated with this fish is not apparent in commercially available farm raised species. It can be poached, steamed, or grilled.

FIGURE 5-62 Trout

Tilefish/Golden Bass This fish has an off-white, flaky flesh and delicate flavor. Tilefish can be cooked by any technique and is occasionally smoked.

Trigger Fish Trigger is a tropical or subtropical fish, occasionally harvested in cooler climates. (See Figure 5-61.) It is sold as turbot in the Bahamas, Bermuda, and Florida. The tough skin should be removed before cooking. The firm flesh is best when poached or sautéed.

Trout Along with catfish, salmon, oysters, mussels, and clams, trout are farm raised in large quantities. (See Figure 5-62.) In fact, with the exception of some special trout species, such as the Dolly Varden or brown, all trout sold in restaurants come from commercial hatcheries. Rainbow trout is the most readily available type of trout. It is excellent when pan-fried in a manner similar to catfish, roasted, or poached. *Truite au bleu* is a famous trout preparation: freshly caught trout is poached in a vinegar court bouillon until the blue color is barely set. Smoked trout is also widely available.

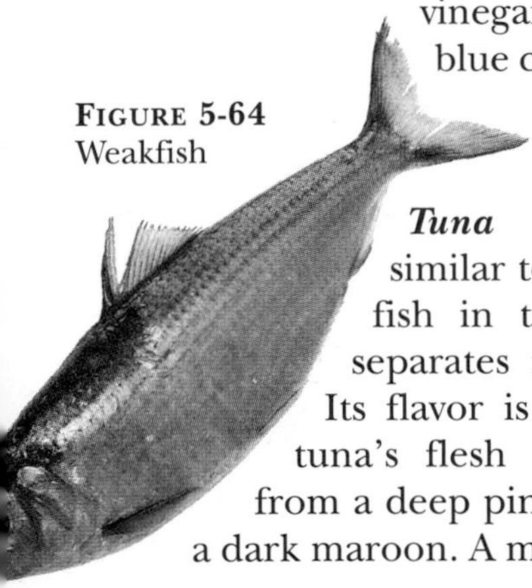

FIGURE 5-63 Tuna

FIGURE 5-64 Weakfish

Tuna Tuna's flesh is similar to that of swordfish in texture, but it separates more readily. Its flavor is unique, and tuna's flesh color ranges from a deep pinkish-beige to a dark maroon. A member of the mackerel family, tuna has the distinctive strip of dark-colored flesh along its back. Tuna is often roasted or cut into steaks and grilled. (See Figure 5-63.) Also popular is canned tuna—albacore (white) or light meat, packed in either oil or water. Canned tuna is essential for *tonnato* sauce and *salade Niçoise*.

Weakfish The weakfish is harvested in the United States from Massachusetts to Florida. It is also marketed as squeteaque, drum, croaker, and sea trout. Its lean and flaky flesh makes it a popular fish for grilling and pan-frying. The spotted squeteaque is most abundant in North Carolina and the southern states. (See Figure 5-64.)

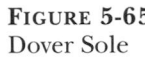

FIGURE 5-65 Dover Sole

FIGURE 5-66 Flounder

Flat Fish

Dover Sole One of the only true soles is the Dover sole, a flat fish with a compact, oval shape (see Figure 5-65) and firmly textured, delicately, flavored flesh. Dover sole was so highly esteemed that hundreds of different dishes were devised to feature it in the classical repertoire. Dover sole is available fresh or frozen. Note that although many species of flounder have been dubbed "sole," they should not be confused with Dover sole.

Flounder Flounder is often sold in the United States under the market name of "sole": lemon sole, gray sole, white sole are all forms of flounder, a flat, disk-shaped fish with both eyes on the same side of its head. (See Figure 5-66.) Plaice, another flounder species, is often sold as dab (sand dab, roughback). Flounder is generally

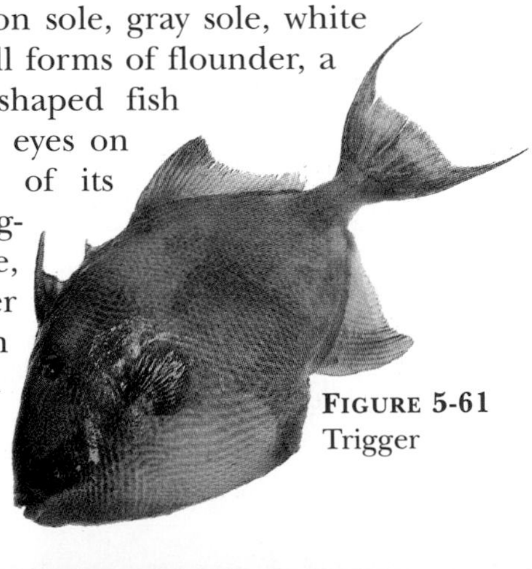

(1) Top

(2) Bottom

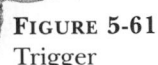

FIGURE 5-61 Trigger

FIGURE 5-67   Halibut

(1) Top

(2) Bottom

quite delicate, with a tendency to flake readily. It is particularly suited to shallow-poaching and steaming and is also commonly cut into "fingers" and deep-fried. Readily available whole, flounder is also sold cut into quarter fillets and skinned.

Halibut   Halibut has firm, white meat with a delicate flavor. The halibut can grow to be quite large and may be cut into steaks or fillets. A halibut of 10 to 40 pounds is considered market-size; they can grow to be over 200 pounds. This fish is now being farm raised, as over-fishing has greatly reduced its availability. (See Figure 5-67.)

Turbot   A disk-shaped fish esteemed for its snowy-white, moist, finely textured flesh, turbot may grow large enough to cut into steaks or fillets. It is generally steamed or poached to highlight its delicacy and whiteness. This fish, although a northern Atlantic species, is being successfully farm raised in Chile.

FIGURE 5-68
Land Snails

Shellfish

Univalves

Abalone   The abalone has one shell and a suction cup that attaches firmly to rocks; it must be pried loose. Available from California, state law prohibits the exportation of live abalone, so most of the country must rely on frozen or canned abalone. The meat, which is cut into steaks and pounded before sautéing or grilling, becomes extremely tough if overcooked. Advances in raising aqua-cultured abalone may help increase its availability.

Conch   True conch comes from the Caribbean and is more accurately classified as a gastropod—a large class of mollusk. Conch is sold out of the shell and may be available ground. It is used in salads, *ceviche*, chowders, and fritters. Further north, the whelk, which is much smaller and grayish in color, is sold as conch, although it is more accurately termed a sea snail.

FIGURE 5-69   Clams

FIGURE 5-70 Mussels

FIGURE 5-72 Scallops

FIGURE 5-71 Oysters

Snails Fresh snails, or *escargots*, are imported from France. They average 32 snails per pound and are classically served in their shells with a compound garlic butter as an appetizer. Fresh snails are far superior to canned snails, and are increasingly available from farms in this country. (See Figure 5-68.)

Bivalves

Clams Clams are available in the shell, shucked (and possibly frozen), and canned. Clams sold as "live" should definitely be checked for tightly closed shells, to make sure they are alive. They should have a sweet smell.

Clams, like oysters, may be marketed by the name of the bed from which they were taken and local preferences for species will vary. (See Figure 5-72.) The following terms are commonly applied to clams:

Littlenecks (1-to-1 ½-inches) are small hardshell clams often eaten raw on the half shell. *Topnecks* (1 ½-to-2-inches) and *cherrystones* are the next largest sizes and are also commonly eaten raw. If hardshell clams are more than 3 inches in diameter, they are generally referred to as *quahogs* and are used for chowder or fritters.

Pacific littleneck clams, also known as *manilla clams*, are found on the Pacific coast and are generally steamed.

Soft-shell clams, or "steamers," are generally steamed or used in fritters.

Mussels Most commercially available mussels are farm raised and are sold live in the shell. (See Figure 5-70.) Mussels are commonly prepared *à la* *marinière* (steamed with wine, garlic, and lemon) or as the major component of Billi-bi soup (a velouté soup garnished with mussels), although there are a great many other presentations.

Mussels steamed and served in the shell should be debearded first.

Oysters   Oysters are sold live in the shell or shucked. (See Figure 5-71.) As with clams, they are generally marketed by the name of the beds from which they were harvested, and local preference will vary greatly. Some of the most famous presentations include raw on the half shell, oyster stew, oyster omelets, and oysters Rockefeller, a dish that includes spinach and Pernod.

Scallops   Three species of scallop are of commercial importance: bay scallops, sea scallops, and calico scallops. Sea scallops can become quite large (2 to 3 inches in diameter); bay and calico scallops are smaller. True bay scallops (northern) are generally considered superior in quality to calicos.

Most scallops are sold shucked. (See Figure 5-72.) Occasionally, shucked scallops with the roe attached may be found. Even less frequently, they are sold still in the shells, though farm-raised scallops in the shell are increasingly available.

Coquilles St. Jacques is customarily thought of as a cream-based scallop gratin; it is also the name for scallop in French, and refers to the fact that St. James wore the shell of the scallop as his personal emblem.

Crustaceans

Crab   Common kinds of crab include blue, Dungeness, king, and spider. Blue crab, which is found on the Atlantic Coast, especially around the Chesapeake Bay, is sold live, or as pasteurized or canned meat. (See Figure 5-73.)

In the spring through late summer, when the crab molts, blue crab are sold as "soft-shelled crabs," which are commonly pan-fried or sautéed. Hard-shelled crab may be boiled or steamed. The meat may be removed and used in a variety of preparations, including one of the most famous, crab cakes.

She-crab soup is made from the roe and meat of female crabs, identifiable by their broad "aprons."

Dungeness crab is common on the Pacific Coast. King crab and spider crab are valued mainly for their legs, although the whole crab can be used.

FIGURE 5-73   Crustaceans

(1) Clockwise from left: Dungeness, American lobster, Crayfish, Shrimp (head on) Shrimp, Blue crab.

(2) Spider crab

Spider crab is common to the Adriatic and the Mediterranean. Only one claw per stone crab measuring at least 2 3/4 inches can be harvested, however, in order to help save the species. Fishermen simply twist off the claws (which grow back) and return the crab to the sea. Legs and claws are cooked and frozen on the ship in most cases and the claw may be cracked (especially in the case of stone crab).

Jonah crab is a larger relative of the stone crab. It is found only from Nova Scotia to Florida. The meat of the crab is excellent for crab cakes and can be fried or baked.

Crayfish   Freshwater crayfish is widely available

TABLE 5-8 SHRIMP SIZE AND COUNT

Commercial Name	Type I: Raw, Chilled or Frozen, Not Peeled	Peeled, Deveined	Type II: Cooked, Chilled or Frozen, Peeled, Deveined
Colossal	15 or fewer	10 or fewer	30 or fewer
Extra jumbo	16–20	20–25	31–40
Jumbo	21–25	26–31	41–60
Extra large	26–30	32–38	61–90
Large	31–35	39–44	91–125
Medium large	36–42	45–53	126 up
Small	51–60	64–75	
Extra Small	61 and over	76 and over	

Commercial names apply to Type I only.

year-round because it can be farmed. Crayfish may be purchased live or precooked and frozen (whole, or tail meat only). Crayfish are used extensively in Creole and Cajun cooking and are also a classic garnish. *Etouffé* and *jambalaya* are two of the most popular crayfish dishes.

Lobster American lobster is generally the most prized; it is available live or cooked and canned. The meat is firm and succulent and virtually the entire lobster is edible. The female may contain the egg sac, known as the roe. It is considered a delicacy; however, lobsters with visible egg sacs cannot be legally harvested. Both sexes possess the green tomalley, or liver, another prized part.

To determine the sex of the lobster, feel the appendages where the tail meets the body. In the female they will be soft and feathery, whereas in the male they are rigid. The female's tail or abdomen is generally broader.

Other types of lobster include the rock lobster (often sold as frozen tails, rock lobster is the market name for spiny lobster), Dublin prawn, and lobsterette.

Shrimp Shrimp is probably one of the most popular crustaceans. Shrimp are most commonly available frozen, as they are often processed and flash-frozen either on the boat or as soon as boats are unloaded at shore in order to preserve flavor and quality. Fresh shrimp are highly perishable, but they may be available in some regions of the United States, notably the Gulf of Mexico and Chesapeake Bay regions, and there are both saltwater and freshwater species. The flesh has a sweet flavor and a firm, almost crisp texture.

Shrimp are sold according to the number in a pound, known as the "count." The count ranges include 3 per pound; 10 to 15; 21 to 25; 26 to 30; 31 to 35; and on up to over 100 per pound. (See Table 5-8.)

Some common presentations include cold "cocktails," deep-fried (tempura), baked, sautéed, and grilled.

Cephalopods

Octopus Octopus is firmly textured with a sweet "marine" flavor. It is generally sold fresh, and

FIGURE 5-74 Cephalopods

(1) Cuttlefish

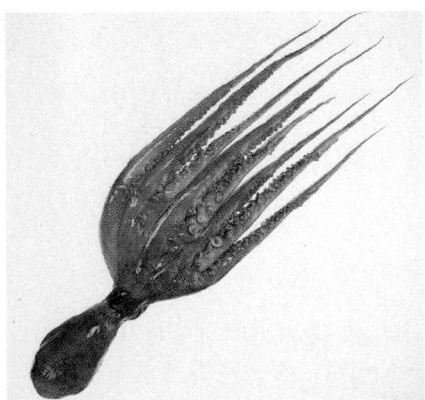

(2) Octopus

cleaned of its ink and beak, but may also come frozen. Octopus may be prepared in a number of dishes, including ceviche, chowders, and salads. (See Figure 5-74.)

Squid   Squid is one of the most widely available forms of seafood. It has always been an established part of Mediterranean and Asian cuisines and is continuing to gain popularity in the United States. Squid are available in a range of sizes; small squid are frequently stuffed and cooked whole in a sauce, whereas large squid are cut into rings, fried, and served with a spicy sauce. There are many different presentations, however, because squid are suited to most cooking techniques. Squid over nine inches long are too tough for culinary use.

Miscellaneous Items

Caviar   "Caviar" is defined by the FDA as the salted roe from the sturgeon. It is available fresh (it must be refrigerated carefully) or pasteurized and canned. Fresh caviar should be bright, shiny, and whole. It should not appear smashed or dull. The four varieties (ranging from the most expensive and desirable to the least expensive) are: Beluga (has a large grain and is light in color), ship (medium grain, also light in color), sevruga (small grain and dark colored), and osetra (also small-grained and dark). The best quality caviar is served perfectly plain. Lesser-quality (but still good) caviar is traditionally served with toast or blinis and lemon, hard-boiled eggs, and finely chopped onions.

Frogs' Legs   These are the hind legs of frogs that are usually farm raised. Frogs' legs are sold in pairs. One classic dish is frogs' legs sautéed *à la provençale.*

Fruits and Vegetables

Fruits

For the chef, the term "fruits" means a fresh product that is sweet. They are customarily used in sweet dishes, such as pies, puddings, ice creams, and dessert sauces. Other spots held by fruits on the menu are as a plate of fresh seasonal fruits, fruit salads, or fruit soups. They are the classic end to most meals, with or without a plate of cheese. Table 5-9 provides general information about basic fruits.

Historically, fruits have been used as ingredients in savory dishes as well as sweet ones. You can find recipes both old and new that pair a variety of fresh and dried fruits with meat, poultry, and fish. There are several reasons that these pairings have such enduring popularity. Fruits can be an excellent foil for richly flavored or oily foods. Rhubarb, for instance, is traditionally served with mackerel. Dried fruits find their way into compotes, stuffings, and sauces served with game meats, pork, and even some cuts of beef. Applesauce is served with crisp, buttery potato pancakes. The bright flavors of citrus fruits and grapes are frequently used in combination with poultry, veal, or fish preparations.

Apples

Apples are perhaps America's favorite fruit. According to surveys from the International Apple Institute, apples account for nearly 14 percent of all tree fruits (including both fruit and nuts) sold in this country. The most commonly available varieties consist of Golden and Red Delicious, MacIntosh, Granny Smith, and Rome Beauty. Examples of popular varieties of apples are see in Figure 5-75. There are, however, thousands of other varieties grown in orchards throughout the country. A little searching can result in a find that may make your apple tart uniquely flavorful.

Different varieties of apples have particular characteristics. Some are best for eating out of hand or in other preparations where they are left fresh and uncooked. Many apples will begin to turn brown once they come in contact with air. Dousing them in water that has a little lemon juice added will help prevent browning, but may not be desirable if a truly pure apple taste is important. Other types are considered best

FIGURE 5-75   Apples

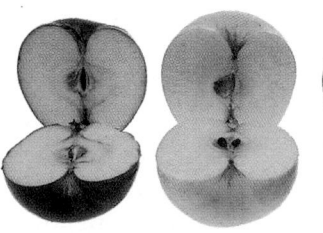

(1) Rome Beauty, Golden Delicious, Red Delicious (whole)

(2) Rome Beauty, Golden Delicious, Red Delicious (cut)

TABLE 5-9 GENERAL FRUIT INFORMATION

Fruit type	Grades Available	Pack, Count, and/or Weight	Yield %	Available Forms
Apples	U.S. Extra Fancy, U.S. No. 1, No. 2	Carton/box (variable count, cell-packed or loose, 34–43#)	76%	Fresh, (see Table 5-10), sliced, frozen, dried, canned
Apricots	U.S. No. 1, No.2	Lug (22#)	80%	Fresh, dried (sulphured, unsulphered)
Bananas	U.S. No. 1, No. 2	Box (40#: average count for No. 1 grade is 115 each)	75%	Fresh, dried
Berries	U.S. No. 1	Basket (½ pint, pint, or quart); Flats (12 baskets, 10#)	90–100%	Fresh (see Table 5-11), dried, IQF frozen frozen in syrup
Cherries	U.S. No. 1	Lugs, 20# California lugs, 18#; Flats, 12#	80%	Fresh, dried, frozen, canned
Citrus, U.S. fruits	U.S. Fancy, No. 1, Combination, or No. 2	Case (count varies by variety from 32 to 100)	65% (varies by use)	Fresh (see Table 5-12), frozen juice concentrate
Figs	U.S. No. 1	Case (35 ea.)	80%	Fresh, dried, IQF frozen
Grapes	U.S. Fancy, Extra No. 1, No.1	Lug/carton (weight ranges: 12, 17, or 23#)	93%	Fresh (see Table 5-13), dried (raisins)
Kiwi	U.S. Fancy, No. 1, No. 2	Case, (39 each)	89%	Fresh
Mango	No Federal grades	Case (12 each)	62%	Fresh, purée
Melons	U.S. No. 1, Commercial, No. 2	Case (5 each)	65 to 70%	Fresh (see Table 5-14)
Nectarines	U.S. Extra No. 1, No. 1	Case (25#)	87%	Fresh, IQF frozen
Papayas	U.S. No. 1, No. 2	Carton/flat (8 to 14 each)	84%	Fresh, purée
Peaches	U.S. Extra Fancy No. 1, Fancy No. 2	Lug/case (35#)	75%	Fresh, IQF frozen slices, frozen in syup, canned, halves, or slices
Pears	U.S. Extra Fancy No. 1, Fancy No. 2	Case (40 to 90 each, by variety)	87%	Fresh (see Table 5-15), dried, canned, sliced, IQF frozen slices
Persimmons	No Federal grades	Flat (11–13#, 25 each)	85%	Fresh
Pineapples	U.S. Fancy No. 1, No. 2	Case (5 each)	62%	Fresh, canned (sliced, crushed, chunks), juice
Plums	U.S. No. 1	Lug/case (28#)	78%	Fresh (see Table 5-16)
Pomegranates	No Federal grades	Case (24 each)	58%	Fresh
Rhubarb	U.S. No. 1	Case (20#); Box (5#); Bulk (varies)	90%	Fresh, IQF pieces

for pies and baking. These fruits tend to retain a recognizable shape and some texture even when baked. Still others are selected for their ability to cook down into a rich, smooth purée for applesauce. Apples for the best cider are usually a blend of apples chosen to give the finished drink a full, well-balanced flavor, achieved by combining several varieties during pressing.

Apple varieties are considered both summer fruits (at their best for only a short season) and winter fruits (which can be held in cold storage for many months without significant loss of quality).

This quality makes it possible to get good fresh apples throughout the year. The climate, temperature, and humidity in warehouses are carefully controlled. Ethylene gas is pumped into storage rooms to assure that the ripening process does not escalate into spoilage.

Dried apples, prepared applesauce, apple juice (bottled or frozen concentrate), cider, spiced or plain pie fillings, and a host of prepared items made from apples can be purchased.

This quintessentially North American fruit is found in thousands of recipes, from soups to

TABLE 5-10 APPLE VARIETIES

Variety*	Description	Peak Season/Fresh	Uses
Crabapple	Very small, tart, red with blush of yellow or white	Fall	In sauces, pickles, as relish
Golden Delicious	Golden skin with freckling. Flesh is sweet, juicy, and crisp	September to May	All-purpose fruit. Stays white after cutting longer than other varieties
Granny Smith	Green skin and white-light green flesh. Extremely crisp and finely textured flesh; tart	April to July	All-purpose fruit
Greening	Green skin. Firm flesh with mild, sweet-tart flavor	October to March	Used for pies, sauces, baked; can be frozen
Jonathan	Bright red, flecked with yellow-green. Tender flesh, semi-tart	September to January	Eating out-of-hand; used for pies, sauces, can be frozen
McIntosh	Primarily red, streaked with yellow or green. Flesh is very white. Crisp,	September to June	Eating out-of-hand; used for sauces, cider, can be frozen
Northern Spy	Firm texture, juicy, sweet-tart taste	October to November	Excellent in pies
Red Delicious	Bright red speckled with yellow. Flesh is a yellow-white, with firm texture and sweet taste	September to June	All-purpose
Rome Beauty	Bright red skin. Flesh is firm with a milk tart-sweet flavor	October to June	All-purpose
Winesap	Bright red skin with some yellow green. Flesh is firm, tart-sweet, aromatic	October to June	Eating out-of-hand; used for pies, sauces, baking, or can be frozen

*There are many varieties of apples available only within smaller regions. These apples share eating and cooking characteristics with those described here. If you have any questions, ask your purveryor or other reputable source for the best use for a particular variety.

breads to classic apple pie. They can be found in puddings, savory and sweet dishes, and sauces. See Table 5-10 to determine which varieties are best for eating out of hand, cooking, and baking.

Berries

Strawberries, raspberries, blueberries, and blackberries are so seasonal that for most people, they mean that spring has arrived or that summer is at its height. Some varieties can be found virtually any time of the year, but it only takes one bite to convince most people that locally grown berries, picked that day, outshine any foreign import.

They tend to be highly perishable (with the exception of cranberries) and

FIGURE 5-76 Berries

(1) Group

(2) Strawberries

(3) Golden gooseberries

are susceptible to bruising, mold, and overripening in fairly short order. Inspect all berries and their packaging carefully before you accept them. Juice-stained cartons or juice leaking through the carton is a clear indication that the fruit has been mishandled or is old. Once berries begin to turn moldy, the entire batch goes quickly.

Cranberries are almost always cooked. Other berries can be featured as fresh fruit, used as a flavoring, purée, or sauce in a number of dishes. They may also be used to flavor vinegars, marinades, or dressings. When fresh berries are out of season, IQF berries are often a perfectly fine substitute.

Dried berries can be used to great advantage in winter fruit compotes, stuffings, breads, or other sweet and savory dishes. Some classic dishes that

(4) Cranberries

TABLE 5-11 BERRIES

Variety	Description	Peak Season/Fresh	Uses
Blueberry	Blue/purple with dusty silver-blue "bloom"	Late summer	Eaten fresh, in baked goods, jams, dried, as flavoring for vinegar
Boysenberry	Hybrid of various types of raspberry, with similar flavor and texture		Eaten fresh, jams and jellies, made into wine or syrup
Cloudberry	Orange-red, similar to raspberry		
Cranberry	Shiny red berry, some with white blush; dry and sour	Fall	Generally cooked; although there are some raw chopped relishes; sauces, jellies, in breads, dried
Currant	May be red, black, or white. Red is generally sweetest, black is very dark	Midsummer	Generally cooked for use in relishes, jams, jellies, wines, cordials, or syrups
Elderberry	Small purple-black berry		Jams, jellies, wines, or cordials
Gooseberry	Smooth skin (some with papery husk still attached. May be green, golden, red, purple or white. Some have fuzzy skins		Used crushed in "fools" or in compotes, relishes, jams, jellies
Mulberry	Resembles but is unrelated to raspberry; juicy with slightly musty aroma	Midsummer	Wines, syrups, cordials
Raspberry	Actually clusters of tiny fruits (drupes), each containing a seed. May have "hairs" on surface. May be red, black, or white. Sweet, juicy fruit. Dewberry is type of raspberry	Two seasons: early summer, late summer	Eaten fresh, used in baked items, syrups, purées/sauces, cordials, syrups, to flavor vinegars
Strawberry	Red shiny, heart-shaped berry, seeds on exterior	Late spring into early summer	Eaten fresh, shortcakes, baked goods, as purée, jams, jellies

use berries include strawberry shortcake, fresh berry cobblers, pies, jams, jellies, and ice creams. (See Figure 5-76 and Table 5-11.)

Cherries Cherries are grown in numerous varieties and come in many shades of red, from the light crimson of Queen Anne to the almost black Bing. They vary in texture from hard and crisp to soft and juicy, and flavors run the gamut from sweet to sour. Cherries are available in a number of different forms. They may be found fresh throughout their growing season, and are also sold canned or dried. Fillings for Danish, pies, and other pastries can also

be found, as well a cherry syrups, cherry-flavored cordials. Kirschwasser, a clear cordial, is one of the most often used in bake shops and kitchen.

Citrus Fruits

Citrus fruits are characterized by their thick skins, which contain aromatic oils, and their segmented flesh, which is extremely juicy. Grapefruits, lemons, limes, oranges, and tangerines are the most common citrus fruits. They range in flavor from the sweetness of oranges to the tartness of lemons. Four common citrus fruits are shown in

FIGURE 5-77 Citrus Fruit

(1) Blood orange   *(2) Lemon and lime*   *(3) White grapefruit*   *(4) Pink grapefruit*

TABLE 5-12 CITRUS VARIETIES

Variety	Description	Uses
Navel orange	Orange skin, relatively smooth; seedless	Eating fresh, juice, zest (zest may be candied)
Temple orange	Orange skin, slightly pebbled texture. Juicy, slightly tart flavor	Eating fresh
Seville orange	Sour flavor	Marmalade
Blood orange	Orange skin with blush of red; pockets of dark red/maroon pigmented flesh. Aromatic	Eating fresh, juicing, in sauces, as flavoring ingredient
Tangerine	Orange, lightly pebbled to smooth skin, loosely attached to fruit. Usually has many seeds. Juicy, sweet-tart flavor	Eating fresh, juice
Mandarin	Deep-orange, smooth skin with "nipple" on one end. Skin loosely attached to flesh, seedless	Eating fresh
Meyers lemon		Juice, flavoring, baked items, zest (zest may be candied)
Lemon	Yellow green to deep yellow skin; extremely tart flesh, seeds	Juice, flavoring, zest (zest may be candied)
Persian lime	Dark green, smooth skin. Flesh is tart, seedless	Juice, flavoring, zest (zest may be candied)
Key lime	Light green	Juice, flavoring (most famous use is Key Lime pie)
Red grapefruit	Yellow flesh, possible red blush. Flesh is deep red, seedless, mellow sweet-tart flavor	Eating fresh, juice
White grapefruit	Yellow flesh, sometimes with green blush. Flesh is pale yellow; seedless varieties available	Eating fresh, juice, flavoring, zest (zest may be candied)
Ugli fruit	Hybrid citrus, with wrinkled yellow-green skin, pink-yellow flesh, seedless	Eating fresh
Juice orange	Orange skin, mottled with green; extremely juicy, smooth sweet flavor	Juice

FIGURE 5-78 Exotic and Tropical Fruit

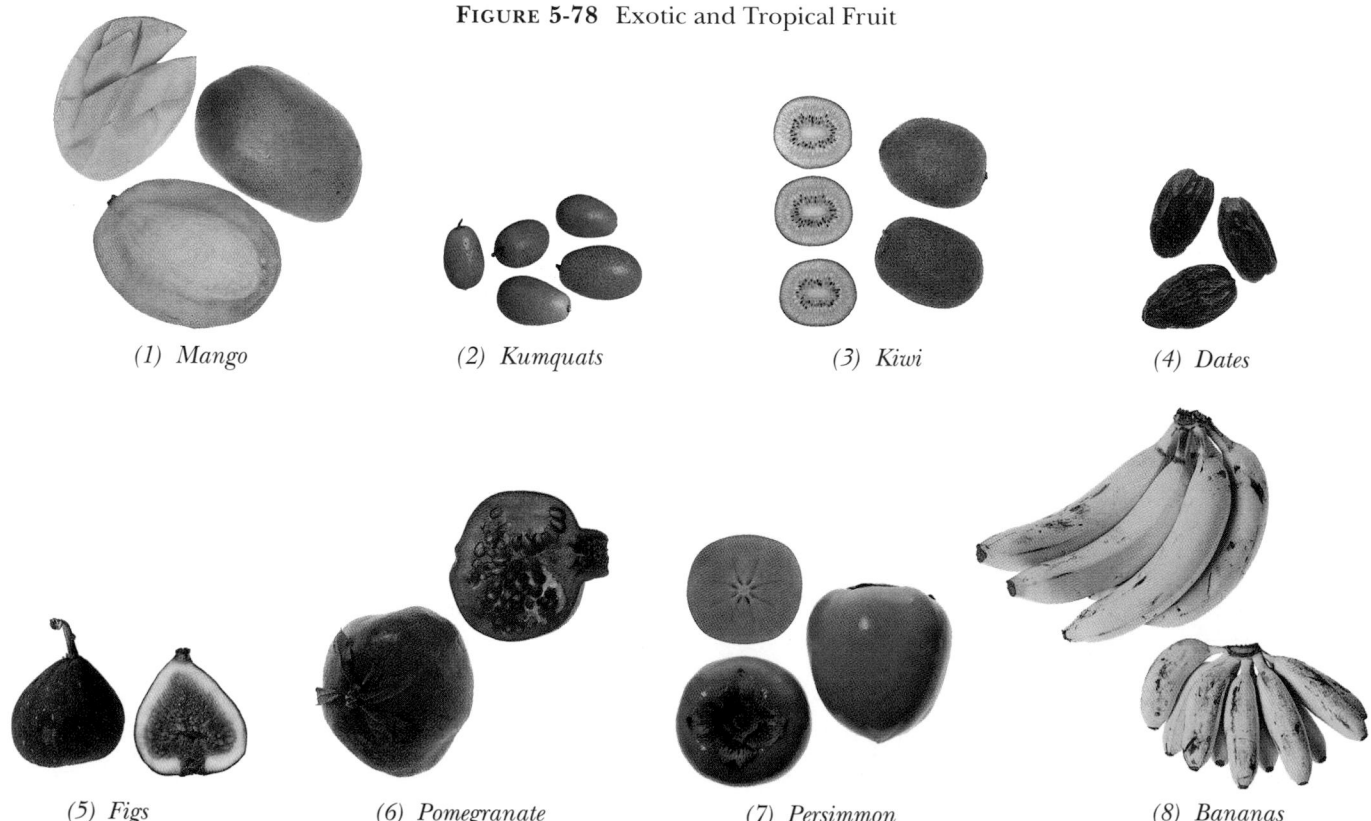

(1) *Mango*　　(2) *Kumquats*　　(3) *Kiwi*　　(4) *Dates*

(5) *Figs*　　(6) *Pomegranate*　　(7) *Persimmon*　　(8) *Bananas*

FIGURE 5-79 Pineapple

FIGURE 5-80 Grapes

(1) Red table   *(2) White/seedless*

(3) Purple/black   *(4) Champagne*

Figure 5-77. See Table 5-12 for additional informatio about citrus fruits.

Oranges come in three basic varieties: thin-skinned, thick-skinned, and bitter. Thin-skinned oranges have smooth skin that is somewhat difficult to peel. They are usually plump and sweet, which makes them ideal for juicing. Varieties include the small Valencia and the blood orange (with orange skin and red pulp). Thick-skinned oranges include the navel, which is large, seedless, and easy to peel, and consequently makes the best eating orange. Bitter oranges like Seville and Bigarade are used almost exclusively for making marmalade. Bigarade sauce—a classic hollandaise-style sauce—is flavored with the juice and rind of the Bigarade.

Grapefruits have yellow skin with an occasional rosy blush where the sun hits them. They are juicy and tart-sweet and are available with either white

(actually yellow) or pink flesh. Pink grapefruits are generally slightly sweeter than white varieties.

Tropical Fruits A wide variety of fruits fall into this category, which is named for the general climatic conditions under which the fruits are grown. Bananas and pineapples are the most common. Un-

	TABLE 5-13 GRAPE VARIETIES		
Variety	*Description*	*Peak Season/Fresh*	*Uses*
Thompson Seedless	Green, with thin skin, seedless	Year-round	Table grape, also dried as raisins
Concord	Thick skin, which may be deep purple, red, or white. Skin "slips" easily from flesh	Late summer, fall	Juices, jams, jellies, syrups, preserves
Black	Deep-purple skin, usually with seeds	Summer (may be available sporadically at other times, especially winter)	Table grape
Red Emperor	Light to deep red, occasionally with green streaking. Thin, tightly adhering skin. Seeds	Summer (available year-round, as imported item)	Table grape
Champagne	Small grape, red to light purple, seedless	Late summer	Table grape

TABLE 5-14 MELON VARIETIES

Variety	Description	Peak Season/Fresh	Signs of Maturity
Cantaloupe	Netting or veining over surface of skin; flesh is smooth, orange, juicy, and fragrant	Summer	Full slip; netting coarse, ground color is yellow to buff, has pleasant melon aroma
Casaba	Skin is light green to yellow green	Early fall	Smooth, velvety feel to skin. Melon aroma
Cranshaw	Salmon-colored, very fragrant flesh	Early fall	Rich melon aroma, slight softening near stem
Gallia	Green flesh that tastes and smells like cantaloupe	Early summer	
Honeydew	Green flesh, juicy	Summer	Velvety to slightly sticky feel of skin. Skin is yellow with no greenish cast
Muskmelon	Deeply ridged melon with bright orange, aromatic flesh	Mid-to-late summer	Ground color is yellow to buff (not green). Full slip
Persian	Dark green skin with yellow marking, flesh is yellow-orange	Summer	Heavy for size, some yielding when pressed
Watermelon	Large, oblong-shape melon with red or yellow flesh. Some seedless varieties	Mid-to-late summer	Underside of fruit should have some color, not dead white

FIGURE 5-81　Melons

(1) Watermelon　　*(2) Honeydew*　　*(3) Cantaloupe*

(4) Muskmelon　　*(5) Casaba*　　*(6) Cranshaw*

like most fruits, they are almost always picked green and allowed to ripen *en route* from the plantation to the ultimate buyer. In this category are found dates, figs, kiwis, mangos, papayas, plantains, pomegranates, and passion fruit. (See Figures 5-78 and 5-79.)

Grapes Grapes, either with seeds or seedless, are juicy fruits that grow in clusters on vines. Technically, they are berries, but because they include so many varieties and have so many different uses, they are grouped separately. (See Figure 5-80.) Of the many kinds available for both eating and wine making, two of the most popular are Californian or Thompson Seedless, which are appropriate for both cooking and eating out of hand, and Napoleon Red, a good table variety. Grapes are dried to form raisins, and they can be purchased throughout the year.

There are some classic dishes that make use of grapes as an ingredient. The most famous is Sole Véronique, a poached fillet of sole in a cream sauce garnished with peeled seedless grapes. For the most part, they are used in fruit platters, as an accompaniment to chccsc plates, or in salads. (See Table 5-13.)

Melons Melons are fragrant, succulent fruits, most of which are related to squashes and cucumbers. They also come in many varieties and range from the size of an orange to that of a watermelon. The four major types are cantaloupes, watermelons, winter melons (honeydew, casaba, crenshaw), and muskmelons. (See Figure 5-81.)

The ability to determine when a melon is ripe is one that eludes some people. Depending upon the type, you will look for a variety of different signs. Cantaloupe melon should have a "full slip." This means that the melon ripened on the vine and grew

away from the stem, leaving no rough edge. Unripe cantaloupes usually have a scarred or rough end. Some melons may become slightly soft at the stem end, though for other melons that could indicate that they are over-the-hill. Aroma is one of the best keys to determining ripeness. (See Table 5-14.)

Peaches, Apricots, and Nectarines

Peaches Sweet and juicy, having a distinctively fuzzy skin, they come in many varieties. All peaches fall into one of two categories—clingstone or freestone. Clingstone peaches have flesh that clings to the pit, whereas the flesh of freestone peaches separates easily. Peach flesh comes in a range of color, from white to creamy yellow to yellow-orange to red, with a whole host of combinations possible.

Apricots. They resemble peaches in some ways. They have slightly fuzzy skin but are smaller, with somewhat drier flesh. They range in color from yellow to golden-orange and some have rosy patches.

Nectarines. They are similar in shape, color, and flavor to peaches, but they have smooth skin and their flesh may closely resemble the flesh of plums in texture in some varieties.

All three of these fruits are popular for use as fresh fruits, as well as in shortcakes, pies, cobblers, and other desserts. They are frequently canned or frozen. Dried versions of these fruits are also available, and make an excellent addition to dried fruit fillings or compotes. (See Figure 5-82.)

Pears Pears are to the French what apples are to the Americans. They also come in many varieties, although fewer than apples. The most commonly available are Bartlett, Bosc, d'Anjou, and Seckel. (See Figure 5-83.) The flesh of pears is extremely

FIGURE 5-82 Peaches, Nectarines, and Apricots

(1) Apricot   *(2) Peach and Nectarine*   *(3) White Peach*

TABLE 5-15 PEARS

Variety	Description	Peak Season/Fresh	Uses
Bartlett	Green skin, turning yellow as fruit ripens, some red varieties	Fall	Eating fresh, poached
Bosc	Long neck, dark russeted skin, brown when ripe	Late fall	Eating fresh, poached, baked
d'Anjou	Green skin, becoming yellow as it ripens, may have brown scarring	Fall	Eating fresh, poached, baked
Seckel	Small pear, green skin with red blush, crisp flesh	Fall	Eating out of hand
William	Long neck, yellow skin, strong perfume	Fall	Preserves, used to flavor cordial "Poire William"

FIGURE 5-83   Pears

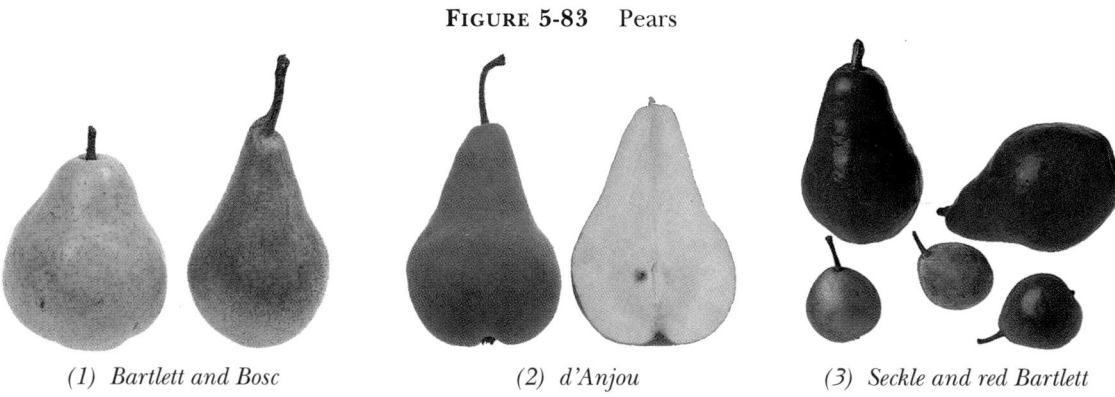

(1) *Bartlett and Bosc*   (2) *d'Anjou*   (3) *Seckle and red Bartlett*

FIGURE 5-84   Plums

(1) *Santa rosa*   (2) *Black amber*

TABLE 5-16 PLUM VARIETIES

Variety	Description	Peak Season/Fresh	Uses
Santa Rosa	Red, with light-yellow flesh	Fall	Eating fresh
Black Friar	Dark-purple with silvery bloom, deep red to purple flesh	Fall	Eating fresh
Damson	Small, with red to light-purple skin, green flesh	Fall	Eating fresh, preserves, conserved, pies
Greengage	Green skin, with yellow-green flesh	Fall	Eating fresh
Prune	Small, purple skin with green flesh, flesh is relatively dry, and pit comes cleanly away	Fall	Eating fresh, dried as prunes. Also known as "prune plum"

fragile. Because they are usually picked for shipping before they have ripened, it is sometimes difficult to find perfectly ripe pears in the market. They will become softer after picking but will not actually continue to ripen. For this reason, pears are often poached whole or used in a sorbet to compensate for their underdeveloped flavor. (See Table 5-15.)

Plums Plums can be anywhere in size from as small as an apricot to as large as a peach. The possible colors include green, red, purple, and various shades in-between. (See Figure 5-84.) When ripe, they are sweet and juicy, and some have sour skins that contrast nicely with their succulent flesh. Cooking plums are generally drier and more acidic than dessert plums, but both types can be eaten raw. Greengage, a sweet plum with green skin and flesh, is a popular dessert variety. Damson, which has purple skin with a silver-blue bloom (faint blush on the skin), is probably the most well-known cooking plum. (See Table 5-16.)

Rhubarb Although technically a vegetable, rhubarb has been classified here as a fruit because of the way it is used. Known as "pie plant," it grows in long stalks with broad, somewhat curly leaves. Only the reddish-green stalks are eaten. (The leaves should not be used because they contain large quantities of oxalic acid, a toxic compound.) Rhubarb is crisp and very sour, so it is usually cooked and sweetened. In addition to being served as a dessert, it is classically combined with rich, oily fish, such as mackerel or bluefish. (See Figure 5-97.)

TABLE 5-17   GENERAL VEGETABLE INFORMATION

Vegetable by Type	Grades Available	Pack/Weight and/or Count	Yield %	Available Forms
Artichoke, globe	U.S. No. 1, No. 2	½ carton (20#, 18, 24, 48 or 60 count)	40%	Fresh, frozen (hearts) marinated, canned in brine
Asparagus	U.S. No. 1, No.2	Case/pyramid (30#)	varies	Fresh, (green, white), canned, frozen, pieces
Avocados	U.S. No. 1; U.S. Combination; U.S. No. 2	Case (36 count)	50%	Fresh, purée, canned
Beans	U.S. Fancy No.1; U.S. Combination; U.S. No. 2	Case (varies by type)	varies	Fresh (see Table 5-25), frozen, canned
Beets	U.S. No. 1; U.S. No. 2	Case, (25# carton: 24-bunch count)	75%	Fresh (see Table 5-27), frozen, canned
Broccoli	U.S. Fancy; U.S. No. 1; U.S. No. 2	Case (14 bunches)	65%	Fresh, frozen: pieces, spears, chopped
Brussels Sprouts	U.S. No. 1; U.S. No. 2	Flat (12 pints)	75%	Fresh
Cabbage	U.S. . No. 1; U.S. Commercial	Case (varies by type)	75%	Fresh (see Table 5-18)
Carrots	U.S. Extra No. 1; U.S. No. 1; U.S. No. 1 Jumbo; U.S. No. 2	Case (varies by type)	85%	Fresh
Cauliflower	U.S. No. 1	Case (12 heads)	58%	Fresh, frozen: florets
Celeriac	U.S. No. 1	Case (12#)	75%	Fresh
Celery	U.S. Extra; U.S. No. 1; U.S. No. 2	Carton (weight and count varies)	75%	Fresh
Corn (sweet)	U.S. Fancy; U.S. No. 1; U.S. No. 2	Case, crate, or bag	48%	Fresh, frozen kernels, canned kernels
Cucumbers	U.S. Fancy; U.S. Choice; U.S. Extra No. 1; U.S. No. 1 Small; U.S. No. 1 Large	Carton, bushel, or LA lug (count and weight varies)	93% (peeled) or 68% (peeled & seeded)	Fresh (see Table 5-20)
Eggplant	U.S. Fancy; U.S. No. 1; U.S. No. 2	Case (count and weight varies)	81%	Fresh (see Table 5-20)
Fennel	U.S. No. 1	Case (24 each)	45%	Fresh

(Table continued on following page)

	TABLE 5-17 *(CONTINUED)*			
Vegetable by Type	*Grades Available*	*Pack/Weight and/or Count*	*Yield %*	*Available Forms*
Greens (cooking)	(Varies by type)	Case (weight varies)	average of 65%	Fresh (see Table 5-19)
Kohlrabi	No Federal grades	Case (24#)	58%	Fresh
Lettuces	(Varies by type)	Case, flat (weight varies)	average of 70%	Fresh (see Table 5-21)
Mushrooms	(Grading for domestic only) U.S. No. 1; U.S. No. 2	Basket (3#); case or flat (weight varies), or bulk, by #	average of 95%	Fresh (see Table 5-22), dried, canned
Onions (cured/dry)	U.S. No. 1, Export; Commerical; U.S. No. 1; U.S. No. 1 Picklers; U.S. No. 2	Bag (25 to 50#)	85%	Frozen, sliced Fresh (see Table 5-23)
Onions (green/fresh)	U.S. No. 1; U.S. No. 2	Case (48 bunches)	90%	Fresh
Parsnip	U.S. No. 1; U.S. No. 2	Case (12#)	80%	Fresh, frozen
Peas	U.S. No. 1; U.S. Fancy	Case or bunch (weight varies)	varies by type	Fresh (see Table 5-25), frozen, canned
Peppers, sweet	U.S. Fancy; U.S. No. 1; U.S. No. 2	Case (weight varies)	average of 80%	Fresh
Peppers, chili	No Federal grades	Case or bulk by #	85%	Fresh (see Table 5-24)
Potatoes	(Varies by type)	Case or bag (weight varies)	varies by use	Fresh (see Table 5-26) Frozen, canned
Squashes (summer)	U.S. No. 1; U.S. No. 2	Case (count and weight varies)	80%	Fresh (see Table 5-20)
Squashes (winter)	U.S. No. 1; U.S. No. 2	Case (count and weight varies)	75%	Fresh (see Table 5-20), frozen, pieces, canned
Tomatoes	U.S. No. 1; U.S. Combination; U.S. No. 2; U.S. No.3	Case (count and weight varies)	100% (varies by use)	Fresh (see Table 5-28), canned, dried
Turnips	U.S. No. 1; U.S. No. 2	Case (25#)	80%	Fresh
Rutabagas	U.S. No. 1; U.S. No. 2	Case (50#)	80%	Fresh

Vegetables

Vegetables include a number of foods, even some that might be botanically classified as "fruits." Tomatoes, for example, are really fruits. Their culinary application is the guiding principle for placing them in this section, rather than the previous one.

As we continue to explore other cuisines, and to reexamine the more familiar dishes of the regions of our own country, we are becoming more adventurous in our selection of vegetables to serve either with meats, or on their own, as appetizers, salads, and entrées. Table 5-17 provides general information about basic vegetable types.

Avocados These egg-to-pear-shaped vegetables have green to black leathery skin, which can be smooth or bumpy.

(See Figure 5-85.) Avocado flesh is buttery smooth, delicately flavored, green near the skin, and yellow toward the center. Cut surfaces must be treated with lemon or lime juice to prevent browning.

Haas avocados have dark, pebbly skin and a more pronounced pear shape than other varieties. Florida varieties are smoother and brighter green in color. If avocados are not ripe when you purchase them, hold them at room temperature (around 70°F/21°C) until they soften. Use ripe avocados as soon as possible, and avoid refrigerating them. If they must be stored in the refrigerator, allow them enough time to warm slightly before serving them, so that their full flavor is allowed to develop.

Cabbage Family The cabbage family *(brassicas)* includes broccoli, Brussels

FIGURE 5-85   Avocado

TABLE 5-18 CABBAGE VARIETIES

Variety	Description	Peak Season/Fresh	Quality Indicators
Broccoli	Usually dark green, some have purple cast	Summer. Also available year-round through imports	Flowers are tight, stems ends not split; leaves firm.
Broccoli rabe (also broccoli raab, rapini)	Stemmed, green, with small florets, leafy	Summer to fall	No yellowing of flowers, leaves firm and stems bright white to light green.
Brussels Sprouts	Small, round, cabbage-shaped, light green	Late fall to winter. Can be found year-round from storage or imports	Leaves firmly attached, stem ends bright.
Cabbage, bok choy	Loose head, deep-green glossy leaves and green-to-white stems	Summer into fall. Available year-round	Stems should be fresh and firm, leaves unwithered.
Celery	Long, heading cabbage with light, yellow, green color	Summer into fall. Available year-round	Free from browning of withering of leaves. Relatively heavy for size.
Cabbage (green)	Tight, round, heading cabbage. Color may range from light to medium green	Late summer to fall. Available year-round	May have loose "wrapper leaves" that should be firm, unwithered. Free from browning or bore holes. Heavy for size. Early varieties are less tight. Winter or storage cabbage are more firmly packed.
Cabbage (red)	Tight, round heading cabbage ranging from deep purple to maroon. Stems on individual leaves are white, giving marbled appearance when cut	Late summer to fall. Available year-round	May have loose wrapper leaves with greenish cast. Head should be very glossy with creamy-white veining.
Cabbage, Savoy	Moderately tight round heading cabbage. Leaves are textured, giving a "waffled" appearance	Summer to fall	Color can range from moderate to light green, but should appear fresh. Loose "wrapper" leaves should be firm.
Cauliflower	Snowy-to creamy-white flowering head with green leaves	Late summer to fall. Available throughout the year in most areas	No evidence of yellowing, browning, or opened flowers. Wrapper leaves should be firmly attached, no wilting.
Kohlrabi (also known as cabbage turnip)	Round, turnip-shaped bulb with stems and leaves attached	Early summer, periodically throughout the year	Bulbs should be firm, no evidence of cracking. Leaves should be firm and green, no evidence of yellowing.

FIGURE 5-86 Cabbages

(1) Green, napa and red

(2) Red, cut

(3) Bok choy, savoy

(4) Kohlrabi, broccoli, broccoli rabe, cauliflower

(5) Brussels sprouts

TABLE 5-19 COOKING GREENS

Variety	Description	Peak Season/Fresh	Uses
Beet greens	Flat leaf, red ribbing	Year-round, especially summer into fall	Steamed, sautéed (especially with garlic), braised
Collards	Large, flat, rounded leaves	Fall	Steamed, sautéed (especially with garlic), braised
Dandelion greens	Narrow leaves with deep teeth on edges	Spring	Steamed, sautéed (especially with garlic), braised
Kale	Ruffled leaves	Late fall	Steamed, sautéed (especially with garlic), braised, soups
Mustard greens	Deeply scalloped, narrow leaves	Summer	Steamed, sautéed (especially with garlic), braised
Spinach	Leaves may be deeply lobed or flat, depending upon variety; deep green	Year-round	Steamed, sautéed (especially with garlic), braised, served raw in salads
Swiss chard	Deeply lobed, glossy leaves, dark green, stems and ribs may be white or deep ruby	Fall	Steamed, sautéed (especially with garlic), braised
Turnip greens	Broad flat leaves with coarse texture, green	Summer into fall	Steamed, sautéed (especially with garlic), braised

FIGURE 5-87 Cooking Greens

(1) Collards, dandelion, beet green, turnip, arugula *(2) Ruby chard* *(3) Kale* *(4) Spinach*

sprouts, cauliflower, kale, kohlrabi, collard greens, and many kinds of cabbage. (See Figure 5-86.) All have a similar flavor. Turnips and rutabagas are also members of the *brassica* family, but they are more commonly thought of as root vegetables. Various cooking greens are shown in Figure 5-87 and described in Table 5-19.

Cooking Greens Chefs across the country are beginning to make use of the wide variety of cooking greens. A resurgence of interest in authentic regional dishes from this country and other cuisines around the world is partly responsible. Another important factor is the public's awareness of the potent vitamin and mineral "cocktails" they deliver.

Cooking greens can be eaten raw, as long as they have been harvested while still quite young. In fact, many mesclun mixes include one or two of these greens. Still, as the name implies, the most common way to serve greens is as a cooked dish.

Cooking greens have a rather limited shelf life, and should be used as soon after they are purchased as possible. Some types are perfect for quick stir-fries. Others are best when treated to a long slow simmer, with or without the addition of ham hocks, bacon, or other smoked pork items. (See Table 5–19 and Figure 5-87.)

Cucumbers, Squashes, and Eggplant Cucumbers, eggplant, and the many squash varieties are all

FIGURE 5-88 Cucumber and Squash

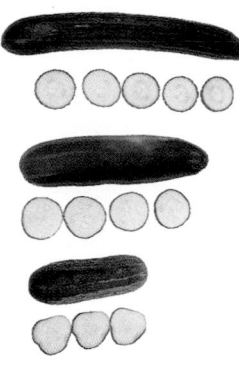

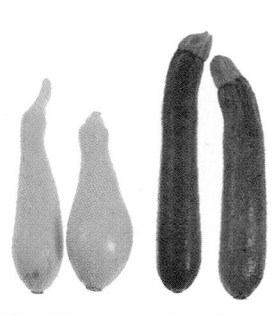

(1) Three cucumbers *(2) Yellow squash and zucchini* *(3) Chayote* *(4) Zucchini with blossom* *(5) Baby pattypan*

FIGURE 5-89 Winter Squashes

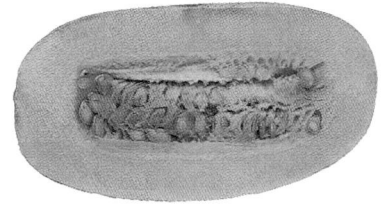

(1) Spaghetti squash *(2) Hubbard, mini-pumpkins, cheese squash*

(3) Acorn *(4) Butternut*

TABLE 5-20 CUCUMBER, SQUASH, AND EGGPLANT VARIETIES

Variety	Description	Uses
Cucumbers		
Slicing	Long, narrow, green, occasionally with pale-green or yellow underside	Salads, pickling, relishes, uncooked sauces
Kirby	Short, chubby cylinder with green skin, deep ridges, warts	Eating fresh, pickles
English/Burpless	Long, even cylinder with some ridging, no seeds	Salads, crudités
Squash, Summer		
Pattypan	Yellow (may be mottled or streaked with green) flattened ball shape	Generally steamed, sautéed, pan-fried
Chayote	Pear-shape, green, with deep ridging between halves	Steamed, sautéed, stir-fried, stuffed, pan-fried
Crookneck	Yellow skin with bent narrow neck	As for pattypan
Yellow	Yellow, elongated pear shape	As for pattypan
Zucchini	Green, with flecks of yellow, cylinder shape. Golden variety is deep yellow with green at stem end	As for pattypan, also in breads, fritters
Squash, Winter		
Acorn	Dark green (some varieties may have orange blush or be virtually all orange) with deep ridges and acorn shape	Baked, puréed, simmered, glazed with honey or maple syrup, soups
Butternut	Tan, orange, or light brown skin, elongated pear shape	Baked, puréed, simmered, glazed with honey or maple syrup, soups
Hubbard	Dusty green, very warty	Baked, puréed, simmered, glazed with honey or maple syrup, soups
Pumpkin	Deep orange with deep ridges	Baked, puréed, simmered, glazed with honey or maple syrup, soups, pies, breads
Spaghetti	Yellow, "zeppelin" shape	Steamed or roasted, flesh may be served with herbs, sauces, etc.
Eggplant		
Purple (standard)	May have rounded or elongated pear shape, deep glossy purple/black skin. Green leaves attached	Stewed, braised, roasted, grilled
Japanese	Long, narrow, cylinder shape with deep glossy purple black shape	Stewed, braised, roasted, grilled
White	May be long or round (egg shape) Some are streaked with purple	Stewed, braised, roasted, grilled

members of the gourd family. They have fairly tough rinds, thick flesh, and flat, oval seeds. Summer squashes (zucchini, yellow, crookneck, pattypan) are picked when they are immature to insure a delicate flesh, tender seeds, and thin skins. Winter squashes (acorn, butternut, hubbard, pumpkin, spaghetti) are characterized by their hard rind and seeds. (See Figure 5-88 and Table 5-20.)

Cucumbers are a common ingredient in salad bowls, crudité platters, and as part of uncooked sauces or soups, such as salsa or gazpacho. They can also be served cooked, or as a part of a creamed soup.

Summer squashes have relatively subtle flavors, which make them popular for use in vegetable

stews or soups or as a vehicle for other flavors. Zucchini is probably the most familiar of the summer squashes. It is also used in fritters and quickbreads.

Winter squash finds its way into all categories of food as well, from soups to cakes and pies, from quickbreads to side dishes. These squash have a more pronounced flavor than summer squash. Frozen and canned squashes are often available, as well as fresh squash. (See Figure 5-89.)

Eggplant comes in a range of shapes and sizes from the slender, glossy black Japanese varieties, to very large specimens. Although many people swear by their own technique for removing the bitterness from eggplant, the best advice is to choose eggplant that are mature, but not overlarge by type. Roasted

TABLE 5-21   LETTUCE VARIETIES

Variety	Description	Flavor
Arugula	Tender leaves, rounded "teeth"	Pungent, peppery, becoming very biting as it ages
Belgian endive	Tight, oblong head, white leaves with some yellow or green at tips	Slightly bitter; often prepared as a braised. vegetable, in addition to use as salad item.
Boston lettuce (butterhead)	Soft, tender leaves. Heading lettuce	Mild, delicate flavor. May also be braised as vegetable.
Curly endive	Heading lettuce; sharp "teeth" on curly leaves. Interior leaves light yellow	Slightly to very bitter.
Escarole	Heading lettuce, with scalloped edges on leaves	Slightly to very bitter. Often served as cooking green, in soups, stews.
Iceberg lettuce	Tight heading lettuce with pale-green leaves	Very mild
Leaf lettuce	May be green or red-tipped. Loose heading lettuce w/tender leaves	Usually mild, becoming bitter with age.
Oak leaf lettuce	Deep scalloping on leaves, tender	Nutty flavor
Mâche	Loose bunches, very tender leaves, rounded	Very delicate flavor
Radicchio	Heading form of endive, deep-red to purple leaves with white veining	Bitter
Watercress	Bunching green, with rounded scallops on leaves	Peppery

FIGURE 5-90   Lettuces

(1) Iceberg, Boston, and Romaine   *(2) Red/green leaf*

(3) Arugula   *(4) Mesclun mix (wild)*

TABLE 5-22 MUSHROOM VARIETIES

Variety	Description	Peak Season/Fresh	Uses
Button (Parisian)	Standard white-to-buff-colored mushroom	Year-round	Raw or cooked, marinated, in sauces, soups, stews
Boletus (also bolete)	Rounded golden cap, bulbous stem	Fall	Raw or cooked, marinated, in sauces, soups, stews; may be dried
Cepe (also Cep)	Type of boletus	Fall	Raw or cooked, marinated, in sauces, soups, stews
Chanterelles	Golden to apricot (black and ivory sometimes available)	Fall	Raw or cooked, marinated, in sauces, soups, stews
Cremini	Round cap, buff to brown	Year-round	Raw, cooked, sauces
Enoki (enokidake)	White to buff, long slender stalk-like mushrooms	Year-round	Salads, Asian dishes, soups and consommés as garnish
Lobster mushroom	Deep red, mottled color	Fall	Sautéed, used in some sauces
Morels	Cone-shaped cap, deeply pitted, hollow stem and cap	Early spring	Sauces, in cream sauce, may be dried
Porcini	Type of boletus		Raw or cooked, marinated, in sauces, soups, stews; may be dried
Portobello	Large tan-to-brown caps, opened from stem, like a parasol	Fall	Sautéed or grilled
Oak mushroom	Creamy to silvery gray cluster of shell-shaped mushrooms, very delicate	Year-round (farm-raised)	Sautéed, used in some sauces, ragouts, etc.
Oyster mushroom	See Oak mushroom		
Shiitake	Parasol-shaped with light-brown cap, tough stems (usually cut away before cooking)	Year-round	Sautéed or grilled; frequently dried
Straw mushrooms	Conical cap, usually gray to nearly black with white "fringe" and slender stems	Year-round	Sautéed, used in some sauces, ragouts, etc.
Truffles	Ball-shaped fungus, may be black or white	Black, fall; white, spring into summer	Sautéed, used in some sauces, ragouts; sold canned, as essence, or as truffle-flavored oil

eggplant is used in numerous dishes, ranging from a Middle Eastern dip to a luscious soup. It is wonderful grilled, pan-fried, braised, or stewed. Ratatouille, a famous French vegetable stew, makes liberal use of eggplant.

Lettuces Salads are one of the most neglected parts of many menus. Today's chef has more options regarding the type and quality of greens featured in the salad bowl than at any other time, however. Guests at your restaurant are growing less and less likely to be satisfied with a wedge of iceberg and Thousand Island dressing. (See Figure 5-90.)

Some lettuces are better "keepers" than others. Special mixes can be purchased, some with the addition of edible flowers, such as nasturtiums, chrysanthemums, or pansies. (See Table 5-21.)

Mushrooms Mushrooms are a type of fungus. Some varieties are edible and delicious, some are edible but of little culinary consequence. Still others are toxic, producing a host of unpleasant effects ranging from cramps and headaches to death. Knowing your purveyor is of great importance when you have wild mushroom varieties on the menu. Domestically raised mushrooms include familiar domestic button mushrooms, as well as wild varieties, including shiitakes and portobellos. There are other varieties that are not yet successfully farm raised, and are offered to either the purveyor or the chef by professional "foragers." (See Figure 5-91.)

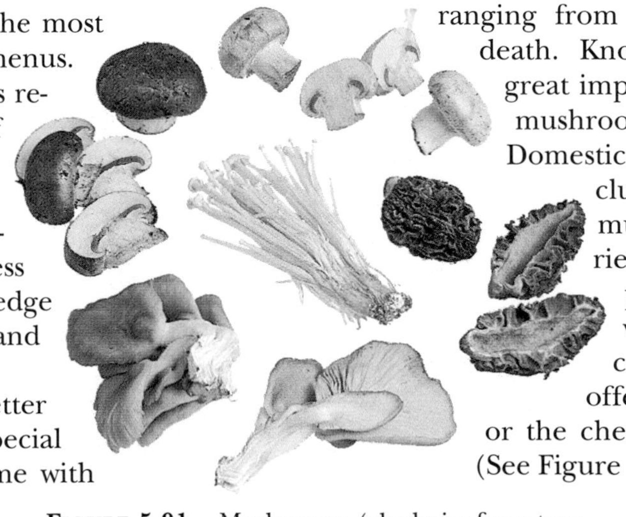

FIGURE 5-91 Mushrooms (clockwise from top: Button, Morel, Oyster, Cremini, Enoki)

TABLE 5-23 ONION VARIETIES

Variety	Description	Uses
Boiling onions	Small round onions with white skin	Stews, soups, compotes
Cippolini onions	Small round, flattened onions with yellow papery skin	Baked, grilled, casserole
Garlic (standard, elephant)	Bulb, with white or red-streaked papery skin, encasing individual cloves, also covered with papery skin	Flavoring ingredient; may be roasted into purée
Leeks	Long, fresh onion with white root end gradually becoming a dark green at tops	Grilled, steamed, serve "à la grecque" or other cold preparation. Used extensively in soups, stews, and sauces; main ingredient or flavoring
Pearl onions	Small, oval onions. May be white or red.	Boiled, pickled, or brined. Often served in stews and braises
Ramps	Wild leeks, small white stem ends with flat green tops	Stewed or sautéed
Red onions	Small, round flattened onions with red papery skin. Flesh is red and white	Eaten raw in salads, grilled, in compotes or marmalades
Scallions (green onions)	Fresh onions, with white root ends becoming green at tops. Entire plant is used, except for roots	Eaten raw as crudité, in salads, as ingredient in uncooked sauces
Shallots	May be cloves bunched together or single shallots, with light-brown papery skin. Flesh is white/purple	Used primarily as flavoring ingredient
Spanish onions	Large onions with yellow to yellow-brown skin. Flesh is milder than yellow onion	Used as a aromatic or ingredient in soups, stews, sauces, braises. Basic component of mirepoix
Sweet onions (Walla Walla, Vidalia, Maui)	Generally has flattened shape. Skin varies by type from white to tan. Flesh is very sweet	Eaten raw in salads, grilled, sautéed
Yellow onions	Moderate size, with yellow brown, papery skin. Pungent flesh	Used as an aromatic or ingredient (see Spanish onions)
White onions	Moderate size, with white, papery skin	Used as an aromatic or ingredient (see Spanish onions)

FIGURE 5-92 Onions

(1) *(Clockwise from top) Leeks, red onion, pearl, cippolini, shallots, Spanish, and garlic*

(2) *Vidalia*

(3) *Ramp*

Most mushrooms are completely edible, but if the stem is tough or has a sticky skin it should be trimmed away. Many wild mushrooms are available dried as well as fresh. Dried versions of morels, shiitake, and wood ears are sometimes preferred for certain dishes, as they deliver an even more intense flavor than when fresh. (See Table 5-22.)

Onion Family Onions and their relations belong to the *allium*, or lily, family. All varieties share a pungent flavor and aroma. It is hard to imagine a kitchen without a good supply of this basic item. Garlic, shallots, dry and green onions are used in so many dishes, and in so many guises, that they are quite rightly considered indispensable. (See Figure 5-92.)

Onions are part of that most fundamental aromatic combination—mirepoix. Garlic is called for in so many preparations that it is nearly taken for granted. Roasted, chopped, or slivered, it can be found as a topping for flatbreads, a flavoring for sauces, or the main ingredient in soups or sauces. Over the last several years, sweet onions have become widely available at certain times of the year. These varieties are often featured either raw or as grilled or broiled dishes.

Onions fall into two main categories, reflecting the state in which they are used: cured (dried) and fresh (green). Dry onions

FIGURE 5-93
Chilies

(1) Anaheim/New Mexico

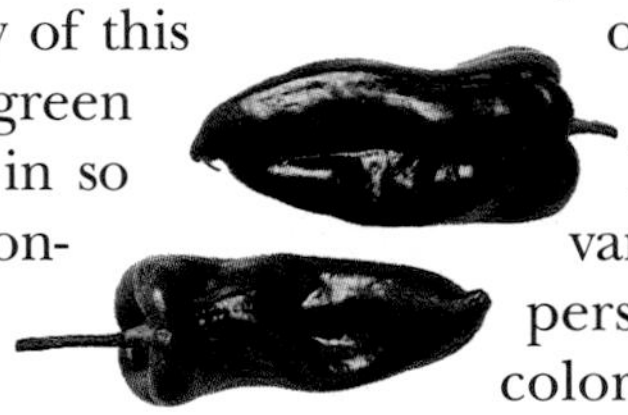

(2) Poblano

(3) Scotchbonnet

should be stored in a relatively cool, dry area of the kitchen in the bags or boxes in which they are received. (See Table 5-23.) Fresh onions should be stored under refrigeration. One additional member of this family that has not been included here is chives. They are discussed with other fresh herbs below.

Peppers, Bell Bell, or sweet, peppers are named for their shape and come in many colors—green, red, yellow, even creamy white and purple-black. All peppers start out green, but special varieties will ripen into rich vibrant colors. Sweet peppers have similar flavors, though red and yellow varieties tend to be sweeter than green peppers. Still, it is acceptable to substitute one color for another. The only big difference in most dishes will be appearance.

Bell peppers are hollow, except for whitish ribs and a core with a cluster of small seeds. Generally, both ribs and core are removed before use. One of the most popular ways to prepare sweet peppers is to roast them, and toss them with a good-quality oil, fresh herbs, and cracked peppers. The are featured in sauces such as coulis, in antipastos, as the topping for grilled breads or pizzas, and in salads.

Look for firm peppers when examining a delivery or the offerings in the local farmer's market. The skin should be

TABLE 5-24 CHILI PEPPER VARIETIES*		
Variety	*Description*	*Forms*
Anaheim (also California)	Tapered deep-green chili, glossy	Fresh, dried
Banana (also Hungarian Wax)	Small tapered chili, pale yellow to yellow green. Considered one of the hottest peppers	Used in sauces, stews, may be pickled
Habanero (also Scotch Bonnet)	Ball-shaped, wrinkled pepper, about the size of cherry pepper. Possibly the hottest pepper	Used in sauces, bottled condiments, as dried flakes
Jalapeño	Compact tapered chili, may be deep green, or red	Chipotle (roasted, usually packed in adobo sauce); pickled; canned whole or chopped)
Poblano (also ancho, pasilla)	Very-deep green to black, tapered and flattened shape. Relatively mild	Often used for stuffing
Serrano	Tiny, skinny, dark green, and very hot	May be used in place of jalapeños, or use jalapeños in their place

*Peak season occurs during the summer months, but are generally available fresh throughout the year.

tight and glossy, with no puckering or wrinkling. The flesh should be thick and crisp. Depending upon the variety, the color may be mottled or streaked and the pepper may be more or less deeply ridged. Peppers will keep well for several days, but if some peppers in a box begin to soften or develop brown spots, check the entire box immediately and use all acceptable peppers as soon as possible. Once peppers start to lose quality, they go quickly.

Peppers, Chili Chili peppers (*chiles* in Spanish) are related to bell peppers, but they are usually smaller and contain spicy, volatile oils. There are numerous books devoted to chili peppers, and a whole host of fresh and dried chilies are available throughout the entire country. (See Figure 5-93.) The hotter the pepper, the more important it is to handle them carefully. Use sensible precautions when working with such powerhouses as habaneros or banana chilies—wear gloves, wash and rinse your cutting surface and knives, and avoid contact with sensitive tissues, such as the eyes.

Chilies are available fresh, canned, and dried (whole, flaked, and ground). Popular varieties include anaheim, ancho/poblano, jalapeño, and serrano. (See Table 5-24.)

Pod and Seed Vegetables These vegetables include fresh legumes, such as peas, beans, and bean sprouts, as well as corn and okra. All are best eaten young and fresh, when they are at their sweetest and most tender. Once picked, they begin to convert their natural sugars into starch. Garden peas and sweet corn are especially prone to flavor loss. There is a perceptible difference in the quality of these items within only hours of picking. They can lose their sweetness as soon as a day after being harvested. After a few days, they become mealy.

If possible, purchase pod and seed vegetables from local growers to minimize lag time between

TABLE 5-25 PEA AND BEAN VARIETIES

Variety	Description	Peak Season/Fresh	Uses
Beans, Edible Pods			
Green beans	Long green beans, slender, with even, matte color	Mid-to late summer	As side dish, pickled, may be fresh or frozen
Haricot verts	Smaller and more slender than regular regular beans, velvety skin	Mid-to late summer	Side dish
Romano	Similar in color to regular beans, but wider and more flattened with more developed flavor	Mid-to late summer	As for regular beans, often braised with ham or bacon
Burgundy/purple	Similar in shape to regular beans, but with deep purple to maroon skin that turns green as it is cooked	Mid-to late summer	As for regular beans
Beans, Inedible Pods*			
Fava	Pods are long, large, and light green, beans are a delicate green color, almost kidney shaped	Spring to early summer	Cooked, puréed, may be cooked and eaten cold. Large beans must be peeled before eating
Cranberry	Pods are white streaked with red, beans are mottled with red	Midsummer	Cooked, puréed, soups, braised
Borlotti	Pods are green to buff, beans are creamy white	Early to midsummer	Cooked, puréed, soups, braised
Flagelot	Pods are green, beans are a light green	Midsummer	Cooked, puréed, soups, braised
Black-eyed pea	Pods are green often mottled with brown, beans are round, tan, with black "eye"	Throughout summer and into fall	Cooked, puréed, soups, braised; Hoppin' John is most famous dish
Peas			
Garden pea/ petit pois	Pods are tapered, rounded, and should "squeak" when rubbed together, peas are round, light-drab green when raw	Early spring to summer	Steamed, stewed (petits pois à la Française), chilled, puréed, in soups
Snow pea	Pods are flat, drab green when raw	Early spring to summer	Steamed, stir-fried
Sugar snap	Pods are deeper green than garden or snow peas	Early spring to summer	Steamed, stir-fried

*All beans in this section are available fresh and also dried.

FIGURE 5-94   Pod Vegetables

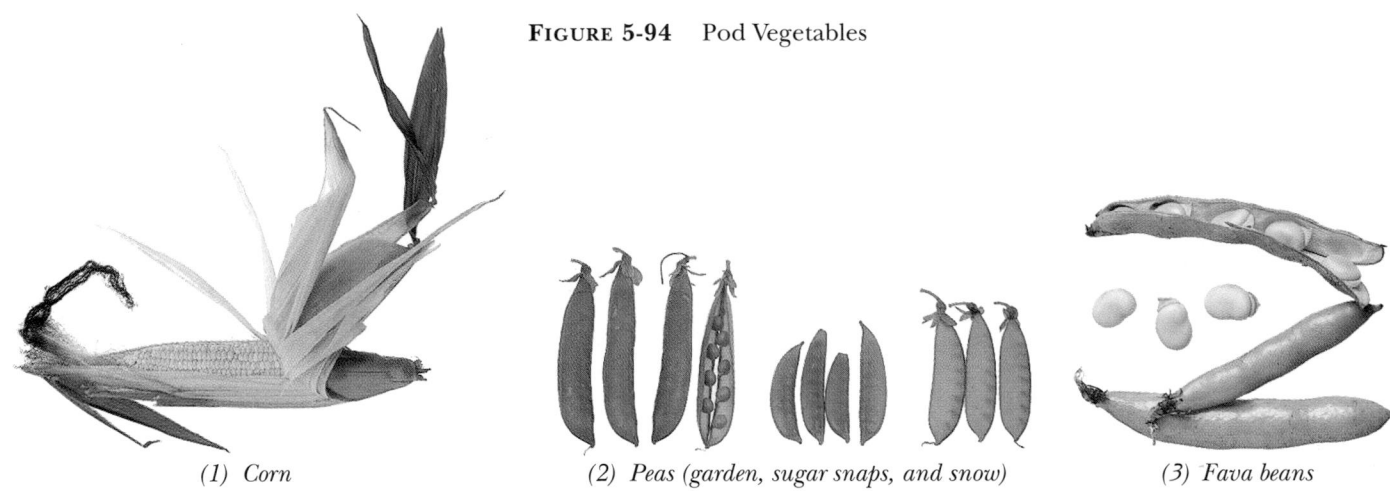

(1) Corn   *(2) Peas (garden, sugar snaps, and snow)*   *(3) Fava beans*

picking and serving. This is especially important with peas and corn, which are highly perishable. Peas, beans, and corn are also available in dried form, as discussed later in this chapter.

Some fresh peas and beans are eaten whole, when the pods are still fleshy and tender—for example, sugar snap peas, snow peas, green beans, and wax beans. In other cases, the peas or beans (such as limas, scarlet runners, and black-eyed peas) are removed from their inedible pods. (See Figure 5-94 and Table 5-25.)

Potatoes   Potatoes have gone from being America's favorite side dish, to an item that weight-watchers and sophisticates shunned as too filling and pedestrian, back to the limelight as a terrific source of various nutrients. Today, you can choose from a wide variety of special potatoes, as well as the more familiar favorites to establish a repertoire of potato dishes that belong in virtually every category of the menu. (See Figure 5-95 and Table 5-26.)

This sweet, subtly flavored tuber was originally grown in South America. The potato, along with the tomato, were thought to be poisonous. After a long period of distrust in European countries, it was finally established as a standard item in cuisines around the world. A French physician, Antoine-August Parmentier, was perhaps most responsible for changing the public opinion. Without his efforts, some classic dishes developed by French chefs might still be undiscovered.

Sweet potatoes and yams, unrelated botanically to each other, are also not closely related to the white potato. Still, they are covered here, since they are handled in the same basic way in the

kitchen. Sweet potatoes tend to be a little moister and more deeply colored than yams. Yams have a more understated flavor than sweet potatoes, but both are noticeably sweeter than white potatoes.

While potatoes are among the vegetables referred to as "winter" vegetables, they do require proper storage in order to retain quality. Potatoes should be kept dry, away from excess heat or sunlight, and in a well-ventilated area.

Roots and Tubers   Roots and tubers serve as nutrient reservoirs for their plants. Consequently, they are rich in sugars, starches, vitamins, and minerals. Popular root vegetables include beets, carrots, celeriac, parsnips, radishes, rutabagas, and turnips. (See Figure 5-96.) Salsify, a relatively unfamiliar

FIGURE 5-95   Potatoes (clockwise from top left: Russet, Chef's, New Red, Red Bliss, and Yams)

TABLE 5-26 POTATO VARIETIES

Variety	Description	Peak Season/Fresh	Uses
Chef's potato	Firm, smooth, relatively round with white to light tan skin, shallow eyes. Available in range of sizes (chef can specify)	Year-round (fresh in late summer into fall)	The younger the potato, the waxier it is. Used for salads, purées, soups, and other dishes. Tends to be too moist for baking
Red potato	Firm, smooth, relatively round with light-pink to dark-red skin, shallow eyes. Available in range of sizes (chef can specify)	Year-round (fresh in late summer into fall)	The younger the potato, the waxier it is. Used for salads, purées, soups, and other dishes. Excellent for oven roasting.
Russet/Idaho	Oblong, with brown, russeted skin	Year-round (fresh in late summer into fall)	Best for baking and for frying
Purple/caribe	Deep-purple skin with purple flesh	Midsummer	Salads, home-fries, other preparations to showcase color and flavor
Yukon gold/ Yellow Finn	Brown, tan, or red skin with buttery golden flesh	Year-round (fresh in late summer into fall)	Baked, puréed, casseroles, salads
Irish	Relatively round, but generally "misshapen," deep eyes	Late summer	Boiling
Salt	Small, no more than 1 inch in diamiter	Year-round (fresh in late summer into fall)	Boiling, steaming
"New" potatoes	Same as chef's, but no more than 1–1½ inches in diameter	Early summer	Steaming, oven-roasting with herbs
Bliss potatoes	Same as red, but no more than 1–1½ inches in diameter	Early summer	Steaming, oven-roasting with herbs
Sweet potatoes	Light to deep-orange skin with deep orange, moist flesh, may be rounded or tapered, dense texture, quite sweet	Year-round (fresh in late summer into fall)	Roasted, boiled, puréed, used in casseroles, soups
Yam	Tan to light-brown russeted skin with pale to deep yellow flesh, dryer and less sweet than sweet potato	Year-round (fresh in late summer into fall)	Roasted, boiled, puréed, used in casseroles, soups

FIGURE 5-96   Roots and Tubers

  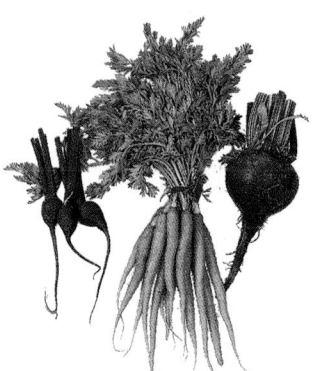  

(1) Carrots (baby cello, horse, and fresh)

(2) Radish

(3) Beets, bunch of baby carrots, baby beets

(4) Black salsify

(5) Parsnips

root to most Americans, is also part of this group. It may be white or black, and has a flavor some consider similar to oysters, others to asparagus, and still others compare to artichoke hearts.

Tubers are enlarged, bulbous roots capable of generating a new plant. In addition to potatoes, described above, this category includes Jerusalem artichokes, a vegetable that is not native to Jerusalem and which is not technically an artichoke.

Roots and tubers should be stored dry and unpeeled. If they come with greens attached, these should be fresh at the time of purchase and cut off

TABLE 5-27 VARIEITES OF ROOTS AND TUBERS

Variety	Description	Peak Season/Fresh	Uses
Beets			
Baby	Small, red ball-shaped	Throughout summer and into fall (greens are available from mid-spring)	Cooked, served hot, in salads, glazed
Red	Medium to large deep red/maroon root vegetable. May be sold w/ or w/out tops	Throughout summer and into fall (greens are available from mid-spring)	Cooked, served hot, in salads, glazed, pickled, in soup (borscht)
Golden	Small, yellow to golden-orange ball-shaped	Throughout summer and into fall	Cooked, served hot, in salads, glazed (do not bleed)
Turnips			
Purple-topped or white	White, similar in shape to beets, with purple "blush" on stem end	Late fall into early winter months, throughout winter from storage	Cooked, as vegetable side dish
Rutabagas/ Swedes	Large, ball-shaped vegetable, usually coated with wax	Late fall into early winter months, throughout winter from storage	Cooked, as vegetable side dish, often puréed
Radish			
Red	Small, ball-shaped or slightly elongated root vegetable, may be cherry red, striped, white, or specialty colors (purple, orange, etc.) (may be sold in cello packs or with green tops)	Early spring and fall crops (available throughout the year from storage or imports)	Salads, crudité platter
Daikon	Carrot-shaped, white radish with mild radish flavor	Late summer and early fall (available year round)	Cooked, raw, grated as garnish
Salsify Oyster Plant			
White	Similar in appearance to parsnip	Fall into winter	Cooked as side vegetable, often creamed
Black	Long, stick-shaped, dark-black matte skin	Fall into winter	Cooked as side vegetable, often creamed

as soon thereafter as possible. When they are properly stored, most roots and tubers will retain good quality for several weeks. (See Table 5-27.)

Shoots and Stalks This family consists of plants that produce shoots and stalks used as vegetables. Globe artichokes, asparagus, celery, and fennel are examples. Globe artichokes are thistles. Asparagus is part of the growth cycle of a fern. The stalks should be firm, fleshy, and full, and should have no evidence of browning or wilting. (See Figure 5-97.)

Tomatoes These succulent "vegetables" are actually berries.

They are grown in hundreds of varieties, in colors from green to yellow to bright red. Basic types include small, round cherry tomatoes, oblong plum tomatoes, and large beefsteak tomatoes. All have smooth, shiny skin, juicy flesh, and small, edible seeds. Most tomatoes grown commercially are picked green-ripe and allowed to ripen in transit. Most chefs prefer to find locally grown varieties whenever possible, since vine-ripened tomatoes have especially rich flavors and juiciness.

Recently, growers have been able to produce several spe-

FIGURE 5-97 Shoots and Stalks (Rhubarb, Fennel, and Celery)

TABLE 5-28 TOMATOES

Variety	Description	Peak Season/Fresh	Uses
Beefsteak	Large, deep red, deeply ridged, juicy	Late summer	Serve fresh in salads, sandwiches
Cherry tomatoes	Small red or yellow tomatoes that grow in clusters. Yellow version is low acid	Mid- to late summer	Salads, crudité platters
Currant (or Cranberry) tomatoes	Very small red or yellow tomatoes that grow in clusters. Yellow version is low acid	Mid- to late summer	Specialty items, usually served fresh
Pear tomatoes	Pear-shaped, small red or yellow tomatoes	Mid- to late summer	Usually served fresh in salads or crudité
Plum tomatoes (Roma)	Egg-shaped tomato, red with relatively greater proportion of flesh	Late summer	Sauces, purées, soups, and other cooked dishes
Yellow slicing tomatoes	Large, round, smooth-skinned tomatoes; low acid	Mid- to late summer	Sliced fresh in salads and other uncooked preparations
Tomatillos	Small, green, round berry, tastes like a green tomato, with a light-green-to-brown papery husk	Mid- to late summer	Usually cooked before used in sauces (pico de gallo, *e.g.*)

FIGURE 5-98   Tomatoes

(1) Slicing, plum, and cherry

(2) Yellow, green, and beefsteak

(3) Tomatillo

cial varieties of tomatoes for the market, including special low-acid golden varieties of both slicing and cherry tomatoes. Heirloom species can also be found occasionally.

There are no hard and fast rules about which tomatoes work best under which circumstances, but there is a certain etiquette. Slicing tomatoes, including deeply ridged beefsteaks and other varieties, are favored for use in salads and other uncooked preparations. Plum, or Roma, tomatoes with their relatively drier flesh are preferred for sauces and purées. (See Figure 5-98 and Table 5-28.)

Herbs

Herbs are the leaves of aromatic plants and are used primarily to add flavor to foods. (See Table 5-29 for basic information on each of the most common culinary herbs.)

Selection

Most herbs are available both fresh and dried, although some (thyme, bay leaf, rosemary) dry more successfully than others. Aroma is a good indicator of quality in both fresh and dried herbs. An herb's scent can be tested by using your fingers to crumble a few leaves and then smelling those leaves. A weak or stale aroma indicates old and less-potent herbs. Fresh herbs also may be judged by appearance. They should have good color (usually green), fresh-looking leaves and stems, and no wilt, brown spots, sunburn, or pest damage. (See Figure 5-99.)

TABLE 5-29 CULINARY HERBS

Variety	Description	Peak Season/Fresh	Uses/Affinities
Basil	Leaves are pointed, green. Purple varieties, large or small-leafed varieties available, also specialty types with cinnamon, clove, and other flavors	Summer/year-round	Flavoring for sauces, pesto sauce, dressings, infusing oils, vinegars etc. Also available in dried-leaf form. Chicken, fish, and pasta dishes
Bay leaf	Smooth, rigid leaf	Summer	Available dried year-round. Used to flavor soups, stews, stocks, sauces, and grain dishes
Chervil	Similar in shape to parsley, with finer leaves, licorice flavor	Summer	Component of "fines herbes" often used in "pluches" to garnish dishes. Egg, chicken, shellfish, dishes
Cilantro	Similar in shape to parsley, with pronounced, unique flavor	Mid to late summer	Component of Asian and South/Central American dishes; flavoring for salsa and other uncooked sauces
Dill	Feathery shape with strong aroma	Late summer	Fresh is used to flavor sauces, stews, braises (especially Central and Eastern European dishes). Seeds used in pickles
Marjoram	Small, rounded leaves with a flavor similar to oregano	Throughout summer	Used in Greek, Italian, and Mexican dishes. Especially suitable for vegetable dishes
Mint	Pointed, textured leaves. Size varies by type, as does particular flavor	Throughout summer	Used to flavor sweet dishes, beverages, as a "tisane" and in some sauces. Mint jelly is traditional with lamb
Oregano	Small, oval leaves	Throughout summer	Used with a variety of sauces, with poultry, beef, veal, lamb, and vegetables
Parsley	Feathered leaves; may be curly or flat	Year-round	Component of "fines herbs" and of bouquet garni. Flavoring for sauces, soups, dressings, and other dishes. Garnish
Rosemary	Leaves shaped like pine needles with a pine aroma and flavor	Year-round	Large branches used as skewers. Popular in Middle Eastern dishes, grilled foods, and in marinades. Dried is nearly as intense in flavor as fresh
Sage	Large leaves, may be furry or velvety. Sage-green color	Summer	Popular as flavoring in stuffings, sausages, and some stews. Dried, rubbed sage also available
Savory	Summer savory has flavor similar to thyme. Winter savory is more like rosemary	Summer and fall	Used in salads, stuffings, sauces
Tarragon	Narrow leaves with pronounced licorice flavor	Summer	Another component of "fines herbs." Used with chicken, fish, veal, and egg dishes
Thyme	Very small leaves. Varieties available with special flavors (nutmeg, mint, lemon, etc.)	Summer	Part of bouquet garni. Dried leaves may occasionally be used in place of fresh. Used to flavor soups, stocks, stews, and braises

Proper Use

Herbs can be used to flavor numerous preparations. They should enhance and balance, not overpower, a dish's flavors. Only occasionally, and with a purpose, should the herb's flavor be dominant.

When used with discretion, herbs can transform the taste of plain foods into something special. Overuse or inappropriate use can cause, at best, a dish that tastes of nothing but herbs and, at worst, a culinary disaster.

FIGURE 5-99   Herbs

(1) Thyme

(2) Curly and flat parsley

(3) Dill

(4) Sage

(5) Mint

(6) Cilantro

(7) Basil

(8) Oregano

(9) Rosemary

(10) Tarragon

Certain herbs have a special affinity for certain foods. Guidelines stating which herbs are most effectively paired with which foods are not cast in stone, but following them can familiarize the chef with the way herb–food combinations work and can serve as a springboard for future experimentation.

Fresh herbs should be minced or cut in chiffonade as close to serving time as possible. They are usually added to a dish toward the end of the cooking time, to prevent the flavor from cooking out. Dried herbs are usually added early in the process. For uncooked preparations, fresh herbs should be added well in advance of serving, to give them a chance to blend with the other elements.

Storage In general, herbs should be stored by wrapping loosely in damp paper or cloth. If desired, the wrapped herbs may then be placed in plastic bags to help retain freshness and reduce wilting of leaves, and should be stored at 35 to 45°F (2 to 7°C). Some herbs, especially watercress and parsley, may be held by trimming the stems and placing the bunch in a jar of water. Wrap damp toweling around the leaves to prevent wilting.

Foodservice operations that grow herbs may have an excess at certain times of the season. These may be used for making compound butters, pestos, and flavored vinegars and oils.

Dairy, Cheese, and Egg Identification

A concentrated source of many nutrients—especially protein and calcium—dairy products and eggs hold a prominent place on menus. Milk and milk products are not only used as beverages but as ingredients in many dishes. Béchamel sauce, for example, is based on milk. Cream, crème fraîche, sour cream, and yogurt are used to finish sauces, to prepare salad dressings, and in many baked goods.

Cheeses may be served as is, perhaps as a separate course with fruit, or as part of another dish. Fondue, raclette, and Welsh rarebit are classic dishes from around the world that feature cheese.

Eggs appear on menus throughout the day—from morning breakfast dishes to dessert soufflés

TABLE 5-30 PROPER STORAGE TIMES AND TEMPERATURES OF DAIRY PRODUCTS AND EGGS

Product	Storage Time	Temperature
Milk, fluid, pasteurized (whole, low-fat, skim, other unfermented)	1 week	35–40°F/2-4°C
Milk, evaporated		
Unopened	6 months	60–70°F/16–21°C
Opened	3–5 days	35–40°F/2-4°C
Milk, sweetened, condensed		
Unopened	2–3 months	60–70°F/16–21°C
Opened	3–5 days	35–40°F/2-4°C
Milk, nonfat dry		
Unopened	3 months	60–70°F/16–21°C
Reconstituted	1 week	35–40°F/2-4°C
Buttermilk	2–3 weeks	35–40°F/2-4°C
Yogurt	3–6 weeks	35–40°F/2-4°C
Cream		
Table or Whipping	1 week	35–40°F/2-4°C
Ultrapasteurized	6 weeks	35–40°F/2-4°C
Whipped, Pressurized	3 weeks	35–40°F/2-4°C
Ice cream	4 weeks	–10–0°F/ –23– –18°C
Butter	3–5 days	35°F/2°C
Margarine	5–7 days	35°F/2°C
Cheese, unripened, soft	5–7 days	35–40°F/2-4°C
Cheese, ripened, soft, semisoft	5–7 days	35–40°F/2-4°C
Cheese, ripened, hard	2–3 months	35–40°F/2-4°C
Cheese, very hard	2–3 months	35–40°F/2-4°C
Cheese foods	2–3 weeks	35–40°F/2-4°C
Cheese, processed		
Unopened	3–4 months	60–70°F/16–21°C
Opened	1–2 weeks	35–40°F/2-4°C
Eggs, whole, in shell	5–7 days	33–38°F/1–3°C
Eggs, whole, fluid	2–3 days	29–32°F/–1–0°C
Eggs, frozen	1–2 months	–10–0°F/ –23– –18°C
Eggs, dried	1–2 months	40°F/4°C

Adapted from Eva Medved, *Food Preparation and Theory*, which was adapted from various USDA publications.

served at midnight. Eggs' unique composition makes them useful in the preparation of numerous sauces, especially emulsified ones, such as hollandaise and mayonnaise.

Purchasing and Storage

Although dairy products and eggs are two separate kinds of products, freshness and wholesomeness are important for both. Both are also highly perishable. For these reasons, careful purchasing and storage procedures are extremely important.

Table 5-30 provides holding temperatures and average shelf life of eggs and various dairy products. Milk and cream containers customarily are dated to indicate how long the contents will remain fresh enough to use. Because the freshness period will vary, the chef should not combine, or "marry," milk and cream from separate containers, to avoid contamination.

When used in hot dishes, milk or cream should be brought to a boil before being added to other ingredients. If milk curdles, it should not be used. Unfortunately, detecting spoilage by simply smelling or tasting unheated milk is often impossible.

When considering storage arrangements for dairy products, flavor transfer is a particular concern. Storing all milk, cream, and butter away from foods with strong odors is preferable, when feasible. Cheeses should be carefully wrapped, both to maintain moistness and to prevent the odor from permeating other foods and vice versa.

Eggs should be refrigerated and the stock rotated to assure that only fresh, wholesome eggs are served. The chef should inspect eggs carefully upon delivery, making sure that shells are clean and free of cracks. Eggs with broken shells should be discarded because of the high contamination risk.

Dairy Products

Milk Milk is invaluable in the kitchen, whether it is served as a beverage or used as a component in dishes. U.S. federal regulations govern how milk is produced and sold, to assure that it is clean and safe to use.

Most milk sold in the United States has been pasteurized. In pasteurization, the milk is heated to 145°F (63°C) for 30 minutes, or to 161°F (72°C) for 15 seconds in order to kill bacteria or other organisms that could cause infection or contamination. Milk products with a higher percentage of milkfat are heated to either 150°F (65°C) for 30 minutes or to 166°F (74°C) for 30 seconds for ultrapasteurization.

The date stamp on milk and cream cartons is 10 days from the point of pasteurization. For example, if milk was pasteurized on October 10, the date on the carton would read October 20. If the product

TABLE 5-31 FORMS OF MILK AND CREAM

Form	Description	Type of Container
Milk		
Whole	Contains no less than 3% milkfat	Bulk, gallon, half-gallon, quart, pint, ½ pint
Low-fat	Usually contains 1 or 2% milkfat and is generally labeled accordingly	Same as whole milk
Skim	Contains less than 0.1% milkfat	Same as whole milk
Powdered or Dry	Milk from which water is completely removed. Made from either whole or skim milk and labeled accordingly	50# bulk, 24 oz. bulk
Evaporated	Milk that has been heated in a vacuum to remove 60% of its water. May be made from whole or skim milk and is labeled accordingly	14.5 oz., 10 oz., or 6 oz. cans
Condensed	Evaporated milk that has been sweetened	Same as above
Cream		
Heavy or Whipping	Must contain at least 35% milkfat. Light whipping cream is occasionally available, containing 30 to 35% fat	Quarts, pints, ½ pints
Light	Contains between 16 and 32% fat	Same as heavy cream
Half-and-half	Contains between 10.5 and 12% fat. Used as a lightener for coffee	Same as heavy cream and in portion sizes

has been properly stored and handled, it should still be fresh and wholesome on the stamped date.

Milk is also generally homogenized, which means that it has been forced through an ultrafine mesh at high pressure in order to break up the fat globules it contains. This fat is then dispersed evenly throughout the milk, preventing it from rising to the surface. Milk may also be fortified with vitamins A and D. Lowfat or skim milk is almost always fortified, because removing the fat also removes fat-soluble vitamins.

FIGURE 5-100   Milk and Cream

State and local government standards for milk are fairly consistent. Milk products are carefully inspected before and after production. Farms and animals (cows, sheep, and goats) are also inspected, to assure that sanitary conditions are upheld. Milk that has been properly produced and processed is labeled "grade A."

Milk comes in various forms and is classified according to its percentage of fat and milk solids. (See Table 5-31 and Figure 5-100.)

Cream   Milk, as it comes from the cow, goat, or sheep, contains a certain percentage of fat, known alternately as milkfat or butterfat. Originally, milk was allowed to settle long enough for the cream, which is lighter than the milk, to rise to the surface. Today, a centrifuge is used to spin the milk. The cream is driven to the center where it can be easily drawn off, leaving the milk behind.

Cream, like milk, is homogenized and pasteurized, and may also be stabilized to help extend shelf life. Some chefs prefer cream that has not been stabilized or ultrapasteurized because they believe it will whip to a greater volume. Two forms of cream are used in most kitchens: heavy (whipping) cream and light cream. Half-and-half, a combination of whole milk and cream, does not contain enough milkfat to be considered a true cream. Its milkfat content is approximately 10.5 percent. (See Table 5-31.)

Ice Cream   In order to meet government standards, any product labeled as ice cream must contain a certain amount of milkfat. For vanilla, it is no less than 10 percent milkfat. For any other flavor, the requirement is 8 percent. Stabilizers can make up no more than 2 percent of ice cream. Ice creams that contain less fat should be labeled "ice milk."

Premium brand ice cream may contain several times more fat than is required by these standards. The richest ice creams have a custard base (a mixture of cream and/or milk and eggs), which gives them a dense, smooth texture. It should readily melt in the mouth. When the ice cream is allowed to melt at room temperature, there should be no separation. The appearance of "weeping" in melting ice cream indicates an excessive amount of stabilizers.

Other frozen desserts similar to ice cream are: sherbet, sorbet, granité, gelatin, frozen yogurt, and frozen tofu. Sherbet does not contain cream, and so it is far lower in butterfat than ice creams. It does contain a relatively high percentage of sugar in order to achieve the correct texture and consistency during freezing. Some sherbets will contain a percentage of either eggs or milk, or both.

Although the word "sherbet" is the closest English translation of the French word "sorbet," sorbets are commonly understood to contain no milk.

Granités, the simplest forms of "ices," are basically flavored syrups that are allowed to freeze. Once solid, they are scraped to produce large crystals or flakes.

Frozen yogurts and tofu often contain stabilizers and a high percentage of fat. They may be lower in total fat than ice cream or even fat-free, but some brands are still high in calories due to a high sugar content.

Test a variety of these products to determine which brand offers the best quality for the best price.

Refer to Chapter 12 for information about preparing frozen desserts in your own kitchen.

Butter   Anyone who has accidentally over-whipped cream has been well on the way to producing butter. Historically, butter was churned by hand. Today it is made mechanically by mixing cream that contains between 30 and 45 percent milkfat at a high speed. Eventually, the milkfat clumps together, separating out into a solid mass, that leaves a fluid referred to as buttermilk. The solid mass is butter.

The best-quality butter has a sweet flavor, similar to very fresh heavy cream. If salt has been added, it

FIGURE 5-101 Butter/Cream Cheese

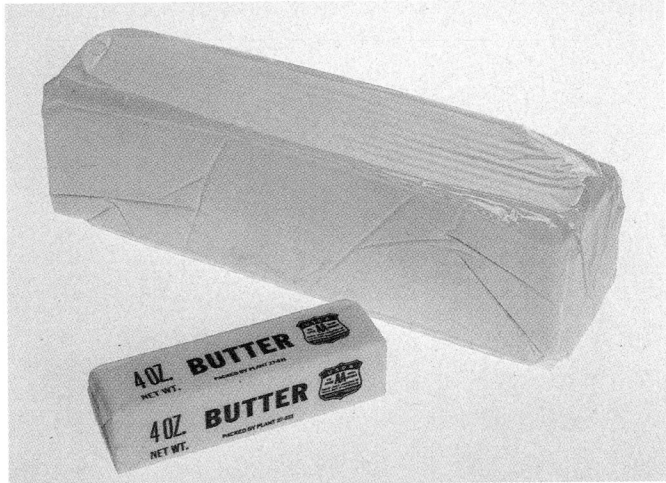

FIGURE 5-102 Crème Fraîche, Cottage Cheese, Ricotta, and Yogurt

should be barely detectable. The color of butter will vary depending upon the breed of cow and time of year, but is usually a pale yellow. The cow's diet will vary from season to season, affecting the color and flavor of the butter.

The designation "sweet butter" indicates only that the butter is made from sweet (as opposed to sour) cream. It does not mean necessarily that the butter is unsalted. If unsalted butter is desired, be sure that the word "unsalted" appears on the package.

Salted butter may contain no more than a maximum of 2 percent salt. This added salt will aid in extending butter's shelf life. It may also mask a slightly "old" flavor or aroma. Old butter will take on a very faintly cheesy flavor and aroma, especially when heated, as it is for cooking and baking. As it continues to deteriorate, the flavor and aroma can become quite pronounced, and extremely unpleasant, much like sour or curdled milk.

The best-quality butter, labeled "grade AA," is made from sweet cream. It has the best flavor, color, aroma, and texture. Grade A butter also is of excellent quality. Both grades AA and A contain a minimum of 80 percent fat. Grade B may have a slightly acidic taste, as it is made from sour cream. (See Figure 5-101.)

Fermented and Cultured Milk Products Yogurt, sour cream, crème fraîche, and buttermilk are all produced by inoculating milk or cream with a bacterial strain that causes fermentation to begin. The fermentation process thickens the milk and gives it

a pleasantly sour flavor. A variety of these products are illustrated in Figure 5-102.

Yogurt is made by introducing the proper culture into milk (whole, lowfat, or skim may be used). Available in a variety of container sizes, yogurt can be purchased plain or flavored with different fruits, honey, coffee, or other ingredients.

Sour cream is a cultured sweet cream that contains about 16 to 22 percent fat. It comes in containers of various sizes, beginning with a half-pint. Low, reduced, and nonfat versions of sour cream are also available.

Crème fraîche is similar to sour cream but has a slightly more rounded flavor, with less bite. It is often preferred in cooking, since it curdles less readily than sour cream in hot dishes. This product is made from heavy cream with a butterfat content of approximately 30 percent. This high butterfat content helps account for its higher cost.

Although crème fraîche is available commercially, many operations make their own. They heat heavy cream, add a small amount of buttermilk, and allow the mixture to ferment at room temperature until thickened and lightly soured.

Buttermilk, strictly speaking, is the by-product of churned butter. Despite its name, it contains only a

	TABLE 5-32 FRESH CHEESE		
Type/Milk Used	*Shape and Color*	*Flavor*	*Texture*
Bucheron (raw goat's)	Log, white	Slightly tangy	Soft, creamy
Chevre (general) (goat's)	Block, pyramid, button, wheel, log	Mild to tangy (depending on age), may be flavored with herbs or peppercorns	Soft to crumbly (depending on age)
Cottage (whole or skim cow's*)	Curds, white	Mild	Soft, moist
Cream (whole cow's, plus cream)	Block, white	Mild, slightly tangy	Soft, cream
Feta (sheep's, goat's, or cow's)	Block, white	Tangy, salty	Soft, crumbly
Fromage Blanc (whole or skim cow's)	Soft, white	Mild, tangy	Soft, slightly crumbly
Mascarpone (whole cow's milk/cream)	Soft, pale yellow	Buttery, slightly tangy	Soft, smooth
Montrachet (raw goat's)	Log, white	Slightly tangy	Soft, creamy
Mozzarella (whole or skim cow's, buffalo's)	Irregular sphere, white	Mild, sometimes smoked	Tender to slightly elastic (depending on age)
Neufchâtel (whole or skim cow's**)	Block, white	Mild, slightly tangy	Soft, creamy
Ricotta (whole, skim, or low-fat cow's***)	Soft curds, white	Mild	Soft, moist to slightly dry, grainy

* Cream may be added to finished curds.
**May have added cream.
***May have added whey.

very small amount of butterfat. Most buttermilk sold today is actually skim milk to which a bacterial strain has been added. Usually sold in pints or quarts, buttermilk is also available as a dried powder for baking uses.

Cheese

The variety of cheeses produced throughout the world is extensive, ranging from mild, fresh cheeses (pot cheese or cottage cheese) to strongly flavored, blue-veined cheeses (Roquefort or Gorgonzola) to hard grating cheeses (Parmesan or Romano). Cheeses are used in many dishes and require careful handling and selection. Some cheeses are excellent for cooking, while others will become a hopelessly stringy mass when subjected to heat. Selecting the right cheese for the intended effect is important, because cheese can be quite expensive.

In general, the procedure for making cheese is this: Milk is combined with the appropriate starter (generally rennet, an enzyme), which causes milk solids to coagulate into curds. The liquid left after curds are formed is known as the whey.

The curds are then processed in various ways, depending on the type of cheese desired. They may be drained and used immediately, as fresh cheese, or they may be pressed, shaped, inoculated with a special mold, and aged. Whey is also used to make some cheeses.

Cheese is made from a variety of different milks—cow's milk, goat's milk, sheep's milk, even buffalo's milk. The type of milk used will help to determine the cheese's ultimate flavor and texture.

Natural cheeses are considered "living" in much the same way that wine is considered living. The cheese will continue to grow, developing or aging to maturity (ripening), and finally spoiling (overripening). Processed or pasteurized cheeses and cheese foods, on the other hand, do not ripen and their character will not change.

Cheese may be grouped according to the type of milk from which they are made, their texture, age, or ripening process. The terms used are:

- Fresh cheese
- Soft, or rind-ripened cheese
- Semi-soft cheese

FIGURE 5-103 Brie, Camembert, and Assorted Fresh and Aged Goat Cheeses

FIGURE 5-104 Edam, Gruyère, Jarlsburg, Gouda, Morbier, and Colby Cheeses

	TABLE 5-33 SOFT AND RIND-RIPENED		
Type/Milk Used	*Shape and Color*	*Flavor*	*Texture*
Brie (pasteurized, whole or skim cow's, goat's, sometimes cream)	Disk, light yellow	Buttery to pungent	Soft, smooth, with edible rind
Camembert (raw or pasteurized whole cow's, goats)	Disk, light yellow	Slightly tangy	Soft, creamy, with edible rind
Explorateur (whole cow's and cream)	Wheel, pale yellow	Rich, mild	Soft and creamy
Limburger (whole or low–fat cow's)	Block, light yellow, brown exterior	Very strong flavor and aroma	Soft, smooth, waxy
Pont-l'Évêque (whole cow's)	Square, light yellow	Piquant, strong aroma	Soft, supple, with small holes and edible golden-yellow crust

- Hard cheese
- Grating cheese
- Blue-veined cheese

These cheeses are shown in Figures 5-103 to 5-107.

Fresh Cheese

Fresh cheeses include cottage cheese or fresh goat's cheese, mozzarella, fromage blanc, ricotta, and quark. These cheese are moist and very soft.

They have a flavor that is generally termed "mild," but fresh cheese made from goat's or sheep's milk may seem strong to some tastes. (See Table 5-32.)

Soft or Rind-ripened Cheese

Soft cheeses, such as Brie or Camembert, usually have a surface mold. This soft, velvety skin is often edible, though some people find it too strong to enjoy. The cheese ripens from the outside to the center. When fully ripe, a soft cheese should be nearly runny, with a full flavor. (See Table 5-33.)

TABLE 5-34 SEMI-SOFT CHEESES

Type/Milk Used	Shape and Color	Flavor	Texture
Bel Paese (whole cow's)	Wheel, light yellow	Mild, buttery	Semi-soft, creamy, waxy
Brick (whole cow's)	Block, light yellow	Mild to pungent (depending on age)	Semi-soft, elastic, with many tiny holes
Edam (whole or part-skim cow's)	Loaf or sphere (may be coated with wax)	Mild to tangy (depending on age)	Hard, may be slightly crumbly with tiny holes
Fontina (whole cow's or sheep's)	Wheel, medium yellow	Nutty flavor, strong aroma	Hard
Harvarti (cream-enriched cow's)	Loaf or wheel, medium yellow	Buttery (may be flavored with dill or caraway	Semi-soft, creamy, with small holes
Morbier (whole cow's)	Wheel, light yellow with edible ash layer	Mild	Semi-soft, smooth
Monterey Jack (whole cow's)	Wheel or block, light yellow	Mild to pungent (may be flavored with jalapeño peppers)	Semi-soft to very hard (depending on age)
Muenster (whole cow's)	Wheel or block, light yellow (rind may be orange)	Mild to pungent (depending on age)	Semi-soft, smooth, waxy with small holes
Port-Salut (whole or low-fat cow's)	Wheel or cylinder, white with russet exterior	Buttery, mellow to sharp	Semi-soft, smooth
Taleggio (raw cow's)	Square, light yellow	Creamy	Semi-soft with holes

Semi-soft Cheese

Semi-soft cheeses are more solid than soft cheeses but do not grate easily. They can be sliced, however. An inedible wax rind is used to coat the cheese, in order to preserve moisture and extend shelf life. Edam, Muenster, and Port Salut are among the better known semi-soft cheeses. These cheeses are allowed to age for specified periods of time, though not quite as long as hard or grating cheeses. (See Table 5-34.)

Hard, or Cheddar-type, Cheeses

Hard cheeses, such as Gruyère, Cheshire, and Cheddar, have a drier texture than semi-soft cheeses and a firm consistency. They will slice and grate easily. (See Table 5-35.)

Cheddar cheese, though it originated as a farmhouse cheese in England, is extremely popular in the United States. In fact, its popularity is so widespread that some people refer to it as American cheese. Be aware, however, that the sliced processed cheese also known as American cheese is not the same product.

An aged version of Monterey Jack cheese, known as Dry Jack, is produced in this country and is gaining in popularity.

Grating Cheeses

Parmesan, Romano, and Sap Sago cheese are typically grated or shaved rather than cut into slices because of their crumbly texture. The best-quality Parmesan is imported from the Reggiano region of Italy. It is used as a table or eating cheese.

FIGURE 5-105   Hard/Cheddar Cheese

TABLE 5-35 HARD AND CHEDDAR-TYPE CHEESES

Type/Milk Used	Shape and Color	Flavor	Texture
Cantal (whole cow's)	Cylinder, light yellow	Mild to sharp, slightly nutty	Hard
Cheddar (whole cow's)	Wheel, light or medium yellow	Mild to sharp (depending on age)	Hard
Cheshire (whole cow's)	Cylinder, light or medium yellow (may have blue marbling)	Mellow to piquant	Hard
Derby (whole cow's)	Cylinder, honey colored	Mild (may be flavored with sage)	Firm
Double Gloucester (whole cow's)	Large wheel, bright yellow-orange, colored with annatto	Full flavored	Firm, smooth, creamy
Emmenthaler (Swiss); (raw or pasteurized, part-skim cow's)	Wheel, light yellow	Mild, nutty	Hard, smooth, shiny with large holes
Gjetost (whole cow's and goat's)	Small block, light brown	Butter, caramel, slightly tangy	Hard
Gouda (whole cow's)	Wheel (may be coated with wax)	Mild, creamy, slightly nutty	Hard, smooth, may have tiny holes
Jarlsberg (whole cow's)	Wheel, light yellow	Sharp, nutty	Hard with large holes
Manchego (whole sheep's)	Cylinder, light yellow	Full and mellow	Semisoft to firm (depending on age) with holes
Provolone (whole cow's)	Pear, sausage, round, other, light yellow to golden-brown	Mild to sharp (depending on age), may be smoked	Hard, elastic

TABLE 5-36 GRATING CHEESES

Type/Milk Used	Shape and Color	Flavor	Texture
Asiago (whole or part-skim cow's)	Cylinder or flat block, light yellow	Mild to sharp	Semisoft to hard (depending on age)
Parmigiano Reggiano/Parmesan (part-skim cow's)	Cylinder, light yellow	Sharp, nutty	Very hard, dry, crumbly
Ricotta Salata (whole sheep's)	Cylinder, off-white	Pungent	Hard
Romano, Pecorino (whole sheep's, goat's, or cow's)	Cylinder	Very sharp	Very hard, dry, crumbly
Sap Sago (buttermilk, whey, and skim cow's)	Flattened cone, light green	Piquant, flavored with clover leaves	Very hard, granular

Domestically produced versions of these cheeses are available, as are blends of Parmesan and Romano. These cheeses are almost inescapably linked in the public mind with pasta dishes, and may actually be referred to as "pasta cheese." (See Table 5-36.)

Blue-veined Cheeses

Blue-veined cheeses, such as Roquefort and Gorgonzola, have consistencies that range from smooth and creamy to dry and crumbly. Their blue veining is the result of injecting a special mold into the cheese before ripening. (See Table 5-37.)

FIGURE 5-106   Sap Sago, Parmigiano-Reggiano, and Pecorino Romano Cheeses

FIGURE 5-107   Roquefort, Gorganzola, and Maytag Blue Cheeses

TABLE 5-37 BLUE CHEESES

Type/Milk Used	Shape and Color	Flavor	Texture
Bleu/Blue (whole cow's or goat's)	Cylinder, white with blue-green veins	Piquant, tangy	Semisoft, possibly crumbly
Blue Brie (whole cow's, goat's with added cream)	Wheel, white with patches of blue	Rich, piquant, but mild for blue	Soft, creamy
Bleu de Bresse (whole cow's or goat's)	Wheel, light yellow with blue veins	Piquant but mild for blue	Soft, creamy, slightly crumbly
Danish Blue (whole cow's)	Blocks, drums, white	Strong, sharp, salty	Firm, crumbly
Fourme D'Ambert (whole cow's)	Cylinder, medium yellow with blue-green marbling and reddish yellow rind	Sharp, pungent	Semisoft, crumbly
Gorgonzola (whole cow's and/or goat's)	Wheel, medium yellow with blue marbling	Tangy, piquant	Semisoft, dry for blue
Maytag Blue (whole cow's)	Cylinder, medium yellow with blue marbling	Strong, salty	Hard, crumbly
Roquefort (raw sheep's)	Cylinder, white with blue-green marbling	Sharp, pungent	Semisoft, crumbly
Stilton (whole cow's)	Cylinder, medium yellow with blue-green marbling	Piquant, but mild for blue	Hard, crumbly

Eggs

Eggs are one of the kitchen's most important items. From mayonnaise to meringues, soups to sauces, appetizers to desserts, they are prominent on any menu. Today's consumer is well aware of the potential for foodborne illness through eggs. Therefore, we will look first at basic rules for safe handling here.

• All eggs in the shell should be free from cracks, leaking, or obvious holes.

FIGURE 5-108 Flat of Eggs

• Eggs should be cooked to a minimum of 165°F(74°C) to kill the salmonella bacteria. Fried eggs or poached eggs with runny yolks should be prepared only at customer request.

• Any foods containing eggs must be kept within safe temperatures throughout handling, cooking, storage. Cooling and reheating must be done quickly over direct heat.

The egg is composed of two parts: the white and the yolk. Each is able to play a number of important culinary roles. Whole eggs are used as the main component of many breakfast dishes and can be prepared by scrambling, frying, poaching, baking, or in custards. Eggs are also used to glaze baked goods, and add nourishment, flavor, and color. Despite concerns over safe handling, the egg remains one of the most adaptable and functional ingredients in the chef's larder. (See Figure 5-108.)

Egg Whites

The white consists almost exclusively of protein and water. The protein is known as "albumen." Its ability to form a relatively stable foam is crucial to the development of proper structure in many items: angel food cakes, soufflés, meringues. They are a key ingredient in clarifying stocks and broths to produce consommés. Egg whites may replace some or all of other binders used in some forcemeats, especially mousselines made from fish, poultry, or vegetables.

Egg Yolks

The yolk also has the ability to foam. This function, plus its ability to form emulsions, make egg yolks crucial to the preparation of items including mayonnaise, hollandaise, and genoise. Yolks are also responsible for providing additional richness to foods, as when they are included as a liaison in sauces or soups. The yolk contains protein and, in addition, significant amounts of fat and a natural emulsifier called lecithin.

Grating, Sizes, and Market Forms

Eggs are graded by the U.S. Department of Agriculture on the basis of external appearance and freshness. The top grade, AA, indicates that the egg is fresh, with a white that will not spread unduly once the egg is broken. The yolk should ride high on the white's surface. The yolk is anchored in place by twisted white membranes known as the *chalazae*.

Eggs come in a number of sizes: jumbo, extra large, large, medium, small, and pee wee.

Younger hens produce smaller eggs, which are often regarded to be of a better quality than larger eggs. Medium eggs are best for breakfast cookery, where the cooked egg's appearance is important. Large and extra-large eggs are generally used for cooking and baking, where the whole egg's appearance is less critical.

Eggs are also sold in several processed forms: bulk, or fluid, whole eggs (which sometimes includes a percentage of extra yolks to obtain a specific blend), egg whites, and egg yolks. Pasteurized eggs are used in preparations such as salad dressings, eggnog, or desserts where the traditional recipe may have indicated that the eggs should be raw. These products generally are available in liquid or frozen form.

Dried, powdered eggs are also sold and may be useful for some baked goods or in certain specific circumstances. For instance, on shipboard, it may not be possible to properly store fresh eggs for the duration of a voyage.

Egg substitutes may be entirely egg free or may be produced from egg whites, with dairy or vegetable products substituted for the yolks. These substitutes are important for people who require a reduced-cholesterol diet.

Nonperishable Goods Identification

The term "nonperishable goods" is somewhat misleading. Although the staple items covered in this section do have long shelf lives, most of them are of the best quality when they are relatively fresh. A broad spectrum of nonperishable goods, also known as "dry goods," forms part of any foodservice operation's basic day-to-day needs. The following products are discussed:

- grains, meals, and flours
- dried legumes
- dried pastas and noodles
- oils and shortenings
- vinegars and condiments
- dried herbs and spices
- salt and pepper
- extracts and other flavorings
- nuts and seeds
- dried fruits and vegetables
- sugars, syrups, and other sweeteners
- chocolate
- coffee, tea, and other beverages
- thickeners
- prepared, canned, and frozen foods

Purchasing and Storage

Well-organized kitchens maintain a parstock of dry goods. This assures that there is enough of an item to assure that all menu offerings, as well as any items for special events, can be prepared from what is on hand. There should also be a slight overstock, in case of an unusually busy weekend or for other contingencies. Excessive overstock, however, can monopolize valuable storage space. Nonperishable goods may be purchased in bulk, by the case, or in single units.

Inspect all dry goods as they arrive, just as carefully as produce, meats, and fish are inspected, to ensure that the delivery matches the order. Check bags, boxes, cans, or other containers to make sure they are intact and clean and that they are not dented, broken, or in any way below standard.

Store dry goods in an area that is properly dry, ventilated, and accessible. All goods should be placed above floor level, on shelving or pallets. Some nonperishable items, such as whole grains, nuts and seeds, and coffee (if it is not vacuum-packed) are best stored under refrigeration, or even in the freezer.

Grains, Meals, and Flours

This broad category extends from whole grains such as rice and barley to ground cornmeal and pastry flour. Grains are of great importance to many cuisines. Wheat and corn are of primary importance in Western countries, such as the United States and Canada. Rice is fundamental to many Eastern cuisines. In fact, in many Eastern countries, the word for rice is the same as that for food. Other cultures rely upon grains such as oats, rye, and buckwheat.

Whole grains are grains that have not been milled. Whole grains tend to have a shorter life span than milled grains and, therefore, should be purchased in amounts that can be used in a relatively short period of time—two to three weeks.

Milled grains have had the germ, bran, and/or hull removed, or have been polished. When the whole grain is milled, it is essentially crushed into successively smaller particles. Although processed, or milled, grains tend to last longer, some of their nutritive value is lost during processing.

Milled grains that are broken into coarse particles may be referred to as "cracked." If the milling process continues, meals and cereals (cornmeal, farina, cream of rice) are formed. Finally, the grain may be ground into a fine powder, known as "flour." (See Table 5-38 and Figure 5-109.)

TABLE 5-38 GRAINS, MEALS, FLOURS, & OTHER STARCHES

Name	Purchase Form	Major Uses or Dishes
Wheat		
Whole	Unrefined or minimally processed whole kernels	Side dish
Cracked	Coarsely crushed, minimally processed kernels	Side dish, hot cereal
Bulgur	Hulled, cracked hard or soft wheat; parboiled and dried	Side dish, salad (tabbouleh)
Semolina	Polished wheat kernel (bran and germ removed), whole or ground	Pasta, flour, couscous (below)
Couscous	Semolina pellets, often parcooked	Side dish (often served with stew of same name)
Farina	Polished, medium–grind wheat cereals	Breakfast cereal
Bran	Separated outer covering of wheat kernel; flakes	Added to baked goods; prepared cereals, and other foods to increase dietary fiber
Germ	Separated embryo of wheat kernel; flakes	Added to baked goods and cereals to boost flavor and nutrition
Wheat flour (Whole or Graham)	Finely ground, whole kernels	Baked goods
All Purpose	Finely ground, polished kernels; usually enriched; may be bleached	Baked goods, thickener, other kitchen uses
Bread	Finely ground, polished hard wheat kernels; usually enriched; may be bleached	Bread dough
Cake	Very finely ground, polished soft wheat kernels; usually enriched and bleached	Cakes and other delicate baked goods
Pastry	Very finely ground, polished soft wheat kernels; usually enriched and bleached	Pastry and other delicate baked goods
Self–Rising	Very finely ground, polished soft wheat kernels to which baking powder and salt have been added; usually enriched and bleached	Cakes and other baked goods not leavened with yeast
Rice		
Brown	Hulled grains, bran intact; short, medium, or long grain; may be enriched	Side dish, other
White	Polished grains, usually enriched, long or short grain	Long grain: side dish, other. Short grain: pudding
Converted	Parcooked, polished grains, may be enriched	Side dish, other
Basmati	Delicate, extra, long grain, polished	Side dish including pilaf
Italian, short grain, arborio	Short grain, polished; types include Piedmontese and arborio	Risotto
Wild	Long, dark-brown grain not related to regular rice	Side dish, stuffings, other
Glutinous	Round, short grain, very starchy; black (unhulled) or white (polished)	Sushi, other Oriental dishes
Rice Flour	Very finely ground polished rice	Thickener

(Table continued on following page)

TABLE 5-38 *(CONTINUED)*

Name	Purchase Form	Major Uses or Dishes
Corn		
Hominy	Whole, hulled kernels; dry or canned	Side dish including succotash, in soup or stew
Grits	Cracked hominy	Side dish, hot cereal, baked goods
Meal	Medium-fine ground, hulled kernels; white or yellow	Baked goods, coating, polenta
Masa harina	Corn processed with lime to remove hull, medium ground; dry, dough, raw or cooked tortillas	Tortillas and other Mexican dishes
Cornstarch	Very finely ground, hulled kernels	Thickener, coating
Barley		
Pot or Scotch	Coarse, whole kernels; ground (barley meal)	Side dish, hot cereal, soups; meal: baked goods
Pearl	Polished, whole kernels; ground (barley flour)	Side dish, hot cereal, soups; flour: baked goods
Oats		
Oats, whole	Groats or berries	Cereal, stuffing
Oatmeal	Steel cut, rolled, flakes, quick-cooking, instant	Cereal, cakes, cookies, quickbreads
Oat bran	Separated outer covering of grain, flakes	Added to cereals and baked goods for dietary fiber
Others		
Arrowroot	Fine, starchy powder made from a tropical root	Thickener
Buckwheat	Whole, coarsely cracked groats (kashi), flour	Whole: side dish; flour: pancakes, baked goods
Filé	Fine, starchy powder made from sassafras leaves	Thickener (especially in Creole dishes such as gumbo)
Millet	Whole, flour	Side dish, flat breads
Rye	Cracked, flour (whole berries available)	Cracked: side dish; flour: baked goods
Sorghum	Whole, flour, syrup	Porridge, flat breads, beer, syrup and molasses

FIGURE 5-109   Grains, etc.

(1) Flour group (clockwise from top left: graham, bread, unbleached all-purpose, cornmeal, (center) semolina)

(2) Oat group (from top: steel cut, rolled, groats)

(Figure 5-109 continued on facing page)

FIGURE 5-109   *(continued)*

(3) Millet, barley, and buckwheat groats

(4) Wheat group (clockwise from top left: germ, berries, bulgur, cracked)

(5) Starches (rice flour, wheat starch, glutinous wheat flour)

(6) Wild rice and basmati brown rice

Figure 5-110   Dried Legumes

from left to right: (top row) split peas, lima, pinto, flageolot, red/pinto; (middle) yellow split pea, baby lima, black-eyed pea, black/turtle, chickpeas; (bottom) calypso, adzuki, green lentils, red lentils, navy/small white

Various methods are used for milling: crushing between metal rollers, grinding between stones, or cutting with steel blades in an action similar to that of a food processor. Grains ground between stones are called "stone-ground"; they may be preferred in some cases, because they retain more of their nutritive value due to a lower temperature during this milling process than in others.

Dried Legumes

These foodstuffs, seeds from pod-producing plants, have many uses in the contemporary kitchen. Although in theory they have a lengthy shelf life, as do most nonperishable items, they are best when used within six months of purchase. In some cases, they may be dried versions of beans and peas that are also available fresh, canned, or frozen.

Store dried legumes in a cool, dry, well-ventilated area. Before using, discard any beans or peas that appear moldy, damp, or wrinkled. It should be noted that as beans age they will take longer to cook. (See Table 5-39 and Figure 5-110.)

Dried Pasta and Noodles

Dried pasta is a valuable "convenience food." It stores well, cooks quickly, and comes in an extensive array of shapes, sizes, and flavors. This range of shapes and flavors provides a base for a number of preparations, from a simple spaghetti dish to Asian and Middle Eastern specialties.

Pasta and noodles are made from a number of different flours and grains. Good-quality dried pastas from wheat flour are customarily made from durum semolina. Many pastas are flavored or colored with vegetables, such as spinach, peppers, or tomatoes. (See Table 5-40 and Figure 5-111.)

Oils and Shortenings

Oils are produced by pressing a high-oil-content food, such as olives, nuts, corn, avocados, and soybeans. The oil then may be filtered, clarified, or hydrogenated in order to produce an oil or shortening that has the appropriate characteristics for its intended use.

The hydrogenation process causes the oil to remain solid at room temperature, when it is known as shortening. A shortening labeled "vegetable shortening" is made from vegetable oil, whereas one labeled just "shortening" may contain animal products.

Several different oils and shortenings are required in every kitchen. Oils for salads and other cold dishes should be of the best possible quality, with a perfectly fresh flavor. First pressings of olive oil or nut oils are often chosen for these purposes, because of their special flavors.

Cooking oils may have a neutral flavor; those used for frying should have a high smoking point as well. Shortenings used for baking should also be neutral in flavor.

Oils and shortenings should be stored in dry storage away from extremes of heat and light. (See Tables 5-41 and 5-42; Figure 5-112.) For more information about cooking oils and fats, refer to Chapter 9.

Vinegars and Condiments

Vinegars and most condiments are used to introduce sharp, piquant, sweet, or hot flavors into foods. They may be used as an ingredient or served on the side, to be added according to a guest's taste. A well-stocked kitchen should include a full

TABLE 5-39 DRIED BEANS, LENTILS, AND PEAS

Name	Description	Purchase Form	Uses
Beans			
Adzuki	Small, reddish-brown with white ridge on one side, slightly sweet flavor	Dried	Asian dishes
Black/Turtle	Shiny, brownish-black, medium sized, rounded kidney shape	Dried, canned	Mexican dishes
Black-eyed pea	Cream-colored with black patch around hilum, medium-sized, kidney-shaped	Dried, canned, fresh	Caribbean, soul food, and Southern dishes (including Hoppin' John)
Cannelini	Medium-sized, white, smooth, long, kidney-shaped, a type of haricot	Dried, canned	Soups, Italian dishes
Chick pea	Medium-sized, acorn-shaped, light tan to brown	Dried, canned	Middle Eastern and Mediterranean dishes, salads
Fava/Broad bean	Large, flat, green (fresh) to brown (dried)	Fresh, dried; larger, baby	Mediterranean dishes (including *falafel*)
Flageolet	Medium-sized, smooth, flat oval, green or white, a type of haricot	Dried	
Kidney	Long, curved kidney shape, pink to maroon	Dried, canned	Mexican dishes, chili, salads
Lentils	Small, green, brown, yellow, orange, dark green (puy)	Dried, canned soups	Soups, stews, side dishes, purées
Lima	Medium-sized, flat, white light green	Canned, frozen	Side dishes, including succotash
Mung	Small, round, green or yellow	Fresh or dried; whole, skinless, split, sprouted	Asian dishes
Navy	Small, smooth, rounded, white, a type of haricot	Dried, canned	Soups, baked beans
Pigeon pea	Small, nearly round, off-white with orange-brown mottling	Dried, canned	African, Indian, and Caribbean dishes
Pinto	Medium–sized, kidney-shaped mottled pink	Dried, canned	Latin American dishes including refried beans, Italian *pasta e fagioli*
Soissons	Medium-size, oval, white, a type of haricot	Dried	Cassoulet
Soy	Medium-size, rounded, black or yellow	Fresh or dried; salted, fermented, soy sauce, other (see below)	Asian dishes
Bean Products			
Bean paste, soy	Thick sauce of fermented soybeans, flour, and salt	Bottled or canned, whole or ground beans	Asian dishes
Bean paste, hot	Soybean paste with crushed chili peppers	Bottled or canned	Asian dishes
Bean paste, sweet/red	Puréed red beans and sugar	Bottled or canned	Sweet Asian dishes (such as dumplings)
Miso	Japanese soybean paste	Foil pouches, jars	Japanese soups and sauces
Tofu (Soybean curd)	Off-white, soft, curdled bean protein	Cakes, packed in water or pressed	Asian dishes
Peas, Garden	Fresh: (See vegetables) Dried: Green or yellow, smooth or wrinkled	Fresh, frozen, dried split or whole, canned	Fresh/frozen: side dish, purées, soups. Dried: soups, purées

TABLE 5-40 DRIED PASTA AND NOODLES (PATES SECHES, PASTA SECCA)

Name (Italian/English)	Description (Shape, Base Flour)	Major Dish(es)
Acini di pepe/ Peppercorns	Tiny, pellet-shaped; wheat flour	Soups
Anelli/Rings	Medium-small, ridged, tubular pasta cut in thin rings; wheat flour	Soups
Arrowroot Vermicelli	Very thin, Chinese noodles; arrowroot starch dough enriched with egg yolks	Asian dishes
Canneloni/Large Pipes	Large cylinders	Stuffed with cheese or meat, sauced, and baked
Capellini/Hair	Very, fine, solid, cylindrical; the finest is *capelli d'angelo* (angel's hair); wheat flour	With oil, butter, tomato, seafood, or other thin sauce; soup
Cavatappi/Corkscrews	Medium-thin, hollow, ridged pasta twisted into a spiral and cut into short lengths; wheat flour	With medium and hearty sauces
Cellophane Noodles	Very thin, transparent noodles; in bunches or compressed bundles; mung bean starch mung bean starch	Asian dishes: fried crisp for garnish, boiled for lo mein
Conchiglie/Shells	Large or medium, ridged shell shape; *conchigliette* are small shells; wheat flour	Filled with meat or cheese and baked; conchigliette: soups
Cresti di Gallo/ Cocks' Combs	Ridged, hollow, elbow-shaped noodles with a ruffled crest along one edge; wheat flour	With hearty sauces
Ditali/Thimbles	Narrow tubes cut in short lengths; *ditalini* are tiny thimbles; wheat flour	With medium-texture sauces, soups
Egg Flakes	Tiny, flat squares; wheat flour	Soups
Egg Noodles	Usually ribbons in varying widths; may be cut long or short, packaged loose or in compressed bundles; may have spinach or other flavorings; wheat flour dough enriched with egg yolks	Buttered casseroles, some sauces, puddings (sweet and savory)
Elbow Macaroni	Narrow, curved tubes cut in short lengths (about 1 inch); wheat flour	Macaroni and cheese, casseroles, salads
Farfalle/Butterflies	Flat, rectangular noodles pinched in center to resemble butterfly or bow; may have crimped edges; *farfallini* are tiny butterflies	With medium or hearty sauces; baked, soups
Fedeli or Fidelini	Very fine ribbon pasta, similar to capellini; wheat flour	With oil, butter, or light sauce
Fettucini	Long, flat, ribbon-shaped, about 1/4-inch wide; wheat flour	With medium-hearty, rich sauces (*e.g.* alfredo)
Fiochetti/Bowties	Rectangles of flat pasta curled up and pinched slightly in the center to form bow shapes	With medium and hearty sauces sauces
Fusilli/Twists	Long, spring- or corkscrew-shaped strands; thicker than spaghetti	With tomato and other medium-thick sauces
Lasagne	Large, flat noodles about 3-inches wide; usually with curly edges; wheat flour	Baked with sauce, cheese, and meat or vegetables
Linguine	Thin, slightly flattened, solid strands, about 1/8-inch wide; wheat flour	With oil, butter, marinara, or other thin sauces

range of vinegars, mustards, relishes, pickles, olives, jams, and other condiments. In general, vinegars and condiments should be stored in the same manner as oils and shortenings.

Dried Herbs and Spices

Many of the fresh herbs discussed earlier in this chapter, are also available in dried form. Some herbs, such as rosemary, sage, and bay leaves, dry successfully, whereas others will retain very little flavor.

Dried herbs are often stored incorrectly, which compounds the problem of flavor loss. They are frequently stored on the top shelf of the range, are kept for too long, and are purchased in overly large quantities. A chef should buy only the amount of dried herbs that can be used within two or three months, and should store them away from heat. Herbs that have a musty or "flat" aroma should be discarded. If at all possible, the chef should try to find fresh herbs.

Spices are aromatics produced primarily from the bark and seeds of plants. Most spices' flavors are

	TABLE 5-40 *(CONTINUED)*	
Name (Italian/English)	*Description (Shape, Base Flour)*	*Major Dish(es)*
Maccheroni/Macaroni	Thin, tubular pasta in various widths; may be long like spaghetti or cut into shorter lengths	With medium-hearty sauces
Mafalde	Flat, curly-edged, about $^3/_4$-inch wide; sometimes called lasagnette or malfadine; wheat flour	Sauced and baked
Manicotti/Small Muffs	Thick, ridged tubes; may be cut straight or on an angle; wheat flour	Filled with meat or cheese and baked
Mostaccioli/ Small Mustaches	Medium-size tubes with angle-cut ends; may be ridged (rigati); wheat flour	With hearty sauces
Orecchiette/Ears	Smooth, curved rounds of flat pasta; about $^1/_2$-inch in diameter; wheat flour	With oil-and-vegetable sauces or any medium sauce; soups
Orzo/Barley	Tiny, grain-shaped; wheat flour	Soups, salads, pilaf
Pastina/Tiny Pasta	Miniature pasta in any of various shapes, including stars, rings, alphabets, seeds/teardrops	Soups buttered, (as side dish or cereal for children)
Penne/Quills or Pens	Same as mostaccioli	With hearty sauces
Rice Noodles	Noodles in various widths (up to about $^1/_8$ inch); rice sticks are long, straight ribbons; rice vermicelli is very thin; rice flour	Asian dishes
Rigatoni	Thick, ridged tubes cut in lengths of about $1^1/_2$ inches	With hearty sauces; baked
Rotelle/Wheels	Spiral shaped; wheat flour	With medium or hearty sauces
Rotini/Cartwheels	Small, round, 6-spoked wheels; wheat flour	With hearty sauces; soups
Soba (Japanese)	Noodles the approximate shape and thickness of fedeli or taglarini; buckwheat flour	Asian dishes, including soups, hot and cold noodle dishes
Somen (Japanese)	Long, thin, noodles; resemble tagliarini wheat flour	Asian dishes, including soup
Spaghetti/Little Strings	Solid, round strands ranging from very thin to thin; very thin spaghetti may be labeled spaghettini; wheat flour	With oil, butter, marinara, seafood, or other thin sauces
Tagliarini	Ribbon pasta cut about $^1/_8$-inch wide; wheat flour	With rich, medium-hearty sauces
Tagliatelli	Same as fetuccini; may be mixed plain and spinach noodles, called paglia e fieno (straw and hay)	With rich, hearty sauces
Tubetti /Tubes	Medium-small (usually about as thick as elbow macaroni), tubular, may be long or cut in lengths of about an inch; tubettini are tiny tubes	With medium and hearty sauces; soups
Udon (Japanese)	Thick, noodles, similar to somen; wheat flour	Asian dishes
Vermicelli	Very fine cylindrical pasta, similar to capellini; wheat flour	With oil, butter, or light sauce
Ziti/Bridegrooms	Medium-size tubes; may be ridged (rigati); may be long or cut in approximately 2-inch lengths (ziti tagliate); wheat flour	With hearty sauces; baked

*Where base flour is listed as wheat, usually duram semolina is used. Wheat pastas may be made from flours, including whole wheat and buckwheat, and they may be flavored with vegetables and/or herb purées.

quite intense and powerful. Spices are nearly always sold in dried form and may be available whole or ground. In addition, the chef may use spice blends, such as curry powder, quatre épices, chili powder, and pickling spice.

Whole spices will keep longer than ground spices, although most spices will retain their potency for about six months if they are properly stored. They should be kept in sealed containers in a cool, dry spot, away from extreme heat and direct light. Check spices from time to time to be sure they are still potent, discarding any that have lost their flavor or have become stale or musty smelling. For optimum flavor, purchase whole spices and grind them as close as possible to the time they are to be used. (See Table 5-43 and Figure 5-113.)

Salt and Pepper

Salt was once one of the most prized of all seasonings. The expression "below the salt" shows its importance as an indicator of class differences. The nobles, who sat at the head of the table ("above the

FIGURE 5-111   Pasta

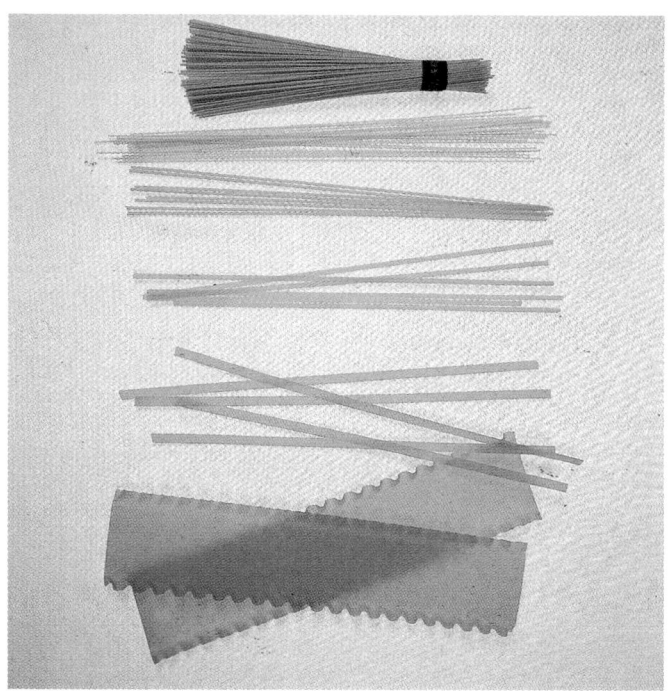

(1) (from top: soba, cappelini, spaghetti, linguini, fettucini, lasagne)

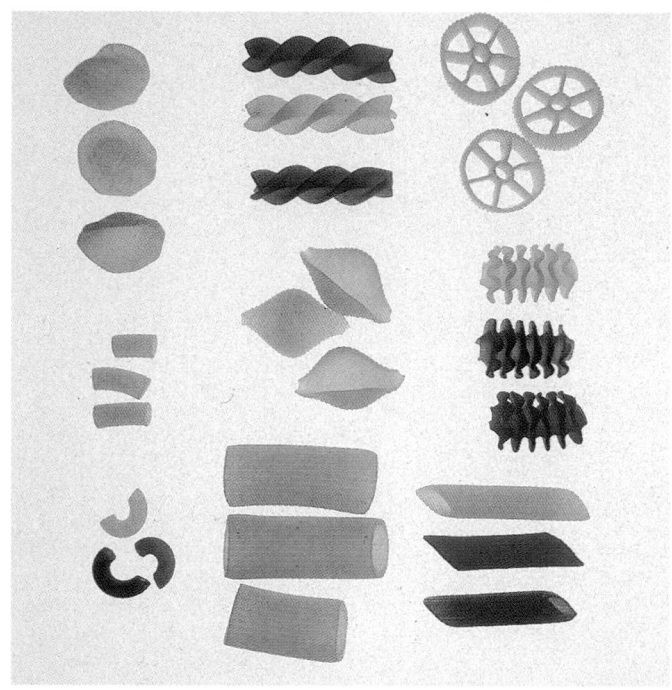

(2) Special and flavored pastas (top row: orechietti, fusilli, pin wheels; middle: tubetti, shells, radiatore; bottom: elbow, rigatoni, penne)

(3) Extruded types (clockwise from top left: orzo, elbow, tubettini, shells)

salt") were allowed to use salt. The lesser folk, sitting "below the salt," relied on herbs to flavor their food. Salt is today readily available in numerous forms.

Pepper was at one time the single most expensive seasoning in the world. Today, most kitchens require a number of different peppers for different uses. Not all of the peppers listed in Table 5-44 are related botanically; however, they all have a pungent, fiery flavor and aroma. Freshly ground pepper is preferable, and should be used when possible.

Bulk stores of salt and pepper should be held in dry storage, away from moisture. In very humid weather, salt may cake together; mixing a few grains of rice in with the salt will help to prevent this. Whole peppercorns will retain their flavor indefinitely, releasing it only when crushed or ground. Check ground or cracked pepper for pungency if its age is in question.

Extracts and Other Flavorings

The chef uses a variety of flavorings for cooking and baking. They may be either extracts, which are alcohol-based, or emulsions, which are oil-based. Herbs, spices, nuts, and fruits are used to prepare both extracts and emulsions. Common flavors include vanilla, lemon, mint, and almond.

Alcohol-based extracts can lose their potency with prolonged exposure to air, heat, or light. To preserve flavor, store in tightly capped dark jars or bottles away from heat or direct light. Oil-based

Name	Description/Uses
Butter-Flavored Oils/ Shortenings	Vegetable oils (usually blended) flavored with real or artificial butter flavor for use on griddles. Hydrogenated shortening used for baked goods, pastries.
Canola Oil (Rapeseed oil)	A light, golden-colored oil, similar to safflower oil. Low in saturated fat. Extracted from the seeds of a variety of turnips (the same plant as the vegetable broccoli rabe). Used in salads and cooking, mostly in the Mediterranean region and India; also used in margarine and blended vegetable oils.
Coconut Oil	A heavy, nearly colorless oil extracted from fresh coconuts. Used primarily in blended oils and shortenings. Used primarily in prepared, processed, packaged foods.
Corn Oil	A mild-flavored refined oil. It is medium-yellow colored, inexpensive, and versatile
Cottonseed Oil	This pale-yellow oil is extracted from seed of the cotton plant. Used for frying.
Frying Fats	Blended oils or shortenings (usually based on processed corn or peanut oils) designed for high smoke point and long fry life. May be liquid or plastic at room temperature.
Grapeseed Oil	This light, medium-yellow, aromatic oil is a by-product of wine making. It is used in salads and some cooking and in the manufacture of margarine.
Lard	Solid animal fat. May be treated to neutralize flavor.
Olive Oil	Oil varies in weight and may be pale-yellow to deep-green depending on fruit used and processing. Cold-pressed olive oil, is superior in flavor to refined. Oil from the first pressing, called "virgin" oilve oil is the most flavorful. Also classified according to acidity: extra virgin, superfine, fine, virgin, and pure, in ascending degree of acidity. "Pure" olive oil, and that labeled just "olive oil" may be a combination of cold-pressed and refined oil; suitable for cooking.
Oil Sprays	Vegetable oils (usually blended) packaged in pump or aerosol sprays for lightly coating pans, griddles.
Peanut Oil	A pale-yellow refined oil, with a very subtle scent and flavor. Some less-refined types are darker with a more pronounced peanut flavor. These are used primarily in Asian cooking.
Safflower Oil	A golden-color oil with a light texture. Made from a plant that resembles the thistle. Usually refined.
Salad Oil	Mild flavored vegetable oils blended for use in salad dressings, mayonnaise, etc.
Sesame Oil	Two types: a light, very mild, Middle Eastern type and a darker Asian type pressed from toasted sesame seeds. Asian sesame oil may be light or dark brown. The darker oil has a more pronounced sesame flavor and aroma. Asian sesame oil has a low smoke point so it is used primarily as a flavoring rather than in cooking.
Shortening/Baking Fat	Blended oil solidified using various processes, including whipping in air and hydrogenation. Designed for plasticity and mild flavor. May have real or artificial butter flavor added. Usually emulsified to enable absorption of more sugar in baked goods. May contain animal fats unless labeled "vegetable shortening."
Soybean Oil	A fairly heavy oil with a pronounced flavor and aroma. More soybean oil is produced than any other type. Used in most blended vegetable oils and margarines.
Sunflower Oil	A light, odorless and nearly flavorless oil pressed from sunflower seeds. Pale yellow and versatile.
Vegetable Oil	Made by blending several different refined oils. Designed to have a mild flavor and a high smoke point.
Walnut Oil	A medium-yellow oil with a nutty flavor and aroma. Cold-pressed from dried walnuts. More perishable than most other oils; should be used soon after purchase. Used primarily in salads. (Other nut oils include almond, hazelnut, and peanut above.)

emulsions are more stable, but should also be stored in cool, well-ventilated areas in tightly capped jars or bottles to preserve freshness and flavor.

Wines, Cordials, and Liqueurs

A general rule of thumb for selecting wines, cordials, and liqueurs for use in cooking and baking is this: If it is not suitable for drinking, it is not suitable for cooking.

Among the common selections for use in the kitchen are brandies and cognacs, champagne, dry red and white wines, port, sauternes, sherry, stouts, ales, beers, and sweet and dry vermouth. For baking purposes, the chef should keep on hand bourbon, cassis, fruit brandies, gin, Kahlua, rum, and Scotch. Items listed for the kitchen can, of course, be used in the bakeshop, and vice versa.

Purchase wines and cordials that are affordably priced and of good quality. Table wines (bur-

TABLE 5-42 SMOKING POINTS OF SELECTED FATS

Name	Uses	Approximate Melting Point	Smoking Point*
Butter, whole	Baking, cooking	95°F/36°C	300°F/150°C
Butter, clarified	Cooking	95°F/36°C	300°F/150°C
Coconut oil	Coatings, confectionary, shortening	75°F/24°C	350°F/175°C
Corn oil	Frying, salad dressings, shortening	12°F/–11°C	450°F/230°C
Cottonseed oil	Margarine, salad dressings, shortening	55°F/13°C	420°F/215°C
Frying fat	Frying	105°F/40°C	465°F/240°C
Lard	Baking, cooking, specialty items	92°F/33°C	375°F/190°C
Olive oil	Cooking, salad dressings	32°F/0°C	375°F/190°C
Peanut oil	Frying, margarine, salad dressings, shortening	28°F/–2°C	440°F/225°C
Safflower oil	Margarine, mayonnaise, salad dressings	2°F/–17°C	510°F/265°C
Shortening, emulsified vegetable	Baking, frying, shortening	115°F/46°C	325°F/165°C
Soybean oil	Margarine, salad dressings, shortening	–5°F/–20°C	495°F/257°C
Sunflower oil	Cooking, margarine, salad dressings, shortening	2°F/–17°C	440°F/225°C

*The smoke point of any oil will be reduced after it is used for cooking. Temperatures are approximate.

FIGURE 5-112   Oils and Vinegars

(1) Top row: vinegars; bottom row: oils

(2) Infused oils

(3) Virgin olive oils

(4) Nut oils

TABLE 5-43 SPICES

Product	Uses/Affinities	Product	Uses/Affinities
Allspice	Braises, forcemeats, fish, pickles, desserts	**Ginger**	Fresh: Asian dishes, curries, braises; ground dry: Some desserts and baked goods
Anise	Desserts and other baked goods, liqueur		
Caraway	Rye bread, pork, cabbage, soups, stews, some cheeses, liqueur *(kummel)*	**Horseradish**	Sauces (for beef, chicken, fish), egg salad, potatoes, beets
Cardamom	Curries, some baked goods, pickling	**Juniper**	Marinades, braises (especially game), sauerkraut, gin, and liqueurs
Cayenne	Sauces, soups, most meats, some fish, and poultry	**Mace**	Some forcemeats, pork, fish, spinach, other vegetables, pickles, desserts, and baked goods
Celery seed	Salads (including cole slaw), salad dressings, soups, stews, tomatoes, some baked goods		
Chili powder	Chili and other Mexican dishes, curries	**Mustard**	Pickling, meats, sauces, cheese and eggs, prepared mustard
Cinnamon	Desserts, some baked goods, sweet potatoes, hot beverages, curries, pickles, and preserves	**Nutmeg**	Sauces and soups (especially cream), veal, chicken, aspics, spinach, mushrooms, potatoes, other vegetables, desserts (especially custards), baked goods
Cloves	Stocks, sauces, braises, marinades, curries, pickling, desserts, some baked goods	**Paprika**	Braises and stews (including goulash), sauces, garnish
Coriander seeds	Curries, some forcemeats, pickling, some baked goods	**Pepper**	Stocks, sauces, meats, vegetables, many other uses
Cumin	Curries, chili, and other Mexican dishes	**Saffron**	Poultry, seafood, rice pilafs, sauces, soups, some baked goods
Dill Seeds	Pickling, sauerkraut		
Fennel seeds	Sausage, fish and shellfish, tomatoes, some baked goods, marinades	**Star anise**	Asian dishes, especially pork and duck
Fenugreek	Curries, meat, poultry, chutney	**Turmeric**	Curries, sauces, pickling, rice

TABLE 5-44 SALT AND PEPPER

Name	Description
Salt	
Rock salt	An unrefined, coarse salt not added directly to foods but used in some ice cream machines.
Table salt	All-purpose salt made by grinding refined rock salt into fine crystals. May be fortified with iodine and treated with magnesium carbonate to prevent clumping.
Sea salt	Made by allowing sea water to evaporate, leaving behind salt crystals. Available refined or unrefined, in whole crystals or ground. In its unrefined state, it may be known as "sel gris," French for "gray salt."
Kosher salt	Pure refined rock salt, also known as "coarse salt" or "pickling salt." Because it does not contain magnesium carbonate, it will not cloud items to which it is added. Kosher salt is required for "koshering" foods that must meet Jewish dietary guidelines.
Curing salt	A blend of 94 percent salt and 6 percent sodium nitrite. Used in a variety of charcuterie items, especially those to be cold-smoked. Usually dyed pink to differentiate it from other salts. Saltpeter, which is potassium nitrate, is occasionally used in place of curing salt.
MSG (Monosodium glutamate)	A flavor enhancer, without a distinct flavor of its own. Associated with the "Chinese Food Syndrome," "MSG" causes severe allergic reactions in some people.
Pepper	
Black peppercorns	Available as whole berries, cracked, or ground. The Telicherry peppercorn is one of the most prized. Mignonette or shot pepper is a combination of coarsely ground or crushed black and white peppercorns.
White peppercorns	Black peppercorns are allowed to ripen and then husks are removed. May be preferred for pale or lightly colored sauces. Available in same form as black peppercorns.
Green peppercorns	Unripe peppercorns that are packed in vinegar or brine; also available freeze-dried (they must be reconstituted in water before use).
Cayenne	A special type of chili, originally grown in Cayenne in French Guiana. The chili is dried and ground into a fine powder. The same chili is used to make hot pepper sauces.
Chili flakes	Dried, whole red chili peppers that are crushed or coarsely ground.
Paprika	A powder made from dried sweet peppers (pimientos). Available as mild, sweet, or hot. Hungarian paprikas are considered superior in flavor.

FIGURE 5-113   Flavoring/Seasonings

(1) Peppercorns (clockwise from top left: green, black, ground cayenne, red)

(2) Powdered seasonings and blends (from top right: ground mustard, ground coriander, ground cumin, poultry seasoning)

(3) Powdered seasonings and blends (from top right: old bay, paprika, tumeric, curry (center), and cardamom)

(4) Seeds (clockwise from top: mustard, celery, dill, fennel)

(5) Saffron

(6) Herbs and spices (clockwise from top left: parsley flakes, pickling spice, bay leaves, cloves)

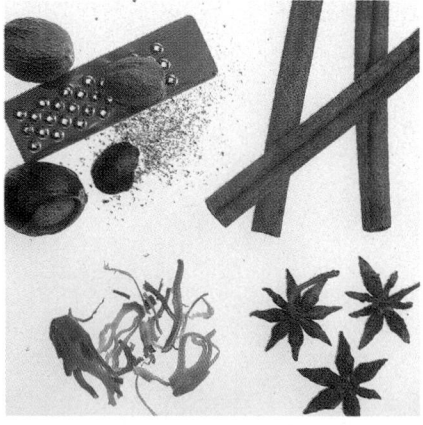

(7) Spices (clockwise from top left: nutmeg, cinnamon, star anise, mace)

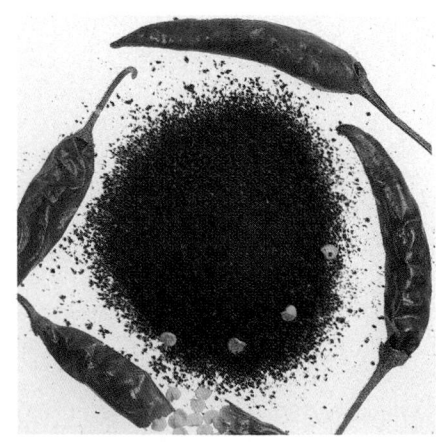

(8) Chili powder

gundies, chablis, and chardonnays, for example) lose their flavor and become acidic once opened, especially when subjected to heat, light, and air. To preserve flavor, keep them in closed bottles or bottles fitted with pouring spouts, and refrigerate when not needed. Fortified wines (madeiras, sherries, and ports, for example) are more stable than table wines and can be held in dry storage if there is not enough room to refrigerate them. The same advice also applies to cordials, cognacs, and liqueurs.

Nuts and Seeds

With the exception of the peanut, which grows underground in the root system of a leguminous plant, nuts are the fruits of various trees. They are available in the following forms—in the shell, roasted, shelled, blanched, sliced, slivered, chopped, and as butters.

Nuts have a number of culinary uses, adding a special flavor and texture to dishes. They are relatively expensive and should be stored carefully to keep them from becoming rancid. Nuts that have not been roasted or shelled will keep longer. Shelled nuts may be stored in the freezer or cooler, if space allows. In any case, they should be stored in a cool, dry, well-ventilated area and checked periodically to be sure they are still fresh.

Some of the seeds used in the kitchen are considered spices (celery or fennel seed, for example), and others, including sesame seeds and poppy seeds, are covered in Table 5-45. Seeds are usually available whole or as a paste and should be stored in the same manner as nuts. (Also see Figure 5-114.)

Dried Fruits and Vegetables

The United States processes over one billion pounds of dried fruit per year. Federal and state standards have been established for some (but not all) types of dried or low-moisture fruits and vegetables. Because the fruit is allowed to fully mature before being harvested and dried, there is greater potential for damage and defects. Low-moisture fruits and vegetables (raisins, sun-dried tomatoes, and so on) are somewhat perishable and should be refrigerated or carefully stored. Purchase no more

FIGURE 5-114 Nuts and Seeds

than a one-month supply. Vacuum- or chemically-dried vegetables (mushrooms) are not as perishable, but should be carefully stored in a cool, dry area. There is a great variety in the price and quality of dried fruits and vegetables. The chef will need to experiment to determine what is the best quality available. (See Figure 5-115.)

Sugars, Syrups, and Other Sweeteners

Once a symbol of wealth and prosperity, sugar is now so commonplace and inexpensive that it takes a good deal of effort to avoid using it. Sugar is extracted from plant sources (sugar beet or sugar cane) and then refined into the desired form. Syrups (maple syrup, corn syrup, molasses, and honey) are also derived from plants.

Table sugar has a number of important roles in the kitchen and bake shop, in addition to being required on the table to sweeten beverages.

Syrups and other sweeteners, such as honey and sugar substitutes, may also be necessary, depending on a particular kitchen's menu and the guests' needs. (See Table 5-46 and Figure 5-116.)

TABLE 5-45 NUTS AND SEEDS

Name	Description	Purchase Form
Almond	Teardrop-shape seed of a fruit that resembles the apricot. Pale-tan, woody, shell. Bitter and sweet types available. Bitter require cooking; sweet may be used raw or cooked	Whole in shell; shelled: whole, blanched, slivered, ground, almond paste, other products
Brazil	Large, oval nut; grows in clusters of segments. Each segment is a hard, wrinkled, three-sided, brown seed containing the rich nut	Whole in shell; shelled
Cashew	Kidney-shape nut that grows as the appendage of an apple-like fruit, which is not usually eaten. It is always sold hulled, as its skin contains irritating oils similar to those in poison ivy	Shelled: raw or toasted
Chestnut	Fairly large, round-to teardrop-shape nut; hard, glossy, dark-brown shell	Raw (whole in shell); canned: whole in water or syrup, puréed
Coconut	Melon-sized fruit that grows on a type of palm. The "nut," its woody, brown "seed," is covered with hairy fibers and surrounds a layer of rich, white nutmeat. The inside of the nut is hollow and contains thin, white juice (coconut water)	Whole in shell, flaked (may be sweetened), coconut cream, other products
Hazelnut	Small, nearly round nut; shiny, hard shell with matte spot where cap was attached. Nutmeat rich and delicately flavored	Whole in shell; shelled: whole, chopped
Macadamia	Nearly round, rich, sweet nut native to Australia	Shelled and roasted in coconut oil
Peanut	Seed grows inside a fibrous pod among the roots of a leguminous plant	Whole in shell; shelled: whole, skinned; raw or roasted; peanut butter
Pecan	Medium-brown, smooth, glossy, oval shaped shell. Two-lobed nutmeat has a rich flavor	Whole in shell; shelled: halved, chopped
Pine Nut	Tiny, cream-colored, elongated kernel is the seed of a Mediterranean pine. Fairly perishable	Shelled: raw or toasted
Pistachio	Cream-colored shell; green nutmeat with distinctive, sweet flavor	Whole in shell: roasted, usually salted, natural or dyed red; occasionally shelled, chopped
Poppy seeds	Tiny, round, blue-black seeds with a rich, slightly musty flavor	Whole
Pumpkin seeds	Flat, oval, cream-colored seeds with semihard hull and soft, oily interior	Whole in shell; shelled: raw or toasted
Sesame seeds	Tiny, flat, oval seeds; may be black (unhulled) or tan (hulled); oily with rich, nutty flavor	Whole: hulled or unhulled; paste (tahini)
Sunflower seeds	Small, somewhat flat, teardrop-shape seeds; oily, light tan seed with woody, black and white shell; grown primarily for oil	Whole in shell; shelled
Walnut	Mild, tender, oily nutmeat; grows in convoluted segments inside hard, light-brown shell. White walnuts, or butternuts, and black walnuts are North American varieties. Butternuts are richer and black walnuts stronger in flavor	Whole in shell; shelled: halved, chopped; pickled (whole)

FIGURE 5-115   Dried Fruits and Vegetables

(1) Chilies (top row: Mulatto/pasilla; middle: bird beak, serranos; bottom: Poblano, chipotle)

(2) Fruit (clockwise from top left: cranberry, blueberry, cherry, strawberry)

(3) Mushrooms (clockwise from top left: shiitake, chaterelle, portabella, morel)

Chocolate

Chocolate is produced from beans, known as cocoa beans, which grow in a pod on the cacao tree. For the ancient Aztecs, cocoa beans served not only to produce drinks and as a component of various sauces, but also as currency. Today the word "chocolate" is usually associated with sweets—cakes, candies, and other desserts—although it is also used in a variety of savory entrées, such as *mole poblano*, a chocolate chicken dish of Mexican origin.

The chocolate extraction process is lengthy, and has undergone a great deal of refinement since the days of the Aztecs. The first stage involves crushing

TABLE 5-46 SUGARS, SYRUPS, AND OTHER SWEETENERS

Name	Description	Purchase Form
Sugar		
Brown	Granular, refined sugar with some impurities left in or some molasses added; light to medium brown; moister than white sugar; slight molasses flavor	Bulk, bags, boxes
Muscovado	Granular, brown sugar, which has undergone little processing; soft and moist; dark brown with pronounced molasses flavor	Bulk, bags
Demerara	Partially refined sugar in large crystals, golden-brown, dissolves slowly	Bulk, boxes
Turbinado	Coarse granular sugar that is slightly more refined than demarara sugar; golden	Bulk, boxes
White, Coarse/Preserving	Pure, refined sugar in large crystals; dissolves slowly	Bulk boxes
White, Granulated	Pure, refined sugar in small, evenly sized crystals	Bulk, bags, individual packets
White, Superfine/Bar	Pure, refined sugar in very small crystals; dissolves quickly	Bulk, bags, boxes
Confectioners, 10X	Very finely powdered, pure refined sugar; usually mixed with a small amount of cornstarch to prevent clumping	Bulk, bags, boxes
White, Lump/Cube	Pure, refined, granulated sugar pressed into small cubes or tablets	Boxes
Syrup		
Corn	Liquified sugar extracted from corn; less sweet than sugar (types: light (pale yellow) and dark (deep amber)	Bulk, jars
Maple	Liquified sugar made from the concentrated sap of the sugar maple, golden brown	Bulk, jars (jugs)
Treacle	A liquid by-product of refining, not widely used in the United States, light or dark, flavor resembles molasses	Bulk, jars
Flavored	Sugar or other syrup with added flavoring (common types: cassis (black currant), grenadine (pomegranate), maple)	Bulk, jars, individual packets
Molasses	Thick, dark-brown liquid by-product of sugar refining; rich flavor but less sweet than sugar (types: sulfured, unsulfured, blackstrap)	Bulk, jars
Honey	Thick, pale-straw to deep-brown liquid (creamed honeys are moist and granular; may be packaged with honeycomb, whole or in pieces; sweeter than sugar	Bulk, jars

the kernel into a paste, called chocolate liquor. The liquor is then further ground to give it a smoother, finer texture, and sweeteners and other ingredients may be added. The liquor may be pressed, causing cocoa butter to be forced out. The cocoa solids that are left are ground into cocoa powder. The remaining cocoa butter may be combined with chocolate liquor to make eating chocolates or it may be flavored and sweetened to make "white chocolate." (See Table 5-47 and Figure 5-117.) Cocoa butter also has numerous pharmaceutical and cosmetic uses.

Chocolate should be stored, well wrapped, in a cool, dry, ventilated area. Under most conditions it should not be refrigerated, since this could cause moisture to condense on the surface of the chocolate. If the weather is hot and humid, however, it may be preferable to refrigerate or freeze the chocolate to prevent loss of flavor. Sometimes stored chocolate develops a white coating, or *bloom*. The bloom merely indicates that some of the cocoa butter has melted and then recrystallized on the surface. Chocolate with a bloom can still be safely used. If properly stored, chocolate will last for several months. Cocoa powder should be stored in tightly sealed containers in a dry place. It will keep almost indefinitely.

Coffee, Tea, and Other Beverages

A good cup of coffee or tea is often the key to a restaurant's reputation. The chef should identify brands and blends that best serve the establishment's specific needs. Whereas some operations prefer to select whole coffee beans, others may be better served by buying preground, portioned, and vacuum-packed coffee. Many restaurants serve brewed, decaffeinated coffee, and some offer

FIGURE 5-116 Sugars and Syrups

(1) Sugars (clockwise from top: light brown, granular white, amber crystals, raw dark brown, and powdered)

FIGURE 5-117 Chocolates and Cocoa

(2) Syrups (from left: maple, pancake, honey, karo, light)

espresso and cappuccino, regular and decaffeinated.

Teas come in many varieties, including decaffeinated and herbal teas. Most are blends and are available in single-serving bags or in loose form.

Although coffee and tea generally keep well, they will lose a lot of flavor if stored too long or under improper conditions. Whole roasted beans or opened containers of ground coffee should be kept cool, ideally, refrigerated. Teas should be stored in cool, dry areas, away from light and moisture.

Prepared mixes (powdered fruit drinks or cocoa mixes, for example) also should be kept moisture-free. Frozen juices and other beverages should remain solidly frozen until needed. Canned juices should be kept in dry storage. Remember to rotate stock, and check all cans, boxes, and other containers for leaks, bulges, or mold. (See Figure 5-118.)

Leaveners

Leaveners are used to give foods a light, airy texture. Chemical leaveners, such as baking soda (sodium bicarbonate) and baking powder (a combination of baking soda, cream of tartar, and talc), work rapidly in the presence of moisture and heat. Baking powder is usually double-acting, which means that an initial reaction occurs in the presence of moisture, when liquids are added to dry ingredients, and a second in the presence of heat, as the item bakes in the oven.

Yeast also leavens foods, by the process of fermentation, which produces alcohol and carbon dioxide. The gas creates a number of small pockets, and the alcohol burns off during baking.

Chemical leaveners should be kept perfectly dry. Dried yeast can be held for extended periods, but

TABLE 5-47   CHOCOLATE AND RELATED PRODUCTS

Type	Description	Purchase Form
Chocolate liquor	The chocolate-flavored portion of chocolate; obtained by grinding and liquefying chocolate nibs	(See unsweetened chocolate)
Cocoa butter	The vegetable fat portion of chocolate; removed for cocoa; added for chocolate	Plastic at room tempertaure
Cocoa	Chocolate from which all but 10–25% of the cocoa butter has been removed	Powder, unsweetened
Cocoa, dutch process	Chocolate from which all but 22–24% of the cocoa butter has been removed; treated with alkali to reduce its acidity	Powder, unsweetened
Cocoa, breakfast	Cocoa (above) with at least 22% cocoa butter	Powder, unsweetened
Cocoa, low-fat	Cocoa (above) with less than 10% cocoa butter	Powder, unsweetened
Cocoa, instant	Cocoa (above) that has been precooked, sweetened (usually about 80% sugar), and emulsified to make it dissolve more easily in liquid; may have powdered milk added	Powder
Chocolate, unsweetened (bitter/baking)	Solid chocolate made with about 95% chocolate liquor and 5% cocoa butter	Blocks or bars
Chocolate, bittersweet	Solid chocolate made with 35–50% chocolate liqour, 15% cocoa butter, and 35–50% sugar; interchangeable with semisweet chocolate; may have added ingredients, such as nuts, fillings, stabilizers, emulsifiers, and/or preservatives	Blocks, bars, chunks, and chips
Chocolate, semisweet	Solid chocolate made with about 45% chocolate liquor, 15% cocoa butter, and 40% sugar; interchangeable with bittersweet chocolate; may have added ingredients. (See above)	Blocks, bars, chunks, and chips
Chocolate, sweet	Solid chocolate made with 15% chocolate liquor, 15% cocoa butter, and 70% sugar; may have added ingredients. (See above)	Blocks, bars, chunks, and chips
Chocolate, milk	Solid chocolate made with 10% chocolate liquor, 20% cocoa butter, 50% sugar, and 15% milk solids; may have added ingredients. (See above)	Blocks, bars, chunks, and chips
Chocolate, coating (couverture)	Solid chocolate made with 15% chocolate liquor, 35% cocoa butter, and 50% sugar; high fat content makes it ideal for coating candy, pastries, and cakes	Blocks, bars, chunks, and chips
Confectionary coating	Solid, artificial chocolate made with vegetable fat other than cocoa butter; usually contains real chocolate flavoring in chocolate-flavored types; other flavors available	Blocks, bars, chunks, and chips
Chocolate, white	Solid chocolate made with cocoa butter or other vegetable fats, sugar, milk solids, and vanilla flavoring; contains no chocolate liquor; may contain artificial yellow color and/or other added ingredients. (See above)	Blocks, bars, chunks, and chips
Chocolate syrup	Chocolate or cocoa, sugar and/or other sweeteners, water, salt, other flavorings	Thick liquid
Chocolate sauce	Same as chocolate syrup but thicker; may have added milk, cream, butter, and/or other thickeners	Thick liquid
Carob	A dark-brown, somewhat chocolate-like flavoring produced from the carob bean; unsweetened carob is somewhat sweet, so it requires less added sugar than chocolate (about $3/4$ usual amount)	Blocks, bars, chunks, powder

fresh yeast has a short shelf life of only a few weeks under refrigeration.

Thickeners

Thickeners are used to give a liquid a certain amount of viscosity. The process of forming an emulsion is one way to thicken a liquid, as is the process of reduction. In addition, various thickening ingredients can be used. These include the following:

• *Arrowroot* is a starchy root that is ground and highly refined. A lesser amount of arrowroot than of cornstarch may be used to achieve the same degree of thickening.

• *Cornstarch* is a refined, finely ground corn flour.

• *Filé gumbo powder,* which is powdered sassafras root, is used in Cajun and Creole cookery.

• *Gelatin* is a protein that, when properly combined with a liquid, will cause the liquid to gel as it cools. It is available in powdered form and in sheets.

Thickeners should be stored in tightly sealed containers in dry storage. They will keep almost indefinitely.

Prepared, Canned, and Frozen Foods

Only you, as the chef can determine how and when to use convenience foods, depending upon the requirements and capabilities of the kitchen and the quality of the convenience foods available. (See Figure 5-119.) It may make sense, for example, to purchase prepared and frozen doughs (puff pastry, brioche, phyllo dough). Other frozen items frequently used are corn, peas, and spinach. As highly skilled craftsmen develop appropriate methods of producing high-quality prepared foods, more products are becoming available. Everything from special breads to custom-made sauces is currently on the market, with new products and lines being developed all the time.

Canned products also have valid uses in the contemporary kitchen. Depending upon the season,

FIGURE 5-118 Coffee/Tea

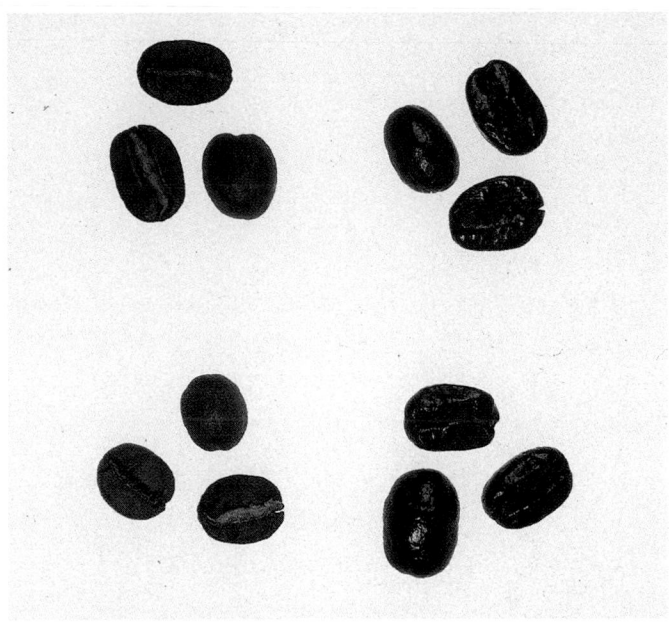

(1) Coffee beans (clockwise from top left: full city (medium-roast), dark (French) roast, Espresso (Italian) roast, ligh roast)

(2) Tea varieties (clockwise from top left: spiced, black, herbal (tisane), green)

TABLE 5-48   COMMON CAN SIZES

Can Size (Industry Term)	Approximate Net Weight or Fluid Measure	Approximate Cups Per Can	Number of Portions	Principal Products
No. 10	6–7 lb 5 oz	12–13	25	Institutional size for fruits, vegetables
No. 5 Squat	4–4 1/4 lb	8	16–20	Institutional size for canned fish, sweet potatoes
No. 3 Cyl	46 or 51 fl oz	5 1/4	10–12	Fruit and vegetable juices, condensed soups
No. 2 1/2	26–30 oz	3 1/2	5–7	Fruits, some vegetables
No. 2	18 or 20 oz	2 1/2	5	Juices, fruits, ready-to-serve soups
No. 303	1 lb	2	4	Fruits, vegetables, ready-to-serve soups
No. 300	14–16 oz	1 3/4	3–4	Some fruits and meat products
No. 1 (Picnic)	10 1/2–12 oz	1 1/4	2–3	Condensed soups
8 oz	8 oz	1	2	Ready-to-serve soups, fruits, vegetables

Note: When substituting one can for another size, one No. 10 can is approximately equivalent to:
   7 No. 303 (1 lb) cans
   5 No. 2 (1 lb 4 oz) cans
   4 No. 2 1/2 (1 lb 13 oz) cans
   2 No. 3 (46 to 50 oz) cans

FIGURE 5-119   Prepared and Miscellaneous Foods

(1) Wonton wrappers

(2) Tahini paste

(3) Seaweed wrappers and rice paper wrappers

(4) Truffles

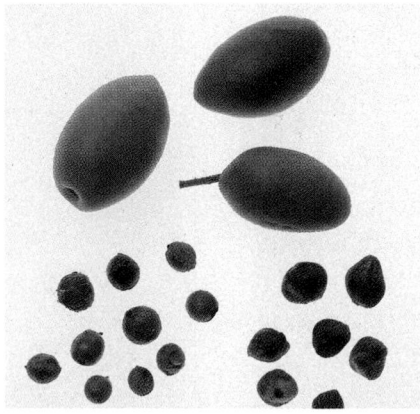

(5) Green peppercorns, olives, capers

(6) Can sizes

some canned items may be of better quality than below standard fresh produce. An obvious example is canned tomatoes, which are often superior to out-of-season fresh tomatoes. Quality, determined by good taste, yield, price, and color, will vary from product to product. (See Table 5-48.)

Other convenience foods that may have a place in the kitchen include mayonnaise and prepared bases. In all cases, remember to choose products that are of good quality.

For storage purposes, frozen goods should be kept solidly frozen until they are needed. Canned goods should be rotated on the shelves to assure that the "first in" is the "first out" (FIFO rule).

Summary

The menu should be evaluated carefully to determine what sorts of dry goods will be required and what the appropriate parstock is. Overstocking is just as costly an error as not having a product on hand. No food is at its best when it has been stored for too long. Proper purchasing and storing procedures should be consistently applied to ensure that all items will be at their peak of flavor, appearance, and freshness.

PART III

Cooking in the Professional Kitchen

A s soon as you hear the term "chef," certain associations immediately spring to mind. You can see the flashing knife and the steam rising like a cloud from a pot of soup. You can feel the velvety texture of a perfect sauce, hear the crackle of foods as they first hit a hot pan.

These are the sights, sounds, and textures of cooking in the professional kitchen. Whether you are a novice or an old hand, there is a sense of excitement and magic whenever you begin to work. Finding a perfect groove, fitting your rhythms with those of the dining room, tackling the day's work—these are the fundamentals of cooking in the professional kitchen.

Throughout this part of the book, the basic cooking methods will be thoroughly explained. Mise en Place covers such things as the basic knife cuts, the preparation of aromatic combinations, including mirepoix, sachet dépices, and bouquet garni. Other tasks that you *will perform—preparing stocks, cutting up poultry, meats, and fish, cleaning salad greens, or grinding spice blends, for instance—are also found in this chapter. A good mise en place is the point from which a good day's work flows.*

The chapter devoted to soups covers a variety of basic soup preparation methods. From broths to consommés, purées to bisques, cold soups to specialty soups, all can be found in this chapter.

Sauces are often regarded as a chef's highest technical challenge. It is true that a silken cream sauce, a light but rich hollandaise, and a complex yet translucent brown sauce is no mean feat. The ability to consistently produce sauces that meet high standards of excellence is the hallmark of the skilled craftsman.

Chapters 9 and 10 define and illustrate the cooking methods used for meats, fish, poultry, grains and pastas, dry and fresh vegetables, fruits, and eggs. Matching the right food with the right technique is the first step. Completing the process with attention to each detail— assembly of mise en place, advance preparation of foods and equipment, care in maintaining the highest standards of safety and cleanliness, cooking just to the exact moment of doneness, and preparing all sauces and garnishes required is the fulfillment of your responsibility as a chef.

The basic dry heat techniques include grilling, roasting, poêléng, sautéing, pan-frying, and deep-frying.

Foods are cooked either through direct radiant heat, or contact with a hot pan, or hot fats. These foods are typically intensely flavored. Many have a crisp exterior texture that offers an interesting contrast. Moist heat and combination cooking methods have different attributes, varying according to the method you select, and the food you are preparing. Steaming, poaching, simmering, stewing, and braising are all examples of these techniques.

Two other areas in the kitchen are also explained in this part of the book: charcuterie and baking. These special pursuits may often form the particular focus of a chef's career. Whether or not you intend to become a charcutière, *any professional must know the correct way of preparing pâtés, sausages, terrines, and other items produced in the cold kitchen. Likewise, the procedure for preparing breads, cakes, simple pastries and cookies, and kitchen desserts ought to be a part of your professional repertoire, even if you have no inclination to become a* pâstissiere.

Once the food has been cooked perfectly, the final task that remains is to prepare the plate for the guest. It is in completing this last detail that you put the finishing touches. The placement of each element, the combinations of colors, textures, and even heights on a plate, the appearance of the plate itself, and the addition of a garnish tell the guest immediately that you have done your job carefully and with pride.

Mise en place is a French phrase that translates as "to put in place." For the true professional, it means far more than simply assembling all the ingredients, pots and pans, plates, and serving pieces needed for a particular period. Mise en place is also a state of mind. Someone who has truly grasped the concept is able to keep many tasks in mind simultaneously, weighing and assigning each its proper value and priority. This assures that the chef has anticipated and prepared for every situation that could logically occur during a service period.

The techniques, terms, basic preparations (or appareils), and skills covered in this chapter represent only the most basic elements of mise en place, gathered together for easy reference. They include knife skills, common seasoning and flavoring combinations, and techniques for mixing, shaping, and cooking a variety of ingredients and preparations, ranging from meat fabrication to stocks and court bouillons. Each of the cooking techniques explained in Part III of this book will impart its own lessons on the meaning of mise en place.

FIGURE 6-1   Three Knife Grips

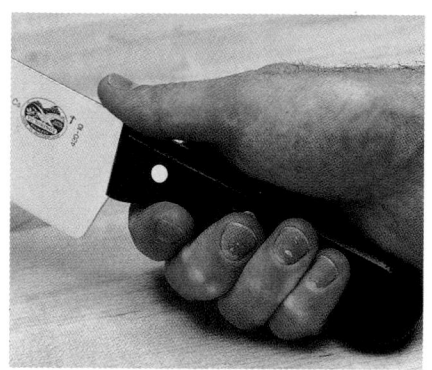

(1) Grasping the handle with thumb along spine of blade.

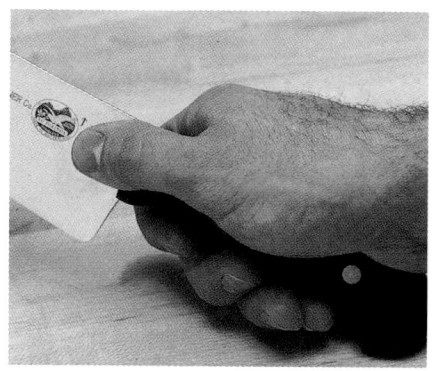

(2) Grasping the handle with thumb along side of blade.

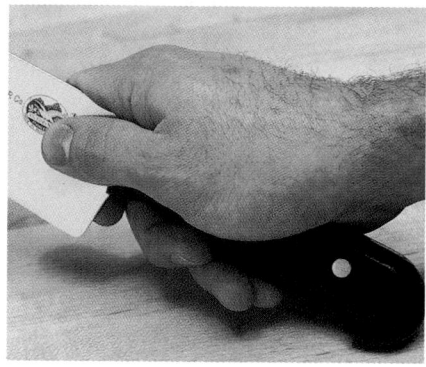

(3) Grasping the handle with the thumb and two fingers along either side of the blade.

Knife Skills

Knife skills include basic and advanced cuts that are used every day to prepare vegetables and other ingredients. Some of these cuts are quite familiar. Others are more unusual and may even require specialized tools or equipment. Some ingredients (onions, peppers, tomatoes, and leeks, for example) may demand special handling or preparation prior to cutting. These advance preparation steps will be discussed in the next section of this chapter.

The information and skills required to select, maintain, store, and sharpen knives and other cutting tools are discussed in Chapter 4, "Equipment Identification."

Holding the Knife

It is important to be comfortable with your knife as you work. There are several different ways a knife can be held. The way you hold the knife will be determined in part by the way your knife and your hand fit one another. The grip you choose will also be determined according to the task at hand. Delicate cutting or shaping techniques will call for greater control, involving the fingertips more than the fist. Coarser chopping and cutting tasks require a firmer grip and more leverage. The three basic grips used with a chef's knife are as follows:

1. Grip the handle with all four fingers and hold the thumb gently but firmly on top of the blade.

FIGURE 6-2
The Guiding Hand

2. Grip the handle with four fingers and hold the thumb firmly against the side of the blade.

3. Grip the handle with three fingers, resting the index finger flat against the blade on one side, and holding the thumb on the opposite side to give additional stability and control for finer cuts.

See Figure 6-1 for examples of these holds.

The Guiding Hand

The guiding hand, the hand not holding the knife, is used to hold the object being cut (see Figure 6-2). This is done to prevent the food from slipping as you cut it. It also makes it easier to control the size of the cut or slice you are making. Your fingertips hold the object, with the thumb held back from the fingertips and the fingertips tucked under slightly, so that your knuckles curl out over your fingertips. The knife blade then rests against your knuckles, preventing your fingers from being cut.

FIGURE 6-3   Basic Vegetables Cuts and Dimensions

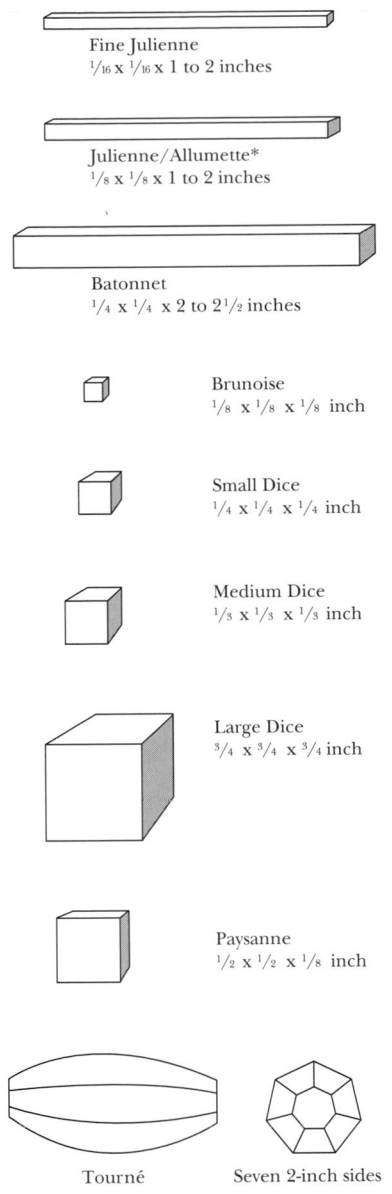

Fine Julienne
1/16 x 1/16 x 1 to 2 inches

Julienne/Allumette*
1/8 x 1/8 x 1 to 2 inches

Batonnet
1/4 x 1/4 x 2 to 2 1/2 inches

Brunoise
1/8 x 1/8 x 1/8 inch

Small Dice
1/4 x 1/4 x 1/4 inch

Medium Dice
1/3 x 1/3 x 1/3 inch

Large Dice
3/4 x 3/4 x 3/4 inch

Paysanne
1/2 x 1/2 x 1/8 inch

Tourné   Seven 2-inch sides

*Allumette normally refers only to potatoes.

FIGURE 6-4   Basic Peeling Techniques

(1) Using a paring knife to scrape carrots.

(2) Using a swivel-bladed peeler.

(3) Using a chef's knife to remove heavy peels.

As you make successive cuts, your fingertips should move back, maintaining a grip and controlling the width of each cut that is made.

Basic Knife Cuts

The basic cuts include:

- Coarse chopping and mincing
- Mincing
- Shredding (chiffonade)
- Julienne and batonnet
- Dicing
- Lozenge
- Rondelle, and oblique or roll cut

Your aim, whenever you cut something, should always be to cut the food into pieces of uniform shape and size. Unevenly cut items give an impression of carelessness that can spoil the dish's look. An even more important consideration is that foods of different sizes and shapes won't cook evenly. The basic cuts are illustrated in Figure 6-3. They are also discussed in the following pages, with step-by-step methods. It should be noted that the dimensions indicated in Figure 6-3 are recommended guidelines and may be modified if necessary. It is important that you be completely familiar with these cuts and able to execute them properly.

Peeling Vegetables and Fruits

Many vegetables and fruits should be peeled before they are cut. Swivel-bladed peelers are commonly used, since they cut only very thin strips from the outside of the vegetable. A paring knife can be used to either scrape or cut away the skin as well. Thicker or tougher skins may require a chef's knife to cut them away—winter squashes, pineapples, rutabagas, or celeriac, for example. Figure 6-4 illus-

FIGURE 6-8   Cutting Julienne Potatoes

FIGURE 6-5
Coarse Chopping

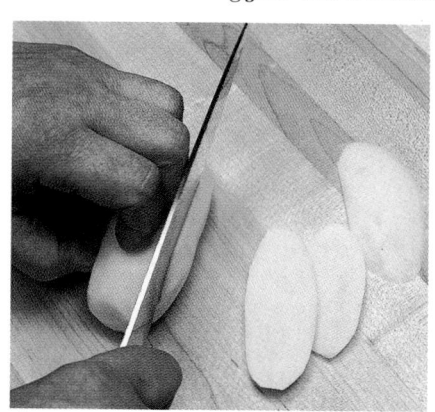

(1) Squaring off the potato to make it stable on cutting surface.

FIGURE 6-6
Mincing Parsley

(2) Cutting even slices, ⅛-inch thick.

FIGURE 6-7
Cutting Belgian Endive into Chiffonade

(3) Stacking slices and cutting at ⅛-inch intervals to make julienne.

trates three basic peeling techniques. Special peeling techniques are explained in the next section.

Coarse Chopping

This method (see Figure 6-5) is usually used for such items as mirepoix which will not be part of the finished presentation. They are normally strained out of the dish and discarded before service. The method for coarse chopping is as follows:

1. Trim the root and stem ends and peel the vegetables if necessary.

2. Slice or chop the vegetables at nearly regular intervals until the cuts are relatively uniform. This need not be a perfectly neat cut, but all the pieces should be roughly the same size.

Mincing

This is a even, very fine cut (see Figure 6-6) that is especially appropriate for herbs and other flavoring ingredients such as garlic and shallots. Usually, the guiding hand is used to hold the item being cut just until a very coarse mince is achieved. As the fineness of the mince becomes greater, the guiding hand is often used to hold the tip of the knife's blade in position. The method is as follows:

1. Gather herbs or roughly chopped garlic or shallots in a pile on a cutting board and position the knife above the pile.

2. Keeping the tip of the blade against the cutting board, raise and lower the knife's heel firmly and rapidly, repeatedly chopping through the herbs or vegetables.

3. Continue chopping until the desired fineness is attained.

Chiffonade/Shredding

The *chiffonade* cut is used for leafy vegetables and herbs (see Figure 6-7). The result is a finely shredded product, often used as a garnish or bed. The method is as follows:

1. When cutting tight heads of greens, such as Belgian endive or head cabbage, core the head and cut it in half, if it is large, to make cutting easier. For greens with large, loose leaves, roll individual leaves into tight cylinders before cutting. For smaller leaves, stack several leaves on top of one another.

2. Use a chef's knife to make very fine, parallel cuts to produce fine shreds. A box grater or mandolin can also be used to cut items such as cabbages or head lettuce, if you prefer.

Julienne and Batonnet

These cuts are long and rectangular (see Figure 6-8). Related cuts are the standard *pommes frites* and *pommes pont neuf* cuts (both are names for French fries) and the *allumette* (or matchstick) cut. The differences between these cuts is the size of the final product. The method is as follows:

1. Trim the vegetable so that the sides are straight, which will make it easier to produce even cuts. (The trimmings can be used, as appropriate, for stocks, soups, purées, or any preparation where shape is not important.)

2. Slice the vegetable lengthwise, using parallel cuts of the proper thickness.

3. Stack the slices, aligning the edges, and make parallel cuts of the same thickness through the stack. To make batonnet, the cuts should be thick. To make a fine julienne, the cuts should be very thin.

Dice

Dicing is a cutting technique that produces a cube shape (see Figure 6-9). Different preparations

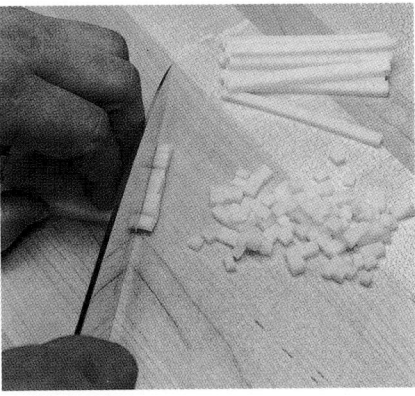

FIGURE 6-9
Cutting Julienned
Potatoes into
Small Dice
(Brunoise)

FIGURE 6-10
Paysanne Cut
Made from
Battonet Potatoes

FIGURE 6-11
Lozenge Cut from
Carrots

require different sizes of dice. The names given to different-sized dice are fine *brunoise*, small, medium, and large dice. The method is as follows:

1. Trim and cut the vegetable as for julienne or batonnet.

2. Gather the julienne or batonnets and cut through them crosswise at evenly spaced intervals.

FIGURE 6-12
Rondelle Cut
Variations:
Straight
(foreground);
Diagonal
(center); Halved
Cut on Diagonal
(backround)

Paysanne/Fermière

This cut resembles the thin, square wooden tile used in the game of Scrabble® (see Figure 6-10), and it is often used for vegetables that are to garnish soups, stews, and braises. Although the size may vary, depending on the vegetable being cut and its intended use, a cut of ½-inch square and ¼-inch thick is customary. The method is as follows:

1. Trim and cut the vegetable as for batonnet.

2. Make even, thin, crosswise cuts in the batonnets, at roughly ¼-inch intervals.

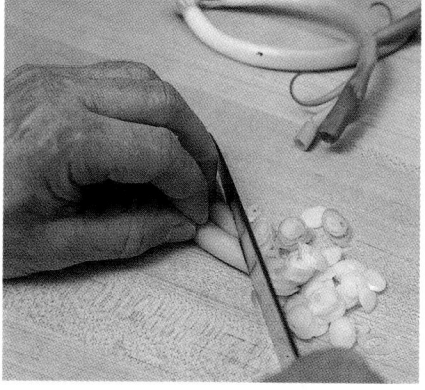

FIGURE 6-13
Diagonal Bias
Cut

Lozenge/Diamond

The lozenge cut (see Figure 6-11) is similar to the paysanne. Instead of cutting battonet, the vegetable is sliced thinly and then cut into strips of the appropriate width, as shown. The method is as follows:

1. Trim and slice the vegetable thinly.

2. Cut the slices into strips of the desired width.

FIGURE 6-14
Oblique or
Roll Cut

3. Make an initial bias cut to begin the process. This will leave some trim that should be reserved for use in preparations that do not require a neat, decorative cut.

4. Continue to make bias cuts, parallel to the first one.

Rounds/Rondelles

These are simple to cut (see Figure 6-12). The shape is the result of cutting a cylindrical vegetable, such as a carrot or cucumber, crosswise. The basic rondelle shape, a round disk, can be varied by cutting the vegetable on the bias to produce an elongated or oval disk, or by slicing it in half for half-moons. If the vegetable is scored with a channel knife, flower shapes are produced. The method is as follows:

1. Trim and peel the vegetable if necessary.

2. Make parallel slicing cuts through the vegetable at even intervals.

Diagonal/Bias Cut

This cut is often used to make vegetables ready for stir-fries and other Asian-style dishes (see Figure 6-13). Because it exposes a greater surface area of the vegetable, employing this cut shortens cooking time. The method is as follows:

1. Place the peeled or trimmed vegetable on the work surface.

2. Make a series of even parallel cuts on the bias.

Oblique or Roll Cut

This cut is used primarily with long, cylindrical vegetables such as parsnips, carrots, and celery (see Figure 6-14). The method is as follows:

1. Place the peeled vegetable on a cutting board. Make a diagonal cut to remove the stem end.

2. Hold the knife in the same position and roll the vegetable 180-degrees (a half-turn). Slice

FIGURE 6-15
Turning
(*Tournéing*)
Carrots

through it on the same diagonal, forming a piece with two angled edges.

3. Repeat until the entire vegetable has been cut.

Tourné/Turned Vegetables

Turning vegetables (*tourner* in French) requires a series of cuts that simultaneously trim and shape the vegetable (see Figure 6-15). The shape may be likened to a barrel or football. Turned vegetables are traditionally given different names, depending on their size. *Printanière* (the size of a large marble) and *jardinière* (the size of a quail's egg) are two of the more common names for turned cuts. The method is as follows:

1. Peel the vegetable, if desired.

2. Cut into pieces of manageable size. Cut large round or oval vegetables, such as beets and potatoes, into quarters, sixths, or eighths (depending on their size), to form pieces slightly larger than 2 inches. Cut cylindrical vegetables, such as carrots, into 2-inch pieces.

3. Using a paring or tourné knife, carve the pieces into barrel or football shapes. The faces should be smooth, evenly spaced, and tapered so that both ends are narrower than the center.

Special and Decorative Cuts Using Special Cutting Tools and Techniques

You can create numerous special cuts using such tools as a Japanese "turner," an apple peeler, mouli

FIGURE 6-16   Fluting Mushrooms

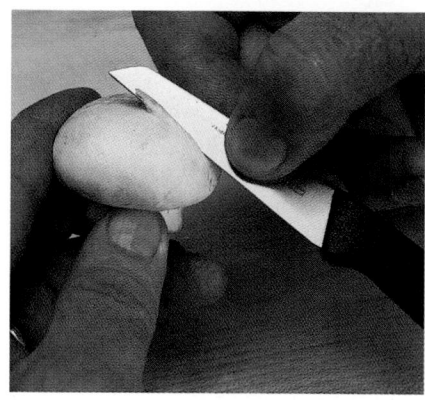

(1) Begin cutting groove, drawing the blade smoothly over the cap.

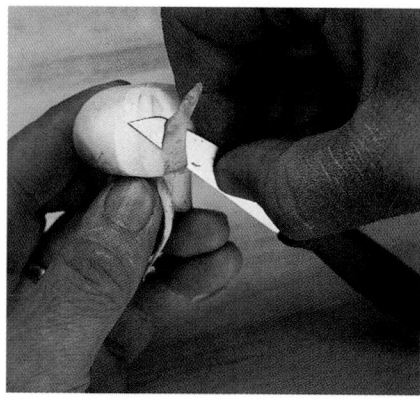

(2) Continue cutting grooves around the caps.

(3) Trim the stem away.

FIGURE 6-17
Cutting a Cornichon into a Fan

Fluting

This technique (see Figure 6-16) takes some practice to master, but the result makes an attractive garnish. It is customarily used on mushrooms. The method is as follows:

1. Hold the mushroom between the guiding hand's thumb and forefinger. Place the blade of a paring knife at an angle against the mushroom cap center. Rest the thumb of the cutting hand on the mushroom and use it to brace the knife.

2. Rotate the knife toward the cap edge, to cut a shallow groove. At the same time the knife blade is cutting, the guiding hand turns the mushroom in the opposite direction.

3. Turn the mushroom slightly and repeat the cutting steps. Continue until the entire cap is fluted. The trimmings should be pulled away.

4. Trim away the stem.

Fanning

The fan (see Figure 6-17) cut uses one basic, easy-to-master cut to produce complicated-looking garnishes. It is used on both raw and cooked foods, such as pickles, strawberries, peach halves, zucchini, avocados, and other somewhat pliable vegetables and fruits. The method is as follows:

1. Leaving the stem end intact, make a series of parallel vertical slices through the item.

cutters, ripple cutters, and box graters. Be sure to read any instructions that come with special cutters and use all the safety guards that are available.

A swivel-bladed peeler can also be used to create special cuts, such as curled or shaved Parmesan to top carpaccio or Caesar salads. Parisienne scoops (melon ballers) can also be used to prepare balls of varying sizes.

FIGURE 6-18 Dicing an Onion

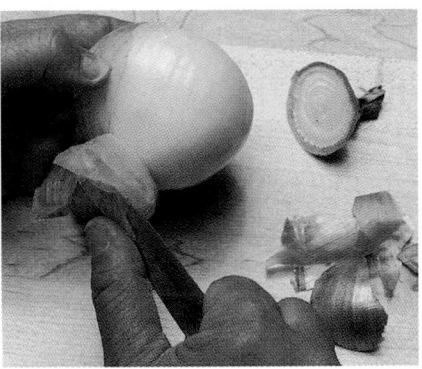

(1) Peel away the skin, leaving root end intact.

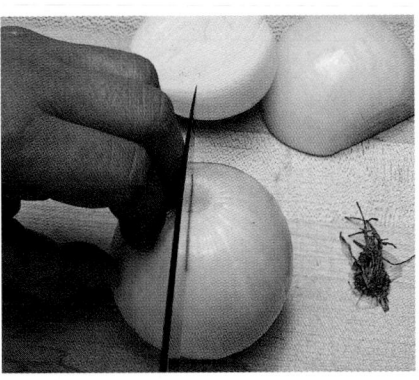

(2) Halve the onion from end to end.

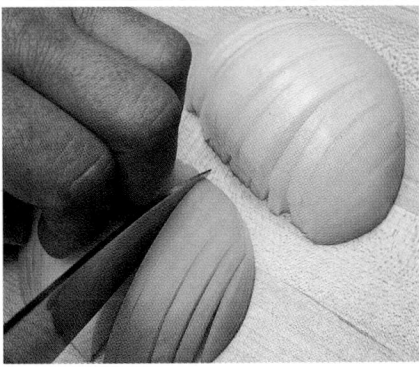

(3) Make a series of parallel cuts, leaving root end intact.

(4) Make horizontal cuts parallel to work surface

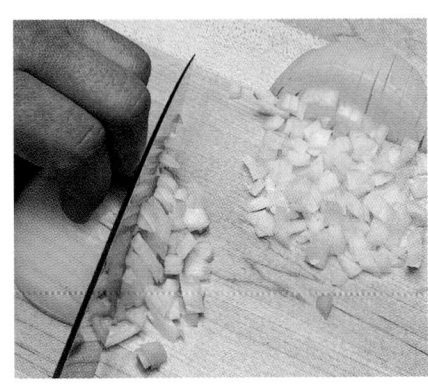

(5) Cut through onion, producing even dice.

2. Spread the cut item into a fan shape.

Waffle/Gaufrette

In order to make *gaufrette* cuts, you will need a mandolin. Potatoes, sweet potatoes, beets, and other large, relatively solid foods can be made into this cut. The blades are set so that the first pass of the vegetable doesn't actually cut away a slice, but only makes grooves. The second pass, made at a 90-degree turn, makes a crosshatch pattern, as well as slicing away the first cut.

Advance Preparation Techniques for Certain Vegetables

The number of ingredients that need to be on hand for a smooth service period will vary. Some menus will require an extensive mise en place setup, including tomato concassé, minced herbs, roasted peppers, plumped sun-dried tomatoes, and other ingredients. The steps involved in preparing foods for cutting or other applications are discussed by type below.

Onions

Onions are among the most indispensable ingredients in any kitchen. They can be cut into a variety of shapes and sizes. It is best to cut onions as close as possible to the time you need them. As cut onions sit, they take on a strong, sulfurous odor.

Peeling and Dicing an Onion

Because onions grow in layers, they require a special technique, instead of that used on solid foods. The method is as follows:

1. Use a paring knife to remove the stem end. Peel off the skin and underlying layer, if it contains brown spots. Trim the root end but leave it intact.

2. Halve the onion lengthwise through the root. Lay it cut-side down and make a series of evenly spaced, parallel, lengthwise cuts with the tip of a chef's knife, again leaving the root end intact. The closer the cuts, the finer the dice will be.

FIGURE 6-19　Peeling and Mashing Garlic

(1) Breaking the skin, using the flat side of a chef's knife.

(2) Pulling away the skin.

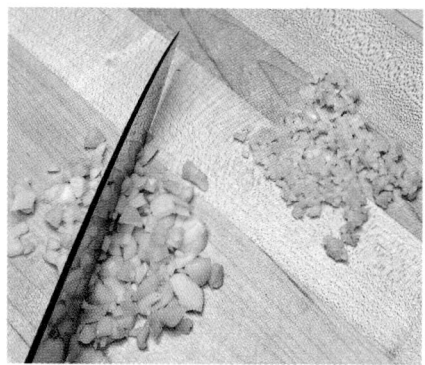

(3) Chopping the cloves into progressively smaller dice.

(4) Hold the blade almost flat to mash the garlic to a paste.

(5) The technique used to mince shallots is similar to that for onions.

ingredients should be cut and used as close as possible to cooking time. In addition to having a better flavor, they are safer. Chopped garlic and shallots that are allowed to sit at room temperature can become infected with potentially harmful pathogens.

Peeling and Mashing Garlic and Shallots

Mashed or minced shallots and garlic are required in many preparations—for example, as a component in the aromatic bed for shallow-poached items, or in the reduction used to flavor emulsion sauces. It is important to have enough prepared to last through a service period. To prevent bacterial growth, store uncooked, minced shallots or garlic covered in oil under refrigeration. The method is as follows:

1. To loosen the skin, crush the garlic clove or shallot bulb between the knife blade's flat side and the cutting board, using the heel of the hand. Peel off the skin and remove the root end and any brown spots.

2. Mince the clove or bulb fairly fine, or coarsely chop, as for herbs. (If desired, sprinkle the garlic or shallot with salt before mincing. This makes mashing easier by providing abrasion and absorbing excess juice and oil.)

3. Make two or three horizontal cuts parallel to the work surface, from the onion's stem end toward the root end, but do not cut all the way through.

4. Make even, crosswise cuts with a chef's knife, all the way through, from stem to root end.

See Figure 6-18 for photos illustrating the method for peeling and dicing an onion.

Aromatic combinations that include onions are explained in the section on Basic Aromatic and Flavoring Combinations, later in this chapter.

Garlic and Shallots

Garlic and shallots can be purchased already chopped, but many chefs feel strongly that these

3. Hold the knife at an angle and use the cutting edge to mash the garlic or shallot against the cutting board. Repeat this step until the item is mashed to a paste. *Note:* Large quantities may be minced in a food processor.

4. To hold, place in a jar, cover with a layer of oil, and refrigerate.

See Figure 6-19 for photos illustrating the method for peeling and mashing garlic and shallots.

Roasting Garlic and Shallots

The flavor of garlic and shallots becomes rich, sweet, and smoky after roasting. This technique is quite popular, and roasted garlic can be found as a component of marinades, glazes, and vinaigrettes, as well as a spread for grilled breads. The method is as follows:

1. Place the unpeeled head of garlic or shallot bulbs in a small pan or sizzler platter. Some chefs like to place them on a bed of salt. The salt holds the heat, roasting the garlic quickly and producing a dryer texture in the finished product.

2. Roast at a moderate temperature until the garlic or shallots are quite soft. Any juices that run from the garlic or shallots should be browned. The aroma should be sweet and pleasing, with no hints of harshness or sulfur.

Leeks

One of the biggest concerns when working with leeks is removing every trace of dirt. A leek grows in layers, trapping grit and sand between each layer (see Figure 6-20). Careful rinsing is essential.

The stringy roots of a leek should be trimmed away, but its end should be left intact. Most of the dark green leaves are cut away as well. The leek is then slit along its length, leaving the root end still intact, if desired. Rinse under running water until there is no dirt remaining.

Tomatoes

Fresh and canned tomatoes are used in a number of dishes. When you use fresh tomatoes, you will often prefer to cut them into *concassé*. This term indicates that the tomato has been peeled, seeded, and then chopped. Canned whole tomatoes may also be seeded and chopped, but they are normally peeled before canning.

Roasting is another advance preparation technique that can be used. While the flavor is deeper and more intense than that of fresh or canned tomatoes, it is not so rich as that of sun-dried tomatoes. For directions regarding the proper use of sun-dried tomatoes (and other dried fruits and vegetables), refer to the next section of this chapter.

Preparing Tomato Concassé

Tomato concassé is required in the preparation or finishing of a number of different sauces and dishes. If required, it should be made in advance, but only enough to last through a single service period. Once peeled and chopped, tomatoes will begin to lose some of their flavor and texture. The

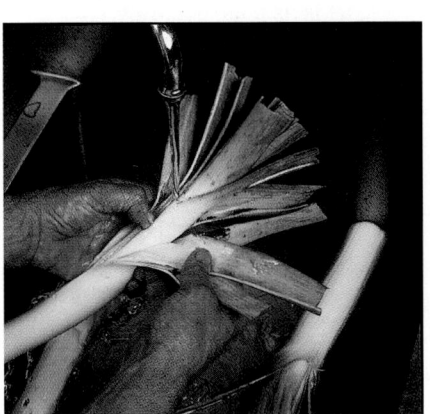

FIGURE 6-20
Cleaning Leeks
Under Running
Water

FIGURE 6-21
Submerging
Tomtoes in Ice
Water to Stop
Cooking

same blanching and peeling method used for tomatoes is also used for peaches and apricots. The method is as follows:

1. Cut an "X" into the bottom of the tomato. Some chefs also like to cut out the stem at this point. Others prefer to wait until the tomato has already been blanched.

2. Bring a pot of water to a rolling boil. Drop the tomatoes into the water. After 10 to 30 seconds (depending on the tomatoes' age and ripeness), remove them with a slotted spoon, skimmer, or spider. Immediately plunge them into very cold or ice water. Pull away the skin.

3. Halve each tomato crosswise at its widest point and gently squeeze out the seeds. (Plum tomatoes are more easily seeded by cutting lengthwise.)

4. Coarsely chop or cut the flesh into dice or julienne, as desired.

See Figure 6-21 for a step in the method for preparing tomato concassé.

Roasting Tomatoes

Roasted tomatoes (sometimes referred to as "oven-dried") can be made by either halving or slicing ripe tomatoes (see Figure 6-22). They can be used to replace sun-dried tomatoes in some dishes. The method is as follows:

1. Core the tomato and cut it into halves or slices.

2. Coat lightly with oil, and add seasonings and aromatics as desired. Salt, pepper, fresh or dried

FIGURE 6-22
Roasted Tomatoes

herbs, plain or infused oils, chopped garlic, or shallots are all good choices.

3. Roast the tomatoes until they are browned and have a rich "roasted" aroma.

Sweet Peppers and Chilies

Peppers and chilies are used in dishes from cuisines as diverse as those of Central and South America, Japan and other Asian countries, Spain, and Hungary. As the interest in chilies and peppers has grown, many special varieties, both fresh and dried, have become available. For more information about working with dried chilies, refer to the next section of this chapter.

Seeding and Cutting Peppers

Make a cut around the stem end of the pepper and then halve the pepper from top to bottom. Pull or cut away the seeds. If you are working with very

FIGURE 6-23 Seeding and Filleting Peppers and Chilis

(1) Cut away both ends, halve, and cut away seeds and stems. Reserve trim for other uses.

(2) Cut flesh away from skin before dicing, a process known as "filleting."

(3) Wear gloves to protect skin when working with chilis.

FIGURE 6-24 Roasting and Peeling Peppers

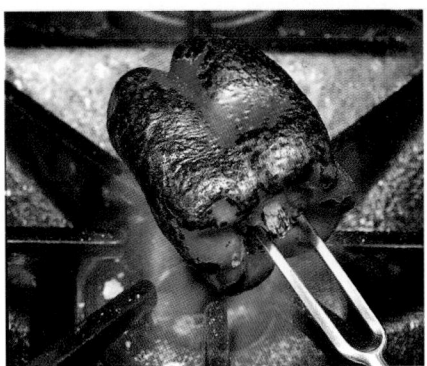

(1) Turn peppers in a gas flame until charred.

(2) Wrap in plastic to allow skin to steam.

(3) Remove skin, using a paring knife if necessary.

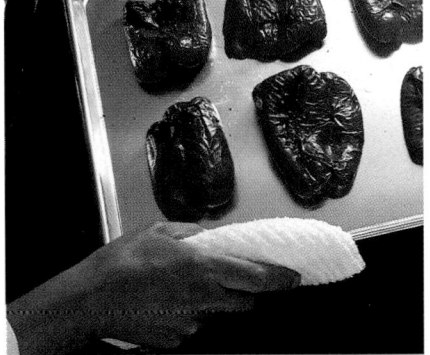

(4) Roast large batches in a very hot oven on a sheet pan.

(5) Once charred, cover with an inverted roasting pan to steam.

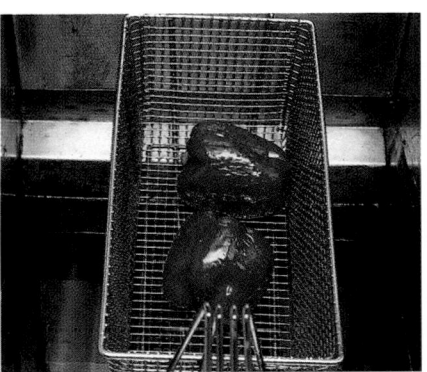

(6) Blister peppers by dropping into hot oil.

hot chilies, you may want to use plastic gloves to protect your skin.

Chilies retain a good deal of their heat in the seeds, ribs, and blossom ends. You can control the degree of heat by adjusting how much, if any, of these parts of the chili you add to a dish.

You can make very regular cuts, even julienne or dice, by "filleting" the pepper before cutting. Cut away the top and bottom of the pepper. Cut the pepper from top to bottom and open it out flat to create an even rectangle. Slice away the flesh from the skin, if desired, and then cut into neat julienne or dice. Reserve any edible scraps to use in coulis or to flavor broths, stews, or court bouillons.

See Figure 6-23 for photos illustrating the method for seeding and cutting peppers.

Roasting and Peeling Peppers

There are four basic methods for peeling peppers. The first method does not roast the pepper, so its sweet, fresh flavor is not changed. The remaining three versions actually cook the pepper. Roasting and grilling peppers make it easy to remove their skin, and also give them a special flavor. See Figure 6-24 for photos illustrating method of peeling peppers.

Peeling with a Swivel Peeler This method is used when peeled, raw peppers are needed.

• Section the pepper with a knife, cutting along the folds to expose the unpeeled skin.

• Remove the core, seeds, and ribs and peel with a swivel peeler.

Peeling Charred Peppers This technique is used to roast and peel small quantities.

• Hold the pepper over the flame of a gas burner with tongs or a kitchen fork or place the pepper on a grill. Turn the pepper and roast it until the surface is evenly charred.

• Place in a plastic or paper bag or under an inverted bowl to steam the skin loose.

• When the pepper is cool enough to handle, remove the charred skin, using a paring knife if necessary.

Peeling Oven- or Broiler-Roasted Peppers This method is used for larger quantities.

• Halve the peppers and remove stems and seeds. Place cut-side down on an oiled sheet pan.

• Place in a very hot oven or under a broiler. Roast or broil until evenly charred.

• Remove from the oven or broiler and cover immediately, using an inverted sheet pan. This will steam the peppers, making the skin easier to remove.

• Peel, using a paring knife if necessary.

Peeling Deep-Fried Peppers This is a quick method for blistering small quantities.

• Using tongs or the double basket method, submerge the peppers in oil that has been heated to 325°F (165°C).

• Deep-fry the peppers for about a minute, until they are blistered all over. The peppers usually will not brown dramatically.

• Remove from the deep fat, drain, and let cool.

• Peel away the skin, using a paring knife if necessary.

Mushrooms

Fresh mushrooms may require some careful cleaning before they are sliced or minced. When-

ever practical, the preferred method is to use a clean cloth or soft brush to wipe away any dirt. Large quantities can be very quickly rinsed in cold water, then drained well on layers of absorbent toweling. Avoid any prolonged contact with water as you clean or hold mushrooms, however. They absorb liquids quickly, and an excess of moisture will cause them to deteriorate rapidly.

Some mushrooms should have the stems removed. Shiitakes, for example, have very tough, woody stems that are rarely served. The stems should be cut away from the cap (see Figure 6-25).

Sliced and minced mushrooms will begin to weep almost as soon as they are cut. When you need cut mushrooms (as a garnish for a sauce, to sauté or grill, or to prepare duxelles), try to cook them as soon as possible after they are cut. Avoid cutting more than you need at a given time.

Leafy Greens

Salad greens, cooking greens, and herbs are often quite sandy and gritty. Removing all traces of

FIGURE 6-26 Preparing Greens

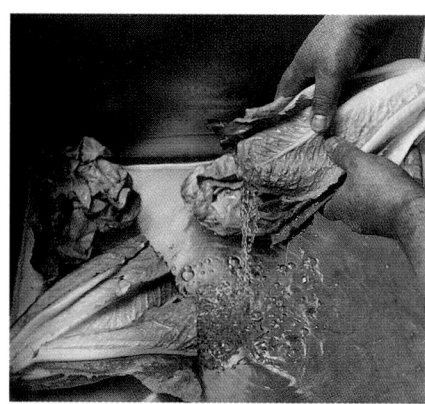

(1) Rinsing lettuces in cold water (romaine and Boston lettuces are shown here).

FIGURE 6-25 Removing Tough Stems from Shiitake Mushrooms

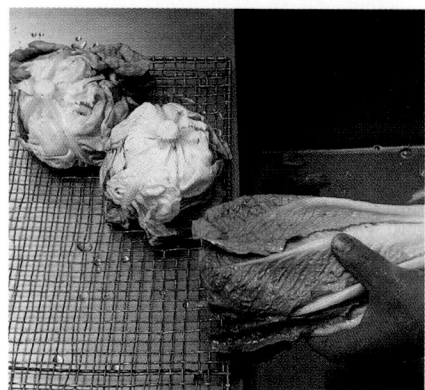

(2) Draining excess water away from greens.

(Figure 6-26 continued on facing page)

FIGURE 6-26   *(continued)*

(3) Removing tough cores from romaine lettuce leaves.

(7) Draining in a colander.

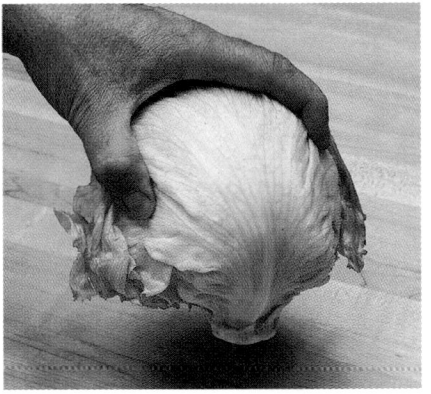

(4) Rapping core of iceberg lettuce on work surface to loosen it.

(8) Removing heavy stems.

(5) Pulling out the core.

(9) Salad greens ready to spin dry.

(6) Rinsing leafy greens (spinach shown here).

(10) Greens after spinning, ready to dress.

dirt from them is a very important part of the mise en place for the pantry and hot line. Greens that are raised hydroponically, prepared mesclun mixes, and prerinsed spinach may need only a quick plunge or rinse with cool water. Other leafy greens should be cleaned as follows:

1. Fill a sink with cool water. Separate or loosen heading greens and dip them into the water. Plunging them in and out of the water will loosen the sand.

2. Lift them out of the water and drain the sink. Repeat the process until there are no signs of grit remaining in the water.

3. Once rinsed, allow the greens to drain briefly and, if necessary, spin them dry using a salad spinner.

To remove the core from iceberg or Boston lettuce, gently rap or push the core down onto a work surface. This will generally break the core away from the leaves. For tighter heads, you may need to use a paring knife to cut out the core.

Loose heads and "bunching" greens such as Romaine or frisée will separate into individual leaves easily. Trim the coarse ribs or stem ends away if necessary. Spinach stems can be pulled away easily.

Refer to Figure 6-26 for photos illustrating preparation of leafy greens.

Fresh Herbs

The procedure for refreshing or rinsing herbs is the same as that described above for leafy greens. Many chefs feel that mincing or cutting fresh herbs is an acceptable practice, as long as it is not done too far in advance. Others, however, prefer to tear or snip herbs to avoid bruising them. Figure 6-27 illustrates the different methods for mincing fresh herbs.

Citrus Fruits

Citrus fruits, including oranges, lemons, limes, and grapefruit, are used to add flavor and color to dishes. They are also served as a functional garnish

FIGURE 6-27   Working with Fresh Herbs

(1) Mincing parsley with scissors.

(2) Tearing basil into small pieces by hand.

with some foods—for instance, a slice of lime with a Cuban-style black bean soup or a wedge of lemon with a broiled fish.

Although citrus fruits keep well, be sure that the fruit you select is not bruised or softened. Before juicing citrus fruits, you should allow them to come to room temperature if possible. Roll the fruit under the palm of your hand on a cutting board or other work surface before juicing to break some of the membranes. This helps to release more juice. Remember to strain out seeds and pith before using the juice, either by covering the citrus fruit with cheesecloth before squeezing it, or by straining it after juicing. There are numerous special tools to juice citrus fruits including reamers, extractors, hand-held and electric juicers.

Zesting Citrus Fruit

The zest, the outer portion of a citrus fruit's peel or rind, is used to add color, texture, and fla-

FIGURE 6-28 Zesting Citrus

(1) Using a zester.

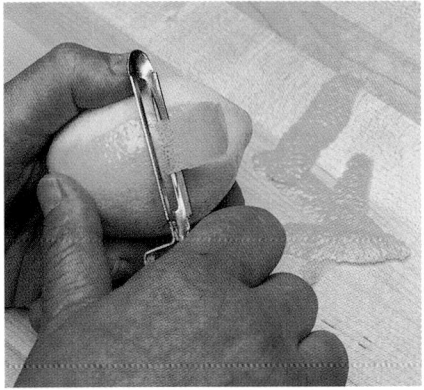

(2) Using a vegetable peeler to remove strips.

(3) Cutting strips into julienne.

FIGURE 6-29 Roasting Chestnuts

(1) Chestnuts ready to come out of the oven.

(2) Peeling chestnuts.

vor to various preparations. The zest includes *only* the skin's brightly colored part, which contains much of the fruit's flavorful and aromatic volatile oils. It does not include the underlying white pith, which has a bitter taste. See Figure 6-28 for photos illustrating the method for zesting citrus fruit. The method is as follows:

1. Use a paring knife, swivel-bladed peeler, or zester to remove only the peel's colored portion.

2. If julienne or grated zest is called for, use a chef's knife to cut or mince the zest. Grated zest can also be prepared using the fine holes of a box grater.

Chestnuts

To peel chestnuts, cut an "X" with a paring knife in the flat side of the nut. Then, they can be either boiled or roasted just until the skin begins to pull away. Work in small batches, keeping the chestnuts warm, and pull and cut away the tough outer skin.

Cooked chestnuts can be left whole, puréed, sweetened, or glazed.

See Figure 6-29 for photos illustrating the method for roasting and peeling chestnuts.

Eggplant

Eggplant is available in a range of shapes and colors, from small white balls to enormous purple-

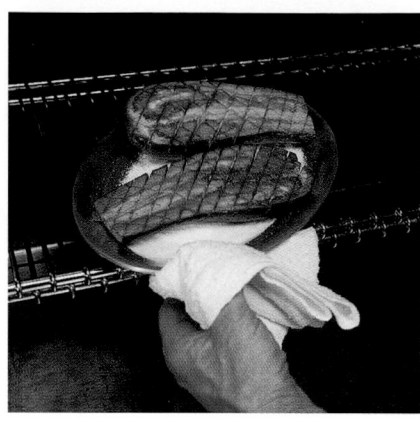

FIGURE 6-30
Roasting Eggplant

black specimens. For the best results, whether you intend to roast, pan-fry, or grill eggplant, be sure the vegetable is properly handled. Eggplant will discolor once cut, so be sure to work quickly.

Salting Eggplant

Large eggplants can become bitter, as can large cucumbers, zucchini, and summer squash. To reduce bitterness, many chefs believe that eggplant (as well as cucumbers and summer squash) should be salted as follows:

1. Slice the ends from the eggplant and discard, or slice it in half from one end to the other (depending on the size of the eggplant). Slice or score the eggplant as required by recipe or desired result.

2. Scatter salt liberally over the eggplant, tossing slices to coat them evenly.

3. Place the eggplant in a colander or perforated hotel pan, and (optional) weight the eggplant to help expel its juices. Generally speaking, a few hours is sufficient to draw off any bitterness.

4. Rinse the eggplant well to remove the salt, dry thoroughly, and then proceed with cooking.

Roasting Eggplant

Eggplant responds well to roasting (see Figure 6-30). The flesh becomes extremely soft with an appetizing flavor and aroma. To prepare the eggplant for roasting, proceed as follows:

1. Slice the eggplant in half.

2. Score it in a diamond pattern, cutting through most of the flesh, but leaving the skin intact.

3. If desired, rub the cut surface with some olive oil.

4. Roast the eggplant cut-side down until softened but not browned.

5. Turn the eggplant cut-side up and continue to roast until the flesh is very soft. It is now ready to purée. If desired, the flesh can be strained after puréeing.

Corn

Sweet corn should be husked and the silk removed just before cooking. To remove the kernels,

FIGURE 6-31   Cutting Corn from the Cob

(1) Use a chef's knife to cut kernels away, before or after cooking.

(2) To "milk" corn, first score rows with a knife.

(3) Use the back of the knife to scrape out the pulp and milk.

FIGURE 6-32   Preparing Potatoes

(1) Pierce with a kitchen fork before baking, to allow steam to vent.

(2) Dry boiled or steamed potatoes after draining for best texture and flavor.

FIGURE 6-33   Preparing an Artichoke

(1) Trim away both ends of the arti choke.

(2) Use scissors to cut away the barbs from ends of leaves.

hold the ear upright and cut down the rows. To "milk" the corn, proceed as follows:

1. Score the rows of kernels with a knife.

2. Use the back of a knife, spoon, or butter curler to scrape out the flesh.

See Figure 6-31 for photos illustrating the method for milking corn.

Potatoes

When you peel or cut potatoes, the exposure to air will cause them to discolor quickly. To prevent this, place the cut potatoes in a container of cool water. If you will be frying the potatoes, you must take the time to blot them dry on absorbent toweling. This will dramatically reduce the splattering that occurs when the potatoes come in contact with hot oil. It will also prolong the life of the oil in deep-fat fryers, since excess moisture encourages fats and oils to break down more quickly.

Baked potatoes can blow apart in the oven, if they are not pierced. Piercing them with the tip of a paring knife or kitchen fork allows the steam to escape before enough pressure builds up to cause an explosion. Baking potatoes on a bed of salt, or rubbing the skin lightly with oil, are methods recommended by some chefs to encourage the development of a crisp skin and delicate, fluffy interior.

Whenever potatoes are boiled or steamed, it is a good idea to dry them briefly before serving them, or going on to make purées, salads, or hash browns. This drives off any excess moisture, improving both flavor and texture. To dry potatoes, place them in a pot or on a sheet pan, and then into the oven or over low heat until the potatoes look dry and "mealy."

See Figure 6-32 for photos illustrating the method for piercing and drying potatoes.

Artichokes

Artichokes are related to thistles and need to have the hairy "choke" removed before they are served. This can be done before or after cooking. Either spread the leaves open and scoop out the

FIGURE 6-35   Coring an Apple

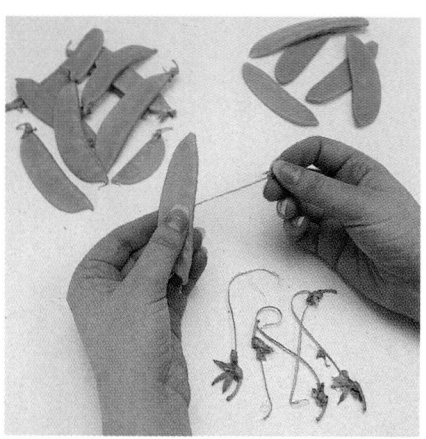

FIGURE 6-34
Pulling Away
Strings from Snow
Peas

(1) Use an apple corer to remove core.

(2) The apple is ready to stuff, bake, or poach.

purple and white leaves, or cut the artichoke in half and then remove the choke.

To "turn" the artichoke bottom, cut away the leaves and stem, and scoop out the choke. This will leave a dish-shaped portion of the artichoke, referred to as the bottom. If the artichoke was not cooked before the leaves and choke are cut away, cook the bottom immediately in lightly acidulated water or rub it with lemon juice to prevent discoloration.

To prepare a whole artichoke for service, trim away the sharp tips of the leaves and the stem as follows:

1. Use a sharp knife to cut away the very top and the stem of the artichoke. Rub the cut surface with lemon to prevent discoloration.

2. Use kitchen shears to snip off the barbs that remain on the leaves. (The choke, visible in Figure 6-33 as the light purple area near the center of the choke, can be scooped out now if desired.)

3. (Optional) Use twine to hold the artichoke's shape. A piece of lemon will give additional protection against any discoloration. Or, lemon slices or juice can be added to the cooking water.

Snow and Sugar Snap Peas

Snow and sugar snap peas have a rather tough string that runs along one seam. This string should

be removed before the peas are cooked. Snap off the stem end and pull (see Figure 6-34). The string will come away easily.

Asparagus

Very slender young asparagus may need no further preparation than simply a trim to remove the very ends of the stalk, and a quick rinse. However, it is often a good idea to trim the stalk a little more and peel the stem partially to remove the "fingernails," which can be a little tough and unpleasant to eat.

As asparagus matures, the stem becomes tough. To remove the woody portion, you can bend the stem gently until it snaps. Use a special asparagus peeler or swivel-bladed peeler. Peeling the stem part-way up the stem not only enhances palatability, it also makes it easier to cook the asparagus evenly, so that the stem and tips are done at the same time.

Asparagus may be tied into loose bundles to make it easier to remove them from boiling water when they are properly blanched or cooked. Don't tie them too tightly, or make the bundles more than a few inches in diameter. Otherwise, the center stalks will not cook properly.

Apples

Apples, as well as pears, peaches, and bananas, will discolor when they are exposed to air. To prevent this, toss them in water that has been acidulated by adding a little lemon juice or vinegar. There shouldn't be so much acid that it overwhelms the flavor of the fruit, however.

To remove the core from apples before baking or slicing them, you can use an apple corer, as shown here in Figure 6-35.

Additional Basic Mise en Place and Appareil

In addition to vegetables and fruits, the chef must also have other ingredients on hand, including thickeners such as those described here. Mixtures of ingredients that are themselves used as components in a dish are referred to as *appareils*. Thickeners are not the only examples of appareils. Aromatic combinations such as those described in the next section are also considered appareils, as are batters, basic sauces, stuffing mixtures, and marinades.

FIGURE 6-36
Dried Fruits Before Plumping (background) and After (foreground).

Working with Dried Fruits and Vegetables

Dried fruits and vegetables have always been an important part of many cuisines. Drying foods makes them suitable for long-term storage. It also concentrates flavors. Today, there are still some vegetables and fruits that are only briefly available as fresh ingredients—morels, for instance. Throughout the rest of the year, they can only be had in a preserved form.

We also enjoy the special flavors of dried chilies, mushrooms, tomatoes, and fruits such as apples, cherries, and raisins, even though we may often be able to purchase those same ingredients fresh. To get the most from these ingredients, recipes may often call for "plumped" or rehydrated dried fruits, vegetables, and mushrooms. The method is as follows:

1. Check the dried ingredient first, to remove any obvious debris or seriously blemished, moldy specimens.

2. Place it in a bowl or other container and add enough boiling or very hot liquid (water, wine, fruit juices, or broth can all be used) to cover.

3. Let the dried ingredient steep in the hot water for several minutes, until softened and plumped as shown in Figure 6-36.

4. Pour off the liquid, reserving it if desired for use in another preparation. If necessary, the liquid can be strained through a coffee filter or cheesecloth to remove any debris.

Dried chilies may be toasted in the same manner as dried spices, nuts, and seeds, by tossing them in a dry skillet over moderate heat. They may also be passed repeatedly through a flame until toasted and softened. The pulp and seeds are then scraped from the skin, or the whole chili may be used, according to individual recipes.

Soaking Beans

Most beans, with a few notable exceptions (lentils, split peas, and black-eyed peas), are easier to prepare and produce a better-quality finished dish if they are allowed to soak. The skins soften slightly, allowing for more rapid and even cook-

FIGURE 6-37
Beans Before Soaking (on right) and After (on left).

ing. Figure 6-37 shows the change in volume after soaking. (For information about beans and soaking times, refer to the bean cookery table in Appendix 2.)

Rinse and sort beans to remove dirt, stones, and moldy specimens. There are two methods commonly used, the long-and quick-soak methods.

The Long-Soak Method

• Place the rinsed and sorted beans in a container and add enough cool water to cover them by a few inches.

• Let the beans soak for the suggested period (time will vary depending on the bean, from 4 to 24 hours).

• Drain the beans and cook as directed.

FIGURE 6-38
Preparing Croutons in the Oven.

Quick-Soak Method

• Place the rinsed and sorted beans in a pot, and add enough water to cover by a few inches. Bring the water to a simmer.

• Remove the pot from direct heat and cover. Let the beans steep for 1 hour.

• Drain and continue cooking as directed by recipe.

Making Bread Crumbs

Bread crumbs may be "dry" or "fresh." Fresh bread crumbs (known as *mie de pain*) are prepared by grating or processing a finely textured bread, such as 1- or 2-day-old hard rolls. Dry bread crumbs can be prepared from slightly stale bread that has been additionally dried or toasted in a warm oven.

Bread crumbs are used as a binder, topping, crust, and as part of the standard breading mise en place.

FIGURE 6-39   Toasting Pine Nuts

(1) Pine nuts in a dry skillet, just starting to brown.

(2) Tossing the nuts to ensure even browning.

Making Croutons

Croutons are commonly used as a garnish for soups and salads. Large croutons, known as rusks, are made to act as the base for sautéed or grilled meats, a reflection of an earlier dining practice, when plates were actually slabs of bread, intended for consumption once they had been well dampened with juices and sauces from the meal.

To prepare croutons, cut bread (crusts removed or not, as desired) into the desired size. You may want to rub or toss the cubes or slices lightly with oil or clarified butter. Seasonings such as salt and pepper, chopped herbs and garlic, or grated Parmesan cheese may also be added.

There are a few different ways to finish croutons. You may bake them in a moderate oven until lightly browned (see Figure 6-38). Turn them from time to time and check them frequently to avoid scorching. Smaller quantities may be tossed in a dry or lightly oiled skillet. Deep-fried croutons will not hold long and tend to become quite oily.

FIGURE 6-40 Making a Slurry Using Wine

(1) Adding wine (a burgundy used here) to arrowroot.

(2) The properly diluted arrowroot, ready to use.

Good croutons should be light in color, relatively greaseless, and appropriately seasoned.

Toasting Nuts and Seeds

Toasting nuts, seeds, and spices improves their flavor, as long as they are not allowed to scorch. To toast small quantities, use a dry skillet (cast iron is an excellent choice, but other materials will also work well). Heat it over direct heat and add the nuts, seeds, or spices (see Figure 6-39). Toss or stir frequently, stopping just as a good color and aroma are achieved. Pour the nuts, seeds, or spices out into a cool container and spread into a thin layer to stop any further browning.

Large quantities can be toasted in a moderate oven. Spread the nuts, seeds, or spices out on a dry sheet pan and toast just until a pleasant aroma is apparent. The oils in nuts, seeds, and spices can scorch quickly so be sure to check frequently. Stir them often to encourage even browning. Be sure to transfer nuts and spices toasted in the oven to a cool container also, so that they don't become scorched from residual heat in the pan.

Thickeners

Thickeners are added to liquids to give a sauce, soup, stew, or braise additional body. The type of thickener you choose will have a definite effect on the overall quality of the finished dish. Some thickeners, such as roux and gelatin, require meticulous care in order to achieve the best results. Others, including beurre manié and slurries, are less demanding in terms of the length of time required for preparation, as well as the "trickiness" of properly incorporating them into a liquid. Recipes for specific thickeners can be found in Part IV, Chapter 13.

Slurries

A slurry is a starch (arrowroot, cornstarch, or rice flour) dissolved in a cool liquid. The mixture should have the consistency of heavy cream (see Figure 6-40). The method is as follows:

1. Blend the starch thoroughly with one to two times its volume of cold liquid. If the slurry has

stood for a while, be sure to stir it well before mixing it into the hot liquid, as the starch tends to settle.

2. Bring the hot liquid to a simmer or low boil.

3. Gradually add the slurry, stirring or whisking constantly to prevent lumping and scorching.

4. Bring the liquid back to a boil and cook just until the sauce reaches the desired thickness and clarity.

Sauces, soups, and other dishes thickened with slurries have limited holding periods. Be sure to check them periodically for quality if they must be held in a steam table. Since slurries work quickly, it is best to thicken items as needed, in batches throughout service whenever possible.

Beurre Manié

A French term for kneaded butter, this is a mixture of equal amounts (by weight) of softened whole butter and flour. Sometimes called "uncooked roux," it is used to quickly thicken sauces and stews. Beurre manié produces a thin to medium consistency and a glossy texture. It is traditionally used in vegetable dishes (peas *bonne femme*, for example) and fish stews (known as *matelotes*). The method is as follows:

1. Allow the butter to soften until it is pliable but not melted—it should still be cool and "plastic."

2. Add an equal weight of flour and work to a smooth paste. Use a wooden spoon when working with small amounts; the friction of the wood against the bowl helps to work the butter and flour together quickly. When making large quantities, use an electric mixer with a paddle attachment.

3. If the beurre manié will not be used right away, store it, tightly wrapped, in the refrigerator.

Roux

Prepared by cooking together a fat and a flour. This mixture is often prepared in advance in large quantities for use as needed. Butter is the most common fat, but chicken fat, vegetable oils, or fats rendered from roasts may also be used. Different

FIGURE 6-41   Preparing Roux

(1) Adding flour to heated clarified butter.

(2) Cooking over moderate heat.

(3) Proper texture.

(4) Blond, brown, and dark brown rouxs.

fats will have a subtle influence on the finished dish's flavor.

The standard proportion of fat to flour is one to one by weight, but depending on the types of fat and flour used, this proportion may need to be adjusted slightly. Cooked roux should be moist but not greasy. A common description is "like sand at low tide." There are four basic types of roux, differing according to the length of time they are cooked and the color of the finished roux:

- White roux
- Pale or blond roux
- Brown roux
- Dark brown or "black" roux

Preparing a Roux   The method for preparing a roux is as follows:

1. Melt the butter or other fat in a pan over moderate to low heat.

2. Add the flour and stir until smooth.

3. If necessary, add a small amount of flour to achieve the proper consistency.

4. Cook, stirring constantly, to the desired color. Roux should be glossy in appearance.

- White roux should be barely colored, or chalky.
- Pale or blond roux should be a golden straw color, with a slightly nutty aroma.
- Brown or black roux should be deep brown, with a strong nutty aroma.

5. If the roux will not be used right away, cool and store it, tightly wrapped, in the refrigerator.

See Figure 6-41 for photos illustrating the method for preparing a roux.

Large quantities of roux may be made in the oven in a rondeau or brazier. The fat is melted and the flour added as in the previous method. The pan is then placed in a moderate (350 to 375°F/175 to 190°C) oven and cooked to the desired color. It should be stirred occasionally during the cooking time.

A so-called "dry roux" may be prepared by gently toasting flour in the oven. This type of roux is often associated with certain Creole and Cajun dishes.

Combining Roux with Liquid   The method for combining a roux with liquid is as follows:

1. Be sure that the roux and liquid temperatures are different—hot liquid and cold roux or cold liquid and hot roux—to help prevent lumping. Add one to the other gradually and whip constantly to work out lumps.

2. Gradually return the soup or sauce to a boil, whisking occasionally.

3. Reduce the heat and simmer, stirring occasionally, for at least 20 minutes, to cook out the taste of the flour.

To test for the presence of starch, press a small amount of the sauce to the roof of the mouth with your tongue. It should not feel gritty or gluey. If it does, continue cooking until the starch is completely cooked out.

Liaison

A liaison is a mixture of egg yolks and cream that is used to both thicken and enrich sauces and soups. A liaison also adds flavor to a sauce or soup and gives it a smooth texture and golden color.

The basic ratio in a liaison is three parts cream to one part egg yolk, by weight. Sour cream or crème fraîche may be substituted for the heavy cream. A combination of 8 ounces (240 milliliters) heavy cream and three egg yolks is sufficient to thicken and enrich 24 ounces (720 milliliters) of liquid.

Liaisons are never added directly to boiling liquids. The heat could cause the yolks to scramble. To avoid this, some of the hot liquid is added to the liaison to raise its temperature gradually. This process is known as "tempering." For a more detailed description of tempering, refer to the section on basic techniques later in this chapter.

Gelatin

Gelatin is used to stabilize foams and thicken liquid-based mixtures that will be served cold. Approximately 2 ounces (75 grams) of any type of gelatin will thicken about 1 gallon (3.75 liters) of liquid. More gelatin will be required if the liquid contains sugar or acidic ingredients, which inhibit gelling. The method for preparing gelatin to add to other foods is as follows:

1. Soak the gelatin in cool liquid before using. This process, called "blooming," allows the gelatin to soften and to begin absorption of the liquid.

2. Melt the dissolved gelatin crystals. This may be done by placing the gelatin–liquid mixture over a warm water bath or by heating it in a microwave oven on a low-power setting. If the gelatin is to be combined with a hot liquid, it may be tempered with some or all of that liquid to melt the crystals.

3. Combine the dissolved gelatin with the liquid. Stir well to disperse throughout the mixture. Chill until the mixture is set.

Pâte à Choux

Pâte à choux, or cream puff dough, is the base for such desserts as profiteroles, éclairs, and Paris-brest. It is also combined with puréed potatoes in savory dishes such as *pommes dauphines* and as a base for savory soufflés. A step-by-step illustration of the procedure for making pâte à choux appears in Chapter 12. The recipes can be found in Part IV, Chapter 30.

Basic Aromatic and Flavoring Combinations

Various seasoning and flavoring ingredients, ranging from single items to more complicated mixtures, are used in many different preparations. Classic seasoning combinations include mirepoix, matignon, marinades, oignon piqué, and oignon brûlé. These combinations of aromatic vegetables, herbs, and spices are meant to enhance and support, not dominate, a dish's flavors. Recipes for these mixtures can be found in Part IV, Chapter 13. Certain basic techniques and ingredient proportions should be observed, as outlined in the following methods.

FIGURE 6-42   Preparing Spice Blends

(1) By hand using a mortar and pestle.

(2) Using a spice grinder.

Salt and Pepper

These two ingredients are so much a part of the final seasoning adjustment made to many dishes that they sometimes are considered a "given." To make it simple to use salt and pepper on the line, many line cooks like to have a mixture ready, either in a small bowl or shaker, to add to dishes.

The ratio of salt to pepper most commonly recommended is four parts salt to one part ground pepper, by volume. This recipe can be changed if kosher or sea salts are used, since they have a different flavor and degree of saltiness than ordinary table salt.

Spice Blends

You can purchase spice blends such as curry powder, garam masala, blackening spices, and chili powders already prepared. However, for customized blends and the freshest flavor, you may prefer to make your own. If desired, the spices can

FIGURE 6-43   White Mirepoix; Finely Cut Regular Mirepoix; and Coarsely Cut Regular Mirepoix

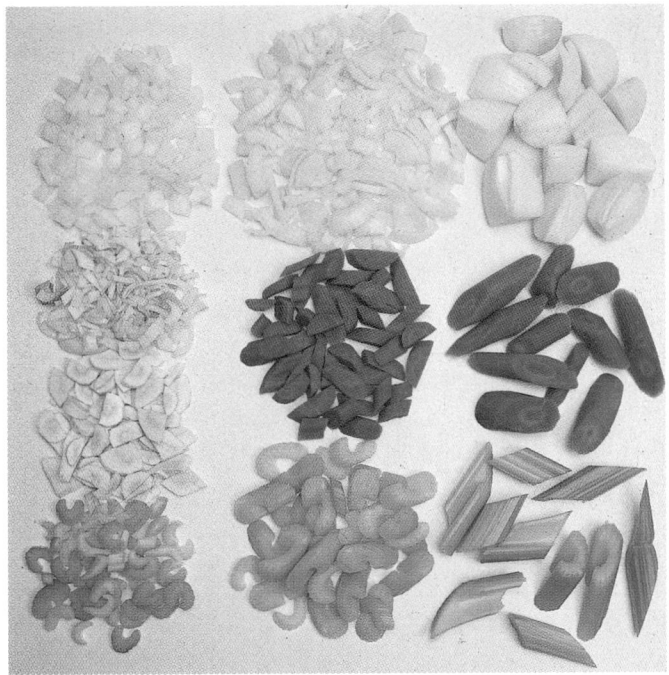

be lightly toasted in a skillet, just until they start to give off an odor.

They can be ground in a mortar and pestle, or in a spice grinder or coffee grinder reserved specifically for use with spices (see Figure 6-42).

Mirepoix

A combination of chopped aromatic vegetables, customarily onion, carrot, and celery, a *mirepoix* is used to flavor stocks, soups, braises, and stews (see Figure 6-43). The basic ratio of ingredients is two parts onion, one part carrot, and one part celery, by weight. When the mirepoix is not part of the finished dish, the vegetables, except the onions, do not have to be peeled.

The size of the cut will depend on how the mirepoix is to be used. For preparations with short cooking times, such as fish fumet, the mirepoix should be sliced or chopped small. For preparations with more than an hour of cooking time, such as brown stock, the vegetables may be cut into larger pieces or even left whole.

Other ingredients may be added to the mirepoix, depending on the needs of a specific recipe.

Leeks are often used in place of all or part of the onion. Other root vegetables, such as parsnips, may be used in addition to, or in place of, the carrots. Bacon and ham are sometimes included.

White Mirepoix

This combination replaces the carrots with parsnips. This is done to be sure that the finished sauce, stock, or soup will have a pale ivory or white color. Leeks may be used in combination with, or in place of, onions.

Matignon

Sometimes referred to as "edible mirepoix," this is intended as part of the finished dish. Consequently, the vegetables are peeled and cut in uniform dice. Diced ham or bacon is also included to enhance the flavor.

Matignons are commonly used in poêléed dishes, such as *poêléed capon*. The ratio of ingredients in a matignon generally is two parts carrot, one part celery, one part leek, one part onion, one part mushroom (optional), and one part pork product (ham or bacon). Various herbs and spices may be included as desired.

Bouquet Garni

Another combination of herbs and vegetables used to flavor stocks and other savory preparations is the *bouquet garni*, the French term for "bouquet of herbs." A bouquet garni is a combination of fresh vegetables and herbs that typically contains fresh thyme, parsley stems, a celery stalk, and a bay leaf, tied into a bundle.

When a bouquet garni has contributed adequate flavor (determined by tasting), it should be removed from the preparation and discarded. If a long end is left on the string used to tie up the bouquet garni, it can be attached to the pot handle. Then, it is easy to pull out the bouquet garni when you are ready to remove it.

See Figure 6-44 for photos illustrating mise en place and assembly for bouquet garni.

FIGURE 6-44   Preparing Bouquet Garni

  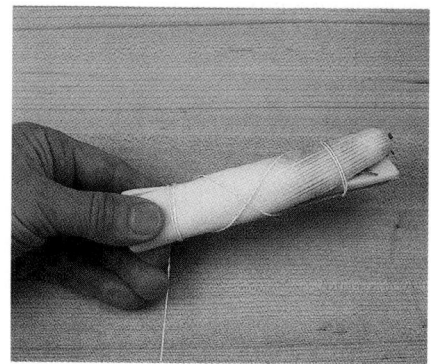

(1) Mise en place.

(2) Assemble by enclosing herbs in leek leaves.

(3) Tied into a bundle, ready to use.

FIGURE 6-45   Preparing a Standard Sachet d'Épices

(1) Mise en place in foreground, completed sachet in background.

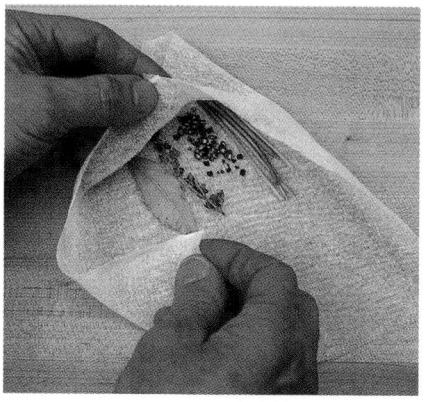

(2) Folding spices and herbs into cheesecloth.

FIGURE 6-46   Onion Piqué and Brûlé

(1) An onion is studded with bay leaf and cloves to prepare onion piqué.

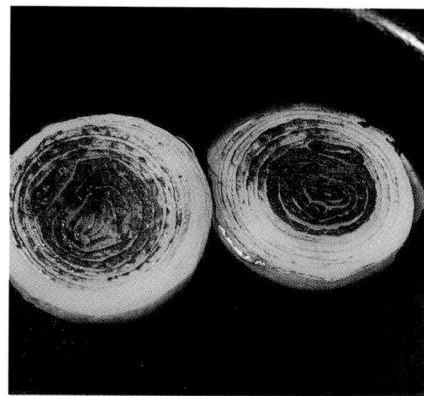

(2) An onion is charred in a dry skillet to prepare onion brûlé.

Sachet d'Épices

A standard *sachet d'épices,* French for "bag of spices," contains parsley stems, dried thyme, bay leaf, and cracked peppercorns in a cheesecloth bag as shown in Figure 6-45. As with the bouquet garni, it should be removed and discarded after enough flavor has been released.

Oignon Piqué and Oignon Brûlé

Both the *oignon piqué* (pricked or studded onion) and *oignon brûlé* (burnt onion) are flavoring ingredients based on whole, halved, or quartered onions (see Figure 6-46). An oignon piqué is made by studding an onion with a whole clove and a bay leaf. It is used to flavor béchamel sauce and some soups. An oignon brûlé is made by peeling an onion, halving it crosswise, and charring the cut edges on a flat top or in a skillet or griswold. Oignon brûlé is used in some stocks and consommés to provide a golden brown color.

Marinades

Originally, marinades were intended to both preserve and tenderize tough meats. These intensely flavored combinations were used to disguise the flavor of meats that had become "high"—meats we would no longer consider suitable or safe to serve our guests. In contemporary kitchens, they are more often used to add flavor to naturally tender meats, fish, and vegetables.

The three components of marinades are oils, acids, and aromatics (spices, herbs, and vegetables). Oils are used primarily to protect and preserve foods, either as they marinate or during cooking. Acids, such as vinegar, yogurt, wine, and citrus juices, change the food's texture. In some cases, it will make foods firmer, as happens when fish is marinated in lime juice to make ceviche. In others, it will break down connective fibers making foods seem more tender, as happens when beef is marinated in red wine for several days to make sauerbraten.

There are four different types of marinades, made from the three basic types of ingredients:

- Oil and acid marinades

- Oil and aromatic marinades

- Acid and aromatic marinades

- Dry marinades and rubs

Recipes for a variety of marinades can be found in Part IV, Chapter 13.

Liquid Marinades

Liquid marinades are used to soak foods before or after cooking, or as a means of cooking foods chemically, by denaturing the proteins in a food. Marinades made from oils and acids are typically used to add flavor and some moisture to foods.

They are prepared using the same ratio of oil to acid as a classic vinaigrette—three parts oil to one part acid. These marinades are often used as a preliminary step when grilling foods. Oil and spice marinades are used for the same purpose. Marinades that include acids and spices, and no oil, are used to flavor foods, as well as to chemically cook them as happens when preparing ceviche.

The ingredients should be selected according to the marinade's intended use. Select the oil, if any, and the acid carefully, plus the desired seasonings and aromatics. Almost any oil can be used, depending on the desired effect. Commonly used acidic ingredients include vinegar, fruit juice, wine, and beer. Aromatics or other flavoring combinations such as a mirepoix may be included.

Some marinades are cooked before use, others are not. In some cases, the marinade is used to flavor an accompanying sauce, or may itself become a dipping sauce.

To use a liquid marinade, the chef should:

1. Prepare the items to be marinated and place them in a hotel pan large enough to hold the ingredients comfortably (see Figure 6-47).

2. Add the marinade and turn the ingredient(s) to coat evenly.

FIGURE 6-47 A Marinade for Fish

FIGURE 6-48   A Tandoori Rub for Chicken

3. Marinate for the length of time indicated by the recipe, type of main product, or desired result.

Dry Marinades and Rubs

A dry marinade is a mixture of salt, crushed or chopped herbs, spices, and occasionally other aromatics, such as citrus zest. In some cases, the marinade is mixed with oil to make a paste. The marinade is rubbed over the food—usually meats and fish—and the coated item is then allowed to stand, under refrigeration, to absorb the marinade's flavors.

Dry marinades may be referred to as "rubs." Once the ingredients have been properly blended, they are packed or rubbed onto the surface of the food. They may be left on the food during cooking to develop a richly flavored crust. Alternately, they may be scraped away before cooking. One classic use for a dry marinade is the preparation of gravad lax, detailed in Chapter 11. Barbecued beef dishes and tandoori chicken are examples of other dishes that may be prepared using a dry rub (see Figure 6-48).

Duxelles

A *duxelles* is a mixture of finely chopped and sautéed mushrooms that also includes shallots, leeks, and white wine. Duxelles may be "dry" or of a sauce consistency. It may be used as a flavoring, stuffing, or coating. It should be moist enough to hold together but not runny.

Pesto and Other Herb Pastes

Pesto is a mixture of an herb and an oil, puréed into a smooth, thick paste. Italy, specifically Genoa, claims to have first developed this sauce. A French version, known as *pistou*, is traditionally added to a vegetable soup.

Pesto customarily contains basil and oil and may also contain grated cheese, nuts, or seeds, depending on the individual recipe. Contemporary renditions may replace some or all of the basil with cilantro, oregano, or other herbs. The recipe for pesto can be found in Part IV, Chapter 13.

Sun-dried tomatoes, olives, and other ingredients are sometimes used in herb pastes or spreads that are made in a similar fashion as pesto.

Pesto and other herb pastes may be used as a sauce for pasta and other foods, as a soup garnish, or as a dressing or sauce ingredient.

Traditionally, pestos and similar herb pastes were made in a mortar and pestle. Some people still feel that this is the best way to prepare them. For large quantities, it may be more efficient to use a food processor, however. Pestos can discolor quickly. You may want to pour a thin layer of oil on top of the pesto to prevent contact with the air from turning it brown or black.

Persillade

Persillade is a mixture of bread crumbs, minced parsley, and garlic used as a coating for roasted and grilled items. It protects the meat, seals in the juices, and provides textural contrast. Usually, a small amount of melted butter or oil is rubbed into the persillade to help the ingredients adhere better. *Persillé* is the French term used to describe items coated with this appareil.

FIGURE 6-49   A Variety of Stocks and Broths

(1) White beef stock (left), chicken stock (center), and brown veal stock (right).

(2) Court bouillon (left), fish stock (center), and fish fumet (right).

(3) Remouillage (left) and broth (right).

(4) Estouffade (left) and glace de viande (right).

Stocks, Broths, and Court Bouillons

Escoffier noted in the first chapter of his classic work *Le Guide Cuilinaire*, the following basic culinary preparations:

• Stocks and broths used for soups

• Brown and white stocks used for sauces and thickened gravies

• Fumets and essences used to flavor the so-called "small sauces"

Not much has changed with regard to these basic items. Although circumstances may force a chef to use shortcuts, such as prepared stock bases, it is still preferable to prepare stocks in house from fresh and wholesome ingredients.

Stocks are flavorful liquids produced by simmering bones, meat trimmings, vegetables, and other "aromatic" ingredients in water (or *remouillage*). Stocks are further categorized as white stock or brown stock, both of which are discussed below. They are used as the foundation for soups, stews, and sauces. They are not served "as is," however. Recipes for a variety of stocks, essences, and court bouillons can be found in Part IV, Chapter 13.

See Figure 6-49 for examples of various stocks, broths, and fumet.

Categories and Types of Stocks

White Stock

White stocks are made from the meaty bones and trim from veal, beef, poultry, some types of game, and fish. The bones are frequently blanched in order to remove any impurities that might cloud or discolor the finished stock. Ordinary white stock is classically prepared from veal meat and bones, with the addition of poultry carcasses.

A white beef stock (sometimes referred to as a "neutral stock") is often prepared by first simmering the stock at a higher temperature than would be used for most stocks for several minutes. The aim is to produce a stock with a nearly neutral fla-

FIGURE 6-50   Mise en Place for White Stocks

(1) White beef stock.

(2) Chicken stock.

FIGURE 6-51
Mise en Place for
Brown Veal Stock

vor. It is often favored for use in vegetable soups or bean dishes. White beef stock can contribute a significant body to these dishes, while still allowing the flavor of the major ingredient to predominate.

See Figure 6-50 for mise en place for chicken and white beef stocks.

Brown Stock

One of the most commonly called-for stocks in the classic and contemporary repertoire of any kitchen is likely to be brown veal stock *(fond de veau brun)*. Brown stocks are prepared by first cooking meaty bones and meat trim to a deep brown color, as well as the mirepoix and a tomato product, before they are simmered. This changes both the flavor and color of the finished stock. Brown stocks are especially valuable in sauce cookery, as they are used as the foundation for brown sauce, jus lié, demi-glace, and pan gravies.

See Figure 6-51 for mise en place for brown stock.

Remouillage

The word translates as a "rewetting," which is a good way to think of the way that remouillage is made. Bones used to prepare a "primary stock" are reserved after the first stock is strained away from the bones. The bones are then covered with water, and a "secondary stock" is prepared.

Some chefs argue that, if the first stock was made properly and simmered for the correct amount of time, there will be little if anything left in the bones to provide either flavor or body in the remouillage. Others feel that this second generation of stock can be used as the basis for other broths or as the cooking liquid for braises and stews. The food being prepared will provide the majority of the flavor in the finished sauce, and a first-rate stock can be reserved for use in dishes where its role is more significant.

Broth (or Bouillon)

Broths share many similarities with stocks. They are prepared in essentially the same fashion: Meaty bones (or in some cases, the entire cut of meat, bird, or fish) are simmered in water (or remouillage or a prepared stock) along with a variety of vegetables and other aromatic ingredients. For a more detailed discussion of broth preparation, refer to Chapter 7.

Many meatless dishes are prepared with a vegetable broth. Some chefs may refer to this preparation as a vegetable stock. For the purposes of this book, vegetable broth will be used, rather than stock. Those stocks made from meat or fish bones will reach a state of clarity and body through the extraction of proteins found in bones and meat. Vegetable broths vary greatly in the degree of body and clarity that they may achieve.

Fumet (or Essence)

The most common fumet is one prepared by sweating fish bones along with vegetables such as leeks, mushrooms, and celery, then simmering these ingredients in water, perhaps with the addition of a dry white wine. The end result is generally not as clear as a stock, but it is highly flavored. Fumets and essences can be prepared from such ingredients as wild mushrooms, tomato, celery or celery root, ginger, and so forth. These essences, nothing more than highly flavored infusions made from especially aromatic ingredients, can be used to introduce flavor to other preparations, such as consommés or broths and a variety of "small sauces."

See Figure 6-52 for mise en place for fish fumet.

FIGURE 6-52
Mise en Place for
Fish Fumet

FIGURE 6-53
Court Bouillon

Estouffade

The classic formula for *estouffade* set down by Escoffier is virtually identical to what was then known as a brown stock. There are some differences to note, however. Estouffade is prepared by simmering together browned meaty veal bones, a piece of fresh or cured pork, and the requisite vegetables and other aromatics.

Contemporary kitchens tend to prepare a brown stock that does not include pork. Today, estouffade is less widely used as a basic preparation, although it is still regarded as a classic preparation.

Court Bouillon

A "short broth" is often prepared as the cooking liquid for fish or vegetables. The basic components of a court bouillon include aromatic vegetables and herbs, an acid such as vinegar, wine, or lemon juice, and water. See Figure 6-53 for an example of a court bouillon. A court bouillon may be prepared as part of the cooking process, or it may be prepared in large batches and used as required, in much the same manner as stocks and broths are prepared.

Ratios for Stocks

When you use these ratios, you will produce stocks that meet all the criteria of a good-quality product: flavor, clarity, aroma, body, and color. This is not to insist that there are no exceptions or modifications that may not also be appropriate, depending on an individual operation's needs. For instance, if veal bones are either unavailable or their cost makes stock production more expensive than it is worth, the chef may then look to other means to reach the desired end: A quantity of lean trim from meats, or a combination of compatibly flavored meats, may be used to replace some of the bones.

A lesser quantity of bones may be used, resulting in a weaker stock. That stock can then be fortified with a commercially prepared base. These are possible responses to a situation that may be beyond the chef's control. It is still best to use the correct ratio and the suggested ingredients, without resorting to bases and the like, of course. Maintaining the proper balance between bones and liquid is crucial if the chef is going to produce an excellent-quality stock. The standards used in most kitchens are as follows:

Beef, Veal, Poultry, Game, or Special Stocks (e.g., Pork or Turkey) For every gallon of stock, use 8 pounds of bones, 6 quarts of water, 1 pound of mirepoix, and 1 standard sachet d'épices or bouquet garni.

Fish Stock or Fumet For every gallon of finished stock, use 11 pounds of bones, 5 quarts of water, 1 pound of mirepoix, and 1 standard sachet d'épices or bouquet garni.

Preparing Stocks

Mise en Place

1. Assemble all ingredients required for stocks.

The basic elements of any stock are:

- Cool water
- The major flavoring components
- Aromatics and other flavoring ingredients

In some restaurants, stock-making goes on constantly, with brown stocks being left to simmer all night in steam kettles, and white stocks prepared during all shifts as space becomes available on the stove top or in a steam kettle. Wholesome trim from meats such as veal, poultry, pork, beef, and game are reserved (separately) to be included in stocks. The same is true of trim from vegetable preparation: Leeks, onions, carrot, celery, parsnip, turnips, tomatoes, mushrooms, and other aromatic vegetables are often cut to a very special size and shape when they will be part of a finished dish presented to a customer. The unused portion is saved to add to stocks.

It is important that all usable trim be wholesome. Storage containers should be clearly labeled, properly covered, stored in the refrigerator. Before you add trim of any type to a stock, check it carefully There is no way to remove the taste of a spoiled ingredient once it is added to the stock.

Major flavoring ingredients for stocks will vary from one formula to another. Some items that are considered aromatics in one recipe may be the principle component of a court bouillon or vegetable broth. There are several steps that may be required to prepare the major flavoring ingredients.

Bones and vegetables are usually cut into an appropriate size. These ingredients may also be roasted or blanched as necessary. The steps for blanching and browning are discussed below.

Large bones from veal, beef, or game animals should be cut into short lengths, about 2 to 3 inches. This will allow the flavor and body to be easily extracted. Bones can usually be purchased precut, and in larger metropolitan areas they are often available fresh. If you do much of your own butchering, you will need to cut the bones yourself using a bandsaw or heavy cleaver. Bones from poultry or fish should also be cut into smaller pieces.

A number of different ingredients may be added to give special flavors or aromas to stocks, court bouillons, and essences. These traditionally include such preparations as mirepoix, sachet d'épices, and bouquet garni. Other options include wines, spices, herbs, vinegars, and a variety of vegetables. These should be prepared in advance and added only as necessary to contribute the desired flavor.

2. Assemble all equipment necessary for preparing stocks.

Pots used for stocks are usually taller than they are wide. Some have spigots that can be used to remove the finished stock without disturbing the bones. Steam-jacketed kettles are often used to produce large quantities of stock. Court bouillons, fumets, and essences that do not have long simmering times are prepared in rondeaus or other wide shallow pots. Tilting kettles are used when available for large-scale production.

Ladles or skimmers should be on hand to remove scum from the stock as it simmers. Sieves, colanders, or other strainers are used to separate bones and vegetables from the stock. The necessary containers for cooling and storing the stock should also be on hand.

Blanching Bones White stocks are made from bones that have been blanched prior to the start of the process. Blanching assures that any impurities that could cloud the stock or give it a too-strong flavor are first cooked out. The technique is almost universal when working with bones that are received in the kitchen frozen or packed in ice:

•Place the bones in a large pot and add enough cool water to cover them by several inches.

FIGURE 6-54
Bones and
Aromatics
Properly
Roasted for a
Brown Stock

• Bring the water to a full boil and skim away any scum that rises to the surface.

• Drain away or pour off the cooking liquid, and rinse the bones to remove any scum that may have been trapped by the bones themselves.

• The bones are now properly blanched and ready to use in preparing a white stock.

Browning Bones and Mirepoix Brown stocks are made by first browning bones and mirepoix and, if required by recipe, tomato paste or purée. This step starts the process of developing the stock's flavor. Allow sufficient time for ingredients to roast properly for the best end product.

Although the steps below explain the procedure for roasting bones, the same steps are used to roast vegetables if you are preparing a roasted vegetable broth:

• Rinse the bones if necessary and dry them well to remove any excess moisture.

Taking the time to do this will shorten the time required to properly brown the bones. If bones go into the oven when they are wet or still frozen, they will steam before the browning process begins. No one can say for sure that there is a distinct and measurable loss of flavor, but certainly it will increase the time the bones need to spend in the oven, as well as increasing the amount of energy required to cook them.

• Heat a roasting pan in a hot oven and add the bones in an even layer.

Some chefs feel that adding a layer of oil in the pan is a good idea to help spur the browning process. However, since there is usually a fair amount of fat left on the meaty trim or scraps, this is not absolutely critical.

• Roast the bones until they are a rich brown color (see Figure 6-54).

The amount of time required will vary, depending on whether or not the bones had time to defrost and dry, how many bones are packed into the pan, and the heat of the oven.

For small quantities, it may be a good idea to heat some oil in a large rondeau over direct heat, add the bones and cook them on the top of the range. This is not recommended for large quantities, but it is a good way to quickly prepare smaller amounts.

• Add the mirepoix and tomato product to the pan.

Although some chefs feel that the best-quality stocks are achieved by first removing the bones and beginning the stock-making process, then browning the vegetables later on in the same roasting pan, others consider the time-saving technique of adding the mirepoix and tomato directly to the bones as they roast to be a fair tradeoff. The recipes in this book follow the first course, where bones and mirepoix are roasted in separate stages.

• Remove the bones from the roasting pan to the stockpot.

• Deglaze the roasting pan to retain as much of the flavor released as drippings in the final stock as possible.

Method

Since stocks are so basic to so many dishes prepared in the professional kitchen, strict adherence to all sanitary and safety standards mush be observed at all times. This means that all equipment must be clean, including cutting boards and knives. Temperature control, particularly during cooling and storage, is also of vital importance.

There are some specific differences between the method for stocks and that used to prepare court bouillons and fumets. Those distinctions will be noted as appropriate throughout the steps below:

1. Combine the bones with cold water and bring the water slowly to a boil.

This slow rise to cooking temperature will allow any blood or other "impurities" that might cloud the finished stock to be released into the water, where they will coagulate and then rise to the surface. Once they have risen to the surface, they can readily be skimmed away. It is this careful and consistent skimming of stocks as they develop that determines how clear the finished stock will be.

Apart from the aesthetics of a clear, limpid stock as opposed to a cloudy one, remember that the same impurities which leave a stock cloudy are the elements that will "turn" most quickly, spoiling and souring a stock. The clearer the stock, the longer its effective shelf life.

Fumets and essences, in contrast, often call for the flavoring ingredient(s) to be allowed to sweat to begin a rapid release of flavor. Once that has happened, the remainder of the liquid ingredients are added and brought slowly to a simmer.

2. Add the flavoring ingredients at the correct point.

The right time to add mirepoix to a simmering stock (except for fish stocks and fumets) is about 1 hour before the end of cooking time. This will allow plenty of time for the best flavor to be extracted, but not so much time that the flavor will be broken down and destroyed.

Spices and herbs will generally release their flavor sufficiently to flavor a stock within 15 to 30 minutes.

There are a number of other ingredients that might be added to stocks as they simmer to give them a special, distinctive flavor. Wines or essences of highly aromatic ingredients (wild mushrooms, celery, tomatoes, or gingerroot, for instance) can also be added close to the end of cooking time. Refer to specific recipes, both those in this book and others you may collect throughout your training and work experience, for guidance.

Fumets, essences, and court bouillons do not have extended cooking times. All the ingredients are normally added at once and remain in the preparation throughout cooking.

3. Simmer the stock long enough to fully develop flavor, body, clarity, color, and aroma.

- Brown or white veal stock normally requires 6 to 8 hours of simmering time.

- White beef stock may be simmered for 8 to 10 hours.
- White and brown poultry stocks (including chicken, duck, turkey, pheasant, and so forth) should be allowed a minimum of 3 hours of simmering time.
- Fish stock and fumet is properly cooked within 30 minutes to an hour.

Smell and taste the stock as it develops so that you can begin to learn the stages that a stock goes through, as well as to gauge when it has reached its peak. Once the stock reaches that peak, its quality will begin to decline, flavors will deaden and become flat, even the color of the stock may be adversely affected if it is allowed to simmer for too long.

4. Properly strain, cool, and store the stock, if it is not intended for immediate use.

The need to handle all foods carefully has been stressed in Chapter 2, "Food and Kitchen Safety." The correct procedure for handling finished stocks is this:

Strain the finished stock through the spigot, if available. Otherwise, ladle the stock out of the pot, disturbing the bones as little as possible to retain the stock's clarity. Once you have gotten as much stock as possible by ladling, drain the remaining bones and stock in a colander, collecting any stock in a bowl. This stock will not be as clear as that which you handled more carefully, but it is still useful for preparing grain pilafs, thick soups, and other dishes where clarity is not as important as flavor.

Cool the stock as explained in Chapter 2 and check it with a thermometer to determine when it has cooled sufficiently. Generally, a temperature of around 40°F(4°C) is desirable. At that point, the stock can be transferred to plastic storage containers, freeing bain-maries for more appropriate uses.

Stocks should also be clearly labeled with their name and the date they were prepared. If you still have some stock in the walk-in or refrigerator, be sure to store the fresh stock behind the older stock so that the next person searching for stock will naturally reach for the older product first.

See Figure 6-55 for photos illustrating the method for preparing chicken stock.

FIGURE 6-55   Preparing Stocks

(1) Add cold water to bones.

(2) Water at proper level in relation to bones.

(3) Skimming surface to remove impurities.

(4) Adding mirepoix.

(5) Cooking at a simmer.

(6) At the end of cooking time, some loss of volume is apparent.

(7) Straining through cheesecloth.

(8) Cooling in an ice water bath.

(9) Placed in storage containers, covered, labeled, and dated.

FIGURE 6-56   Clarifying Butter

(1) Skim surface as butter is heated.

(2) Ladle clarified butter fat from the pan.

(3) Leave the milk solids in the pan.

(4) Whole butter, just melted (left), butter beginning to clarify (center), fully clarified butter (right).

Basic Cooking Techniques

Instead of explaining the most basic cooking techniques each time they appear in a method or recipe, we outline them in this section for easy reference.

Rendering and Clarifying Fats

Rendering Fats

Occasionally, the fat from ducks, geese, or pork may be required for such dishes as confit or cassoulet. Salt pork, another example, should be gently rendered, or melted down, so that the fat can be used to smother the aromatic vegetables used in the preparation of soups, stews, and braises. Properly clarifying a roast's fat and drippings is essential for the preparation of a good pan gravy. The method is as follows:

1. Cube the fat, if necessary.

2. Place the fat in a sauteuse. Add about ½-inch of water to the uncooked fats if there are no drippings present.

3. Cook over low heat until the water evaporates and the fat is released. (This is the actual clarifying process.)

4. Remove the cracklings, if any, with a slotted spoon (they may be reserved for garnish).

5. Use the clarified fat or store it under refrigeration. A caramelized fond from a roast's drippings should remain once the clarified fat is poured away. Deglaze these drippings with stock, wine, or water and use them to prepare a pan gravy. See the discussion on pan gravies in Chapter 9.

Clarifying Butter

Clarified butter is pure butterfat. Ghee is clarified butter that has been simmered longer to highly clarify the butterfat. Drawn butter is clarified butter served with boiled or steamed seafood.

The purpose of clarifying butter is to allow the chef to cook with butter at a higher temperature than would be possible with whole butter. The milk solids in whole butter scorch easily and lower its smoking point.

Because it has some butter flavor, clarified butter is often used for sautéing, sometimes in combination with a vegetable oil to further raise the smoking point. It is also commonly used to make roux.

When whole butter is clarified, some of its volume is lost during skimming and decanting. One pound (455 grams) of whole butter yields approximately 12 ounces (340 grams) of clarified butter. The process of clarifying butter is as follows:

1. Melt the butter in a heavy saucepan over moderate heat.

2. Continue to cook over low heat until the butterfat becomes very clear and the milk solids drop to the bottom of the pot.

3. Skim the surface foam as the butter clarifies.

4. Pour or ladle off the butterfat into another container, being careful to leave all the liquid in the pan bottom. Discard the liquid.

See Figure 6-56 for photos illustrating the method for clarifying butter.

Alternate Method for Clarifying Butter

1. Heat the butter in a saucepan or bain-marie until the butter and milk solids separate.

2. Refrigerate in the bain-marie until the butterfat has hardened.

3. Bore a hole through the hardened butter with a serving spoon handle. Pour away the water and milk solids.

4. Remelt the butter as needed for service.

Separating Eggs

Before beginning this procedure, you should have four separate containers. One is used to catch the whites, a second to receive the yolks, a third to hold clean whites. The fourth is used to hold whites that are contaminated with bits of yolk. Eggs separate most easily when they are cold.

FIGURE 6-57
Separating Eggs

1. Crack open the egg over a small bowl (see Figure 6-57).

2. Transfer the egg back and forth between the halves of the shell, letting the white drop into the small bowl.

3. Place the yolk in its container.

4. Inspect the egg white. If the white is clean, transfer it to the whites' container. If there are traces of yolk, reserve it separately for use in omelets, quiches, and other preparations. Any yolk which remains can prevent the whites from whipping properly.

Whipping Ingredients to Make a Foam

Egg Whites

Science has proven a fact that chefs and cooks have long known: Copper bowls produce a specific reaction with egg whites, producing a foam with greater volume and stability.

In order to obtain the maximum volume from whipped egg whites, with or without a copper bowl, all traces of fat must be eliminated. Fat (including that contained in the yolks and any grease on the bowl or whip) inhibits foaming. Rinse bowls and whips with white vinegar to remove grease and then rinse well with hot water.

Egg whites will whip to a greater volume if they are not very cold. They can either be very gently warmed over simmering water, or they may be allowed to come to room temperature for about 30 to

FIGURE 6-58   Whipping Egg Whites

(1) A thick foam has formed.

(2) Soft peaks.

(3) Stiff peaks.

(4) Egg whites are beginning to dry out, are over whipped.

45 minutes before whipping. The method is as follows:

1. Begin whipping the egg whites by hand or machine at moderate speed. Tilt the bowl to make whipping by hand easier, resting the bowl on a folded towel to prevent slipping.

2. When the whites are quite foamy, increase the speed.

3. Whip to the appropriate stage. Ingredients like cream of tartar or sugar can be added to the foam as it develops. It is generally not recommended that they be added before at least the soft peak stage is reached.

- *Soft peak.* When the whisk or beater is pulled up through the egg whites, a droopy, rounded peak will form. At this stage, the surface of the whites looks moist and glossy.
- *Medium peak.* Whites beaten to the medium peak stage have a moist surface and form a rounded but fairly stable peak. At this stage, sugar and other flavorings may be added.
- *Stiff peak.* When the whisk or beater is lifted out of the egg whites, they will stand up in stiff, stable peaks. It is crucial to stop beating while the surface is still moist and glossy. Over-beaten egg whites may still resemble those at the stiff peak stage, but their surface looks dry and they have lost their elasticity. If the whites are beaten further, the egg protein will gather into globs and the moisture will weep out.

See Figure 6-58 for photos illustrating the method for whipping egg whites.

Making Meringues

Adding sugar to beaten egg whites produces meringues. In addition to sugar, other ingredients may be added for flavor and texture, including cocoa powder and ground nuts. Meringues may be classified as follows:

- *Soft meringue,* made by whipping egg whites with granulated sugar. Some chefs prefer to use superfine or "bar" sugar for the best texture. This

FIGURE 6-59   Whipping Heavy Cream

(1) Cream is beginning to thicken.

(2) Soft peaks are forming.

(3) Firm peaks are forming.

(4) Cream is overwhipped.

meringue is used to top pies and baked Alaska. It is also used to prepare poached meringues.

• *Swiss (or hard) meringue,* made by incorporating a higher proportion of sugar than is required for a soft meringue. This meringue is piped and baked to make shells, mushrooms, and other confections.

• *Italian meringue,* prepared by gradually beating a sugar syrup (cooked to 238°F/114°C) into whites already at the soft peak stage. It is used for many of the same applications as soft meringue and also used as the basis of an Italian buttercream.

For more information about meringues, buttercreams, and other items prepared with meringues, refer to Chapter 12 and the recipes found in Part IV, Chapter 30 of this book.

Whipping Cream

To whip cream, follow the same general technique as for whipping egg whites. The cream should be cold when it is whipped. Chilling the bowl and beaters or whip in advance also aids in achieving the greatest volume. For best results, sugar and other flavorings should be added after the cream is whipped to at least a soft peak.

Like egg whites, cream can be overbeaten. Overbeaten cream first develops a grainy texture. Eventually, lumps will form and, if whipping continues, the cream will turn to butter.

See Figure 6-59 for photos illustrating the method for whipping cream.

Folding Foams into a Base Appareil

The purpose of folding foams into base mixtures is to produce light, delicately textured finished items. Soufflés, mousses, and Bavarian creams are examples of items lightened by incorporating a foam. Folding is a gentle mixing method and is performed as follows:

1. Have the base appareil in a large bowl to accommodate the folding motion. Stir or beat this mixture to soften it, especially if it has been refrigerated for any length of time.

FIGURE 6-60   Folding Ingredients Together

(1) Add the foam (whipped cream shown here) to the batter (pastry cream shown here).

(2) Use a folding motion to gently incorporate.

(3) Cream is blended into pastry cream properly.

2. Add about one-third of the beaten egg whites or cream and fold in, using a circular motion, going from the side to the bottom of the bowl and back up to the surface.

3. Add the remaining whipped item in one or two additional stages, folding just until blended.

See Figure 6-60 for photos illustrating the method for folding whipped items into a base appareil.

Tempering

Tempering is a term used to describe the method of incorporating an egg-and-cream liaison in a hot liquid (see Figure 6-61). It is also the term used for the careful heating of chocolate or fondant for dipping. The process reduces the temperature extremes present in the food or the appareils so that the finished item remains smooth.

Tempering chocolates and fondant is explained in Chapter 12. The method for tempering a liaison (this term was explained earlier in the section on thickeners) is outlined below:

1. Place the liaison in a container and blend until smooth. Placing a towel under the bowl will stabilize it and prevent it from skidding about on the counter.

2. Gradually add the hot liquid, a ladleful at a time, whipping constantly.

3. When enough hot liquid has been added to raise the temperature of the liaison, add it back to the pot.

4. Return the pot to direct heat and bring the mixture up to just below the boiling point. It should thicken slightly.

Reduction

Reduction is the process by which liquids, such as stocks, wine, heavy cream, combinations of liquids and aromatics, and sauces, lose some of their original volume. This not only thickens but also

FIGURE 6-61 Tempering a Liaison

FIGURE 6-62   Straining Sauces

(1) Twisting through cheesecloth, using a kitchen fork.

(2) Using a chinois.

3. When reducing au sec, keep the heat very low near the end of cooking and watch the reduction carefully to prevent scorching.

Straining

There are a number of ways that an item can be strained (see Figure 6-62). A colander is generally used for larger items cooked in liquid, such as pasta or vegetables. Small quantities of food can be lifted out of a liquid or hot oil with a skimmer, spider, or basket.

Sauces and soups are more often strained through conical sieves or chinois. The greater the degree of fineness desired in the finished product, the finer the sieve's mesh should be.

Placing a small ladle in the chinois before pouring in the sauce or soup helps to avoid a buildup of sediment that will slow the straining process. This technique is demonstrated in Figure 6-62.

For very fine sauces, straining through cheesecloth is recommended. The cheesecloth is first rinsed in very hot water, then cool water and wrung dry. Refer to Chapter 8 for the wringing and milking methods. A different technique, shown here, illustrates a technique for straining small amounts without requiring a second pair of hands. The rinsed and wrung-out cheesecloth is draped over a bowl, the sauce is poured in, and the edges of the cloth are gathered up. Pull the ends between the tines of a kitchen fork, twisting as you go, until the sauce is forced through the cloth.

Various ingredients may require draining in order to give them an acceptable consistency. To drain yogurt for a fresh cheese, a chinois is lined with cheesecloth. A colander could be used as well. Suspend the chinois over a container to catch the liquid as it drains away.

Miscellaneous Techniques

There are a number of techniques that have a variety of applications in the kitchen and the bakeshop. For example, a bain-marie setup would be used in the kitchen to prepare terrines or savory custards. In the bakeshop, this same technique is used to prepare steamed puddings and flans.

concentrates the liquid's flavor. Liquids can be reduced to varying degrees, typically defined by how much liquid is cooked off. For example, reducing by half means half of the liquid is cooked off. To reduce by three-fourths means to cook off three-fourths of the liquid, leaving one-fourth of the original volume.

To reduce *au sec* (to dry) means to reduce until nearly all of the liquid has evaporated. Heavy pots are recommended, especially for reductions au sec, because as more water evaporates, the reduction is more likely to scorch. When reducing a large amount, it is advisable to transfer it to a succession of smaller pots as it reduces. This reduces the risk of scorching the reduction. It is often advisable to strain the liquid as it is transferred from one pot to another. The method is as follows:

1. Place the liquid in a heavy pot.

2. Bring it to a simmer and cook until the liquid has reduced to the desired consistency.

FIGURE 6-63
Preparing
Custards in a
Bain-Marie

FIGURE 6-64 Cutting Parchment Lids

(1) Fold a rectangle of parchment paper in half, and then into a triangle.

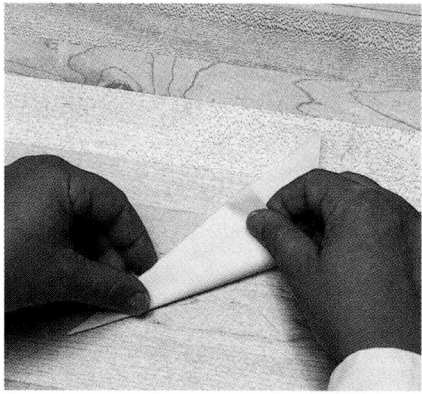

(2) Continue folding the paper into smaller triangles.

(3) Position the tip of the triangle over the center of the pan, and trim the wider end to fit.

(4) The completed lid. Note that the tip was also trimmed to allow steam to escape as foods cook.

Bain-Marie/Water Bath

A bain-marie can be several different things in a professional kitchen. Stainless steel inserts used in steam tables are known as bain-maries. The term is also used to refer to a double boiler, or a bowl set over simmering water so that foods can be gently cooked. A third application of the term is the water bath used to safeguard delicate items such as custards and terrines as they cook in an oven (see Figure 6-63). The steps used to prepare this third type of bain-marie are as follows:

1. Place a deep pan large enough to hold the baking dish comfortably on an oven rack. Add the baking dish.

2. Pour in enough boiling water to come halfway to two-thirds of the way up the side of the dish. (The boiling water is poured in after the baking dish has been placed in the oven to avoid scalding spills.)

3. Adjust the oven temperature as necessary to keep the water temperature between 180 and 190°F (82 and 88°C).

Cutting Parchment Liners

Parchment paper is often used to cover items that will be shallow-poached or braised. The parchment traps some of the steam and allows foods to cook gently and evenly, but does not hold in so much steam that temperature and pressure will build to the point at which delicate foods might

FIGURE 6-65 Cutting Parchment Lids or Liners for Ring Molds

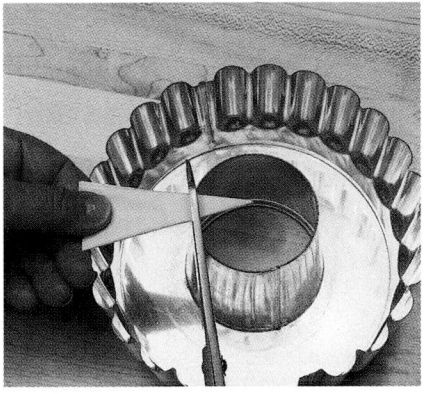

(1) Fold the paper as shown in Figure 6-64. Position the tip of the triangle in the center of the ring mold, and trim as shown.

(2) The proper trimmed liner or lid is ready.

overcook and break apart. The method outlined below and illustrated in Fgure 6-64, is for cutting a round of parchment and lining a sauté pan, casserole, or baking dish.

1. Cut a square of parchment paper a little larger than the pan's diameter.

2. Fold the square in half to form a triangle.

3. Continue folding in half until a long triangle about an inch wide at its widest point is formed.

4. Position the triangle's narrow end above the pan's center and cut away the part that extends beyond the pan edge.

To cut a parchment liner for a ring mold, follow steps 1 to 4 in the method for cutting parchment to line a round pan (above). Then, position the triangle's point above the center of the ring mold and cut off the point at the mold's inner edge as shown in Figure 6-65.

Fabricating Beef, Veal, Lamb, Pork, Poultry, and Game

Very few kitchens have enough refrigeration, storage, or work space to accommodate sides of beef, whole lambs, or entire veal legs. Band-saws and other special tools may be required for some types of butchering. The simple meat fabrication techniques presented in this section for use with beef, veal, lamb, pork, poultry, and game are probably well within the abilities of most chefs, however.

There are definite advantages to fabricating items on the premises. Purveyors may not always be able to cut meat exactly to specification or may be unsure of the exact definition of a particular menu term. For example, they may be familiar with the term "cutlet," but not have a clear idea of what a paillard is. For this reason, the ability to cut paillards, medallions, noisettes, and other "menu cuts" is a skill worth mastering. It also allows you to control portion size and be sure that each portion meets your establishment's standards for quality.

You can generally make use of at least some of the "clean trim" generated by fabrication for other kitchen items (soups, sauces, stocks, salads, and forcemeats, to name a few). The aim is to keep the amount of trim meat to a minimum, however.

Cutting and Pounding Cutlets

When used in reference to meat, the term cutlet means a thin boneless cut of meat that may come from the loin, the tenderloin, or any other sufficiently tender cut, such as the top round. Chicken and turkey cutlets are also common. They are made from the breast, in most cases, although it is possible to prepare cutlets from the thighs of large birds.

These cutlets are often pounded to an even thickness over their entire surface so that they can be rapidly sautéed or pan-fried. Place the cutlet between two pieces of paper or plastic wrap and then gently pound the meat using a meat pounder or mallet, or (in their absence) the side of a cleaver or even the bottom of a skillet or pot. Work from the center of the cut outward.

See Figure 6-66 for photos illustrating the method for cutting and pounding of veal cutlets.

FIGURE 6-66   Preparing Cutlets

(1) Cutting portions from a fully trimmed piece of veal.

(2) Pounding cutlets, a step necessary to prepare cutlets, paillards, and other menu items.

FIGURE 6-67   Cutting Émincé

(1) Small pieces are cut from the a piece of boneless meat, well trimmed to remove fat, sinew, gristle, and silverskin.

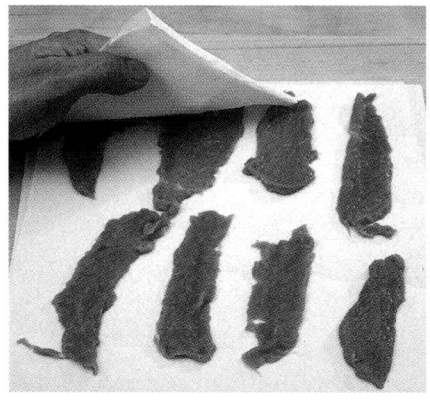

(2) Blot the pounded émincé dry before cooking.

Preparing Paillards

A paillard (derived from the French term for a straw bed) is a pounded cutlet that is grilled, sautéed or pan-fried.

Preparing Émincé

This French word translates as "minced." It is not the same cut as minced herbs or garlic, however. Meats cut into émincé are prepared by first trimming a boneless piece of meat to remove all fat, gristle, or sinew. It is then cut into long strips that have the same diameter as that of the finished cut. Then, slices are made so that each piece is relatively uniform, usually around ¼ inch thick, 1 to 1½ inches wide, and up to 3 inches long (see Figure 6-67).

This cut is generally used with meats that are to be sautéed. This means that the cuts appropriate for preparing émincé should come from tender portions of the animal: the loin, tenderloin, and top round, for instance.

Trimming a Tenderloin

The tenderloin is one of the most expensive cuts, whether from veal, beef, venison, or pork. Great care must be taken when trimming a tenderloin to prevent unnecessary loss.

Your knife should be very sharp. Stop as often as necessary to hone the blade with a steel. Pull away the heavy covering of fat, if it is still on the meat. Use the tip of a boning knife to work the blade under the elastin, also referred to as silverskin. This membrane will shrink and pucker during cooking, causing the meat to cook unevenly. It is extremely tough and unpleasant to bite into as well. Angle the blade as you cut away the silverskin so that only it is removed.

The "chain" is also cut away from a tenderloin of beef, since it contains mainly fat and relatively little usable meat.

See Figure 6-68 for photos illustrating the method for trimming a tenderloin as well as number of 6-ounce portions available from a properly trimmed tenderloin.

Shaping Medallions

Cuts from the boneless loin or the tenderloin of beef, veal, lamb, pork, or venison may be known by a variety of menu terms. Medallions, noisettes, and grenadine are among the most common. Some specific menu terms generally associated only with the beef tenderloin include tournedos and châteaubriand.

These cuts are generally round, and will vary in size depending upon the cut you wish to serve. To give them a uniform appearance and to aid in even cooking, you can gently shape medallions or similar cuts by the following technique:

Dampen a piece of cheesecloth large enough to wrap completely around the medallion, and gather the edges, twisting them until the cheesecloth fits snugly.

Use the flat of your knife blade to hold the meat in place as you continue to twist, tightening the cheesecloth around the meat to make it into an even disk.

See Figure 6-69 for photos illustrating the method for shaping a medallion.

Tying a Roast

This is one of the simplest and most frequently required types of meat fabrication. The chef uses this technique to ensure that the roast will be evenly cooked and that it will retain its shape after roasting. Although simple, the technique is often one of the most frustrating to learn. For one thing, knot tying is not always an easy thing to do. There are no awards given for neatness, however. As long as the string is taut enough to give the roast a compact shape without tying the meat too tightly, the result will be fine. There is one trick to keep in mind that will make initial attempts easier: Leave the string very long so that it will wrap easily around the entire diameter of the meat. In the second technique, the string is left attached to the spool, and is only cut when the entire roast is tied.

Both of the techniques illustrated here are appropriate for tying boneless or bone-in roasts. The choice of technique is largely a matter of personal preference; some chefs find one method easier than the other. See Figures 6-70 and 6-71 for two ways to tie a roast. In both cases, a pork loin is used.

Cleaning a Skirt Steak

Skirt steaks have become a more familiar item on certain menus. They may be purchased already cleaned, but it is an easy process. The basic procedure is demonstrated in the accompanying photos.

See Figure 6-72 for photos illustrating the method for cleaning a skirt steak.

Frenching a Rack of Lamb

This technique is one of the more complicated covered in this chapter, although once it is understood, it is not especially difficult to master. Trimmed and frenched racks or chops can be ordered from a meat purveyor if desired, but you will be able to exercise greater control over the trim loss if you are able to do this yourself.

This same technique can be used to french individual chops of lamb, veal, or pork or the wing bones of a poultry suprême. Any lean trim can be used to prepare a jus, pan-gravy, or for use in a stock.

See Figure 6-73 for photos illustrating the method for frenching a rack of lamb.

Cutting Steaks and Chops

Chops and steaks are similar cuts. Steaks are generally associated with cuts from the rib and loin of beef, while chops are more often used for the same cuts taken from pork, lamb, or venison. There are veal and lamb steaks, usually cut from the "sirloin" or the part of the leg closest to the loin. Some steaks are cut from the chuck or shoulder. These cuts are not as tender as those from the rib, loin, or sirloin, and are generally braised.

To prepare steaks and chops, first trim the cover fat from the subprimal or primal you have purchased. Make cuts straight through the muscle against the grain to make chops or steaks of the size you need for various menu items. If there are still bones in the cut, you may need to use either a cleaver or a handsaw to cut the meat away from the backbone.

See Figure 6-74 for photos illustrating the method for cutting steaks and chops.

Butterflying Meats

Butterflying a cutlet, suprême, shrimp, or leg of lamb opens the item up, so that it is thinner. The

FIGURE 6-68   Trimming and Portioning a Beef Tenderloin

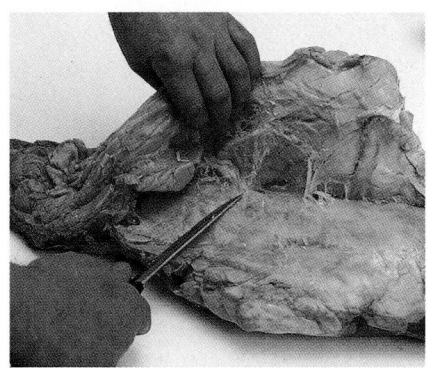

(1) Lift up the fat cap, pulling up with your hand and using the flat of the blade to hold the tenderloin steady.

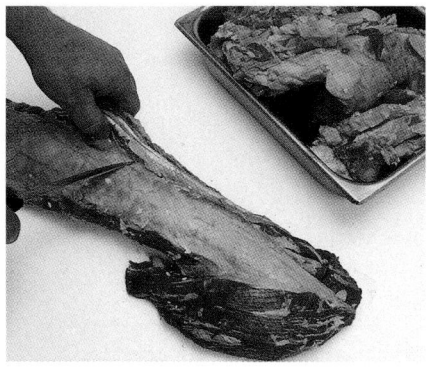

(2) Remove the chain from the tenderloin.

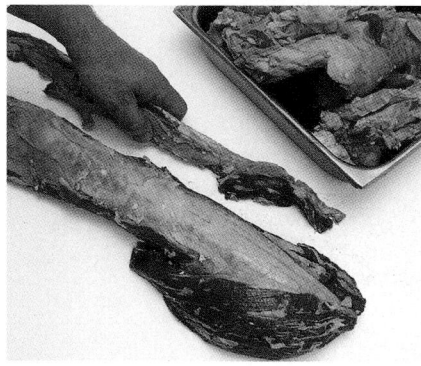

(3) The chain is completely removed from the tenderloin.

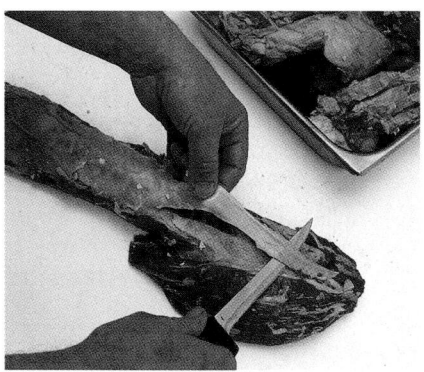

(4) Cutting away the silverskin. Angle the blade upward slightly so that only the silverskin is cut away.

(5) The fully trimmed loin cut into 6-ounce portions.

FIGURE 6-69   Shaping a Medallion

(1) Wrap the meat in a single layer of cheesecloth rinsed in cold water.

(2) Gather the cheesecloth and twist it slightly to begin to shape the meat.

(3) The shaped medallion is in the foreground.

FIGURE 6-70   Tying a Roast

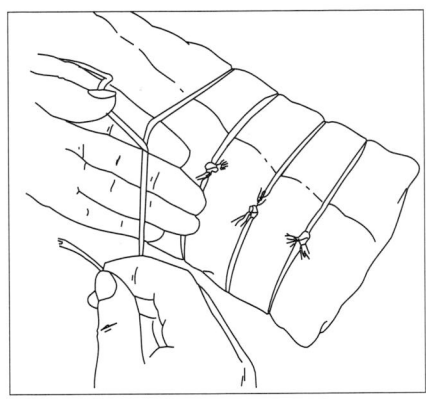

(1) A length of string long enough to wrap completely around the meat is secured by passing it between the fingers and crossing one end over the other end of the string.

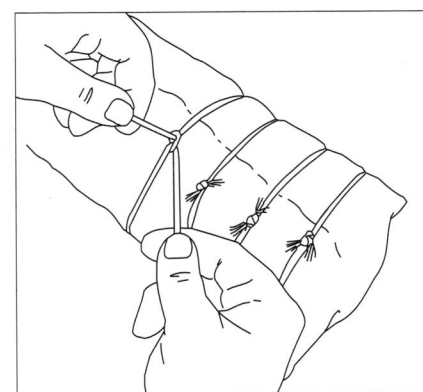

(5) Pull both ends of the string to tighten well. The string should be pressing firmly against the meat.

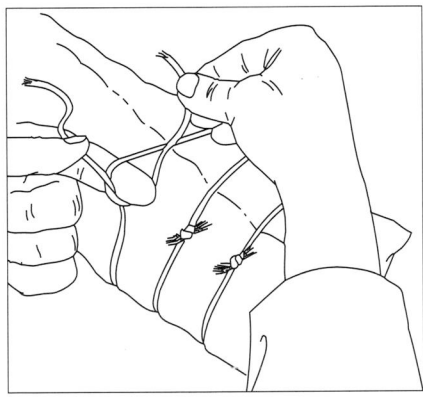

(2) Make a loop by passing the end not held between the fingers underneath the fingertip.

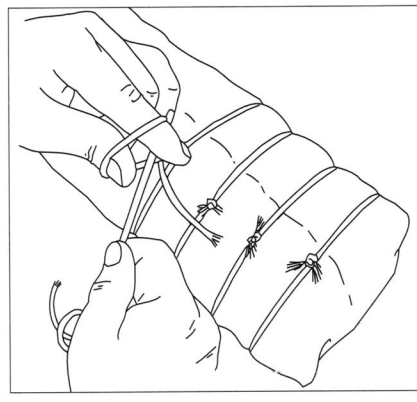

(6) Loop one end of the string completely around the thumb and forefinger, and pull the other end of the string through the loop. Hold the loop's tail firmly between the thumb and forefinger of the other hand.

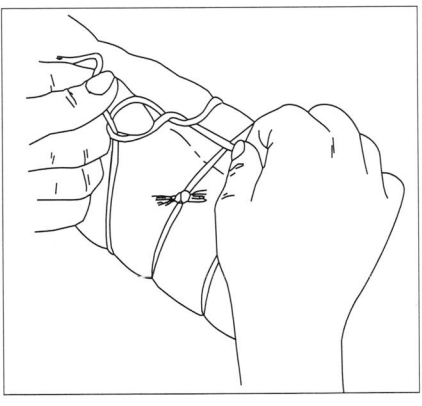

(3) Continuing the same motion, now loop the string back underneath itself.

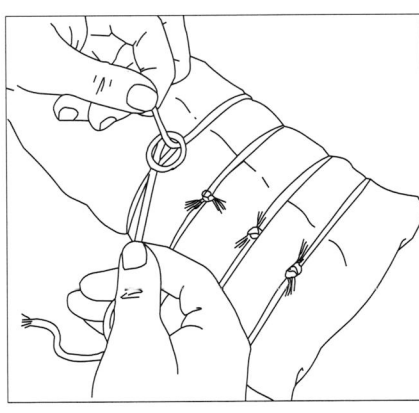

(7) Pull both ends of the string to tighten securely. Trim any long string tails so that the knots are neat.

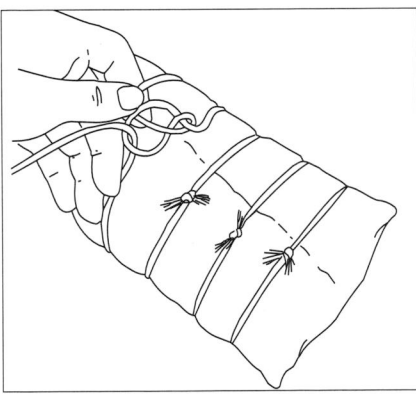

(4) Still working with the same end of the string, pass the tail of the string back through the opening where the fingertip was.

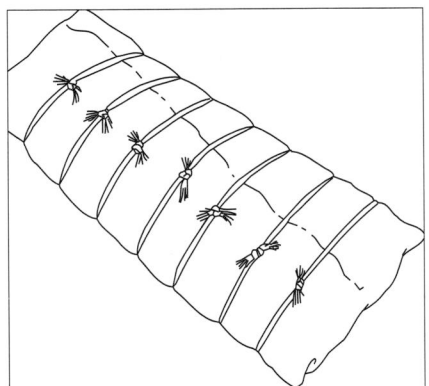

(8) Continue to knot lengths of string at even intervals until the entire piece of meat is securely tied.

FIGURE 6-71   An Alternate Method for Tying a Roast

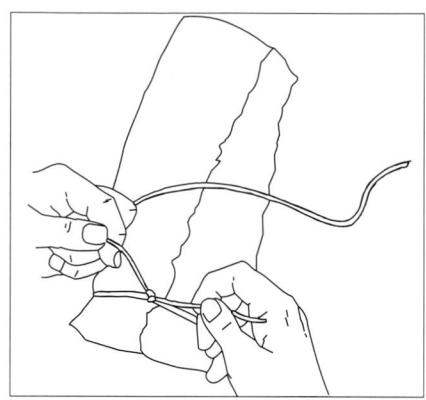

(1) Begin by tying the string around one end of the meat. Leave one end uncut. Any other knot that holds securely may be used.

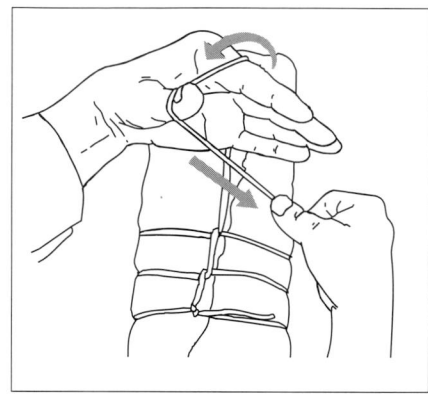

(2) Hold one hand over the meat. Pass the string around the outspread fingers and thumb so that the string comes from behind the fingers, then around the thumb, and back behind itself.

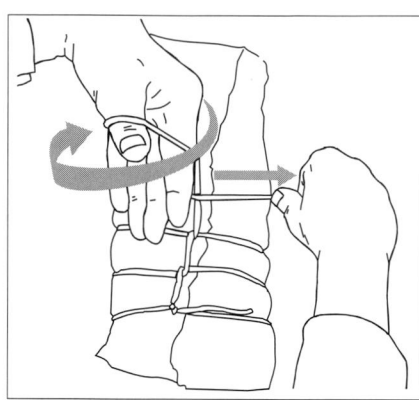

(3) Twist the loop around so that the base of the loop twists back on itself.

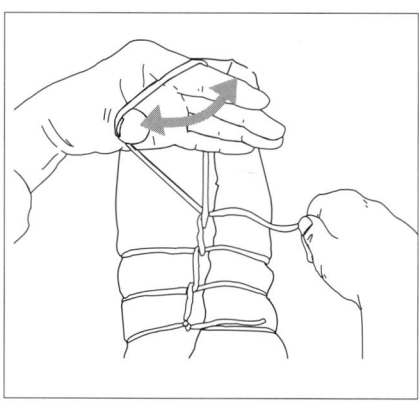

(4) The hand is now spread open so that the loop will enlarge.

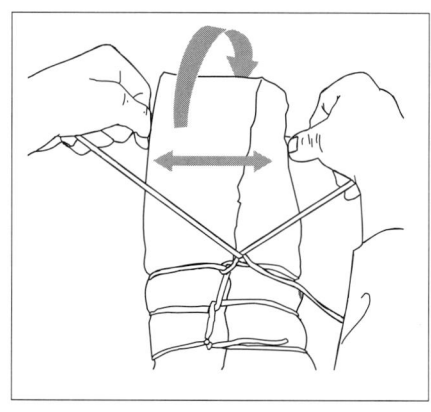

(5) Continue to open the loop wide enough so that it can pass easily around the meat, completely encircling it.

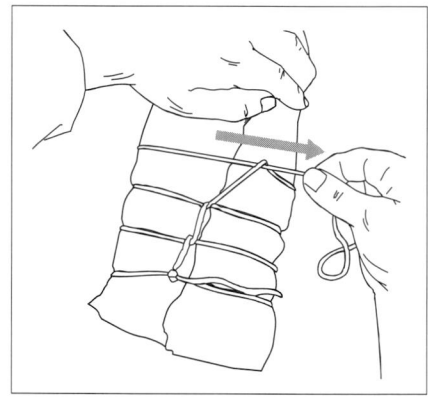

(6) Pull the string's loose end so that the loop is securely tightened around the meat. Continue until the entire piece of meat has been secured with loops.

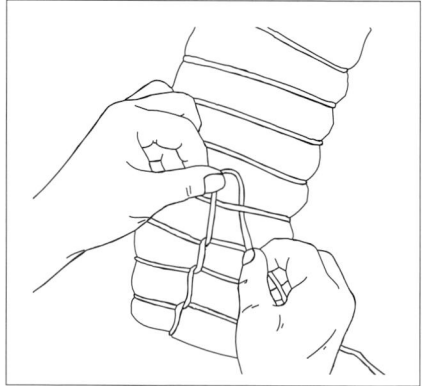

(7) Turn the piece of meat over. Pass the loose end of the string through the loop, then pass it back through underneath the loop. Pull the string tight and continue down the length of the meat.

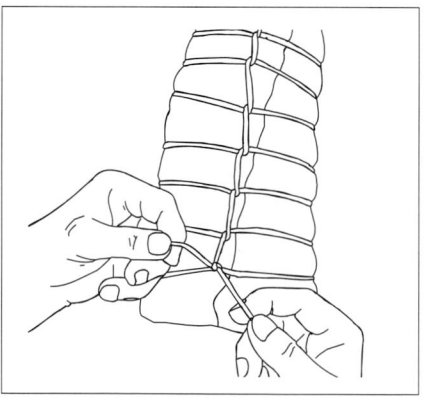

(8) Once the string has been wrapped around each loop from one end to the other, turn the meat back over. Cut the loose end and tie the string securely to the first loop.

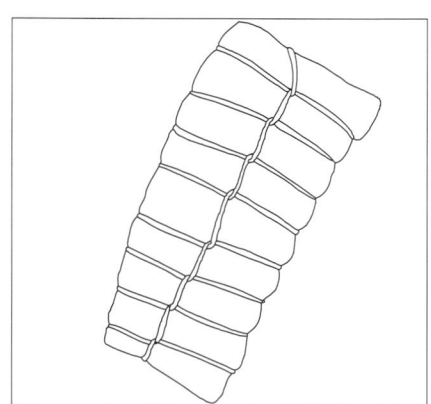

(9) This shows the finished loin. Note that all of the loops are evenly spaced and that the meat is evenly shaped. This photo shows the side of the meat that would be placed down during roasting or braising.

FIGURE 6-72   Cleaning a Skirt Steak

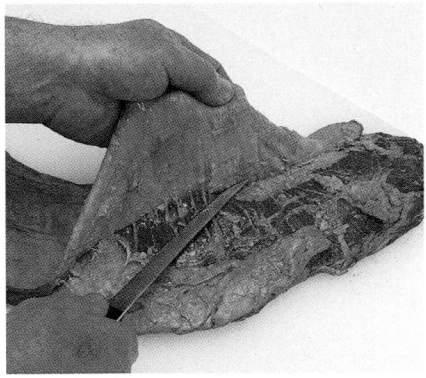

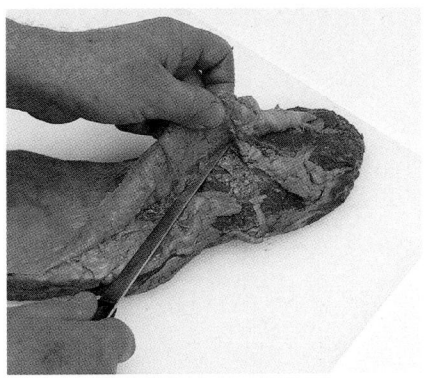

(1) Lift the fat cover away from the steak, holding it steady with the flat side of a knife.

(2) Use the tip of the blade to completely free the fat from the steak.

FIGURE 6-73   Frenching a Rack of Lamb

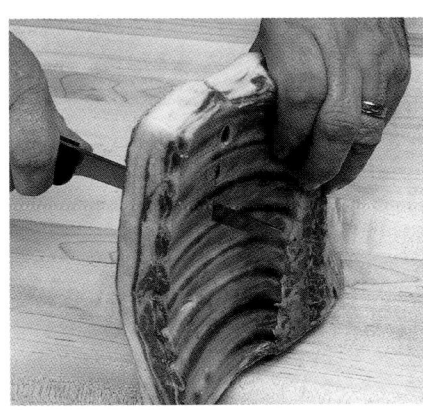

(1) Make an even cut about 3 inches from the meat's eye, through the fat covering, all the way down to the bone.

(2) Set the rack on one end and make a stabbing cut between each bone, using the initial cut as a guide.

(3) Use a boning knife tip to score the membrane covering the bones, which will allow them to break through the membrane easily.

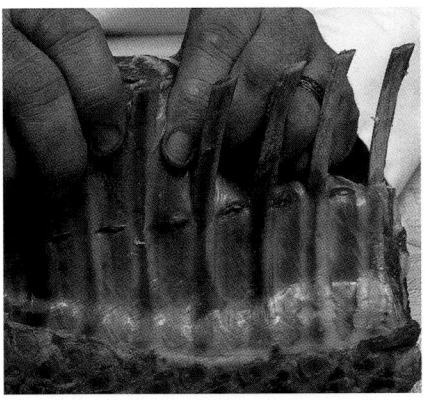

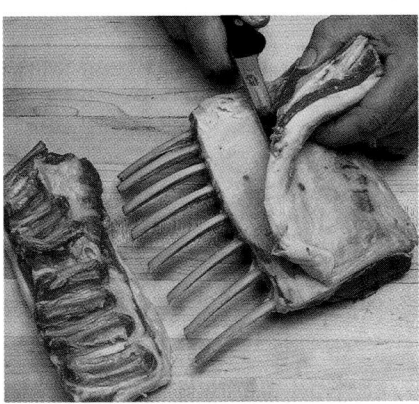

(4) Push the bones through the thin membrane. The thumbs are placed against the fleshy side of the bone and forefingers are positioned between the bones.

(5) Lay the rack so that the bones are facing down. Make an even cut to remove the meat surrounding the bone ends. This should pull away easily.

FIGURE 6-74   Cutting Chops from a Pork Loin

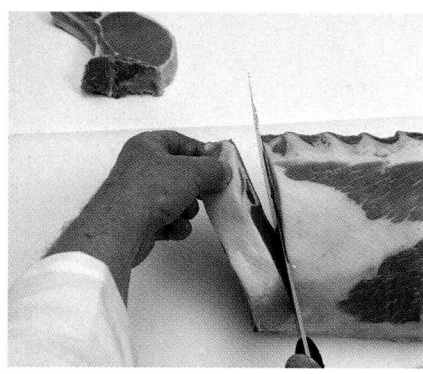

(1) Make an initial cut through the meat to create a chop of the correct thickness and weight.

(2) Continue to cut until reaching the bones. Cut through the bone using either a cleaver...

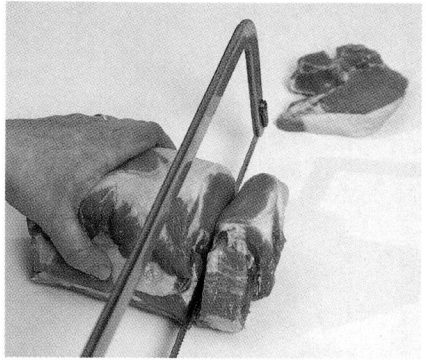

(3) or using a hand saw.

FIGURE 6-75   Boning and Butterflying a Breast Of Veal

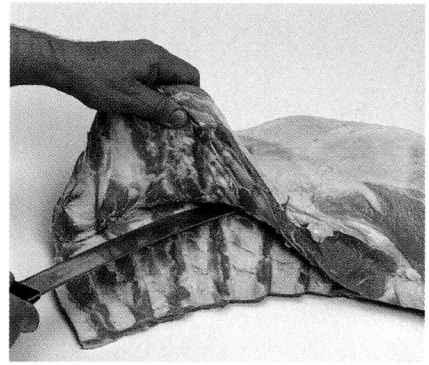

(1) Lay the breastbone side down and cut along the bones to free the meat.

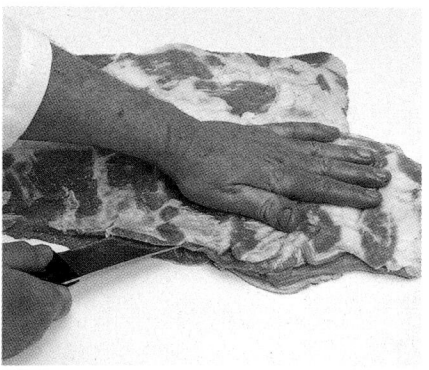

(2) Continue cutting, pulling the meat back as you work, until the bones are cut away.

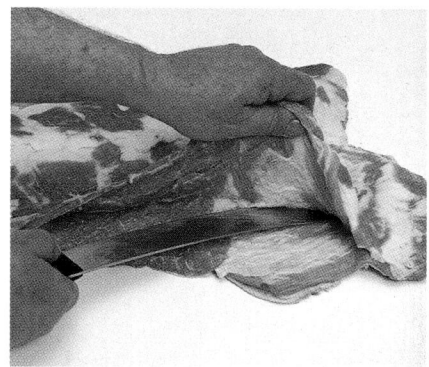

(3) Lay the boned breast on a work surface, and make a horizontal cut through the meat, leaving one length intact.

FIGURE 6-76   Trimming and Boning a Pork Loin

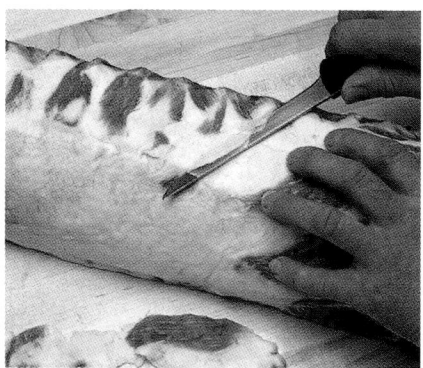

(1) Remove the excess fat covering the edge of the loin to expose the tips of the rib bones.

(2) Make smooth strokes along the bones to free the meat. Pull the meat away to make it easy to see.

(3) When all the meat is freed from one side of the bones, turn the loin over and free the meat from the other side. Here the tenderloin is being gently cut from the bones.

cut is made from one edge of the food up to, but not completely through, the opposite edge. Items are butterflied for a variety of reasons:

- To give them a more uniform thickness so that they will grill evenly
- To make it easier to stuff them
- To give the item a more generous appearance

A breast of veal is being boned and butterflied in Figure 6-75, prior to being stuffed, tied, and roasted or braised.

Trimming and Boning a Pork Loin

The first step is to remove as much of the fat covering as possible. Then, begin making careful cuts, passing the knife as closely as possible to the bones. Use short strokes when you are very close to the bones to scrape the meat away cleanly. Use the tip of the knife to cut around joints and between bones.

See Figure 6-76 for photos illustrating the method for trimming and boning a pork loin.

Boning a Leg of Veal

Although this procedure may look difficult, it is possible to do it successfully by following the natural "seams" in the meat as much as possible. These seams are formed between separate muscles. Follow the seams all the way to the bones and be sure to cut through the ligaments at the joint of the knuckle and leg bones. As you cut with one hand, use the other to pull the meat away. Continue to cut along the seams to separate the remaining meat into several boneless cuts: top round, knuckle, bottom round, and additional trim used for grinding or stew meat.

See Figure 6-77 for photos illustrating the method for boning a leg of veal.

Working with Variety Meats

There are a number of terms used to refer to organ meats, as well as such cuts as the heart, tongue, or stomach. Variety meats, offal, *abats*, and

FIGURE 6-77 Boning a Leg of Veal

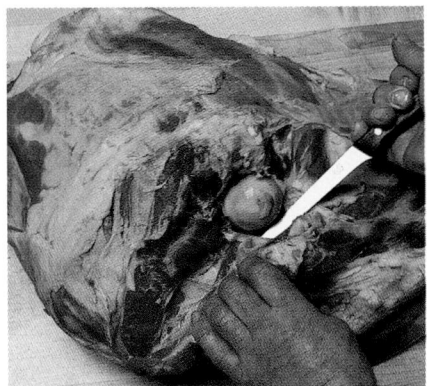

(1) Remove the excess fat covering the edge of the loin to expose the tips of the rib bones.

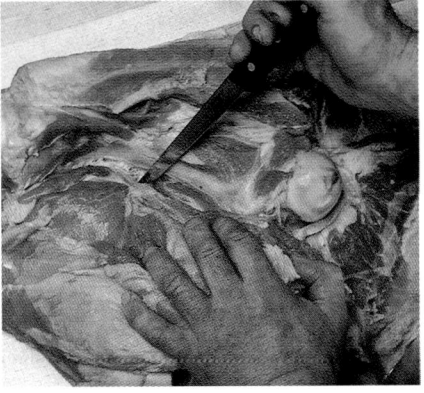

(2) Make smooth strokes along the bones to free the meat. Pull the meat away to make it easy to see.

"innards" are all in use, depending upon the area of the country or the cuisine. In recent years, exports of tongue, liver, kidneys, lungs, sweetbreads, and other variety meats to foreign countries, have reduced supplies in this country. These cuts have been difficult for the ordinary consumer to find for some time. Restaurants and butchers are just as likely to find them in short supply.

If you do have a clientele that appreciates these items, considered delicacies throughout many of the world's cuisines, be sure to give them the correct care and advance preparation.

Sweetbreads

Sweetbreads are the thymus gland of young animals. In some species, this gland gradually atrophies with age, all but disappearing. The meat has a moderately delicate texture and is quite rich.

To prepare sweetbreads for use in these dishes, you must first remove all traces of blood by allowing them to soak in several changes of fresh cool water.

FIGURE 6-78 Cleaning and Pressing Sweetbreads

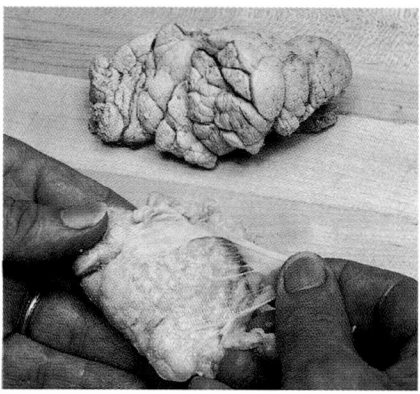

(1) Once the sweetbreads have been properly blanched and cooled, use the fingers to pull away the heavy membrane.

(2) Wrap the sweetbreads in clean cheesecloth and roll them up. Tie the ends with string.

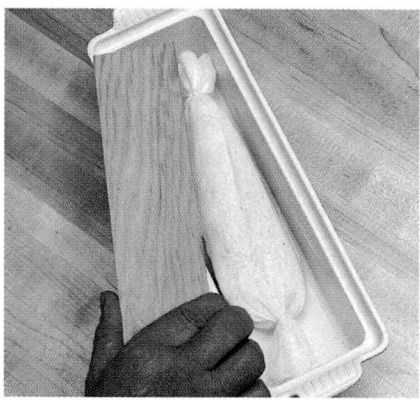

(3) Place the wrapped sweetbreads in a terrine or other container and top with a flat item, such as a clean length of board as used here.

(4) Top the board with a weight. Refrigerate. As the weight pushes out the excess moisture, the sweetbreads will take on a firm, compact texture and shape.

The next step is to blanch them in a court bouillon. After they are peeled, sweetbreads can be pressed to give them a firmer, more appealing texture in certain preparations.

See Figure 6-78 for photos illustrating the method for preparing sweetbreads.

Liver

Calves liver is often featured on menus, smothered with onions and bacon. Pork, lamb, and some types of game liver may also be used. Liver is of course an important ingredient in many pâtés and terrines, as well.

To prepare liver for sautéing or braising, you will need to first remove any veins, sinew, gristle, or silverskin before cooking. The skin pulls away easily, as shown in Figure 6-79.

Kidneys

Steak and kidney pies are still popular in Britain. Other cuisines also feature recipes that call for kidneys. To be sure that the finished recipe does not have an unpleasant taste, kidneys are cleaned.

Split the kidneys and cut out the artery and fat. In some recipes, there may be instructions to blanch the kidneys or soak them in buttermilk to remove any lingering taste of urine.

See Figure 6-80 for photos illustrating how to split and clean kidneys.

Tongue

Tongue is a muscle meat that can be quite tough unless it is gently simmered in a flavorful broth or

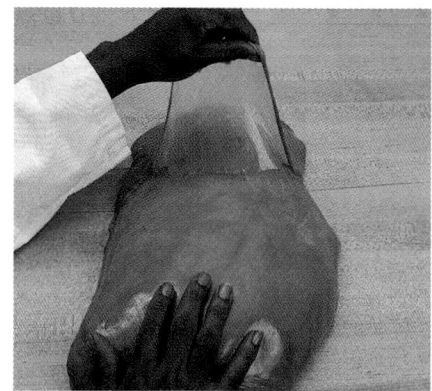

FIGURE 6-79 Cleaning Liver by Pulling Away the Membrane

FIGURE 6-80   Cleaning Kidneys

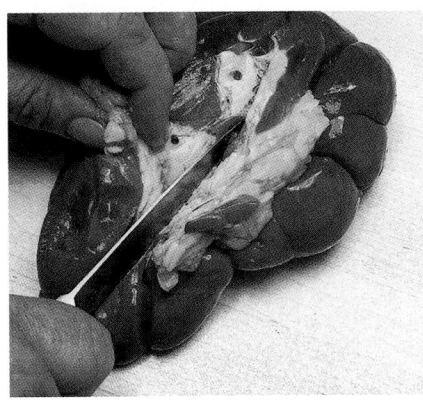

(1) Make a cut through the center of the kidneys, dividing them into two equal pieces.

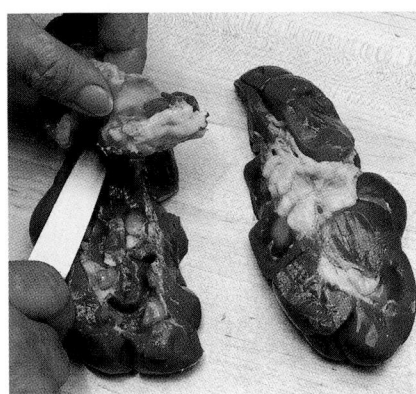

(2) Lift away the kidney fat and use the tip of a sharp knife to cut it away from the kidneys.

FIGURE 6-81   Peeling Tongue

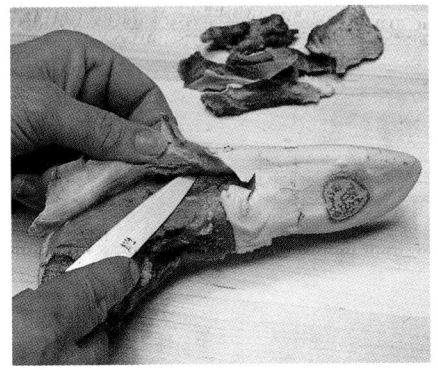

(1) Use the tip of a knife to trim the skin from the underside. Lift it away from the tongue as the cuts are made to prevent removing too much meat.

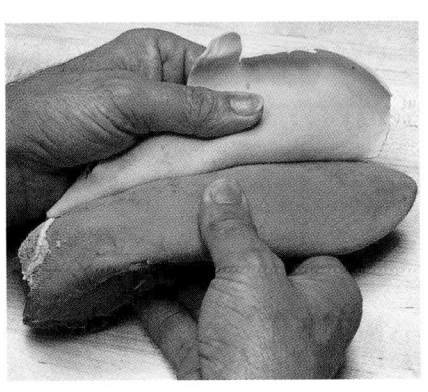

(2) The skin will peel away easily from the tongue's top.

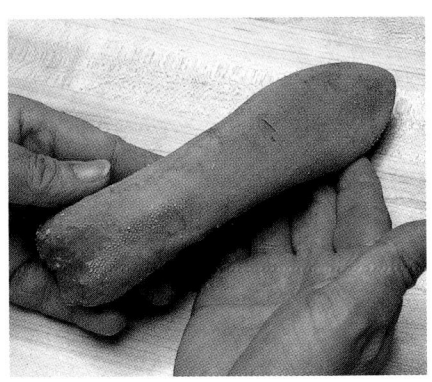

(3) The completely peeled tongue is shown.

bouillon until it is very tender. Allowing the tongue to cool in the liquid will bolster its flavor. Once cooled, the tongue should be carefully peeled to remove the skin. Then, it can be used in a variety of ways: as the garnish for a sauce or soup, or as part of a choucroute or stew. It may also be served on its own.

See Figure 6-81 for photos illustrating the method for peeling tongue.

Removing Marrow

Marrow—the soft, inner substance of bone—is often used as a garnish for a variety of sauces, soups, dumplings, and other dishes. The bones should first be sawed into reasonable lengths to make it easier to remove the marrow. The bones are then rinsed under cool running water until all traces of blood have been eliminated and the water runs clear. The marrow can then be removed from the bone.

See Figure 6-82 for photos illustrating the method for removing bone marrow.

Poultry Fabrication

All kinds of poultry, including chicken, squab, duck, pheasant, and quail, are of great importance to most restaurants. Always popular and readily available, poultry, for the most part, is among the

FIGURE 6-82   Removing Marrow from Bones

(1) *Place the marrow bones in a container and cover with cold water. Add salt to help draw away any excess blood and other impurities.*

(2) *After the marrow bones have soaked for a few hours, push the marrow out using the thumb.*

(3) *The marrow is completely freed.*

least costly of meats used for entrées and other menu items. Throughout this section, the fabrication techniques are demonstrated on a chicken, the bird most commonly used in restaurants. These techniques can be applied to the fabrication of virtually all poultry types.

The younger the bird, the easier it is to cut up. They are usually much smaller and their bones are not completely hardened. The size and breed of the bird will also have some bearing on how easy or difficult it will be to fabricate. Chickens are generally far more simple to cut up, for example, than are pheasant. The tendons and ligaments in chickens are less well-developed, except in the case of free-range birds, which move freely about an enclosed yard or pen.

Although the procedure for boning a duck, for instance, is very similar to that used in boning a Cornish game hen, carcass shapes do differ from breed to breed. A duck has shorter legs and a long, barrel-shaped chest. The game hen, since it is small, will require smaller, more delicate cuts than a turkey. A quail, one of the smallest birds, requires all of a chef's skill and care to avoid mangling the tiny morsels of meat that cling to delicate bones.

The bones and trim remaining after fabrication can be used in a variety of ways: the wings used for hors d'oeuvres, any lean trim for forcemeat preparation, and the bones for making stock.

When working with any type of poultry, the chef should keep all tools and work surfaces scrupulously clean because of the potential for cross-contamination. Follow all of the proper procedures described in Chapter 2 for working with potentially hazardous foods. The following standards must be adhered to strictly:

- Keep poultry iced and under refrigeration when it is not being fabricated.

- Be sure that the cutting board has been thoroughly cleaned and sanitized before and after using it to cut up poultry.

- Clean and sanitize knives, poultry shears, and the steel before and after cutting poultry.

- Store poultry in clean, leak-proof containers, and do not place poultry above any cooked meats. If the poultry drips on the food below it, it will become contaminated. For added safety, it may be a good idea to place a drip pan underneath the container holding the poultry.

The essential tools for cutting up poultry are a clean work surface, a boning knife, and a chef's knife. Some chefs are comfortable using poultry shears to cut through joints and smaller bones. Others may prefer to use a cleaver.

Trussing Birds for Roasting Whole

Roast chicken, turkey, duck, and geese are familiar and popular items. The advance preparation techniques required can vary. Some chefs prefer to leave birds untrussed, in the belief that this permits birds to cook quickly and evenly. Others prefer to

FIGURE 6-83   Trussing a Bird

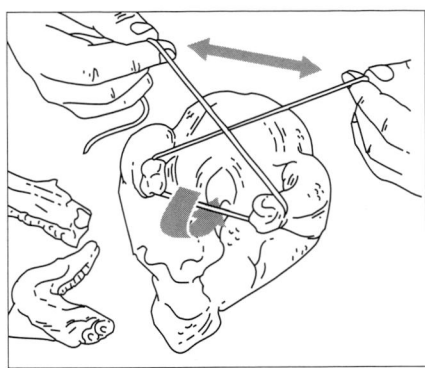

(1) Cut away the first two wing joints. Pass the middle of a long piece of string underneath the joints at the end of the drumstick, and cross the ends of the string to make an X as shown.

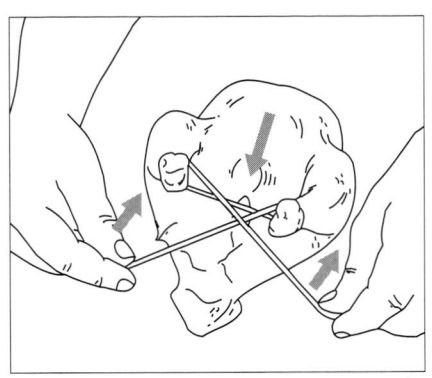

(2) Pull the ends of the string down toward the tail and begin to pull the string back along the body.

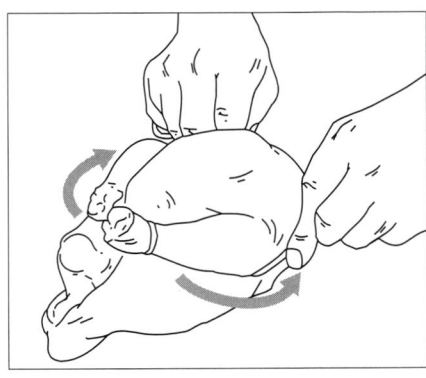

(3) Pull both ends of the string tightly across the joint that connects the drumstick and the thigh and continue to pull the string along the body toward the bird's back, catching the wing underneath the string.

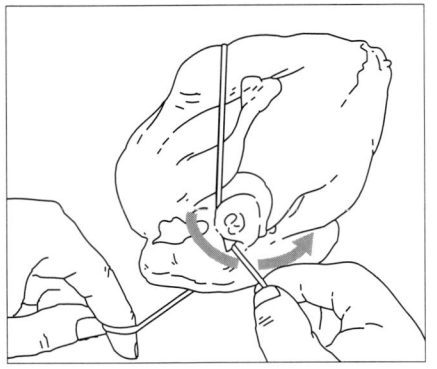

(4) Pull one end of the string securely underneath the backbone at the neck opening.

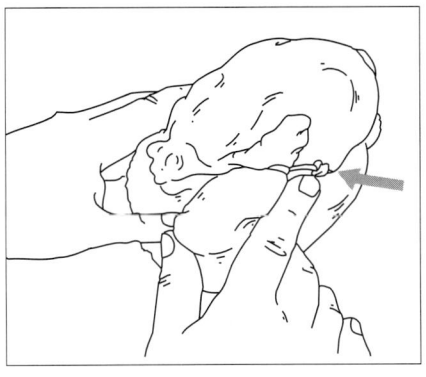

(5) Tie the two ends of the string with a secure knot.

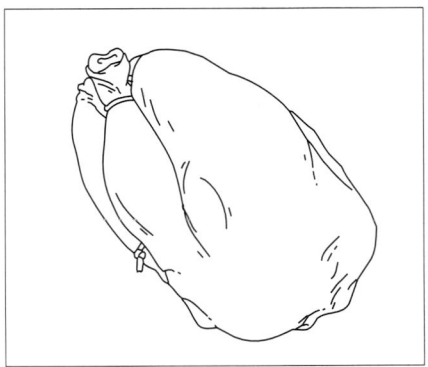

(6) A properly trussed bird.

truss birds, in order to produce roasted birds that are moist, with a better shape and color, and a classic appearance.

Since the wing tips are generally not served, they may be cut away before trussing. Then the bird is ready for trussing either with or without a trussing needle. There are some alterations to these basic techniques that you may learn. The aim of trussing is to produce a neat, compact shape. Figure 6-83 demonstrates one of a number of acceptable ways to truss poultry.

Halving a Bird

Cutting a bird into halves is an especially important technique for use on smaller birds, such as Cornish game hens and broiler chickens, that are

to be prepared by grilling. If the bones are left intact during grilling, they provide some protection against scorching and help to control shrinkage. This technique is also important when birds are roasted whole, but served as semi-boneless halves.

The first step is often removing the wing tips. Then the bird is cut down along the backbone using either a boning knife, a chef's knife, or poultry shears. The wing tips and backbone should be saved to use when you prepare stock.

See Figure 6-84 for photos illustrating the method for removing the backbone.

Removing the Keel Bone

Once the backbone has been cut away, the keel bone is also removed. Lay the bird out flat, bones

FIGURE 6-84   Removing the Wingtips and Backbone

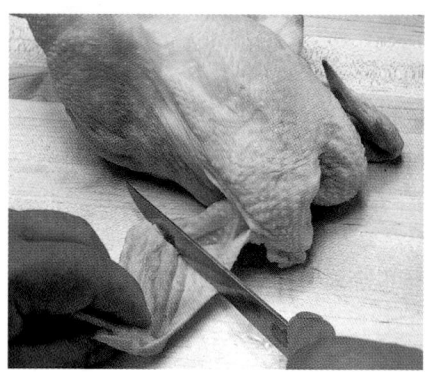

(1) Cut away the first two wing joints by cutting across them with a heavy knife. These wing tips may be reserved for use in stock.

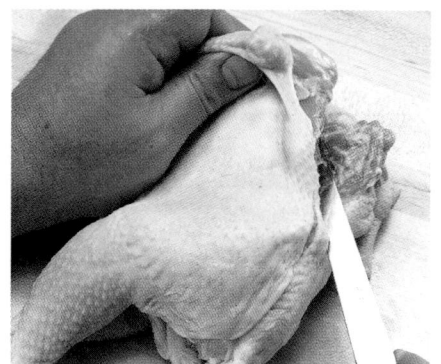

(2) Lay the chicken on one side. Make a cut along one side of the backbone, working from the neck to the tail.

(3) Turn the bird onto its other side. Make another cut along the backbone, this time cutting from the tail toward the neck.

FIGURE 6-85   Removing the Keel Bone and Halving a Bird

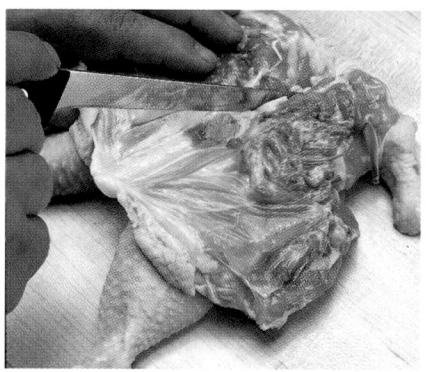

(1) Open the bird out flat, with the skin side facing down. Make a cut through the breast on one side of the keel bone to separate the bird into halves.

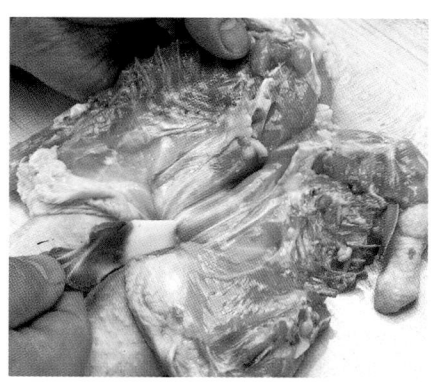

(2) Pull the keel bone away from the chicken completely. The bone may separate into two portions; be sure that it is all removed.

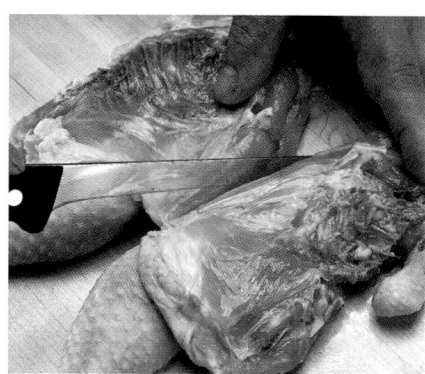

(3) Cut the bird in half through the breast.

FIGURE 6-86   Preparing Halved Birds to Grill or Broil

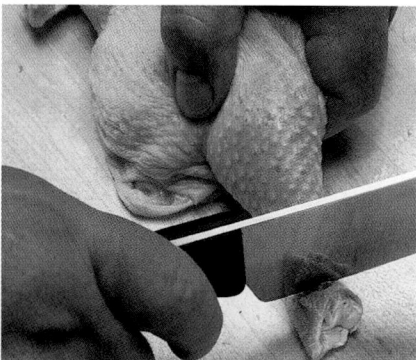

(1) Use the heel of the chef's knife to cut away the end of the drumstick.

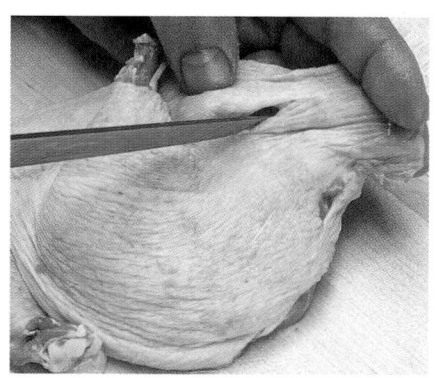

(2) Slit the skin covering the thigh with a boning knife tip to make a pocket.

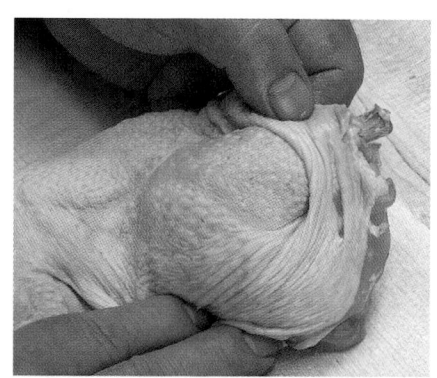

(3) Insert the end of the drumstick into the slit to hold the leg secure during cooking.

facing up. Make an incision just at the top of the keel bone to release it. Then bend the bird so that the keel bone pops out, as shown in Figure 6-85. Cut down the length of the breast to finish dividing the bird into halves.

FIGURE 6-87 Cutting a Bird into Quarters

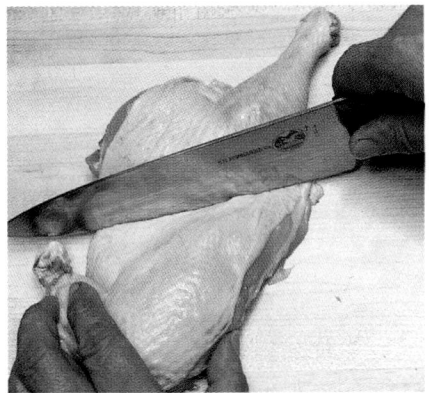

(1) Separate the bird into halves. Then make a diagonal cut to separate the breast from the leg.

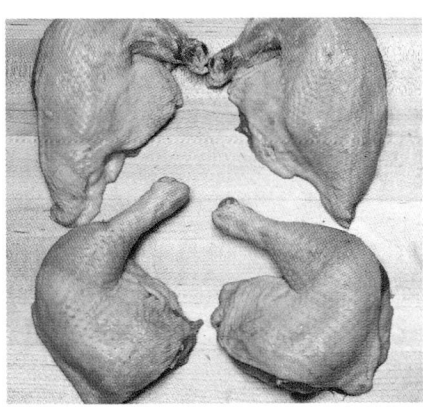

(2) The quartered chicken.

Preparing a Halved Bird to Grill or Broil

Birds that are to be grilled can be given an attractive shape by completing the process shown in Figure 6-86. Here, the chef has removed the end of the drumstick using the heel of the chef's knife. Then, a slit is cut into the skin over the thigh. The end of the drumstick is inserted, creating a neat, compact halved bird that is easy to handle.

Quartering a Bird

Instead of leaving the bird halved, you can continue the cutting process to produce quarters: two leg pieces and two breast pieces. Simply make a cut between the legs and the breast, at the point where the thigh meets the breast, as shown in Figure 6-87(1). A quartered bird is shown in Figure 6-87(2).

Removing the Legs from a Whole Bird

Instead of first removing the backbone, you may opt to remove the legs first. This can be done before or after the wing tips are removed. Make a cut in the skin where the leg and the breast join. Then, bend the leg away from the breast, popping the leg away and exposing the ball joint. Cut through the joint to remove the leg.

The leg can then be separated into two pieces: the drumstick and the thigh. Turn the leg so that you can see a line of fat running over the joint. Use

FIGURE 6-88 Removing the Legs from a Whole Bird

(1) Lay the chicken on its back on a flat work surface. Using a sharp knife, make a cut between the leg and the breast.

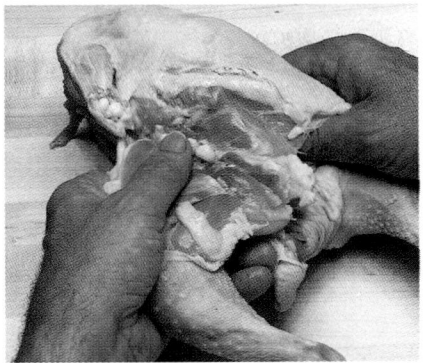

(2) Bend the leg away from the body and press fingertips into the back of the joint to pop the joint loose. Continue to cut the leg away from the breast.

(3) Make a cut completely around the end of the drumstick to sever the flesh, tendons, and skin from the bone.

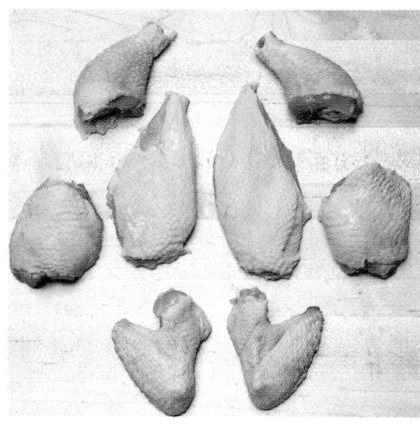

FIGURE 6-89   A Chicken, Cut into Eighths

FIGURE 6-90   Boneless Skinless Breasts

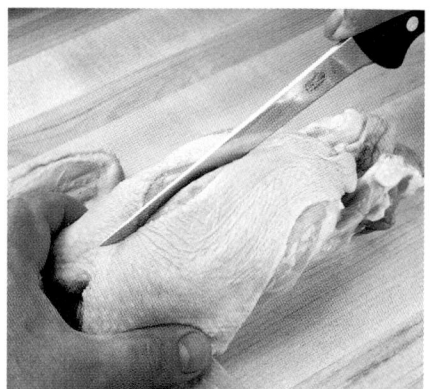

(1) Make a cut along one side of the breastbone to free the breast from the rib cage.

it as a guide to mark the spot where you can easily cut through the joint.

See Figure 6-88 for photos illustrating the method for removing the legs from a whole bird.

Cutting a Bird in Eighths

When a bird is cut into eighths, the chef then has two drumsticks, two thighs, two wing portions, and two breast portions(see Figure 6-89). Broiler or fryer chickens to be pan-fried or deep-fried are usually cut into eighths so that they will cook evenly and thoroughly before their exterior becomes charred. This is also a popular way to cut up poultry for baking, stewing, braising, or barbecuing.

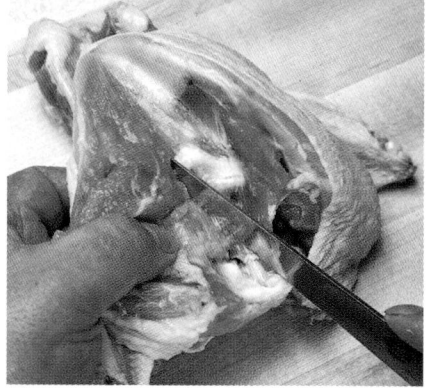

(2) Pull the meat away from the bones as the cut is made so that as little meat as possible is left on the bones.

Boneless, Skinless Chicken Breasts

The breast meat can be cut away from the rib cage before or after the legs are removed. Make a cut along the breast bone, and then carefully cut the meat away from the rib bones. If the wings are still attached, cut through the joint where the wings join the breast.

Be sure to remove the wishbone, if you haven't already. This is removed by either cutting or pushing the bones cleanly from the meat.

Pull the skin away from the breast, and you have completed the process. If desired, the "tenderloin" can be removed from the breast. It is attached by a thin filament, and should pull cleanly away from the breast meat. If necessary, use a paring knife or the tip of a boning knife to completely sever it. The tenderloin has a tendon running through it. This can be removed easily by holding the tendon steady

(3) Make a cut through the joint that attaches the wing to the rib cage. At this point, the chicken breast may be made into suprêmes, or the wings and skin may be completely removed.

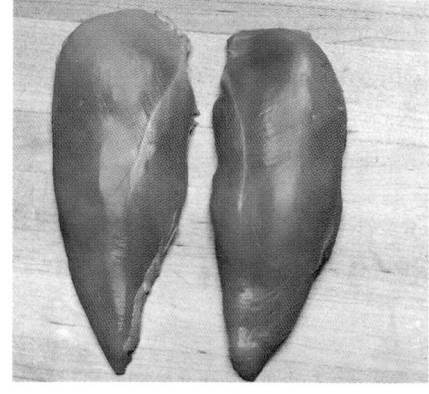

(4) Boneless, skinless chicken breasts.

FIGURE 6-91   Making a Suprême

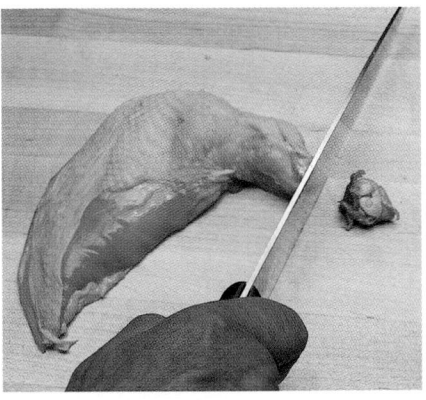

(1) Cut away the first two wing joints. Then use the heel of a chef's knife to cut the end of the remaining wing joint.

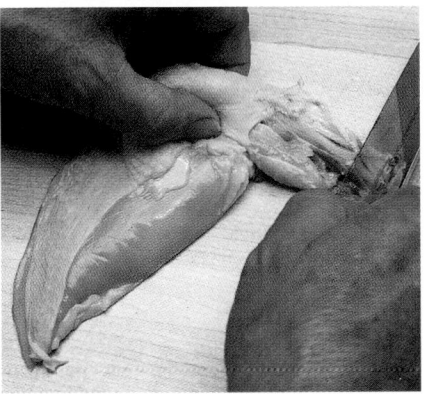

(2) Scrape the meat away from the wing bone, leaving as little meat as possible on the bone.

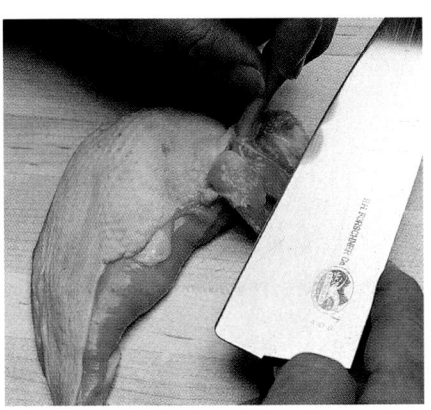

(3) Cut the meat away from the wing bone.

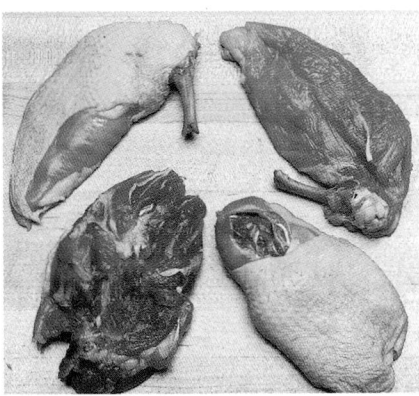

(4) The finished suprême.

with a towel. Press a knife blade at an angle so that the tendon is trapped but not cut, and push the knife away from the hand holding the tendon down, until the entire piece comes out.

See Figure 6-90 for photos illustrating the method for boning and skinning chicken breasts.

Preparing Suprêmes

A suprême is a boneless poultry breast, usually from a chicken, pheasant, partridge, or duck. One wing joint, often frenched, is left attached to the breast meat. The preferred cooking techniques include sautéing, shallow poaching, and grilling.

To prepare a suprême, cut the breast away from the rib cage as you would for a boneless skinless breast. Cut away the wing tips, leaving one section still attached. Use the heel of your chef's knife to french the bone.

See Figure 6-91 for photos illustrating the method for preparing suprêmes.

Boning a Poultry Leg

A boneless leg can be prepared in a number of ways, or it may be cut into strips to use for stir-frys and other dishes. First, make a cut around the end of the drumstick to sever the tendons. Use the tip of a boning knife to cut along the bones, freeing the meat. Then, lift away the bones, cutting through the tendons holding the joint between the drumstick and the thigh.

See Figure 6-92 for photos illustrating the method for boning a poultry leg.

Disjointing a Rabbit

Rabbit is often considered to be similar to chicken, both in terms of its flavor and its relative simplicity to disjoint. The loin and rib sections tend to be dryer than the legs, in much the same way that the chicken breast can be drier than the legs. By first removing the legs and shoulder, as demonstrated in the accompanying photographs, two different cooking methods can be applied to one rabbit—moist heat for the legs, dry heat for the loin—to achieve the most satisfactory results. Or the rabbit can be stewed in pieces.

FIGURE 6-92   Boning a Chicken Leg

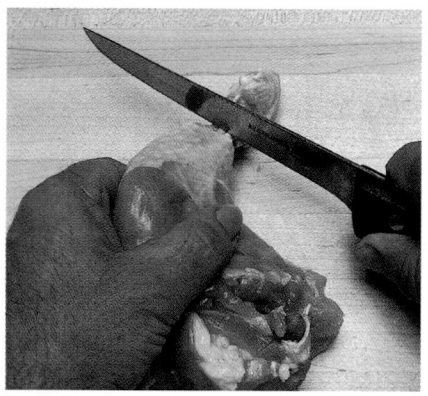

(1) Cut around the end of the drumstick.

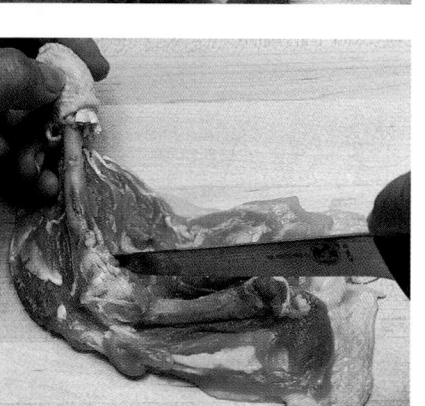

(2) Cut along the natural seams in the meat to expose the drumstick and thighbones. Use the knife tip to cut the meat away from the bone.

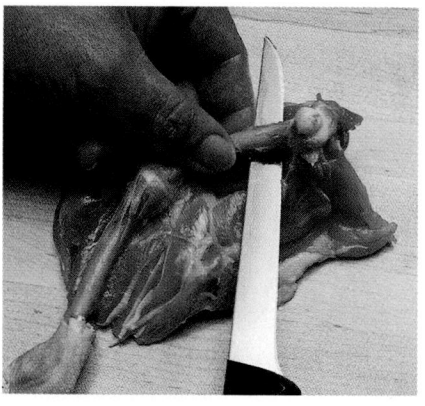

(3) When the bones are completely exposed from the top, run the point of the knife blade underneath them to free them from the meat.

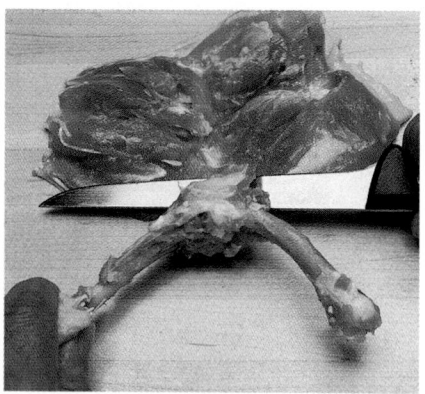

(4) Pull the leg bones away from the meat. Cut the joint that joins the thighbone and the drumstick bone away from the meat. The leg is now completely boneless.

FIGURE 6-93   Disjointing a Rabbit

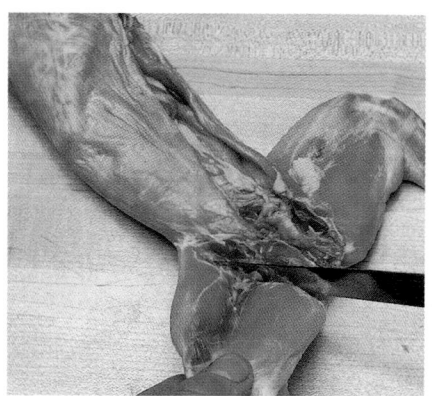

(1) Pull the leg away from the body and then cut through the meat and the joint to separate the leg from the loin.

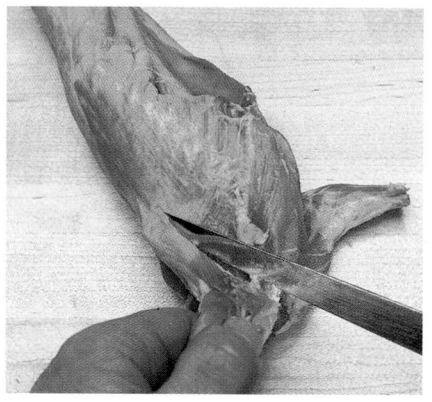

(2) Pull the shoulder away from the body. Cut through the breast and the joint to completely separate the foreleg from the body.

See Figure 6-93 for photos illustrating the method for disjointing a rabbit.

Fish and Shellfish Fabrication

The days of inexpensive fish in great abundance are probably gone. Overfishing of certain species, pollution, and increased demand have made some types of fish difficult or impossible to find. It is, therefore, especially important to make use of this valuable resource in the most profitable way. If whole fish can be cleaned and cut up in-house, with as little trim loss as possible, and if the trim can be put to good use in a mousseline, a filling, canapés, or soups, then fish can still be considered an excellent value.

Fish and shellfish fabrication includes such techniques as scaling, gutting, and cutting round and flat fish into steaks and fillets. Although the more

FIGURE 6-94 Scaling and Trimming Fish

(1) Work in a sink under running water. Hold the fish gently by the head to keep it steady and work from the tail to the head.

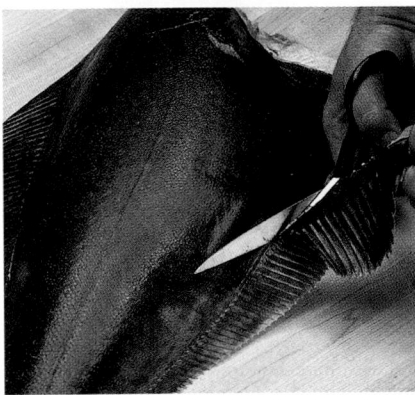

(2) Use scissors to cut fins away.

The best way to remove scales is with a fish scaler. Other tools (the dull side of a table knife, a table crumber, or the handle of a kitchen spoon, for example) can be used if a scaler is not available. Work from the tail toward the head, holding the fish steady by gripping it just behind the eyes. Let the water run as you work so that the scales are less likely to fly around. The fish should not be pinched too tightly, as this could bruise the flesh.

The fins and tail can be cut away at this point, or you may prefer to wait until the fish has been gutted.

See Figure 6-94 for photos illustrating the method for scaling and trimming fish.

Gutting a Fish

Fish may be gutted as soon as it is taken from the water, right on the fishing boat. If you receive fish that have not been gutted yet, you should do this as soon as possible. The gut, or *viscera*, contains enzymes that can begin to break down the flesh rapidly, leading to spoilage. This step may be performed right after the fish has been scaled or, if fish is to be stored on ice, the scales can be allowed to remain until right before cooking. The methods for gutting both round and flat fish are shown in Figure 6-95 a and b.

Pan-Dressed Fish

Pan-dressed fish are those which have been scaled, gutted, and trimmed. In some cases, the head and tail may be removed before cooking. This is not an ironclad rule, however. Depending upon the established practice in your kitchen, or the requirements of a particular dish, you may opt to leave the head and tail on during both cooking and presentation to the guest.

Pan-dressed fish are usually a single portion and their weight is usually no more than 12 ounces after it has been scaled, trimmed, and gutted. Pan-frying and grilling are the most often used techniques for preparing a pan-dressed fish. You may want to add an aromatic filling, such as fresh sprigs of herbs, lemon slices, or scallions to give the fish additional flavor as it cooks.

See Figure 6-96 for photos illustrating two types of pan-dressed fish.

fabrication the chef can do, the more money can be saved, the flip side of this consideration is that if a poor job is done, there will be more waste. If the chef does not have the ability, time, or proper storage space, buying prepared fillets and steaks or already-shucked oysters and clams is more cost-effective.

The techniques shown here are not exceptionally difficult, nor do they require much special equipment. A fish scaler, a sharp flexible filleting knife, needlenose pliers, and a clam and oyster knife are the customary tools.

Scaling and Trimming Fish

Many types of fish, although not all, have scales. Whenever scales are present, the first step in fabricating the fish is to remove them. Scales are difficult to see if they are adhering to flesh rather than to skin.

FIGURE 6-95a   Gutting a Round Fish

(1) Slit the belly of the fish to expose the viscera.

(2) Pull out the viscera.

(3) Rinse the cavity thoroughly under cold running water.

FIGURE 6-95b   Gutting a Flat Fish

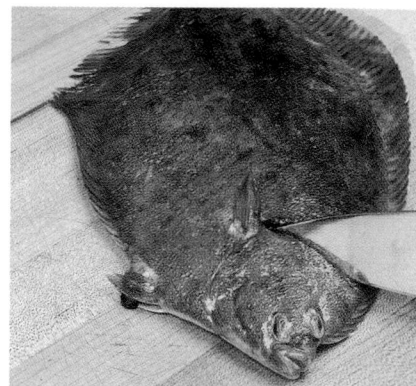

(1) Make a cut as shown.

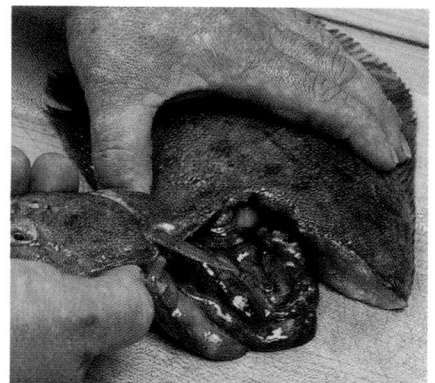

(2) Pull away the head and viscera by hooking your thumb in the head.

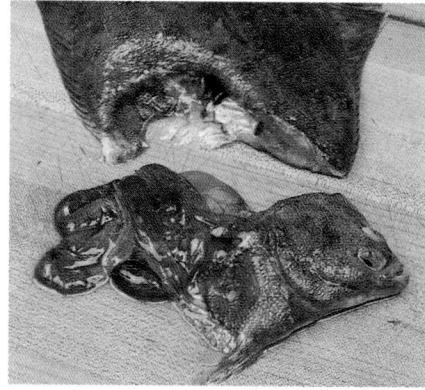

(3) The head and viscera completely removed.

Filleting a Fish

Fillets are one of the most popular cuts of fish. They should be completely boneless. The skin may or may not be removed, depending upon the type of fish. Typical cooking methods for fillets include sautéing, broiling, grilling, baking, and shallow- and deep-poaching. Once fish fillets have been formed, they can be used to prepare *paupiettes, tranches,* or *goujonettes.* These cuts are demonstrated below.

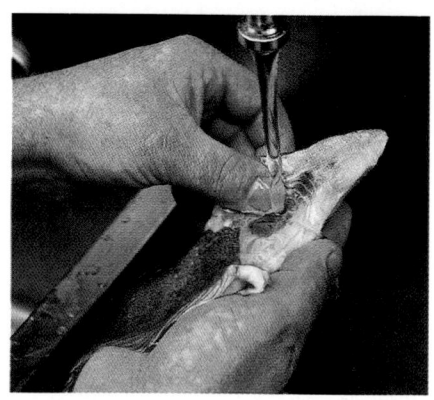

(4) Rinse the cavity thoroughly under cold running water.

FIGURE 6-96   Pan-Dressed Fish

(1) A pan-dressed trout.

(2) Pan-dressed Dover sole.

FIGURE 6-97   Filleting Salmon

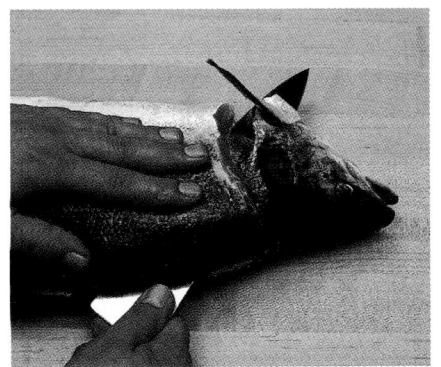

(1) Make a cut behind the head, and run the knife down the length of the fish, working from head to tail on the first side.

(2) Turn the fish to the second side and work from the tail to the head.

(3) Trim away the belly bones.

FIGURE 6-98   Skinning Salmon Fillets

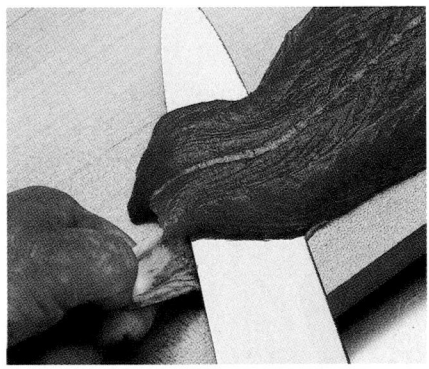

(1) Lay the fillet near the edge of the work surface. Run the blade of a chef's knife between the skin and the flesh, angling the blade downward slightly.

(2) Use a sawing motion, and hold the skin taut to make it easier to remove.

(3) The completely skinned fillet. Note how clean and smooth the flesh is on the skin side.

Round fish, such as salmon, yield two fillets, one from either side. The common approach, for right-handed chefs, is to hold the scaled and gutted fish so that it appears to be swimming away to the right. The second fillet is a little more difficult to remove than the first. See Figure 6-97 for photos illustrating the method for filleting salmon.

Once the fillet is cut away from the fish, you can remove the skin. Be careful that you avoid placing the flesh side down on the cutting surface. There may be some scales or other trim that you would rather not have to rinse or blot away from the fillet.

See Figure 6-98 for photos illustrating the method for skinning salmon.

Some fish, such as salmon, have a number of bones, known as intramuscular, or pin, bones. These are located by gently running your finger down the fillet. Use needlenose pliers or sturdy tweezers to pull them out of the fish. See Figure 6-99 for a photo illustrating the method for removing pin bones.

Flat fish can be cut into two fillets—one from the dark and one from the white side. They can also be made into quarter fillets to make four separate pieces. Figure 6-100 shows how to prepare fillets and quarter fillets from a flounder. The technique for removing the skin from a flounder fillet is shown in Figure 6-101.

Dover sole is handled in a special way. Many chefs like to skin the fish before filleting. The skin is freed from the tail, using a filleting knife, and then it is simply pulled away. See Figure 6-102 for photos illustrating method of skinning Dover sole.

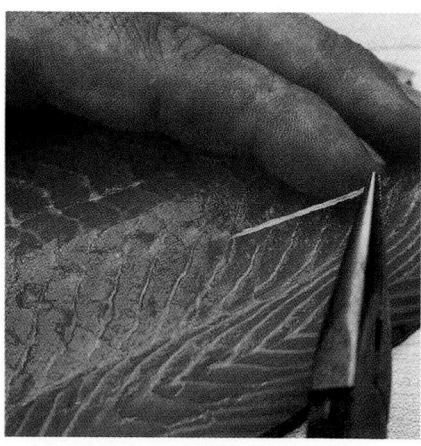

FIGURE 6-99
Removing Pin Bones from Salmon Fillet

Tranche

A *tranche* is simply a slice of the fillet. It is made by holding the knife at an angle while cutting to expose more surface area and give the piece of fish a larger appearance. A tranche can be cut from any relatively large fillet of fish; for example, salmon, halibut, or tuna are often cut into tranches. Though this cut is normally associated with sautéed or pan-fried preparations, it is perfectly acceptable to grill or broil a tranche.

See Figure 6-103 for a photo illustrating cutting a tranche.

Goujonette

The name for this cut is derived from the French name for small fish, *goujon*. *Goujonettes* are small strips cut from a fillet, often breaded or dipped in batter, and then deep-fried. This cut has approximately the same dimensions as an adult's index finger. Goujonettes are normally cut from lean white fish, such as sole or flounder, and may be served with a piquant sauce, such as remoulade or tartar sauce.

See Figure 6-104 for a photo illustrating cutting a goujounette.

Paupiette

A *paupiette* is a thin, rolled fillet, often filled with a forcemeat or other stuffing. It should resemble a large cork or spiral. Paupiettes are generally made from lean fish, such as flounder or sole, although they may also be made from some moderately fatty fish, such as trout or salmon. The most common preparation technique for paupiettes is shallow-poaching.

See Figure 6-105 for a photo illustrating a paupiette.

Cutting Steaks

Steaks are simply cross-cuts of the fish and are relatively easy to make. The fish is scaled, gutted,

FIGURE 6-100   Filleting Flounder

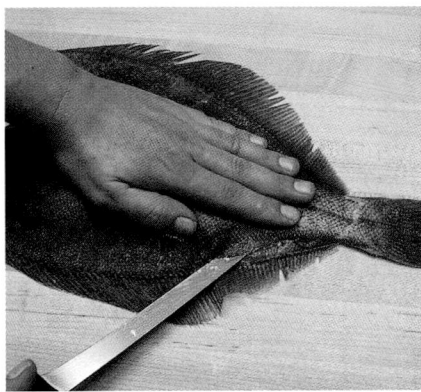

(1) Make the initial cut as shown.

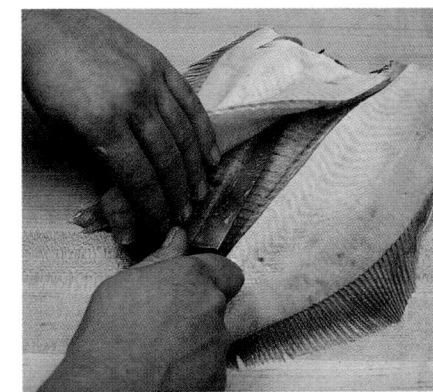

(5) Make cuts from the center working outward.

(2) Continue cutting, lifting the flesh away as you work.

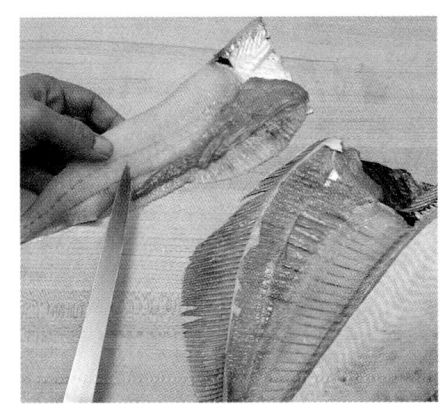

(6) Trim the fillet.

(3) Turn the fish and continue cutting to make a double fillet.

(7) Remove the final quater fillet.

(4) To make quarter fillets, first cut down the center of the fish.

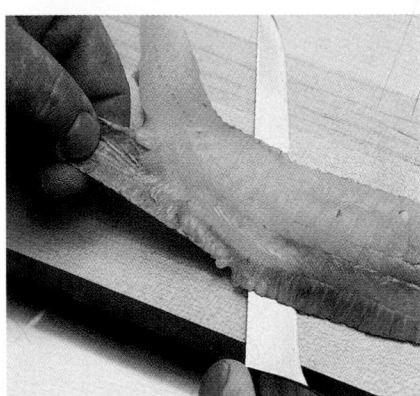

FIGURE 6-101
Skinning
Flounder Fillets

FIGURE 6-102   Trimming and Peeling Dover Sole

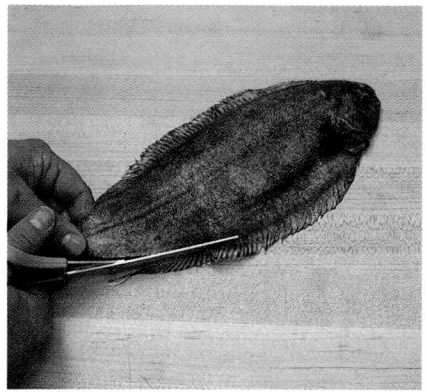

(1) Cut away fins.

(2) Make an initial cut to loosen the skin.

(3) Pull the skin away before filleting the fish, if desired.

FIGURE 6-103   Cutting a Tranche from Salmon Fillets

FIGURE 6-104   Cutting Goujonettes from Flounder Fillets

FIGURE 6-105   Preparing Paupiettes

FIGURE 6-106   Cutting Fish Steaks

(1) Cutting salmon steaks from a gutted and trimmed salmon.

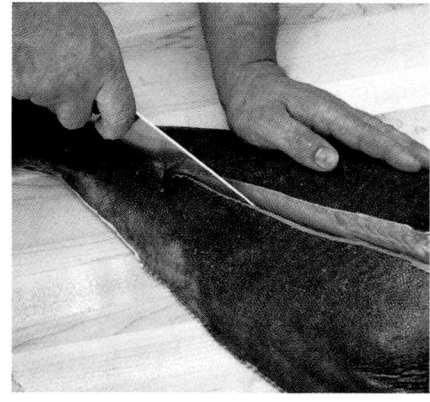

(2) Cutting a halibut in half as first step of preparing steaks.

(3) Cutting the steaks from halibut.

FIGURE 6-107   Cleaning Shrimp

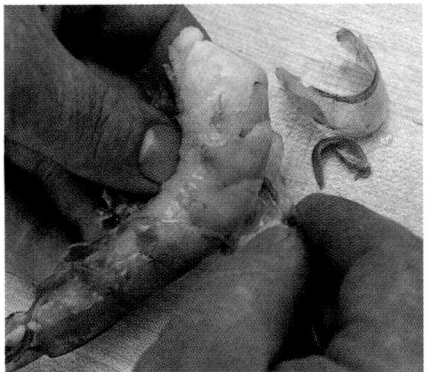

(1) Pulling away the shell.

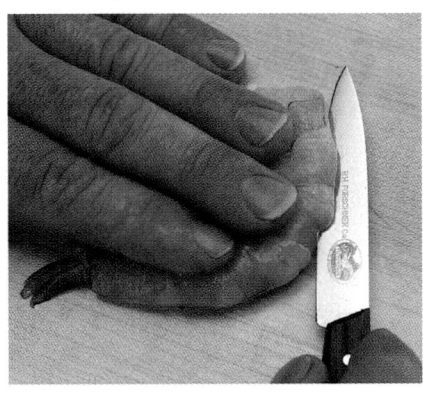

(2) Cutting along the back vein.

(3) Removing the intestinal tract.

and trimmed of its fins. The size of the steak is determined by the cut's thickness. There are a few flat fish large enough to cut into steaks—halibut, and turbot are two examples.

See Figure 6-106 for photos illustrating the method for cutting steaks.

Working with Shellfish

Shrimp

Shrimp are typically peeled, deveined, and occasionally butterflied before cooking.

Peeling and Deveining Shrimp

Shrimp can be cooked in the shell, before peeling and deveining. For many preparations, however, recipes clearly state that shrimp are to be cleaned before cooking. And, in other instances, these operations may be performed after cooking the shrimp.

The greatest advantage to peeling and deveining raw shrimp before cooking is that the shrimp will not be as easy to overcook as they might be if they were left in the shell. There are specific tools available that will lift away the shell and make an incision along the back of the shrimp, pulling away the vein, but a sharp paring knife is all you need.

See Figure 6-107 for photos illustrating the method for peeling and deveining shrimp.

Butterflying Shrimp

To butterfly a shrimp, use a small sharp knife, such as a paring knife, to cut into the shrimp at the same point where the vein was removed. Cut into the shrimp deeply enough to allow the sides to flatten out, but don't cut all the way through the meat.

Lobster

Lobster can be handled in a number of ways before cooking. Some chefs prefer to simply plunge the live lobster into a pot of boiling water. Others believe that it is more humane to kill the lobster. This is generally accomplished by inserting the tip of a knife into the back of the lobster, just behind the "head." This is done to sever the nerve, killing the lobster before boiling, steaming, or broiling. Because lobsters have relatively simple nervous systems, you may see that the lobster continues to move. Keep the bands on the claws to avoid being pinched until the lobster is cooked or stops moving completely.

Working with Cooked Lobster

It is easier to remove the meat from a lobster that has been partially or fully cooked. Cook the lobster by steaming, boiling, or baking. The lobster need not be completely cooked. It is only important that the flesh has begun to firm slightly.

FIGURE 6-108   Working with Cooked Lobsters

(1) Halving a cooked lobster.

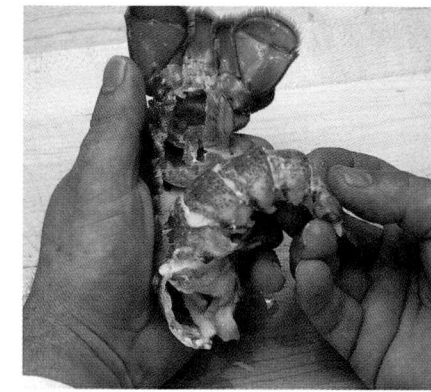

(5) Releasing the meat from the shell.

(2) The halved lobster.

(6) To remove flesh from the claws, you can crack it with a mallet, or...

(3) Pulling the tail away from the body.

(7) Use a nutcracker to break the shell, or...

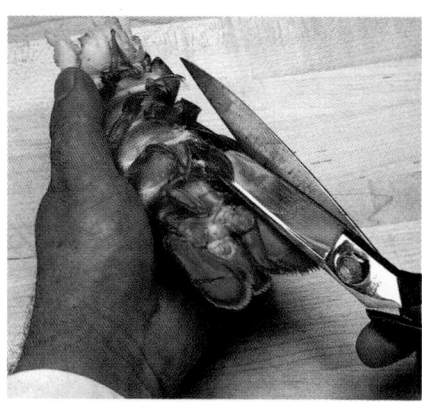

(4) Cutting the shell away with kitchen shears.

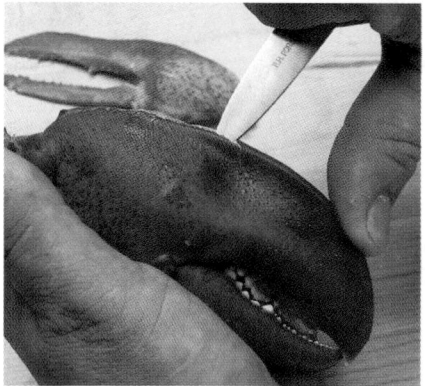

(8) Cut through the shell with the tip of a paring knife.

FIGURE 6-109 Working with Crayfish

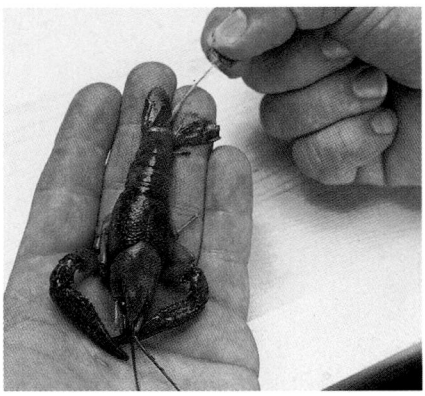

(1) Twist the middle fan of the tail and pull out the intestinal tract, before cooking.

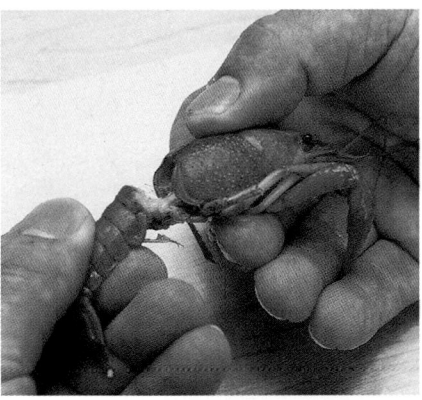

(2) Once cooked, pull the tail away and...

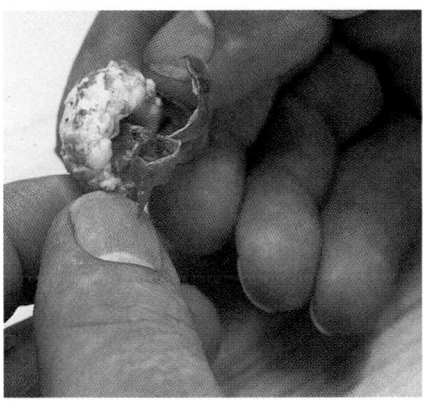

(3) Pull the shell away from the meat.

Techniques for halving a lobster and removing the tail and claw meat are shown in Figure 6-108.

Crayfish

Crayfish share many similarities with lobster, but they are much smaller. Crayfish are especially popular in Cajun and Creole dishes. Like shrimp, they may be simply boiled or steamed and peeled after cooking when the meat is easy to remove from the shell. It is relatively simple to remove the vein from the crayfish before cooking, though this may be done afterward, if preferred.

See Figure 6-109 for photos illustrating how to clean crayfish.

Crab

Blue crab, like lobster, are purchased live. You may prefer to kill them before cooking, as you would do for lobster. Once crabs are cooked, the meat is often removed from the shell. It must be examined carefully, or "picked" to remove any bits of shell or cartilage that remain. This step is important for tinned or frozen crab meat, as well as that which you cook and clean yourself.

Cleaning a Soft-Shelled Crab

A seasonal favorite, soft-shelled crabs are considered a great delicacy. They are not especially difficult to clean once their various parts are identified. Soft-shelled crabs are commonly prepared by sautéing or pan-frying, and the shell may be eaten along with the meat.

See Figure 6-110 for photos illustrating the method for cleaning a soft-shelled crab.

Molluscs

Cleaning and Opening Clams and Oysters

Freshly shucked oysters and clams are required for such classic dishes as oysters Rockefeller or clams casino. Although shucked oysters and clams are available, you may prefer to open them yourself to assure freshness in chowders, gumbos, and other dishes. The practice of serving clams and oysters on the half shell is an important aspect of some establishments.

Clean all molluscs (clams, oysters, and mussels) well by scrubbing them under running water to remove all dirt. Check them carefully. Live clams and oysters will have tightly closed shells. Any that are open, or that feel "heavy" are either dead or close to death, or full of silt. Discard them.

To protect your hands, use a wire mesh glove and/or side towels. Clam and oyster knives should be used, as shown in Figures 6-111 and 6-112.

FIGURE 6-110   Cleaning a Soft-Shelled Crab

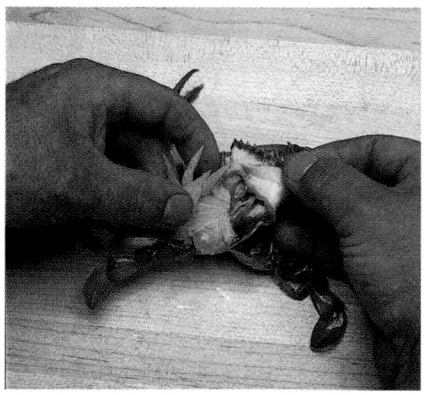

(1) Peel back the pointed shell and scrape away the gill filament on each side.

(2) Cut off the head and carefully squeeze out the green bubble behind the eyes.

(3) Bend back the apron and twist to remove it and the intestinal vein at the same time.

(4) The cleaned crab.

FIGURE 6-111   Cleaning and Opening Oysters

(1) Scrub the oyster well under running water.

(2) Wear a mesh glove to protect your hands. Insert the tip of the oyster knife into the hinge of the shell.

(3) Release the flesh from the shell.

Cleaning and Debearding Mussels

Mussels are rarely served raw, but the method for cleaning them before steaming and poaching is similar to that used for clams. Unlike clams and oysters, mussels have a dark, shaggy beard that is normally pulled away before cooking.

See Figure 6-113 for photos illustrating the method for cleaning and debearding mussels.

FIGURE 6-112 Opening Clams

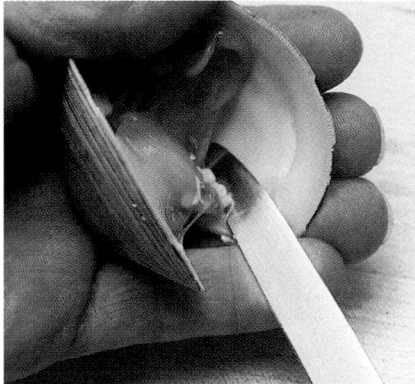

(1) Use the tip of the knife to release the meat from the top shell.

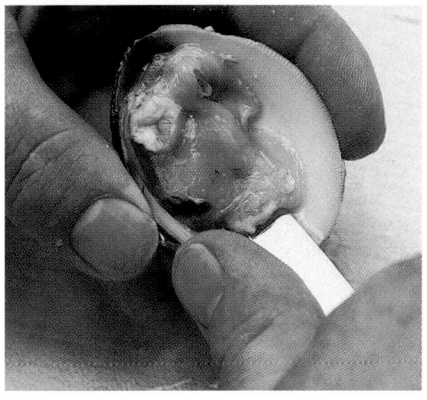

(2) Run the knife under the clam meat to loosen. This clam can now be served "on the half shell."

Cephalopods

This group includes squid, octopus, and cuttlefish. There are some ethnic terms used for these shellfish that may be equally familiar to you and your guests—for instance, *calamari* or *scungilli* are Italian terms. These shellfish are not difficult to prepare, but they do need some advance preparation to remove the ink sac and quill.

When properly fabricated and cooked, they are tender, sweet, and flavorful with a distinctive texture. The mantle can be cut into rings to sauté, pan-fry, or deep-fry; or it may be left whole to grill or braise, with or without a stuffing. If desired, the ink sac can be saved and used to prepare various dishes, such as pasta *(calamares en su tinta)* and rice *(arroz negro)*.

Cleaning Squid and Octopus

Pull away any skin that remains on the mantle and tentacles. Rinse carefully, and pull out the "quill" from the mantle. Cut the tentacles away from the body if desired, by cutting just behind the eye. To remove an octopus's beak, use the tip of a knife or pop it out with your fingers.

See Figure 6-114 for photos illustrating the method for cleaning squid and Figure 6-115 for cleaning octopus.

Miscellaneous Items

Cleaning a Sea Urchin

Sea urchins are a spiny marine fish that may not be available in all areas of the country. They are considered a delicacy in many cuisines, especially French and Japanese. When working with these creatures, the chef should always wear thick rubber gloves to protect his or her hands. Scrape or cut away the spines, which can be quite painful if they pierce the skin. This may be done before cleaning, if desired.

FIGURE 6-113 Cleaning and Debearding Mussels

(1) Scrub well under running water.

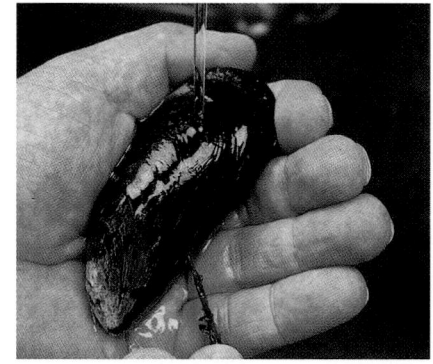

(2) Pull the beard away.

(3) The cleaned and debearded mussel.

FIGURE 6-114   Cleaning Squid

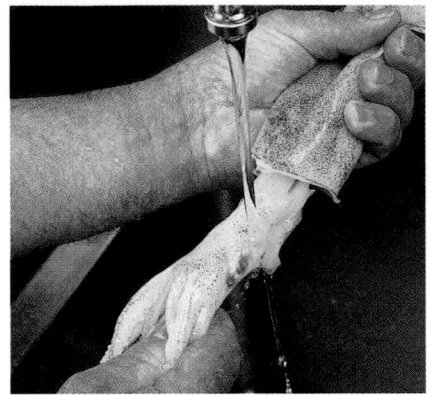

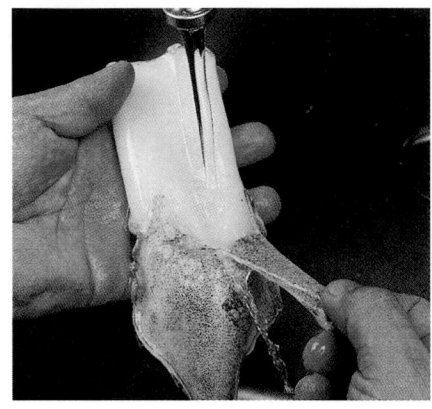

(1) Pull the mantle and tentacles apart under running water.

(2) Pull off the skin from the mantle.

(3) Pull out the quill.

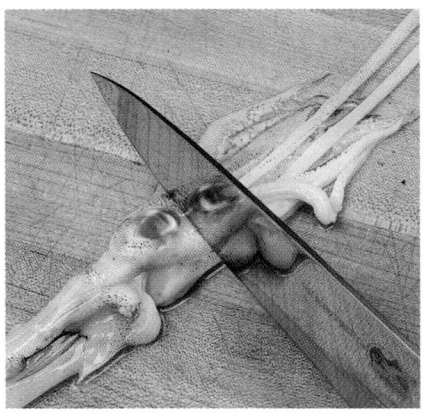

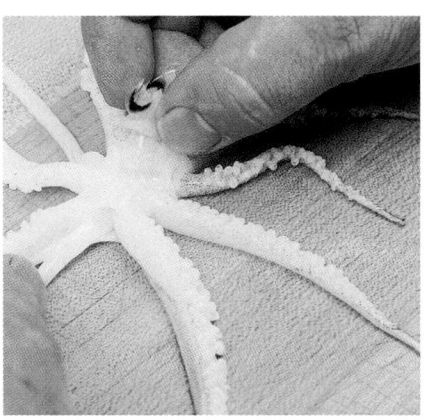

(4) Cut the tentacles away from the head by cutting just above the eye. If desired, the ink sac may be reserved.

(5) Open out the tentacles and pull out the beak.

FIGURE 6-115   Cleaning Octopus

(1) Use the tip of a filleting knife to cut around the eye and lift it from the octopus.

(2) Peel the skin away from the body by pulling firmly.

(3) Pull the suction cups away from the tentacles.

FIGURE 6-116   Cleaning a Sea Urchin

(1) Wear gloves to protect your hands and cut off the shell's top with scissors.

(2) The urchin, cleaned and ready to serve. (Note that you may prefer to shave off the spines before opening and serving.)

FIGURE 6-117   Skinning an Eel

(1) Use a sharp filleting knife to make an incision completely around the fish just behind the fins nearest the head.

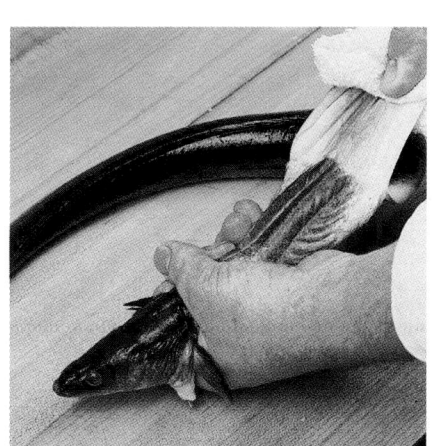

(2) Hold the head securely with one hand and pull the skin away. Hold the skin with a kitchen towel to prevent slipping.

See Figure 6-116 for photos illustrating the method for cleaning a sea urchin.

Skinning an Eel

This is not one of the easiest of tasks, because the eel's skin is firmly attached. It may take several attempts to accomplish the job. The skin must be removed before cooking because it is tough and slippery. The best-known preparation for eel is *matelote,* an eel stew.

See Figure 6-117 for photos illustrating the method for skinning an eel.

Summary

Mise en place is the foundation of all kitchen operations. Any well-schooled chef should be able to produce such commonly used items as mirepoix, bouquet garni, and roux with ease and speed. Assembling properly trimmed steaks, filleted fish, perfectly cleaned salad greens, and minced herbs is as much a part of the chef's daily work as is the preparation of sauces and garnishing of finished plates.

CHAPTER 7 *Soups*

Soups are not only important menu items, they also fulfill several other roles crucial to a restaurant's successful operation. They are an excellent way to show-case a "signature dish" such as a fabulous French onion soup, a robust gumbo or chowder, or a refined consommé with a spectacular garnish. They are a good vehicle for making use of wholesome trim from other kitchen operations: chicken legs, thighs, and backs are used to make rich broth; neatly diced or julienned, cooked meats become a garnish for a soup; even croutons made from the "heels" of loaves of bread are just a few of the cost-savings that can be accomplished when soups are an important part of the menu.

Lunch menus frequently rely on a typically American institution: soup and sandwich, and two important variations on that theme: soup and quiche or soup and salad. It is hard to imagine a lunch menu that has no soup offering. The "soup du jour" has become such a standard that people expect to see it on the menu, or hear about it from their server.

Soups can be hearty, as is the case with regional specialties: chowders, gumbos, thick vegetable or bean soups. They can also be smooth and suave: cream of mushroom, broccoli, or celery. Light broths and consommés tend to do well on dinner menus, when (it is hoped) diners will select a soup that will whet, not overwhelm, their appetite for a more substantial entrée.

The season will have a great deal to do with which soups do well on a menu. In fall, corn chowders, pumpkin bisques, and other soups made from the fullness of the harvest are appropriate. In winter, a filling, steaming bowl of goulash soup or borscht is appealing. Soups in spring can capitalize on tender fresh vegetables, such as

asparagus, green peas, sorrel, and lettuces. In summer, the refreshing, bright flavors and textures of cold soups (gazpacho, vichyssoise, cold fruit soups) are an attractive contrast to the season's heat.

For all these reasons, it is important for the chef to fully master the techniques used to prepare a wide variety of soups. That means learning the fundamentals necessary to produce several distinct styles of soups:

- *Broths*
- *Consommés*
- *Clear vegetable soups*
- *Cream soups and velouté soups*
- *Purée soups*
- *Bisques*
- *Special soups (including international and regional)*
- *Cold soups*

The skills involved in making soups include the proper preparation of excellent-quality basic flavoring and aromatic combinations (covered in Chapter 6: Mise en Place) such as stocks, mirepoix, bouquet garni, and sachet d'épices. A review of any techniques or preparations that are unfamiliar is

TABLE 7-1 SELECTING INGREDIENTS FOR BROTH	
Main item	*Possible choices*
Beef	Shank, chuck, bottom round, oxtail, short ribs/flanken. *Note that a portion of veal shank/shin may also be added.*
Veal	Shank/shin, chuck, bottom round, calves' head.
Pork	Hocks (fresh or smoked), meaty ham bones, boston butt.
Lamb	Shank, leg, shoulder.
Poultry	Stewing hens, necks and backs (meaty portions), legs.
Fish	Lean white fish, including cod, halibut, hake, flounder, pike.
Shellfish	Shrimp, lobster, clams, mussels.
Vegetables	Carrots, onions, parsnips, leeks, mushrooms, tomatoes, celery, celeriac, garlic, shallots, fennel, broccoli stems. Others as deemed appropriate by recipe or intended use.

suggested before undertaking the actual preparation of a particular soup.

For many soups, the fundamental technique and the basic ratio of liquid to principle ingredient (and thickener, if necessary) are all the chef needs in order to produce a wide variety of soups. Once these techniques and ratios are learned, a quick survey of the ingredients on hand or due to arrive from the purveyor or available in the farmer's market can act as the inspiration for the "soup du jour." Recipes, which can be found in Part IV, Chapter 14, offer concrete examples and classic renditions of soups that should be part of any chef's repertoire.

Basic Soup-Making Techniques

Broths

A broth is a clear soup made from meats, poultry, fish, or vegetables. Broths can be used in many of the same applications as a stock: as the basis of other soups, sauces, stews, and braised dishes. Unlike stocks, however, broths may be served "as is."

A perfectly made broth should be translucent, amber to golden brown in color. When you take a spoonful into your mouth, you should sense a perceptible body, as well as a rich, deep, and well-balanced flavor. The aroma of the finished broth should be such that it immediately stimulates the appetite.

In order to produce a broth that has all these characteristics, the chef needs to observe the basic rules of broth preparation:

- Proper selection of ingredients

- Careful monitoring of the broth as it develops

- Safe handling procedures throughout cooking, cooling, reheating, and service.

Mise en Place

1. Assemble all ingredients necessary for making the broth.

The best broths are made from the most flavorful meats, fish, vegetables, and aromatics. This means that you should select from among the ingredients detailed in Table 7-1. Generally speaking, meat cuts should be selected from more exercised parts of the animal. The more fully developed the muscle, the more pronounced the flavor. The same is true of poultry broths. In this case, stewing hens or more mature game birds are the best choice. They have a deeper flavor than younger birds.

Fish should also be carefully selected. Freshness is of tremendous concern, as is the relative leanness or oiliness of the fish. Generally speaking, it is best to use lean, white-fleshed fish, such as sole, halibut, cod, or flounder. Richer or oilier fish tend to lose their fresh savor when the delicate oils found in the fish are subjected to high temperatures for even short periods. Shellfish are generally cooked in a small amount of liquid still in their shells to produce excellent broths. They must be strained very carefully to remove all traces of grit or sand.

Vegetable broths are made from any reasonable combination of vegetables. A selection of wholesome trim from a variety of vegetables (carrots, celery, fennel, onions, leeks, parsnips, tomatoes, broccoli stems, lettuce leaves, for instance) can be combined to make a broth, or a specific recipe can be followed. There are no real hard-and-fast rules about which vegetables to use in preparing a vegetable broth, beyond this simple advice: Do not use any vegetable you would otherwise consign to the compost bucket.

When you select the best ingredients for a broth, you are well on the way to producing the best-quality product. It is equally important to remember that a ratio exists between flavoring ingredients and liquid in order to get a broth that is deep, complex, full-bodied, and flavorful. To produce 1 gallon of broth, you will need:

- 8 to 10 pounds of meat or poultry to 6 quarts of cold water, or
- 10 to 11 pounds of fish or shellfish to 4 quarts of cold water, or
- 6 to 8 pounds of vegetables to 4 quarts of cold water;

plus

- 1 pound of mirepoix;
- 1 standard sachet d'épices or bouquet garni

A number of additional ingredients can be selected to add flavor, aroma, and color to a broth. In addition to herb and vegetable combinations such as mirepoix or bouquet garni, contemporary renditions may call for ingredients such as lemongrass, wild mushrooms, or gingerroot to give a broth its unique character. The recipes found in this book and in many other books illustrate the breadth of possibilities.

A quick glance through any classic or contemporary cookbook will offer endless inspiration for garnishing broths. Simple items, such as chervil "pluches" or a fine brunoise of vegetables, are traditional choices. Other options include diced or julienned meats, pieces of fish or shellfish, dumplings, noodles, rice, croutons, quenelles, and wontons.

2. Assemble all necessary equipment for preparing broth.

Select a pot large enough to accommodate the broth as it cooks. There should be sufficient room at the top of the pot to allow for some expansion during cooking, as well as to make it easy to skim away any impurities on the surface. If available, select a pot with a spigot, to make it easier to transfer the broth from the pot.

You will also need skimmers and ladles, strainers, tasting spoons and cups, and a kitchen fork to remove any large pieces of meat.

If the soup is to be cooled, you will need a clean stainless steel bain-marie (or several) to hold the soup in a cold-water bath. Then, once it is fully cooled (be sure to check it carefully with an instant-reading thermometer), transfer it to clean storage containers with lids. Label and date carefully, along with any additional instructions regarding final seasoning and garnishing.

Method

1. Combine the principle ingredients with a cool liquid and bring the broth to a gentle boil.

Most broths are started with the simplest of all liquids: cool, fresh water. In some cases, you may elect to use a stock or broth as the base liquid. This will produce what is sometimes referred to as a "double broth."

It is important to use cool water (or, if appropriate, cool stock or broth). This will help to gently extract as much flavor as possible. And, in the case of meat-based broths, it will help establish a natural clarification process.

As the broth comes to a boil, be sure to skim the surface carefully to remove as much scum as possible. If this is allowed to remain in the pot, it will eventually cloud the broth. It could even be responsible for the development of an unpleasant aroma or taste. A hard boil should be avoided. It could "cook out" the flavor of the ingredients.

2. Add the remaining ingredients at appropriate intervals.

Some vegetables and herbs will release their best flavor into a broth quickly. Continued cooking, rather than intensifying the flavor, could actually cook away the delicate, volatile oils that hold their flavor essence. Most recipes will indicate which items to add later in the cooking process. The rule of thumb is that the denser the ingredient, the earlier on it is added. Carrots, then, are added near the beginning of cooking time. Parsley stems and branches of fresh thyme are added near the end.

3. Check the flavor of the broth periodically during cooking time.

The only way to be sure that your broth is developing properly is to taste it from time to time as it simmers. This allows you the opportunity to make corrections if necessary. If the clove you added to the sachet d'épices threatens to overwhelm the broth, remove it. If there is a certain lack of rich, roasted flavors, add an oignon brûlé. Final seasoning and flavor adjustments, however, are generally done after the major flavoring ingredients have given up their maximum flavor. Meats, fish, and poultry will usually be fork tender. Vegetables should be extremely soft, but should not have cooked into shreds.

Broths are properly cooked at about the following times:

- For beef, veal, game, or chicken: 2 to 3 hours
- For fish: 30 to 45 minutes
- For vegetables: 30 minutes to 1 hour

4. Strain the broth carefully through a fine sieve or bouillon strainer.

At this stage, the broth is now ready for either service (see below) or proper cooling and storage following the procedures outlined for stock in Chapter 6.

See Part IV, Chapter 14, for specific broth recipes.

Consommés

When they are properly made, consommés are rich, clear soups made by simmering broth or stock with a combination of ingredients known as a clarification. The combination of ingredients in the clarification—lean meat, egg whites, tomatoes or wine, and aromatic vegetables and herbs—removes any particles suspended in the broth. It also serves to fortify the soup's overall flavor.

The best-quality consommés are crystal clear, completely fat free, and amber to brown in color, with a good body. The majority of consommés are served hot, with a special garnish, such as royales, quenelles, perfectly cooked vegetables, or chopped fresh herbs.

Consommés occasionally suffer from a bad reputation. People may tend to think of these soups as weak, even insipid. This may be due in part to the fact that they have become accustomed to consommés made from weakly flavored broths based on bones with very little or no meat left on them. These quality standards need to be remembered:

- Full flavor
- Rich, noticeable body
- A succulence and savor that last in the mouth
- A deep amber to brown color
- Clarity
- Well-balanced flavor

Mise en Place

1. Assemble the ingredients and appareils necessary for the consommé.

Check the quality of broth or stock before preparing consommé as follows: Bring a small amount to a full boil, then smell and taste, checking for fresh, clean, appealing flavors and smells. If there is any doubt about the quality of the broth, use a fresher batch or prepare a new broth.

To reduce the total cooking time, reserve about one-fourth of the total broth required to "temper" the clarification. The remainder of the broth or stock can then be brought to a simmer while preparing the ingredients for the clarification.

The clarification is a combination of lean ground meat, egg whites, mirepoix, herbs and spices, and tomato or another acidic ingredient. This mixture of ingredients is responsible for producing a crystal-clear soup. It also serves as a way to bolster and reinforce the flavor of the finished soup. All these ingredients serve not just one but multiple functions in preparing a well-balanced consommé.

Whenever possible, it is best to freshly grind meat, poultry, or fish, as appropriate. Whether or not you grind the meat in house, be sure to keep it, as well as the egg whites, refrigerated so that they remain wholesome and flavorful. Additionally, when the meat and egg whites are properly chilled, the proteins will begin to coagulate more slowly than if they were warm. This increases their ability to extract impurities present in the broth or stock

Mirepoix vegetables should be cut so that they will become part of the network created as the consommé comes to a simmer and the meat's proteins begin to adhere into a large mass, without being so large and heavy that they fall out of the formed "raft." A variety of aromatic vegetables such as onions, carrots, celery, parsnips, mushrooms, and leeks are typically selected. Other special items are used as necessary or appropriate to achieve a special flavor.

Herbs and spices are also included in the clarification mixture for supporting or starring roles in the big flavor picture. Garlic, cloves, sprigs or stems of tarragon, parsley, chervil, dill, thyme, or other fresh herbs, bay leaf, peppercorns, gingerroot, juniper berries, star anise, and lemongrass are among the many options chefs feature in contemporary renditions of consommé.

An oignon brûlé or oignon piqué is also commonly included in the ingredients selected for flavoring or coloring a consommé.

There are hundreds of classically codified garnishes for consommés, ranging from humble items such as neatly diced root vegetables, to the esoteric edible gold leaf featured in a recipe found in Escoffier's *Le Guide Culinaire*.

Contemporary chefs have extended the range of possibilities even further. They draw on influences as diverse as Eastern Asian cuisines, Caribbean dishes, or Italian provincial cooking styles. No matter what the garnish selected may be, it is important to remember the following guidelines:

- The garnish itself should be as well prepared as the consommé
- Vegetable cuts should be neat and precise
- Royales should be delicately set, soft, and supple in the mouth
- The seasoning selected for the garnish should serve to enhance the flavor of the consommé, not distract from it

2. Assemble all necessary equipment for preparing consommés.

Equipment needs for consommé are the same as those described for broths. Review the information earlier in this chapter.

FIGURE 7-1 Preparing Consommé

(1) The stock and clarification are thoroughly blended.

(2) The consommé is breaking through the raft. An onion brûlé gives additional color and flavor.

(3) The raft has risen to the top.

Method

1. Blend the ingredients for the clarification and add the broth. (See Figure 7-1 for photos illustrating the method for preparing a consommé.)

Mix all the ingredients directly in the pot until the mixture is fairly homogenous. Gradually add the cold broth. Stir the broth into the clarification mixture until evenly blended.

If you need to speed up the process, heat the broth to a simmer, reserving ¼ the total volume of the cold stock to temper the clarification.

2. Bring the consommé slowly to a boil.

Continue to stir the consommé as it comes to a boil. As the temperature rises, the clarification ingredients will begin to adhere into a large, soft mass known as a "raft." Once the raft begins to form, stop stirring the consommé, to allow the raft to come together.

3. Once the raft forms, establish a gentle, even simmer.

As the raft coagulates into a mass, it will rise to the surface of the broth. Since the raft traps the heat, in much the same way that a lid on a pot traps the heat, it is important to adjust the heat to establish a gentle simmer. Many chefs will break a small hole, large enough for a ladle to pass through. This helps to prevent the consommé from coming to a rapid boil. It also makes it possible to baste the raft as the consommé is cooking.

(4) The finished consommé.

Look to see if you have a number of small bubbles breaking on the surface. If there is a strong simmering or boiling action, the raft might break apart before it has properly cleared and flavored the consommé. On the other hand, if the cooking speed is too slow, there may not be sufficient convection within the pot to carry impurities from the bottom of the pot to the top, where they can be "trapped" by the raft. The raft may actually sink below the surface of the consommé before cooking time is completed.

4. Continue to simmer the consommé until it has fully developed.

The goal is to produce a soup that is very rich and smooth, with an even, well-balanced flavor. Recipes will specify a cooking time—(generally, 1 to 1½ hours). When the raft begins to sink slightly, if we assume that this event happens after a reasonable cooking time rather than because the heat wasn't adjusted properly, the consommé is most likely properly simmered.

But, the only way to be sure that the consommé has cooked long enough is to taste it occasionally as it cooks. Once you taste the consommé at different stages, you will be able, with continued practice, to recognize when it has reached a peak of flavor and body. When the consommé is properly cooked, check it again for seasoning and make any necessary adjustments at this point, before straining the soup. Remember to pour a small amount into a soup bowl or plate to assess its clarity as well.

Refer to the section on safe food handling practices in Chapter 2.

5. Strain the finished consommé carefully.

The finished consommé should be strained through either a fine wire mesh sieve (known as a bouillon strainer) or carefully rinsed cheesecloth. If cheesecloth is used, be sure that it has been properly prepared as follows: Rinse it first in very hot water to remove any loose fibers or items that may have been left on the surface of the cheesecloth during its own processing. Then, once the water runs perfectly clear, rinse it with cold water. Rinsing is important not only to remove fibers that could cloud the soup, it also helps the cheesecloth to adhere to the strainer or colander.

Avoid breaking up the raft as you strain the consommé. Allow it to drain out of the pot or steam kettle through a spigot, if there is one. Otherwise, carefully enlarge the opening in the raft, then use a ladle to dip the consommé out of the pot. Don't pour the consommé and raft into a strainer, since it will release some of the impurities you have worked so hard to cook out of the consommé back into the soup.

The consommé is now ready for service or to be properly cooled and stored, following the procedures outlined in Chapter 2.

Refer to Part IV, Chapter 14 for specific consommé recipes.

Clear Vegetable Soups

Clear vegetable soups are based on clear broth or stock. The vegetables are cut into an appropriate and uniform size and the soup is simmered until all ingredients are tender. Meats, grains, and pastas are frequently included to give additional body. Vegetable soups may also be made from a single vegetable, as is done when preparing onion soup. Clear vegetable soups should have a full flavor and be somewhat thicker than broths. Because additional ingredients are cooked directly in the broth, these soups will lack the clarity of either broth or consommé. Croutons are a common garnish, and they may be an integral part of the preparation, as for French onion soup *gratiné*.

Mise en Place

1. Assemble and prepare all ingredients and appareils necessary.

Trim, peel, and cut vegetables as required by type and recipe. Since the vegetables that are cooked in the soup are also part of the finished dish, it is important the cuts are neat and uniform. In this way, you can be certain the items will cook uniformly, and that they will have an attractive appearance.

Some vegetable soups also include meat or fish. Some include a combination—for example, *pot au feu* typically includes beef and chicken. Trim and cut meats, poultry, or fish properly. They may be trussed and cooked whole, rather than cut into pieces. A likely scenario is that meats cooked separately will be diced or julienned, and then returned to the soup near the end of cooking time as a garnish. Be sure that any gristle or excess fat is trimmed from the cooked meat, fish is completely boned, and the skin has been removed from poultry.

Any beans to be included in the soup can be either cooked directly in the soup, or cooked separately and added near the end of cooking time. Whole grains, pastas, rice, or other similar ingredients can also be either cooked directly in the soup, or cooked separately and added during the final minutes of cooking time.

A variety of broths, good-quality stocks, and other liquids, including water, vegetable essences, or juices, are used as the liquid base for vegetable soups. Refer to specific recipes for exact amounts.

As always, be sure to test the quality of any broth or stock that has been stored under refrigeration by bringing a small quantity to a boil, and then tasting it to be sure that it smells and tastes fresh and wholesome.

When you are preparing large quantities of soup, it can be helpful to bring the broth to a simmer over low heat while preparing the other ingredients. This will help reduce overall cooking time, since the soup will come to the correct cooking speed more quickly.

Prepare a sachet d'épices or bouquet garni as required by the recipe. These aromatic combinations are added at specific points during cooking times, so that they will surrender the best flavor. In addition to the traditional ingredients, you may opt to include a variety of other herbs, herb stems, spices, dried or fresh mushrooms and chilies to achieve a particular flavor in the finished soup.

There are several garnishes typically paired with vegetable soups. Croutons, pesto, grated cheese, even beaten eggs can be added to vegetable soups just before they are served. Purées of red peppers, chilies, tomato, or sorrel may also be added at the last moment for a dash of color and flavor.

Fortified wines (for example, a splash of sherry added to a French onion soup), vinegar (added at the last moment to borscht), or citrus juices (lime juice added to a Cuban-style black bean soup) are all common choices for last minute flavor adjustments.

2. Assemble all equipment necessary for cooking.

Most vegetable soups are prepared from start to finish in a single pot. The pot should usually be taller than it is wide to allow the soup to cook gently and evenly at a constant simmer. Review additional information about equipment for cooling and storing soups in Chapter 2.

Method

1. Sweat the aromatic vegetables.

Onions, garlic, leeks, carrots, celery, and parsnips are often included as the basic flavoring ingredients of a vegetable soup. Cooking them gently in a small amount of oil, butter, or rendered salt pork begins the process of releasing their flavors into the soup. Note that some tender vegetables, such as broccoli florets, asparagus tips, and other delicate types, are not generally allowed to sweat. They will be added at staggered intervals, according to individual cooking times.

2. Add the stock, broth, or water and bring the soup slowly to a boil.

A slow simmer is the best cooking speed for most soups. The vegetables and meats will release the best flavor, and the appearance of vegetables will be more attractive when cooked at a simmer. A hard boil tends to cook foods to shreds.

Skim the surface as needed throughout preparation. The scum that is thrown by the soup needs to be removed for the best finished quality.

3. Add any remaining ingredients at appropriate intervals.

Depending on the style of soup you are preparing, additional ingredients, such as chicken pieces, beef brisket, dense vegetables, grains, or legumes, may be added at the same time as the liquid. Keep in mind the overall cooking time of the soup, as well as that required by individual ingredients. Or, refer to recipes for more guidance.

Sachet d'épices and bouquet garni are generally added so that they will cook just long enough to release flavor into the soup. Overcooking these ingredients can deaden their flavor.

Delicate vegetables, such as green peas, kernel corn, asparagus tips, or tomatoes, are usually added near the end of cooking time. Meats, vegetables, pastas, or grains that have been cooked separately are also usually added in the last few minutes of cooking time.

4. Cook until all ingredients are fully cooked and tender and the soup's flavor is developed.

It is important to taste the soup frequently as it cooks. This will allow you to make adjustments if necessary during cooking time. It will also tell you when the soup has reached a peak of flavor. Be sure to follow all safe food-handling practices: Use tasting spoons, and never use the same spoon to taste a soup twice.

5. The soup is now ready for final seasoning, garnishing, and service. Or, it may be properly cooled and stored, following the procedures outlined in Chapter 2.

See Part IV, Chapter 14, for specific vegetable soup recipes.

Cream Soups and Velouté Soups

According to classic definitions, a cream soup is based on a béchamel sauce—milk thickened with roux—and is finished with heavy cream. A velouté soup is based on a light velouté sauce—a stock thickened with roux—and is finished with a liaison of heavy cream and egg yolks. Contemporary menu writers no longer draw a sharp distinction between the two, and in modern kitchens chefs frequently substitute a velouté base for the béchamel in cream soups. True velouté soups are less frequently prepared in professional kitchens than they once were. This is true partly because the addition of a liaison should be done at the last minute. Also, soups finished with a liaison are richer and higher in calories than many guests like.

The major flavoring ingredient for cream and velouté soups is simmered in the velouté until it is tender. The solids are strained out and, in some cases, puréed and returned to the soup. A second straining is often suggested to develop the velvety-smooth texture associated with excellent cream soups. The finished soup should have the thickness of heavy cream.

A garnish is usually included just prior to service. The garnish is frequently diced meat or vegetables that reflect the major flavoring ingredient. For example, cream of broccoli soup may be garnished with lightly blanched broccoli florets.

Mise en Place

1. Assemble and prepare all ingredients and appareils necessary.

Trim, peel, and cut vegetables according to type and recipe requirements. It is less important that the cuts be as neat and uniform for cream soups as was the case for vegetable soups since they are most likely going to be puréed. However, it is still important that the cuts be relatively uniform in size, so that they will cook evenly. Peel broccoli or asparagus stems before using them in soups.

Cream soups based on chicken or fish are typically made from very richly flavored broths or essences. The poultry or fish is then usually added as a garnish at the end of cooking time, or just before the soup is served.

The mirepoix should be cut into relatively small dice, to allow its flavors to be released properly into the soup. If a very pale or ivory-colored cream soup is being made, use a white mirepoix. Other aromatic combinations, including sachet d'épices or bouquet garni, are also used in some formulas.

A full-bodied broth or stock should be available, or a light velouté. In some cases, milk or a light béchamel is appropriate. Refer to specific recipes for guidance. If broth or milk is used, instead of velouté and béchamel, you will also need a sufficient quantity of prepared roux or flour to thicken the soup.

Finishing ingredients, final flavoring and seasonings, and garnishes should be assembled and ready to add at the appropriate point. Fresh sweet cream is the most common finishing ingredient. Liaisons (combinations of egg yolks and heavy or sour cream) and flavored creams (scented with ginger or other aromatics) are also frequently employed.

2. Assemble all equipment necessary for cooking.

It is best to avoid aluminum pots when you are making cream soups, since the action of spoons and whips against the pot could cause the soup to take on a grayish cast. Look also for pots that are of relatively heavy gauge. Because of the presence of starches in the roux or velouté, or in the major flavoring ingredients, cream soups are far more susceptible to scorching than clear soups. If available, a flame-tamer or other similar device should be used to prevent hot spots from developing.

Wooden spoons, ladles, and skimmers are generally required throughout the cooking process. In order to finish the soup properly, you will also need strainers and cheesecloth. Puréeing equipment is also necessary: food mills, blenders, burr mixers, or food processors.

FIGURE 7-2   Preparing a Cream Soup (Cream of Broccoli Soup)

(1) Removing broccoli stems to purée.

(2) Returning puréed broccoli to soup.

(3) Finished soup garnished with broccoli florets.

Review equipment needs for cooling and storing soups in Chapter 2.

Method

1. Sweat the aromatic vegetables. (See Figure 7-2 for photos illustrating the method for preparing a cream soup.)

In addition to a standard or white mirepoix, you may also need to sweat various other vegetables that will act as the major flavoring of the soup: celery, mushrooms, or tomatoes. This should be done gently over low heat in a small amount of oil, butter, or stock until the vegetables begin to release their juices.

Be careful not to undercook the vegetables, since this step is of great importance in determining the quality of the finished soup. On the other hand, avoid cooking them until they become even lightly browned. They should stay light in color. Cook them until they are just limp.

2. Add the liquid base for the soup, and bring it to a gentle simmer.

If you have a prepared velouté or béchamel, add it now and proceed with soup preparation.

Or, add the broth, stock, or milk and bring the soup to a full boil. Then, using a whip, gradually incorporate the correct amount of roux to get the desired consistency. The roux should be cooler than the liquid. Remember to stir or whip constantly as it is incorporated to smooth out any lumps.

At the same time that you add the liquid base, add other ingredients as appropriate, such as peeled broccoli, asparagus stems, or carrots. Working over low heat, bring the soup just up to a simmer.

3. Add the additional ingredients at appropriate intervals.

The time at which certain ingredients are added to the soup will depend on their individual cooking requirements. Tender new peas will become gray and pasty if allowed to cook for too long. A sachet d'épices left in the soup too long may lose its fresh flavor.

4. Simmer the soup gently until it has developed the appropriate flavor, body, and texture.

Skim the surface as needed during cooking time to remove any impurities that could affect the finished soup's flavor. Pulling the pot slightly to the side of the burner will cause the scum to collect on one side of the pot, where it can be more easily skimmed away.

Taste the soup often as it develops. You can remove the soup from the heat once all its ingredients are very tender and the soup has a good flavor.

Stir frequently to prevent scorching. If there is a slight hint of sticking or scorching, immediately transfer the soup to a cool clean pot. Check it again for any scorched taste. If there is none, you can continue cooking the soup. However, if the soup has a burnt aroma or flavor, it is generally beyond repair.

5. Strain the solids from the soup.

For vegetable cream soups, the solids are frequently puréed and returned to the soup. Gradually reincorporate them, adding just enough to achieve the right consistency and flavor. These soups can be strained once more, after the puréed ingredients are reincorporated, for the best consistency.

Cream of chicken soup is generally just strained once to remove all solids.

6. The soup is now ready to be finished, seasoned, and garnished, or it may be properly cooled and stored, following the procedures outlined in Chapter 2.

To finish a cream soup, bring the cream to a simmer and then add it to the soup. Remember that the right amount of cream (liaison, or sour cream) will produce a soup that is delicately flavored, suave, and perfectly smooth. Too much cream will detract from the major flavor of the soup, masking the original taste.

Make any additional adjustments to the soup's consistency or flavor once the cream has been added. If it is too thick, add broth or water. Recheck carefully for flavor, and make additional corrections to the seasoning as needed.

If the cream soup you have prepared is going to be served as a cold soup, be sure that it is completely chilled before adding cold cream. Check the flavoring and consistency when the soup is cold. Foods often need to be more strongly seasoned when they are served cold, since cooling tends to subdue flavors, even that of salt and pepper.

Refer to Part IV, Chapter 14, for individual cream soup recipes.

Purée Soups

Purée soups are slightly thicker than cream soups and have a somewhat coarser texture. They are often based on dried peas, lentils, or beans, or on starchy vegetables such as potatoes, carrots, and squashes.

One of the major complaints about purée soups is that they are served too thick. Remember, the consistency of any soup must be such that it can be eaten easily from a spoon. The spoon should not be able to stand upright in the soup. Observing the relationship between the flavoring ingredient and the liquid should assure that the soup has a pleasing, robust flavor, without becoming watery or too starchy during cooking and reheating.

Mise en Place

1. Assemble and prepare the ingredients.

A great many purée soups are based on dried beans: Great Northerns, navy beans, lentils, black beans, and split peas, for example. Some beans should be soaked for several hours before cooking. This allows the beans to absorb some liquid, shortening the overall cooking time for the soup, as well as allowing them to cook more evenly.

Other purée soups are made from starchy vegetables such as squashes, potatoes, carrots, or turnips. These will normally require peeling and dicing. Since they are puréed before they are served, neatness is not critical. Relative uniformity of size is, however, to allow all the ingredients to cook properly, and at about the same speed.

Water, broth, or stock are the most commonly used base liquids. Check broths or stocks that have been stored carefully before using them in a soup. Bring a small amount to a boil and taste it. If there is any evidence of souring, or off and musty odors, don't use it.

Many purée soups will call for a bit of rendered salt pork, smoked ham, bacon, or other cured pork products. In some instances, you should blanch these ingredients first to remove any excess salt by covering them with cool water, bringing the water to a simmer, and then draining and rinsing. An alternative is to use a ham-based broth.

Onions, garlic, carrots, celery, mushrooms, and tomatoes are all commonly found in puréed soups. Other vegetables are also suggested by specific recipes, such as sweet peppers. They may be puréed during final preparation of the soup, or they may be left as is, to act as a garnish for the soup. Consult specific recipes for preparation and cutting instructions.

FIGURE 7-3   Preparing a Purée Soup (Senate bean soup)

(1) Adding beans to cold liquid to simmer.

(2) Beans and vegetables simmering.

(3) Retuning partially puréed soup to pot.

A variety of ingredients may be used to season puréed soups: chilies, dried mushrooms, diced meats, hot sauces, citrus zests or juices, and vinegars. Garnishes include croutons, diced meats, salsas, dollops of sour cream, and so forth.

2. Assemble all equipment necessary for cooking.

Equipment requirements for purée soups are quite similar to those for cream soups. Review the information earlier in this chapter.

Method

1. Sweat the aromatic vegetables. (See Figure 7-3 for photos illustrating method for preparing a purée soup.)

Occasionally, a recipe will call for minced salt pork or bacon. In that case, it should be rendered to release the fat over low heat. Then add the onions, garlic, shallots, leeks, or other aromatic vegetables called for by the recipe. Cook them over low heat, until a rich aroma develops. It is often appropriate to allow aromatics for a purée soup to cook long enough to take on a rich golden hue. Remember that this should be done over moderate heat to avoid developing a harsh flavor. It can take anywhere from 20 to 30 minutes to properly cook these aromatics.

2. Add the liquid and any additional ingredients required at this point. Bring the soup to a gentle simmer.

Because most purée soups are made from starchy ingredients, it is generally best to start them in a cool liquid. Beans, potatoes, squashes, and other similar ingredients should therefore be added at the same time that the liquid base is added to the soup pot.

3. Add additional ingredients at the correct point and continue to simmer until all the ingredients are soft enough to purée easily.

Purée soups, like all others, should be skimmed throughout cooking time. They also need to be stirred frequently, and to have their cooking speed and temperature carefully monitored.

Another critical point to keep in mind is that the relative dryness of the ingredients featured in purée soups make it impossible to predict how much liquid might be needed to keep the soup at the correct consistency. If a batch of beans are old, for instance, they will require up to one-third more liquid to cook properly than younger, moister beans. If the soup looks thick as it simmers, it may need additional broth, stock, or water.

Add the sachet d'épices or bouquet garni approximately 1 hour before the end of the cooking time and remove them once the soup has extracted the right amount of flavor.

FIGURE 7-4 Using an Immersion Blender

Using an immersion blender or "burr" mixer to purée a pumpkin soup.

Stir the soup frequently to prevent scorching. If there is a slight hint of sticking or scorching, immediately transfer the soup to a cool clean pot. Check it again for any scorched taste. If there is none, continue cooking the soup.

4. Purée the soup.

Some soups, such as Senate bean soup, are only partially puréed. About half the ingredients are left whole to provide textural contrast. Others may be completely puréed. Depending on the quantity of soup you are making and the desired result, you may use a food mill, vertical chopping machine, food processor, blender, or burr mixer (see Figure 7-4).

Some chefs like to control the texture and consistency of the finished soup by straining out the solids, puréeing them until smooth, and then gradually reincorporating the liquid portion of the soup. It may not be necessary to incorporate all this liquid, or it may be necessary to add a little more broth or water.

5. The soup is now ready to serve, or it may be properly cooled and stored.

Purée soups can be garnished and seasoned in a variety of ways. The relatively subtle flavor of many puréed soups makes them good candidates for highly flavored seasonings and garnishes. It is important not to overdo it, however.

Croutons, diced meats, chopped herbs, and other items are typically used. Toasted or deep-fried tortillas are often used with bean soups. Consult specific recipes in this book or others for inspiration.

Refer to Part IV, Chapter 14, for individual purée soup recipes.

Bisques

Bisques, traditionally based on such crustaceans as shrimp, lobster, or crayfish, share characteristics with both purées and cream soups. Lobster, shrimp, and/or crayfish shells are seared in hot oil. Then they are simmered in stock or a fish fumet, along with aromatic vegetables. Rice is the classic thickener. Contemporary renditions often opt for roux in order to achieve a smoother texture and greater stability. A prepared velouté may also be used.

Bisques should have about the same thickness as cream soups and are usually garnished with small pieces of the appropriate shellfish or a combination of shellfish. A dash of sherry may also be added at the last moment.

A vegetable-based bisque is prepared in the same manner as a purée soup. If the vegetable does not contain enough starch to act as a thickener, rice, a roux, or a starchy vegetable such as potatoes may be used to provide additional thickness. After the vegetables are tender, the soup is puréed until a smooth, velvety texture is reached.

Mise en Place

1. Assemble and prepare all ingredients.

Coarsely chop the shellfish and/or shells. It may be a good idea to rinse them in cool water, but allow enough time for them to drain adequately.

A fish fumet or broth is often used to prepare a bisque and should be checked before use if it has been stored. Bring a small amount to a boil and taste it for any sour or off odors. Or, a prepared fish-based velouté may also be used to prepare a bisque, in which case, no additional thickener need be prepared.

Peel, trim, and chop any vegetables to be used in the bisque. Mirepoix is generally a part of the soup. Other ingredients used to add flavor and color include tomato paste, brandy, and dry white wine.

Rice or a prepared roux should be on hand to use to thicken the soup as it simmers.

FIGURE 7-5   Preparing a Bisque (Lobster Bisque)

(1) Searing lobster in hot oil.

(2) Adding the tomato paste to cook out (pinçage).

(3) Garnishing finished bisque with diced cooked lobster meat.

Cream is a common finishing ingredient for most bisques, although some recipes may indicate a liaison of cream and egg yolks for additional richness and a golden hue. Diced poached pieces of shrimp, lobster, crayfish, or other appropriate shellfish are also traditionally used to garnish a bisque.

2. Assemble all equipment necessary for cooking.

The requirements for bisque are identical to those of cream soup; review the information earlier in this chapter.

Method

1. Sear the shells in oil or clarified butter. (See Figure 7-5 for photos illustrating method for preparing a bisque.)

The shells are responsible for developing the flavor of a good bisque, so it is important that they be cooked until they turn a deep red or pink. Stir them frequently to cook well on all sides.

2. Add the aromatic vegetables and allow them to sweat.

Cook the onions, garlic, shallots, leeks, or other aromatic vegetables called for along with the seared shells. This should be done over moderate heat to avoid developing a harsh flavor. It can take anywhere from 20 to 30 minutes to properly cook these aromatics.

3. Add the tomato paste and cook until it takes on a deep rust color.

This process, known as *pinçage*, cooks the tomato paste down so it will contribute a deep, rich flavor that is not excessively sweet. Otherwise, the tomato could give the soup a raw flavor.

4. Add the brandy and cook out.

This step also continues the process of developing a complex, refined flavor base for the finished bisque. Flaming the brandy will quickly reduce it and burn off the raw alcohol, leaving behind the brandy's flavor essence.

5. Add the liquid and additional appropriate ingredients and bring the soup to a simmer.

At this point, add the fumet or broth (or the prepared velouté, if available), along with a sachet d'épices or bouquet garni, if required. Bring the liquid up to a simmer and, if you are not using velouté, add the thickener at this point. Rice is simply stirred into the soup; roux (which should be cooler than the stock) is added carefully and whipped into the soup to prevent lumping.

Wine and additional herbs or other aromatics are generally added at this point. Remember to taste the bisque as it simmers, and remove the sachet or bouquet once the best flavor has been transferred into the soup.

6. Simmer the bisque until it is well flavored and has a good consistency.

Bisques take an average of about 1 hour to cook properly. At that point, all ingredients should be relatively tender, so they will purée easily, except, obviously, the shells.

Bisques should be skimmed throughout cooking time. Stir them frequently and be sure to monitor the heat. Bisques, like any other soup with starchy ingredients, can scorch quickly if left untended for even a few minutes.

Taste the soup (using tasting spoons and cups and following safe food-handling procedures) so that you can make modifications during cooking time. Add additional liquid if necessary to maintain the proper balance between liquids and solids as the soup cooks.

7. Strain and purée the soup.

All the solids strained from the soup, including the shells, should be puréed until a very smooth paste forms. This mixture is then added back to the liquid portion of the soup. Then, the entire soup should be strained once more through a cheesecloth-lined sieve or colander, or a very fine sieve.

If you are using cheesecloth, remember that it must be thoroughly rinsed in hot water to remove any fibers or traces of lint. Rinsing the cheesecloth also helps it to cling to the sides of the sieve or colander better. Squeeze or wring the cheesecloth, or to press the solids left in the sieve to extract as much flavor as possible.

8. The bisque is now ready to serve, or it may be cooled and properly stored.

If you will be serving the soup immediately, add the simmering cream or a tempered liaison, along with any other desired or suggested finishing, seasoning, or garnishing ingredients. See recipes for specific suggestions.

Refer to Part IV, Chapter 14, for individual bisque recipes.

Special Soups

This category of soups includes a number of regional and ethnic specialties that don't fit neatly into any of the basic soup categories outlined above. Despite the fact that they are not strictly de-fined as either purées, vegetable soups, or bisques, the basic techniques used to prepare them do fall within the principles detailed above. A number of recipes for regional and international soups can be found in Part IV, Chapter 14.

A brief and general definition for some of these soups follows: Thick vegetable soups, such as chowders and gumbos, are made with a base of broth, milk, or water, thickened by either a roux and/or the inclusion of a starchy ingredient such as potatoes, rice, or beans. *Chowders* almost invariably contain potatoes; *minestrone* contains beans and pasta; *gumbos* are made with a dark roux, okra, and/or gumbo filé; in a *garbure*, some or all of the ingredients are puréed, or starchy ingredients may be included so that the finished soup will, therefore, have more body than a clear vegetable soup.

Cold Soups

Cold soups may be prepared in a variety of ways. Some, such as vichyssoise, are simply cream soups that are served cold. Others, such as chilled cantaloupe soup or gazpacho, are based on a purée of raw or cooked ingredients that has been brought to the correct consistency by adding a liquid such as a fruit or vegetable juice. Recipes for cold soups can be found in Part IV, Chapter 14.

Soup Service Guidelines

Soup is often the first dish a restaurant's guest will be served. A well-prepared soup will make a positive initial impression. Soups should always be carefully presented—hot soups hot and cold soups cold—in serving dishes that have been properly heated or chilled.

Remember that the more surface area is exposed to the air, the more quickly the soup will cool. This is the reason that consommés and other broth-style soups are traditionally served in cups rather than flatter, wider plates or bowls used for cream soups and purées.

Try, as much as possible, to plate all soups, but especially consommé, only when the waiter is in the kitchen, ready to pick up the order. That way, soups will not lose heat as they sit on the line waiting for the waiter. Remember that the wait staff wants foods to come out of the kitchen as perfectly as possible. Their work depends on yours.

If waiters are responsible for plating soups themselves, be sure that their soup station has adequate space for keeping bowls and plates hot, and that all appropriate garnish is available and at the correct temperature.

Take the time to explain to anyone involved in serving soups the importance of keeping hot soups very hot, and taking them quickly from the kitchen to the guest. Show all waiters or line cooks the way that a soup should look when it is served to the guest: garnishes, additional elements to pass or serve on the side or at table side (grated cheeses, fine oils, etc.).

Reheating Soups

Reheat smaller quantities over direct heat frequently during service if at all possible. Thick soups should be reheated carefully, allowing them sufficient time to "soften" over low heat before bringing them up to a simmer.

Learn the best way to make use of the equipment available for service to determine how to get foods to the optimal service temperature. This aspect of foodservice requires some thought and attention to detail. Getting foods through the danger zone (see Chapter 2) quickly is important to keep the food wholesome. Maintaining food at high temperatures for extended periods often has undesirable effects on the item's flavor.

Check the temperature of foods held in a steam table. If soups and sauces consistently fall short of a desirable temperature (at least 180°F/82°C for soups and most sauces), then adjust the thermostat on the steam table, have it repaired, or learn to compensate by quickly bringing individual servings up to temperature over direct heat or in a microwave. While this may seem awkward or time-consuming, it is a definite improvement over having disgruntled customers send back their soup.

Final Seasoning and Consistency Adjustments

Check the consistency and seasoning of all soups before sending them out to the patron. Storage under refrigeration, as well as holding in a steam table, has the effect of weakening a soup's flavor. And thick soups, especially those made from beans or potatoes, tend to get thicker as they sit. Be sure that you take the time to make all necessary adjustments. Add broth or water to thin a soup that is too thick. Add herbs, salt, pepper, condiments, fortified wines, or other seasoning ingredients to make the flavor come back to life. If nothing seems to work, then discard the soup and replace it with a fresh batch.

Garnishes

Large garnishes, such as dumplings, spring rolls, or wontons, should not be so large that they overwhelm the soup cup or plate selected for service. It is equally important that they not be too difficult for the guest to eat. If your garnish it is not soft enough to "cut through" with the edge of a soup spoon, then it might be a good idea to rethink its use.

Occasionally, garnishes for soups are both prepared and cooked separately. They are generally added to the soup cup individually, so that they will not cloud the consommé you have worked so hard to prepare, for instance. Since service temperature is extremely important for all thin soups, remember to bring the garnish to service temperature before adding it to the soup. There are several ways to do this:

• Heat the garnish in a small quantity of broth, consommé, or water, and hold it in a steam table.

• Cut delicate items into shapes that will allow the heat of the soup to heat them thoroughly. (If they are small and relatively thin, they will not cause the soup's temperature to drop too severely.)

• Keep large items like wontons, dumplings, or quenelles warm and lightly moistened in a steam table or on the shelf over the range.

Summary

Soups that are thoughtfully paired with a menu and carefully prepared and served will inspire your guests to select from among your offerings frequently. For a wide selection of recipes for the soups discussed in this chapter, refer to, Part IV, Chapter 14, of this book.

CHAPTER 8 Sauces

Sauces are often considered one of the greatest tests of a chef's skill. Whether they are classics, such as sauce suprême, or contemporary, such as red pepper coulis, good sauces demand the highest technical expertise. The successful pairing of a sauce with a food demonstrates an understanding of the food and an ability to judge and evaluate a dish's flavors, textures, and colors. Understanding the nuances of pairing a particular sauce with a food is something that develops throughout a chef's career, as lessons are learned about how and why certain combinations have become enduring classics. Uncovering the principles behind these pairings will form the foundation for developing a sensitivity to sauces in particular and the skill and artistry of cooking in general.

Sauces are not just an afterthought—they serve a particular function in a dish's composition. It is in learning to understand why a certain sauce will or will not work with a particular dish that the process of developing culinary judgment begins. Certain sauce combinations endure because the composition is well balanced in all areas: taste, texture, and eye appeal. Some examples of sauces that are classically combined with particular foods will help to illustrate this point.

Sauce suprême is made by reducing a chicken velouté with chicken stock and finishing it with cream. Correctly made, this ivory-colored sauce has a deep chicken flavor and a velvety texture. When served with chicken meat, the sauce's subtle color, smooth flavor, and creamy texture complement the chicken and help to intensify the meat's flavor. The addition of cream to the sauce serves to "round out" the flavors.

Sauce Robert is prepared by finishing demi-glace with mustard and a garnish of julienned cornichons. Its sharp flavors are traditionally paired with pork to cut the meat's richness. The contrast of both flavor and texture produces an effect that is pleasing, but not startling, to the palate. This pungent, flavorful sauce brings out the pork's flavor but might overwhelm a more delicate meat, such as veal.

Naturally leaner foods, such as poultry or fish, are often prepared by quick cooking methods, such as grilling, sautéing, shallow poaching, or steaming. These methods are well suited to these tender cuts but, unlike slower moist heat methods, add no additional moisture. That is why grilled steaks are commonly served with a compound butter or a butter-emulsion sauce such as a béarnaise. The same rationale applies to serving beurre blanc with a delicate white fish that has been shallow poached. These sauces are rich, buttery, creamy preparations that add a layer of suavity and succulence to foods that, left unsauced, might seem dry or bland.

Contemporary dishes take a different approach to counteracting any potential dryness that could result from dry heat methods. Various hot and cold compotes, relishes, chutneys, or marmalades may be substituted for the classic choices.

Lightly coating a sautéed medallion of lamb with a jus lié gives the lamb a glossy finish that gives the entire plate more eye appeal. Pooling a red pepper coulis around
a grilled swordfish steak gives the dish a degree of visual excitement by adding an element of color. Brushing ribs or chicken breasts with a barbecue sauce also enhances the look of the finished dish, glazing the item with color and flavor.

Here are some of the points to consider when selecting the appropriate sauce:

The Sauce Should be Suitable for the Style of Service In a banquet setting, or for any situation where large quantities of food must be served rapidly and at their flavor peak, it is usually best to rely on the traditional grand sauces or a contemporary sauce that shares some of the same characteristics. One of a grand sauce's fundamental benefits is that it may be prepared in advance and held in large quantities at the correct temperature. In an à la carte kitchen, this advantage is less important.

The Sauce Should be Suitable for the Main Ingredient's Cooking Technique A cooking technique that produces flavorful drippings *(fond)*, such as roasting or sautéing, should logically be paired with a sauce that makes use of those drippings. Beurre blancs are suitable for foods that have been shallow poached, because the cooking liquid *(cuisson)* can become a part of the sauce instead of being discarded.

The Sauce's Flavor Should be Appropriate for the Flavor of the Food with Which it is Paired Make sure the flavor of the sauce does not overpower the main ingredients flavor and vice versa. Although a delicate cream sauce complements the flavor of Dover sole, it would be overwhelmed by the flavor of grilled tuna steak. By the same token, a sauce flavored by rosemary would completely overpower a delicate fish but nicely complements lamb.

The Grand Sauces

Demi-glace, velouté, béchamel, tomato, and (in at least some instances) hollandaise are often referred to as the "grand sauces" or "mother sauces." A sauce is considered to be a grand sauce if it met some basic criteria: It can be prepared in large batches, and then flavored, finished, and garnished in great variety, producing the hundreds and thousands of so-called "small sauces." This principle was still considered revolutionary in Carême's time. Escoffier's codification of sauces was considered a major advance.

Some chefs argue that because hollandaise cannot be made in advance in a large quantity and stored, and it is not intended as a base sauce used to prepare a variety of derivative sauces, it does not qualify as a grand sauce. Others feel that it should be counted as one of the grand sauces. Not only do they feel that this sauce can be used to prepare derivatives, but it can also be used as the basic technique to yield a variety of other sauces.

Contemporary Sauces

The broad category of contemporary sauces includes jus lié, beurre blanc, coulis, compound butters, and a variety of miscellaneous sauces, such as relishes, salsas, and compotes. The primary factors distinguishing contemporary sauces from the grand sauces are the following:

- They usually take less time to prepare.

- They are more likely to be specifically tailored to a given food or technique.

- They have a lighter color, texture, and flavor than some of the grand sauces.

- They are more likely to be thickened and finished using emulsions, modified starches, or reduction and less likely to contain roux.

Techniques for Classic and Contemporary Sauces

(Brown Sauce) Sauce Espagnole

The classic method of preparing a brown sauce, as written by Carême, is a lengthy and involved process that calls for Bayonne ham, veal, and partridges. The contemporary version has been greatly simplified and the cooking time reduced.

Sauce espagnole, though it is rarely served on its own in today's restaurants, is still an important preparation. It is used to prepare demi-glace, and may be used to prepare derivative sauces or gravies. It is believed that this is one of the sauces that arrived with Catharine of Aragon and the chefs in her entourage when she married Henry VIII.

Mise en Place

1. Assemble the ingredients and preparations necessary to prepare brown sauce.

The four basic elements of this sauce are:

- Brown veal stock or estouffade
- Mirepoix, cut into large dice
- Tomato purée
- Brown roux

The stock is directly responsible for the ultimate success of this sauce. It must be of excellent quality, with a rich appealing flavor and aroma. The flavor should be well balanced with no strong notes of mirepoix, herbs, or spices that might overwhelm the finished sauce. On the other hand, if the stock has a weak flavor, the sauce will be similarly lacking in taste.

The addition of mirepoix to the sauce is made at the chef's discretion. If there is sufficient flavor in the stock, then it may be unnecessary.

If tomato purée is unavailable, tomato paste, concasséed tomatoes, or plain tomato sauce may be substituted. Be sure to allow whatever tomato product you select sufficient time to cook out properly.

Brown roux contributes to the flavor, color, and texture of the finished sauce. Some chefs like to make this particular roux in the oven to avoid developing a bitter taste.

2. Assemble and prepare the equipment necessary for preparing brown sauce.

Brown sauce is generally prepared in a saucepan or pot that is taller than it is wide. You will also need a whip to incorporate the roux into the stock (or vice versa), kitchen spoons or skimmers to skim the developing sauce, tasting spoons, fine strainers, and containers to hold the finished sauce. Additional containers are necessary for both cooling and storing the sauce.

Method

1. Sweat the mirepoix in a little oil or clarified butter until juices are released and onions are translucent.

"Sweating" implies that aromatic vegetables are being cooked gently over low heat, usually in a covered pot, to encourage them to begin releasing their flavor. This is an important step in flavor development and should be given enough time.

2. Add the tomato purée and sauté until caramelized.

Allowing the tomato to "cook out" reduces any excessive sweetness, acidity, or bitterness, which might affect the finished sauce. It also encourages the development of a deep rich note that, while it should remain a subtle influence, still has a role to play in the sauce's overall flavor and aroma. This process is referred to in French as *pinçage,* a culinary term which indicates that an ingredient (usually tomatoes) is browned in fat.

3. Add brown stock to the mirepoix, bring it to a boil, and gradually incorporate the brown roux.

In order for roux to properly thicken the sauce, it is important that the sauce be at a boil as the roux is incorporated. Once the roux has been whipped into the stock, allow the stock to return once more to a full boil. This allows the starches in the flour to expand quickly, beginning the process of thickening almost immediately.

Stir or whip the sauce constantly while adding the roux a little at a time. There will be a tendency for the roux to form lumps and fall to the bottom of the pot. To counteract this, keep the sauce in motion.

The correct ratio of roux to stock for a sauce is 12 ounces of roux to 1 gallon of stock. Because of the long simmering time of this stock, it is acceptable to slightly reduce the amount of roux. If too much roux is added, be sure to adjust the consistency early on in the cooking process by adding additional stock or water. In that way, the sauce's

natural reduction will allow the best possible flavor to develop, despite any miscalculation with regard to roux.

4. Simmer the sauce for approximately 2 to 3 hours, skimming the surface throughout the cooking time.

Once the roux has been fully incorporated, reduce the heat until a slow, gentle simmer is established. A cooking time of up to 3 hours allows the starchy taste and feel of the roux to completely cook out of the sauce. It also permits all the flavors to properly develop.

Skim the surface of the sauce frequently throughout simmering time. Pulling the pot slightly off the center of the burner will allow the natural convection of the simmering liquid to throw the impurities to one side of the pot. This makes it easier to skim away the scum.

The flour present in the roux may easily settle on the bottom of the pot. Be sure to stir carefully with a wooden spoon from time to time during cooking. This will prevent the flour from sticking and scorching.

Taste the sauce frequently as it develops, so that you can stop cooking at the moment that the sauce has the best flavor, texture, and color. It should have a deep rich flavor and aroma, a lustrous sheen, some translucence, and a well-balanced taste. Hold a small amount of the sauce on your tongue, pressed against the roof of your mouth. If the sauce is properly cooked, there should be no tacky or gluey sensation.

Remember that this sauce is often reduced further, so don't add extra seasonings now.

5. Strain the sauce through a sieve.

At this point, the sauce is ready for use in other preparations, or it may be properly cooled and stored for later use. Refer to proper cooling techniques in Chapter 2.

See Part IV, Chapter 15, for the pagnole recipe.

Demi-Glace

It is important to learn the procedure for making a demi-glace, a highly flavored, glossy sauce,

Sauce	Garnish	Sauce	Garnish
Bercy	Shallots, pepper, white wine, butter, dice of marrow, parsley	**Moscovite**	Poivrade sauce with an infusion of juniper berries, toasted sliced almonds, plumped currants, marsala
Bordelaise	Red wine reduction, glace de viande, poached marrow	**Périgueux**	Truffle essence, chopped truffles, Madeira
Charcutière	Robert sauce, julienne of cornichons	**Périgourdine**	Foie gras purée, sliced truffles
Chasseur	Mushrooms, shallots, white wine, tomato concassé	**Piquante**	Reduction of white wine, vinegar, shallots, strained and garnished with gherkins, chervil, tarragon, pepper
Chateaubriand	Shallots, thyme, bay leaves, mushroom parings, white wine, butter, tarragon, parsley	**Poivrade**	Reduction of red wine marinade, peppercorns, butter
Diable	White wine reduction, pepper mignonette, shallots, cayenne	**Porto**	Reduction of port with shallots, thyme, lemon and orange juice and zest, salt, cayenne
Diane	Poivrade with cream	**Robert**	White wine, onions, mustard, butter
Estragon	Tarragon	**Romaine**	Pale caramel dissolved with vinegar, demi and game stock, reduced, strained through tamis, garnished with toasted pignolis, plumped sultanas and currants
Financière	Madeira sauce with truffle essence		
Fines Herbes	White wine, fines herbes, lemon juice		
Lyonnaise	Onions fried in butter, deglazed with white wine and vinegar; add demi, strain	**Solférino**	Shallots, maître d'hôtel butter, tomato essence, cayenne, lemon
Madère/Madeira	Madeira wine	**Zingara**	Tomatoes, mushroom julienne, truffles, ham, tongue, cayenne, Madeira

even though in contemporary kitchens a jus de veau lié is often used in its place. The name "demi-glace" translates literally as "half-glaze." There are a number of derivatives based on demi-glace that have an important place in the chef's repertoire, some of which can be found in Table 8-1.

A demi-glace of excellent quality will have several characteristics. Demi-glace should have a full, rich flavor. The sauce is prepared from equal quantities of good brown sauce and brown veal stock (or estouffade). The flavor should be that of roasted veal. The aromatics, mirepoix, and tomatoes used in the base preparations should not overpower the main flavor of the finished sauce, but should contribute to a well-balanced taste.

Demi-glace should have a deep brown color. When properly simmered, skimmed, and reduced, demi-glace is translucent and highly glossy. Because of the reduction and also the use of roux in the brown sauce, demi-glace has noticeable body, although it should never feel tacky in the mouth. It is at the correct consistency when it will evenly coat the back of a spoon (a condition known as *nappé*).

A meatless version of "demi-glace" is a great boon to those trying to achieve the greatest possible flavor for a vegetarian entree. Its preparation is similar to that outlined for jus de veau lié, found later in this chapter. It is made by preparing a vegetable stock, simmering it with roasted vegetables and aromatics, and then thickening the "demi-glace" with arrowroot.

Mise en Place

1. Assemble the ingredients and preparations necessary for demi-glace.

Only two base preparations are required for demi-glace.

- Brown veal stock *(fond de veau brun)* or estouffade
- Brown sauce (sauce espagnole)

FIGURE 8-1   Reducing Demi-Glace

(1) The sauce is ready to begin reducing. Note that it pours freely from the spoon.

(2) The sauce has reduced by half. The color has changed and the sauce is noticeably thicker.

No additional seasonings or aromatics are called for. Both the brown sauce and stock have already been flavored. The reduction of this sauce intensifies those flavors significantly.

2. Assemble the equipment necessary for preparing demi-glace.

The shape of the pan, as well as its gauge, are of some importance. A pan that is wider than it is tall will encourage even, rapid reduction by bringing more of the sauce into contact with the source of the heat. The greater surface area also encourages the sauce to reduce. If necessary, have some smaller pots on hand to hold the sauce as it continues to reduce.

A fine strainer and cheesecloth are also necessary for the preparation of this sauce, as well as the usual containers for holding, cooling, or storing. Tasting spoons, skimmers or ladles, and kitchen spoons should also be available.

Method

1. Combine equal parts of the brown veal stock and brown sauce in a heavy-bottomed pot and bring to a boil, then reduce the heat slightly to maintain a simmer.

A moderate cooking speed is important, to avoid scorching the sauce as it reduces. Keep an eye on this sauce as it develops, and rely on not only your eyes but also your nose to act as a watch-keeper. Depending on the quantity of demi-glace being prepared, you may want to begin transferring the sauce into successively smaller pots. This will have the effect of preventing the sauce from scorching as it cooks.

Pull the pot slightly off the center of the heat source to encourage any impurities and fat that might remain in either the brown sauce or stock to collect on one side of the pot. Skim them away as they collect. This helps to produce a sauce that is extremely translucent and glossy.

2. Simmer until the sauce is reduced to half its original volume.

The photos in Figure 8-1 show demi-glace as it begins to reduce and then when it is fully reduced. When demi-glace has the correct consistency, it will feel slightly tacky when you take a small amount into your mouth. This is acceptable. To test another way, pour a small amount of the demi-glace onto a plate. Blow on the sauce. A rose pattern that remains in the sauce should develop. (Remember to discard this test portion. Do not reintroduce it to the pot.)

3. Strain, using either the wringing or milking techniques (see Figures 8-2 and 8-3).

The sauce is now ready to serve, or to use to prepare various derivatives, or it may be properly cooled and stored, following the techniques described in Chapter 2.

See Part IV, Chapter 15, for the demi-glace recipe.

Preparing Demi-Glace Derivatives

There are a number of recipes for sauces derived from demi-glace included Chapter 15. The three main ways of finishing demi-glace to create a variety of special sauces are:

FIGURE 8-2   The Wringing Method for Straining Sauces

(1) The rinsed cheesecloth is draped over a bowl and the sauce is poured into it.

(2) Two people, one working on either side of the bowl, should now gather up the cheesecloth, each twisting in the opposite direction from the other.

(3) Continue until all the sauce has been wrung from the cheesecloth.

FIGURE 8-3   The Milking Method for Straining Sauces

(1) Drape rinsed cheesecloth over a pot or bowl. Pour the sauce into the lined pot. Two people should hold onto the corners of the cloth, as shown.

(2) Lift one corner at a time, alternating from one side to another. The other corners should be held steady. Notice that the upper left corner has been lifted.

(3) The upper right-hand corner has been lifted. Continue alternating corners until the sauce is strained through the cheesecloth into the container.

- Finishing with a fortified wine
- Reduction
- Finishing with butter *(monté au beurre)*

FIGURE 8-4   Adding Fortified Wine

Add Madeira to demi-glace at the last minute for the best flavor.

Fortified wines, such as port (see Figure 8-4), Madeira, marsala, or sherry, are frequently used to give a sauce a special flavor. Because these wines are so intensely flavored, it is not recommended that they be allowed to reduce. Instead, the appropriate quantity of wine is added to the simmering sauce and blended in. Then, the sauce is served as soon as possible for the best flavor.

Figure 8-5   Preparing Sauce Chasseur

(1) Wine is added to sautéed mushrooms.

(2) The wine is cooking away (reducing) over high heat.

(3) Demi-glace is added to the sauce chasseur. All garnish and flavoring ingredients have been reduced and cooked completely.

Reduction sauces are made by using a wine or other flavorful liquid (brandies, cognacs, juices, or essences) to deglaze a sauté pan, along with the specified aromatic or garnishing ingredients. (This may also be done independently of the sautéing process, as in the case of preparing a large batch of a special sauce for banquet service.) In some cases, especially when garnish or flavoring ingredients such as mushrooms, shallots, or tomatoes are added, they are allowed to sauté briefly to bring out their flavors. The wine, if not already added, is added at this point and allowed to reduce to intensify the flavor. Demi-glace is added to the sauce. The sauce simmers briefly, usually about 5 to 10 minutes, so that the flavors can develop fully. Then, the final seasoning adjustments are made.

See Figure 8-5 for photos illustrating the method for preparing sauce chasseur.

Finishing with butter is a step that can be employed either on its own, or as a finishing step for fortified wine sauces or reduction sauces. Whole, unsalted butter is diced and kept firm. It is swirled into the sauce, emulsifying and thickening the sauce. It is important to remember that the pan should be kept in motion the entire time that the butter is blending into the sauce.

Figure 8-6 shows butter being used to finish a sauce chasseur. This final addition of butter gives the sauce a slightly more opaque appearance as well as blending all its flavors into one, rich harmonious taste.

See Part IV, Chapter 15, for demi-glace derivative recipes.

Jus Lié

Jus lié, frequently referred to simply as "jus," is a thickened sauce made from stock (usually brown veal stock, although other stocks may be used). Some chefs prefer a relatively strict interpretation of this term. To them, it should be nothing more than either a stock or drippings from a roast lightly thickened with arrowroot.

Other chefs use it as a replacement for the classic grand sauce, demi-glace. Although similar to a demi-glace in appearance and use, jus lié requires less cooking time because it contains a modified starch (arrowroot, for example) as a thickener. It also has a greater degree of clarity, translucence,

Figure 8-6
Adding Butter to Sauce Chasseur (*Monté au Beurre*).

and sheen, but a less deep and complex flavor and a somewhat lighter texture and color. It may be used in the preparation of many other sauces, in the same way as demi-glace is employed. Jus lié is often used to deglaze pans to create sauces that are specifically tailored to sautés or roasts. It may be flavored or finished using any of the methods described above for demi-glace.

Another way in which jus lié can be varied is to introduce the flavor of a special spice or herb. Since this sauce does not require the lengthy simmering called for with demi-glace, it is more appropriate to make smaller, more customized batches. For example, sprigs of rosemary or tarragon may be added to the jus lié as it develops. This would rarely be done as a step in preparing demi-glace, since the object of demi-glace is to produce a foundation sauce where a single, pronounced flavor might be inappropriate for some uses.

Jus de veau lié indicates a sauce made with a brown veal stock as its base. It is possible to use an array of other base stocks, to further vary the range of possibilities with jus lié. Brown stocks based on poultry, game, pork, or even vegetable stocks are made in kitchens today.

FIGURE 8-7
Adding diluted arrowroot to prepare jus de veau lié.

Mise en Place

1. Assemble the ingredients and preparations necessary to prepare jus lié.

The four basic elements of jus lié are:

- Brown stock
- Mirepoix, cut into large dice
- Tomato purée
- Arrowroot, diluted in a cold liquid

The stock is directly responsible for the ultimate success of this sauce. It must be of excellent quality, with a rich appealing flavor and aroma. The flavor should be well balanced with no strong notes of mirepoix, herbs, or spices that might overwhelm the finished sauce. On the other hand, if the stock has a weak flavor, the sauce will be similarly lacking in taste. Jus lié is prepared with a brown stock: veal, chicken, game, pork, or vegetable.

The addition of mirepoix to the sauce is made at the chef's discretion. If there is sufficient flavor in

the stock, then it may be unnecessary.

If tomato purée is unavailable, tomato paste, chopped tomatoes, or plain tomato sauce may be substituted. Be sure to allow whatever tomato product you select sufficient time to cook out properly.

There are a number of possible additions to the basic list. Wine (a dry table wine, red or white according to the desired result) is a frequent addition. It may be added to the sauce as it simmers, or it may be used in place of water to dilute the arrowroot. Mushroom trimmings, herbs (whole sprigs or stems), ginger, garlic, shallots, or dried fruits and vegetables may also be added to the sauce as it develops. Many chefs also like to add a quantity of well-browned meaty bones or lean trim meat.

2. Assemble and prepare the equipment necessary for preparing jus lié.

Jus lié sauce is generally prepared in a saucepan or pot that is wider than it is tall. This is the most effective means of extracting flavors fully and quickly into the finished sauce. You will also need kitchen spoons or skimmers to skim the developing sauce, tasting spoons, fine strainers, and containers to hold the finished sauce. Additional containers are necessary for both cooling and storing the sauce.

Method

1. Sweat the mirepoix in a little oil or clarified butter until juices are released and onions are golden.

Sweating implies that aromatic vegetables are being cooked gently over low heat, usually in a covered pot, to encourage them to begin releasing their flavor. This is an important step in flavor development and should be given enough time. It is best to let the mirepoix develop a deep golden color.

An alternative to sweating the vegetables is to roast them. This eliminates the need to add extra fat to the sauce.

2. Add the tomato purée and sauté until caramelized.

Allowing the tomato to "cook out" (*pincé*) reduces any excessive sweetness, acidity, or bitterness, which might affect the finished sauce. It also encourages the development of the sauce's overall flavor and aroma. If you are roasting the vegetables to brown them, add the tomato purée to the roasting pan as well.

3. Add brown stock to the mirepoix, bring it to a boil, and simmer over low heat for about 4 to 6 hours.

In order for the sauce to develop the richest flavor, it is important that the sauce simmer long enough for the best possible flavor to develop.

Skim the surface of the sauce frequently throughout simmering time. Pulling the pot slightly off the center of the burner will allow the natural convection of the simmering liquid to throw the impurities to one side of the pot. This makes it easier to skim away the scum.

Taste the sauce frequently as it develops, so that you can stop cooking at the moment that the sauce has the best flavor, texture, and color. It should have a deep rich flavor and aroma, a lustrous sheen, some translucence, and a well-balanced taste.

4. Add the diluted arrowroot to the simmering sauce, and continue to cook for another 2 to 3 minutes.

The arrowroot (or cornstarch) should lightly thicken the sauce, so that it will coat the back of a spoon. Add arrowroot gradually, so that you don't inadvertently overthicken the sauce.(see Figure 8-7).

5. Strain the sauce through a sieve. At this point, the sauce is ready for use in other preparations, or it may be properly cooled and stored for later use. Refer to proper cooling techniques in Chapter 2.

See Part IV, Chapter 15, for recipes for Jus Lié and derivatives.

TABLE 8-2 VELOUTÉ DERIVATIVES

Sauce	Base stock	Garnish
Albufera	Veal	Suprême with meat glaze and pimento butter
Allemande	Veal	Mushrooms
Anchois	Fish	Normande, anchovy butter, minced anchovy fillets
Aromates	Veal	Infusion of thyme, basil, marjoram, chives, shallots, pepper, garnished with chervil, blanched tarragon, lemon juice
Aurore	Veal/fish	Suprême flavored with tomato
Bercy	Fish	Shallots, butter, white wine, parsley
Bonnefoy	Veal	Tarragon
Bretonne	Veal/fish	Julienned leeks, celery, onions, mushrooms, all cooked in butter
Chivry	Chicken	Infusion of chervil, parsley, tarragon, chives, pimpernel, white wine, strained, chivry butter added
Crevettes	Fish	Shrimp butter
Curry	Veal	Onions, apple, curry powder, coconut milk, strained, cream added
Diplomate	Fish	Normande, lobster butter, garnished with lobster and truffles
Hongroise	Veal	Suprême, onions, paprika, white wine
Huîtres	Fish	Normande, oyster juice, poached oysters
Ivoire	Veal	Suprême, pale meat glaze
Joinville	Fish	Crayfish and shrimp coulis, julienne of truffles
Livonienne	Fish	Julienne of truffles and carrots, parsley
Normande	Fish	Mushroom/oyster essence, yolks, butter, cream
Ravigote	Veal	Reduction of white wine and vinegar, shallot butter, garnished with chervil, chives, tarragon
Suprême	Chicken	Reduced with heavy cream
Vin Blanc	Fish	Shallots, butter, fines herbes

Velouté

This sauce, used to prepare numerous white sauces, has a name that translates from French as "velvety, soft, and smooth to the palate." A truly excellent velouté should meet several criteria. The flavor of a velouté should reflect the stock used in its preparation: white veal, which will be nearly neutral in flavor; chicken; or fish. It should have a pale ivory color, with absolutely no hint of gray. Although a velouté will never be transparent, it should be translucent, lustrous, and have a definite sheen. Velouté should be perfectly smooth, with no hint of graininess. The sauce should have a noticeable body, thick enough to coat the back of a spoon, yet still easy to pour from a ladle.

The number of sauces that can be derived from velouté is second only to those derived from demi-glace. Some classic examples of this sauce can be found in Table 8-2. In addition to its use as a base sauce, veloutés are also used to prepare soups, as we have seen in Chapter 7.

Mise en Place

1. Assemble the necessary ingredients and preparations to prepare velouté.

Velouté is prepared by thickening a white stock (veal, chicken, or fish) with an appropriate amount of pale roux,

Assemble the following items to prepare a velouté:

- White stock (veal, chicken, fish, or vegetable)
- Pale roux
- Optional seasoning or flavoring ingredients as desired

TABLE 8-3 RATIOS FOR LIGHT, MEDIUM, AND HEAVY VELOUTÉ AND BÉCHAMEL		
Consistency	Roux	Liquid
Light	10–12 ounces	1 gallon
Medium	12–16 ounces	1 gallon
Heavy	18–20 ounces	1 gallon

Mushroom trimmings (about 5 ounces per gallon of velouté) are occasionally added to velouté for additional flavor, if they are available. A standard sachet d'épices or bouquet garni may also be included. If used, add these ingredients at the point indicated in the method below.

The amount of roux required varies according to the desired consistency of the finished velouté. A medium consistency is used for most sauces. A light consistency is required for soups. A heavy consistency is used for a binder, such as would be required to prepare a croquette. See Table 8-3 for the correct ratio of roux to liquid.

A broth or stock can also be thickened with diluted arrowroot or cornstarch to create a lighter sauce. This will eliminate the additional fat found in traditional roux-thickened veloutés. This sauce has a more limited shelf-life, however, and does not stand up well to being held in a steam table.

2. Assemble the necessary equipment to prepare velouté.

When selecting a pot, avoid aluminum pans, which might cause the finished velouté to take on a grayish cast. Wooden spoons are less likely to impart an off color to this delicately colored sauce. Remember that you will also need tasting spoons, a skimmer, a fine sieve or cheesecloth for straining, and storage or service containers for the finished sauce.

Method

1. Bring the stock to a simmer. Gradually whip in the roux.

In order for roux to properly thicken the sauce, it is important that the stock be at a boil as the roux is incorporated. Once the roux has been whipped into the stock, allow the stock to return once more to a full boil. This allows the starches in the flour to expand quickly, beginning the process of thickening almost immediately.

Stir or whip the sauce constantly while adding the roux a little at a time. There will be a tendency for the roux to form lumps and fall to the bottom of the pot. To counteract this, keep the sauce in motion.

If you are making the roux as part of the sauce-making procedure, it can be prepared directly in

FIGURE 8-8   Preparing Velouté

(1) The pot is slightly off the center of the burner, and a kitchen spoon is used to push the impurities to one side.

(2) Lifting the scum from the surface of the sauce.

(3) Straining the sauce. Note the skin that has formed.

(4) The texture, color, and sheen of a finished velouté.

the pot you are using. Then add the stock gradually to the roux. The stock should be cooler than the roux, but it does not have to be cold. To make the process go more efficiently, bring the stock to a simmer, then remove it from the heat as you make the pale roux. Add the stock gradually, whipping constantly, to work out all lumps from the sauce.

2. Bring to a full boil, then reduce the heat to establish a simmer.

Once the roux has been fully incorporated and a true boil reached, reduce the heat until a slow, gentle simmer is established. If you plan to add extra flavoring ingredients, they should be added now. A cooking time of at least 30 minutes (some chefs prefer to simmer up to 1 hour) will effectively cook away any residual starches in the roux's flour. It also permits any impurities that might affect the final flavor, texture, and appearance of the sauce to be thrown to the surface where they can be skimmed away.

Pulling the pot slightly off the center of the burner will allow the natural convection of the simmering liquid to throw the impurities to one side of the pot. As you can see in Figure 8-8, the chef has placed the pot properly. Then a kitchen spoon is used to first push these impurities to one side and lift them from the surface of the sauce.

Stir the sauce carefully, using a wooden spoon. Make sure that the spoon scrapes the bottom of the pot, releasing any thicker layer before it scorches.

Taste the sauce frequently as it develops, so you can stop cooking at the moment that the sauce has the best flavor, texture, and color. It should have the distinct flavor of the stock you have selected. The aroma and taste will have a very slight nuttiness from the addition of roux. Any optional additions, such as mushroom trimmings or a bouquet garni, should serve to enhance the overall flavor of the sauce.

A good-quality velouté should have a discernable body and aroma, a lustrous sheen, some translucence, and a well-balanced taste. Hold a small amount of the sauce on your tongue, pressed against the roof of your mouth. If the sauce is properly cooked, there should be no tacky or gluey sensation.

3. Strain the sauce through a fine sieve.

As the sauce simmers, it will almost inevitably develop a thick skin on its surface, as well as a heavy,

TABLE 8-4 BÉCHAMEL DERIVATIVES

Sauce	Garnish
Aomard à l'Anglaise	Anchovy essence, cayenne, diced lobster
Bohémienne	Cold, made into mayonnaise, finished with tarragon vinegar
Cardinal	Fish stock, truffle essence, cream, lobster butter
Céleri	Celery hearts cooked in white consommé, onion stuck with clove, drained and sieved, cream sauce mixed in
Crème	Cream, lemon juice
Ecossaise	Thin béchamel with julienned hard-boiled egg white and sieved hard-boiled yolks
Mornay	Butter, grated Gruyère and Parmesan
Oeufs à l'Anglaise	Diced hard-boiled egg, nutmeg
Shrimp	Fish stock, shrimp, butter
Soubise	Chopped onions, puréed

gluey layer on the bottom and sides of the pot. Straining the sauce at this point removes any of these impurities. For a truly velvety texture, use either the milking or wringing method to strain the sauce once more through cheesecloth. The sauce is now ready to be served or it may be properly cooled and stored for later use, following the steps outlined in Chapter 2.

See Part IV, Chapter 15, for the recipes for veloulé and its derivatives.

Béchamel

According to legend, the Marquis Louis de Béchameil (noted for his financial acumen) was responsible for the development of this classic sauce. Whether or not it was he, this sauce has become a permanent part of the basic repertoire of sauces. Originally, a béchamel sauce was made by adding cream to a relatively thick velouté sauce, thinning and finishing it. Today, it is made by thickening milk with a white roux and simmering it with aromatics.

When properly prepared, béchamel should have a creamy flavor, reflecting its base liquid—milk. There should be no taste of roux remaining if the sauce has been allowed to simmer for a sufficient time. Béchamel should have the color of heavy cream—slightly ivory. Although béchamel is essentially opaque, the finished sauce will have a definite sheen. It should be perfectly smooth, with no graininess.

Béchamel and velouté may both be prepared with light, medium, or heavy consistencies. (Refer to Table 8-3 for ratios of roux to liquid.) Light béchamel can be used as the basis for cream soups. Medium béchamel is used as a sauce. Heavy béchamel can be used as a binder for fillings, stuffings, or baked macaroni dishes.

The number of derivative or small sauces made with béchamel is not as extensive as that for either demi-glace or velouté. There are some classic sauces that sould be part of your repertoire, however. Table 8-4 gives the basic garnishes required for béchamel-based sauces.

Mise en Place

1. Assemble the ingredients and preparations necessary for béchamel.

Relatively few ingredients are required to make a good béchamel sauce. They are:

- Milk
- White roux, prepared with oil
- Aromatics

Be sure to check the milk's quality before beginning the process. When milk is very cold, it is often easy to miss the early signs of souring. It is also nearly impossible to tell if the milk has absorbed odors from other foods in the reach-in or walk-in. Bring a small amount to a boil and check it carefully. The milk should smell sweet and have a smooth appearance, with no curdling evident.

If you prefer to make the roux as part of the overall process, you will need to have vegetable oil and all-purpose flour on hand, instead of a prepared roux. This technique is illustrated in Figure 8-9.

The selection of aromatics can make a distinct difference in the finished sauce. In Figure 8-9, the béchamel is being prepared with diced onions that have been allowed to sweat. Some chefs prefer to use an oignon piqué, a whole or halved onion that has been studded with whole cloves and a piece of bay

FIGURE 8-9 Preparing Béchamel Sauce and Mornay Derivative

(1) The flour for the roux is being cooked along with the diced onions.

(2) Adding the cool milk to the roux gradually.

(3) Adding grated Gruyerè to strained béchamel for Mornay sauce.

(4) The finished Mornay sauce.

leaf. Even if you do not use a oignon piqué, you may want to add a whole clove or two, a piece of bay leaf, or even a sprig of fresh thyme to give extra depth to the flavor of this sauce. A final addition of grated nutmeg is considered essential by many. Be wary, however, since nutmeg has a strong flavor and cannot be removed from the sauce once you have put it in.

2. Assemble the equipment necessary to prepare béchamel.

When selecting a pot, avoid aluminum pans, which might cause the finished velouté to take on a grayish cast. A pot that is relatively heavy is important for this sauce, since it, more than any other, is likely to scorch as it simmers.

Wooden spoons are less likely to impart an off color to this delicately colored sauce. Remember that you will also need tasting spoons, a skimmer, a fine sieve or cheesecloth for straining, and storage or service containers for the finished sauce.

Method

1. Sweat the minced onion in a small amount of oil. (See Figure 8-9 for photos illustrating the method for preparing béchamel.)

Since you want the finished sauce to have a distinctly white color, be sure that the onion is allowed to smother in a covered pot over low heat until it softens and becomes translucent. There should be no browning, but the onion should be fully cooked, so that it will not give a sulfurous aroma to the finished sauce.

2. Add the flour to the onion and prepare a white roux.

Stir the flour into the onions until it is evenly blended and allow the roux to cook over low heat for several minutes. This will begin to remove the raw flavor from the flour. It also allows an understated aroma of nuts to be imparted to the finished sauce. For a perfectly white or very pale sauce, do not allow the roux to become even slightly golden at this stage.

If you have a prepared roux on hand, then this step is not necessary. Instead, you would proceed as described for velouté: Add the milk to the smothered onions and bring it to a boil, and gradually whip in the roux.

3. Gradually add the milk to the roux and bring the sauce to a simmer.

As always when working with roux and a liquid, be sure that they are not the same temperature. If you intend to make the roux, as illustrated in the accompanying photographs, the milk can be brought to a simmer, then pulled off the heat to cool while preparing the roux. If you do use oignon piqué, it can be added to the milk as it comes to a simmer, then allowed to steep in the milk as it rests off the heat.

Use a whip or wooden spoon to gradually mix together the liquid and roux. Add any additional ingredients you have selected—thyme, bay leaf, cloves, or oignon piqué now.

Simmer the sauce for 30 minutes to 1 hour. Scorching is even more of a concern with béchamel than any other sauce. Not only will the starches in the flour try to settle out, so will the milk solids. Use a flame diffuser, if you have one, to help prevent scorching.

Follow the same skimming procedure as for velouté and remember to taste the sauce as it develops. As soon as the taste of the flour is cooked away, the sauce has cooked enough.

4. Add the grated nutmeg to taste before straining the sauce.

To many chefs, nutmeg is an indispensable component of béchamel. Remember, however, that it should only be added if it will not interfere with the intended flavor of the finished sauce. Nutmeg is a powerful flavoring and should be added judiciously, a little at a time.

5. The sauce is now ready for service, or it may be cooled and stored properly as explained in Chapter 2.

See Part IV, Chapter 15, for recipes for béchamel sauce and its derivatives.

Tomato Sauce

Although the number of derivative sauces made from a basic tomato sauce are not as great as for demi-glace, béchamel, or velouté, it is an important sauce in any kitchen. There are several approaches to making tomato sauce. In some versions, olive oil is used as the only cooking fat. For others, rendered

TABLE 8-5 TOMATO SAUCES

Tomato	Garnish
Chaudfroid	Aspic jelly
Meat	Cooked ground beef, veal, and/or pork
Nantua	Mirepoix fried with crayfish butter, white wine, cognac, fresh tomatoes, fish velouté, cayenne
Portugaise	Fried onions, concassé, salt, pepper, thin tomato sauce, meat glaze, garlic, parsley
Provençale	Sliced mushrooms, oil, salt, pepper, sugar, garlic, parsley

salt pork or bacon is required. Some recipes indicate the use of roasted veal or pork bones; others are made strictly from tomatoes and the desired vegetables. Refer to Table 8-5 for a listing of some typical tomato sauces.

Tomato sauce is frequently found as an accompaniment to crisp fried foods, vegetable dishes, pastas, or certain sautéed foods. It has a distinctive texture, less smooth and refined than the sauces we have discussed to this point. It was a relative latecomer to the society of grand sauces, since tomatoes had first to arrive in Europe from the New World. Once there, they had to overcome the serious prejudice against them. Many people actually feared that they were poisonous. Still, once assimilated (most likely at some point in the nineteenth century), tomatoes became critical in not only this sauce, but also, as you have seen, as a flavoring ingredient in other sauces.

Tomato sauce should have a deep, rich tomato flavor, with no trace of bitterness, excess acidity, or sweetness. Any of the optional ingredients selected to flavor the sauce should provide underpinnings for the flavor of tomatoes. Once the sauce is properly made, it is perfectly acceptable to add garnishing, finishing, or seasoning ingredients that will lend a special flavor, of course.

Tomato sauce will be opaque, but proper simmering, puréeing, and straining will lend it some sheen. This sauce should be slightly coarser than any other of the grand sauces because of the degree of texture that remains even after puréeing and straining the tomatoes. The sauce should be relatively smooth, thick enough to coat the back of a spoon, and thin enough to pour easily.

Mise en Place

1. Assemble the ingredients and preparations necessary for tomato sauce.

Because of the number of different recipes for tomato sauce, there is a wide range of ingredients and preparations that might be required. Review the recipe or formula you have selected and use that as a guide. The basic components are outlined below:

- Plum tomatoes (fresh or canned)
- Tomato purée (fresh or canned)
- Ground salt pork, oil, or clarified butter
- Stock: veal, chicken, beef, or pork as desired
- Aromatic vegetables, cut into a medium dice
- Standard sachet d'épices or bouquet garni
- Additional or optional flavoring or seasoning items

Plum tomatoes, sometimes referred to as Romas, are generally preferred for tomato sauces, since they have a relatively good ratio of flesh to skin and seeds. When fresh tomatoes are at their peak, it may be a good idea to use fresh tomatoes exclusively. At other times of the year, good-quality canned tomatoes are preferred. Fresh tomatoes should be chopped. Canned tomatoes may be peeled and whole, puréed, or a combination of the two. In some cases, you may want or need to add tomato paste as well.

Roasted bones of veal or pork or browned lean trimmings of these meats are sometimes included in a tomato sauce. One classic tomato sauce, Bolognese, includes a good quantity of beef and is considered a *ragu* by most Italians. The presence of meat is not an absolute requirement for all tomato sauces, however. A marinara sauce, the foundation of many dishes found throughout various regions of Italy, is described in many traditional renditions as a simple, quickly prepared sauce made of olive oil, garlic, onions, and chopped tomatoes.

Some recipes may indicate a standard mirepoix as the aromatic vegetable component. Others may rely more simply on garlic and onions. Let your recipe or your palate be your guide.

A variety of herbs and spices pair well with tomatoes. This makes it easy to "customize" a sauce to suit a particular need. You might want to use only basil for a sauce destined to accompany a dish of pasta. Or, you may want to introduce a more exotic palate to serve with a Middle Eastern-style stuffed vegetable entrée.

2. Assemble the equipment necessary for preparing tomato sauce.

Tomatoes are high-acid foods, so it is best to select a pot that is nonreactive, such as stainless steel or anodized aluminum. The gauge of the pot is important also. Because of the high sugar content of tomatoes, you need to establish even heat with as few hot spots as possible so the sauce won't scorch.

A food mill or sieve is used to do the initial purée-ing of the sauce. For a very smooth texture, you may wish to use a blender, food processor, or immersion blender.

Method

1. Heat the oil, butter, or ground salt pork in a pot over low heat. Then, add the aromatic vegetables and allow them to sweat.

The onions should become translucent, and juices should begin to be released from all the vegetables. It is acceptable to cook the onions until a rich golden brown, especially if you need to develop a sweet flavor to counteract any excess acidity present in the tomatoes.

2. Add the remaining ingredients and bring to a simmer.

Add the tomatoes along with any stock or broth required by the recipe. Any vegetables or flavoring ingredients not already added to the saucepan should be added now.

3. Simmer the sauce until the flavor is fully developed and strain the sauce.

Depending on the type of tomatoes (fresh or canned, for instance) as well as the type of sauce you are preparing, there may be distinct differences in cooking times. The drier the tomatoes, the more quickly the sauce will complete cooking.

Stir frequently throughout preparation and check the flavor occasionally. It may be necessary to correct a harsh or bitter flavor by sweating a small amount of additional chopped onion and carrots and adding them. If the flavor is weak, add a small amount of reduced tomato paste or purée. A too-sweet sauce may be corrected by adding more tomatoes, stock, or water.

Strain the sauce through a colander or coarse sieve once it has the desired flavor. Remove and discard any bones and the sachet or bouquet, if you have used them. Press well on the solids remaining in the colander to extract all the juices.

4. Purée the sauce through a food mill fitted with a fine disk.

Using a food mill is the best way to produce a sauce with the correct consistency. If you prefer a really smooth sauce, you may wish to purée the sauce a second time using a food processor, blender, or immersion blender.

5. The sauce is ready to serve now or it may be properly cooled and stored as explained in Chapter 2.

See Figure 8-10 for photos illustrating the method for preparing tomato sauce. Refer to Part IV, Chapter 15, for individual tomato sauce recipes.

Coulis

Before the codification of sauces into the grand sauces and their derivatives, any sauce would most likely have gone by the name of coulis. Certain soups were also known as coulis, especially those based on game and game birds.

Today, coulis generally indicates a sauce that is essentially a purée of a vegetable, such as red peppers, broccoli, or tomatoes. In fact, the method of preparation is quite similar to that described for a tomato sauce, explained above: Aromatic vegetables and herbs are allowed to sweat; the major flavoring ingredient is added along with a liquid such as broth, stock, vegetable or fruit juices, or water. The sauce is simmered until tender enough to purée.

A coulis may be finished with cream or butter, flavored or garnished with a variety of ingredients, such as chopped fresh herbs, julienne, concassé or dice of the main flavoring ingredient, and so forth. Refer to specific coulis recipes found in Part IV, Chapter 15, for specific information about mise en place, ingredients, and method.

FIGURE 8-10   Preparing Tomato Sauce

(1) The sauce has simmered and is ready to purée.

(2) Using a food mill to purée the sauce.

(3) This portion of the purée should be scraped from the food mill and stirred into the sauce.

(4) Finishing a puréed tomato sauce with chopped fresh oregano, basil, and parsley.

FIGURE 8-11   Preparing Red Pepper Coulis

(1) The diced peppers, ready to cook.

(2) The finished, puréed coulis, being flavored with fresh herbs.

See Figure 8-11 for photos illustrating the method for preparing red pepper coulis.

Hollandaise

This sauce received its name as a recognition of the high quality of the butter and other dairy products produced in Holland. Since the largest proportion of a hollandaise is butter, the sauce will succeed or fail according to not only the skillful balance between egg yolks, reduction, and butter, but also the quality of the butter itself.

Hollandaise belongs to a group of sauces known as emulsion sauces. An emulsion is formed when one substance is suspended in another—in this case, melted or clarified butter is suspended in partially cooked egg yolks. It is fragile because it is not a true mixture and could separate easily into its distinct components. In other words, it could "break." Other examples of emulsion sauces include mayonnaise, beurre blancs, vin blancs, and vinaigrettes.

Hollandaise should be a pale lemon color with a satin smooth texture and appearance. The hol-

landaise-style sauces described in Table 8-6 may have slightly different colors. Sauce choron, for instance, contains tomato purée, which will give the finished sauce a pale orange color. A grainy texture indicates that the egg yolks have overcooked and begun to scramble. The sauce should have the aroma of good butter. For this reason, some chefs like to use melted, rather than clarified, butter so they can incorporate a small amount of the milk solids. A good hollandaise should have a light, almost frothy consistency.

Mise en Place

1. Assemble the ingredients and preparations necessary for hollandaise. To prepare a hollandaise you will need:

- Unsalted butter, melted or clarified and warm
- Egg yolks
- Reduction
- Water
- Fresh lemon juice
- Additional or optional seasoning, flavoring, or garnish ingredients

Opinions differ on whether to use clarified or melted whole butter. Some chefs feel that clarified

TABLE 8-6 WARM BUTTER EMULSION SAUCES (HOLLANDAISE-STYLE)	
Sauce	*Garnish*
Bavaroise	Reduction of pepper, horseradish, thyme, bay leaves, parsley, vinegar, crayfish, garnish with crayfish tails
Béarnaise	Tarragon and chervil
Choron	Béarnaise with tomato
Foyot	Béarnaise with meat glaze
Maltaise	Blood orange
Mousseline	Whipped cream
Noisette	Brown butter
Paloise	Mint
Rubens	Reduction of white wine, mirepoix, and fish stock, strain, add crayfish butter, anchovy sauce

FIGURE 8-12 Preparing Hollandaise

(1) Egg yolks in a bowl with refreshed reduction.

(2) Whipping the egg yolks over simmering water until thickened and frothy.

(3) A clean side towel is used to steady the bowl while the butter is incorporated.

(4) Butter is added in a thin stream while the chef is whipping constantly.

(5) Hollandaise at the proper consistency. Note the ribbons left in the sauce by the whip.

(6) A broken hollandaise.

butter results in a more stable sauce. Others prefer melted whole butter. Then some of the milk solids can be blended into the sauce, giving it a creamier flavor. Whichever approach you take, remember that the best results are achieved when the butter and properly cooked egg yolks are at the same temperature.

The reduction for a hollandaise is prepared as outlined in step 1 of the method for hollandaise below. It consists of water and/or dry white wine, white wine vinegar, minced shallots, and cracked peppercorns.

The seasonings and consistency adjustments needed for this sauce are generally quite simple: Freshly squeezed lemon juice, salt, finely ground white pepper, and a bit of water, if necessary.

2. Assemble all equipment necessary to prepare a hollandaise.

As shown in Figure 8-12, hollandaise is frequently prepared by mixing the sauce in a bowl set over a pot of simmering water. A small saucepan is necessary to make the reduction, and a small fine strainer to strain the finished reduction (if desired). If necessary, the finished sauce can be strained through rinsed cheesecloth.

A whip is used to incorporate the butter and a ladle is necessary to add the butter to the egg yolks in a gradual stream. Once the sauce is prepared, it may be kept warm directly in the container used to prepare it, or it may be transferred to a clean bain-marie or wide-necked vacuum bottle.

Method

1. Make the reduction and add a small amount of water to cool it. Transfer the reduction (strained,

if desired) to a stainless steel bowl. (See Figure 8-12 for photos illustrating the method for preparing a hollandaise.)

Cook the ingredients for the reduction over moderate heat until the liquid is almost completely cooked away *(au sec)*. This initial reduction of water and/or wine, vinegar, shallots, and cracked peppercorns gives the sauce a certain brightness of flavor. Without it, the combination of egg yolks and butter would result in a sauce that is almost deadeningly rich.

The reduction must be cooled down to avoid overcooking the egg yolks. Be careful not to add too much water, however. Usually, a teaspoon or so is enough to moisten and cool the reduction sufficiently. To avoid the need to strain the sauce later, strain the reduction now into the bowl or pot you will use to prepare the sauce.

The stainless steel bowl can be replaced with the top of a double boiler, if you have one. Some chefs may prefer to make the sauce directly in the pan used for the reduction, working carefully over direct heat. This calls for extreme care and attention throughout cooking to avoid scrambling the eggs. It is also a good idea to use a pan that is not made of a reactive metal, such as aluminum, that might cause the sauce to become a little gray.

2. Add egg yolks to the reduction and whip over barely simmering water until they are thickened and frothy.

A successful hollandaise is most easily prepared when the egg yolks are cooked to the exact point—thickened and frothy but still very liquid. They should be very warm, but not hot enough to scramble. The yolks will increase in volume as they cook.

If they seem to be getting too hot and coagulating slightly around the sides and bottom of the bowl or pot, remove it from the heat. Set the bowl on a cool surface and continue to whip until the mixture has cooled very slightly. Then continue cooking the sauce over simmering water.

Be sure that the water is just barely simmering. There should be no visible signs of boiling, just plenty of steam rising from the surface.

3. Add warm butter gradually in a thin stream, whipping constantly. Season to taste as desired.

You will need both hands free to whip and ladle the butter into the egg yolks. Therefore, it is a good

precaution to stabilize the bowl over the simmering water. Drape a clean side towel between the bottom of the bain-marie and the bowl to steady it, if you have not already done so.

Add the butter a little at a time, whipping constantly as it is incorporated. The sauce will begin to thicken as more butter is blended in. Continue adding butter and whipping until the sauce is thickened and all the butter is incorporated. Figure 8-12 shows the sauce as it develops.

Add salt, pepper, or lemon juice to taste as the sauce is nearly finished. Lemon juice will lighten the sauce's flavor and texture, but do not let it become a dominant taste. Add just enough to lift the flavor. If the sauce is too thick, you may want to add a little warm water to regain the desired light texture.

You may want to strain the sauce at this point through cheesecloth or a fine sieve, especially if the reduction was not already strained. If care is taken throughout preparation, straining the sauce should be unnecessary, however.

4. The sauce is now ready to serve. Keep it warm (at around 160°F/70°C).

Hollandaise is a delicate sauce in more ways than one. Not only is it easy to break the emulsion by letting the sauce become too warm, it is also easy to inadvertently create a situation that might encourage the growth of pathogens (*e.g.*, the salmonella bacteria) that could cause a food-borne illness. The quantity of egg yolks and butter in the sauce makes it a likely target. Be sure that any containers you transfer the cooked sauce into are perfectly clean. Stainless steel bain-maries or vacuum bottles with wide necks are good choices.

Keep all spoons and ladles used to serve the sauce meticulously clean and never reintroduce a used tasting spoon, bare fingers, or other sources of cross contamination into the sauce.

Hollandaise should never be held longer than 2 to 3 hours. Discard any unused hollandaise after that point.

See Part IV, Chapter 15, for recipes for hollandaise and hollandaise-style sauces.

Special Tips to Rescue a Broken Hollandaise

The butter and eggs should be at about the same temperature for the best results during mixing the sauce. If the eggs are cooler than the butter, it could cause the sauce to take on a curdled appearance since the egg yolks might further cool the butter. If that happens, continue to whip the sauce over the simmering water until the sauce loses its oily, curdled appearance before adding more butter.

If the butter is a great deal hotter than the eggs (or if the water is allowed to come to a boil under the sauce), then it is possible that the eggs might begin to overcook. In that case, the sauce will develop a "scrambled-eggs" appearance. To counteract this, immediately add a little cold water to the sauce and remove it from the heat. Set the bowl on a cool surface, such as a stainless steel work table, and continue to whip until the sauce looks smooth once more. If it does not become smooth, you will need to strain the sauce before continuing with its preparation.

Look at the amount of cooked yolks left in the sieve after you have strained the sauce. If it is significant, you may need to add another egg yolk or two to regain what you have lost.

Beurre Blanc

There are many stories about how and when, and by whom, beurre blanc was first made. One such story makes the claim that a renowned female chef in France created the sauce. According to Mapie, the Countess de Toulouse-Lautrec, in her book *La Cuisine de France*, she claimed Mme. Clémence first created the sauce as an accompaniment to the salmon and other freshwater fish that abounded in the Loire River.

Beurre blanc is a sauce in which butter forms an emulsion with a reduction. Occasionally, a quantity of reduced heavy cream is added to this sauce to stabilize it, so that it can be held during a service period. Traditionally, the reduction consists of the cooking liquid *(cuisson)* used to prepare shallow-poached dishes. These poaching liquids often contain wine, which makes this sauce similar in nature to a *sauce vin blanc* (see below). It is also possible to prepare a reduction separately, as is done for hollandaise.

Mise en Place

1. Assemble the ingredients and preparations necessary for beurre blanc. To make beurre blanc, you should have:

- Whole unsalted butter, diced and chilled
- Reduction
- Reduced heavy cream (optional)
- Additional or optional seasoning, flavoring, or garnish ingredients as needed

Just as the quality of the butter is critical to the success of a hollandaise, it is equally important to a beurre blanc. Unsalted butter is best, since the presence of extra salt is not necessarily good. You can always add additional salt to taste later on. Check the butter carefully for a rich, sweet, creamy texture and aroma.

The reduction for a beurre blanc may include a variety of ingredients. Those ingredients most commonly used include an acid such as a dry wine, vinegar, or citrus juice; minced shallots, garlic, or ginger; chopped herbs including tarragon, basil, chives, or chervil; the cooking liquid used to poach fish or chicken (especially when the court bouillon contains wine or vinegar); cracked peppercorns; diced tomatoes; saffron; and others as indicated in a specific preparation. Be sure that the reduction is allowed to cook to the proper consistency—syrupy but not dry.

If cream is used to stabilize this sauce, it should be reduced separately. Carefully simmer the cream (don't let it boil over) until it is thickened and takes on a rich, ivory-yellow color.

The seasonings and consistency adjustments needed for this sauce are generally quite simple: freshly squeezed lemon juice, salt, finely ground white pepper, and a bit of water, if necessary.

2. Assemble all equipment necessary to prepare a beurre blanc.

A *sauteuse* is generally used to prepare a beurre blanc, since the greater the surface of the pan in direct contact with the heat, the easier it is to prepare this sauce quickly. Be sure that the pan is of a non-reactive metal. Bi-metal pans, such as copper or anodized aluminum lined with stainless steel, are excellent choices for this sauce. The ingredients used in the reduction are typically left in the sauce, adding texture and garnish, so it is unnecessary to strain it after cooking.

A whip may be used to incorporate the butter in the sauce, but many chefs prefer to use the motion of the pan, swirling it over the burner or flat top, to incorporate the butter. Once the sauce is prepared,

FIGURE 8-13
Whipping Butter
into Beurre Blanc

it may be kept warm directly in the container used to prepare it, or it may be transferred to a clean bain-marie or wide-necked vacuum bottle.

Method

1. Make the reduction and add a small amount of cream, if desired.

This initial reduction of cooking liquids, wine, and/or vinegar, shallots, and cracked peppercorns gives the sauce most of its flavor. Allow all the ingredients to reduce over fairly brisk heat until enough of the liquid has cooked away to create a consistency similar to syrup.

Add a little reduced cream at this point, if desired. Don't overdo the cream, however, since the sauce should have the flavor of fresh sweet butter, not heavy cream.

2. Add chilled diced butter to the reduction and incorporate over low heat until the sauce is the correct consistency.

Temperature control is the key to preparing this sauce. The cooking temperature should be quite low. The butter should be a little cooler than room temperature. Some chefs prefer to have the butter slightly softened, but this requires extra vigilance to be sure that the sauce won't break as it is prepared. Melted or runny butter will rarely produce a good sauce.

Beurre blanc is blended either with a fork, a whip, or by keeping the pan in constant motion as the butter is added a little at a time. The action is quite similar to that used in finishing a sauce with butter.

If the sauce appears to be separating, and the butter is becoming oily rather than creamy, it has gotten too hot. Immediately pull the pan away from the heat and set it on a cool surface. Continue to add chilled butter a little at a time, whipping until the mixture regains the proper appearance (see Figure 8-13). Then continue to incorporate the remainder of the butter over low heat.

If the butter takes a very long time to become incorporated into the sauce, you may need to increase the heat under the pan very slightly. If the sauce appears broken, you may be able to save it by blending in a little additional reduced cream or chilled butter.

3. The sauce is now ready to serve. Keep it warm (at around 160°F/70°C).

In many operations, beurre blanc is considered an *a la minute* sauce. This means that it is not generally held throughout service. If you are intending to prepare a large batch and hold it, use the same techniques described for hollandaise.

See Part IV, Chapter 15, for recipes for beurre blanc.

Sauce Vin Blanc

This sauce can often cause a great deal of confusion. Indeed, it is one of the few sauces that has three distinctly different preparation methods. Since they rely on techniques already described for other sauces, notably velouté, hollandaise, and beurre blanc sauces, we will look at them quickly and refer to more detailed explanations of method as necessary.

Method 1 for Sauce Vin Blanc   A poaching liquid containing wine (usually for the fish being served with this sauce), is reduced and then this reduction is used as the basis for a hollandaise sauce: Egg yolks are cooked with the reduction and melted or clarified butter is gradually whipped into the yolks.

Method 2 for Sauce Vin Blanc   The poaching liquid (as described in method 1) is reduced along with an equal quantity of fish velouté. The sauce is then finished by adding egg yolks and cooking until the sauce thickens slightly. Diced chilled butter is worked into the sauce, using the same technique as you would to prepare a beurre blanc.

According to both Escoffier and *Larousse Gastronomique,* this method is best for use as a glaze.

Method 3 for Sauce Vin Blanc A hollandaise is prepared in the usual manner, and then the reduced poaching liquid used to prepare fish is added. The sauce is then strained.

A recipe for sole vin blanc can be found in Part IV, Chapter 18.

Compound Butters

These flavored butters may be considered as a kind of sauce used to finish grilled or broiled meats, fish, poultry, or game. Compound butters may be flavored with a wide variety of ingredients, including herbs, nuts, citrus zest, garlic, shallots, ginger, and vegetables.

They are easy to prepare and can be stored, wrapped in parchment and/or plastic, for several days without loss of quality. They may also be frozen for extended storage.

In addition to their use as the "sauce" for grilled or broiled foods, they can also be used to flavor grain dishes, pasta, or as a finishing ingredient in another sauce. Boiled or steamed vegetables may be tossed in compound butter just before service. One classic dish, Chicken Kiev, calls for a compound butter to be well chilled, shaped into fin-

gers, and then rolled into a chicken breast. Thus, when the breaded and fried chicken breast is cut into, the "sauce" is released.

Mise en Place

1. Assemble the ingredients necessary for compound butter.

You will need to refer to specific recipes or your own inspiration for the exact ingredients and ratios. The recipes found in Part IV, Chapter 15, will give a general sense of the quantity of flavoring ingredients 1 pound of butter can accommodate as well as the wide range of possible flavoring options.

The butter used must be perfectly fresh. Let the butter soften to room temperature, or use the paddle attachment of a mixer to soften it. As noted, unsalted butter is preferred, but you can use salted butter if that is all you have on hand. Just use extra caution when adding the final seasonings.

Many compound butters are flavored with chopped fresh herbs. There are a host of other options: rendered bacon, puréed and reduced tomatoes or bell peppers, roasted garlic, lemon juice and zest, and so on.

2. Assemble the necessary equipment for compound butter.

Small batches of compound butter are mixed in a bowl with a wooden spoon, larger batches are prepared in a mixer with a paddle attachment. Parch-

FIGURE 8-14 Rolling a Compound Butter into a Cylinder

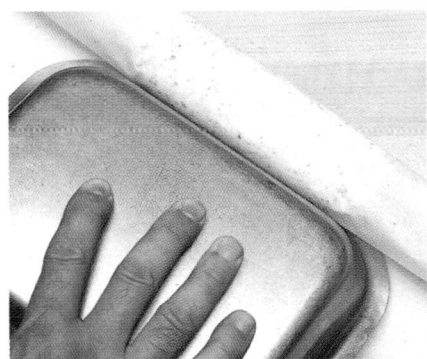

(1) Using the edge of a pan to tighten compound butter into an even cylinder.

(2) Twisting ends of the parchment paper.

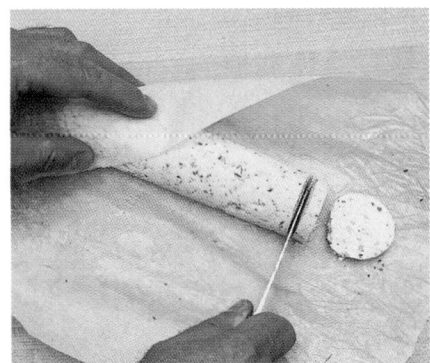

(3) Slicing the chilled compound butter for service.

ment paper is necessary to roll the compound butter after mixing.

Method

1. Prepare the flavoring agents by type or according to individual recipes.

This sauce is not cooked, so be sure that any item that needs cooking is properly prepared and well chilled before it is worked into the butter.

2. Incorporate the flavoring agents into the softened butter working by hand with a spoon, or with a mixer or food processor.

Be sure that all ingredients are thoroughly incorporated and evenly distributed throughout the butter.

3. Roll the butter into a cylinder in parchment paper or pipe it into individual rosettes. Thoroughly chill the butter before service.(See Figure 8-14 for photos illustrating the method for preparing compound butter.)

Butters that are rolled into cylinders can be sliced into medallions before they are used to top broiled items. Rosettes are often added at the last moment and allowed to melt delicately from the heat of the food. The idea is that the rosette will still retain enough of its shape to act as a pleasing and functional garnish on the plate.

See Part IV, Chapter 15, for recipes for compound butters.

Miscellaneous Sauces

Several other items are commonly found on contemporary plated dishes that fill in for traditional sauces, though they may not themselves fit the classic definition of a sauce.

- Broths and essences
- Pilafs, risottos, ragouts, and stews
- Barbecue sauces and glazes

FIGURE 8-15
Salsa: A Sauce Alternative

- Compotes, marmalades, confits, and chutneys
- Salsas (see Figure 8-15) and other "raw sauces"
- Cold emulsion sauces (mayonnaise, vinaigrettes, and marinades)
- Infused oils

A quick look through some menus today will make it apparent that demi-glace sauce and its derivatives are more and more giving way to preparations as diverse as bean ragouts, compotes, chutneys, relishes, and vegetable stews.

Though not true sauces, these items do fulfill some of the classic functions of sauces: They add flavor, moisture, texture, and color to another item. Beyond that, they also allow the chef greater freedom to accomplish other things. Turning to a sauce alternative, such as those discussed here, allows the chef to breath new life into old standards by introducing new flavors or preparations from other ethnic cuisines.

Salsas, broths, stews, compotes, and vinaigrettes served instead of butter-based or finished sauces also makes it easy for chefs to lighten the overall calorie and fat content of a dish without leaving guests wondering where the flavor and excitement went. Selecting these sauce alternatives, in place of a hollandaise or sauce vin blanc, encourages you to increase the variety of grains, legumes, fruits, and vegetables offered to the guest, without belaboring the shift toward a more nutritional focus. Some of these same issues were initially addressed in Chapter 3.

One "sauce" gaining favor in contemporary restaurants is a broth. The broth (or, as it may also be known on menus, fumet or essence) should be extremely flavorful. It is still light in body, although some broths may have a light purée added for color and flavor. The broth is often used as a pool beneath the food being served. It is not intended to turn every main course into a soup, however. An example might be a rich salmon broth flavored with a purée of fresh peas. A piece of pan-seared or grilled salmon would be served on a puddle of broth.

Other options that appear to have moved from the status of fad to established trend include relishes, salsas, compotes, and even beds of vegetables and grains such as ratatouille or hash.

Cold vinaigrettes and mayonnaise may be used as a sauce for hot sautéed items or as a marinade. Relishes and compotes based on fruits and/or vegetables may be served hot or cold. An example is a confit of red onion, consisting of onions stewed in butter and finished with a small amount of honey and vinegar. Another example is a dried-fruit compote, composed of dried fruits stewed in wine, stock, or a combination of the two.

Rice and other grains, such as bulgur and barley, are prepared by the pilaf or risotto method and used as a bed for other foods. Beans and other dried legumes, such as lentils, may be stewed and served in lieu of a standard sauce. Recipes for these sauces can be found throughout Part IV of this book, as well as in numerous other books and magazines.

Serving Sauces

Reheating Sauces

As you have seen, most of the grand sauces and some contemporary sauces can be prepared in advance, then cooled and stored. When you are ready to serve them, you will need to reheat the sauce quickly and safely. This is most easily accomplished over direct heat, although in the case of some very delicate cream sauces, you may prefer to use a double boiler.

Once the sauce is at the correct temperature, check it carefully for the best possible flavor, aroma, texture, color, and appearance. Make any necessary adjustments to the sauce either now, or after the sauce has been finished according to need.

Holding a Finished Sauce

Some sauces are suitable for holding in a steam table during service. As noted, they must be brought as quickly as possible through the danger zone and up to service temperature. Then, they are generally transferred to clean bain-maries and placed in a hot water bath.

Those sauces that have been thickened with a starch will be prone to developing a skin if they are left uncovered. Some chefs like to top the sauce with clarified butter. This creates an airtight seal that prevents a skin from forming on the surface of the sauce. Others prefer to use a fitted cover for the bain-marie or a piece of parchment paper cut to fit directly onto the surface of the sauce. Plastic wrap can also be used.

Emulsion sauces, such as hollandaise-type sauces and beurre blancs, need special care. They may not hold up in a steam table, since temperatures could be high enough to cause the sauce to break. Find another warm spot in the kitchen, or use a vacuum bottle (preferably one with a wide neck). Be sure that any emulsified sauces that remains after service are discarded to avoid foodborne disease.

Plating and Presentation

Sauces do add flavor, moisture, and texture to a dish. They also serve to enhance its visual appeal. There are some principles used in applying sauces to foods.

Maintain the temperature of the sauce. Be sure that hot sauces are extremely hot, warm emulsions sauces are as warm as possible without danger of breaking, and cold sauces remain cold until they come in contact with hot foods. The temperatures of the sauce, the food being sauced, and the plate should all be carefully monitored.

If the food being served has a crisp or otherwise interesting texture, it is generally best to pool the sauce beneath the food, spreading it in a layer directly on the plate. If an item could benefit from a little "cover" or the sauce has more visual appeal, spoon or ladle it evenly over the top of the food.

Use common sense when you determine portion sizes for sauces. There should be enough for the guest to enjoy the flavor of the sauce with each bite, but not so much that the dish looks swamped. Not only does this disturb the balance between the items on the plate, it also makes it difficult for the waiter to carry the food from the kitchen to the guest's table without at least some of the sauce running onto the rim, or worse, over the edge of the plate.

Sauces should be artfully applied to foods, but they should never look as if they were "touched" or labored over. Foods should appear fresh and as natural as possible.

Summary

Far more than a simple test of technical skill, sauces demand the best from the chef who prepares them, selects them, and crafts them to meet the needs of a special dish, menu, or foodservice operation.

CHAPTER 9 Dry-Heat Cooking Methods

The cooking methods explained in the chapter are known collectively as the dry-heat methods. They include:

- *Grilling, broiling, and barbecuing*
- *Roasting and baking*
- *Poêléing*
- *Sautéing (and variations)*
- *Pan-frying*
- *Deep-frying*

The dry heat techniques discussed in this chapter produce a range of results. Grilled and broiled items should have a highly flavored exterior, smoky and slightly charred. Their interiors should be evenly moist and juicy. Roasted foods should develop a rich roasted aroma, a well-developed color and texture. Sautéed and stir-fried foods should also develop the appropriate degree of browning; their textures will vary according to the food being prepared, but in general, they remain resilient but tender enough to produce a pleasing effect when eaten. Pan-fried and deep-fried items have a tender interior and a crisp exterior.

Understanding how these techniques actually cook the food makes it clear that the reason for selecting a particular cooking medium depends on the desired result. In sautéing, for example, the butter or oil chosen for a preparation contributes flavor as well as pan lubrication. Pan-fried and deep-fried foods tend not to depend upon the flavor of the cooking oil to develop a particular effect. Oils that have specific cooking properties, such as their high smoking point, are best. These oils are nearly neutral in flavor, for the most part.

Certain kinds or cuts of meat, poultry, and fish are best prepared using certain techniques. Consider the food's characteristics: What is the texture—firm, delicate, dense? Are there bones? Is the food naturally lean or oily? What is the size, shape, and thickness of the food? Because dry heat does not have a tenderizing effect, any food prepared by one of these techniques must be naturally tender or should be prepared in a way that will introduce additional moisture. This can be done by barding or marinating foods. These techniques are also outlined in this chapter.

No matter what food you are preparing or which cooking technique you intend to use, two abilities are of great importance: it is extremely important to select the proper cuts, shapes, and sizes of foods for grilling, roasting, sautéing, or frying. You also must be adept at gauging the exact point at which foods are perfectly cooked—a skill acquired only through experience.

The Dry-Heat Cooking Methods

Grilling, Broiling, and Barbecuing

Broiling, barbecuing, and pan-broiling are all forms of grilling. The difference between the methods lies in the source of the heat.

Grilled foods are cooked by radiant heat from a source located below the food. They should have a smoky, slightly charred flavor resulting from the flaring of the juices and fats that are rendered out as the item cooks. The drippings that might have collected or reduced in a sauté pan are actually reducing directly on the food's surface. This creates an intensely flavored exterior.

Hardwoods such as grapevines, mesquite, hickory, or apple are frequently used to introduce a special flavor. Branches of herbs may also be allowed to smolder on the fire to lend their distinct flavor.

Broiled foods are generally considered to be those cooked by a heat source located above the food. The broiler is used to perform other types of cooking, however, and this can result in a little confusion.

Frequently, delicate items such as lean white fish are first brushed with butter and then placed on a heated sizzler platter before being placed on the rack below the heat source. This is not broiling in the strictest sense of the word; it is actually closer to baking. Items prepared in this manner may still be referred to as "broiled" on a menu. Similarly, the broiler or a salamander can be used to prepared glazed or "gratinéed" foods, such as stuffed tomatoes, Sole Véronique with glaçage, or a gratin of salmon (see Figure 9-1).

Barbecuing is a term that can cause confusion. In some parts of the country, it signifies a food that has been basted repeatedly with a barbecue sauce during grilling. In others, it refers to pit- or spit-roasted items. On some menus, it may have little if anything to do with either a pit, spit, or grill. A "barbecued beef sandwich" may simply be roasted beef that has been thinly sliced and simmered in a barbecue sauce.

Pan-broiled foods are cooked on top of the stove in a heavy cast-iron or other warp-resistant metal pan over intense heat. Any fat or juices released during

FIGURE 9-1   Salmon Gratin

Glaçage is used to coat a piece of salmon, then browned in a broiler or salamander.

cooking are removed as they accumulate; otherwise the result is a sauté or a stew. Special pans made to simulate a grill's effect may be used. These pans have thick ridges that hold the food up and away from any juices or fat that might collect.

Mise en Place

1. Assemble all ingredients and preparations used for grilling.

There are relatively few items necessary to create good grilled foods. Those that are selected should be of a size, shape, and quality that will stand up to intense heat without losing their natural tenderness. Refer to either Chapter 5 or specific recipes for additional guidance in selecting:

- Meats, fish, poultry, breads, vegetables, fruits
- Oils for lubricating both the food and the grill's rods
- Seasonings and flavorings
- Additional and optional items, as desired

Foods should be of relatively even thickness and cut thinly enough to allow them to cook properly without excessive exterior charring. Cut them into the appropriate size. Trim away any fat, silverskin, and gristle from meats. Pound meats and fish

FIGURE 9-2   Preparing Skewered Items

(1) Be sure to soak wooden skewers first.

(2) Note that some space is left between items to allow even, rapid cooking.

lightly to even their thickness, if appropriate. Some foods are cut into strips, chunks, or large dice and then threaded on skewers (see Figure 9-2).

The oil you select can be neutral in flavor. Or, depending upon the item you are grilling, you may wish to incorporate a flavored oil to add a special taste.

Salt and pepper are, of course, the mainstay seasoning. But, remember that marinades may be used to introduce additional flavor or moisture. Some marinades are also intended to improve the texture of foods that might otherwise become too soft to handle easily on the grill (see Figure 9-3).

There are numerous ways to enhance the flavor, texture, and color of foods being grilled. A protective coating of melted butter and bread crumbs, known as *à l'anglaise,* may be applied to foods. A glaze or barbecue sauce can be added as well.

2. Assemble and prepare all equipment necessary for grilling.

FIGURE 9-3   Marinated Foods for Grilling

(1) Vegetables in a marinade prior to cooking.

(2) Marinated flank steak and zucchini being grilled.

FIGURE 9-4   Preparing the Grill

(1) Scrub grill well to remove any burned-on particles.

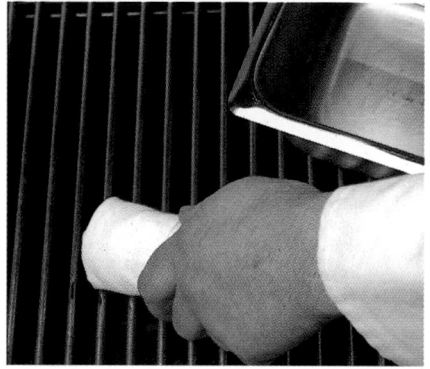

(2) Rub the grill lightly with oil .

Grills and broilers should be carefully maintained (see Figure 9-4). The rods should be scoured or brushed well between service periods. Rub the rods lightly with a vegetable oil to season them before preheating the grill.

Remember that it is best to establish temperature "zones" on the grill (see Figure 9-5). Learn which is the "hot" area and which is cool. Developing a system for placing foods on the grill, whether by food type or by range of doneness, will help speed your work on the line.

Some restaurants have special procedures so that potential problems created by foods that might drip through the grill can be avoided. For instance, cheese may not be applied to burgers while still on the grill. Instead, the burger might be cooked to just a few degrees less than requested, and then transferred to a sizzler platter. The sliced cheese is used to top the burger, and a quick pass under a broiler or salamander completes the cooking process. A special "zone" of the grill may have to be established for foods brushed with barbecue sauce to prevent a flavor transfer from the sauce to all the other grilled items.

FIGURE 9-5   Zones on a Grill

Mentally divide the grill so that you avoid flavor transfers. Cook the foods at their best temperatures.

Hand racks for delicate items, or those that might be awkward to turn easily, should be similarly cleaned between uses. A light brushing or coating of oil will help prevent the skin of delicate fish or poultry from sticking and tearing. Be sure that the collar on the handle is well secured once the food has been properly positioned (see Figure 9-6).

Tongs, offset spatulas, flexible spatulas, and sizzler plates are almost universally required at the

FIGURE 9-6   Placing Fish in a Hand Grill

(1) Brush the fish's skin (red snapper shown) lightly with oil to prevent tearing.

(2) Close the hand grill, and push the metal collar until it is securely fastened.

FIGURE 9-7   Grilling Chicken Paillards

(1) Using tongs, dip the chicken in plain or seasoned oil, and allow the excess to drain away before placing it on the grill.

(2) Grill on the first side until the edges begin to change color.

FIGURE 9-8   Releasing Fish from Hand Grill

Use a spatula to gently release the fish from the grill without tearing the skin. A black bass is shown.

grill station (see Figures 9-7 and 9-8). You should also have a collection of spoons or other utensils for serving sauces, brushes to apply glazes, marinades, or barbecue sauces. Hot plates are also a requirement, so that the food can be quickly and correctly plated and served to the guest.

Method

1. Place the food on the grill to start cooking and "mark" it.

It does make a difference which side of the food goes onto the grill first. The best looking, or "presentation" side always goes face down on the grill first. Once the item is turned to the second side, it should not usually be turned again.

Most patrons expect to see the familiar cross-hatch marks on grilled food at a restaurant. While it is certainly possible to grill foods correctly without giving them the trademark "grid," it is not difficult to do. It has the added advantage of "releasing" the food from the grill before the presentation side sticks and tears.

To mark foods on a grill or broiler, gently work the spatula under the food and give it a quarter turn (90°F/32°C). Let it continue to cook on the first side another minute or two before turning the food completely over.

Whenever a barbecue sauce is used, it is usually a good idea to apply several thin coats, rather than one heavy coat (see Figure 9-9). The more light coats, the better the finished color, flavor, and appearance of the food.

FIGURE 9-9 Applying Barbecue Sauce

Brush the meat after it has been partially cooked for the best results.

2. Turn once to cook on second side.

Since most foods cooked by grilling or broiling are relatively thin and tender, they should not require much more cooking time, once they have been turned. Thicker cuts, or those that must be cooked to a higher internal doneness may need to move to the cooler portion of the grill, so that they don't develop a charred exterior. Or, they may be removed from the grill altogether and allowed to finish cooking in the oven.

For banquets, it may be helpful to quickly mark foods on the grill, just barely cooking the outer layers of the food. Then, they can be laid out on sheet or hotel pans, and finished in the oven. This allows you to greatly expand the potential output of your grill. Exercise extreme care in chilling the food quickly if it is to be held for any appreciable amount of time.

If you are using a barbecue sauce or glaze, you will probably need to turn the item more than once, however. Brush barbecue sauce on the top of the food and turn it repeatedly, until a good shiny glaze and crust have developed.

3. Finish to desired doneness and serve at once.

Most red meats, some fish, and duck breasts may be prepared to a range of doneness. Most other foods are cooked until they are cooked through. In either case, a deft touch and a sixth sense about when a food is properly cooked is a

FIGURE 9-10 Degrees of Doneness in Red Meats

(1) Very rare.

(2) Rare.

(3) Medium.

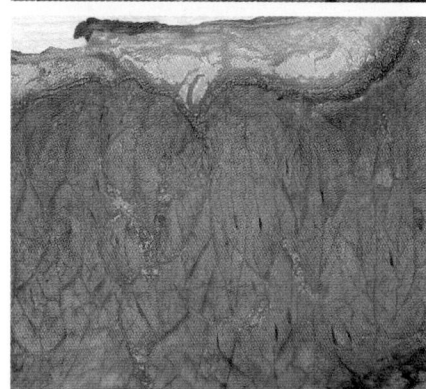

(4) Medium-well.

FIGURE 9-11 Spit-Roasting Chickens

FIGURE 9-12 Spit-Roasting Setup

great boon to a grill chef. Rely on a combination of previous experience and sensory data—the way a food looks, feels, and smells—to guide you. Figure 9-10 shows red meats cooked to different degrees of doneness.

Roasting and Baking

Spit-roasting was one of the earliest cooking methods. This technique involves placing the food on a rod that is turned either manually or with a motor (see Figure 9-11). The radiant heat, given off by a fire or gas jets, cooks the item in much the same manner as grilling or broiling. Constant turning assures that the food cooks evenly and develops a good crust on all sides. The tradition of serving roasted and grilled foods on toasted bread or a croûton began when pieces of bread were placed below the cooking food to trap escaping juices. In contemporary kitchens, drip pans are placed under the spit, as shown in Figure 9-12.

Roasting, as it is most commonly practiced today, however, is more similar to baking than it is to the original form of roasting.

Roasted foods are cooked through contact with dry, heated air held in a closed environment—an oven. As the outer layers become heated, the food's natural juices turn to steam and penetrate the food more deeply. The rendered juices, or pan-drippings, are the foundation for sauces prepared while the roast rests.

The flavor and aroma of a roasted food should contribute to an overall sensation of fullness, richness, and depth. This is due in part to the nature of the food and in part to the browning process. They should normally have a rich color, ranging from delicate gold colors to the nearly black color of a perfectly roasted rib of beef. The proper development of color has a direct bearing on the flavor. Items that are too pale lack not only eye appeal but also the depth of flavor associated with properly roasted foods.

Baking is the term associated with most portion-size foods that are cooked according to the techniques outlined here, including pork chops, potatoes, and squash. Still, this is not an ironclad rule. Garlic is roasted, hams are baked, and potatoes cooked in their skins are baked while those peeled and added to the roast's drippings or coated with oil are "oven-roasted."

Smoke-roasting is an adaptation of roasting that allows foods to take on a rich, smoky flavor (see Figure 9-13). The food cooks in a smoke bath, in a tightly closed roasting pan or smoking setup. This can be done over an open flame or in the oven.

Unlike smoked foods made in traditional charcuterie operations, the food does not have to be brined and cured before smoking. There are limitations and drawbacks, of course. Smoke-roasting does not preserve foods. Any food left too long in the smoke bath can develop an acrid, unappetizing aroma and taste.

FIGURE 9-13   Smoke-Roasting

(1) Corn is being smoke-roasted in a hotel pan setup.

(2) Chicken is given a light "smoking" using disposable pans and a rack.

FIGURE 9-14
Roasted Bones for
Jus de Veau Lié

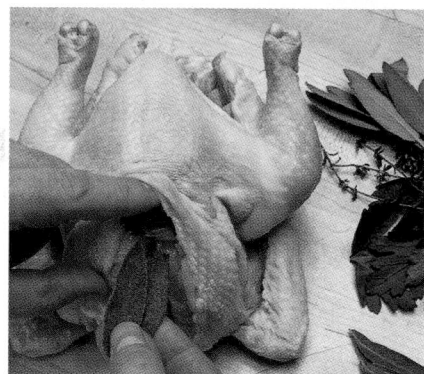

FIGURE 9-15
Stuffing Herbs
Under a
Chicken's Skin

FIGURE 9-16
Using Flavored
Bread Crumbs to
Coat Tenderloin
Steaks

Mise en Place

1. Assemble all ingredients and preparations for roasting.

In some cases, roasting is used as a preliminary step in other preparations. For example, bones are often roasted for stocks (see Figure 9-14). Be sure that the bones are cut into the correct lengths. Allow them sufficient time to drain and dry before placing them in the oven for the best results. Mirepoix and tomato products are also roasted in many types of brown stocks.

Select tender meats from the rib and loin areas for the best results. The more tender cuts from the legs of certain animals, such as top round, are also excellent when roasted. Young, tender birds may be roasted, as may whole fish. Whole chickens are roasted, or cut into pieces and "baked."

Vegetables and fruits are roasted or baked, the terminology varies according to custom. Vegetables cooked whole and in their skins are pierced or scored. This allows the steam that builds up as the food cooks to escape. If this step is omitted, you will find that you have exploding potatoes and squash shrapnel to clean up.

A layer of fat or poultry skin is traditionally allowed to remain. It is felt that this bastes foods naturally, as they roast. For additional flavor during roasting, herbs or aromatic vegetables may be used to stuff the cavity, or they may be inserted just under the skin (see Figure 9-15).

Today, with an increased concern over the amount of fat in diets, every trace of visible fat or skin is often removed in an effort to keep foods "fat-free." Should the natural protection of fat or skin be removed, then, foods might become dry and lose flavor. In that case, an alternative "skin"

FIGURE 9-17   Preparing Stuffed Pork Chops

(1) Cutting a pocket in the chop.

(2) Chops are secured by tying with twine or with skewers.

(3) The stuffed chops.

FIGURE 9-18
Filled and Flavored Apples Ready to Bake in Cider

FIGURE 9-19   Baking Squash

(1) Cut side of the squash being brushed with butter.

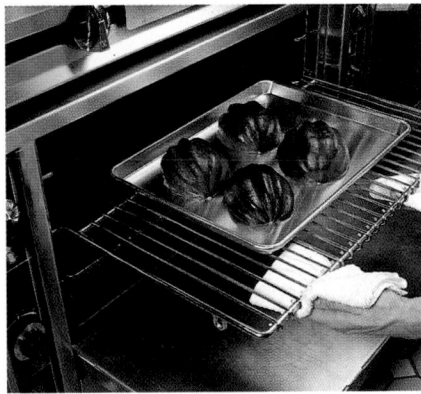

(2) Place cut side down on the baking sheet before baking.

should be added, in the form of coatings or crusts (see Figure 9-16). You should be aware, however, that it has been determined that the amount of fat released from skin or fat layers as foods roast does not penetrate far into the meat. Since it does provide some protection from the drying effects of an oven without dramatically changing the amount of fat, you may opt to leave it in place or remove the fat or skin before the item is served.

Barding—tying thin sheets of fatback, bacon, or caul fat—and *larding*—inserting small strips of fatback into a food—have been the traditional preparation techniques for roasted foods that are naturally lean. Venison, wild boar, game birds, and certain cuts of beef or lamb may be candidates. These same techniques, using different products, are used today. Rather than larding a roast with fatback, today you may find a roast has been studded with slivers of garlic. A "robe" of shredded potatoes may be applied in place of the bacon.

Foods such as chicken breasts, chops, squashes, tomatoes, peppers, or apples are frequently stuffed before roasting (see Figures 9-17 and 9-18). These stuffings should be properly prepared. Remember that adding a hot stuffing to a cold food could result in food poisoning. Keep all foods at the correct temperature at each stage of preparation.

Some vegetables are halved and baked, as is the squash shown in Figure 9-19. It is often a good idea to baste and season them before and during cooking.

Mirepoix is used to flavor the jus or pan gravy for roasted items. It should be cut into a size that allows it to brown properly. If it will be added during roasting, take into account the overall cooking time. The longer a roast cooks, the larger the cut should be. If you will add it at the last moment, cut the mirepoix small, so that it will brown properly in a much shorter amount of time. To complete the pan gravy or jus, a rich stock, or brown sauce should be on hand. Pan gravy calls for flour to make a roux, while a jus is usually thickened with arrowroot or cornstarch.

2. Assemble all equipment necessary for preparation and service.

Roasting pans or baking sheets should be of the right size and shape to hold the food correctly. There should be enough room for air to circulate freely, but not so much that any juices that render from the food are likely to scorch.

The less that comes between the food and direct contact with the heated air, the more successfully the food will roast. To that end, you may want to set foods on roasting racks, beds of mirepoix, or even bones. Or you may prefer to set the foods directly on very shallow roasting or baking pans. The food should remain uncovered. Covering the pan will trap the steam that escapes from the meat. Roasting pans that are too deep for the food will also create a steam bath that could affect the finished quality of the dish.

You may also need butcher's twine or skewers, instant-reading thermometers, and a kitchen fork. You will need an additional pan to hold the roasted food while you make a sauce from the pan drippings. Strainers and skimmers or ladles are necessary to prepare the sauce. A carving board and extremely sharp carving knife should be nearby for final service.

Method

1. Sear the food as appropriate and baste throughout cooking time.

Searing is an initial step for certain foods. This may be done by cooking small items in a little hot oil or other fat over direct heat. Or, you may opt to

begin the roasting process at a very high temperature, then reduce the heat once the food takes on a good color. Chefs often prefer to allow a deep color to develop gradually over the course of roasting larger items, rather than searing them. They feel that avoiding extreme temperatures produces a food that is moister and has lost less volume during cooking. As long as the finished dish has a rich and appealing color, it matters little which approach you take.

Roasted and baked foods may be basted during roasting. The fats and juices released by the food itself are the traditional basting liquid. Foods, such as vegetables or fruits, may call for a special basting liquid, prepared separately. A marinade, glaze, flavored or plain butter, or fruit juices are possible choices.

Adjust the temperature of the oven if necessary throughout the roasting period. Or, if you typically have ovens pre-set to specific temperatures, be prepared to move foods from one oven to another. Some foods roast best at high temperatures for very short periods. Others may need an initial period at high temperature, then a more extended period at moderate to low temperatures. Failure to watch the cooking speed and to regulate the temperature accordingly will result in foods that are uneven in color, taste, and texture.

2. Cook foods to the correct doneness, and allow them to rest briefly.

Meats, fish, poultry, and game are generally cooked to a specified internal temperature. An instant-reading thermometer is the most accurate gauge (see Figure 9-20). Other tests, including the

FIGURE 9-20
Determining Doneness with an Instant-Reading Thermometer

FIGURE 9-21
Checking Juices
from a Roast
Chicken for
Doneness

FIGURE 9-22   Preparing a Pan Gravy

(1) Add flour to released drippings and cook to form a roux.

(2) Add the stock and simmer until thickened.

(3) Strain the gravy to remove mirepoix.

"skewer" test, touch, or fork-tenderness may also be used for meats and other foods.

To test whole roasted birds for doneness, pierce them at the point where the thigh is thickest (see Figure 9-21). The juices should run nearly clear. Any juices that have accumulated in the cavity should no longer have a red or pink hue.

Allow a few minutes for small items or up to 15 or 20 minutes for larger foods, so that the food can "rest" before it is served. While this might seem to run counter to the constant refrain of serving hot foods hot, it is an important step in properly roasting foods. A brief period to rest after they come out of the oven allows the food's temperature to equalize. This benefits the texture, aroma, and flavor of the foods. It also plays a key role in carryover cooking, which should be thought of as the last stage of cooking (see below).

3. Prepare the pan gravy or jus, if desired (see Figure 9-22). Steps in preparing granes follow.

4. Carve (optional) and serve with appropriate sauce and garnish.

Carryover Cooking

Carryover cooking refers to the fact that the heat retained by foods, even after they come out of the oven, is enough to continue "cooking" the food. The internal temperature will rise, and this can change the degree of doneness dramatically.

The larger the item, the greater the amount of heat it will retain and the more its internal temperature will rise. Cornish game hen or quail may show an increase in its internal temperature of 5 to 10°F (3 to 6°C). A top round of beef's temperature may increase as much as 15°F (8°C) and the temperature of a steamship round of beef by up to 20°F (-11C). In order to achieve the correct doneness, the main item should be removed from the oven when the internal temperature is lower than the desired service temperature.

Preparing Jus or Pan Gravy for Roasted Foods

The sauce made from the accumulated drippings is frequently referred to as a *jus* or pan gravy. When the jus made from drippings is thickened with arrowroot or cornstarch, it may be referred to as *jus lié*. If a sauce is made with a roux incorporating the fat rendered from a roast, it is usually called pan gravy.

For both jus and gravy, add the mirepoix to the rendered fat and drippings in the roasting pan (if the drippings are not scorched). They may be added during the roasting period, or they can be allowed to brown in the dripping. Place the roasting pan over direct heat. Cook the mirepoix until it is browned, the fat is clarified, and the drippings are reduced.

To make a pan gravy, pour off the excess fat, leaving only enough to prepare an adequate amount of roux. Add flour to the roasting pan for pan gravy, and stir it well. Cook this roux for a few minutes. Add the appropriate stock to the pan. Be sure to add the liquid gradually and stir it continuously to work out all the lumps in the roux.

Simmer the gravy until it is well flavored and properly thickened. This will usually take around 15 to 20 minutes. Strain the gravy. Adjust the seasoning if necessary, and skim any fat floating on the surface before serving. Hold pan gravies in a steam table as you would any sauce, taking the necessary precautions to keep a skin from forming: a layer of clarified butter, a piece of parchment, or a tight-fitting cover.

For jus, add stock to the reduced drippings and mirepoix. There is no roux necessary. Simmer for the same amount of time as you would a regular gravy. Skim the jus as it cooks to remove fat from the surface. Then, just before you are ready to strain the sauce, it may be thickened with a little diluted arrowroot or cornstarch if desired.

Carving

Once the food is properly roasted, the chef's task may not be complete. The food must be carved correctly to make the most of the item. Some meats, poultry, and fish are cut into serving-sized portions before they are cooked. In other instances, it is more appropriate to prepare a large roast or an entire bird

FIGURE 9-23 Carving a Rib Roast

(1) Make cuts parallel to the cutting board until you reach the bone.

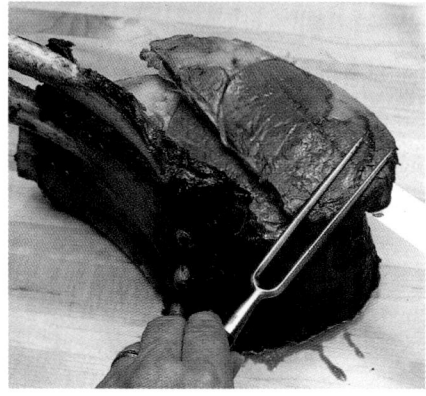

(2) Use the tip of the knife to release the cut from the bone.

or fish. The rib roast of beef, leg of lamb, and whole duck may be considered prototypes. For example, because they are similar in structure, a ham would be carved in the same manner as a leg of lamb.

Standing Rib Roast

This carving method could also be used for a rack of veal or venison or a crown roast of lamb or pork (see Figure 9-23).

1. Lay the rib roast on its side.

Using a sharp meat slicer, make parallel cuts from the outer edge toward the bones.

2. Use the knife tip to cut the slice of meat away from the bone and serve it.

Leg of Lamb

1. To steady the leg, hold the shank bone firmly in one hand with a clean side towel. Make parallel cuts from the shank end down to the bone (see Figure 9-24).

FIGURE 9-24   Carving a Leg of Lamb

(1) Cut away the end piece. This is usually served only by special request.

(2) The initial cuts are made vertically, until the bone is reached.

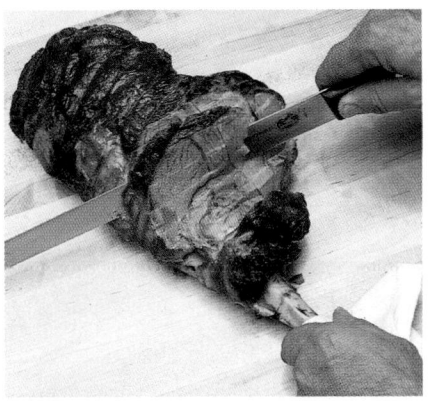

(3) Angle the knife as you continue cutting, so that cuts stay properly sized.

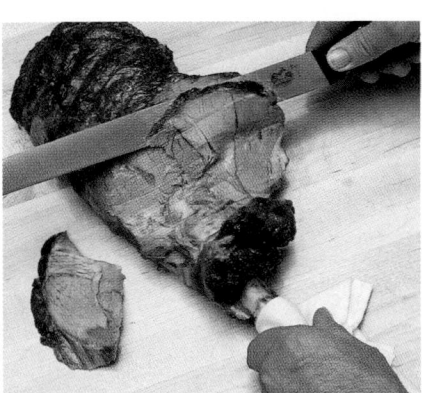

(4) Reverse the angle to get the most cuts.

2. Continue cutting slices of meat from the leg, cutting away from the bone to make even slices.

3. When the slices become very large, begin to cut the meat at a slight angle, first from the left side, then from the right side, alternating until the leg is entirely sliced.

Birds

Although a duck is used to demonstrate these carving techniques, they could be applied to any bird (see Figure 9-25).

1. Use a knife tip to cut through the skin at the point where the leg meets the breast. Use the tines of a kitchen fork to gently press the leg away from the body. A properly roasted bird's leg will come away easily.

2. Use one kitchen fork to hold the breast steady. Insert another kitchen fork at the joint between the drumstick and the thigh. Pull the leg away from the body. Repeat for the other leg.

3. Cut the leg into two pieces through the joint between the thigh and the drumstick.

4. Cut through the skin on the breast on either side of the breastbone to begin to remove the breast meat.

5. Use the tines of a kitchen fork to gently pull the breast meat away from the rib cage. Make short, smooth strokes with the knife tip to cut the meat cleanly and completely away.

Poêléing

Poêléing, a technique most often associated with white meats and game birds, is sometimes known as "butter-roasting." Meats are allowed to cook in their own juices in a covered vessel on a bed of aromatic vegetables known as a *matignon*. The matignon then becomes a garnish served as part of the sauce. Stock or jus is often used to prepare a sauce from the pan drippings.

Because the food's surface is not browned as deeply as it would be in roasting, the flavor tends to be more delicate. An initial searing, or removing the cover during the final cooking stage, will allow

FIGURE 9-25 Carving a Roasted Duck

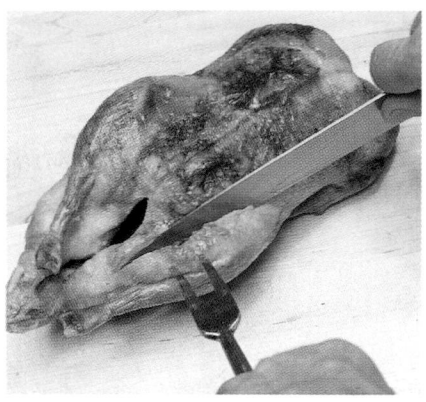

(1) Cut through the skin to expose the thigh joint.

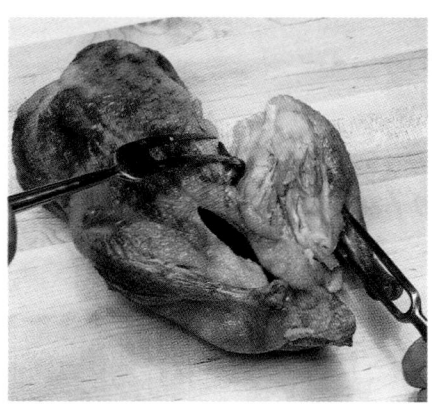

(2) Pull the leg away from the body completely.

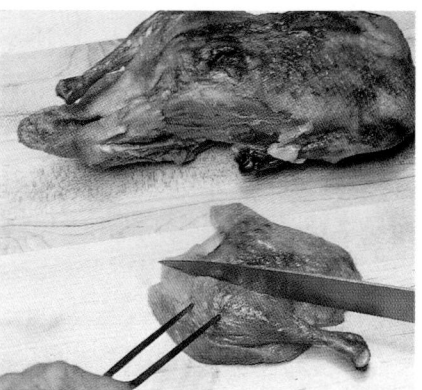

(3) Cut through the leg to separate it into thigh and drumstick.

(4) Cut the breast over the breastbone.

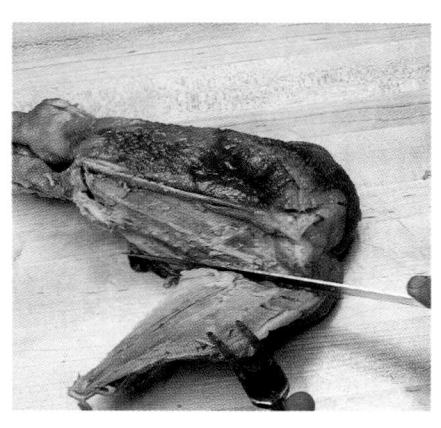

(5) Cut the meat away from the bones.

the surface of the poêléed item to brown slightly. In general, however, poêléed items should have a less pronounced color than that of roasted items. The surface should appear moist. Poêléed items should be tender and moist. The should develop a slight crust, which offers some contrast in textures.

Mise en Place

1. Assemble all ingredients and preparations for poêléing.

- Main item
- Matignon
- Butter (melted)
- Stock or a prepared jus for sauce
- Thickener if necessary

Veal, capon, and small game are often prepared by this method. The addition of butter, as well as the matignon, furnishes additional moisture during cooking. As in other dry-heat techniques, the meats should be trimmed of excess fat, and they are frequently tied to help retain their shape and to promote even cooking.

A matignon is a mirepoix (sometimes referred to as "edible mirepoix") in which the vegetables are peeled and cut into a uniform dice or julienne. Ham is traditionally included. The matignon becomes the garnish for the finished sauce.

Whole, unsalted butter is used both to smother the matignon and to baste the bird, if desired.

Other ingredients may be required to prepare a variety of stuffings, fillings, or garnishes. Refer to specific recipes for guidance.

2. Assemble all equipment necessary for preparation and service.

The equipment necessary for poêléing is nearly identical to that for roasting. There is one special piece required: a tight-fitting cover for a casserole or ovenproof earthenware dish. If there is no cover available, then cover the baking or roasting pan tightly with aluminum foil.

FIGURE 9-26   Poussin Poêlé

(1) The matignon is allowed to sweat in butter.

(2) Cover the pot when ready to go in the oven. The birds have been basted with additional butter.

(3) Poêlé, covered, in the oven.

(4) Add a thickener to the sauce after it has been degreased.

Method

1. Sear or "seize" the main item. See Figure 9-26 for photos illustrating the method for poêléing.

Cook the main item on all sides in the hot oil, just until the surface begins to turn color. This is known as "seizing." Remove the main item. This is done to begin the development of flavor. Whether or not the food should be allowed to just lightly stiffen or if it should begin to take on a rich golden hue is a decision made according to the desired end result.

2. Sweat/smother matignon.

Cook the matignon in melted whole butter over medium heat, stirring frequently until the onions are translucent. This is a crucial step in development of flavor for the finished dish, especially the sauce made from the pan drippings. The matignon will be a part of this sauce, so it is important that it be properly cooked.

3. Baste with additional butter (optional), cover and cook in oven until properly cooked.

Butter-roasting implies that there is a significant amount of butter used throughout cooking. In addition to its contribution to flavor, the butter also acts as a way to add moisture to lean white meats, the foods most traditionally prepared by this technique—veal, chicken, game birds, squab, and pheasant.

The same tests for doneness applied to roast meats are used for poêléed dishes. An instant-reading thermometer, inserted in the thickest part of the meat or the thigh of birds is the surest method. It should be used in conjunction with other evaluations, such as the correct color of the food's exterior. Juices running from meats or the cavity of birds should be nearly clear. The bird's leg should move freely when wiggled, If the leg pulls away or falls away, then the bird is overcooked. There should be a pleasing and appropriate aroma as well. Remember to allow a sufficient margin for carryover cooking as the meat rests.

4. Carve and serve with the sauce. Prepare the sauce as you would a pan gravy:

Place the casserole over high heat and add the stock or jus. Simmer until it is well flavored and slightly reduced. Pull the casserole slightly off-center to allow the fat to collect on one side; skim.

Thicken the stock or jus with diluted arrowroot or cornstarch. Add any additional ingredients to finish or garnish the sauce. Adjust the seasoning to taste.

Sautéing

The object of sautéing foods is to produce a flavorful exterior with the best possible texture and color. The proper color and texture will vary, of course, depending upon the food you are sautéing. Red meats and game should have a deep-brown exterior. White meats, such as veal, pork, and poultry, should have a golden or amber exterior. Lean white fish will be pale gold when sautéed as skinless fillets, whereas steaks of firm fish, such as tuna, will take on a darker color. Onions can be sautéed to a variety of stages: limp and translucent, crisp and deep brown, or a rich mahogany with a melting texture.

Because sautéing is a rapid technique and does not have the tenderizing effect of some of the moist-heat methods described in Chapter 10, any food to be sautéed must be naturally tender. This technique cooks food rapidly in a small amount of fat over relatively high heat. The juices released during cooking form the base for a sauce made in the same pan and served with the sautéed item.

The sauce serves three purposes:

• It captures the food's flavor that is lost during cooking

• It introduces additional flavor (an important factor because tender foods often have a subtle flavor). It counteracts the dryness resulting from the sautéing process.

Stir-frying, generally associated with Asian styles of cooking and successfully borrowed by innovative Western chefs, shares many similarities with sautéing. Foods to be stir-fried are customarily cut into small pieces and cooked rapidly in a small amount of oil.

Mise en Place

1. Assemble all ingredients and preparations for sautéing.

Cut the main item into an appropriate size. Trim away the fat, silverskin, and gristle from meats For poultry suprêmes and fillets of fish, remove the skin and bones. Pound or butterfly the meats to achieve an even thickness.

Vegetables and fruits are generally sliced, but this should be a decision made with respect to the nature of the food itself. For instance, you would certainly slice or chunk pineapple before sautéing it, but you may not need to do so with small button mushrooms.

Marinades, stuffings, or seasonings may be required by specific recipes. Marinades should be allowed a sufficient amount of time to add the correct degree of flavor. Stuffings must be properly prepared, allowed to cool if necessary, then incorporated correctly and secured so that they do not escape during cooking.

Dredging or dusting the item with flour is another common advance preparation technique. This is generally recommended for meat cut into strips (*émincé*) and for chicken and fish. One particular application of sautéing, *à la meunière*, requires dusted fish and meats (see Figure 9-27). Dusting is optional, otherwise, and many chefs feel that it is not always desirable. If you wish, seasoning can be added to the flour. If it is not, it is generally a good idea to season the food lightly with salt, pepper, or other items just prior to sautéing.

The cooking medium must be able to reach relatively high temperatures without breaking down or smoking. Clarified butter, neutral-flavored oil, olive oil, or rendered fats such as bacon, goose fat, or lard are often used.

A base sauce (demi-glace, jus lié, essences, broths, or a coulis, for instance) is usually necessary. There are a number of possible ingredients you may need to have on hand to flavor or finish the sauce. Wine, stock, cognac or liqueur, fortified wine, or water is often used to deglaze the pan.

Additional aromatic ingredients, such as shallots, mushrooms, capers, tomatoes, or peppers might be required. Butter may be used to finish the sauce; it should be whole butter, diced and either chilled or softened to room temperature.

For additional suggestions, refer to specific recipes in Part IV of this book, or other classic and contemporary recipe collections.

2. Assemble all equipment necessary for preparation and service.

FIGURE 9-27 Dredging Trout with Flour

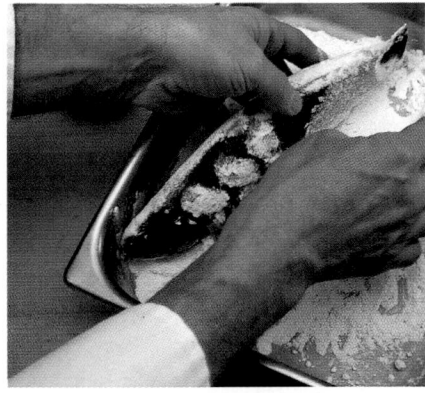

(1) Coat first one side and then the other of a pan-ready trout with flour.

(2) Shake off any excess before sautéing.

A sauté pans may be referred to as a "sauteuse" or "sautoir." They also variously are referred to, depending upon the size, shape, and material used to make the pan, as griswolds (cast iron), bi-metals (copper lined with tin or stainless steel), or rondeaus (if they are quite large).

Bear in mind that certain materials are better at conducting heat quickly with quick reaction to changes in temperature, while others offer a more constant heat that does not react as quickly. There are benefits to both types of pans, and you will learn quickly which pan works best in which situation and with which food.

The quantity of food you will be sautéing should be taken into account when selecting an appropriate pan. It is important that the pan be of an appropriate size, to avoid overcrowding. If too much is put in the pan, the pan's temperature will drop quickly and a good crust will not form on the food. Equally important, the pan must not be too large. This can cause the drippings to scorch, rendering them unsuitable for the sauce.

A selection of small tools, holding containers, and serving pieces are also necessary. Spatulas, tongs, spoons (slotted and solid metal spoons, wooden spoons, and tasting spoons), sizzler platters or sheet pans, bain-maries and steam tables for holding sauce, and strainers should be close at hand.

Method

1. Place food into preheated oil and let it cook until browned or golden (see Figures 9-28, 9-29, and 9-30).

The cooking medium (e.g. butter or oil) helps assure an even heat transfer from the pan to the item. The amount you add to the pan will depend upon the type of food being prepared. The more natural marbling or fat present in the food, the less fat you really need. Well-seasoned or non-stick pans may not require any fat beyond that which is already present in the food.

Red meats and/or very thin meat pieces will sauté best when fat is at, or nearly at, the smoking point. Less-intense heat is required for white meats, fish, shellfish, most vegetables, fruits, and eggs.

Both pan and the cooking medium must be allowed to reach the correct temperature before the main item is added. This assures that, as soon as the food hits the hot pan, the cooking process begins. The juices released by the food should cook down quickly, coating and glazing the food, as well as forming a rich *fond*, used to flavor the sauce.

It is important that the best-looking side of the food, or the side you want facing up to the customer, should go down onto the heated pan first. Do not crowd the food, and avoid overlapping pieces. Direct contact with the pan is critical to the proper development of color and flavor.

2. Turn item once.

Sautéed foods should be thin enough to cook properly in no more than a few minutes on each side. Turning foods repeatedly during cooking can disturb the process of flavor development. There are exceptions to this general piece of wisdom, however. Stir-frying is one such instance. Sautéed vegetables and fruits may repeatedly be tossed or turned to cook properly as well. Common sense and experience should offer guidance. For even more specific details, refer to recipes, here or elsewhere.

FIGURE 9-28   Trout à la Meunière

(1) Add fish to a pan with preheated oil, clarified butter, or a mixture of both.

(2) Turn the trout when the first side is golden brown. Note the use of both an offset spatula and a flexible spatula for greater control.

(3) Pour off the clarified butter, add fresh whole butter, and allow it to cook until lightly browned.

(4) Add the lemon juice and parsley.

Very thin pieces of meat are generally cooked completely on top of the stove, over high heat. Larger cuts of meat that must be cooked through (veal, chicken, and pork, for example), may need to have the heat beneath them lowered slightly during the final phases of sautéing. Another option is to finish them in the oven, either in the sauté pan or in a baking dish, sizzler platter, or sheet pan.

Determining doneness in sautéed foods is an imprecise science. It might seem helpful to indicate that a strip loin steak, for example, will be cooked to medium rare in 6 to 7 minutes. Such an instruction ignores some crucial factors which will alter the actual cooking time: the intensity of the heat beneath the pan, the pan's material, the number of meat pieces in the pan, how well aged the meat is, the conditions under which the meat was raised and/or harvested, and so on. In general, the thinner, moister, and more delicate the food, the more quickly it will cook.

3. Remove the food from the pan while preparing the sauce (if any), add the appropriate flavoring or garnishing ingredients, and serve at once on heated plates.

Sautéed foods will not, as a rule, hold as much heat as roasted items. They will, however, continue to cook a little once removed from the pan, as a result of carryover cooking. Be sure to allow a slight margin, so that foods are not overdone by the time you are ready to put them on a plate.

Making Sauces for Sautéed Foods

The basic technique for making a sauce that incorporates the fond found in sauté pans is this: Remove any excess fat or oil. Add aromatic ingredients or garnish items that need to be cooked, such as garlic, shallots, mushrooms, ginger, and so forth. Then, deglaze the pan, releasing the reduced drippings from the pan. Wines, cognac, water, or broths can be used for this step. Whatever liquid is added now is allowed to reduce. That means that fortified wines should be reserved until later, since their flavors are best when not allowed to reduce.

The base sauce (brown sauce, demi-glace, jus de veau lié, for example) is added at this point, along

FIGURE 9-29   Swiss-Style Shredded Veal

(1) Sauté the veal émincé in a sauté pan that holds the meat comfortably. Do not overcrowd or the color and flavor will not develop.

(2) Remove the veal once it has a good color on both sides.

(3) After the sauce is finished (directly in the pan) return the veal to coat with the sauce and briefly reheat.

FIGURE 9-30   Sautéed Pork with Winter Fruits

(1) Pork medallions are sautéed until browned. Note the color change on the unturned piece, which indicates that it is ready to be turned.

(2) Deglaze the sauté pan with stock.

(3) Add the garnishing ingredients to the sauce.

with any other ingredients as desired to add flavor, texture, and color. Finishing ingredients, such as cream, butter, purées of vegetables or herbs, or fortified wines are all appropriate.

In many cases, chefs opt to return the main item (a chicken breast or veal scallop, for example) to the finished sauce briefly. This glazes and coats the item, as well as reheats it very gently. The sauce may be ladled directly onto the plate, forming a pool; the sautéed item is placed on the sauce. Or, the sauce may be ladled over the food. Be sure that any stray spots or drips are carefully wiped from the plate using a clean cloth wrung out in hot water.

Scrambling Eggs and Preparing Omelets

Scrambled eggs and omelets are made by whisking together the eggs so that the yolks and whites are evenly blended. They are then cooked over gentle heat, keeping the pan and the eggs in motion constantly, until the eggs begin to form a soft, thickened mass. The photos in Figure 9-31 show the various stages of scrambling eggs. The classic rolled omelet (see Figure 9-32) is also shown. According to Escoffier: "In a few words, what is an omelet? It is really a special type of scrambled egg enclosed in a coating or envelop of coagulated egg and nothing else."

FIGURE 9-31   Scrambling Eggs

(1) Add the beaten eggs to a pan, preheated over moderate heat.

(2) Keep the eggs in constant motion, so that soft curds form slowly.

(3) At this point the eggs are almost fully scrambled.

FIGURE 9-32   Making a Rolled Omelet

(1) Stop stirring the eggs when they reach a softly set state (see Figure 9-31(3)) and allow a skin to form. Then, release the eggs from the skillet by jarring the handle.

(2) Roll the omelet out of the pan onto a heated plate.

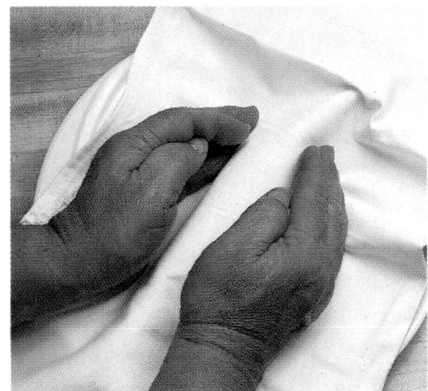

(3) If desired, shape the omelet using a clean towel or napkin.

(4) Lightly "glaze" the omelet with butter for added sheen.

Stir-Frying

Stir-frying is associated with Asian cooking styles. A wok is the traditional tool for stir-frying, because of its construction and shape. The wok concentrates heat in the bottom of the pan. The sides of the pan have varying degrees of heat, creating zones that allow a variety of foods to be prepared in a single pan, without overcooking or undercooking any single item.

Foods must be cut properly, usually into small strips, dice, or shreds. They are added to the pan in sequence, with foods requiring the longest cooking time added first, and those that cook very quickly or are simply added for flavor and texture added at the last moment.

Rather than turning the food once, you should keep stir-fried foods constantly in motion. Push them up to the sides of the wok out of the most intensely heated part of the pan. This makes room for items to be added to the bottom of the wok in their turn.

Sauces are frequently part of stir-fried dishes. They are generally combinations of intensely flavored liquids and oils such as soy sauce and sesame oil, occasionally thickened with a small amount of diluted arrowroot or cornstarch.

Pan-Frying

The object of pan-frying is to produce a flavorful exterior with a crisp, brown crust, which acts as a barrier to retain juices and flavor. Because the product itself is not browned, the flavor will be different than if the item had been sautéed. The proper color depends upon the type of item, the coating that is used and, to a certain extent, the item's thickness. The color of relatively thin and delicate meats, fish, shellfish, and poultry should be golden to amber. Thicker pieces may take on a deeper color, resulting from the longer cooking time. In all cases, the product should not be extremely pale. As with sautéing, a lack of color indicates that improper heat levels or the incorrect pan size were used.

Only naturally tender foods should be pan-fried and, after cooking, the product should still be tender and moist. Excessive dryness means the food was allowed to overcook, was cooked too far in advance and held too long, or was cooked at a temperature higher than required.

Although this technique shares similarities with sautéing, it has some important differences. Whereas a sautéed item is often lightly dusted with flour and quickly cooked over high heat in a small amount of oil, a pan-fried food is usually coated with batter or breaded and cooked in a larger amount of oil over less-intense heat. The product is cooked more by the oil's heat than by direct contact with the pan. In pan-frying, the hot oil seals the food's coated surface and thereby locks the natural juices inside instead of releasing them. Because no juices are released and a larger amount of oil is involved, any accompanying sauce is made separately.

Mise en Place

1. Assemble all ingredients and preparations for pan-frying:

- Breadings, batters, or other coatings
- Oil
- Stuffings, marinades, or seasoning mixtures
- Ingredients for sauce or gravy

Cut the food you are pan-frying into an appropriate size. A whole chicken, for instance, may be cut into eighths (see Figure 9-33). Pork loins can be made into cutlets, which are pounded to an even thickness. Veal is prepared in a similar fashion for scallopine or wiener schnitzel (see Figure 9-34). Zucchini, eggplant, and green tomatoes are usually sliced. Trim away any fat, silverskin, and gristle on meat. Remove the skin and bones for poultry suprêmes and fillets of fish, if necessary or desired.

Items for standard breading include flour (with seasoning added if desired), milk and/or beaten eggs, and bread crumbs. Batters, such as beer batter, are prepared according to the formula or recipe being used. They should be held at the correct temperature, if they are made in advance. Refer to recipes for guidance.

The oil for pan-frying should have the ability to reach high temperatures without breaking down or smoking. Vegetable oils, olive oil, and shortenings are all appropriate. Rendered animal fats have a place in certain regional and ethnic dishes. You should understand that many people have not grown up with these dishes on their daily table, however. Today's guest may find chicken fried in lard a taste that is too heavy. Oils with particular flavors, especially olive oil or rendered bacon, pork, or goose fats, should be selected with an understanding that they will have an influence on the flavor of the finished dish.

Fillings, stuffings, or sauces are all commonly a part of the pan-frying technique. Some dishes will

FIGURE 9-33   Southern Fried Chicken

(1) Chicken is marinated in seasoned milk or buttermilk and then coated with flour.

(2) Add the pieces in a single layer to hot oil. Turn periodically until the chicken is evenly browned and fully cooked.

(3) Make a roux using some of the cooking oil.

(4) Add stock to make a gravy and simmer, then finish with cream if desired.

FIGURE 9-34   Wiener Schnitzel

(1) Breaded cutlets are pan-fried in hot oil and turned carefully.

(2) Note the color of the properly cooked schnitzel, as well as the quantity of oil used for pan-frying.

call for a sauce made separately. At least one classic dish, the gravy for Southern fried chicken, is made directly in the pan used to fry the food.

2. Assemble all equipment necessary for preparation and service:

- Pan
- Tongs, kitchen fork, skimmer, spider
- Holding or finishing pans
- Setup to blot/drain after frying
- Heated plates

The pan must be large enough to avoid overcrowding. If the pan is crowded, the oil's temperature will drop quickly and a good seal will not form. If this happens, the food may absorb the oil and the breading can become soggy or even fall away in places.

Method

Optional first step: standard breading procedure
This process, while optional, is a common way to

prepare foods for pan-frying. If it is done correctly, the finished item will have an even coating that is extremely crisp, golden, and delicious.

Breading needs a little time to firm up before it is pan-fried for the best possible results. If you bread an item, then immediately put it into hot oil, there is a good chance that the breading will fall away. Not only will this have a negative impact on the dish's finished texture, it will also make the cooking oil break down quickly. Then, subsequent batches cooked in the same oil will blacken without cooking properly.

1. Dry the main item well, then hold it in one hand (left hand if you are right-handed, and right hand if you are left-handed) and dip it in flour. Shake off any excess flour, and transfer the food to the container of egg wash.

2. Switch hands, pick up the food and turn it if necessary to coat it on all sides. Transfer it to the container of bread crumbs. Use your dry hand to pack bread crumbs evenly around the food. Shake off any excess, then transfer the food to a holding tray.

3. Let the food rest under refrigeration for about 1 hour or longer before continuing on with pan-frying.

4. Discard any unused flour, egg wash or bread crumbs.

The presence of juices, drippings, or particles of the food you just coated will contaminate these products, making them unsafe for use with other foods. Even sifting the flour or crumbs or straining the egg wash will not be sufficient to prevent cross-contamination and eliminate the potential for food poisoning.

1. Heat oil to correct temperature for food being cooked.

In general, there should be enough cooking oil in the pan to allow the food to swim in the oil. As a rule of thumb, add enough oil so that the oil comes one-quarter to one-half the way up the sides of the food; the thinner the main item, the less oil is required.

The pan and the cooking oil must reach the correct temperature before you add the food. Otherwise, the development of the crust will be slowed,

FIGURE 9-35 Potato Pancakes

(1) The prepared batter is dropped by spoonfuls into heated oil. A cast iron skillet is often used for its ability to produce crisp crusts.

(2) Turn the cakes carefully to avoid splashing.

and it may never achieve the desired state. When a faint haze or slight shimmer is noticeable, the oil is usually hot enough.

2. Add food to hot oil and keep oil and/or food in motion.

Getting all surfaces of pan-fried foods evenly browned and crisped requires that the food be in direct contact with the hot oil (see Figure 9-35). If foods are crowded, then they may not develop good colors and textures.

If there is not enough oil in the pan, the food may stick to the pan and tear, or the coating may come away. Keep the oil and/or the pan gently in motion, either by using tongs to gently move the food around in the pan or by using an easy circular motion to keep the oil in the pan moving.

When pan-frying a large quantity of food in batches, remember to skim away any loose particles between batches. Add more fresh oil, or replace all of the oil, to keep the level constant and to prevent smoking or foaming.

FIGURE 9-36
Pan-Frying Batter-
Coated Zucchini
Slices

3. Brown on first side, then turn the food.

Once a good crust and a pleasing color develops on the first side, turn the food. Continue to cook the food until a rich golden color develops on the second side. If the food is of the right size and shape, it will be completely cooked at this point (see Figure 9-36).

4. Finish in pan or uncovered in oven.

Some foods can be cooked completely in the pan. Others, because they are thick, include bones, or a stuffing, may need to finish cooking in the oven. If they do need to go into the oven, be sure that they are left uncovered to prevent steam from softening the crisp coating you have developed. Ideally, they should be placed on a rack.

Foods that can finish cooking in the pan over direct heat should be watched carefully. If they are becoming too brown, turn the heat down.

5. Sauce and serve.

Deep-Frying

In this technique, foods are cooked by being completely submerged in hot fat. The food is almost always given a coating—a standard breading, a batter such as a tempura or beer batter or, in some instances, simply a flour coating. The coating acts as a barrier between the fat and the product and also contributes flavor and texture contrast. One notable exception is potatoes.

As with the other dry-heat methods that use cooking fats and oils, the foods must be naturally tender and of a shape and size that allow them to cook quickly without becoming tough or dry. Poultry, fish, and potatoes are among the most commonly selected foods for deep-frying. Vegetables, coated with breading or a tempura batter, are also popular choices. Cooked foods are often chopped fine, bound with a heavy béchamel or velouté, shaped into croquettes and then deep-fried.

Mise en Place

1. Assemble all ingredients and preparations for deep-frying:

- Batters, breading, coatings (optional)
- Item being prepared
- Oil
- Separately prepared sauce

Cut the item into the appropriate size. Foods should be fairly thin, with a uniform size and shape so that they can cook rapidly and evenly. Remove the skin (especially from fish), as desired or as indicated in the recipe. Remove any gristle, fat, and silverskin or any inedible shells. Cut the food into chunks or fingers, or butterfly and pound it, depending upon the food's nature and the desired result.

Breading may be done up to one hour in advance of deep-frying and chilled to allow the breading to firm (refer to notes in Mise en Place for pan-frying). Batters or plain flour coatings should be applied immediately before cooking.

The cooking medium must be able to reach a high temperature without smoking or breaking down. Have available a neutral-flavored oil with a high smoking point. A rendered fat, such as lard, may be used to create a special flavor or effect, as in certain regional dishes. The careful selection and maintenance of cooking oils for deep-fat frying is discussed below.

In addition to the usual salt-and-pepper seasoning mixture, spice blends, marinades, stuffings, or fillings are also commonly used to add interest to fried foods.

2. Assemble all equipment necessary for preparation and service:

- Frying kettle or fryolator

- Basket, spider, skimmer
- Tongs
- Container for blotting/draining
- Container to finish in oven or hold warm
- Serving pieces

Electric or gas deep-fryers are excellent choices if you do a great deal of deep-frying, since they maintain even temperatures. They are also put together in such a way that it is relatively easy to clean them and care for the oil properly. If you fry many different types of foods, it is generally a good idea to reserve different fryers to handle different foods. This will help prevent flavor transfer. No one wants an apple fritter to taste like a piece of fish.

If you do not have a free-standing fryer, deep kettles or pots, such as stock pots, can be used. A thermometer will help control temperatures. Once the correct frying temperature is reached, adjust the flame so that the temperature remains relatively constant.

A collection of other equipment, baskets, spiders, tongs, and containers lined with absorbent toweling are all important.

Fat and Oil Selection and Maintenance Both fats and oils may be used as a cooking medium for deep-frying, although vegetable oil is most commonly used. Fats and oils differ in specific properties such as flavor, color, or smoking point, but they are all basically the same compound. They contain fatty acids, flavor compounds, and glycerin. The amount of saturated, monounsaturated, or polyunsaturated fats in an oil or shortening give it a particular set of characteristics.

For deep-fat frying, the ideal oil is one with a neutral flavor and color and a high smoking point (around 425°F/218°C). Several practices, in addition to selecting the proper oil, will help prolong the product's life. Follow these steps to get the best from your frying oil:

- Store oils in a cool, dry area and keep them away from strong lights, which leach vitamin A.
- Use a high-quality oil.
- Prevent the oil from coming in contact with copper, brass, or bronze, because these metals hasten breakdown.
- When frying moist items, dry them as thoroughly as possible before placing them in oil, because water breaks down the oil and lowers the smoking point.
- Do not salt products over the pan because salt breaks down the oil.
- Fry items at the proper temperature. Do not overheat the oil.
- Turn off the fryer after using it and cover when it is not used for long periods of time.
- Constantly remove any small particles (such as loose bits of breading or batter) from the oil during use.
- Filter the kettle's entire contents after each shift, if possible, or at least once a day. After the oil has been properly filtered, replace 20 percent of the original volume with fresh oil, to extend the life of the entire amount.
- Discard the oil if it becomes rancid, smokes below 350°F (176°C), or foams excessively. As oil is used, it will darken; if it is a great deal darker than when it was fresh, it will brown the food too rapidly. The food may appear properly cooked but actually be underdone.

Method

1. Place prepared items directly into hot oil.

When foods are added to hot oil, the oil will lose temperature for a brief time. The more food added, the lower the temperature will drop and the longer it will take to come back to the proper level. This period of time is known as "recovery time."

There are three distinct approaches to introducing foods to the hot oil. The method chosen depends upon the food, any coating it may or may not have, and the intended result.

Swimming Method In the swimming method of frying, used for tempura and other batter-coated items (see Figure 9-37), the food is gently dropped into hot oil using tongs. Then, it falls to the bottom of the fryer. As it cooks, it "swims" back to the surface. It may be necessary to turn it once it reaches the surface, to allow it to brown evenly. It is then removed with a skimmer.

Basket Method The foods are placed in a basket that is lowered into the hot oil, and then they are lifted out in the basket once properly cooked. This

FIGURE 9-37
Vegetable
Tempura
Prepared by the
Swimming
Method

FIGURE 9-38
Breaded Shrimp
Prepared by the
Basket Method

FIGURE 9-39   Lorette Potatoes

(1) The lorette appareil is piped into shapes on parchment strips.

(2) The strip is lowered into the hot oil and the lorette potatoes release from the parchment.

(3) The properly cooked lorette potatoes.

method is generally used for breaded items (see Figure 9-38) and French fries.

Double-basket method   Certain types of food, in order to develop a good color, need to be fully submerged in hot oil for a fairly long time. Foods that would tend to rise to the surface too rapidly are placed in a basket, which is lowered into the hot oil, and are then held under the oil's surface by the bottom of a second basket. A variation on this method is used to produce nests from julienned potatoes.

2. Cook foods to the proper color and doneness.

Some foods are fried in two stages. The first stage, known as *blanching*, gives foods a preliminary cooking at a lower temperature. This is typically done for French fries. During the initial cooking, the food cooks evenly but the surface does not brown completely. Then, once they are properly blanched, they are finished just at the time of service by submerging them in oil heated to a higher temperature.

Foods that are properly fried may rise to the surface, indicating that they are fully cooked. Or, you may rely on their appearance. A deep golden brown is appropriate (see Figures 9-39 and 9-40). Cutting foods into small pieces, or blanching them, or using precooked items as for croquettes are all ways to assure that fried foods are fully cooked.

If it is necessary, some foods, such as chicken pieces, can be partially cooked by deep-frying, and then allowed to finish in the oven. To prevent the

FIGURE 9-40 Making Souffléd Potatoes

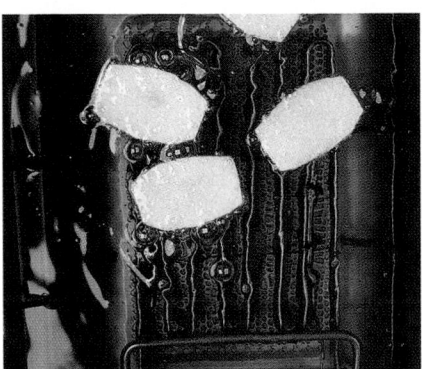

(1) Thinly sliced and shaped potatoes are placed in hot oil.

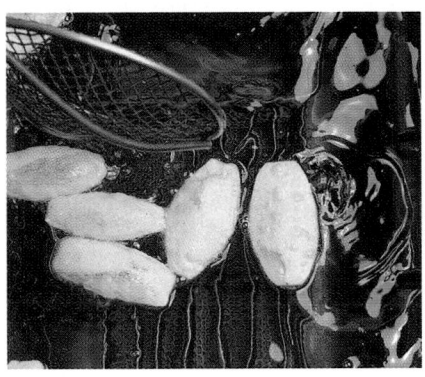

(2) The potatoes are beginning to "soufflé."

(3) Golden-brown souffléd potatoes being removed from the fryer.

crust from becoming too soggy or oily during this finishing, place the food on a rack in a sheet pan. That way, any excess oil will drain away, and no steam that could dampen the crust will develop.

3. Drain or blot foods and serve them while very hot.

Fried foods retain their best quality for only a short time. The best approach is to drain them briefly, salt or season as desired, and then serve at once. Sometimes foods may be held for very short periods in a warm oven or under a heat lamp, but the shelf life of any fried food is short.

If the food tastes heavy, oily, or strongly of another food, it means that the oil was not properly handled. It may have been at the wrong temperature. If the color has not developed properly, it may mean that the oil was not hot enough, or that too many items were added at once. With the exception of tempura, which will be light gold in color, most deep-fried foods should have a strong golden color.

Another possibility is that it is old, or has started to break down through extended use or improper care. Or, the oil may have been used to cook a strongly flavored food such as fish.

A properly deep-fried food's texture is moist and tender on the interior, with a crisp, delicate crust. If

the crust has become soggy, the food may have been held too long after cooking or the coating may have been applied too heavily.

Summary

The dry heat methods covered in this chapter include cooking techniques that every chef must master. The ability to match-up foods with their most appropriate cooking methods—pan-frying meaty chicken thighs, sautéing a tender cutlet from a top round of veal, roasting an eggplant—is the starting point. No one can make a wonderful sauté or stir-fry with a tough grizzled piece of meat.

Next in importance is properly executing every phase of advance preparation. Seasoning, trimming, butterflying, pounding, and stuffing items must be done in advance, with care and attention. Too much or too little will result in a less-than-wonderful end product.

The final test of skill is accurately determining doneness. The exact moment of perfect doneness is a fleeting thing. Whether you are grilling a steak to medium rare, roasting a chicken, or frying an egg, a slight miscalculation in either direction can drastically affect the quality of the finished dish.

CHAPTER *10* *Moist-Heat and Combination Cooking Techniques*

The moist-heat techniques—steaming, poaching, simmering, and boiling—result in products that have a distinctly different flavor, texture, and appearance from those prepared with dry-heat methods. The foods prepared by these methods are generally subtly flavored with a simple, straightforward appeal. These techniques typically require the use of naturally tender meats, poultry, or fish. The proper selection of a flavorful liquid is an important point for many preparations. Careful monitoring of cooking temperatures and times and the ability to determine doneness are also critical to a mastery of moist-heat methods.

The combination methods—stewing and braising—are so known because foods are usually given a preliminary preparation step, such as the initial searing of a pot roast or blanching of veal for a blanquette. A properly prepared braise or stew has a complexity and flavor concentration that is simply not possible with other cooking techniques. The dish's finished consistency should be smooth, suave, and meltingly tender, because of the slow cooking needed to soften the main item's tough connective tissues. Braising and stewing are frequently regarded as "peasant" techniques, often associated with regional or home-style cooking.

The successful execution of these techniques depends, as do all cookery methods, on the proper choice of main ingredients and careful attention to proper technique throughout each step of preparation and service. Contemporary renditions of classic dishes, such as a navarin *made with lobster instead of mutton, are clear examples that no cooking technique need become outmoded.*

Steaming and Its Variations

There are any number of foods that can be prepared by steaming or one of the techniques based on steaming. The cooking methods covered in this section include:

- Steaming

- Preparing foods "en papillote"

- Shallow-poaching

- Pan-steaming

All of these techniques cook foods by surrounding them with a vapor bath. In some cases, the food is suspended above a simmering or boiling liquid or stew. Foods prepared en papillote rely on the moisture naturally present in the food or that introduced through the use of sauces or ingredients, such as mushrooms or tomatoes, that have high moisture contents. Shallow-poaching and pan-steaming call for the food to be cooked directly in a small amount of liquid in a covered pan. The cover traps steam, cooking the portion of the food that is not submerged in the poaching liquid.

Ingredient Selection Foods prepared by any of the steaming methods should be naturally tender, or they should be cut or prepared so that they will have the best possible consistency when fully cooked. Steaming does not tenderize tough foods as it cooks them, so cuts of meat from the shoulder or shank are rarely steamed.

Preparation techniques can include skinning, boning, filleting, trimming, slicing, or grinding. Vegetables are peeled and cut if necessary. Remember that the size of the cut and the thickness of the food will influence total cooking time. Steaming is best when foods are not cooked for extended periods.

Determining Doneness for Moist-Heat Methods

Steamed foods should be plump, moist, tender to the bite, and just cooked. Any excessive cooking will cause the food to take on an inappropriate texture. Vegetables that should have been just barely tender may become soft enough to mash, and they may well lose their best color. Foods meant to be puréed, however, should be cooked until they no longer offer any resistance when pierced or cut. In some cases, it should be possible to mash them with a fork or spoon.

The desired degree of doneness, and terms used to refer to those stages include:

- Blanched—foods are cooked just long enough to set colors or make them easy to peel.

- Par-cooked—foods are cooked to partial doneness, as might be appropriate for vegetables or grains to be finished by sautéing or stewing.

- *Al dente* or tender-crisp—foods are cooked until they can be bitten into easily, but still offer a slight resistance and sense of texture. There should be no audible crunch, and foods should not fly off the plate when a guest tries to cut them.

- Fully cooked—foods are quite tender, though they should still retain their shape and color.

Any juices from poultry should be nearly colorless. Meats and poultry should offer a little resistance when pressed with a fingertip and should take on an evenly opaque appearance.

The flesh of fish and shellfish will lose its translucency when properly cooked, taking on a nearly opaque appearance.

Mussels, clams, and oysters will open when properly cooked and the edges of the flesh should curl.

Shrimp, crab, and lobster should have a bright pink or red color.

Vegetables and fruits should have a good color, with no dulling or graying evident. They should be tender to the bite, if they are being served directly from the steamer.

Grains should be fluffy and tender to the bite. Beans should be tender enough to mash easily, yet still retain their shape.

Steaming

Steaming is an efficient and highly effective way to prepare naturally tender foods. It is unfortunate that, to many minds, steaming has become synonymous with the bland foods suggested by diet plans for patients on a low-fat, low-cholesterol, and low-sodium regime. It is true that this technique has many properties that make it an admirable choice for those concerned with healthful cooking methods. That does not mean that steamed foods are, or need to be, tasteless and uninteresting.

Foods that are steamed include such standard offerings as steamed lean fish, vegetables, poultry breasts, and some fruits. It also includes more exotic and unusual fare such as tamales or dim sum. (See Figure 10-1.) The success or failure of any steamed food rests upon the same criteria as that applied to sautéed or roasted foods. Is the dish moist, flavorful, appealing from both a visual and textural stance? Are the flavors fully developed? Have the accompanying seasonings, garnishes, and sauces been selected with care and prepared with the same attention to detail as the main item?

Steamed foods are cooked by surrounding them with a vapor bath in a closed cooking vessel. Tiered aluminum or bamboo steamers, small inserts, couscoussières, gas or electric pressure or convection steamers can all be used to steam foods. The food should not come into direct contact with the liquid used to create the steam, and the container should stay closed until the food is properly cooked.

FIGURE 10-1   Making Dim Sum

(1) Filling the dough wrappers.

(2) Arranging the dim sum in a steamer.

(3) The steamer is set over simmering water.

(4) The steamed dumplings with a dipping sauce.

FIGURE 10-2   Steaming Couscous

(1) The top of the couscousière is filled with couscous and set over a simmering stew.

(2) Steam is being released and clumps are being broken up by stirring with a kitchen fork.

To add more interest to steamed foods, they may be stuffed, wrapped in aromatic leaves, marinated, or sauced. There is no excuse for serving uninteresting steamed vegetables, when the judicious application of some simple seasonings would make all the difference.

Overcooking foods in a steamer is a common problem. Once foods have gone from properly cooked to overdone, they become as dry and uninteresting as a roast that was left untended for too long. Properly steamed foods do not generally lose much of their original volume, and they are exceptionally plump, moist, and tender. Just as a roast will continue to cook even after it is removed from the oven, so will steamed fish or poultry after they come out of the steamer. This makes timing of great importance.

Mise en Place

1. Assemble all ingredients and preparations for steaming:

- Main ingredient(s)
- Steaming liquid
- Additional or optional items for flavoring, finishing, and garnishing
- Sauce or items necessary to prepare sauce

Items to be steamed should be naturally tender and of a size and shape that will allow them to cook in a short amount of time. Cut the main item into the appropriate size, if necessary. Fish is generally made into fillets, though there are some classic presentations of whole steamed fish. Poultry breast is often made into a suprême, or a boneless skinless piece. Vegetables and fruits should be handled appropriately. Remove tough skins that could slow down cooking. Cut them into even, regular shapes, so that they will all finish cooking at the same time. Leave shellfish in the shells, unless otherwise indicated (scallops are customarily removed from the shell, for example).

Relatively few grains are appropriate for steaming, although two exceptions come to mind. Couscous, not a true grain, is often steamed over a flavorful stew, or prepared on its own over simmering water (see Figure 10-2). Short grain rice may also be steamed. The length of time required to steam raw rice is considerable, however.

Any liquid may be used for steaming. Water is the most common. If you want to serve the steaming liquid as a flavorful broth along with the steamed food, you may prefer to select from other more highly flavored items: broths or stocks, wine, beer, court bouillon. Adding aromatic ingredients to the liquid will also boost the flavor of the liquid, as well as adding flavor to the food being steamed. Herbs, spices, citrus rind, or gingerroot, garlic, or mushrooms could be added.

Stuffings or fillings, marinades or wrappers can all be used in preparing steamed foods. Refer to recipes in Part IV, Chapter 13, or in other resources, for specific suggestions.

2. Assemble all equipment necessary for cooking and serving:

- Steamer, steamer insert, or other equipment for steaming
- Steamer racks, pans, or inserts
- Tongs, spoons, spatulas
- Serving pieces

The quantity of food being steamed will guide you to the correct equipment. Small amounts of food can be steamed using a small insert [see Figure 10-3(1)]. Larger quantities, or foods that require different cooking times, are better prepared in tiered steamers. Remember that it is important to allow enough room for steam to circulate completely around foods as they cook. This will encourage even, rapid cooking.

Convection or pressure steamers are good choices for steaming large quantities of foods. They allow the chef to have steamed foods prepared in appropriate batch sizes throughout a meal period, or to handle the more intense demands of a banquet or institutional feeding situation.

In addition to steamers, you will also need to have on hand the necessary tools for handling foods, transferring them from the steamer to serving pieces, containers to hold sauces, and spoons, ladles, and other serving utensils.

Method

1. Bring the liquid to a full boil in a covered vessel.

Add enough liquid to the bottom of the steamer to last throughout cooking. Each time you need to add more liquid to the pot, you will lower the cooking temperature, and affect the overall time necessary to prepare steamed foods.

If you need to open the lid during cooking time, remember to tilt the lid away from your face and hands, so the steam will not burn you.

2. Add the main item to the steamer on a rack in a single layer.

To ensure even cooking, foods should be placed in a single layer, not touching one another, so that the steam can circulate completely. Foods may be placed on plates or in shallow dishes on the rack in order to collect any juices that might escape.

3. Replace the lid and allow the steam to build up again.

It is a good idea to adjust the heat to maintain even, moderate cooking speed. Liquids do not need to be at a rolling boil in order to produce steam. Rapid boiling may cause the liquid to cook away too quickly.

FIGURE 10-3 Steaming Vegetables

(1) A small steamer with broccoli florets.

(2) A steamer insert ready to go into a pressure or convection steamer.

Once the food is in the steamer and the cover has been replaced, avoid removing the lid unnecessarily. The drop in temperature can be significant. This makes it a little more difficult to gauge how long foods need to cook, so it may be a good idea to refer to some standard cooking times. Most recipes will include some information about how long specific foods take to steam to the correct doneness. Still, it is important to check the foods, starting at the earliest point at which they might be done.

4. Steam the main item to the correct doneness.

Steamed foods should be cooked until they are just done. Since steaming is used as a preliminary cooking technique in many cases, remember to stop cooking earlier for par-cooked foods. Foods that are to be puréed once steamed should be cooked until they are easy to pierce with a kitchen fork or paring knife, so they will mash easily. In general, check steamed foods for doneness by applying the tests described above, taking texture, color, consistency, shape, and aroma into account.

5. Serve the food immediately on heated plates with an appropriate sauce, as desired or as indicated by the recipe.

Cooking Foods en Papillote

In this variation of steaming, the main item and accompanying ingredients are encased in parchment paper and cooked in a hot oven. The main item rests on a bed of herbs, vegetables, or sauce and the combination of these ingredients and their natural juices serves as the sauce. The steam created by the food's natural juices cooks the food. As the steam volume increases, the paper puffs up.

Foods that have been properly prepared en papillote will demonstrate the same characteristics of flavor, appearance, and texture as other steamed foods.

Mise en Place

1. Assemble all ingredients and preparations for en papillote:

- Main item(s)
- Broth or sauce
- Additional or optional flavoring, seasoning, or garnishing items

In addition to the preparation techniques for steaming, there is an optional first step. Sear thicker meat cuts in advance to ensure that they will be adequately cooked during the relatively short cooking times associated with this technique as well as to provide additional color and flavor.

Vegetables can be included to provide moisture for steam. They also add color, flavor, and texture. Cut the vegetables into a fine julienne or dice. Sweat or blanch the vegetables, if necessary, to ensure that they will cook in the same amount of time as the main item.

Prepare herbs and spices according to type. Some herbs may be left in sprigs; others are cut into a chiffonade or minced. Have a prepared sauce, reduced heavy cream, wine, or citrus juices on hand if your recipe calls for them.

2. Assemble all equipment necessary for cooking and serving:

- Parchment paper
- Sizzler platters or baking sheets
- Serving pieces

Method

1. Assemble the packages.

The method for cutting the parchment and making the individual packages is shown in Figure 10-4. Cut the parchment into a heart shape large enough to allow the food and any additional ingredients to fit comfortably without overcrowding. The paper needs to have enough "give" to expand during cooking. Oil or butter the paper on both sides to prevent it from burning.

Place a bed of aromatics, vegetables, or sauce (if you are using these optional components) on one half of the heart and top it with the main item.

Fold the empty half of the heart over the main item and fold and crimp the edges of the paper to form a tight seal.

2. Place the bag on a preheated sizzler platter and put it in a very hot oven.

The oven temperature may need to be carefully monitored, since delicate foods such as fish fillets can be overcooked quickly at a high temperature. A thicker cut may be best if cooked slowly at a moderate temperature and "puffed" in a very hot oven.

Foods prepared en papillote should be cooked until they are just done. This is difficult to gauge without experience, since you cannot apply the senses of sight and touch in determining doneness. If the item has been cut to the correct size or if it has been partially cooked before being placed en papillote, it should be done when the bag is very puffy and the paper is brown.

Shallow-Poaching

Shallow-poaching, like sautéing and grilling, is an à la minute technique suited to foods that are cut into portion size or smaller pieces. This method cooks foods using a combination of steam and a liquid bath: The food is partially submerged in a liquid that often contains an acid, such as wine or

FIGURE 10-4   Snapper en Papillote

(1) Preparing the parchment heart.

(2) Arranging the ingredients on the oiled paper.

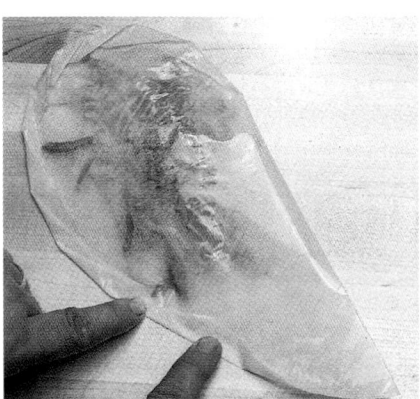

(3) Folding, crimping, and sealing the package.

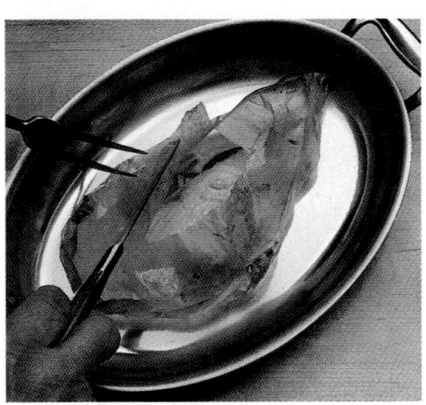

(4) The fully cooked snapper being opened.

lemon juice, and aromatics, such as shallots and herbs. The pan is covered to capture some of the steam released by the liquid during cooking. The captured steam cooks the portion of the food not directly in the liquid.

In shallow-poaching, a significant amount of flavor is transferred from the food to the cooking liquid. This cooking liquid (or *cuisson*) is frequently used as the base for a sauce served with the main item. Adding acids, such as wine or lemon juice, to the cooking liquid gives the finished sauce a bright flavor. Those same ingredients also make it easier for butter to be emulsified in the sauce, thus a beurre blanc is often the sauce of choice.

Mise en Place

1. Assemble all ingredients and preparations for shallow-poaching:

- Main ingredient(s)
- Liquid
- Additional or optional items for flavoring, finishing, and garnishing
- Items necessary to prepare the sauce

Items to be shallow-poached should be naturally tender and of a size and shape that will allow them to cook in a short time. Remove the skin and bones from poultry and game birds to make them into suprêmes. Remove the skin and bones from fish to prepare fillets. The fillets may be rolled or folded to form paupiettes. The "meat" side of the fish should show on the exterior. Remove shellfish from its shell, if desired.

The liquid should contribute flavor to the food as well as to the sauce prepared from the cooking liquid. Chose rich broths or stocks, and add wine, vinegar, and/or citrus juice.

Cut shallots, garlic, or gingerroot finely or mince them. Other ingredients you wish to serve along with the sauce as a garnish should be cut neatly, into strips, dice, julienne, or chiffonade. These ingredients are often allowed to smother or par-cook in advance of shallow-poaching the main item. This is done to develop the best possible flavor, as well as to make certain that all of the ingredients in the finished dish are fully cooked at the same time.

The sauce you prepare may be a beurre blanc, sauce vin blanc, or simply the reduced cooking liquids served as a broth.

If you need butter for a beurre blanc, it should be diced and kept cool. Sauce vin blanc may require a velouté, egg yolks, and/or butter. Refer to specific recipes for additional suggestions or guidance.

2. Assemble all equipment necessary for cooking and serving:

- Sauté pan, or other suitable cooking vessel
- Parchment or loose-fitting lid
- Serving pieces as needed: strainers, whip, tongs, etc.

Select the pan or baking dishes carefully for shallow-poached dishes. If there is too much space left around the food, then you will need to add a significant quantity of poaching liquid. This will have several adverse effects: It will make it easier to overcook the food. Sauce preparation will take longer, since you will have more liquid to reduce. Cooking speed can be more difficult to control properly.

Parchment is generally used to loosely cover the pan as the food cooks. It traps enough of the steam to cook the unexposed part of the food, but not so much that the cooking speed increases. Maintaining a gentle, low cooking temperature is the best way to produce the most delicious results.

Method

1. Add the ingredients to the pan. (The method for shallow-poaching is shown in Figure 10-5.)

Although not always essential, a coating of butter is generally spread in an even layer in a cold pan or baking dish. Then, the aromatic ingredients (shallots, garlic, vegetables, herbs, or mushrooms) are added in an even layer. They may be allowed to smother lightly in the butter at this point, or they may have been cooked separately. If they can cook completely in the time required by the main item and the sauce preparation steps, they can be added raw.

2. Add the main item and the cooking liquid.

Set the main item on top of the aromatics, and then pour in the liquid. It is not necessary in most

FIGURE 10-5   Shallow-Poaching Fillet of Sole

(1) The sole is placed in a pan of the correct size and lightly covered with parchment.

(2) Adding velouté to the reduced cooking liquid to prepare a sauce vin blanc.

cases to have the liquid already heated. For large items, it may be helpful, however. Be careful that it is not at a full boil, however.

The liquid's level should be no higher than halfway up the item; generally, less liquid is required. If too much is used, either a great deal of time will be needed for it to reduce properly or only part of it will be usable in the sauce. This is undesirable and could result in a loss of flavor in both the main item and the sauce.

3. Bring the liquid to a bare simmer over direct heat.

The liquid is typically brought up to the correct cooking speed over direct heat. There may be some occasions when it is preferable to perform the entire cooking operation in the oven, however. The quantity of food being prepared and available equipment will dictate where it is most logically done. Do not allow the liquid to boil at any time. A rapid boil will cook the food too quickly, affecting the quality of the dish. Fish might easily break apart or poultry and game suprêmes may toughen if they are not cooked at the correct temperature—never more than 170°F(75°C).

4. Lightly cover the sauté pan with parchment paper and finish cooking the main item either over direct heat or in a moderate oven.

Acceptable results can be achieved by finishing the cooking over direct heat; however, the heat in an oven, which is more even and gentle, is preferable. In addition, finishing shallow-poaching in the oven makes burner space available for other purposes. Shallow-poached foods should be cooked until they are just done. Apply the tests outlined above for steamed foods.

5. Remove the main item to a holding dish. Moisten it with a small amount of the cooking liquid. Cover the item and keep it warm while completing the sauce.

6. Prepare a sauce from the cooking liquid.

7. Ladle the sauce over the food and serve it while still very hot.

To Make a Sauce from the Cooking Liquid

Allow the cooking liquid to reduce rapidly over direct heat until it is thickened. This concentrates the flavors and will form the foundation for the sauce.

Add the additional ingredients for the sauce, including any seasoning or garnish ingredients. Butter is often added for a beurre blanc. Keep the pan in motion as the butter is added, a little at a time. Velouté or béchamel may be required for a vin blanc sauce.

Finishing ingredients, such as liaisons, must be added carefully so that they cook properly. It is usually safest to add egg yolk and cream liaisons away from direct heat. With experience, however, many chefs find it possible to add these delicate ingredients without any problem over direct heat.

For additional information about beurre blanc or sauce vin blanc, refer to Chapter 8 on Sauces. For additional suggestions and recommendations to prepare sauces for shallow-poached items, refer to specific recipes, either in Part IV of this book or other sources.

Pan-Steaming

Pan-steaming cooks foods by placing them directly in a liquid, such as water, broth, or court bouillon. There is not enough water to completely submerge the food, however. This technique is often used to prepare vegetables.

The mise en place for ingredients and equipment is similar to that required for shallow-poaching, with the following difference: A tight-fitting lid is essential in order to pan-steam foods fully and quickly. Speed is one of this technique's most valuable assets, since even green vegetables can be prepared quickly enough that any acids that might have caused discoloration are not allowed enough time to have any effect.

The amount of liquid required is determined by the texture of the food being pan-steamed. For denser foods, such as carrots or turnips, you may need more liquid. Delicate items, including new peas or asparagus tips, may require relatively little liquid.

Mise en Place

1. Assemble all ingredients and preparations for pan-steaming.

Refer to the information for both shallow-poaching and steaming (above). Since the liquid used in pan-steaming is often discarded, water is the most ordinary choice. In pan-steaming, the addition of aromatics, such as chopped shallots or additional minced vegetables is common.

Once foods are pan-steamed, the liquid may be drained away and a little cream or butter added to finish the dish. This is an optional component.

2. Assemble all equipment necessary for cooking and serving.

Apart from the usual serving pieces, the only requirement for pan-steaming is a sautoir or rondeau with a tight-fitting lid. Remember that the food should be added to the pan in a single, even layer (see Figure 10-6). It is important to select a pan that can comfortably hold the food being pan-steamed without crowding.

Method

1. Bring the liquid to a boil in a pan.

If you are adding any special aromatics, they should be added to the liquid as it comes to a boil so that they can release their flavors.

2. Add the food being pan-steamed in a single layer.

Some foods, such as peas, may be allowed to pile up in the pan but, in general, there should be only enough food added so that the liquid comes up about one-quarter to one-third of the depth of the food, with enough head room between the top of the food and the lid to allow steam to build up.

3. Cover the pan and cook until the food is properly done.

Refer to the tests for doneness outlined in the section on determining doneness above.

The Submersion Techniques

Poaching, simmering, and boiling are techniques that call for a food to be completely submerged in a liquid that is kept at a constant, moderate temperature. The distinction between them is a slight difference in cooking temperatures. At one end of the temperature range, from around 160 to 185°F (70° to 82°), foods are considered "poached." There should be relatively little flavor lost from the food to the cooking liquid.

At the middle range, from 185 to 200°F (82 to 85°C), foods may be referred to as either simmered or "boiled." Simmering temperatures encourage a greater transfer of flavor from the food being prepared into the liquid, but it is important to monitor these temperatures in order to properly cook foods such as less-tender cuts of meat, stewing hens, and some vegetables. This is the same approximate temperature necessary to make rich broths or stocks, where the goal is producing a richly flavored liquid.

Boiling, done either at or close to a true boil (212°F/100°C), is best for grains, beans, pasta, and some vegetables. Often, foods are referred to as boiled when it might be more accurate to say that

FIGURE 10-6
Pan-Steaming Cauliflower

they are simmered. Simmering and boiling will be considered together, however, since they are used with the same types of foods.

The major areas of concern with all of these methods are proper development of flavor, color, and texture in the finished dish, a proper balance between the main ingredients and any aromatic, seasoning or flavoring ingredients, and careful monitoring of cooking speed. As you become more comfortable with these skills, you will be able to produce perfectly poached, boiled, and simmered foods that have rich, full, satisfying flavors, textures, aromas, and colors.

Ingredient Selection   Poaching is typically associated with naturally tender foods. Simmering and boiling are reserved for foods that require some substantial softening to occur during cooking—meats with significant amounts of connective tissue, dried beans and grains, vegetables rich in natural fibers.

Determining Doneness   The desired degree of doneness, and terms used to refer to those stages include all of those previously described for the steaming method. Some foods are cooked when they are *fork tender*. This means they are cooked to the point at which they slide from a kitchen fork easily with lifted or pierced.

For many foods, an instant-reading thermometer can be used to gauge doneness. A thermometer is also helpful to monitor the temperature of the cooking liquid. It can be difficult to see the difference between a liquid at a perfect poaching temperature and one that is a degree or two away from a slow boil. The difference to the food can be quite important.

Poaching

Poached foods are usually naturally tender. Eggs, fruits, chickens, and fish all come to mind instantly when poaching is under consideration.

The liquid used for poaching must be well flavored. Stock, broth, or court bouillon are all appropriate, depending upon the type of food and the desired result. Poaching is done within a range of 160 to 185°F (70 to 82°C). The surface of a poaching liquid should show some motion, sometimes called "shivering," but no air bubbles should break the surface.

Mise en Place

1. Assemble all ingredients and preparations for poaching:

- Main ingredient(s)
- Liquid
- Additional or optional items for flavoring, finishing, and garnishing
- Items necessary to prepare sauce

Items to be poached are generally naturally tender. Wrap whole fish in cheesecloth to protect it from breaking apart during cooking. Stuff poultry or meats, if desired, and truss or tie them to help retain their shape.

The liquid used in poaching should be appropriate to the food and well flavored in order to compensate for any flavor lost during cooking. It is important to use good-quality stocks and enough aromatic ingredients, such as herbs, wines, spices, and vegetables, to produce a full, pleasing flavor in both the finished product and any sauce prepared from the poaching liquid.

Poached items may also be served with a pungent sauce prepared separately, as in the custom of serving "boiled" beef with a horseradish sauce.

2. Assemble all equipment necessary for cooking and serving:

- Poacher or other pot

- Ladles or skimmers
- Holding containers to keep foods warm (optional)
- Carving boards and slicers (optional)
- Instant-reading thermometer

The pot used for poaching should be selected with attention to the size and shape of the food being prepared. The pot should hold the food, the liquid, and aromatics comfortably, with enough room to allow the liquid to expand as it heats. There should also be enough space so that the surface can be skimmed if necessary throughout cooking. Racks or trivets may be necessary to protect the food from sticking to the bottom of the pot during cooking. Specially designed fish poachers can be used if available.

Method

1. Combine the food to be poached with the liquid and bring to the correct cooking temperature. The method for poaching salmon is shown in Figure 10-7.

Some foods are allowed to start off in cool water. Others are placed into water that is already at poaching temperature. The choice is made according to the needs of the item itself, as well as the overall cooking time. Eggs, for instance, should be started in water already at about 160° to 170°F (70° to 75°C) (see Figure 10-8). Dense fruits, such as pears, might be allowed to come up to temperature along with the cooking liquid, to ensure that they are evenly and fully cooked. (See Figure 10-9.)

Be sure that the item is completely submerged in the liquid. This is especially important for poultry. If a part of the food is above the cooking liquid's level, cooking will be uneven, and the finished product will probably not have the proper color or texture.

2. Maintain the desired cooking speed throughout the poaching process.

Make sure the liquid does not boil. The temperature should be checked periodically with an instant-reading thermometer and the heat adjusted as necessary. If a cover is used on a fish poacher, the

FIGURE 10-7 Poaching Salmon

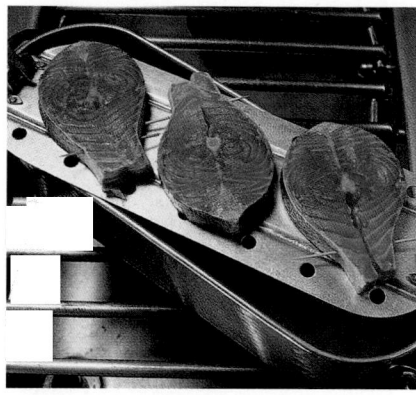

(1) The salmon is set on a poaching rack to protect it from breaking up during cooking.

(2) The court bouillon's temperature should now be reduced to the correct cooking speed.

(3) The salmon in the poaching liquid. Thermometer now reads 160°F (70°C).

(4) Removing the center bone from the poached salmon.

cooking speed must be monitored regularly. Covering a pot has the effect of creating pressure, which allows the liquid's temperature to become higher. Setting the lid just slightly ajar may be a good precaution against the liquid's coming to a boil without anyone noticing.

As is true for shallow-poached items, it is sometimes desirable to complete poaching in the oven, once the proper cooking temperature has been reached over direct heat. Common sense will indicate which items can be placed in the oven and which should remain on top of the stove. For instance, it would be difficult and dangerous to lift a large pot full of hot liquid off the stove and into the oven.

Skim the surface of the liquid throughout cooking time, if necessary. This will help the dish to develop appropriate and attractive colors, as well as keeping the broth from becoming too cloudy.

3. Carefully remove the main item to a holding container and moisten it with some of the liquid to prevent it from drying out while the sauce is being prepared.

Poached foods should be cooked just until the food is set and a safe internal temperature is reached. Refer to the section above regarding degrees of doneness and tests for determining when a food is properly poached.

If a poached or simmered item is to be served cold, it may be desirable to slightly undercook it. Then, the pot can be removed from the heat and the food allowed to cool in the poaching liquid. The liquid will retain enough heat to complete the cooking process.

Once it has reached room temperature, the item and the broth should be carefully cooled and stored for later use. The liquid is customarily used in a sauce or as the basis of another dish.

5. Cut or slice the main item, as necessary, and serve it immediately on heated plates with the appropriate sauce.

Simmering and Boiling

Simmered foods are often referred to as being boiled ("boiled" beef, for example); however, this is not an accurate description of the cooking speed. In

FIGURE 10-8   Poaching Eggs

(1) Adding the eggs to heated water.

(2) Stopping the cooking to hold for later service.

(3) Blotting the egg after it is reheated, to remove excess water.

fact, the liquid's temperature should be kept as close to a boil as possible without ever reaching a true boil. A vigorous boil causes most meats, fish, and poultry to become tough and stringy. The temperature should be high enough to allow connective tissues to soften, however. Usually the required cooking time is deliberately extended to allow even well-exercised cuts of meat to become tender to the bite.

Dried beans and grains, meals, and some vegetables are more often boiled. The additional heat is necessary to soften the fibers and coatings that make these foods such excellent candidates for extended storage. Boiling both rehydrates and cooks the food, changing the texture from dry and hard into something agreeable to the palate.

FIGURE 10-9
Poaching Pears in
Red Wine

Mise en Place

1. Assemble all ingredients and preparations for simmering and boiling:

-   Main ingredient(s)
-   Liquid
-   Additional or optional items for flavoring, finishing, and garnishing
-   Items necessary to prepare sauce

Some items to be simmered are generally naturally tender. Wrap whole fish in cheesecloth to protect it from breaking apart during cooking. Stuff the poultry, if desired, and truss it to help retain its shape. Stuff meats, if desired, and tie them to maintain their shape. Proper tying or trussing of the item will ensure that its natural shape is preserved.

Most dried beans and some grains may require an initial soaking to begin softening them. This can be a longer soaking, done in enough cool water to cover them for several hours. The "quick-soak" method calls for beans to be combined with water, brought up to a boil, and allowed to steep in the hot water for about 1 hour. In either case, they should be drained before beginning the actual boiling process.

The liquid used for simmering should be appropriate to the food and well flavored in order to compensate for any flavor lost during cooking. It is important to use good-quality stocks and enough aromatic ingredients, such as herbs, wines, spices, and vegetables, to produce a full, pleasing flavor in both the finished product and any sauce prepared from the liquid. Most boiled foods are prepared in plain or salted water.

Boiled foods are often served with a pungent sauce prepared separately—pasta served with a tomato sauce, for instance. Others are simply dressed with butter and seasoned.

2. Assemble all equipment necessary for cooking and serving:

- Poacher or other pot
- Ladles or skimmers
- Strainers or colanders
- Holding containers to keep foods warm or to hold once cooled (optional)
- Carving boards and slicers (optional)
- Instant-reading thermometer

The pot used for simmering and boiling should be selected with attention to the size and shape of the food being prepared. The pot should hold the food, the liquid, and aromatics comfortably, with enough room to allow the liquid to expand as it heats. There should also be enough space so that the surface can be skimmed if necessary throughout cooking. A tight-fitting lid is necessary for some types of simmering and boiling, such as pilafs (see below). The method for boiling lobsters is shown in Figure 10-10.

Method

1. Combine the food to be simmered or boiled with the liquid and bring to the correct cooking temperature.

Some foods are allowed to start off in cool water—potatoes or heavily salted or brined meats, for instance. Others, such as pastas or vegetables, are added to a liquid that is already at the correct temperature. This allows the liquid to return to the correct temperature shortly after the item is added to ensure proper cooking.

In general, the amount of liquid in the pot should be sufficient to keep the item completely submerged throughout cooking time. Grains and beans will absorb significant amounts of liquid as they cook. Add more water or stock if necessary to keep the pot from cooking dry. By the end of cooking time, there may be no free liquid at all.

FIGURE 10-10 Boiling Lobsters

(1) Killing the lobster.

(2) Adding the lobster to rapidly boiling water.

(3) The color is beginning to change.

(4) Removing the cooked lobster to a holding container.

FIGURE 10-12   Cooking Pasta

FIGURE 10-11
Carving Boiled
Corned Beef

(1) Salt is being added to boiling water.

For more specific details, refer to the recipes in Part IV.

2. Maintain the proper cooking speed throughout the simmering or boiling process.

Maintain an even cooking temperature throughout cooking time. Skim the surface of the liquid to remove any impurities, if necessary. This will help the dish to develop appropriate and attractive colors, as well as keeping any broth from becoming too cloudy—an important point if the broth is to be used as a sauce or served separately.

(2) Add the pasta and separate the strands to prevent clumps from forming.

The tests for doneness will vary from one food type to another. Polenta for instance, should pull cleanly away from the sides of the pot. Risotto should be creamy. Rice pilafs should be fluffy and separate easily into distinct grains. Pasta is cooked to the point at which it is tender enough to bite into easily, although it should not be mushy. Meats should be fork tender. Refer to the section above on determining doneness.

3. Carefully remove the main item as appropriate.

(3) Draining the pasta in a colander.

The food is ready to finish as desired, or it may be properly cooled and stored for later service. Figure 10-11 shows boiled corned beef being carved.

Special Boiling Methods

Pasta

Pasta is traditionally cooked in boiling or near-boiling water. (See Figure 10-12.) Most chefs like to add salt to the water. If it is added, there should be

(4) Rinsing the pasta with cold water to stop cooking.

FIGURE 10-13   Making Spaetzle

(1) Using a spaetzle board and a spatula.

(2) Using a spaetzle-maker.

(3) Using a ricer.

enough so that the taste of salt is just barely discernible.

Add dry or fresh pasta to simmering or boiling water. Stir the pasta with a fork to separate the strands. If this step is ignored, the pasta will clump together as it cooks. Fresh pasta should be cooked at a slightly slower speed than dried pasta to keep it from falling apart. Filled pastas, such as tortellini and ravioli, should be cooked at a bare simmer so that they do not separate.

Once the pasta has cooked sufficiently, drain it immediately, and then process as necessary. If it is to be served right away, combine it with any sauce or garnish ingredients suggested by the recipe. To hold pasta for later service, drain it in a colander, rinse it in cool water, and allow it to drain well. If desired, you can rub a little oil through it to help keep the pieces separated.

To reheat pasta that has been cooled, drop it into simmering water long enough to reheat. Then drain well before combining it with sauces or garnish.

Spaetzle

Spaetzle is a kind of soft noodle. Once the batter is prepared, it can be added to water or broth that is at a lazy simmer. Three techniques for shaping spaetzle are shown in Figure 10-13. The recipe can be found in Part IV, Chapter 22.

Pilaf

The best pilafs are grain dishes that are light, fluffy, and relatively dry. To achieve this, it is important to observe the correct ratio of grain to liquid. For specific information, refer to the chart included in Appendix 2. Figure 10-14 shows the proper method for preparing rice pilaf.

Any aromatic vegetables, such as onions or leeks, should be smothered in fat or oil. The grain is added and stirred until it is coated with oil. Then, the correct amount of liquid is added and brought to a simmer. Herbs, spices, or other seasonings can also be added now. To prevent the grain from becoming sticky, it is not stirred again once a simmer is reached.

At this point, the pot should be covered. The pilaf can be finished either over direct heat or in the oven. When properly cooked, the grains should separate easily.

Polenta and Other Cereals

Polenta (see Figure 10-15), and other cereals, are prepared as follows: Bring the liquid to a simmer. Gradually add the cereal, stirring constantly so that lumps don't form. Many traditionalists feel that polenta should be added so slowly that you can see

FIGURE 10-14   Making Rice Pilaf

(1) Onions are allowed to cook until the flavor is developed.

(2) The rice is added and stirred until coated with oil.

(3) The stock and aromatics are added and brought to a simmer before the pot is covered and cooking finishes.

(4) The rice has absorbed all of the stock and is ready to serve.

FIGURE 10-15   Preparing Polenta

(1) Add the cornmeal gradually to simmering water. Stir constantly with a wooden spoon throughout cooking time.

(2) The polenta is at the correct consistency.

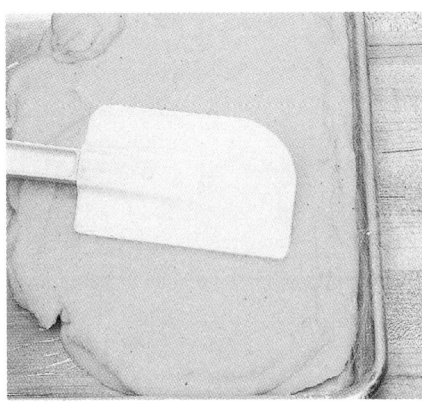

(3) Spread the polenta into an even layer and cool to use later.

(4) Polenta can be cut into a variety of shapes, then grilled, pan-fried, baked, or broiled before serving.

through the stream as it is poured into the pot. Others like to add a handful at a time.

Once the cereal is added, it is generally stirred constantly as it returns to a simmer. Some cereals require less stirring (oatmeal or farina, for instance); others demand constant stirring (polenta and grits). Continue to cook, stirring as needed, until the correct consistency and doneness is reached. Polenta is properly cooked when the cereal forms a mass that pulls away from the sides of the pot.

Risotto

Risotto, like pilaf, demands careful attention to ratios between grain and liquid. Unlike pilaf, risotto cannot be successfully prepared with a wide variety of grains. Instead, a short grain rice, such as arborio, is generally specified. This rice has the best properties for preparing a creamy dish, since the starch is released more readily during cooking.

The aromatic vegetables, spices (e.g. saffron), and rice are given a preliminary sauté in oil or butter, as is done for pilaf. However, rather than adding all of the liquid at once and coming immediately to the correct cooking speed, the liquid is added in smaller quantities, usually in thirds. The risotto is stirred constantly as each addition is absorbed by the grain. For the final addition of liquid, some recipes indicate the addition of a wine. This cannot be added earlier, since the acids in wine would prevent the grain from softening properly. Figure 10-16 shows the method for preparing risotto. Figure 10-17 shows a fully cooked risotto in the pot.

The Combination Cooking Methods

Stewing

Stewing is similar to braising and can use the same meat cuts, but the main item is cut into bite-size pieces. The amount of liquid used in relation to the amount of the item varies from one style of preparation to another. Some stews call for very little additional liquid; others may call for proportion-

FIGURE 10-16   Making Risotto

(1) Adding heated stock gradually to the short grain rice.

(2) Stirring the risotto constantly as it absorbs successive additions of stock and broth, to develop the correct, creamy consistency.

ately more liquid than the main item. A stew's basic components do not differ to any substantial degree from those of a braise(see below).

The technique for stewing is also nearly identical to that for braising, although a few optional steps in stewing allow the cook to vary the results. For example, initial blanching of veal or chicken, instead of searing, results in a pale, almost ivory-colored fricassée. Because the main item is cut into small pieces (see Figure 10-18), the cooking time for stewing is shorter than for braising. The following is a partial listing of the stews featured in different ethnic cuisines.

FIGURE 10-17 A Properly Cooked Saffron Rissotto

Blanquette This white stew is traditionally made from white meats (veal or chicken) or lamb, and is garnished with mushrooms and pearl onions. The sauce is always white and is finished with a liaison of egg yolks and heavy cream (see Figure 10-19).

Bouillabaisse This is a Mediterranean-style fish stew combining a variety of fish and shellfish.

Fricassée Fricassée is a white stew, often made from veal, poultry, or small game (rabbit, for example).

Goulash (gulyas) This stew originated in Hungary and is made from beef, veal, or poultry, seasoned and colored with paprika, and generally served with potatoes and dumplings.

Navarin This is a stew traditionally prepared from mutton or lamb, with a garnish of root vegetables, onions, and peas. The name probably derives from the French word for turnips, *navets*, which is the principle garnish.

Ragout A French term for stew, this translates literally as "restores the appetite."

Matelote This is a special type of fish stew, typically prepared with eel, although other fish may be used. Other fish stews that are served as main courses include bouillabaisse, cioppino, and bourride.

Mise en Place

1. Assemble all ingredients and preparations for stewing:

- Main item(s)
- Cooking fat or oil (optional in some cases)
- Cooking liquid
- Additional or optional flavoring, seasoning, or garnishing items
- Thickener for sauce (optional in some cases)

Foods to be stewed are typically cut into bite-sized pieces. Meats, poultry, and fish should be trimmed and seasoned. It may be appropriate to dust these items with flour. Peel and cut fruits and vegetables as necessary. Beans and grains may require soaking or par-cooking.

FIGURE 10-18 Vegetable Stew

(1) Vegetables are undercooked at an early stage.

(2) Vegetables are tender and fully cooked. The final seasonings are being added now.

FIGURE 10-19 Veal Blanquette

(1) Adding hot stock to blanch the veal. A carrot, bouquet garni, and an oignon piqué are added as the aromatics.

(2) The finished stew, with a final addition of chopped parsley.

Select the appropriate cooking liquid according to the foods you are stewing or the recipe's recommendation. Water, broth, stock, vegetable and fruit juices, or milk may be used.

Refer to the recipes in Part IV for seasoning, garnishing and finishing ingredients.

2. Assemble all equipment necessary for cooking and serving:

- Deep pot with lid (or other cooking vessel)
- Kitchen fork to test doneness
- Equipment as needed to finish sauce

Method

1. Sear the main item in hot oil or blanch it by placing it in a pot of cold stock or water and bringing the liquid to a boil.

Searing the main item assists in developing color and flavor. In order to develop a good color, the main item should not be added to the pot in quantities so large that the pieces are touching one another. If they are touching, the pan's temperature will be lowered significantly, hindering proper coloring. Instead, the item should be seared in batches, and each batch should be removed when it has developed a good color. The main item is generally dredged in flour prior to searing, to assist in lightly thickening the cooking liquid.

Blanching also improves the color and flavor of the finished stew. In addition, skimming the surface of the blanching liquid removes any impurities that could give the stew a gray color or off flavor. Once the boil is reached, drain the main item.

2. Remove the main item from the pot and add the mirepoix.

Lightly brown the mirepoix or, for stews that should remain pale in color, sweat it until the vegetables begin to release their juices and become translucent.

3. Return the main item to the mirepoix in the pot; add the appropriate cooking liquid and bring it to a simmer.

Some stews call for only a small amount of liquid, relying on the main item's natural juices to provide moisture. This is especially true for stews made from naturally tender foods such as fish or shellfish. Other stews may include proportionately more liquid than main item. See the specific recipes for guidance.

4. Cover the pot and place it in a moderate oven, or cook it over direct heat on the stove top.

5. Add the aromatics and vegetable garnish, if necessary or desired, at the appropriate time to ensure proper cooking and extraction of flavor.

6. Stew the food until a piece of the main item is tender to the bite.

Because the main item is cut into small pieces, it is possible and advisable to test for doneness by biting into the food rather than applying the fork-tender test.

7. Finish the stew by adding any additional thickeners or liason, garnish ingredients, or final seasoning adjustments.

8. Serve the stew on heated plates with the sauce and the appropriate garnish.

Braising

This technique is considered appropriate for foods that are portion-sized or larger, or cuts from more-exercised areas of large animals, mature whole birds, or large fish. Relatively little liquid (stock or jus) is used in relation to the main item's volume. A bed of mirepoix, which should be peeled if it is to be served, also introduces additional moisture and flavor.

One of braising's benefits is that less tender cuts of meat become tender as the moist heat gently penetrates the meat and causes tough connective tissues to soften. Another bonus is that any flavor from the item is released into the cooking liquid, and becomes the accompanying sauce; thus, virtually all flavor and nutrients are retained.

Tender foods, even delicate fish and vegetables, can also be braised. To properly braise these kinds of foods, the chef must use less cooking liquid, and must cook the food at a lower temperature and for a shorter time.

The first step for most braises is to sear the main item in a small amount of hot fat. This develops the proper flavor and color and is done in a rondeau or brazier over direct heat on the stove top. Braised vegetables, however, are usually blanched before they are braised. Mirepoix is then allowed to lightly brown or sweat in the same pot and the cooking liquid is added and brought to a simmer. Once these steps are completed, the pot is usually covered and placed in a moderate oven.

Braising in the oven tends to result in a better product without danger of causing the food to scorch from prolonged contact with a pot in direct contact with an open flame. Air is a less efficient conductor than metal—the result is a gentler transfer of heat. There is also less chance of inadvertently overcooking (and thereby toughening) the item. Finally, burner space is kept open for other needs.

If the entire braising operation is to be done on the stove top, certain precautions must be taken. The cooking speed must be carefully regulated because the liquid can easily become too hot. If this happens, the portion of the main item covered by the liquid will cook more quickly than any exposed areas and could become tough or stringy. Scorching could also be a problem.

The following is a partial listing of braising techniques and specific names for braised dishes of various types and nationalities:

Daube   A daube is a braise customarily made from red meats, often beef, and includes red wine. The main item is often marinated beforehand. The name is derived from the French pot used to prepare a daube, the *daubière*, which has an indentation in the lid to hold hot pieces of charcoal.

Estouffade   This is a French term used to refer to the braising method and the dish itself.

Pot Roast   This common American term for braising is also the name of a traditional braised dish.

Swissing   This is a braising technique often associated with portion-size meat cuts. The main item is repeatedly dredged in flour and pounded to tenderize the flesh (Swiss steak, for example).

Braised foods should have an intense flavor as the result of slow, gentle cooking. The main item's natural juices, along with the braising liquid, become concentrated, providing both a depth of flavor and a full-bodied sauce.

If a braised food does not have a robust flavor, it may have been undercooked or perhaps was allowed to braise at an overly high temperature for an insufficient time. Another possibility is that the main item was not seared properly, with inadequate time allowed for browning the product before liquids were introduced. Finally, if the lid was not removed from the pot during the final stage of cooking, the sauce may not have reduced properly and a glaze may not have been allowed to form on the main item's surface.

Braised foods should have a deep color appropriate to the type of food being prepared. They should retain their natural shape, although a significant amount of volume is lost during cooking.

To maintain the proper shape throughout the cooking time, the main item can be trussed or tied. Braised foods should be extremely tender, almost to the point at which they can be cut with a fork. They should not, however, fall into shreds; this would indicate that the main item has been overcooked.

Mise en Place

1. Assemble all ingredients and preparations for braising:

- Main item(s)
- Cooking fat or oil (optional in some cases)
- Braising liquid
- Additional or optional flavoring, seasoning, or garnishing items
- Thickener for sauce (optional in some cases)

Foods to be braised are traditionally more mature, less tender, and more flavorful than foods prepared by dry-heat and moist-heat techniques. Tender foods, especially fish, should be cooked the minimum amount of time necessary to achieve the best flavor. Trim away all fat, silverskin, and gristle on the main item. Marinate red meats and poultry, if desired; truss or tie. Stuff whole fish with an aro-

FIGURE 10-20   Braising Beef

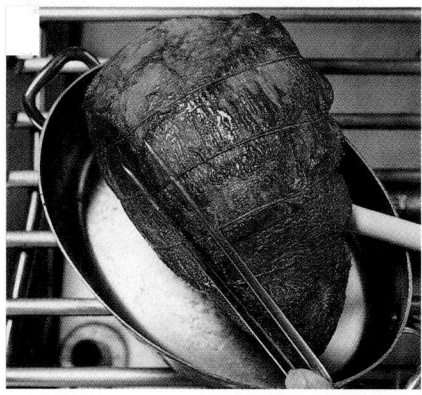

(1) The meat has been seared on all sides, and is being removed from the pan.

(2) Allowing the tomatoes to "cook out" after the mirepoix has already been sautéed.

(3) Adding the broth and sachet to the pan and bringing the liquid to a simmer.

(4) The meat is returned to the pan, ready to braise until fork-tender.

matic filling and then wrap it in lettuce leaves or other coverings to help maintain shape and prevent it from breaking apart during cooking, if desired. Dredge the main item in flour. This will help to thicken the sauce during cooking.

A mirepoix used in braising should be peeled if it is to be puréed and used in the sauce. Cut the vegetables into an appropriate size, depending on the cooking time required for the main item.

Use a white mirepoix for "white" braises. Use a well-flavored stock or jus appropriate to the main item's flavor. Broths, essences, or vegetable juices may be used.

2. *Aromatics.* Prepare a sachet d'épices or bouquet garni, including spices, herbs, and other aromatic ingredients, as desired or required by the recipe.

Braised items often include some sort of pork product. Have available ham, bacon, or salt pork according to recipes. Blanch these ingredients to remove excess salt, if necessary.

Tomatoes are included frequently in braised dishes. They act as a tenderizer to break down the tough tissues of less tender meats and also give the finished dish additional flavor and color. Have available tomato purée, tomato concassée, or tomato paste, as necessary.

Vegetable garnishes may be added for color, flavor, and texture to the dish as it braises. They should be added in a timely fashion, so that they will finish cooking at the same time as the main item.

Various thickeners may be used to prepare a sauce from the braising liquid (see Figure 10-21): Dilute arrowroot or cornstarch in a cold liquid and add it to the sauce at the end of the cooking time; prepare a roux and add it to the braised item at the start of the cooking time; or puree the mirepoix and return it to the sauce.

3. Assemble all equipment necessary for cooking and serving.

- Deep pot with lid (or other cooking vessel)
- Kitchen fork to test doneness
- Carving knife, if necessary
- Equipment as needed to finish sauce

Method

1. Sear the main item in hot oil or blanch.

This initial searing helps the item develop color and flavor. White meat and poultry should be seared only to the point at which the skin begins to turn color. Red meats should be seared to a deep brown color. Fish may not require an initial searing. Blanch vegetables by boiling or steaming.

2. Remove the main item and add the mirepoix.

For white meats, fish, poultry, and game birds, sweat the mirepoix until the onions are translucent. For red meats and large game, sweat until the onions are golden-brown. If a roux is being used as a sauce thickener, it may be added at this point.

3. Add the mirepoix to the pot and allow it to cook properly.

The mirepoix furnishes both moisture and flavor. If you will be including it in the finished sauce, cut it evenly and neatly to the desired shape and size.

4. Add the appropriate amount of liquid.

There should be just enough liquid to keep the main item moistened throughout the cooking time and to produce an adequate amount of sauce to serve with the finished dish. The more tender the product, the less liquid will be required, because the cooking time will be shorter and there will be less opportunity for the liquid to reduce properly. In general, the liquid should cover the main item only by one-third. Bring the liquid to a simmer over direct heat.

5. Return the main item, cover the pot, and place it in a moderate oven.

The more tender the item, the lower the oven's temperature should be. Covering the pot allows the steam to condense on the lid and fall back onto the main item, moistening the food's exposed surfaces. The main item should be turned from time to time during cooking to keep all surfaces evenly moistened with the braising liquid.

6. Add the sachet d'épices or bouquet garni and vegetable garnish at the appropriate times, to ensure proper flavor extraction and cooking.

FIGURE 10-21 Finishing the Sauce for Braised Foods

(1) Transfer the braising liquid to another pot if necessary, and reduce it over direct heat. Skim the surface to degrease.

(2) Add a thickener (diluted arrowroot is used here) to give the sauce additional body if necessary.

7. Remove the lid during the final portion of the cooking time.

This will cause the braising liquid to reduce adequately so that the sauce will have the proper consistency and flavor. Also, if the main item is turned frequently after the lid has been removed and is thus exposed to hot air, a glaze will form on its surface, providing a glossy sheen and a good flavor.

8. Remove the main item from the braising liquid when it is fork-tender.

Properly cooked braised foods are fork-tender. This means that they will slide easily from a kitchen fork inserted at the food's thickest part. For foods that are portion-size or smaller, check for doneness by "cutting" them with the side of a fork.

9. Place the pot over direct heat and continue to reduce the sauce to develop its flavor, body, and consistency.

FIGURE 10-22
Adding Herbs to Braised Endive Wrapped with Bacon

along with the sachet d'épices or bouquet garni. Return the sauce to the heat and bring it to a boil. Add diluted arrowroot or cornstarch to lightly thicken the sauce, if desired. Add any final finishing or garnishing ingredients (see Figure 10-22). Adjust the seasoning with salt and pepper.

11. Carve or slice the main item and serve it on heated plates with the sauce and an appropriate garnish.

This additional reduction fortifies the sauce's flavor and provides an opportunity to skim away any surface fat. Add additional garnish or finishing ingredients at this point, as appropriate.

10. Strain the sauce.

If mirepoix is strained out, it may be puréed and returned to the sauce if it is still flavorful. Otherwise, simply strain it out of the sauce and discard it

Summary

The moist heat and combination cooking methods detailed in this chapter, combined with the dry heat methods in Chapter 9, are the basic techniques used to build numerous specific recipes. Just as a painter must learn the basics of form and color, a chef must fully master these fundamentals of the kitchen. Once you have all these methods firmly within your grasp, you can begin the process of refining and creating virtually endless variations.

11 : *Charcuterie and Garde-Manger*

In its strictest interpretation, the term charcuterie *refers to items made from a pig. These include sausages, smoked hams, bacon, pâtés, terrines, and head cheeses. Translated from the French, the word literally means "cooked flesh." Garde-manger refers to the kitchen's pantry or larder section, where foods were kept cold. Various preparations completed in this "cold kitchen" came to be known as part of the garde-manger repertoire. Over time, because of the similarities in their products, the seemingly separate areas of charcuterie and garde-manger have become closely joined. In this chapter, the various responsibilities of the garde-manger and charcuterie kitchen areas and the types of items they produce will be covered.*

This chapter will touch on only a small number of the vast array of items that fall within the scope of the charcuterie and garde-manger stations. These "cold kitchen" areas hold the primary responsibility for several courses on the standard menu, as well as for various special events, including buffets and receptions.

The garde-manger station, or pantry, is generally given responsibility for the preparation of all cold appetizers, including cold salads, soups, and any first course item to be served cold. This might include chilled seafood cocktails, mixed green or composed salads, vinaigrettes, and other special cold preparations. While the pantry may not necessarily be responsible for the actual production of sausages, pâtés, terrines, smoked meats, and fish, they are often called upon to plate and present these items for menus or buffets. Recipes and preparation notes for salads and salad dressings can be found in Part IV, Chapter 25. Information about selecting and preparing greens and other ingredients is contained in Chapters 5 and 6. Appetizer and hors d'oeuvre recipes, including dips and spreads, may be found in Part IV, Chapter 26.

The subject of this chapter is focused primarily on the preparation of forcemeats, as well as a few additional charcuterie items, including gravad lax and cold daubes.

Pâtés, sausages, terrines, and galantines allow the chef to make full use of all food items brought into the kitchen, whether as the foundation for a mousseline forcemeat or as the garnish for a pâté.

The change in eating style of most contemporary diners has reduced the emphasis on rich, high-fat terrines and other delicacies. This does not mean that the role of the cold kitchen has been greatly diminished. It simply offers a new challenge to chefs to update classic preparations, making them lighter and more appealing to modern tastes.

Background

The need to preserve foods of all sorts to last over long periods of time has been felt throughout the world. Fruits, grains, and vegetables have been dried and stored in virtually every culture. Methods for preserving meats, fish, and poultry, always

FIGURE 11-1   A Selection of Specialties

(1)   Clockwise from top left: Kielbasi, stuffed derma, jambonneau, head cheese, lieberkaese, rolled pressed pig's head. Kiszka, a polish blood sausage, is in the center.

among the most-prized and difficult-toobtain food items, have also been developed.

Preparations as diverse as pemmican and jerky, prepared by Native Americans, to dried Chinese-style sausages, presumably one of the earliest of all sausages made, to gravlax (also referred to as "gravad lax") from Scandinavia, to the *boudin noir* made throughout France, have been relished for years. This chapter owes a large debt to the methods employed by French charcutières over the years, so most of the terminology will bear a distinctly Gallic stamp. See Figure 11-1 for a selection of charcutèrie and garde-manger specialties.

The history of charcuterie extends back to the workers' guilds at the end of the Middle Ages, when the *charcutières* were granted a charter allowing them to sell products from the pig, including cooked items. Since those times, the role of the charcutière has expanded greatly. Sausages, pâtés, and terrines today are made from a wide range of ingredients, including poultry, fish, shellfish, and vegetables. In contemporary kitchens, especially large ones, there may still be a separate area for the

(2) *Clockwise from top left: bacon, English bacon, tasso, smoked loin of pork.*

(3) *Fresh sausages (clockwise from top): Tuscan, merguez, Mexican chorizo, and hot Italian.*

(4) *Semidry sausages (clockwise from top): salami, hard smoked salami, Lyonerwurst, Swiss pantli.*

(5) *A selection of smoked and cooked sausages.*

preparation and production of charcuterie and garde-manger items. Smaller kitchens may rely on outside purveyors for some or all of these products or may incorporate their production into other kitchen areas.

Historically, charcuterie and garde-manger products provided a way of preserving meat over the winter by using spices and herbs, smoking, and curing with salt. The use of salts, spices, and fats was noticeably more liberal than is the case today, but not because tastes were so radically different. These ingredients all have the ability to aid in preserving foods by slowing or preventing various types of spoilage or food-borne illness.

Salts dry out foods, creating an environment that is not suitable to many types of pathogens. Salt combined with nitrites or nitrates is even more effective. It is no longer such a great necessity that ingredients such as curing salts, saltpeter, or pot ash be added to foods to prevent the growth of botulism. Introducing curing salts or lavish quantities of other types of salt is more often a matter of personal preference today, an option exercised in order to obtain a specific color or flavor in the finished dish.

The addition of what might be seen as excessive spices to foods also had a function beyond simple flavoring: it was a way to mask the taste of foods that became increasingly "high" or "gamey" as the months wore on. Fat also has a preservative effect by limiting the amount of exposure to air a food will have. In addition, it added flavor, moisture, and gave a sense of fullness and satisfaction to those who ate foods cooked or preserved in fats. Now that refrigeration is available, the flavoring is somewhat lighter and less fat is used, but the result should still be a rich, well-flavored product.

Forcemeats

One of the basic components of charcuterie and garde-manger items is a preparation known as a forcemeat. In the following sections, five distinct forcemeat styles are explained and a variety of items prepared from forcemeats is also discussed.

Figure 11-2 illustrates mise en place for charcuterie items.

A forcemeat is a lean meat and fat emulsion that is established when the ingredients are forced together by grinding, sieving, or puréeing. Depending on the grinding and emulsifying methods and the intended use, the forcemeat can have a smooth consistency or be heavily textured and coarse. The result must not be just a mixture but an emulsion, so that it will hold together properly when sliced and have a rich and pleasant taste and feel in the mouth.

Forcemeats are used in the hot kitchen (see Figure 11-3), as well as in the cold kitchen. They can be found as fillings or stuffings for a variety of dishes, ranging from mousseline spread on a fish fillet to gratin forcemeat used to stuff mushroom caps. Shown here are two additional uses of forcemeat in the contemporary kitchen.

Basic Forcemeat Types

Forcemeats may be used for quenelles, sausages, pâtés, terrines, and galantines or to prepare stuffings for other items (a salmon forcemeat may be used to fill a paupiette of sole, for example). Each forcemeat style will have a particular texture.

FIGURE 11-2 Mise en Place for Contemporary and Classic Charcuterie Items

FIGURE 11-3 Forcemeats in the Hot Kitchen

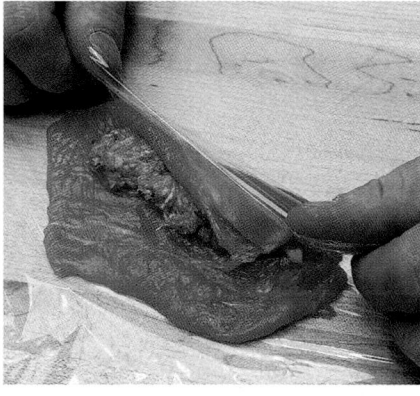

(1) Filling a chicken breast.

(2) Preparing filled pastas, such as the cappelletti shown here.

Straight forcemeats combine pork and pork fat with a dominant, or flavoring, meat in equal parts, through a process of progressive grinding and emulsification. The meats and fat are cut into strips, seasoned, cured, rested, progressively ground, and then processed with a binder, such as egg.

A *country-style forcemeat* is rather coarse in texture. It is traditionally made from pork and pork fat, with a percentage of liver and other garnish ingredients.

In a *gratin forcemeat*, some portion of the dominant meat is sautéed and cooled before it is ground. The term *gratin* means "browned" and doesn't imply that cheese is included in the recipe.

A very light forcemeat, *mousseline* is based on white meats (veal or poultry) or fish. The inclusion of cream and eggs gives a mousseline its characteristic light texture and consistency.

Emulsified forcemeats (also referred to as 5/4/3 forcemeats) combine meat, fat, and seasonings into a very finely textured forcemeat. Careful temperature control must be maintained throughout the mixing of this forcemeat. The basic mixture is five parts meat/four parts fat/three parts ice. This forcemeat is used for frankfurters, bockwurst, and knockwurst.

Basic Preparation Guidelines

1. Maintain proper sanitation and temperature at all times.

All necessary ingredients and tools used in preparing any forcemeat must be scrupulously clean and well chilled at all times. If the forcemeat is to be a true emulsion, it must be kept quite cold throughout its preparation so that the proteins and fats can combine properly.

Ingredients should be refrigerated until they are ready to be used and, if necessary, held over a container of ice to keep the temperatures low during actual preparation. Maintaining the correct temperature is important for more than the proper formation of an emulsion.

These foods are often highly susceptible to contamination, due to the amount of handling they receive, their increased contact with equipment, and greater exposure to air. Pork, poultry, seafood, and dairy products can begin to lose their quality and safety rapidly when they rise above 40°F (4°C). If the forcemeat seems to be approaching room temperature, it is too warm. Work should be stopped and all ingredients and equipment refrigerated. Work may be resumed only after everything is below 40°F (4°C) once more.

2. Grind foods properly.

The technique used to prepare most forcemeats is known as *progressive grinding*. The following procedures should be observed:

- Cut all solid foods into dice or strips that will fit easily through the grinder's feed tube.
- Do not force the foods through the feed tube with a tamper. If they are the correct size, they will be drawn easily by the worm.
- Be sure that the blade is sharp. Meats should be cut cleanly, never mangled or mashed, as they pass through the grinder.
- For all but very delicate meats (fish or some types of organ meats, for example), begin with a die that has large or medium openings.

Continue to grind through progressively smaller dies until the correct consistency is achieved.
- Remember to chill ingredients and equipment between successive grindings.
- When using a food processor to finish grinding the meat, be sure that the blade is very sharp and the meat is not overprocessed.
- Mousseline or other very delicate forcemeats may be pushed through a sieve (tamis) for the smoothest possible texture.

Special Preparations

There are some distinct preparations used in the production of forcemeats. They are panadas or binders, pastry for items prepared "en croûte," and aspic gelée.

Thickeners and Binders Specific ingredients or mixtures (often referred to as *panadas*) are added to forcemeats once the meat(s) has been properly ground. This is done to assure that pâtés, terrines, and other items do not fall apart or crumble when sliced. Whenever a panada is required, it should comprise no more than 20 percent of the forcemeat's total volume, not including garnish ingredients. The type of binder used will vary, depending on the type of meat, fish, or vegetable used as a flavoring. The three types most often called for are bread panada, flour panada, or pâte à choux. Panadas may also be based on rice and potatoes, although these are less frequently used. In some forcemeats, heavy cream or a liaison of heavy cream and eggs may act as a thickener.

Bread panadas are made as follows: Cubed bread is soaked in milk, in an approximate ratio of one part bread to one part milk. The bread cubes and milk are combined and allowed to soak until the bread has absorbed the milk. If necessary, the bread may be squeezed to remove any excess milk before the panada is added to the forcemeat.

A flour panada is essentially a very heavy béchamel. A roux is prepared and milk added, in an approximate ratio of one part roux to one part milk. Three to four egg yolks per pound of béchamel may be added. The panada must be chilled completely before it is added to the forcemeat.

Pâte à choux is sometimes used as a binder for forcemeats as well. The recipe and directions for preparing pâte à choux are found in Chapter 30. The pâte à choux must also be completely chilled before it is added to the forcemeat.

Pâté Dough Pâté dough is by necessity a stronger dough than a normal pie dough, although its preparation technique is identical to that used for more delicate pastry doughs. (Refer to Part IV, Chapter 30.) Other flours, herbs, ground spices, or lemon zest may be added to change the dough's flavor. Instructions for lining a mold with pâté dough are included in the step-by-step illustrations of preparing a pâté en croûte later in this chapter.

Aspic Gelée Aspic gelée is a well-seasoned, highly gelatinous, perfectly clarified stock. It is frequently strengthened by adding a quantity of gelatin (either sheets or granular gelatin may be used). The aspic is applied to foods to prevent them from drying out, preserving their moisture and freshness.

When properly prepared, aspic should set firmly but still melt in the mouth. The recipe and ratios for aspic are included in Part IV, Chapter 27. Aspic gelée made from white stock will be clear, with practically no color. When the base stock is brown, the result is amber or brown in color. Other colors may be achieved by adding an appropriate spice, herb, or vegetable purée.

Straight Forcemeat

Mise en Place

1. Assemble all ingredients and preparations necessary for a straight forcemeat.

This is a basic forcemeat that can be used to prepare a variety of items, including sausages, pâtés, terrines, and galantines, illustrated later in this chapter. The main components are:

- Dominant or theme meat
- Fat
- Panada or other binder
- Seasoning, flavoring, and garnish

"Dominant meat" need not necessarily mean pork. It might just as easily be veal, beef, lamb, game, poultry, fish, shellfish, or even a combination of meats. The ratio of dominant meat to other ingredients will vary, depending on the desired result (see the specific recipes which can be found in Part IV, Chapter 27).

Cut the meat into cubes or strips. Combine it with spices and/or a marinade, if desired. Chill it well before proceeding with grinding or mixing.

Pork fat is traditionally used for most straight forcemeats. It should be cut into cubes or strips, then chilled until needed. Chilled heavy cream may be more appropriate for delicately flavored forcemeats based on white meats, poultry, or fish.

Different forms of binders can be used, depending on the type of forcemeat. In some cases, the proteins naturally present in the dominant meat may bind the forcemeat sufficiently to permit the cooked forcemeat to be sliced neatly after it is cooked. In other cases, it may be necessary to add a panada, additional eggs, or sometimes a combination of binders to prevent the slices from crumbling.

Forcemeats, especially those to be served cold, should have a full flavor. Salt, in addition to acting as a preservative, as discussed earlier, is one of the most common flavorings used in seasoning a forcemeat. Ground pepper (black or white), green peppercorns, various ground seeds and spices, and spice blends, fresh herbs, liqueurs and cordials can also be used to season forcemeats.

Curing salt, also known as tinted curing mix (TCM), is a special compound that combines salt with sodium nitrate. The ratio is 94 percent salt and 6 percent nitrite. Its primary function is to prevent botulism in forcemeat items such as sausages that are to undergo lengthy smoking at extremely low temperatures. Today it is most often used to produce a pink color found desirable in sausages, pâtés, and other items.

A variety of garnishes may be included to provide additional texture, flavor, or color. The choices include diced meats (usually the same as the dominant meat), vegetables (dices, purées, juliennes), herbs and spices, nuts, and dried fruits.

Aspic may be used to coat charcuterie items once they are cooked and completely cooled. Although aspic adds visual appeal by giving sheen and luster, its basic function is to protect the product from moisture loss during storage.

Method

1. Have all ingredients and equipment at the correct temperature, under 40°F/4°C. See Figure 11-4 for photos illustrating method for preparing straight forcemeat.

2. Combine the dominant meat, fat, and (if appropriate) the garnish ingredients with a marinade and refrigerate them.

Marinating the meat and fat is the way in which the chef gets as much flavor as possible into the finished product. Refer to specific recipes. The marinade may be complex, including wines, spices, and herbs, or relatively simple, nothing more than cognac or port.

3. Run the meats and fat through a meat grinder, using a die with large openings (coarse die).

The degree of fineness of the finished forcemeat is determined by the number of successive grindings, as well as the opening size of the die used on the grinder. Be sure that you start with the largest hole and proceed through progressive grindings until the desired texture is achieved. Hold the ingredients over ice or refrigerate them before continuing.

4. Place the ground meat in a food processor and add the panada. Process the mixture to a smooth consistency.

Not always essential, this final "grinding" step, shown in the accompanying illustration, gives the finished item a smooth texture and encourages it to hold together well when sliced. To test the forcemeat's quality, prepare a test quenelle as explained later in this chapter. Make any necessary adjustments to correct the consistency or seasoning.

5. Gently fold the garnish into the forcemeat by hand, working over ice. The forcemeat is now ready to use for a variety of applications.

FIGURE 11-4   Preparing Straight Forcemeat

(1) Marinating the meats and fat.

(2) First stage: grinding through a coarse die.

(3) Second stage: grinding through a medium die.

(4) Third stage: grinding with the egg in a food processor.

(5) Adding the garnish.

photos illustrating the method for preparing country-style forcemeat.

Cut the meats and fat into dice or strips. Marinate the ingredients if desired or appropriate. Keep them chilled at all times.

2. Grind the meats once through a coarse die and again through a medium die, and hold over ice or keep them refrigerated.

3. Push the liver through a sieve (tamis) to remove all sinews, membranes, and fibers.

Refer to Chapter 27, pages 000 through 000, for specific recipes.

Country-Style Forcemeat

Mise en Place

For a description of essential and optional components, refer to the mise en place for straight forcemeat.

Method

1. Prepare all meats, fat, and garnish ingredients as indicated by the recipe. See Figure 11-5 for

4. Gently work the sieved liver and panada into the ground meats and fat by hand.

Do this over ice to keep all ingredients at the correct temperature. Prepare a test quenelle to check consistency and seasoning as explained later in this chapter. Any garnish should be added after making any necessary adjustments. The forcemeat is now ready to be used in a variety of applications.

Refer to Part IV, Chapter 27, for specific recipes.

Gratin Forcemeat

Mise en Place

Review information for straight forcemeat earlier in this chapter.

FIGURE 11-5   Preparing Country-Style Forcemeat

(1) Pushing the liver through a drum sieve.

(2) Adding the liver and panada (cream and eggs) to the ground meat.

FIGURE 11-6   Preparing Gratin Forcemeat

(1) Cooking chicken livers with spices and aromatics.

(2) Adding cream to the ground meats while working over ice.

The dominant meat used to flavor this forcemeat is quickly seared before being marinated, to give this forcemeat its distinctive flavor. Livers are often used today, but rabbit, veal, game birds, and pork would all be equally appropriate as the theme meat.

Method

1. Sear the theme meat first to give it the proper flavor.See Figure 11-6 for photos illustrating the method for preparing gratin forcemeat.

Allow the meat to cool completely before proceeding with the method.

2. Grind the other meats (cut into dice or strips of the appropriate size), pork fat, and cooked meat first through a coarse die and then through a medium or fine die. Hold the ground mixture over ice or refrigerate it between grindings.

3. Stir the panada into the ground meats, working over ice.

To test the forcemeat's quality, prepare a test quenelle as explained later in this chapter. Make any necessary adjustments to correct the consistency or seasoning. The forcemeat is now ready to be used in a variety of applications.

Refer to Part IV, Chapter 27, for specific recipes.

Mousseline Forcemeat

Mise en Place

Review the information for essential and optional components in the mise en place for straight forcemeat.

Method

1. Cut the meat into dice, and keep it very cold until it is time to prepare the forcemeat.See Figure 11-7 for photos illustrating the method for preparing mousseline forcemeat.

2. Grind the meat to a paste in a cold food processor.

If eggs are included, add them at this time, and pulse the machine on and off to incorporate them into the meat. Do not overwork the meat.

3. With the machine running, add cold heavy cream in a thin stream.

Once the cream is incorporated, add aspic gelée in the same manner, if desired or necessary. The forcemeat should be very smooth, but not rubbery. Add seasonings according to recipes or desired result at this point.

4. Push the forcemeat through a drum sieve with a rigid plastic scraper to remove any sinews and membranes that may remain. This assures the correct texture.

Work with a small quantity of the forcemeat, keeping the remainder over ice or refrigerated. To test the forcemeat's quality, prepare a test quenelle as explained later in this chapter. Make any necessary adjustments to correct the consistency or seasoning.

5. The forcemeat is ready to be used at this point as a stuffing or to prepare sausages, terrines, or quenelles.

Refer to Part IV, Chapter 27, for specific recipes.

5/4/3, or Emulsion, Forcemeat

Mise en Place

A typical emulsion forcemeat will always contain five parts meat, four parts fat, and three parts ice, hence, the name "5/4/3." See Fig. 11-8 for emulsion forcemeat's mise en place. Refer to the mise en place for straight forcemeat for additional information regarding essential and optional components.

Method

1. Cut all meats and fat into dice or strips. Hold the meats and fat separately and keep them very cold.

See Figure 11-9 for photos illustrating the method for preparing 5/4/3, or emulsified, forcemeat.

FIGURE 11-7 Preparing Mousseline Forcemeat

(1) Grinding the chicken in a food processor.

(2) Adding the cream with the machine running.

(3) The correct consistency before pushing the forcemeat through a drum sieve.

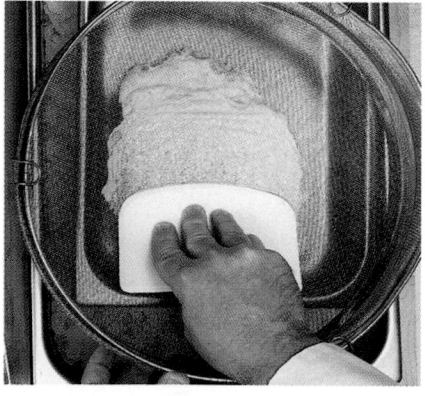

(4) Pushing the forcemeat through a drum sieve.

FIGURE 11-8 Mise en Place for 5/4/3, or Emulsion, Forcemeat

(1) Adding a curing mix.

(2) Grinding the meats through a fine die.

(3) Grinding jowl fat through a fine die.

2. Add curing salt to the meat only; do not add it to the fat.

3. Grind the meats separately through the fine die once.

Place them in the bowl of a chopping machine or a food processor. Add the ice along with the spices and other ingredients and blend the mixture until it reaches 40°F (4°C) for the second time. The temperature will drop below 40°F (4°C) and then gradually regain the same temperature. At this point, the fat can be added. It is important that the temperature be correct in order for the correct emulsion to form.

4. Grind the fat through a fine die.

Add this to the meat mixture. Continue to blend the mixture until it reaches a temperature of 58°F (14°C).

5. Make a quenelle to test for binding and taste, and adjust these accordingly.

This forcemeat can be used in a variety of preparations: Stuff the mixture into casings and hot-smoke them (see the information later in this chapter about smoking). These sausages are usually smoked only until they have a good color; they must be poached to an internal temperature of 155°F (68°C) and then prepared as desired, (*e.g.*, grilled) or cooled before service.

Refer to Part IV, Chapter 27, for specific emulsified forcemeat recipes.

Garde-Manger and Charcuterie Specialties

This section includes step-by-step instructions for preparing a number of different items produced in the garde-manger kitchen, including various forcemeat-based preparations such as quenelles, sausages, pâté en croûte, galantines, and items such as daubes and cured salmon.

Quenelles

Quenelles are poached dumplings made from a forcemeat. Any forcemeat can and should be checked for flavor, texture, color, and consistency by preparing a test quenelle. This is, in fact, an excellent safeguard against producing sausages, terrines, or pâtés that have poor quality.

A mousseline forcemeat, shaped into a quenelle and gently poached, is often served as an appetizer or a garnish for soups. There are many ways to form a quenelle. Different techniques are described in the method below. A richly flavored stock or court bouillon is used as the poaching liquid. Properly prepared quenelles should be light and tender, with a good flavor.

Method

1. Prepare the forcemeat and keep it chilled until it is time to poach the quenelles. The method

FIGURE 11-9   Preparing 5/4/3, or Emulsion, Forcemeat

(1) Combining the meats with ice and spices in the bowl of a chopper.

(2) Chopping the meat until it reaches a temperature of 40° F/4°C.

(3) Adding the ground fat to the mixture.

(4) The correct consistency.

for preparing quenelles from a forcemeat is illustrated in Figure 11-10.

2. Bring the poaching liquid to 150°F (65°C).

The liquid must not be at a rolling boil; this could cause the quenelles to fall apart as they cook. Cooking quenelles at high temperatures will give a false impression of the forcemeat's quality. Even an excellent mousseline can become rubbery if improperly cooked.

3. Shape the quenelles.

There are many ways to do this, one of which employs spoons. The spoons are first dipped in cold water; an appropriate amount of the forcemeat is scooped up with one of the spoons, and the second spoon is used to smooth and shape the mixture. The quenelle is pushed from the spoon into the poaching medium. Other shaping methods include using ladles or piping the mixture through a plain-tipped pastry bag.

4. Poach the quenelles in the poaching liquid. The cooking time will vary, depending on the quenelles' diameter. They should appear completely cooked through when broken open.

5. When making a test quenelle, be sure to test it at serving temperature.

If the forcemeat is to be served cold, let the sample cool completely before tasting it. Make any necessary adjustments in the forcemeat. If it has a rubbery or tough consistency, add heavy cream; if it does not hold together properly, additional panada or egg whites may be necessary. Adjust the seasoning and flavoring ingredients as needed.

See Part IV, Chapters 26 and 27, for specific recipes.

Pâté de Campagne, or Country-Style Pâté

Pâté de campagne is made from a country-style forcemeat. Many traditional garnishes may be added, including nuts, marinated meats, or dried fruits. Traditionally, the mold for a pâté de campagne would be lined with sheets of fatback. Con-

FIGURE 11-10
Preparing
Quenelles from
a Forcemeat

temporary versions may call for other liners, including romaine leaves, plastic wrap, or leek leaves.

Method

1. Line the mold completely with thin slices of fatback. There should be a 2- to 3-inch overhang on all sides. See Figure 11-11 for photos illustrating the method for preparing pâté de campagne, or country-style pâté.

2. Add the garnished country-style forcemeat to the lined mold and press it down with a spatula to remove any air pockets.

3. Fold the overhanging fatback onto the top of the pâté to completely encase the forcemeat.

4. Lay various herbs and spices over the top of the pâté, if desired. Place the lid on the mold or cover tightly with foil. Cook the pâté in a bain-marie in order to maintain the correct temperature. This will yield a product that is smooth, moist, and flavorful.

5. After the pâté has cooked to the correct internal temperature, allow it to cool to room temperature. Pour off all the fat and liquid that may have collected in the mold. Pour aspic gelée into the mold to fill it to the top. Then chill it completely before slicing.

Refer to Part IV, Chapter 27, for specific pâté recipes.

FIGURE 11-11   Pâté de Campagne, or Country-Style Pâté

(1) Filling a lined mold.

(2) Folding the fatback overhang.

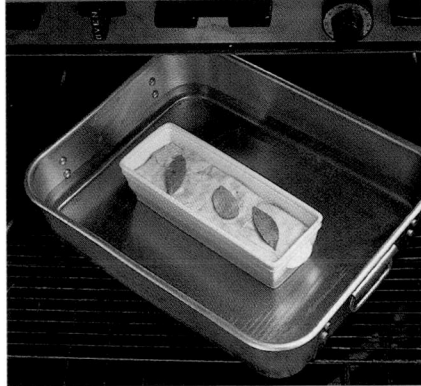

(3) The pâté is shown without its cover, to illustrate the water's height in relationship to the terrine.

(4) Adding aspic to the cooled pâté.

Pâté en Croûte

This is a more elaborate style of pâté in which the mold is lined with a pastry crust. The procedure for lining the mold, baking the pâté, cutting the chimney, and filling the pâté with aspic is explained here. Various forcemeats, including straight and country-style, may be used. Some chefs like to use elaborate in-lays and garnishes to create decorative effects, especially for competitions and display pieces.

Method

1. Prepare the forcemeat as necessary, according to the type. Keep the forcemeat and garnish cold until it is time to fill the mold.

2. Line the mold.

Roll out sheets of dough to approximately ⅛-inch thick. Cut the sheets to fit the mold: Measure the mold's bottom and sides and lightly score the dough. The corners may be cut out, and will eventually be pinched together as a seam, or the excess can be pinched away when the pastry is laid into the mold. An overhang of about 2 inches on the sides and ends of the pâté is necessary.

A second piece, known as the cap piece, should be measured out large enough to completely cover the mold's top and extend down into the mold about 2 to 2½ inches.

The method for measuring dough for pâté en croûte is illustrated in Figure 11-12.

3. Lay the pieces into the mold and press them into place.

FIGURE 11-12 Measuring Dough for Pâté en Croûte

(1) Measure cutting lines as shown. Allow sufficient dough to create a generous overhang.

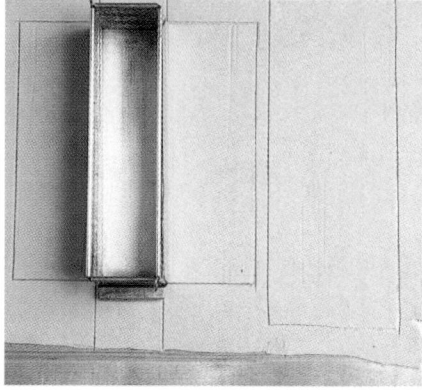

(2) The excess dough can be cut out of the corners by making cuts as shown here, if desired.

If a single large rectangle has been used, fit the dough gently into the corners and use a ball of scrap dough to press out any air pockets. If the pieces have been cut to fit, lay them in the mold and press them into place.

4. Use egg wash to "glue" the pastry together in the corners and pinch the seams closed or pinch away the excess in the corners.

FIGURE 11-13 Lining the Mold with Dough

(1) Laying pieces of dough into the mold and forming seams.

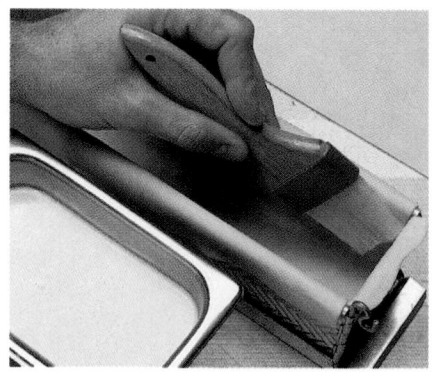

(2) Using egg wash to "glue" the seams closed.

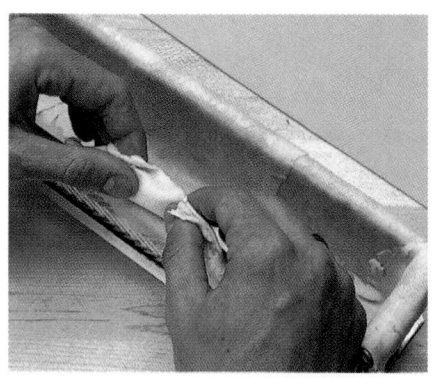

(3) Lining the pastry dough with thin fatback sheets.

Save dough scraps to make the chimney and any desired decorations.

5. Line the bottom and sides of the pastry-lined mold with sheets of fatback, thinly sliced prosciutto, or other sliced meats.

The method for lining the mold with dough is illustrated in Figure 11-13.

6. Garnish the forcemeat as desired, if the garnish has not already been folded in. Add the forcemeat to the lined mold and press out any air pockets with a spatula, smoothing the surface.

7. Fold the fatback, prosciutto, or other sliced meat over the top of the forcemeat. Then fold over the pastry sheets and trim the top layers with scissors so that the edges just meet. Pull the pâté away from the mold's edges with a spatula.

At this point, some chefs prefer to invert the pâté mold. This bottom piece of the mold should be removed and replaced, so that the bottom piece of dough becomes the top layer. This eliminates the need for a cap piece.

8. Add the cap piece to seal the pâté, and tuck the edges down into the mold.

The method for filling and capping the pâté is illustrated in Figure 11-14.

9. Cover the pâté with aluminum foil and bake it (see Figure 11-15) until it is approximately half-done (about 45 minutes). Remove the pâté from the oven and remove the foil.

The dough should have just begun to lose its moist appearance. Egg wash can be brushed onto the dough now with a reduced danger of the surface appearing cracked or checkered.

10. Using round cutters, cut one or two vent holes in the pastry to allow steam to escape.

Cut a ring of pastry to go around the chimney's opening base. Use aluminum foil rolled into a tube to keep the hole from closing during the final baking. This "chimney" will allow steam to escape and will prevent the crust from rupturing. Add any decorative pieces, as desired, using egg wash to secure them to the top crust.

11. Complete the baking in a moderate oven (about 350°F/170°C) to an internal temperature of

FIGURE 11-14 Filling and Capping the Pâté

(1) Filling the prepared mold.

(2) Trimming the excess dough.

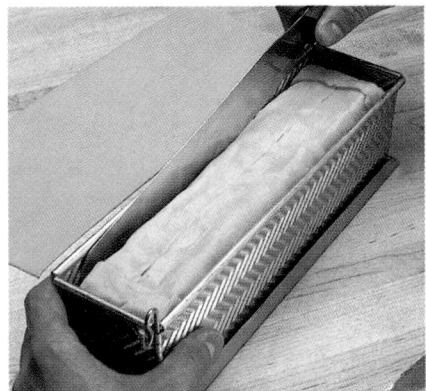

(3) Freeing the dough from the mold sides.

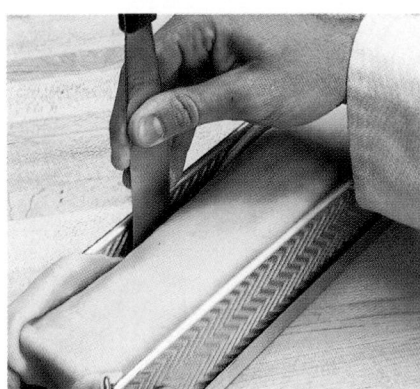

(4) Putting the cap piece in place.

FIGURE 11-15   Baking Pâté en Croûte

(1) Covering the pâté with foil before the first stage of baking.

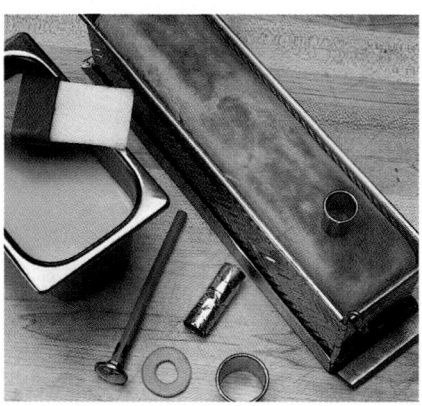

(2) Cutting a hole in the crust and brushing with egg wash.

(3) Filling the cooled pâté with aspic.

(4) A sliced pâté en croûte.

150°F (65°C) for meat and 145°F (63°C) for fish and vegetables.

12. Remove the pâté from the oven and let it cool for about 1 hour. Drain away any cooking liquid. Fill the mold with aspic, pouring the liquid through the holes that have been cut in the crust.

13. Chill the pâté thoroughly before slicing and service. Excessive shrinkage or gaps between the pastry and the pâté itself usually means that the pâté has been baked too long or in an oven that was too hot.

See Part IV, Chapter 27 for specific pâté en croûte recipes.

Terrines

Like pâtés, terrines are loaves of straight, country-style, or gratin forcemeats baked in a mold. The difference is that terrines are traditionally placed in a covered earthenware mold, called a terrine, and cooked in a hot-water bath. Although pâtés are traditionally unmolded before they are served, terrines would customarily have been served from the mold. The strict interpretation of a terrine has been somewhat modified for contemporary service; they are usually unmolded and sliced. To vary the presentation, the mold can be filled with two forcemeats of different colors—for example, layers of a forcemeat flavored and colored with green herbs could be alternated with layers of a forcemeat flavored and colored with saffron.

Method

1. Prepare a forcemeat as desired or necessary according to the recipe. Chill it until it is time to fill the mold.

Meat and game terrines may be made from straight or country-style forcemeats. Fish, chicken, and vegetable terrines may be prepared from mousseline forcemeats.

2. Prepare any garnishes as desired or necessary. Keep them refrigerated until they are ready to be used.

3. Prepare the mold. Line it first with plastic wrap and then with a "liner" ingredient, of which the following are the most common: thin sheets of fatback, blanched vegetables, blanched romaine leaves, or thin slices of ham or smoked fish.

4. Fill the mold, adding the garnish as described for pâtés.

5. Fold all liners over the mold's surface.

6. Cover the terrine with its lid.

7. Place the terrine in a roasting pan. Set the pan on the rack of a moderate (about 300°F/150°C) oven. Add enough boiling water to come up nearly to the level of the top of the forcemeat.

8. Bake the terrine to an internal temperature of 150°F (65°C) for meats and 140°F (60°C) for fish.

Regulate the temperature of the oven throughout cooking time. The water temperature should remain at approximately 160°F (70°C) throughout cooking time.

9. Remove the terrine from the bath and allow it to cool. Weight the terrine and refrigerate it overnight. If desired, fill the mold with aspic once it has been cooled and the weight has been removed.

To weight terrines, remove the lid and cover the terrine with foil or plastic. Fit a press plate over the surface, or use a board cut to the mold's dimensions and set a 2-pound weight on the board.

10. Chill the terrine thoroughly before slicing and serving it.

See Part IV, Chapter 27 for specific terrine recipes.

Sausages

There are almost countless types of sausages. Each ethnic group and cuisine tends to have its own favorite examples. Sausages popular in France include such classics as *andouilles, boudins blancs* and *noirs, saucisson,* and *crepinettes.* Dishes that feature sausages include venerable favorites such as cassoulet and choucroute. In the British Isles, sausages are equally important; *haggis* is popular in Scotland, bangers in England, and white puddings are made in Wales. Spain and Portugal produce *chorizo* and *linguiça.* In Italy, *cotechino, salamis* (both dried and smoked), and *pepperoni* find their way into sauces, soups, baked dishes, and breads. Germany and Switzerland make a prodigious quantity of sausages, including *bratwurst, knockwurst, leberwurst,* and *landjaeger.*

Sausage meat may be used either in bulk (loose) form or to fill casings, natural or synthetic, which are then usually formed into links. From this point, they may be used fresh (poached, grilled, fried, or baked) or, if appropriate, they may be dried and smoked or cured. Smoked or cured sausages generally do not require additional cooking. The following method describes the procedure for filling sausage casings using a sausage-stuffing machine. The same general guidelines apply to hand stuffing. See Figure 11-1 (3) and (4) for examples of sausages.

Method

1. Prepare and garnish the forcemeat as desired or required by the recipe used. The method for filling sausage casings and tying them into links is illustrated in Figure 11-16, and that for twisting sausage into links in Figure 11-17.

2. Rinse the casings thoroughly in tepid water to remove the salt and to make them more pliable.

3. Be sure that all parts of the sausage stuffer that will come in contact with the forcemeat are clean and chilled.

4. Tie a double knot in the casing end. Depending on the type of casing, as well as the type of sausage, the casing may be cut into appropriate lengths.

5. Gather the casing over the nozzle of the sausage stuffer.

6. Support the casing as the forcemeat is expressed through the nozzle and into the casing.

7. If the sausage is to be made into links, use either of the following methods:
Press the casing into links at the desired intervals and then twist the link in alternating directions for each link; or, tie the casing with twine at the desired intervals.

FIGURE 11-16   Filling Sausage Casings and Tying Them into Links

(1) Filling the casing with forcemeat.

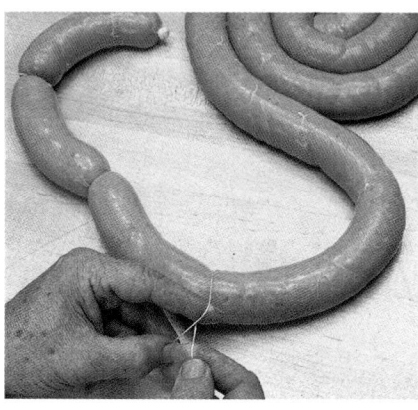

(2) Tying the sausages into even links.

FIGURE 11-17   Twisting Sausage into Links

(1) Using fingers to press the sausage into even links.

(2) Twisting the links to keep them separate; no twine is used here.

8. At this point, fresh sausages may be cooked or stored under refrigeration. Other types of sausage may undergo additional curing, smoking, or drying.

See Part IV, Chapter 27, for specific sausage recipes.

Galantines

The term *galantine* derives from an Old French word, *galin*, meaning "chicken." Originally, galantines were made exclusively from poultry and game birds and were stuffed and tied in the bird's natural shape. Today, however, they are made from a wide range of products, including fish, shellfish, and meats. The skin, if available, is used as a casing to hold the forcemeat.

Method

1. Remove the skin, keeping it as intact as possible. See Figure 11-18 for photos illustrating the method for preparing a galantine, specifically a chicken galantine.

Make an incision through the skin down the middle of the back and pull the entire skin away from the bird. Use a small knife to help loosen it, if necessary.

2. Bone out the dominant meat, reserving intact any pieces that will be used for garnish.

All other meat should be cut into dice or strips of the appropriate size to prepare the forcemeat. The bones and any nonusable trim should be used to prepare a rich stock you can use to poach the galantine.

3. Trim the skin to form a large rectangle.

Lay out the skin or other casing for the galantine on a large cheesecloth square. Mound the forcemeat down the rectangle's center and position any garnish (the tenderloin or diced, marinated breast meat, for example) as desired. Use the cheesecloth to roll the galantine into a tight cylinder.

4. Tie the ends with butcher's twine and use a strip of cheesecloth to secure it at even intervals in order to maintain the shape of the cylinder.

5. Place the galantine on a perforated rack and then lower it into a simmering stock.

Be sure that the galantine is completely submerged. Maintain the liquid at constant 150–155°F (65–67°C) even simmer throughout the cooking time—generally 1 to 1½ hours or until an internal temperature of 150°F (65°C) for meats and 140°F (60°C) for fish has been reached.

6. Let the galantine cool in the cooking liquid. (If cheesecloth or plastic wrap has been used, remove the casing.) Rewrap the galantine in fresh plastic wrap, reroll it to form a tight cylinder, and refrigerate it.

7. Unwrap the galantine before slicing and serving it.

Refer to Part IV, Chapter 27, for individual galantine recipes.

Cured and Smoked Items

Before they are used in other charcuterie preparations, many foods undergo a cure, usually by allowing the meats to marinate briefly in either a brine, or wet or dry cure. (See Figure 11-1 (2) and (5) for a selection of smoked and cured items.) Curing is especially important as the first step for items that are to be smoked. Meat, fish, and sausage cures and brines often call for curing salt, a preservative that helps prevent the growth of botulism. Curing salt (tinted curing mix or TCM) is composed of 94 percent salt and 6 percent sodium nitrite. Today its use may be optional for all but items smoked or air-cured for long periods at low temperatures.

Curing may be accomplished by using a *dry cure* (dry salts, spices, and herbs) or a brine (a combination of water, salt, spices, and other flavorings). Dry cures are packed around the item to be cured. Instructions for ratios and times used in dry curing are given in specific recipes. In a *wet cure*, the food is completely immersed in a brine and allowed to cure for a specified amount of time, depending on the nature and size of the item.

FIGURE 11-18 Preparing a Chicken Galantine

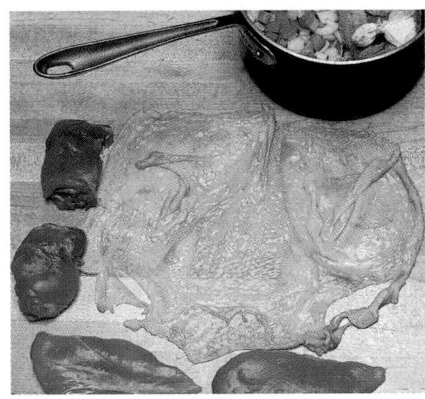

(1) Mise en place.

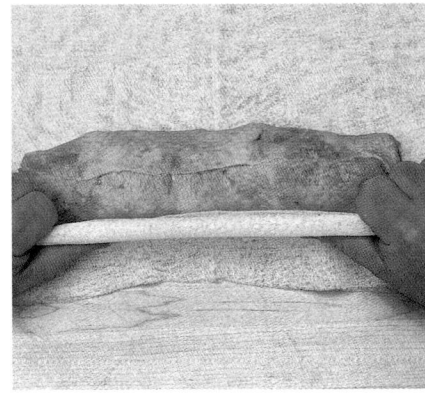

(2) Filling and rolling the galantine.

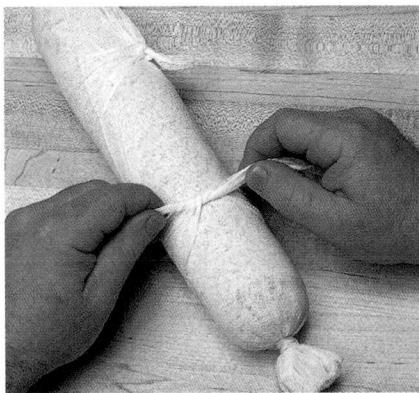

(3) Tying the galantine.

(4) Placing the galantine on a rack before poaching it.

Again, ratios and times for curing by brine are given in specific recipes. After the food has been properly cured or brined, it is allowed to air-dry, making it more receptive to smoke. Smoking flavors foods and preserves their colors. A variety of smoking methods can be used. Even kitchens too small to have a smoker can produce foods with a smoked flavor.

Smoking takes place in an enclosed structure—a smokehouse—where smoke from hardwood chips (hickory, mesquite, apple) circulates freely and reaches all sides of the product. Depending on the nature of the items, they may be hung from the ceiling or placed on racks. The smokehouse temperature and the time needed for smoking depend on the product's nature and the desired outcome. The common ways of smoking are cold smoking, hot smoking, and smoke roasting or pan smoking. (For more information about smoke roasting or pan roasting, see Chapter 9.)

Cold smoking is done within a specified temperature range, less than 100°F (37°C). The food should take on a smoky flavor and color but will not be fully cooked during the process. It is usually necessary to complete the cooking of the product before it is served. This method is commonly used for smoked salmon, landjager, classic French garlic sausage, and all other hard-salami sausage types. Cold smoking will give the food a smoky flavor and darker color.

Hot smoking, at temperatures above 145°F (63°C), will fully cook the food. Smoke roasting is not a traditional smoking method, but it offers a wide range of possibilities for smaller kitchens with no access to a smokehouse.

See Part IV, Chapter 26, for specific smoked and cured item recipes.

Cured Salmon

Cured salmon is commonly referred to as "gravad lox" or "gravlax." This dish of Swedish origin, is essentially raw salmon allowed to marinate in a dry cure of salt, sugar, and dill. Numerous interpretations of this dish can be found today, some made with tequila and cilantro, others with vodka and caraway. It is the classic accompaniment to bagels and cream cheese.

FIGURE 11-19   Preparing Cured Salmon

(1) Coating salmon fillets with a spice mixture.

(2) Wrapping the salmon tightly in cheesecloth.

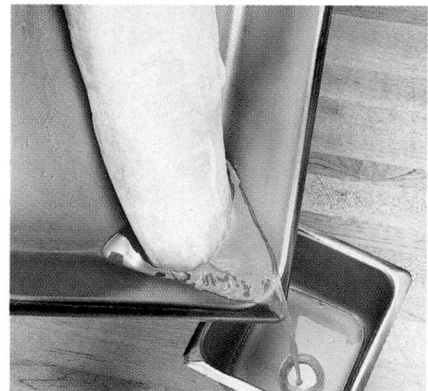

(3) Draining away the drippings.

(4) Unwrapping the salmon and scraping away the cure.

Method

1. Coat trimmed salmon fillets with a dry-cure-and-herb mixture. Wrap them tightly in cheesecloth, place them in a hotel pan, and weight them with a press plate. Allow the salmon to cure for several hours or days, according to the recipe.The method for preparing cured salmon is illustrated in Figure 11-19, and that for slicing and serving gravad lox in Figure 11-20.

2. Drain away any drippings that have accumulated in the pan and reserve them to make a mayonnaise-style sauce to serve with the cured salmon.

3. Unwrap the salmon and scrape away the cure. Slice the salmon very thinly on the diagonal to serve.

4. Prepare a mayonnaise (optional).

See Part IV, Chapter 26 page for a gravad lox recipe.

Daube

A daube, when prepared by a charcutière, is a cold preparation of a variety of meats, usually including the tongue, head, and feet of veal and/or pork. The hot version of the dish is also known as a daube—a rich, slowly cooked braise prepared in a *daubière.* The cold version is slowly simmered, like the hot version. Then it is chilled until the proteins of the meat set the cooking liquid into a gel firm enough to slice. Head cheese and similar cold meat in aspic preparations are made in much the same manner as the daube described here.

Method

1. Gently simmer the meats in an aromatic broth enriched with vegetables and herbs. Once the meats are tender, trim and cut them into julienne or dice .See Figure 11-21 for photo illustrating the method for preparing a daube.

2. Line the mold, usually an earthenware terrine, with plastic wrap. Leave enough overhang to ensure that the mold can be fully sealed.

3. Place the prepared meats, along with the desired herbs and other garnishes, in the mold. An aspic, made by clarifying and enriching the stock

FIGURE 11-20 Slicing and Serving Cured Salmon

(1) Slicing the salmon thinly on the diagonal.

(2) Preparing a mayonnaise.

used to simmer the meats, is added to completely fill the mold.

4. Fold back the overhanging plastic wrap over the top of the mold to seal the daube, and refrigerate the entire dish until the aspic is firmly set.

5. Once the daube is thoroughly chilled, it is ready to be sliced and served.

Refer to Part IV, Chapter 27, for the daube recipe.

Summary

Sausages, pâtés, terrines, galantines, smoked, and cured foods are consistently well received on virtually any menu. Recipes that are based on the preparation of the five basic forcemeats can be found in Part IV, Chapter 27. For further information about smoking foods, refer to the recommended reading list in the appendix.

FIGURE 11-21   Preparing a Daube

(1) Simmering the meats.

(3) Filling the mold with meats and aspic.

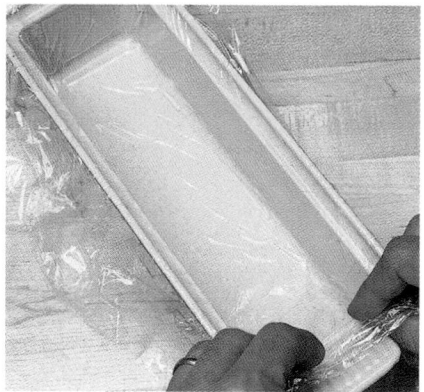

(2) Lining the mold with plastic wrap.

(4) Sealing by folding back the overhanging plastic wrap.

12 Baking and Pastry

Freshly baked breads and desserts make a good and lasting impression on the guests and contribute significantly to an operation's success. Although baking and pastry can be a specialization in itself, every chef must learn basic procedures and be able to produce items such as pie dough, puff pastry, and simple, pleasing desserts.

The function of various ingredients and how they will affect the finished product by giving it a tender "crumb," a well-developed crust, or a very light texture are examined in this chapter. Also included are the six basic functions of ingredients and the techniques of measuring (known as scaling), proper pan preparation, sifting, tempering chocolate, and working a pastry bag. The chef should always bear in mind that baking is a science that depends on exact measurements and the proper handling of ingredients and tools in order to ensure the same results consistently.

Although baking is not a difficult process, understanding the role that a given ingredient will play in the finished product is important. Baking ingredients will generally fall into six basic categories of function:

- Strengtheners, such as flour and eggs

- Shorteners, such as butters and oils

- Sweeteners, or liquifiers, including a variety of sugars and syrups

- Chemical and organic leaveners

- Thickeners, such as cornstarch, flour, and eggs

- A number of different flavorings

As this list demonstrates, one ingredient may fulfill a number of different functions; for example, eggs and flour can each be categorized as both a strengthener and a thickener.

Strengtheners

Strengtheners provide stability, ensuring that the baked good does not collapse once it is removed from the oven. For most baked items, the major strengthener is flour, often referred to as the "backbone" of baked goods, because it provides the structure or framework.

Flours include wheat flours of varying "strengths" or hardness, from soft pastry flours to hard wheats used for breads and pastas, as well as special flours and meals including whole grain flours, rye, pumpernickel, oat, rice, or cornmeal.

Flour functions as a strengthener because of its proteins and starches. The proteins present in eggs (found in the whites and yolks) allow them to serve as a strengthener as well. Eggs are used in this way for cakes, such as genoise, angel food, and chiffon, made by the foaming method.

Starches are also important to many baked goods' overall structure. The starch granules first swell in the presence of liquid. Then, as they are heated, they swell even more, trapping liquid or steam within their expanded frame. As heat continues to set the starch into a stable structure, texture is also affected.

Shorteners

Shorteners make baked goods tender and moist. This occurs when the shortener (butter, oil, hydrogenated shortening, or lard) is incorporated into the batter. The fat tends to surround the flour and other ingredients, breaking the long strands of gluten in the batter or dough into shorter units—hence the term "shorteners."

The way in which the fat is incorporated will affect the item's overall texture. Fats that are rubbed or rolled into doughs tend to separate the dough into large layers, creating a flaky texture. When the fat is thoroughly creamed together with sugar so that it can be mixed evenly throughout the batter, the resulting item's texture will be more cake-like and tender.

Fat also helps to retain moisture in the finished product. In addition to the fats and oils commonly considered shorteners, egg yolks, soft cheeses, cream, and milk may also fall into this category because they contain a relatively high percentage of fat.

Sweeteners

Sweeteners (sugars, syrups, honey, and molasses) perform other functions in addition to providing flavor. Sugars in any form tend to attract moisture, so baked goods containing sweeteners generally are moist and tender. They also have a longer shelf-life than unsweetened baked goods.

The caramelization of sugar is responsible for the appealing brown color on the surface of many baked products. Heat applied to the sugar causes this browning reaction. Besides affecting the color, caramelization also gives a product a deep, rich, and complex flavor. An obvious example is the difference in taste between simple syrup, made by dissolving a sugar in water, and a caramel syrup.

Leaveners

Leaveners produce a desirable texture by introducing a gas, carbon dioxide, into the batter or dough by one of three means: chemical, organic, or physical.

Chemical Leaveners

Baking soda and baking powder are the primary *chemical leaveners.* In these leaveners, an alkaline ingredient (baking soda or baking powder) interacts with an acid (already present in baking powder, or an ingredient such as buttermilk, sour cream, yogurt, or chocolate). The alkalies and acids produce a gas, carbon dioxide, when combined in the batter.

As the item is baked, this gas expands, giving the baked goods their characteristic texture, known as "crumb." This process of expansion happens rapidly; hence, many items prepared with chemical leaveners are called "quick breads."

Double-acting baking powder is so called because a first action occurs in the presence of moisture in the batter and a second action is initiated by the presence of heat. That is, it reacts once when it is mixed with the batter's liquids and again when the batter is placed in a hot oven.

Organic Leaveners

Organic leaveners, are living organisms that feed on sugars present in flours or as added sweeteners, producing alcohol and carbon dioxide. Unlike chemical leaveners, organic leaveners take a substantial amount of time to do their job. They have to grow and reproduce sufficiently to fill the dough with air pockets.

Yeast and sourdoughs are organic leaveners, which means that they must be "alive" in order to be effective. Organic leaveners can be killed by overly high temperatures and, conversely, cold temperatures can inhibit their action. The temperature of the dough and its environment must be controlled carefully. Yeast will not function well below approximately 65 to 70°F (18 to 21°C), and above 110°F (43°C) yeast is destroyed.

Two types of yeast are used in the professional bakeshop: dry (or granulated) yeast and fresh (compressed) yeast. Dry yeast, in bulk or packets, should be refrigerated. It will keep for several months, which makes it suitable for kitchens that only occasionally make their own bread. Fresh yeast, on the other hand, is quite perishable and can be held under refrigeration for only 7 to 10

days. It may be frozen for longer storage. Cold yeast should be allowed to return to room temperature before it is used.

Proofing Yeast If there is any doubt about whether or not the yeast is still alive, it should be "proofed" before it is added to the other ingredients. Proofing is accomplished as follows:

1. Combine the yeast with warm liquid and a small amount of flour or sugar.

2. Let the mixture rest at room temperature until a thick surface foam forms.

3. The foam indicates that the yeast is alive and can be used. If there is no foam, the yeast is dead and should be discarded.

Sourdough starters are used to leaven a variety of country-style breads, biscuits, and even pancakes. Sourdough starters are essentially cultures produced by blending flour and water. This mixture is then inoculated with an existing yeast, or is left exposed so that wild yeast, naturally present in the air, will begin the process of fermentation.

Starters can be kept alive for extended periods, by replenishing the flour and water as some of the starter is removed to prepare baked goods. This long life has become the stuff of legend in some bakeries where the culture has been kept alive for years, even decades.

Different parts of the world have different types of wild yeasts, which lend a particular flavor to the sourdough starter. In addition, the degree of sourness considered appropriate varies from one region or country to another. San Francisco sourdough is different from that produced in France.

The preparation of various starters and instructions for keeping them alive can be found in Part IV, Chapter 28, of this book.

Physical Leaveners

The basic physical leavener is steam, which is produced when liquids in a batter or dough are heated. This causes the air pockets to expand. Steam leavening is critical in sponge cakes and soufflés. It also plays a vital role in the production of puff pastry, croissant, and Danish. In these products, the steam is trapped, causing the layers to separate and rise.

Thickeners

Sauces and puddings can be thickened by using various ingredients, including eggs, gelatin, and starches, such as flour, cornstarch, arrowroot, or rice flour. These thickeners may be used to lightly thicken a mixture, as for a sauce, or to produce an item that is firmly set, such as a Bavarian cream.

The quantity and type of thickener, as well as the amount of stirring or other manipulation, will determine the finished product's properties. For example, if a custard is cooked over direct heat and stirred constantly, the result will be a sauce that pours easily. The same custard cooked in a bain-marie with no stirring at all will set into a firm custard that can be sliced.

Arrowroot and cornstarch are generally preferred for thickening sauces, puddings, and fillings where a translucent effect is desired. If these thickeners are to be diluted before incorporation with other ingredients, they should be mixed with a small amount of a cool liquid.

Flour is commonly used to thicken items such as crème pâtissière. In order to prevent lumping, the flour and sugar are often stirred together before they are combined with the liquid. Flour-thickened sauces are also often additionally thickened and enriched with eggs. The eggs must be tempered to prevent the sauce from curdling.

Eggs (whole eggs or yolks) may be used either alone or in conjunction with other thickeners. As the egg proteins begin to coagulate, the liquid becomes trapped in the network of set proteins, producing a *nappé* texture, in which the sauce will coat the back of a spoon when the spoon is dipped into the sauce and withdrawn.

Gelatin, when added in the desired amount, can produce light, delicate foams (Bavarian creams, mousses, and stabilized whipped cream, for example) that are firmly set. Such foams will retain a mold's shape and can be sliced. Gelatin is an animal protein found in bones. (It is this protein that causes stock to gel as it cools.) Gelatin powder or sheets are frequently used for a variety of bakeshop items. Before use, gelatin must first be softened

(also known as "bloomed") in a cool liquid. Once the gelatin has absorbed the liquid, it is then gently heated to melt the crystals. This is accomplished either by adding the softened gelatin to a hot mixture, such as a hot custard sauce, or by gently heating the gelatin over simmering water.

Flavorings

Flavoring ingredients can range from extracts and essences to chocolate chips and chopped nuts. Whole vanilla beans along with other whole and ground spices are also used. Various forms of fruit including juices, zest, purées, and dried fruits also can be considered flavorings. In general, flavoring ingredients do not have a great impact on the characteristics of the batter or dough as it is mixed, shaped, and baked. Specific recipes throughout the book indicate appropriate flavorings, as well as how and when to add them.

Techniques Used to Prepare Ingredients and Equipment

Scaling

Careful measuring, known as scaling, is more important in baking than in other types of cookery. The most accurate way to measure ingredients is to weigh them. Even liquid ingredients are often, though not always, weighed.

Various scales may be used in the bakeshop, including balance-beam, spring-type, or electronic scales. Other measuring tools, including volume measures and measuring spoons, are also required.

After the batter or dough is mixed, it is scaled once more, to ensure that the proper amount is used for the pan size. Not only does this contribute to the uniformity of products, but it also decreases the possibilities of uneven rising or browning caused by too much or too little dough in the pan.

Sifting Dry Ingredients

Dry ingredients used for most baked goods should be sifted before they are incorporated into

FIGURE 12-1
Sifting Dry
Ingredients

the dough or batter (see Figure 12-1). Sifting aerates flour and confectioners' sugar, removing lumps and filtering out any impurities. Leavening ingredients and some flavoring ingredients (cocoa powder, for example) are more evenly distributed after sifting.

Sifting should take place after the ingredients have been properly scaled. They are passed through a sifter onto a sheet of parchment paper. The paper can then be used to transfer the dry ingredients to the batter or dough.

Selecting and Preparing Pans and Molds

In addition to measuring devices and ovens, which were discussed in Chapter 4, pans of various sizes and shapes make up the major category of baking equipment. Pans are available in several gauges (metal thicknesses). Heavy-gauge pans are usually preferred; some very delicate items, such as wafer-type cookies, may even be baked on doubled pans.

Pans also come with different surfaces. Shiny pans are used for items containing large amounts of sugar and fat, which could burn or scorch easily during cooking. The shiny surface tends to reflect some of the heat away from the pan, slightly slowing down the cooking process. Darker surfaces hold the heat better and are used for items in which a well-developed crust and a deeper color are desirable.

A variety of pans are used in the bakeshop. The correct shape and size are important to ensure that the baked item's texture and appearance are correct. If the pan is too large, the item may not rise properly during baking and the edges may quickly

become overbaked. Conversely, a pan that is too small will result in items that may not be properly baked through; their appearance will also suffer.

Lean doughs, such as pizza dough, hard rolls, and French and Italian breads, are baked in pans or directly on a hearth that has been dusted with cornmeal or other coarse meals. The meal very slightly elevates the dough so that a good crust can form on all surfaces. It also allows the bread to release easily from the baking surface. A "peel" is used to load shaped and proofed breads onto the hearth. This peel should also be dusted with cornmeal so that the breads slide off easily.

Delicate batters, especially those for soufflés sponge cakes, jelly rolls, or cookies that include a high proportion of eggs, sugar, and butter, are baked in pans that have been liberally greased (usually with a hydrogenated shortening or a blend of shortening and flour), lined with parchment paper, and then greased again and dusted with flour or sugar (see Figure 12-2).

To coat a pan with flour or sugar, shake a handful of flour into the pan and spread it around to

FIGURE 12-2 Preparing Molds

(1) Coating soufflé molds.

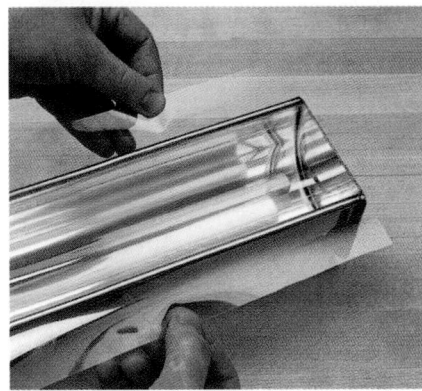

(2) Lining mold with acetate.

coat all surfaces. To release the excess flour, rap the pan sharply on a work surface and shake it out. Many operations prefer to use a spray or spread that has already combined shortening with flour, simplifying the process.

Angel food cakes are baked in ungreased tube pans. An exception to the general rule of greasing pans, this is critical in producing tall cakes. The batter must be able to adhere to the pan sides in order to give the cake stability until it is fully baked and cooled.

Parchment may be called for as a liner for delicate items. Delicate cookies, muffins, or loaf cakes may be baked in pans or tins that have been lined with parchment or fluted paper liners. Frozen desserts or molded items can be chilled in molds lined with acetate sheets (see Figure 12-2). Mixers, kneading equipment, sheeters, and proof boxes are also important pieces of equipment when baking is done frequently.

Selecting and Preparing Ovens

The final quality of baked goods depends on baking them at the right temperature and in the appropriate oven. In all cases, the oven should be fully preheated to the correct temperature.

Items that will rise during baking, such as vol-au-vents made from puff pastry or éclairs made from pâte à choux, should be prepared in standard ovens. The oven must not be overloaded because the air will not be able to circulate evenly in a crowded space. For even baking and browning in a conventional oven, the racks should be inserted in the oven's center. It may be necessary to rotate or rearrange the pans for even baking.

Some cakes, muffins, and cookies may be baked in a convection oven, the advantage being that larger batches may be baked in a single load. The forced movement of air allows each item to bake evenly.

Yeast-Raised Breads

The earliest breads were nothing like the light, airy breads we know today. Leavened bread did not become possible until the Egyptians, using the wheat that flourished in the fertile Nile River valley, dis-

covered why some of their baked dough seemed to have a different texture.

Few foods appeal so directly to the guest as bread. As more specialty or "artisanal" bakeshops open up around the country, Americans are re-learning the pleasures of good breads. Whole grains, organically grown flours, hearth-style ovens, and old-fashioned techniques are gaining favor. If you are able to produce breads on-site, so much the better.

Several factors should be kept in mind when deciding whether or not to bake breads on the premises. The first is the amount of space available—there should be room to accommodate each stage of the process. Second, there should be adequate and appropriate baking equipment, with enough oven space to avoid "competing" against other kitchen needs.

Although baking is meticulous work, requiring careful measuring and proper handling of doughs, the rewards can be significant, especially if quality baked goods are not readily available through a reliable purveyor.

Mixing Yeast Doughs

Yeast breads are divided into two categories: lean doughs and rich doughs (see Figure 12-3). A lean dough, the type used to prepare hard rolls or pizza dough, can be produced with only flour, yeast, and water. In fact, that is the formula for a classic French baguette. This dough can be varied by including additional ingredients, such as spices, herbs, special flours, and/or dried nuts and fruits. These additions will not greatly change the basic texture. Breads made from lean dough tend to have a chewier texture, more bite, and a crisp crust. Hard rolls, French- and Italian-style breads, and whole-wheat, rye, and pumpernickel breads are considered lean.

A rich dough, such as brioche or challah, is produced by the addition of shortening or tenderizing ingredients, such as sugars or syrups, butter or oil, whole eggs or egg yolks, milk or cream. When these fats are introduced, they will give the bread a cake-like texture after baking. The doughs are usually softer and a little more difficult to work with during kneading and shaping than lean doughs.

FIGURE 12-3 A Selection of Breads

(1) Lean dough breads.

(2) Rich dough and quick breads.

Mise en Place

1. Assemble and prepare all ingredients.

Select the appropriate flour for the type of bread being prepared. Yeast doughs made with low-gluten flours (rye, oat, pumpernickel) must include at least some wheat flour, to introduce the necessary gluten for proper rise and texture.

The liquid most often used for lean doughs is water. Milk is used for most rich doughs. The liquid should be at the correct temperature.

Salt controls the yeast's activity and, with the exception of sodium-free breads, it is an essential component. It also helps to give bread the correct texture and flavor.

As with any baked item, it is important to scale all ingredients correctly. An additional concern with yeast-raised doughs is that the temperature of the ingredients be carefully monitored. The overall temperature of the dough and the bakeshop will affect the way that the dough behaves during all phases of mixing, proofing, shaping, and final rise.

2. Assemble all the necessary equipment.

The equipment required for preparing yeast doughs will vary depending upon the size of the batch you intend to make. A variety of bowls, a scale, a drum sieve (or tamis), a bench scraper, a clean working surface (wood is traditional) a mixer with a dough hook, clean cloths to cover the dough as it rises, molds to use during rising, pans or a hearth stove, and a correctly preheated stove are all important.

Other tools that may be necessary, or simply helpful, include a proofing box, a dough or instant-reading thermometer, and a dough "divider" used to separate scaled dough into rolls, if available.

Method

There are a few points at which the chef or baker can vary the method for preparing yeast doughs (see Figure 12-4), and these will be described throughout the method below.

1. Blend fresh yeast with some or all of the liquid and mix until it is evenly blended. Instant dry yeast should be thoroughly blended with the dry ingredients before adding liquids.

If it is necessary, you may want to "proof" the yeast as described earlier to be sure that it is vigorous. Remember that temperature control is important at this stage and throughout the bread-baking process.

Sourdough starters may be used to replace all or some of the yeast.(See recipes in Part IV, Chapter 28.)

Sponge Mixing Method A sponge should not be confused with a sourdough starter. A sponge is prepared by combining the yeast and liquid with a por-

FIGURE 12-4   Mixing Yeast Dough

(1) Dissolving fresh yeast in water.

(2) Dry ingredients are added to yeast mixture.

(3) The dough has formed a shaggy mass.

(4) Properly kneaded dough.

tion of the flour and allowing it to ferment until the mixture is light and spongy. This method is often needed to produce a good texture when using low-gluten flours such as rye or oat.

2. Add all the remaining ingredients—except the salt—to the yeast mixture. Once all the dry ingredients have been added, add the salt on top of them. This will prevent the salt from killing the yeast.

3. Mix on low speed until the dough starts to "catch." It should look like a shaggy mass at this point. Scrape down the bowl's sides and bottom once or twice so that the dough will mix evenly.

4. Increase the mixing speed to medium and continue to knead until the dough develops a smooth appearance and feels springy when touched.

Proper kneading is essential to the full development of the gluten. Gluten is what provides the dough enough strength and elasticity to allow it to rise properly. As the yeast feeds on the sugars in the flour, it gives off gas, which when trapped by the dough, causes the dough to rise. If the dough could not expand, it would not rise. If the dough is either under or overkneaded, the finished product will have a coarse texture, full of large tunnels and holes.

Kneading is generally done directly in the mixing machine using a dough hook. Small batches may be kneaded by hand. If you are kneading a dough by hand, be sure to allow plenty of time. It is difficult to overknead when you are supplying the power. When using a machine be sure to adhere to recommended kneading times.

5. Remove the dough to a clean bowl that has been lightly oiled. Cover the dough with plastic wrap or a clean cloth and let it rise (see Figure 12-5).

It is a good idea to take the temperature of the dough at this point (78°F/26°C) so that you can make any adjustments necessary for a slow rise. Generally speaking, a slow rise results in a better finished item.

As the dough rises, it will grow in volume. To test the dough to see if it has risen sufficiently, press your finger into the dough. The hole should remain visible. The dough should not spring back in place.

Doughs should be allowed to rise sufficiently so the finished bread will have the correct texture.

FIGURE 12-5   First Rise for Dough

(1) Shaped dough before the first rise.

(2) Dough has risen and is ready to punch down.

Dough that has not risen sufficiently (considered underfermented) will have a coarse texture and poor volume after it is baked. Underproofed breads often have a dull appearance and a tight texture. Dough that has risen too much due to overfermentation may have a sour taste, sometimes described as "yeasty" or as tasting like beer.

6. When the dough has risen sufficiently, punch it down (see Figure 12-6).

Hold and Press the dough down in a few places. This will gently expel the carbon dioxide, even out the overall temperature, and redistribute the yeast evenly. It also introduces a fresh supply of oxygen, essential to continued yeast activity.

7. Remove the dough to a prepared work surface.

A clean wooden surface is often used to work with doughs. Use a bench knife to cut the dough into pieces of the correct size. The way to be most accurate is to use a scale.

If you are making individual loaves, each piece should be enough for one loaf. If you are making rolls and will be using a dough divider, refer to the instructions available for scaling a single "press," as it is known.

At this point, you will round gently the dough into smooth balls before the dough goes on for its second rise (see Figure 12-7), sometimes referred to as "bench proofing."

Shaping Doughs

Properly shaping the dough helps to achieve an attractive appearance; but, more important, proper shaping will ensure that the items bake evenly.

The first step is to cut and scale the dough into pieces of the appropriate weight. Use a slapping action to punch the dough into a rectangle of an even

FIGURE 12-6
Punching Down
Dough

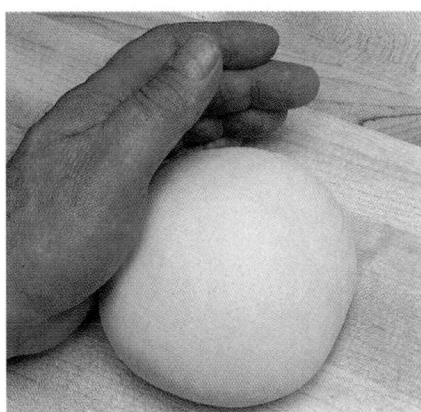

FIGURE 12-7
Rounding Off
Dough

FIGURE 12-8   Shaping Baguettes

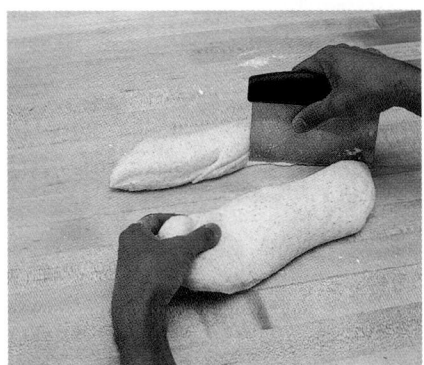

(1) Dividing the dough into pieces.

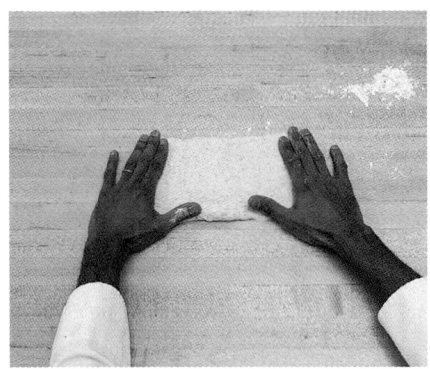

(2) Stretching the dough.

(3) Rolling into a baguette.

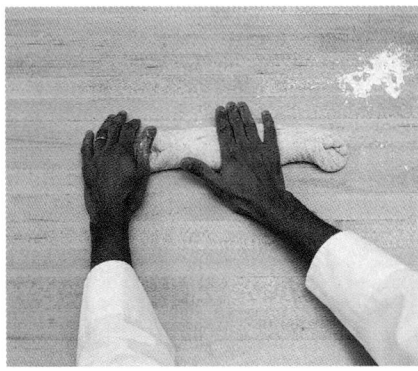

(4) Sealing the seams and stretching baguette.

(5) The baguette is ready to go into bread form.

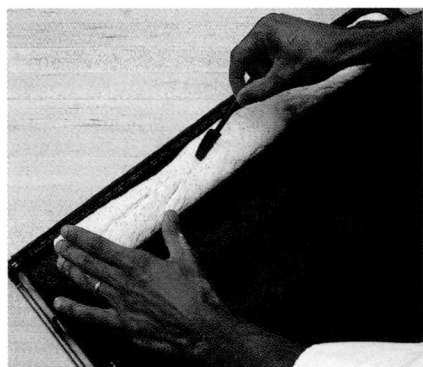

(6) Docking baguettes.

thickness. Once the dough is flattened, fold it in half and flatten it once more. Now grasp both ends of the dough and gently stretch it. Lift the ends up from the work table and allow the dough's weight to stretch itself out.

For some breads, such as baguettes or pan loaves, you will now fold the dough into thirds, and then begin the process of rolling each loaf or roll. (See Figure 12-8.) Use the heel of your palm to firmly seal the seams as the dough is rolled into a cylinder. Hard rolls are often prepared in the same way as long loaves. (Special equipment may be required to prepare large quantities of Kaiser rolls or other specialty items, such as bagels.) They should be transferred to prepared pans.

For round loaves (see Figure 12-9), shaped in molds or linen-lined baskets, stretch the dough as described above, and then round it off once more, rather than folding it into thirds and rolling it into

a cylinder. Once the dough is rounded, place it into prepared molds.

For flatbreads, such as ciabatta (see Figure 12-10), the dough is formed very gently into a rectangle. Then, you will lift it onto a prepared pan or sheet, and flatten it with your fingertips. The dough is then typically brushed with olive oil or a sauce (as for pizza). Herbs or other flavoring ingredients may be added at this point as well.

The Final Rise/Pan-Proofing   The shaped dough is allowed to rise once more. Some breads should be allowed to complete this second rise in a steam-filled proof box, while others react best to being left to rise on the table or in their forms, covered, but not in a proof box.

Docking Breads and Rolls   After shaping, many products will need to be "docked," meaning that

FIGURE 12-9 Shaping Round Loaves

(1) Dough is allowed to rise after rounding. A special basket is used to give crust additional interest.

(2) Docking round loaves.

(3) Baking in a hearth oven.

FIGURE 12-10 Preparing Ciabatta

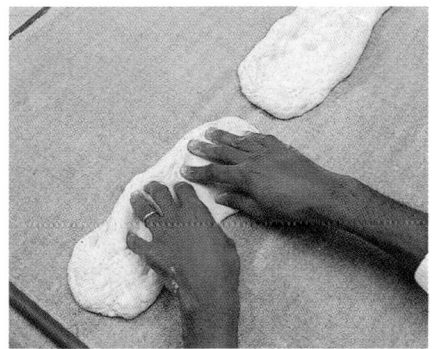

(1) Forming ciabatta into cylinders.

(2) Brushing ciabatta with olive oil.

(3) Baked ciabatta.

the dough's surface is punctured so that the steam that builds up inside the product during baking will not cause it to split or rupture in an uncontrolled manner. The surface may be simply slashed with a sharp knife. Round loaves may be punctured with a wooden skewer or spoon handle.

Baking Yeast Breads

Once the dough has risen for the final time, it should be baked at the appropriate temperature. Doneness is determined by examining the item. Look for a rich color on the exterior, both top and bottom crusts. Thumping the item to see if it has a hollow sound is not always effective, although it is a commonly used test.

Cooling and Storing Yeast Breads

Once the bread or rolls have been baked, they should be allowed to cool on a rack before they are cut or wrapped for storage (see Figure 12-11). If

FIGURE 12-11
Cooling on a
Rack

you do hold baked goods, remember that it is not always the best idea to wrap them in a completely airtight fashion. The character of some whole grain and dark rye breads develops more slowly than others and a few days at room temperature, covered but not tightly wrapped, actually will enhance the product. Crisp crusts do not stand up well to plastic wraps, which tend to trap moisture.

Quick Breads, Cakes, and Other Batters

Quick breads differ from yeast breads in that they use chemical leaveners rather than organic ones and thus do not require a rising period. Muffins, biscuits, and scones are examples of quick breads that have a place on the breakfast menu as well as in the breadbasket at lunch or dinner. These simple baked items allow the chef to offer homemade breads and cakes without the time needed for yeast doughs.

There are four basic methods for preparing the batters used to create cakes, muffins, and quick-breads:

• *The straight mixing method* calls for all ingredients to be combined at once and blended into a batter.

• *The creaming method* is used to prepare products with more refined crumb and texture—pound cakes, butter cakes, and most drop cookies. A fat is creamed together with sugar. Eggs, other liquids, and flavoring extracts are added in stages. The last step is blending the dry ingredients into the batter.

• *The "two-stage" method* is used to prepare cakes that contain a very high percentage of sugar. The dry ingredients are first blended with all of the shortening and half of the liquid until smooth, then the remaining wet ingredients are gradually added.

• *The foaming method,* which produces the lightest texture, is used for genoise (sponge cakes), angel food, and chiffon cakes. Eggs and sugar are beaten until very light, and flour is carefully folded into the batter.

The Straight Mixing Method

The straight mix method is used when making such popular items as pancakes, popovers, cornsticks, bran muffins, pumpkin bread, and carrot cake. Once the basic technique is understood, they are simple to produce, requiring little special equipment.

All ingredients are combined at once in this method and blended into a batter. The important thing to remember is that the batter should not be overworked; unlike yeast doughs, these batters should be mixed as briefly as possible to ensure a light, delicate texture in the finished item.

Mise en Place

1. Assemble all ingredients required for the batter.

Specific recipes may indicate the use of a number of different flours—for example, unbleached flour, whole wheat flour, pastry flour, or cornmeal—according to the desired result. The flour should be carefully weighed, then properly sifted.

A variety of liquids may be used in preparing a batter. Milk, buttermilk, water, oil, the moisture from vegetables, such as zucchini, and other liquids can all be appropriate, according to the recipe. The liquid should be properly measured, either by weight or by volume; both methods of measure will be accurate.

The leavener for most quickbreads and many other batters is a chemical leavener: either baking soda, baking powder, or a combination of the two. Because the leavener is used in very small amounts, it may be appropriate to measure it by volume rather than by weight; a teaspoon or tablespoon measure may be more accurate than a scale at very small measures. The leavener should be sifted with the flour, the salt, and any other dry ingredients required by the recipe.

The amount of shorteners used in a dough will determine its final texture. Refer to the specific recipe for directions to prepare the shortener. In some cases, it may need to be melted and cooled; for others, it should be left cold, but still smooth and pliable.

The number and types of flavoring ingredients that can be used in batters is almost limitless: cocoa, chopped nuts, grated vegetables, berries, citrus zest, and spices and herbs, for example. Refer to the specific recipe for information regarding the advanced preparation of these ingredients.

Method

1. Sift together all of the dry ingredients, and have them ready.

A standard procedure is to sift the flour, leavener, and other dry ingredients through a drum sieve directly into a bowl or onto parchment. This makes it easy to pick up the dry ingredients and add them to the rest of the batter.

2. Combine all the liquid or pourable ingredients (eggs, milk or buttermilk, oil or melted butter, for example) in a mixing bowl. Blend them well to achieve a relatively uniform mixture.

3. Combine the dry ingredients with the liquid ingredients all at once.

Mix the ingredients by hand or in a mixer with a paddle attachment, just until the dry ingredients are moistened. The appearance and consistency of the batter will differ from product to product.

4. Scale off the batter into prepared baking pans. Use paper liners, if available, to line pans and muffin tins, or butter the pans and dust them with flour.

5. Bake the batter at the appropriate temperature until it is baked through.

When properly baked, the item's surface should spring back when pressed with a fingertip and a skewer inserted near the center should come away clean.

During baking, muffins and quick breads should rise to create a dome-shaped upper crust. The crust may develop a crack. The edges may become slightly darker than the center, but they should not shrink too far away from the pan's sides.

6. Remove the item from the oven, then cool it on racks before serving and/or storing.

The texture should be even throughout the product's interior, with a cake-like crumb. Quick breads should be moist but not wet or unduly heavy.

The Creaming Method

Creaming together fat and sugar produces an exceptionally fine crumb and a dense, rich texture that holds up well and slices evenly. Pound cakes are the primary example of the results of this method. Many cookies are also made by creaming, although the ingredient proportions differ—cakes have less butter and more eggs, whereas cookies usually have greater amounts of butter and sugar.

A leavener, such as baking powder or baking soda, is not always required for pound cake and cookies. However, use of a leavener will result in lighter, less-dense products. Refer to the specific recipes for guidelines.

Mise en Place

Refer to the basic mise en place for the straight mixing method, earlier in this chapter.

Method

1. Combine the room temperature butter (or other shortening) and sugar and blend them together until the mixture is smooth, light, and creamy (see Figure 12-12).

This is generally done in a mixer, using a paddle attachment. Scrape down the bowl's sides and bottom as needed throughout mixing to be sure that the mixture is evenly creamed together. It should be light in both color and texture and relatively smooth. Do not undermix at this stage, because the final texture will depend upon this step. If you have begun with cold butter, you may need to allow some extra time at this stage to allow the friction of the paddle and the sugar to gently warm and soften the butter.

2. Gradually add the eggs, which should be at room temperature.

FIGURE 12-12   Creaming Method

(1) Combine butter and sugar.

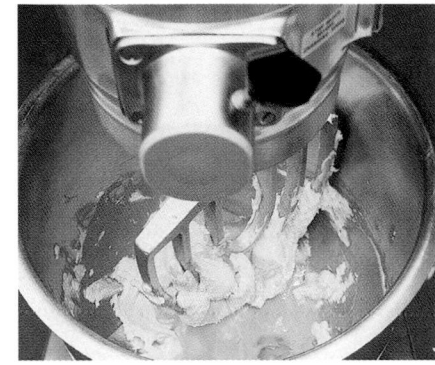
(2) Add eggs.

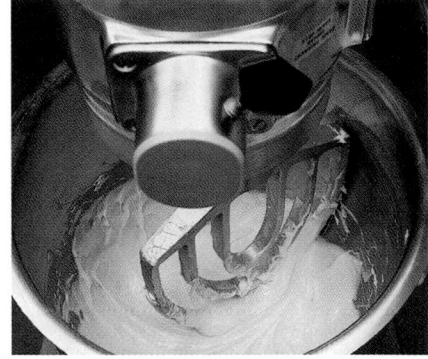
(3) Blend.

(4) Add sifted dry ingredients.

(5) Alternate with liquid ingredients.

(6) Finished batter.

If either the eggs or the butter mixture are too cool, the batter may appear curdled, like a broken hollandaise. If this should happen, continue to mix, without adding more eggs, until the mixture looks completely smooth again. If your kitchen or bakeshop is exceptionally cold, you may need to allow the batter to heat up very slightly over warm water before returning it to the mixing machine for further beating. If the room is warm, have eggs cool when they are added.

3. Once the eggs are incorporated, add the sifted dry ingredients, alternating with the liquid ingredients. Continue to mix until the batter is very smooth.

It is not necessary to divide the dry and liquid ingredients into exact thirds, but they should be added, alternately, to the batter in three batches. Scrape down the bottom and sides of the bowl to be sure that the finished batter is perfectly blended. The finished batter should be extremely smooth and light, with no trace of lumps.

If you are adding fruits, nuts, or other ingredients, they should be incorporated according to the recipe or formula you have selected.

4. Pour the batter into pans that have been greased and floured or lined with parchment paper.

Bake the batter until the cake springs back when pressed lightly with a fingertip and the edges have begun to shrink from the pan's sides. Tests for doneness may vary from one type of item to another, but in general a wooden skewer inserted near the center of the item should come out clean.

5. Remove the cake from the oven and the pan, and cool it properly before serving and/or storing.

Specific items may require special handling at this point, but a general rule is this: Allow the cake, muffin, or quickbread to cool briefly still in the pan, then unmold it onto a rack and allow it to continue to cool to room temperature.

FIGURE 12-13 Glazes

(1) Brushing pound cake with apricot glaze.

(2) Ladling on confectioners' sugar glaze.

The crust of these products is usually slightly darker than the interior. The higher proportion of eggs, butter, and sugar causes this browning action. The cake should rise evenly, without a noticeable center hump or dip. If the cake has been properly mixed, it should not have tunnels or air pockets.

At this point, many items may be given a glaze, frosting, or other coating. Figure 12-13 shows a pound cake being glazed.

The Two-Stage Method

This technique is used to prepare what are referred to as "high-ratio cakes." This means that the weight of the sugar given in the recipe is either equal to or greater than the weight of the flour. In order for these cakes to be successfully prepared, it is necessary to use an emulsified shortening.

A high-ratio cake has a tender texture, a fine crumb, and excellent keeping qualities. The sugar acts as a moisturizing agent, and prevents the cake from becoming stale and dry too rapidly.

Mise en Place

Refer to the basic mise en place for the straight mixing method, earlier in this chapter.

Method

1. Place all of the sifted dry ingredients in the bowl of a mixer.

2. Add all of the shortening and approximately half of the liquid to the dry ingredients, and mix them using the paddle attachment, at a low speed. The batter should be smoothly blended but stiff and fairly thick.

3. Combine the eggs with the remaining liquid ingredients and blend them with a whip to a smooth consistency. Add this mixture to the batter in two or three parts.

Mix the batter well between additions and remember to scrape the sides and bottom of the bowl in order to blend the batter smoothly. This process should usually be accomplished in 3 minutes of actual mixing time.

The characteristics of the finished baked item will depend a great deal on how the batter is handled during mixing. Overmixing can result in cakes that have a rapid initial rise, only to collapse as they continue baking. Under mixed batters may not rise evenly, or they may develop large tunnels or air pockets.

4. After all of the wet ingredients have been incorporated, increase the speed of the mixer to medium and mix the batter for another 3 minutes.

It is important to scrape the bowl down repeatedly during this process. This is the only way to be certain that the batter is properly and fully blended.

5. Scale the batter as desired and place it into prepared pans. Bake the cake at an appropriate temperature, usually 350°F (176°C).

These cakes are baked until the surface of the cake springs back when it is lightly pressed with a fingertip. The top crust should be lightly browned, with an even, uncracked surface. The texture and crumb throughout the cake should be quite fine and very even, with no evidence of air pockets or tunnels. When properly prepared and baked, the taste of the cake should reflect the dominant flavoring ingredients (butter, vanilla, or chocolate, for instance).

Cool the cake completely before going on to fill, frost, or decorate.

The Foaming Method

A foam of whole eggs, yolks, or whites provides the structure for genoise, angel food cake, and chiffon cakes, and some special small cakes or cookies, such as madeleines and ladyfingers. These extremely delicate cakes are also quite resilient; in some cases, cakes made by this method may be rolled, as in the classic holiday dessert, *bûche de Noël.*

There are two versions of the foaming method. In one method, used for genoise, the eggs and sugar are heated before they are beaten into a foam. In the other, used for angel food and chiffon cakes, a basic meringue is prepared using just egg whites. In the method outlined below, requirements for angel food and chiffon cakes are given as variations of the genoise technique.

The foaming method is also used for preparing meringue, a mixture made of egg whites and sugar beaten until thickened. Recipes for meringues can be found in Part IV, Chapter 30.

Mise en Place

Refer to the basic mise en place for the straight mixing method earlier in this chapter for a discussion of ingredients and equipment.

If you are using egg whites as the foundation of a cake, be sure that they are completely free of all traces of yolk.

Method

1. Combine the eggs (whole, yolk, or whites) with sugar in a bowl. Place the bowl over a hot-water bath and heat it to approximately 100°F (38°C) whipping constantly.

This is done to completely dissolve the sugar, increase the volume, and develop a finer grain. Use a whip to blend together the sugar and eggs.

FIGURE 12-14   Foaming Method

(1) Combine eggs and sugar in bowl.

(2) Beating mixture with whip.

(3) Folding in sifted dry ingredients.

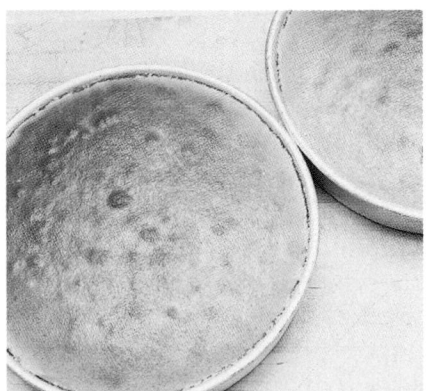

(4) Finished genoise sponge cake.

For angel food and chiffon cakes, especially those made with only egg whites, it may be preferable to omit this stage and start by whipping the room-temperature whites into a thick foam and then gradually incorporating the sugar (see Figure 12-14).

2. Remove the mixture from the heat and beat it with the whip attachment until the eggs form a stable foam that has tripled in volume.

Mixing time is generally 15 minutes on third speed and five minutes on second speed. The mixture should form a ribbon as it falls from the whip.

3. Gently fold in the sifted dry ingredients. This can be done by hand, using a spatula or whisk, or at a low speed using the whip attachment. Do not overwork the batter at this point, as the foam could start to deflate, resulting in a flat, dense product.

4. Add any flavorings or additional ingredients at this point.

If butter or chocolate is required, it should be melted and slightly cooled. Add it after the dry ingredients have been properly incorporated. These ingredients should be warm enough to liquefy, to ensure that they are evenly distributed throughout the batter.

Be sure that any garnish ingredients added to the batter, such as nuts or chips, are small enough to stay trapped in the batter as it bakes.

5. Immediately pour the batter into pans that have been prepared correctly. Bake the batter until the surface springs back when lightly pressed with a fingertip and the cake has begun to shrink from the pan's sides.

6. Remove the cake from the oven and let it cool. Some cakes should be allowed to remain in the pan as they cool to help them retain the correct structure once they are unmolded. Others need to be removed from the pans and allowed to cool on cooling racks.

These cakes should rise evenly during baking. When they are properly baked, they will begin to shrink away from the pan's sides. When cut, the cake should have no large tunnels or air pockets. Cakes prepared by the foaming method are often more spongy than other cakes, although they do have a discernible crumb.

Angel food and chiffon cakes are the most spongy of these types. The limited amount of fats (e.g., butter) used gives these cakes a slightly dry texture, which is why they often are flavored and moistened with simple syrup. Even though there is a large proportion of eggs in foamed cakes, there should not be a marked egg flavor.

Biscuits, Scones, and Soda Breads

Although biscuits, scones, and soda breads are considered quick breads, the technique for preparing their batters is different from the straight mixing method, more similar to that used for either the creaming mixing method, or that used to prepare pie dough or blitz puff pastry.

They are more often referred to as being made from doughs than batters. Their texture will vary, depending upon the mixing method used and the ingredients selected.

Some biscuits, are light and cakey, such as shortcake biscuits made with eggs and buttermilk, mixed by a creaming method. Other biscuits are flakier, because the shortening is rubbed, not creamed, into the dough. These biscuits will separate easily into layers once baked.

Pastry Doughs for Pies and Pastries

All chefs should be able to prepare and work with a variety of doughs including flaky and mealy pie doughs; blitz puff pastry; "rolled-in" doughs such as classic puff pastry, croissant, and Danish doughs; phyllo dough and pâte à choux. These doughs are certainly not retained for exclusive use in the bakeshop. They are used as components in such savory dishes as cheese straws or pot pies. Phyllo dough is frequently used to make savory strudels and turnovers, and such special items as spanakopita or beurrecks.

Cookies, including shortbreads and tuiles, are important elements in many of the more elaborate plated desserts and cakes you might want to offer on your dessert menu. You may want to use them to decorate cakes you purchase from elsewhere, if you do not make the majority of your own desserts. This

FIGURE 12-15   Pie Dough

(1) Combining flour and fat.

(2) Flaky pie dough.

(3) Mealy pie dough.

is one way to make sure that your dessert menu is not exactly the same as the restaurant down the street.

Basic Pie Dough

Basic pie dough is often called 3–2–1 dough, because it is composed of three parts flour, two parts fat, and one part water (by weight). When properly made, the crust is flaky and crisp. This dough is also referred to a pâte brisée.

Pie dough may be referred to as either "flaky" or "mealy." The difference has to do with how the fat or shortening is incorporated into the flour. When the shortening is allowed to remain in large pieces, the finished pie dough will separate easily into layers, hence the descriptive term, flaky. When the fat is worked more thoroughly into the flour, the result will be a pie crust with a very small flake. It will be more similar to a shortbread or cookie dough, with short fine grain referred to as mealy.

Mise en Place

1. Assemble all ingredients.

Many formulas suggest the use of pastry flour to keep the dough tender. Since it has a tendency to clump together, pastry flour must be properly sifted. Special flours may also be used to prepare a variety of pastry doughs and cookies, according to

the specific recipe. In some instances, notably the dough for Linzertortes, the flour is partially replaced by ground toasted nuts.

The type of fat selected will have an effect on the finished item. Lard is a traditional choice among some chefs (and talented home cooks as well). Hydrogenated vegetable shortenings are a common choice, and they should be chilled for best results. Butter is often used for its flavor. If you do use butter, remember that it contains a small but significant quantity of moisture (water). You should adjust the formula slightly to account for that. Cream cheese or sour cream may be required in some doughs. They contain a good deal of fat, which will affect the amount of other fats used in the dough. The amount of fat in the overall formula should be decreased if these ingredients are used.

The liquid used in pie doughs is customarily water, but milk or cream may also be used for very tender crusts. In some cases, the liquid should be very cold to achieve the proper flaky texture in the finished item. It is a good idea in some formulas—notably for pie doughs—to completely dissolve the salt in the liquid to ensure that it will be evenly distributed throughout.

When sugar is added to the dough, it will also have an effect, changing not only the flavor but also the texture and color of the baked dough. This dough is known as *pâte sucrée*. Eggs give doughs a golden color and a firmer texture. Refer to the formulas in Part IV of this book for specific quantities.

FIGURE 12-16 Rolling Pie Crust

(1) Roll with pin in one direction on a diagonal.

(2) Switch hands and roll in the opposite direction.

2. Assemble all equipment necessary.

This type of dough can be prepared by hand or in a mixer with a paddle or dough hook. In addition to a variety of bowls, you will also need a rolling pin, pastry cutters, crimpers, knives or scissors, a brush to apply egg wash, and pie or tart pans.

Method

1. Combine the flour and the fat.

Cut the fat into the dough either by hand, by using a mixer with a paddle attachment, or with a pastry knife (see Figure 12-15). For flaky pie dough, leave the fat pieces rather large, about the size of marbles. For mealy pie dough, continue to blend the mixture until it resembles a coarse meal and has begun to take on a slightly yellow color.

2. Add the cold water all at once; mix it quickly into the flour-and-fat mixture.

Keep mixing just until a shaggy mass forms. It is not necessary to create a completely homogeneous dough at this point. In fact, for flaky pie dough, you may be startled at first to see large lumps of shortening or butter still visible. This is desirable, and not a matter for concern.

3. Gather the dough into a smooth ball and chill it until it is firm.

You may have to knead the dough very briefly by hand to get it gathered into a smooth ball. A few turns ought to be sufficient. Any more and you may warm the dough too much. Proper chilling allows the dough to relax and also firms up the fat.

4. Turn the chilled dough onto a floured work surface. Scale the dough into the correct size.

As a general rule, you will need about one ounce of pie dough for every inch of the pan's diameter, plus an additional ounce or two to allow for an adequate overhang. If the dough is extremely cold and hard, you may need to give it a little time to soften very slightly.

5. Using even strokes, roll the dough into the desired thickness and shape.

Turn it occasionally to produce an even shape and to keep it from sticking to the work surface (see Figure 12-16).

Dust the working surface very lightly with flour, if necessary, as you work. Try to avoid adding a lot of flour. This will affect the quality of the baked dough. Work from the center toward the edges, rolling in different directions. Try not to let the rolling pin run off the edges of the dough.

Preparing Pies and Tarts

Although pies and tarts are alike in terms of the doughs and fillings that are used, there are some differences. Pies are generally double-crusted (having top and bottom crusts) and are baked in a relatively deep pan with sloping sides to accommodate large amounts of filling. Tarts are usually prepared in thin, straight-sided pans, often with removable bottoms. Tarts (and tartlets) most often have a single crust and are not as deep as pies.

Lining a Pie Plate or Tart Mold

The dough should be rolled out in a circle that is large enough to fit into the pan, covering the bottom and sides, with an inch or so of overhang (see Figure 12-17). Brush away all flour from the upper surface, then fold the dough in half, and brush away any excess flour on the bottom.

With the dough still folded in half or draped over the rolling pin, transfer the dough to a pan and fit it gently into the pan's corners. Use a ball of scrap dough to press out any air pockets. Trim away the excess dough. At this point, the pie is ready to fill, or you may want to bake the crust "blind." Both procedures are outlined below.

Baking Blind

The procedure for preparing a prebaked pie shell is known as baking blind. The dough is prepared, rolled out, and fitted into the pan. The dough is pierced in several places with the tines of a fork (known as docking) to prevent blisters from forming in the dough as it bakes.

The pastry is then covered with parchment paper and an empty pie pan is set on top of the paper (this is known as "double panning"). The pans are placed upside down in the oven. This procedure prevents the dough from shrinking back down the pan's edges and keeps it from blistering. The dough is baked in a moderate oven until it is set, appears dry, and has a light golden color.

Another method is to place a sheet of parchment paper over the dough after docking and then fill it with pie weights or dried beans before baking.

Once the shell is baked, it may be coated with melted chocolate or an apricot glaze to prevent the crust from becoming soggy. This also adds additional flavor to the finished pie or tart. Be sure however, that the flavor you introduce is appropriate to the particular item.

Fillings for Pies and Tarts

Most fruit fillings and some custard fillings for American-style pies are added to the pie crust be-

FIGURE 12-17 Lining a Pie Plate with the Bottom Crust

(1) Transferring bottom pie crust into pan.

(2) A scrap of dough is used to gently press the dough into the pan's corners.

fore baking. Some special tarts (a jam-filled linzertorte, for instance) are also filled before baking.

Other pies and tarts are made by first prebaking the crust and then adding a filling. Cream fillings, such as a pastry cream, Bavarian or a mousse, are usually added to prebaked crusts. Fresh-fruit or cream-filled tarts are also generally made with prebaked crusts.

Fruit-filled pies and tarts may be uncooked or cooked, depending upon the type of fruit you are using—fresh, frozen, or dried. Thickeners may be added to the fruit to tighten the filling, giving it additional body and making the finished product easier to slice into portions. Toasted breadcrumbs may also be used to trap the juices and prevent the bottom crust from becoming soggy. For filling recipes, refer to Part IV, Chapter 30, of this book.

Topping Pies and Tarts

Many pies and tarts will receive a topping of some sort. There are many possibilities, including a

FIGURE 12-18 Preparing a Lattice Top

(1) Cut even strips of pie dough.

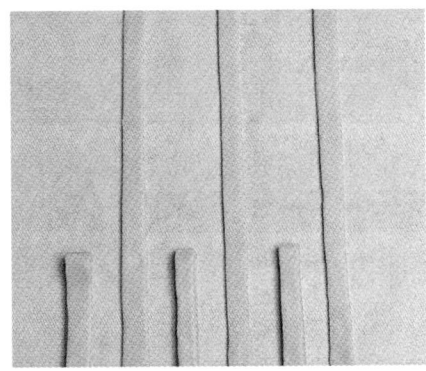

(2) Lay out vertical strips, folding back every other one.

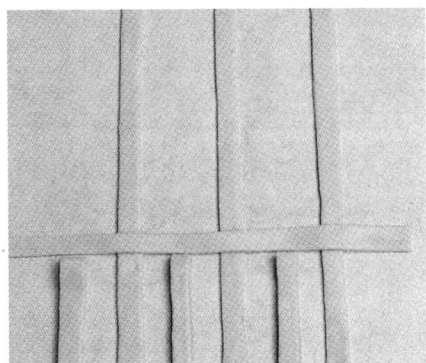

(3) Lay in a horizontal strip.

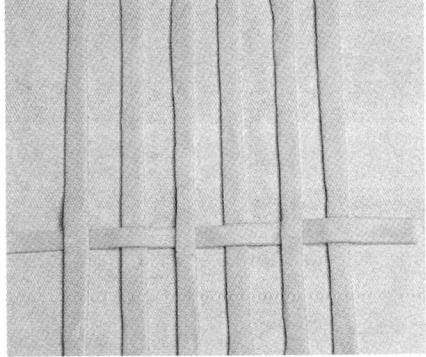

(4) Unfold vertical strips to create lattice. Repeat until all horizontal strips are interwoven

(5) The lattice is ready to transfer to the filled pie.

(6) The cherry pie is ready to bake.

standard top crust, a lattice top, or a crumb topping. Other topping choices include meringues, whipped cream, or glazes.

To make a top crust, roll out the dough in the same manner as for the bottom crust. You will need slightly less dough for the top layer than the bottom, however. Cut slashes or a circular vent in the top crust to allow steam to escape. Eggwash the edge of the bottom layer or brush it lightly with water or milk to help seal the bottom and top crusts together. Pinch or cut away any excess dough, and finally, turn the edges and crimp or flute to seal.

Brush the top crust very lightly with egg wash if desired, or sprinkle it with sugar. You may opt to decorate the pie with cutouts made from scraps of dough. Brush both the tops and bottoms of these decorations so that they will stick well.

Lattice tops are made by cutting even strips of pie dough, and arranging them in a basketweave pattern. For the most evenly spaced lattice, you can use the method demonstrated in Figure 12-18.

Another common pie topping is a meringue, which is piped onto the pie in a decorative pattern or simply mounded and peaked. Meringues are quickly browned in a very hot oven. If properly applied, they should not lift away from the filling, nor should there be visible moisture beads on the meringue's surface.

Fresh-fruit tarts are generally brushed with a glaze, such as apricot, to enhance their appearance and extend their shelf life.

Baking Pies and Tarts

Filled and trimmed pies and tarts should be placed on sheet pans and baked at a high temperature until the dough is browned. To enhance the finished product's appearance, milk or an egg wash may be brushed on the dough to make a shiny, darker, and perhaps golden (if egg yolk is used) surface.

Roll-In Doughs

Danish, croissant, and puff pastry doughs are used to prepare a number of special pastries. These are considered by many to be among the most technically advanced and time-consuming doughs to prepare correctly. Proper mixing methods, rolling techniques, and temperature control are important in order to produce doughs that are flaky and delicate after baking. Pastries based on these doughs, especially those made from puff pastry, are often referred to as French pastries.

The techniques for preparing these three doughs are similar. Danish and croissant doughs use yeast, but puff pastry (pâte feuilletée) does not include an added leavener. In all three, the dough is layered with butter (referred to as a "roll-in") in such a manner that several layers are produced after the dough is properly folded and rolled.

Phyllo dough, though itself not considered a roll-in dough, is also discussed here. A very lean dough is prepared, kneaded, and stretched into very thin sheets. Before the dough is used, it is frequently brushed with melted butter. The effect is similar to that created by the layers of butter in laminated doughs.

Excellent-quality doughs can be purchased, usually as frozen sheets. This makes is possible to create special Danish and other pastries, especially in operations where space is too limited to support full-scale pastry production. To use the frozen doughs, allow the dough to thaw in the refrigerator before rolling, cutting, shaping, and baking.

Mise en Place

1. Assemble all ingredients necessary to prepare the dough.

The ingredients for puff pastry are few: butter or shortening, flour, and water. Croissant dough and Danish doughs are both made from a yeast-raised dough and a roll-in, made from butter or shortening blended with flour.

FIGURE 12-19   Blitz Puff Pastry

(1) Combining ingredients for dough.

(2) Blending into rough dough.

(3) Gathering dough into ball.

(4) Rolling dough into rectangle.

FIGURE 12-20
Initial Three-Fold (Letter-Fold) Blitz.

FIGURE 12-21 Blitz Puff Pastry

(1) Book-fold blitz.

(2) Repeating book-fold.

The proper mixing methods for the basic roll-in dough components have been discussed in earlier sections of this chapter. Blitz puff pastry is made in the same way as flaky pie dough. Classic puff pastry, croissant and Danish dough are prepared in the same way as yeast dough. All three of these doughs include a separately prepared "roll-in" made by working together butter, shortening, or a combination of the two with flour.

2. Assemble all equipment necessary.

These doughs can be mixed by hand or by using a mixer. A work surface, rolling pin, knives, or special cutters are also required. Sheet trays are necessary, as is an adequate refrigerator.

Method for Blitz Puff Pastry

1. Combine ingredients and blend into a rough dough. Turn the dough onto a floured surface, gather into a ball, and dust lightly with flour (see Figure 12-19).

2. Roll dough out into a rectangle, and fold into thirds (a letter-fold—see Figure 12-20). If the dough is not cool, stop at this point and let it firm in the refrigerator.

3. Turn dough so the longest edge is parallel to the edge of the work surface. Roll the dough out again into a rectangle, and make a "book-fold" as follows (see Figure 12-21):

Fold the narrow edges of the rectangle inward until they meet in the center of the rectangle. Now fold the rectangle in half again, as shown in the accompanying photographs. Repeat the book-fold another three or four times, allowing the dough sufficient time to firm between rolling out the dough and folding it.

Method for Doughs with Separate Roll-Ins

1. Working on a floured surface, roll the prepared dough out into a rectangle, about ½-inch thick. It should be cool but not stiff. Use a brush to remove any excess flour from the dough (see Figure 12-22).

2. Roll out the roll-in between two pieces of parchment paper to form a rectangle that will cover two-thirds of the dough; it should be the same approximate thickness (½-inch) and consistency as the dough.

3. Position the roll-in on the dough so that one-third of the dough is uncovered and there is a one-half-inch border on the other three sides. Fold the uncovered third of the dough over the roll-in. Next,

FIGURE 12-22 Classic Puff Roll-In

(1) Rolling dough into rectangle.

(2) Removing excess flour from dough.

(3) Roll-in encased in dough.

(4) Marking the number of turns completed.

(5) Refrigerating the dough before continuing to roll out.

dough is worked long enough for the butter (or other fat) to become warm, it will be absorbed into the dough, instead of remaining in a separate layer. This will reduce the number of layers and could give the finished product a rubbery or gummy texture.

To work with these doughs after they are completely prepared, or with purchased frozen doughs that have been gently thawed, observe the following guidelines.

fold the opposite third on top of the dough. The dough should appear stacked in the five layers, with alternating layers of dough and roll-in. Use your fingertips to weld the seams together.

Once the roll-in has been encased in the dough, it is rolled out and given a three- or letter-fold. This initial fold is then followed with the recommended number of three or four folds. Be sure to brush away any excess flour from the dough. Left on the dough, this flour might interfere with proper layer formation. Once the dough has received all the necessary turns, it should be allowed to rest under refrigeration overnight before rolling, shaping, and baking.

Rolling and Shaping the Finished Dough

It is essential to completely chill the dough between the rolling out and folding stages. If the

• Keep the dough chilled, taking out only the amount to be worked with at a given time. If the dough is too warm, the flakiness of the finished product will be reduced.

• Use a sharp knife when shaping or cutting the dough. Clean cuts will ensure that the baked item rises evenly. This is especially important for high, straight-sided items such as *vol-au-vent* and *bouchée*.

• Do not run the roller over the dough's edge; this will destroy the layers.

• Chill puff-pastry items before baking them. This keeps the layers of dough and roll-in separate, ensuring the best rise and flakiness in the finished product.

• Save puff-pastry scraps. They can be piled together and rolled out to use for items such as *napoléons* where a substantial rise is not necessary.

FIGURE 12-23 Pâte à Choux

(1) Pâte à choux in progress.

(2) Ready to come off the heat.

(3) Adding eggs gradually.

(4) Working the dough.

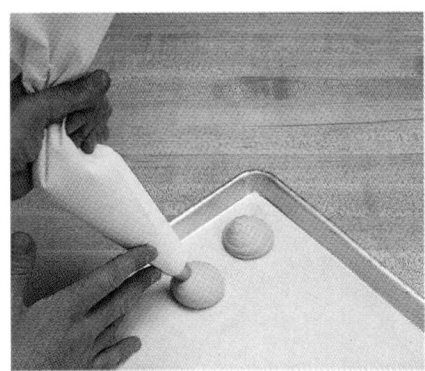

(5) Piping dough onto sheet pan.

Nut- and seed-paste fillings can be purchased, as in the case of almond paste and poppy-seed paste.

It is generally best to allow filled and shaped pastry doughs some time to firm or chill again before they are baked. For the best results, bake the pastries at the correct temperature; usually parchment-lined baking sheets are used.

Handling Method for Phyllo Dough

This dough should be covered lightly with plastic wrap and dampened towels as you work with it. Otherwise, it can become brittle and shatter. Melted butter, bread crumbs, or a combination of both are spread evenly over the dough to keep the layers separate as they bake. This creates a flaky finished product. A brush or spray bottle is generally used to apply the butter or oil in an even coat.

Fillings for Pastries

There are a number of fillings that are appropriate for pastries made from Danish, croissant, and puff-pastry doughs, including fresh or cooked fruits, chocolate, custards and other creams, jams, and savory ingredients, such as cheese or sliced ham. Recipes for some commonly used fillings are included in Part IV, Chapter 30, of this book.

Pâte à Choux

Pâte à choux is made by combining water, butter, flour, and eggs into a smooth batter. When properly prepared and baked, it will expand during baking, creating a delicate shell with an essentially hollow center. Pâte à choux is soft enough so that the chef can use a pastry bag to pipe it into different shapes. Among the most common shapes are cream puffs, *profiteroles*, and *éclairs*.

Mise en Place

1. Assemble and prepare all ingredients.

This includes the basic components: water, or a combination of water and milk, butter or shortening, eggs, and flour. Sugar, ground spices, or grated cheese may be added according to specific recipes.

2. Assemble all equipment.

The dough is mixed in a pan over direct heat. The eggs can be incorporated with a spoon or a mixer fitted with a paddle attachment. Pastry bags or parchment cones are used to pipe out the pâte à choux onto parchment-lined sheet pans.

Method

1. Bring the liquid and butter to a full boil. Add the flour and cook it until the mixture pulls away from the pan, forming a ball (see Figure 12-23.)

2. Place the dough in the bowl of a mixer. Use the paddle attachment to mix it for a few minutes, allowing the dough to cool slightly. This will prevent the dough's heat from cooking the eggs as they are worked into the mixture.

3. Add the eggs gradually, in three or four additions, working the dough until it is smooth each time. Scrape down the bowl's sides and bottom as necessary. Continue to do so until all the eggs are incorporated. Mix the dough just until a smooth heavy paste forms. Do not overmix.

4. The dough is ready to use at this point. It should be piped onto sheet pans lined with parchment paper, according to the desired result.

To properly bake pâte à choux, begin the baking process at a high temperature (375 to 400°F/190 to 204°C). Reduce the heat to 250°F (120°C) once the pâte à choux begins to take on color. Continue to bake until they are golden brown, and there are no visible beads of moisture on their exteriors.

Remove the items from the oven as soon as they are fully baked. Slash eclairs, cream puffs, and other large items with a sharp knife to allow the steam to escape. This will ensure that the shells remain crisp.

If the item is to be filled, slice it open and pull away any loose dough from the interior. Spoon or pipe the filling into the shell. Glaze or sauce as desired.

Creams, Bavarians, and Mousses

Vanilla Sauce

This sauce has been included in the creams section of this chapter, since it is the foundation of many other dessert items, including ice cream, mousses, Bavarians, and a buttercream. A baked custard is based on the same ingredients, combined in the same ratio as a vanilla sauce. Instead of stirring the sauce as it cooks over direct heat, a custard is placed in an appropriate mold and baked in a bain-marie until it is firmly set. As a dessert sauce, it is a classic accompaniment to soufflés and other hot desserts, such as steamed puddings.

Mise en Place

1. Assemble all ingredients for the sauce.

Differences do exist between various vanilla sauce formulas. Some recipes may include whole milk, whereas others will call for heavy cream, light cream, or a combination of cream and milk. Some recipes will use only egg yolks; others will use whole eggs or a ratio of whole eggs to egg yolks.

Vanilla sauce can be flavored by adding a number of other ingredients, including liqueurs, cordials, chocolate, or fruits.

2. Assemble all equipment necessary to prepare the sauce.

Since this is a delicate sauce that can curdle easily if it is allowed to overheat, select a heavy gauge pot, a double-boiler, or a bain-marie. The sauce should be prepared in a nonreactive pot, such as stainless steel, to prevent it from becoming even slightly gray. Wooden spoons are suggested for stirring the sauce as it cooks. A fine chinois or cheesecloth is used to strain the sauce into a clean container. Prepare an ice or cold water bath to quickly cool the sauce once it is cooked.

Method

1. Combine the eggs with half of the sugar in a stainless steel bowl. Blend them well, using a whip. (See Figure 12-24.)

FIGURE 12-24 Vanilla Sauce

(1) Blend eggs and sugar, and heat milk or cream.

(2) Tempering egg-and-sugar mixture with hot milk.

(3) Adding the remainder of the egg mixture.

(4) Creating soft "gel" that will coat wooden spoon.

(5) Adding desired flavoring.

5. Add any desired flavoring ingredients at this point. For specific suggestions, refer to the recipes in Part IV, Chapter 29, of this book.

6. Once the sauce has reached the correct consistency, strain it immediately through a fine chinois or cheesecloth into a bain-marie or other container set in an ice water bath. Wrap or cover tightly, if the cream is to be stored for any length of time.

2. Combine the milk with half of the sugar in a large pot and heat it just to the boiling point. If you are using a vanilla bean to flavor the sauce, it should be added now, to steep in the milk as it heats. Be sure to keep an eye on the milk as it heats. There is a great likelihood that it will boil over as it nears the boiling point.

3. Temper the egg and sugar mixture with the hot milk; return it to the pot. Continue to cook the sauce over low heat until it begins to thicken. Stir the sauce constantly to prevent it from overcooking. The sauce should never come to a boil, because egg yolks and whites coagulate well below the boiling point. The idea is to create a soft "gel" that will coat the back of a wooden spoon. The sauce's temperature should not go above 180°F (82°C).

Pastry Cream

Pastry cream (*crème patisserie*) is often required for the production of napoléons, éclairs, and Boston cream pie. It may also be used as a soufflé base or to prepare steamed puddings.

Mise en Place

1. Assemble all ingredients required for pastry cream.

The basic ingredients are quite similar to those used to prepare vanilla sauce: eggs, milk, sugar, and flavoring. In addition, a thickener, such as flour or cornstarch may be required in some formulas.

FIGURE 12-25   Pastry Cream

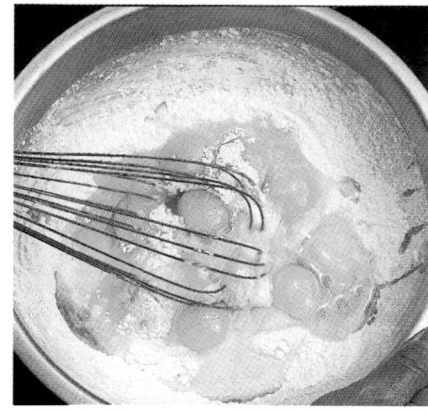

(1) Mixing flour, sugar, and eggs.

(2) Passing the whip through the cream.

(3) Adding whole butter.

FIGURE 12-26   Preparing Apricot Soufflé

(1) First addition of beaten whites to puréed apricots.

(2) Blending purée and whites with a whip.

(3) Folding final additions of egg whites in with a rubber spatula.

(4) Level the top of filled soufflé molds.

(5) Run your thumb around the dish's rim to promote an even rise during baking.

2. Assemble all equipment required for pastry cream. Refer to the information regarding vanilla sauce above.

Method

1. Mix the flour, half of the sugar, and the whole eggs together in one bowl and blend them to a smooth consistency (see Figure 12-25.)

2. Bring the milk and the remaining sugar to a boil. If a vanilla bean is used to flavor the sauce, it may be added at this point.

3. Use part of the milk mixture to temper the egg mixture. Be sure to blend it thoroughly at this point, so that there will not be any lumps of starch in the finished pastry cream. Return the tempered eggs to the pot and continue to cook the mixture until it reaches a full boil. Stir or whip the pastry cream constantly while it cooks. It will become very thick; when the whip passes through the cream, the wires will leave traces.

4. After removing the pastry cream from the heat, add flavorings and whole butter.

Remove the cream to a clean bowl and cool it quickly over an ice bath. Some chefs sprinkle sugar on the cream's surface to prevent the formation of a skin; others dot it with additional butter or place a sheet of plastic wrap or parchment paper directly on the surface.

Preparing Dessert Soufflés

Classic dessert soufflés are made by combining a pastry cream (plain or flavored) with beaten egg whites. This mixture is then baked in a hot oven until the soufflé expands and is just barely cooked. As an alternative to a pastry cream base, a purée of cooked or raw fruits may be used, as demonstrated in the method for an apricot soufflé (see Figure 12-26).

The soufflé should rise evenly, without requiring a collar. Because soufflés are fragile, they must be served immediately upon removing them from the oven. This means that both the kitchen and wait staffs need to be completely prepared with a total mise en place—including all sauces, garnishes,

serving pieces, and a tray—so that there is no delay in taking the finished soufflé to the guest. Careful timing and clear communication are critical.

Bavarian Creams

These delicate creams are made by stabilizing a vanilla sauce with gelatin, and then lightening the mixture with whipped cream and beaten egg whites (see Figure 12-27). They may be used on their own or as a filling for a variety of pastries, tortes, pies, and cakes.

Bavarians are incredibly versatile and lend themselves well to a wide range of flavors. Among the possible flavorings are various fruits (raspberries, bananas, and mangoes, to name a small sampling), chocolate, nuts, and many liqueurs, such as Grand Marnier or Kahlúa.

FIGURE 12-27 Bavarian Cream

(1) An alternate folding sequence is to add the purée to the beaten whites.

(2) Folding gently until mixture appears homogeneous.

FIGURE 12-28   White Chocolate Mousse

(1) Cooking eggs.

(2) Adding syrup.

(3) Folding in melted white chocolate.

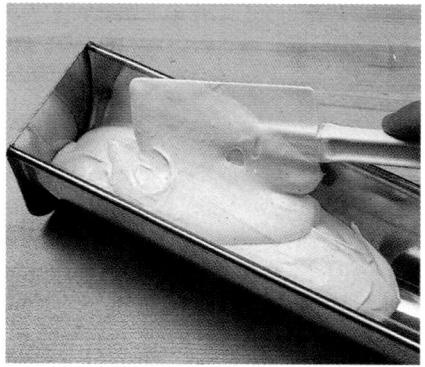

(4) Filling mold.

(5) Finished plated dessert.

Mousse

Although quite similar to a Bavarian, a mousse (see Figure 12-28) usually does not contain gelatin as a stabilizer. For the best texture in the finished mousse, the eggs and sugar are beaten to a foam over a hot water bath. They should be allowed to reach at least 165°F(74°C) to be sure that the finished mousse will remain wholesome. The cooked eggs are then beaten until they form ribbons.

Flavoring ingredients are added, and then the mousse is lightened with whipped cream. A well-prepared mousse may often become the signature dessert for a restaurant. The presentation may be varied by using different containers, such as tuile cups, hollowed fruits, or special molds or glasses.

Buttercreams

Buttercreams are made by several methods. They are referred to as Italian, French, German, and Swiss, depending upon their ingredients. Most versions follow one of two basic methods:

- A pastry cream or vanilla sauce is prepared, flavored, and allowed to cool. Softened butter is whipped into this base.

- The second method requires a syrup made by heating sugar and water. The hot syrup is beaten into eggs (whole, yolks, or whites) to make a meringue or foam, and then softened butter is added gradually, as shown in the step-by-step photos for Italian buttercream (see Figure 12-29).

Refer also to the recipes for buttercreams in Part IV of this book.

Sauces and Glazes

The sauces described here are used to add flavor, moisture, and eye appeal to various desserts. In addition to their role as a dessert adornment, they are also used as a basic component or ingredient in other items, as we have already seen in the previous discussion of vanilla sauce. Other sauces and glazes include chocolate sauce, sugar-based items, such as simple syrup, butterscotch and caramel, and various fruits sauces. Sabayons and "curds" are also included here.

FIGURE 12-29 Preparing Italian Buttercream

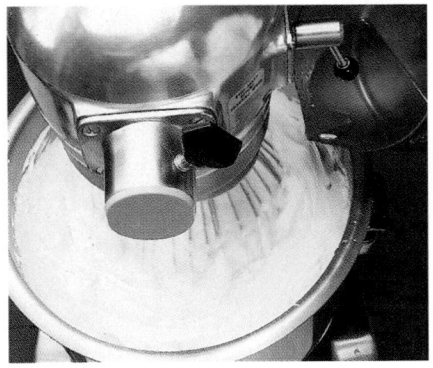

(1) The meringue is whipped to full volume.

(2) Add softened butter to the meringue.

(3) The finished buttercream.

Chocolate Sauce

The success of any chocolate glaze or sauce depends primarily on the chocolate's quality. Chocolate must be melted carefully to prevent it from scorching or becoming grainy. Any liquid that is to be added should be incorporated carefully. A small amount of water can cause chocolate to "seize" or stiffen.

There are numerous formulas for chocolate sauces and syrups, some of which are found in Part IV of this book. Ganache, made by heating chocolate with cream and butter, can also be used as a sauce, a glaze, or to prepare truffles. Once shaped, truffles can be rolled in cocoa powder or dipped in chocolate.

Fondant

Fondant is basically a sugar-and-water syrup that has been cooked to the correct temperature, cooled, and worked repeatedly until it is smooth, creamy, opaque, and thick. Although it is made in some bakeshops, good-quality fondant can be purchased from purveyors.

For use as a glaze, fondant must be heated to approximately 105°F (40°C) and poured evenly over the product. The product may also be dipped directly into the fondant. The fondant provides a protective coating that is especially beneficial for cakes that need to be held or that could dry out easily—petits fours, for example.

Syrups and Glazes

Simple syrup (see Figure 12-30) is make by cooking together sugar and water, along with any flavorings you like, until the sugar is completely dissolved. This preparation is then used to moisten layer cakes or genoise, or it may be used to poach fruits. It has many uses, and can be prepared in quantity and held under refrigeration for extended periods.

Glazes made from preserves or jellies are often brushed onto fresh fruit tarts or tartlets to give the fruit a sheen. The glazes also help to prevent the darkening of fruits that might discolor in the presence of air. The jelly or preserves should be heated gently to a liquid state, and then strained if necessary to remove seeds or fibers. The glaze should be applied lightly with a pastry brush.

FIGURE 12-30
Cooking Simple
Syrup

There are other glazes that may be used with baked items. Many are made by stirring together confectioner's sugar with some water and possibly a flavoring, such as an extract or concentrated fruit purée. These should be room temperature, or possibly warm, so that they flow easily when applied to the baked item.

A pound cake in Figure 12-13, can be glazed first with apricot preserves and then with a confectioner's sugar glaze.

Fruit Sauces

These sauces may be made from a variety of fruits, which may be fresh, frozen, or dried. Some of the most popular fruit sauces include fresh berry coulis, in varieties such as raspberry and strawberry, and compotes made by simmering dried fruits, such as apricots, currants, and raisins.

Fresh berry sauces or puréed fruit compotes can be used as a base for flourless soufflés, as noted above. They may also be used to flavor Bavarian creams, buttercreams, and other fillings and frostings.

Caramel/Butterscotch Sauces

These sauces are based on a richly flavored sugar syrup that has been allowed to cook to a deep, golden color. If no additional ingredients are added to the caramelized syrup, the mixture can be used to coat the mold for a classic dessert—*crème caramel*. To make a smooth sauce, cream and butter are often added. Butterscotch sauce contains these same ingredients plus a small amount of an acid, such as apple-cider vinegar, to provide its distinctive flavor.

Sabayon (Zabaglione)

This fragile sauce is one of the few dessert sauces that cannot easily be made ahead and held. It is a delicate foam of egg yolks, sugar, and wine, customarily Marsala. The mixture is whipped constantly as it cooks over simmering water until it becomes thick and light.

Sabayon may be flavored as desired. If chocolate is added, the sauce will lose some of its airiness. For this reason, melted chocolate should be stirred in at the very end of the preparation time. Traditionally, a sabayon is served over peeled and sliced fresh fruit or on its own, with delicate cookies. It may also be stabilized with gelatin and used in the same manner as a Bavarian cream.

Fruit Curds

Curds are made in much the same manner as a hollandaise sauce. Egg yolks are cooked together with sugar and a fruit juice or purée over low heat or in a bain-marie. Softened butter is added, and the sauce is allowed to cook until thickened. Unlike a hollandaise, the sauce may be allowed to reach a gentle simmer. Once prepared, the sauce should be cooled rapidly, and kept refrigerated if it will not be used immediately.

This sauce may be used on its own, folded together with whipped cream. It is also used to fill tarts and other pastries.

Frozen Desserts

Frozen desserts have always been extremely popular. The actual production of most of these desserts requires no special equipment beyond the usual assortment of cooking utensils.

Some frozen desserts such as ice creams, gelatos, and sherbets, are made in an ice cream freezer that churns the base mixture to produce a smooth creamy product. This means that the mixture is agitated as it is cooled, incorporating additional air so that the end result is light and smooth, making them easy to eat with a spoon.

Others, such as granité and frozen soufflés, are "still-frozen." This means that the basic mixture is prepared, placed in a mold, and then allowed to freeze. The presence of various ingredients such as sugar and alcohol ensures that the end result will be smooth, light, and not rock-hard. Whipped cream and beaten egg whites will naturally introduce enough air to prevent the frozen soufflés and mousses from becoming too hard.

Frozen Soufflés and Mousses

Frozen soufflés, parfaits, and mousses are made by preparing a mousse or Bavarian cream (as outlined in the section covering creams), and using it to fill an appropriate mold or other container. It is then "still-frozen" until it becomes solid. To give the appearance of a classic hot soufflé, a parchment collar may be attached to the container, so that the mousse or Bavarian appears to have "risen" above the rim of the dish. A frozen soufflé or mousse is often allowed to "temper" briefly in the refrigerator before it is served.

Ice Cream and Gelato

Ice creams and gelato may be made in various ways and with different equipment. Essentially, a vanilla sauce is prepared, flavored, and then chilled. Once it is cooled, it is placed in an ice cream freezer along with appropriate flavorings and garnishes. The freezer is chilled to temperatures below 32°F (0°C), and a paddle churns the custard as it freezes. Gelato is an Italian specialty. It is generally lower in fat than many ice creams, and may be prepared with or without the addition of eggs.

Sorbets/Sherbets

Sorbets are based on liquids, such as fruit juices, wine, or coffee. The liquid is sweetened and may be combined with milk or cream and, in some cases, egg whites. The base mixture is then frozen in the same manner as ice cream. The result is a sorbet with a texture similar to that of ice cream. The far lower percentage of butterfat and absence of egg yolks, however, gives sorbets a more "icy" texture.

Sorbets that are not heavily sweetened and do not, as a rule, contain cream or milk frequently are served between a formal meal's courses as an *intermezzo* ("between the work") to cleanse the palate.

Granité

Granité (or *granita* in Italian) is a special type of frozen dessert. In these "icy" preparations, the base mixture is prepared in the same manner as for a sorbet, although it customarily does not contain any milk, cream, or eggs. The mixture is placed in the freezer and allowed to still-freeze until service. At that time, the granité is scraped to produce large flakes or granules.

Simple Cookies, Candies, and Confections

The practice of offering a small confection at the end of a meal lends a special touch to a guest's dining experience. Truffles, petits fours, and other simple candies can be a mark of distinction between your establishment and others.

Candy-making, especially for fine chocolate, is demanding and can even be quite expensive. The range of confections shown here are simple to prepare, however, even in restaurants where special equipment may not always be on hand:

• Candied citrus peels may be dipped in chocolate.

• A simple nougat mixture, made by blending almonds and sugar with a melted chocolate, is tempered, shaped, and dusted with cocoa powder (see Figure 12-31).

• Flavored fondant is shaped using a mat then dipped in chocolate and simply decorated.

• Nuts may be coated with a caramelized sugar, then glazed with melted chocolate and or cocoa powder (see Figure 12-32).

There are many other examples and recipes you may find suitable for your needs and level of skill.

Preparing Cookies, Petits Fours, and Other Small Pastries

The range of items known as cookies is so large that no single definition is appropriate. The recipes included in Part IV of this book demonstrate the number of different styles possible, including drop, bar, spritz, filled, and icebox cookies.

FIGURE 12-31   Nougat Candies

(1) Working confection on marble.   *(2) Shaping in a plastic-lined form.*   *(3) Coating nougat with cocoa.*

FIGURE 12-32   Chocolate-Covered Almonds

(1) Coating almonds with caramelized sugar.

(2) Covering with chocolate.

FIGURE 12-33   Various Cookies and Petits Fours

In general, cookies should be bite-size. They contain a high percentage of sugar, so the oven temperature must be regulated during baking. Convection ovens, which produce evenly baked items, are especially good for baking many kinds of cookies.

Cookies are often served at receptions, as part of a dessert buffet, or with ice cream or sorbet. An assort-ment of cookies might be presented at the end of a meal, as an appealing "extra." Cookies may be elaborate, with frostings and fillings, or plain (see Figure 12-33). Some cookies—tuiles for example—are used as shells for various fillings (see Figure 12-34).

Tempering Chocolate for Coating

The process of preparing chocolate for glazing or coating items is known as tempering. Chocolate

FIGURE 12-34 Tuiles

(1) Drop the batter onto a prepared baking sheet.

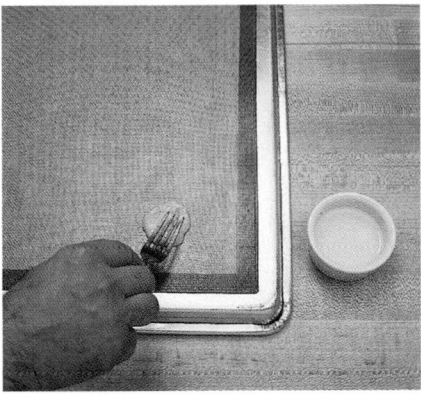

(2) Use the back of a spoon to spread the batter out.

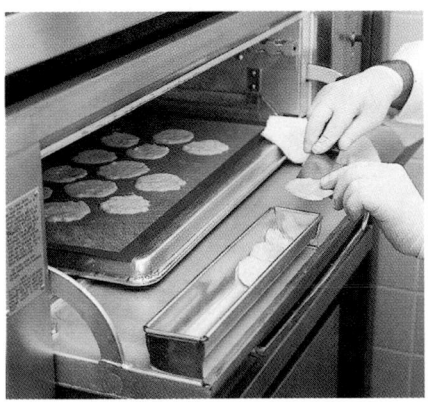

(3) Remove the tuiles from the baking sheet when the edges are browned.

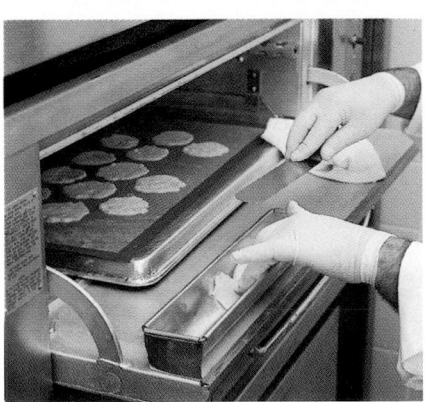

(4) To shape tuiles, lay in a mold and press down while they are still very hot.

contains two distinct types of fat, which melt at different temperatures. In order to ensure that the chocolate will melt smoothly and harden evenly with a good shine, it must be handled carefully.

Method

1. Chop the chocolate coarsely with a chef's knife and place it in a stainless steel bowl. Place the bowl over very low heat or barely simmering water, making sure that no moisture comes in contact with the chocolate. Stir the chocolate occasionally as it melts to keep it at an even temperature throughout (see Figure 12-35.)

2. Continue to heat the chocolate until it reaches a temperature of between 105 to 110°F (40° to 43°C). Use an instant-reading thermometer for the most accurate results.

3. Remove the chocolate from the heat. Add a large piece of unmelted chocolate and stir it in until the temperature drops to approximately 87 to 92°F (30 to 33°C). If the chocolate drops below 85°F (29°C) while working with it, it will be necessary to repeat the steps described here to retemper it. If the chocolate scorches or becomes grainy, it can no longer be used. If any moisture comes in contact with the chocolate as it is being tempered, it will "seize."

Tempered chocolate will coat the back of a spoon with an even layer and then harden into a shiny shell. The item can be either dipped directly into the tempered chocolate with a dipping fork, or placed on a rack over a clean sheet tray and the chocolate poured over it.

(5) Dark chocolate mousse in tuilles.

FIGURE 12-35 Tempering Chocolate

(1) Chopping chocolate coarsely.

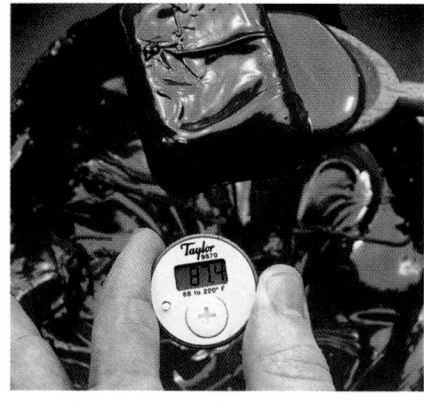

(2) Testing temperature of chocolate.

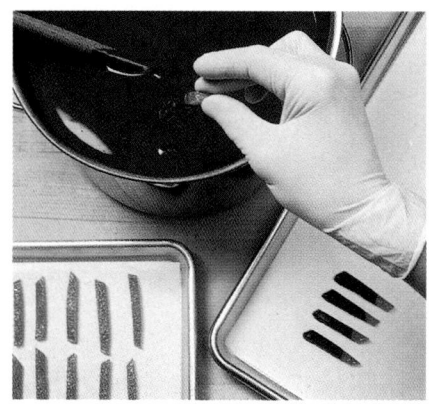

(3) Dipping candied orange peel into the chocolate.

FIGURE 12-36 Fondant

(1) Preparing fondant for candies.

(2) Molding fondant.

(3) Dipping the fondant into the chocolate.

(4) Decorating chocolate-dipped fondant.

Preparing Candies from Fondant

Fondant for candies should be heated to 160°F (70°C). Then it can be molded or shaped as desired. Once cooled, fondant confections can be dipped in chocolate and decorated, as shown in Figure 12-36.

FIGURE 12-37 Parchment Cones

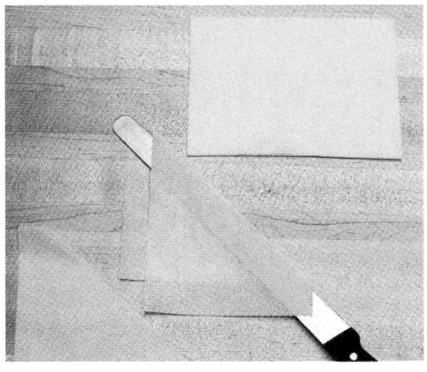

(1) Folding parchment on the diagonal.

(2) Making a pivot point.

(3) Rolling into funnel shape.

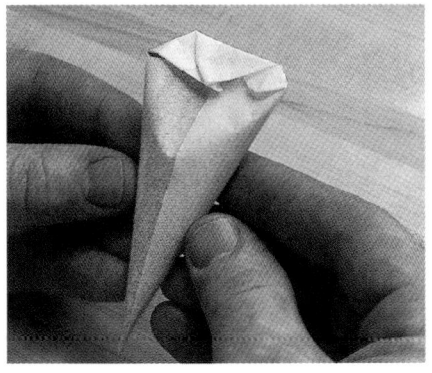

(4) Sealing the filled cone.

(5) Creating small opening.

Special Tools and Techniques for Decorating Pastries and Cakes

There are some tools used to create cakes and tortes that are readily available in virtually any kitchen or bakeshop—pastry bags and parchment cones.

Parchment Cones

Parchment cones are used to decorate pastries with delicate designs of chocolate, fondant, or special piping gels. To prepare a cone, complete the following steps (see Figure 12-37):

1. Fold a sheet of parchment paper on the diagonal, slightly overlapping. Do not form a perfect triangle. Use a nonserrated knife to cut through the fold.

2. Hold the uneven corner between the thumb and forefinger of one hand. Use the other thumb and forefinger to make a "pivot point" by holding the parchment at the diagonal's midpoint.

3. Roll the parchment into a funnel shape, keeping the point closed as the paper is rolled. This may require some practice. It is important to keep the paper taut as it is rolled.

4. When the entire triangle has been rolled into a cone, fold the point on the top so that it is on the interior of the cone.

5. Hold the cone so that the tip is pointing downward, and fill the cone no more than half full. Do not add too much, or it will ooze out of the top. Fold the outer points in toward the cone's center and fold the last corner over the top of the other points, sealing the cone completely.

6. Hold the cone so that the tip is resting on a cutting surface and use scissors or a sharp knife to nick away a small amount of the paper, creating a small opening. The deeper the cut, the larger the opening and, therefore the lines of piping, will be.

When working with a parchment cone, make sure that the seam is on the side of the cone away from you. This will keep the seam from buckling open as you pipe.

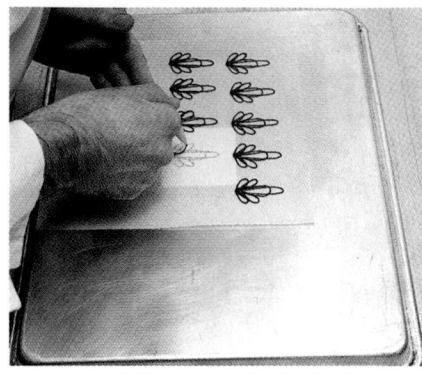

FIGURE 12-38
Sample Design for Tracing

FIGURE 12-39 Pastry Bags

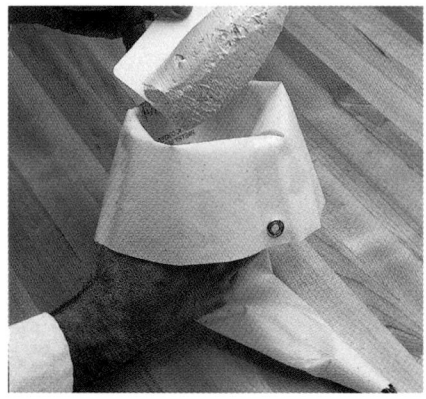

(1) Filling pastry bag.

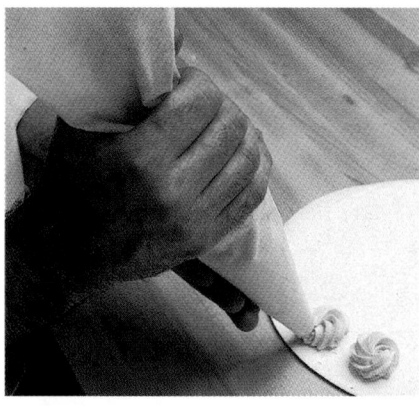

(2) Hand position for piping.

(3) Caring for pastry bag.

Parchment cones are used to create a variety of finely worked designs or filigree work. To prepare decorative filigree, use the following method:

Secure a stencil to the back of a sheet pan, near the center of the pan. Position a parchment sheet over the stencil so that it can be used as a guide for piping the chocolate. The parchment can then be easily slid to a clean spot once the initial design is completed, until the desired amount of designs have been traced onto the sheet (see Figure 12-38). Use your fingers to gently pinch the top of the cone, expressing the chocolate out through the tip. Use the fingertips of your other hand to steady the cone.

Pastry Bags and Tips

Pastry bags are important throughout the kitchen for a number of different applications. To properly fill, use, and care for a bag, use the following procedures (see Figure 12-39):

1. Select the desired tip and position it securely in the pastry bag's opening. A coupler makes it easy to change tips as you work.

2. Fold down the bag's top to create a cuff, then transfer the buttercream or other preparation to the bag with a spatula or spoon. Support the bag with your free hand while filling it.

3. Unfold the bag's cuff, and use one hand to gather together and twist the top of the bag. Press on the bag first to expel any air pockets. Once these have been removed, the bag is ready to use. With one hand, press the buttercream down and out of the bag. Use the other hand to support and guide the bag.

When the design is finished, first release the pressure on the bag, then gently twist the tip while simultaneously lifting it cleanly away from the rosette or other design. This will prevent the formation of tails and threads that could spoil the effect.

4. Remove all the excess buttercream or other filling or frosting from the bag and wash it carefully with warm, soapy water after each use. Turn the bag inside out. Wipe the bag dry with absorbent toweling before storing it to keep it in good condition, safe, and sanitary between uses.

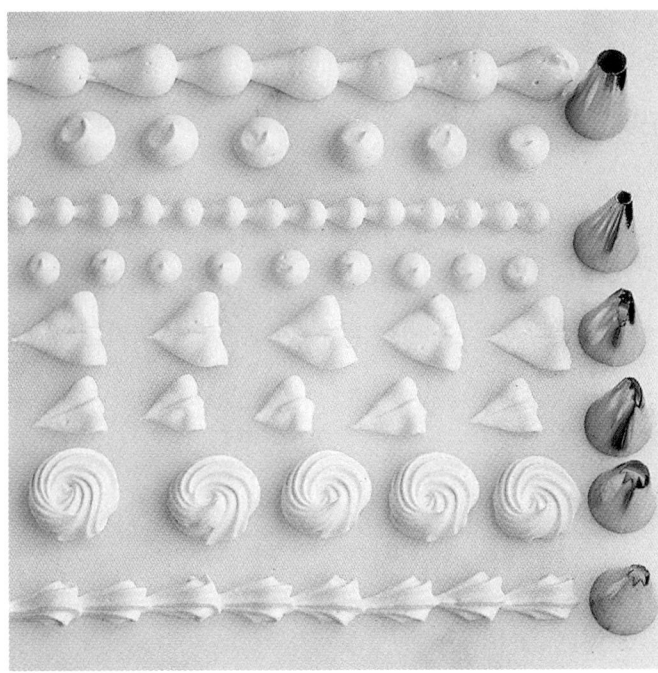

FIGURE 12-40 Various Tips and Their Effects

Various effects can be created using a selection of tips. In Figure 12-40 the top rows 1 and 2 show a border design and individual rosettes made with a plain opening. Rows 3 and 4 show the same technique using a plain tip with a smaller opening. Rows 5 and 6 show the effect of two different-sized leaf tips. Rows 7 and 8 show rosettes made with a star tip and a shell border from the same tip. A number of other tips are available.

Assembling and Decorating Tortes

The elaborate wedding cakes, tortes, and other fancy cakes prepared by bakeshops have a definite place. They are not included here, however, since they represent a very specific type of pastry work. Instead, we will look at the ways that a restaurant can produce beautiful, simple, high-quality cakes and tortes.

1. Prepare all the basic components and have them at the correct temperature. Some will need to

FIGURE 12-41 Tortes

(1) Assembling torte—splitting layers.

(2) Building torte.

(3) Brushing layers with melted jam or preserves.

(4) Adding filling.

(5) Glazing torte.

FIGURE 12-42   Frosting Cake

(1) Adding icing.

(2) Using cake comb to create decorative edge.

(3) The finished cake.

be warmed or held at room temperature in order to spread properly. Others may need to be held under refrigeration (see Figure 12-41.)

2. To separate a cake into layers, use a knife with a long blade to cut the sponge cake horizontally. Be sure to use the entire knife to make the cut. Trim the cake's edges, if necessary, and brush away any loose crumbs.

3. Moisten the layers with simple syrup or brush them with melted jam or preserves. Place the first layer on a cake circle, or in the bottom of a round mold.

If desired, you can cut additional pieces to line the walls of the mold. This will give the finished cake a neat, attractive appearance, as well as making it easier to decorate later on.

4. Spread the filling evenly on each layer, building the cake as you go. You may use a Bavarian cream, as shown here, a mousse, pastry cream, or custards. Add garnish or flavoring ingredients, such as poached or fresh fruit, as you work.

The amount of filling spread between each layers will vary, depending upon the type you select. However, as a general rule, its thickness should not exceed that of the cake layer.

5. Once the final layer has been added and smoothed off, a glaze or topping should be applied evenly. If the glaze is at the correct consistency, it is easy to spread it by tilting it, as shown, or with a spatula.

After the cake is filled and glazed, it can be refrigerated to firm up if necessary before any additional frostings or decorations are applied. A traditional approach to frosting a cake is shown in Figure 12-42.

Set the assembled cake on a turntable. Spread an even layer of icing on the cake's top and sides. Use level, even strokes to smooth it out. Hold the palette knife parallel to the cake's edge and turn the cake into the palette knife to even the coating on the sides. Smooth the top surface once more. Occasionally dip the palette knife into hot water for the smoothest finish. Use a cake comb to create a decorative edge if desired, or use other techniques for decorating the torte:

• Use fine cake crumbs, or sliced or chopped nuts to create an edge for the cake. Gently press them along the cake's bottom. Scatter the crumbs evenly over the top of the cake, if desired.

• Very lightly score the cake's top by pressing the edge of a palette knife into the icing to mark the slices. Place decorations, such as chocolate circles and whipped cream or buttercream rosettes, so that each slice will have a share of the decoration.

Summary

The careful production of hearth-style breads, muffins, cakes, biscuits, and scones permits you to offer an interesting range of baked goods to your guests at every meal. A bountiful bread basket might feature your signature breadsticks, an array of special flat breads, pizzas, and calzones can be either main course or appetizer menu selections.

Several of the items discussed in this chapter are used as the components to "build" finished pastries or plated desserts. The ability to assemble many components into a pleasing plate presentation is also important. While certain stylistic touches may change, these fundamentals remain the same.

• Each item must be of high quality, in terms of taste, texture, and appearance.

• All of the elements on the plate or in the pastry should work together to produce a pleasing effect.

• Contrasting textures, colors, and flavors can be successfully combined, but the overall effect should be pleasing, not jarring.

PART *IV*

The Recipes

Mise en Place and Stock Recipes   *419*

Soup Recipes   *449*

Sauce Recipes   *521*

Meat Entrées   *555*

Poultry Entrées   *621*

Fish Entrées   *657*

Vegetarian Entrées   *709*

International Entrées   *733*

Vegetable Side Dishes   *791*

Potato, Grain, and Pasta Dishes   *817*

Breakfast Recipes   *857*

Salads and Salad Dressings   *881*

Sandwiches and Pizzas   *917*

Hors d'Oeuvres and Appetizers   *935*

Sausages, Pâtés, and Terrines   *993*

Breads   *1025*

Kitchen Desserts   *1045*

Pastries and Cakes   *1079*

CHAPTER *13* Mise en Place
and Stock Recipes

*Each day, for each recipe, you will need to prepare the basic in-
gredients and mixtures used to season, flavor, and garnish
foods.*

The recipes in this chapter include the following categories:
- *Vegetable combinations, such as mirepoix and matignon*
- *Thickeners, such as roux*
- *Aromatics and spice blends*
- *Marinades*
- *Croutons*
- *Stocks, broths, essences, fumets, and court bouillons*

*These recipes can be scaled to produce the quantities you re-
quire.*

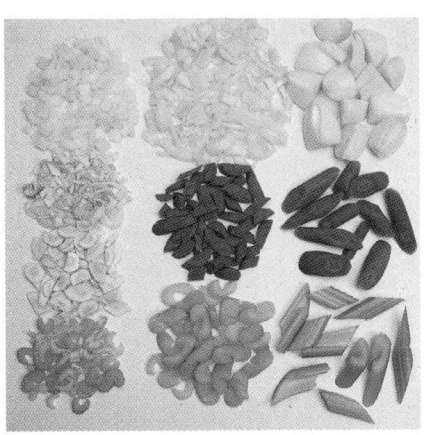

Mirepoix (regular and white) can be cut to the appropriate size, depending upon overall cooking time.

For more information on preparing Mirepoix see Chapter 6.

Mirepoix

Yield: 1 pound (450 grams)

Onions, chopped	*8 ounces*	*225 grams*
Carrots, chopped	*4 ounces*	*115 grams*
Celery, chopped	*4 ounces*	*115 grams*

1. Cut the vegetables into an appropriate size based on the cooking time of the dish.

2. Add mirepoix to the recipe as directed.

White Mirepoix

Yield: 1 pound (450 grams)

Onions, chopped	*4 ounces*	*115 grams*
Leeks, chopped	*4 ounces*	*115 grams*
Celery, chopped	*4 ounces*	*115 grams*
Parsnips, chopped	*4 ounces*	*115 grams*
Mushroom trimmings (optional)	*2 to 3 ounces*	*60 to 85 grams*

White mirepoix is used for white stocks and sauces.

1. Cut the vegetables into an appropriate size, based on the cooking time of the dish.

2. Add mirepoix to the recipe as directed.

Matignon

Yield: 1 pound (450 grams)

Matignon is generally required for poêléed items and for braised vegetables.

For more information on poêléing, read Chapter 9, pages 313 through 316.

Onions, small dice	*4 ounces*	*115 grams*
Carrots, small dice	*4 ounces*	*115 grams*
Celery, small dice	*4 ounces*	*115 grams*
Mushrooms, small dice	*2 ounces*	*60 grams*
Bacon or ham, small dice or minced	*2 ounces*	*60 grams*
Whole butter	*1 ounce*	*30 grams*

1. Cut all the vegetables and the bacon or ham into a neat, small dice and combine.

2. Sweat in whole butter, or use as directed in specific recipes.

Sofrito

Yield: 12 ounces (340 grams)

Onions, chopped	5 ounces	140 grams
Green pepper, chopped	5 ounces	140 grams
Garlic cloves, chopped	2 each	2 each
Cilantro, chopped	2 tablespoons	2 tablespoons
Parsley, chopped	1 tablespoon	1 tablespoon
Olive oil	2 tablespoons	2 tablespoons

1. Combine the onions, green pepper, garlic, cilantro, and parsley in a food processor and grind coarsely. The sofrito may be prepared in advance to this point. Store in the refrigerator.

2. When ready to use, heat the olive oil in a sauté pan. Sweat the sofrito for approximately 5 minutes.

Sofrito is an aromatic vegetable-and-herb blend used in the Spanish Caribbean.

Seeded, minced jalapeño chilies may be added. If desired, add 8 fluid ounces (240 milliliters) of white wine at the end of the cooking time.

Dry Duxelles

Yield: Approximately 1 pound (450 grams)

Clarified butter	3 ounces	85 grams
Shallots, chopped	2 ounces	60 grams
Mushrooms, chopped fine	1 1/2 pounds	680 grams
Parsley, chopped	1 tablespoon	1 tablespoon
Salt, (to taste)	1/2 teaspoon	1/2 teaspoon
Pepper, (to taste)	1/4 teaspoon	1/4 teaspoon

1. Heat butter in a small sauté pan.

2. Add the shallots and sweat.

3. Add the mushrooms to the pan and cook until they are browned and dry.

4. Add parsley; add salt and pepper to taste.

VARIATION

Duxelles Sauce: Add enough demi-glace and tomato purée for a good sasuce consistency. Add chopped parsley just before serving.

It is believed that duxelles are so named because they were created by Chef La Varenne, while working in the household of Marquis d'Uxelle.

Add dry bread crumbs and a little tomato sauce for a vegetable stuffing.

Pesto is believed to have originated in Genoa, but this herb paste is used throughout much of the Mediterranean as a sauce and a condiment.

Two ounces of basil equals 1 pint of tightly packed basil leaves.

Pesto loses its color and fresh flavor quickly, so make only enough for service time.

To hold or freeze pesto, do not add the Parmesan cheese. Cover the pesto with a thin layer of olive oil. The cheese should be added just prior to service.

Pesto

Yield: Approximately 10 ounces (285 grams)

Basil leaves, fresh	*2 ounces*	*60 grams*
Garlic cloves	*3 each*	*3 each*
Pine nuts, toasted	*1 1/2 ounces*	*45 grams*
Parmesan cheese	*2 ounces*	*60 grams*
Olive oil, as needed	*2 to 4 fluid ounces*	*60 to 120 milliliters*

1. Place all ingredients in a blender or food processor.

2. Purée gradually add enough oil to reach the desired consistency.

3. Serve immediately or refrigerate.

VARIATIONS

Arugula Pesto: Replace half of the basil with rinsed and dried spinach leaves. Use almonds to replace the pine nuts.

Cilantro Pesto: Replace the basil with an equal quantity of cilantro. Use Dry Jack cheese, or omit the cheese completely.

Spinach and Sun-Dried Tomato Pesto: Replace the basil with an equal amount of spinach leaves. Add 2 ounces (60 grams) of drained, oil-packed sun-dried tomatoes.

The mixture should be moist enough to adhere when pressed lightly, but not so moist that it packs tightly.

Persillade

Yield: Approximately 1 pound (450 grams)

Garlic, minced	*2 ounces*	*60 grams*
Parsley, chopped	*2 ounces*	*60 grams*
Bread crumbs, fresh	*10 ounces*	*285 grams*
Butter, melted	*approximately 2 ounces*	*approximately 60 grams*

1. Combine garlic, parsley, and bread crumbs.

2. Gradually add the melted butter until the desired consistency is reached.

Basic Roux

Yield: 2 pounds (900 grams)

Clarified butter or oil	*1 pound*	*450 grams*
Flour	*1 pound*	*450 grams*

1. Heat the clarified butter or oil in a rondeau over moderate heat.

2. Add the flour all at once. Stirring constantly, cook over low heat until the roux is a very pale ivory, for approximately 8 minutes.

VARIATIONS

White Roux: Always use oil to maintain the color. Cook as directed above.

Blonde/Pale Roux: Cook the roux for an additional 2 to 3 minutes, until roux becomes golden in color.

Brown Roux: Continue to cook the roux until it is browned and has a pronounced nutty aroma.

For more information on how to make a roux or other thickeners, see Chapter 6.

Brown and black roux are used extensively in Acadian/Creole cuisine; in gumbos, stews, and gravies.

Beurre Manié

Yield: 6 ounces (170 grams)

Butter	*3 1/2 ounces*	*100 grams*
Flour	*2 1/2 ounces*	*70 grams*

1. Allow the butter to soften until pliable.

2. Add the flour and, using a wooden spoon, work to a smooth paste. (An electric mixer may be used for larger quantities.)

3. Use immediately or wrap tightly and refrigerate.

For more information on Beurre Manié or other thickeners, see Chapter 6.

Beurre manié is used to thicken vegetable stews (petits pois à la Française) and matelotes.

Liaison

Yield: Approximately 8 fluid ounces (240 milliliters)

Heavy cream	*1/2 pint*	*240 milliliters*
Egg yolks	*3 each*	*3 each*

1. Combine ingredients. Temper the liaison before adding to a hot liquid by adding a little of the hot liquid to the liaison to gradually raise the temperature. Then add the tempered liaison to the remainder of the hot liquid.

VARIATION

Sour Cream or Crème Fraîche Liaison: Substitute equal quantities of these ingredients for the heavy cream.

This quantity of liaison is sufficient to thicken 24 fluid ounces (720 milliliters) of liquid.

For more information on liaisons and tempering, see Chapter 6.

To make it easy to pull a bouquet garni out of a soup or stew once it has added a good flavor, leave the string tail extra long and tie it to the handle.

For more information about the preparation of and uses for Bouquet Garni, see Chapter 6.

One sachet or bouquet garni is enough to flavor 1 gallon (3.75 liters) of liquid.

For more information on the preparation of and uses for Sachet d'Épices see Chapter 6, page 210.

Standard Bouquet Garni

Yield: 1 each

Celery, trimmed, whole stalk	*4 ounces*	*115 grams*
Parsley stems	*3 or 4 each*	*3 or 4 each*
Thyme sprig, fresh	*1 each*	*1 each*
Bay leaf	*1 each*	*1 each*
Leek leaves	*2 or 3 each*	*2 or 3 each*

1. Halve the celery stalk crosswise. Sandwich herbs between celery pieces and fold leek leaves around the herbs and celery.

2. Tie the bundle securely with butcher's twine.

VARIATION

Savory, sage, rosemary, or other fresh herbs may be used in addition to or in place of the ingredients called for above, depending on the recipe or desired result.

Standard Sachet d'Épices

Yield: 1 each

Parsley stems	*3 or 4 each*	*3 or 4 each*
Thyme leaves	*1/2 teaspoon*	*1/2 teaspoon*
Bay leaf	*1 each*	*1 each*
Peppercorns, cracked	*1/2 teaspoon*	*1/2 teaspoon*
Garlic clove, crushed (optional)	*1 each*	*1 each*

1. Place all ingredients on a piece of cheesecloth approximately 4-inches square. Gather up the edges and tie with butcher's twine, leaving a long tail of string to tie to the stockpot handle.

VARIATION

Cloves, dill, tarragon stems, juniper berries, star anise, allspice, and other herbs and spices may be included, according to the recipe or desired result.

Barbecue Spice Mix

Yield: About 2 ounces (60 grams)

Paprika	*1/2 ounce*	*15 grams*
Chili powder	*1/2 ounce*	*15 grams*
Salt	*1/2 ounce*	*15 grams*
Cumin, ground	*2 teaspoons*	*2 teaspoons*
Sugar	*2 teaspoons*	*2 teaspoons*
Dry mustard	*1 teaspoon*	*1 teaspoon*
Pepper	*1 teaspoon*	*1 teaspoon*
Thyme, dried	*1 teaspoon*	*1 teaspoon*
Oregano, dried	*1 teaspoon*	*1 teaspoon*
Curry powder	*1 teaspoon*	*1 teaspoon*
Cayenne	*1/2 teaspoon*	*1/2 teaspoon*

1. Combine all spices and mix well.

2. Rub evenly over the surface of meats, poultry, or fish. Allow them to marinate for several hours before cooking.

There are many spice blends available already prepared. It is simple, though, to prepare them to your own specifications from whole toasted spices in a coffee grinder.

Chili Powder

Yield: About 2 ounces (60 grams)

Chilies, dried and ground	*1 1/2 ounces*	*45 grams*
Cumin	*1/2 ounce*	*15 grams*
Oregano leaves, dried	*1 teaspoon*	*1 teaspoon*
Garlic powder	*1/2 teaspoon*	*1/2 teaspoon*
Coriander, ground	*1/4 teaspoon*	*1/4 teaspoon*

1. Combine all spices. Keep in a tightly covered jar or other container until needed.

2. Use as required by recipe.

Ancho, pasilla, and mulato chilies are all good choices.

Dried thyme and cloves may also be added.

Chili powder blend should not be confused with the chili powder called for in some recipes. Be sure to use pure powdered chilies in recipes that call for them. Commercially prepared chili powder is actually a blend similar to this one. This blend can be used as a seasoning for chili con carne, soups, and as a rub for meats.

Chinese Five Spice

Yield: 2 1/2 ounces (70 grams)

Star anise	*1/2 ounce*	*15 grams*
Cloves	*1/2 ounce*	*15 grams*
Szechwan pepper	*1/2 ounce*	*15 grams*
Fennel seeds	*1/2 ounce*	*15 grams*
Cinnamon (or cassia)	*1/2 ounce*	*15 grams*

1. Grind the spices in a spice mill or with a mortar and pestle.
2. Store tightly covered until needed.

Curry Powder

Bird's eye or other small chilies may be used.

Add paprika, cloves, saffron, fenugreek, cardaomom, or fresh curry leaves to the blend.

Toast seeds or spices in a dry skillet, when working with small quantities.

Yield: about 1 ounce (30 grams)

Cumin seeds	*3/4 ounce*	*20 grams*
Coriander seeds	*1/4 ounce*	*10 grams*
Mustard seeds, whole	*1 teaspoon*	*1 teaspoon*
Dried red chilies, to taste	*4 each*	*4 each*
Cinnamon	*1 tablespoon*	*1 tablespoon*
Turmeric, ground	*1/4 ounce*	*10 grams*
Ginger, ground	*1 tablespoon*	*1 tablespoon*

1. Combine all the seeds and chilies. Roast them in a 300°F (150°C) oven for 5 minutes. Remove and cool slightly. Split the chilies and remove the seeds.
2. Grind the whole spices, ground spices, and chilies in a spice mill or with a mortar and pestle until blended evenly.

Dry Cure for Smoked Fish

Yield: 3 pounds (1.3 kilograms)

Brown sugar	*1 pound*	*450 grams*
Kosher salt	*2 pounds*	*900 grams*
Bay leaves	*12 each*	*12 each*
Black pepper, coarsely ground	*2 tablespoons*	*2 tablespoons*
Onion powder	*2 tablespoons*	*2 tablespoons*
Garlic powder	*1 tablespoon*	*1 tablespoon*
Cloves, ground	*1 tablespoon*	*1 tablespoon*
Allspice, ground	*1 tablespoon*	*1 tablespoon*
Mace, ground	*1 tablespoon*	*1 tablespoon*

1. Purée all ingredients in a food processor. Reserve until needed.

See Chapter 12, for information about using this cure to prepare gravad lox.

Salmon may be cured for three days. For a shorter curing period, use equal parts sugar and salt.

Fines Herbes

Yield: 4 ounces (115 grams)

Chervil leaves, chopped	*1 ounce*	*30 grams*
Chives, chopped	*1 ounce*	*30 grams*
Parsley leaves, chopped	*1 ounce*	*30 grams*
Tarragon leaves, chopped	*1 ounce*	*30 grams*

1. Combine all herbs. Use according to specific recipes.

VARIATIONS

Add burnet, marjoram, savory, lovage, or watercress.

Herbes de Provence: Combine basil, fennel seed, lavender, marjoram, rosemary, sage, savory, and thyme for this classic blend from the South of France.

Fines herbes is a classic combination of fresh herbs used to season sauces, flavor omelets and soufflés, and to fill fresh pastas.

Garam Masala

Yield: 2 ounces (60 grams)

Garam masala is a spice blend used in Indian cuisines. The ratio of ingredients may be varied to suit individual preference.

Cardamom pods, green or black	*10 each*	*10 each*
Coriander seeds, whole	*1 tablespoon*	*1 tablespoon*
Cumin seeds	*1 tablespoon*	*1 tablespoon*
Cinnamon stick, **broken into small pieces**	*1 each*	*1 each*
Cloves, whole	*1 teaspoon*	*1 teaspoon*
Black peppercorns	*2 teaspoons*	*2 teaspoons*
Bay leaves	*2 each*	*2 each*
Nutmeg, ground	*1/4 teaspoon*	*1/4 teaspoon*

1. Break open the cardamom pods and remove the seeds. Combine all the ingredients except the nutmeg and bay leaves. Roast them in a 300°F (150°C) oven for 5 minutes. Remove and cool slightly.

2. Grind the spices with the nutmeg and bay leaves in a spice mill or with a mortar and pestle.

Seasoning Mix for Spit Roasted Meats and Poultry

Yield: About 2 1/2 ounces (75 grams)

Pack or rub this spice blend evenly over meats or poultry. Allow it to rest several hours under refrigeration before roasting.

Kosher salt	*1 1/2 ounces*	*45 grams*
Dry mustard	*1/2 ounce*	*15 grams*
Black pepper, coarsely ground	*1 tablespoon*	*1 tablespoon*
Thyme, dried	*2 teaspoons*	*2 teaspoons*
Oregano, dried	*2 teaspoons*	*2 teaspoons*
Coriander, ground	*2 teaspoons*	*2 teaspoons*
Celery seed or salt	*2 teaspoons*	*2 teaspoons*

1. Combine all and mix well.

Quatre Épices

Yield: About 4 ounces (120 grams)

Peppercorns	*5 tablespoons*	*5 tablespoons*
Nutmeg, ground	*2 tablespoons*	*2 tablespoons*
Cinnamon, ground	*1 tablespoon*	*1 tablespoon*
Cloves, whole	*1 tablespoon*	*1 tablespoon*
Ginger (optional)	*1 tablespoon*	*1 tablespoon*

1. Grind the spices in a spice mill or with a mortar and pestle.

Red Curry Paste

Yield: 24 ounces (680 grams)

Coriander seeds	2 teaspoons	2 teaspoons
Fennel seeds	1 teaspoon	1 teaspoon
Cumin seeds	1 teaspoon	1 teaspoon
Black peppercorns	1 teaspoon	1 teaspoon
Red peppers, roasted, seeded, and peeled	4 each	4 each
Jalapeño peppers, seeded and peeled	6 each	6 each
Chipotle peppers	2 each	2 each
Olive oil	2 fluid ounces	60 milliliters
Shallots, chopped	2 each	2 each
Garlic cloves	5 each	5 each
Lemongrass, bottom 4 inches, minced	1 each	1 each
Ginger, minced	2 tablespoons	2 tablespoons
Nutmeg, ground	1/4 teaspoon	1/4 teaspoon
Lime zest	from 1 lime	from 1 lime
Salt	1 teaspoon	1 teaspoon

Curry pastes are used frequently in Thai and Vietnamese dishes. This blend is particularly good with seafood.

1. Roast the coriander, fennel, cumin, and black pepper in a 300°F (150°C) oven for 5 minutes. Remove and cool slightly.

2. Grind them in a spice mill or with a mortar and pestle.

3. Combine all the ingredients in a food processor or blender and purée very fine.

4. Refrigerate.

Standard Reduction

Yield: 3 to 4 fluid ounces (90 to 120 milliliters)

Mushroom stems, chopped	4 ounces	115 grams
Parsley stems	10 to 12 each	10 to 12 each
Bay leaves	3 each	3 each
Peppercorns	1 teaspoon	1 teaspoon
Thyme sprigs, fresh	2 each	2 each
Shallots, minced	2 each	2 each
Garlic cloves, minced	3 each	3 each
Wine, dry (red or white)	6 fluid ounces	180 milliliters
Water	1 fluid ounce	30 milliliters

For more information on the preparation of and uses for Standard Reduction, see Chapter 6.

This reduction can be used for flavoring beurre blanc, see page 545; as essence for shallow-poached item; and as a flavoring for mayonnaise-style dressings, see page 911.

1. Combine all ingredients with enough wine to cover by 1/2 inch.

2. Reduce over moderate heat by half. Add the water.

3. Strain, cool, and reserve.

Asian-Style Marinade

Yield: 1 pint (480 milliliters)

Hoisin sauce	*6 fluid ounces*	*180 milliliters*
Sherry	*6 fluid ounces*	*180 milliliters*
Rice wine vinegar	*2 fluid ounces*	*60 milliliters*
Soy sauce	*2 fluid ounces*	*60 milliliters*
Garlic cloves, minced	*4 each*	*4 each*

1. Mix together all the ingredients. Pour over the meat or fish. Refrigerate until service.

Hot bean paste, sesame oil, and/or fresh ginger may be added.

Allow meats to marinate at least 3 hours, up to overnight. Fish should marinate 30 minutes to 2 hours. Refrigerate meats throughout marination.

Barbecue Marinade

Yield: 1 pint (480 milliliters)

Vegetable oil	*10 ounces*	*285 grams*
Cider vinegar	*5 fluid ounces*	*150 milliliters*
Worcestershire sauce	*1 fluid ounce*	*30 milliliters*
Brown sugar	*1 tablespoon*	*1 tablespoon*
Dry mustard	*2 teaspoons*	*2 teaspoons*
Tabasco sauce	*1 teaspoon*	*1 teaspoon*
Garlic powder	*1 teaspoon*	*1 teaspoon*
Onion powder	*1 teaspoon*	*1 teaspoon*
Garlic cloves, minced	*2 each*	*2 each*

1. Mix together all the ingredients. Pour over the meat or fish. Refrigerate until service.

Bourbon, powdered chilies, and/or tomato paste are additional flavorings to consider.

Allow poultry to marinate a minimum of 2 hours, up to overnight.

Basic Meat Marinade

Yield: 8 fluid ounces (240 milliliters)

Vegetable oil	*7 fluid ounces*	*200 milliliters*
Worcestershire sauce	*1 fluid ounce*	*30 milliliters*
Thyme, fresh, chopped	*1 bunch*	*1 bunch*
Garlic cloves, minced	*8 each*	*8 each*
Black pepper, coarse ground	*2 teaspoons*	*2 teaspoons*

1. Combine all the ingredients of the marinade. Pour the marinade over the meat. Refrigerate until service.

Add other herbs as desired—sage, rosemary, parsley, and tarragon are all good choices.

Wild game, such as bear, boar, or elk, should be allowed to marinate at least 12 hours, up to 36 hours, before cooking.

Cumin-Lime Marinade (Adobo)

Yield: 8 fluid ounces (240 milliliters)

Lime juice	*8 fluid ounces*	*240 milliliters*
Garlic cloves, minced	*5 each*	*5 each*
Cilantro (optional)	*1 tablespoon*	*1 tablespoon*
Salt	*1 teaspoon*	*1 teaspoon*
Cumin, ground	*1 teaspoon*	*1 teaspoon*
Cracked black pepper	*1/2 teaspoon*	*1/2 teaspoon*

1. Mix together all the ingredients. Pour over the meat or fish. Refrigerate until service.

Vegetables need only a brief marinade before they are grilled for a flavor boost. Brush some on them during grilling for additional flavor.

Add chopped fresh parsley, chives, or ground coriander to this marinade. Use it to marinate fish, chicken, or vegetables.

Fish Marinade

Yield: 8 fluid ounces (240 milliliters)

Olive oil	*6 fluid ounces*	*180 milliliters*
Lemon juice	*2 ounces*	*60 milliliters*
Garlic cloves, minced	*2 each*	*2 each*
Salt	*1 teaspoon*	*1 teaspoon*
Pepper	*1 teaspoon*	*1 teaspoon*

1. Mix together all the ingredients. Pour over the fish. Refrigerate until service.

VARIATION

Wine Marinade: Replace the lemon juice with a dry white wine or white vermouth. Substitute shallots for the garlic.

Substitute grapefruit or tangerine juice in this marinade if you prefer.

Marinate fish under refrigeration for 30 minutes up to 2 hours.

Lamb and Game Marinade

Yield: 1 pint (480 milliliters)

Hot bean paste, sesame oil, and/or fresh ginger may be added.

Replace up to half of the red wine with gin for red game meats such as venison, boar, bear, or elk.

Dry red wine	*4 fluid ounces*	*120 milliliters*
Vinegar	*4 fluid ounces*	*120 milliliters*
Olive oil	*2 fluid ounces*	*60 milliliters*
Sugar	*1 tablespoon*	*1 tablespoon*
Dried mint flakes	*1 tablespoon*	*1 tablespoon*
Salt	*1 teaspoon*	*1 teaspoon*
Juniper berries	*1 teaspoon*	*1 teaspoon*
Bay leaves	*2 each*	*2 each*
Onion	*2 slices*	*2 slices*
Parsley sprig	*1 each*	*1 each*
Thyme sprig	*1 each*	*1 each*
Garlic clove, minced	*1 each*	*1 each*
Nutmeg, ground	*pinch*	*pinch*

1. Combine all ingredients. Pour over the lamb or game and refrigerate. Venison can be marinated for three days for maximum flavor.

Latin Citrus Marinade

Yield: 10 fluid ounces (300 milliliters)

This marinade could be used to prepare ceviche. Or, add it to cooked beans (black, pink, or pinto) as part of a salad "sampler."

Orange juice	*6 fluid ounces*	*180 milliliters*
Lemon juice	*3 fluid ounces*	*90 milliliters*
Lime juice	*1 fluid ounce*	*30 milliliters*
Achiote paste	*1 tablespoon*	*1 tablespoon*
Garlic clove, chopped	*1 each*	*1 each*
Salt	*1 teaspoon*	*1 teaspoon*
Oregano, dried	*1/2 teaspoon*	*1/2 teaspoon*
Cumin, ground	*1/2 teaspoon*	*1/2 teaspoon*
Cloves, ground	*1/4 teaspoon*	*1/4 teaspoon*
Cinnamon, ground	*1/4 teaspoon*	*1/4 teaspoon*
Pepper	*1/4 teaspoon*	*1/4 teaspoon*

1. Combine all the ingredients in a bowl. Pour over poultry, fish, or vegetables and marinate in the refrigerator.

Red Wine Game Marinade

Yield: 1 quart (1 liter)

Dry red wine	*12 fluid ounces*	*360 milliliters*
Olive oil	*2 fluid ounces*	*60 milliliters*
Red wine vinegar	*2 fluid ounces*	*60 milliliters*
Thyme, dried	*2 teaspoons*	*2 teaspoons*
Juniper berries	*1 teaspoon*	*1 teaspoon*
Savory, dried	*1 teaspoon*	*1 teaspoon*
Pepper	*1 teaspoon*	*1 teaspoon*
Parsley sprigs	*3 each*	*3 each*
Garlic cloves, minced	*2 each*	*2 each*
Carrot, diced	*1 each*	*1 each*
Onion, diced	*1 each*	*1 each*
Celery, diced	*1 each*	*1 each*
Bay leaf	*1 each*	*1 each*

1. Combine all ingredients. Pour over the game and refrigerate.

Game meats should be marinated several days before cooking.

Red Wine Marinade

Yield: 1 pint (480 milliliters)

Red wine	*8 fluid ounces*	*240 milliliters*
Olive oil	*6 fluid ounces*	*180 milliliters*
Lemon juice	*2 fluid ounces*	*60 milliliters*
Garlic cloves, minced	*3 each*	*3 each*
Salt	*1 teaspoon*	*1 teaspoon*
Pepper	*1 teaspoon*	*1 teaspoon*

1. Combine all ingredients. Pour over the meat and refrigerate.

Use this marinade for sauerbraten or other marinated and braised red meat dishes.

Rosemary and Gin Marinade for Game Meats

Yield: 1 pint (480 milliliters)

This marinade is especially good for cuts from the venison haunch.

Gin	8 fluid ounces	240 milliliters
Dry vermouth	8 fluid ounces	240 milliliters
Bay leaf	1 each	1 each
Peppercorns	8 each	8 each
Mirepoix	5 ounces	140 grams
Garlic clove, minced	1 each	1 each
Rosemary leaves, chopped	1 tablespoon	1 tablespoon

1. Combine all ingredients. Pour over the game and refrigerate.

Teriyaki Marinade for Game Meats

Yield: 1 pint (480 milliliters)

The beer you select will affect the final flavor. For the richest taste, use a dark beer, or stout.

Soy sauce	8 fluid ounces	240 milliliters
Beer	4 fluid ounces	120 milliliters
Brown sugar	2 ounces	60 grams
Onion, minced	1 ounce	30 grams
Ginger, ground	1 tablespoon	1 tablespoon
Garlic cloves, minced	3 each	3 each

1. Combine all ingredients. Pour over the game and refrigerate. Wild venison can be marinated for three days for maximum flavor. Farm-raised venison has a milder flavor and should be marinated overnight.

Teriyaki Marinade

Yield: 1 pint (480 milliliters)

Star anise cloves and/or cinnamon may be added.

Brush or baste foods with this marinade as they cook.

Soy sauce	6 fluid ounces	180 milliliters
Corn or peanut oil	6 fluid ounces	180 milliliters
Dry sherry	3 fluid ounces	90 milliliters
Honey	1 ounce	30 grams
Garlic cloves, minced	2 each	2 each
Gingerroot, grated	1/4 ounce	10 grams
Orange zest (optional)	2 tablespoons	2 tablespoons

1. Combine all ingredients. Blend well.
2. Pour over meats, shellfish, or poultry. Marinate under refrigeration for up to 8 hours.

Croutons

Yield: 1 pound (450 grams)

White bread	*1 pound*	*450 grams*
Butter, melted or olive oil, as needed	*4 ounces*	*115 grams*
Salt, to taste	*1 teaspoon*	*1 teaspoon*
Pepper (optional), to taste	*1/2 teaspoon*	*1/2 teaspoon*
Garlic cloves (optional), mashed to a paste, or minced fine	*2 each*	*2 each*

1. Slice and cube the bread into desired size. If it is very fresh, let the bread cubes dry out in the oven for five minutes before continuing.
2. Toss the bread, butter or oil, seasoning, and garlic together on a baking sheet or in a hotel pan.
3. Bake for 8 to 10 minutes until lightly golden.

VARIATIONS

Herb Croutons: Chopped fresh or dried herbs (such as oregano or rosemary) can be tossed with the croutons.

Parmesan Cheese Croutons: Grated Parmesan cheese can be added to taste near the end of cooking time. Toss to coat evenly.

Croutons can be prepared in advance and stored in an airtight container for several days.

For smaller batches, the croutons can be cooked on top of the stove in a skillet or sauté pan.

Whole wheat, pumpernickel, or rye breads may be substituted.

Bean and Cheese Croutons

Yield: 20 croutons

Bacon, chopped	*4 slices*	*4 slices*
Onions, minced	*4 ounces*	*115 grams*
Serrano pepper, minced	*1 each*	*1 each*
Garlic cloves, mashed	*2 each*	*2 each*
Pinto beans, cooked, mashed	*8 ounces*	*225 grams*
Salt, to taste	*1/2 teaspoon*	*1/2 teaspoon*
Pepper, to taste	*1/4 teaspoon*	*1/4 teaspoon*
French bread, sliced 1/2 inch thick, lightly toasted	*20 slices*	*20 slices*
Monterey Jack cheese, grated	*6 ounces*	*170 grams*

These can be prepared in advance, and gratinéed per order.

Serve these with the Sante Fe Chili Soup (page 499) or other Southwestern-style soups or salads.

Chopped fresh cilantro may be added. Substitute jalapeño Jack cheese for the Monterey Jack and Serrano peppers.

1. Combine the bacon, onions, serrano pepper, garlic, beans, salt, and pepper. Spread on French bread slice, top with cheese, and bake until cheese is melted.

Cheddar Cheese Rusks

Yield: 20 each

French bread, sliced 1/3 inch thick	*20 each*	*20 each*
White cheddar cheese, grated	*8 ounces*	*225 grams*
Heavy cream	*2 fluid ounces*	*60 milliliters*
Cayenne, to taste	*1/8 teaspoon*	*1/8 teaspoon*

1. Lightly toast the bread in a 325°F (165°C) oven. Combine the rest of the ingredients and spread onto the croutons. Gratinée under the broiler.

These can be prepared well in advance and warmed slightly before serving. Or they can be prepped in advance and gratinéed per order.

Goat Cheese Croutons

Yield: 20 each

French bread, sliced 1/3 inch thick	*20 each*	*20 each*
Goat cheese, log	*10 ounces*	*285 grams*
Fresh herbs, to taste	*1/8 teaspoon*	*1/8 teaspoon*

1. Dry the croutons in a 325°F (165°C) oven. Slice the goat cheese log 1/4-inch thick. Place a piece of the cheese on each crouton. Garnish with chopped fresh herbs (rosemary, basil, or thyme) or fresh-ground black pepper. Heat in the oven. Do not brown.

Serve with soups (Butternut Squash, page 474, French Lentil, page 481) or on a bed of field greens. If serving with a salad, drizzle olive oil on the crouton at service.

For a smoother spread, the goat cheese may be blended with 2 fluid ounces (60 milliliters) of heavy cream, sour cream, or crème fraiche, and then spread on the crouton.

Rye Bread Croutons

Yield: 20 each

Rye bread, cut in 2-inch rounds	*20 each*	*20 each*
Butter, softened	*2 ounces*	*60 grams*
Cheddar cheese, sharp, grated	*4 ounces*	*115 grams*
Parmesan cheese, grated	*2 ounces*	*60 grams*
Dijon mustard	*2 tablespoons*	*2 tablespoons*
Cayenne, to taste	*1/8 teaspoon*	*1/8 teaspoon*

1. Toast rye bread circles on both sides in broiler.

2. Mix butter, cheeses, mustard, and cayenne pepper together. Spread cheese mixture on top of each crouton; brown lightly in the broiler.

Brown Veal Stock (Jus de Veau)

Yield: 1 gallon (3.75 liters)

Veal bones,		
including knuckles and trim	*8 pounds*	*3.6 kilograms*
Oil, as needed	*4 fluid ounces*	*115 milliliters*
Cold water or Remouillage	*6 quarts*	*5.75 liters*
Mirepoix	*1 pound*	*450 grams*
Tomato paste	*6 fluid ounces*	*180 milliliters*
Standard Sachet d'Épices	*1 each*	*1 each*
Salt (optional)	*to taste*	*to taste*

1. Rinse the bones and dry them well.

2. Brown the bones in oil.

3. Combine the bones and water.

4. Bring the stock to a boil over low heat.

5. Simmer for a total of about 6 hours, skimming the surface as necessary.

6. Brown the mirepoix and tomato paste; add to the stock after the stock has simmered for about 5 hours. Deglaze the reduced drippings with water and add to the stock. Add sachet d'épices (and salt, if used).

7. Simmer an additional hour.

8. Strain the stock.

VARIATION

Brown Game Stock (**Jus de Gibier**): Replace the veal bones with an equal weight of venison bones and lean trim (or bones of other game animals). Include fennel seeds and/or juniper berries in standard sachet d'épices, if desired.

The mirepoix can be browned with the bones in step 2 (see page 420). A larger cut of mirepoix can be used, if this procedure is followed.

For information on preparing stock see Chapter 6, page 212. For information on the proper handling and storage of stock, see Chapter 2, page 38.

For Standard Sachet d'Épices, see page 424.

Estouffade

Yield: 1 gallon (3.75 liters)

Veal bones	*4 pounds*	*1.8 kilograms*
Beef bones	*4 pounds*	*1.8 kilograms*
Unsmoked ham knuckle	*1 each*	*1 each*
Cold water	*6 quarts*	*5.75 liters*
Mirepoix	*1 pound*	*450 grams*
Tomato paste	*10 ounces*	*300 milliliters*
Standard Sachet d'Épices	*1 each*	*1 each*
Salt (optional)	*to taste*	*to taste*

Estouffade is a traditional component of Espagnole/brown sauce, a sauce that is further reduced and refined to make demiglace. Most often, brown veal stock, and specialty brown stocks (game, pork, or poultry) are used today.

Estouffade is also the term for a savory stew of French origin which is featured in Acadian cuisine.

For Standard Sachet d'Épices, see page 424.

1. Rinse all the bones and dry them well.

2. Brown the veal and beef bones.

3. Combine ham knuckle and the veal and beef bones with water.

4. Bring the mixture to a boil slowly.

5. Simmer for 5 hours, skimming the surface as necessary.

6. Brown the mirepoix and tomato paste; add to the stock. Deglaze the reduced drippings with water and add to the stock. Add sachet d'épices (salt, if used).

7. Simmer an additional hour.

8. Strain the stock.

Glace de Viande

Yield: 4 to 8 fluid ounces (120 to 240 milliliters)

Yield will vary depending on cooking time and desired consistency.

Brown Veal Stock or Remouillage	*1 quart*	*1 liter*

1. Place the stock or remouillage in a heavy gauge pot over moderate heat.

2. Bring to a simmer and let reduce until volume is halved, then transfer to a smaller pot.

3. Continue to reduce, transferring to successively smaller pots until very thick and syrupy.

VARIATIONS

Glace de Gibier: Substitute game stock for brown veal stock.

Glace de Volaille: Substitute chicken stock for brown veal stock.

Glace de Poisson: Substitute fish stock for brown veal stock.

Veal Stock

Yield: 1 gallon (3.75 liters)

Veal bones, cut into 3-inch lengths, blanched (optional)	*8 pounds*	*3.6 kilograms*
Cold water or Remouillage	*6 quarts*	*5.75 liters*
Mirepoix	*1 pound*	*450 grams*
Standard Sachet d'Épices	*1 each*	*1 each*
Salt (optional)	*to taste*	*to taste*

1. Rinse the bones.
2. Combine the bones and water.
3. Bring the stock to a boil over low heat.
4. Skim the surface, as necessary.
5. Simmer the stock for a total of 6 hours.
6. Add mirepoix and sachet d'épices (salt, if used) in the last hour of simmering.
7. Strain the stock.

This stock was originally called "ordinary stock."

White Beef Stock

Yield: 1 gallon (3.75 liters)

Beef bones, cut into 3-inch lengths, blanched (optional)	*8 pounds*	*3.6 kilograms*
Cold water or Remouillage	*6 quarts*	*5.75 liters*
Mirepoix	*1 pound*	*450 grams*
Standard Sachet d'Épices	*1 each*	*1 each*
Salt (optional)	*to taste*	*to taste*

1. Rinse the bones.
2. Combine the bones and water.
3. Bring the stock to a boil over low heat.
4. Skim the surface, as necessary.
5. Simmer the stock for a total of 8 hours. Add more water if necessary.
6. Add mirepoix and sachet d'épices (and salt, if used) in the last hour of simmering.
7. Strain the stock.

Veal shank or feet are sometimes added to bolster its body.

This stock is a good choice for preparing vegetable or bean soups.

Pork Stock

Yield: 1 gallon (3.75 liters)

Pork or ham bones		
blanched (optional), and lean trim	*8 pounds*	*3.6 kilograms*
Cold water or Remouillage	*6 quarts*	*5.75 liters*
Mirepoix	*1 pound*	*450 grams*
Standard Sachet d'Épices	*1 each*	*1 each*
Salt (optional)	*to taste*	*to taste*

For Standard Sachet d'Épices, see page 424.

This is a special stock that might be used in the preparation of bean soups or stews. When using to cook beans, add smoked neck bones or ham hocks.

1. Rinse the bones.

2. Combine the bones and water.

3. Bring the stock to a boil over low heat.

4. Skim the surface, as necessary.

5. Simmer the stock for a total of about 6 hours.

6. Add mirepoix and sachet d'épices (and salt, if used) in the last hour of simmering.

7. Strain the stock.

VARIATION

Brown Pork Stock (**Jus de Pork**): Rinse the bones and dry them. Brown the bones in a roasting pan. Combine them with the water and bring to a boil over low heat. Simmer for 5 hours. Brown the mirepoix and 2 ounces (60 grams) tomato paste in the roasting pan; add to the stock. Deglaze the pan with water and add to the stock. Simmer an additional hour. If desired, add one or more of the following herbs or spices to the standard sachet d'épices: red pepper flakes, caraway seeds, oregano stems, and mustard seeds.

White Lamb Stock

Yield: 1 gallon (3.75 liters)

Lamb bones, blanched (optional)	*8 pounds*	*3.6 kilograms*
Cold water or Remouillage	*6 quarts*	*5.75 liters*
Mirepoix	*1 pound*	*450 grams*
Standard Sachet d'Épices	*1 each*	*1 each*
Salt (optional)	*to taste*	*to taste*

For information on preparing stock see Chapter 6, page 212. For information on the proper handling and storage of stock see Chapter 2, page 38.

1. Rinse the bones.

2. Combine the bones and water.

3. Bring the stock to a boil over low heat.

(Recipe continued on facing page)

4. Skim the surface, as necessary.

5. Simmer the stock for a total of about 6 hours.

6. Add mirepoix and sachet d'épices (and salt, if used) in the last hour of simmering.

7. Strain the stock.

VARIATION

***Brown Lamb Stock* (Jus d'Agneau):** Rinse the bones and dry them. Brown the bones in a roasting pan. Combine them with the water and bring to a boil over low heat. Simmer for 5 hours. Brown the mirepoix and tomato paste in the roasting pan; add to the stock. Deglaze the pan with water and add to the stock. Simmer an additional hour. If desired, add one or more of the following herbs or spices to the standard sachet d'épices: mint stems, juniper berries, cumin seed, caraway seeds, and rosemary.

For Standard Sachet d'Épices, see page 424.

This is a special stock, which might be used in the preparation of Scotch Broth, page 513, or Irish Stew, page 747.

Remouillage

Yield: 1 gallon (3.75 liters)

Bones, reserved from preparing stock	*8 pounds*	*3.6 kilograms*
Cold water	*6 quarts*	*5.75 liters*
Mirepoix	*1 pound*	*450 grams*
Standard Sachet d'Épices	*1 each*	*1 each*

1. Combine all ingredients, and simmer for approximately 6 hours.

2. Strain the stock.

Remouillage will not have the same depth of body or flavor as normal stock.

For information on preparing Remouillage see Chapter 6, page 212. For information on the proper handling and storage of stock see Chapter 2, page 38.

For Standard Sachet d'Épices, see page 424.

Chicken Stock

Yield: 1 gallon (3.75 liters)

For information on preparing stock see Chapter 6, page 212. For information on the proper handling and storage of stock see Chapter 2, page 38.

For a very rich stock, substitute stewing hens.

Chicken bones, cut into 3-inch lengths, blanched (optional)	*8 pounds*	*3.6 kilograms*
Cold water or Remouillage	*6 quarts*	*5.75 liters*
Mirepoix	*1 pound*	*450 grams*
Standard Sachet d'Épices	*1 each*	*1 each*
Salt (optional)	*to taste*	*to taste*

1. Rinse the bones.

2. Combine the bones and water.

3. Bring the stock to a boil over low heat.

4. Skim the surface, as necessary.

5. Simmer the stock for a total of 4 to 5 hours.

6. Add the mirepoix and sachet d'épices (and salt, if used) in the last hour of simmering.

7. Strain the stock.

VARIATIONS

Brown Chicken Stock: Rinse the bones and dry them. Brown the bones in a roasting pan. Combine them with the water and bring to a boil over low heat. Simmer for about 4 hours. Brown the mirepoix and up to 4 ounces (115 grams) tomato paste in the roasting pan; add to the stock. Deglaze the pan with water and add to the stock. Simmer an additional hour.

Asian-style Chicken Stock: Add gingerroot, lemongrass, scallions, and fresh or dried chilies to the sachet d'épices.

Turkey Stock: Replace chicken bones with meaty turkey bones.

Game Bird Stock

Yield: 1 gallon (3.75 liters)

Use duck, pheasant, goose, partridge, or any other other game birds. Because of the size of rabbit bones, rabbit stock can also be prepared in this manner.

Bones from game birds, blanched (optional)	*8 pounds*	*3.6 kilograms*
Cold water	*6 quarts*	*5.75 liters*
Mirepoix	*1 pound*	*450 grams*
Standard Sachet d'Épices	*1 each*	*1 each*
Salt (optional)	*to taste*	*to taste*

1. Rinse the bones.

2. Combine the bones and water.

(Recipe continued on facing page)

3. Bring the stock to a boil over low heat.

4. Skim the surface, as necessary.

5. Simmer the stock for a total of 5 hours.

6. Add the mirepoix and sachet d'épices (and salt, if used) in the last hour of simmering.

7. Strain the stock.

For information on preparing stock see Chapter 6, page 212. For information on the proper handling and storage of stock see Chapter 2, page 38.

This is a special stock for use in game soups, sauces, and entrées. For added richness, use chicken or white stock instead of water.

VARIATION

Brown Game Bird Stock: Rinse the bones and dry them. Brown the bones in a roasting pan. Combine them with the water and bring to a boil over low heat. Simmer for about 4 hours. Brown the mirepoix and up to 4 ounces (115 grams) tomato paste in the roasting pan; add to the stock. Deglaze the pan with water and add to the stock. Simmer an additional hour. If desired, add one or more of the following herbs and spices to the standard sachet d'épices: rosemary, caraway seed, tarragon stems, and sage.

Fish Fumet

Yield: 1 gallon (3.75 liters)

Oil	4 ounces	120 milliliters
Fish bones or crustacean shells	11 pounds	5 kilograms
White Mirepoix	1 pound	450 grams
Mushroom trimmings	10 ounces	285 grams
Cold water	4 quarts	4.75 liters
White wine	1 quart	1 liter
Bouquet Garni	1 each	1 each
Salt (optional)	to taste	to taste

1. Heat the oil; add the bones and mirepoix.

2. Sweat the bones or shells and mirepoix.

3. Add the mushroom trimmings.

4. Add water, wine, and bouquet garni (and salt, if used); bring to simmer.

5. Simmer for 35 to 40 minutes, skimming the surface as necessary.

6. Strain the stock.

White wine is included in this fumet recipe, but it can be omitted if you prefer.

For Bouquet Garni, see page 424.

The fumet is prepared using the "sweating method." For more information, read Chapter 6, page 212.

443

Fish Stock

Yield: 1 gallon (3.75 liters)

For information on preparing stock see Chapter 6, page 212. For information on the proper handling and storage of stock, see Chapter 2, page 38.

For Standard Sachet d'Épices, see page 424.

This stock is prepared when clarity is important (for consommé, broth, etc.) It has been called the "swimming method" to distinquish from fumet, which is referred to as the "sweating method."

Add the fish's head only if it is extremely fresh.

Be sure to remove all traces of visceral blood from the bones.

Fish bones, trimmings (optional)	*11 pounds*	*5 kilograms*
Cold water	*5 quarts*	*4.75 liters*
White Mirepoix	*1 pound*	*450 grams*
Standard Sachet d'Épices	*1 each*	*1 each*
Mushroom trimmings, (optional)	*10 ounces*	*285 grams*
Salt (optional)	*to taste*	*to taste*

1. Combine all ingredients.

2. Bring the mixture to a simmer over low heat.

3. Skim the surface, as necessary.

4. Simmer for 30 to 40 minutes.

5. Strain the stock.

Shellfish Stock

Yield: 1 gallon (3.75 liters)

Use shrimp, crab, lobster, or crayfish shells, alone, or in combination.

Some chefs recommend a simmering time of 1 1/2 to 2 hours for lobster shells.

Use this stock to prepare fish soups or bisque. It can also be used to prepare a veloute or to poach shellfish.

Crustacean shells	*11 pounds*	*5 kilograms*
Oil	*2 ounces*	*60 milliliters*
Mirepoix	*1 pound*	*450 grams*
Tomato paste	*3 to 4 fluid ounces*	*90 to 120 milliliters*
Cold water	*5 quarts*	*4.75 liters*
Standard Sachet d'Épices	*1 each*	*1 each*
White wine	*1/2 pint*	*240 milliliters*

1. Sauté the crustacean shells in oil until deep red.

2. Add the mirepoix and continue to sauté another 10 to 15 minutes.

3. Add tomato paste and sauté briefly.

4. Add water, seasonings, and wine and simmer 30 minutes.

5. Strain the stock.

Vegetable Stock

Yield: 1 gallon (3.75 liters)

Vegetable oil	*2 ounces*	*60 milliliters*
Onions, sliced	*4 ounces*	*115 grams*
Leeks, green and white parts, chopped	*4 ounces*	*115 grams*
Celery, chopped	*2 ounces*	*55 grams*
Green cabbage, chopped	*2 ounces*	*55 grams*
Carrots, chopped	*2 ounces*	*55 grams*
Turnip, chopped	*2 ounces*	*55 grams*
Tomato, chopped	*2 ounces*	*55 grams*
Garlic cloves, crushed	*3 each*	*3 each*
Cold water	*4 1/2 quarts*	*4.25 liters*
Standard Sachet d'Épices, plus	*1 each*	*1 each*
Fennel seeds	*1 teaspoon*	*1 teaspoon*
Whole cloves	*3 each*	*3 each*

This stock can be used in any recipe calling for stock, particularly when a meatless version is preferred.

For information on preparing stock see Chapter 6, page 212. For information on the proper handling and storage of stock see Chapter 2, page 38.

1. Heat the oil.

2. Add the vegetables and sweat them for 3 to 5 minutes.

3. Add water and sachet d'épices and simmer for 30 to 40 minutes.

4. Strain the stock.

VARIATION

Roasted Vegetable Stock: Roast the vegetables in a large pan, turning to make sure all sides are evenly roasted. Combine them with the water and simmer for 30 to 40 minutes. If desired, fresh or dried chilies may be roasted with the other vegetables.

White Wine Court Bouillon

Yield: 1 gallon (3.75 liters)

For more information on the preparation of and uses for Court Bouillon, see Chapter 6, page 212 and Chapter 10 (on poaching), page 339.

Court Bouillon is a savory fish stew featured in Acadian cuisine. It is a court bouillon base containing aromatic vegetables and regional fish (snapper is most commonly used), thickened with brown roux and served over steamed rice.

If desired, include coriander and fennel seeds in the Court Bouillon.

Cold water	2 1/2 quarts	2.4 liters
White wine	2 1/2 quarts	2.4 liters
Salt (optional)	2 teaspoons	2 teaspoons
Carrots, sliced	12 ounces	340 grams
Onions, sliced	1 pound	450 grams
Thyme leaves, dried	pinch	pinch
Bay leaves	3 each	3 each
Parsley stems	1 bunch	1 bunch
Peppercorns	1/2 ounce	15 grams

1. Combine all ingredients except the peppercorns.
2. Simmer for 50 minutes.
3. Add the peppercorns and simmer for an additional 10 minutes.

V A R I A T I O N

Red Wine Court Bouillon: Replace half of the white wine with an equal amount of dry red wine.

Court bouillon is used to poach fish and vegetables.

Vinegar Court Bouillon

Yield: 1 gallon (3.75 liters)

Cold water	5 quarts	4.75 liters
White wine vinegar	1/2 pint	240 milliliters
Salt (optional)	2 teaspoons	2 teaspoons
Carrots, sliced	12 ounces	340 grams
Onions, sliced	1 pound	450 grams
Thyme leaves, dried	pinch	pinch
Bay leaves	3 each	3 each
Parsley stems	5 to 6 each	5 to 6 each
Peppercorns	1/2 ounce	15 grams

1. Combine all ingredients except the peppercorns.
2. Simmer for 50 minutes.
3. Add the peppercorns and simmer for an additional 10 minutes.

Wild Mushroom Essence

Yield: 1 gallon (3.75 liters)

Olive oil	*1 tablespoon*	*1 tablespoon*
Mushrooms	*3 pounds*	*1.3 kilograms*
Wild mushrooms, dried	*2 ounces*	*60 grams*
Celery	*5 ounces*	*140 grams*
Leeks	*3 ounces*	*85 grams*
Shallots	*1 ounce*	*30 grams*
Water	*1 gallon*	*3.75 liters*
Vermouth	*10 ounces*	*300 milliliters*
Bouquet Garni, plus		
Thyme	*1 teaspoon*	*1 teaspoon*
Chervil	*1 teaspoon*	*1 teaspoon*
Juniper berries	*5 each*	*5 each*
Peppercorns, cracked	*1 teaspoon*	*1 teaspoon*
Garlic cloves	*4 each*	*4 each*
Bay leaves	*2 each*	*2 each*

1. Combine all ingredients in a stock pot, bring to a simmer.

2. Simmer 45 minutes.

3. Strain the stock.

VARIATION

Add different herbs to get a particular flavor, such as oregano or basil.

An essence is prepared in a manner similar to that of a stock. For information on preparing stock see Chapter 6, page 212. For information on the proper handling and storage of stock, see Chapter 2, page 38.

For Bouquet Garni, see page 424.

This essence can be used in any recipe calling for a rich or game-style broth or stock, particularly when a nonmeat stock is desired. Use it in soups and sauces that will be complemented by the mushroom and herb flavor.

Blanc

Yield: 2 quarts (2 liters)

Blanc is used to cook vegetables such as mushrooms, cardoons, celeriac, or salsify to keep them white.

Water	2 quarts	2 liters
Flour	1 ounce	30 grams
Onion	1 slice	1 slice
Cloves, whole	2 each	2 each
Bouquet Garni	1 each	1 each
Salt	2 teaspoons	2 teaspoons
Lemon juice	2 fluid ounces	60 milliliters

1. Combine the ingredients and bring them to a boil.

2. Use as necessary to cook vegetables.

CHAPTER 14 *Soup Recipes*

Soups are an important part of most menus. They may be served as a separate course, or as a combination luncheon item: soup and salad, soup and quiche, or soup and sandwich. Some soups are even good as a main course.

Be sure to check the seasoning and flavor of all soups before they are served, especially if you reheat batches of soup. Bring hot broth-based soups to a full boil over direct heat. Cream soups and veloutés need careful handling to prevent them from breaking. Do not allow them to boil, but bring them up to at least 180°F (82°C).

The recipes in this chapter have been grouped as follows:

- *Broths and Consommés*
- *Vegetable Soups*
- *Cream Soups*
- *Purée Soups*
- *Bisques*
- *Cold Soups*
- *American Regional Soups*
- *International Soups*
- *Asian Soups*

Adding different garnishes to a perfectly prepared broth gives you great flexibility in preparing special soups for your menu.

Use chicken, diced or julienned, as a garnish, or try one of the garnishes suggested in the variations.

For Mirepoix see page 420; for Standard Sachet d'Épices see page 424.

Double Chicken Broth

Yield: 1 gallon (3.75 liters)

Stewing hen	*6 pounds*	*2.7 kilograms*
Chicken Stock	*1 1/2 gallons*	*5.75 liters*
Mirepoix	*1 pound*	*450 grams*
Chopped tomatoes	*8 ounces*	*225 grams*
Standard Sachet d'Épices	*1 each*	*1 each*
Garlic clove, sliced	*1 each*	*1 each*
Salt, to taste	*1 teaspoon*	*1 teaspoon*
Pepper, to taste	*1/2 teaspoon*	*1/2 teaspoon*

1. Bring the stewing hen and stock to a simmer, skim the surface, and simmer very gently for 2 hours.

2. Add the mirepoix and tomatoes and simmer for 1/2 hour.

3. Add the sachet d'épices and garlic; simmer for an additional 1/2 hour.

4. Degrease, remove the chicken, and strain thoroughly.

5. Adjust the seasoning with salt and pepper to taste and garnish as desired.

VARIATIONS

Chicken Broth with Garden Vegetables: Garnish each portion with fine-diced, blanched vegetables (carrots, celery, leeks, peas, turnips) and diced, cooked beef.

Chicken Broth with Barley: Garnish with diced, cooked vegetables and 1 tablespoon of cooked barley per portion.

Chicken Broth with Spaetzle: Garnish with plain, herbed, or spinach spaetzle.

Chicken Noodle Soup: Cook egg noodles (broad or fine) in the broth. Garnish with assorted vegetables.

Beef Broth

Yield: 1 gallon (3.75 liters)

Beef hind shank	*8 pounds*	*3.6 kilograms*
Cold water	*1 1/2 gallons*	*5.75 liters*
Mirepoix	*1 pound*	*450 grams*
Tomatoes, chopped	*8 ounces*	*225 grams*
Standard Sachet d'Épices	*1 each*	*1 each*
Garlic clove, sliced	*1 each*	*1 each*
Salt, to taste	*1 teaspoon*	*1 teaspoon*
Pepper, to taste	*1/2 teaspoon*	*1/2 teaspoon*

1. Bring the beef shank and water to a simmer, skim the surface, and simmer very gently for 3 hours.

2. Add the mirepoix and tomatoes; simmer for 1/2 hour.

3. Add the sachet d'épices and garlic, and simmer for an additional 1/2 hour.

4. Degrease, remove the beef shank, and strain thoroughly.

5. Adjust the seasoning with salt and pepper to taste; garnish as desired.

VARIATIONS

Beef Broth with Garden Vegetables: Garnish each portion with fine-diced, blanched vegetables (carrots, celery, leeks, peas, turnips) and diced, cooked beef.

Beef Broth with Barley: Garnish with diced, cooked vegetables and 1 tablespoon of cooked barley per portion.

Beef Broth with Spaetzle: Garnish with plain, herbed, or spinach spaetzle.

For a deeper flavor, roast the mirepoix or add 1/2 oignon brûlé.

Use lean beef, diced or julienned, as a garnish, or try one of the garnishes suggested in the variations.

For Mirepoix, see page 420; for Sachet d'Épices, see page 424; and for Spaetzle, see page 852.

Lamb Broth

Yield: 1 gallon (3.75 liters)

Garnish with diced or brunoise-cut root vegetables and cubed, cooked lamb.

Lamb hind shank	*8 pounds*	*3.6 kilograms*
Cold water	*1 1/2 gallons*	*5.75 liters*
Mirepoix, roasted	*1 pound*	*450 grams*
Tomatoes, chopped	*8 ounces*	*225 grams*
Garlic clove, sliced	*1 each*	*1 each*
Standard Sachet d'Épices	*1 each*	*1 each*
Salt	*1 teaspoon*	*1 teaspoon*
Pepper	*1/2 teaspoon*	*1/2 teaspoon*

1. Bring the lamb shank and water to a simmer, skim the surface, and simmer very gently for 2 hours.

2. Add the mirepoix, tomatoes, and garlic; simmer for 1/2 hour.

3. Add the sachet d'épices and garlic, and simmer for an additional 1/2 hour.

4. Degrease, remove the lamb shank, and strain thoroughly. Dice lean lamb and add to broth.

5. Season with salt and pepper to taste.

6. Bring to service temperature.

7. Adjust the seasoning with salt and pepper to taste and garnish portions individually or add to batch.

Smoked Turkey Broth

Yield: 1 gallon (3.75 liters)

Turkey legs, smoked	*8 pounds*	*3.6 kilograms*
Chicken stock	*1 1/2 gallons*	*5.75 liters*
Mirepoix	*1 pound*	*450 grams*
Tomatoes, chopped	*8 ounces*	*225 grams*
Standard Sachet d'Épices	*1 each*	*1 each*
Garlic clove, sliced	*1 each*	*1 each*
Salt, to taste	*1 teaspoon*	*1 teaspoon*
Pepper, to taste	*1/2 teaspoon*	*1/2 teaspoon*

Use turkey meat, diced or julienned, as a garnish, or try one of the garnishes suggested in the variations.

For Mirepoix, see page 420; for Standard Sachet d'Épices, see page 424; and for Spaetzle, see page 852.

1. Bring the turkey legs and stock to a simmer, skim the surface, and simmer very gently for 2 hours.

2. Add the mirepoix and tomatoes; simmer for 1/2 hour.

3. Add the sachet d'épices and garlic, and simmer for an additional 1/2 hour.

4. Degrease, remove the turkey leg, and strain thoroughly.

5. Adjust the seasoning with salt and pepper to taste and garnish as desired.

VARIATIONS

Turkey Broth with Garden Vegetables: Garnish each portion with fine-diced, blanched vegetables (carrots, celery, leeks, peas, turnips) and diced, cooked turkey.

Turkey Broth with Barley: Garnish with diced, cooked vegetables and 1 tablespoon of cooked barley per portion.

Turkey Broth with Spaetzle: Garnish with plain, herbed, or spinach spaetzle.

Turkey Broth with Tortilla Strips: Season with 8 ounces of dry sherry immediately before service, if desired. Garnish with Toasted Tortilla Strips, diced green chilies, and grated Monterey Jack cheese.

Beef Consommé

Yield: 1 gallon (3.75 liters)

For a more detailed explanation of the method for preparing a Consommé, refer to Chapter 8, page 262.

For information on preparing Onion Brûlé, see Chapter 6.

For White Beef Stock see page 439; for Standard Sachet d'Épices, see page 424.

Add celeriac and turnips to the clarification if desired.

Clarification		
Onion Brûlé	1 each	1 each
Mirepoix	1 pound	450 grams
Ground shank	3 pounds	1.35 kilograms
Egg whites, beaten	10 each	10 each
Tomatoes, chopped	12 ounces	340 grams
White Beef Stock	5 quarts	4.75 liters
Standard Sachet d'Épices, plus	1 each	1 each
Whole cloves	1 each	1 each
Allspice berries	2 each	2 each
Kosher salt, to taste	1 teaspoon	1 teaspoon
White pepper, top taste	1 teaspoon	1 teaspoon

1. Mix the ingredients for the clarification and blend with stock. Mix well.

2. Bring the mixture to a slow simmer, stirring frequently until raft forms.

3. Add the sachet d'épices and simmer for 45 minutes, or until the appropriate flavor and clarity are achieved. Baste raft occasionally.

4. Strain the consommé; adjust the seasoning with salt and white pepper to taste.

VARIATIONS

Beef Consommé Julienne: Garnish with a julienne of vegetables, blanched until tender.

Beef Consommé Paysanne: Garnish with paysanne-cut vegetables, blanched until tender.

Beef Consommé Printanière: Garnish with tourné vegetables, blanched until tender.

Beef Consommé with Wild Mushrooms: Garnish with sliced wild mushrooms that have been sautéed quickly in hot butter.

Fish Consommé

Yield: 1 gallon (3.75 liters)

Clarification

Fish, whiting or pike, ground	*3 pounds*	*1.35 kilograms*
Egg whites, beaten	*8 each*	*8 each*
Leeks, rough julienne	*4 ounces*	*115 grams*
Celery, rough julienne	*4 ounces*	*115 grams*
Parsley stems	*5 to 6 each*	*5 to 6 each*
White wine	*1 pint*	*.5 liter*
Lemons, juiced	*2 each*	*2 each*
Fish Stock	*5 quarts*	*4.75 liters*
Standard Sachet d'Épices	*1 each*	*1 each*
Salt, to taste	*1 teaspoon*	*1 teaspoon*
Ground white pepper, to taste	*1/2 teaspoon*	*1/2 teaspoon*

1. Mix the ingredients for the clarification and blend with fish stock. Mix well.

2. Bring the mixture to a slow simmer, stirring frequently until raft forms.

3. Add the sachet d'épices and simmer for 45 minutes, or until the appropriate flavor and clarity are achieved. Baste raft occasionally.

4. Strain the consommé; adjust the seasoning with salt and white pepper to taste.

VARIATIONS

Asian Fish Consommé: Flavor with lemongrass, chili pods, or gingerroot, and serve with spring rolls or wontons.

Fish Consommé with Seafood and Fresh Dill: Garnish with small-diced, cooked seafood (shrimp, lobster, crab, scallops) and chopped, fresh dill.

Fish Consommé with Quenelles: Garnish each portion with small quenelles made from fish mousseline forcemeat.

The quantity of fish in the clarification can be reduced by 1 pound (450 grams). This will still produce acceptable results.

For a more detailed explanation of the method for preparing a Consommé, refer to page 262.

Instead of adding the garnish directly to the soup, it should be added to individual portions.

For Standard Sachet d'Épices, see page 424; for Fish Stock, see page 444.

455

As the consommé comes slowly to a boil, the ingredients for the clarification begin to form a mass that will rise to the top of the pot.

For a more detailed explanation of the method for preparing a Consommé, refer to page 262.

For Standard Sachet d'Épices, see page 424; for White Mirepoix, page 420.

The recipes for crepes, used in the garnish of the Chicken Consommé Celestíne, is found on page 872.

Chicken Consommé

Yield: 1 gallon (3.75 liters)

Clarification		
White Mirepoix, chopped	*1 pound*	*455 grams*
Chicken, lean, ground	*3 pounds*	*1.35 kilograms*
Egg whites, beaten	*10 each*	*10 each*
Tomatoes, chopped	*12 ounces*	*340 grams*
Onion Brûlé	*1 each*	*1 each*
Chicken stock, cold	*5 quarts*	*4.75 liters*
Standard Sachet d'Épices, plus:	*1 each*	*1 each*
Whole clove	*1 each*	*1 each*
Allspice berries	*2 each*	*2 each*
Kosher salt, to taste	*1 teaspoon*	*1 teaspoon*
White pepper, to taste	*1/2 teaspoon*	*1/2 teaspoon*

1. Mix the ingredients for the clarification and blend with chicken stock. Mix well.

2. Bring the mixture to a slow simmer, stirring frequently until raft forms.

3. Add the sachet d'épices and simmer for 45 minutes, or until the appropriate flavor and clarity are achieved. Baste raft occasionally.

4. Strain the consommé; adjust the seasoning with salt and white pepper to taste.

VARIATIONS

Chicken Consommé with Julienned Vegetables: Garnish each portion with blanched, julienned leeks, carrots, celery, and potatoes; include a fine julienne of cooked chicken breast, if desired.

Chicken Consommé Paysanne: Garnish each portion with blanched paysanne- cut leeks, turnips, carrots, celery, and potatoes.

Chicken Consommé with Quenelles: Garnish with small quenelles make of chicken mousseline forcemeat.

Chicken Consommé with Garden Vegetables: Garnish with fresh peas, tomato concassée, and other garden vegetables cut into brunoise, if desired.

Chicken Consommé Celestíne: Garnish each portion with julienned strips of a plain or herb-flavored crepe.

Mushroom Consommé

Yield: 1 gallon (3.75 liters)

Clarification

Chicken, lean, ground	*3 pounds*	*1.35 kilograms*
Egg whites, beaten	*10 each*	*10 each*
White Mirepoix, chopped	*1 pound*	*450 grams*
Tomatoes, chopped	*12 ounces*	*340 grams*
Onion Brûlé	*1 each*	*1 each*
Mushroom Essence, cold	*5 quarts*	*4.75 liters*
Standard Sachet d'Épices, plus:	*1 each*	*1 each*
Whole clove	*1 each*	*1 each*
Allspice berries	*2 each*	*2 each*
Kosher salt, to taste	*1 teaspoon*	*1 teaspoon*
White pepper, to taste	*1/2 teaspoon*	*1/2 teaspoon*

1. Prepare the clarification and blend with the essence. Mix well.

2. Bring the mixture to a slow simmer, stirring frequently until raft forms.

3. Add the sachet d'épices and simmer for 45 minutes, or until the appropriate flavor and clarity are achieved. Baste raft occasionally.

4. Strain the consommé; adjust the seasoning with salt and white pepper to taste.

Dried mushrooms give a special, deep flavor to dishes, which some people find as appealing as that of fresh mushrooms.

For a more detailed explanation of the method for preparing a Consommé, refer to Chapter 7, page 262.

The recipe for Standard Sachet d'Épices is on page 424; Mushroom Essence is on page 447.

Garnish the consommé individually at service time with chopped, cooked, fresh or dried, mushrooms.

Game Hen Consommé with Roasted Garlic Custard

Yield: 1 gallon (3.75 liters)

Custards, or royales, should be handled with care. To reheat, it is generally sufficent to place them in the bowl or cup and ladle extremely hot consommé over the custard. A 3/4-ounce (23 grams) portion of royale is appropriate for each serving. Cut the royale into various shapes if desired: diamonds, rounds, squares, or strips.

The recipe for crêpes is found on page 872.

Clarification		
Game hen meat, ground	*2 pounds*	*900 grams*
Egg whites, whipped	*10 each*	*10 each*
Mirepoix, ground	*3/4 pound*	*450 grams*
Tomatoes, chopped	*8 ounces*	*225 grams*
Dry white wine	*2 fluid ounces*	*60 milliliters*
Game hen stock	*5 quarts*	*4.75 liters*
Standard Sachet d'Épices	*1 each*	*1 each*
Salt, to taste	*1 teaspoon*	*1 teaspoon*
White pepper, to taste	*1/2 teaspoon*	*1/2 teaspoon*
Custard		
Milk	*1 1/2 pints*	*.75 liter*
Heavy cream	*8 fluid ounces*	*240 milliliters*
Eggs	*5 each*	*5 each*
Egg whites	*3 each*	*3 each*
Garlic, roasted	*2 heads*	*2 heads*
Ground white pepper	*1/2 teaspoon*	*1/2 teaspoon*
Garnish		
Game hen breast meat, poached, brunoise	*10 ounces*	*285 grams*
Prosciutto, brunoise	*10 ounces*	*285 grams*
Wild rice, cooked	*10 ounces*	*285 grams*

1. Mix the ingredients for the clarification and blend with stock. Mix well.

2. Bring the mixture to a slow simmer, stirring frequently until raft forms.

3. Add the sachet d'épices and simmer for 45 minutes to an hour, or until the appropriate flavor and clarity are achieved. Baste raft occasionally.

4. Strain the consommé; adjust the seasoning with salt and white pepper to taste.

5. To make the custard, combine all ingredients until well blended. Strain, pour into buttered 2-ounce (60-gram) timbale molds.

6. Bake custards in a 170°F (75°C) water bath until set.

7. Add the custard and remaining garnish to the soup immediately before service.

VARIATION

Game Hen Consommé with Plain or Herbed Crepes: Instead of a royale, you can prepare plain or herbed crepes and cut them into strips.

Smoked Turkey Consommé with Fennel Ravioli

Yield: 1 gallon (3.75 liters)

Clarification

Turkey, ground	*3 pounds*	*1.35 kilograms*
Egg whites, beaten	*10 each*	*10 each*
Mirepoix, chopped	*1 pound*	*450 grams*
Onion Brûlé	*1 each*	*1 each*
Sage, leaves	*2 each*	*2 each*
Bay leaf	*1 each*	*1 each*
Thyme, sprig	*1 each*	*1 each*
Peppercorns	*1/2 teaspoon*	*1/2 teaspoon*
Tomato Concassé	*12 ounces*	*340 grams*
Smoked turkey broth, cold	*5 quarts*	*4.75 liters*
Standard Sachet d'Épices	*1 each*	*1 each*
Salt	*to taste*	*to taste*
White pepper	*to taste*	*to taste*

Filling

Garlic, minced	*1/2 ounce*	*15 grams*
Shallots, minced	*1/2 ounce*	*15 grams*
Olive oil	*1 tablespoon*	*1 tablespoon*
Fennel, brunoise	*1 pound*	*450 grams*
Chervil leaves, chopped	*1 teaspoon*	*1 teaspoon*
Fennel, leaves	*2 teaspoons*	*2 teaspoons*
Ground chicken meat	*3 1/2 ounces*	*100 grams*
Heavy cream	*2 fluid ounces*	*60 milliliters*
Pernod	*2 fluid ounces*	*60 milliliters*
Pasta Dough	*14 ounces*	*400 grams*

Garnish

Tomatoes, peeled, seeded, julienne	*1 pound*	*455 grams*
Chervil, pluches	*as needed*	*as needed*

The recipe for Pasta Dough may be found on page 846. The recipe for Smoked Turkey Broth is on page 453.

For a more detailed explanation of the method for preparing a Consommé, refer to page 262.

When rolling out the pasta dough, you may want to place fennel leaves between two sheets then run through the machine to give a decorative effect.

1. Mix the ingredients for the clarification and blend with broth. Mix well.

2. Bring the mixture to a slow simmer, stirring frequently until raft forms.

3. Add the sachet d'épices and simmer for 45 minutes, or until the appropriate flavor and clarity are achieved. Baste raft occasionally.

4. Strain the consommé; adjust the seasoning with salt and white pepper to taste.

5. Prepare filling for ravioli: sauté garlic and shallots in olive oil. Add fennel, and cook until tender, using stock if needed. Add chervil, fennel leaves, and salt. Cool.

(Recipe continued on following page)

459

6. Prepare a mousseline forcemeat with chicken and cream; Fold in cooled fennel mixture and Pernod.

7. Roll out the pasta dough (with fennel leaves, see note). Cut in ravioli shape. Fill with fennel mixture and seal.

8. Blanch ravioli in boiling salted water until tender. Drain and reserve.

9. Serve consommé garnished with ravioli, tomatoes, and chervil.

Clear Oxtail Soup

Yield: 2 gallons (7.5 liters)

Oxtails, disjointed	*10 pounds*	*4.5 kilograms*
Mirepoix, coarse chop	*2 pounds*	*900 grams*
Beef Stock	*2 gallons*	*7.5 liters*
Tomatoes, chopped	*5 pounds*	*225 kilograms*
Standard Sachet d'Épices	*1 each*	*1 each*
Egg whites	*12 each*	*12 each*
Water	*8 fluid ounces*	*240 milliliters*
Vinegar	*2 tablespoons*	*2 tablespoons*
Salt, to taste	*2 teaspoons*	*2 teaspoons*
Garnish		
Celery, small dice, cooked	*2 pounds*	*900 grams*
Carrots, small dice, cooked	*2 pounds*	*900 grams*
Turnips, small dice, cooked	*2 pounds*	*900 grams*
Sherry wine, dry	*4 fluid ounces*	*120 milliliters*

1. Brown the oxtails.

2. Add mirepoix and cook until the vegetables are tender.

3. Add stock, tomatoes, and sachet d'épices. Simmer until oxtails are tender.

4. Strain liquid and cool. Remove meat from oxtails and cut into small dice.

5. Whisk eggs whites, water, vinegar, and salt together.

6. Degrease liquid and whisk the egg white mixture in.

7. Bring to a simmer and strain through a double cheesecloth.

8. Add garnish ingredients. Heat thoroughly.

9. Stir in sherry and season with salt to taste.

American Bounty Vegetable Soup

Yield: 1 gallon (3.75 liters)

Beef shank, sliced 3 inches thick	*3 pounds*	*1.3 kilograms*
White Beef Stock	*1 gallon*	*3.75 liters*
Leeks, white only, sliced thin	*4 ounces*	*115 grams*
Onions, 1/4-inch dice	*8 ounces*	*225 grams*
Carrots, peeled, 1/4-inch dice	*4 ounces*	*15 grams*
Celery, 1/4-inch dice	*4 ounces*	*115 grams*
Turnips peeled, 1/4-inch dice	*6 ounces*	*170 grams*
Green cabbage, chiffonade	*4 ounces*	*15 grams*
Clarified butter, as needed	*2 ounces*	*60 grams*
Garlic cloves, minced	*3 each*	*3 each*
Standard Sachet d'Épices	*1 each*	*1 each*
Potatoes, 1/4-inch dice	*4 ounces*	*15 grams*
Lima beans	*4 ounces*	*15 grams*
Corn kernels	*4 ounces*	*15 grams*
Tomato Concassé	*4 ounces*	*15 grams*
Salt, to taste	*1 teaspoon*	*1 teaspoon*
Pepper, to taste	*1/2 teaspoon*	*1/2 teaspoon*
Nutmeg, ground, to taste	*1/4 teaspoon*	*1/4 teaspoon*
Parsley, flat leaf, chopped	*1/4 cup*	*1/4 cup*

The recipe for White Beef Stock may be found on page 439.

Some chefs prefer the flavor of chicken broth in this soup.

Garnish the soup with Croutons (page 435) or Cheddar Cheese Rusks (page 436).

1. Simmer the beef shank in the stock until the meat is very tender. Strain and degrease the broth.

2. When the meat is cool enough to handle, cut it into neat dice and reserve for garnish.

3. Sweat the leeks, onions, carrots, celery, turnips, and cabbage in clarified butter until limp.

4. Add garlic and sauté until aroma is apparent.

5. Add the reserved beef broth and sachet d'épices; simmer for approximately 10 minutes.

6. Add the potatoes, beans, corn, and tomato concassé. Continue to simmer for another 20 minutes.

7. Adjust the seasoning with salt, pepper, and nutmeg to taste.

8. Garnish with parsley.

Amish-Style Chicken Corn Soup

Yield: 1 gallon (3.75 liters)

The Amish are renowned for their use of herbs. Saffron, featured here, is part of a crocus. It has a distinct flavor that can overpower other ingredients.

The recipe for Mirepoix may be found on page 420.

Spaetzle (page 852) may be used instead of egg noodles.

Stewing hen, quartered	*1 each*	*1 each*
Standard Sachet d'Épices	*1 each*	*1 each*
Chicken stock	*5 quarts*	*4.75 liters*
Mirepoix	*12 ounces*	*340 grams*
Saffron threads, crushed	*1 teaspoon*	*1 teaspoon*
Garnish		
Chicken meat, diced	*5 ounces*	*140 grams*
Corn kernels, cooked	*8 ounces*	*225 grams*
Celery, diced, cooked	*4 ounces*	*115 grams*
Parsley, chopped	*2 ounces*	*60 grams*
Egg noodles, cooked	*10 ounces*	*285 grams*
Salt, to taste	*1 teaspoon*	*1 teaspoon*
Pepper, to taste	*1/2 teaspoon*	*1/2 teaspoon*

1. Combine the hen, sachet d'épices, and stock. Simmer for 1 1/2 hours, skimming as necessary.

2. Add the mirepoix and saffron and simmer for an additional 1 1/2 hours.

3. Remove the hen, let stand until cool enough to handle, then remove the meat and dice.

4. Strain the broth.

5. Bring the soup to service temperature.

6. Add the garnish and adjust the seasoning with salt and pepper to taste.

Minestrone

Yield: 1 gallon (3.75 liters)

Salt pork, ground	*2 ounces*	*60 grams*
Olive oil	*2 fluid ounces*	*60 milliliters*
Onions, paysanne	*1 pound*	*455 grams*
Celery, paysanne	*8 ounces*	*225 grams*
Carrots, paysanne	*8 ounces*	*225 grams*
Green peppers, paysanne	*8 ounces*	*225 grams*
Green cabbage, chiffonade	*8 ounces*	*225 grams*
Garlic cloves, minced	*3 each*	*3 each*
Tomato Concassé	*1 1/2 pounds*	*680 grams*
Chicken Stock	*1 gallon*	*3.75 liters*
Chickpeas, cooked	*4 ounces*	*115 grams*
Black-eyed peas, cooked	*6 ounces*	*170 grams*
Ditalini, cooked	*6 ounces*	*170 grams*
Salt, to taste	*1 teaspoon*	*1 teaspoon*
Pepper, to taste	*1/2 teaspoon*	*1/2 teaspoon*
Parmesan cheese, grated	*5 ounces*	*140 grams*

The recipe for Chicken Stock may be found on page 442.

Replace the ditalini with other types of pasta: vermicelli, tubettini, or spaghetti. Break long strands of pasta into shorter lengths before cooking them.

To bolster the flavor, add up to 4 ounces (115 grams) of tomato paste.

1. Render the salt pork in the oil. Do not brown.

2. Add the onions, celery, carrots, peppers, cabbage, and garlic and sweat until the onions are translucent.

3. Add the Tomato Concassé and stock.

4. Simmer until the vegetables are tender. Do not overcook them.

5. Add the chickpeas, black-eyed peas, and ditalini. Simmer the soup until all ingredients are hot.

6. Adjust the seasoning with salt and pepper to taste.

7. Garnish with grated Parmesan cheese just prior to service.

Other stocks, including white stock, chicken stock, or combinations of stocks, can be used to prepare a good onion soup. Each will have a different flavor and color.

White wine is often used instead of Calvados in this soup. Or, if preferred, some apple juice may be used.

Sherry may be used to finish the soup just before it is served, if desired.

White Onion Soup is made by gently cooking the onions in butter or oil until they are limp but not colored, over low heat. If desired, up to 6 ounces (170 grams) of flour may be added as a thickener. In some classic recipes, the onions are puréed, then either returned to the soup or spread on a crouton.

You will need approximately 20 croutons for 20, 6-fluid ounce (120-milliliter) servings.

Onion Soup Gratiné

Yield: 1 gallon (3.75 liters)

Onions, sliced thin	*3 pounds*	*1.35 kilograms*
Clarified butter	*2 ounces*	*60 grams*
Calvados (optional)	*4 fluid ounces*	*120 milliliters*
White Beef Stock	*1 gallon*	*3.75 liters*
Salt, to taste	*1 teaspoon*	*1 teaspoon*
Pepper, to taste	*1/2 teaspoon*	*1/2 teaspoon*
Croutons or rusks	*1 per portion*	*1 per portion*
Gruyère cheese, grated	*1 1/4 pounds*	*570 grams*

1. Sauté the onions in clarified butter until browned. Add a little butter, if necessary, to prevent burning.

2. Deglaze the pan with the Calvados; add the stock.

3. Simmer until the onions are tender and the soup is properly flavored.

4. Adjust the seasoning with salt and pepper to taste.

5. Garnish each portion with a crouton. Top generously with grated Gruyère and brown under a salamander or broiler, or bake in a moderate oven until lightly browned.

Potage au Pistou

Yield: 1 gallon (3.75 liters)

Chicken stock	*3 quarts*	*2.8 liters*
Potatoes, small dice	*1 pound*	*450 grams*
Vermicelli pasta, broken into pieces	*4 ounces*	*115 grams*
Green beans, cut in 1/4-inch pieces	*1 pound*	*450 grams*
Plum tomatoes, small concassé	*1 pound*	*450 grams*
Aillade Paste		
Garlic cloves, crushed or chopped	*2 each*	*2 each*
Basil leaves	*1 ounce*	*30 grams*
Olive oil	*2 tablespoons*	*2 tablespoons*
Chicken Stock	*2 tablespoons*	*2 tablespoons*
Salt, to taste	*1/2 teaspoon*	*1/2 teaspoon*
Pepper, to taste	*1/2 teaspoon*	*1/2 teaspoon*
Gruyère cheese, shredded	*for garnish*	*for garnish*

(Recipe continued on facing page)

1. Bring stock to a boil. Add potatoes, pasta, and green beans, and cook until done.

2. Add tomato concassé, cook for 5 minutes and remove from heat.

3. Purée aillade ingredients in a blender.

4. Add aillade paste to individual portions. Adjust seasoning, top with Gruyère cheese, and serve.

Potage Garbure

Yield: 1 gallon (3.75 liters)

Salt pork, ground	*4 ounces*	*115 grams*
Olive oil	*2 ounces*	*60 milliliters*
Onion, 1/4-inch dice	*8 ounces*	*225 grams*
Carrots, 1/4-inch dice	*12 ounces*	*340 grams*
Leeks, 1/4-inch dice	*12 ounces*	*340 grams*
Potatoes, 1/4-inch dice	*12 ounces*	*340 grams*
Green cabbage, 1/4-inch dice	*12 ounces*	*340 grams*
Zucchini, 1/4-inch dice	*12 ounces*	*340 grams*
Tomato Concassé, 1/4-inch dice	*1 pound*	*450 grams*
Salt, to taste	*1 teaspoon*	*1 teaspoon*
Pepper, to taste	*1/2 teaspoon*	*1/2 teaspoon*

A garbure is a traditional French soup that typically includes cabbage, potatoes, and an assortment of root vegetables.

1. Render the salt pork. Add the olive oil and heat.

2. Sauté onions, carrots, and leeks in olive oil and salt pork, add chicken stock and bring to a simmer, cook for 10 minutes.

3. Add turnips, potatoes, cabbage, and zucchini, simmer 10 minutes longer.

4. Add tomato concassé, salt, and pepper to soup and simmer 10 minutes; adjust seasoning.

Adding the purée to the soup base gives greater control of the flavor and consistency of the finished soup.

See method for Cream Soups, Chapter 8, page 267.

Prepare a thin velouté, using the ratio as in Table 8-3. The recipe is on page 531.

Fines Herbes is explained on page 427.

Cream of Broccoli Soup

Yield: 1 gallon (3.75 liters)

Onions, chopped	*8 ounces*	*225 grams*
Celery, chopped	*4 ounces*	*115 grams*
Leeks, chopped	*4 ounces*	*115 grams*
Broccoli stems, chopped	*3 pounds*	*1.3 kilograms*
Butter	*3 ounces*	*85 grams*
Chicken Stock	*3 quarts*	*3 liters*
Velouté	*12 ounces*	*340.2 grams*
Salt, to taste	*1 teaspoon*	*1 teaspoon*
Pepper, to taste	*1/2 teaspoon*	*1/2 teaspoon*
Heavy cream, heated	*1 pint*	*.5 liter*
Broccoli florets, blanched	*1 pound*	*450 grams*

1. Sweat the onions, celery, leeks, and broccoli stems in butter.

2. Add the velouté and cook until all ingredients are tender.

3. Purée the solids until they are completely smooth. Return the purée to the velouté and simmer slowly for 10 minutes.

4. Adjust the seasoning with salt and pepper to taste.

5. Add hot cream immediately before service.

6. Strain through either a cheesecloth or chinois.

7. Garnish to order with broccoli florets before serving.

VARIATIONS

Cream of Asparagus (**Crème Argenteuil**): Replace the broccoli with an equal weight of asparagus stems. Garnish with blanched asparagus tips.

Cream of Lettuce (**Crème Choisy**): Replace the broccoli with an equal weight of shredded lettuce (Romaine, Boston, etc.). Garnish with a chiffonade of fines herbes.

Cream of Celery (**Crème Céleri**): Replace the broccoli with an equal weight of celery or celeriac. Garnish with diced blanched celery.

Cream of Cauliflower

Yield: 1 gallon (3.75 liters)

Cauliflower, trimmed and coarsely chopped	2 pounds	900 grams
Potatoes, large dice	3/4 pound	340 grams
Onions, chopped	6 ounces	170 grams
Leeks, chopped	6 ounces	170 grams
Celery, chopped	4 ounces	115 grams
Chicken Stock	2 quarts	2 liters
Standard Sachet d'Épices	1 each	1 each
Milk, boiling	1 pint	480 milliliters
Salt, to taste	1/2 teaspoon	1/2 teaspoon
Pepper, to taste	1/4 teaspoon	1/4 teaspoon
Cauliflower florets, blanched	1 pound	450 grams

1. Combine the cauliflower, potatoes, onions, leeks, celery, and 8 ounces (240 milliliters) of chicken stock and smother until the vegetables begin to soften.

2. Add the remainder of the stock and the sachet d'épices. Simmer the soup until all ingredients are very tender.

3. Drain, reserving the liquid, and purée the vegetables until smooth.

4. Combine the purée with enough soup liquid to correct the consistency.

5. Add the hot milk and adjust the seasoning with salt and pepper to taste.

6. Garnish with cauliflower before serving.

VARIATION

Cream of Cauliflower Soup with Cheddar: Add 12 ounces (340 grams) of grated Cheddar cheese to the soup, in step 5.

For Chicken Stock see page 442.

If desired, finish the soup by whipping in 1/2 teaspoon of butter per portion immediately prior to service time.

Serve with Goat Cheese Croutons, see page 436 or Rye and Cheese Croutons, page 436.

This soup may be referred to as Crème DuBarry, a reference to one of the Sun King's consorts, Comtesse du Barry. She was considered an excellent cook, and especially favored dishes that featured cauliflower. Today, DuBarry generally indicates the presence of cauliflower in a dish.

Cream of Chicken Soup

Yield: 1 gallon (3.75 liters)

This soup is also known as Purée à la Reine, *or Queen's Soup.*

Use a thin chicken Velouté (page 531) to prepare this soup, if you prefer. In that case, omit the onion, carrots, celery, butter, flour, and bay leaf.

Onions, medium dice	*8 ounces*	*225 grams*
Celery, medium dice	*4 ounces*	*115 grams*
Carrots, medium dice	*4 ounces*	*115 grams*
Butter	*9 ounces*	*250 grams*
Flour	*7 ounces*	*200 grams*
Chicken Stock, heated	*1 gallon*	*3.75 liters*
Bay leaf	*1 each*	*1 each*
Chicken breasts, diced	*3 1/4 pounds*	*1.5 kilograms*
Milk, heated	*24 fluid ounces*	*720 milliliters*
Half and half, heated	*12 fluid ounces*	*360 milliliters*
Salt, to taste	*1 teaspoon*	*1 teaspoon*
Pepper, to taste	*1/2 teaspoon*	*1/2 teaspoon*

1. Sauté the onions, celery, and carrots in butter until tender.

2. Add the flour and cook out the roux for 8 to 10 minutes.

3. Add the stock gradually, stirring until thickened and smooth.

4. Add the bay leaf and chicken; simmer for 30 minutes.

5. Remove the chicken and purée it. Return to the soup.

6. Add the milk and half and half. Simmer 10 minutes and strain through a fine sieve.

7. Adjust the seasoning with salt and pepper to taste.

Cream of Tomato Soup

Yield: 1 gallon (3.75 liters)

Bacon, diced	*2 ounces*	*60 grams*
Oil, as needed	*2 ounces*	*60 grams*
Carrots, diced	*8 ounces*	*225 grams*
Celery, diced	*8 ounces*	*225 grams*
Onions, diced	*8 ounces*	*225 grams*
Garlic cloves, minced	*2 each*	*2 each*
Flour	*6 ounces*	*170 grams*
Chicken Stock	*2 quarts*	*2 liters*
Tomatoes, chopped	*2 pound*	*900 grams*
Tomato purée	*24 fluid ounces*	*720 milliliters*
Pepper, to taste	*1/2 teaspoon*	*1/2 teaspoon*
Parsley stems	*4 each*	*4 each*
Bay leaf	*1 each*	*1 each*
Clove, whole	*1 each*	*1 each*
Light cream, hot	*1 1/2 pints*	*720 milliliters*

Use fresh tomatoes when they are in season. Otherwise, canned plum tomatoes are the best choice.

For a Roasted Tomato Soup, slice fresh tomatoes and roast them at 400°F (205°C) until browned.

1. Render the bacon in the oil. Add carrots, celery, onions, and garlic, reduce heat and sweat about 8 to 10 minutes. Add flour and blend well to make a roux. Cook out about 3 to 4 minutes.

2. Add stock, blend well. Add chopped tomatoes, tomato purée, and pepper; simmer about 30 minutes. Add the parsley stems, bay leaf, and clove; continue to simmer another 30 minutes. Strain well.

3. Blend hot cream into strained base soup. Adjust consistency and seasoning.

VARIATION

Cream of Tomato with Rice: Add 1 pound (450 grams) of cooked long grain white rice to the tomato soup, immediately prior to serving, or garnish individual portions of soup with 3 tablespoons of cooked rice.

Cheddar Cheese Soup

Yield: 1 gallon (3.75 liters)

The quality of the cheese plays a distinct role in this soup. Select an aged Cheddar for the best results.

Add the cheese just before serving the soup; it may take on a curdled appearance if held too long.

For Chicken Stock see page 442; for White Mirepoix, see page 420.

Use a prepared Velouté (page 531) and begin this soup at step 4.

Replace the wine with a lager beer, if you prefer.

White Mirepoix	12 ounces	340 grams
Garlic cloves, minced	2 each	2 each
Clarified butter	4 ounces	115 grams
Flour	4 ounces	115 grams
Chicken Stock	3 quarts	3 liters
Cheddar cheese, grated	2 pounds	900 grams
White wine	8 fluid ounces	240 milliliters
Dry mustard	2 tablespoons	2 tablespoons
Heavy cream	1 pint	480 milliliters
Tabasco, to taste	1/2 teaspoon	1/2 teaspoon
Worcestershire sauce, to taste	1/2 teaspoon	1/2 teaspoon
Salt, to taste	1/2 teaspoon	1/2 teaspoon
White pepper, to taste	1/4 teaspoon	1/4 teaspoon
Green peppers, julienne, blanched	4 ounces	115 grams
Red peppers, julienne, blanched	4 ounces	115 grams

1. Sweat the mirepoix and garlic in the butter until it is limp.

2. Add the flour to make a roux and cook out for 5 minutes.

3. Add the stock gradually, whipping to work out lumps, and simmer for 45 minutes.

4. Add the Cheddar cheese and wine (reserving 1 ounce to dilute the mustard) and continue to heat the soup gently until cheese melts. Do not allow the soup to boil.

5. Blend the dry mustard and wine. Add this mixture along wih the cream. Heat gently for 2 to 3 minutes, and adjust consistency with stock if necessary. Season to taste with Tabasco and Worcestershire sauces, salt, and pepper.

6. Add the peppers to the soup or use them to garnish individual portions.

Wild Mushroom Soup

Yield: 1/2 gallon (2 liters)

Assorted wild mushrooms	*2 pounds*	*900 grams*
Shallots, minced	*3 each*	*3 each*
Thyme, sprigs	*2 each*	*2 each*
Bay leaf	*1/2 each*	*1/2 each*
Butter	*1 1/2 ounces*	*40 grams*
Mushroom Essence	*2 quarts*	*2 liters*
Salt, to taste	*1/2 teaspoon*	*1/2 teaspoon*
Pepper, to taste	*1/4 teaspoon*	*1/4 teaspoon*
Heavy cream	*1 1/2 pints*	*720 milliliters*
Cornstarch (optional)	*1 teaspoon*	*1 teaspoon*

Garnish individual portions with profiteroles filled with Duxelles. The recipe for Duxelles is on page 421.

The recipe for Mushroom Essence is on page 447.

1. Chop the mushrooms, reserving 1/2 pound for garnish.

2. Sauté shallots, add chopped mushrooms, thyme sprigs, and bay leaf in butter for 5 minutes.

3. Add the Mushroom Essence and cook another 20–30 minutes, then purée.

4. Add remaining Mushroom Essence and heavy cream; simmer for 10 minutes.

5. Strain.

6. Sauté mushrooms for garnish and add to soup.

7. Season and adjust consistency with cornstarch slurry.

Use a single variety of mushroom, or a combination of varieties. Save some good-looking examples to use as a garnish.

For an elegant presentation, top with puff pastry. Seal edges and bake until the pastry is golden.

If desired, finish the soup with a little white wine or sherry instead of the lemon juice.

The recipe for Velouté is on page 531.

Cream of Mushroom Soup

Yield: 1 gallon (3.75 liters)

Mushrooms, chopped	*2 1/2 pounds*	*1.15 kilograms*
Leeks, whites, thinly sliced	*8 ounces*	*225 grams*
Celery, finely chopped	*4 ounces*	*115 grams*
Butter	*3 ounces*	*85 grams*
Chicken Velouté	*2 1/2 quarts*	*2.5 liters*
Thyme, sprigs	*2 each*	*2 each*
Heavy cream, heated	*24 fluid ounces*	*720 milliliters*
Salt, to taste	*1 teaspoon*	*1 teaspoon*
Pepper, to taste	*1/2 teaspoon*	*1/2 teaspoon*
Lemon juice, to taste	*1 tablespoon*	*1 tablespoon*
Garnish		
Mushrooms, diced, cooked	*10 ounces*	*285 grams*
Chervil pluches	*20 each*	*20 each*

1. Sweat the chopped mushrooms, leeks, and celery in butter.

2. Add velouté and thyme; simmer for 10 minutes. Discard thyme.

3. Purée in blender, strain through cheesecloth or a fine chinois.

4. Add heavy cream, return to a simmer, season with salt, pepper, and lemon juice to taste.

5. Garnish with the cooked, diced mushrooms and chervil pluches.

Watercress Soup

Yield: 1 gallon (3.75 liters)

Watercress, rinsed, stemmed, and blanched	*3 bunches*	*3 bunches*
Leeks, chopped	*6 ounces*	*170 grams*
Onions, chopped	*8 ounces*	*225 grams*
Butter, as needed	*4 ounces*	*115 grams*
White Beef Stock	*1 gallon*	*3.75 liters*
Potatoes, sliced thin	*2 1/2 pounds*	*1.2 kilograms*
Salt, to taste	*1 teaspoon*	*1 teaspoon*
Pepper, to taste	*1/2 teaspoon*	*1/2 teaspoon*
Sour cream	*1 pound*	*450 grams*
Garnish		
Watercress sprigs	*to taste*	*to taste*

To blanch watercress, bring a large pot of salted water to a boil. Drop in watercress and cook for 20 to 30 seconds. Drain and rinse with cool water.

For Cream Soups see page 267.

The recipe for White Beef Stock is on page 439.

1. Purée the watercress. Reserve it.
2. Sweat the leeks and onions in butter.
3. Add the stock and bring it to a boil.
4. Add the potatoes and simmer them until they are tender.
5. Purée the soup and add the watercress. Return the soup to a simmer. Add the sour cream to finish, and heat through but do not boil again.
6. Adjust the seasoning with salt and pepper to taste.
7. Garnish the soup with watercress sprigs.

473

Garnish the finished soup with toasted pumpkin or squash seeds and a little puff of cream.

Clean and wash the squash seeds as you cut the squash. Lightly oil them and dry them in an oven on low heat.

For Chicken Stock, see page 442.

A vegetable stock can be used in place of the chicken stock to prepare a meatless version.

Butternut Squash Soup

Yield: 1 gallon (3.75 liters)

Gingerroot, minced	*3/4 ounce*	*20 grams*
White wine	*12 fluid ounces*	*360 milliliters*
Vegetable oil, as needed	*1 fluid ounce*	*30 milliliters*
Onions, medium dice	*6 ounces*	*170 grams*
Celery, medium dice	*6 ounces*	*170 grams*
Garlic clove, chopped	*1 tablespoon*	*1 tablespoon*
Butternut squash, cooked	*2 pounds*	*900 grams*
Chicken Stock	*3 quarts*	*3 liters*
Heavy cream	*8 fluid ounces*	*240 milliliters*
Salt, to taste	*1 teaspoon*	*1 teaspoon*
White pepper, to taste	*1/2 teaspoon*	*1/2 teaspoon*

1. Heat the ginger and wine until nearly at a boil. Remove from the heat; steep until cooled to room temperature. Strain. Reserve wine.

2. Heat the oil; sweat the onion, celery, and garlic until limp.

3. Peel, seed, and dice the squash. Add it to the pot along with the infused wine and chicken stock.

4. Simmer until the vegetables are soft; about one hour.

5. Purée and strain through a medium chinois, if necessary.

6. Add the heavy cream. Return the soup to just below a simmer. Adjust seasoning to taste with salt and pepper.

VARIATION

Other squashes: This soup can be prepared with any of a variety of puréed squashes: butternut, hubbard, pumpkin, or acorn.

Wild Rice Soup

Yield: 1 gallon (3.75 liters)

Butter, clarified	2 ounces	60 grams
Leeks, fine dice	12 ounces	340 grams
Carrots, fine dice	4 ounces	115 grams
Celery, fine dice	4 ounces	115 grams
Flour	1 ounce	30 grams
Chicken Stock	1 gallon	3.75 liters
Wild rice	9 ounces	250 grams
Heavy cream	1 pint	480 milliliters
Salt, to taste	1 teaspoon	1 teaspoon
Chives, minced	2 ounces	60 grams
Parsley, chopped	1 ounce	30 grams
Dry sherry	2 fluid ounces	60 milliliters

Wild rice is available in varying quality grades. If you can find "broken" rice, this is a good place to use it.

Garnish the soup with chopped toasted walnuts or pecans.

Evaporated skimmed milk can replace heavy cream to finish soup.

If this soup seems thin as you are preparing it, you may need to add some prepared Roux (page 422), but remember the soup will continue to thicken as it simmers.

1. Heat the butter over medium heat. Add the leeks, carrots, and celery; sweat them until soft.

2. Add the flour and stir it well to make a roux. Cook the roux gently over low heat for approximately 3 minutes, stirring constantly.

3. Add the chicken stock gradually, whipping well with each addition to eliminate lumps. Bring it to a simmer.

4. Add the wild rice and continue to simmer the soup until the rice is done. Add the heavy cream.

5. Garnish the soup with chives and parsley immediately before serving. Add the sherry, and serve the soup immediately.

Purée of Split Pea

Yield: 1 gallon (3.75 liters)

For Chicken Stock, see page 442; for Standard Sachet d'Épices see page 424; for Croutons see page 435.

A pale roux may be incorporated into the stock in step 4. This will give the soup greater stability if it must be held on a steam table.

For a heartier version, purée half of the soup and return the purée with the meat in step 7.

Garnish individual portions at service with croutons that have been fried in butter and garlic.

Bacon, chopped fine	6 slices	6 slices
Vegetable oil	2 fluid ounces	60 milliliters
Onions, chopped	12 ounces	340 grams
Celery, chopped	4 ounces	115 grams
Garlic, crushed	1 tablespoon	1 tablespoon
Chicken Stock	1 gallon	3.75 liters
Potatoes, large dice	1 pound	450 grams
Green split peas	1 1/2 pounds	680 kilograms
Smoked ham hocks	1 pound	455 grams
Bay leaves	2 each	2 each
Salt, to taste	1 teaspoon	1 teaspoon
Whole black peppercorns	1/2 teaspoon	1/2 teaspoon

1. Render the bacon in the oil.

2. Add the onions and celery and sauté until the onions become transparent.

3. Add the garlic and sauté until an aroma develops; do not brown.

4. Add the stock, potatoes, split peas, ham hocks, and bay leaves and bring to a simmer. Allow the soup to simmer for 1 1/2 hours or until the peas are very tender.

5. Remove the ham hocks and bay leaves.

6. Purée the soup until smooth. Adjust consistency with additional stock if necessary.

7. Dice the lean meat from the ham hock and return it to the soup.

8. Bring the soup back to a boil. Adjust the seasoning with salt and pepper to taste.

VARIATIONS

Yellow Split Pea Soup: Replace the green split peas with yellow split peas.

Vegetarian Split Pea Soup: The chicken stock can be replaced with vegetable stock, if desired. Omit the ham hocks and bacon.

Purée of Black Bean

Yield: 1 gallon (3.75 liters)

Black beans, dried	*1 1/2 pounds*	*680 grams*
Bacon fat, rendered	*4 ounces*	*115 grams*
Onions, medium dice	*12 ounces*	*340 grams*
Chicken Stock	*1 gallon*	*3.75 liters*
Standard Sachet d'Épices	*1 each*	*1 each*
Smoked ham hocks	*2 each*	*2 each*
Dry sherry	*6 fluid ounces*	*180 milliliters*
Allspice, ground (optional)	*1/2 teaspoon*	*1/2 teaspoon*
Salt, to taste	*1 teaspoon*	*1 teaspoon*
Pepper, to taste	*1/2 teaspoon*	*1/2 teaspoon*
Garnish		
Sour cream	*8 ounces*	*225 grams*
Tomato concassé	*12 ounces*	*340 grams*
Scallions, minced	*5 ounces*	*140 grams*

For Chicken Stock, see page 442. The Standard Sachet d'Épices is on page 424.

For a meatless version, replace the chicken stock with vegetable stock and omit the ham hocks. Replace the bacon fat with vegetable oil.

Chopped cilantro, diced jicama, chopped hard-boiled eggs, grated Monterey Jack cheese, and/or toasted tortilla strips also make excellent garnishes for this soup.

Additional seasonings to consider for this soup include garlic, cilantro, chipotle peppers, and lemon or lime juice (in place of the sherry).

1. Soak the beans overnight in enough cold water to cover them. Drain.
2. Heat bacon fat in soup pot; add the onions and sweat until translucent.
3. Add chicken stock.
4. Add beans, Sachet d'Épices, and ham hocks.
5. Simmer until the beans are very tender.
6. Remove ham hocks. Dice lean meat and reserve. Remove sachet.
7. Remove half of the beans and purée until smooth. Return the purée to the soup.
8. Finish soup with sherry and allspice. Add diced ham, if desired.
9. Adjust the seasoning with salt and pepper to taste.
10. Garnish individual portions at the time of service with sour cream, tomato concassé, and minced scallions.

White Bean Soup

1 gallon (3.75 liters)

For Chicken Stock see page 442; for White Beef Stocks see page 439.

Serve with Croutons page 435, or Cheddar Cheese Rusks page 436.

This soup is also known as Purée Faubonne.

Great northern or navy beans	2 pounds	900 grams
Bacon, chopped fine	6 ounces	170 grams
Leeks, julienne	6 ounces	170 grams
Red onions, dice	8 ounces	225 grams
Garlic, minced	1/2 ounce	15 grams
White Beef or Chicken Stock	1 gallon	3.75 liters
Thyme, sprig	1 each	1 each
Bay leaves	2 each	2 each
Salt, to taste	1/2 teaspoon	1/2 teaspoon
Pepper, to taste	1/4 teaspoon	1/4 teaspoon

1. Soak beans overnight in cool water to cover. Drain.
2. Render bacon in a soup pot; sweat leeks, onions, and garlic until tender.
3. Add beans, stock, thyme, and bay leaves. Simmer until beans are tender, about 1 1/2 hours.
4. Remove thyme and bay leaf. Season with salt and pepper.

VARIATION

Red Bean Purée (**Purée Soissonnaise**): Prepare the soup as directed, substituting red beans for great northern beans.

Senate Bean Soup

Yield: 1 gallon (3.75 liters)

Navy beans, dried	*1 1/2 pounds*	*680 grams*
Chicken Stock	*1 gallon*	*3.75 liters*
Smoked ham hocks	*2 each*	*2 each*
Vegetable oil	*2 ounces*	*60 milliliters*
Onions, diced	*6 ounces*	*170 grams*
Carrots, diced	*6 ounces*	*170 grams*
Celery, diced	*6 ounces*	*170 grams*
Garlic cloves, minced	*2 each*	*2 each*
Oignon Piqué (optional)	*1 each*	*1 each*
Standard Sachet d'Épices	*1 each*	*1 each*
Chef's potatoes, large dice	*1 pound*	*450 grams*
Tabasco, to taste	*1 teaspoon*	*1 teaspoon*
Salt, to taste	*1 teaspoon*	*1 teaspoon*
Pepper, to taste	*1/2 teaspoon*	*1/2 teaspoon*

For Chicken Stock, see page 442; for Oignon Piqué see page 210; for Standard Sachet d'Épices see page 424.

Garnish individual portions at service time with Croutons, see page 435.

Replace the Chicken Stock with Vegetable Stock and omit the ham hocks. Replace the bacon fat with vegetable oil.

1. Soak the beans overnight. Drain.

2. Combine the beans, stock, and ham hocks. Simmer for 2 hours. Strain this broth. Dice meat from ham hocks and reserve.

3. Heat the oil. Add the onions, carrots, and celery; sweat for 4 to 5 minutes, or until the onions are translucent. Add the garlic; sauté it until an aroma is apparent.

4. Add the beans, broth, Oignon Piqué, Sachet d'Épices, potatoes, and ham hocks; simmer until the beans and potatoes are tender.

5. Remove and discard the Oignon Piqué and the Sachet d'Épices.

6. Purée half of the soup. Recombine the purée and reserved ham with the remaining soup. Adjust the consistency with additional broth or water if necessary.

7. Return the soup to a simmer and adjust the seasoning with Tabasco, salt, and pepper to taste.

VARIATION

Alternate method of preparation: Simmer the beans with the stock and ham hocks for 1 hour. Add the potatoes, Oignon Piqué, and Sachet d'Épices; continue to simmer until they are very tender. Remove and discard the Oignon Piqué and Sachet d'Épices. Purée half of the soup and recombine. Sweat the vegetables in bacon fat, lard, or oil. Add them to the soup, with the diced ham, at service time.

Purée of Lentils

Yield: 1 gallon (3.75 liters)

Esaü is acknowledged to have sold his inheritance for a bowl of this soup.

For White Beef Stock see page 439; for Standard Sachet d'Épices see page 424; for Croutons see page 435.

The White Beef Stock can be replaced with Vegetable Stock if desired. To adjust the seasoning or change the flavor slightly, add lemon juice.

Lentils	*1 pound*	*450 grams*
White Beef Stock	*1 gallon*	*3.75 liters*
Bacon, medium dice	*6 ounces*	*170 grams*
Carrots, medium dice	*4 ounces*	*115 grams*
Onions, medium dice	*8 ounces*	*225 grams*
Standard Sachet d'Épices	*1 each*	*1 each*
Butter	*3 ounces*	*85 grams*
Salt, to taste	*1 teaspoon*	*1 teaspoon*
Pepper, to taste	*1/2 teaspoon*	*1/2 teaspoon*
Garnish		
Croutons, as needed	*8 ounces*	*225 grams*
Chervil, chopped	*1 bunch*	*1 bunch*

1. Combine the lentils, stock, and bacon. Bring the mixture to a simmer and skim it.

2. Add the carrots and onions; simmer for 45 minutes.

3. Add the Sachet d'Épices; simmer for another 30 minutes.

4. Strain the mixture. Reserve the stock; discard the Sachet d'Épices.

5. Purée the solids and add the reserved stock to achieve the proper consistency.

6. Finish with butter.

7. Adjust the seasoning with salt and pepper to taste.

8. Garnish each portion with a bit of whole butter, croutons, and chervil.

VARIATION

Potage Esaü: Prepare lentil soup and add cooked rice.

French Lentil Soup

1 gallon (3.75 liters)

Vegetable oil	2 fluid ounces	60 milliliters
Onions, small dice	8 ounces	225 grams
Garlic cloves, minced	2 each	2 each
Carrots, brunoise	6 ounces	170 grams
Leeks, brunoise	4 ounces	115 grams
Celery, brunoise	4 ounces	115 grams
Tomato paste	1 ounce	30 grams
French lentils	1 1/4 pounds	575 grams
Chicken Stock	3 quarts	3 liters
Standard Sachet d'Épices	1 each	1 each
Bay leaf	1 each	1 each
Thyme leaves, dried	1/2 teaspoon	1/2 teaspoon
Caraway seeds	1/2 teaspoon	1/2 teaspoon
Lemon, sliced	1 each	1 each
Sherry wine vinegar	1 fluid ounce	30 milliliters
Riesling wine	4 fluid ounces	120 milliliters
Salt, to taste	1 teaspoon	1 teaspoon
White pepper, to taste	1/2 teaspoon	1/2 teaspoon

For Chicken Stock see page 442; for Standard Sachet d'Épices see page 424.

As this soup is held, it may become thicker. Adjust as necessary by adding more water or stock. Be sure to check the seasoning if you make a consistency adjustment.

The Chicken Stock can be replaced with Vegetable Stock if desired.

1. Heat oil, and add onions and garlic; sauté until translucent.

2. Add carrots, leeks, and celery; sweat until limp.

3. Add tomato paste; sauté but do not brown.

4. Add lentils, stock, Sachet d'Épices, bay leaf, thyme, caraway and lemon. Simmer until lentils are tender; remove Sachet d'Épices and lemon.

5. Adjust seasoning with vinegar, wine, and salt and pepper.

Crecy is the name given to various dishes that are either made from or garnished with carrots, in honor of the excellent carrots harvested at Crecy, a small town in the Seine-et-Marne.

Potage Crecy is a classic puréed soup. For more detail on preparing Puréed Soups see Chapter 7, page 269.

For Chicken Stock see page 442. The Standard Sachet d'Epices is on page 424.

Three-quarters of a pound of potatoes can be used in place of the rice if desired.

Potage Purée Crecy

Yield: 1 gallon (3.75 liters)

Butter	2 ounces	60 grams
Onions, minced	2 ounces	60 grams
Carrots, diced	3 pounds	1.3 kilograms
Chicken Stock	3 quarts	3 liters
Rice, uncooked	6 ounces	170 grams
Standard Sachet d'Épices, plus		
Tarragon, fresh	2 tablespoons	2 tablespoons
Parsley	2 tablespoons	2 tablespoons
Peppercorns, crushed	2 teaspoons	2 teaspoons
Heavy cream, heated	8 fluid ounces	240 milliliters
Salt, to taste	1/2 teaspoon	1/2 teaspoon
Pepper, to taste	1/4 teaspoon	1/4 teaspoon

1. Sauté onions and carrots until onions are translucent.

2. Add chicken stock, rice, and Sachet d'Épices; simmer until rice and carrots are extremely tender.

3. Remove Standard Sachet d'Épices and purée soup.

4. Finish soup by adding heavy cream.

5. Adjust seasoning to taste with salt and pepper.

Sweet Potato Soup

Yield: 1 gallon (3.75 liters)

Vegetable oil, as needed	*2 fluid ounces*	*60 milliliters*
Garlic cloves, minced	*2 each*	*2 each*
Celery, medium dice	*6 ounces*	*170 grams*
Onions, fine dice	*6 ounces*	*170 grams*
Leeks, fine dice	*6 ounces*	*170 grams*
Chicken Stock	*3 quarts*	*3 liters*
Sweet potatoes, medium dice	*3 pounds*	*1.35 kilograms*
Cinnamon stick	*1 each*	*1 each*
Nutmeg, whole, fresh ground	*1/4 teaspoon*	*1/4 teaspoon*
Maple syrup	*2 ounces*	*60 grams*
Salt	*1 teaspoon*	*1 teaspoon*
Heavy cream, heated	*12 fluid ounces*	*360 milliliters*
Garnish		
Heavy cream	*4 fluid ounces*	*120 milliliters*
Currants, dried	*2 ounces*	*60 grams*
Almonds, sliced, toasted	*2 ounces*	*60 grams*

This soup reinforces the subtly sweet flavor of the sweet potato with maple syrup and nutmeg.

1. Heat the oil. Add the garlic, celery, onions, and leeks; sweat them until the onions are translucent.

2. Add the stock and sweet potatoes. Bring to a boil, reduce the heat, and simmer until the sweet potatoes are extremely tender.

3. Purée the soup until it is smooth. Return it to the soup pot. Add the remaining ingredients. Return the soup to a boil.

4. Thin the soup with stock or water, if necessary. Remove and discard the cinnamon stick.

5. Prior to service time, whip the heavy cream. Put a dollop on each serving.

For Chicken Stock see page 442.

Garnish individual portions with whipped heavy cream, currants, and almonds.

VARIATION

Vegetarian version: A vegetable stock can be used to prepare a meatless version.

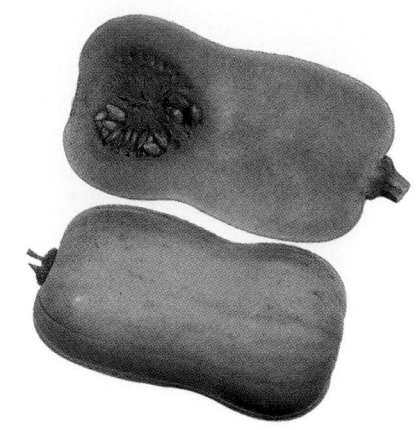

Butternut squash makes an excellent soup, but use other squashes or pumpkin in its place if you prefer.

For Chicken Stock see page 442. To reduce sodium, adjust the seasoning with citrus juices: lemon or lime. A Vegetable Stock can be used to prepare a nonmeat soup. The Standard Sachet d'Épices is on page 424.

To serve, ladle into soup bowls. Garnish with chopped chestnuts and a sprinkle of cinnamon, with toasted squash seeds or almond slices, or with diced Granny Smith apples, if desired. Or dust lightly with ground cumin and a dollop of sour cream.

Autumn Squash Apple Cider Soup

Yield: 1 gallon (3.75 liters)

Butternut squash, flesh only, diced	2 1/2 pounds	1 kilogram
Vegetable oil	3 fluid ounces	90 milliliters
Onions, chopped	12 ounces	340 grams
Leeks, chopped	12 ounces	340 grams
Carrots, chopped	6 ounces	170 grams
Celery, chopped	6 ounces	170 grams
Ginger, ground	1 teaspoon	1 teaspoon
Allspice, ground	1/4 teaspoon	1/4 teaspoon
Nutmeg, ground	1/2 teaspoon	1/2 teaspoon
Cumin, ground	1/2 teaspoon	1/2 teaspoon
Salt	1 teaspoon	1 teaspoon
Dry white wine	6 fluid ounces	180 milliliters
Cider	1 1/2 pints	720 milliliters
Chicken Stock	2 quarts	2 liters
Standard Sachet d'Épices, plus:		
Star anise	4 each	4 each
Parsley stems	5 each	5 each
Whole black peppercorns	10 each	10 each
Thyme, sprigs	2 each	2 each
Salt,	to taste	to taste
Pepper,	to taste	to taste

1. Roast squash in 425°F (220°C) oven until soft. Purée and reserve.

2. Heat oil in large stock pot and sauté onions, leeks, carrots, and celery with ground spices until soft.

3. Deglaze with wine and cider. Add squash, stock, and Sachet d'Épices; simmer until all ingredients are tender.

4. Remove sachet. Purée the soup and pass through fine chinois. Adjust consistency with additional cider or stock. Add salt and pepper to taste.

VARIATION

Butternut, hubbard, pumpkin, or acorn squashes can be used. Use sweet potato to replace 1 pound (450 grams) of the squash.

Shrimp Bisque

Yield: 1 gallon (3.75 liters)

Shrimp shells	1 1/2 pounds	680 grams
Onions, minced	1 pound	450 grams
Butter	2 ounces	60 grams
Garlic cloves, minced	2 each	2 each
Paprika	3 tablespoons	45 milliliters
Tomato paste	2 ounces	60 grams
Brandy	3 fluid ounces	90 milliliters
Velouté (made with Shellfish Stock)	3 quarts	3 liters
Heavy cream, heated	1 quart	1 liter
Shrimp, peeled and deveined	26 ounces	750 grams
Salt, to taste	1/2 teaspoon	1/2 teaspoon
Pepper, to taste	1/4 teaspoon	1/4 teaspoon
Old Bay Seasoning, to taste	1/2 teaspoon	1/2 teaspoon
Tabasco, to taste	1/4 teaspoon	1/4 teaspoon
Worcestershire sauce, to taste	1/2 teaspoon	1/2 teaspoon
Dry sherry	4 fluid ounces	120 milliliters

Add cooked diced shrimp meat to garnish the finished soup.

A more detailed explanation of bisque preparation can be found in Chapter 7 on page 271.

Make a Velouté (page 531) using either Shellfish Stock (page 444) or Fish Fumet (page 443).

1. Sauté the shrimp shells and onions in butter.

2. Add the garlic, paprika, and tomato paste. Cook out for a few minutes.

3. Add the brandy and deglaze. Let the brandy reduce until dry.

4. Add the Velouté. Simmer for 45 minutes. Strain the bisque through a fine chinois or cheesecloth.

5. Return the bisque to a simmer. Add the heavy cream.

6. Dice the shrimp, sauté, and add to the bisque, simmering gently for 5 minutes. Adjust the seasoning to taste with salt, pepper, Old Bay Seasoning, Tabasco, and Worcestershire sauce.

7. Add the sherry immediately before serving.

VARIATION

Lobster Bisque: Replace shrimp shells and shrimp with lobster shells and lobster tail meat.

Pumpkin Bisque

Yield:1 gallon (3.75 liters)

Other winter squashes may be substituted for part or all of the pumpkin.

Serve the soup in hollowed mini pumpkins if desired.

Gingerroot, grated	*1 teaspoon*	*1 teaspoon*
White wine	*2 fluid ounces*	*60 milliliters*
Garlic, chopped	*1 tablespoon*	*1 tablespoon*
Celery, medium dice	*5 ounces*	*140 grams*
Onion, medium dice	*6 ounces*	*170 grams*
Leeks, white only, medium dice	*3 ounces*	*85 grams*
Butter, unsalted	*1 ounce*	*30 grams*
Pumpkin flesh	*2 pounds*	*900 grams*
Chicken stock	*1 gallon*	*3.75 liters*
Salt, to taste	*1 teaspoon*	*1 teaspoon*
Nutmeg, ground (optional)	*1 teaspoon*	*1 teaspoon*
Heavy cream, whipped	*10 fluid ounces*	*300 milliliters*

1. Steep the gingerroot in the wine. Strain. Reserve wine.

2. Sauté the garlic, celery, onions, and leeks in butter.

3. Add the pumpkin and stock and simmer until all the vegetables are tender.

4. Purée the solids with enough liquid to achieve the desired consistency.

5. Add the wine to the soup, season with salt and nutmeg, and finish with a dollop of whipped heavy cream.

Oyster Bisque

Yield: 1 gallon (3.75 liters)

Oysters, washed	*60 each*	*60 each*
Fish stock	*3 quarts*	*2.85 liters*
Onions, diced	*8 ounces*	*225 grams*
Butter	*4 ounces*	*115 grams*
Converted long-grain rice	*12 ounces*	*340 grams*
Heavy cream, heated	*1 1/2 pints*	*720 milliliters*
Tabasco, to taste	*1 teaspoon*	*1 teaspoon*
Worcestershire sauce, to taste	*1 tablespoon*	*1 tablespoon*
Salt	*1/2 teaspoon*	*1/2 teaspoon*
Parsley, chopped	*2 tablespoons*	*2 tablespoons*

(Recipe continued on facing page)

1. Place oysters in a pot with the stock; steam until they open.

2. Immediately strain broth and remove oyster meat from shell. Reserve both.

3. Sauté the onions in butter, add rice and oyster broth, and simmer until rice is soft.

4. Purée the soup, chop half the oysters, add to soup. Reserve the remaining oysters for the garnish.

5. Add heavy cream, adjust consistency and seasoning to taste with Tabasco, Worcestershire sauce, and salt.

Oysters must be alive when they are cooked. For more information on selecting and cleaning oysters see Chapter 5. This bisque is thickened with rice, in the classic manner. For more detail about bisques see Chapter 7, page 271.

For Fish Stock see page 444.

Garnish individual portions with the remaining whole oysters and chopped parsley, thyme, or other fresh herbs.

Chilled Red Plum Soup

Yield: 1 gallon (3.75 liters)

Red plums, pitted, peeled, and chopped	5 pounds	2.25 kilograms
Apple juice	2 quarts	2 liters
Standard Sachet d'Épices, plus		
Ginger, fresh, large slices	2 each	2 each
Cinnamon stick	1 each	1 each
Allspice, grains	8 to 10 each	8 to 10 each
Black peppercorns	6 to 8 each	6 to 8 each
Honey	4 ounces	115 grams
Arrowroot, as needed	1/2 teaspoon	1/2 teaspoon
Lemon juice, to taste	1 fluid ounce	30 milliliters
Garnish per serving		
Sour cream	2 teaspoons	20 grams
Almonds, slivered and toasted	1/2 teaspoon	1/2 teaspoon

1. Simmer the plums in enough apple juice to cover, along with the Sachet d'Épices and the honey, until the plums are tender. Discard the Sachet d'Épices.

2. Purée the soup until it is very smooth. Strain if desired.

3. Return the soup to a simmer.

4. Thicken with diluted arrowroot if necessary.

5. Adjust the flavor with lemon juice to taste.

6. Chill the soup thoroughly.

7. At service, garnish each portion with sour cream and toasted, slivered almonds.

Chilled Apple Soup

Yield: 1 gallon (3.75 liters)

Replace the apples with pears. Substitute pear cider for the apple juice.

Golden Delicious apples, medium, quartered	16 each	16 each
White wine, dry	24 ounces	720 milliliters
Apple juice	8 ounces	240 milliliters
Sugar	8 ounces	225 grams
Cinnamon stick	1 each	1 each
Gingerroot, large slices	3 each	3 each
Sour cream	8 fluid ounces	240 milliliters
Heavy cream	8 fluid ounces	240 milliliters
Lemon juice, fresh	as needed	as needed

1. Combine the apples, wine, half of the apple juice, the sugar, cinnamon, and gingerroot; bring the mixture to a boil.

2. Simmer the mixture until the apples are tender.

3. Remove the cinnamon and ginger.

4. Purée the mixture through a food mill or sieve.

5. Blend the sour cream and heavy cream, and add to the apple purée. Stir to combine. Adjust the consistency with the remaining apple juice.

6. Chill the soup thoroughly.

7. Adjust the seasoning with a few drops of lemon juice.

Beet Fennel Ginger Soup

Yield: 1 gallon (3.75 liters)

Beets, diced	*3 1/2 pounds*	*1.6 kilograms*
Savoy cabbage, chopped	*1 3/4 pounds*	*.800 kilograms*
Fennel, chopped (reserve the tops)	*1 3/4 pounds*	*.800 kilograms*
Garlic cloves, chopped	*5 each*	*5 each*
Gingerroot, fine dice	*3 ounces*	*85 grams*
Vegetable Stock	*1 gallon*	*3.75 liters*
Salt, to taste	*1 teaspoon*	*1 teaspoon*
Pepper, to taste	*1/2 teaspoon*	*1/2 teaspoon*
Nonfat yogurt	*10 ounces*	*285 grams*
Fennel leaves, reserved from above	*20 each*	*20 each*

The recipe for Vegetable Stock may be found on page 445.

This soup could also be served chilled.

Replace yogurt with sour cream or a combination of sour cream and yogurt, if desired.

To shorten overall cooking time for soup, cook beets in advance in simmering water until tender, peel, dice, and then proceed with method.

1. Combine beets, cabbage, fennel, garlic, and ginger; add vegetable stock to cover.

2. Bring to a boil, cover, and simmer the soup until all of the ingredients are very tender.

3. Strain the soup through a sieve, and purée the vegetables in a food processor, adding some of the liquid as necessary.

4. Combine the broth with the puréed vegetables until the desired consistency is reached.

5. Serve in heated soup cups or plates. Garnish with a tablespoonful of yogurt and a sprig of fennel leaf.

Chilled Gazpacho

Yield: 1 gallon (3.75 liters)

For Croutons, see page 435.

Serve individual portions garnished with chopped herbs or scallions and Croutons. Add a pinch of clove to the croutons when frying them, for additional flavor.

Gazpacho has a short refrigeration shelf-life. The tomatoes will sour very quickly. It is best when prepared on a daily basis.

Tomato concassé	2 1/2 pounds	1 kilogram
Cucumbers, peeled, seeded, and diced	10 ounces	285 grams
Onions, diced	10 ounces	285 grams
Green peppers, diced	10 ounces	285 grams
Red peppers, diced	10 ounces	285 grams
White bread, cubed	8 ounces	225 ounces
Olive oil	6 fluid ounces	180 milliliters
Red wine vinegar	4 fluid ounces	120 milliliters
Salt, to taste	1 teaspoon	1 teaspoon
White pepper, to taste	1/2 teaspoon	1/2 teaspoon
Garnish		
Tomato, small dice	2 ounces	60 grams
Red pepper, small dice	2 ounces	60 grams
Green pepper, small dice	2 ounces	60 grams
Cucumber, small dice	2 ounces	60 grams
Croutons	8 ounces	225 grams

1. Combine the ingredients, except the garnish; chill the soup. Let the soup rest overnight.

2. Purée the soup and strain.

3. Garnish each portion or serve garnish ingredients separately.

New England-Style Clam Chowder

Yield: 1 gallon (3.75 liters)

Cherrystone clams, washed	20 each	20 each
Water	1 quart	1 liter
Salt pork, minced to a paste	4 ounces	115 grams
Onions, minced	4 ounces	115 grams
Celery, fine dice	4 ounces	115 grams
Flour	3 1/2 ounces	100 grams
Potatoes, 1/4-inch dice	3/4 pound	340 grams
Milk, scalded	1 quart	1 liter
Heavy cream, scalded	12 fluid ounces	360 milliliters
Salt, to taste	1/2 teaspoon	1/2 teaspoon
White pepper, to taste	1/2 teaspoon	1/2 teaspoon
Tabasco, to taste	1/2 teaspoon	1/2 teaspoon
Worcestershire sauce, to taste	1/2 teaspoon	1/2 teaspoon

Clams must be alive at the time they are to be cooked. For more information on selecting clams, see Chapter 5. For information on preparing Tomato Concassé, see Chapter 6, page 193.

1. Steam the clams in water in a covered pot until they open.
2. Strain the broth through a filter or cheesecloth and reserve it.
3. Pick, chop, and reserve the clams.
4. Render the salt pork in the soup pot; add the onions and celery and sweat until they are translucent.
5. Add the flour; cook to make a blond roux.
6. Add reserved broth and milk gradually and incorporate it completely, working out any lumps that might form.
7. Simmer for 30 minutes, skimming the surface as necessary.
8. Add the potato to the soup and simmer until tender.
9. Add the reserved clams and cream.
10. Adjust the seasoning to taste with salt, white pepper, Tabasco, and Worcestershire sauce.

Manhattan-Style Clam Chowder

Yield: 1 gallon (3.75 liters)

The recipe for Manhattan-Style Clam Chowder has a tomato broth base. New England-Style Clam Chowder has a creamy base and has no tomatoes at all.

Clams must be alive at the time they are to be cooked. For more information on selecting clams, see Chapter 5.

Chowder clams, washed	30 each	30 each
Water	1 quart	1 liter
Salt pork, minced to a paste	3 ounces	85 grams
Onions, medium dice	8 ounces	225 grams
Carrots, medium dice	4 ounces	115 grams
Celery, medium dice	8 ounces	225 grams
Leeks, white only, medium dice	4 ounces	115 grams
Green peppers, medium dice	4 ounces	115 grams
Garlic, mashed to a paste	1 teaspoon	1 teaspoon
Tomato Concassé	1 pound	450 grams
Bay leaf	1 each	1 each
Thyme, sprig	1 each	1 each
Oregano, sprig	1 each	1 each
Potatoes, medium dice	3/4 pound	340 grams
Salt, to taste	1 teaspoon	1 teaspoon
White pepper, to taste	1/2 teaspoon	1/2 teaspoon
Tabasco, to taste	1/2 teaspoon	1/2 teaspoon
Worcestershire sauce, to taste	1/2 teaspoon	1/2 teaspoon
Old Bay Seasoning, to taste	1/2 teaspoon	1/2 teaspoon

1. Steam the clams in water in a covered pot until they open.

2. Pick, chop, and reserve the clams. Strain and reserve the clam broth.

3. Render the salt pork in the soup pot.

4. Sweat the onions, carrots, celery, leeks, and green peppers in the rendered salt pork until limp.

5. Add the garlic; sauté until an aroma is apparent.

6. Add the reserved clam broth, tomato concassé, bay leaf, thyme, and oregano; simmer for 30 minutes.

7. Add the potatoes; simmer until they are tender.

8. Remove the herbs and discard.

9. Degrease the soup. Add the clams and adjust the seasoning to taste with salt, white pepper, Tabasco, Worcestershire sauce, and Old Bay Seasoning.

Corn Chowder

Yield: 1 gallon (3.75 liters)

Salt pork, ground	*4 ounces*	*115 grams*
Onions, small dice	*6 ounces*	*170 grams*
Celery, small dice	*6 ounces*	*170 grams*
Green peppers, small dice	*4 ounces*	*115 grams*
Red peppers, small dice	*4 ounces*	*115 grams*
Flour	*4 ounces*	*115 grams*
Chicken Stock	*2 quarts*	*2 liters*
Corn kernels	*2 pounds*	*900 grams*
Potatoes, small dice	*2 pounds*	*900 grams*
Bay leaf	*1 each*	*1 each*
Heavy cream, scalded	*1 pint*	*480 milliliters*
Milk, scalded	*1 pint*	*480 milliliters*
Salt, to taste	*1/2 teaspoon*	*1/2 teaspoon*
White pepper, to taste	*1/2 teaspoon*	*1/2 teaspoon*
Tabasco, to taste	*1/2 teaspoon*	*1/2 teaspoon*
Worcestershire sauce, to taste	*1 teaspoon*	*1 teaspoon*

Fresh corn gives this soup a rich, sweet flavor.

For Chicken Stock, see page 442.

Substitute evaporated milk for the heavy cream in the recipe for a lower cholesterol soup.

1. Render the salt pork.

2. Sweat the onions, celery, and peppers in the rendered salt pork.

3. Add the flour and cook to make a blond roux.

4. Add the chicken stock gradually, whipping to work out lumps. Bring the soup to a simmer. Cook for 30 to 40 minutes.

5. Purée half of the corn and add it to the soup with the potatoes.

6. Add the whole corn kernels and bay leaf and simmer until the corn and potatoes are tender.

7. Combine the heavy cream and milk; add to the soup.

8. Remove and discard the bay leaf.

9. Adjust the seasoning with salt, white pepper, Tabasco, and Worcestershire sauce, to taste.

Fish Chowder

Yield: 1 gallon (3.75 liters)

Other fish and chopped shellfish can be added to the soup. Garnish with croutons or oyster crackers.

For Fish Stock, see page 444.

Substitute evaporated milk for the heavy cream in the recipe.

Salt pork, ground	*4 ounces*	*115 grams*
Onions, medium dice	*4 ounces*	*115 grams*
Celery, medium dice	*4 ounces*	*115 grams*
Carrots, medium dice	*4 ounces*	*115 grams*
Flour	*4 ounces*	*115 grams*
Fish Stock	*2 quarts*	*2 liters*
Potatoes, medium dice	*10 ounces*	*285 grams*
Cod fillet, cubed	*20 ounces*	*570 grams*
Milk, hot	*1 pint*	*480 milliliters*
Heavy cream, hot	*1 pint*	*480 milliliters*
Parsley, chopped	*2 tablespoons*	*2 tablespoons*
Salt, to taste	*1/2 teaspoon*	*1/2 teaspoon*
Tabasco, to taste	*1/2 teaspoon*	*1/2 teaspoon*
Worcestershire sauce, to taste	*1 teaspoon*	*1 teaspoon*

1. Render salt pork; add onions, celery, and carrots. Sauté until onions are translucent.

2. Add flour and cook 2 to 3 minutes.

3. Add fish stock, bringing to a simmer.

4. Add potatoes; simmer until potatoes are tender.

5. Add cod; simmer 3 minutes longer.

6. Finish soup by adding milk, heavy cream, and parsley.

7. Season to taste with salt, Tabasco, and Worcestershire sauce.

Chicken and Shrimp Gumbo

Yield: 1 gallon (3.75 liters)

Andouille sausage, chopped	3 ounces	85 grams
Chicken meat, lean, chopped	5 ounces	140 grams
Onions, diced	8 ounces	225 grams
Green peppers, chopped	5 ounces	140 grams
Celery, chopped	5 ounces	140 grams
Jalapeños, chopped	1/2 ounce	15 grams
Scallions, split and cut on bias	4 ounces	115 grams
Garlic, chopped	1/2 ounce	15 grams
Okra, sliced	5 ounces	140 grams
Tomato Concassé	8 ounces	225 grams
Flour, baked to dark brown	5 ounces	140 grams
Chicken Stock	3 quarts	3 liters
Bay leaves	2 each	2 each
Oregano, dried	1 teaspoon	1 teaspoon
Onion powder	1 teaspoon	1 teaspoon
Thyme, dried	1/2 teaspoon	1/2 teaspoon
Basil, dried	1/2 teaspoon	1/2 teaspoon
Shrimp, peeled, deveined, and chopped	12 ounces	340 grams
Converted long grain rice, cooked	20 ounces	570 grams
Filé powder	1 tablespoon	1 tablespoon
Salt, to taste	1 teaspoon	1 teaspoon
Pepper	1/4 teaspoon	1/4 teaspoon

Filé powder is the powdered root of the sassafras plant. The word filé *translates from French as "stringy." When added to a gumbo at the correct point, filé powder thickens the soup slightly. If, however, it is allowed to boil, the powder becomes stringy and gummy. Never allow a filé-thickened soup to return to a full boil.*

Instead of adding the rice directly to the soup, it can be added by individual portions. Use about 2 tablespoons cooked rice per portion.

For information about peeling and deveining shrimp see Chapter 6, page 251.

1. Sauté the sausage and add the chicken. Sauté until chicken loses its raw appearance.

2. Add the onion, green pepper, celery, jalapeños, scallions, garlic, okra, and tomato concassé. Sauté until tender and translucent.

3. Add the flour and cook out for several minutes.

4. Add the stock, stirring to work out any lumps.

5. Add the seasonings; simmer for half an hour.

6. Add the shrimp and rice, simmer for 2 minutes.

7. Add the filé powder, whipping well. Do not allow the soup to return to a boil.

8. Adjust the seasoning to taste with salt and pepper, if necessary.

Use smoked ham hocks, as shown here, neck bones, or other smoked pork cuts to make a broth. This broth can then be used to prepare beans, soups, stews, or sauces.

Eliminate the cream if desired. Replace salt pork with 1 fluid ounce (30 milliliters) vegetable oil.

For information about blanching green vegetables see Chapter 10, page 341.

For Standard Sachet d'Épices see page 424; for Chicken Stock see page 442.

If collards are unavailable, escarole, dandelion, turnip, and kale may be used.

Ham Bone and Collard Greens Soup

Yield: 1 gallon (3.75 liters)

Salt pork	*4 ounces*	*115 grams*
Onions, small dice	*8 ounces*	*225 grams*
Celery, small dice	*4 ounces*	*115 grams*
Flour	*5 ounces*	*140 grams*
Chicken Stock	*3 quarts*	*3 liters*
Ham hock	*2 each*	*2 each*
Standard Sachet d'Épices	*1 each*	*1 each*
Collard greens, chopped, blanched	*2 pounds*	*900 grams*
Heavy cream	*8 fluid ounces*	*240 milliliters*

1. Render the salt pork.

2. Sweat the onions and celery.

3. Add the flour and make a roux. Cook out for several minutes.

4. Add the chicken stock gradually, whipping to work out any lumps.

5. Add the ham hock and sachet d'épices; simmer for 1 hour.

6. Cut collard greens into small dice or chiffonade and add to soup. Simmer until tender.

7. Remove hocks and sachet d'épices, remove meat from hocks, and dice.

8. Finish with heavy cream and garnish with diced reserved ham hock meat.

Maryland Crab Soup

Yield: 1 gallon (3.75 liters)

Water	1 gallon	3.75 liters
Salt	2 tablespoons	2 tablespoons
Blue crabs	24 each	24 each
Old Bay Seasoning	1 teaspoon	1 teaspoon
Butter	6 ounces	170 grams
Onions, minced	8 ounces	225 grams
Flour	7 ounces	200 grams
Fish Fumet	2 1/2 quarts	2.5 liters
Milk	1 quart	1 liter
Heavy cream	1 pint	480 milliliters
Dry sherry	3 fluid ounces	90 milliliters
Parsley, chopped	1 ounce	30 grams
Salt, to taste	1/2 teaspoon	1/2 teaspoon
Pepper, to taste	1/2 teaspoon	1/2 teaspoon
Mace	1/4 teaspoon	1/4 teaspoon

She-crabs are female crabs with the roe in evidence. This coral-colored part of the crab is highly prized, and is added just at the last moment, as you would a liaison.

1. Bring water, salt, and Old Bay Seasoning to a boil; add crabs, boil 6 minutes.

2. Drain crabs, pick meat, and reserve.

3. Sweat onion in butter, add flour, cook out roux.

4. Incorporate fumet, milk, and cream, simmer 30 to 45 minutes.

5. Add crab meat, sherry, parsley, and season to taste with salt, pepper, mace and additional Old Bay Seasoning, if desired.

Peanut Soup

Yield: 1 gallon (3.75 liters)

For Chicken Stock see Chapter 13, page 442.

Peanuts are not true nuts. They are actually legumes. Peanuts have been used to prepare a variety of dishes throughout the world. Booker T. Washington, one of America's great inventors, is credited with fostering an increased appreciation of the ground nut, or "goober."

Servings may be garnished with chopped parsley or chopped roasted peanuts.

Fresh-roasted peanuts can be substituted for some or part of the peanut butter. Purée them with some chicken stock before adding to the soup.

Celery, medium dice	*6 ounces*	*170 grams*
Onions, fine dice	*2 ounces*	*60 grams*
Green peppers (optional), fine dice	*1 ounce*	*30 grams*
Butter	*4 ounces*	*115 grams*
Flour	*3 ounces*	*85 grams*
Chicken Stock, heated	*2 1/2 quarts*	*2 1/2 liters*
Peanut butter, unsalted, without sugar	*10 ounces*	*285 grams*
Milk	*1 quart*	*1 liter*
Salt, to taste	*1 teaspoon*	*1 teaspoon*
Sugar (optional)	*1 teaspoon*	*1 teaspoon*

1. Sweat celery, onions, and green peppers in butter until tender. Add the flour and make a roux. Cook lightly, but do not brown.

2. Gradually add the hot stock; blend until smooth. This will be quite thin.

3. Place this béchamel in a bain-marie and add peanut butter and milk. Blend well. Cook until heated and smooth. Adjust consistency and seasoning with sugar and salt to taste.

VARIATION

Spicy Peanut Soup: For a spicier version, add 1 or 2 teaspoons of chili powder, or substitute hot sesame oil for the butter.

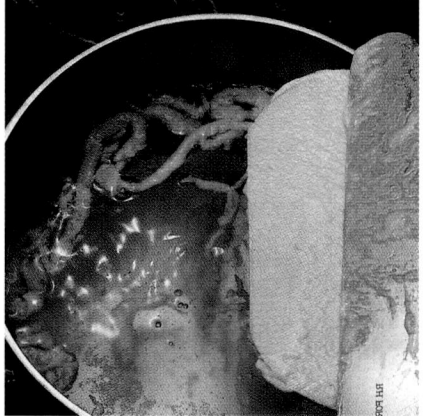

This is one of three ways to prepare spaetzle. For more information about cooking spaetzle, refer to the recipe on page 852.

Philadelphia Pepper Pot Soup

Yield: 1 gallon (3.75 liters)

Mirepoix, medium dice	*1 pound*	*450 grams*
Butter, or beef fat	*2 ounces*	*60 grams*
White Beef Stock	*1 gallon*	*3.75 liters*
Tripe, small dice	*1 pound*	*450 grams*
Veal shank, meat only, small dice	*4 ounces*	*115 grams*
Potatoes, medium dice	*8 ounces*	*225 grams*
Green peppers, medium dice	*2 ounces*	*60 grams*
Standard Sachet d'Épices	*1 each*	*1 each*
Black peppercorns, cracked	*1 tablespoon*	*1 tablespoon*
Spaetzle (1/2 ounce per portion)	*10 to12 ounces*	*300 to 350 grams*

(Recipe continued on facing page)

1. Caramelize the mirepoix in the butter or beef fat.

2. Add the beef stock, tripe, and veal shank. Simmer for 1 hour.

3. Add the potatoes, green peppers, and sachet d'épices. Simmer the mixture until the vegetables are tender and the soup is adequately flavored. Degrease it if necessary. Remove the sachet d'épices and discard it. Add the peppercorns.

4. Prepare the spaetzle according to the recipe (see reference). Using a spaetzle press or colander, push the spaetzle into the simmering soup. Simmer the spaetzle until it floats to the top, about 3 to 5 minutes.

According to legend, this soup was prepared by the cook at Valley Forge under orders of General Washington, who hoped to warm and feed the troops, who were suffering from a harsh, cold winter. If desired, the amount of peppercorns can be doubled.

To prevent the spaetzle from overcooking, it can be cooked separately in broth or salted water. Drain thoroughly and add to individual portions. Add about 2 tablespoons to each portion.

Santa Fe Chile Soup

Yield: 1 gallon (3.75 liters)

Oil	*1 fluid ounce*	*30 milliliters*
Onions, small dice	*10 ounces*	*285 grams*
Beef shanks, meat only, 1/4-inch cubes	*1 1/4 pounds*	*570 grams*
Ground cumin	*1/4 ounce*	*8 grams*
Chili powder	*1/2 ounce*	*15 grams*
Garlic cloves, mashed	*4 each*	*4 each*
Tomato purée	*8 ounces*	*225 grams*
Brown Sauce	*10 fluid ounces*	*300 milliliters*
Brown Stock	*1 1/4 quarts*	*1.2 liters*
Tomato Concassé	*8 ounces*	*225 grams*
Cayenne, to taste	*1/8 teaspoon*	*1/8 teaspoon*
Red pepper flakes, to taste	*1/4 teaspoon*	*1/4 teaspoon*
Tabasco, to taste	*1/4 teaspoon*	*1/4 teaspoon*
Salt, to taste	*1 teaspoon*	*1 teaspoon*

Use a variety of chilies to give this soup your personal stamp.

Use a commercially made chili powder, or prepare the version on page 425.

Serve with Bean and Cheese Croutons, see Chapter 13, page 435, Corn Muffins page 435, or Tortilla Chips.

1. Sauté onions in oil until translucent.

2. Add beef, cumin, and chili powder and brown lightly.

3. Add garlic and cook out for about 30 seconds.

4. Add tomato purée, brown sauce, and brown stock and simmer until meat is tender (about 1 to 1 1/4 hours).

5. Add tomato concassé, simmer 10 minutes longer. Degrease. Adjust consistency with stock. Add remaining seasonings to taste.

VARIATION

Santa Fe Chile Stew: Add 8 ounces (225 grams) each of sautéed red and green peppers and 1 pound (450 grams) of cooked beans (black, pinto, or kidney). Garnish with grated Monterey Jack cheese or sour cream, diced jalapeño, and chopped cilantro. Serve over brown rice.

Seafood Gumbo

Yield: 1 gallon (3.75 liters)

For peeling and deveining shrimp see Chapter 5; for cooking rice see Chapter 10; for Tomato Concassé see Chapter 6.

For Roux see page 423; for Shellfish Stock see page 444; for Mirepoix see page 420.

Gumbo is a term derived from one of the African words for okra. Gumbos are generally thickened with one or a combination of the following: roux, filé powder, or okra.

Instead of preparing a separate broth, it is fine to use a previously prepared shellfish broth. Reserve shells from this recipe for use in broths, soups, or fumets.

Instead of adding the rice directly to the soup, it can be added by individual portions. Use about 2 tablespoons cooked rice per portion.

Shrimp, 31 to 35 count	2 pounds	900 grams
Crabs, cut in half	10 each	10 each
Mirepoix	1 1/2 pounds	680 kilograms
Butter	4 ounces	115 grams
Fish Stock	1 gallon	3.8 liters
Seafood seasoning	1 tablespoon	1 tablespoon
Bacon, chopped	6 slices	6 slices
Onions, fine dice	4 ounces	115 grams
Celery, fine dice	2 ounces	60 grams
Green peppers, fine dice	2 ounces	60 grams
Garlic, minced	2 tablespoons	2 tablespoons
Thyme, dried	2 teaspoons	2 teaspoons
Basil, dried	2 teaspoons	2 teaspoons
Oregano	2 teaspoons	2 teaspoons
Marjoram	2 teaspoons	2 teaspoons
Bay leaf	1 each	1 each
Brown roux	8 ounces	225 grams
Tomato Concassé	8 ounces	225 grams
Okra, sliced 1/2-inch thick	1 pound	450 grams
Vegetable oil, as needed	1 fluid ounce	30 milliliters
Long-grain rice, boiled	8 ounces	225 grams
Worcestershire sauce, to taste	1/2 teaspoon	1/2 teaspoon
Tabasco, to taste	2 dashes	2 dashes
Cayenne pepper, to taste	1/8 teaspoon	1/8 teaspoon
Salt, to taste	1/2 teaspoon	1/2 teaspoon

1. Peel and devein the shrimp. Dice the shrimp. Reserve the shells and meat separately.

2. Sauté shrimp shells, crabs, and mirepoix in butter until shells turn bright red.

3. Add stock and seafood seasoning. Simmer for 45 minutes, then strain. Reserve this broth.

4. Pick crabmeat from shells. Reserve.

5. Render bacon until limp, not browned. Add onions, celery, green peppers, garlic, and spices; sauté until onions are lightly browned.

6. Add stock, bring to a simmer.

(Recipe continued on facing page)

7. Thicken soup with roux; add tomato concassé and seasonings.

8. Sauté okra in oil until softened, add to soup.

9. Simmer the soup until okra is tender, add rice.

10. Dice shrimp, sauté, and add to soup, adjust seasonings.

Bergen Fish Soup

Yield: 1 gallon (3.75 liters)

Carrots, medium dice	*4 ounces*	*115 grams*
Parsnips, medium dice	*4 ounces*	*115 grams*
Leeks, medium dice	*4 ounces*	*115 grams*
Potatoes, medium dice	*6 ounces*	*170 grams*
Butter	*3 ounces*	*85 grams*
Fish Velouté	*3 quarts*	*3 liters*
Cod fillet, diced	*1 pound*	*450 grams*
Sour cream	*12 ounces*	*340 grams*
Egg yolks	*2 each*	*2 each*
Dill, chopped	*1/2 ounce*	*15 grams*
Parsley, chopped	*1/2 ounce*	*15 grams*
Salt, to taste	*1/2 teaspoon*	*1/2 teaspoon*
Pepper, to taste	*1/2 teaspoon*	*1/2 teaspoon*

This is a true velouté soup, as explained in Chapter 7, pages 267 through 269.

The recipe for Velouté is found on page 531.

1. Sweat the vegetables in the butter until they are limp.

2. Add the velouté and simmer until the vegetables are very tender.

3. Add the cod to the soup. Continue to cook at just below a simmer for 5 minutes.

4. Combine the sour cream and egg yolks to make a liaison. Temper and add to the soup. Return to a bare simmer, but do not allow the soup to boil.

5. Add the dill and parsley. Adjust the seasoning to taste with salt and pepper.

Mussels should be very fresh, with tightly closed shells.

For Fish Fumet see page 443.

This soup, like all other velouté soups, will not hold well. It can be prepared as a base soup, then finished with liaison as needed by batch throughout service.

The chef at Maxim's in Paris, Louis Parthe, is said to have created this soup for the American tin tycoon, William B. Leeds.

Billi Bi Soup

Yield: 1 gallon (3.75 liters)

Onions, sliced	*12 ounces*	*340 grams*
Parsley stems	*6 each*	*6 each*
Whole black peppercorns, cracked	*6 each*	*6 each*
Mussels	*4 pounds*	*1.8 kilograms*
White wine, dry	*1 1/2 quarts*	*1.5 liters*
Fish Fumet	*1 1/2 quarts*	*1.5 liters*
Saffron threads, crushed	*1/2 teaspoon*	*1/2 teaspoon*
Roux	*5 ounces*	*140 grams*
Egg yolks	*3 each*	*3 each*
Heavy cream	*12 fluid ounces*	*360 milliliters*
Salt	*to taste*	*to taste*
Pepper	*to taste*	*to taste*

1. Combine onions, parsley, peppercorns, mussels, wine, fish stock, and saffron; cover and bring to a simmer.

2. When the mussels open, remove the meat and reserve. Discard shells. Strain the soup and return to a simmer.

3. Thicken liquid with roux, simmer 20 minutes.

4. Combine egg yolks and heavy cream to make a liaison. Temper with the hot soup, return liaison to soup, and bring soup back to a bare simmer. Strain through a fine chinois or cheesecloth.

5. Adjust the consistency of the soup and season to taste with salt and pepper. Add mussels to the soup.

Borscht

Yield: 1 gallon (3.75 liters)

Butter, unsalted	*2 ounces*	*60 grams*
Onions, julienne	*3 ounces*	*85 grams*
Leeks, julienne	*4 ounces*	*115 grams*
Green cabbage, julienne	*3 ounces*	*85 grams*
Celery, julienne	*3 ounces*	*85 grams*
Beets, fresh, julienne	*2 1/2 pounds*	*1.125 kilograms*
Tomato Concassé	*8 ounces*	*225 grams*
White Beef Stock	*1 gallon*	*3.8 liters*
Beef brisket, cooked, julienne	*1 pound*	*455 grams*
Duck breast, cooked, julienne	*8 ounces*	*225 grams*
Standard Sachet d'Épices, plus	*1 each*	*1 each*
Fennel seed	*1/4 teaspoon*	*1/4 teaspoon*
Clove, whole	*1 each*	*1 each*
Red wine vinegar	*6 fluid ounces*	*180 milliliters*
Salt	*1 teaspoon*	*1 teaspoon*
Pepper	*1/2 teaspoon*	*1/2 teaspoon*
Garnish		
Sour cream	*11 fluid ounces*	*330 milliliters*
Dill, sprigs, fresh	*as needed*	*as needed*

There are numerous recipes for borscht throughout Eastern Europe. This version is adapted from a Polish-style soup. Other renditions are meatless, or served cold, or puréed and finished with yogurt.

1. Heat the butter; add onions, leeks, cabbage, celery, and beets. Sweat.

2. Add the tomatoes, stock, beef, duck, and Sachet d'Épices. Simmer 30 minutes or until all ingredients are fully cooked.

3. Adjust seasoning to taste with vinegar, salt, and pepper. Top each portion with sour cream and sprinkle with dill.

Budnersuppe—Barley Soup with Air-Dried Beef

Yield: 1 gallon (3.75 liters)

This is a Swiss soup, made with an air-dried, salt-cured beef, known as "bundner fleisch." The flavor is extremely strong.

Carrots, brunoise	4 ounces	115 grams
Leeks, brunoise	4 ounces	115 grams
Celeriac, brunoise	4 ounces	115 grams
Onions, brunoise	6 ounces	170 grams
Air-dried beef, brunoise	4 ounces	115 grams
Barley	8 ounces	225 grams
Butter	2 ounces	60 grams
Flour	4 ounces	115 grams
White Beef Stock	3 quarts	3 liters
Smoked pork knuckle	1 each	1 each
Egg yolks	3 each	3 each
Heavy cream	8 fluid ounces	240 milliliters
Pepper, to taste	1/2 teaspoon	1/2 teaspoon
White wine	2 fluid ounces	60 milliliters
Chives, minced	1/2 bunch	1/2 bunch
Salt, to taste	1/2 teaspoon	1/2 teaspoon

1. Sauté brunoise vegetables (carrots, leeks, celeriac, and onions) in butter, add barley to vegetables and sauté in butter, add the flour and sauté for 2 minutes.

2. Add stock and pork knuckle; simmer for 45 minutes; remove meat from knuckles; dice and return to soup.

3. Temper egg yolks and heavy cream (liaison) into soup. Adjust consistency and finish soup with pepper, white wine, chives, and salt.

Cock-a-Leekie Soup

Yield: 1 gallon (3.75 liters)

This soup originates in Scotland, where oatmeal would have been used to thicken the soup.

The prunes can be plumped in hot water, or allowed to macerate in brandy overnight.

Stewing hen, whole	3 pounds	1.3 kilograms
Water	1 gallon	3.75 liters
Mirepoix	12 ounces	340 grams
Leeks, julienne	8 ounces	225 grams
Potatoes, julienne	1 pound	450 grams
Salt, to taste	1/2 teaspoon	1/2 teaspoon
Pepper, to taste	1/4 teaspoon	1/4 teaspoon
Prunes, plumped, cooked, and pitted	6 ounces	170 grams

(Recipe continued on facing page)

1. Wash fowl. Cover with cold water in stockpot. Add mirepoix and simmer until fowl is tender. Remove fowl from pot and cool.

2. Strain stock through chinois and cheesecloth back into pot. Skim off fat.

3. Add leeks and potatoes to stock and bring to boil. Reduce to simmer and continue to cook until vegetables are done.

4. Remove the chicken from the bone and add to soup. Season to taste.

5. Garnish with cooked, pitted prunes.

Corned Beef and Barley Soup

Yield: 1 1/2 gallons (5.75 liters)

Corned beef	*3 1/2 pounds*	*1.6 kilograms*
Oil, to sear	*as needed*	*as needed*
White or Brown Stock	*1 gallon*	*3.75 liters*
Salt, to taste	*1/2 teaspoon*	*1/2 teaspoon*
Standard Sachet d'Épices	*1 each*	*1 each*
Onions, small dice	*8 ounces*	*225 grams*
Celery, small dice	*4 ounces*	*115 grams*
Pearl barley	*8 ounces*	*225 grams*
Tomato Concassé	*12 ounces*	*340 grams*
Parsley, chopped	*5 tablespoons*	*5 tablespoons*

This soup will generate more corned beef than is probably necessary for garnishing the soup. Use the remainder for a boiled dinner, sandwiches, or in other preparations.

Other vegetables, especially root vegetables such as parsnips, turnips, rutabagas, or potatoes, can be added to this soup. Prepare the vegetables according to type, and add them in a staggered manner, so that all of the ingredients finish cooking at the same time.

1. Sear corned beef in oil.

2. Add stock, salt, and sachet d'épices. Simmer for 2 hours skimming as necessary throughout cooking. Remove meat and cut it into small dice for garnish.

3. Strain and degrease the broth thoroughly and reserve.

4. Sweat the onions and celery in oil. Add the broth and barley to the soup, and simmer until all ingredients are tender.

5. Return the diced corned beef, add the tomatoes, and simmer another 10 to 15 minutes.

6. Adjust the seasoning to taste. Add parsley to soup or add to individual portions.

Finnish Salmon Soup

Yield: 1 gallon (3.75 liters)

Prepare Fish Fumet as directed on page 443 using salmon bones.

This soup is traditionally served as a meal and would use more salmon and potatoes to make it heartier.

Onions, medium dice	*8 ounces*	*225 grams*
Butter	*2 ounces*	*60 grams*
Potatoes, diced	*12 ounces*	*340 grams*
Fish Fumet	*3 quarts*	*3 liters*
Salmon fillet, cut in 1-inch cubes	*1 1/2 pounds*	*700 grams*
Heavy cream	*1 pint*	*480 milliliters*
Salt, to taste	*1 teaspoon*	*1 teaspoon*
Pepper, to taste	*1/2 teaspoon*	*1/2 teaspoon*
Dill, chopped	*2 teaspoons*	*2 teaspoons*

1. Sweat the onions in butter until limp.

2. Add potatoes, sauté briefly, add stock, and bring to a simmer.

3. Simmer until potatoes are tender, add salmon; simmer until salmon is cooked (approximately 20 minutes total cooking time).

4. Add heavy cream, salt and pepper, and dill.

Goulash Soup

Yield: 1 gallon (3.75 liters)

Bacon, chopped	*4 ounces*	*115 grams*
Onions, diced	*2 pounds*	*900 grams*
Garlic cloves, minced	*6 each*	*6 each*
Beef shank, small dice	*2 pounds*	*900 grams*
Sweet Hungarian paprika	*1/2 ounce*	*15 grams*
Flour	*2 ounces*	*60 grams*
Tomato paste	*2 ounces*	*60 grams*
Brown Veal Stock	*1 gallon*	*3.75 liters*
Standard Sachet d'Épices, plus	*1 each*	*1 each*
Caraway seeds	*1 teaspoon*	*1 teaspoon*
Bay leaves	*2 each*	*2 each*
Marjoram leaves	*1 teaspoon*	*1 teaspoon*
Potatoes, medium dice	*1 1/2 pounds*	*650 grams*
Salt, to taste	*1/2 teaspoon*	*1/2 teaspoon*
Pepper, to taste	*1/4 teaspoon*	*1/4 teaspoon*

(Recipe continued on facing page)

1. Render the bacon over low heat. Remove it from the pot.

2. Raise the heat to medium. Add the onions and garlic and sauté until light brown.

3. Add the beef and paprika and sauté the mixture briefly.

4. Add the flour and tomato paste and stir them in well.

5. Add the stock and sachet d'épices. Bring the mixture to a simmer. Simmer slowly for 45 minutes.

6. Add the potatoes and continue simmering the soup until all of the ingredients are very tender.

7. Adjust the seasoning to taste with salt and pepper on the day of service.

This soup's flavor improves if it is allowed to rest for 24 hours before it is served. Adjust seasoning and consistency after the soup is reheated for service.

Erwtensoep (Holland)—Green Split Pea Soup

Yield:1 gallon (3.75 liters)

Vegetable oil	*1 fluid ounce*	*30 milliliters*
Leeks, 1/4-inch dice	*6 ounces*	*170 grams*
Celeriac, 1/4-inch dice	*6 ounces*	*170 grams*
Onions, diced	*8 ounces*	*225 grams*
Green split peas	*1 pound*	*450 grams*
Potatoes, medium dice	*1 pound*	*450 grams*
Ham hock	*1 each*	*1 each*
White Beef Stock	*1 gallon*	*3.75 liters*
Kielbasa, sliced	*1/2 pound*	*225 grams*
Salt, to taste	*1/2 teaspoon*	*1/2 teaspoon*
Pepper, to taste	*1/2 teaspoon*	*1/2 teaspoon*

1. Heat the oil, add the leeks, celeriac, and onions and sweat until limp.

2. Add the split peas, potatoes, ham hocks, and stock. Simmer until peas are tender.

3. Remove ham hocks, cut lean meat from bones, dice 1/4-inch dice.

4. Purée the soup until very smooth, and return diced meat to soup.

5. Add kielbasa to soup, simmer 5 minutes, adjust consistency and seasonings before serving.

This set-up is an efficient way to serve soups in a banquet setting.

The recipe for White Beef Stock is on page 439.

507

Menudo is a spicy Mexican soup combining tripe, posole (hominy), and peppers that is often served on New Year's morning as a hangover cure.

Menudo—Tripe Soup

Yield: 2 gallons (7.5 liters)

Hominy	*8 ounces*	*225 grams*
Garbanzo beans	*8 ounces*	*225 grams*
Tripe, blanched	*4 pounds*	*1.8 kilograms*
Chicken Stock	*6 quarts*	*5.75 liters*
Pork butt, blanched	*2 pounds*	*900 grams*
Onions, 1/4-inch dice	*2 each*	*2 each*
Garlic cloves, mashed	*4 each*	*4 each*
Green pepper, 1/4-inch dice	*4 each*	*4 each*
Red pepper, 1/4-inch dice	*4 each*	*4 each*
Jalapeños, minced	*2 each*	*2 each*
Olive oil	*6 ounces*	*180 milliliters*
Salt, to taste	*1/2 teaspoon*	*1/2 teaspoon*
Pepper, to taste	*1/2 teaspoon*	*1/2 teaspoon*
Chili powder	*1/2 ounce*	*15 grams*
Cumin, ground	*1/2 ounce*	*15 grams*
Tomato Concassé	*1 pound*	*455 grams*
White wine	*4 ounces*	*120 grams*
Cilantro, chopped	*2 tablespoons*	*30 grams*
Oregano, dried	*1 tablespoon*	*15 grams*
Cider vinegar	*2 fluid ounces*	*60 milliliters*

The recipe for Chicken Stock is on page 442.

1. Soak hominy and garbanzo beans separately overnight in enough cold water to cover. Cook them separately in water until tender. Drain and reserve.

2. Simmer tripe for approximately 1 hour in the stock; add pork and continue cooking until all meats are fork tender. Remove the meats, and cut into 1/4-inch dice. Reserve.

3. Sweat all vegetables in oil until tender.

4. Add spices, diced pork and tripe, stock, hominy, and garbanzo beans, simmer for 15 minutes.

5. Add tomato concassé, wine, herbs, and vinegar and bring to a boil. Adjust seasoning.

Minestrone Genovese

Yield: 1 gallon (3.75 liters)

Pancetta, paysanne	*1 ounce*	*30 grams*
Olive oil	*2 fluid ounces*	*60 milliliters*
Onions, paysanne	*8 ounces*	*225 grams*
Carrots, paysanne	*4 ounces*	*115 grams*
Celery, paysanne	*3 ounces*	*85 grams*
Green peppers, paysanne	*3 ounces*	*85 grams*
Zucchini, paysanne	*6 ounces*	*170 grams*
Eggplant, paysanne	*6 ounces*	*170 grams*
Potatoes, paysanne	*6 ounces*	*170 grams*
Tomato Concassé	*8 ounces*	*225 grams*
Chicken Stock	*1 gallon*	*3.75 liters*
Elbow macaroni, cooled	*5 ounces*	*140 grams*
Kidney beans, cooked and cooled	*5 ounces*	*140 grams*
Salt, to taste	*1/2 teaspoon*	*1/2 teaspoon*
Pepper, to taste	*1/4 teaspoon*	*1/4 teaspoon*
Pesto	*5 to 6 ounces*	*140 to 170 grams*

1. Render pancetta in olive oil without browning.
2. Add onions, carrots, celery, and peppers; sweat until halfway cooked.
3. Add zucchini and eggplant; sweat.
4. Add potatoes, tomato concassé, and stock; bring to a simmer.
5. Simmer soup until vegetables are tender; add pasta and beans.
6. Season soup with salt, pepper, and pesto.

Pesto is a traditional sauce from Genoa, used here to finish a soup. The recipe is found on page 422.

The recipe for Chicken Stock is on page 442.

There are numerous versions of minestrone. Chickpeas, green beans, and red peppers could also be added. The pancetta indicated above is a special kind of bacon, with slightly more lean meat than our traditional sliced or slab bacon. Replace pancetta with other bacon, if pancetta is unavailable.

Mansahari Mirchi Soup—Mulligatawny Soup

Yield: 1 gallon (3.75 liters)

"Mulligatawny" derives from a word meaning "pepper water" and is from the southern part of India.

Cardamom, fenugreek, Garam Masala (page 428), Curry Powder (page 426), and/or cinnamon can also be added. Finish the soup with a bit of unsweetened coconut milk, if desired.

Fresh green chilies, seeded and chopped	6 each	6 each
Coriander, ground	2 tablespoons	2 tablespoons
Turmeric, ground	4 teaspoons	4 teaspoons
Cumin, ground	1 1/2 teaspoons	1 1/2 teaspoons
Nutmeg, ground	1 teaspoon	1 teaspoon
Clove, ground	1/2 teaspoon	1/2 teaspoon
Black pepper, ground	1/2 ounce	15 grams
Garlic cloves	5 each	5 each
Gingerroot, grated	4 teaspoons	4 teaspoons
Onions, chopped	4 each	4 each
Ghee (clarified butter)	1 ounce	30 grams
Lamb, 1/3-inch dice	2 pounds	900 grams
Salt, to taste	1/2 teaspoon	1/2 teaspoon
Tomato paste	6 ounces	180 grams
White Stock	3 quarts	3 liters
Carrots, 1/4-inch dice	4 each	4 each
Granny Smith apples, peeled, 1/4-inch dice	4 each	4 each

1. Using a food processor, grind all chiles, spices, garlic, and gingerroot into a fine paste.

2. Sauté onions in ghee until golden brown; add spice paste and lamb and sauté for 5 minutes. Add lamb and brown lightly.

3. Add salt, tomato paste, and stock; simmer until meat is almost cooked.

4. Add carrots and apples, simmer soup until everything is tender.

VARIATION

Chicken Mulligatawny: Chicken can replace lamb in this soup. Add cooked white or brown rice before serving.

Oxtail Soup à l'Anglaise

Yield: 1 gallon (3.75 liters)

Oxtails, cut in 1-inch pieces	*4 pounds*	*1.8 kilograms*
White Beef Stock	*5 quarts*	*4.75 liters*
Onions, medium dice	*8 ounces*	*225 grams*
Turnips, medium dice	*4 ounces*	*115 grams*
Carrots, medium dice	*4 ounces*	*115 grams*
Celery, medium dice	*3 ounces*	*85 grams*
Leeks, medium dice	*2 ounces*	*60 grams*
Beef fat, rendered	*3 ounces*	*85 grams*
Vegetable oil, if necessary	*2 fluid ounces*	*60 milliliters*
Flour	*4 ounces*	*115 grams*
Tomato Concassé	*8 ounces*	*225 grams*
Potatoes, medium dice	*8 ounces*	*225 grams*
Salt, to taste	*1/2 teaspoon*	*1/2 teaspoon*
Pepper, to taste	*1/4 teaspoon*	*1/4 teaspoon*
Dry sherry, as needed	*2 fluid ounces*	*60 milliliters*
Parsley, chopped	*1/2 ounce*	*15 grams*

Oxtail has a full-bodied flavor and enough natural gelatin to produce a soup with an appealing body.

1. Brown oxtails in oven, reserve the rendered fat. (Or oxtails may be seared on the stove.)

2. Transfer the browned oxtails to stockpot, cover with beef stock, and bring to a boil. Reduce heat and simmer 3 to 4 hours or until meat is tender enough to remove from the bone easily. Strain and reserve stock and oxtails separately.

3. Sauté the onions, turnips, carrots, celery, and leeks in the rendered beef fat. Add oil if necessary. Add flour and cook out the roux for 3 to 4 minutes.

4. Add the hot stock, gradually, stirring until smooth.

5. Add tomato concassé and potatoes. Simmer until all ingredients are tender.

6. Remove meat from bones, cut into dice and add to soup. Season to taste with salt, pepper, and wine. Garnish with chopped parsley.

This soup is a thick soup, unlike the clear broth version of Oxtail Soup on page 460.

This soup is known in Portugal as *caldo verde,* or green soup.

White Beef Stock is on page 439.

Replace chorizo with kielbasa or other sausages if you wish. Or substitute small dice of a good-quality air-dried ham.

This soup makes an excellent vegetarian dish, simply by omitting the ham hocks and sausage. Use vegetable broth instead of beef stock.

Potato Kale Soup (Caldo Verde)

Yield: 1 gallon (3.75 liters)

White mirepoix	*12 ounces*	*340 grams*
Olive oil	*2 fluid ounces*	*60 milliliters*
Potatoes, cut in chunks	*7 pounds*	*3.15 kilograms*
White Beef Stock	*3 quarts*	*3 liters*
Ham hocks, fresh	*1 each*	*1 each*
Bay leaf	*1 each*	*1 each*
Salt, to taste	*1 teaspoon*	*1 teaspoon*
Kale, fresh, julienne	*1 pound*	*450 grams*
Chorizo, sliced, blanched	*4 ounces*	*15 grams*
Pepper, to taste	*1/2 teaspoon*	*1/2 teaspoon*

1. Sweat the mirepoix in oil.

2. Add the potatoes, stock, ham hocks, bay leaf, and salt; simmer until the potatoes and ham hocks are tender.

3. Remove the bay leaf and ham hocks, and cut the ham into a fine dice; reserve.

4. Purée the soup. Return the diced ham and puréed soup to the pot. Simmer for 30 minutes.

5. Add the kale and chorizo and simmer for 5 minutes.

6. Adjust the seasoning with salt and pepper to taste.

Scotch Broth

Yield: 1 gallon (3.75 liters)

Lamb, 1/3-inch cubes	*2 pounds*	*900 grams*
White Beef Stock	*3 quarts*	*3 liters*
Barley	*8 ounces*	*225 grams*
Salt, to taste	*1/2 teaspoon*	*1/2 teaspoon*
Carrots, brunoise	*4 ounces*	*115 grams*
Turnips, brunoise	*4 ounces*	*115 grams*
Onions, brunoise	*4 ounces*	*115 grams*
Leeks, brunoise	*4 ounces*	*115 grams*
Celery, brunoise	*4 ounces*	*115 grams*
Savoy cabbage, diced	*4 ounces*	*115 grams*
Salt, to taste	*to taste*	*to taste*
Pepper, to taste	*to taste*	*to taste*
Parsley, chopped	*as needed*	*as needed*

The method in this recipe is a traditional approach to making this soup. Instead of blanching the lamb, you may prefer to "sweat" it in 2 fluid ounces (60 milliliters) of oil. Add the vegetables to the lamb and smother. Then add the broth and barley, and simmer. The flavor will be slightly different.

See White Beef Stock, page 439.

Add a Bouquet Garni (page 424) during simmering, if desired.

1. Blanch the lamb in simmering water for 5 minutes. Drain.

2. Combine meat, stock, barley, and salt in a soup pot, simmer for 45 minutes.

3. Add the carrots, turnips, onions, leeks, celery brunoise, and cabbage to the soup and simmer until all ingredients are very tender.

4. Adjust seasoning to taste with salt and pepper; finish with chopped parsley.

VARIATION

Use a lamb broth to replace white stock if desired; see this Chapter, page 452.

Seafood Minestrone

Yield: 1 gallon (3.75 liters)

If desired, use the shrimp shells to make a stock to replace some of the necessary fish stock.

Diced cod or haddock or other white fish may also be included.

The recipe for Fish Fumet is on page 443; for Pesto, see page 422.

White wine	5 fluid ounces	150 milliliters
Mussels, cleaned and debearded	30 each	30 each
Fish Fumet	3 quarts	3 liters
Olive oil	2 fluid ounces	60 milliliters
Bacon slices, chopped	4 each	4 each
Garlic, minced	1/2 ounce	15 grams
Leeks, small dice	10 ounces	285 grams
Onions, small dice	6 ounces	170 grams
Celery, small dice	4 ounces	115 grams
Tomato paste	3 fluid ounces	90 milliliters
Salt, to taste	1 teaspoon	1 teaspoon
Rosemary leaves, dried	1 teaspoon	1 teaspoon
Thyme leaves, dried	1 teaspoon	1 teaspoon
Pepper, to taste	1/4 teaspoon	1/4 teaspoon
Bay leaves	2 each	2 each
Lemon slices	2 each	2 each
Kidney beans, red, soaked	4 ounces	115 grams
Arborio rice	6 ounces	170 grams
Tomato Concassé	1 1/4 pounds	570 grams
Shrimp, peeled, deveined, and chopped	6 ounces	170 grams
Pesto	5 to 6 ounces	150 to 170 grams

1. Heat the wine over high heat in a saucepan with a tight-fitting lid. Add the mussels. Cover the pan and steam the mussels just until the shells open.

2. Remove the mussels from their shells; reserve them.

3. Strain the steaming liquid through a cheesecloth. Add enough fish fumet to equal 2 quarts. Reserve the liquid.

4. Heat the oil in a soup pot. Add the bacon and cook it until it is limp and translucent. Do not brown it. Add the garlic, leeks, onions, and celery. Sauté the vegetables until the onion is translucent.

5. Add the tomato paste and pincé.

6. Add the remaining ingredients (except the mussels and shrimp) and the reserved fish stock. Bring the liquid to a boil; reduce the heat and simmer the soup until the beans and rice are tender.

7. Add the mussels and shrimp; salt to taste. Remove the soup from the heat immediately. Serve it in heated bowls garnished with 1/2 teaspoon of pesto.

Velouté Dieppoise

Yield: 1 gallon (3.75 liters)

Leeks, sliced	*8 ounces*	*225 grams*
Mushrooms, sliced	*10 ounces*	*285 grams*
Butter	*2 ounces*	*60 grams*
Fish Velouté	*3 quarts*	*3 liters*
Standard Sachet d'Épices	*1 each*	*1 each*
Mussels	*40 each*	*40 each*
White wine, dry	*10 fluid ounces*	*300 milliliters*
Heavy cream	*1 pint*	*480 milliliters*
Egg yolks	*4 each*	*4 each*
Shrimp, cooked, diced	*12 ounces*	*340 grams*
Salt, to taste	*1/2 teaspoon*	*1/2 teaspoon*
Pepper, to taste	*1/4 teaspoon*	*1/4 teaspoon*
Worcestershire sauce, to taste	*1/2 teaspoon*	*1/2 teaspoon*
Butter	*4 ounces*	*115 grams*

1. Sweat leeks and mushrooms in butter.

2. Add velouté and sachet; simmer 30 minutes.

3. Heat the wine over high heat in a saucepan with a tight-fitting lid. Add the mussels. Cover the pan and steam the mussels just until the shells open.

4. Remove the mussels from their shells; reserve them.

5. Strain the steaming liquid through a cheesecloth. Add it to the soup.

6. Combine heavy cream and egg yolks.

7. Temper the liaison, return it to the soup, and bring to a bare simmer. Strain the soup.

8. Add mussels and shrimp.

9. Adjust seasoning to taste and finish with butter.

The recipe for Velouté is on page 531. Use fish fumet or stock for this recipe.

Fish prepared "à la Diepoisse" is traditionally steamed in white wine, then served with a white sauce made from reducing the cooking liquid and finishing it with cream.

The method for velouté soups is described in Chapter 7, page 267.

Waterzooi de Poulet (Chicken Soup)

Yield: 1 gallon (3.75 liters)

The procedure for preparing roux is found in the recipe on page 423.

Waterzooi is a Flemish word that means flowing water spout. It was originally made from fish, but now is generally made from poultry, specifically that raised around Ghent.

This is a classic velouté soup, finished with a liaison.

Chickens, whole	*3 1/2 pounds*	*1.575 kilograms*
Chicken Stock	*1 gallon*	*3.8 liters*
Standard Sachet d'Épices	*1 each*	*1 each*
Pale roux	*12 ounces*	*340 grams*
Carrots, allumette	*5 ounces*	*140 grams*
Celeriac, allumette	*5 ounces*	*140 grams*
White turnips, allumette	*3 ounces*	*85 grams*
Potatoes, allumette	*8 ounces*	*225 grams*
Leeks, whites only, allumette	*4 ounces*	*115 grams*
Egg yolks	*3 each*	*3 each*
Half and half	*20 fluid ounces*	*600 milliliters*
Salt, to taste	*1 teaspoon*	*1 teaspoon*
White pepper, to taste	*1/2 teaspoon*	*1/2 teaspoon*
Parsley, fresh, chopped	*3 ounces*	*85 grams*

1. Combine the chicken, stock, and sachet d'épices. Bring the mixture to a boil. Simmer it for 45 minutes, skimming if necessary. Remove the chicken.

2. Strain the broth and keep it hot.

3. Remove the chicken meat from the bones and dice it.

4. Combine the broth with the roux.

5. Simmer the soup for 1 hour.

6. Add the vegetables to the soup and continue to simmer until they are tender.

7. Combine the egg yolks with the half and half. Temper the liaison with the hot velouté. Add this liaison to the velouté with the vegetables and reserved chicken meat.

8. Bring the soup to serving temperature. Adjust the seasoning with salt and pepper to taste. Serve, garnished with parsley.

Chicken Egg Drop Soup

Yield: 1 gallon (3.75 liters)

Oil, vegetable or peanut	*1 tablespoon*	*1 tablespoon*
Ginger, minced	*1 tablespoon*	*1 tablespoon*
Scallions, sliced thin	*2 ounces*	*60 grams*
Chicken Stock	*3 quarts*	*3 liters*
Cornstarch, as needed	*2 ounces*	*60 grams*
Eggs, beaten	*8 to 10 each*	*8 to 10 each*
Salt, to taste	*2 teaspoons*	*2 teaspoons*
White pepper, to taste	*1 teaspoon*	*1 teaspoon*
Egg shade color, diluted (optional)	*1/4 teaspoon*	*1/4 teaspoon*
Garnish		
Green scallion, chopped	*2 ounces*	*60 grams*

Egg shade is a food coloring. Its use is optional, but it is traditionally added to particular recipes, such as this one, to provide a rich golden color.

1. Heat oil, add ginger and scallion, stir-fry. Add chicken stock and bring to a boil.

2. Combine cornstarch and some water or cold stock; add half to the soup, stirring constantly; return to a boil. Check consistency, add more diluted cornstarch if desired.

3. Stir in eggs, add seasonings and color (optional).

4. Garnish individual portions with scallion greens.

Hot and Sour Soup

Yield: 1 gallon (3.75 liters)

Oil, vegetable or peanut	2 tablespoons	2 tablespoons
Ginger, minced	1 tablespoon	1 tablespoon
Scallion or cilantro, chopped	2 tablespoons	2 tablespoons
Pork butt, shredded or ground	8 ounces	225 grams
Bamboo shoots, shredded	4 ounces	115 grams
Black fungus, soaked and diced	3 tablespoons	3 tablespoons
Tiger lily bud, soaked, tied in knot	3 tablespoons	3 tablespoons
Chinese cabbage, shredded	8 ounces	225 grams
Chicken stock	3 quarts	3 liters
Bean curd, diced	1 pound	450 grams
Black soy sauce, to taste	2 tablespoons	2 tablespoons
Salt, to taste	1 teaspoon	1 teaspoon
White vinegar	2 fluid ounces	60 milliliters
White pepper, to taste	2 teaspoons	2 teaspoons
Black pepper, to taste	2 teaspoons	2 teaspoons
Cornstarch	2 ounces	60 grams
Eggs, beaten lightly	2 each	2 each
Sesame oil	2 tablespoons	2 tablespoons
Garnish		
Scallion	3 ounces	85 grams
Cilantro leaves	1 ounce	30 grams

1. Heat oil, add ginger and scallion, stir-fry. Add pork, continue to stir-fry until pork is cooked through.

2. Add bamboo shoots, black fungus, tiger lily, and Chinese cabbage, stir-fry until cabbage is tender.

3. Add stock, reserving 2 cups (480 milliliters) to dilute cornstarch, and bean curd, bring to a simmer. Add soy sauce, salt, vinegar, and peppers; thicken with cornstarch slurry.

4. Slowly add eggs to soup, return to a simmer; add sesame oil.

5. Garnish individual portions with scallion or cilantro.

Wonton Soup

Yield: 1 gallon (3.75 liters)

Wonton wrappers (thin skin)	*2 packs*	*2 packs*
Eggs, beat in a bowl lightly	*2 each*	*2 each*
Wonton stuffing		
Ground pork	*1 pound*	*450 grams*
Chinese cabbage, chopped	*1/2 pound*	*225 grams*
Scallions, chopped	*4 each*	*4 each*
Ginger, minced	*1/2 tablespoon*	*1/2 tablespoon*
Soy sauce	*2 tablespoons*	*2 tablespoons*
Salt	*1 teaspoon*	*1 teaspoon*
White pepper	*1/2 teaspoon*	*3 grams*
Sesame oil	*2 tablespoons*	*2 tablespoons*
Chicken stock	*8 fluid ounces*	*240 milliliters*
Soup		
Chicken stock	*1 gallon*	*3.75 liters*
Black soy sauce	*2 tablespoons*	*2 tablespoons*
Salt, to taste	*1 teaspoon*	*1 teaspoon*
Pepper, to taste	*1/2 teaspoon*	*1/2 teaspoon*
Garnish		
Ham, fine julienne	*4 ounces*	*115 grams*
Eggs	*4 each*	*4 each*
Cello spinach or watercress, blanched for 30 seconds, rough cut	*1 pack*	*1 pack*

The method for filling and folding wontons is similar to that for preparing tortellini. Fold in half to make a triangle and overlap two points.

Wontons can be cooked, shocked in cold water, and held for service. Wontons would be placed in cup and hot soup would be added.

1. To make the wontons, combine all ingredients for the stuffing and mix together. Place 1/2 teaspoon stuffing on each wonton wrapper, brush edges with egg wash, and fold.

2. Sauté scallion and ginger in oil, add chicken stock, bring to a boil, add soy sauce, salt, and pepper.

3. Cook wontons in boiling salted water for 2 minutes, drain, and add to soup.

4. Add garnish to individual portions.

CHAPTER *15* Sauce Recipes

This chapter contains recipes for the grand sauces and many classic variations. In addition, you will find recipes for contemporary sauces such as vegetable coulis. The recipes are grouped as follows:

- *Basic Brown Sauces*
- *Small Brown Sauces*
- *Velorito Sauce and Derivatives*
- *Bechamel Sauce and Derivatives*
- *Tomato Sauces*
- *Warm Butter Sauces*
- *Beurre Blanc*
- *Coulis and Vegetable Sauces*
- *Barbecue Sauces*

As you read through the entrée recipe chapters which follow, however, you may also find additional sauces contained within an individual recipe. Look at the various cold sauces in Chapters 24 and 26, as well.

This demi-glace has cooked sufficiently to coat a spoon.

See Chapter 8, pages 278 to 280.

For Jus de Veau Lié, see page 523.

Often, Jus de Veau Lié, or other types of lié sauces are used to replace Demi-Glace in contemporary cooking. Any variation indicating Demi-Glace can be prepared with a jus of the appropriate flavor. Similarly, any derivative of a jus lié can be prepared using Demi-Glace.

Demi-Glace

Yield: 1 quart (1 liter)

Brown Veal Stock	2 quarts	2 liters
Brown Sauce	2 quarts	2 liters

1. Reduce the Brown Veal Stock by one-third.

2. Add the Brown Sauce; continue to reduce to 1 quart. Skim the surface as necessary.

3. Strain the sauce.

VARIATION

Demi-Glace may be finished with 2 to 3 fluid ounces (60 to 90 milliliters) Glace de Viande if desired.

See Chapter 8, pages 277 to 278.

Another method for preparing this sauce is as follows: Add half of the stock to the browned Mirepoix and tomato. Thicken the other half of the stock with all of the roux. Combine and simmer.

Brown Sauce (Sauce Espagnole)

Yield: 1 gallon (3.75 liters)

Mirepoix	1 pound	455 grams
Vegetable oil, hot	3 fluid ounces	90 milliliters
Tomato paste	4 ounces	115 grams
Brown Veal Stock, hot	1 1/2 gallons	5.75 liters
Pale roux	12 ounces	340 grams
Standard Sachet d'Épices	1 each	1 each

1. Brown the onions from the Mirepoix in the hot oil; add the remainder of the Mirepoix and continue to brown.

2. Add the tomato paste; cook out for several minutes.

3. Add the brown stock; bring up to a simmer.

4. Whip the roux into the stock. Return to a simmer and add the Standard Sachet d'Épices.

5. Simmer for approximately 1 hour; skim the surface as necessary.

6. Strain through cheesecloth.

Jus de Veau Lié

Yield: 1 gallon (3.75 liters)

Brown Veal Stock	*4 1/2 quarts*	*4.5 liters*
Veal bones and trim, roasted	*4 pounds*	*1.8 kilograms*
Mirepoix, caramelized	*1 pound*	*450 grams*
Standard Sachet d'Épices	*1 each*	*1 each*
Arrowroot or cornstarch, **diluted with cold water** **or dry wine**	*1 ounce*	*30 grams*

1. Combine all the ingredients except the arrowroot and bring to a simmer.

2. Simmer for a minimum of 2 1/2 to 3 hours, skimming the surface as necessary, to extract full body and flavor from the bones and trim.

3. Strain the sauce, pressing well. Return the strained sauce to the heat and bring to a full boil. Add diluted arrowroot or cornstarch to thicken the sauce enough to coat the back of a wooden spoon.

VARIATIONS

Jus de Volaille Lié: Replace the Brown Veal Stock with a Brown Chicken Stock and replace the veal bones and trim with an equal weight of chicken bones and trim.

Jus de Canard Lié: Replace the Brown Veal Stock with a Brown Duck Stock and replace the veal bones and trim with an equal weight of duck bones and trim.

Jus d'Agneau Lié: Replace the Brown Veal Stock with a Brown Lamb Stock and replace the veal bones and trim with an equal weight of lamb bones and trim.

Jus de Gibier Lié: Replace the Brown Veal Stock with a Brown Venison Stock and replace the veal bones and trim with an equal weight of venison bones and trim.

Adding diluted arrowroot to thicken jus de veau.

See Chapter 8, pages 282 to 285 for more information about preparing Jus de Veau Lié.

Add various fresh herbs or spices to the Jus (either loose or in a Standard Sachet d'Épices or Bouquet Garni) to give the sauce a particular flavor.

Another way to customize a Jus is to add an Essence or "Fumet" made from such ingredients as tomatoes, celery, or mushrooms.

Wild Mushroom Jus

Yield: 1 quart (1 liter)

This Jus may be used on its own as a "vegetarian" sauce, or it may be used to flavor other sauces.

Select from any cultivated wild mushrooms. When they are not in season, substitute dried mushrooms that have been properly reconstituted in hot water or wine.

Sweet onion, small dice	*2 each*	*2 each*
Garlic clove, minced fine	*1 each*	*1 each*
Extra-virgin olive oil	*1 tablespoon*	*15 milliliters*
Shiitake mushrooms, sliced	*12 ounces*	*340 grams*
Portabello mushrooms, sliced	*12 ounces*	*340 grams*
Cremini mushrooms, sliced	*12 ounces*	*340 grams*
Oregano	*2 teaspoons*	*2 teaspoons*
Water or Vegetable Stock	*1 pint*	*480 milliliters*
Tamari sauce	*4 fluid ounces*	*120 milliliters*
White wine	*4 fluid ounces*	*120 milliliters*
Whole wheat flour, roasted	*2 tablespoons*	*2 tablespoons*
Salt, to taste	*1/2 teaspoon*	*1/2 teaspoon*
Pepper, to taste	*1/2 teaspoon*	*1/2 teaspoon*

1. Sauté onions and garlic in olive oil.

2. Add mushrooms, oregano, tamari, and wine.

3. Thicken with roasted flour slurry.

4. Season to taste.

Marsala Sauce

Yield: 1 quart (1 liter)

Demi-Glace	*1 quart*	*1 liter*
Shallots, minced	*3 tablespoons*	*45 grams*
Marsala	*3 fluid ounces*	*90 milliliters*

1. Combine the Demi-Glace, shallots, and peppercorns.

2. Simmer the mixture until it has reduced, so that the sauce coats the back of a spoon.

3. Strain the sauce.

4. Add the marsala and return to a simmer. Do not boil.

VARIATIONS

Marsala Sauce: Marsala Sauce may be used as the basis of other sauces.

Finish with butter: A small amount of whole unsalted butter can be used to finish the sauce immediately before service if desired.

See page 522 for Demi-Glace.

If necessary, you may need to add salt and pepper to taste.

Marsala and Madeira are fortified wines. Therefore it is usually not allowed to reduce during sauce production. Unlike table wines, which benefit from the flavor intensification of reduction, fortified wines become unpalatable if overcooked.

Sauce Madeira

Yield: 1 quart (1 liter)

Demi-Glace	*1 quart*	*1 liter*
Madeira	*8 fluid ounces*	*240 milliliters*
Butter, cold, cut into small pieces	*3 ounces*	*85 grams*

1. Reduce the Demi-Glace by 8 ounces (240 milliliters). Add the Madeira and heat briefly. Do not boil.

2. At service, finish the sauce with butter.

Truffles are an integral garnish for a number of special Demi-Glace derivatives.

Reduce the base sauce (e.g. Demi-Glace) by an amount equal to the amount of fortified wine you intend to add to the sauce.

Sauce Perigeaux

Yield: 1 quart (1 liter)

Demi-Glace	*1 quart*	*1 liter*
Truffles, black, chopped	*2 ounces*	*60 grams*
Truffles, black, essence	*3 fluid ounces*	*90 milliliters*
Madeira	*4 fluid ounces*	*120 milliliters*
Butter	*2 to 3 ounces*	*60 to 85 grams*

1. Combine Demi-Glace, truffles, and essence, and simmer the mixture until reduced slightly.

2. Add the Madeira and finish with butter just prior to service.

Fines Herbes Sauce

Yield: 1 quart (1 liter)

White wine	*10 fluid ounces*	*300 milliliters*
Parsley, stems	*6 each*	*6 each*
Chervil leaves, dried	*1 1/2 tablespoons*	*1 1/2 tablespoons*
Tarragon leaves, dried	*1 1/2 tablespoons*	*1 1/2 tablespoons*
Chives	*1 1/2 tablespoons*	*1 1/2 tablespoons*
Shallots, minced	*1 ounce*	*30 grams*
Demi-Glace	*1 quart*	*1 liter*
Lemon juice	*1 teaspoon*	*1 teaspoon*
Fines Herbes, chopped per portion	*1 teaspoon*	*1 teaspoon*
Butter	*2 to 4 ounces*	*60 to 115 grams*

1. Reduce the wine, parsley stems, chervil, tarragon, chives, and shallots by half.

2. Add the Demi-Glace; reduce until the sauce coats the back of a spoon.

3. Add the lemon juice and strain the sauce.

4. At service, adjust the seasoning to taste, add the Fines Herbes, and finish with butter.

VARIATION

Tarragon Sauce: For a tarragon sauce, use only dried tarragon in the initial reduction and add chopped, fresh tarragon leaves at service.

Sauce Marchand de Vin

Yield: 1 quart (1 liter)

Shallots, minced	*2 ounces*	*60 grams*
Thyme, sprigs	*2 each*	*2 each*
Bay leaf	*1 each*	*1 each*
Cracked peppercorns	*1/2 teaspoon*	*1/2 teaspoon*
Red wine	*1 pint*	*480 milliliters*
Demi-Glace	*1 quart*	*1 liter*
Unsalted butter, diced	*4 ounces*	*115 grams*

1. Combine the shallots, thyme, bay leaf, pepper, and red wine; reduce the mixture until syrupy.

2. Add the Demi-Glace; reduce until the sauce coats the back of a spoon. Strain the sauce.

3. Finish the sauce with the butter.

This sauce may also be finished with Glace de Viande. See Chapter 13, page 438, for more information about Glace de Viande.

Mushroom Sauce

Yield: 1 quart (1 liter)

Shallots, minced	*2 ounces*	*60 grams*
Clarified butter	*1 ounce*	*30 grams*
Mushrooms, trimmings	*8 ounces*	*225 grams*
Thyme, sprigs	*2 each*	*2 each*
Bay leaves, crumbled	*1 each*	*1 each*
Whole black peppercorns	*8 each*	*8 each*
Burgundy	*4 fluid ounces*	*120 milliliters*
Demi-Glace or Jus de Veau Lié	*1 quart*	*1 liter*
Mushrooms, sliced thick and sautéed in clarified butter	*12 ounces*	*340 grams*

1. Sauté the shallots in the clarified butter until they are translucent.

2. Add the mushroom trimmings and sauté until moisture is released.

3. Add the thyme, bay leaf, pepper, and Burgundy; reduce by half.

4. Add the Demi-Glace; reduce until the sauce coats the back of a spoon.

5. Degrease the sauce and strain.

6. Add the sautéed mushrooms; adjust the seasoning with salt and pepper to taste.

Choose a firm mushroom, whether you opt for wild or domestic mushrooms, with no blemishes or soft spots.

Piquant Sauce

Yield: 1 quart (1 liter)

This is a reduction sauce. For more information about reduction sauces, read Chapter 8, pages 280 to 282.

White wine	*12 fluid ounces*	*360 milliliters*
Cider vinegar	*6 fluid ounces*	*180 milliliters*
Shallots, minced	*1 1/2 ounces*	*45 grams*
Demi-Glace or Jus Lié	*1 quart*	*1 liter*
Pickles, gherkins	*2 ounces*	*60 grams*
Tarragon, fresh, chopped	*1 teaspoon*	*1 teaspoon*
Chervil, fresh, chopped	*1 teaspoon*	*1 teaspoon*
Parsley, fresh, chopped	*1 teaspoon*	*1 teaspoon*
Salt, to taste	*1/2 teaspoon*	*1/2 teaspoon*
Pepper, to taste	*1/4 teaspoon*	*1/4 teaspoon*
Butter, cut into small pieces	*2 ounces*	*60 grams*

1. Reduce the white wine, vinegar, and shallots by three-quarters.

2. Add the Demi-Glace or Jus Lié and reduce until the sauce coats the back of a spoon. Strain the sauce. Return to a simmer.

3. Add the remaining ingredients, adjust the seasoning to taste with salt and pepper, and finish with butter.

Robert Sauce

Yield: 1 1/2 quarts (1 1/2 liters)

Onions, fine dice	*14 ounces*	*400 grams*
Clarified butter	*2 ounces*	*60 grams*
White wine	*1 pint*	*480 milliliters*
Demi-Glace	*1 quart*	*1 liter*
Dry mustard, ground, dissolved in warm water	*2 teaspoons*	*2 teaspoons*
Salt, to taste	*1/2 teaspoon*	*1/2 teaspoon*
Pepper, to taste	*1/4 teaspoon*	*1/4 teaspoon*
Butter	*2 ounces*	*60 grams*

(Recipe continued on facing page)

1. Sauté the onions in butter until they are translucent.

2. Add the wine and reduce to 2 ounces (60 milliliters).

3. Add the Demi-Glace; reduce until the sauce coats the back of a spoon, and remove from heat.

4. Add the dissolved mustard; strain the sauce. Adjust the seasoning to taste with salt and pepper.

5. Finish with butter.

VARIATION

Sauce Charcutière: To serve with pork, add 2 to 3 cornichons cut in a short julienne.

This sauce is typically served with sautéed, grilled, or roasted pork.

Sauce Bordelaise

Yield: 1 quart (1 liter)

Shallots, minced	*1 ounce*	*30 grams*
Thyme, sprigs	*2 each*	*2 each*
Bay leaf	*1 each*	*1 each*
Whole black peppercorns, mignonette	*1/2 teaspoon*	*1/2 teaspoon*
Red wine	*1 pint*	*480 milliliters*
Demi-Glace	*1 quart*	*1 liter*
Bone marrow, poached, diced	*4 ounces*	*115 grams*
Lemon, juiced, to taste	*1/2 each*	*1/2 each*
Glace de Viande (optional)	*1 tablespoon*	*1 tablespoon*
Butter, cold	*5 ounces*	*140 grams*

1. Combine the shallots, thyme, bay leaf, pepper, and red wine; reduce the mixture to 1 cup (240 milliliters).

2. Add the Demi-Glace; reduce until the sauce coats the back of a spoon. Strain the sauce.

3. Finish the sauce with the bone marrow, lemon juice, and Glace de Viande. Adjust the seasoning to taste and finish with butter.

Read about preparing marrow in Chapter 6.

Be sure to allow the mushrooms to cook down sufficiently for the best flavor and texture.

The recipe for Glace de Viande is on page 438.

Sauce Chasseur

Yield: 1 quart (1 liter)

Clarified butter	*1 ounce*	*30 grams*
Olive oil	*1/2 fluid ounce*	*15 milliliters*
Mushrooms, sliced thick	*10 ounces*	*285 grams*
Shallots, minced	*1 ounce*	*30 grams*
Garlic clove, minced	*1 each*	*1 each*
Tomato paste	*3 ounces*	*85 grams*
White wine	*8 fluid ounces*	*240 milliliters*
Brandy	*3 fluid ounces*	*90 milliliters*
Demi-Glace	*1 quart*	*1 liter*
Tomato Concassé	*1 pint*	*480 milliliters*
Parsley, fresh, chopped	*1 tablespoon*	*1 tablespoon*
Glace de Viande	*1 fluid ounce*	*30 milliliters*
Tarragon, chopped	*1 tablespoon*	*1 tablespoon*
Salt, to taste	*1/2 teaspoon*	*1/2 teaspoon*
Pepper, to taste	*1/4 teaspoon*	*1/4 teaspoon*
Butter, cold	*2 ounces*	*60 grams*

1. Heat the butter and olive oil until smoking.

2. Add the mushrooms and sauté them until they are browned.

3. Add the shallots and garlic; sauté them until an aroma is released. Add the tomato paste and pincé.

4. Add the wine and brandy; reduce the mixture by half.

5. Add the Demi-Glace and Tomato Concassé; reduce until the sauce coats the back of a spoon.

6. Finish the sauce with the Demi-Glace, parsley, and tarragon.

7. Adjust the seasoning with salt and pepper to taste.

8. Finish with butter.

Sauce Châteaubriand

Yield: 1 quart (1 liter)

White wine	*1 pint*	*480 milliliters*
Shallots, minced	*2 each*	*2 each*
Thyme, sprigs	*3 each*	*3 each*
Mushrooms, trimmings	*4 ounces*	*115 grams*
Bay leaf	*1 each*	*1 each*
Glace de Viande	*1 quart*	*1 liter*
Tarragon, chopped	*1 tablespoon*	*1 tablespoon*
Salt, to taste	*1/2 teaspoon*	*1/2 teaspoon*
Pepper, to taste	*1/4 teaspoon*	*1/4 teaspoon*
Maître d'Hôtel butter, chilled, small pieces	*3 ounces*	*85 grams*

1. Combine the white wine, shallots, thyme, mushroom trimmings, and bay leaf; reduce by half.

2. Add the Glace de Viande and simmer. Strain the sauce and reserve.

3. At service, add the tarragon, adjust the seasoning with salt and pepper to taste, and finish with the maître d'hôtel butter.

Velouté

Yield: 2 quarts (2 liters)

White Veal, Chicken, or Fish Stock	*2 1/2 quarts*	*2 1/2 liters*
White Roux	*8 ounces*	*225 grams*
Salt, to taste	*1/2 teaspoon*	*1/2 teaspoon*
Pepper, to taste	*1/4 teaspoon*	*1/4 teawpoon*

1. Bring the stock to a boil.

2. Whip the roux into the stock: work out all the lumps.

3. Simmer for 30 to 40 minutes, skimming the surface as necessary.

4. Season with salt and pepper to taste and then strain the sauce.

See Chapter 8, pages 280 to 282 for more information about reduction sauces.

Straining the sauce is a critical step in order to produce the best texture in the finished sauce.

There are a number of optional aromatics that can be added to this sauce as it simmers to give it a special flavor: bay leaf, thyme, mushroom trimmings, or a Standard Sachet d'Épices. However, if the sauce is to be further reduced or flavored to make a special sauce, it is best to keep this base as plain as possible.

Some chefs prefer to add the stock to the roux. See Chapter 6 for information on working with roux.

Fresh dill is rather perishable, so be sure to use it before the leaves begin to wilt.

The recipe for Velouté is on page 531.

Dill Sauce

Yield: 1 quart (1 liter)

Onions, fine dice	*4 ounces*	*115 grams*
Clarified butter	*1 ounce*	*30 grams*
Velouté	*1 quart*	*1 liter*
Sour cream	*10 ounces*	*285 grams*
Dill, fresh, chopped	*3 tablespoons*	*3 tablespoons*
Salt, to taste	*1/2 teaspoon*	*1/2 teaspoon*
Pepper, to taste	*1/4 teaspoon*	*1/4 teaspoon*

1. Sweat the onions in the butter.

2. Add the Velouté and simmer until the sauce coats the back of a spoon.

3. At service, add the sour cream and dill. Add salt and pepper; adjust the seasoning to taste.

Horseradish Sauce

Yield: 1 quart (1 liter)

Horseradish, grated	*4 ounces*	*115 grams*
White wine vinegar, as needed	*2 fluid ounces*	*60 milliliters*
Water, as needed	*2 fluid ounces*	*60 milliliters*
Chicken Velouté	*24 fluid ounces*	*720 milliliters*
Sour cream	*12 ounces*	*340 grams*
Egg yolks (optional)	*3 each*	*3 each*
Salt, to taste	*1/2 teaspoon*	*1/2 teaspoon*
Pepper, to taste	*1/4 teaspoon*	*1/4 teaspoon*
Sugar, as needed	*1 tablespoon*	*1 tablespoon*

There are a variety of cold horseradish sauces as well as this hot version.

1. Hold the grated horseradish in enough vinegar and water to cover it.

2. Bring the Velouté to a simmer; let it reduce until the sauce coats the back of a spoon.

3. Combine the sour cream and egg yolks. Temper with Velouté, then add to the remainder of the Velouté. Return to just below a simmer.

4. Drain and squeeze the horseradish and add it to the sauce. Adjust the seasoning to taste with salt, pepper, vinegar, and sugar.

Sauce Albuféra

Yield: 1 quart (1 liter)

White Veal Stock	*1 quart*	*1 liter*
White Roux	*4 ounces*	*115 grams*
Chicken Stock	*1 quart*	*1 liter*
Heavy cream	*4 fluid ounces*	*120 milliliters*
Glace de Viande	*4 to 6 ounces*	*115 to 170 grams*
Pimiento Butter	*2 ounces*	*60 grams*

1. Combine the White Veal Stock and the roux. Cook the mixture until it is smooth and thickened.

2. Add the Chicken Stock. Reduce the mixture by half. Simmer it for 45 to 60 minutes.

3. Temper the heavy cream with some of the hot sauce. Add the tempered cream to the rest of the sauce.

4. Add the Glace de Viande and Pimiento Butter to the sauce.

This sauce is excellent with poached or braised poultry.

For Pimento Butter, see page 548.

Use a prepared Sauce Suprême (page 534) and finish with Glace de Viande and Pimento Butter.

Nantua Sauce

Yield: 1 quart (1 liter)

Béchamel	*24 fluid ounces*	*720 milliliters*
Heavy cream	*16 fluid ounces*	*480 milliliters*
Crayfish Butter	*10 ounces*	*285 grams*
Salt, to taste	*1/2 teaspoon*	*1/2 teaspoon*
Pepper, to taste	*1/4 teaspoon*	*1/4 teaspoon*

1. Combine the Béchamel with the cream; simmer and reduce to 1 quart (1 liter).

2. Finish the sauce with the crayfish butter just prior to service.

3. Adjust the seasoning with salt and pepper to taste.

VARIATION

To prepare this sauce *à la minute*, heat 2 ounces (60 milliliters) of Béchamel per portion, add 1 tablespoon heavy cream, and finish with a small piece of crayfish butter.

To make Crayfish Butter, follow the recipe for Shellfish Butter on page 549, using only crayfish shells.

This sauce is classically garnished with crayfish tails.

The recipe for Béchamel is on page 535.

Suprême Sauce

Yield: 1 quart (1 liter)

If desired, this sauce may be finished with 3 ounces (85 grams) of butter.

Chicken Velouté	*1 quart*	*1 liter*
Heavy cream, heated	*8 fluid ounces*	*240 milliliters*
Mushroom infusion (optional)	*4 fluid ounces*	*120 milliliters*
Salt, to taste	*1/2 teaspoon*	*1/2 teaspoon*
Pepper, to taste	*1/4 teaspoon*	*1/4 teaspoon*

1. Combine the Velouté and heavy cream. If desired, add the optional mushroom infusion at this point (see Note). Simmer until the sauce coats the back of a spoon.

2. Strain the sauce and adjust the seasoning to taste with salt and pepper.

Note: To make a mushroom infusion, sweat sliced mushrooms in a small amount of butter. Add enough water to cover and simmer over low heat for about 10 minutes. Remove from the heat and allow the liquid to cool. Strain the liquid and reserve. Or, to make an infusion from dried mushrooms, cover the dried mushrooms with boiling water and let the mushrooms steep for 20 to 30 minutes. Then, strain carefully through cheesecloth. Discard the mushrooms.

Shrimp Sauce

Yield: 2 quarts (2 liters)

If desired, you may add 2 ounces (60 milliliters) of dry sherry in step 6.

The recipe for Velouté is on page 531. Prepare this sauce with Shellfish Stock (page 444).

Shrimp shells	*2 pounds*	*900 grams*
Butter	*2 ounces*	*60 grams*
Shallots, minced	*1/2 ounce*	*15 grams*
Garlic cloves, minced	*2 each*	*2 each*
Sweet Hungarian paprika	*1 tablespoon*	*1 tablespoon*
Brandy	*2 fluid ounces*	*60 milliliters*
Heavy cream	*1 quart*	*1 liter*
Velouté	*1 1/2 quarts*	*1.5 liters*

(Recipe continued on facing page)

1. Sauté the shells in the hot butter until they are red.

2. Add the shallots and garlic; sauté until an aroma is apparent.

3. Add the paprika; cook out for several minutes.

4. Deglaze with the brandy.

5. Add the heavy cream and reduce by half until the sauce coats the back of a spoon. Add the Velouté and simmer until a sauce consistency is reached.

6. Strain the sauce. Adjust the seasoning.

VARIATION

Lobster Sauce: Substitute 1 lobster, cut for sauté, for the shrimp shells. Reserve the coral and tomalley to finish the sauce.

Béchamel

Yield: 2 quarts (2 liters)

Milk	*2 1/2 quarts*	*2.375 liters*
White Roux	*8 ounces*	*225 grams*
Onions, fine dice, smothered in clarified butter	*2 ounces*	*60 grams*
Salt, to taste	*1/2 teaspoon*	*1/2 teaspoon*
White pepper, to taste	*1/4 teaspoon*	*1/4 teaspoon*
Nutmeg, ground to taste	*1/4 teaspoon*	*1/4 teaspoon*

1. Scald the milk (do not boil) and pour it over the roux. Bring to a boil.

2. Add the smothered onions.

3. Simmer for 30 minutes.

4. Adjust the seasoning to taste with salt, white pepper, and nutmeg.

5. Strain through a double thickness of cheesecloth.

VARIATIONS

Heavy Béchamel: A heavy Béchamel is often used as a binder for croquettes and similar preparations. Increase the amount of roux to 12 ounces (340 grams) per gallon (3.75 liters).

Mornay Sauce: Combine Béchamel with 1 quart (1 liter) cuisson (cooking liquid). Simmer until reduced to 2 quarts (2 liters). Add 8 ounces (225 grams) each of Gruyère and Parmesan cheese to the sauce. Finish with up to 2 ounces (60 grams), if desired.

Some chefs like to whisk heated milk into the roux, working gradually to avoid lumps.

You may see some older versions of the Béchamel recipe that call for the addition of a whole onion or oignon piqué as the sauce simmers. However, leaving an onion whole in the sauce as it cooks could cause it to sour in a relatively short period of time. However, you may add the bay leaf and clove as it simmers; or thyme, as some chefs prefer.

Cheddar cheese is grated and added to a Béchamel. Use a well-aged cheese for the best flavor.

Use to prepare Macaroni and Cheese, page 726; as a sauce for various omelets and poached egg dishes; to dress steamed or boiled vegetables.

Cheddar Cheese Sauce

Yield: 2 1/2 quarts (2.5 liters)

Béchamel, medium consistency	2 quarts	2 liters
Cheddar cheese, grated	1 pound	450 grams
White wine, dry	2 ounces	60 milliliters
Mustard seed, ground	1 tablespoon	1 tablespoon
Sweet Hungarian paprika (optional)	1 teaspoon	1 teaspoon
Salt, to taste	1 teaspoon	1 teaspoon
White pepper, to taste	1/2 teaspoon	1/2 teaspoon

1. Heat Béchamel gently over low heat.

2. Add the grated cheese and continue to heat, stirring often, until cheese melts. Do not allow the sauce to boil.

3. Combine the wine with ground mustard and paprika. Add to the sauce, and stir until combined.

4. Season the sauce to taste with salt and white pepper.

5. Strain the sauce through a fine sieve.

For Béchamel, see page 535.

To reduce fat and calories, this sauce can be "creamed" with evaporated skimmed milk. Replace whole milk in a Béchamel with skim milk and thicken Béchamel with arrowroot or cornstarch rather than roux.

Cream Sauce

Yield: 1 quart (1 liter)

Béchamel, medium	1 quart	1 liter
Heavy cream, hot	8 fluid ounces	240 milliliters
Salt, to taste	1/2 teaspoon	1/2 teaspoon
White pepper, to taste	1/2 teaspoon	1/2 teaspoon

1. Combine the Béchamel and heavy cream. Simmer until the sauce coats the back of a spoon.

2. Adjust the seasoning to taste with salt and pepper. Strain the sauce, if desired.

Fresh Tomato Sauce

Yield: 1 quart (1 liter)

Onions, brunoise	*8 ounces*	*225 grams*
Celery, brunoise	*4 ounces*	*115 grams*
Carrots, brunoise	*8 ounces*	*225 grams*
Garlic, mashed to a paste	*1 tablespoon*	*1 tablespoon*
Olive oil	*3 fluid ounces*	*90 milliliters*
Butter	*2 ounces*	*60 grams*
Tomato Concassé	*4 pounds*	*1.8 kilograms*
Parsley, chopped	*2 tablespoons*	*2 tablespoons*
Basil, chiffonade (optional)	*1 tablespoon*	*1 tablespoon*
Oregano, chopped (optional)	*1 tablespoon*	*1 tablespoon*
Salt, to taste	*1 teaspoon*	*1 teaspoon*
Pepper, to taste	*1/2 teaspoon*	*1/2 teaspoon*

1. Sweat the onion, celery, carrots, and garlic in the oil and butter until they are translucent.

2. Add the Tomato Concassé; simmer for 45 minutes to 1 hour, until the flavor is fully developed and the correct consistency is reached.

3. Add the parsley, basil, and oregano as desired. Adjust the seasoning to taste with salt and pepper.

Plum tomatoes are often preferred when preparing tomato sauce.

Some chefs prefer to purée the sauce in step 3.

There are a number of ways to season this sauce. Use fresh herbs and spices, including rosemary, thyme, bay leaves, and red pepper flakes that are compatible with the menu items this is to accompany.

Other finishing ingredients might include black olives, sun-dried tomatoes, or wild or domestic mushrooms.

Marinara Sauce

Yield: 2 quarts (2 liters)

This is a classic accompaniment to light pastas and fried seafood dishes such as fried calamari. For a spicier sauce, add a few red pepper flakes. Canned tomatoes should be used when good fresh tomatoes are not available.

Olive oil	*1 fluid ounce*	*30 milliliters*
Onions, small dice	*8 ounces*	*225 grams*
Garlic cloves, minced	*4 each*	*4 each*
Tomato Concassé	*7 pounds*	*3.5 kilograms*
Tomato purée	*20 fluid ounces*	*600 milliliters*
Basil, fresh, chopped	*1/2 cup*	*1/2 cup*
Oregano, fresh, chopped	*1 tablespoon*	*1 tablespoon*

1. Sweat the onions in the olive oil until they are translucent.
2. Add the garlic and sauté it until an aroma is apparent.
3. Add the Tomato Concassé, tomato purée, and oregano to the onions.
4. Simmer the mixture to achieve a heavy consistency.
5. Add the basil and adjust the seasoning to taste.

Tomato Sauce

Yield: 2 quarts (2 liters)

To read more about Tomato Sauce, refer to pages 289 to 292.

Salt pork, minced	*4 ounces*	*115 grams*
Clarified butter	*2 ounces*	*60 grams*
Carrots, medium dice	*2 ounces*	*60 grams*
Onions, small dice	*4 ounces*	*115 grams*
Garlic cloves, minced	*2 each*	*2 each*
Flour	*4 ounces*	*115 grams*
Plum Tomato Concassé	*2 quarts*	*2 liters*
White Beef Stock	*1 quart*	*1 liter*
Tomato purée	*1 pint*	*480 milliliters*
Pork bones	*1 pound*	*450 grams*
Bay leaf	*1 each*	*1 each*
Thyme, sprig	*1 each*	*1 each*
Sugar, to taste	*1 tablespoon*	*1 tablespoon*
Salt, to taste	*1 teaspoon*	*1 teaspoon*

(Recipe continued on facing page)

1. Render the salt pork in the butter.

2. Add the carrots and onions; sauté until the onions are translucent.

3. Add the garlic and sauté until an aroma is apparent.

4. Add the flour; cook out for 5 minutes.

5. Combine the Tomato Concassé, stock, and tomato purée. Add the onion mixture in thirds. Return to a simmer after each addition.

6. Add the pork bones, bay leaf, thyme, and sugar. Simmer on the stove top for 1 1/2 hours, or cook in a 300°F (150°C) oven.

7. Remove the bones and bay leaf. Purée the sauce and adjust the seasoning with salt to taste.

There are many variations possible for tomato sauces. This version is often referred to as a "French" tomato sauce, since it is thickened with a roux. The ultimate yield of the sauce will vary according to the quality of tomatoes, simmering time, and the way in which the sauce is strained. The roux may be omitted if desired.

Meat Sauce

Yield: Approximately 2 quarts (2 liters)

Olive oil	*2 tablespoons*	*30 milliliters*
Garlic cloves, minced	*2 each*	*2 each*
Onion, minced	*3 ounces*	*85 grams*
Chuck, ground (or combination of ground veal and chuck)	*2 1/2 pounds*	*115 kilograms*
Tomato purée	*1 quart*	*1 liter*
Tomato paste	*1 1/2 ounces*	*45 grams*
Salt, to taste	*1 teaspoon*	*1 teaspoon*
Pepper, to taste	*1/2 teaspoon*	*1/2 teaspoon*
Basil, fresh, chopped	*1 tablespoon*	*15 grams*
Oregano, fresh, chopped	*1 tablespoon*	*15 grams*
Thyme, fresh, chopped	*1 tablespoon*	*15 grams*

The classic "spaghetti sauce" loved by children and adults; this sauce also works well with lasagna and heavier pasta dishes. See pasta recommendations in Table 5-40.

1. Heat the olive oil in a large skillet.

2. Add the garlic and onion and sauté them until the onions are tender and light and brown.

3. Add the ground meat. Sauté the mixture, stirring it with a wooden spoon to break up any lumps, until the meat is browned, about 5 minutes.

4. Add the tomato purée and 2 tablespoons (30 grams) of the tomato paste. Mix well.

5. Season the sauce to taste with the salt and pepper. Add the herbs.

6. Degrease the sauce if necessary.

7. Adjust the seasoning or consistency with additional tomato paste if necessary.

Cook the yolks until they are frothy and have reached the same temperature as the butter.

See Chapter 8, pages 292 to 295.

When making Hollandaise Sauce, the butter may be increased slightly; consider a ratio of 2 to 3 ounces (60 to 85 grams) of butter per egg yolk.

Hollandaise Sauce

Yield: 20 ounces (600 milliliters)

Cider vinegar	*2 fluid ounces*	*60 milliliters*
Whole black peppercorns, fresh-cracked	*1/2 teaspoon*	*1/2 teaspoon*
Water	*4 fluid ounces*	*120 milliliters*
Egg yolks	*6 each*	*6 each*
Clarified butter, warm	*12 ounces*	*340 grams*
Lemon juice	*2 teaspoons*	*2 teaspoons*
Salt, to taste	*1/2 teaspoon*	*1/2 teaspoon*
Pepper, to taste (optional)	*1/4 teaspoon*	*1/4 teaspoon*

1. Combine the vinegar and peppercorns; reduce until the liquid has almost cooked away. Cool the reduction slightly.

2. Add hot water to the reduction. (The reduction may be strained at this point, if desired.)

3. Add the reduction to the egg yolks. In a stainless steel bowl, whip over simmering water until the yolks ribbon and triple in volume. They should have a light but firm consistency.

4. Gradually add the warm clarified butter, whipping constantly.

5. Add the lemon juice, and adjust the seasoning to taste with salt and pepper.

6. Strain through a cheesecloth, if necessary, to remove any pieces of cooked egg.

VARIATION

Sauce Maltaise: Finish the Hollandaise with zest and juice from a blood orange.

Béarnaise

Yield: 20 fluid ounces (600 milliliters)

Reduction

Shallots, chopped	*1 tablespoon*	*1 tablespoon*
Whole black peppercorns, fresh-cracked	*1/2 teaspoon*	*1/2 teaspoon*
Tarragon leaves, dried	*1 tablespoon*	*1 tablespoon*
Tarragon vinegar	*3 fluid ounces*	*90 milliliters*
Dry white wine	*3 fluid ounces*	*90 milliliters*
Water	*4 fluid ounces*	*120 milliliters*
Egg yolks	*6 each*	*6 each*
Clarified butter, warm	*12 ounces*	*340 grams*
Tarragon, pluches, coarsely chopped	*2 tablespoons*	*2 tablespoons*
Chervil, pluches, coarsely chopped	*1 tablespoon*	*2 tablespoons*
Salt, to taste	*1/2 teaspoon*	*1/2 teaspoon*

A pinch of cayenne is added for a classic presentation.

If your kitchen prepares Béarnaise often, or other warm-butter sauces that are based on a reduction, you may want to prepare reductions separately, in advance. The recipe for a Béarnaise Reduction follows.

1. Combine the shallots, peppercorns, dried tarragon, vinegar, and wine. Reduce to sec.

2. Add the water to the reduction; strain if desired.

3. Combine the reduction and the egg yolks in a stainless steel bowl. Whip over a bain-marie until the yolks form ribbons and triple in volume. They should be light but firm.

4. Add the clarified butter gradually, whipping constantly. Strain if necessary to remove any cooked egg particles.

5. Add the chopped tarragon and chervil; adjust the seasoning to taste with salt.

Béarnaise Reduction

Yield: 3 to 4 fluid ounces (90 to 120 milliliters)

Shallots, chopped	*2 tablespoons*	*2 tablespoons*
Black peppercorns, fresh-cracked	*1 teaspoon*	*1 teaspoon*
Tarragon, chopped	*2 tablespoons*	*2 tablespoons*
Tarragon vinegar	*4 fluid ounces*	*120 milliliters*
Dry white wine	*4 fluid ounces*	*120 milliliters*
Water	*2 fluid ounces*	*60 milliliters*

The amount of shallots can be increased if desired.

1. Combine the shallots, peppercorns, tarragon, vinegar, and wine in a saucepan. Bring to a simmer, then reduce until nearly dry.

2. Refresh the reduction with water. Strain if desired.

Choron Sauce

Yield: 1 quart (1 liter)

Also called Sauce Béarnaise Tomatée, this sauce often accompanies grilled meats and poultry.

The amount of butter may be reduced by as much as 10 ounces (285 grams).

Shallots, chopped	1 ounce	30 grams
Black peppercorns, fresh-cracked	12 each	12 each
Tarragon leaves, dried	3 tablespoons	7 grams
Tarragon vinegar	4 fluid ounces	120 milliliters
Dry white wine	4 fluid ounces	120 milliliters
Water	2 fluid ounces	60 milliliters
Egg yolks	9 each	9 each
Clarified butter, warm	27 ounces	.750 kilograms
Tomato paste	1 1/2 ounces	40 grams
Salt, to taste	1/2 teaspoon	1/2 teaspoon

1. Combine the shallots, peppercorns, dried tarragon, vinegar, and wine. Reduce to sec.

2. Add the water to the reduction; strain.

3. Combine the strained reduction and egg yolks in a stainless steel bowl. Cook over a bain-marie until the yolks form ribbons and triple in volume.

4. Add the clarified butter gradually, whipping constantly.

5. Add the tomato purée; adjust the seasoning to taste with salt.

Creole Mustard Sauce

Yield: 1 quart (1 liter)

Select from among the many mustard varieties (dry, whole, ground, or prepared) to make this sauce.

Shallots, minced	2 ounces	60 grams
Cider vinegar	4 fluid ounces	120 milliliters
Black peppercorns, fresh-cracked	2 teaspoons	2 teaspoons
Bay leaves	2 each	2 each
Dry white wine	1 pint	480 milliliters
Heavy cream, reduced by half	8 fluid ounces	240 milliliters
Butter, diced	1 1/2 pounds	680 grams
Dijon mustard, to taste	1 ounce	30 grams
Creole mustard, to taste	1 ounce	30 grams
Mild mustard, to taste	1 ounce	30 grams

(Recipe continued on facing page)

1. Combine the shallots, vinegar, peppercorns, bay leaves, and wine. Reduce the mixture to 6 ounces (180 milliliters).

2. Add the heavy cream and reduce the mixture by half. Strain the sauce and return it to the heat.

3. Whisk in the butter gradually over low heat. Do not allow the sauce to boil.

4. Add the mustards, to taste.

The butter should be cut into small cubes, slightly softened, but still cold as it is added into the sauce in step 3.

This sauce should be held in the same manner as Hollandaise and Béarnaise, pages 540 and 541.

Sauce Mousseline

Yield: 20 ounces (600 milliliters)

Cider vinegar	*1 fluid ounce*	*30 milliliters*
Black peppercorns, fresh-cracked	*1/4 teaspoon*	*1/4 teaspoon*
Water	*2 fluid ounces*	*60 milliliters*
Egg yolks	*4 each*	*4 each*
Clarified butter, warm	*12 ounces*	*360 milliliters*
Lemon juice	*1 teaspoon*	*1 teaspoon*
Salt, to taste	*1/2 teaspoon*	*1/2 teaspoon*
Pepper, to taste	*1/4 teaspoon*	*1/4 teaspoon*
Heavy cream, whipped to soft peaks	*4 fluid ounces*	*115 milliliters*

Sauce Mousseline, also known as Sauce Chantilly, is a variation of the classic Hollandaise Sauce served with poached fish and boiled or steamed vegetables such as asparagus. To read about preparing Hollandaise-style sauces, see pages 292 to 295.

1. Combine the vinegar and peppercorns; reduce until the liquid has cooked away. Cool the reduction slightly.

2. Add water to the reduction. (The reduction may be strained at this point, if desired.)

3. Add the reduction to the egg yolks. Whip over simmering water until the yolks ribbon.

4. Gradually add the warm clarified butter, whipping constantly.

5. Add the lemon juice, salt, and pepper to taste.

6. Fold in the whipped cream immediately prior to service and keep warm.

Royal Glaçage

Yield: 24 fluid ounces (720 milliliters)

For the best results, have all of the Hollandaise and Velouté (pages 531 and 540) at the same temperature when they are combined. Fold in the cream just before using.

Hollandaise sauce, warm	*8 fluid ounces*	*240 milliliters*
Velouté, warm	*8 fluid ounces*	*240 milliliters*
Heavy cream, whipped to soft peaks	*8 fluid ounces*	*240 milliliters*

1. Fold together all of the ingredients gently.

2. Coat the item to be glazed with the glacage.

3. Brown lightly under a salamander or broiler.

Sauce Paloise is made in the same way as Béarnaise, substituting mint for the tarragon both in the reduction and as a final garnish ingredient.

Sauce Palois

Yield: 20 fluid ounces (600 milliliters)

Shallots, chopped	*1 tablespoon*	*1 tablespoon*
Black peppercorns, fresh-cracked	*4 each*	*4 each*
Mint sprigs, fresh, chopped	*2 tablespoons*	*2 tablespoons*
Cider vinegar	*3 fluid ounces*	*90 milliliters*
Dry white wine	*3 fluid ounces*	*90 milliliters*
Water	*2 fluid ounces*	*60 milliliters*
Egg yolks	*6 each*	*6 each*
Clarified butter, warm	*16 ounces*	*450 grams*
Mint, pluches, chiffonade	*4 tablespoons*	*4 tablespoons*
Salt, to taste	*1/2 teaspoon*	*1/2 teaspoon*
Pepper, to taste	*1/4 teaspoon*	*1/4 teaspoon*

1. Combine the shallots, peppercorns, mint sprigs, vinegar, and wine. Reduce until syrupy.

2. Add the water and wine to the reduction; strain the reduction into a stainless steel bowl, then combine it with the egg yolks. Cook the mixture over a bain-marie until the yolks form ribbons when dropped from the whip.

3. Add the clarified butter gradually, whipping constantly until all the butter is incorporated and the sauce is thick.

4. Add the chiffonade of mint; adjust the seasoning to taste with salt and pepper.

Lemon Beurre Blanc

Yield: 1 1/2 pints (720 milliliters)

Shallots, minced	2 ounces	60 grams
Dry white wine	8 fluid ounces	240 milliliters
Lemon juice	3 fluid ounces	90 milliliters
Cider vinegar	3 fluid ounces	90 milliliters
Heavy cream (optional)	8 fluid ounces	240 milliliters
Butter, softened	1 1/2 pounds	680 grams
Salt, to taste	1/2 teaspoon	1/2 teaspoon
Pepper, to taste	1/4 teaspoon	1/4 teaspoon
Lemon zest	1 tablespoon	1 tablespoon

1. Reduce the cream by half.
2. Combine the shallots, wine, lemon juice, and vinegar. Reduce until nearly dry.
3. Add the reduced heavy cream and continue to reduce slightly.
4. Gradually whisk in the butter.
5. Adjust the seasoning to taste with salt and pepper.
6. Lemon zest may be added for additional color and texture.

Mise en place for beurre blanc.

Traditionally, a Beurre Blanc does not contain cream. However, the cream serves as a stabilizer here. The more the cream is reduced, the greater its stabilizing effect, and therefore the longer it will last during service. As with all warm emulsion sauces, it is best not to hold the sauce where it could become hot enough to break. Some chefs keep it in a bain-marie in a warm water bath, above the line. Others hold it in a vacuum bottle. If you choose not to use cream, it is best to make it à la minute.

Mustard Tarragon Sauce with Green Peppercorns

Yield: Approximately 1 quart (1 liter)

Shallots, minced	2 ounces	60 grams
Cider vinegar	1 fluid ounce	30 milliliters
Tarragon leaves, dried	2 tablespoons	2 tablespoons
Dry white wine	8 fluid ounces	240 milliliters
Butter, cut into pieces	1 1/2 pounds	680 grams
Dijon Mustard	4 tablespoons	60 grams
Green peppercorns, in brine, drained, crushed	3 tablespoons	45 grams
Salt, to taste	1/2 teaspoon	1/2 teaspoon
Pepper, to taste	1/4 teaspoon	1/4 teaspoon

1. Combine the shallots, vinegar, tarragon, and wine. Reduce to 3 ounces. Strain (optional).
2. Add the mustard and green peppercorns.
3. Whisk in the butter gradually over low heat.
4. Adjust the seasoning with salt and pepper to taste.

Tarragon Beurre Blanc

Yield: 1 1/2 pints (720 milliliters)

This sauce is a good accompaniment to poached chicken breast or lean white fish. Use the cooking liquid to replace some or all of the wine in the reduction.

Shallots, minced	*2 ounces*	*60 grams*
Tarragon vinegar	*2 1/2 fluid ounces*	*75 milliliters*
Black peppercorns, fresh-cracked	*8 each*	*8 each*
Bay leaf	*1 each*	*1 each*
Dry white wine	*12 fluid ounces*	*360 milliliters*
Heavy cream, reduced by half (optional)	*8 fluid ounces*	*240 milliliters*
Butter, softened	*1 1/2 pounds*	*.680 kilograms*
Tarragon, fresh, chopped	*1 tablespoon*	*1 tablespoon*

1. Combine the shallots, vinegar, peppercorns, bay leaf, and wine. Reduce to 2 ounces (60 milliliters). Strain.

2. Reduce the cream by half and add it to the reduction.

3. Gradually whisk in the butter over low heat.

4. Add the tarragon leaves.

Roll the compound butter into a tight cylinder before chilling.

For a spicier version, add a chipotle pepper and a tablespoon of Adobe sauce in which the chipotle pepper is packed; purée.

See Chapter 8, pages 297 to 298.

Chili Butter

Yield: Approximately 1 pound (450 grams)

Chili powder	*1 tablespoon*	*7 grams*
Cumin, ground	*1/2 teaspoon*	*1 gram*
Sweet Hungarian paprika	*1/2 teaspoon*	*1 gram*
Chili powder, Hot	*1 tablespoon*	*7 grams*
Oregano	*1 tablespoon*	*7 grams*
Worcestershire sauce	*1/2 teaspoon*	*1/2 teaspoon*
Tabasco sauce	*1/4 teaspoon*	*1/4 teaspoon*
Garlic powder	*1/4 teaspoon*	*1/4 teaspoon*
Onion powder	*1/4 teaspoon*	*1/4 teaspoon*
Butter, softened	*1 pound*	*455 grams*

1. Heat the chili powder, cumin, and paprika in a dry pan to release their flavors. Cool.

2. Combine the spices with the remaining ingredients.

3. Pipe the butter into rosettes, using a pastry bag, or roll into a cylinder.

4. Refrigerate or freeze until needed.

Maître d'Hôtel Butter

Yield: 1 1/4 pounds (570 grams)

Butter, softened	*1 pound*	*450 grams*
Parsley bunch, finely chopped	*1/2 each*	*1/2 each*
Lemon juice	*2 to 3 tablespoons*	*45 milliliters*
Salt, to taste	*1/2 teaspoon*	*1/2 teaspoon*
Pepper, to taste	*1/4 teaspoon*	*1/4 teaspoon*

1. Combine all the ingredients.

2. Pipe into rosettes, using a pastry bag, or roll in parchment paper.

3. Refrigerate or freeze until needed.

VARIATIONS

Basil Compound Butter: Add chopped fresh basil to replace parsley. Add grated Parmesan cheese and minced garlic to taste. For best flavor, sweat the garlic in olive oil or butter, and cool, before adding to the butter.

Sun-Dried Tomato-and-Oregano Butter: Add about 3 tablespoons (60 grams) of minced fresh oregano in addition to the parsley. Add 2 ounces (60 grams) of minced sun-dried tomatoes.

Rosemary-and-Ginger Butter: Replace the parsley with about 2 to 3 tablespoons of minced fresh rosemary leaves; add 1 tablespoon of grated fresh gingerroot (or more to taste). If desired, add soy or tamari sauce to replace the lemon juice.

Cilantro-and-Lime Butter: Replace the parsley with chopped cilantro leaves. Replace the lemon juice with fresh lime juice. Add dried red pepper flakes, to taste, if desired.

This is one of the most commonly prepared compound butters. It can be held under refrigeration for several days, but be sure to check it carefully for any souring as a result. It is best held in the freezer.

When serving with some grilled meat and fish, consider adding 1 to 2 tablespoons of prepared mustard to the blend.

Pimiento Butter

Yield: 1 1/4 pounds (570 grams)

Roast the garlic in butter for additional flavor.

Butter, softened	*1 pound*	*450 grams*
Pimientos, sweet, minced	*4 ounces*	*115 grams*
Garlic, minced	*1/4 teaspoon*	*1/4 teaspoon*
Lemon juice	*1 tablespoon*	*1 tablespoon*
Salt, to taste	*1/2 teaspoon*	*1/2 teaspoon*
Pepper, to taste	*1/4 teaspoon*	*1/4 teaspoon*

1. Combine all ingredients.

2. Pipe the butter into rosettes using a pastry bag, or roll in parchment paper.

3. Refrigerate or freeze until needed.

VARIATIONS

Roasted Red Pepper Butter: Use puréed roasted red peppers, that have been sautéed over medium heat to dry, instead of pimientos. Add chopped chipotle peppers if desired.

Roasted Yellow Pepper Butter: Use puréed roasted yellow pepper. Add 1/2 teaspoon chopped fresh majoram.

Scallion Butter

Yield: 1 pound (450 grams)

For an Asian flavor, grated gingerroot and diced lemongrass may also be included in this butter.

Butter, softened	*1 pound*	*450 grams*
Scallions, minced	*4 each*	*4 each*
Garlic, minced	*1/4 teaspoon*	*1/4 teaspoon*
Parsley, chopped	*1 ounce*	*30 grams*
Soy sauce	*1 tablespoon*	*1 tablespoon*
Lemon juice	*1 tablespoon*	*1 tablespoon*
Salt, to taste	*1/2 teaspoon*	*1/2 teaspoon*
Pepper, to taste	*1/4 teaspoon*	*1/4 teaspoon*

1. Combine all ingredients.

2. Pipe the butter into rosettes, using a pastry bag, or roll in parchment paper.

3. Refrigerate or freeze until needed.

Shellfish Butter

Yield: 1 pound (450 grams)

Shallots, minced	*1/2 ounce*	*15 grams*
Sweet Hungarian paprika	*4 teaspoons*	*4 teaspoons*
Crustacean shells (shrimp, lobster, crab), coarsely chopped	*8 ounces*	*225 grams*
Dry white wine	*8 fluid ounces*	*240 milliliters*
Butter, softened	*16 ounces*	*455 grams*

1. Sauté the shallots, paprika, and shells until they are bright red.

2. Deglaze with the wine and reduce to 2 ounces (60 milliliters).

3. Strain the reduction into a bowl set over an ice bath. Press the shells to extract the flavor.

4. Whip the butter and the reduction together.

5. Roll into a cylinder; refrigerate or freeze until needed.

Traditionally, shellfish shells would be baked until they were very dry, pounded into a fine powder, and incorporated into sauces and butters such as this one.

This butter can be used to finish various sauces, including Sauce Nantua, Shrimp Sauce, or as a way to create specialty beurre blancs prepared from the poaching liquid for various fish or shellfish.

Red Chili Sauce

Yield: 1 quart (1 liter)

Vegetable oil	*3 tablespoons*	*3 tablespoons*
Onions, finely chopped	*3 ounces*	*85 grams*
Garlic cloves, minced	*2 each*	*2 each*
Oregano	*1/2 teaspoon*	*1/2 teaspoon*
Cumin, ground	*2 teaspoons*	*2 teaspoons*
Chili powder	*4 ounces*	*115 grams*
Chicken or Beef Stock	*1 1/4 quarts*	*1.2 liters*
Salt, to taste	*1/2 teaspoon*	*1/2 teaspoon*

1. Sweat the onions in the oil. Add the garlic and cook 30 seconds more. Add the oregano and the cumin and continue to cook. Add the chili powder and cook briefly, stirring constantly. Do not let mixture burn.

2. Add the stock, whisking to remove any lumps. Simmer for about 30 minutes and reduce to sauce consistency. Strain if desired. Adjust seasoning.

VARIATIONS

Red Chili Sauce with Tomatoes: For a sweeter sauce, replace 1 pint (480 milliliters) of the stock with 10 ounces (285 grams) of Tomato Concassé. Increase the onions to 6 ounces (170 grams).

Chipotle Chili Sauce: For a smoky flavor, add 2 or 3 chipotle peppers and Adobe sauce (depending on desired heat) to the cooking sauce.

The sauce can be finished with butter for added richness.

Almost any whole dried chilies can be used in place of, or in addition to, the chili powder. To use dried chilies first roast the chilies in a skillet for 3 or 4 minutes. Soak them in boiling water, seed, and then purée them. The purée can be added to the sauce with the stock. Strain the sauce in the final step.

Green Chili Sauce

Yield: 1 quart (1 liter)

Three tablespoons of flour can be added to the onion-oil mixture to make a roux for a thicker, more stable sauce.

Fresh green chilies (New Mexico, Anaheim, or Poblano) or canned chilies may be used for the sauce.

Vegetable oil	*3 tablespoons*	*3 tablespoons*
Onions, finely diced	*3 ounces*	*85 grams*
Garlic cloves, minced	*2 each*	*2 each*
Cumin, ground	*1 teaspoon*	*1 teaspoon*
Chicken or Pork Stock	*1 quart*	*1 liter*
Green chilies, roasted and peeled	*1 pound*	*450 grams*
Oregano	*1/2 teaspoon*	*1/2 teaspoon*
Salt, to taste	*1/2 teaspoon*	*1/2 teaspoon*
Jalapeños (optional)	*2 teaspoons*	*2 teaspoons*

1. Sweat the onions in the oil until tender. Add the garlic and cumin and cook briefly. Add the remaining ingredients.

2. Simmer the sauce about 30 minutes; adjust the consistency. Season to taste. For a smooth consistency, purée the sauce.

VARIATIONS

Green Chili Sauce with Tomatoes: Replace 1 pint (480 milliliters) of the stock with 10 ounces (285 grams) of Tomato Concassé.

Green Chili Sauce with Tomatillas: Replace 1 pint (480 milliliters) of the stock with 10 ounces (285 grams) of blanched, peeled, and seeded tomatillas.

Green Chili Sauce with Cream: Add 4 to 8 fluid ounces (120 to 240 milliliters) of heavy cream at the end. Enchiladas prepared with this sauce are called "Swiss Enchiladas."

Red Pepper Coulis

Yield: 2 quarts (2 liters)

Red peppers, roasted and chopped	*3 pounds*	*1.35 kilograms*
Olive oil	*2 fluid ounces*	*60 milliliters*
Shallots, chopped	*1 ounce*	*30 grams*
White wine	*8 fluid ounces*	*240 milliliters*
Chicken Stock	*16 fluid ounces*	*480 milliliters*
Salt, to taste	*1/2 teaspoon*	*1/2 teaspoon*
Pepper, to taste	*1/4 teaspoon*	*1/4 teaspoon*

(Recipe continued on facing page)

1. Sweat the peppers in the olive oil until they are tender; remove the peppers and purée. Reserve the oil used to sweat the peppers.

2. Sweat the shallots in the reserved oil.

3. Deglaze with wine.

4. Add the stock; reduce by half. Purée the sauce. Adjust the consistency.

5. Adjust the seasoning with salt and pepper to taste.

See Chapter 8, page 291 for more information about Coulis.

This sauce can be finished in a number of ways: add a small amount of heavy cream or crème fraîche, additional chopped fresh herbs, or a julienne of other bell peppers (red, green, yellow, etc.).

Tomato Coulis

Yield: 2 quarts (2 liters)

Olive oil	*2 fluid ounces*	*60 milliliters*
Onions, minced	*8 ounces*	*225 grams*
Garlic, minced	*1/2 ounce*	*15 grams*
Tomato paste	*8 fluid ounces*	*240 milliliters*
Red wine	*12 fluid ounces*	*360 milliliters*
Plum tomatoes, flesh only	*2 1/2 pounds*	*1.2 kilograms*
Chicken Stock	*1 quart*	*1 liter*
Basil, sprigs	*2 each*	*2 each*
Thyme, sprig	*1 each*	*1 each*
Bay leaf	*1 each*	*1 each*
Pepper, to taste	*1/4 teaspoon*	*1/4 teaspoon*

Roasted garlic and roasted red peppers may be included in this purée for a more intense flavor.

1. Heat the olive oil; sauté the onions until they are tender. Add the garlic; sauté it briefly. Add the tomato paste; caramelize it lightly.

2. Add the red wine, tomatoes, stock, basil, thyme, and bay leaf. Simmer the mixture for approximately 45 minutes. Remove and discard the herbs.

3. Run the mixture through a food mill with a coarse plate. Adjust the consistency if necessary.

4. Finish the sauce with the pepper. Cool the sauce and hold it under refrigeration.

Barbecue Sauce

Yield:1 quart (1 liter)

Additional seasonings for barbeque sauce include, but are not limited to: bourbon, rum, molasses, honey, maple syrup, ketchup, cocktail sauce, A-1 Steak Sauce, mustard, cumin, cracked black peppercorns, salt, oregano, chipotle peppers or other peppers, additional vinegars, and infused oils.

The recipe for Chili Powder is on page 425, or use a good-quality commercially prepared blend.

Butter, unsalted	*1 tablespoon*	*15 grams*
Onions, chopped	*4 ounces*	*115 grams*
Garlic, minced	*1 tablespoon*	*1 tablespoon*
Chili Powder	*2 tablespoons*	*2 tablespoons*
Jalapeño chilies, minced	*1 tablespoon*	*1 tablespoon*
Coffee	*4 fluid ounces*	*120 milliliters*
Worcestershire sauce	*4 fluid ounces*	*120 milliliters*
Tomato paste	*4 ounces*	*115 grams*
Apple cider vinegar	*2 fluid ounces*	*60 milliliters*
Brown sugar	*2 ounces*	*60 grams*
Apple cider	*2 tablespoons*	*30 milliliters*
Stock	*as needed*	*as needed*

1. Heat the butter in a saucepan over medium heat. Add the onion and garlic. Sauté them for 2 or 3 minutes until an aroma is apparent.

2. Add the chili powder and jalapeños. Sauté the mixture for another 30 to 45 seconds.

3. Add the coffee, Worcestershire sauce, tomato paste, vinegar, brown sugar, and cider. Simmer the sauce for 20 minutes, or until it is somewhat thickened. Keep it warm until it is needed.

Mango/Bourbon Barbecue Sauce

Yield: 1 quart (1 liter)

Vegetable oil	*1 tablespoon*	*1 tablespoon*
Onion, minced	*6 ounces*	*170 grams*
Garlic cloves, chopped	*5 each*	*5 each*
Ketchup	*1 pint*	*480 milliliters*
Chicken Stock	*8 fluid ounces*	*240 milliliters*
Mango, diced	*8 ounces*	*225 grams*
Hoisin sauce	*4 fluid ounces*	*120 milliliters*
Cider vinegar	*4 fluid ounces*	*120 milliliters*
Bourbon	*2 fluid ounces*	*60 milliliters*
Ancho chilies, stemmed, seeded, and chopped	*2 each*	*2 each*
Brown sugar	*2 tablespoons*	*2 tablespoons*
Lemon juice	*2 tablespoons*	*2 tablespoons*
Worcestershire sauce	*1 tablespoon*	*1 tablespoon*
Lemon zest	*1 teaspoon*	*1 teaspoon*
Old Bay Seasoning	*1/2 teaspoon*	*1/2 teaspoon*
Black pepper	*1/2 teaspoon*	*1/2 teaspoon*
Cayenne pepper	*dash*	*dash*

This barbeque sauce has a unique flavor well-suited to seafood such as skate wings, shrimp, and swordfish. It is also good with chicken and pork.

1. Heat the oil over medium-high heat. Add the onions and garlic and sauté for about 6 minutes, or until the onions are tender and have a sweet aroma.

2. Add the rest of the ingredients and simmer for one hour.

3. Purée the barbecue sauce in a blender until very smooth. It is ready for use, or it can be cooled and stored in the refrigerator until needed.

CHAPTER *16* *Meat Entrées*

There are numerous possibilities when it comes to devising the menu selections for entrées. The recipes here, plus those in the following four chapters, offer a wide range of options. You will find them arranged both by the type of meat and the cooking method.

- *Beef*
- *Veal*
- *Lamb*
- *Pork*
- *Game*
- *Variety Meats*
- *Ground Meats*

Please look at the selections in the International Entrées chapter for additional options.

Beef Tournedos Sauté à la Niçoise

Yield: 10 servings

Garnish the plate with black niçoise olives and julienned pimientos if desired.

To read about Demi-Glace, see page 522.

Beef tenderloin medallions	10 each	10 each
Clarified butter	1 ounce	30 grams
Garlic cloves, minced	1 tablespoon	1 tablespoon
Anchovy fillets	2 each	2 each
Tomato Concassé	12 ounces	340 grams
Demi-Glace	12 fluid ounces	360 milliliters
Niçoise olives	20 each	20 each
Tarragon, chopped	2 teaspoons	2 teaspoons
Salt, to taste	1/2 teaspoon	1/2 teaspoon
Pepper, to taste	1/4 teaspoon	1/4 teaspoon

1. Sauté the beef in the clarified butter to the desired doneness. Keep the beef warm.
2. Heat the water. Sauté the garlic and anchovies until brown.
3. Add the Tomato Concassé and Demi-Glace. Let the mixture reduce slightly.
4. Add the olives and tarragon and adjust the seasoning with salt and pepper to taste.
5. Portion the sauce (about 2 fluid ounces/60 milliliters) onto the tournedos.

Beef Stroganoff

Yield: 10 servings

Beef Stroganoff is traditionally served over egg noodles or Spaëtzle.

Two ounces (60 grams) of tomato paste may be added to the cooked onions if desired. Sauté briefly to develop flavor.

The recipe for Jus de Veau Lié may be found on page 523.

Tenderloin of beef émincé, or beef tips	4 pounds	1.8 kilograms
Vegetable oil, as needed	3 fluid ounces	90 milliliters
Mushrooms, sliced	1/2 pound	225 grams
Butter	2 ounces	60 grams
Onions, minced	8 ounces	225 grams
Jus de Veau Lié	1 pint	480 milliliters
Sour cream	8 fluid ounces	240 milliliters
Dijon mustard	1 tablespoon	1 tablespoon
Lemon juice	1 tablespoon	1 tablespoon
Salt, to taste	1/2 teaspoon	1/2 teaspoon
Pepper, to taste	1/2 teaspoon	1/2 teaspoon

1. Sauté beef in hot oil to desired doneness. Remove meat and keep warm.
2. Sauté mushrooms in butter for 2 to 3 minutes and remove.
3. Sauté onions in butter until translucent. Add Jus de Veau Lié and simmer 10 minutes. Add sour cream to pan, stirring constantly. Reduce until proper consistency is reached.
4. Add mustard, lemon juice, and adjust seasoning to taste with salt and pepper.
5. Reheat meat and mushrooms in sauce (do not boil meat in sauce).

Tenderloin of Beef with Red Chili Sauce and Jalapeño Cheese

Yield: 10 servings

Beef tenderloin, 6 ounces	10 each	10 each
Red Chili Sauce	20 fluid ounces	600 milliliters
Monterey Jack jalapeño cheese	5 ounces	140 grams
Polenta, grilled	2 pounds	900 grams
Zucchini, tourné, blanched	1 1/2 pounds	680 grams

1. Sauté beef in a dry cast iron skillet to desired doneness.

2. Heat Chili Sauce with a small amount of stock.

3. Cut cheese into the same shape as polenta (1/2-ounce/15-gram disk) or grate the cheese. Place on top of polenta and brown under a salamander.

4. To serve, place beef with sauce in middle of plate; arrange grilled polenta and heated and seasoned zucchini around plate.

Wrapping medallions in cheesecloth gives them a uniform shape and allows for even and uniform cooking.

The beef may be grilled if you prefer.

For Red Chili Sauce, see page 549

Roast Prime Rib au Jus

Yield 10 servings

Beef, rib eye roast, boneless	4 pounds	1.8 kilograms
Salt, to taste	1 teaspoon	1 teaspoon
Pepper, coarse-ground, to taste	1 teaspoon	1 teaspoon
Mirepoix, medium dice	8 ounces	225 grams
Brown Veal Stock	1 1/2 quarts	1.5 liters
Arrowroot, diluted, as needed	1/2 ounce	15 grams

1. Rub roast with salt and pepper; tie the roast.

2. Place roast on a wire rack in a roast pan.

3. Roast in a 300 to 315°F (150 to 157°C) oven, until the roast reaches an internal temperature of 100°F (35°C); add Mirepoix.

4. Remove roast when it has reached an internal temperature of 125°F (50°C); allow to rest.

5. To make jus, clarify fat in a roast pan, then discard all fat.

6. Add stock and simmer until reduced by one-half; degrease.

7. Strain through a fine chinoise, and adjust seasonings.

8. Remove string, slice meat against the grain, and serve with jus.

Rib cuts are tender, and well-suited to dry-heat cooking methods such as roasting.

The recipe for Brown Veal Stock may be found on page 437.

When roasting, be sure to watch the cooking speed and to regulate the temperature accordingly for correct doneness.

The recipe for Jus de Veau Lié may be found on page 523.

If the roast is removed at an internal temperature of 125°F (60°C), it should reach a final service temperature of 135°F (58°C) as a result of carry-over cooking. This will produce a medium-rare roast.

Roast Top Round of Beef au Jus

Yield: 10 servings

Beef top round roast	*4 pounds*	*1.8 kilograms*
Salt, to taste	*1/2 teaspoon*	*1/2 teaspoon*
Pepper, cracked, to taste	*1 teaspoon*	*1 teaspoon*
Garlic clove, mashed to a paste	*1 each*	*1 each*
Oil	*1 fluid ounce*	*30 milliliters*
Mirepoix, medium dice	*8 ounces*	*225 grams*
Tomato paste (optional)	*1 ounce*	*30 grams*
Jus de Veau Lié	*1 1/2 quarts*	*1.5 liters*
Worcestershire sauce	*to taste*	*to taste*
White or red wine (optional)	*2 fluid ounces*	*60 milliliters*

1. Rub roast with salt, pepper, and garlic; tie the roast.

2. Brown roast on all sides in hot oil; place on a wire rack in a roast pan.

3. Place roast in a 300 to 315°F (150 to 157°C) oven, roast until it reaches an internal temperature of 100°F (35°C); add Mirepoix, and continue to roast.

4. Remove roast when internal temperature is 125°F (50°C); allow to rest.

5. To make sauce, clarify fat in roast pan, then discard all fat.

6. Add Jus de Veau Lié and simmer until reduced slightly. Degrease thoroughly.

7. Strain through a fine chinoise; adjust seasonings with salt, pepper, Worcestershire sauce, and wine. Adjust consistency.

8. Remove string, slice meat against the grain, serve with jus.

Standing Rib Roast au Jus

Yield: 25 to 30 servings

The recipe for Brown Veal Stock may be found on page 437.

Beef rib roast	*14 pounds*	*6.3 kilograms*
Salt, to taste	*1 teaspoon*	*1 teaspoon*
Pepper, cracked, to taste	*1 teaspoon*	*1 teaspoon*
Mirepoix	*1 1/2 pounds*	*680 kilograms*
Brown Veal Stock	*2 quarts*	*2 liters*
Arrowroot or cornstarch, (optional), diluted in cold stock or water	*2 1/2 ounces*	*70 grams*

(Recipe continued on facing page)

1. Season the beef with the salt and pepper and roast it at 300 to 315°F (150 to 157°C) for 2 1/2 hours. Add the Mirepoix to the pan.

2. Continue to roast to an internal temperature of 130 to 135°F (55 to 58°C)

3. Remove the roast and let it rest for one-half hour.

4. Clarify the fat and reduce the pan drippings. Drain off the fat and reserve it.

5. Deglaze the roasting pan with the stock. Simmer briefly and strain. Adjust the consistency with the arrowroot or cornstarch (optional). Adjust the seasoning with salt and pepper to taste.

To make Yorkshire Pudding, prepare the batter for popovers. Place 1 teaspoon of rendered fat from the roast into ramekins. Add batter and bake at 400°F (205°C) for 20 to 25 minutes.

Roast Strip Loin au Jus

Yield: 10 servings

Strip loin, oven-ready	5 pounds	2.25 kilograms
Salt, to taste	1/2 teaspoon	1/2 teaspoon
Pepper, to taste	1/2 teaspoon	1/2 teaspoon
Mirepoix, chopped coarsely	8 ounces	225 grams
Brown Veal Stock, hot	1 1/2 quarts	1.5 liters

1. Season the loin with salt and pepper. Begin roasting the loin with the fat side down in a very hot oven (400 to 415°F/205 to 210°C). Turn the loin when the fat starts to crackle and reduce the heat to 350°F (175°C).

2. Roast the loin to the desired doneness (internal temperature of 125°F/50°C); remove it from the pan and let it rest for 20 minutes before carving it.

3. Add the Mirepoix to the roasting pan and cook it over direct heat until the Mirepoix is browned, the drippings are reduced, and the fat is clarified.

4. Deglaze the roasting pan thoroughly with the brown stock and simmer to achieve good flavor. Strain the jus.

5. Slice the roast and serve it with the jus.

VARIATION

Roast Strip Loin with Pepper Crust: Rub a good quantity of cracked peppercorns over the beef before roasting. Serve with Sauce Marchand de Vin (page 527).

If desired, add 1 to 2 ounces (30 to 60 grams) of tomato paste to the Mirepoix and pincé.

To make Brown Veal Stock, see page 437.

Tenderloin of Beef with Blue Cheese Herb Crust

Yield: 10 servings

Medallions of beef are typically cut at 5 to 6 ounces (140 to 170 grams) each.

The recipe for Jus de Veau Lié may be found on page 523.

Crumb mixture		
Bread crumbs, white	*4 ounces*	*115 grams*
Blue cheese	*2 1/4 ounces*	*75 grams*
Parsley, chopped	*1/2 ounce*	*15 grams*
Chives, chopped	*1/2 ounce*	*15 grams*
Garlic cloves, minced	*3 each*	*3 each*
White pepper, to taste	*1/4 teaspoon*	*1/4 teaspoon*
Beef tenderloin medallions	*10 each*	*10 each*
Jus de Veau Lié	*1 1/4 pints*	*600 milliliters*

1. Process the bread crumbs, blue cheese, parsley, chives, garlic, and white pepper to a fine crumb.

2. At service, sear the tenderloin in a nonstick pan.

3. Pack 1/2 ounce (15 grams) of the crumb mixture on top of each medallion. Bake in a medium oven to the desired doneness. Brown the medallions under a salamander, if necessary.

4. Heat the Jus de Veau Lié and pool it around the medallion.

Beef Wellington

Yield: 10 to 12 servings

To make this classic dish a lighter entrée, replace the puff pastry with phyllo. Some formulas may also call for either Pâté Brisée (pages 30 to 32) or brioche.

There is a version of Beef Wellington in which forcemeat is prepared by blending 10 ounces (285 grams) of pork and 2 eggs with the Duxelles, Foie Gras, and truffles.

For Sauce Madeira, see page 525.

Beef tenderloin	*4 pounds*	*1.8 kilograms*
Salt, to taste	*1 teaspoon*	*1 teaspoon*
Pepper, to taste	*1/2 teaspoon*	*1/2 teaspoon*
Duxelles	*8 ounces*	*225 grams*
Foie Gras, diced	*8 ounces*	*225 grams*
Truffles, diced	*1 1/2 ounces*	*50 grams*
Puff Pastry, sheet	*1 each*	*1 each*
Egg wash	*4 fluid ounces*	*120 milliliters*
Sauce Madeira	*20 fluid ounces*	*600 milliliters*

1. Season and sear tenderloin. Cool.

2. Combine the Duxelles, Foie Gras, and truffles. Spread it evenly on the tenderloin.

3. Roll out dough to 3/16-inch thickness. Wrap around tenderloin. Brush with egg wash, sealing seams. Decorate with pastry scraps as desired. Bake at 350°F (175°C) about 40 minutes. Dough should be cooked thoroughly and golden brown. Meat should have an internal temperature of 130°F (55°C).

4. Cut in 3/4-inch slices. Serve the Sauce Madeira on the side.

Broiled Sirloin Steak with Chili Butter

Yield: 10 servings

Sirloin steak, 10 ounces (285 grams)	*10 each*	*10 each*
Salt, to taste	*1/2 teaspoon*	*1/2 teaspoon*
Black pepper, fresh-ground, to taste	*1/4 teaspoon*	*1/4 teaspoon*
Vegetable oil	*as needed*	*as needed*
Chili Butter	*5 ounces*	*140 grams*

1. Season steak with salt and pepper; brush with oil.

2. Broil in hot broiler until desired doneness.

3. Turn steak at 45-degree angles during broiling to achieve grill marks.

4. Serve with compound butter and other accompaniments.

The recipe for Chili Butter is on page 546.

For a selection of compound butter recipes, see page 546 to 549.

For information on broiling and grilling meat, see Chapter 9, pages 302 to 307.

Beef Tenderloin with Scallion Butter

Yield: 10 servings

Beef tenderloin medallions	*10 each*	*10 each*
Salt, to taste	*1/2 teaspoon*	*1/2 teaspoon*
Pepper, to taste	*1/4 teaspoon*	*1/4 teaspoon*
Vegetable oil	*as needed*	*as needed*
Scallion Butter	*10 ounces*	*300 grams*

1. Season the tenderloin with the salt and pepper; brush it with the oil.

2. Broil or grill the tenderloin to the desired doneness.

3. Top the tenderloin with a slice of the scallion butter, about 1/2 ounce (15 grams) per portion.

VARIATION

Tenderloin Steak with Spice Rub: Rub the shaped tenderloin with the Spice Rub on page 425 and marinate for 2 to 3 hours. Serve with Jus de Veau Lié.

The recipe for Scallion Butter is on page 548.

Shape the tenderloin medallions as illustrated in Figure 6-69 on page 230.

Broiled Sirloin Strip Steak
with Sauce Marchand de Vin

Yield: 10 servings

The recipe for Sauce Marchand de Vin can be found on page 527.

Beef strip steaks, well-trimmed	*10 each*	*10 each*
Salt, to taste	*1/2 teaspoon*	*1/2 teaspoon*
Black peppercorns, cracked, to taste	*1/4 teaspoon*	*1/4 teaspoon*
Vegetable oil	*as needed*	*as needed*
Sauce Marchand de Vin	*20 fluid ounces*	*600 milliliters*
Butter, chilled	*4 ounces*	*115 grams*

1. Season the steak with the salt and pepper; brush it with the oil.
2. Broil the steaks to the desired doneness.
3. Heat the sauce; finish with butter.
4. Serve the steak with the Sauce Marchand de Vin.

Barbecued Sirloin Steak "Star of Texas"

Yield: 10 servings

A recipe for Barbecue Sauce can be found on page 552.

Bread crumb topping		
Garlic cloves, minced	*2 each*	*2 each*
Parsley, fresh chopped	*1/2 ounce*	*15 grams*
Bread crumbs	*6 ounces*	*170 grams*
Butter, melted	*6 ounces*	*170 grams*
Salt, to taste	*1/2 teaspoon*	*1/2 teaspoon*
Pepper, to taste	*1/4 teaspoon*	*1/4 teaspoon*
Sirloin steak	*10 each*	*10 each*
Garlic, minced	*1 tablespoon*	*1 tablespoon*
Salt, to taste	*1/2 teaspoon*	*1/2 teaspoon*
Peppercorns, cracked, to taste	*1/4 teaspoon*	*1/4 teaspoon*
Vegetable oil	*as needed*	*as needed*
Barbecue Sauce, as needed	*12 fluid ounces*	*360 milliliters*

1. Combine all of the ingredients for the bread crumb topping; blend them well.
2. Rub the steaks with garlic and season them with salt and pepper.
3. Brush the steaks with vegetable oil, and broil them until they are rare. Glaze both sides of the steak with barbecue sauce.
4. Top the steak with the bread-crumb mixture and finish it in a hot oven until it is brown.
5. Serve additional barbecue sauce on the side.

Strip Steak "Provençale"

Yield: 10 servings

Marinade

Dry white wine	*8 fluid ounces*	*240 milliliters*
Garlic cloves, mashed	*1 tablespoon*	*1 tablespoon*
Bay leaves	*2 each*	*2 each*
Black peppercorns, cracked	*1 teaspoon*	*1 teaspoon*
Rosemary leaves	*2 teaspoons*	*2 teaspoons*
Beef strip loin steaks	*10 each*	*10 each*
Olive oil, as needed	*3 fluid ounces*	*90 milliliters*

Sauce

Olive oil	*2 fluid ounces*	*60 milliliters*
Mushrooms, sliced	*16 ounces*	*450 grams*
Tomato Concassé	*16 ounces*	*450 grams*
Niçoise olives, pitted and sliced	*30 each*	*30 each*
Scallions, sliced	*4 each*	*4 each*
Salt, to taste	*1/2 teaspoon*	*1/2 teaspoon*
Pepper, to taste	*1/2 teaspoon*	*1/2 teaspoon*

Crush the garlic clove between the work surface and the flat edge of the blade.

1. Combine all ingredients for the marinade, pour over the steak, and marinate at least 1 hour.

2. Drain steak, brush with olive oil, and place on the grids of a preheated hot broiler or grill.

3. Mark and turn steak at a 45° angle; mark and turn over; finish cooking to proper degree of doneness.

4. Sauté mushrooms in olive oil until almost dry. Add the Tomato Concassé and heat through.

5. Add remaining marinade, niçoise olives, and scallions; reduce until desired sauce consistency is reached. Season with salt and pepper, to taste.

6. Portion sauce on a plate and arrange steak on top.

Cut the steaks into 6- to 8-ounce (170- to 225-gram) portions depending on use.

Increase the garlic in the sauce if desired. You may also want to add capers and sliced cornichon.

Although the sauce may be prepared in advance, broil the steaks to order.

563

Beef Tenderloin with Garlic Glaze

Yield: 10 servings

Cut the beef tenderloin into 6-ounce (170-gram) steaks. if you choose smaller medallions, do not butterfly the steak before glazing it.

Rosemary or other fresh herbs may be added to the glaze. To read about roasting garlic, see page 193.

The recipes for Glace de Viande can be found on page 438, Demi-Glace on page 522, and Jus de Veau Lié on page 523.

Garlic glaze

Glace de Viande	4 fluid ounces	120 milliliters
Garlic cloves, roasted and puréed	6 ounces	170 grams
Beef tenderloin steaks	10 each	10 each
Salt, to taste	1/2 teaspoon	1/2 teaspoon
Pepper, to taste	1/4 teaspoon	1/4 teaspoon
Demi-glace or Jus de Veau Lié	1 pint	480 milliliters
Burgundy	4 fluid ounces	120 milliliters

1. Combine the ingredients for the garlic glaze.

2. Grill the tenderloin briefly on both sides; butterfly it. Season it with salt and pepper to taste.

3. Spread 1 ounce (15 milliliters) of the garlic glaze on the tenderloin. Gratiné it under a broiler.

4. Heat the Demi-Glace or Jus Lié. Add the burgundy and reduce slightly.

5. Serve the tenderloin with the hot burgundy sauce.

Blackened Beef with Corn-and-Pepper Sauce

Yield: 10 servings

Sauce

Corn, cob with husks on	5 each	5 each
Onions, large dice	6 ounces	170 grams
Olive oil	2 teaspoons	2 teaspoons
Tomato paste	2 ounces	60 grams
Red wine	10 fluid ounces	300 milliliters
Beef Stock, as needed	1 1/2 pints	720 milliliters
Bay leaf	1 each	1 each
Thyme, sprig	1 each	1 each
Butter	1 tablespoon	1 tablespoon
Red peppers, brunoise	6 ounces	170 grams
Green peppers, brunoise	6 ounces	170 grams
Jalapeño pepper, diced	1 teaspoon	1 teaspoon
Garlic cloves, minced	4 each	4 each
Shallots, minced	2 ounces	60 grams
Turmeric	1/2 teaspoon	1/2 teaspoon
Curry powder, to taste	1 teaspoon	1 teaspoon
Beef tenderloin, steaks	10 each	10 each

(Recipe continued on facing page)

Blackening mixture

Curry powder	*1 teaspoon*	*1 teaspoon*
Fennel seed, ground	*1 tablespoon*	*1 tablespoon*
Cayenne, ground	*pinch*	*pinch*

1. Dampen the corn husks and roast the corn in a 375°F (190°C) oven for 15 minutes. Remove the corn from the oven. Shuck the ears, slice the kernels from the cob with a knife, and reserve the kernels and the cobs separately.

2. Grill the cobs over hot coals until they are evenly browned and reserve them.

3. Sauté the onions in the olive oil until they are browned. Add the tomato paste and sauté. Add the wine; reduce until nearly dry.

4. Add the stock, bay leaf, thyme, and grilled cobs. Simmer until the sauce is reduced by one-quarter. Strain the sauce, adjust seasoning, and reserve it.

5. Return the pan to medium heat and melt the butter. Add the red and green peppers, reserved corn kernels, jalapeño pepper, garlic, shallots, turmeric, and curry. Sauté the mixture until the peppers are tender.

6. Add the strained sauce to the pan and simmer it until all the vegetables are tender.

7. Season each medallion with the blackening mixture. Grill the beef over hot coals to the desired doneness. Pool the hot sauce on the heated plates and top each serving with a medallion.

4 to 5 ounces (115 to 140 grams) is an adequate portion size for a steak served with such a hearty sauce.

Use the blackening mixture below or consider one of the spice blends on pages 425 to 429, especially the Curry Powder, Garam Masala, or Barbecue Spice Mix.

London Broil

Yield: 10 servings

Flank steak	*4 pounds*	*1.8 kilograms*
Marinade		
Vegetable oil	*4 fluid ounces*	*120 milliliters*
Salt, to taste	*1/2 teaspoon*	*1/2 teaspoon*
Pepper, to taste	*1/4 teaspoon*	*1/4 teaspoon*
Paprika	*2 teaspoons*	*2 teaspoons*
Jus de Veau Lié or Demi-Glace	*20 fluid ounces*	*600 milliliters*

1. Trim the flanks and remove all skin, membrane, and fat, if necessary.

2. Pour marinade over steaks and marinate under refrigeration for 2 to 3 hours or overnight.

3. Broil 3 to 5 minutes on each side.

4. Cut in very thin diagonal slices across the grain.

Flank steaks usually range from 1 1/2 to 3 pounds (680 grams to 1.3 kilograms). You will needed 2 to 3 for 10 servings. Use any extra for salads and sandwiches.

Minced shallots, garlic, chopped cilantro, or other fresh herbs may be added to the marinade.

London Broil is also often served with Mushroom Sauce page 527 or Bordelaise Sauce page 529.

Braised Beef Bourgignonne

Yield: 10 servings

The recipe for Red Wine Marinade is on page 433. The Standard Sachet d'Epices recipe is on page 424.

The traditional version of this dish would be larded with strips of salt pork marinated in brandy.

Boneless bottom round or chunk	4 pounds	1.8 kilograms
Salt, to taste	1/2 teaspoon	1/2 teaspoon
Pepper, to taste	1/2 teaspoon	1/2 teaspoon
Oil	as needed	as needed
Salt pork, cut into lardons	4 ounces	115 grams
Mirepoix	8 ounces	225 kilograms
Flour	2 ounces	60 grams
Tomato purée	6 fluid ounces	180 milliliters
Red Wine Marinade	1 pint	480 milliliters
Demi-Glace	1 pint	480 milliliters
Brown Veal Stock	1 quart	1 liter
Standard Sachet d'Épices	1 each	1 each

1. Trim, tie, and season the meat. Place in a pan with the marinade; cover and marinate for 2 hours, turning occasionally. Drain and reserve marinade.

2. Fry the lardons in hot oil until brown on all sides; remove and reserve. Sear the meat on all sides; remove.

3. Add the Mirepoix; sauté it until it is brown.

4. Add the flour; cook it out for 3 to 4 minutes.

5. Add the tomato purée and cook it out for 2 minutes.

6. Return the meat to the pan; add the marinade, stock, Demi-Glace, and Standard Sachet d'Épices. Bring the liquid to a simmer. Cover the pan and braise the meat until it is fork tender, about 2 to 3 hours.

7. Remove the meat and keep it warm. Degrease the sauce and strain it. Simmer the sauce to reduce it, if necessary. Adjust the seasoning with salt and pepper. Return the fried lardons.

8. Slice and serve the meat with the sauce.

VARIATION

Beef Stew à la Bourgignonne: Cut the meat into large pieces (2 to 3 inches/5 to 7.5 centimeters). Marinate and prepare as directed above. Add blanched pearl onions and butter mushrooms if desired.

Yankee Pot Roast

Yield: 10 servings

Beef, chuck or brisket	*4 pounds*	*1.8 kilograms*
Salt, to taste	*1 teaspoon*	*1 teaspoon*
Pepper, to taste	*1/2 teaspoon*	*1/2 teaspoon*
Vegetable oil	*as needed*	*as needed*
Mirepoix	*8 ounces*	*225 grams*
Flour	*2 ounces*	*60 grams*
Tomato purée	*6 fluid ounces*	*180 milliliters*
Dry red wine	*8 fluid ounces*	*240 milliliters*
Brown Veal Stock	*1 1/2 quarts*	*1.5 liters*
Standard Sachet d'Épices	*1 each*	*1 each*

Additional vegetables such as turnips and green peppers may be added. An Oignon Piqué, chopped garlic, and a bay leaf will also bolster the flavor.

Serve the pot roast with potato pancakes, roasted, braised, or boiled potatoes, bread dumplings, or egg noodles.

1. Trim the beef and season it with salt and pepper.
2. Sear the beef in hot oil; remove it and keep it warm.
3. Add the Mirepoix; sauté it until it is browned.
4. Add the flour; cook it out for 3 to 4 minutes.
5. Add the tomato purée and cook out for several seconds.
6. Place the beef on a bed of mirepoix.
7. Add the wine, stock, and Standard Sachet d'Épices. Bring the liquid to a simmer. Cover the pan and braise the beef until fork tender.
8. Remove the beef and keep it warm. Degrease the sauce and strain it. Simmer the sauce to reduce it, if necessary. Adjust the seasoning with salt and pepper to taste.
9. Slice the beef and serve it with the sauce.

Shaker Stuffed Flank Steak

Yield: 10 servings

Selecting 2-pound steaks (9-kilogram) will allow you to make 2 rolls, each serving 5.

For more information about braising, refer to Chapter 10, pages 346 to 350.

Ingredient	US	Metric
Flank steak	4 pounds	1.8 kilograms
Bread, white, sliced, cut into 1/2 inch cubes	10 slices	10 slices
Butter	2 ounces	60 grams
Onions finely chopped	8 ounces	225 grams
Celery, finely chopped	6 ounces	170 grams
Mushrooms, diced	8 ounces	225 grams
Ground beef	8 ounces	225 grams
Ground pork	8 ounces	225 grams
Ground veal	8 ounces	225 grams
Eggs	2 each	2 each
Parsley, chopped	1/2 ounce	15 grams
Rosemary leaves, dried	1/2 teaspoon	1/2 teaspoon
Basil, fresh	1/2 teaspoon	1/2 teaspoon
Savory, dried	1/2 teaspoon	1/2 teaspoon
Sage	1/2 teaspoon	1/2 teaspoon
Salt, to taste	2 teaspoons	2 teaspoons
Pepper, to taste	2 teaspoons	2 teaspoons
Vegetable oil, as needed	4 fluid ounces	120 milliliters
Mirepoix	6 ounces	170 grams
Tomato purée	2 teaspoons	2 teaspoons
Red wine	6 fluid ounces	180 milliliters
Brown Veal Stock	30 fluid ounces	900 milliliters
Arrowroot, diluted	as needed	as needed
Tarragon, fresh, chopped	1/2 teaspoon	1/2 teaspoon
Chervil, fresh, chopped	1/2 teaspoon	1/2 teaspoon

1. Butterfly flank steak, pound lightly, reserve.
2. Brown bread cubes in half the butter and remove from pan.
3. Add remaining butter to pan and sauté onion, celery, and mushrooms until tender; chill.
4. Mix bread cubes, vegetables, meats, eggs, and spices.
5. Spread on flank steak, roll up the steak and stuffing like a jelly roll, and tie.
6. Sear flank steak in oil and remove.

(Recipe continued on facing page)

7. Add Mirepoix to pan and sauté.

8. Add tomato purée and brown lightly.

9. Deglaze with red wine and brown stock.

10. Return meat, bring to a simmer, and cover. Braise at 350°F (175°C) until tender, approximately 1 1/2 hours.

11. Remove meat, strain, and degrease liquid.

12. Season with tarragon and chervil; adjust salt and pepper to taste.

13. Add arrowroot to thicken as necessary.

14. Serve sauce over sliced flank.

Braised Short Ribs

Yield: 10 servings

Short ribs	*10 each*	*10 each*
Vegetable oil	*as needed*	*as needed*
Mirepoix	*8 ounces*	*225 grams*
Tomato paste	*2 ounces*	*60 grams*
Brown Stock	*8 fluid ounces*	*240 milliliters*
Brown Sauce	*1 1/4 pints*	*600 milliliters*
Bay leaves	*2 each*	*2 each*
Thyme, leaves	*pinch*	*pinch*
Madeira or sherry	*3 fluid ounces*	*90 milliliters*
Salt, to taste	*1/2 teaspoon*	*1/2 teaspoon*
Pepper, to taste	*1/2 teaspoon*	*1/2 teaspoon*

1. Brown short ribs on all sides in hot oil.

2. Remove ribs, add mirepoix and caramelize.

3. Add tomato paste, and caramelize.

4. Add Brown Stock, sauce, bay leaves and thyme; bring to a simmer.

5. Return ribs, cover. Braise in oven at 350°F (175°C) until fork tender.

6. Remove ribs, degrease the sauce, simmer until correct consistency is reached. Strain, add wine, and season with salt and pepper to taste.

Savory Swiss Steak

Yield: 10 servings

The steaks should be cut into portions 4 to 6 ounces (115 to 170 grams) in size.

"Swissing" requires steaks to be dredged in flour, pounded, dredged again and pounded, so that a crust of seasoned flour is worked onto the surface of the steaks.

Flour	*6 ounces*	*170 grams*
Salt, to taste	*1 teaspoon*	*1 teaspoon*
Pepper, to taste	*1/2 teaspoon*	*1/2 teaspoon*
Beef bottom round, cut into steaks	*10 each*	*10 each*
Vegetable oil	*as needed*	*as needed*
Seasoned stock		
Beef Stock	*1.5 quarts*	*1.5 liters*
Tomato purée	*6 fluid ounces*	*180 milliliters*
Soy sauce	*3 fluid ounces*	*90 milliliters*
Peppercorns	*4 to 5 each*	*4 to 5 each*
Cloves, whole	*2 each*	*2 each*
Bay leaf	*1 each*	*1 each*
Thyme, sprig	*1 each*	*1 each*
Savory, stem	*1 each*	*1 each*
Onions, small dice	*1 pound*	*450 grams*
Garlic cloves, crushed	*2 each*	*2 each*
Celery, small dice	*3 ounces*	*85 grams*
Vegetable oil, as needed		

1. Season the flour (reserve 2 ounces/60 grams for sauce) with the salt and pepper and dredge the steaks; shake off any excess flour.

2. Heat 1/8-inch of oil in a skillet. Add the steaks and brown them on both sides. Remove the steaks to a brazier or roasting pan.

3. Combine all of the ingredients for the stock and simmer it for 20 minutes.

4. Sauté the onions, garlic, and celery in the oil in a saucepot until the vegetables are tender.

5. Add the flour and cook it to make a light brown roux.

6. Strain the hot stock and add it gradually to the roux, stirring it until it is thickened and smooth. Adjust the seasoning with salt, if desired, and pour the sauce over the steaks.

7. Braise the steaks at 350°F (175°C) until they are tender, about 1 to 1 1/2 hours.

Beef Rouladen in Burgundy Sauce

Yield: 10 servings

Bottom round, trimmed	3 pounds	1.3 kilograms
Bacon, chopped	8 ounces	225 grams
Ham, lean raw smoked scraps, chopped	4 ounces	115 grams
Beef, ground	2 ounces	60 grams
Onions, chopped and sautéed	3 ounces	85 grams
Eggs, beaten	2 each	2 each
Bread crumbs, dry	6 ounces	170 grams
Parsley, chopped	1 tablespoon	1 tablespoon
Sweet pickles, julienne	20 each	20 each
Flour, for dredging	as needed	as needed
Salt, to taste	1/2 teaspoon	1/2 teaspoon
Pepper, to taste	1/4 teaspoon	1/4 teaspoon
Vegetable oil, as needed	2 fluid ounces	60 milliliters
Tomato purée	4 fluid ounces	120 milliliters
Garlic cloves, minced	1 each	1 each
Brown Sauce	1 quart	1 liter
Red wine	4 fluid ounces	120 milliliters

The recipe for Brown Sauce is found on page 552.

Serve this dish with spaëtzle, bread dumplings, or broiled potatoes. Tournéed root vegetables are also a nice accompaniment.

1. Slice the beef into ten 4 to 5 ounce (115 to 150 grams) portions, approximately 3-by-4 inches. Flatten with cleaver, or meat pounder; butterfly if necessary.

2. Combine bacon, ham, ground beef, onions, eggs, bread crumbs, and parsley; mix well.

3. Fill beef slices with the filling and pickle. Roll up and secure with toothpicks or tie.

4. Dredge rolls in flour seasoned with salt and pepper. Brown on all sides in hot oil. Place the browned rolls in braiser.

5. Sauté the tomato paste and garlic in the same oil. Add the brown sauce and wine. Bring to a simmer. Cover tightly and braise at 350°F (175°C) 1 1/2 hours or until the meat is tender. Turn once during braising.

6. Pour the sauce over the rouladen.

7. Strain the sauce, adjust consistency, and season.

8. Serve two rouladen with the sauce.

Estouffade of Beef (Beef Stew)

Yield: 10 servings

Cubes for stew should be roughly 1 1/2 inches (almost 4 centimeters) square.

If you prefer, you can dredge the beef cubes in flour before searing in the oil. Delete the roux in step 4.

For a more home-style presentation, you may add the vegetable garnish to the braising liquid near the end of cooking time. Braise until the beef and vegetables are tender.

Beef shank, or chuck, cut into cubes	4 pounds	1.8 kilograms
Salt, to taste	1/2 teaspoon	1/2 teaspoon
Pepper, to taste	1/2 teaspoon	1/2 teaspoon
Vegetable oil	1 fluid ounce	30 milliliters
Mirepoix	12 ounces	340 grams
Tomato paste	2 ounces	60 grams
Flour	2 1/2 ounces	70 grams
Brown Veal Stock	1 quart	1 liter
Standard Sachet d'Épices,	1 each	1 each
Garnish		
Peas	4 ounces	115 grams
Carrots, tourné	20 each	20 each
Celery, tourné	20 each	20 each
Turnips, tourné	20 each	20 each
Pearl onions	10 each	10 each

1. Season the beef with the salt and pepper and sear it in hot oil. Remove and reserve it.

2. Add the Mirepoix and let the onions brown. Add the tomato paste and cook out for several seconds.

3. Add the flour to the Mirepoix. Cook out the roux.

4. Add one-third of the stock; whip out the lumps and bring it to a simmer. Add the remaining stock and return it to a simmer.

5. Add the beef and Mirepoix. Return it to a simmer; add the Sachet d'Épices.

6. Cover the beef and braise it in an oven until it is very tender.

7. Cook the vegetables for the garnish separately until they are tender; reserve them.

8. Degrease the stew; discard the Sachet d'Épices.

9. Adjust the seasoning with salt and pepper to taste; reheat the vegetable garnish. Serve the stew garnished with the vegetables.

Chili Con Carne

Yield: 15 servings

Pinto or kidney beans, dried	*1 pound*	*450 grams*
Beef shank, diced	*4 pounds*	*1.8 kilograms*
Salt, to taste	*1/2 teaspoon*	*1/2 teaspoon*
Pepper, to taste	*1/2 teaspoon*	*1/2 teaspoon*
Onions, minced	*10 ounces*	*285 grams*
Red peppers, chopped	*4 ounces*	*115 grams*
Green peppers, chopped	*4 ounces*	*115 grams*
Anaheim peppers, chopped	*2 ounces*	*60 grams*
Vegetable oil	*as needed*	*as needed*
Garlic cloves, minced to a paste	*3 each*	*3 each*
Chili powder, mild	*1 ounce*	*30 grams*
Cumin, ground	*1 ounce*	*30 grams*
Oregano, dried	*1/2 ounce*	*15 grams*
Tomato purée	*3 fluid ounces*	*90 milliliters*
Brown Stock	*1 pint*	*480 milliliters*
Beer	*12 fluid ounces*	*340 milliliters*
Tomato Concassé	*1 1/2 pounds*	*680 grams*
Garnish		
Onions, chopped	*4 ounces*	*115 grams*
Cilantro, chopped	*3 tablespoons*	*3 tablespoons*
Cheddar or Jack cheese, grated	*8 ounces*	*225 grams*

1. Soak the beans overnight. Drain. Cover with water and cook until tender

2. Season the beef with the salt and pepper.

3. Sweat the onions in hot oil. Add the red, green, and Anaheim peppers and cook until almost tender. Add the garlic and cook it until an aroma is apparent.

4. Add the meat. Sauté it until lightly seared.

5. Add the spices and sauté briefly. Add the tomato purée, beef stock, and beer. Mix them together with the meat.

6. Bring the chili to a simmer; cover the pan and braise the meat on the stove in a moderate oven until it is very tender to the bite.

7. Add the Tomato Concassé and the cooked beans; heat the chili thoroughly. Adjust the consistency. Adjust the seasoning with salt and pepper to taste.

8. Garnish each serving with chopped onions, grated cheese, and chopped cilantro.

Use pinto, kidney, black beans, or a combination of any cooked beans. Different types of beans should be cooked separately as they cook at different times and black beans will color other beans.

Chipotle, ancho, or other chilies may be added. You may prefer the use of the Chili Powder blend on page 425.

Serve over rice or with cornbread.

Cincinnati Chili *Include one or more of the following: cinnamon, allspice, nutmeg, ginger, clove, mace, coriander, cardamom, or mustard to taste.*

Two-way: Serve the chili over spaghetti.

Three-way: Spaghetti, chili, Cheddar cheese.

Four-way: Spaghetti, chili, Cheddar cheese, chopped onions.

Five-way: Beans, spaghetti, chili, Cheddar cheese, chopped onions.

Big Jim's Chili

Yield: 15 servings

Serve with Warm Black-eyed Pea Salad, page 905 and Cornbread, page 1027.

Lean beef (chuck or round), diced small	5 pounds	225 kilograms
Onions, diced small	1 1/2 pounds	680 grams
Garlic cloves, minced	6 each	6 each
Vegetable oil	4 fluid ounces	120 milliliters
Beef Stock	1 quart	1 liter
Tomato purée	20 ounces	570 grams
Green chilies, diced	8 ounces	225 grams
Fresh jalapeños, minced	2 to 3 each	2 to 3 each
Chili Powder, pure, mild	2 ounces	60 grams
Hot Chili Powder	2 tablespoons	2 tablespoons
Cumin, ground	6 tablespoons	6 tablespoons
Oregano, dried	3 tablespoons	3 tablespoons
Salt, to taste	1 teaspoon	1 teaspoon

1. Brown meat in oil and remove from pan, leaving excess oil in pan.

2. Smother onions and garlic in remaining oil until soft.

3. Add stock, beef, and tomato purée and bring to a boil.

4. Reduce to a simmer and cook 1 hour. Add the remaining ingredients and simmer 1 more hour, stirring frequently. When adding the seasonings, use only two-thirds of the ground cumin. Add remaining ground cumin during the last 15 to 20 minutes of cooking.

5. Adjust seasonings.

Corned Beef with Cabbage and Boiled Vegetables

Yield:12 to 14 servings

This is traditionally served with Horseradish Sauce, page 532.

Corned beef brisket, trimmed	1 each	1 each
Water or White Beef Stock	2 quarts	2 liters
Green cabbage, cut into wedges	3 heads	3 heads
Carrots, 3-inch pieces, cut on the bias	2 pounds	.9 kilograms
Turnips, peeled, cut in 1/4 or 1/2	2 pounds	.9 kilograms
Onions, small whole	2 pounds	.9 kilograms
Beets, small	2 pounds	.9 kilograms
Potatoes, small, peeled, cut in 1/4 or 1/2	24 each	24 each

(Recipe continued on facing page)

1. Split the brisket along the natural seam into two pieces.

2. Cover the meat with water or White Beef Stock, bring to a boil, simmer until meat is tender (approximate cooking time 3 hours).

3. Cook beets with skins on until tender, in boiling water; reserve water, peel, cut, return to cooking liquid, and keep warm.

4. Cook remaining vegetables in corned beef stock until tender; keep warm.

Corned beef remaining from this dish can be used to prepare Red Flannel Hash, page 875 or Reuben Sandwiches, page 921.

Poached Tenderloin with Green Peppercorn Sabayon

Yield: 10 servings

Beef tenderloin, trimmed and tied	*3 pounds*	*1.3 kilograms*
Beef Stock, as needed	*1 quart*	*1 liter*
Standard Bouquet Garni	*1 each*	*1 each*
Dry white wine	*2 fluid ounces*	*60 milliliters*
Egg yolks	*5 each*	*5 each*
Green peppercorns, drained	*2 ounces*	*60 grams*
Salt, to taste	*1/2 teaspoon*	*1/2 teaspoon*

Add any broth left over from cooking the tenderloin to soups or braises.

1. Season the beef well.

2. Bring the stock to a simmer in a fish poacher or rondeau.

3. Add the tenderloin and Standard Bouquet Garni. Poach the tenderloin until it reaches an internal temperature of 130°F (51°C) for medium rare. Remove the tenderloin from the stock and keep it warm.

4. At the time of service, slice the tenderloin.

5. Combine 3 ounces (90 milliliters) of cooking liquid with the egg yolks in a stainless steel bowl. Add the wine.

6. Cook the yolks over simmering water, whipping them constantly until they are thick and foamy. Add the green peppercorns and adjust the seasoning with salt.

7. Serve the sauce with the sliced tenderloin.

New England Boiled Dinner

Yield: 25 servings

The recipe for the Standard Sachet d'Épices is on page 424.

To read more about boiling as a cooking method, refer to chapter 10, pages 339 to 341.

The recipe for Béchamel is on page 539; White Beef Stock is on page 439.

Corned beef brisket	10 pounds	4.5 kilograms
Beef tongue	2 pounds	900 grams
White Beef Stock	1 gallon	3.75 liters
Standard Sachet d'Épices	1 each	1 each
Vegetable garnish, per serving		
Red Bliss potatoes	50 each	50 each
Green cabbage, cut into wedges	50 each	50 each
Pearl onions	50 each	50 each
Carrots, tourné	50 each	50 each
Parsnips, tourné	50 each	50 each
Rutabaga, tourné	50 each	50 each
Beets, tourné	50 each	50 each
Green beans, cut in 2-inch lengths	5 ounces	140 grams
Sauce		
Béchamel	1 1/2 quarts	1.5 liters
Heavy cream	12 fluid ounces	360 milliliters
Horseradish, grated minced, to taste	6 ounces	170 grams

1. Place the beef and tongue in a pot with enough cold stock to cover them. Bring the stock to a slow simmer.

2. Add the Sachet d'Épices; continue to simmer the liquid gently for approximately 3 hours or until the meats are very tender. Remove the meats; keep them warm and moist.

3. Cook the vegetables separately in the stock or reserved cooking liquid.

4. Combine the ingredients for the sauce and heat the mixture.

5. Slice the meats and serve them with the vegetables and sauce.

Veal Scaloppine Marsala

Yield: 10 servings

Veal, top round,		
trimmed scaloppine	*3 pounds*	*450 grams*
Flour, seasoned	*as needed*	*as needed*
Butter	*3 ounces*	*85 grams*
Shallots, minced	*4 each*	*4 each*
Marsala, dry	*10 fluid ounces*	*300 milliliters*
Jus de Veau Lié	*10 fluid ounces*	*300 milliliters*
Butter	*4 ounces*	*115 grams*
Salt, to taste	*1/2 teaspoon*	*1/2 teaspoon*
Pepper, to taste	*1/4 teaspoon*	*1/4 teaspoon*

Cut the scaloppini into 2-ounce (60-gram) portions. This is especially good if you are using the loin.

The recipe for Jus de Veau Lié is on page 523. Substitute Demi-Glace, page 522, if you prefer.

1. Cut veal into scaloppini. Flatten veal with a mallet to an even thickness.

2. Dredge veal in flour and sauté on both sides in butter until lightly browned.

3. When veal is done, remove from pan and keep warm.

4. Add shallots to pan and sauté until translucent.

5. Add wine and reduce to one-half.

6. Add Jus de Veau Lié and reduce until sauce consistency is reached.

7. Remove from heat and finish with butter. Season.

8. Serve sauce over the veal.

VARIATIONS

Pork Scaloppine Marsala: Cut pork tenderloins into 2-ounce (60-gram) portions and prepare in the same manner.

Chicken Marsala: Lightly pound one boneless, skinless breast portion to an even thickness.

Sautéed Veal with Lump Crabmeat and Asparagus

Yield: 10 servings

Princesse-*style veal dishes call for a garnish of artichoke bottoms filled with asparagus tips.* Argenteuil *is another name given to dishes garnished with asparagus. The Argenteuil area of the Val d'Oise has been famous for its asparagus since the 17th century.*

The recipe for Velouté is on page 531.

Sauce

Chicken Stock	*4 fluid ounces*	*120 milliliters*
White wine	*2 fluid ounces*	*60 milliliters*
Tarragon vinegar	*1 fluid ounce*	*30 milliliters*
Tarragon, fresh, bunch	*1 each*	*1 each*
Shallots, minced	*1/2 ounce*	*15 grams*
Worcestershire sauce	*1/2 teaspoon*	*1/2 teaspoon*
Black peppercorns, cracked	*1 teaspoon*	*1 teaspoon*
Bay leaf	*1 each*	*1 each*
Velouté	*20 fluid ounces*	*600 milliliters*
Glace de Viande	*3 1/2 fluid ounces*	*105 milliliters*
Heavy cream	*1 fluid ounce*	*30 milliliters*
Veal loin, medallions,	*3 pounds*	*1.3 kilograms*
Flour, as needed	*4 ounces*	*115 grams*
Butter	*2 ounces*	*60 grams*
Crabmeat, lump, picked, heated slightly	*7 ounces*	*200 grams*
Asparagus, peeled, blanched	*1 1/4 pounds*	*570 grams*

1. Make a reduction of the Chicken Stock, wine, vinegar, tarragon, shallots, Worcestershire, pepper, and bay leaf.

2. Add the Velouté, cream, and Glace de Viande to the reduction. Bring this mixture to a boil and let it reduce slightly. Keep warm.

3. Cut the veal into medallions (2 ounces/60 grams) each, shape lightly and season.

4. Dust the medallions in flour, shaking away any excess.

5. Heat the butter in a sauté pan, add the veal, and sauté on both sides until just cooked through.

6. Reheat the asparagus until very hot.

7. Fan the asparagus on heated plates and mound the crabmeat at the base of the asparagus. Place the sautéed veal on top of the asparagus and lightly coat with the sauce.

Swiss-Style Shredded Veal

Yield: 10 servings

Veal, top round	*3 pounds*	*1.3 kilograms*
Salt, to taste	*1/2 teaspoon*	*1/2 teaspoon*
Pepper, to taste	*1/4 teaspoon*	*1/4 teaspoon*
Vegetable oil, as needed	*2 fluid ounces*	*60 milliliters*
Flour, as needed	*3 ounces*	*85 grams*
Shallots, minced	*1/2 ounce*	*15 grams*
Mushrooms, sliced	*1 pound*	*450 grams*
Dry white wine	*5 fluid ounces*	*150 milliliters*
Demi-Glace	*10 ounces*	*285 grams*
Brandy	*1 ounce*	*30 milliliters*
Lemon juice, to taste	*1 teaspoon*	*1 teaspoon*

The traditional accompaniment to this dish is Roësti Potatoes, page 824.

1. Cut the veal into émincé; blot dry and season with salt and pepper.

2. Heat the oil in a sauteuse; dredge the veal and sauté until just cooked through. Remove the veal and keep warm. Pour off any excess oil.

3. Add shallots and mushrooms to the pan. Sauté until the mushroom juices have cooked away.

4. Deglaze the pan with white wine.

5. Add the Demi-Glace, heavy cream, and any juices released by the veal. Simmer until reduced to a good sauce consistency. Degrease if necessary.

6. Add the brandy; flame. Season the sauce to taste with lemon juice, salt, and pepper.

7. Return the veal to the pan and reheat briefly. Do not allow the sauce to boil. Serve.

DRY-SAUTÉ TECHNIQUE

1. Heat pan, remove from heat, and spray with vegetable oil; wipe out excess.

2. Place pan back on heat; add meat.

3. Allow meat to sauté until moisture appears on its surface; stir to loosen.

4. When meat is done, remove; finish cooking process.

Sautéed Veal with Wild Mushrooms and Marsala Sauce

Yield: 10 servings

Cut the top round into 2-ounce (60-grams) medallions.

Serve with Basic Risotto, page 833, which has been cooked with stock and has a creamy consistency. Adjust the seasoning with fresh lemon zest to taste.

Recipes for Vinaigrettes can be found on pages 906 to 910.

If Japanese or fingerling eggplant is available, it may be acceptable to either leave them whole or slice them.

Veal loin	3 pounds	1.3 kilograms
Clarified butter	2 ounces	60 grams
Salt, to taste	1/2 teaspoon	1/2 teaspoon
Pepper, to taste	1/4 teaspoon	1/4 teaspoon
Flour, as needed	3 ounces	85 grams
Jus de Veau Lié	20 fluid ounces	600 milliliters
Eggplant, sliced	2 pounds	900 grams
Vinaigrette	5 fluid ounces	150 milliliters
Cremini mushrooms, sliced	1 pound	450 grams
Marsala	2 fluid ounces	60 milliliters
Butter, whole	1 to 2 ounces	30 to 60 grams

1. Cut the veal loin into medallions (approximately 2 ounces/60 grams each). Shape lightly and season well with salt and pepper. Dredge in the flour and shake off any excess.

2. Sauté the medallions in clarified butter, turning once. Remove from the pan and keep warm. Pour off the excess butter from the pan.

3. Add the Jus de Veau Lié to the pan and simmer until slightly reduced. Strain.

4. Marinate the eggplants briefly in the vinaigrette, then grill until very soft. (Time will vary according to eggplants' thickness).

5. At service, sauté the mushrooms. Add the strained sauce. Finish with Marsala and butter. Adjust seasoning to taste.

6. Serve 2 veal medallions per portion with the eggplant and sauce.

Veal Cordon Bleu

Yield: 10 servings

Veal, top round	*3 pounds*	*1.3 kilograms*
Ham, cut very thin	*6 ounces*	*285 grams*
Gruyère, cut very thin	*6 ounces*	*285 grams*
Flour	*as needed*	*as needed*
Egg wash	*as needed*	*as needed*
Bread crumbs, fresh, white	*as needed*	*as needed*
Oil	*as needed*	*as needed*
Butter	*1 ounce*	*30 grams*
Shallots, minced	*2 ounces*	*60 grams*
Mushrooms, small, sliced	*6 ounces*	*170 grams*
White wine	*4 fluid ounces*	*120 milliliters*
Jus de Veau Lié	*1 1/2 pints*	*720 milliliters*
Heavy cream	*4 fluid ounces*	*120 milliliters*
Parsley, chopped	*1 tablespoon*	*1 tablespoon*
Salt, to taste	*1/2 teaspoon*	*1/2 teaspoon*
Pepper, to taste	*1/4 teaspoon*	*1/4 teaspoon*

The term cordon bleu *has its earliest origin in a society of knights established by Henri III of France in 1578. This dish is one of many taught to students at the Cordon Bleu cooking schools.*

1. Cut the veal into 5- to 6-ounce (140- to 170-gram) cutlets. Flatten veal cutlet with a meat mallet.

2. Place ham and cheese together; fold in thirds.

3. Place ham roll in center of the veal cutlet, fold meat around the ham, and chill.

4. Dredge the veal in flour, dip in egg wash, and roll in bread crumbs. Allow to rest in the refrigerator for 30 to 60 minutes.

5. Brown veal in oil; place on a sheet pan.

6. Bake veal in a 350°F (175°C) oven, until an internal temperature of 150°F (66°C) is reached.

7. To make sauce, sauté shallots in butter, add mushrooms, and continue to sauté.

8. Add wine and reduce by one-half, add Jus de Veau Lié, and simmer 15 to 20 minutes.

9. Finish with heavy cream; add parsley and season. Portion sauce on a plate; slice veal in 3 pieces on the bias; fan out on sauce.

Veal Medallions with Red Pepper Sauce

Yield: 10 servings

Try these medallions with the Tomato Coulis shown on page 551.

The method for shaping medallions is shown on page 228.

Serve with polenta or a hearty grain such as bulgar.

Veal, loin, boneless	3 pounds	1.3 kilograms
Salt, to taste	1/2 teaspoon	1/2 teaspoon
Pepper, to taste	1/4 teaspoon	1/4 teaspoon
Flour	as needed	as needed
Butter, clarified	2 ounces	60 grams
Sauce		
Shallots, minced	3 each	3 each
Dry white wine	8 fluid ounces	240 milliliters
Dry vermouth	2 fluid ounces	60 milliliters
Red peppers, roasted, and puréed	8 ounces	225 grams
Heavy cream, reduced	6 fluid ounces	180 milliliters
Butter, diced	2 ounces	60 grams
Red peppers, julienne, blanched	2 ounces	60 grams
Green peppers, julienne, blanched	2 ounces	60 grams
Yellow peppers, julienne, blanched	2 ounces	60 grams
Whole butter	1/2 ounce	15 grams

1. Cut the veal into 2-ounce (60-gram) medallions. Flatten veal medallions slightly with a mallet to shape.

2. Season and dredge veal in flour; shake off excess.

3. Sauté veal in butter, remove from sauté pan and reserve. Pour off excess butter.

4. Dice roasted peppers; purée in blender until smooth.

5. Combine shallots, wine, and vermouth in the sauteuse, reduce to one-fourth of original volume.

6. Add pepper purée and heavy cream; reduce to sauce consistency; strain if desired.

7. Finish the sauce with butter and pepper. Adjust seasoning with salt and pepper.

8. Sauté julienned peppers in butter to reheat.

9. Pool sauce around veal. Garnish with julienned peppers.

Sautéed Veal Scalopine with Tomato Sauce

Yield: 10 servings

Veal, top round	4 pounds	1.8 kilograms
Salt, to taste	1/2 teaspoon	1/2 teaspoon
White pepper, to taste	1/2 teaspoon	1/2 teaspoon
Flour, as needed	3 ounces	85 grams
Clarified butter, as needed	6 ounces	170 grams
White wine	10 fluid ounces	300 milliliters
Tomato Sauce	20 fluid ounces	600 milliliters
Whole butter	1 ounce	30 grams

Use any of the Tomato Sauces on pages 537 to 539.

When preparing the Tomato Sauce, try roasting the garlic and tomatoes in the oven first.

1. Cut the veal into 6-ounce (170-gram) cutlets and pound thin. Dry the veal and season it with the salt and pepper; dredge it in the flour, shake off the excess.
2. Sauté the veal in the butter until it is golden brown on both sides.
3. Remove the veal and keep it warm.
4. Degrease the pan; deglaze it with the wine.
5. Add the tomato sauce and bring it to a simmer. Monté au beurre to finish.
6. Serve the sauce pooled around the veal.

Veal Scalopine Shaker Village

Yield: 10 servings

Veal, top round	4 pounds	1.8 kilograms
Salt, to taste	1/2 teaspoon	1/2 teaspoon
Pepper, to taste	1/4 teaspoon	1/4 teaspoon
Flour, as needed	3 ounces	85 grams
Clarified butter, as needed	2 ounces	60 grams
Shallots, minced	2 tablespoons	30 grams
White wine	8 fluid ounces	240 milliliters
Jus de Veau Lié, heated	1 pint	480 milliliters
Fresh herbs, minced	2 tablespoons	2 tablespoons
Tomato Concassé	16 ounces	450 grams
Whole butter	1 ounce	30 grams

The method for pounding scalopine is illustrated on page 226.

1. Cut and dry the veal and season it with salt and pepper; dredge it in the flour and shake off the excess.
2. Sauté the veal in the clarified butter until it is golden brown on both sides.
3. Degrease the pan. Add the shallots and sauté them briefly.
4. Deglaze the pan with the wine.
5. Add the Jus de Veau Lié and herbs; reduce to nappé consistency.
6. Add the Tomato Concassé and heat through.
7. Finish the sauce with whole butter and adjust the seasoning to taste.

Sautéed Veal Scalopine with Sauce Zingara

Yield: 10 servings

Zingara is a classic sauce composed of Demi-Glace and Tomato Sauce garnished with ham, pickled tongue, and mushrooms, and seasoned with paprika. Truffles, though usually associated with this sauce, are optional. Zingara means "gypsy" in Italian.

To read more about the technique of sautéing, refer to Chapter 9, pages 316 to 319.

Veal, top round	*4 pounds*	*1.8 kilograms*
Flour, as needed	*3 ounces*	*85 grams*
Clarified butter	*as needed*	*as needed*
Sauce		
Olive oil	*3/4 ounce*	*20 milliliters*
Onions, chopped	*2 ounces*	*60 grams*
Garlic, minced	*1 ounce*	*30 grams*
Tomato Concassé	*12 ounces*	*30 grams*
Tomato Sauce	*12 fluid ounces*	*360 milliliters*
Demi-Glace, heated	*12 fluid ounces*	*360 milliliters*
Tarragon leaves, fresh-chopped	*1/2 teaspoon*	*1/2 teaspoon*
Ham, julienne	*3 ounces*	*85 grams*
Tongue, julienne	*3 ounces*	*85 grams*
Mushrooms, julienne	*3 ounces*	*85 grams*
Black Truffles, julienne	*1/2 ounce*	*15 grams*
Salt, to taste	*1/2 teaspoon*	*1/2 teaspoon*
Pepper, to taste	*1/2 teaspoon*	*1/2 teaspoon*

1. Cut the veal into 6-ounce (170-gram) cutlets. Season the veal, dredge it with flour (optional), and sauté it in the clarified butter. Remove the veal and keep it warm.

2. Add the olive oil and sauté the onions until transparent.

3. Add the garlic and sauté it until it is aromatic.

4. Add the Tomato Concassé and cook for 3 to 4 minutes.

5. Add the Tomato Sauce and Demi-Glace; reduce to a sauce consistency.

6. Add the tarragon, ham, tongue, mushrooms, and truffles. Bring the sauce to a simmer and adjust the seasonings.

7. Serve approximately 2 ounces (60 grams) of sauce per serving with the scalopine.

Breaded Veal Cutlet Gruyère

Yield: 10 servings

Veal cutlet, breaded	*10 each*	*10 each*
Vegetable oil	*4 fluid ounces*	*120 milliliters*
Tomatoes, slices	*30 each*	*30 each*
Gruyère cheese, slices	*10 each*	*10 each*
Parsley, chopped	*4 tablespoons*	*4 tablespoons*
Mushroom Sauce	*20 fluid ounces*	*600 milliliters*

Six ounces (170 grams) is an adequate portion size.

Substitute Jack cheese for the gruyère. Sprinkle with cilantro and serve with a Red Chili Sauce, page 549, or Fresh Tomato Salsa, page 936.

1. Panfry the breaded veal cutlet in the oil until it is golden brown on both sides. Place the cutlet on a sizzler platter. Arrange the tomato slices on the cutlet; cover these with a slice of cheese.

2. Place the cutlet under a broiler to melt and lightly brown the cheese.

3. Sprinkle the cutlet with the parsley and serve it with Mushroom Sauce, page 527.

Veal Shoulder Poêlé

Yield: 10 servings

Veal shoulder roast	*4 pounds*	*8 kilograms*
Rosemary	*1/4 teaspoon*	*1/4 teaspoon*
Basil	*1/2 teaspoon*	*1/2 teaspoon*
Thyme	*1/2 teaspoon*	*1/2 teaspoon*
Garlic cloves	*2 each*	*2 each*
Marjoram	*1/2 teaspoon*	*1/2 teaspoon*
Salt, to taste	*1/2 teaspoon*	*1/2 teaspoon*
Pepper, to taste	*1/4 teaspoon*	*1/4 teaspoon*
Bacon, slices, diced	*3 each*	*3 each*
Butter	*1/2 ounce*	*15 grams*
Matignon, fine dice	*4 ounces*	*113 grams*
Dry white wine	*8 fluid ounces*	*240 milliliters*
Bay leaves	*2 each*	*2 each*
Brown Veal Stock,	*8 fluid ounces*	*240 milliliters*
Cornstarch, as needed	*1 tablespoon*	*1 tablespoon*

To learn more about poêléing, read Chapter 9, pages 313 to 316

1. Trim and butterfly the roast.

2. Mix herbs together and chop fine. Spread them over the veal, shape into a roast, and tie. Season with salt and pepper.

3. Render bacon in butter, add Matignon and sauté lightly.

(Recipe continued on next page)

4. Place veal in pot on top of Matignon and baste with some of the fat.

5. Cover pot and pôelé in 300°F (150°C) oven, basting every 20 minutes; remove lid for the last 30 minutes to allow veal to brown.

6. Check for doneness; meat should have an internal temperature of 140°F (60°C) and be tender when pierced with a fork. When done, remove veal and keep warm.

7. Add wine, bay leaves, and stock to pan; simmer 20 minutes. Degrease if necessary.

8. Thicken with cornstarch, reduce more if necessary.

9. Decrease sauce and season with salt and pepper to taste.

10. Slice the veal and serve with the sauce.

Fricassée de Veau

Yield: 10 servings

Veal shank, cubed	*4 pounds*	*1.8 kilograms*
Flour, as needed	*3 ounces*	*85 grams*
Vegetable oil, as needed	*2 fluid ounces*	*60 milliliters*
White Veal Stock	*1 1/2 pints*	*720 milliliters*
Pearl onions	*20 each*	*20 each*
Mushroom caps	*20 each*	*20 each*
Egg yolks	*3 each*	*3 each*
Heavy cream	*6 fluid ounces*	*180 milliliters*
Salt, to taste	*1/2 teaspoon*	*1/2 teaspoon*
Pepper, to taste	*1/4 teaspoon*	*1/4 teaspoon*

Other vegetables such as fresh peas, tourné carrots, and asparagus tips may be added at the appropriate cooking time or cooked separately and added as garnish.

There are numerous versions of fricassée with a wide variety of garnish options. This version is based on Fricassée à l'Ancienne.

1. Flour veal and sauté in oil without browning the meat.

2. Add stock and bring to a simmer; stir occasionally.

3. Cover and stew until tender, about 1 1/2 hours.

4. Add onions in the last 20 minutes.

5. Add mushrooms in the last 10 minutes.

6. Temper liaison of heavy cream and egg yolks, and add to the sauce. (Do not allow to boil once liaison is added.)

7. Adjust seasoning with salt and pepper to taste. Serve the stew with the sauce and vegetable garnish

Veal Blanquette

Yield: 10 servings

Veal breast, boned, cut in a large dice	*4 pounds*	*1.8 kilograms*
Water, cold	*as needed*	*as needed*
White Beef Stock	*2 quarts*	*2 liters*
Standard Sachet d'Épices	*1 each*	*1 each*
Roux, white	*4 ounces*	*113.4 grams*
Mushrooms	*1 1/2 pounds*	*.68 kilograms*
Butter	*1 ounce*	*30 grams*
Lemon juice, as needed	*2 tablespoons*	*2 tablespoons*
Egg yolks	*2 each*	*2 each*
Heavy cream	*8 fluid ounces*	*240 milliliters*
Pearl onions	*20 each*	*20 each*
Salt, to taste	*1/2 teaspoon*	*1/2 teaspoon*
Pepper, to taste	*1/4 teaspoon*	*1/4 teaspoon*

At service, do not boil the sauce. Simmer only until thickened and add garnish.

1. Cover the veal with cold water and blanch it. Drain and rinse the veal.

2. Combine the veal with the stock; simmer the veal until it is tender, about 1 1/2 hours. Add the Sachet d'Épices during the final half-hour of cooking time. Remove and discard the Sachet d'Épices and reduce the stock briefly.

3. Combine the roux with the stew; simmer the mixture until it is thickened.

4. Stew the mushrooms and pearl onions in butter until they are tender. Add the lemon juice, salt, and pepper to taste; reserve.

5. At service, heat the blanquette to just below a boil. Combine the egg yolks and cream for a liaison. Temper the mixture and add it to the blanquette. Simmer the sauce until it is thickened, but do not boil it.

6. Add the reserved mushrooms and pearl onions. Adjust the seasoning with salt and pepper to taste.

VARIATIONS

Chicken Blanquette: Substitute 4 pounds (1.8 kilograms) of chicken for the veal. Include fresh thyme in the Sachet d'Épices.

Lamb Blanquette: Substitute 4 pounds (1.8 kilograms) lamb for the veal. Include fresh rosemary in the Sachet d'Épices.

Braised Veal Breast with Mushroom Sausage

Yield: 10 servings

The method for preparing a veal breast is illustrated in Chapter 6, page 232.

The recipe for Pâté Spice may be found on page 997.

Forcemeat

Veal shank, or pork, lean, diced	*2 1/4 pounds*	*1 kilogram*
Long-grain rice, cooked	*12 ounces*	*340 grams*
Onions, minced	*7 ounces*	*200 grams*
Heavy cream	*5 fluid ounces*	*150 milliliters*
Egg whites	*3 each*	*3 each*
Onion powder	*1 tablespoon*	*1 tablespoon*
Garlic powder	*1/2 teaspoon*	*1/2 teaspoon*
Pâté Spice	*1 1/2 teaspoons*	*1 1/2 teaspoons*
Salt, to taste	*1 teaspoon*	*1 teaspoon*
Spanish paprika	*3/4 teaspoon*	*3/4 teaspoon*
Anise seed	*1 teaspoon*	*1 teaspoon*
Cayenne, ground	*1/4 teaspoon*	*1/4 teaspoon*
Mushrooms, diced	*14 ounces*	*400 grams*
Veal, breast, boned, trimmed, and pounded	*2 each*	*2 each*
Mirepoix	*8 ounces*	*225 grams*
Tomato paste	*2 ounces*	*60 grams*
Demi-Glace	*1 pint*	*480 milliliters*

1. Prepare a forcemeat by grinding the veal through a coarse die. Grind once more with all of the remaining ingredients for the sausage except the mushrooms. Working over an ice bath, fold the mushrooms into the forcemeat. Make a test quenelle to check for flavor and consistency.

2. Divide the forcemeat evenly between the two pounded veal breasts. Roll the breast around the forcemeat, rolling with the grain. Tie the breasts to form roulades.

3. Sear the roulades on all sides in a casserole. Remove them.

4. Add the Mirepoix to the casserole and sweat until the onions become limp and slightly golden.

5. Add the tomato paste and sauté it until there is a sweet aroma and the paste has begun to lose its bright red color.

6. Add the veal stock and Demi-Glace; stir well to release the fond. Return the roulades to the casserole.

(Recipe continued on facing page)

7. Bring the liquid just to a simmer. Cover the casserole and braise in a moderate oven until the veal is fork tender.

8. Remove the roulades and let them rest briefly. Strain the sauce and degrease it. If necessary, adjust the consistency of the sauce by reducing it further or thinning it with a small amount of additional stock.

9. Slice the roulades and shingle on heated plates. Coat the sliced veal lightly with the sauce.

Emincé of Lamb with Green Peppercorns

Yield: 10 servings

Lamb leg, cut into thin strips	2 1/4 pounds	1 kilogram	*The dry-sauté technique is described on page 579.*
Shallots, chopped	3 tablespoons	3 tablespoons	
Jus de Veau Lié	1 pint	480 milliliters	*For information about various grains and cooking times, refer to the table in Appendix 2.*
Heavy cream	6 fluid ounces	170 milliliters	
Dijon mustard	1 tablespoon	1 tablespoon	
Green peppercorns	1 ounce	30 grams	
Red wine	8 fluid ounces	14 milliliters	
White port wine	8 fluid ounces	14 milliliters	
Brown rice pilaf	2 pounds	900 grams	

1. Dry-sauté the lamb in a seasoned cast iron pan and remove from pan. The lamb should be well browned.

2. Deglaze pan with red wine and shallots.

3. Add jus, cream, and mustard.

4. Simmer the sauce to the correct consistency.

5. Return the lamb to the pan, along with any juices that have accumulated. Reheat but do not boil.

6. Finish with the green peppercorns and white port; adjust the seasoning to taste with salt.

7. Serve on a bed of rice.

Noisettes of Lamb Judic

Yield: 10 servings

The noisettes should be cut into 3-ounce (85-gram) portions. Serve 2 noisettes per plate.

A traditional garnish consists of braised lettuce, Château Potatoes, page 823, and baked tomatoes stuffed with mushroom Duxelle.

Use Demi-Glace if you do not have Jus d'Agneau Lié.

Lamb leg, cut into noisettes	20 each	20 each
Salt, to taste	1/2 teaspoon	1/2 teaspoon
Pepper, coarse ground, to taste	1/4 teaspoon	1/4 teaspoon
Vegetable oil, as needed	1 fluid ounce	30 milliliters
White wine	2 fluid ounces	60 milliliters
Jus d'Agneau Lié, heated	20 fluid ounces	600 milliliters
Butter	1 ounce	30 grams

1. Season the noisettes with salt and pepper. Sauté them in oil over high heat for 2 minutes on each side. Remove the lamb from the pan and keep it warm on the rack.

2. Deglaze the pan with the wine. Add the Jus d'Agneau Lié and reduce the sauce.

3. Finish the sauce with the butter; adjust the seasoning.

4. Serve the sauce over the lamb.

Because the lamb is slaughtered when still quite young, it is tender, and most cuts can be cooked by any method.

Boulangère refers to dishes baked in the baker's oven, not necessarily dishes involving bread, as might be expected. Traditionally, in France, on wash day (usually Monday), villagers would prepare their dinner and leave it at the local boulangerie to be baked off in the oven. This tradition of having special wash-day meals seems to be common throughout the world.

Roast Leg of Lamb Boulangère

Yield: 16 servings

Lamb leg, tied	10 pounds	4.5 kilograms
Salt, to taste	1 teaspoon	1 teaspoon
Pepper, to taste	1 teaspoon	1 teaspoon
Garlic cloves, slivered	2 each	2 each
Idaho potatoes, sliced 1/8-inch thick	4 pounds	1.8 kilograms
Onions, sliced thin	1 pound	450 grams
Brown Veal Stock, hot, as needed	20 fluid ounces	600 milliliters
Jus de Veau Lié, hot	1 quart	1 liter

1. Season the lamb with salt and pepper to taste; stud it with the slivered garlic.

2. Roast the lamb for 1 1/2 hours. Remove; pour off grease.

3. Layer the sliced potatoes and onions in the roasting pan. Season the layers with salt and pepper to taste. Add enough stock to moisten well.

4. Place the lamb on the potatoes. Continue to roast to an internal temperature of 130 to 135°F (55 to 57°C). The potatoes should be tender.

5. Let the leg rest before carving it.

6. Serve the sliced lamb on a bed of potatoes. Serve it with the hot jus lié.

VARIATION

If desired, stud the lamb with rosemary leaves along with the garlic.

Roast Rack of Lamb Persille

Yield: 10 servings

Lamb rack, frenched	*4 each*	*4 each*
Rosemary, sprigs	*6 each*	*6 each*
Thyme, sprigs	*8 each*	*8 each*
Salt, as needed	*1 teaspoon*	*1 teaspoon*
Pepper, as needed	*1 teaspoon*	*1 teaspoon*
Vegetable oil, as needed	*3 fluid ounces*	*90 milliliters*
Mirepoix	*8 ounces*	*225 grams*
Brown Veal or Lamb Stock	*8 fluid ounces*	*240 milliliters*
Bread crumbs, fresh, white	*10 ounces*	*285 grams*
Garlic cloves, mashed to a paste	*2 each*	*2 each*
Parsley, chopped	*1 tablespoon*	*1 tablespoon*
Butter, melted	*2 ounces*	*60 grams*

Each rack will contain 7 bones. To cut into portions, divide between the bones.

1. Season rack of lamb with rosemary, thyme, salt, and pepper, and rub with oil.

2. Place in roasting pan with Mirepoix.

3. Roast in 375°F (190°C) oven until 125 to 130°F (52 to 54°C) internal temperature is reached.

4. Remove lamb and keep warm.

5. Caramelize Mirepoix more, if desired.

6. Pour off excess fat and deglaze pan with stock.

7. Simmer 10 to 15 minutes, strain and season.

8. Mix bread crumbs, garlic, parsley, butter, salt, and pepper together and spread this mixture on top of the lamb rack.

9. Return the lamb to the oven until crumbs lightly brown.

10. Cut lamb into portions (2 to 3 chops per portions); serve with jus.

Mediterranean in origin, mint is an aromatic herb which compliments the flavor of the lamb.

Roast Leg of Lamb with Mint Sauce

Yield: 10 servings

Salt herbs (see below)	*2 tablespoons*	*30 grams*
Lamb leg, boneless, rolled and tied	*6 pounds*	*2.7 kilograms*
Garlic cloves, mashed to paste	*3 each*	*3 each*
Mirepoix, medium dice	*4 ounces*	*113 grams*
Brown Stock	*1 1/2 quarts*	*1.5 liters*
Salt, to taste	*1/2 teaspoon*	*1/2 teaspoon*
Mint, chopped	*1 tablespoon*	*1 tablespoon*
Arrowroot, or cornstarch, diluted	*as needed*	*as needed*

1. Combine all ingredients for spice mixture; grind to a fine powder in a blender.

2. Rub roast with seasoning mixture and garlic paste; marinate overnight.

3. Rub roast with oil; place on a wire rack in a roast pan.

4. Roast in a 325 to 350°F (160 to 175°C) oven, to an internal temperature of 110°F (40°C); add Mirepoix.

5. Remove roast at 135°F (55°C); allow to rest.

6. To make mint sauce, clarify fat in roasting pan, then discard all fat.

7. Add Mirepoix, Brown Stock, and mint; simmer until reduced by one-third; degrease.

8. Thicken with arrowroot, strain through a fine chinoise, and adjust seasonings.

9. Remove string, slice meat against the grain, and serve with jus.

Note: For salt herbs, combine 2 tablespoons of salt with 1 tablespoon each of rosemary and thyme, 3 bay leaves, and 1 teaspoon of pepper. Let rest 12 hours before using.

Grilled Lamb Chops with Mint Sauce

Yield: 10 servings

Double lamb rib chops	*20 each*	*20 each*
Olive oil, as needed	*2 fluid ounces*	*60 milliliters*
Salt, to taste	*1/2 teaspoon*	*1/2 teaspoon*
Pepper, to taste	*1/4 teaspoon*	*1/4 teaspoon*
Jus d'Angeau Lié	*20 fluid ounces*	*600 milliliters*

(Recipe continued on facing page)

Vegetables, brunoise, blanched (carrot, celery, leek, onion)	1 1/4 pounds	570 grams
Mint pluches, chiffonade	1 ounce	30 grams

1. Pound the lamb chops lightly to shape them to an even thickness.

2. Season with salt and pepper, Brush the chops with oil; grill the chops to desired doneness. Hold the chops on a sizzler platter.

3. Heat the Jus d'Agneau Lié to reduce it slightly. Add the brunoise vegetables and chiffonade of mint. Adjust the seasoning with salt and pepper.

4. Serré the chops with the sauce and serve.

Lamb Chops with Arizona Chili Butter

Yield: 10 servings

Arizona Chili Butter

Butter	1 pound	450 grams
Chili powder	1 tablespoon	1 tablespoon
Cumin, ground	1/2 teaspoon	1/2 teaspoon
Paprika	1 1/2 teaspoons	1 1/2 teaspoons
Chili Powder, hot	1 tablespoon	1 tablespoon
Oregano, fresh, chopped	1 tablespoon	1 tablespoon
Chipotles, chopped, to taste	1 teaspoon	1 teaspoon
Worcestershire sauce	1 1/2 teaspoons	1 1/2 teaspoons
Tabasco	1/4 teaspoon	1/4 teaspoon
Garlic powder	1/4 teaspoon	1/4 teaspoon
Onion powder	1/4 teaspoon	1/4 teaspoon
Lamb chops, 3 per portion	30 each	30 each
Salt, to taste	1/2 teaspoon	1/2 teaspoon
Pepper, to taste	1/4 teaspoon	1/4 teaspoon
Vegetable oil	as needed	as needed

The Chili Butter may be made in advance and held under refrigeration for 2 or 3 days or held in the freezer.

To read about making compound butters see pages 546 to 549.

1. Combine all the ingredients for the Chili Butter; roll and chill.

2. Season the chops; brush them lightly with the oil.

3. Grill or broil the chops to the desired doneness, to an internal temperature of 140°F (60°C) for medium.

4. Top each chop with a slice of Chili Butter; flash the chops under a broiler just before serving.

Grilled Lamb Chops with Whole Cloves of Garlic

Yield: 10 servings

To make a garlic-infused oil, combine the sliced cloves from one head of garlic, 8 ounces (240 milliliters) of olive oil. Heat over medium heat. Remove from heat; cool; strain. The oil is now ready to use, or maybe held under refrigeration for up to one week. Additional sliced garlic cloves may be added to the refrigerated portion.

Garnish the chops with whole roasted garlic cloves. To read about roasting garlic see page 191.

Garlic, whole cloves	*30 each*	*30 each*
Lamb chops, double, from rib	*20 each*	*20 each*
Garlic-infused oil	*as needed*	*as needed*
Salt, to taste	*1/2 teaspoon*	*1/2 teaspoon*
Pepper, to taste	*1/4 teaspoon*	*1/4 teaspoon*
Butter	*2 ounces*	*60 grams*
White wine	*8 fluid ounces*	*240 milliliters*
Jus d'Agneau Lié	*1 pint*	*480 milliliters*
Basil, minced	*1 ounce*	*30 grams*
Tomato Concassé	*8 ounces*	*225 grams*

1. Blanch the garlic cloves in salted water; shock and peel them. Cook them in three successive changes of water until they are tender. (This will remove any bitter taste.)

2. Brush the chops with the garlic-infused oil and season them with the salt and pepper. Broil the chops to the appropriate doneness. Hold them on a sizzler platter.

3. Sauté the blanched garlic cloves in the butter until they are lightly browned. Deglaze the pan with the white wine; reduce to sec.

4. Add the Jus d'Agneau Lié and any juices from the sizzler platter; reduce the mixture lightly.

5. Add the basil and Tomato Concassé. Monté au beurre. Adjust the seasoning to taste.

6. Nappé the sauce over the chops and serve.

Lamb Chops with Artichokes

Yield: 10 servings

Lamb chops, rib or loin	*20 each*	*20 each*
Salt, to taste	*1/2 teaspoon*	*1/2 teaspoon*
Pepper, to taste	*1/2 teaspoon*	*1/2 teaspoon*
Marinade		
Olive oil	*4 fluid ounces*	*120 milliliters*
Lemon juice	*2 fluid ounces*	*60 milliliters*
Soy sauce	*2 fluid ounces*	*60 milliliters*
Thyme, chopped	*1 tablespoon*	*1 tablespoon*
Artichoke mixture		
Shallots, minced	*3 tablespoons*	*3 tablespoons*
Garlic, minced	*2 teaspoons*	*2 teaspoons*
Olive oil	*2 fluid ounces*	*60 milliliters*
Zucchini, julienne	*3/4 pound*	*340 grams*
Tomato Concassé	*5 ounces*	*140 grams*
Artichoke bottoms, cooked and sliced	*10 each*	*10 each*
Pepperoncini, chopped	*1 tablespoon*	*1 tablespoon*

When grilling lamb chops, select a hardwood such as grapevines, mesquite, hickory, or apple to introduce a special flavor.

To read about cleaning and preparing artichoke hearts see page 199.

The artichoke may be prepared in advance. After preparation, it should be cooled thoroughly, refrigerated, and reheated to order.

1. Trim the chops and season with salt and pepper. Combine all the ingredients for the marinade and brush liberally onto the chops. Marinate them under refrigeration for 1 to 2 hours.

2. To prepare the artichoke mixture, sauté the shallots and garlic in the oil. Add the zucchini first, then the Tomato Concassé and artichokes. Season the mixture with the pepperoncini, salt, and pepper to taste.

3. Grill or broil the chops to desired doneness.

4. Serve the chops on a bed of the artichoke mixture. Garnish with them with artichoke leaves.

Lamb Stew

Yield: 10 servings

Additional vegetables such as fresh peas, parsnips, and rutabagas might be added. Roasted garlic, rosemary, thyme, or other seasonings could also be included.

Serve the Lamb Stew with Irish Soda Bread, page 1031.

The technique for tournéeing vegetables is explained in Chapter 6, page 187.

Lamb, cubed	*4 pounds*	*1.8 kilograms*
Vegetable oil, as needed	*4 fluid ounces*	*120 milliliters*
Onions, chopped	*6 ounces*	*170 grams*
Tomato paste	*2 ounces*	*60 grams*
Brown Stock or red wine	*8 fluid ounces*	*240 milliliters*
Brown Sauce	*20 fluid ounces*	*600 milliliters*

Standard Sachet d'Épices, plus
     bay leaf
     thyme
     peppercorn
	1 each	*1 each*

Carrots, tourné	*20 each*	*20 each*
Potatoes, tourné	*20 each*	*20 each*
Celery, tourné	*20 each*	*20 each*
Turnips, tourné	*20 each*	*20 each*
Mushrooms	*20 each*	*20 each*
Tomato Concassé	*8 ounces*	*225 grams*
Salt, to taste	*1/2 teaspoon*	*1/2 teaspoon*
Pepper, to taste	*1/2 teaspoon*	*1/2 teaspoon*

1. Brown the lamb on all sides in hot oil.

2. Remove meat, add onions, and sauté until translucent.

3. Add tomato paste; sauté 2 to 3 minutes.

4. Add stock, sauce, and sachet; bring to a simmer.

5. Add meat; cover.

6. Braise in 350°F (175°C) oven until fork tender.

7. About 20 minutes before done, add carrots, potatoes, celery, and turnips.

8. About 5 minutes before done, add mushrooms, and Tomato Concassé.

9. When finished, degrease the sauce.

10. Adjust consistency and seasonings with salt and pepper to taste.

Braised Lamb Shanks

Yield: 10 servings

Lamb shanks, well-trimmed	10 each	10 each
Salt, to taste	1/2 teaspoon	1/2 teaspoon
Pepper, to taste	1/4 teaspoon	1/4 teaspoon
Vegetable oil, as needed	4 fluid ounces	120 milliliters
Mirepoix	1 pound	450 grams
Garlic cloves, minced	3 each	3 each
Tomato paste	1 ounce	30 grams
White wine (optional)	1 pint	480 milliliters
Brown Sauce or Brown Lamb Stock	2 quarts	1.9 liters
Standard Sachet d'Épices	1 each	1 each

Select lamb shanks that average 1 pound (450 grams) each.

To read more about the braising cooking method, refer to Chapter 10, pages 346 to 350.

1. Season the lamb with the salt and pepper. Sear it in hot oil on all sides and remove it.

2. Add the Mirepoix to the same oil and caramelize it.

3. Add the garlic, tomato paste, and wine; reduce the sauce.

4. Add the Brown Sauce and reduce it slightly.

5. Add the lamb shanks and Sachet d'Épices and adjust the seasoning with salt and pepper to taste. Cover the pan and braise the lamb until it is fork tender, about 1 1/4 hours.

6. Remove the lamb shanks. Strain the sauce, degrease it, adjust the consistency, and return the meat to the sauce.

VARIATION

Lamb Shanks Printanière: Garnish the lamb with tournéed carrots, turnips, potatoes, glazed pearl onions, peas, and green beans. The vegetables and lamb should be prepared separately.

Pork Cutlet Sauce Charcutière

Yield: 10 servings

Fabricate the cutlets into 4- to 5-ounce (115- to 140-gram) portions.

This sauce also works well with grilled pork chops and other grilled or sautéed meats.

Pork loin	4 1/2 pounds	1.8 kilograms
Salt, to taste	1/2 teaspoon	1/2 teaspoon
Pepper, to taste	1/4 teaspoon	1/4 teaspoon
Flour, for dredging	as needed	as needed
Butter	3 ounces	85 grams
Shallots, minced	4 each	4 each
White wine	4 fluid ounces	120 milliliters
Jus de Veau Lié	12 fluid ounces	360 milliliters
Dijon mustard	1 tablespoon	1 tablespoon
Cornichons, julienne	1 1/2 ounces	42 grams
Lemon juice	1 teaspoon	1 teaspoon
Whole butter, diced	2 ounces	60 grams

1. Cut the pork into 5-ounce (140-gram) cutlets. Pound to an even thickness.

2. Season pork cutlets and dredge in flour.

3. Sauté in butter until lightly browned and cooked. Remove them from the pan and keep warm. Pour off any excess butter from the pan.

4. Add shallots to pan and sauté until translucent.

5. Deglaze pan with white wine and reduce by half.

6. Add Jus de Veau Lié and reduce to sauce consistency.

7. Add mustard, cornichons, and lemon juice to finish sauce. Season with salt and pepper to taste. Finish with whole butter.

8. Serve the cutlets with the sauce.

Pork Scalopine with Herb Sauce

Yield: 10 servings

Pork scallopini	*20 each*	*20 each*
Salt, to taste	*1/2 teaspoon*	*1/2 teaspoon*
Pepper, to taste	*1/4 teaspoon*	*1/4 teaspoon*
Clarified butter	*4 ounces*	*115 grams*
Shallots, finely minced	*4 each*	*4 each*
Tomato Concassé	*8 ounces*	*225 grams*
Fresh herbs	*1 tablespoon*	*1 tablespoon*
White wine	*6 fluid ounces*	*180 milliliters*
Jus de Veau Lié	*20 fluid ounces*	*600 milliliters*
Butter	*4 ounces*	*115 grams*

1. Season pork and sauté in clarified butter until light brown.

2. Remove meat and keep warm.

3. Remove excess butter from pan, add shallots, and sauté.

4. Deglaze with white wine, and add the herbs and Jus de Veau Lié.

5. Reduce to a good consistency, add Tomato Concassé and herbs; heat through.

6. Finish with the butter.

7. Season to taste with salt and pepper. Garnish the plate with additional fresh herbs if desired.

Use fresh herbs to add flavor and color to this dish.

Pork Medallions with Red Onion Confit

Yield: 10 servings

Pork loin or tenderloin medallions	*4 1/2 pounds*	*1.8 kilograms*
Sherry wine vinegar	*2 fluid ounces*	*60 milliliters*
Jus de Veau Lié	*20 fluid ounces*	*600 milliliters*
Red Onion Confit, warmed	*1 1/4 pounds*	*570 grams*

1. Cut the loin into 20, 2-ounce (65-gram) medallions.

2. Sear the medallions in a sauté pan on both sides and finish them in the oven.

3. Combine the vinegar and Jus de Veau Lié in a saucepan; bring to a quick boil.

4. Deglaze the sauté pan with the vinegar; add the Jus de Veau Lié and simmer to reduce.

5. Place the warm Red Onion Confit (see recipe at right) onto the center of a heated serving platter or plate. Pour the sauce around the confit and place two medallions on the plate.

Red Onion Confit *Sweat 6 ounces (170 grams) of sliced red onions in 1 to 2 teaspoons of butter. Add 1 tablespoon of honey or brown sugar and caramelize the onions. Add 1 fluid ounce (30 milliliters) each of red wine and red wine vinegar; reduce au sec. Season with salt and pepper. Serve warm at room temperature. Sweet white onions (Vidalia) may be used in place of the red onions.*

599

Tenderloin of Pork with Apples and Caraway

Yield: 10 servings

Cut the noisettes into 5-ounce (140-gram) portions.

A variety of apples makes this dish very appealing; however, feel free to use any seasonal or local cooking apples that you have on hand.

Pork tenderloin, noisettes	*10 each*	*10 each*
Caraway seeds, as needed	*2 teaspoons*	*2 teaspoons*
Salt, to taste	*1/2 teaspoon*	*1/2 teaspoon*
Pepper, to taste	*1/4 teaspoon*	*1/4 teaspoon*
Clarified butter	*as needed*	*as needed*
Applejack	*5 fluid ounces*	*150 milliliters*
Jus de Veau Lié	*20 fluid ounces*	*600 milliliters*
Butter	*2 ounces*	*60 grams*
Granny Smith apples, sliced and sautéed	*3 each*	*3 each*
Golden Delicious apples, sliced and sautéed	*3 each*	*3 each*
Red Delicious apples, sliced and sautéed	*3 each*	*3 each*

1. Shape the noisettes and pound them to a uniform shape. Rub them with the caraway seeds; season them with the salt and pepper.

2. Sauté the noisettes in the clarified butter until they are barely cooked through. Remove them and keep them warm.

3. Deglaze the pan with the applejack and reduce. Add the Jus de Veau Lié and simmer it. Monté au beurre.

4. Return the noisettes to the pan to coat them with the sauce, along with any accumulated drippings. Serve them on heated plates, garnished with the warm, sautéed apple slices.

Sautéed Medallions of Pork with Warm Fruits

Yield: 10 servings

Pork loin, trimmed	4 pounds	1.8 kilograms
Red Delicious apples, tournéed or large dice	5 ounces	140 grams
Bartlett pears, tournéed or large dice	4 ounces	115 grams
Dry white wine	32 fluid ounces	1 liter
Cherries, dried	1 3/4 ounces	50 grams
Dried apricots	3 1/2 ounces	100 grams
Chicken Stock, hot	1 quart	1 liter
Demi-Glace	1 quart	1 liter
Brandy, apple-flavored	1 3/4 fluid ounces	52 milliliters
For service		
Pumpkin pasta	1 1/2 pounds	680 grams
Haricots verts, steamed	1 1/4 pounds	570 grams

Dry-sautéeing is explained on page 579.

To make pumpkin pasta, sauté 4 ounces (115 grams) of puréed pumpkin until it is reduced to 3 ounces (85 grams). Cool and add to Basic Pasta Dough, page 846.

Pork chops, venison, game birds, duck, turkey, or goose will all work well with this sauce.

1. Cut the pork into medallions, about 2 ounces (60 grams) each. One portion is 3 medallions.

2. Poach the apple and pear in the white wine until tender. Let cool in the poaching liquid.

3. Reconstitute the dried fruits in Chicken Stock. Strain and reserve the stock.

4. At service, dry-sauté the pork in a properly seasoned sauté pan. Remove the pork from the pan and keep it warm.

5. Deglaze the pan with a small amount of the reserved Chicken Stock. Add the fruits and heat well. Add the Demi-Glace and the brandy and flame the sauce to burn off some of the alcohol.

6. Return the pork to the sauté pan to coat lightly with the sauce.

7. Serve the pork on a bed of pumpkin pasta with the haricots verts. Coat the pork with the sauce and garnish with the fruit.

Pork Cutlets with Wild Mushrooms and Crabmeat

Yield: 10 servings

Use pork cutlets weighing about 5 ounces (140 grams) each.

If fresh wild mushrooms are not available, use dried reconstituted mushrooms or fresh button mushrooms.

Pork cutlet	4 pounds	1.8 kilograms
Salt, to taste	1/2 teaspoon	1/2 teaspoon
Pepper, to taste	1/4 teaspoon	1/4 teaspoon
Clarified butter, as needed	4 ounces	115 grams
White wine	20 fluid ounces	600 milliliters
Heavy cream, reduced, as needed	8 fluid ounces	240 milliliters
Wild mushrooms, diced	1 pound	450 grams
Butter	3 ounces	85 grams
Crabmeat, lump	10 ounces	285 grams
Fresh herbs, as available or desired	2 teaspoons	2 teaspoons

1. Season the cutlets with the salt and pepper.
2. Heat the clarified butter. Add the cutlets and sauté them until they are nearly cooked through. Remove them from the pan and keep them warm.
3. Deglaze the pan with the wine and reduce.
4. Add the reduced heavy cream and reduce the sauce to nappé a good consistency.
5. In a separate pan, sauté the mushrooms in the whole butter until they are tender.
6. Add the crabmeat and fresh herbs and heat through.
7. Place the crabmeat mixture on top of the cutlets.
8. Add any accumulated drippings to the sauce.
9. Reheat the sauce and pool it on a warm plate. Serve the cutlets on the pool of sauce.

Panfried Breaded Pork Cutlets

Yield: 10 servings

Pork cutlets	4 pounds	1.8 kilograms
Flour	as needed	as needed
Salt, to taste	1/2 teaspoon	1/2 teaspoon
Pepper, to taste	1/4 teaspoon	1/4 teaspoon
Oregano	1 teaspoon	1 teaspoon
Egg wash	6 fluid ounces	180 milliliters
Bread crumbs, dry	as needed	as needed
Vegetable oil	8 fluid ounces	240 milliliters
Lard	8 ounces	225 grams
Lemon wedges	10 each	10 each

(Recipe continued on facing page)

1. Pound the pork cutlets to an even thickness.

2. Season the flour with salt, pepper, and oregano.

3. Dredge the cutlets in flour and dip in egg wash.

4. Dredge in dry bread crumbs; allow cutlets to rest 30 minutes in refrigerator.

5. Shallow-fry in oil and lard until lightly browned. Drain on absorbent paper.

6. Serve with a lemon wedge.

The pork cutlets should weigh 4 to 5 ounces (115 to 140 grams) each.

Other dried herbs may be used to season the flour or the bread crumbs.

If you prefer you may delete the lard and fry the pork cutlets in vegetable oil only.

Pan-Fried Pork Chop Forestière

Yield: 10 servings

Pork chops, frenched	*10 each*	*10 each*
Salt, to taste	*1/2 teaspoon*	*1/2 teaspoon*
Pepper, to taste	*1/4 teaspoon*	*1/4 teaspoon*
Flour	*as needed*	*as needed*
Vegetable oil	*as needed*	*as needed*
Butter	*1 ounce*	*30 grams*
Shallots, minced	*2 ounces*	*60 grams*
Mushrooms, assorted, sliced	*1 pound*	*450 grams*
White wine	*4 fluid ounces*	*120 milliliters*
Jus de Veau Lié	*10 fluid ounces*	*300 milliliters*

Use pork chops weighing approximately 7 to 8 ounces (200 to 225 grams).

Rosemary, thyme, caraway or other herbs may be added to the sauce.

1. Season the chops with salt and pepper.

2. Dredge chops in flour and pan-fry in oil.

3. When chops are done, remove and keep warm.

4. Pour excess fat from pan, add butter, and sauté shallots until translucent.

5. Add mushrooms and sauté; deglaze with white wine, and reduce until almost dry.

6. Add Jus de Veau Lié and reduce to sauce consistency; season to taste with salt and pepper.

7. Place the pork chop on a plate. Spoon the sauce and the mushrooms around the chop.

Baked Stuffed Pork Chops

Yield: 10 servings

Serve Robert Sauce, page 528, or Sauce Charcutière, page 529, with these chops, if desired.

The chops you cut should be at least 3/4-inch (2-centimeters) thick. For more information about cutting chops, refer to Chapter 6, page 234.

Pork chops, center, thick-cut	*10 each*	*10 each*
Salt, to taste	*1/2 teaspoon*	*1/2 teaspoon*
Pepper, to taste	*1/4 teaspoon*	*1/4 teaspoon*
Stuffing		
Vegetable oil or rendered bacon fat	*2 ounces*	*60 grams*
Onion, minced	*4 ounces*	*115 grams*
Celery, minced	*3 ounces*	*85 grams*
Garlic cloves, minced	*2 each*	*2 each*
Bread cubes, dried	*24 ounces*	*680 grams*
Parsley, chopped	*1 tablespoon*	*1 tablespoon*
Sage, rubbed, to taste	*1 teaspoon*	*1 teaspoon*
Chicken Stock, as needed	*6 fluid ounces*	*180 milliliters*
Jus de Veau Lié	*20 fluid ounces*	*600 milliliters*

1. Cut a pocket into the chops. Season with salt and pepper. Refrigerate until stuffing is properly prepared and cooled.

2. Heat the oil or bacon fat in a pan. Add the onion and cook until it is golden brown. Add the celery and garlic, and cook until the celery is limp. Remove them from the pan, spread out on a baking sheet, and allow this mixture to cool completely.

3. Combine the onion mixture with bread cubes, parsley, and sage. Add enough of the stock to make a stuffing that is moist but not wet. Chill the stuffing until it is 40°F (4°C).

4. Place the stuffing inside the pork chops. Secure the chops by tying or closing with skewers.

5. Sear the pork chops in a sauté pan until golden on both sides. Remove to a baking sheet and finish cooking in a 350°F (166°C) oven to an internal temperature of 150°F (65°C).

6. Pour off any excess oil or bacon fat from the pan. Add the Jus de Vea Lié and bring to a simmer. Degrease the sauce if necessary. Adjust the seasoning to taste with salt and pepper.

7. Serve the chops with the sauce.

Pork Roast with Jus Lié

Yield: 10 servings

Pork loin roast, boneless	*3 1/2 pounds*	*1.3 kilograms*
Salt, to taste	*1/2 teaspoon*	*1/2 teaspoon*
Black peppercorns, coarse-ground	*1/2 teaspoon*	*1/2 teaspoon*
Garlic cloves, mashed to paste	*2 each*	*2 each*
Rosemary, sprigs	*1 each*	*1 each*
Thyme, sprigs	*2 each*	*2 each*
Vegetable oil, as needed	*3 fluid ounces*	*90 milliliters*
Mirepoix, medium dice	*4 ounces*	*115 grams*
White wine (optional)	*4 fluid ounces*	*120 milliliters*
Bay leaves	*2 each*	*2 each*
Brown Pork Stock	*1 quart*	*1 liter*
Arrowroot, as needed	*2 tablespoons*	*2 tablespoons*
Salt, to taste	*1/2 teaspoon*	*1/2 teaspoon*
Pepper, to taste	*1/4 teaspoon*	*1/4 teaspoon*

For additional flavor when boning the pork loin, save the bones and use them as a rack to roast the loin.

To prepare Brown Pork Stock, refer to page 445.

Tomato paste may be added to Mirepoix and browned if a darker gravy is desired. One ounce (30 grams) should be sufficient.

1. Season pork loin with salt, pepper, garlic, herbs, and spices; tie. Sear the pork in the oil until browned.

2. Place pork loin on a rack in a roasting pan. Add the Mirepoix.

3. Roast at 325°F (160°C) to an internal temperature of 160°F (80°C); remove roast and allow to rest. This should take 30 to 45 minutes.

4. To make stock, clarify fat from drippings in the roasting pan; pour off all fat.

5. Deglaze pan with wine, add Brown Pork Stock and bay leaves, and simmer until reduced by half; degrease.

6. Mix arrowroot and water, whisk into simmering sauce; return to a simmer.

7. Strain through a fine chinoise, adjust seasonings.

8. Remove string, slice pork against the grain, serve with jus lié.

Pork Loin Stuffed with Apples and Prunes

Yield: 12 Servings

Reserve the bone and trim from the loin to make the sauce.

Pork loin, center cut, trimmed, rib bones in	*6 pounds*	*3 kilograms*
Granny Smith apples, 1/4-inch dice	*3 each*	*3 each*
Prunes, pitted, diced	*6 ounces*	*170 grams*
Gingerroot, grated	*1/2 ounces*	*15 grams*
Salt, to taste	*1/2 teaspoon*	*1/2 teaspoon*
Pepper, to taste	*1/4 teaspoon*	*1/4 teaspoon*
Vegetable oil	*4 fluid ounces*	*120 milliliters*
Mirepoix	*8 ounces*	*225 grams*
Dry red wine	*8 fluid ounces*	*240 milliliters*
Brown Stock	*1 quart*	*1 liter*
Arrowroot, diluted	*as needed*	*as needed*

1. Cut a pocket in the eye of the loin.

2. Combine the apples, prunes, and ginger. Season them to taste with salt and pepper. Stuff the loin with the mixture and tie it with a string.

3. Season the loin with salt and pepper and sear it in oil on all sides.

4. Roast the loin to an internal temperature of 160°F (65°C).

5. Meanwhile, brown the bones in a rondeau. Add the Mirepoix and brown it; deglaze the rondeau with the red wine. Add the Brown Stock; simmer it for about 1 hour, until it is reduced and well flavored.

6. Remove the loin and let it rest for 15 to 20 minutes.

7. Strain the stock. Thicken it with the arrowroot; adjust the seasoning to taste.

Roast Tenderloin of Pork with Honey and Thyme

Yield: 10 servings

Pork tenderloin	*3 1/2 pounds*	*1.6 kilograms*
Vegetable oil	*2 fluid ounces*	*60 milliliters*
Shallots, minced	*1 tablespoon*	*1 tablespoon*
Garlic, minced	*1/2 teaspoon*	*1/2 teaspoon*
Tomato paste	*1 ounce*	*30 grams*
Dijon mustard	*1/2 ounce*	*15 grams*
Red wine vinegar	*1 1/2 fluid ounces*	*45 milliliters*

(Recipe continued on facing page)

Honey	1 3/4 ounces	50 grams
Thyme, minced	1 teaspoon	1 teaspoon
Whole black peppercorns, cracked	1 teaspoon	1 teaspoon
Brown Pork Stock	22 fluid ounces	660 milliliters
Arrowroot	1/2 ounce	15 grams
Salt, to taste	1/2 teaspoon	1/2 teaspoon
Pepper, to taste	1/4 teaspoon	1/4 teaspoon

1. Sear the pork in the oil until browned. Remove it. Pour off any excess grease.

2. Add the shallots, garlic, tomato paste, and mustard to the pan and sauté.

3. Deglaze the pan with the red wine vinegar, and add the honey, thyme, and cracked peppercorns.

4. Roll the tenderloin in the glaze. Transfer the meat to a roasting pan.

5. Roast the meat in a medium oven to an internal temperature of 160°F (70°C). Brush the glaze over the tenderloin occasionally as it roasts.

6. Deglaze the roasting pan with the Brown Pork Stock. Add diluted arrowroot; simmer the mixture until it is thickened. Adjust the seasoning to taste with salt and pepper.

7. Slice the pork on a bias. Serve it with the sauce.

Broiled Pork Chop

Yield: 6 servings

Pork chops, thick-cut	10 each	10 each
Salt, to taste	1/2 teaspoon	1/2 teaspoon
Pepper, to taste	1/4 teaspoon	1/4 teaspoon
Vegetable oil	as needed	as needed

Marinate the chops in the Teriyaki Marinade, page 434. Brush the chops with the marinade as they broil.

1. Season pork chops and dip in oil.

2. Broil on medium heat broiler until done.

3. Turn at 45-degree angles during broiling to achieve grill marks.

4. Serve with compound butter or other accompaniments.

Broiled Pork Chops with Sesame Ginger Butter

Yield: 10 servings

The pork chops should weigh approximately 6 ounces (170 grams).

Prepare the Five Spice Powder on page 426 or use a commercially prepared blend.

The compound butter can be made in advance and be refrigerated or frozen.

If you prefer a sauce, you can easily prepare one by boiling the marinade, adding Pork or Chicken Stock, and reducing to a simmer. Thicken with a slurry and season to taste. Serve the sauce over the pork chop. Garnish with toasted sesame seeds.

Pork chops	*10 each*	*10 each*
Compound Butter		
Butter, softened	*10 ounces*	*285 grams*
Sesame seeds, hulled	*1 tablespoon*	*1 tablespoon*
Gingerroot, grated	*1 tablespoon*	*1 tablespoon*
Sherry wine	*1 fluid ounce*	*30 milliliters*
Five Spice Powder	*2 teaspoons*	*2 teaspoons*
Soy sauce	*1 1/2 fluid ounces*	*45 milliliters*
Scallions, sliced thin	*2 each*	*2 each*
Marinade		
Sesame oil	*3 fluid ounces*	*90 milliliters*
Vegetable oil	*3 fluid ounces*	*90 milliliters*
Soy sauce	*3 fluid ounces*	*90 milliliters*
Rice wine vinegar	*2 fluid ounces*	*60 milliliters*
Gingerroot, grated	*1 tablespoon*	*15 grams*
Garlic, minced	*2 teaspoons*	*2 teaspoons*
Sherry wine	*3 fluid ounces*	*90 milliliters*
Honey	*1 tablespoon*	*1 tablespoon*
Hot bean paste (optional)	*1 tablespoon*	*1 tablespoon*
Hoisin sauce (optional)	*1 tablespoon*	*1 tablespoon*
Plum sauce (optional)	*1 tablespoon*	*1 tablespoon*
Five Spice Powder	*2 teaspoons*	*2 teaspoons*
Scallions, sliced	*3 each*	*3 each*

1. Trim the pork chops to remove excess fat. French the bones if desired.

2. Mix all compound butter ingredients together, roll up in parchment paper or plastic wrap, and chill.

3. Combine the marinade ingredients. Add the pork chops and marinate 1 to 2 hours, refrigerated.

4. Drain pork chops, place on the grids of a preheated hot broiler.

5. Mark and turn at a 45° angle; mark and turn over. Finish cooking on the lower temperature side of the broiler.

6. Cut the compound butter into 1/2-ounce (15-gram) portions.

7. Garnish each pork chop with a slice of compound butter. Quickly flash under the broiler.

Pork Goulash

Yield: 10 servings

Pork shoulder, boneless	*3 pounds*	*1.3 kilograms*
Hungarian paprika	*3 tablespoons*	*45 grams*
Vegetable oil or lard	*3 fluid ounces*	*90 milliliters*
Salt, to taste	*1/2 teaspoon*	*1/2 teaspoon*
Pepper, to taste	*1/4 teaspoon*	*1/4 teaspoon*
Onions, diced	*3 pounds*	*1.3 kilograms*
Garlic cloves, minced	*2 each*	*2 each*
Dry white wine	*8 fluid ounces*	*240 milliliters*
Brown Pork or Veal Stock	*1 pint*	*480 milliliters*
Jus de Veau Lié	*1 pint*	*480 milliliters*
Standard Sachet d'Épices	*1 each*	*1 each*
Caraway seeds	*1 teaspoon*	*5 milliliters*
Marjoram leaves, chopped	*1/2 teaspoon*	*1/2 teaspoon*
Savory leaves, chopped	*1/2 teaspoon*	*1/2 teaspoon*
Lemon zest	*1 teaspoon*	*1 teaspoon*
Sour cream	*8 ounces*	*240 milliliters*

1. Cut the pork into 1-inch (2.5-centimeter) cubes. Rub pork with paprika and season with salt and pepper.

2. Brown pork in hot oil or lard; remove.

3. Add onions, cover, and sweat lightly. Add garlic and cook briefly

4. Add wine and deglaze; reduce slightly.

5. Return pork, add stock, Jus de Veau Lié, and sachet, caraway, marjoram, and savory; bring to a simmer.

6. Cover and braise at 350°F (175°C) until meat is tender, about 1 1/4 hours.

7. When meat is done, degrease and check consistency of sauce. Remove sachet and discard.

8. Add lemon zest and adjust seasonings with salt and pepper to taste.

9. Serve each portion garnished with sour cream.

You may replace the pork with beef or veal.

If you prefer a smoother sauce, place the caraway seeds, marjoram, and savory in the sachet.

Goulash is traditionally served with spaëtzle or bread dumplings.

North Carolina-Style Barbecued Pork

Yield: 10 servings

Other ingredients may be added to the Barbecue Sauce; see page 552 for ideas.

There are as many recipes for barbecue as there are pleats in a chef's toque. This is one version.

If desired and if time allows, you may want to smoke pork before braising.

Serve about 5 ounces (140 grams) per portion as an entrée. Or for a sandwich, place 3 ounces (85 grams) on a grilled bun and top with coleslaw (or serve it on the side).

Pork shoulder	3 1/2 pounds	1.6 kilograms
Marinade		
Malt vinegar	6 fluid ounces	80 milliliters
Worcestershire sauce	2 tablespoons	2 tablespoons
Onions, rough chopped	4 ounces	115 grams
Jalapeño peppers, seeded and rough-chopped	1 ounce	30 grams
Dry mustard	1 tablespoon	1 tablespoon
Garlic, chopped	1 ounce	30 grams
Peppercorns, cracked	2 teaspoons	2 teaspoons
Braising liquid		
Onions, chopped	4 ounces	115 grams
Oil	1 fluid ounce	30 milliliters
Tomato paste	1 ounce	30 grams
Brown Stock	12 fluid ounces	360 milliliters
Barbecue sauce		
Braising liquid, reduced to sauce consistency		
Brewed coffee	8 fluid ounces	240 milliliters
Balsamic vinegar	1 fluid ounce	30 milliliters
Molasses	2 tablespoons	30 milliliters
Frank's Hot Sauce	2 tablespoons	30 milliliters

1. Trim the pork and remove excess fat.

2. Combine ingredients for marinade. Pour over and rub into pork. Marinate 24 hours, turning occasionally.

3. Sear the pork on a grill. Sweat the onions in the oil in a rondeau. Add the tomato paste and pincé. Add pork and stock; bring to a simmer. Braise in a 325°F (165°C) oven for 2 to 3 hours or until pork pulls apart easily with a fork.

4. Remove the pork and let it cool. Strain the braising liquid. Reduce slightly.

5. Combine the braising liquid with the coffee and molasses. Reduce to sauce consistency. Add hot sauce and salt and pepper to taste.

6. Shred the pork. Add enough of the Barbecue Sauce to thoroughly moisten the pork.

Stewed Rabbit with Prunes

Yield: 10 servings

Rabbits	*3 to 4 each*	*3 to 4 each*
Flour	*6 ounces*	*170 grams*
Lard	*2 ounces*	*60 grams*
Shallots, minced	*2 ounces*	*60 grams*
Mirepoix, fine dice	*1 1/2 pounds*	*.68 kilograms*
White wine	*12 fluid ounces*	*360 milliliters*
Brown Sauce	*12 fluid ounces*	*360 milliliters*
Salt, to taste	*1/2 teaspoon*	*1/2 teaspoon*
Pepper, to taste	*1/4 teaspoon*	*1/4 teaspoon*
Thyme, sprig	*1 each*	*1 each*
Bay leaves	*2 each*	*2 each*
Arrowroot, diluted	*as needed*	*as needed*
Prunes, pitted	*1 pound*	*450 grams*
Red currant jelly	*6 ounces*	*170 grams*

1. Clean the rabbits thoroughly. Remove all sinews and tendons. Cut each rabbit into pieces. Reserve the trim meat and bones.

2. Dredge the rabbit pieces in flour. Shake off the excess.

3. Sauté the rabbit in hot lard in a brazier until it is light brown. Remove it and keep it warm.

4. Add the shallots and Mirepoix to the pot along with the reserved trim meat and bones. Sauté briefly.

5. Add the wine, Brown Sauce, salt, pepper, and herbs with the reserved rabbit. Bring the mixture to a boil.

6. Cover the pot and braise the rabbit in a 300°F (150°C) oven until it is tender. Remove the rabbit, moisten with a little braising liquid, and keep warm.

7. Strain and skim the sauce. Return to the heat, simmer, and degrease.

8. Adjust the sauce consistency with the diluted arrowroot if necessary.

9. Add the prunes and currant jelly and simmer the sauce for 5 minutes. Adjust the seasoning to taste.

10. Serve the rabbit with the sauce.

Rabbit and Oyster Étouffé

Yield: 10 servings

Rabbit	*2 each*	*2 each*
Seasoning Mixture		
Paprika	*1 teaspoon*	*1 teaspoon*
Garlic powder	*3/4 teaspoon*	*4 grams*
Onion powder	*1/2 teaspoon*	*1/2 teaspoon*
Black pepper	*1/2 teaspoon*	*1/2 teaspoon*
Basil, dried	*1/2 teaspoon*	*1/2 teaspoon*
Filé Powder	*1/2 teaspoon*	*1/2 teaspoon*
Cayenne, ground	*1/8 teaspoon*	*1/8 teaspoon*
Vegetable oil, as needed	*3 fluid ounces*	*90 milliliters*
Onions, minced	*4 ounces*	*115 grams*
Green peppers, minced	*4 ounces*	*115 grams*
Celery, diced	*2 ounces*	*60 grams*
Scallions, sliced thin	*2 ounces*	*60 grams*
Tomato Concassé	*2 ounces*	*60 grams*
Garlic cloves, minced	*2 each*	*2 each*
Chicken Stock	*1 quart*	*1 liter*
Oysters, shucked, liquor reserved	*1 pound*	*450 grams*
Flour, toasted	*7 ounces*	*200 grams*
Garnish		
Scallions, sliced	*4 tablespoons*	*60 grams*
Long-grain rice, cooked	*1 pound*	*450 grams*

1. Disjoint the rabbit.

2. Combine the ingredients for the seasoning mix. Coat the rabbit evenly in this mixture.

3. Heat the oil in a rondeau. Add the rabbit and sear until it is evenly browned on all sides. Remove.

4. Add the onions and sweat lightly; add the pepper, celery, and scallions, Tomato Concassé, and garlic. Cover the pot and sweat until the onions are translucent.

5. Remove the cover from the pot and allow the onions to brown slightly.

6. Add the stock, bring to a simmer, return the rabbit, and cover the pot.

7. Complete cooking either on top of the oven or in a moderate oven (350°F/175°C) until the rabbit is tender.

8. Remove the rabbit from the sauce and keep it warm.

(Recipe continued on facing page)

9. Skim the surface of the sauce; reduce slightly to adjust consistency if necessary.

10. Add the rabbit to the sauce along with the oysters and the reserved liquor and simmer just until the edges of the oysters begin to curl.

11. Serve the étouffé on a bed of rice topped with sliced scallions.

Coniglio in Umido (Liquarian Rabbit Stew)

Yield: 10 servings

Rabbits, cut in pieces	*3 each*	*3 each*
Salt, to taste	*1/2 teaspoon*	*1/2 teaspoon*
Pepper, cracked	*1/2 teaspoon*	*1/2 teaspoon*
Vegetable oil	*2 fluid ounces*	*60 milliliters*
Butter	*1 ounce*	*30 grams*
Mirepoix	*1 pound*	*450 grams*
Garlic cloves, minced	*3 each*	*3 each*
Rosemary	*1/2 teaspoon*	*1/2 teaspoon*
Bay leaves	*2 each*	*2 each*
Thyme	*1/2 teaspoon*	*1/2 teaspoon*
White wine	*12 fluid ounces*	*360 milliliters*
Nutmeg, ground, to taste	*pinch*	*pinch*
Tomatoes, crushed, include juices	*1 pound*	*450 grams*
Pine nuts, toasted	*3 ounces*	*85 grams*
Brown Sauce	*12 fluid ounces*	*360 milliliters*

Liquaria is a region of Italy on the northern side of the Mediterranean.

This stew incorporates many elements of this traditional peasant cuisine: rabbits, herbs, and pine nuts. It may be preferable to reserve the pine nuts as a garnish scattered over the finished stew.

For a smoother finish, the sauce may be strained.

If the sauce is not strained, be sure to peel the Mirepoix and cut it evenly.

1. Season the rabbit with salt and pepper. Brown rabbit on all sides in oil and butter, remove; keep warm.

2. Add Mirepoix and sauté until lightly colored; add garlic, rosemary, bay leaves, thyme and pepper; sauté.

3. Add the white wine to deglaze; reduce to half of original volume.

4. Add nutmeg. Return rabbit to the pan; add tomatoes, pinenuts, and brown sauce; bring to a simmer.

5. Braise the rabbit, covered, in a 350°F (175°C) oven, until meat is fork-tender (approximately 1/2 hour). Remove the rabbit and keep warm.

6. Reduce the sauce over direct heat. Degrease sauce; season to taste with salt and pepper.

Coniglio Alla Molisanta (Rabbit, Sausage, and Prosciutto on Skewer)

Yield: 10 servings

Rabbit	*2 each*	*2 each*
Sage, leaves, chopped small	*4 each*	*4 each*
Parsley, chopped	*2 teaspoons*	*2 teaspoons*
Rosemary, chopped	*2 teaspoons*	*2 teaspoons*
Sausage, Italian, Hot	*10 each*	*10 each*
Prosciutto, sliced thin	*20 slices*	*20 slices*
Olive oil	*2 fluid ounces*	*60 milliliters*
Jus	*6 fluid ounces*	*180 milliliters*

1. Cut the rabbit meat into 1-inch (2.5-centimeter) cubes. Combine the herbs and rub into the meat; allow to marinate at least 1 hour. Reserve the bones.

2. Prepare a jus from the rabbit bones; reduce to 6 fluid ounces (180 milliliters).

3. Cut the prosciutto into strips and wrap one strip around each piece of rabbit.

4. Cut the sausage into 1-inch (2.5-centimeter) pieces.

5. Thread the rabbit and sausage on skewers (alternate rabbit and sausage meat), rub with oil.

6. Grill the skewers until just done; brush with jus.

Roast Venison with Mustard Sauce

Yield: 10 servings

Serve the roast with spaëtzle or noodles. Braised red cabbage would work well with this.

Venison roast, from loin or leg, boneless, tied	*4 pounds*	*1.8 kilograms*
Salt, to taste	*1/2 teaspoon*	*1/2 teaspoon*
Pepper, to taste	*1/2 teaspoon*	*1/2 teaspoon*
Vegetable oil, as needed	*2 fluid ounces*	*60 milliliters*
Jus de Veau Lié or Gibier Lié	*1 1/4 pints*	*600 milliliters*
Heavy cream, reduced	*8 fluid ounces*	*240 milliliters*
White wine	*2 fluid ounces*	*60 milliliters*
Creole mustard	*2 ounces*	*60 grams*

1. Season the roast with the salt and pepper. Sear it on all sides in hot oil.

2. Roast it in a moderate oven to the desired doneness. (About 140°F (60°C).)

3. Let the roast rest for 15 minutes before carving it.

4. To prepare the sauce, heat the rendered juices over direct heat. Pour off the fat.

(Recipe continued on facing page)

5. Deglaze the roasting pan with the white wine; stir it well to release the fond. Add the jus and simmer.

6. Strain the sauce into a saucepan. Add the heavy cream and mustard; simmer until it has reduced.

7. Adjust the seasoning to taste with salt and pepper.

8. Carve the roast; serve each portion with approximately 2 ounces (60 milliliters) of sauce.

VARIATIONS

Roast Venison with Garlic Glaze: Mix together 1 part Glace de Viande and 2 parts puréed roasted garlic. Spread the glaze on the roast during the final part of roasting. Serve with Mushroom Sauce, page 527.

Roast Venison with Sauce Marsala: Serve with Marsala Sauce, page 524.

Roast Venison with Tarragon Sauce: Infuse the venison stock with fresh rosemary. Finish the sauce to order with Tarragon Beurre Blanc, page 546, or Mustard Tarragon Sauce with Green Peppercorns, page 545.

Indian Grilled Buffalo

Yield: 10 servings

Marinade

Yogurt	*4 fluid ounces*	*120 milliliters*
Onions, minced	*3 ounces*	*85 grams*
Gingerroot, minced	*3/4 ounces*	*20 grams*
Garlic cloves, minced	*4 each*	*4 each*
Cumin seed, toasted and freshly ground	*1 teaspoon*	*1 teaspoon*
Pepper	*1 teaspoon*	*1 teaspoon*
Nutmeg, ground	*1/2 teaspoon*	*1/2 teaspoon*
Buffalo, round, trimmed	*3 pounds*	*1.3 kilograms*
Zucchini, sliced, grilled	*2 pounds*	*.4 kilograms*
Basmati rice, pilaf-style	*40 ounces*	*1.3 kilograms*
Mango chutney	*1 pint*	*480 milliliters*

1. Cut the meat into cubes of about 1 inch (2.5 centimeters).

2. Combine all of the ingredients for the marinade.

3. Add the buffalo meat to the marinade and coat evenly. Marinate under refrigeration for 24 hours.

4. Thread the buffalo on skewers (if using bamboo skewers, be sure to soak them in cold water before using). Grill the skewers to the desired doneness.

5. Serve the skewers with grilled zucchini slices on a bed of basmati rice with mango chutney.

Additional seasonings may be added to the recipe. Add 1 teaspoon of one of the spice blends in Chapter 13, pages 425 to 429.

Beef or pork may be substituted for the buffalo meat.

To read about grilling vegetables, see page 300. To prepare the rice pilaf, follow the recipe on pages 22 to 30.

If desired, baste the buffalo with Mango Bourbon Barbeque Sauce, page 553, as it grills.

Raita (Cucumber Yogurt Salad) (see pages 24 to 25) is a cooling accompaniment to this dish.

Calf's Liver with Bacon Cream Sauce

Yield: 10 servings

Consider a portion size of 6 to 8 ounces (170 to 225 grams) when preparing this recipe.

This dish may be garnished with crisp, fried, thinly sliced onions.

A tossed green salad is a good accompaniment to this dish.

Bacon Cream Sauce		
Bacon, diced	*1 1/4 pounds*	*570 grams*
Onions, chopped fine	*10 ounces*	*285 grams*
Heavy cream	*40 fluid ounces*	*1.2 liters*
Calves' livers, 6 to 8 ounces	*10 each*	*10 each*
Salt, to taste	*1/2 teaspoon*	*1/2 teaspoon*
Pepper, to taste	*1/4 teaspoon*	*1/4 teaspoon*
Vegetable oil or rendered bacon fat	*as needed*	*as needed*

1. Sauté the bacon until it is crisp; remove and drain it. Strain the bacon grease and reserve the fat.

2. Sauté the onions in the strained bacon fat until they are lightly browned, drain the excess fat, and add the cooked bacon.

3. Add the heavy cream and reduce to sauce consistency. Keep the sauce hot until needed.

4. Season the liver with the salt and pepper.

5. Sauté the liver in the oil or rendered bacon fat until it is medium-rare and browned on both sides.

6. Serve the liver with 2 ounces (60 grams) of Bacon Cream Sauce per serving.

Braised Oxtails

Yield: 12 servings

Oil, as needed	*2 fluid ounces*	*60 milliliters*
Oxtails, trimmed, cut in pieces	*10 pounds*	*4.5 kilograms*
Mirepoix	*1 pound*	*450 grams*
Dry red wine	*1 quart*	*1 liter*
Thyme, ground	*1 teaspoon*	*1 teaspoon*
Bay leaf	*2 each*	*2 each*
Peppercorns	*1 teaspoon*	*1 teaspoon*
Garlic cloves, minced	*3 each*	*3 each*
Parsley stems	*4 each*	*4 each*
Tomato purée	*6 fluid ounces*	*180 milliliters*
Brown Veal Stock, as needed	*1 quart*	*1 liter*

(Recipe continued on facing page)

Garnish

Carrots, tournée, cooked	48 each	48 each
Celeriac, tournée, cooked	48 each	48 each
Turnip, white, tournée, cooked	48 each	48 each
Turnip, yellow, tournée, cooked	48 each	48 each
Onion rings	6 each	6 each

To prepare Onion Rings, slice quartered onions thinly and separate them. Dredge in flour, shake off any excess, and deep-fry until crisp and deep brown.

1. Heat a large rondeau, add a small amount of oil, and sear oxtails until browned on all sides; remove, reserve.

2. Add Mirepoix and caramelize and add tomato purée; cook out for 2 to 3 minutes. Add wine, reduce by one-half, and add aromatics; return oxtails.

3. Add enough stock to come halfway up meat. Bring to a simmer, cover, and braise in a 300°F(150°C) oven until tender, turning occasionally during cooking.

4. When meat is tender, remove, cover, and keep warm, strain and degrease sauce, and reserve fat.

5. Heat the carrots, celeriac, and turnips in reserved fat.

6. Serve the oxtails surrounded by the garnish and coated with the sauce. Top with onion rings.

Smoked Beef Tongue Madeira Sauce

Yield: 10 servings

Smoked beef tongue	4 to 5 pounds	1.8 to 2.25 kilograms
Pickling spice	1 tablespoon	1 tablespoon
Jus de Veau Lié	1 1/4 pints	600 milliliters
Madeira	2 fluid ounces	60 milliliters
Butter	2 1/2 ounces	70 grams
Salt, to taste	1/2 teaspoon	1/2 teaspoon
Pepper, to taste	1/4 teaspoon	1/4 teaspoon

To read about preparing tongue, see Chapter 6, page 235.

1. Cover beef tongue with cold water and bring to a simmer. Add pickling spice.

2. Simmer until tongue is tender.

3. When tongue is soft, shock in cold water, peel outer skin, trim fat, and remove bones.

4. For sauce, reduce Jus de Veau Lié by one-third. Add Madeira and monté au beurre. Adjust with salt and pepper to taste.

5. Thinly slice the tongue. Arrange the slices on a plate and serve the sauce over the tongue.

Italian Meatballs

Yield: 10 servings

Tomato purée, fennel seeds, rosemary, and basil are other seasoning ingredients that might be added.

When combining the ingredients, handle them gently. Be careful not to overmix or compress the mixture.

A combination of ground beef, pork, and veal may be used.

To hold the meatballs for service, dish them into a hotel pan and cover with hot stock, or refrigerate.

For Italian Meat Loaf, place in loaf pan and roast in oven.

Onions, finely chopped	*1 pound*	*450 grams*
Celery, finely chopped	*6 ounces*	*170 grams*
Oil	*2 fluid ounces*	*60 milliliters*
Garlic, minced	*2 teaspoons*	*2 teaspoons*
Bread crumbs, fresh	*6 ounces*	*170 grams*
Stock or milk	*10 fluid ounces*	*300 milliliters*
Ground beef	*4 1/2 pounds*	*2 kilograms*
Eggs	*3 each*	*3 each*
Parmesan cheese, grated	*1 ounce*	*30 grams*
Parsley, finely chopped	*1/2 ounce*	*15 grams*
Oregano, minced	*1 teaspoon*	*1 teaspoon*
Salt, to taste	*1/2 teaspoon*	*1/2 teaspoon*
Pepper, to taste	*1/4 teaspoon*	*1/4 teaspoon*

1. Sauté onions and celery in oil. Add the garlic and sweat. Cool.

2. Combine bread and stock or milk in large mixing bowl; mix well. Add the remaining ingredients, including the onions, and blend thoroughly.

3. Form into balls and roast at 350°F (175°C) for about 30 minutes.

VARIATION

Swedish Meatballs: Use ground veal; omit oregano. Season with nutmeg and serve in a cream sauce with leeks.

Meat Loaf

Yield: 10 servings

White bread, 1/4-inch dice	*6 ounces*	*170 grams*
Milk, as needed	*8 fluid ounces*	*480 milliliters*
Ground beef	*3 1/2 pounds*	*1.6 kilograms*
Onions, minced, sautéed	*10 ounces*	*285 grams*
Ketchup	*6 ounces*	*180 grams*
A-1 Steak Sauce	*10 fluid ounces*	*300 milliliters*
Salt, to taste	*1/2 teaspoon*	*1/2 teaspoon*
Pepper, to taste	*1/4 teaspoon*	*1/4 teaspoon*
Eggs	*3 each*	*3 each*
Bread crumbs, fresh	*6 ounces*	*170 grams*

(Recipe continued on facing page)

1. Place cubed bread into a mixing bowl. Add milk to soak the bread. Squeeze out excess liquid; discard.

2. Add the remaining ingredients and mix gently.

3. Place in loaf pan or form into shape in a roasting pan.

4. Bake in a 350°F (175°C) oven until meat loaf is firm and evenly browned, approximately 1 1/2 hours.

VARIATIONS

Asian Meat Loaf: Replace the A-1 Steak Sauce with 2 fluid ounces (60 milliliters) of soy sauce; add diced water chestnuts; replace half the bread with cooked rice.

Italian Meat Loaf: Substitute 1 1/2 pounds (680 grams) sweet or hot Italian sausage for 1 1/2 pounds (680 grams) ground beef. Add 1/2 ounce (15 grams) of chopped parsley.

For an American classic, serve with mashed potatoes and buttered peas and carrots. Or offer Meat Loaf sandwiches on white pullman bread.

Glaze the Meat Loaf with ketchup in the final 20 minutes of roasting.

Lay parcooked bacon over the top of the meat loaf in the final 30 minutes of roasting.

This is a basic Meat Loaf. Additional seasonings, such as chopped parsley, oregano, sautéed garlic or green peppers, and chili powder can be included in the preparation.

Roast Beef Hash

Yield: 10 servings

Onions, chopped fine	*6 ounces*	*170 grams*
Celery, chopped fine	*3 ounces*	*85 grams*
Vegetable oil, as needed	*2 ounces*	*60 milliliters*
Potatoes, cooked, 3/8-inch dice	*2 pounds*	*900 grams*
Roast beef, cooked and chopped	*2 pounds*	*900 grams*
Salt, to taste	*1/2 teaspoon*	*1/2 teaspoon*
Pepper, to taste	*1/4 teaspoon*	*1/4 teaspoon*

1. Sauté onions and celery in oil in a hot skillet until tender.

2. Add the potatoes and roast beef and heat thoroughly. Season with salt and pepper to taste.

Preparation notes: The onions and celery may be cooled down and added to the potatoes and roast beef. Pan-fry in hot frying pan with very little oil at service time. Hash should be golden brown. Top with a poached egg, if desired.

Hash may be prepared in advance, portioned and fried as above and placed on a sheet pan. Immediately prior to service, heat in the oven and top with poached egg.

Any beef or other meat may be substituted for the roast beef. This is a good use of wholesome usable trim from roasted meats.

C H A P T E R 17 : *Poultry Entrées*

It was once a sign of great prosperity to be able to provide a meal that included chicken. Today, this enormously adaptable bird is prepared in almost endless ways. In this chapter, you will find chicken recipes for

- *Sautéed and Pan-Fried*
- *Roasted*
- *Grilled and Broiled*
- *Braised and Stewed*

In addition you will find recipes for:

- *Game Birds*
- *Turkey*

Remember to review the options in Chapter 20, as well.

Chicken Provençal

Yield: 10 servings

Dishes referred to as "provençal" typically include olive oil, garlic, and herbs. Provence is a region of France along the Mediterranean.

For more information about sautéeing, read Chapter 8, pages 316 to 319.

Tomato Concassé is explained in Chapter 6, page 191.

Chicken suprêmes	*10 each*	*10 each*
Salt, to taste	*1/2 teaspoon*	*1/2 teaspoon*
Pepper, to taste	*1/4 teaspoon*	*1/4 teaspoon*
Flour, as needed	*3 ounces*	*85 grams*
Vegetable oil, as needed	*3 fluid ounces*	*90 milliliters*
Butter	*5 ounces*	*140 grams*
Garlic cloves, minced	*3 each*	*3 each*
White wine	*10 fluid ounces*	*300 milliliters*
Tomato Concassé	*1 3/4 pound*	*800 grams*
Black olives, sliced or julienne	*4 ounces*	*115 grams*
Anchovy fillets, mashed to a paste	*3 each*	*3 each*
Basil, chiffonade	*2 tablespoons*	*2 tablespoons*

1. Season the chicken suprêmes with salt and pepper. Dredge them lightly with the flour, shaking off excess.

2. Heat the vegetable oil in a sauté pan and sauté the chicken breasts until golden brown and cooked through. Remove the breasts from the pan and keep warm.

3. Pour off excess fat from the sauté pan; add the butter. Return the pan to the heat. Add the garlic to the melted butter and sauté it briefly.

4. Deglaze the pan with the wine, stirring well to release all of the drippings. Add the Tomato Concassé, olives, and anchovy paste. Bring this mixture to a simmer and cook it for a few minutes or until the flavor is developed.

5. Return the chicken breasts along with any released juices to the sauté pan and toss to coat the chicken with the sauce.

6. Serve the chicken with the sauce on a heated plate. Garnish with the basil.

VARIATION

Olives, Capers, and Chicken Breast with Herbs: You may elect to use different olives in this dish, introduce some capers, add other herbs, either in addition to or as a replacement for the basil. Oregano, marjoram, chives, chervil, and thyme are all good choices.

Chicken Suprêmes with Fines Herbes Sauce

Yield: 10 servings

Chicken suprêmes	*10 each*	*10 each*
Salt, to taste	*1/2 teaspoon*	*1/2 teaspoon*
Pepper, to taste	*1/4 teaspoon*	*1/4 teaspoon*
Flour (optional)	*3 ounces*	*85 grams*
Clarified butter, as needed	*2 ounces*	*60 grams*
Shallots, minced	*2 tablespoons*	*2 tablespoons*
Dry white wine	*12 fluid ounces*	*360 milliliters*
Chicken Stock	*14 fluid ounces*	*360 milliliters*
Glace de Volaille	*3 ounces*	*90 milliliters*
Heavy cream	*6 fluid ounces*	*180 milliliters*
Fine herbes	*2 ounces*	*60 grams*

1. Blot chicken suprêmes to dry. Season well. Dredge in flour, if desired.

2. Sauté the chicken in the clarified butter until almost cooked through. Remove and keep warm.

3. Degrease the pan. Add the shallots and sauté them until they are translucent.

4. Deglaze the pan with the white wine; reduce the sauce au sec.

5. Add the stock and Glace de Volaille.

6. Add the cream; reduce the sauce until thickened.

7. Add the Fines Herbes and adjust the sauce's consistency by additional reduction if necessary. Serve the sauce over the chicken.

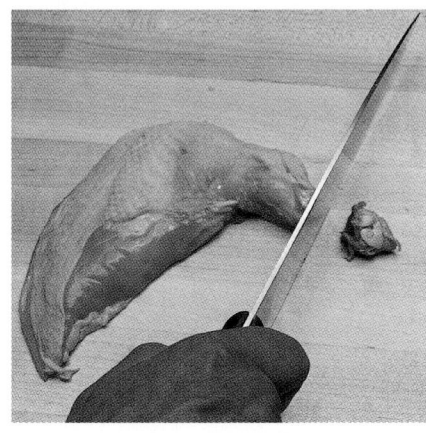

To prepare a suprême: Leave one wing-joint, frenched, attached to the meat. Preferred cooking techniques include sautéing, shallow poaching, and grilling.

"Fines herbes" is a French term for a classic herb combination of tarragon, parsley, chive, and chervil. Herb combinations may be found in Chapter 13 on page 427.

The recipe for Chicken Stock is on page 442; Glace de Volaille, page 438.

Breast of Chicken Chardonnay

Yield: 10 servings

Chicken suprêmes are the boneless breast with one wing bone (usually frenched) still attached. For more information and illustrations of preparing suprêmes, refer to Chapter 6, page 243, and page 623.

For a stronger mustard flavor, add 1 tablespoon of prepared Dijon mustard with the mustard seeds.

Serve with spaëtzle or egg noodles.

Chicken suprêmes	10 each	10 each
Salt, to taste	1/2 teaspoon	1/2 teaspoon
Pepper, to taste	1/4 teaspoon	1/4 teaspoon
Flour, as needed	3 ounces	85 grams
Clarified butter, as needed	3 ounces	85 grams
Mushrooms, sliced	2 pounds	900 grams
Chardonnay	1 pint	480 milliliters
Chicken Stock, reduced	1 1/2 pints	720 milliliters
Heavy cream	12 fluid ounces	360 milliliters
Mustard seeds	1 tablespoon	1 tablespoon
Leeks, cut into triangles, blanched	1 1/4 pound	570 grams

1. Dry the chicken, season with salt and pepper, and dredge in flour.

2. Sauté the chicken in the clarified butter until done. Remove the chicken and keep it warm.

3. Sauté the mushrooms in the same pan.

4. Deglaze the pan with the wine; add the stock and reduce it by half.

5. Add the heavy cream and reduce the sauce by half.

6. Add the mustard seeds and reduce until thickened.

7. Add the leeks and heat them through. Serve the sauce over the chicken.

Sautéed Chicken Breast with Tarragon Sauce

Yield: 10 servings

Chicken breasts	*10 each*	*10 each*
Salt, to taste	*1/2 teaspoon*	*1/2 teaspoon*
Pepper, to taste	*1/4 teaspoon*	*1/4 teaspoon*
Flour, as needed	*3 ounces*	*85 grams*
Clarified butter, as needed	*3 ounces*	*85 grams*
Shallots, minced	*2 teaspoons*	*2 teaspoons*
Dry white wine	*10 fluid ounces*	*300 milliliters*
Demi-Glace or Jus de Volaille	*1 1/2 pints*	*720 milliliters*
Tarragon, chopped coarse	*2 tablespoons*	*2 tablespoons*
Butter, diced	*3 ounces*	*85 grams*

The recipe for Demi-Glace is on page 522. The Jus de Volaille is a variation of Jus de Veau Lié, page 523.

One cup of flour weighs 3 1/2 ounces (100 grams). A scant cup is generally enough to coat 10 chicken breasts adequately.

1. Season the chicken with salt and pepper; dredge it in the flour if desired.

2. Sauté the chicken in the clarified butter until golden. Finish in the oven.

3. Degrease the sauté pan.

4. Add the shallots and sweat them. Do not brown them.

5. Deglaze the pan with the white wine and reduce to sec.

6. Add the Demi-Glace or jus; simmer it until the sauce has the proper consistency.

7. Add the chopped tarragon; finish the sauce with the whole butter.

8. Serve the sauce with the chicken.

Breast of Chicken with Mushroom and Ham Stuffing

Yield: 10 servings

The recipe for Sauce Suprême is on page 534.

You can use fresh white bread crumbs to tighten the stuffing. In that case, omit the flour.

The standard breading procedure is explained on pages 322 to 323.

Stuffing

Onions, minced	1 ounce	30 grams
Butter	1 ounce	30 grams
Mushrooms, minced	12 ounces	340 grams
Dry white wine	4 fluid ounces	120 milliliters
Flour	1 tablespoon	1 tablespoon
Heavy cream	4 fluid ounces	120 milliliters
Ham, minced	4 ounces	115 grams
Parsley, chopped	1 tablespoon	1 tablespoon
Salt, to taste	1/2 teaspoon	1/2 teaspoon
White pepper, to taste	1/4 teaspoon	1/4 teaspoon
Chicken breasts	10 each	10 each
Salt, to taste	1/2 teaspoon	1/2 teaspoon
Pepper, to taste	1/4 teaspoon	1/4 teaspoon
Flour, as needed	4 ounces	115 grams
Bread crumbs, dry, as needed	6 ounces	170 grams
Walnuts, chopped	2 ounces	60 grams
Egg wash, as needed	6 fluid ounces	180 milliliters
Clarified butter, as needed	2 ounces	60 grams
Sauce Suprême, heated	1 1/2 pints	720 milliliters

1. To prepare the stuffing: Sweat the onion in the butter. Add the mushrooms and sauté briefly. Add the wine and reduce by half. Add the flour and cook for 3 minutes.

2. Add the heavy cream, ham, and parsley. Bring the mixture to a boil. Remove the mixture from the heat. Adjust the seasoning with the salt and white pepper. Cool.

3. Flatten the chicken breasts with a mallet. Season with salt and pepper and dredge in flour; shake off the excess.

4. Place 2 tablespoons of stuffing on each suprême. Roll it up tightly. If necessary, cover each suprême with more breading. Chill for 30 minutes.

5. Combine the bread crumbs and chopped walnuts. Bread the chicken using the standard breading procedure.

6. Pan-fry the chicken in clarified butter until golden on all sides. Finish the chicken in a moderate oven (350°F/175°C). Serve with the sauce suprême.

Chicken Suprême Maréchal

Yield: 10 servings

Chicken breasts, boneless and skinless	10 each	10 each
Salt, to taste	1/2 teaspoon	1/2 teaspoon
Pepper, to taste	1/4 teaspoon	1/4 teaspoon
Flour, as needed	3 ounces	85 grams
Egg wash, as needed	6 fluid ounces	180 milliliters
Bread crumbs, dry, as needed	8 ounces	225 grams
Vegetable oil, as needed	5 fluid ounces	150 milliliters
Sauce Suprême, heated	1 1/2 pints	720 milliliters
White asparagus, tips only, blanched	30 each	30 each
Black truffles, sliced thinly	10 each	10 each

The recipe for Sauce Suprême is on page 534.

White asparagus is specially grown. As the spears emerge from the ground, soil is mounded around them. This prevents the plant's development of chlorophyll (the element responsible for green plants' color.)

Use the remaining trim from the asparagus to prepare Cream of Asparagus Soup, page 466.

1. Trim each breast and pound lightly to an even thickness. Season the chicken breasts with salt and pepper; bread according to the standard breading procedure.

2. Pan-fry breasts in hot oil. If necessary, finish in the oven.

3. Reheat the sauce, as needed, to order. Serve the chicken with the sauce, asparagus tips, and a truffle slice.

VARIATIONS

Pan-Fried Chicken Breast with Fresh Tomato Coulis: Replace the Sauce Suprême with Tomato Coulis (page 551). Garnish each portion with basil chiffonade.

Pan-Fried Chicken Breast with Eggplant: Pan-fry the chicken as directed above. Top each portion with slices of grilled eggplant and mozzarella. Heat briefly in a hot oven and serve with Tomato Sauce (page 538).

Southern Fried Chicken with Country Style Gravy

Yield: 8 servings

Chickens (fryers)	*4 each*	*4 each*
Salt, as needed	*1 teaspoon*	*1 teaspoon*
Pepper, as needed	*1 teaspoon*	*1 teaspoon*
Buttermilk	*1 quart*	*1 liter*
Dijon mustard	*4 ounces*	*115 grams*
Tarragon leaves, chopped	*1 tablespoon*	*1 tablespoon*
Flour, as needed	*8 ounces*	*225 grams*
Vegetable oil	*1 pint*	*240 milliliters*
Milk	*24 fluid ounces*	*360 milliliters*

The technique for cutting a chicken into eighths is shown in Chapter 6, pages 238 to 239.

The traditional accompaniments are whipped potatoes and biscuits.

Southern Fried Chicken may also be served cold with potato salad and cole slaw.

1. Cut chicken in eighths, trim, and season well with salt and pepper to taste.

2. Combine buttermilk, mustard, and tarragon. Add chicken pieces and turn until coated evenly. Let chicken pieces marinate for at least 4 hours, up to overnight.

3. Remove the chicken from the buttermilk and let it drain.

4. Roll the chicken in flour until well coated.

5. Heat the oil in a rondeau. Add the chicken pieces without crowding. Cook, turning occasionally, until well browned and cooked through.

6. Remove the chicken from the oil; drain on absorbent toweling.

7. Pour off most of the oil from the pan, leaving about 2 ounces (60 milliliters) in the pan. Add 2 ounces (60 grams) of flour to make a roux. Cook the roux for 5 to 6 minutes.

8. Add the milk, stirring well to remove all lumps. Let this gravy simmer at least 15 minutes. Adjust seasoning with salt and fresh ground pepper.

9. Serve the chicken with the gravy.

VARIATIONS

Chicken-Fried Steak with "Cream" Gravy: Substitute 8 steaks (shell, top round, or chuck) for the chicken. The steaks should weigh 4 to 5 ounces (115 to 140 grams) per portion. Marinate the steaks in buttermilk (omit the mustard and tarragon) or "swiss" the steaks by flouring and pounding them until tender. Fry them as directed above. The gravy is prepared in the same manner, with plenty of salt and fresh ground pepper. Serve with mashed potatoes.

Chicken-Fried Chicken: This is prepared like Chicken-Fried Steak, using 8 pounded chicken breasts in place of the steak.

Roast Chicken with Pan Gravy

Yield: 10 servings

Chickens, wing tips removed	*5 each*	*5 each*
Salt, to taste	*3/4 teaspoon*	*3/4 teaspoon*
White pepper, to taste	*1/2 teaspoon*	*1/2 teaspoon*
Thyme, sprigs	*5 each*	*5 each*
Rosemary, sprigs	*5 each*	*5 each*
Garlic cloves, bruised	*5 each*	*5 each*
Bay leaves	*5 each*	*5 each*
Chervil, sprigs	*10 each*	*10 each*
Vegetable oil, as needed	*2 fluid ounces*	*60 milliliters*
Mirepoix, diced	*8 ounces*	*225 grams*
Flour	*2 ounces*	*60 grams*
Chicken Stock, hot	*1 pint*	*480 milliliters*
Tomato paste (optional)	*1/2 ounce*	*15 grams*

The recipe for Chicken Stock may be found on page 442.

Serve with whipped potatoes or roasted potatoes seasoned with garlic and rosemary.

1. Season chicken, and place thyme, rosemary, garlic, bay leaves and chervil in the cavity of each bird.

2. Rub skin with oil; truss chickens with twine.

3. Place chicken, breast side up, on a rack in a roasting pan.

4. Roast at 375°F (190°C) until the thigh meat registers an internal temperature of 150°F (65°). Add the Mirepoix after the chicken has roasted 30 to 40 minutes.

5. Remove chicken and Mirepoix and allow the chicken to rest.

6. Clarify fat in the roasting pan; discard all but 3 ounces (90 milliliters).

7. Add flour, cook out roux, incorporate stock, and whisk until smooth.

8. Simmer gravy until proper consistency and flavor is reached; degrease thoroughly.

9. Strain the gravy through a fine chinoise, season to taste.

10. Carve the chicken into portions and serve with gravy.

Poêlé of Capon with Tomatoes and Artichokes

Yield: 10 servings

The recipe for Matignon can be found on page 420.

Advance preparation techniques for Tomato Concassé and artichoke bottoms can be found in Chapter 6.

Parsley, chives, chervil, and tarragon make up the classic herb blend, fines herbes. For other herb blends, see Chapter 13.

Capon (12 pounds)	1 each	1 each
Salt, to taste	1 teaspoon	1 teaspoon
Pepper, to taste	1/2 teaspoon	1/2 teaspoon
Fresh herbs, as available or desired	1 bunch	1 bunch
Matignon	8 ounces	225 grams
Butter, as needed	2 ounces	60 grams
Chicken Stock or Jus de Volaille Lié	1 quart	1 liter
Arrowroot	2 teaspoons	2 teaspoons
Tomato Concassé	8 ounces	225 grams
Artichoke bottoms, poached and sliced	8 ounces	225 grams
Parsley, chopped	2 tablespoons	2 tablespoons
Chives, chopped	2 tablespoons	2 tablespoons
Chervil, chopped	2 tablespoons	2 tablespoons
Tarragon, chopped	2 tablespoons	2 tablespoons

1. Season the bird with the salt and pepper and stuff the cavity with a bundle of the fresh herbs. Truss the bird.

2. Sweat the Matignon in butter. Arrange the capon on the Matignon. Brush liberally with butter. Cover it in a casserole and poêlé the bird in a moderate (350°F/175°C) oven for approximately 2 hours, or until it is fully cooked; internal temperature of the thigh should be approximately 140°F (60°C). Remove the cover during the final half-hour of cooking time to brown the skin.

3. Place the casserole on direct heat and bring the liquid to a boil; let it reduce slightly.

4. Add the Chicken Stock or Jus de Volaille Lié and bring the mixture to a boil.

5. Dilute the arrowroot and add it to the stock to thicken the stock lightly. Add the Tomato Concassé, artichoke bottoms, and chopped herbs. Adjust the seasoning to taste. Skim the excess butter from the surface as necessary.

6. Carve the capon and serve it with the sauce.

VARIATIONS

Poêlé Poussins: Substitute poussins (baby chickens) or squash for the capon. Use one or two per portion, depending upon the bird's size.

Poêlé of Rabbit with Prunes: Substitute approximately 5 rabbits for the capon. Each rabbit will make 2 servings. Substitute 1 pound (450 grams) of prunes plumped in cognac for the tomatoes and artichokes.

Pan-Smoked Chicken with Apples and Green Peppercorns

Yield: 10 servings

Chicken breast cutlets	*10 each*	*10 each*
Marinade		
Apple cider	*8 fluid ounces*	*240 milliliters*
Apple cider vinegar	*2 fluid ounces*	*60 milliliters*
Shallots, minced	*1/2 ounce*	*15 grams*
Garlic cloves, minced	*3 each*	*3 each*
Reduction		
Apple cider	*1 pint*	*480 milliliters*
Shallots	*3/4 ounce*	*20 grams*
Garlic, cloves	*3 each*	*3 each*
Green peppercorns	*3/4 ounce*	*20 grams*
Jus de Veau Lié	*1 1/2 pints*	*720 milliliters*
Apples, peeled and sliced	*3 each*	*3 each*

1. Lightly pound chicken cutlets, pat dry, and place in shallow hotel pan.

2. Combine ingredients for the marinade, pour over the chicken, turn to coat evenly. Marinate under refrigeration for up to 3 hours.

3. Make the reduction to flavor the sauce by combining the cider, shallots, garlic, and peppercorns until reduced to about 2 ounces (60 milliliters).

4. Add the Jus de Veau Lié, bring to a simmer, and reduce slightly to proper consistency.

5. Place the chicken on a rack, and set it in a pan over lightly dampened hardwood chips. Cover tightly and heat until the smell of smoke is apparent. Pan-smoke for 3 minutes from that point.

6. Remove the chicken from the pan. Finish cooking by grilling or baking.

7. Add the apples to the sauce, adding apple cider to thin if necessary.

8. To serve, arrange sliced chicken on a plate over apples and sauce.

Use disposable pans to create a smoke roaster.

Use cutlets that are 4 to 5 ounces (115 to 140 grams) each.

Jus de Veau Lié may be found on page 523.

The set up for pan-smoking may be found in Chapter 9 on page 306.

Granny Smith apples will give a tart-sweet flavor to this dish.

Smoked Chicken Breast with Barbecue Sauce

Yield: 10 servings

Either of the Barbeque Sauces in Chapter 15 (pages 552 and 553) would be good on the chicken.

Chicken breast	*10 each*	*10 each*
Marinade		
Fresh apple cider	*8 fluid ounces*	*240 milliliters*
Cider vinegar	*1 fluid ounce*	*30 milliliters*
Shallots, minced	*1/2 ounce*	*15 grams*
Garlic, minced	*1/2 teaspoon*	*1/2 teaspoon*
Barbecue Sauce, as needed	*1 1/2 pints*	*720 milliliters*

1. Place the chicken breasts in a pan or shallow bowl. Combine the ingredients for the marinade. Pour the marinade over the breasts; let the poultry marinate for 1 to 2 hours.

2. Pan-smoke the chicken breasts until the surface turns light golden, 2 to 3 minutes; finish it in a moderate oven (350°F/175°C). Or, grill the chicken, turning it frequently and basting it occasionally with Barbecue Sauce until it is done.

3. Heat the remaining Barbecue Sauce and thin it with a little stock, if necessary. Serve the chicken breasts with the sauce.

V A R I A T I O N

Cumin-Lime Grilled Chicken: Use the Cumin-Lime Marinade (page 431) to replace the marinade. Grill or bake the chicken if you would rather not pan-smoke it. Omit the Barbeque Sauce.

Chicken Legs with Duxelles

Yield: 10 servings

Chicken legs, whole	10 each	10 each
Shallots, minced	6 ounces	170 grams
Clarified butter	2 ounces	60 grams
Mushrooms, small dice	2 pounds	900 grams
Salt, to taste	1 teaspoon	1 teaspoon
Pepper, to taste	1/2 teaspoon	1/2 teaspoon
Heavy cream, reduced	8 fluid ounces	240 milliliters
Bread crumbs, fresh	8 ounces	225 grams
Parsley, chopped	2 teaspoons	2 teaspoons
Butter, melted, as needed	2 ounces	60 grams
Sauce Suprême, heated	1 1/2 pints	720 milliliters

For method for boning chicken legs is illustrated on page 242.

The recipe for Sauce Suprême is on page 534.

1. Bone out the chicken legs. Pound flat with mallet and chill.

2. To make the Duxelles, sweat the shallots in the clarified butter. Add the mushrooms and sauté them until dry. Season with salt and pepper.

3. Add the heavy cream, bread crumbs, and parsley to the Duxelles. Combine well and chill.

4. Portion 3 ounces (85 grams) of the stuffing mixture onto each chicken leg. Fold the meat over the stuffing.

5. Brush each chicken leg with melted butter.

6. Bake the legs at 375°F (190°C) until they have an internal temperature of 140°F (60°C).

7. To serve, pool 2 ounces (60 milliliters) of Sauce Suprême on a heated plate; place a chicken leg on top of the sauce.

Breast of Cornish Game Hen

Yield: 10 servings

After removing the suprêmes from the birds, you should have about 1/2 pound (225 grams) of lean meat to prepare the filling. If necessary, augment with additional chicken leg meat.

The recipe for Jus de Volaille Lié is a variation of Jus de Veau Lié, page 523. Add thyme, sage, and bay leaf to the sachet.

Cornish game hens	*10 each*	*10 each*
Forcemeat filling		
Bacon, minced	*2 1/2 ounces*	*70 grams*
Butter	*6 ounces*	*170 grams*
Mushrooms, domestic, minced	*10 ounces*	*285 grams*
Morels, minced	*10 ounces*	*285 grams*
Shallots, minced	*2 teaspoons*	*2 teaspoons*
Garlic cloves, minced	*2 each*	*2 each*
Thyme, sprigs	*5 each*	*5 each*
Bay leaves	*2 1/2 each*	*2 1/2 each*
Sage, leaves	*5 each*	*5 each*
Madeira	*4 fluid ounces*	*120 milliliters*
Egg white	*4 ounces*	*115 grams*
Heavy cream	*10 fluid ounces*	*300 milliliters*
Salt, to taste	*1/2 teaspoon*	*1/2 teaspoon*
Pepper, to taste	*1/4 teaspoon*	*1/4 teaspoon*
Jus de Volaille Lié	*1 1/2 pints*	*720 milliliters*

1. Make suprêmes from the Cornish game hens.

2. Cut all leg meat and other lean trim away from the carcass. Trim well, cut into dice. Refrigerate until needed.

3. Render the bacon in a sauteuse over medium heat. Add 3/4 ounce (22 grams) of the butter and heat. Add the mushrooms and sweat until barely tender.

4. Add the shallots and garlic and sauté. Add the thyme, bay leaves, sage, and Madeira. Reduce until thickened. Discard the bay leaves, thyme, and sage. Chill the mixture to below 40°F (4°C).

5. Process the diced game hen in a food processor to a paste (20 to 30 seconds). Scrape down the sides of the bowl. Add the heavy cream and pulse until just incorporated.

6. Remove the leg meat to a bowl. Fold in the cooled mushroom mixture and season with salt and pepper.

7. Loosen the skin from the breast meat. Pipe about 2 ounces (60 grams) of the meat/mushroom mixture between the skin and breast meat on each side of the breast. Smooth out the surface to spread filling evenly.

8. Place the suprêmes in a baking dish. Brush them lightly with the remaining butter and season well with salt and pepper. Bake at 350°F (175°C) oven for 25 minutes or to an internal temperature of 140°F (60°C).

9. To serve, slice the breast on a slight diagonal into 4 slices. Fan the slices out on a warm plate. Serve with heated jus.

Breast of Chicken with Oyster Stuffing and Roasted Garlic Sauce

Yield: 10 servings

Chicken breasts	*10 each*	*10 each*
Salt, to taste	*1/2 teaspoon*	*1/2 teaspoon*
Pepper, to taste	*1/4 teaspoon*	*1/4 teaspoon*
Stuffing		
Butter	*1 ounce*	*30 grams*
Scallions, fine dice	*3 each*	*3 each*
Red pepper, fine dice	*3 ounces*	*85 grams*
Green pepper, fine dice	*3 ounces*	*85 grams*
Celery stalk, fine dice	*1 each*	*1 each*
Oysters, shucked, juices reserved	*20 each*	*20 each*
Cornbread	*6 ounces*	*170 grams*
Tomato paste	*1 ounce*	*30 grams*
Garlic cloves, roasted	*3 each*	*3 each*
Red wine	*4 fluid ounces*	*120 milliliters*
Jus de Veau Lié	*1 pint*	*480 milliliters*
Heavy cream	*3 fluid ounces*	*90 milliliters*

To read about roasting garlic, refer to Chapter 6, page 191.

The recipe for Jus de Veau Lié may be found on page 523.

1. Cut a pocket in each chicken breast from the wing end. Season with salt and pepper.

2. For the stuffing: Heat the butter in a sauteuse. Add the scallions, red and green peppers, and celery; sweat. Remove them from the heat.

3. Poach oysters gently for about 1 minute, just until the edges begin to curl. Remove the oysters from the liquor. Reserve the oyster liquor. Dice the oysters and reserve.

4. Crumble the cornbread and combine it with the oysters and liquor. Season the stuffing with pepper.

5. Place a portion of the oyster stuffing into each breast, stuffing loosely into the pocket.

6. Bake the chicken breasts at 350°F (175°C) until juices from the breasts run clear when pierced with a skewer.

7. To prepare the sauce, combine the tomato paste and garlic in a saucepan over high heat; sauté briefly.

8. Add the red wine and reduce until nearly dry.

9. Add the Jus de Veau Lié and reduce it.

10. Add the heavy cream. Continue to simmer the sauce until thickened.

11. To serve the chicken, remove and discard the skin. Add any pan juices to the sauce. Slice the breasts into medallions and place them on warm plates, nappé with the sauce, and serve immediately.

Grilled Paillards of Chicken with Tarragon Butter

Yield: 10 servings

To prepare Tarragon Butter, proceed as for Maître d'Hôtel Butter (page 541), substituting tarragon for the parsley.

To read more about grilling, refer to Chapter 9, pages 300 to 305.

Chicken paillards	*10 each*	*10 each*
Oil	*2 fluid ounces*	*60 milliliters*
Salt, to taste	*1 teaspoon*	*1 teaspoon*
Pepper, to taste	*1/2 teaspoon*	*1/2 teaspoon*
Lemon juice	*2 teaspoons*	*2 teaspoons*
Tarragon, fresh, chopped	*2 teaspoons*	*2 teaspoons*
Tarragon Butter	*1 tablespoon*	*1 tablespoon*

1. Trim and lightly pound the chicken paillards. Combine the oil, salt, pepper, lemon juice, and tarragon, and brush the mixture on the chicken.

2. Grill the chicken until it is barely cooked through.

3. Top each paillard with a rosette or a slice of the tarragon butter and serve it immediately.

VARIATIONS

Grilled Chicken Sandwich: Serve the chicken on a sliced baguette or club roll. Garnish the sandwich as desired.

Grilled Chicken with Basil and Fresh Mozzarella: Grill the chicken as indicated in the recipe, substituting chopped, fresh basil for the tarragon in the marinade. Top each grilled paillard with a fresh basil leaf and a slice of fresh mozzarella. Place the chicken under a broiler briefly before serving.

Grilled Chicken Fajitas: Add ground cumin and chili powder to the marinade. Slice the chicken breasts on a diagonal. Serve them with steamed flour tortillas, salsa, chopped onions, tomato, lettuce, and other condiments as desired.

Grilled Chicken Breast with Fennel

Yield: 10 servings

Marinade

Olive oil	*4 ounces*	*120 milliliters*
Garlic cloves, crushed	*3 each*	*3 each*
Fennel seeds, cracked	*1/4 teaspoon*	*1/4 teaspoon*
Salt, to taste	*1/2 teaspoon*	*1/2 teaspoon*
Pepper, to taste	*1/4 teaspoon*	*1/4 teaspoon*
Chicken breasts, pounded	*10 each*	*10 each*
Shallots, minced	*1 tablespoon*	*1 tablespoon*
Butter, as needed	*2 ounces*	*60 grams*
Fennel, julienne and cooked	*10 ounces*	*285 grams*
Sun-dried tomatoes, julienne	*2 ounces*	*60 grams*
Lemon juice, to taste	*2 teaspoons*	*2 teaspoons*
Salt, to taste	*1/4 teaspoon*	*1/4 teaspoon*
Pepper, to taste	*1/8 teaspoon*	*1/8 teaspoon*

This is an oil-and-spice marinade. To learn more about marinades, read Chapter 6, pages 209 to 210.

Instead of a marinade, rub the chicken breasts with a spice blend, such as those in Chapter 13, pages 425 to 429.

Serve with rice.

1. Combine the olive oil, garlic, fennel seeds, salt, and pepper. Add the chicken and marinate briefly.

2. Grill the chicken breast, basting it occasionally with marinade until it is done.

3. Sweat the shallots in the butter. Add the fennel and sun-dried tomatoes; sauté it until heated through.

4. Season the fennel to taste with lemon juice, salt, and pepper.

5. Serve the chicken on a bed of fennel. Garnish it with fennel leaves, if desired.

Grilled Chicken with Black Bean Sauce

Yield: 10 servings

The recipe for Barbeque Spice Blend is on page 425. Or use the Chili Powder Blend, also on page 425.

You may prefer to grill the breasts still on the bone. To make presentation neater, however, remove the bones before plating the chicken.

Top the chicken with Fresh Tomato Salsa (page 267) and sour cream. Garnish with a wedge of lime.

Chicken breasts	10 each	10 each
Barbecue Spice Blend	2 ounces	60 grams
Black Bean Sauce		
Bacon slices, minced	3 each	3 each
Onions, diced	3 ounces	85 grams
Garlic cloves, minced	3 each	3 each
Oregano, chopped	1/4 teaspoon	1/4 teaspoon
Cumin seeds, toasted and ground	1/2 teaspoon	1/2 teaspoon
Jalapeños, chopped	1/2 teaspoon	1/2 teaspoon
Dried chili, toasted	1 each	1 each
Chicken stock	4 fluid ounces	120 milliliters
Black beans, cooked	10 ounces	285 grams
Sun-dried tomatoes, chopped	1/2 ounce	15 grams
Salt, to taste	1/2 teaspoon	1/2 teaspoon
Lemon juice, to taste	1 fluid ounce	30 milliliters
Sherry wine vinegar	1 teaspoon	1 teaspoon

1. Rub the chicken with the spice blend. Let marinate about 2 hours.

2. For Black Bean Sauce, render bacon; add onion, garlic, oregano, cumin, jalapeños, and chili.

3. Add stock, beans, and sun-dried tomatoes and cook an additional 10 to 15 minutes. Remove chili and discard.

4. Purée one-third of the beans. Add purée back to the sauce. Season to taste with lemon juice, vinegar, salt, and pepper.

5. Serve the chicken on a pool of the Black Bean Sauce.

Asian-Style Broiled Chicken Breast

Yield: 10 servings

The recipe for Asian-Style Marinade is on page 430; Scallion Butter is on page 548.

Serve on a bed of Cilantro Lime Rice, page 832.

Chicken breasts, boneless, skin on	10 each	10 each
Salt, to taste	1/2 teaspoon	1/2 teaspoon
Pepper, to taste	1/4 teaspoon	1/4 teaspoon
Asian-Style Marinade	1 pint	480 milliliters
Scallion Butter, 10 slices	5 ounces	140 grams

(Recipe continued on facing page)

1. Season chicken breasts and place in marinade for up to 3 hours. Remove and drain.

2. Broil on medium heat until done.

3. Turn at 45-degree angles during broiling to achieve grill marks.

4. Serve with Scallion Butter.

Broiled Chicken Tex Mex

Yield: 10 servings

Compound butter

Butter, softened	*10 ounces*	*285 grams*
Cilantro, chopped	*3 ounces*	*85 grams*
Garlic, minced	*1 teaspoon*	*1 teaspoon*
Jalapeño peppers, chopped fine	*1 teaspoon*	*1 teaspoon*
Chili powder	*3/4 teaspoon*	*3/4 teaspoon*
Cumin, ground	*3/4 teaspoon*	*3/4 teaspoon*
Salt, to taste	*1/2 teaspoon*	*1/2 teaspoon*
Pepper, to taste	*1/2 teaspoon*	*1/2 teaspoon*
Lime juice	*2 fluid ounces*	*60 milliliters*
Tequila (optional)	*1 fluid ounce*	*30 milliliters*
Chicken breasts, bone in	*10 each*	*10 each*

Marinade

Vegetable oil	*4 fluid ounces*	*120 milliliters*
Vinegar (optional)	*2 fluid ounces*	*60 milliliters*
Lime juice	*2 fluid ounces*	*60 milliliters*
Cilantro, chopped	*1 tablespoon*	*1 tablespoon*
Garlic, minced	*1 teaspoon*	*1 teaspoon*
Jalapeño peppers, chopped fine	*1 tablespoon*	*1 tablespoon*
Chili powder	*1 teaspoon*	*1 teaspoon*
Cumin, ground	*1 teaspoon*	*1 teaspoon*
Salt, to taste	*1/2 teaspoon*	*1/2 teaspoon*
Pepper, to taste	*1/4 teaspoon*	*1/4 teaspoon*

The method for preparing a Compound Butter is illustrated on pages 295–296.

1. Mix all compound butter ingredients together, roll up in parchment paper or plastic wrap and chill.

2. Combine all ingredients for the marinade, pour over the chicken breasts, and marinate 1 to 2 hours under refrigeration.

3. Drain chicken breasts; place on grids of a preheated hot broiler.

4. Mark and turn chicken at a 45° angle, mark and turn over; finish cooking on the lower temperature side of the broiler.

5. Garnish chicken breast with a slice of compound butter.

Chicken Fricassée

Yield: 10 servings

This dish has the best flavor when prepared with a stewing hen. Increase the cooking time to 1 1/2 hours.

Chickens, whole	2 each	2 each
Salt, to taste	1/2 teaspoon	1/2 teaspoon
Pepper, to taste	1/4 teaspoon	1/4 teaspoon
Vegetable oil	4 fluid ounces	120 milliliters
Onions, diced	1 pound	450 grams
Garlic cloves, minced	2 each	2 each
Flour	2 ounces	60 grams
Dry white wine	8 fluid ounces	240 milliliters
Chicken Stock	1 pint	480 milliliters
Bay leaves	2 each	2 each
Thyme leaves	1 teaspoon	1 teaspoon
Heavy cream	8 fluid ounces	240 milliliters
Carrots, diced and blanched	1 pound	450 grams
Leeks, diced and blanched	1 pound	450 grams

1. Cut chicken into pieces. Rinse and blot dry. Season well with the salt and pepper.

2. Heat the oil and sauté the chicken until it stiffens slightly, but does not brown. Remove and reserve.

3. Add the onions and garlic to the pan; cover and sweat.

4. Add the flour to the pan and cook, stirring frequently, for about 5 minutes.

5. Add the wine, Chicken Stock, bay leaves, and thyme. Bring to a simmer and return the chicken, along with released juices.

6. Cover the pan and braise the chicken until it is fork tender, about 35 to 45 minutes.

7. To finish the sauce, remove the chicken and keep warm. Strain the sauce and degrease. Add the heavy cream and simmer until the sauce has thickened slightly. Add the carrots and leeks. Adjust the seasoning.

8. Return the chicken to the sauce, simmer about 2 minutes and serve.

Chicken Legs Hunter-Style

Yield: 10 servings

Chicken legs and thighs, disjointed	*10 each*	*10 each*
Salt, to taste	*1/2 teaspoon*	*1/2 teaspoon*
Pepper, to taste	*1/4 teaspoon*	*1/4 teaspoon*
Vegetable oil	*2 fluid ounces*	*60 milliliters*
Shallots, minced	*1/2 ounce*	*15 grams*
Garlic cloves, mashed to paste	*4 each*	*4 each*
Mushrooms, cut in quarters	*20 each*	*20 each*
Dry white wine	*12 fluid ounces*	*360 milliliters*
Tomato Concassé	*8 ounces*	*225 grams*
Jus de Veau Lié	*32 fluid ounces*	*1 liter*
Parsley, chopped	*2 tablespoons*	*30 grams*

The recipe for Jus de Veau Lié may be found on page 523.

To read about preparing Tomato Concassé, see Chapter 6, page 191.

1. Chicken should be seasoned with salt and pepper and browned on all sides in hot oil; remove and reserve.

2. Discard half the oil, add shallots and garlic; sauté until they have a good aroma.

3. Add mushrooms, sauté until juices are released. Deglaze with wine and reduce by half.

4. Add Tomato Concassé, Jus de Veau Lié, and chicken.

5. Cover and place in a 350°F (175°C) oven, until chicken is done (35 to 45 minutes).

6. Remove the chicken pieces and excess fat, adjust consistency of sauce and season.

7. Finish with chopped parsley.

Chicken Pot Pie

Yield: 10 servings

The recipe for Chicken Velouté is on page 531.

Other vegetables such as turnips, rutabagas, and green beans may be added. You may season the Velouté with fresh herbs if desired.

Chicken, white and dark meat, cooked	*2 pounds*	*900 grams*
Pearl onions, cooked	*20 each*	*20 each*
Mushrooms caps, sautéed	*20 each*	*20 each*
Carrots, cubed, blanched	*4 each*	*4 each*
Potatoes, parisienne	*4 each*	*4 each*
Green peas	*8 ounces*	*225 grams*
Chicken Velouté	*1 1/2 quarts*	*1.4 liters*
Puff pastry	*2 sheets*	*2 sheets*
Egg wash	*as needed*	*as needed*

1. Cut the chicken into large bite-size pieces. Divide evenly and place into 10 portion-sized casserole or soup bowls; add the vegetables.

2. Pour the Velouté over the chicken and vegetables.

3. Roll out the puff pastry 1/4-inch thick. Cut a circle slightly larger than the casserole. Lay it over the casserole, seal, and brush with egg wash.

4. Bake at 425°F (220°C) until crust is done and chicken is heated thoroughly.

Poule au Pot (Chicken with Vegetables)

Yield: 10 servings

The recipe for Bouquet Garni is on page 424.

Chicken Stock can be found on page 442.

Chickens, whole	*13 pounds*	*5.85 kilograms*
Chicken stock, as needed	*2 1/2 quarts*	*2.4 liters*
Bouquet Garni	*1 each*	*1 each*
Vegetable garnish		
Carrots, tourné or battonet	*30 pieces*	*30 pieces*
Pearl onions	*30 pieces*	*30 pieces*
Celery, battonet	*30 pieces*	*30 pieces*
Parsnips, tourné or battonet	*30 pieces*	*30 pieces*
Peas	*10 ounces*	*285 grams*
Fennel, batonnet	*30 pieces*	*30 pieces*
Mushrooms	*20 each*	*20 each*
Salt, to taste	*1/2 teaspoon*	*1/2 teaspoon*
Pepper, to taste	*1/4 teaspoon*	*1/4 teaspoon*
Fresh herbs, as available or desired, chopped	*2 ounces*	*60 grams*

(Recipe continued on facing page)

1. Truss the chicken.

2. Cover the chicken with cold stock. Bring the stock to a simmer. Add the Bouquet Garni. Poach the chicken until it is tender and cooked through. Skim the surface, as necessary, throughout the poaching procedure.

3. Cook the vegetables separately (in additional stock, if available) until they are tender. Refresh and hold them.

4. At service, portion the chicken and serve it with the broth and vegetables heated in the broth. Add the salt, pepper, and chopped, fresh herbs, if desired.

Poached Chicken Florentine

Yield: 10 servings

Butter, as needed	*3 ounces*	*85 grams*
Shallots, minced	*4 each*	*4 each*
Chicken breasts, boneless, skinless	*10 each*	*10 each*
Dry white wine	*10 fluid ounces*	*300 milliliters*
Chicken Stock	*1 pint*	*480 milliliters*
Mornay Sauce	*1 1/2 pints*	*720 milliliters*
Spinach, cooked, coarse-chopped	*1 3/4 pound*	*800 grams*
Parmesan cheese	*3 ounces*	*85 grams*

This recipe has its roots in the cuisine of Tuscany. According to culinary legend, the recipe for this dish traveled to France with Caterina di Medici.

Mornay Sauce is a variation of Béchamel Sauce (page 535).

1. Butter pan and sprinkle with shallots.

2. Add chicken breasts, wine, stock, and bring to a simmer.

3. Cover with a parchment-paper cover; poach in a 350°F (175°C) oven until done (about 15 minutes).

4. Remove chicken breasts to a serving platter and keep warm.

5. Strain poaching liquid and reduce until syrupy. Add Mornay sauce and reduce until correct consistency.

6. Sauté spinach in butter to reheat and arrange on a platter.

7. Place chicken on top of spinach and coat with the Mornay sauce.

8. Top with Parmesan cheese and brown lightly under a salamander or broiler.

Poached Chicken Breast with Tarragon Sauce

Yield: 10 servings

Make a Velouté Sauce with Chicken Stock. The recipe is on page 531.

This recipe calls for chicken breasts to be shallow-poached. For more information about this cooking method, refer to Chapter 10, page 332 to 335.

Butter, as needed	*2 ounces*	*60 grams*
Shallots, minced	*3 each*	*3 each*
Chicken suprêmes	*10 each*	*10 each*
Chicken Stock	*4 fluid ounces*	*120 milliliters*
Dry white wine	*6 fluid ounces*	*180 milliliters*
Chicken Velouté	*20 fluid ounces*	*600 milliliters*
Tarragon, fresh, chopped	*1 tablespoon*	*1 tablespoon*
Heavy cream, reduced	*4 fluid ounces*	*120 milliliters*
Salt, to taste	*1/2 teaspoon*	*1/2 teaspoon*
Pepper, to taste	*1/4 teaspoon*	*1/4 teaspoon*

1. Butter shallow pan and sprinkle with shallots.

2. Add chicken breasts, stock, and wine.

3. Bring to a simmer; cover with a parchment-paper cover.

4. Poach in oven at 350°F (175°C) until done.

5. Remove chicken to serving platter; cover with the paper and keep warm.

6. Strain poaching liquid and reduce to one-quarter of original volume.

7. Add Velouté and tarragon and reduce until sauce consistency.

8. Add heavy cream and season to taste.

9. Serve sauce over chicken breast.

Poached Cornish Game Hen with Star Anise

Yield: 10 servings

Rock Cornish game hens	*10 each*	*10 each*
Salt, to taste	*1/2 teaspoon*	*1/2 teaspoon*
Pepper, to taste	*1/4 teaspoon*	*1/4 teaspoon*
Bay leaves	*10 each*	*10 each*
Thyme, sprigs	*10 each*	*10 each*
Caraway seeds	*1/4 teaspoon*	*1/4 teaspoon*
Parsley stems	*30 each*	*30 each*
Chicken Stock or Consommé	*as needed*	*as needed*
Star anise	*20 each*	*20 each*
Carrots, battonet, blanched	*10 ounces*	*285 grams*
Turnips, battonet, blanched	*10 ounces*	*285 grams*
Parsnips, battonet, blanched	*10 ounces*	*285 grams*
Yellow squash, battonet, blanched	*10 ounces*	*285 grams*
Cucumbers, battonet, blanched	*10 ounces*	*285 grams*
Rice, cooked	*1 1/4 pounds*	*570 grams*
Scallions, 3-inch lengths	*10 ounces*	*285 grams*
Chives, chopped	*2 ounces*	*60 grams*

For the most flavorful broth, allow the vegetables to cook completely in the broth.

To make timing of service easier, poach the hen in advance for approximately 30 minutes. Chill quickly and keep refrigerated. At service, place one hen, broth, and garnish into individual casseroles. Reheat for 20 minutes at 375°F (190°C).

1. Trim the game hens; rub with salt and pepper. Season each hen cavity with the bay leaves, thyme, caraway seeds, and parsley stems. Truss hens.

2. Place the hens in casseroles. Cover with stock or Consommé. Add the star anise.

3. Cover hens with parchment paper. Simmer gently for about 40 minutes.

4. When hens are nearly done, add the vegetables; simmer until heated through.

5. Add the rice just before service. Sprinkle hens with the scallions and chives. Serve each in the casserole, if appropriate.

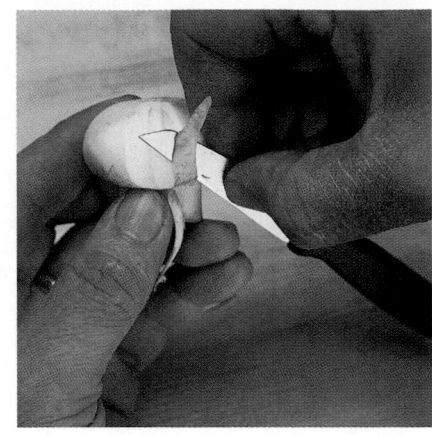

Use a tourné knife to flute mushroom caps.

The use of Beurre Manié is explained in Chapter 6, page 204.

You may prefer to use Chicken Velouté to prepare the glaçage instead of thickening the cuisson with Beurre Manié.

The recipe for Hollandaise is on page 540.

Chicken Eugene

Yield: 10 servings

Shallots, minced and sweated	*2 tablespoons*	*2 tablespoons*
Chicken suprêmes	*10 each*	*10 each*
Chicken Stock	*1 pint*	*480 milliliters*
Dry white wine	*5 fluid ounces*	*150 milliliters*
Salt, to taste	*1/2 teaspoon*	*1/2 teaspoon*
Pepper, to taste	*1/4 teaspoon*	*1/4 teaspoon*
Beurre Manié, as needed	*3 ounces*	*85 grams*
Heavy cream, whipped	*10 fluid ounces*	*300 milliliters*
Hollandaise	*10 fluid ounces*	*300 milliliters*
French bread, slices	*10 each*	*10 each*
Butter, as needed	*10 ounces*	*285 grams*
Mushroom caps, fluted	*10 ounces*	*285 grams*
Ham, thin slices, heated	*10 each*	*10 each*

1. Place the shallots in a buttered sauteuse. Place the suprêmes over the shallots. Add the chicken stock, white wine, salt, and pepper.

2. Bring the liquid to a simmer and poach it until the chicken is done. Remove chicken, reserve the liquid. Keep the chicken warm.

3. Prepare a glaçage: Thicken the reserved cuisson with Beurre Manié. Fold in the whipped cream and then the Hollandaise.

4. Coat the chicken breasts with the sauce. Place them under a broiler or salamander until they are golden.

5. Sauté the French bread in butter until it is golden. Sauté the mushroom caps in butter.

6. Place bread on the plates. Top each with a ham slice, then the chicken. Garnish with a mushroom cap.

Roast Duckling with Sauce Bigarade

Yield: 10 servings

Ducklings	5 each	5 each
Salt, to taste	1/2 teaspoon	1/2 teaspoon
Pepper, to taste	1/4 teaspoon	1/4 teaspoon
Parsley stems	15 each	15 each
Thyme, sprigs	5 each	5 each
Bay leaves	5 each	5 each
Sauce Bigarade		
Sugar	3/4 ounce	20 grams
Water	1 tablespoon	1 tablespoon
White wine	1 fluid ounce	30 milliliters
Cider vinegar	1 fluid ounce	30 milliliters
Blood orange juice	3 fluid ounces	90 milliliters
Demi-Glace	1 quart	1 liter
Brown Veal Stock	1 pint	480 milliliters
Blood orange, zest, julienned and blanched	1 each	1 each
Blood orange, segment flesh only	1 each	1 each

1. Place duckling, breast side up, on a rack. Season with salt and pepper. Place the parsley stems, thyme, and bay leaves into the cavity.

2. Roast the duckling until the thigh has an internal temperature of 140°F (60°C). Remove the duckling from the pan; and let it cool. Split and partially debone the duckling.

3. Degrease the pan and reserve the drippings.

4. To prepare the gastrique: Combine the sugar and water. Caramelize carefully.

5. Add the wine, vinegar, and orange juice, and reduce by half.

6. Add the Demi-Glace and Brown Veal Stock; bring sauce to a boil.

7. Add the pan drippings. Reduce the heat and simmer until the mixture is reduced to 1 quart (1 liter). Strain through a cheesecloth. Reserve.

8. For each serving, brush the duckling with a small amount of the sauce and reheat it until it is crisp in a very hot oven (450°F/230°C).

9. Reheat approximately 2 ounces (60 milliliters) of sauce per serving and finish it with the blanched orange zest and orange segments. Pool the sauce on a plate and place the duckling on the sauce.

A gastrique is defined by Larousse Gastronomique *as a mixture of vinegar and sugar cooked until nearly dry and used to flavor fruit sauces such as the one here.*

Brown Veal Stock can be found on page 437.

If blood oranges are not available, substitute tangerines or juice oranges and adjust the flavor with lemon or lime juice.

Roast Duckling with Red Pears, Ginger, and Green Peppercorns

Yield: 10 servings

Use Jus de Canard, prepared according to the variation for Jus de Veau Lié on page 523.

The recipe for Demi-Glace is on page 522.

Ducklings, trimmed	5 each	5 each
Parsley stems	15 each	15 each
Thyme, sprigs	5 each	5 each
Bay leaves	5 each	5 each
Sauce		
Cider vinegar	2 fluid ounces	60 milliliters
Sugar	2 ounces	60 grams
Red Bartlett pears, cooked, puréed	3 ounces	85 grams
Demi-Glace, flavored with ginger	1 quart	1 liter
Ginger, minced	1 ounce	30 grams
Green peppercorns	1 ounce	30 grams
Plum brandy	4 fluid ounces	120 milliliters
Butter	4 ounces	115 grams

1. Place duckling, breast up, on a rack. Season with salt and pepper. Place herbs in cavity of the bird.

2. Roast duckling until juices run barely pink. Remove duckling from the oven. Cool, split, and partially debone it. Reserve.

3. For the sauce: Combine vinegar and sugar; bring the mixture to a boil and cook until it is barely golden.

4. Add the pear purée and Demi-Glace, ginger, and peppercorns; let the mixture reduce slightly. Adjust seasoning to taste.

5. Coat each duckling with a small amount of the sauce and reheat it until crisp in a very hot oven (450°F/230°C).

6. Reheat approximately 2 ounces (60 milliliters) of the sauce per serving and finish with plum brandy and whole butter. Pool the sauce on the plate and top with the duckling.

Roast Duckling with Plum Sauce

Yield: 10 servings

Ducklings	5 each	5 each
Salt, to taste	1/2 teaspoon	1/2 teaspoon
Pepper, to taste	1/2 teaspoon	1/2 teaspoon
Parsley stems	10 each	10 each
Thyme, sprigs	5 each	5 each
Bay leaves	5 each	5 each
Glaze		
Soy sauce	12 fluid ounces	360 milliliters
Honey	3 ounces	85 grams
Peppercorns, cracked	6 each	6 each
Orange zest, grated	1 each	1 each
Ginger, grated	1 ounce	30 grams
Garlic, cloves, split	2 each	2 each
Cilantro, chopped	1 ounce	30 grams
Sauce		
Cider vinegar	2 fluid ounces	60 milliliters
Sugar	2 1/2 ounces	70 grams
Red plums, puréed	4 ounces	115 grams
Jus de Canard Lié	1 pint	480 milliliters
Kirsch, to taste	1 fluid ounce	30 milliliters
Butter, as needed	2 1/2 ounces	70 grams
Garnish		
Red plums	20 slices	20 slices
Mint leaves	20 each	20 each

Jus de Canard Lié is a variation of Jus de Veau Lié, page 523.

1. Place each duckling, breast up, on a rack. Rub with salt and pepper. Place the parsley, thyme, and half of bay leaf in each duck's cavity.

2. Mix all ingredients together for the glaze; brush each duckling with it.

3. Roast ducklings in a very hot oven (450°F/230°C) for 15 minutes. Turn down to 350°F (175°C). Roast ducklings, brushing occasionally with more glaze, until done. Total roasting time is approximately 1 hour and 15 minutes.

4. Remove ducklings and let rest while completing sauce.

5. Combine the vinegar and sugar. Bring the sauce to a boil; cook it until golden. Add the plum purée and return to boil. Add the Jus de Canard Lié, return the mixture to a boil; simmer to reduce slightly. Adjust the seasoning with the kirsch, salt, and pepper, if necessary. Finish with butter at service.

6. Split each duckling and partially debone the breast. Reheat in a very hot oven to crisp the skin.

7. Serve each duckling (one-half bird per serving) on a pool of the sauce; garnish each dish with sliced plums and mint leaves.

Marinated Grilled Duck Breast

Yield: 10 servings

Serve the sliced duck breast with
Dauphinoise Potatoes (page 821) and
Green Beans with Walnuts (page 797).

Another way to serve this duck is as part
of a composed salad on a bed of mixed
greens tossed with Georgia Peanut Salad
(page 909).

Duck breasts, boned and halved	*10 each*	*10 each*
Marinade		
Soy sauce	*8 fluid ounces*	*240 milliliters*
Water	*8 fluid ounces*	*240 milliliters*
Sesame oil, dark	*1/2 ounce*	*15 grams*
Hoisin sauce	*1/2 ounce*	*15 grams*
Ginger, coarsely chopped	*1 tablespoon*	*1 tablespoon*
Garlic, minced	*1 tablespoon*	*1 tablespoon*
Salt, to taste	*1/2 teaspoon*	*1/2 teaspoon*
Pepper, to taste	*1/4 teaspoon*	*1/4 teaspoon*

1. Trim the duck breasts if necessary; place in a hotel pan.

2. Combine all of the ingredients for the marinade and pour the mixture over the duck. Turn the breasts to coat evenly. Let marinate in the refrigerator for several hours or overnight.

3. Grill the duck until it has cooked to the desired doneness. Brush with marinade during the grilling.

4. At service, slice the breast on the diagonal and finish on a grill.

Roast Pheasant with Cranberry-Peppercorn Sauce

Yield: 10 servings

Pheasant	5 each	5 each
Salt, to taste	1/2 teaspoon	1/2 teaspoon
Pepper, to taste	1/4 teaspoon	1/4 teaspoon
Bay leaves	5 each	5 each
Thyme, sprigs	5 each	5 each
Mirepoix	10 ounces	285 grams
Sauce		
Chicken Stock	1 quart	1 liter
Red wine	4 fluid ounces	120 milliliters
Peppercorns, cracked	1/2 teaspoon	1/2 teaspoon
Shallots, minced	1 ounce	30 grams
Bay leaf	1 each	1 each
Cranberries, fresh or frozen	7 ounces	200 grams
Sugar	1 ounce	30 grams
Arrowroot, diluted	1 tablespoon	1 tablespoon
Port wine	2 fluid ounces	60 milliliters
Butter, as needed	4 ounces	115 grams

To substitute dried cranberries for fresh or frozen ones, plump 3 ounces (85 grams) in the port. Drain the cranberries, reserving the port to finish the sauce.

1. Trim each pheasant. Season the cavity with the salt, pepper, thyme, and bay leaf. Truss pheasant.

2. Roast at 450°F (230°C) until juices run pink. Remove pheasant and let rest.

3. Add the Mirepoix to the roasting pan and caramelize. Add the Chicken Stock and simmer until well flavored. Strain jus.

4. Combine the wine, pepper, shallots, and bay leaf; reduce by half and strain.

5. Add the reduction to the pheasant jus, bring it to a boil, and simmer it for 5 minutes.

6. Add the cranberries and sugar. Simmer for 15 minutes or until thickened.

7. Add the arrowroot and thicken the sauce. Remove it from the heat.

8. Finish the sauce with the port.

9. To serve, halve and partially debone each pheasant, brush each half with sauce, and reheat in a hot oven.

10. Bring the remaining sauce to a boil and finish with whole butter. Adjust seasoning to taste. Serve each pheasant half on a pool of sauce.

Roast Turkey with Chestnut Stuffing

Yield: 12 servings

If desired, add 4 ounces (115 grams) sautéed celery to the stuffing. The egg may be omitted. Add more Chicken Stock to bind the mixture. Thyme, rosemary, and oregano may be added for additional seasoning.

The recipe for Turkey Broth may be found on page 453. A rich Chicken Stock or Chicken Broth may be substituted.

Turkey, whole	*15 pounds*	*6.75 kilograms*
Salt, to taste	*1/2 teaspoon*	*1/2 teaspoon*
Pepper, to taste	*1/4 teaspoon*	*1/4 teaspoon*
Mirepoix	*1 pound*	*450 grams*
Chestnut stuffing		
Onions, minced	*4 ounces*	*115 grams*
Bacon fat	*4 ounces*	*115 grams*
Bread cubes, dried	*1 1/2 pounds*	*680 grams*
Chicken Stock, hot	*4 fluid ounces*	*120 milliliters*
Egg, beaten	*1 each*	*1 each*
Parsley, chopped	*2 tablespoons*	*2 tablespoons*
Salt, to taste	*1/2 teaspoon*	*1/2 teaspoon*
Pepper, to taste	*1/2 teaspoon*	*1/2 teaspoon*
Sage, rubbed	*1 teaspoon*	*1 teaspoon*
Chestnuts, roasted and chopped	*8 ounces*	*225 grams*
Flour	*3 ounces*	*85 grams*
Turkey Broth	*1 1/2 quarts*	*1.5 liters*

1. Season the outside of the turkey with the salt and pepper. Place it on a rack in a roasting pan. Roast it at 425°F (220°C) for 15 minutes. Reduce the heat to 350°F (175°C) and roast the turkey to an internal temperature of 150°F (65°C). Add the Mirepoix when the turkey has roasted for about 3 hours.

2. To make the stuffing, sauté the onion in bacon fat until tender.

3. Combine the bread cubes, chicken stock, and eggs; add to the onion.

4. Add the parsley, pepper, sage, and chestnuts. Mix them well.

5. Place the stuffing in a buttered hotel pan and cover it with parchment paper. Bake the stuffing at 350°F (175°C) for 45 minutes.

6. Pour off most of the fat from the roasting pan. Let the drippings reduce until syrupy over direct heat.

7. Add the flour, stir well to combine, and cook out for 5 to 6 minutes. Add the broth and whisk to remove any lumps. Simmer for 20 minutes; strain, degrease, and adjust the seasoning.

8. Let the turkey stand 20 minutes before carving it. Serve it with pan gravy and the chestnut stuffing.

Roast Turkey Suprême with Pan Gravy

Yield: 10 servings

Turkey breast, boned	*4 pounds*	*1.8 kilograms*
Salt, to taste	*1/2 teaspoon*	*1/2 teaspoon*
Pepper, to taste	*1/4 teaspoon*	*1/4 teaspoon*
Poultry seasoning, to taste	*1/2 teaspoon*	*1/2 teaspoon*
Vegetable oil, as needed	*2 ounces*	*60 grams*
Mirepoix, diced small	*4 ounces*	*115 grams*
Flour	*2 ounces*	*60 grams*
Tomato paste	*1 ounce*	*30 grams*
Dry white wine	*3 fluid ounces*	*90 milliliters*
Turkey Broth	*20 fluid ounces*	*600 milliliters*

1. Season turkey breast, rub with oil and tie.

2. Place turkey on a rack in a roasting pan.

3. Roast turkey in a 350°F (175°C) oven. Add mirepoix after the turkey has roasted about 30 minutes.

4. Remove turkey when it has reached an internal temperature of 150°F (65°C), and allow to rest.

5. To make gravy, clarify fat in the roasting pan, discard all but 2 ounces (60 milliliters).

6. Add flour, cook out roux, incorporate stock, and whisk until smooth.

7. Simmer gravy until proper consistency is reached; degrease; strain through a fine china cap, season.

8. Remove string, carve turkey against the grain and serve with the gravy.

To make a stuffed boneless turkey breast, butterfly the breast and spread a stuffing such as those for Breast of Chicken with Mushroom and Ham (page 626) or Chicken Legs with Duxelles (page 633).

Pan-Smoked Turkey with Port Wine Sauce

Yield: 10 servings

The set-up for pan-smoking is in Chapter 9, page 306.

Fabricate the cutlets into 6-ounce (170-gram) portions.

The recipe for Jus de Veau Lié can be found on page 523.

Turkey breast cutlets	*10 each*	*10 each*
Stuffing		
Shallots, chopped	*2 teaspoons*	*2 teaspoons*
Garlic, minced	*1/2 teaspoon*	*1/2 teaspoon*
Butter	*2 teaspoons*	*2 teaspoons*
Wild rice, cooked	*3 ounces*	*85 grams*
Apples, peeled and julienned	*3 ounces*	*85 grams*
Ground chicken	*4 ounces*	*115 grams*
Heavy cream	*2 fluid ounces*	*60 milliliters*
Salt, to taste	*1/2 teaspoon*	*1/2 teaspoon*
Wild mushrooms, sliced	*1 pound*	*450 grams*
Sage, fresh, chopped	*2 teaspoons*	*2 teaspoons*
Jus de Veau Lié	*1 pint*	*480 milliliters*
Port wine	*2 fluid ounces*	*60 milliliters*

1. Butterfly the cutlets and reserve.

2. For the stuffing, sauté the shallots and garlic in the butter.

3. Add the wild rice and apple; heat thoroughly.

4. Purée the ground chicken in a food processor. Remove from the machine and fold in the heavy cream over an ice bath.

5. Add the salt and wild rice mixture to the puréed chicken.

6. Stuff the turkey breasts with the chicken-rice mixture. Tie or skewer to secure.

7. Pan-smoke the turkey breasts for 2 or 3 minutes. Finish cooking in the oven at 325°F (160°C).

8. Sweat the wild mushrooms in their own juices and season with the sage.

9. Add the Jus de Veau Lié and bring to a simmer. Finish with the port wine.

10. Serve turkey with the sauce.

Turkey Cutlet California

Yield: 10 servings

Turkey breast cutlets	*10 each*	*10 each*
Salt, to taste	*1/2 teaspoon*	*1/2 teaspoon*
Pepper, to taste	*1/4 teaspoon*	*1/4 teaspoon*
Flour, as needed	*4 ounces*	*115 grams*
Olive oil, as needed	*3 fluid ounces*	*90 milliliters*
Guacamole		
Avocados, coarsely mashed	*1 pound*	*450 grams*
Tomato Concassé	*5 ounces*	*140 grams*
Cilantro, chopped	*1 ounce*	*30 grams*
Garlic cloves, minced	*2 each*	*2 each*
Monterey Jack cheese, sliced or grated	*5 ounces*	*140 grams*

1. Pound the cutlets to an even thickness.

2. Season each cutlet with the salt and pepper. Dredge in the flour and shake off the excess.

3. Sauté cutlet in the olive oil until golden on both sides. Remove and keep warm.

4. Combine the avocado, Tomato Concassé, cilantro, and garlic for the guacamole.

5. Place guacamole on each cutlet and top with the cheese. Heat it in an oven or under a broiler until the cheese is melted. Serve at once.

Avocado flesh is buttery smooth and delicately flavored in this mix.

The cutlets should weigh 4 to 5 ounces (115 to 140 grms) per portion.

Serve with Cilantro Lime Rice, black beans or Refried Beans, and Fresh Tomato Salsa.

Jalapeño Monterey Jack may be used for more spice.

CHAPTER *18* *Fish Entrées*

Fish has become increasingly popular on menus in all types of establishments. The fish you select for a particular recipe can be varied readily, as long as the basic texture (lean or oily, firm or flaky)

remains the same. The recipes in this chapter have been grouped by cooking method:

- Sautéed and Pan-Fried
- Deep-Fried
- Grilled and Broiled
- Roasted and Baked
- Braised and Stewed
- Poached and Simmered

There are additional recipes for fish in Chapter 20, International Entrées.

Sauté Trout Meunière

Yield: 10 servings

Trout, pan-dressed	10 each	10 each
Lemon juice, as needed	1 lemon	1 lemon
Salt, to taste	1/2 teaspoon	1/2 teaspoon
Pepper, to taste	1/4 teaspoon	1/4 teaspoon
Flour, for dredging	2 ounces	60 grams
Clarified butter	2 ounces	60 grams
Lemon slices, skinless, seedless	20 each	20 each
Lemon juice	2 fluid ounces	60 milliliters
Parsley, chopped (blanched, optional)	3 tablespoons	3 tablespoons
Butter, whole	6 ounces	170 grams

Some chefs prefer to add the lemon juice and the parsley to the browned butter, creating a slightly thickened sauce to pour over the trout.

This technique may be applied to most pan-dressed fish or fillets cut from larger fish.

Meunière-style means "in the manner of the miller's wife." The method of preparing this dish is illustrated on pages 315 and 316.

1. Season trout with lemon juice, salt, and pepper; dredge in flour.

2. Sauté in clarified butter over moderate heat until lightly browned and cooked through, about 8 to 10 minutes.

3. When trout is done remove to a serving platter and keep warm.

4. Sprinkle with lemon juice and parsley.

5. Wipe out pan and add whole butter. Heat butter until lightly browned and pour over fish. Garnish trout with lemon slices.

Trout Amandine

Yield: 10 servings

Trout, pan-dressed	10 each	10 each
Salt, to taste	1/2 teaspoon	1/2 teaspoon
Pepper, to taste	1/4 teaspoon	1/4 teaspoon
Milk (optional), as needed	8 fluid ounces	240 milliliters
Flour, for dredging	2 ounces	60 grams
Clarified butter	6 fluid ounces	180 milliliters
Butter, whole	5 ounces	140 grams
Almonds, slivered	5 ounces	140 grams
Lemon juice	2 fluid ounces	60 milliliters
Parsley, chopped	3 tablespoons	3 tablespoons

Brown the butter until it develops a nutty aroma and flavor. This is called beurre noisette.

This recipe works with most pan-dressed fish or fillets and is especially appropriate for soft-shelled crabs.

1. Season the trout with salt and pepper.

2. Dip the fish in the milk and dredge in the flour.

3. Sauté the trout in the clarified butter until cooked through. Remove it and keep it warm.

(Recipe continued on facing page)

4. Pour off the excess butter. Add the whole butter and let it brown slightly.

5. Add the almonds and brown them.

6. Add the lemon juice and parsley.

7. Pour the sauce over the trout while it is very hot and foamy.

Sautéed Sole with Mango Chutney and Grilled Bananas

Yield: 10 servings

Sole fillet, trimmed	*2 1/4 pounds*	*1 kilogram*
Milk	*12 fluid ounces*	*360 milliliters*
Bread crumbs, dry	*12 ounces*	*340 grams*
Butter	*2 ounces*	*60 grams*
Mango Chutney, prepared	*1 pound*	*450 grams*
Bananas, sliced on bias and grilled	*1 1/2 pounds*	*680 grams*

1. Portion the sole at about 5 ounces (140 grams). Dip the sole in the milk.

2. Place the sole immediately into the bread crumbs and coat evenly. Press the crumbs in place to form a crust. Let coating firm under refrigeration 1 hour.

3. Sauté the breaded sole in the butter over high heat until just done.

4. Serve at once with Mango Chutney and grilled bananas.

Garnish with toasted coconut if desired.

To grill bananas, select relatively firm specimens. Slice them on an exaggerated diagonal. Brush them lightly with vegetable oil and grill until just marked. Season with lemon or lime juice, salt, and pepper.

Seared Sea Scallops with Saffron Rice, Asparagus, and a Light Tomato Sauce

Yield: 10 servings

Sea scallops, muscle tabs removed	*2 1/2 pounds*	*1 kilogram*
Butter	*4 ounces*	*115 grams*
Garlic, minced	*1 ounce*	*30 grams*
Tomato Concassé	*8 ounces*	*225 grams*
Jus de Veau Lié	*1 pint*	*480 milliliters*

1. Dry scallops as thoroughly as possible.

2. Sear the scallops in a seasoned cast-iron skillet or a nonstick pan. Remove them from the pan and keep them warm.

3. Add the whole butter and let heat. Add the garlic to the butter and sauté over moderate heat until the aroma becomes sweet.

4. Add the Tomato Concassé and sauté briefly. Add the Jus de Veau Lié and bring to a simmer. Adjust the seasoning and serve with the scallops.

Serve the scallops with a saffron rice and fresh asparagus. This would also be good over angel hair pasta.

659

Stir-Fried Scallops, San Francisco-Style

Yield: 10 servings

If bay scallops are not available, use sea scallops sliced on half. To read more about scallops, refer to page 120.

Sliced water chestnuts, onions, bamboo shoots, bean sprouts, and Chinese cabbage or bok choy cut in chiffonade can also be added in step 5.

The recipe for Fish Stock is on page 443. Basic Boiled Rice is on page 831.

Bay scallops	3 pounds	1.3 kilograms
Peanut oil	4 fluid ounces	120 milliliters
Gingerroot, minced	1 tablespoon	1 tablespoon
Garlic, minced	1 tablespoon	1 tablespoon
Celery, sliced on bias	5 ounces	140 grams
Red peppers, cut in diamonds, blanched	2 ounces	60 grams
Yellow peppers, cut in diamonds	2 ounces	60 grams
Green peppers, cut in diamonds, blanched	2 ounces	60 grams
Snow peas, cut in half	4 ounces	115 grams
Mushrooms, cut in quarters	2 ounces	60 grams
Zucchini, split, cut in very thin slices	4 ounces	115 grams
Fish Stock, hot	12 fluid ounces	360 milliliters
Hot bean paste	1 1/2 teaspoons	1 1/2 teaspoons
Red bean paste	1 tablespoon	1 tablespoon
Cornstarch	2 tablespoons	2 tablespoons
Oyster sauce	2 tablespoons	2 tablespoons
Winter or Brown Rice, cooked	1 1/2 to 2 pounds	680 to 900 grams
Scallions, sliced thin	4 each	4 each
Sesame seeds, black, toasted	1 ounce	30 grams

1. Blot excess moisture from bay scallops with a paper towel.

2. Heat a well-seasoned wok, add a small amount of oil.

3. Add some scallops; sauté until browned, tossing or turning frequently. Remove to a platter, keep warm; repeat this process until all scallops are cooked.

4. Add all remaining oil to the pan; lightly sauté the ginger and garlic.

5. Add celery, peppers, peas, mushrooms, and zucchini; stir-fry until zucchini is halfway cooked.

6. Mix Fish Stock, bean pastes, cornstarch, and oyster sauce together; add vegetables; bring to a boil, stirring constantly.

7. Add bay scallops, mix together, and season.

8. Serve with rice.

9. Garnish with scallions and sesame seeds.

Panfried Halibut with Puttanesca Sauce

Yield: 10 servings

Halibut, skinless fillets	*10 each*	*10 each*
Salt, to taste	*1/2 teaspoon*	*1/2 teaspoon*
Pepper, to taste	*1/4 teaspoon*	*1/4 teaspoon*
Flour, as needed	*3 ounces*	*85 grams*
Egg wash, as needed	*8 fluid ounces*	*240 milliliters*
Bread crumbs, fresh	*4 ounces*	*115 grams*
Almonds, slivered and coarse-chopped	*6 ounces*	*170 grams*
Vegetable oil, as needed	*6 fluid ounces*	*180 milliliters*
Sauce		
Olive oil, as needed	*2 tablespoons*	*2 tablespoons*
Garlic cloves, mashed to a paste	*3 each*	*3 each*
Anchovy paste	*1 tablespoon*	*1 tablespoon*
Red pepper flakes	*1/4 teaspoon*	*1/4 teaspoon*
White wine	*6 ounces*	*170 grams*
Capers, rough-chopped	*2 tablespoons*	*2 tablespoons*
Tomato Concassé	*1 1/2 pounds*	*680 grams*
Black olives, pitted	*3 ounces*	*85 grams*
Lemon juice, as needed	*2 teaspoons*	*2 teaspoons*
Parsley, chopped	*1 ounce*	*30 grams*

Coarse-ground pecans or walnuts may be used instead of almonds.

Puttanesca Sauce is reputed to have first been devised by the prostitutes of Naples. It is a quickly made sauce of pungent, salty ingredients.

1. Portion the filets at approximately 6 ounces (170 grams) each. Season the halibut with salt and pepper.

2. Dredge the fish in the flour, dip in the egg wash, and coat with a combination of the bread crumbs and almonds. Allow to rest, refrigerated, at least 30 minutes.

3. Pan-fry the halibut in hot vegetable oil. Finish in a 325°F (165°C) oven, if necessary.

4. For the sauce, heat the olive oil; add the garlic, anchovy paste, and red pepper flakes; sauté briefly.

5. Add the wine and reduce the mixture. Add the capers and Tomato Concassé. Cook until the liquid is reduced slightly. Adjust the seasoning with the salt, pepper, and lemon juice. Add the parsley.

6. Pool the coulis on a heated plate. Arrange the halibut on the coulis and serve.

Fisherman's Platter

Yield: 10 servings

To read about the standard breading procedure, see pages 320 to 321. Tartar and Rémoulade Sauces can be found on pages 915 to 916. The technique for cutting fish into goujonettes is illustrated on page 248.

You may prefer to deep fry the fish and shellfish.

Other breadings that might be used include cornmeal, cracker or corn flake crumbs, or flour and ground nut mixes.

Cocktail sauce and lemon slices may be preferred by some customers.

Fish, cut in goujonettes	1 1/4 pounds	570 grams
Oysters, shucked	20 each	20 each
Little Neck clams, shucked	20 each	20 each
Shrimp, 16 to 20 count, peeled, deveined, and butterflied	20 each	20 each
Sea scallops, muscle tabs removed	10 ounces	285 grams
Salt, to taste	1/2 teaspoon	1/2 teaspoon
Pepper, to taste	1/4 teaspoon	1/4 teaspoon
Lemon juice, to taste	4 fluid ounces	120 milliliters
Standard breading	as needed	as needed
Vegetable oil, as needed	1 pint	480 milliliters
Tartar or Rémoulade Sauce	1 pint	480 milliliters

1. Season the fish and shellfish with the salt, pepper, and lemon juice.

2. Bread the fish and shellfish. Refrigerate for at least 30 minutes.

3. Pan-fry them until they are cooked through.

4. Drain the fish and shellfish briefly on absorbent paper.

5. Serve the fish immediately with the Tartar or Rémoulade Sauce.

Flounder Stuffed with Crabmeat with Lemon Beurre Blanc

Yield: 10 servings

Other fish suitable for this dish include halibut, trout, and grouper.

If you prefer a dish that is not quite so rich, serve the stuffed flounder with a Vegetable Coulis such as those found on pages 550 and 551.

Stuffing:

Shallots, minced	2 each	2 each
Scallions, minced	2 each	2 each
Butter	1 ounce	30 grams
Flour	1 1/2 ounces	40 grams
White wine	8 fluid ounces	240 milliliters
Heavy cream	8 fluid ounces	240 milliliters
King crabmeat, rough chopped	14 ounces	400 grams
Parsley, chopped	1 tablespoon	1 tablespoon
Salt, to taste	1/2 teaspoon	1/2 teaspoon
Pepper, to taste	1/4 teaspoon	1/4 teaspoon
Flounder fillet	10 each	10 each
Flour	2 ounces	60 grams
Salt, to taste	1/2 teaspoon	1/2 teaspoon

(Recipe continued on facing page)

Pepper, to taste	1/4 teaspoon	1/4 teaspoon
Eggs, beaten	5 each	5 each
Vegetable oil	6 ounces	180 milliliters
Lemon Beurre Blanc	20 ounces	570 milliliters

The recipe for Lemon Beurre Blanc is on page 545.

1. To make stuffing, sauté shallots and scallions in butter.

2. Add flour; cook 1 minute.

3. Add wine, cream, and crabmeat; bring to a boil, and cook until mixture is thick, stirring occasionally.

4. Add parsley; season and chill.

5. Portion the flounder at about 5 ounces (140 grams) per portion. Spread stuffing on fillet, and roll up, completely encasing the filling.

6. Dip fish in seasoned flour; shake off excess. Dip fish in egg, brown in oil, and finish in a 350°F (175°C) oven 8 to 10 minutes.

7. Serve with Lemon Beurre Blanc.

Pan-Fried Trout with Bacon

Yield: 10 servings

Bacon	20 slices	20 slices
Brook trout, whole, boned	10 each	10 each
Salt, to taste	1/2 teaspoon	1/2 teaspoon
Pepper, to taste	1 teaspoon	1 teaspoon
Cornmeal, as needed	2 ounces	60 grams
Lemons	2 each	2 each
Parsley	3 bunches	3 bunches

Serve with Hush Puppies (page 836) or Cornbread (page 1027).

Almonds may be added in the manner of Amandine; see page 658.

1. Crisp bacon in skillet. Remove from pan, and keep warm.

2. Season the inside of the trout with salt and pepper, dip in milk. Dredge in cornmeal.

3. Pan-fry trout in the bacon fat until golden brown on both sides.

4. Drain on absorbent paper. Deep fry small bunches of parsley, stems partially removed.

5. Garnish with bacon pieces, lemon wedges or slices, and deep-fried parsley.

Pan-Seared Black Sea Bass with Ratatouille

Yield: 10 servings

Five to 6 ounces (140 to 170 grams) makes an adequate portion size for this recipe.

Crisp-seared salmon also works well with the ratatouille. Sautéed monkfish (without the skin) is another good choice.

The recipe for Maître d'Hôtel Butter is on page 547.

Black Sea Bass fillets	*10 each*	*10 each*
Salt, to taste	*1/2 teaspoon*	*1/2 teaspoon*
Pepper, to taste	*1/4 teaspoon*	*1/4 teaspoon*
Lemon juice, to taste	*2 tablespoons*	*2 tablespoons*
Flour, for dredging	*2 ounces*	*60 grams*
Ratatouille		
Olive oil	*1 fluid ounce*	*30 milliliters*
Onions, julienne	*2 ounces*	*60 grams*
Garlic cloves, minced	*1 each*	*1 each*
Green peppers, julienne	*2 ounces*	*60 grams*
Eggplant, large dice	*6 ounces*	*170 grams*
Tomato Concassé	*6 ounces*	*170 grams*
Tomato purée	*2 fluid ounces*	*60 milliliters*
Basil	*1/4 teaspoon*	*1/4 teaspoon*
Oregano	*1/4 teaspoon*	*1/4 teaspoon*
Thyme	*pinch*	*pinch*
Yellow squash, julienne	*4 ounces*	*115 grams*
Zucchini, julienne	*4 ounces*	*115 grams*
Salt, to taste	*1/2 teaspoon*	*1/2 teaspoon*
Pepper, to taste	*1/4 teaspoon*	*1/4 teaspoon*
Maître d'Hôtel Butter	*5 ounces*	*140 grams*

1. Season the fish with salt, pepper, and lemon juice.

2. Lightly dredge in flour, shake off the excess.

3. In a very hot pan, sear the fish, skin side down, until lightly browned.

4. Turn fish, and finish in the pan in a 350°F (175°C) oven.

5. For ratatouille: Sauté onion, garlic, and green pepper in oil. Add eggplant, Tomato Concassé, purée, and spices; simmer 10 minutes. Add squashes, simmer 5 minutes longer; season.

6. Serve on a bed of ratatouille; fold the skin back to expose the flesh.

7. Garnish with Maître d'Hôtel Butter.

Deep-Fried Flounder with Rémoulade Sauce

Yield: 10 servings

Flounder fillets, cut into goujonettes	3 pounds	1.3 kilograms
Salt, to taste	1/2 teaspoon	1/2 teaspoon
Pepper, to taste	1/4 teaspoon	1/4 teaspoon
Lemon juice, to taste	1 ounce	30 grams
Flour	2 ounces	60 grams
Egg wash	8 fluid ounces	240 milliliters
Bread crumbs, dry	2 ounces	60 grams
Rémoulade Sauce	20 fluid ounces	600 milliliters

1. Season the fish with salt, pepper, and lemon juice.

2. Bread the fish using the standard breading procedure.

3. Deep-fry the fish at 350°F (175°C) until golden brown.

4. Drain well on absorbent paper.

5. Serve the fish with the sauce.

Flounder's taste is delicate. Its texture flakes easily and can be cut into "fingers" and deep-fried.

The recipe for Rémoulade Sauce may be found on page 915.

Deep-Fried Squid (Calamari)

Yield: 10 servings

Squid, cleaned, cut in rings	4 pounds	1.8 kilograms
Salt, to taste	1/2 teaspoon	1/2 teaspoon
Pepper, to taste	1/4 teaspoon	1/4 teaspoon
Lemon juice, to taste	1 fluid ounce	30 milliliters
Worcestershire sauce, to taste	1 tablespoon	1 tablespoon
Flour, as needed	2 ounces	60 grams
Egg wash, as needed	1 pint	480 milliliters
Bread crumbs, dry	as needed	as needed
Marinara Sauce	20 fluid ounces	600 milliliters

1. Season squid with salt, pepper, lemon juice, and worcestershire sauce; dredge in flour.

2. Dip in egg wash; dredge in dry bread crumbs. (This entire step may be omitted for a lighter coating.)

3. Deep-fry until golden brown; drain on absorbent paper.

4. Serve squid with Marinara as a dipping sauce.

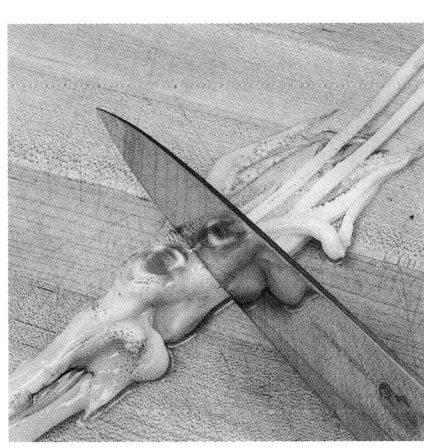

The tentacles may be left whole if they are small or cut into pieces appropriately for various preparations.

Serve 3 to 4 ounces (85 to 115 grams) per porion as an appetizer.

If desired, serve 4 ounces (115 grams) of the squid over linguini with Marinara Sauce, found on page 538.

Flounder à la Orly

Yield: 10 servings

Beer Batter: Combine 5 ounces (140 grams) of flour, 2 tablespoons baking powder, 1 tablespoon sugar, and salt and pepper to taste. Stir in 12 fluid ounces (360 milliliters) beer to form a batter. Use immediately.

This fish can also be served with French fries and malt vinegar in the classic "fish and chips."

Flounder fillets	*10 each*	*10 each*
Salt, to taste	*1/2 teaspoon*	*1/2 teaspoon*
Pepper, to taste	*1/4 teaspoon*	*1/4 teaspoon*
Lemon juice, to taste	*1 fluid ounce*	*30 milliliters*
Flour, as needed	*4 ounces*	*115 grams*
Beer Batter	*1 recipe*	*1 recipe*
Parsley, sprigs	*20 each*	*20 each*
Tomato sauce	*20 fluid ounces*	*600 milliliters*
Lemon wedges	*10 each*	*10 each*

1. Portion the flounder at 6 ounces (170 grams). Season fillets with salt, pepper, and lemon juice..

2. Dredge the fish in flour and shake off excess.

3. Dip in batter.

4. Deep-fry at 350°F (175°C) degrees until lightly browned.

5. Drain on absorbent paper.

6. Deep-fry parsley sprigs at 350°F (175°C) (swimming method) until crisp, 45 seconds; drain.

7. Serve fried fish with tomato sauce; garnish with lemon wedge and fried parsley.

Deep-Fried Breaded Shrimp

Yield: 10 servings

Shrimp, peeled and deveined	*3 1/2 pounds*	*1.6 kilograms*
Flour, as needed	*4 ounces*	*115 grams*
Egg wash, as needed	*6 fluid ounces*	*180 milliliters*
Bread crumbs, fresh, white	*4 ounces*	*115 grams*
Salt, to taste	*1/2 teaspoon*	*1/2 teaspoon*
Rémoulade or Tartar Sauce	*1 pint*	*480 milliliters*

For Rémoulade or Tartar Sauce see pages 915 to 916.

Another option is to dip the shrimp in a beer batter and fry. See facing page for Beer Batter recipe.

1. Bread the shrimp according to the standard breading procedure: First, dip them into the flour and shake off any excess. Then, coat the shrimp with the egg wash. Finally, evenly coat the shrimp with the bread crumbs.

2. Place the shrimp in a fryer basket and lower them into a deep fryer set at 375°F (190°C).

3. Deep-fry the shrimp until they are evenly browned and thoroughly cooked. Lift the basket and allow the excess oil to drain back into the fryer. Drain the shrimp very briefly on absorbent toweling, and season them to taste with salt as desired.

4. Serve the shrimp on a heated plate with Rémoulade or Tartar Sauce, or as desired.

VARIATION

Popcorn Shrimp: Season very small shrimp with a seasoning blend such as Barbecue Spice Blend or Chili Powder (page 425). Bread and fry; serve as an appetizer with Black Bean Salsa (page 936) or Pineapple Salsa (page 676).

Deep-Fried Sole Anglaise

Yield: 10 servings

Sole fillets	*10 each*	*10 each*
Salt, to taste	*1/2 teaspoon*	*1/2 teaspoon*
Pepper, to taste	*1/4 teaspoon*	*1/4 teaspoon*
Lemon juice, to taste	*1 fluid ounce*	*30 milliliters*
Flour, as needed	*2 ounces*	*60 grams*
Egg wash	*6 fluid ounces*	*180 milliliters*
Bread crumbs, fresh	*4 ounces*	*115 grams*
Parsley	*20 sprigs*	*20 sprigs*
Lemon wedges	*10 each*	*10 each*

Five ounces (140 grams) is a sufficient portion size.

Offer cocktail sauce, Tartar Sauce, or Rémoulade Sauce on the side (see pages 915 to 916). Traditional accompaniments include cole slaw, French fries, and Hush Puppies.

(Recipe continued on next page)

1. Season sole with salt, pepper, and lemon and dredge in flour.

2. Dip the pieces of the fish in the egg wash, drain, and dredge in bread crumbs.

3. Deep-fry 350°F (175°C) until lightly browned. Drain on absorbent paper.

4. Deep-fry parsley sprigs until crisp, about 45 seconds; drain on paper.

5. Serve fish garnished with lemon wedge and fried parsley.

Broiled Salmon Steaks

Yield: 10 servings

Salmon steaks	*10 each*	*10 each*
Salt, to taste	*1/2 teaspoon*	*1/2 teaspoon*
Pepper, to taste	*1/4 teaspoon*	*1/4 teaspoon*
Lemon juice, to taste	*1 fluid ounce*	*30 milliliters*
Vegetable oil	*4 fluid ounces*	*120 milliliters*
Bread crumbs, fresh	*8 ounces*	*225 grams*
Compound butter	*5 ounces*	*140 grams*

The steaks should weigh approximately 6 ounces (170 grams).

Prepare the Dill Compound Butter using the recipe for Maître d'Hôtel Butter (page 547). Substitute dill for parsley in the recipe.

1. Season salmon steak with salt, pepper, and lemon juice.

2. Dip in oil and dredge in bread crumbs.

3. Place in hand grill and broil in medium-heat broiler, turning when golden brown. Cooking time is 6 to 8 minutes.

4. Serve with compound butter.

Bluefish with Creole Mustard Sauce

Yield: 10 servings

Bluefish fillets	*3 1/2 pounds*	*1.6 kilograms*
Salt, to taste	*1/2 teaspoon*	*1/2 teaspoon*
Pepper, to taste	*1/4 teaspoon*	*1/4 teaspoon*
Vegetable oil, as needed	*2 fluid ounces*	*60 milliliters*
Creole mustard sauce	*1 1/2 pints*	*720 milliliters*

Use whole fish such as pompano, mullet, or black sea bass instead of fillets.

The recipe for Creole Mustard Sauce is on page 542.

1. Portion the bluefish at 5 ounces (140 grams).

2. Season the bluefish with salt and pepper to taste and brush with oil. Place the fish in a hand grill.

3. Grill or broil the fish until it is just cooked.

4. Serve the fillets with the sauce.

Broiled Stuffed Lobster

Yield: 10 servings

Lobsters, 1 to 1 1/2 pounds each, split and cleaned	*5 each*	*5 each*
Stuffing		
Butter	*2 ounces*	*60 grams*
Onions, minced	*10 ounces*	*285 grams*
Celery, minced	*5 ounces*	*140 grams*
Red peppers, minced	*1 1/2 ounces*	*43 grams*
Green peppers, minced	*1 1/2 ounces*	*43 grams*
Bread crumbs	*8 ounces*	*225 grams*
Lemon wedges	*20 each*	*20 each*
Butter, melted	*10 fluid ounces*	*285 grams*

1. Place lobsters on a grill rack, shell side up. Grill until the shells are red. Remove from the rack.

2. Melt the butter in a sauté pan. Sweat the vegetables. Remove from the heat. Add the bread crumbs and spoon the mixture into each cavity. (Do not place it over the tail meat.)

3. Place lobsters on a sheet pan and finish in a 400°F (205°C) oven.

4. Crack the claws but leave the meat inside. Serve the lobster with lemon wedges and drawn butter.

Broiled Mackerel with a Pimiento Butter

Yield: 10 servings

Mackerel, 5- to 6-ounce portions	*10 each*	*10 each*
Salt, to taste	*1/2 teaspoon*	*1/2 teaspoon*
Pepper, to taste	*1/4 teaspoon*	*1/4 teaspoon*
Lemon juice, to taste	*1 fluid ounce*	*30 milliliters*
Flour, as needed	*4 ounces*	*115 grams*
Vegetable oil, or butter, as needed	*4 fluid ounces*	*120 milliliters*
Pimiento Butter	*6 ounces*	*170 grams*

1. Season the fish with salt and pepper and lemon juice to taste.

2. Brush or dip the fish in oil or butter. Dredge in the flour.

3. Broil the fish in an oiled hand grill until it is just cooked.

4. Before serving, flash the fish under a salamander or broiler; serve immediately with the pimiento butter.

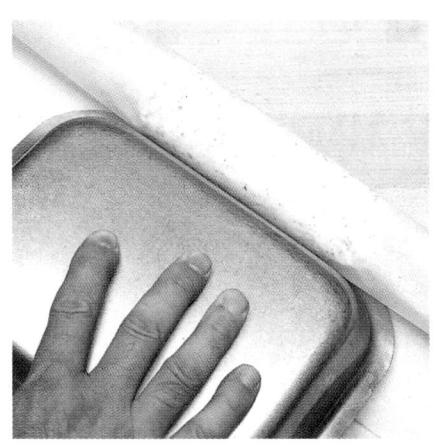

Use a flavored butter as a kind of sauce to finish broiled fish dishes.

The recipe for Pimiento Butter can be found on page 548.

Basil is a pungent herb and is often combined with tomato for coulis or sauce.

Cut the shark into 6- to 8-ounce (170- to 225-gram) portions.

To prepare pinchots, *cut the shark into 1-inch cubes placed on skewers and grill. If using wooden skewers, be sure to soak them first.*

Swordfish and tuna steaks also work with this sauce.

Broiled Mako Shark with Grilled Scallions and Tomato-Basil Coulis

Yield: 10 servings

Coulis

Olive oil	1 tablespoon	1 tablespoon
Butter	1 tablespoon	1 tablespoon
Shallots, minced	4 each	4 each
Garlic cloves, mashed to paste	2 each	2 each
Tomato paste	2 tablespoons	2 tablespoons
Tomato Concassé	2 pounds	900 grams
Chicken Stock	10 fluid ounces	300 milliliters
Standard Sachet d'Epices	1 each	1 each
Red wine vinegar	2 tablespoons	2 tablespoons
Basil, chopped	2 tablespoons	2 tablespoons
Salt, to taste	1/2 teaspoon	1/2 teaspoon
Sugar, to taste (optional)	1/2 teaspoon	1/2 teaspoon
Mako shark steaks	10 each	10 each
Scallions, trimmed	4 pounds	1.8 kilograms
Vegetable oil	20 fluid ounces	60 milliliters
Salt, to taste	1/2 teaspoon	1/2 teaspoon
Pepper, to taste	1/4 teaspoon	1/4 teaspoon
Lemon juice, to taste	2 fluid ounces	60 milliliters

1. To prepare coulis: Sauté shallots, garlic, and tomato paste in oil and butter.

2. Add Tomato Concassé, stock, and sachet; simmer for 20 minutes.

3. Remove sachet and purée the tomato mixture.

4. Add vinegar and basil. Adjust seasoning to taste with salt and sugar.

5. Season shark with salt, pepper, and lemon juice.

6. Lard with scallions; cut shark into steaks.

7. Rub steaks and scallions with oil. Cook on a grill for 5 to 7 minutes. (Turn steaks 45-degree angles during cooking to achieve grill marks.)

8. Put the steak on a warm platter; pool the coulis around the steak. Top with grilled scallions.

Broiled Lemon Sole on a Bed of Leeks

Yield: 10 servings

Lemon sole or flounder fillets	*4 pounds*	*1.8 kilograms*
Lemon juice, as needed	*2 fluid ounces*	*60 milliliters*
Vegetable oil, as needed	*2 fluid ounces*	*60 milliliters*
Bread crumbs, fresh, as needed	*4 ounces*	*115 grams*
Leeks, paysanne or fermière cut	*10 ounces*	*285 grams*
Butter, as needed	*2 ounces*	*60 grams*
Heavy cream	*10 fluid ounces*	*300 milliliters*

For more information about broiling, refer to Chapter 9, pages 300 to 304.

The fillets should weigh about 6 ounces (170 grams) each.

Paysanne and fermière cuts are described on page 186.

1. Season the fish with the lemon juice, salt, and pepper to taste. Brush it with the oil.
2. Dredge the fish in the crumbs; shake off the excess crumbs.
3. Place the fish on a sizzler platter. Broil it until it is cooked through.
4. Stew the leeks in the butter and cream until they are tender. Season them with salt and pepper. Serve the fish on a bed of leeks.

Broiled Tuna with Salsa Cruda

Yield: 10 servings

Lime juice	*2 fluid ounces*	*60 milliliters*
Shallots, minced	*1 ounce*	*30 grams*
Garlic cloves, mashed to a paste	*3 each*	*3 each*
Tuna steaks	*10 each*	*10 each*
Salsa cruda		
Tomato concassé, fine dice	*14 ounces*	*400 grams*
Jalapeño peppers, fine dice	*3/4 ounce*	*20 grams*
Cherry peppers, fine dice	*3/4 ounce*	*20 grams*
Cilantro, chopped	*1 bunch*	*1 bunch*
Scallions, whites, chopped fine	*3 ounces*	*60 grams*
Garlic cloves, mashed	*3 each*	*3 each*
Lime juice	*3 fluid ounces*	*90 milliliters*
Olive oil, as needed	*2 fluid ounces*	*60 milliliters*
Green, yellow, and red peppers, roasted	*6 ounces*	*170 grams*

Steaks should be cut in 4- to 6-ounce (115- to 170-gram) portions.

The tuna may be grilled if you prefer. Broiled or grilled, the tuna may be finished in the oven if necessary.

1. Combine lime juice, shallots, and garlic. Rub tuna steaks with mixture. Let rest under refrigeration for an hour.
2. Combine ingredients for salsa. Refrigerate the salsa for at least an hour.
3. Broil the tuna until cooked through but still moist and tender. Turn once during cooking time.
4. Serve the tuna with the salsa.

Tuna's flesh color is unique, ranging from pinkish beige to dark maroon. Cut into 4-ounce steaks (115-gram) portions.

Substitute swordfish or mahi-mahi or other firm "meaty" fish for the tuna.

To read about roasting peppers, see page 193.

Serve the tuna on a bed of penne pasta sautéed in hot olive oil and garlic. Mound the peppers on top of the tuna and ladle the sauce over the assembled dish.

Grilled Tuna with Roasted Peppers and Balsamic Vinegar Sauce

Yield: 10 servings

Balsamic vinegar sauce		
Balsamic vinegar	*3 fluid ounces*	*90 milliliters*
Fish Stock or fumet	*8 fluid ounces*	*240 milliliters*
Tomato Concassé	*2 ounces*	*60 grams*
Herbs, chopped (combination of thyme, tarragon, cilantro)	*1 ounce*	*30 grams*
Arrowroot, as needed	*1 tablespoon*	*1 tablespoon*
Enoki mushrooms	*2 ounces*	*60 grams*
Tuna steaks	*10 each*	*10 each*
Salt, to taste	*1/2 teaspoon*	*1/2 teaspoon*
Pepper, to taste	*1/4 teaspoon*	*1/4 teaspoon*
Green peppers, roasted, julienne	*4 ounces*	*115 grams*
Red peppers, roasted, julienne	*4 ounces*	*115 grams*
Yellow peppers, roasted, julienne	*4 ounces*	*115 grams*
Butter	*as needed*	*as needed*

1. Combine the vinegar, stock, Tomato Concassé, and herbs. Heat the mixture and thicken it lightly with the arrowroot.

2. Add the mushrooms to the sauce.

3. Rub the tuna steak with salt and pepper.

4. Grill the steak to the desired doneness; butterfly it.

5. Sauté the peppers until they are hot but still firm.

6. Arrange the tuna steaks on the peppers. Nappé them with the sauce.

Grilled Tuna with Pecan-Lime Butter

Yield: 10 servings

Pecan-lime butter

Butter, softened	*8 ounces*	*225 grams*
Pecans, toasted and crushed fine	*1 1/2 ounces*	*43 grams*
Lime juice, to taste	*1 1/2 fluid ounces*	*45 milliliters*
Oyster sauce	*1 tablespoon*	*1 tablespoon*
Garlic, minced	*1 teaspoon*	*1 teaspoon*
Lovage leaves, chopped	*1 tablespoon*	*1 tablespoon*
White wine	*1 tablespoon*	*1 tablespoon*
Salt, to taste	*1/4 teaspoon*	*1/4 teaspoon*
Pepper, to taste	*1/4 teaspoon*	*1/4 teaspoon*

Marinade

Peanut oil	*6 fluid ounces*	*180 milliliters*
Champagne vinegar	*4 fluid ounces*	*120 milliliters*
Garlic cloves, minced	*3 each*	*3 each*
Scallions, minced	*2 each*	*2 each*
Dry white wine	*4 fluid ounces*	*120 milliliters*
Celery or lovage leaves, minced	*2 tablespoons*	*2 tablespoons*
Tuna steaks	*10 each*	*10 each*

Cut the tuna into 6-ounce (170-gram) steaks.

The fish can also be marinated in the Cumin-Lime Marinade or the Latin-Citrus Marinade found on pages 430 to 434.

Swordfish or shark may be substituted.

An illustration of toasting nuts is found on page 202.

1. Mix all ingredients for the pecan-lime butter together, roll up in parchment paper or plastic wrap; chill until firm.

2. Combine the ingredients for the marinade, pour over the tuna steaks, and marinate 45 minutes.

3. Drain tuna steaks, place on grids of a hot grill.

4. Mark and turn at a 45° angle, mark and turn over, finish cooking on the lower-temperature side of the grill.

5. Garnish steak with a 1/2 ounce (15-gram) slice of pecan-lime butter.

Grilled Swordfish with Pepper Cream Sauce

Yield: 10 servings

Cut the steaks into 5- to 6-ounce (140- to 160-gram) portions.

The recipe for Fish Fumet can be found on page 443.

Mahi-mahi steaks may be substituted for the swordfish.

Cracked rose peppercorns may be added to the sauce as well.

Swordfish steaks	10 each	10 each
Salt, to taste	1/2 teaspoon	1/2 teaspoon
Pepper, to taste	1/4 teaspoon	1/4 teaspoon
Lemon juice	2 fluid ounces	60 milliliters
Oil, as needed	2 fluid ounces	60 milliliters
Pepper cream sauce		
White wine	14 fluid ounces	420 milliliters
Fish Fumet	14 fluid ounces	420 milliliters
Green peppercorns, drained and mashed	3 tablespoons	3 tablespoons
Black peppercorns, cracked	3 tablespoons	3 tablespoons
White peppercorns, cracked	3 tablespoons	3 tablespoons
Thyme, sprig	1 each	1 each
Bay leaves	2 each	2 each
Heavy cream, reduced	6 fluid ounces	180 milliliters
Chives, chopped	2 ounces	60 grams

1. Season the swordfish with the salt and pepper to taste. Brush with the lemon juice and oil. Let the fish marinate 30 minutes.

2. For the sauce: Combine the wine, fumet, peppercorns, thyme, and bay leaves. Reduce the mixture by half. Remove the thyme and bay leaves. Add the cream and reduce it to the desired consistency. Adjust the seasoning to taste with salt.

3. Grill the fish to the correct doneness at the time of service.

4. Add chives (1 tablespoon or 2 grams per portion) to the sauce immediately prior to service. Pool the sauce on the plate and top it with grilled swordfish.

Grilled Salmon with Roasted Pepper Salad

Yield: 10 servings

Salmon steaks	*3 1/2 pounds*	*1.6 kilograms*
Marinade		
Limes, juiced	*2 each*	*2 each*
White wine vinegar	*1 tablespoon*	*1 tablespoon*
Honey	*1 teaspoon*	*1 teaspoon*
Onions, fine mince	*1 3/4 ounces*	*50 grams*
White pepper, to taste	*1/4 teaspoon*	*1/4 teaspoon*
Pepper salad		
Red peppers, roasted, julienne	*12 ounces*	*340 grams*
Green peppers, roasted, julienne	*12 ounces*	*340 grams*
Yellow peppers, roasted, julienne	*12 ounces*	*340 grams*
Red onions, julienne	*2 ounces*	*60 grams*
Golden raisins, plumped	*2 ounces*	*60 grams*
Black olives, cut in strips	*20 each*	*20 each*
Tomatoes, peeled, seeded, and cut in strips	*7 ounces*	*200 grams*
Pine nuts, toasted	*1 ounce*	*30 grams*
Jalapeño peppers, seeded and finely chopped	*1 ounces*	*30 grams*
Garlic, chopped fine	*1 ounces*	*30 grams*
Cayenne, ground	*pinch*	*pinch*
Balsamic Vinaigrette	*10 fluid ounces*	*300 milliliters*
Parmesan cheese, shaved, as needed	*2 ounces*	*60 grams*

The recipe for Balsamic Vinaigrette is contained in notes on Basic Vinaigrette (see page 906).

For a summer menu, serve the Pepper Salad cold on a bed of lettuce. Boiled red potatoes marinated in the Balsamic Vinaigrette could accompany the salad along with a quartered hard boiled egg in the Niçoise style. Add the warm grilled swordfish right before service.

This Pepper Salad can be served on a bed of grilled eggplant or as an ccompaniment to other grilled fish or poultry.

1. Cut the salmon into 6-ounce (170-gram) steaks.

2. Prepare marinade with lime juice, vinegar, honey, onions, and pepper. Lightly marinate fish for about 45 minutes. Grill the fish to the desired doneness.

3. Prepare roasted pepper salad: Combine peppers, onions, raisins, olives, tomatoes, jalapeños, garlic, and cayenne.

4. Warm the vinaigrette and roasted pepper salad in a sauteuse (do not overcook).

5. To serve, arrange fish on a bed of warmed salad. Finish salad with shaved Parmesan.

Grilled Spanish Mackerel
with Tomato Fondue

Yield: 10 servings

Spanish mackerel fillets	3 1/2 pounds	1.6 kilograms
Salt, to taste	1/2 teaspoon	1/2 teaspoon
Pepper, to taste	1/2 teaspoon	1/2 teaspoon
Vegetable oil, as needed	2 fluid ounces	60 milliliters
Tomato fondue		
Olive oil	1 fluid ounce	30 milliliters
Garlic, minced	2 ounces	60 grams
Onions, diced	7 ounces	200 grams
Tomato Concassé	2 1/4 ounces	64 grams
Fresh herbs, including: basil, chives, sage, tarragon, parsley	1 ounce	30 grams
Tomato juice	4 fluid ounces	120 milliliters
Lime juice	1 fluid ounce	30 milliliters
Pepper, to taste	1/4 teaspoon	1/4 teaspoon

1. Cut the mackerel into 5-ounce (140-gram) portions.

2. Prepare the fondue as follows: Heat the oil and sauté the garlic and onions until they lose their harsh aroma. Add the Tomato Concassé and cook quickly over high heat, tossing frequently, until most of the free moisture reduces. Add the herbs, tomato juice, lime juice, and black pepper. Reduce very briefly if necessary. Adjust the seasoning to taste with salt.

3. Grill the mackerel, and serve with the tomato fondue pooled around it.

Fillet of Mahi-Mahi with Pineapple Chutney

Yield: 10 servings

To prepare the chutney, place the pineapple and juice in a pot. Reduce slightly. Add the pepper and simmer just to develop flavor. Season with brown sugar and vinegar to taste.

Mahi-Mahi, fillets or steaks	10 each	10 each
Lime juice	1 tablepoon	1 tablepoon
Pineapple chutney	20 ounces	570 grams
Pineapple chunks	12 ounces	340 grams
Pineapple juice	8 fluid ounces	240 milliliters
Red pepper, diced	3 ounces	85 grams
Green pepper, diced	3 ounces	85 grams
Jalapeño pepper, fine dice	1 ounce	30 grams
Brown sugar, as needed	2 tablespoons	2 tablespoons
Rice wine vinegar	2 tablespoons	2 tablespoons

(Recipe continued on facing page)

1. If desired, cut mahi-mahi into 5- to 6-ounce (140- to 170-gram) tranches. Sprinkle with lime juice. Let marinate briefly.

2. Grill mahi-mahi. Serve immediately with warm salsa.

Scallion-Studded Swordfish with a Red Pepper Coulis

Yield: 10 servings

Red pepper coulis:

Red peppers, roasted, peeled, and seeded	*6 ounces*	*170 grams*
Shallots, minced	*2 each*	*2 each*
White wine	*4 fluid ounces*	*120 milliliters*
Heavy cream	*4 fluid ounces*	*120 milliliters*
Butter, cut into cubes	*2 ounces*	*60 grams*
Salt, to taste	*1/2 teaspoon*	*1/2 teaspoon*
Swordfish, skin on	*3 pounds*	*1.3 kilograms*
Scallions, cut into quarters	*10 each*	*10 each*
Lemons, juiced	*2 each*	*2 each*
Salt, to taste	*1/2 teaspoon*	*1/2 teaspoon*
Pepper, to taste	*1/4 teaspoon*	*1/4 teaspoon*
Vegetable oil	*2 fluid ounces*	*60 milliliters*
Scallion fans	*10 each*	*10 each*
Red peppers, fine julienne, blanched	*1 ounce*	*30 grams*

To prepare scallion fans as a garnish, trim root ends and cut the white end into fringe.

Halibut steaks or fillets or pompano fillets would work well with this recipe.

1. Purée peppers in blender.

2. In a saucepan, combine shallots and wine, reduce by half.

3. Add pepper purée and heavy cream; reduce until sauce consistency.

4. Remove from heat; monté au beurre and adjust seasoning with salt to taste.

5. Lard swordfish with scallion quarters: Use a wooden skewer to pierce the swordfish. Work a piece of scallion into the fish, leaving both ends of the scallion exposed.

6. Portion fish into 10 steaks and season with salt, pepper, and lemon juice.

7. Brush with oil; broil for 5 to 7 minutes; turn to achieve grill marks.

8. Remove skin (optional) and serve with red pepper coulis, julienned peppers, and scallion fan.

Broiled Seafood Platter

Yield: 10 servings

Serve with lemon wedges, cocktail sauce, and Tartar Sauce. Use any lean, flaky white fish that is available: cod, haddock, halibut, turbot, or flounder.

Hake fillets	2 pounds	900 grams
Shrimp, peeled, deveined, butterflied	20 each	20 each
Oysters, shucked, on the halfshell	20 each	20 each
Clams, shucked, on the halfshell	30 each	30 each
Sea scallops	20 each	20 each
Salt, to taste	1/2 teaspoon	1/2 teaspoon
Pepper, to taste	1/2 teaspoon	1/2 teaspoon
Lemon juice, to taste	2 fluid ounces	60 milliliters
Clarified butter	2 ounces	60 grams
Bread crumbs, dry	3 ounces	85 grams

1. Season fish and seafood with salt, pepper, and lemon juice, dip in oil, dredge in bread crumbs, and place on a sizzler platter.

2. Top the seafood with bread crumbs and drizzle with butter.

3. Broil on medium heat in the broiler until browned and cooked (approximately 6 minutes).

Salmon Baked in Phyllo with Saffron Sauce

Yield: 10 servings

To read about preparing mousseline forcemeats, see page 361.

The recipe for Duxelles may be found on page 421.

Fish Velouté may be found on page 531.

Puff pastry sheets may be used in place of phyllo. Increase the baking time until the pastry reaches a light golden brown.

Salmon fillet	24 ounces	680 grams
Salt, to taste	1/2 teaspoon	1/2 teaspoon
Pepper, to taste	1/4 teaspoon	1/4 teaspoon
Egg white, chilled	1 each	1 each
Heavy cream, chilled	2 fluid ounces	60 milliliters
Tarragon leaves, chopped	1/2 teaspoon	1/2 teaspoon
Basil leaves, chopped	1/2 teaspoon	1/2 teaspoon
Salt	1/4 teaspoon	1/4 teaspoon
Duxelles	10 ounces	285 grams
Phyllo dough sheets	10 each	10 each
Clarified butter, as needed	3 ounces	85 grams
Bread crumbs, dry	3 ounces	85 grams

(Recipe continued on facing page)

Saffron sauce

Dry white wine	*2 fluid ounces*	*60 milliliters*
Saffron threads, crushed	*1 pinch*	*1 pinch*
Fish Velouté	*1 pint*	*480 milliliters*
Tomato Concassé	*5 ounces*	*140 grams*
Chives, chopped	*as needed*	*as needed*

1. Cut the salmon into 5-ounce (140-gram) pieces. Reserve all trim for the mousseline filling. You will need 5 ounces (140 grams). Chill the fish thoroughly.

2. Make a mousseline as follows: Purée the salmon in the chilled bowl of a food processor to a smooth paste. Add the egg white, cream, herbs, and salt. Pulse the machine off and on, until the ingredients are all just incorporated. Keep chilled until needed.

3. Spread the forcemeat on the salmon and top with the duxelles.

4. Wrap the salmon in the phyllo (brush with butter, scattering bread crumbs between each sheet) and bake in a 400°F (205°C) oven for 20 minutes. Salmon should have an internal temperature of 150°F (65°C) and pastry should be a golden brown.

5. To prepare the sauce, heat the wine and steep the saffron in it. Add it to the velouté and simmer until the sauce is a deep golden color and reduced to a good consistency. Add the Tomato Concassé and the chives. Pool the sauce on heated plates and serve the salmon on top of the sauce.

Potato-Roasted Cod

Yield: 10 servings

Cod fillets	*10 each*	*10 each*
Salt, to taste	*1/2 teaspoon*	*1/2 teaspoon*
Pepper, to taste	*1/4 teaspoon*	*1/4 teaspoon*
Lemon juice	*to taste*	*to taste*
Spinach	*2 1/4 pounds*	*1 kilogram*
Butter, as needed	*2 ounces*	*60 grams*
Garlic cloves, mashed to a paste	*3 each*	*3 each*
Idaho potatoes	*5 each*	*5 each*
Clarified butter, as needed	*5 ounces*	*140 grams*

Portion the cod into 4- to 5-ounce (115- to 140-gram) pieces.

Turbot, halibut, grouper, and tilapia are other good choices.

A thin layer of Duxelles may be added between the fish and the spinach.

The potatoes may be grated, squeezed dry, and molded around the fish. Carefully pan-fry the fish. Add an egg to the grated potatoes to bind if desired.

1. Season fillets with lemon, salt, and pepper.

2. Sauté the spinach in the butter and garlic. Chill well.

3. Spread a layer of spinach over fillet. Refrigerate until needed.

4. Peel potatoes and slice very thin on a mandoline; blanch in a deep-fryer at 325°F (162°C) and drain on paper towels.

5. Arrange blanched potatoes in a scale pattern on top of the spinach; brush with butter.

6. Bake in a 400°F (205°C) oven until potatoes brown and fish is cooked.

Baked Lemon-Stuffed Trout

Yield: 10 servings

Trout, pan-dressed and deboned	*10 each*	*10 each*
Shallots, minced, smothered	*2 teaspoons*	*2 teaspoons*
Lemons, sliced thin	*3 each*	*3 each*
Parsley, sprigs	*1 ounce*	*30 grams*
Thyme, sprigs	*1 ounce*	*30 grams*
Salt, to taste	*1/2 teaspoon*	*1/2 teaspoon*
Pepper, to taste	*1/4 teaspoon*	*1/4 teaspoon*
Butter	*as needed*	*as needed*

Serve lemon wedges on the side. You may prefer to dot the fish with a Compound Butter when baking. If a sauce is desired, Hollandaise (page 541) would be a good choice.

To smother the shallots, heat a small amount of butter over moderate heat. Add the shallots and cook slowly, covered, until they are tender.

1. Rub the fish with shallots and lemon juice to help dissolve any remaining bone. Add the lemon slices, parsley, and thyme.
2. Fold the fish closed and season well.
3. Place the fish in a buttered baking dish.
4. Dot the fish with butter.
5. Bake in a 400°F (205°C) oven until it is done, about 10 to 12 minutes.
6. Serve the trout with lemon slices.

Roasted Monkfish with Niçoise Olives and Pernod Sauce

Yield: 10 servings

Marinade

Lime juice	*2 fluid ounces*	*60 milliliters*
Green peppercorns, mashed	*1 tablespoon*	*1 tablespoon*
Tarragon, chopped	*1 tablespoon*	*1 tablespoon*
Shallots, minced	*1 tablespoon*	*1 tablespoon*
Monkfish, trimmed of connective tissue	*3 1/2 pounds*	*1.5 kilograms*
Vegetable oil, as needed	*2 fluid ounces*	*60 milliliters*
Tomato paste	*1 ounce*	*30 grams*
Pernod, as desired	*1 to 2 fluid ounces*	*30 to 60 milliliters*
Tarragon Beurre Blanc	*1 pint*	*480 milliliters*
Niçoise olives, pitted and split	*1 ounce*	*30 grams*
Salt, to taste	*1/2 teaspoon*	*1/2 teaspoon*
Pepper, to taste	*1/4 teaspoon*	*1/4 teaspoon*

The recipe for Tarragon Beurre Blanc can be found on page 546. You may wish to reduce the amount of lemon.

1. Combine all ingredients for the marinade. Add the monkfish and marinate for 15 to 30 minutes.

2. Coat a griswold or heavy sautoir with oil. Sear the monkfish in the hot pan on all sides.

3. Finish in a 350°F (175°C) oven. Remove the monkfish and keep it warm.

4. Sauté the tomato paste in the pan for 2 minutes to cook it down. Deglaze the pan with the Pernod. Add the Tarragon Beurre Blanc and olives. Adjust the consistency and seasoning with salt and pepper.

5. Slice the monkfish and fan it on plate. Coat the fish with the sauce.

Salmon Fillet with Smoked-Salmon-and-Horseradish Crust

Yield: 10 servings

Cut the fillet into 5-ounce (140-gram) portions.

If desired, serve with Horseradish Sauce, page 532, or prepare a cold horseradish sauce by combining equal parts mayonnaise and whipped heavy cream and adding prepared horseradish to taste.

Salmon fillets	10 each	10 each
Limes, juiced	2 each	2 each
Shallots, mashed, as needed	2 teaspoons	2 teaspoons
Garlic, mashed, as needed	2 teaspoons	2 teaspoons
Black peppercorns, crushed, as needed	2 teaspoons	2 teaspoons
Crumb mixture		
Butter	3 ounces	85 grams
Shallots, minced	1/2 teaspoon	1/2 teaspoon
Garlic, minced	1/2 teaspoon	1/2 teaspoon
Bread crumbs, fresh	5 ounces	140 grams
Smoked salmon	5 ounces	140 grams
Horseradish, prepared	1 ounce	30 grams

1. Rub the salmon fillets with the lime juice, shallots, garlic, and crushed peppercorns.

2. To make the crumb mixture: Sauté the shallots and garlic in the butter until they are aromatic.

3. Combine all of the ingredients for the crumb mixture in a food processor and process them to a fine consistency.

4. Portion 1 ounce (30 grams) of the crumb mixture onto each salmon fillet.

5. Bake the fillets in a medium oven until done. Brown fillets under a salamander, if necessary, to brown the crumbs. Serve fillets on heated plates.

Noisettes of Salmon
with Cucumber-Dill Sauce

Yield: 10 servings

Salmon fillets, cut into noisettes	*20 each*	*20 each*
Fish Marinade	*1 pint*	*480 milliliters*
Salt, to taste	*1/2 teaspoon*	*1/2 teaspoon*
Cucumber-dill sauce		
Vegetable oil, as needed	*1 fluid ounce*	*30 milliliters*
Sweet onions (Vidalia), sliced	*4 ounces*	*115 grams*
Cucumber, peeled, halved, sliced	*14 ounces*	*400 grams*
White vinegar, as needed	*6 fluid ounces*	*180 milliliters*
Sugar, to taste	*2 tablespoons*	*2 tablespoons*
Dill, fresh	*2 ounces*	*60 grams*

Portion size should be 4 to 5 ounces (115 to 140 grams) per serving.

The recipe for Fish Marinade can be found on page 431.

You may substitute lemon juice or white wine for some or all of the white vinegar.

If using large cucumbers, you may want to seed and salt them first.

1. Marinate the salmon 30 to 45 minutes. Drain.
2. Finish cooking the salmon in a hot oven for about 8 to 10 minutes.
3. Add some oil to the sauté pan. Lightly sauté the onions. Add the cucumbers, vinegar, and sugar. Reduce slightly.
4. Add the dill; adjust seasoning with salt and sugar.
5. Serve the salmon on a bed of the cucumber-dill sauce.

Hot Smoked Salmon Fillet with
Sun-Dried Tomato Coulis

Yield: 10 servings

Salmon fillets	*17 1/2 ounces*	*500 grams*
Lime, juiced	*1 each*	*1 each*
Garlic cloves, mashed	*2 each*	*2 each*
Shallots, minced	*1 ounce*	*30 grams*
Peppercorns, cracked	*1/4 teaspoon*	*1/4 teaspoon*
Hickory chips	*as needed*	*as needed*
Sun-Dried Tomato Coulis	*20 ounces*	*570 grams*

The set-up for smoke-roasting may be found on page 306.

Use 3 ounces (85 grams) of sun-dried tomatoes in the Sun-Dried Tomato Coulis (page 551).

1. Mix together lime juice, garlic, shallots, and peppercorns. Marinate salmon fillets 30 to 45 minutes.
2. Drain the salmon. Place it on a rack or steamer.
3. Place hickory, apple, or other hardwood chips in a heavy skillet. Place the skillet over high heat. When the chips are smoking, place the salmon in the skillet and cover it tightly. Smoke the salmon for 2 to 3 minutes.
4. Finish cooking the salmon in a hot oven for about 8 to 10 minutes.
5. Plate the salmon and pool the sauce around the fish.

Smoked-Roasted Bluefish with Leek Compote and Horseradish Sauce

Yield: 10 servings

Bluefish is a slightly oily fish with a distinctive flavor. If it is unavailable, use salmon or mackerel. Whole pan-dressed trout may also be used.

The recipe for Horseradish Sauce is on page 532. If you prefer, substitute a Compound Butter and serve horseradish separately.

The set-up for smoke-roasting is on page 306.

Bluefish fillets	3 1/2 pounds	1.6 kilograms
Salt, to taste	1/2 teaspoon	1/2 teaspoon
Pepper, to taste	1/4 teaspoon	1/4 teaspoon
Lemon juice	2 fluid ounces	60 milliliters
Hickory chips	as needed	as needed
Leek Compote		
Garlic clove, mashed to a paste	1 each	1 each
Leeks, sliced	1 pound	455 grams
Butter	2 ounces	60 grams
Dry white wine	2 fluid ounces	60 milliliters
Chicken Stock	4 fluid ounces	120 milliliters
Parsley, chopped	1/2 teaspoon	1/2 teaspoon
Tomato Concassé	6 ounces	170 grams
Salt, to taste	1/2 teaspoon	1/2 teaspoon
Horseradish Sauce	20 fluid ounces	600 milliliters

1. Season fish with salt, pepper, and lemon.

2. Spread a quarter inch of hickory chips in the bottoms of disposable foil hotel pans.

3. Place the fish on wire racks; set racks on top of hickory chips. Do not allow fish to touch the hickory chips.

4. Cover pans with foil or a second foil pan.

5. Place pans with fish on burner with high heat; when smoke starts to show, lower heat slightly.

6. Smoke fish for 5 to 6 minutes. Move pans occasionally to be sure to burn all chips.

7. Remove pans from heat and let pans sit for 2 minutes before opening.

8. To make the leek compote: Sweat garlic and leeks in butter until wilted.

9. Add wine and stock, reduce until leeks are tender and liquid has almost evaporated; stir occasionally.

10. Add parsley and Tomato Concassé; season to taste with salt.

11. Remove fish from smoker, remove skin, set each fish on a portion of leek compote, and nappé with horseradish sauce.

Cioppino

Yield: 10 servings

Olive oil	1 fluid ounce	30 milliliters
Onions, diced fine	6 ounces	170 grams
Scallions, diced	2 bunches	2 bunches
Green peppers, diced	2 each	2 each
Fennel, diced	5 ounces	140 grams
Garlic, cloves, minced	5 each	5 each
Fish Fumet	1 quart	1 liter
Tomato Concassé	6 pounds	150 grams
Tomato purée	4 fluid ounces	120 milliliters
Dry white wine	8 fluid ounces	240 milliliters
Bay leaves	2 each	2 each
Pepper, to taste	1/4 teaspoon	1/4 teaspoon
Salt, to taste	1/2 teaspoon	1/2 teaspoon
Little Neck clams	20 each	20 each
Crabs, disjointed	3 each	3 each
Shrimp, 21 to 25 count, peeled and deveined	20 each	20 each
Swordfish, diced	1 1/4 pounds	570 grams
Basil, chopped	3 tablespoons	3 tablespoons
Croutons, garlic-flavored	10 each	10 each

This fish stew and others like it are derived from dishes prepared by fishermen returning to shore. The selection of seafood would vary from day to day.

To prepare the croutons, spread 10 slices of Italian bread with an olive oil-garlic mixture. Toast in the oven until crisp.

1. Heat the oil in a soup pot. Add the onions, scallions, peppers, and fennel. Sauté until the onions are translucent.

2. Add the garlic and sauté it until an aroma is apparent. Add the white wine and reduce by half.

3. Add the fish fumet, Tomato Concassé, tomato purée, white wine, and bay leaves. Cover the pot and simmer the mixture slowly for about 45 minutes. Add a small amount of water, if necessary. Cioppino should be more of a broth than a stew.

4. Remove and discard the bay leaves.

5. Add the whole clams and crabs. Simmer for about 10 minutes. Add the shrimp and swordfish; simmer them until the fish is just cooked through.

6. Add the chopped basil; adjust the seasoning to taste with salt and pepper. Ladle the cioppino into heated bowls and garnish each bowl with a crouton.

Seafood Newburg

Yield: 4 servings

Select lobsters that weigh approximately 1 1/2 to 2 pounds (800 to 900 grams). Reserve the coral and tomalley to add to the sauce.

This dish, as originally prepared by Charles Ranshofer of Delmonico's, contained only lobster, Madeira, cream, and egg yolks.

One classic presentation of this dish is in a piped-out border of Duchesse Potatoes (see page 827).

Scallops, cleaned	*5 ounces*	*140 grams*
Lobsters, blanched	*2 each*	*2 each*
Shrimp, shelled and deveined	*6 ounces*	*170 grams*
Olive oil	*1 fluid ounce*	*30 milliliters*
Shallots, chopped	*1 tablespoon*	*1 tablespoon*
Brandy	*2 fluid ounces*	*60 milliliters*
Clarified butter	*1 ounce*	*30 grams*
Madeira	*6 fluid ounces*	*180 milliliters*
Heavy cream	*12 fluid ounces*	*360 milliliters*
Egg yolks	*4 each*	*4 each*
Salt, to taste	*1/2 teaspoon*	*1/2 teaspoon*
White pepper, to taste	*1/4 teaspoon*	*1/4 teaspoon*

1. Cut the lobster into pieces. Reserve the coral and tomalley.

2. Heat the olive oil and butter over high heat.

3. Sauté the seafood until the scallops and shrimp are stiffened. Remove the lobster pieces from their shells and return.

4. At service, add the brandy; flame it. Add the Madeira and simmer until nearly reduced.

5. Blend the heavy cream and yolks. Add this to the pan and cook over very gentle heat until thickened. Season to taste with salt and pepper and serve immediately.

Shrimp Jambalaya

Yield: 10 servings

Salt pork, minced	*6 ounces*	*170 grams*
Onions, diced	*6 ounces*	*170 grams*
Green pepper, diced	*6 ounces*	*170 grams*
Red pepper, diced	*6 ounces*	*170 grams*
Celery, diced	*6 ounces*	*170 grams*
Ham, diced	*8 ounces*	*225 grams*
Garlic cloves, minced	*5 each*	*5 each*
Long-grain rice	*8 ounces*	*225 grams*
Salt, to taste	*2 teaspoons*	*2 teaspoons*
Tabasco, to taste	*several drops*	*several drops*
Thyme, leaves	*1 teaspoon*	*1 teaspoon*
Fish Stock	*3 pints*	*1.5 liters*
Garbanzo beans, cooked and drained	*8 ounces*	*225 grams*
Olives, ripe, pitted	*3 ounces*	*85 grams*
Tomato Concassé	*1 1/2 pounds*	*680 grams*
Shrimp, peeled and deveined	*2 1/4 pounds*	*1 kilogram*
Okra	*20 each*	*20 each*
Parsley, chopped	*3 tablespoons*	*3 tablespoons*

The recipe for Fish Stock can be found on page 443.

The okra may be left whole if it is very small. Slice larger okra about 1/2 inch (1 centimeter) thick.

It is thought that the term jambalaya *has its origins in the French word for ham (*jambon*), an important ingredient in any good version of this dish.*

1. Render the salt pork until it is lightly browned.

2. Add the onions, peppers, celery, ham, and garlic; cook them over high heat until an aroma is apparent.

3. Add the rice; cook until the rice is coated with the rendered fat. (It should appear shiny.) Add the salt, Tabasco, thyme, and stock. Bring the mixture to a boil.

4. Add the garbanzos, olives, and Tomato Concassé. Cover the pot and cook the mixture over low heat for 20 minutes, or until the rice is nearly tender.

5. Add the shrimp; cover the pot again and cook the jambalaya until the shrimp are barely cooked through and the rice is tender.

6. Sauté the okra quickly and add it to the jambalaya. Adjust the seasoning to taste with salt, pepper, and Tobasco.

7. Garnish with chopped parsley.

Shrimp Creole

Yield: 10 servings

Both this dish and jambalaya (preceding page) incude the Acadian "Holy Trinity," green peppers, onions, and celery. These aromatic vegetables are allowed to smother in pork fat or butter until tender.

Bacon, chopped	*4 ounces*	*115 grams*
Onions, diced	*10 ounces*	*285 grams*
Green peppers, diced	*6 ounces*	*170 grams*
Celery, diced	*6 ounces*	*170 grams*
Garlic cloves, minced	*3 each*	*3 each*
Tomato Concassée	*1 1/2 pounds*	*680 grams*
Fish Stock	*1 pint*	*480 milliliters*
Bay leaf	*1 each*	*1 each*
Paprika	*1 tablespoon*	*1 tablespoon*
Cayenne, ground	*1/2 teaspoon*	*1/2 teaspoon*
Fish Stock	*3 fluid ounces*	*90 milliliters*
Cornstarch	*2 tablespoons*	*2 tablespoons*
Shrimp, 16 to 20 count, peeled, deveined	*3 pounds*	*1.35 kilograms*
Salt, to taste	*1/2 teaspoon*	*1/2 teaspoon*
Pepper, to taste	*1/4 teaspoon*	*1/4 teaspoon*
Rice, cooked	*24 ounces*	*680 grams*

1. Render bacon until almost crisp, add onion, pepper, celery, and garlic. Sauté until onions are translucent.

2. Add tomatoes, stock, bay leaf, paprika and cayenne; bring to a simmer.

3. Simmer 20 minutes.

4. Mix cornstarch with water or cold stock and add to a simmering sauce.

5. Add shrimp and simmer only long enough to cook shrimp. Adjust seasonings to taste with salt, pepper, and cayenne.

6. Serve over rice.

Fillet of Snapper en Papillote

Yield: 10 servings

Red snapper fillets	*4 pounds*	*1.8 kilograms*
Salt, to taste	*1/2 teaspoon*	*1/2 teaspoon*
Pepper, to taste	*1/4 teaspoon*	*1/4 teaspoon*
Clarified butter	*2 ounces*	*60 grams*
Fish Velouté	*1 pint*	*480 milliliters*
Dry white wine	*4 fluid ounces*	*120 milliliters*
Shallots, minced	*2 tablespoons*	*2 tablespoons*
Scallions, sliced	*5 ounces*	*140 grams*
Mushrooms, sliced	*5 ounces*	*140 grams*

1. Cut the fillets into 6-ounce (170-gram) portions; season well with salt and pepper.

2. (Optional): Heat the clarified butter in a sauteuse. Quickly sear the fish on both sides until stiffened. Remove from the pan.

3. Cut 10 pieces of parchment into heart shapes large enough to enclose the fillets. Brush lightly with oil or butter.

4. Place the Velouté on one side of each parchment heart. Place the fish on top. Sprinkle with the wine, shallots, and scallions. Shingle the mushrooms on top.

5. Fold the paper over and seal the sides tightly.

6. Place each bag on a hot, buttered sizzler platter. Shake it to prevent burning.

7. Finish in a hot oven (400 to 425°F/205 to 220°C) for 5 to 8 minutes. Serve immediately.

The procedure for preparing fish en papillote is illustrated in Figure 10-4 on page 333.

The vegetable garnish can be varied according to the season: peas in early summer, tomatoes and squash in the fall. For an elegant spring entrée, use asparagus tips and morels.

If you cook the fish in clarified butter (step 2), be sure you cool the fish properly before storing them.

Orange Roughy en Papillote with Shrimp and Scallions

Yield: 10 servings

The recipe for Latin Citrus Marinade is on page 432.

Orange roughy fillets	*4 pounds*	*1.8 kilograms*
Salt, to taste	*1/2 teaspoon*	*1/2 teaspoon*
Pepper, to taste	*1/2 teaspoon*	*1/2 teaspoon*
Latin Citrus Marinade	*10 fluid ounces*	*300 milliliters*
Vegetable oil	*1 fluid ounce*	*30 milliliters*
Scallions, sliced	*2 ounces*	*60 grams*
Garlic clove, mashed to a paste	*1 each*	*1 each*
Tomato Concassé	*8 ounces*	*225 grams*
Dry white wine	*10 fluid ounces*	*300 milliliters*
Fish stock	*16 fluid ounces*	*480 milliliters*
Shrimp, diced	*10 ounces*	*285 grams*
Cilantro, minced	*2 tablespoons*	*2 tablespoons*
Lemon juice	*1 tablespoon*	*1 tablespoon*
Parchment paper hearts	*10 each*	*10 each*

1. Trim the fillets; cut into 6-ounce (170-gram) portions. Season with salt and pepper.

2. Combine the fish with the marinade. Marinate for 30 minutes

3. Heat the oil; sauté scallions and garlic until they have a good aroma.

4. Add the Tomato Concassé and wine; bring to a simmer.

5. Add shrimp, cilantro, and lemon to taste. Sauté until the shrimp is cooked. Cool completely before assembling fish.

6. Brush parchment hearts with oil.

7. Remove the fish from the marinade and place on paper. Top with the shrimp and scallions.

8. Fold paper over fish, start in the top corner folding the paper to seal in the fish.

9. Bake on a tray in a hot oven (400 to 425°F/205 to 220°C) oven 6 to 8 minutes.

Salmon Fillet and Cucumbers en Papillote

Yield: 10 servings

Salmon fillets	4 pounds	1.8 kilograms
Cucumbers, seeded, sliced thin	24 ounces	680 grams
Tomato Concassé	8 ounces	225 grams
Dill, chopped	3 tablespoons	3 tablespoons
Shallots, minced	1/2 ounce	15 grams
Salt, to taste	1/2 teaspoon	1/2 teaspoon
Pepper, to taste	1/4 teaspoon	1/4 teaspoon

To cut the cucumbers, peel them, then cut in half lengthwise. Scoop out the seeds and slice thinly.

1. Cut the salmon into 6-ounce (170-gram) portions. Season well with salt and pepper.

2. Cut parchment paper into heart shapes. Scatter the cucumbers, tomatoes, and dill on one side to make a bed for the salmon.

3. Seal papillotes, securing edges well.

4. Bake in hot oven (400 to 425°F/205 to 220°C) for 8 to 10 minutes.

Poached Turbot with Lemon Beurre Blanc

Yield: 10 servings

Salt, to taste	1/2 teaspoon	1/2 teaspoon
Pepper, to taste	1/4 teaspoon	1/4 teaspoon
Turbot fillet or steaks	4 pounds	1.8 kilograms
Butter, softened, as needed	1 ounce	30 grams
Shallots, minced	1 ounce	30 grams
Fish Fumet	1 pint	480 milliliters
Dry white wine	4 fluid ounces	120 milliliters
Lemon juice, to taste	1 tablespoon	1 tablespoon
Lemon Beurre Blanc	1 recipe	1 recipe

Reduce the cooking liquid from the fish until it is syrupy. Use this reduction when preparing the Lemon Beurre Blanc (page 545).

To read more about shallow-poaching, refer to chapter 10, pages 332 to 335.

1. Cut the turbot into 6-ounce (170-gram) portions. Season with salt and pepper.

2. Butter shallow pan; sprinkle with shallots.

3. Place turbot in pan and add fumet and lemon juice.

4. Bring to a simmer over direct heat; cover with parchment.

5. Poach in 300°F (150°C) oven until fish is firm and opaque (about 8 minutes).

6. When done, remove turbot, cover with paper, and keep warm.

7. Prepare the Lemon Beurre Blanc with the reduced cooking liquid. Season to taste and serve turbot with the sauce.

Mussels Mariner-Style (Moules à la Marinère)

Yield: 10 servings

"A la marinère" or mariner's style dishes arew prepared with shellfish prepared with white wine and herbs.

Serve about 1 pound (450 grams) of mussels per portion. Present them in a large, shallow soup plate, on a bed of pasta if desired. This is also a good appetizer served simply with French bread.

The recipe for Red Curry Paste can be found on page 429.

Mussels	*8 pounds*	*3.6 kilograms*
Shallots, minced	*3 each*	*3 each*
White wine	*8 fluid ounces*	*240 milliliters*
Fish Stock	*8 fluid ounces*	*240 milliliters*
Chopped herbs: tarragon, thyme, basil, chives, parsley	*2 tablespoons*	*2 tablespoons*
Butter, diced	*4 ounces*	*115 grams*
Salt, to taste	*1/2 teaspoon*	*1/2 teaspoon*
Pepper, to taste	*1/4 teaspoon*	*1/4 teaspoon*
Lemon juice, to taste	*1 fluid ounce*	*30 milliliters*

1. Scrub the mussels well and remove the beards.

2. Place the mussels in a pan, add shallots, wine, and stock; cover tightly.

3. Bring to a simmer on top of the stove and cook over low heat until the mussels open.

4. When done remove the mussels with a slotted spoon; keep warm.

5. Strain poaching liquid, return to the heat; reduce.

6. Add herbs and whisk in the butter to emulsify the sauce.

7. Season the sauce to taste with salt, pepper, and lemon juice.

8. Serve the mussels with the sauce.

VARIATION

Thai Curried Mussels: Add Red Curry Paste and coconut milk to the strained cooking liquid. Use mint, cilantro, and Thai basil in place of tarragon, thyme, chives, and parsley. Serve on a bed of noodles.

Cold Poached Salmon Steak with Green Mayonnaise

Yield: 10 servings

Salmon	*4 pounds*	*1.8 kilograms*
Court Bouillon, as needed	*1 quart*	*1 liter*
Bouquet Garni	*1 each*	*1 each*
Lemons, sliced	*3 each*	*3 each*
Green Mayonnaise	*20 fluid ounces*	*600 milliliters*

1. Rinse the salmon and blot dry. Wrap in cheesecloth if desired. Place on a fish-poacher rack.

2. Bring the court bouillon, bouquet garni, and lemon slices to a bare simmer.

3. Lower the salmon into the court bouillon. Monitor the cooking speed carefully, maintaining a poaching temperature of 155°F (67°C).

4. Cook the salmon just until it is barely cooked through (internal temperature should be 150°F/65°C); the flesh should still hold together. Allow it to cool in the Court Bouillon.

5. Remove the salmon from the Court Bouillon; unwrap, and carefully remove skin and bones. Chill thoroughly and serve with mayonnaise.

The liquid used for poaching must be well flavored. It is important to use good-quality stocks and aromatic ingredients.

Recipes for Court Bouillon may be found on page 446. Bouquet Garni is on page 424. The recipe for Green Mayonnaise is on page 911.

Poached Salmon with Bearnaise Sauce

Yield: 10 servings

Salmon fillets	*4 pounds*	*1.8 kilograms*
Court Bouillon	*2 quarts*	*2 liters*
Béarnaise Sauce	*20 fluid ounces*	*600 milliliters*

The recipe for Béarnaise Sauce may be found on page 541.

1. Cut the salmon into 5- to 6-ounce (140- to 170-gram) portions.

2. Make court bouillon by combining all ingredients and simmering for 20 minutes.

3. Strain, pour in a shallow pan and bring to a very gentle simmer.

4. Add salmon and poach 8 to 10 minutes, or until just cooked.

5. Remove, serve with sauce.

VARIATION

Poached Salmon with Mousseline Sauce: Replace the Béarnaise Sauce with mousseline. Glaze under a broiler or salamander if desired.

Coquilles St. Jacques au Gratin

Yield: 10 servings

To read more about preparing a mousseline forcemeat, read Chapter 11, page 361.

The recipes for Duchesse Potatoes is on page 827.

Scallop varieties (bay, sea, and calico) are discussed on page 120.

Scallops	3 1/2 pounds	1.6 kilograms
Butter, softened	2 ounces	60 grams
White wine	3 fluid ounces	900 milliliters
Shallots, minced	1 tablespoon	1 tablespoon
Parsley stems, chopped	1/2 bunch	1/2 bunch
Salt	1 teaspoon	1 teaspoon
Pepper, to taste	1/4 teaspoon	1/4 teaspoon
Duchesse Potatoes	2 pounds	900 grams
Duxelles	10 oumces	285 grams
Mornay Sauce	20 fluid ounces	600 milliliters
Parmesan cheese, grated	6 ounces	60 grams

1. Remove the muscle tabs from the scallops. Butter a pan and place the scallops in a layer.

2. Add the wine, shallots, and parsley. Season well; cover with parchment.

3. Bring to a gentle simmer over direct heat, then poach 5 minutes; maintain poaching liquid at a simmer.

4. Remove the scallops, moisten, and keep warm. Reduce the cooking until nearly dry. Strain the reduced cooking into the Mornay Sauce. Simmer and reduce.

5. Pipe the potatoes to make a border. Make a base of duxelles; top with poached scallops.

6. Coat the scallops with Mornay Sauce and parmesan cheese.

7. Brown the scallops under a broiler until very hot and golden.

Poached Salmon and Asparagus with Basil Sauce

Yield: 10 servings

Salmon fillets	*4 pounds*	*1.8 kilograms*
Asparagus, trimmed and blanched	*1 1/2 pounds*	*680 grams*
Butter, softened	*2 ounces*	*60 grams*
Salt, to taste	*1 teaspoon*	*1 teaspoon*
Pepper, to taste	*1/4 teaspoon*	*1/4 teaspoon*
White wine	*4 fluid ounces*	*120 milliliters*
Fish Fumet	*4 fluid ounces*	*120 milliliters*
Shallots, minced	*1 ounce*	*30 grams*
Garlic clove, minced	*1 each*	*1 each*
Dry vermouth	*3 fluid ounces*	*90 milliliters*
Bay leaf	*1 each*	*1 each*
Fish Velouté	*1 pint*	*480 milliliters*
Chives, cut	*1 tablespoon*	*1 tablespoon*
Basil, chiffonade	*2 tablespoons*	*2 tablespoons*
Heavy cream, reduced	*3 fluid ounces*	*90 milliliters*
Garnish		
Tomatoes, peeled, seeded, and julienned	*5 ounces*	*140 grams*
Basil, chiffonade	*as needed*	*as needed*

The recipe for Fish Fumet may be found on page 443. Fish Velouté is on page 531.

To read more about shallow-poaching, read Chapter 10, pages 332 to 335.

1. Cut the salmon into 5-ounce (140-gram) portions on the diagonal or butterfly the portioned salmon. Wrap salmon portion around each 2-ounce (60-gram) bundle of asparagus. Tie to secure.

2. Butter a sauteuse and scatter with shallots and garlic. Place fish in the pan, season well, and add wine and Fish Fumet. Cover with parchment.

3. Bring to a gentle simmer over direct heat; finish cooking in a 350°F (175°C) oven.

4. Remove the fish, moisten, and keep warm. Add the vermouth and bay leaf to the cooking liquid. Reduce to sec.

5. Add the velouté, chives, and basil to finish the sauce. Simmer approximately 5 minutes.

6. Strain and finish with heavy cream and salt.

7. Garnish with julienned tomato and additional basil.

8. Remove the string from the salmon bundles. Serve fish with sauce.

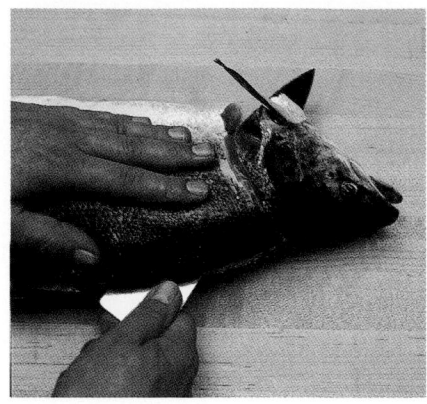

Fillets are the most common form of fabrications for fish. Use a filleting knife to make the initial cut down the backbone.

Vin Blanc Sauce may be prepared in three different ways. After the fish is properly poached, you may

(1) reduce the cooking liquid and add it to prepared Velouté, or

(2) reduce the cooking liquid and use it to replace the standard reduction for Hollandaise Sauce, or

(3) prepare a Hollandaise (without a reduction), gradually incorporating the reduced cooking liquid.

Poached Sole Vin Blanc

Yield: 10 servings

Sole fillets	*4 pounds*	*1.8 kilograms*
Salt, to taste	*1/2 teaspoon*	*1/2 teaspoon*
Pepper, to taste	*1/4 teaspoon*	*1/4 teaspoon*
Butter, as needed	*1 ounce*	*30 grams*
Shallots, minced	*1/2 ounce*	*15 grams*
Dry white wine	*4 fluid ounces*	*120 milliliters*
Fish Stock	*8 fluid ounces*	*240 milliliters*
Velouté, béchamel, or butter	*20 fluid ounces*	*600 milliliters*
Egg yolks, beaten	*3 each*	*3 each*
Butter, diced	*2 ounces*	*30 grams*

1. Portion the sole at 6 ounces (170 grams) each. Season the sole with the salt and pepper and fold into thirds.

2. Butter a pan; sprinkle with the shallots. Place the sole on the bed of shallots. Add the wine and stock.

3. Bring the liquid to a bare simmer over direct heat.

4. Cover the sole with buttered parchment paper; finish it in a 350°F (175°C) oven.

5. Remove the sole and keep it warm.

6. Reduce the cooking liquid and add the Velouté; Simmer until reduced to a good sauce consistency.

7. Temper the yolks with the hot sauce; return the sauce to the heat and cook until thickened. Do not boil the sauce.

8. Finish the sauce with the butter, season to taste, and coat the fish with the sauce.

Poached Halibut with Saffron Sauce

Yield: 10 servings

Halibut steaks	4 pounds	1.8 kilograms
Butter, as needed	1 ounce	30 grams
Shallots, minced	2 each	2 each
Dry white wine	8 fluid ounces	240 milliliters
Fish Fumet	10 fluid ounces	300 milliliters
Fish Velouté	1 pint	480 milliliters
Heavy cream	4 fluid ounces	120 milliliters
Saffron threads, crushed	as needed	as needed
Salt, to taste	1/2 teaspoon	1/2 teaspoon
Pepper, to taste	1/4 teaspoon	1/4 teaspoon
Garnish		
Zucchini, small dice	1 pound	450 grams
Butter, as needed	2 ounces	60 grams
Fleurons	20 pieces	20 pieces

The recipe for Fish Fumet may be found on page 443. To read about preparing Velouté, see pages 283 to 285.

To make the fleurons: Roll puff pastry 1/8-inch thick. Brush with egg wash; score with a fork. Sprinkle with herbs, cut out with a crescent cutter. Bake on parchment paper in a 400°F (205°C) oven until crisp and browned.

1. Butter a shallow pan; sprinkle with shallots.
2. Add halibut steaks, wine, and Fumet.
3. Cover pan with buttered paper; bring to a simmer on top of the stove.
4. Poach fish in a 350°F (175°C) oven, 6 to 8 minutes.
5. Remove fish, cover and keep warm.
6. Add the saffron to the poaching liquid; reduce by half.
7. Add Velouté and heavy cream and reduce until sauce consistency.
8. Adjust the sauce's seasoning with salt and pepper. Strain.
9. Glace the zucchini in butter over moderate heat; season to taste with salt and pepper.
10. Serve sauce over fish, garnish with zucchini and fleurons.

Green grapes add a delicate flavor to the dish.

Cut the fillets into 6-ounce (170-gram) portions.

The recipe for Hollandaise Sauce may be found on page 540.

The method for preparing paupiettes is illustrated in Figure 6-105, page 248.

Paupiettes of Sole Véronique

Yield: 10 servings

Sole fillets	*4 pounds*	*1.8 kilograms*
Egg white	*1 each*	*1 each*
Heavy cream	*4 fluid ounces*	*120 milliliters*
Salt, to taste	*1/2 teaspoon*	*1/2 teaspoon*
Pepper, to taste	*1/4 teaspoon*	*1/4 teaspoon*
Shallots, minced	*1 tablespoon*	*1 tablespoon*
Parsley stems, chopped	*8 each*	*8 each*
Dry white wine	*4 fluid ounces*	*120 milliliters*
Fish Fumet	*5 fluid ounces*	*150 milliliters*
Beurre Manié	*2 ounces*	*60 grams*
Heavy cream, whipped	*4 fluid ounces*	*120 milliliters*
Hollandaise Sauce	*4 fluid ounces*	*120 milliliters*
Green grapes, peeled, 3 to 4 per order	*10 ounces*	*285 grams*

1. Trim the fillets and refrigerate them. Save all the trim for the filling.

2. To prepare the mousseline filling: Purée the diced trim in a food processor. Add egg white to the purée and process until it is just blended. Work in the heavy cream by hand over an ice bath; season the mixture to taste with salt and pepper.

3. Divide the filling evenly between the fillets and roll them in paupiettes.

4. Butter a sauteuse and add the shallots and parsley stems. Arrange the paupiettes in the sauteuse.

5. Add the wine and Fumet; cover the fish with buttered parchment paper. Bring the liquid to a simmer over direct heat and finish the fish in a moderate oven. Remove the paupiettes and keep them warm while finishing the sauce.

6. Return the sauteuse to the heat and thicken the cooking liquid with the Beurre Manié. Remove the pan from the heat. Add the heavy cream and Hollandaise; mix them in thoroughly and adjust the seasoning to taste to make glaçage.

7. Place the paupiettes on a sizzler platter. Coat each portion completely with 2 fluid ounces (60 milliliters) of glaçage. Brown them under a salamander or broiler.

8. Serve the fish immediately with heated grapes.

Tilapia with Capers and Tomatoes

Yield: 10 servings

Tilapia fillets	*4 pounds*	*1.8 kilograms*
Shallots, chopped	*1 ounce*	*30 grams*
Butter, softened, as needed	*3 ounces*	*85 grams*
Dry white wine	*6 fluid ounces*	*180 milliliters*
Fish Fumet	*6 fluid ounces*	*180 milliliters*
Capers, drained	*2 tablespoons*	*2 tablespoons*
Tomato Concassé	*4 ounces*	*115 grams*
Mushrooms, sliced	*20 each*	*20 each*
Fines Herbes, chopped	*1 tablespoon*	*1 tablespoon*
Fish Velouté	*12 fluid ounces*	*360 milliliters*
Heavy cream, reduced	*4 fluid ounces*	*120 milliliters*
Brandy (optional)	*1 fluid ounce*	*30 milliliters*
Salt, to taste	*1/2 teaspoon*	*1/2 teaspoon*
Cayenne, ground	*pinch*	*pinch*

Fines Herbes is a classic French herb blend. The recipe for Fines Herbes may be found on page 427.

1. Trim the fish into 6-ounce (170-gram) portions. Season with salt and pepper. Butter a sautoir, and add shallots and seasoned fish fillets.

2. Add wine, fumet, capers, Tomato Concassé, mushrooms, and Fines Herbes; cover with a paper cover.

3. Bring to a simmer over direct heat; place in a 350°F (175°C) oven until done (flesh turns opaque), 6 to 8 minutes.

4. Remove fish and garnish with a slotted spoon; cover and keep warm while finishing the sauce.

5. Reduce poaching liquid by half. Add velouté and cream; reduce to a good sauce consistency.

6. Add brandy if desired, season to taste with salt and cayenne and finish with butter.

7. Return the garnish to the sauce. Serve the fish coated with the sauce.

Perch Bordelaise-Style

Yield: 10 servings

The recipe for Sauce Bordelaise is on page 529.

Perch fillets	*10 each*	*10 each*
Salt, to taste	*1/2 teaspoon*	*1/2 teaspoon*
Pepper, to taste	*1/4 teaspoon*	*1/4 teaspoon*
Shallots, minced	*1 ounce*	*1 ounce*
Dry red wine (Bordeaux)	*10 fluid ounces*	*300 milliliters*
Fish Fumet	*10 fluid ounces*	*300 milliliters*
Sauce Bordelaise	*20 fluid ounces*	*600 milliliters*
Butter, diced	*2 ounces*	*60 grams*
Parsley, chopped	*1 ounce*	*30 grams*

1. Portion the perch at 6 ounces (170 grams). The skin may be left on if desired. Season the perch with salt and pepper.

2. Butter the pan and scatter the shallots over the bottom. Place the perch on top of the shallots.

3. Add the wine and stock. Cover the fish with buttered parchment paper and bring to a simmer over direct heat. Finish the fish in a 350°F (175°C) oven, about 5 minutes. Remove the fish and keep it warm.

4. Reduce the cooking liquid until nearly dry.

5. Add the Sauce Bordelaise, capers, and mushrooms.

6. Finish the sauce with the butter. Adjust the seasoning with salt and pepper to taste.

7. Serve the sauce with the fish.

Poached Sea Bass with Clams, Bacon, and Peppers

Yield: 10 servings

Butter, softened	3 ounces	85 grams
Sea bass fillets	3 pounds	1.3 kilograms
Little Neck clams, scrubbed	1 dozen	1 dozen
White wine	4 fluid ounces	120 milliliters
Chicken Stock	5 fluid ounces	150 milliliters
Clam juice	5 fluid ounces	150 milliliters
Green peppers, julienned and blanched	8 ounces	225 grams
Bacon, minced, rendered crisp	10 ounces	285 grams
Salt, to taste	1/2 teaspoon	1/2 teaspoon
Pepper, to taste	1/4 teaspoon	1/4 teaspoon
Chives, chopped	1 tablespoon	1 tablespoon

1. Cut the fish into 3-ounce (85-gram) portions. Season well with salt and pepper.
2. Lightly butter a sauteuse. Add the fish and clams.
3. Add the wine, chicken stock, and clam juice.
4. Cover the fish with buttered parchment paper.
5. Bring the liquid just barely to a simmer over direct heat. Place in a 350°F (175°C) oven and poach the fish and clams until the fish is slightly underdone and the clams just barely open. Remove the fish and clams; keep them warm.
6. Strain the cooking liquid and reduce it.
7. Whip in the remaining butter to lightly thicken the sauce.
8. Add the peppers and bacon to the sauce. Adjust the seasoning with salt and pepper to taste.
9. Ladle the sauce over the fish and clams. Garnish with the chives.

Always check live clams for a tightly closed shell and sweet smell.

Use monkfish, grouper, Mako shark, or other roughy to replace the sea bass.

To read more about clams, see Chapter 5, page 119.

Poached Red Snapper Veracruz

Yield: 10 servings

Spanish sauce	*1 quart*	*1 liter*
Poblano chili, roasted and peeled	*2 each*	*2 each*
Garlic cloves, peeled	*2 each*	*2 each*
Red onion, peeled and quartered	*1 each*	*1 each*
Safflower oil	*2 tablespoons*	*2 tablespoons*
Tomato Concassé	*1 pound*	*450 grams*
Oregano	*1/2 teaspoon*	*1/2 teaspoon*
Tomato purée	*8 fluid ounces*	*240 milliliters*
Sugar	*1 teaspoon*	*15 grams*
Vinegar	*1 teaspoon*	*15 milliliters*
Salt	*1/2 teaspoon*	*1/2 teaspoon*
Black pepper	*1/4 teaspoon*	*1/4 teaspoon*
Lime juice	*3 limes each*	*3 limes each*
Red snapper, fillets	*3 1/2 pounds*	*1.6 kilograms*
Salt	*to taste*	*to taste*
Pepper	*to taste*	*to taste*
White wine	*6 fluid ounces*	*180 milliliters*
White Stock	*12 fluid ounces*	*360 milliliters*
Jalapeño chilies, chiffonade (optional)	*2 each*	*2 each*
Black olives, sliced (optional)	*3 ounces*	*85 grams*
Capers	*2 tablespoons*	*2 tablespoons*

1. To prepare the sauce: Remove stems and seeds from peppers. Purée garlic, onions, and peppers in food processor.

2. Heat oil, add purée and sauté. Add other ingredients for the sauce. Heat sauce and cook for 20 to 25 minutes.

3. Adjust seasoning and keep warm for service.

4. Sprinkle the lime juice over fish and season lightly with salt and pepper.

5. Shallow-poach the fish in the white wine and stock, remove, and keep warm.

6. Reduce cuisson and add Spanish sauce. Adjust seasoning.

7. Pool some sauce on a plate, place fish on top, garnish with chili strips, olives, and capers.

Poached Striped Bass with Watercress Sauce

Yield: 10 servings

Sea bass fillets	*3 1/2 pounds*	*1.6 kilograms*
Watercress leaves	*2 pounds*	*900 grams*
Butter, as needed	*3 ounces*	*85 grams*
Salt, to taste	*1/2 teaspoon*	*1/2 teaspoon*
Pepper, to taste	*1/4 teaspoon*	*1/4 teaspoon*
Fish Fumet, as needed	*5 fluid ounces*	*150 milliliters*
White wine, as needed	*5 fluid ounces*	*150 milliliters*
Heavy cream, reduced	*6 fluid ounces*	*180 milliliters*
Lemon juice, to taste	*1/2 fluid ounce*	*15 milliliters*

The recipe for Fish Fumet is on page 443.

To read more about filleting fish, read Chapter 6, pages 244 to 247.

1. Portion the sea bass at 5 to 6 ounces (140 to 170 grams) and season with salt and pepper.

2. Blanch the watercress leaves in boiling salted water; cook them until they are bright green. Drain, shock, and purée the watercress.

3. Butter a sauteuse. Place the fish in the pan. Add equal parts of the Fish Fumet and white wine to barely cover the fish.

4. Cover the pan with buttered parchment paper.

5. Heat the liquid to a simmer over direct heat. Finish poaching the fish in a 350°F (175°C) oven. Remove the bass, moisten it with cooking liquid, and keep it warm.

6. Reduce the cooking liquid by one-half to three-quarters.

7. Add the reduced heavy cream. Reduce the sauce until thickened. Add the watercress purée and the lemon juice, salt, and pepper to taste.

8. Ladle the sauce around the fish and serve.

Paupiettes of Trout with Saffron Filling

Yield: 10 servings

To make the blanc, follow the recipe for Lemon Beurre Blanc, page 545. Substitute the reduced poaching liquid (step 9) for the lemon and white wine in the recipe.

Trout	10 each	10 each
Saffron threads, pulverized, to taste	1/4 teaspoon	1/4 teaspoon
Heavy cream	1 fluid ounce	30 milliliters
Egg white	1 tablespoon	1 tablespoon
Salt, to taste	1/2 teaspoon	1/2 teaspoon
White pepper, to taste	1/4 teaspoon	1/4 teaspoon
Dry white wine	2 fluid ounces	60 milliliters
Fish Stock	4 fluid ounces	120 milliliters
Spinach, blanched	10 ounces	285 grams
Beurre blanc	1 pint	480 milliliters
Tomato Concassé	7 ounces	200 grams
Chives, chopped	2 tablespoons	2 tablespoons

1. Fillet the trout, reserving about 4 ounces (115 grams) to make the filling. Keep the fish well chilled.

2. Heat the saffron in the cream and let it steep for 30 minutes. Chill well.

3. Place the trout trim and egg whites in a food processor with a steel blade. Process them to a fine paste, scraping down the sides of the bowl as needed.

4. Add the saffron-cream infusion, salt, and pepper, pulsing until just incorporated.

5. Spread the trout fillets evenly with the mousseline. Roll the fillets into paupiettes.

6. At service, shallow-poach the paupiettes in the white wine and Fish Stock in a 350°F (175°C) oven. Remove them from the pan, moisten, and keep warm.

7. Reduce the poaching liquid until syrupy to flavor the beurre blanc.

8. Sauté the spinach in butter until very hot. Season well.

9. Prepare the beurre blanc with the reduced poaching liquid, Tomato Concasse, and chopped chives. Ladle the sauce around the edge of the spinach.

10. Place the spinach on warmed plates. Place two paupiettes over the spinach on each plate.

Catfish Topped with Crabmeat and Cornbread Crumbs

Yield: 10 servings

Onions, minced	*3 ounces*	*85 grams*
Butter	*1 ounce*	*30 grams*
Béchamel, thick	*6 fluid ounces*	*180 milliliters*
Crabmeat Jonah, picked	*4 ounces*	*115 grams*
Catfish fillets	*3 pounds*	*1.3 kilograms*
Salt, to taste	*1/2 teaspoon*	*1/2 teaspoon*
Pepper, to taste	*1/4 teaspoon*	*1/4 teaspoon*
Cornbread, crumbs	*4 ounces*	*115 grams*
Shallots, minced and sweated	*1 tablespoon*	*1 tablespoon*
White wine	*4 fluid ounces*	*120 milliliters*
Fish Stock	*8 fluid ounces*	*240 milliliters*
Heavy cream	*2 fluid ounces*	*60 milliliters*
Ham, julienne	*4 ounces*	*115 grams*
Dry sherry, to taste	*2 fluid ounces*	*60 milliliters*
Butter	*3 ounces*	*85 grams*

The recipe for Béchamel is on page 535.

1. Sweat the onions in butter.

2. Add the Béchamel and heat it through. Fold in the crabmeat and cool the mixture.

3. Cut the fillets into 4- to 5-ounce (115- to 140-gram) portions. Season the fish with salt and pepper.

4. Top each fillet with the crab mixture. Top the crab mixture with the cornbread crumbs, about 2 tablespoons (30 grams) of crumbs per portion.

5. Butter the pan and add a layer of shallots. Place the fish on top of the shallots.

6. Add the white wine and Fish Stock and poach the fish until done. Remove the fish and keep it warm.

7. Add the heavy cream to the poaching liquid and reduce it.

8. Add the ham and sherry.

9. Monté au beurre to finish.

10. Serve the catfish on a heated plate with the sauce.

Boiled Lobster with Drawn Butter

Yield: 10 servings

For cold-boiled lobster or when lobster meat will be removed from the shell for another use, cool the cooked lobster in cold running water. (This makes handling easier and prevents further cooking.)

Lobsters	*10 each*	*10 each*
Butter, melted and drawn	*20 ounces*	*570 grams*
Lemon wedges	*as needed*	*as needed*
Parsley, sprigs (optional)	*10 each*	*10 each*

1. Plunge the live lobsters head-first into a large pot of boiling, salted water.

2. When the water returns to a boil, simmer the lobster for 6 to 8 minutes for a 1-pound lobster (larger lobsters may take up to 20 minutes, depending on their weight). Do not overcook or the flesh will become tough.

3. Serve the lobster immediately with lemon wedges and drawn butter.

4. Garnish with parsley sprigs.

New England Shore Dinner

Yield: 10 servings

Cut the cod fillet into 2-ounce (60-gram) portions.

Onions, small dice	*10 ounces*	*285 grams*
Butter	*3 ounces*	*85 grams*
Garlic cloves, minced	*3 each*	*3 each*
Thyme leaves	*1 teaspoon*	*1 teaspoon*
Bay leaves	*2 each*	*2 each*
Chicken Stock, as needed	*1 pint*	*480 milliliters*
Corn on the cob, husked and quartered	*3 each*	*3 each*
Lobsters, quartered	*3 each*	*3 each*
Clams, topneck	*20 each*	*20 each*
Mussels, cleaned	*20 each*	*20 each*
Red Bliss potatoes, cooked	*10 each*	*10 each*
Cod fillet	*1 1/4 pounds*	*570 grams*
Leeks, split	*5 each*	*5 each*
Onions, boiling, parcooked	*5 each*	*5 each*
Sea scallops	*5 ounces*	*140 grams*
Zucchini, thick batonnet	*2 each*	*2 each*
Parsley, chopped	*2 teaspoons*	*2 teaspoons*

(Recipe continued on facing page)

1. Sweat the onion in the butter. Add the garlic and sauté until the aroma is apparent.

2. Add the thyme, bay leaves, and stock; simmer the liquid.

3. Arrange the following ingredients in a flameproof casserole. Bottom layer: corn, lobster, clams, mussels, potatoes. Top layer: cod, leeks, boiling onions, scallops, zucchini.

4. Cover and steam all of the ingredients over direct heat or in a 350°F (175°C) oven until the seafood is cooked through, about 20 to 25 minutes.

5. Arrange the fish, seafood, and vegetables on a heated platter, or serve it directly from the casserole.

Seafood Poached in a Tomato Broth with Fennel

Yield: 10 servings

Fish Consommé	*1 quart*	*1 liter*
Standard Sachet d'Épices	*1 each*	*1 each*
Pernod	*4 fluid ounces*	*120 milliliters*
White wine	*4 fluid ounces*	*120 milliliters*
Fennel, julienne	*1 pound*	*450 grams*
Tomato Concassé	*1 pound*	*450 grams*
Assorted seafood	*50 ounces*	*1.4 kilograms*

The recipe for Fish Consommé is on page 455.

Select a variety of seafood. Use one or more of the following: clams, crabs, lobster tail, cod or hake, shark, tuna, or monkfish.

1. Combine the consommé, Sachet d'Épices, Pernod, wine, fennel, and Tomato Concassé; simmer the liquid until the fennel is barely tender and the broth is well flavored.

2. At the time of service, heat to a bare simmer 8 ounces (240 milliliters) of the broth per serving. Add the seafood and poach it until it is just cooked through.

CHAPTER 19 *Vegetarian Entrées*

An increasing number of individuals are looking for vegetarian options on the menu. In this chapter you will find recipes in the following groups:

- *Egg and Crêpe Dishes*
- *Nut, Bean, and Tofu Dishes*
- *Vegetable Loaves and Burgers*
- *Roulades and Strudels*
- *Pasta and Rice*
- *Vegetable Stews*
- *Tex-Mex Specialties*

In addition, you may wish to adapt recipes from chapters devoted to vegetable, potato, rice, and grain dishes, breakfast recipes, and salads and sandwiches (Chapters 21 and 25).

To "turn" the artichoke bottom, cut away the leaves and stem, and scoop out the choke.

Skim or low-fat milk may replace the whole milk.

To check soufflés for doneness, look at the sides of the soufflés. They should appear set. The soufflé should rise easily.

Artichoke Soufflé

Yield: 10 servings

Artichoke bottoms	*10 ounces*	*285 grams*
Eggs, separated	*1 dozen*	*1 dozen*
Gruyère cheese, grated	*10 ounces*	*285 grams*
Milk	*1 1/2 pints*	*720 milliliters*
Cornstarch	*2 tablespoons*	*2 tablespoons*
Salt, to taste	*1/2 teaspoon*	*1/2 teaspoon*
Pepper, to taste	*1/4 teaspoon*	*1/4 teaspoon*
Butter, softened	*2 ounces*	*60 grams*
Almonds, ground	*3 ounces*	*85 grams*

1. Trim artichokes; cook in acidulated water until tender. Chop very fine or purée.

2. Bring the milk to a simmer; thicken with cornstarch. Stir in egg yolks and cheese off the heat.

3. Blend the artichokes into the milk mixture. Season to taste.

4. Whip egg whites to a firm peak; fold into artichoke mixture.

5. Brush soufflé molds with butter and dust with ground almonds.

6. Pour mixture into greased soufflé molds. Place in a 170°F (75°C) water bath; bake in a 350°F (175°C) oven until done, approximately 20 minutes.

VARIATIONS

Souffléed Crêpes: Prepare crêpes (see page 872). Place a spoonful of filling in the center of the crêpe. Fold in half and then into quarters. Bake in a buttered dish for 10 to 12 minutes.

Artichoke Soufflé in Red Pepper Shells: Hollow red peppers, fill with soufflé mixture and bake as directed above.

Artichoke Spinach Ricotta Pie

Yield: 10 servings

Crust

Wild rice, cooked until quite soft	*2 pounds*	*900 grams*
Duxelles	*4 ounces*	*115 grams*
Egg whites, beaten	*2 each*	*2 each*
Walnuts, chopped	*3 ounces*	*85 grams*
Soy sauce	*1 tablespoon*	*1 tablespoon*

Filling

Olive oil	*1 tablespoon*	*1 tablespoon*
Garlic cloves, minced	*2 each*	*2 each*
Spinach, stemmed	*3 1/2 pounds*	*1.6 kilograms*
Artichoke bottoms, cooked and sliced thin	*3 each*	*3 each*
Ricotta cheese	*8 ounces*	*225 grams*
Nutmeg, ground	*1/8 teaspoon*	*1/8 teaspoon*
Marjoram leaves, dried	*1 tablespoon*	*1 tablespoon*
Salt, to taste	*2 teaspoons*	*2 teaspoons*
Pepper, to taste	*1 teaspoon*	*1 teaspoon*
Parmesan cheese, grated	*5 ounces*	*140 grams*
Egg whites, beaten lightly	*6 each*	*6 each*
Tomato Sauce	*20 ounces*	*570 grams*
Red pepper flakes	*1 tablespoon*	*1 tablespoon*

For Tomato Sauce see page 538.

1. Preheat oven to 375°F (190°C). To prepare crust: Combine all ingredients in a bowl and mix well. Adjust seasonings. Press into well-oiled individual tart pans. Chill while preparing filling.

2. Heat oil until hot and sauté garlic until it is golden. Add the spinach and sauté over high heat until it is tender.

3. Combine artichokes, spinach, ricotta, Parmesan, and egg whites. Stir in the nutmeg and marjoram, reserving some artichoke slices for garnish. Adjust seasoning to taste with salt and pepper.

4. Spoon filling into prepared rice shells; garnish top with artichoke slices.

5. Bake in bottom oven until crust is golden and filling is set.

6. Serve either directly in the pan or carefully unmold.

Stuffed Spinach Rolls

Yield: 10 servings

The recipe for Vegetable Stock can be
found on page 445. Mushroom Essence is
on page 447.

Use smaller leaves for bite-sized rolls
suitable for appetizer portions or canapés.

If desired, 6 ounces (170 grams) of
Duxelles (page 421) can be added to the
mix. Ricotta cheese may replace some of
the required cheese.

Spinach leaves (large)	40 each	40 each
Parmesan cheese, grated	10 ounces	285 grams
Mozzarella cheese, grated	10 ounces	285 grams
Barley, cooked	12 ounces	340 grams
Garlic, cloves, chopped	3 each	3 each
Butter	1 tablespoon	1 tablespoon
Walnuts, toasted and chopped	6 ounces	170 grams
Bread crumbs, fresh	2 ounces	60 grams
Pepper, to taste	1/4 teaspoon	1/4 teaspoon
Chives, chopped	1 teaspoon	1 teaspoon
Thyme, dried	1/2 teaspoon	1/2 teaspoon
Scallions, chopped	2 each	2 each
Vegetable Stock or Mushroom Essence	8 fluid ounces	240 milliliters

1. Blanch spinach leaves carefully in boiling water. Drain well and spread out, ready to use.

2. Combine the parmesan and mozzarella with the barley.

3. Sweat the garlic lightly in butter, add the walnuts, bread crumbs, and a little pepper to taste.

4. Combine the garlic–bread-crumbs–walnuts mixture with chives, thyme, and scallions into the cheese mix, stirring just enough to blend them together. Do not overmix.

5. Take 2 spinach leaves and lay them out flat on a board. Place a spoonful of the cheese mix onto the spinach leaves.

6. Fold the sides of the spinach leaf in toward the center first then roll up the spinach leaf into a roll, keeping it reasonably taut.

7. Place the spinach rolls into a greased gratin dish (2 per portion). Add enough vegetable stock to just cover the bottom of the pan. Cover with a tight-fitting lid and shallow-poach for a few minutes over a medium-high heat on the range until the stock has disappeared. Serve at once.

Spinach Crêpes with Wild Mushrooms and Roasted Red Pepper Coulis

Yield: 10 servings

Spinach crêpes	*10 each*	*10 each*
Shallots, minced	*4 each*	*4 each*
Wild mushrooms, small dice	*2 pounds*	*900 grams*
Butter	*2 ounces*	*60 grams*
White wine	*6 fluid ounces*	*180 milliliters*
Flour	*1 tablespoon*	*1 tablespoon*
Vegetable Stock	*12 fluid ounces*	*360 milliliters*
Parsley, chopped	*2 tablespoons*	*2 tablespoons*
Salt, to taste	*1/2 teaspoon*	*1/2 teaspoon*
Pepper, to taste	*1/2 teaspoon*	*1/2 teaspoon*
Roasted red pepper coulis		
Shallots, minced	*4 each*	*4 each*
White wine	*12 fluid ounces*	*360 milliliters*
Red peppers, roasted and puréed	*1 1/2 pounds*	*680 grams*
Heavy cream	*6 fluid ounces*	*180 milliliters*
Butter	*4 ounces*	*115 grams*
Salt to taste	*1/2 teaspoon*	*1/2 teaspoon*

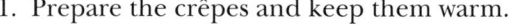

If a mushroom stem is tough or has a sticky skin, be sure to trim it away.

1. Prepare the crêpes and keep them warm.

2. Sauté shallots and mushrooms in butter, and add wine; reduce until almost dry.

3. Stir in flour and cook 2 to 3 minutes; add Vegetable Stock and bring to boil, add parsley and cook until thick; season to taste with salt and pepper. Reserve the mushroom filling.

4. Combine shallots and wine and reduce to half the original volume.

5. Add the peppers to the shallots.

6. Add the heavy cream and reduce until the coulis has a good consistency. Finish with butter and seasoning to taste.

7. Fill crêpes with mushroom filling and heat to order in a 375°F (190°C) oven.

8. Serve the crêpes very hot with the roasted red pepper coulis.

Falafel

Yield: 10 servings

Falafels are traditionally served in pitas with lettuce, tomato, onion, and Yogurt Tahini Sauce (page 939).

Mediterranean Sampler Plate: Include Humus B'Tahini (page 939), Baba Ghannouj (page 937), pita triangles, Stuffed Grape Leaves (page 990) and any of the Mediterranean salads on pages 894 to 898.

Garbanzo or fava beans, soaked overnight	1 pound	450 grams
Garlic cloves, coarse-chopped	3 each	3 each
Large onions, coarse-chopped	1 each	1 each
Parsley, flat-leaf	1/4 bunch	1/4 bunch
Cumin, roasted	1 tablespoon	1 tablespoon
Coriander, roasted	1 tablespoon	1 tablespoon
Cayenne, as desired	1 teaspoon	1 teaspoon
Salt	1 tablespoon	1 tablespoon
Baking soda	1 teaspoon	1 teaspoon
Water	4 fluid ounces	120 milliliters

1. Drain the garbanzo beans and rinse. Grind beans, garlic, onions, and parsley through a fine die or grinder.

2. Add spices and mix.

3. Dissolve salt and baking soda in water. Add to chick pea mixture and mix.

4. Mold into flat round disks.

5. Heat oil to 350°. Deep-fry falafel until golden brown. Drain.

Grilled Marinated Tofu with Black Bean Salsa

Yield: 10 servings

The recipe for Black Bean Salsa may be found on page 936.

Remember to soak the skewers if you are using wooden ones.

To press tofu, place it in a hotel pan between several layers of cheesecloth. Top with a board or a second hotel pan. Weight with canned goods or weights (5 pounds/2.25 kilograms) for several hours.

Tofu, drained and pressed	36 ounces	1 kilogram
White wine	6 fluid ounces	180 milliliters
Vegetable oil	1 tablespoon	1 tablespoon
Salt	1/4 teaspoon	1/4 teaspoon
Pepper	1/2 teaspoon	1/2 teaspoon
Rosemary, sprigs	2 each	2 each
Black Bean Salsa	20 ounces	570 grams

1. Cut tofu into 2-inch (5-centimeter) cubes.

2. Combine wine, oil, salt, pepper, and rosemary to make a marinade. Add the tofu.

3. Allow to marinate for about 30 minutes.

4. Remove the tofu from marinade and thread on skewers.

5. Mark the tofu squares on the grill.

6. Serve with Black Bean Salsa on the side.

Pecan-Herb Loaf with Tomato-Tahini Sauté

Yield: 10 servings

Vidalia onions	2 ounces	60 grams
Olive oil	1 teaspoon	1 teaspoon
Mushrooms, chopped fine	4 ounces	115 grams
Garlic, mashed to a paste	1 ounce	1 ounce
Pecans, toasted and chopped fine	4 ounces	115 grams
Almonds, toasted and chopped fine	4 ounces	115 grams
Sesame seeds, toasted	2 ounces	60 grams
Flour	1 ounce	30 grams
Arrowroot	2 tablespoons	2 tablespoons
Salt, to taste	2 teaspoons	2 teaspoons
Pepper, to taste	1/4 teaspoon	1/4 teaspoon
Basil, chopped fine	1/2 teaspoon	1/2 teaspoon
Oregano, chopped fine	1/4 teaspoon	1/4 teaspoon
Savory	1/4 teaspoon	1/4 teaspoon
Tofu	1 1/4 pounds	570 grams
Tomato-tahini sauce		
Olive oil	1 teaspoon	1 teaspoon
Tahini	2 ounces	60 grams
Onions, chopped	3 ounces	85 grams
Tomato Concassé	1 pound	450 grams
Soy sauce	1 teaspoon	1 teaspoon
Pepper, to taste	1/4 teaspoon	1/4 teaspoon
Garlic cloves, chopped fine	1 each	1 each
Basil, chopped fine	1/2 teaspoon	1/2 teaspoon

Other sweet onions may be substituted for the Vidalia.

1. Sauté the onions in olive oil until browned. Add the garlic; sauté until the aroma is apparent. Add the pecans, almonds, and sesame seeds. Remove the mixture to a bowl and allow it to cool.

2. Stir in the flour, then add the arrowroot. Add the salt, pepper, basil, oregano, and savory. Blend well.

3. Purée the tofu and add it to the nut mixture.

4. Pack the mixture into a loaf mold and bake at 350°F (175°C) for about 1 hour, or to an internal temperature of 150°F (65°C).

5. Heat the olive oil for the sauce in a sauteuse. Sauté the onions until limp. Add the garlic, and sauté until the aroma is apparent.

6. Add the tahini, tomatoes, soy sauce, salt, and pepper to taste. Simmer the sauce briefly.

7. Slice the loaf and serve with the sauce. Scatter the basil over the top just before serving.

Vegetable Burger

Yield: 10 servings

Garnish with yogurt seasoned with lemons and roasted garlic cloves. Top with alfalfa sprouts.

The burger can also be served as a sandwich or a Kaiser roll topped with melted cheese, lettuce, and tomato.

Carrots, ground	*1 1/2 pounds*	*680 grams*
Celery, ground	*4 ounces*	*115 grams*
Onions, ground	*4 ounces*	*115 grams*
Red pepper, ground	*2 ounces*	*60 grams*
Green pepper, ground	*2 ounces*	*60 grams*
Walnuts, ground	*3 ounces*	*85 grams*
Mushrooms, chopped fine	*8 ounces*	*225 grams*
Scallions, chopped fine	*8 ounces*	*225 grams*
Eggs	*2 each*	*2 each*
Tabasco, to taste	*1/4 teaspoon*	*1/4 teaspoon*
Salt, to taste	*1/2 teaspoon*	*1/2 teaspoon*
Pepper, to taste	*1/4 teaspoon*	*1/4 teaspoon*
Sesame oil, to taste	*1/2 teaspoon*	*1/2 teaspoon*
Cracker or matzoh meal, as needed to bind	*2 ounces*	*60 grams*

1. Mix together the carrots, celery, onions, and peppers. Press out any excess liquid. Add walnuts, mushrooms, scallions, eggs, Tabasco, and seasonings.

2. Add enough cracker meal to make a firm mixture. Form into patties (6 ounces/170 grams).

3. Roll in additional cracker meal, if desired, then panfry both sides to golden brown. Finish cooking in a 350°F (175°C) oven, about 30 minutes.

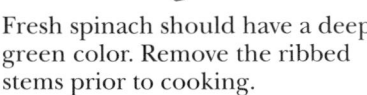

Fresh spinach should have a deep green color. Remove the ribbed stems prior to cooking.

Spinach Roulades with Mushrooms and Sour Cream

Yield: 10 servings

Spinach, fresh	*3 pounds*	*1.4 kilograms*
Butter	*1 tablespoon*	*1 tablespoon*
Salt, to taste	*1/2 teaspoon*	*1/2 teaspoon*
Pepper, to taste	*1/4 teaspoon*	*1/4 teaspoon*
Eggs, separated	*6 each*	*6 each*
Filling		
Mushrooms, sliced	*8 ounces*	*225 grams*
Butter	*1 tablespoon*	*1 tablespoon*
Sour cream	*1 pint*	*480 milliliters*
Nutmeg, ground	*pinch*	*pinch*
Parmesan cheese, grated	*2 ounces*	*60 grams*

(Recipe continued on facing page)

1. Cook spinach until tender; drain and chop. Add the butter, salt, pepper, and egg yolks; mix thoroughly.

2. Line a 7–by–11-inch jelly-roll pan with parchment paper or wax paper that has been greased.

3. Beat the egg whites until stiff but not dry. Fold them into the spinach mixture. Carefully pour this mixture into the pan and place in the oven at 400°F (205°C) for 10 to 15 minutes. When it has risen and is springy to the touch, remove.

4. To prepare the filling, sauté the mushrooms in the butter. Add the sour cream and heat. Do not boil. Season with salt and pepper.

5. Unmold the spinach mixture onto parchment that has been sprinkled with Parmesan cheese. Spread the filling on the spinach, roll it up to create an 11-inch long log, and place in oven for an additional 5 minutes.

6. Slice into 10 portions.

Vegetable Strudel

Yield: 10 servings

Snow peas, julienned and blanched	*8 ounces*	*225 grams*
Carrots, julienned and blanched	*8 ounces*	*225 grams*
Yellow squash, julienned	*8 ounces*	*225 grams*
Zucchini, julienned	*8 ounces*	*225 grams*
Yellow pepper, julienned	*8 ounces*	*225 grams*
Red pepper, julienned	*8 ounces*	*225 grams*
Ricotta cheese	*8 ounces*	*225 grams*
Garlic cloves, roasted	*6 each*	*6 each*
Salt, to taste	*1/2 teaspoon*	*1/2 teaspoon*
Basil, shredded	*3 tablespoons*	*3 tablespoons*
Phyllo, large sheets	*5 each*	*5 each*
Vegetable oil or melted butter	*2 fluids ounces*	*60 milliliters*
Bread crumbs, fresh	*4 ounces*	*115 grams*
Tomato Coulis	*20 fluid ounces*	*600 milliliters*

Authentic strudel dough is made by stretching a ball of dough carefully into a delicate, almost translucent sheet. This recipe calls for machine-made phyllo dough.

1. Combine all vegetables with roasted garlic, salt, and pepper to taste and mix well. Gently fold in the basil.

2. Stack the phyllo sheets, brushing them with oil or melted butter, and dusting with bread crumbs between each layer.

3. Spread the vegetable mixture evenly along one edge of the sheets. Roll the sheets into a log. Brush the top with a little butter.

4. With a serrated knife, score lines where you will cut the strudel after it is baked.

5. Place seam-side down on a parchment-lined sheet pan, and bake at 400°F (200°C) about 15 to 20 minutes, or to an even golden brown.

6. Slice the strudel, and place it in a pool of coulis.

Escarole-Feta Turnovers

Yield: 10 servings

Cut the squares into 6-inch (15-centimeter) squares. Dust the work surface with flour; this is a sticky dough.

To read about preparing pastry doughs, see pages 392 to 398.

Basic Pie Crust dough or Puff Pastry dough may be substituted for the Cream Cheese Pastry.

Serve the turnovers with any of the tomato sauces or vegetable coulis suggested in Chapter 15. Prepared mango chutney and toasted coconut would work well with the Vegetable Curry Turnover.

Cream cheese pastry		
Cream cheese, softened	*8 ounces*	*225 grams*
Butter, softened	*8 ounces*	*225 grams*
Flour	*20 ounces*	*570 grams*
Salt	*1 teaspoon*	*1 teaspoon*
Milk	*as needed*	*as needed*
Olive oil	*1 tablespoon*	*1 tablespoon*
Garlic cloves, minced	*2 each*	*2 each*
Escarole	*1 1/2 pounds*	*680 grams*
Sun-dried tomatoes, diced	*5 each*	*5 each*
Scallions, chopped	*3 each*	*3 each*
Feta cheese, crumbled	*8 ounces*	*225 grams*
Salt, to taste	*1/2 teaspoon*	*1/2 teaspoon*
Pepper, to taste	*1/4 teaspoon*	*1/4 teaspoon*
Egg wash	*as needed*	*as needed*

1. Blend the cream cheese and butter. Cut in the flour and add the salt. Mix until the butter is pea-sized. Form into a ball and chill.

2. Heat the olive oil, sauté the garlic, and add the escarole. Cover and steam. Add the sun-dried tomatoes and scallions. Drain. Cool. Add the feta cheese. Season to taste with salt and pepper.

3. Roll out the dough into squares. Place a portion of the filling in the center; fold over to create a triangle. Seal with egg wash, crimp edges. Brush surface with egg wash. Bake at 325°F (165°C) until golden brown, approximately 30 minutes.

VARIATIONS

Vegetable Curry Turnover: Heat 2 tablespoons olive oil; add 4 ounces (115 grams) chopped onions and 2 mashed garlic cloves. Cover and sweat. Add 2 tablespoons Curry Powder Blend or Garam Masala Blend. Cook briefly. Add 1/2 pound (225 grams) each of blanched, chopped cauliflower, broccoli, potatoes, and peas. Toss to blend. Add 8 fluid ounces (225 milliliters) Vegetable Stock or 4 fluid ounces (115 milliliters) coconut milk and cook out. Fill as above.

Roasted Pepper with Gorgonzola Turnover: Prepare Roasted Pepper Salad (page 675) and chill. Add 8 ounces (225 grams) crumbled gorgonzola. Fill as directed above.

Wild Mushroom Mille Feuille

Yield: 10 servings

Mushroom ragout

Olive oil	*2 fluid ounces*	*60 milliliters*
Garlic cloves, minced	*5 each*	*5 each*
Shiitakes, quartered	*1 pound*	*450 grams*
Cèpes, quartered if large	*1 pound*	*450 grams*
Chanterelles, whole	*1 pound*	*450 grams*
Rosemary, sprigs	*4 each*	*4 each*
Thyme, sprigs	*4 each*	*4 each*
Salt, to taste	*1/2 teaspoon*	*1/2 teaspoon*
Pepper, to taste	*1/4 teaspoon*	*1/4 teaspoon*
Balsamic vinegar	*3 fluid ounces*	*90 milliliters*
White wine	*10 fluid ounces*	*300 milliliters*
Vegetable Stock	*1 pint*	*480 milliliters*
Parsley, chopped	*1/2 ounce*	*15 grams*
Pasta dough, sheets	*2 pounds*	*2 pounds*
Shallots	*2 pounds*	*680 grams*
Vinegar	*1 fluid ounce*	*30 milliliters*
Honey	*2 fluid ounces*	*60 milliliters*
Tomato slices	*20 each*	*20 each*
Rosemary, sprigs	*10 each*	*10 each*

1. Prepare mushroom ragout: Heat olive oil; sauté garlic and mushrooms with sprigs of herbs in small batches.

2. Remove herbs. Deglaze with vinegar and wine; reduce liquid by half and add stock. Cook and reduce to sauce consistency. Stir in chopped parsley just before serving. Season to taste with salt and pepper.

3. Roast the shallots in a 350°F (175°C) oven. Peel and slice or chop, as desired. Combine with vinegar and honey and cook out slightly. Keep warm.

4. Roll out pasta dough, sprinkle with parsley, fold into thirds, and roll to very thin sheets. Cut into 3-inch (7.5-centimeter) squares. Drop into salted boiling water and cook until al dente. Rinse to stop the cooking process.

5. To assemble, reheat the ragout, shallots, pasta squares, and tomatoes. Layer with 2 ounces (60 grams) mushroom ragout, 2 ounces (60 grams) shallots, and 2 roasted tomato halves between pasta squares. Serve 2 layered pastas per portion. Garnish with fresh rosemary sprigs.

Canneloni with Swiss Chard and Walnuts, Piedmont Style

Yield: 10 servings

To prepare crêpes for this dish, use the recipe on page 872, adding 2 tablespoons of minced fresh parsley.

The Cream Sauce is on page 536.

Canneloni is prepared in this manner in the Piedmont region of Italy. The traditional filling includes veal, prosciutto, and Parmesan. Elsewhere, they are pasta sheets filled with tomato sauce and mozzarella.

Swiss Chard, rinsed, stems removed	2 pounds	9 kilograms
Butter	2 ounces	60 grams
Onions, minced	4 ounces	115 grams
Brandy	2 fluid ounces	60 milliliters
Heavy cream	1 fluid ounces	30 milliliters
Walnuts, toasted	3 ounces	85 grams
Gruyére cheese, grated	1 ounce	30 grams
Egg, beaten well	1 each	1 each
Salt, to taste	1 teaspoon	1 teaspoon
Pepper, to taste	1/2 teaspoon	1/2 teaspoon
Nutmeg, ground, to taste	1/8 teaspoon	1/8 teaspoon
Crêpes	20 each	20 each
Cream Sauce	8 fluid ounces	240 milliliters

1. Blanch the Swiss chard in rapidly boiling salted water. Drain, squeeze dry, and coarsely chop.

2. Melt the butter in a skillet. Add the shallots and allow them to sweat.

3. Add the brandy and flame. Add the cream and reduce slightly. Add the Swiss chard and cook over mediun heat for five minutes.

4. Away from the heat, mix in the nuts, grated cheese, and beaten egg. Add salt, pepper, and nutmeg to taste. Let this mixture cool and keep refrigerated until needed.

5. Add the filling to the crêpes and roll into canneloni. Place in a baking pan or individual gratin dishes.

6. Blend the cream sauce and egg yolk and ladle over the canneloni.

7. Bake at 375°F (190°C) for about 20 to 30 minutes, or until heated throughly. Serve at once.

Vegetable Lasagna

Yield: 10 servings

Eggplant, peeled, 1/8-inch slices	*2 pounds*	*900 grams*
Flour, as needed	*4 ounces*	*115 grams*
Egg wash	*5 ounces*	*140 grams*
Bread crumbs	*6 ounces*	*170 grams*
Vegetable oil, as needed	*6 ounces*	*180 milliliters*
Zucchini	*1 pound*	*450 grams*
Yellow squash	*1 pound*	*450 grams*
Mushrooms, sliced	*1 pound*	*450 grams*
Garlic, cloves, minced	*3 each*	*3 each*
Salt, to taste	*1/2 teaspoon*	*1/2 teaspoon*
Pepper, to taste	*1/2 teaspoon*	*1/2 teaspoon*
Ricotta cheese	*1 pound*	*450 grams*
Eggs, beaten	*2 each*	*2 each*
Parmesan cheese, grated	*8 ounces*	*225 grams*
Mozzarella, grated	*12 ounces*	*340 grams*
Tomato sauce	*1 quart*	*1 liter*

Tomato Sauce recipes may be found on page 537 and 538. For a spicier finish, add up to 1 tablespoon red chili flakes to the tomato paste.

To read about the standard breading procedure, see pages 320 to 321.

If you pefer, you may grill or blanch the eggplant rather than bread and fry it.

Include other vegetables, as available: sautéed onions, red and green peppers (roasted or blanched), blanched broccoli, Swiss chard, or spinach are all good choices.

Prepared lasagna noodles may also be added.

1. Coat eggplant with flour, egg wash, and bread crumbs using standard breading procedure.

2. Fry eggplant in very hot oil and drain well.

3. Slice zucchini and yellow squash lengthwise into 1/8-inch thick slices to make "lasagna noodles." Blanch, shock, and drain well. Reserve.

4. Sauté mushrooms, add the garlic and season to taste. Drain off excess liquid.

5. Mix ricotta, eggs, and half the Parmesan.

6. In a baking pan, place a thin layer of tomato sauce, a layer of eggplant, then the ricotta mixture, zucchini, yellow squash, mushrooms and mozzarella. Repeat the process until all ingredients are used, ending with a layer of eggplant and tomato sauce. Cover the pan.

7. Bake at 350°F (175°C) until all ingredients are thoroughly cooked, about one hour. Remove cover, top with the remaining Parmesan cheese and place back in the oven to bake another 15 to 20 minutes. Allow to rest about 15 minutes before cutting.

Roasted Eggplant Ravioli

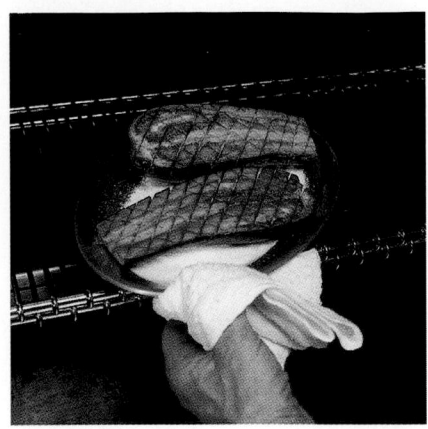

Eggplant responds well to roasting, The flesh becomes extremely soft with an appetizing flavor and aroma.

To read about roasting eggplant, see page 198. To read about roasting garlic, see page 191.

To make spinach pasta, purée 4 ounces (115 grams) of spinach; reduce to 3 ounces (85 grams). Add to the basic pasta dough recipe, page 846.

Yield: 10 servings

Eggplant filling		
Eggplant, roasted, peeled, seeded, and puréed	*2 pounds*	*900 grams*
Garlic bulbs, roasted, pulp puréed	*2 each*	*2 each*
Onions, minced, sweated, and cooled	*10 ounces*	*285 grams*
Bread crumbs, as needed	*6 ounces*	*170 grams*
Parsley, minced	*1 tablespoon*	*1 tablespoon*
Chives, minced	*2 tablespoons*	*2 tablespoons*
Salt, to taste	*1/2 teaspoon*	*1/2 teaspoon*
Pepper, to taste	*1/4 teaspoon*	*1/4 teaspoon*
Spinach pasta	*1 1/2 pounds*	*680 grams*
Olive oil, as needed	*4 fluid ounces*	*120 milliliters*
Chanterelles, cut in half	*1 pound*	*450 grams*
Shiitake mushrooms, caps, cut in half	*1/2 pound*	*225 grams*
Red onions, sliced thin	*2 each*	*2 each*
Balsamic vinegar	*1 fluid ounce*	*30 milliliters*
Parmesan cheese, grated	*2 ounces*	*60 grams*
Roasted red peppers, cut into strips	*6 ounces*	*140 grams*

1. Combine ingredients for filling, season to taste with salt and pepper. Chill filling, place into a pastry bag.

2. Cut pasta into 2 1/2-inch (6.3 centimeter) disks. Brush edges with water. Pipe filling onto pasta disk, top and seal edges with second pasta disk.

3. Bring a large pot of salted water to a simmer.

4. Boil ravioli gently until cooked through. (This is best done to order.)

5. Heat olive oil, add the mushrooms and sauté until they are partially caramelized. Add the red onions and cook until caramelized, add the balsamic vinegar and season to taste with salt and pepper.

6. Drain ravioli, set on a bed of the mushrooms, onion, and mix.

7. Garnish with red pepper strips. Serve with Parmesan cheese.

Vegetable Curry with Brown Rice Pilaf

Yield: 10 servings

Vegetable or peanut oil	*2 ounces*	*60 mililiters*
Onions, sliced	*12 ounces*	*40 grams*
Garlic, mashed to a paste	*1 ounce*	*30 grams*
Celery, bias cut	*4 ounces*	*115 grams*
Potatoes, small dice	*10 ounces*	*285 grams*
Green beans, blanched	*10 ounces*	*285 grams*
Scallions, bias cut	*1 bunch*	*1 bunch*
Curry Powder	*1 ounce*	*30 grams*
Cumin, ground	*1/2 teaspoon*	*1/2 teaspoon*
Coriander, ground	*1/2 teaspoon*	*1/2 teaspoon*
Vegetable Stock	*1 pint*	*480 milliliters*
Tomato Concassé	*8 ounces*	*225 grams*
Salt, to taste	*1 teaspoon*	*1 teaspoon*
Pepper, to taste	*1/2 teaspoon*	*1/2 teaspoon*
Brown Rice Pilaf	*2 pounds*	*900 grams*
Garden peas, shelled, blanched	*8 ounces*	*225 grams*

1. Heat the oil over high heat. Add the onions and garlic and sauté until well browned.

2. Add the celery, potatoes, and green beans. Sauté, stirring frequently, until the green beans are blistered.

3. Add the scallions, curry powder, cumin, and coriander. Sauté briefly.

4. Add the vegetable stock and bring it to a simmer. Stew the ingredients until they are all very tender and the liquid is thickened. Adjust the seasoning to taste with salt and pepper.

5. Add the green peas to the pilaf. Make a ring of pilaf and serve the curry in the center.

The recipe for Curry Powder is on page 426. Prepare Rice Pilaf (page 831) using brown rice.

Thinly sliced Granny Smith apples may be added in step 3.

Garnish with toasted coconut, toasted pumpkin seeds, currants, and prepared mango chutney.

Finish with unsweetened coconut milk, if desired.

Eggplant Parmesan

Yield: 10 servings

Prepare the Eggplant Parmesan in a hotel pan or in individual gratin dishes.

To read about the standard breading procedure, see pages 320 to 321.

Recipes for Tomato Sauce may be found on pages 537 to 539.

Eggplant, peeled, 1/2-inch slices	2 pounds	1.15 kilograms
Vegetable oil, as needed	4 fluid ounces	120 milliliters
Salt, to taste	1/2 teaspoon	1/2 teaspoon
Pepper, to taste	1/2 teaspoon	1/2 teaspoon
Tomato Sauce	1 quart	1 liter
Mozzarella cheese, grated	12 ounces	340 grams
Parmesan cheese, grated	4 ounces	115 grams

1. Bread eggplant using the standard breading procedure.

2. Fry eggplant until golden, and drain well. Season with salt and pepper.

3. Pour a thin layer of tomato sauce into a gratin dish, then top with the eggplant slices. Cover with additional sauce. Top with mozzarella cheese. Cover and bake in the oven for 15 minutes. Remove the cover and bake for an additional 6 to 8 minutes to brown the cheese. Serve with Parmesan cheese.

There are several approaches to making tomato sauce. Learn different techniques to vary standard offerings.

Serve this dish with fresh Tomato Sauce, page 537.

The recipe for Risotto may be found on page 833.

Cheese-Filled Risotto Croquettes with Tomato Sauce

Yield: 10 servings

Risotto, cooked	2 pounds	900 grams
Heavy cream	2 fluid ounces	60 milliliters
Parmesan cheese, grated	2 ounces	60 grams
Egg yolks	2 each	2 each
Mozzarella or fontina cheese, cut into 20 cubes	10 ounces	285 grams
Standard breading	as needed	as needed
Tomato sauce, heated	1 1/4 pints	600 milliliters

1. Combine the risotto with the cream, Parmesan cheese, and egg yolks.

2. Form the mixture into croquettes by making a ball of risotto around the cubed cheese (about 2 ounces/60 grams of risotto per croquette).

3. Bread the croquettes according to the standard breading procedure. Chill them thoroughly to firm the breading.

4. Fry until evenly browned. Serve 2 croquettes per person on a pool of heated tomato sauce.

Whole Wheat Pasta Primavera with Basil Cream Sauce

Yield: 10 servings

Linguini pasta, fresh	*1 1/2 pounds*	*680 grams*
Basil chiffonade	*1/2 ounce*	*1/2 ounce*
Cream Sauce	*1 1/2 pints*	*720 milliliters*
Salt, to taste	*1 teaspoon*	*1 teaspoon*
Pepper, to taste	*1 teaspoon*	*1 teaspoon*
Asparagus tips	*8 ounces*	*225 grams*
Broccoli florets	*8 ounces*	*225 grams*
Peas, fresh	*8 ounces*	*225 grams*
Morels, chopped	*6 ounces*	*170 grams*
Parmesan cheese	*3 ounces*	*85 grams*
Peppercorns, fresh-cracked	*as needed*	*as needed*

Prepare the pasta using the recipe for Basic Pasta on page 846. Substitute whole wheat flour for half the required flour.

1. Cook the pasta in boiling salted water. Shock. Reserve.

2. Prepare the sauce by adding the basil to the Cream Sauce. Bring to service temperature. Season to taste with salt and pepper.

3. Steam the vegetable until just cooked.

4. Reheat the pasta in boiling water. Toss the pasta with the basil sauce. Serve in a soup plate. Garnish each dish with asparagus, broccoli, peas, and morels.

5. Finish with grated Parmesan cheese and freshly cracked pepper.

VARIATION

Whole Wheat Pasta with Broccoli Rabe: Trim, blanch, and chop 1 1/2 pounds (680 grams) broccoli rabe. Sauté 4 slivered garlic cloves in 2 ounces (60 milliliters) of olive oil until golden. Add broccoli rabe to finish cooking. Season with salt, pepper, and balsamic vinegar to taste. Heat the whole wheat pasta; top with broccoli rabe. Finish with Parmesan cheese and fresh-cracked pepper.

VEGETARIAN ENTRÉES

Pasta Pomodoro

Yield: 6 servings

Angel hair pasta	2 pounds	900 grams
Olive oil	2 fluid ounces	120 milliliters
Garlic, minced	2 tablespoons	2 tablespoons
Basil, chiffonade	1/2 ounce	15 grams
Tomato Concassé	4 pounds	1.8 kilograms
Pepper	1 tablespoon	1 tablespoon
Salt	1 tablespoon	1 tablespoon

1. Cook the pasta in boiling salted water until nearly tender. Drain, rinse with cool water, and reserve.

2. Heat the oil. Add the garlic and cook until golden. Do not scorch.

3. Add the basil, tomatoes, and pepper. Sauté for a few minutes.

4. Reheat the pasta if necessary, and drain well. Serve in heated plates, topped with the tomato mixture.

In summer, when very fresh tomatoes are available, prepare as follows: Combine the oil, garlic, tomatoes, basil, salt, and pepper, and 1 tablespoon crushed red pepper flakes. Let this mixture rest for 2 hours under refrigeration to allow flavors to develop.

Serve with freshly grated Parmesan if desired.

Macaroni and Cheese

Yield: 10 servings

Macaroni, uncooked	2 1/4 pounds	1 kilogram
Salt	1/2 teaspoon	1/2 teaspoon
Cheddar Cheese Sauce	1 quart	1 liter
Bread crumbs, fresh (optional)	6 ounces	170 grams

1. Bring a large pot of salted water to a boil on the stove. Add the macaroni and return to a boil. Cook the pasta al dente, 7 to 9 minutes. Do not overcook.

2. Drain the pasta and shock. Mix the pasta with the Cheddar Cheese Sauce.

3. Pour into a gratin or hotel pan. If desired, sprinkle bread crumbs over the surface. Bake at 300°F (175°C) until heated through and the surface is crisp. Lower the temperature if necessary. The cheese will separate if baked at too high a temperature.

Cheddar Cheese Sauce can be found on page 536.

Other cheeses may be blended with the Cheddar cheese: Monterey Jack, fontina, or Swiss. Grate some over the surface near the end of baking time.

Other ingredients may be precooked and included with the macaroni and cheese. Try blanched broccoli florets, peas, diced red and green peppers, chopped onions, and canned tuna.

Other pasta shapes can replace the macaroni: rotini, fusili, and shells all work well.

Stuffed Cabbage Roll on a Lentil Ragout

Yield: 10 servings

Savoy cabbage, blanched	3 heads	3 heads
Brown rice, uncooked	12 ounces	340 grams
Onion, minced	1 ounce	30 grams
Vegetable oil	1 fluid ounce	30 milliliters
Vegetable Stock	20 fluid ounces	600 milliliters
Orange, zested	1 each	1 each
Thyme, sprig	1 each	1 each
Salt, to taste	1/2 teaspoon	1/2 teaspoon
Pepper, to taste	1/2 teaspoon	1/2 teaspoon
Lentil ragout		
Vegetable oil	1 fluid ounce	30 milliliters
Onion, minced	2 ounces	60 grams
Green lentils	5 ounces	140 grams
White vinegar	2 tablespoons	2 tablespoons
Vegetable Stock	1 1/2 pints	680 milliliters
Thyme, sprig	1 each	1 each
Italian parsley, chopped	2 tablespoons	2 tablespoons
Dijon mustard, to taste	1/2 teaspoon	1/2 teaspoon
Salt, to taste	1/2 teaspoon	1/2 teaspoon
Pepper, to taste	1/4 teaspoon	1/4 teaspoon
Garnish		
Fried jerusalem artichoke chips	30 pieces	30 pieces
Tomato Concassé, heated	1 pound	450 grams
Chives, finely cut	1 bunch	1 bunch

To make Fried Jerusalem Artichoke Chips: Slice Jerusalem artichokes very thin using a mandolin. Deep-fry in 375°F (190°C) oil until very crisp. Drain on absorbent paper and season with salt to taste.

1. Separate the blanched Savoy cabbage heads. Chop the inner leaves and reserve the larger ones.

2. Sauté the rice and onion in the vegetable oil. Add the stock, orange zest, thyme, salt, pepper, and chopped cabbage leaves. Bring to a simmer, cover and place into a 325°F (165°C) oven until rice is tender. Drain if necessary. Remove the thyme.

3. Fill the large leaves with the rice and roll up.

4. Place in a hotel pan, add a little stock, cover and put into the oven to finish cooking.

5. For lentil ragout: Sweat onion in the oil; add lentils, vinegar, vegetable stock, and thyme.

6. Cover and cook until lentils are done.

7. Finish with parsley and mustard. Season to taste with salt and pepper. Remove the thyme.

8. Place ragout on plate, put cabbage rolls on top, sprinkle chips on top, and garnish with Tomato Concassé and chives.

727

Casablanca Stew over Couscous

Yield: 20 servings

The recipe for Couscous may be found on page 838.

Turnips, tomato concassé, fennel, artichoke bottoms, saffron, and other seasonings may be added.

Serve prepared Harissa sauce or similar hot sauce on the side.

Additional garnishes include more currants, almonds, and parsley.

Olive oil	3 fluidounces	90 mililiters
Onions, diced	1 1/4 pound	570 grams
Garlic cloves, minced	5 each	5 each
Leeks, brunoise	1 pound	450 grams
Spice blend		
Ground cumin	1 teaspoon	1 teaspoon
Ginger, fresh-minced	1/2 ounce	15 grams
Turmeric	1 teaspoon	1 teaspoon
Dry mustard	1 teaspoon	1 teaspoon
Coriander, ground	1 teaspoon	1 teaspoon
Cinnamon, ground	1 teaspoon	1 teaspoon
Cayenne	1/2 teaspoon	1/2 teaspoon
Spanish paprika	2 teaspoons	2 teaspoons
Cardamom seeds, toasted	1 teaspoon	1 teaspoon
Pumpkin, brunoise	1 pound	450 grams
Butternut squash, brunoise	1 pound	450 grams
Zucchini squash, diced, brunoise	1/2 pound	225 grams
Vegetable stock, as needed	3 quarts	3 liters
Carrots, brunoise	1/2 pounds	225 grams
Tomato purée	6 fluid ounces	180 mililiters
Celery, diced, brunoise	1/2 pound	225 grams
Eggplant, peeled, diced, brunoise	1 pound	450 grams
Chickpeas, cooked	10 ounces	170 grams
Fava beans, cooked	8 ounces	225 grams
Currants, plumped	8 ounces	225 grams
Lemons, zested	2 lemons	2 lemons
Salt, to taste	1 teaspoon	1 teaspoon
Pepper, to taste	1 teaspoon	1 teaspoon
Lemon, juiced	1 each	1 each
Couscous, steamed	4 pounds	1.8 kilograms

1. Heat oil; sauté onion, garlic, and leeks over moderate heat until soft. Cook another 2 minutes; stir frequently.

2. Briefly toast the spices over low heat; add them to the onions.

3. Add pumpkin and squash; add stock as necessary to cover; cook another five minutes. Add carrots, celery, eggplant, tomato purée, currants, and the remaining stock.

4. Add chickpeas and fava beans. Cover and simmer until flavors are developed. Adjust seasonings with salt, pepper, and lemon. Serve piping hot, garnished with lemon zest, and accompanied with couscous.

Rice and Beans, Mexican Style

Yield: 10 servings

Pinto beans, presoaked	1 pound	450 grams
Salt, to taste	1 teaspoon	1 teaspoon
Hungarian paprika	1 teaspoon	5 milliliters
Vegetable oil	2 fluid ounces	60 mililiters
Onions	4 ounces	115 grams
Green peppers, chopped fine	6 ounces	170 grams
Red peppers, chopped fine	6 ounces	170 grams
Yellow peppers, chopped fine	4 ounces	115 grams
Tomato Concassé	6 ounces	170 grams
Capers (Spanish if available)	1 tablespoon	1 tablespoon
Golden seedless raisins	2 ounces	60 grams
Cayenne, ground, to taste	pinch	pinch
Pepper, to taste	1/4 teaspoon	1/4 teaspoon
Vegetable Stock, as needed	1 pint	480 milliliters
Lemon juice	to taste	to taste
White rice, cooked	2 pounds	900 grams

1. Simmer the beans in salted water with paprika.

2. Heat the oil; sauté onions and peppers; cook until the onions are golden brown.

3. Add Tomato Concassé, capers, raisins, cayenne, and salt.

4. Cover with stock and cook to stew consistency; add beans and adjust seasoning to taste with lemon juice.

5. Serve over rice.

VARIATION

Rice and Beans, Puerto Rican Style: Sauté 8 ounces (225 grams) of Sofrito (page 421). Substitute 8 ounces (225 grams) each of peeled, cubed potatoes and pumpkin for the peppers, capers, and raisins. Cook as directed. Add 2 ounces (60 grams) green olives stuffed with pimientos. Serve over short-grain white rice. Garnish with fried plantains or any of the suggestions above. Pink beans may be substituted for the pinto beans. Pigeon peas and garbanzo beans may also be included.

This dish is traditionally garnished with sautéed bananas and chopped hard-boiled egg whites.

Deep-fried thinly sliced plantains, sweet potatoes, or yucca or beet chips would also be appropriate. See note on page 727.

Brown rice may be substituted.

Reduce the liquid from the stew until almost dry. Use the mixture as a classic filling for Empenadas, turnovers, or tamales.

Black Bean and Cornmeal Loaf with Fresh Salsa

Yield: 10 servings

The recipe for Salsa may be found on page 936.

Eight ounces (225 grams) of grated Cheddar or Monterey Jack cheese can be added to the cornmeal mixture.

Vegetable Stock	1 quart	1 liter
Salt	1 teaspoon	1 teaspoon
Vegetable oil, as needed	2 fluid ounces	60 mililiters
Cornmeal	8 ounces	225 grams
Red peppers, diced	5 ounces	140 grams
Green peppers, diced	5 ounces	140 grams
Red onions, diced	6 ounces	170 grams
Garlic, minced	4 ounces	115 grams
Sun-dried tomatoes, softened and diced	3 ounces	85 grams
Cilantro, chopped	1/4 ounce	8 grams
Black beans, cooked	12 ounces	340 grams
Tabasco, to taste	1/4 teaspoon	1/4 teaspoon
Salt, to taste	1/2 teaspoon	1/2 teaspoon
Pepper, to taste	1/2 teaspoon	1/2 teaspoon
Flour, as needed	2 ounces	60 grams
Salsa	20 fluid ounces	60 milliliters

1. Heat a skillet with half of the oil. Add peppers, onions, and garlic; sweat until softened. Remove from heat and add tomatoes, cilantro, beans, and Tabasco. Season to taste with salt and pepper and Tabasco. Reserve.

2. Heat stock; add salt and 1 tablespoon of oil. Slowly whisk in the cornmeal, reduce heat, and cook 20 minutes, stirring constantly. Mixture should pull away from the sides of the pot. Set aside. Fold in bean mixture.

3. Turn mixture into a greased loaf pan. Refrigerate overnight.

4. Unmold loaf and slice into 15 equal slices. Cut each slice on the diagonal to make 30 triangles.

5. Lightly dust triangles with flour. Sauté triangles in oil until brown.

6. Serve 3 triangles per portion; top with freshly made salsa.

Vegetarian Chili

Yield: 10 servings

Pinto beans, cooked	*1 pound*	*450 grams*
Black beans, cooked	*1 pound*	*450 grams*
Kidney beans, cooked	*8 ounces*	*225 grams*
Garbanzo beans, cooked	*8 ounces*	*225 grams*
Adobo sauce, from canned chipotles	*2 tablespoons*	*2 tablespoons*
Chipotles	*3 each*	*3 each*
Vegetable oil	*as needed*	*as needed*
Onions, chopped	*1 pound*	*450 grams*
Garlic cloves, minced	*3 each*	*3 each*
Oregano leaves, chopped	*1 tablespoon*	*1 tablespoon*
Cumin, seed, to taste, ground	*2 tablespoons*	*2 tablespoons*
Chili powder	*1 ounce*	*30 grams*
Green chilies, roasted, peeled, and seeded (or canned)	*3 each*	*3 each*
Vegetable Stock, or water, as needed	*1 quart*	*1 liter*
Tomato Concassé, juice reserved	*1 1/2 pounds*	*680 grams*
Salt, to taste	*1/2 teaspoon*	*1/2 teaspoon*
Pepper, to taste	*1/4 teaspoon*	*1/4 teaspoon*
Lime juice, to taste	*1 fluid ounce*	*30 milliliters*

1. Heat the oil in a large rondeau. Add onions and sweat. Add the red and green peppers. Cook until soft.

2. Add the oregano, cumin, and chili powder; cook for a minute. Do not let the spices burn. Add the garlic and cook briefly. Add the green chilies, chipotle peppers, and Adobo sauce.

3. Add the Tomato Concassé and stock. Simmer approximately 30 minutes. Add the beans; continue to simmer. Adjust consistency and season to taste with salt, pepper, and lime juice.

Serve over brown rice with cornbread, or as a filling for burritos and enchiladas.

Twelve fluid ounces (360 mililiters) of beer may replace part of the vegetable stock.

If chipotles are not available, use diced, fresh jalapeños or add any dried red chilies. Remove dried chilies at the end of cooking time.

Chopped carrots, zucchini, celery, or jicama may be added in step 2.

You may use Red Chili Sauce (page 549) as the base of the chili if you prefer. Prepare it according to the recipe and add the onions and peppers, or use the Chili Powder Spice Blend (page 425) to replace the spices.

Vegetarian Tamales

Yield: 10 servings

The amount of chili powder, cumin, and oregano you want to add will depend on the flavor of the enchilada sauce you are using.

Red or Green Chili Sauce (pages 549 and 550) can be used instead of the enchilada sauce.

Add 8 ounces (225 grams) of cooked mashed beans to the mixture if desired.

Cooked corn kernels may be added to the vegetable mix or the tamale dough.

The filling and the dough can be prepared one day in advance. The tamales can be rolled up to 6 hours in advance. Once steamed, they hold for a very short time. If they must be cooked in advance, it is better to cool them down and reheat them in the oven rather than to try to hold them on a steam table.

Onions, finely diced	6 ounces	170 grams
Vegetable oil	2 fluid ounces	60 milliliters
Yellow squash, diced	8 ounces	225 grams
Zucchini, diced	8 ounces	225 grams
Tomato Concassé	5 ounces	140 grams
Prepared enchilada sauce	4 fluid ounces	120 milliliters
Chili powder, roasted to taste	1/2 teaspoon	1/2 teaspoon
Salt, to taste	1/2 teaspoon	1/2 teaspoon
Cumin, roasted	1/2 teaspoon	1/2 teaspoon
Oregano	1/4 teaspoon	1/4 teaspoon
Corn husks (Mexican, dried)	4 ounces	115 grams
Masa harina	12 ounces	340 grams
Water or stock	14 fluid ounces	420 milliliters
Vegetable shortening	4 fluid ounces	115 grams
Baking powder	3/4 teaspoon	3/4 teaspoon
Salt	1/4 teaspoon	1/4 teaspoon

1. Sweat the onions in the oil about 5 minutes. Add the squashes and continue to cook until tender. Add the Tomato Concassé and enchilada sauce and cook until almost dry. Season to taste with chili powder, cumin, and oregano and salt. Cool and reserve.

2. Soak the corn husks in hot water to make them pliable.

3. Mix masa harina with water, shortening, baking powder, and salt. Beat until smooth and fluffy.

4. Drain the corn husks. Lay 1 or 2 husks on the work surface. The husks should be about 5 inches (13 centimeters) wide.

5. Place 2 tablespoons of masa mixture on the smooth side of each corn husk and spread over the lower two-thirds of the husk, leaving 1 inch (2 1/2 centimeters) of space on each side.

6. Place one generous tablespoon of vegetable mixture lengthwise down the center of the masa. Roll tightly so the edges of masa fit together. Fold the excess husk under. Tie each with a strip of corn husk if necessary.

7. Steam the tamales, folded side down, for about 40 to 50 minutes. Serve immediately, in the husk, slightly opened, with enchilada sauce, if desired.

C H A P T E R **20** *International Entrées*

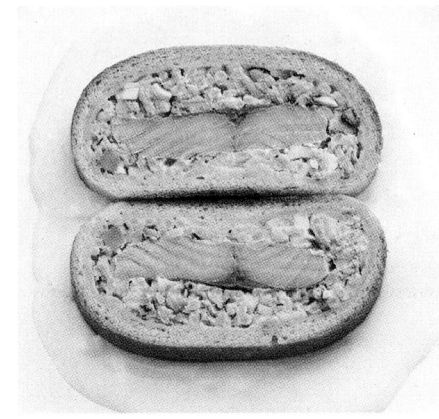

The constant interchange of recipes, ingredients, and cooking styles from one group to another has made it difficult to draw strict lines around any single cuisine. There are "international" recipes to be found throughout this book, many of which are so familiar that they are no longer regarded as foreign.

As the availability of special ingredients favored in Asian, Latin American, Caribbean, Mediterannean, and Middle Eastern cuisines has increased, so has the appearance of those dishes on many menus throughout this country. Add to that the increased awareness of the potential health benefits associated with ethnic cuisines, and it is easy to understand the growing demand on the part of your guests for a broader spectrum of offerings from around the world.

The recipes in this chapter have been loosely grouped as follows:

- *Europe: Beef*
- *Europe: Veal*
- *Europe: Lamb*
- *Europe: Poultry*
- *Europe: Fish*
- *Europe: Mixed*

- *Latin: Beef*
- *Latin: Pork*
- *Latin: Poultry*
- *Latin: Fish*

- *Asia: Beef*
- *Asia: Pork*
- *Asia: Lamb*
- *Asia: Poultry*
- *Asia: Fish*

Beef Tenderloin with Spicy Tomato Sauce
(Medaglione di Bue alla Pizzaiola)

Yield: 10 servings

Sauce infusion

White wine	*1 pint*	*480 milliliters*
Oregano, sprig	*1 each*	*1 each*
Basil, leaves	*5 each*	*5 each*
Pepperoncini, chopped	*2 each*	*2 each*
Bay leaf	*1 each*	*1 each*
Parsley, sprig	*1 each*	*1 each*

Sauce

Olive oil	*2 fluid ounces*	*60 milliliters*
Onions, fine dice	*3 ounces*	*85 grams*
Garlic cloves, minced	*3 each*	*3 each*
Tomato Concassé	*1 3/4 pounds*	*800 grams*
Salt, to taste	*1/2 teaspoon*	*1/2 teaspoon*
Pepper, to taste	*1/4 teaspoon*	*1/4 teaspoon*
Beef tenderloin, trimmed	*4 pounds*	*1.8 kilograms*
Clarified butter, as needed	*2 to 3 ounces*	*60 to 85 grams*

Garnish

Oyster mushrooms, sliced	*4 ounces*	*115 grams*
Porcini mushrooms, sliced	*4 ounces*	*115 grams*
Parsley, chopped	*1 teaspoon*	*1 teaspoon*

1. To make the infusion: Reduce the wine to 6 fluid ounces (180 milliliters), add the herbs and allow to steep for 1 to 2 hours; strain.

2. To make the sauce: Sauté the onions and garlic in oil, add the Tomato Concassé and simmer to a thick consistency.

3. Add the strained infusion and purée in a food processor; season. Reduce consistency if necessary.

4. Sauté the beef medallions to desired degree of doneness; portion 2 ounces (60 grams) of sauce on a plate; arrange 2 medallions of beef on top.

5. Sauté the mushrooms in clarified butter, add parsley and season to taste with salt and pepper. Place the mushrooms on top of the beef.

Beef Goulash

Yield: 10 servings

Onions, sliced or diced	2 pounds	900 grams
Lard or oil	2 ounces	60 grams
White wine vinegar	1 fluid ounce	30 milliliters
Sweet Hungarian paprika	4 tablespoons	4 tablespoons
Marjoram, powdered	1 teaspoon	1 teaspoon
Garlic cloves, minced	3 each	3 each
Lemon zest	1 teaspoon	1 teaspoon
Salt, to taste	1/2 teaspoon	1/2 teaspoon
White Beef Stock	1 quart	1 liter
Tomato paste	4 ounces	120 grams
Beef shank, cut in large cubes	5 pounds	2.25 kilograms

1. Sauté the onions in lard or oil until they are brown.

2. Add the vinegar, spices, garlic, lemon zest, and salt; Cook over moderate heat until nearly dry.

3. Add the stock and tomato paste and bring the mixture to a simmer.

4. Add the beef shank, cover the pan, and braise it until fork-tender, approximately 1 1/2 hours. Degrease the sauce and adjust the seasoning with salt and pepper to taste.

There are many goulash recipes, with each region of Central Europe favoring its own style. Serve goulash with Bread Dumplings (page 855) or broad egg noodles. Garnish with heavy cream and chopped dill.

Goulash is best when it is prepared a day in advance to allow the flavors to "marry."

Sauerbraten

Yield: 10 servings

Marinade

Dry red wine	8 fluid ounces	240 milliliters
Red wine vinegar	8 fluid ounces	240 milliliters
Water	2 quarts	2 liters
Onions, sliced	2 each	2 each
Whole black peppercorns	8 each	8 each
Juniper berries	10 each	10 each
Bay leaves	2 each	2 each
Whole cloves	2 each	2 each
Salt, to taste	2 teaspoons	2 teaspoons
Vegetable oil	3 fluid ounces	90 milliliters
Mirepoix, diced	1 pound	450 grams
Tomato paste	4 ounces	115 grams
Flour	2 ounces	60 grams
Brown Veal Stock	3 quarts	3 liters
Gingersnaps, pulverized	3 ounces	85 grams
Beef bottom round	4 pounds	1.8 kilograms

(Recipe continued on next page)

Braising may be done in the oven at 300°F (150°C) or on the stove top.

"Fork-tender" means that meats will slide easily from a kitchen fork when lifted, or that they can be "cut" with a fork.

1. Trim the beef to remove any gristle or silverskin.

2. Combine all the ingredients for the marinade and bring the mixture to a boil. Cool it to room temperature.

3. Season the beef with salt and place it in the marinade; marinate it under refrigeration for 3 to 5 days, turning it twice per day.

4. Remove the meat from the marinade. Strain and reserve the marinade; reserve the onions and herbs separately.

5. Bring the strained marinade to a boil and skim off the scum.

6. Heat the oil in a brazier. Add the beef and sear it on all sides. Remove the meat and reserve it.

7. Add the mirepoix and reserved onions and herbs from the marinade. Let them brown lightly.

8. Add the tomato paste and cook out for several seconds.

9. Deglaze the pan with the strained marinade and reduce the liquid by half.

10. Add the flour and combine the mixture thoroughly.

11. Add the brown stock, whip out any lumps, and bring to a simmer. Return the meat to the pan, cover it and braise until fork-tender.

12. Remove the meat and reduce the sauce. Degrease thoroughly.

13. Add the gingersnaps and cook the sauce for 10 minutes, until the gingersnaps dissolve. Strain the sauce through cheesecloth.

Zwiebel Rostbraten

Yield: 10 servings

Strip loin steaks, lightly pounded	4 pounds	1.8 kilograms
Salt, to taste	1/2 teaspoon	1/2 teaspoon
Black pepper, freshly ground	1/4 teaspoon	1/4 teaspoon
Oil, as needed	2 fluid ounces	60 milliliters
Onions, sliced	5 each	5 each
Balsamic vinegar	4 fluid ounces	120 milliliters
Demi-Glace	1 quart	1 liter
Crisp-fried onions	as needed	as needed

Portion the steaks into 6-ounce (170-gram) cuts.

Crisp-fried onions are prepared by sautéeing thinly sliced onions in very hot oil over high heat.

This dish is also known as Wiener Rostbraten, or Viennese Minute Steak.

1. Season meat with salt and pepper, sauté quickly to desired doneness in a small amount of oil in a hot pan.

2. Remove steaks, keep warm.

3. Add onions to the pan and cook until dark brown. Deglaze with vinegar; add Demi-Glace and reduce to proper sauce consistency; adjust seasonings.

4. Coat the steaks with the sauce. Garnish with crisp-fried onions.

Veal Saltimbocca

Yield: 10 servings

Veal top round	*4 pounds*	*1.8 kilograms*
Prosciutto, 1/2-ounce slices	*5 ounces*	*140 grams*
Sage leaves	*10 each*	*10 each*
Flour, as needed	*4 ounces*	*115 grams*
Clarified butter, as needed	*1 3/4 ounce*	*50 grams*
Demi-Glace or Jus de Veau Lié	*20 fluid ounces*	*150 milliliters*
Salt, to taste	*1/2 teaspoon*	*1/2 teaspoon*
Pepper, to taste	*1/4 teaspoon*	*1/4 teaspoon*
Marsala	*10 fluid ounces*	*300 milliliters*

1. Cut the veal into 2- to 3-ounce (60- to 85-gram) scaloppine. To assemble the saltimbocca, pound the veal, lay a piece of prosciutto amd a sage leaf on one side of the veal, and fold in half. Secure the veal with a toothpick. Season with salt and pepper.

2. Dredge the veal in the flour; shake off excess.

3. Heat the butter in a sauté pan. Add the veal and sauté on both sides.

4. Remove the veal from the pan and keep warm.

5. Pour off the butter from the pan. Add the Demi-Glace and bring the sauce to a simmer; reduce by about one-fourth. Finish the sauce with the Marsala; adjust seasoning to taste with salt and pepper.

6. Pool the sauce on a heated plate and place the veal in the pool of sauce. Remove the toothpicks.

Although not essential, some people like to add a small slice of cheese to the veal along with the prosciutto and sage. Use mozzarella or smoked provolone.

Saltimbocca means "to jump in the mouth," an apt name for this quickly prepared sauté.

Veal Piccata, Milanese-Style

Yield: 10 servings

Occasionally, dishes called Piccata are similar in preparation to those known as "à la meunière." The item is floured, quickly sautéed, topped with lemon zest, minced garlic, and parsley. Whole butter is cooked until it is very hot and foamy, then poured over the sautéed food.

Madeira Sauce	20 fluid ounces	600 milliliters
Ham, julienne	2 ounces	60 grams
Beef tongue, julienne	1 ounce	30 grams
Mushrooms, julienne, cooked	2 ounces	60 grams
Parsley, chopped	2 teaspoons	2 teaspoons
Salt, to taste	1/2 teaspoon	1/2 teaspoon
Pepper, to taste	1/4 teaspoon	1/4 teaspoon
Veal top round	3 1/2 pounds	1.6 kilograms
Flour, for dredging	4 ounces	115 grams
Eggs, beaten	4 each	4 each
Parmesan cheese, grated, as needed	2 ounces	60 grams
Olive oil	3 fluid ounces	90 milliliters

1. To make the sauce: Combine the Madeira Sauce with the ham, tongue, and mushrooms. Bring to a simmer.

2. Finish the sauce with the parsley; season to taste with salt and pepper. Reserve.

3. Cut the veal into scaloppine, about 2 ounces (60 grams) each; pound. Dredge the veal in flour and shake off the excess.

4. Combine the eggs and Parmesan cheese; mix well.

5. Dip the veal in the egg-cheese mixture; panfry in oil until golden brown on both sides; blot briefly.

6. Ladle 2 ounces (60 milliliters) of sauce on a plate and place veal scaloppini on top of the sauce.

Wiener Schnitzel

Yield: 10 servings

Veal top round	*3 1/2 pounds*	*1.6 kilograms*
Salt, to taste	*1/2 teaspoon*	*1/2 teaspoon*
Pepper, to taste	*1/4 teaspoon*	*1/4 teaspoon*
Flour, as needed	*4 ounces*	*115 grams*
Eggs, whole	*4 each*	*4 each*
Milk	*4 fluid ounces*	*120 milliliters*
Breadcrumbs	*12 ounces*	*340 grams*
Vegetable oil, as needed	*3 to 4 ounces*	*90 to 120 milliliters*
Whole butter	*3 ounces*	*85 grams*
Lemon wedges or slices	*10 each*	*10 each*
Parsley sprigs	*10 each*	*10 each*

The method for cutting and pounding scaloppine is found in Chapter 6 on page 226. Pan-frying Wiener Schnitzel is illustrated on page 320.

To read more about standard breading, refer to pages 320 and 321.

The butter and veal must be extremely hot. In fact, the butter should still be bubbly when the dish is presented to the guest.

Rolled anchovies are another classic garnish for this dish.

1. Cut the veal into cutlets of about 5 to 6 ounces (140 to 170 grams). Pound them to an even thickness. Season well with salt and pepper.

2. Bread the veal cutlets: Dredge in flour, dip in egg wash (made by blending eggs and milk), and coat in bread crumbs. Refrigerate the cutlets until firm.

3. Panfry the cutlets in the hot oil until golden brown on both sides and cooked through. Shake the pan occasionally to keep the cutlets moving.

4. Heat the butter in a separate pan until hot and foamy.

5. Serve the cutlet topped with foaming butter and garnished with a lemon wedge and parsley.

VARIATION

Holstein Schnitzel: Top the Wiener Schnitzel with a soft-cooked fried egg.

Scaloppine of Veal with Stuffing
(Scaloppine di Vitello Porta Foglia)

Yield: 10 servings

Veal scaloppine	3 1/2 pounds	1.6 kilograms
Salt, to taste	1/2 teaspoon	1/2 teaspoon
Pepper, to taste	1/2 teaspoon	1/2 teaspoon
Stuffing		
Shallots, minced	1 ounce	30 grams
Ham, chopped fine	6 ounces	170 grams
Italian sweet sausage	6 ounces	170 grams
Spinach, blanched, rough chop	5 ounces	140 grams
Ricotta cheese	3 ounces	85 grams
Romano cheese, grated	2 ounces	60 grams
Nutmeg, ground	1/4 teaspoon	1/4 teaspoon
Sage, chopped	2 teaspoons	10 grams
Flour, as needed	3 ounces	85 grams
Olive oil	2 fluid ounces	60 milliliters
Dry white wine	8 fluid ounces	240 milliliters
Demi-Glace or Jus de Veau Lié	20 fluid ounces	600 milliliters
Sage leaves	10 each	10 each

1. Cut the veal into scaloppine, about 5 to 6 ounces (140 to 170 grams) each. You should have 20 pieces. Pound the scaloppine. Season with salt and pepper before filling.

2. Combine the shallots with the ham, sausage, spinach, ricotta, romano, nutmeg, and sage. Season with salt and pepper; mix well.

3. Spread 1 ounce (30 grams) of stuffing on each scaloppine. Fold over and secure with a toothpick.

4. Dredge scaloppine in flour and shake off excess.

5. Sauté in oil until lightly browned on both sides; remove to a serving platter, discard toothpick and keep warm.

6. Pour off excess fat from the pan; add wine; reduce until syrupy.

7. Add the Demi-Glace and simmer briefly.

8. Arrange the scaloppine on a plate, coat with the sauce, and top with a sage leaf.

Ossobuco alla Milanese

Yield: 10 servings

Veal shank	*10 each*	*10 each*
Salt, to taste	*1/2 teaspoon*	*1/2 teaspoon*
Pepper, to taste	*1/4 teaspoon*	*1/4 teaspoon*
Flour, as needed	*3 ounces*	*85 grams*
Vegetable oil, as needed	*2 fluid ounces*	*60 milliliters*
Dry white wine	*8 fluid ounces*	*240 milliliters*
Tomato paste	*6 ounces*	*170 grams*
Brown Sauce	*2 quarts*	*2 liters*
Gremolata		
Garlic cloves, minced	*2 each*	*2 each*
Lemon zest	*2 tablespoons*	*2 tablespoons*
Parsley, flat-leaf, chopped	*2 tablespoons*	*2 tablespoons*
Anchovy fillets, chopped	*5 each*	*5 each*

1. Season the meat with the salt and pepper; dredge in the flour, and sear on all sides in hot oil. Remove the meat and reserve.

2. Degrease the pan and deglaze it with the wine; reduce the wine by three-quarters.

3. Add the tomato paste and sauté briefly. Add the brown sauce; return the meat to the pan and bring the sauce to a simmer.

4. Cover the pan and braise the meat until it is fork tender, approximately 2 to 3 hours. Remove the meat to moisten and keep it hot.

5. Return the pan to the heat and reduce the sauce to the proper thickness. Adjust seasoning to taste with salt and pepper. Degrease well.

6. Combine all of the ingredients for the gremolata.

7. Serve the ossobuco with the sauce and top with the gremolata.

A veal shank generally weighs 1 to 3 pounds (450 grams to 1.3 kilograms). Use one small shank per portion. Cut larger shanks into crosscuts and serve 1 to 1 1/2 pounds (450 to 680 grams) per portion.

In Milan, ossobuco is served with risotto, one of the rare occasions in Italy that risotto is served as a side dish.

For additional flavor, sauté 8 ounces (225 grams) of mirepoix and 2 cloves of minced garlic in the pan before deglazing it with wine. Prior to service, strain the sauce and reduce to proper consistency.

Grilled Pork Chop with Spicy Sauce
(Lombata di Maiale Grigliata con Piccante)

Yield: 10 servings

The pork chops should be cut into 7- to 8-ounce (200- to 225-gram) portions. Trim the fat as desired.

Anchovy pesto		
Anchovy paste	*1 ounce*	*30 grams*
Parsley, chopped	*1 ounce*	*30 grams*
Basil, chopped	*1 ounce*	*30 grams*
Capers, small	*3 tablespoons*	*3 tablespoons*
Garlic, minced	*3 tablespoons*	*3 tablespoons*
Spicy sauce		
White wine	*3 fluid ounces*	*90 milliliters*
White wine vinegar	*3 fluid ounces*	*90 milliliters*
Shallots, minced	*2 each*	*2 each*
Rosemary, sprig	*1 each*	*1 each*
Bay leaf	*1 each*	*1 each*
Brown Sauce	*1 quart*	*1 liter*
Dijon mustard	*1/2 ounce*	*15 grams*
Salt, to taste	*1/2 teaspoon*	*1/2 teaspoon*
Pepper, to taste	*1/4 teaspoon*	*1/4 teaspoon*
Pork chops, center cut	*10 each*	*10 each*
Vegetable oil	*2 fluid ounces*	*60 milliliters*
Garnish		
Cornichons, julienne	*2 tablespoons*	*2 tablespoons*

1. To prepare pesto, combine ingredients, and pulse in a food processor until very fine mince.

2. To prepare the sauce: Combine the wine, vinegar, shallots, rosemary, and bay leaf; reduce to one-third of original volume.

3. Add the sauce and simmer 10 minutes; strain.

4. Add the mustard and season.

5. Season the pork chops with salt and pepper; brush with oil and broil until done, turning once.

6. Remove the chops and brush each side with pesto.

7. Arrange each chop on a plate and garnish with cornichons; pool the sauce around the pork.

Pork Chops with Fennel
(Costatine al Finocchio)

Yield: 10 servings

Pork chops, center cut, frenched	*10 each*	*10 each*
Salt, to taste	*1/2 teaspoon*	*1/2 teaspoon*
Pepper, to taste	*1/4 teaspoon*	*1/4 teaspoon*
Vegetable oil, as needed	*2 fluid ounces*	*60 milliliters*
Garlic, minced	*1 tablespoon*	*1 tablespoon*
Tomato paste	*1 tablespoon*	*1 tablespoon*
Dry red wine	*4 fluid ounces*	*120 milliliters*
Fennel seeds, crushed	*1/4 teaspoon*	*1/4 teaspoon*
Brown Sauce or Demi-Glace	*2 fluid ounces*	*60 milliliters*
Marsala	*2 fluid ounces*	*60 milliliters*
Fennel, fresh, sliced on the bias, **and blanched**	*12 ounces*	*340 grams*
Butter	*1 ounce*	*30 grams*
Parsley, chopped	*1 tablespoon*	*15 grams*

The pork chops should be cut into 7- to 8-ounce (200- to 225-gram) portions.

1. Season the pork chops and sauté in oil.

2. When pork chops are done, remove to a serving platter and keep warm.

3. Drain excess oil from the pan, add garlic and tomato paste; sauté briefly.

4. Add red wine and fennel seeds; reduce until nearly dry. Add the Brown Sauce or Demi-Glace. Simmer to a good sauce consistency. Add the Marsala to finish the sauce.

5. Sauté fennel in butter to reheat, arrange on a hot platter.

6. Set pork chops on top of the fennel; pool sauce around the chops.

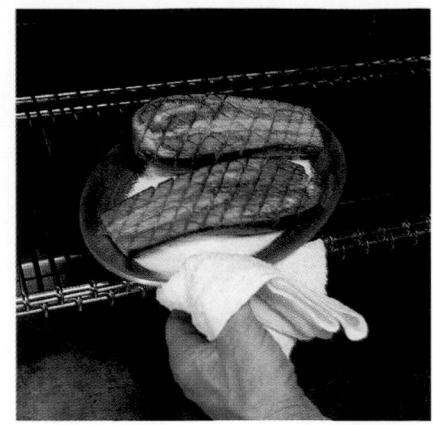

Pork Medallions with Eggplant
(Nodini di Maiale con Melanzane)

Yield: 10 servings

Olive oil	*4 fluid ounces*	*120 milliliters*
Onions, diced	*5 ounces*	*140 grams*
Shallot, minced	*1 each*	*1 each*
Eggplant, peeled, diced	*1 pound*	*450 grams*
Tomato Concassé	*5 ounces*	*140 grams*
Basil, chopped	*1 teaspoon*	*1 teaspoon*
Oregano, chopped	*1 teaspoon*	*1 teaspoon*
Parsley, chopped	*2 teaspoons*	*2 teaspoons*
Salt, to taste	*1/2 teaspoon*	*1/2 teaspoon*
Pepper, to taste	*1/4 teaspoon*	*1/4 teaspoon*
Pork, loin or tenderloin	*4 pounds*	*1.8 kilograms*
Flour, as needed	*2 ounces*	*60 grams*
Dry white wine	*2 fluid ounces*	*60 milliliters*
Demi-Glace or Jus de Veau Lié	*20 fluid ounces*	*600 milliliters*
Oregano sprigs, for garnish	*10 each*	*10 each*

The eggplant can be roasted instead of sautéed if you prefer. Score the flesh and brush liberally with oil, shallots, and onions. Roast until tender as explained on page 198.

Veal medallions or chicken cutlets may be substituted for the pork.

1. Sauté the onions and shallots in olive oil.

2. Add the eggplant; sauté in oil until tender; add Tomato Concassé and herbs; simmer just long enough to cook the tomatoes; season to taste with salt and pepper.

3. Cut the pork into 2- to 3-ounce (60- to 85-gram) medallions. Lightly pound pork medallions with a meat mallet; dredge in seasoned flour and shake off the excess.

4. Sauté pork medallions in olive oil until lightly browned; remove to a serving platter, keep warm.

5. Remove excess oil from the pan; deglaze with stock.

6. Add the Demi-Glace. Simmer a few minutes and strain.

7. Place a portion of eggplant on a plate and set the pork medallions on top, covering half the eggplant; pool 2 ounces (60 grams) of sauce around the pork.

Roasted Stuffed Pork Loin Genoa-Style with Garlic-Flavored Jus

Yield: 10 servings

Stuffing

Pork, lean, ground	6 ounces	170 grams
Italian sausage	6 ounces	170 grams
Bread crumbs, fresh	3 ounces	85 grams
Heavy cream	1 1/2 fluid ounces	45 milliliters
Egg, beaten	1 each	1 each
Pesto	10 ounces	285 grams
Pork loin, boneless, well-trimmed	3 1/2 pounds	1.6 kilograms
Salt, to taste	1/2 teaspoon	1/2 teaspoon
Pepper, to taste	1/4 teaspoon	1/4 teaspoon
Caul fat, as needed	4 ounces	115 grams
Mirepoix, medium dice	4 ounces	115 grams
Tomato paste	2 ounces	60 grams
Garlic cloves, minced	3 each	3 each
Bay leaf	1 each	1 each
Pork or Veal Stock	18 fluid ounces	540 milliliters

Prepare the pesto as directed on page 422, using Romano cheese.

For a roasted garlic jus, roast a garlic bulb, unpeeled, in the oven until softened. Peel and mash. Use as much garlic as desired.

1. Combine the ingredients for the stuffing; mix well.

2. Butterfly the pork loin; pound lightly with a meat mallet.

3. Spread the pesto mixture on the pork, then spread the stuffing over the pesto.

4. Roll up the pork loin, jelly-roll fashion; wrap in caul fat and secure with butcher's twine.

5. Roast the pork to an internal temperture of 160°F (70°C) in a 350°F (175°C) oven.

6. When the pork is done, remove; allow to rest. Pour off excess fat.

7. Add the Mirepoix and tomato paste to the roast pan; caramelize lightly.

8. Add the garlic, bay leaf, and stock; simmer until approximately 20 ounces (600 milliliters) remain; strain and season to taste with salt and pepper.

9. Portion 2 fluid ounces (60 milliliters) of jus on a plate and arrange 2 to 3 slices of pork on top.

Portuguese Stuffed Leg of Lamb
(Pierna de Cordero)

Yield: 12 to 14 servings

For a darker sauce, add 2 ounces (60 grams) of tomato paste to the browned Mirepoix in step 6; pincé. Deglaze with sherry.

Lamb leg	*8 pounds*	*3.6 kilograms*
Salt, to taste	*1/2 teaspoon*	*1/2 teaspoon*
Pepper, to taste	*1/2 teaspoon*	*1/2 teaspoon*
Forcemeat		
Mushrooms, chopped coarse	*3 ounces*	*85 grams*
Lemon juice	*1 tablespoon*	*1 tablespoon*
Olive oil	*1 fluid ounce*	*30 milliliters*
Pork butt, ground	*1 1/2 pounds*	*680 kilograms*
Dry sherry	*6 fluid ounces*	*180 milliliters*
Bread crumbs, dry	*2 ounces*	*60 grams*
Egg, beaten	*1 each*	*1 each*
Oregano, chopped	*1/4 teaspoon*	*1/4 teaspoon*
Basil, chopped	*1/4 teaspoon*	*1/4 teaspoon*
Mint, chopped	*1/2 teaspoon*	*1/2 teaspoon*
Cilantro, chopped	*1 teaspoon*	*1 teaspoon*
Heavy cream	*6 fluid ounces*	*180 milliliters*
Mirepoix	*6 ounces*	*170 grams*
Brown Veal or Lamb Stock	*1 1/2 quarts*	*1.5 liters*
Bay leaves	*2 each*	*2 each*
Arrowroot, diluted with water	*as needed*	*as needed*
Cilantro, chopped	*1 tablespoon*	*1 tablespoon*

1. Bone the leg of lamb (reserve the bones to prepare the jus). Butterfly, pound, and season each half with salt and pepper to taste.

2. Sprinkle the mushrooms with lemon juice and sauté in hot oil; let cool.

3. Combine the ground pork, half the sherry, the bread crumbs, and egg in a food processor until smooth. Add the herbs and cream; pulse until all are incorporated. Adjust the seasoning to taste. Fold the mushrooms, by hand, into the forcemeat. Chill if necessary.

4. Place the forcemeat on the lamb, roll up jelly-roll style and tie with string.

5. Sear the lamb on all sides in hot oil.

6. Brown the bones in a hot oven; add the mirepoix and brown for 10 minutes more.

7. Deglaze the pan with the remaining sherry and add the brown stock and bay leaves.

8. Set the leg of lamb on a rack (it should not touch the liquid) and glaze it every 10 minutes. Cook to an internal temperature of 150°F (65°C). Remove the lamb and reserve it.

9. Degrease the pan drippings and reduce if necessary to bolster flavor. Thicken it with diluted arrowroot and strain. Adjust the seasoning to taste. Add cilantro to the sauce.

10. Slice the lamb and serve it with sauce.

Irish Stew

Yield: 10 servings

Lamb shoulder	*4 pounds*	*1.8 kilograms*
White Veal or Lamb Stock	*1 1/2 quarts*	*1.5 liters*
Bouquet Garni	*1 each*	*1 each*
Onions, large dice	*1 pound*	*450 grams*
Potatoes, large dice	*1 pound*	*450 grams*
Celery, large dice	*1/2 pound*	*225 grams*
Carrots, large dice	*1/2 pound*	*225 grams*
Parsnips, large dice	*1/2 pound*	*225 grams*
Turnips, large dice	*1/2 pound*	*225 grams*
Salt, to taste	*1/2 teaspoon*	*1/2 teaspoon*
White pepper, to taste	*1/2 teaspoon*	*1/2 teaspoon*
Parsley, chopped	*1 tablespoon*	*1 tablespoon*

1. Combine the lamb and stock and bring to a simmer. Skim the surface throughout cooking time as necessary. Continue to cook over low heat for an hour; maintain a very gentle simmer.

2. Add the Bouquet Garni and the vegetables. Simmer slowly for another 1 to 1 1/2 hours or until all of the ingredients are fork-tender.

3. Season to taste with salt and pepper and add parsley.

4. Serve in crocks or shallow soup plates.

To make Shepherd's Pie, place a portion of stew in a crock or individual casserole. Top with Duchesse Potatoes (page 827). Brush the potatoes lightly with egg wash. Bake until browned.

Pearl onions may be used instead of chopped onions.

Serve with Irish Soda Bread, page 1031.

Chicken Breast with Ham and Sherry

Yield: 10 servings

Use cured hams, especially those from Spain. Substitute Parma or Smithfield.

Chicken suprêmes	*10 each*	*10 each*
Salt, to taste	*1/2 teaspoon*	*1/2 teaspoon*
Pepper, to taste	*1/4 teaspoon*	*1/4 teaspoon*
Flour, as needed	*2 ounces*	*60 grams*
Olive oil, as needed	*2 fluid ounces*	*60 milliliters*
Onions, julienne	*10 ounces*	*285 grams*
Garlic cloves, mashed	*4 each*	*4 each*
Red pepper, julienne	*10 ounces*	*285 grams*
Green peppers, julienne	*10 ounces*	*285 grams*
Ham, julienne	*8 ounces*	*225 grams*
Tomatoes, peeled, seeded, and julienne	*8 ounces*	*225 grams*
Ripe olives, pitted and sliced	*40 each*	*40 each*
Dry sherry	*5 fluid ounces*	*150 milliliters*
Jus de Volaille or Demi-Glace	*20 fluid ounces*	*600 milliliters*
Thyme, chopped	*2 teaspoon*	*2 teaspoon*
Marjoram, chopped	*1 teaspoon*	*1 teaspoon*

1. Dry the suprêmes and season with salt and pepper. Dredge in flour and shake off excess.

2. Sauté the chicken in the oil until just cooked through. Remove and keep it warm.

3. In the same oil, sauté the onions, garlic, and peppers. Add the ham, tomatoes, and olives; deglaze with the sherry.

4. Add the Jus de Volaille or Demi-Glace; bring it to a boil and adjust the seasoning with the thyme, marjoram, salt and pepper to taste.

5. Serve the sauce over the chicken.

Roast Chicken with Walnut Sauce (Kotmis Satsivi)

Yield: 10 servings

Broiler chickens	5 each	5 each
Butter, melted	3 ounces	85 grams
Salt, to taste	1/2 teaspoon	1/2 teaspoon
Pepper, to taste	1/4 teaspoon	1/4 teaspoon
Walnut sauce		
Onions, minced	4 ounces	115 grams
Butter, unsalted	1 ounce	30 grams
Red wine vinegar	2 fluid ounces	60 milliliters
Garlic, minced	3 tablespoons	3 tablespoons
Cloves, ground	1/4 teaspoon	1/4 teaspoon
Cinnamon, ground	3/4 teaspoon	3/4 teaspoon
Cayenne, ground	3/4 teaspoon	3/4 teaspoon
Bay leaf	1 each	1 each
Saffron threads, crushed	3/4 teaspoon	3/4 teaspoon
Red wine	4 fluid ounces	120 milliliters
Brown Chicken Stock	48 fluid ounces	1.5 liters
Roux	5 ounces	140 grams
Walnuts, roasted and chopped	10 ounces	285 grams
Parsley, chopped	1/4 ounce	2 grams

Broiler chickens average about 1 1/2 pounds (680 grams). You may wish to substitute Cornish game hens in this dish.

1. Truss the chickens, brush with butter, and season with salt and pepper.

2. Roast on a rack in a 375°F (190°C) oven until internal temperature of 160°F (70°C), baste occasionally with drippings.

3. Remove chickens, and reserve pan drippings.

4. To make the sauce: Sauté onions in butter until translucent, add vinegar, reduce until almost dry.

5. Add garlic, cloves, cinnamon, cayenne, bay leaf, and saffron; sauté 2 to 3 minutes.

6. Add red wine, reduce by half, add stock and pan drippings, and bring to a simmer. Degrease the sauce.

7. Thicken with roux; simmer 20 minutes, and add walnuts, parsley, and adjust seasonings to taste with salt and pepper.

8. Cut chicken into halves or quarters. Serve one half or 2 pieces of quartered chicken per serving with 2 ounces (60 grams) of the sauce.

Roast Stuffed Spring Cornish Hens with Garlic Sauce (Pollastrino Farcito Arrosto al Sugo d'Aglio)

Yield: 10 servings

The recipe for Glace de Viande is on page 438. For Glace de Volaille, use chicken stock. Or, use Jus de Volaille Lié, found on page 523, as a variation.

Use the livers reserved from the game hens in the stuffing.

Cornish game hens, 1 1/2 pounds	*5 each*	*5 each*
Stuffing		
Chicken livers	*10 ounces*	*285 grams*
Butter	*3 ounces*	*85 grams*
Scallions, sliced on the bias	*5 each*	*5 each*
Garlic cloves, minced	*2 each*	*2 each*
Brandy	*2 fluid ounces*	*60 milliliters*
Chicken Stock	*6 fluid ounces*	*180 milliliters*
Croutons, sautéed in butter, cooled	*6 ounces*	*170 grams*
Porcini mushrooms, reconstituted, fine dice	*3 ounces*	*85 grams*
Chicken breasts sautéed in butter, cooled, diced	*10 ounces*	*285 grams*
Rosemary, chopped	*1 teaspoon*	*1 teaspoon*
Salt, to taste	*1 teaspoon*	*1 teaspoon*
Pepper, to taste	*1/2 teaspoon*	*1/2 teaspoon*
Spinach leaves, blanched	*20 each*	*20 each*
Jus de Volaille, as needed	*1 pint*	*480 milliliters*
Shallots, minced	*1 ounce*	*30 grams*
Garlic, minced	*2 teaspoons*	*2 teaspoons*
White wine	*8 fluid ounces*	*240 milliliters*
Marsala	*2 fluid ounces*	*60 milliliters*

1. Halve the birds, removing the backbone and breastbone, retaining the leg bones. Refrigerate until needed.

2. To make the stuffing: Sauté the livers in butter just until stiffened. Remove; dice and cool completely.

3. Add scallions and garlic to the same pan and sauté, add brandy and chicken stock and reduce to half of the original volume. Cool.

4. Combine the reduction with the liver mixture, croutons, mushrooms, diced chicken, and herbs, mix gently; season.

5. Divide the stuffing mixture into 10 portions and wrap each portion in 2 spinach leaves.

6. Place the stuffing in the cavity of the Cornish hens; place cut side down in a roast pan.

(Recipe continued on facing page)

7. Roast hens 15 to 20 minutes in a 350°F (175°C) oven until the thigh has an internal temperature of 160°F (70°C). When done, brush with Jus de Volaille; remove and allow to rest; keep warm.

8. To make the sauce: Drain excess fat from the roast pan and add the shallots and garlic; sauté without browning.

9. Add the white wine and reduce until one-third of original volume. Add the remaining Jus de Volaille and simmer briefly.

10. Finish the sauce with Marsala and season to taste with salt and pepper. Serve one-half hen on a plate, and pool with 1 1/2 ounces (45 milliliters) of sauce.

Chicken Cacciatore

Yield: 10 servings

Chicken, fryers	*5 each*	*5 each*	
Salt, to taste	*1/2 teaspoon*	*1/2 teaspoon*	
Pepper, to taste	*1/4 teaspoon*	*1/4 teaspoon*	
Flour, as needed	*4 ounces*	*115 grams*	
Olive oil	*2 fluid ounces*	*60 milliliters*	
Onions, medium dice	*10 ounces*	*285 grams*	
White wine	*5 fluid ounces*	*150 milliliters*	
Mushrooms, sliced	*1 pound*	*450 grams*	
Tomato Concassé	*10 ounces*	*285 grams*	
Garlic cloves, minced	*3 each*	*3 each*	
Lemon zest, grated	*2 teaspoons*	*2 teaspoons*	
Brown Sauce	*30 fluid ounces*	*900 milliliters*	

Frying chickens average about 2 1/2 pounds (1 kilogram). Refer to Chapter 6, pages 238 to 240, for more information about cutting a chicken into eighths.

1. Cut the chickens into eight pieces.

2. Season the chicken with salt and pepper and dredge it in the flour.

3. Sauté the chicken in the olive oil until it is lightly browned. Remove and reserve it.

4. Sauté the onion in the same oil.

5. Add the mushrooms, Tomato Concassé, garlic, and lemon zest. Sauté until the mushrooms have begun to release their juices.

6. Deglaze the pan with the wine and reduce the liquid.

7. Add the Brown Sauce and return the chicken pieces. Bring the sauce to a simmer.

8. Cover and braise in a 300°F (150°C) oven until fork-tender. Remove the chicken. Degrease the sauce. Serve one half per order, coated with the sauce.

Salmon meat ranges from very pale to deep orange red, depending on species and habitat. The meat is firm, rich, and flavorful.

Salmon in Brioche

Yield: 10 servings

Brioche dough

Yeast, instant	*1 ounce*	*30 grams*
Milk, warm	*24 fluid ounces*	*720 milliliters*
Flour	*2 pounds*	*1 kilogram*
Eggs, beaten	*2 each*	*2 each*
Salt	*1 teaspoon*	*1 teaspoon*
Nutmeg, ground	*pinch*	*pinch*
Butter, melted	*2 1/2 ounces*	*70 grams*

Filling

Butter	*1 ounce*	*30 grams*
Onions, minced	*4 ounces*	*115 grams*
Mushrooms, minced	*4 ounces*	*115 grams*
Lemon juice, to taste	*2 teaspoons*	*2 teaspoons*
Rice, cooked	*8 ounces*	*225 grams*
Eggs, hard-cooked and chopped	*3 each*	*3 each*
Vesiga, soaked and chopped	*8 ounces*	*225 grams*

Salmon steaks or fillets	*3 pounds*	*1.3 kilograms*
Salt, to taste	*1/2 teaspoon*	*1/2 teaspoon*
Pepper, to taste	*1/2 teaspoon*	*1/2 teaspoon*

Vesiga is a traditional component of coulbiac. It is the dried spinal cord of the sturgeon. If you are using dried vesiga, it must be soaked in cool water for 5 to 6 hours, then simmered in fish stock for 3 to 4 hours. It should then be chopped before it is added to the rice mixture. Although traditional, vesiga may be omitted if it is unavailable.

1. To prepare the brioche, dissolve yeast in milk.

2. Add one-half of the flour, mix together and rest in a warm place for 15 minutes.

3. Add the eggs, salt, nutmeg, and butter to the yeast mixture; mix well.

4. Add the remaining flour, mix until a smooth dough is formed.

5. Proof dough 20 minutes (covered), press flat and chill until firm (about 15 minutes).

6. Roll out dough and cut into two fish shapes 12 inches (30 centimeters) long.

7. Heat the butter and sauté the onions and mushrooms until tender. Remove from the heat and cool.

8. Combine all of the remaining ingredients for the filling. Season to taste with salt and pepper.

9. Spread a layer of the filling on one piece of dough. Place the salmon fillet on the filling. Top the salmon with the remaining filling and cover with the second piece of dough.

10. Decorate with fins, eyes, and scales sculpted from the remaining dough; brush with egg wash.

11. Bake in a 350°F (175°C) oven to an internal temperature of 145°F (60°C), rest 15 minutes before slicing.

Stuffed Squid (Calamares Rellenos)

Yield: 10 servings

Squid, cleaned	4 1/2 pounds	2 kilograms
Ham, chopped fine	10 ounces	285 grams
Green olives, chopped	30 each	30 each
Tomato Concassé	8 ounces	225 grams
Salt, to taste	1/2 teaspoon	1/2 teaspoon
Pepper, to taste	1/4 teaspoon	1/4 teaspoon
Parsley, fresh-chopped	2 tablespoons	2 tablespoons
Onions, chopped	8 ounces	225 grams
Garlic cloves, minced	6 each	6 each
Olive oil	3 fluid ounces	90 milliliters
White wine	8 fluid ounces	240 milliliters
Tomato sauce	1 pint	480 milliliters
Flour, as needed	2 ounces	60 grams
Cilantro, chopped	1 ounce	30 grams

Squid can grow to be very large. However, once they are more than 10 ounces (285 grams), they became quite tough. An 8-ounce (225-gram) squid is best for this dish.

The recipe for Tomato Sauce is on page 538.

1. Remove the squid tentacles. Reserve half the tentacles, leaving them whole. Finely chop the remaining tentacles and mix them with the ham, olives, Tomato Concassé, salt, pepper, and parsley. Stuff each squid three-quarters full with this mixture, close the ends, and secure them with toothpicks.

2. Sauté the onion and garlic in the olive oil until soft. Place the squid on top of the onion mixture.

3. Add the wine and bring the mixture to a boil.

4. Pour the tomato sauce over the squid and braise it in a moderate oven until it reaches an internal temperature of 140°F (60°C). Remove the toothpicks.

5. Dredge the reserved tentacles in flour, shake off the excess, and fry in hot oil until crisp.

6. Serve the squid and sauce topped with the fried tentacles and sprinkled with cilantro.

Shellfish Soup Flavored with Fennel and Saffron (Zuppa di Pesce alla Modenese)

Yield: 10 servings

The recipe for Fish Consommé is on page 455. Use a very rich, clear broth or stock if you prefer.

The procedure for preparing croutons may be found on page 435.

Butter	*1 ounce*	*30 grams*
Fennel, julienne	*3 ounces*	*85 grams*
Celery root, julienne	*2 ounces*	*60 grams*
Leeks, julienne	*4 ounces*	*115 grams*
Carrots, julienne	*4 ounces*	*115 grams*
Saffron threads, crushed	*1/2 teaspoon*	*1/2 teaspoon*
Fish Consommé, hot	*1 3/4 quarts*	*1.6 liters*
Sea bass fillet	*20 ounces*	*600 grams*
Shrimp, peeled and deveined	*20 each*	*20 each*
Littleneck clams, washed	*20 each*	*20 each*
Mussels, cleaned	*30 each*	*30 each*
Squids, cut in thin slices	*2 each*	*2 each*
Parsley, chopped	*2 tablespoons*	*2 tablespoons*
Salt, to taste	*1/2 teaspoon*	*1/2 teaspoon*
Pepper, to taste	*1/4 teaspoon*	*1/4 teaspoon*
Croutons, large	*20 each*	*20 each*

1. Heat the butter. Sauté fennel, celery, leek, and carrot in butter until limp.

2. Add saffron to the hot Fish Consommé and allow to infuse for 5 minutes.

3. Cut the sea bass into 2-ounce (60-gram) portions. Arrange the fish and shellfish on the fennel mixture.

4. Carefully pour the Fish Consommé over the fish, simmer gently, covered, until the fish is cooked. Season to taste with salt and pepper.

5. Serve the fish stew with croutons and sprinkle with chopped parsley.

Sea Bass with Vegetables *(Branzino alla Verdure)*

Yield: 10 servings

Topping

Red onions, julienne	*5 ounces*	*140 grams*	*Cut the onions, tomatoes, and zucchini into an even julienne, about 2 inches long.*
Garlic cloves, mashed to paste	*2 each*	*2 each*	
Olive oil	*2 fluid ounces*	*60 milliliters*	*Cut the sea bass into 6-ounce (170-gram) portions.*
Tomatoes, skinned, seeded, and julienne	*12 ounces*	*240 grams*	
Zucchini, julienne	*10 ounces*	*285 grams*	*To read about poaching fish, see pages 332 to 335.*
Sea bass fillets	*3 1/2 pounds*	*1.6 kilograms*	
Salt, to taste	*1/2 teaspoon*	*1/2 teaspoon*	
Pepper, to taste	*1/4 teaspoon*	*1/4 teaspoon*	
Butter	*2 ounces*	*60 grams*	
White wine	*6 fluid ounces*	*180 milliliters*	
Fish Fumet	*8 fluid ounces*	*240 milliliters*	
Squid, sliced thin, cooked	*30 slices*	*30 slices*	
Oregano, chopped fine	*1 teaspoon*	*1 teaspoon*	
Parsley, chopped fine	*1 teaspoon*	*1 teaspoon*	
Basil, chopped fine	*1 teaspoon*	*1 teaspoon*	

1. To prepare the topping: Sauté onions and garlic in oil until translucent.

2. Add tomatoes and zucchini and sauté briefly; season and cool.

3. Place the fish portions in a buttered shallow pan; top each piece with a portion of vegetable topping.

4. Add wine and Fish Fumet, bring to a simmer and cover with a parchment paper cover; poach in a 350°F (175°C) oven until done, approximately 5 to 8 minutes.

5. When the fish is done, remove to a serving platter, cover; keep warm.

6. Reduce poaching liquid to 6 ounces (180 milliliters); season to taste with salt and pepper.

7. Place the fish on a plate and ladle some of the poaching liquid over the fish; arrange a few slices of squid on top of each portion and sprinkle with herbs.

Stuffed Swordfish (Bracilolo di Pescespada)

Yield: 10 servings

Mahi-mahi or salmon may be substituted for the swordfish. If using salmon, replace the parsley in the stuffing with dill and add to the herb seasonings.

Portion the swordfish into 5-ounce (140-gram) pieces.

Stuffing

Onions, minced	*4 ounces*	*115 grams*
Swordfish, small dice	*1 pound*	*450 grams*
Olive oil	*2 fluid ounces*	*60 milliliters*
Brandy	*3 fluid ounces*	*90 milliliters*
Bread crumbs, fresh	*8 ounces*	*225 grams*
Parsley, chopped	*2 teaspoons*	*2 teaspoons*
Salt, to taste	*1/2 teaspoon*	*1/2 teaspoon*
Pepper, to taste	*1/4 teaspoon*	*1/4 teaspoon*
Swordfish, sliced	*3 1/2 pounds*	*1.8 kilograms*
Basil, sprigs, chopped	*2 tablespoons*	*2 tablespoons*
Thyme, chopped	*2 teaspoons*	*2 teaspoons*
Lemon juice, to taste	*2 teaspoons*	*2 teaspoons*
Mozzarella cheese, sliced thin	*10 ounces*	*285 grams*
Olive oil	*2 fluid ounces*	*60 milliliters*

1. To make the stuffing: Sauté onions and swordfish in oil, add brandy and reduce to almost dry.

2. Add bread crumbs and parsley, mix gently; season to taste with salt and pepper and chill.

3. Season swordfish slices with basil, thyme, lemon, salt, and pepper.

4. Spread each slice of swordfish with stuffing, top with a slice of mozzarella cheese.

5. Roll swordfish slices so that stuffing is enclosed; secure with twine.

6. Dip swordfish in oil and broil until done, approximately 10 minutes.

Paella

Yield: 10 servings

Pork, lean, diced	*24 ounces*	*680 grams*
Chicken legs, cut into thighs and drumsticks	*2 pounds*	*900 grams*
Olive oil	*5 fluid ounces*	*150 milliliters*
Garlic cloves, chopped	*3 each*	*3 each*
Onions, small dice	*8 ounces*	*225 grams*
Red peppers, small dice	*8 ounces*	*225 grams*
Green peppers, small dice	*8 ounces*	*225 grams*
Rice, short-grain	*1 1/2 pound*	*680 grams*
Saffron, crushed	*1 teaspoon*	*1 teaspoon*
Salt	*1/2 teaspoon*	*1/2 teaspoon*
Chicken Stock, hot	*1 1/2 pints*	*720 milliliters*
Clams, fresh, cleaned	*20 each*	*20 each*
Mussels, fresh, cleaned	*20 each*	*20 each*
Shrimp, peeled and deveined	*20 each*	*20 each*
Chorizo, cooked and sliced	*8 ounces*	*225 grams*
Tomato Concassé, small dice	*8 ounces*	*225 grams*
Carrots, small dice	*4 ounces*	*115 grams*
Peas (garden)	*4 ounces*	*115 grams*
Niçoise olives, pitted	*6 ounces*	*170 grams*
Green olives, pitted	*6 ounces*	*170 grams*
Scallions, sliced	*4 ounces*	*115 grams*
Lemons	*4 each*	*4 each*

There are many variations of this traditional Spanish dish. Garnish with strips of roasted red peppers and serve it directly in a paella pan for an authentic presentation.

Cut the onions, peppers, and Tomato Concassé into 1-inch (2 1/2 centimeter) dice.

1. Brown the chicken and pork in the olive oil. Remove and reserve.

2. Sauté the garlic, onions, and peppers in the reserved oil.

3. Add the rice, saffron and salt. Stir until the rice is coated with oil.

4. Add the stock and bring the mixture to a boil. Cover the pan and place it in a 400°F (205°C) oven; cook the rice mixture for 8 minutes.

5. Place the clams and mussels on top of the rice. Check the rice periodically and add more stock or water if necessary. Replace the cover and return the pan to the oven for 5 minutes.

6. Add the shrimp, chorizo, Tomato Concassé, carrots, and peas. Return the pan to the oven and cook the paella until the shrimp is cooked through and all ingredients are very hot.

7. Garnish the paella with the olives and scallions. Drizzle with the juice of 2 lemons. Cover the paella pan and allow the paella to rest for 10 minutes. Wedge the remaining lemons and serve with the paella.

Cassoulet

Yield: 12 to 14 servings

Cassoulet is a classic dish from the South of France. As with other traditional dishes, ingredients vary from region to region and from season to season. The one common ingredient is white beans. Mutton is often used, though goat is not unheard of in France. Lamb is preferred, especially in this country.

    This recipe is essentially a combination of three separate preparations: duck confit, bean stew, and braised meats. These components are combined and baked with a crust.

    Although the whole process can take several days when done correctly, it is well worth the effort and is a popular item on any menu.

Select a duck that weighs approximately 6 pounds (2.75 kilograms).

Cut the pork and lamb into 2-inch (5-centimeter) cubes.

Confit		
Kosher salt	2 ounces	60 grams
Curing salt	1/4 teaspoon	1/4 teaspoon
Pepper, ground	1/4 teaspoon	1/4 teaspoon
Juniper berries, crushed	2 each	2 each
Bay leaf, crushed	1 each	1 each
Garlic, chopped	1/2 teaspoon	1/2 teaspoon
Duck, cut in 6 pieces	1 each	1 each
Duck fat, rendered, as needed	1 pint	480 milliliters
Bean stew		
Chicken Stock	3 quarts	3 liters
Navy beans, dried, soaked overnight	2 pounds	900 grams
Garlic sausage	1 pound	450 grams
Slab bacon, battonet	1 pound	450 grams
Onions, whole	2 each	2 each
Garlic, chopped	1 ounce	30 grams
Bouquet Garni	1 each	1 each
Meat stew		
Pork loin, cut into cubes	1 1/2 pounds	680 grams
Lamb shoulder, or leg, cut into cubes	1 1/2 pounds	680 grams
Olive oil	3 fluid ounces	90 milliliters
White Mirepoix	1 pound	450 grams
Salt, to taste	1/2 teaspoon	1/2 teaspoon
Garlic, mashed to a paste	1/2 teaspoon	1/2 teaspoon
White wine	3 fluid ounces	90 milliliters
Tomato Concassé	8 ounces	225 grams
Standard Sachet d'Épices	1 each	1 each
Demi-Glace	1 pint	480 milliliters
Brown Stock, as needed	1 quart	1 liter
Salt, to taste	1/2 teaspoon	1/2 teaspoon
Pepper, to taste	1/2 teaspoon	1/2 teaspoon
Bread crumbs, fresh	12 ounces	340 grams
Parsley, chopped	2 tablespoons	2 tablespoons

(Recipe continued on facing page)

1. To prepare the confit: Mix all the seasonings, coat the duck with the mixture, and place it in a container with a weighted lid. Press the duck for 72 hours under refrigeration.

2. Brush off the excess seasoning mixture and stew the bird in the duck fat until it is very tender.

3. When ready to use the confit, scrape away excess fat and broil the duck on a rack until the skin is crisp. Debone and slice the duck.

4. To prepare the beans: Bring the chicken stock to a boil and add the beans.

5. Add the bacon and return to a boil; cook for 30 minutes.

6. Add the sausage, onions, garlic, and Bouquet Garni; return the mixture to a boil and cook it until the sausage reaches a 150°F (65°C) internal temperature and the bacon is fork-tender.

7. Remove the sausage, bacon, onion, and Bouquet Garni. Reserve the sausage and bacon.

8. Continue to cook the beans until they are tender but still hold their shape. Strain the beans and reserve; reduce the stock.

9. To prepare the meats: Sear the pork and lamb in hot olive oil until they are brown. Remove and reserve them.

10. Degrease the pan and sauté the White Mirepoix. Add the garlic and salt.

11. Deglaze the pan with the white wine.

12. Add the Tomato Concassé, Sachet d'Épices, Demi-Glace, and Brown Stock. Bring the sauce to a boil; return the meat to the sauce.

13. Cover the pan and braise the meat in an oven at 300°F (150°C) until fork-tender.

14. Remove the meat and reduce the braising liquid. Adjust the seasoning and strain the sauce. Combine the reduced braising liquid with the bean stock.

15. Peel the sausage and slice it.

16. Cut the bacon in 1/4-inch (.5-centimeter) slices.

17. Layer the sausage, bacon, pork, and lamb into individual casseroles. Cover with the beans and duck confit.

18. Pour the combined braising liquid and bean stock over all and sprinkle it with the bread crumbs and parsley.

19. Bake the cassoulet in a moderate oven (350°F/175°C) until it is heated through and a good crust has formed, about 45 to 50 minutes.

Choucroute Garni

Yield: 16 to 18 servings

"Choucroute" actually refers only to the sauerkraut. Choucroute Garni is a more elaborate dish composed of meats and sauerkraut. Like paella, there are numerous variations throughout France and Germany.

Choucroute is a traditional Sunday lunch in Alsace, France. It is accompanied by mustard and plenty of bread.

If sausage is not used, increase the amount of pork loin or other pork by 2 1/2 pounds (1.6 kilograms).

Salt-cured ham such as Smithfield can be included. Adjust the seasoning accordingly

Onions, sliced	*10 ounces*	*285 grams*
Garlic, minced	*1 ounce*	*30 grams*
Granny Smith apples, peeled and diced	*2 each*	*2 each*
Goose fat	*6 ounces*	*170 grams*
Sauerkraut, prepared	*4 pounds*	*1.8 kilograms*
Chicken Stock	*1 pint*	*480 milliliters*
White wine	*8 fluid ounces*	*240 milliliters*
Standard Sachet d'Épices, plus 6 juniper berries	*1 each*	*1 each*
Carrot, whole	*1 each*	*1 each*
Pork loin, smoked	*5 pounds*	*2.25 kilograms*
Pork sausages with garlic (optional)	*2 1/2 pounds*	*1.125 kilograms*
Salt, to taste	*1/2 teaspoon*	*1/2 teaspoon*
Black pepper, fresh-ground	*1/2 teaspoon*	*1/2 teaspoon*
Idaho potatoes or other high-starch potatoes, grated fine	*2 each*	*2 each*
Chef potatoes, peeled and boiled	*3 pounds*	*1.3 kilograms*

1. Sauté the onions, garlic, and apples in the goose fat until tender.

2. If the sauerkraut is very salty, rinse it in several changes of water and squeeze it dry. Add the sauerkraut to the onions, garlic, and apples.

3. Add the Chicken Stock, wine, Sachet d'Épices, and carrot; stir.

4. Place the pork loin on top of the sauerkraut, cover the pan, and braise the meat for approximately 45 minutes.

5. Prick the skins of the sausages in 5 to 6 places and add them to the pan with the sauerkraut. Cover the pan and cook the pork loin and sausages until they reach 150°F (65°C) internal temperature, approximately 15 to 20 minutes.

6. Remove the carrot, Sachet d'Épices, pork loin, and sausages. Season the sauerkraut with salt and pepper.

7. Add the grated potato to the sauerkraut and cook it for 2 minutes to bind it.

8. Slice the pork loin and sausages; serve on a bed of sauerkraut. Serve the hot boiled potatoes on the side.

Polish Stuffed Cabbage

Separate the cabbage into leaves; blanch and cool them.

The recipe for Matignon may be found on page 420

Yield: 10 servings

Savoy cabbage	2 each	2 each
Veal breast, cubed	12 ounces	340 grams
Pork, cubed	12 ounces	340 grams
Beef bottom, cubed	12 ounces	340 grams
Onions, diced, sautéed, and cooled	10 ounces	285 grams
Heavy cream	8 fluid ounces	240 milliliters
Eggs	3 each	3 each
Salt, to taste	1/2 teaspoon	1/2 teaspoon
Pepper, to taste	1/4 teaspoon	1/4 teaspoon
Nutmeg, ground, to taste	pinch	pinch
Bread crumbs, dry	6 ounces	170 grams
Matignon, sliced thin	6 ounces	170 grams
Bay leaf	1 each	1 each
Beef Stock, hot	1 quart	1 liter
Bacon, sliced	10 pieces	10 pieces
Demi-Glace, heated	1 pint	480 milliliters

1. Separate the cabbage into leaves; blanch and cool them.

2. Combine the meat, onions, cream, and eggs. Season them with the salt, pepper, and nutmeg; mix well.

3. Run the mixture through a grinder twice.

4. Add the bread crumbs to the ground meat mixture.

5. Remove the large veins from each cabbage leaf. Place the meat in the center of each leaf and roll them up.

6. Place the cabbage rolls on top of the Matignon and bay leaf. Add the hot stock and place the sliced bacon on top of the cabbage rolls.

7. Braise the cabbage rolls in a 350°F (175°C) oven, basting occasionally, to an internal temperature of 150°F (65°C).

8. Remove the cabbage rolls and keep them warm. Degrease the sauce; add the Demi-Glace and let the sauce reduce to the correct consistency and flavor. Adjust the seasoning with salt and pepper to taste.

Beef and Pork Tamales

Yield: 10 servings

Steam the tamales folded side down for about 40 to 50 minutes. Serve immediately, with Red Chili Sauce (page 550), Green Chili Sauce (page 550), or enchilada sauce, if desired.

The filling and the dough can be prepared one day in advance. The tamales can be rolled up to 6 hours in advance. Once steamed, they hold for a very short time. If they must be cooked in advance, it is better to cool them down and reheat them in the oven than to try to hold them on a steam table.

The tamale filling can be filled in banana leaves, if available.

Cooked mashed pinto beans can replace some of the meat in the filling.

Beef, lean, diced	*3/4 pound*	*340 grams*
Pork, lean, diced	*3/4 pound*	*340 grams*
Enchilada sauce, prepared	*8 fluid ounces*	*240 milliliters*
Chili Powder, to taste	*1/2 teaspoon*	*1/2 teaspoon*
Salt, to taste	*1/2 teaspoon*	*1/2 teaspoon*
Corn husks (Mexican, dried)	*4 ounces*	*115 grams*
Masa harina	*12 ounces*	*340 grams*
Water or stock	*14 fluid ounces*	*415 milliliters*
Lard or shortening	*4 ounces*	*115 grams*
Baking powder	*3/4 teaspoon*	*3/4 teaspoon*
Salt	*1/4 teaspoon*	*1/4 teaspoon*

1. Combine beef, pork and enchilada sauce in a heavy pot. Cook over medium heat until meat is nearly done and add stock, if necessary. Season to taste with chili powder and salt. Meat should be tender and mixture should be fairly dry. Reserve and cool.

2. Soak the corn husks in hot water to make them pliable.

3. Mix masa harina with water, lard, baking powder and salt. Beat until smooth and fluffy.

4. Drain the corn husks. Lay one or two husks on the work surface. The husks should be about 5-inches (13-centimeters) wide.

5. Place two tablespoons of masa mixture on the smooth side of acorn husk and spread over the lower 2/3 of the husk, leaving 1 inch (2.5 centimeters) of space on each side.

6. Place one generous tablespoon of meat mixture lengthwise down center of masa. Roll tightly, so the edges of the masa fit together. Fold the excess husk under. Tie with a strip of corn husk if necessary.

VARIATION

Pork and Beef Tamales with Mole: Substitute 8 fluid ounces (240 milliliters) of the sauce in Mole Poblano de Pollo (page 765) for the enchilada sauce. Serve with additional Mole Sauce or Red Chili Sauce.

Braised Stuffed
Flank Steak (Matambre)

Yield: 10 servings

Flank steaks, trimmed	*4 pounds*	*1.8 kilograms*
Salt, to taste	*1/2 teaspoon*	*1/2 teaspoon*
Pepper, to taste	*1/4 teaspoon*	*1/4 teaspoon*
Marinade		
Garlic cloves, mashed	*4 each*	*4 each*
Cilantro, chopped	*2 tablespoons*	*2 tablespoons*
Basil, chopped	*2 tablespoons*	*2 tablespoons*
Olive oil	*1 pint*	*480 milliliters*
Red wine vinegar	*8 fluid ounces*	*240 milliliters*
Stuffing		
Bread crumbs, fresh	*8 ounces*	*225 grams*
Eggs, hard-boiled and chopped	*3 each*	*3 each*
Corn kernels	*6 ounces*	*170 grams*
Spinach leaves, blanched, squeezed dry, and chopped	*1 pound*	*450 grams*
Carrots, cut lengthwise, parboiled	*3 each*	*3 each*
Onions, sliced	*4 ounces*	*115 grams*
Cilantro, chopped	*1 ounce*	*30 grams*
Olive oil	*4 fluid ounces*	*120 milliliters*
Red wine	*10 fluid ounces*	*300 milliliters*
Demi-Glace	*1 quart*	*1 liter*
Brown Veal Stock	*1 quart*	*1 liter*
Standard Sachet d'Épices, plus oregano	*1 each*	*1 each*

1. Butterfly the steak, slitting it horizontally in the direction of the grain. Season to taste with salt and pepper.

2. Combine all of the ingredients for the marinade. Add the meat and marinade it under refrigeration for 24 hours. Drain the meat and dry it.

3. Mix the bread crumbs and eggs and spread a layer over the opened butterflied steak. Sprinkle the corn kernels over the breading.

4. Place the spinach on the breading mixture. Add a layer of carrots.

5. Sprinkle the onions, cilantro, salt, and pepper on top.

6. Roll the flank steak in jelly-roll fashion and tie it with butcher's twine.

7. Brown the steak rolls evenly in hot oil.

8. Deglaze the pan with wine. Add the Demi-Glace, stock, and Sachet d'Épices; braise the meat until it is fork-tender

9. Reduce the sauce, degreasing as necessary. Adjust the seasoning and strain it.

10. Slice the steak rolls crosswise. Serve them with the sauce.

Pork in Orange and Lemon Sauce with Sweet Potatoes

Yield: 10 servings

Although not traditional, you can purée the cooked sweet potatoes and pipe them to form a border. Serve the stew in the center.

Pork cubes should be approximately 1-inch (2.5-centimeters) thick.

The sweet potatoes may be baked in their skin, or boiled and then peeled.

Marinade

Cider vinegar	1 pint	480 milliliters
Annatto seeds, crushed fine	3 tablespoons	45 milliliters
Cumin, ground	2 tablespoons	30 milliliters
Garlic, chopped	2 tablespoons	30 milliliters
Salt	1 tablespoon	1 tablespoon
Pepper	1 teaspoon	1 teaspoon
Pork loin, cut in 1-inch cubes	3 1/2 pounds	1.6 kilograms
Vegetable oil	4 fluid ounces	120 milliliters
White Beef Stock	1 1/2 quarts	1.5 liters
Oranges juiced, fresh	1 1/2 pints	720 milliliters
Lemon juice, fresh	2 fluid ounces	60 milliliters
Arrowroot, diluted in water, as needed	1 teaspoon	1 teaspoon
Salt, to taste	1/2 teaspoon	1/2 teaspoon
Pepper, to taste	1/4 teaspoon	1/4 teaspoon
Sweet potatoes, cooked	5 each	5 each

1. Combine all of the ingredients for the marinade. Add the pork and marinate overnight.

2. Remove the pork and dry it; reserve the marinade.

3. Brown the pork in the oil. Remove and reserve the pork. Pour off the excess oil.

4. Add the pork, reserved marinade, and Beef Stock. Bring it to a stew over low heat and simmer until the meat is tender.

5. Add the orange and lemon juices, bring the mixture to a simmer, and cook for 3 minutes.

6. Adjust the consistency and seasoning with the arrowroot (dilute in cold water), salt, and pepper.

7. Slice the sweet potatoes 1/4-inch (.5-centimeter) thick; reheat them. Arrange the potatoes on a plate and serve the pork and sauce over them.

Chicken Mole (Mole Poblano de Pollo)

Yield: 10 servings

Sesame seeds	*3 ounces*	*85 grams*
Almonds, chopped	*1 ounce*	*30 grams*
Chili powder	*2 ounces*	*60 grams*
Anise seeds	*1 teaspoon*	*1 teaspoon*
Cinnamon, ground	*1/2 teaspoon*	*1/2 teaspoon*
Oregano, dried	*1 teaspoon*	*1 teaspoon*
Chicken breasts, boneless	*10 each*	*10 each*
Peanut oil	*4 fluid ounces*	*120 milliliters*
Onions, fine dice	*8 ounces*	*225 grams*
Garlic cloves, mashed	*6 each*	*6 each*
Green peppers, fine dice	*8 ounces*	*225 grams*
Jalapeño peppers, chopped fine	*10 each*	*10 each*
Corn tortilla, toasted	*1 each*	*1 each*
Tomato Concassé	*1 pound*	*450 grams*
Chicken Stock	*1 pint*	*480 milliliters*
Mexican chocolate, chopped	*4 ounces*	*115 grams*
Salt, to taste	*1/2 teaspoon*	*1/2 teaspoon*
Pepper, to taste	*1/4 teaspoon*	*1/4 teaspoon*

1. Toast the sesame seeds, almonds, chili powder, anise, cinnamon, and oregano in a dry skillet until very aromatic. Remove and set aside. Brown the onions; add the garlic, peppers, and jalapeños and sauté for a few minutes.

2. Return the seasonings and sauté the mixture briefly. Add the tortilla and Tomato Concassé. Sauté until nearly dry. Allow the sauce to cool, then purée until smooth.

3. Sear the chicken in oil in a braising pan. Deglaze the pan with the stock and add the puréed sauce. Blend until smooth.

4. Add the chicken and bring to a boil. Cover the pan and braise the chicken in a moderate oven 325°F (165°C) until tender. Remove the chicken and keep it warm.

5. Adjust the consistency of the sauce by simmering to reduce. Add the chocolate, simmer the sauce, and adjust the seasoning with salt and pepper to taste.

6. Pour the sauce over the chicken and reheat it in the oven. Garnish it with additional toasted sesame seeds if desired.

It is said that Mole Poblano was first created by nuns in Mexico in anticipation of a visit by the bishop. Originally prepared with turkey, it is still served with turkey at fiestas in Mexico, especially at Christmas and weddings.

For restaurant service, individual chicken breast portions may be more practical.

Watch the seasonings carefully as you toast them. If they burn, it will give the sauce a very bitter flavor.

As with most sauces (mole *cames from the Nahuatl word for "concoction"*), mole varies from region to region in Mexico, each immensely proud of their variation. A mix of chilies (fresh and dried), seeds, (sesame, pumpkin), nuts and breads can be included. Chocolate is most well known but not required. If Mexican chocolate is not available, use bittersweet chocolate and a touch of sugar and cinnamon.

With the time and care required to prepare this sauce, you may wish to double the amount to have extra on hand for burritos and enchiladas, or to freeze for later use.

Chicken Enchiladas

Yield: 10 servings

The recipe for Green Chili Sauce may be found on page 549.

To make cheese enchiladas, cut "fingers" of fresh white cheese. Make the enchiladas smaller. Bake in Red Chili Sauce or prepared enchilida sauce.

Green Chili Sauce	*1 pint*	*480 milliliters*
Chicken Stock	*3 fluid ounces*	*90 milliliters*
Chicken meat, cooked and shredded	*1 1/4 pounds*	*570 grams*
Sour cream	*6 ounces*	*170 grams*
Monterey Jack, grated cheese	*12 ounces*	*340 grams*
Corn tortillas	*20 each*	*20 each*

1. Simmer the sauce until it is very hot. Adjust the consistency with the chicken stock, if necessary.

2. Combine the chicken with the sour cream and half of the cheese.

3. Dip the tortillas in the sauce to coat them evenly. Portion the chicken onto the tortillas. Fold or roll them.

4. Place the enchiladas in a baking dish. Cover them with more of the sauce. Sprinkle the cheese on top. Bake the enchiladas at 350°F (175°C) until the cheese has melted and the enchiladas are very hot.

VARIATIONS

Chicken and Spinach Enchiladas: Add 1 pound (450 grams) of blanched chopped spinach to the chicken.

Beef Enchiladas: Use Red Chili Sauce (page 549). Replace the chicken with braised beef that has been shredded. Omit the sour cream from the filling and serve it as a garnish.

Chili Enchiladas: Use Red Chili Sauce and fill the enchiladas with the Vegetarian Chili (page 731).

Vatapa

Yield: 10 servings

Shrimp, peeled and deveined, shells reserved	2 pounds	900 grams
Olive oil, as needed	2 fluid ounces	60 milliliters
Onions, diced	8 ounces	225 grams
Garlic cloves, minced	2 each	2 each
Jalapeño peppers, diced	4 each	4 each
Fresh coconut, shredded, water reserved	1/2 each	1/2 each
Peanuts, chopped	2 ounces	60 grams
Gingerroot, grated	2 ounces	60 grams
Tomato paste	2 ounces	60 grams
White wine	4 fluid ounces	120 milliliters
Fish Stock	1 quart	1 liter
Roux	2 ounces	60 grams
Heavy cream	8 fluid ounces	225 milliliters
Salt, to taste	1/2 teaspoon	1/2 teaspoon
Pepper, to taste	1/4 teaspoon	1/4 teaspoon
Monkfish, cut into cubes	2 pounds	1 kilogram
Garnish		
Tomato Concassé, small dice	6 ounces	170 grams
Coconut, shredded and toasted	1/2 each	1/2 each
Peanuts, roasted and chopped	3 ounces	85 grams
Cilantro, chopped	2 tablespoons	2 tablespoons

When coconuts are fresh, there is a watery liquid that can be collected by boring through the eyes and allowing it to drain out.

Vatapa is a seafood stew from Brazil.

Cut the monkfish into 2-inch (5-centimeter) cubes.

1. Sauté shrimp shells in very hot oil and flambé with brandy.

2. Add onions, garlic cloves, jalapeños, coconut, peanuts, and ginger to shrimp shells, and sauté for 3 minutes.

3. Add tomato paste and sauté for a few minutes, deglaze with wine, add stock and coconut water, and bring to a boil; reduce by one-half, add roux, and simmer for 20 minutes.

4. Add cream and reduce until a good consistency is achieved. Season and strain.

5. Sauté shrimp in hot oil; add monkfish, sauté until done. Add the sauce to the fish, and check consistency and seasonings.

6. Garnish with tomato, coconut, peanuts, and cilantro.

Beef Teriyaki (Yakiniku)

Yield: 10 servings

This would make about 25 tasting portions as part of a combination platter.

Beef tenderloin, trimmed	3 1/2 pounds	1.6 kilograms
Vegetable oil, as needed	2 fluid ounces	60 milliliters
Sesame oil	2 fluid ounces	60 milliliters
Teriyaki sauce		
Japanese soy sauce	3 fluid ounces	90 milliliters
Sugar	1 ounce	30 grams
Shire-mirin	1 fluid ounce	30 milliliters
Scallions, minced	2 ounces	60 grams
Ginger, minced	1/2 teaspoon	1/2 teaspoon
Garlic, minced	1/2 teaspoon	1/2 teaspoon
Chicken Stock	8 fluid ounces	240 milliliters
Rice vinegar	1 tablespoon	1 tablespoon
Sake (rice wine)	2 tablespoons	2 tablespoons
Cornstarch, diluted in water	2 teaspoons	2 teaspoons

1. Trim the beef and cut it into 2-ounce (60-gram) pieces.

2. To make the sauce, combine the soy sauce, sugar, mirin, scallions, ginger, garlic, and stock, bring to a simmer, cook 10 minutes. Season to taste with salt and pepper.

3. Rub oil on beef, grill to medium-rare. Add vinegar, sake, and adjust thickening with cornstarch.

4. Serve sauce with beef.

Beef with Red Onions and Peanuts

Yield: 10 servings

Coating		
Egg	1 each	1 each
Cornstarch	3 tablespoons	3 tablespoons
Oil	3 tablespoons	3 tablespoons
Beef top butt, shredded	3 1/2 pounds	1.6 kilograms
Sauce		

(Recipe continued on facing page)

Vinegar	4 fluid ounces	120 milliliters
Sugar	2 ounces	60 grams
Fish Sauce	2 fluid ounces	60 milliliters
Sake	2 fluid ounces	60 milliliters
Pepper	1/2 teaspoon	1/2 teaspoon
Stock	8 fluid ounces	240 milliliters
Cornstarch, as needed	1 teaspoon	1 teaspoon
Oil, to sauté	2 fluid ounces	60 milliliters
Garlic, minced	2 teaspoons	2 teaspoons
Gingerroot, grated	2 teaspoons	2 teaspoons
Lemongrass, sliced thin	1 stalk	1 stalk
Red onions, sliced	1 pound	450 grams
Peanuts, whole, dry-roasted	2 ounces	60 grams

1. Combine ingredients for coating and mix with beef.

2. To make sauce: Combine all ingredients and bring to a simmer; thicken with cornstarch slurry.

3. To finish the beef, heat oil, and add ginger, garlic, and lemongrass; stir-fry lightly; add beef and stir-fry until done.

4. Add onions and stir-fry until translucent.

5. Add peanuts and sauce; mix together. Serve.

Skewered Beef and Scallions

Yield: 10 servings

Marinade

Soy sauce	3 fluid ounces	90 milliliters
Sugar	1 ounce	30 grams
Sesame oil	2 fluid ounces	60 milliliters
Garlic, minced	1 ounce	30 grams
Gingerroot, minced	2 teaspoons	2 teaspoons
Black pepper, ground	2 teaspoons	2 teaspoons
Beef top butt, or flank steak trimmed	3 1/2 pounds	1.6 kilogram
Scallions, cut into pieces	2 bunches	2 bunches

Bamboo skewers should be soaked in water for several minutes before using them to skewer the meat and scallions.

This dish can also be sautéed or stir-fried.

1. Combine the ingredients for the marinade.

2. Cut the beef into strips 1 by 4 inches (2.5 by 10 centimeters), about 1/8-inch (2.5-centimeters) thick.

3. Add the beef to the marinade and marinate for several hours or overnight.

4. Thread beef on skewer, alternating with scallions.

5. Broil until medium-rare and serve.

Sateh of Beef with Spicy Peanut Sauce

Yield: 10 servings

A good relish to accompany this recipe is made by slicing cucumbers and red onions and combining them with rice wine vinegar and adding sugar or red pepper flakes if desired.

To prepare lemongrass, peel away the tough outer layer. Chop the tender heart for use.

Cut beef into 1 by 5 inch (2 by 13 centimeter) thin strips.

Top round of beef	3 1/2 pounds	1.6 kilograms
Marinade		
Peanut oil	4 fluid ounces	120 milliliters
Lemongrass, minced	1 stalk	1 stalk
Garlic, minced	1 tablespoon	1 tablespoon
Chili peppers, crushed	1/2 teaspoon	1/2 teaspoon
Curry Powder	1 tablespoon	1 tablespoon
Honey	1 tablespoon	1 tablespoon
Fish sauce	2 fluid ounces	60 milliliters
Spicy peanut sauce		
Peanut oil	2 tablespoons	2 tablespoons
Garlic, minced	1 tablespoon	1 tablespoon
Onion, minced	3 ounces	85 grams
Chili peppers, crushed	1/2 teaspoon	1/2 teaspoon
Kaffir lime leaf	1 each	1 each
Curry powder	1/2 teaspoon	1/2 teaspoon
Lemongrass, sliced	1 stalk	1 stalk
Coconut milk	2 fluid ounces	60 milliliters
Milk	1 cup	240 milliliters
Tamarind paste	1 teaspoon	1 teaspoon
Fish Sauce	1 tablespoon	1 tablespoon
Dark brown sugar	1 tablespoon	1 tablespoon
Lemon juice	2 teaspoons	2 teaspoons
Peanut butter	2 ounces	60 milliliters
Chicken Stock, as needed	2 to 3 fluid ounces	60 to 90 milliliters

1. Cut the beef into strips 1 by 5 inches(2.5 by 13 centimeters).
2. Combine ingredients for the marinade; marinate meat for at least 2 hours, up to 12 hours.
3. To make peanut sauce: Heat oil, add garlic, onion, chili pepper, lime leaf, curry powder, and lemongrass; stir-fry.
4. Add coconut milk, milk, tamarind, fish sauce, sugar, lemon juice, and peanut butter, simmer 15 to 20 minutes.
5. Adjust consistency with Chicken Stock.
6. Grill just before service; serve with spicy peanut sauce.

Chinese-Style Barbecued Spareribs

Yield: 10 servings

Marinade

Hoisin sauce	*4 fluid ounces*	*120 milliliters*
Bean sauce	*4 fluid ounces*	*120 milliliters*
Applesauce	*4 ounces*	*115 grams*
Ketchup	*8 ounces*	*240 grams*
Soy sauce	*4 fluid ounces*	*120 milliliters*
Sake	*8 fluid ounces*	*240 milliliters*
Peanut oil	*4 fluid ounces*	*120 milliliters*
Ginger, minced	*2 tablespoons*	*2 tablespoons*
Scallions, minced	*6 each*	*6 each*
Garlic cloves, minced	*6 each*	*6 cloves*
Sugar	*2 ounces*	*60 grams*
Salt	*1 tablespoon*	*1 tablespoon*
Spareribs, trimmed	*10 racks*	*10 racks*
Honey	*8 fluid ounces*	*240 milliliters*

To serve as an appetizer, cut the racks into 2- to 3-ounce (60- to 85-gram) portions.

1. Combine all of the ingredients for the marinade.

2. Score the ribs with a sharp knife. Place the ribs in the marinade. Marinate them for at least 4 hours.

3. Place the ribs in a smoker at 425°F (220°C) for 30 minutes. Reduce the heat to 375°F (190°C). Smoke the ribs for 50 minutes more.

4. Brush the honey on the ribs during the last 5 minutes. Slice the ribs between the bones and serve.

Braised Pork Stew with Chestnuts

Yield: 10 servings

To read about peeling chestnuts, refer to Chapter 6, page 197.

To make a cornstarch slurry, dilute cornstarch with enough water to make a very thin paste. If the cornstarch "settles," be sure to recombine it before using.

Pork butt, trimmed	3 1/2 pounds	1.6 kilograms
Vegetable oil	2 fluid ounces	60 milliliters
Ginger root, minced	1 tablespoon	1 tablespoon
Scallion, chopped	4 each	4 each
Soy sauce	4 fluid ounces	120 milliliters
White wine	2 fluid ounces	60 milliliters
Chicken Stock	1 pint	480 milliliters
Sugar	1 tablespoon	1 tablespoon
Black pepper, crushed	2 teaspoons	2 teaspoons
Star anise seed	1 each	1 each
Cornstarch, as needed	1 teaspoon	1 teaspoon
Chestnuts, peeled	1 pound	450 grams
Pine nuts, lightly toasted	2 ounces	60 grams
Pearl onions, parcooked	10 ounces	285 grams
Garnish		
Leeks, sliced, blanched	2 each	2 each

1. Trim the pork and cut it into 3/4-inch (2-centimeter) cubes.

2. Heat oil, add ginger, and scallion, stir-fry; add pork; stir-fry until white and set.

3. Add soy sauce and wine and enough stock to cover pork by one-half.

4. Add sugar, pepper, and star anise; simmer pork until it is very tender, stirring often.

5. Remove pork, and thicken liquid to medium consistency with cornstarch slurry; return pork and reheat.

6. Add chestnuts, pine nuts, and pearl onions, and adjust seasonings to taste.

7. Garnish with leeks.

Stir-Fried Pork

Yield: 10 servings

Pork butt	*3 1/2 pounds*	*1.6 kilograms*
Scallions	*1 bunch*	*1 bunch*
Cornstarch	*1 tablespoon*	*1 tablespoon*
Oyster sauce	*1 fluid ounce*	*30 milliliters*
Sugar	*2 teaspoons*	*2 teaspoons*
Soy sauce	*1/2 fluid ounce*	*15 milliliters*
Water	*1 fluid ounce*	*30 milliliters*
Vegetable oil	*1 fluid ounce*	*30 milliliters*
Garlic cloves, minced	*2 each*	*2 each*
Dry sherry	*1 fluid ounce*	*30 milliliters*
Stock	*12 fluid ounces*	*360 milliliters*
Salt, to taste	*1/2 teaspoon*	*1/2 teaspoon*

Substitute other meats for the pork: beef, lamb, or chicken.

Include vegetables such as broccoli florets, julienned carrots, or snow peas, if desired.

1. Cut pork in to strips or shreds. Reserve.

2. Split scallions and cut into 1-inch (2.5-centimeters) sections.

3. Mix cornstarch, oyster sauce, sugar, soy sauce, and water into a paste.

4. Heat oil, add garlic and stir-fry, add pork, and stir-fry for 3 more minutes.

5. Add sherry wine and remaining soy sauce; stir-fry for 1 to 2 minutes; add stock and bring to a boil.

6. Add reserved cornstarch paste and return to a boil, just until the juices are thickened.

7. Add scallions and season.

Indian or Malayan in origin, the mango is a luscious fruit in color and taste. Use it in chutneys.

Chutney may be cooked or fresh. In this version, a ripe mango is allowed to macerate in lime juice with chilies.

Indian Grilled Lamb with Fresh Mango Chutney

Yield: 10 servings

Marinade

Green cardamom seeds	*1 teaspoon*	*1 teaspoon*
Cumin seeds	*1 teaspoon*	*1 teaspoon*
Vegetable oil, as needed	*1 tablespoon*	*1 tablespoon*
Onions, minced	*4 ounces*	*115 grams*
Garlic, mashed to a paste	*3/4 ounce*	*21 grams*
Gingerroot, grated	*3/4 ounce*	*21 grams*
Nutmeg, ground	*1/2 teaspoon*	*1/2 teaspoon*
Cinnamon, ground	*1/2 teaspoon*	*1/2 teaspoon*
Yogurt, nonfat	*4 fluid ounces*	*120 milliliters*
Black pepper, to taste	*1 teaspoon*	*1 teaspoon*
Lamb leg, boneless	*3 1/2 pounds*	*1.6 kilograms*
Zucchini squash, grilled	*1 3/4 pounds*	*800 grams*
Fresh mango chutney		
Mangoes, small dice	*1 pound*	*450 grams*
Lime juice	*1 fluid ounce*	*30 milliliters*
Cilantro, chopped	*2 teaspoons*	*2 teaspoons*
Jalapeño peppers, minced	*1/2 teaspoon*	*1/2 teaspoon*
Gingerroot, minced	*1 teaspoon*	*1 teaspoon*

1. Toast the cardamom and cumin seeds, then grind. Prepare marinade: In a sauteuse, heat the oil and add the onions, garlic, ginger, and black pepper; sauté until limp.

2. Cool the onion mixture, and add with the ground spices to the yogurt.

3. Cut lamb along the grain. Season to taste with salt and pepper. Marinate overnight in yogurt mixture.

4. Thread lamb on skewers. Grill lamb to desired doneness.

5. Prepare mango chutney: Mix together all ingredients. Let marinate for several hours.

Pakistani-Style Lamb Patties

Yield: 10 servings

Onions, minced	2 ounces	60 grams
Vegetable oil	1 fluid ounce	30 milliliters
Garlic cloves, minced	8 each	8 each
Bread crumbs, fresh	2 ounces	60 grams
Lamb, lean, ground	3 pounds	1.3 kilograms
Pine nuts, toasted	3 ounces	85 grams
Eggs, beaten	2 or 3 each	2 or 3 each
Sesame tahini	1 ounce	30 grams
Parsley, chopped	3 tablespoons	45 milliliters
Salt, to taste	1/2 teaspoon	1/2 teaspoon
Pepper, to taste	1/4 teaspoon	1/4 teaspoon
Coriander, ground	1 teaspoon	1 teaspoon
Cumin, ground	2 tablespoons	2 tablespoons
Fennel seed, ground	1 teaspoon	1 teaspoon
Gingerroot, grated	2 tablespoons	2 tablespoons

For the fullest flavor, toast whole spices in a dry skillet and then grind as directed on page 206.

1. Sauté the onions in hot oil until they are translucent.

2. Add the garlic and sauté it briefly. Remove the mixture from the heat and allow it to cool.

3. Soak the bread crumbs in water. Squeeze out any excess moisture.

4. Combine the bread crumbs, onions, and garlic.

5. Add the lamb, pine nuts, beaten eggs, tahini, parsley, salt, pepper, and spices. Mix together gently but thoroughly.

6. Shape the mixture into patties and chill.

7. Grill or broil the patties to the desired doneness.

Spicy Hunan Lamb

Yield: 10 servings

Eggs	*2 each*	*2 each*
Cornstarch	*1 ounce*	*30 grams*
Oil	*3 fluid ounces*	*90 milliliters*
Lamb roast, boneless	*3 1/2 pounds*	*1.6 kilograms*
Sauce and vegetables		
Gingerroot, chopped	*1 tablespoon*	*1 tablespoon*
Garlic, chopped	*1 tablespoon*	*1 tablespoon*
Scallion, chopped	*3 ounces*	*85 grams*
Hot bean paste	*1 ounce*	*30 grams*
Mushrooms, sliced	*2 pounds*	*900 grams*
Red peppers, sliced	*1/2 pound*	*225 grams*
Dried black fungus, soaked	*1 ounce*	*30 grams*
Leeks, jullienne	*4 ounces*	*115 grams*

1. Cut the lamb into fine strips.

2. Combine the eggs, half of the oil, and the cornstarch.

3. To prepare sauce and vegetables: Heat oil, add ginger, garlic, scallion, and hot bean paste; stir-fry until scallions are bright green.

4. Add lamb; stir-fry until lamb is done; add mushrooms, peppers, fungus, and leeks, stir-fry until vegetables are tender.

Couscous with Lamb Stew

Yield: 10 servings

Lamb, shoulder or leg, cut in large cubes	*2 pounds*	*900 grams*
Onion, diced	*8 ounces*	*225 grams*
Garlic cloves, chopped	*8 each*	*8 each*
Saffron threads, crushed	*pinch*	*pinch*
Gingerroot, grated	*1 tablespoon*	*1 tablespoon*
Cloves, ground	*dash*	*dash*
Cumin, ground	*1 teaspoon*	*1 teaspoon*
Coriander, ground	*1 teaspoon*	*1 teaspoon*
Nutmeg, ground	*1/2 teaspoon*	*1/2 teaspoon*
Turmeric, ground	*3 tablespoons*	*3 tablespoons*

(Recipe continued on facing page)

Bay leaves	2 each	2 each
Olive oil	3 fluid ounces	90 milliliters
Chicken or Lamb Stock	1 quart	1 liter
Carrots, large dice	8 ounces	225 grams
Turnips, large dice	4 ounces	115 grams
Chicken legs	4 each	4 each
Couscous	1 pound	450 grams
Salt, to taste	1/2 teaspoon	1/2 teaspoon
Zucchini, large dice	8 ounces	225 grams
Green peppers, large dice	8 ounces	225 grams
Chickpeas, cooked	8 ounces	225 grams
Tomatoes, peeled, wedged	1 pound	450 grams
Artichoke bottoms, quartered	10 each	10 each
Lima beans, cooked	2 ounces	60 grams
Arabic white truffles, (if available), sliced	4 ounces	115 grams
Garnish		
Almonds, sliced and toasted	2 ounces	60 grams
Raisins or currants	2 ounces	60 grams
Harissa sauce (hot sauce), diluted with 1 ounce water	2 fluid ounces	60 milliliters
Parsley, chopped, as needed	2 ounces	60 grams

Substitute Jerusalem artichokes for white truffles.

1. In the lower pan of a couscousière, sauté the lamb with the onion, garlic, and spices in the olive oil. Cover with the stock and simmer until the lamb is nearly cooked.

2. Add the carrots, turnips, and chicken legs and stew over low heat for 15 minutes.

3. Rinse and soak the couscous in warm water for 90 seconds and place it in the top pan of the couscousière.

4. Steam the couscous over the simmering stew for 20 minutes.

5. Remove the top pan and season the couscous with salt to taste. Reserve warm while finishing the stew.

6. Add the zucchini and green peppers to the lower pan and cook the stew for 4 minutes.

7. Add the chickpeas, tomatoes, artichoke bottoms, lima beans, and truffles and return the stew to a boil. Adjust the seasonings to taste.

8. Mound the couscous on a heated plate or platter and place the meat stew in the center of the mound. Serve the garnishes separately.

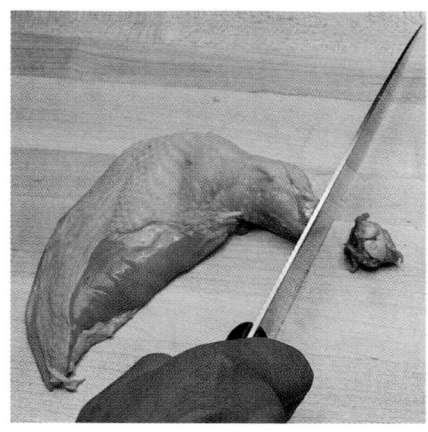

A suprême is a boneless, skinless, poultry breast. One wing joint, often frenched, is left attached to the breast meat.

Tandoori-Style Chicken

Yield: 10 servings

Chicken suprêmes	*10 each*	*10 each*
Yogurt, nonfat	*8 ounces*	*225 grams*
Water	*1 fluid ounce*	*30 milliliters*
Saffron threads, crushed	*1/2 teaspoon*	*1/2 teaspoon*
Cumin, ground	*1 tablespoon*	*1 tablespoon*
Cardamom, ground	*1 tablespoon*	*1 tablespoon*
Coriander, ground	*3 teaspoons*	*3 teaspoons*
Gingerroot, minced	*2 ounces*	*60 grams*
Garlic cloves, minced	*4 each*	*4 each*
Cayenne, ground, to taste	*1/2 teaspoon*	*1/2 teaspoon*
Lime juice, to taste	*2 teaspoons*	*2 teaspoons*

1. Trim the chicken breasts.

2. Mix the yogurt, water, seasonings, and lime juice together.

3. Place the chicken in the yogurt mixture and marinate for 12 hours.

4. Remove and grill the chicken breasts until cooked through.

Aromatic Chicken

Yield: 10 servings

To make a cornstarch slurry, add enough cold water to the cornstarch to make a very thin paste.

Chicken legs	*10 each*	*10 each*
Oil, as needed	*2 fluid ounces*	*60 milliliters*
Gingerroot, minced	*1/2 ounce*	*15 grams*
Garlic, mashed	*1/2 ounce*	*15 grams*
Scallion, chopped	*1/2 bunch*	*1/2 bunch*
Orange skin	*1 ounce*	*30 grams*
Cinnamon stick	*1 each*	*1 each*
Szechuan peppercorns	*1 teaspoon*	*1 teaspoon*
Star anise	*2 each*	*2 each*
Salt, to taste	*1 teaspoon*	*1 teaspoon*
Black pepper, to taste	*1/2 teaspoon*	*1/2 teaspoon*
Soy sauce	*4 fluid ounces*	*120 milliliters*
Dry sherry	*2 fluid ounces*	*60 milliliters*
Sugar, to taste	*1 tablespoon*	*1 tablespoon*
Chicken Stock, as needed	*6 fluid ounces*	*180 milliliters*
Cornstarch slurry, as needed	*1 tablespoon*	*1 tablespoon*

(Recipe continued on facing page)

1. Halve the chicken legs and remove the skin.

2. Heat the oil in a wok, and add ginger, garlic, and scallion. When golden brown, add the chicken pieces and all spices; add soy sauce, sherry, and sugar.

3. Stir-fry until aromatic; cover the chicken legs by three-fourths with stock and stew gently for 45 minutes.

4. When the chicken is done, remove to a hotel pan.

5. Degrease the stewing liquid and bring to a boil. Thicken with cornstarch slurry to make a medium-thick sauce and strain.

6. Serve the chicken coated with the sauce.

Chicken in Curry Sauce

Yield: 10 servings

Chicken, boneless, skinless	*3 pounds*	*1.3 kilograms*	*The recipe for Red Curry Paste is on page 429.*
Oil	*2 fluid ounces*	*60 milliliters*	
Garlic, chopped	*1 ounce*	*30 grams*	
Spanish onion, diced	*12 ounces*	*340 grams*	
Red Curry Paste	*2 ounces*	*60 grams*	
Salt	*1 tablespoon*	*1 tablespoon*	
White pepper	*1/2 tablespoon*	*1/2 tablespoon*	
Chicken Stock, as needed	*1 quart*	*1 liter*	
Red Bliss potatoes, diced, parcooked	*2 pounds*	*900 grams*	
Cornstarch slurry	*1 tablespoon*	*1 tablespoon*	
Brown sugar, to taste	*1 tablespoon*	*1 tablespoon*	
Coconut milk	*12 fluid ounces*	*360 milliliters*	
Basil leaves, coarse-chopped	*2 tablespoons*	*2 tablespoons*	
Cilantro leaves, whole	*1 tablespoon*	*1 tablespoon*	
Scallion or toasted coconut, as needed	*2 ounces*	*60 grams*	

1. Cut the chicken into large cubes.

2. Heat oil, add garlic and onions, stir-fry until golden brown.

3. Add curry paste, salt, white pepper; heat briefly to release the flavor.

4. Add chicken and stock, bring to a simmer. Stew over low heat for 15 to 20 minutes.

5. When chicken is done, add potatoes and cook until tender.

6. Thicken liquid with cornstarch slurry if necessary.

7. Add sugar and coconut milk.

8. Garnish as desired.

Chicken Teriyaki (Yakitori)

Yield: 10 servings

Teriyaki sauce

Oil, to sauté	*1 ounce*	*30 milliliters*
Ginger, minced	*2 teaspoons*	*2 teaspoons*
Garlic, minced	*2 teaspoons*	*2 teaspoons*
Scallions, chopped	*2 ounces*	*60 grams*
Japanese soy sauce	*6 fluid ounces*	*180 milliliters*
Sake	*2 fluid ounces*	*60 milliliters*
Rice vinegar	*1 fluid ounce*	*30 milliliters*
Chicken Stock	*1 pint*	*480 milliliters*
Sugar, to taste	*1 ounce*	*30 grams*
Shiro-mirin	*2 fluid ounces*	*60 milliliters*
Cornstarch slurry, as needed		
Sesame oil	*1 fluid ounce*	*30 milliliters*
Chicken, fryers	*3 each*	*3 each*
Salt, to taste	*1/2 teaspoon*	*1/2 teaspoon*
Pepper, to taste	*1/4 teaspoon*	*1/4 teapoon*
Eggs, beaten	*2 each*	*2 each*
Cornstarch	*2 ounces*	*60 grams*
Oil	*4 fluid ounces*	*120 milliliters*
Gingerroot, minced	*1/2 teaspoon*	*1/2 teaspoon*
Garlic, minced	*1/2 teaspoon*	*1/2 teaspoon*
Scallions, chopped	*1 ounce*	*30 grams*
Mushrooms, diced	*2 pounds*	*900 grams*
Red peppers, diced	*1 pound*	*450 grams*
Snow peas, diced	*1 pound*	*450 grams*

1. To make the sauce: Heat oil, add ginger, garlic, and scallions and cook until golden brown. Add soy sauce, sake, vinegar, stock, sugar, and shiro-mirin; bring to a boil. Thicken with cornstarch (medium consistency). Finish with sesame oil.

2. Cut the chickens into large pieces. Season to taste.

3. Coat the chicken with eggs, cornstarch, and half of the oil.

4. Heat remaining oil; add ginger, garlic, and scallions. Cook until light brown.

5. Add chicken and stir-fry until chicken is done; add vegetables. When the vegetables are tender, add sauce.

6. Thicken with cornstarch to a medium consistency. Mix well and season to taste with sesame oil.

Chicken with Cashews

Yield: 10 servings

Coating

Eggs	*2 each*	*2 each*
Cornstarch	*2 ounces*	*60 grams*
Oil	*3 fluid ounces*	*90 milliliters*
Chicken, boneless, skinless	*3 1/2 pounds*	*1.6 kilograms*
Vegetable oil	*2 fluid ounces*	*60 milliliters*
Gingerroot, minced	*1 teaspoon*	*1 teaspoon*
Garlic, minced	*1 teaspoon*	*1 teaspoon*
Scallion, chopped	*1 tablespoon*	*1 tablespoon*
Vegetable mixture		
Snow peas, diced	*8 ounces*	*225 grams*
Red peppers, diced	*4 ounces*	*115 grams*
Baby corn, diced	*2 ounces*	*60 grams*
Straw mushrooms, whole	*4 ounces*	*115 grams*
Salt, to taste	*1/2 teaspoon*	*1/2 teaspoon*
White pepper, to taste	*1/4 teaspoon*	*1/4 teaspoon*
Black soy sauce	*2 tablespoons*	*2 tablespoons*
Hoisin sauce	*2 tablespoons*	*2 tablespoons*
Cashews, toasted	*3 ounces*	*85 grams*

1. Cut the chicken into 3/4-inch (2-centimeter) cubes.

2. Combine ingredients for coating and mix with chicken, set aside.

3. Heat the oil in a wok; add ginger, garlic, and scallion; stir-fry. Add chicken and stir-fry until chicken is done.

4. Add vegetable mixture, and stir-fry until vegetables are very hot and tender-crisp. Add black soy sauce, hoisin sauce, and seasonings; mix until combined.

5. Garnish each portion with cashews.

INTERNATIONAL ENTRÉES

Hot Sesame Chicken

Yield: 10 servings

This recipe would serve 25 as part of a combination platter or hors d'oeuvre selection.

Chickens, boneless, skinless	3 1/2 pounds	1.6 kilograms
Eggs	2 each	2 each
Cornstarch	2 ounces	60 grams
Oil, as needed	3 fluid ounces	90 milliliters
Gingerroot, minced	1 teaspoon	1 teaspoon
Garlic, minced	1 teaspoon	1 teaspoon
Scallion, chopped	1 tablespoon	1 tablespoon
Mushrooms, diced	12 ounces	340 grams
Red peppers, diced	6 ounces	170 grams
Celery, diced	12 ounces	340 grams
Gingko nuts, drained	4 ounces	115 grams
Sesame seeds	1 ounce	30 grams
Black pepper, to taste	1 teaspoon	1 teaspoon
Hot bean paste	2 tablespoons	2 tablespoons
Chili powder	1 tablespoon	1 tablespoon
Soy sauce	2 fluid ounces	60 milliliters
Garnish:		
Sesame seeds, toasted	2 ounces	60 grams

1. Cut the chicken into 1-inch (2.5-centimeter) chunks.

2. Combine the eggs, cornstarch, and half of the oil; mix with chicken.

3. Heat the remaining oil in a wok; add garlic, ginger, scallion, and stir-fry until very hot. Add chicken; stir-fry until chicken is done.

4. Add mushrooms, red pepper, celery, and gingko nuts; stir-fry until vegetables are just tender-crisp.

5. Add sesame seeds, pepper, bean paste, and soy sauce, mix together.

6. Check seasonings, and garnish with sesame seeds.

782

Miso Chicken

Yield: 10 servings

Chicken, boneless and skinless	*3 1/2 pounds*	*1.6 kilograms*
Eggs	*2 each*	*2 each*
Cornstarch	*2 ounces*	*60 grams*
Vegetable or peanut oil, as needed	*5 fluid ounces*	*150 milliliters*
Miso sauce		
Gingerroot, minced	*1 tablespoon*	*1 tablespoon*
Garlic, minced	*1 tablespoon*	*1 tablespoon*
Scallions, chopped fine	*3 ounces*	*85 grams*
Miso bean paste	*6 ounces*	*170 grams*
Japanese soy sauce	*6 fluid ounces*	*180 milliliters*
Sake	*3 fluid ounces*	*90 milliliters*
Sugar	*2 ounces*	*60 grams*
Chicken Stock	*1 pint*	*480 milliliters*
Cornstarch slurry, as needed	*2 tablespoons*	*2 tablespoons*
Sesame oil	*2 tablespoons*	*2 tablespoons*
Ginger root, minced	*1/2 teaspoon*	*1/2 teaspoon*
Garlic, minced	*1/2 teaspoon*	*1/2 teaspoon*
Mushrooms, diced	*12 ounces*	*340 grams*
Asparagus tips	*12 ounces*	*340 grams*
Red peppers, diced	*12 ounces*	*340 grams*
Celery, diced	*4 ounces*	*115 grams*

Miso is fermented bean paste, which may be labeled as red, yellow, or brown.

To make a slurry, dilute cornstarch with cold water until a very thin paste forms.

1. Cut the chicken into 1-inch (2.5-centimeter) chunks.

2. Combine the eggs, cornstarch, and 3 tablespoons of oil; mix together with chicken.

3. To make sauce: Heat a little of the oil in a wok; add ginger, garlic, and scallions, stir-fry until aromatic.

4. Add miso paste and soy sauce and bring to a boil; add sake, sugar, and stock, return to a boil; thicken with cornstarch to medium consistency.

5. Finish sauce with sesame oil and hold for service.

6. To finish the preparation, heat the remaining oil in a wok; add ginger and garlic, stir-fry until aromatic; add chicken and stir-fry until chicken is done.

7. Add mushrooms, asparagus or broccoli, pepper, and celery; stir-fry until vegetables are tender-crisp; add sauce, and mix well.

Roast Chicken with Lemongrass

Yield: 10 servings

Prepare a jus lié by degreasing the pan drippings, adding enough stock or broth to get about 2 fluid ounces (60 milliliters) per portion. Thicken lightly with cornstarch or arrowroot.

Chickens, broilers	*5 each*	*5 each*
Lemongrass stalks, thinly sliced	*4 each*	*4 each*
Garlic cloves, mashed	*3 each*	*3 each*
Shallots, sliced	*1 ounce*	*30 grams*
Chili peppers, seeded and sliced	*4 each*	*4 each*
Sugar	*1 tablespoon*	*1 tablespoon*
Salt	*1/2 teaspoon*	*1/2 teaspoon*
Fish sauce	*3 fluid ounces*	*90 milliliters*

1. Trim the chickens, rinse, pat dry, and reserve.
2. Combine lemongrass, garlic, shallots, chili peppers, and sugar; purée to a paste, and add salt and fish sauce.
3. Loosen skin of the chickens at the breast and legs, rub half the paste between meat and skin, and rub the rest on the skin and in the cavity.
4. Truss chickens and roast on a rack at 425°F (220°C) for 15 minutes. Reduce the heat to 375°F (190°C) and roast until the thigh has an internal temperature of 160°F (70°C). Baste often with pan drippings.
5. Remove from the oven; allow to rest before carving.

Hot and Sour Fish

Yield: 10 servings

Ghee is clarified butter that has been allowed to heat until milk solids just begin to brown.

Filet of sole	*4 pounds*	*1.8 kilograms*
Salt, to taste	*1/2 teaspoon*	*1/2 teaspoon*
Pepper, to taste	*1/4 teaspoon*	*1/4 teaspoon*
Batter		
Cold water	*24 fluid ounces*	*720 milliliters*
Baking powder	*3 tablespoons*	*3 tablespoons*
Flour, all-purpose	*1 pound*	*450 grams*
Sesame oil	*2 fluid ounces*	*60 milliliters*
Hot and sour sauce		
Peanut oil, as needed	*2 fluid ounces*	*60 milliliters*
Garlic cloves, minced	*2 each*	*2 each*
Assorted vegetables, fine dice	*1 pound*	*450 grams*
Tomato paste	*4 ounces*	*115 grams*
Water	*12 fluid ounces*	*360 milliliters*
Fish sauce	*2 tablespoons*	*2 tablespoons*
Sugar	*1 tablespoon*	*1 tablespoon*
Worcestershire sauce	*1 tablespoon*	*1 tablespoon*
Red wine vinegar	*1 fluid ounce*	*30 milliliters*
Red chili pepper flakes	*1 teaspoon*	*1 teaspoon*
Soy sauce	*1 tablespoon*	*1 tablespoon*
Cilantro, chopped fine	*2 tablespoons*	*2 tablespoons*
Oil (for deep-frying)	*1 pint*	*480 milliliters*

(Recipe continued on facing page)

1. Cut the fish into portions (5 to 6 ounces/140 to 170 grams).

2. Combine all of the ingredients for the batter; mix until smooth. Chill until needed.

3. To make the sauce: Heat the oil in a wok; add the garlic, and fine-dice vegetables; stir-fry briefly.

4. Add tomato paste, water, fish sauce, and sugar; mix together.

5. Add remaining ingredients for the sauce. Simmer 15 to 20 minutes, and adjust consistency with water if necessary. Keep hot for service.

6. To fry the fish: season lightly with salt and pepper, dip fish in batter, deep-fry in 350°F (175°C) oil until golden brown, and drain on absorbent paper. Serve with hot sauce.

Indian Prawn Curry (*Jheenga Shorwedder*)

Yield: 10 servings

Cloves, ground	*1/4 teaspoon*	*1/4 teaspoon*
Cardamom seeds	*1/2 teaspoon*	*1/2 teaspoon*
Bay leaves	*3 each*	*3 each*
Cumin seeds	*1 teaspoon*	*1 teaspoon*
Turmeric, ground	*1 teaspoon*	*1 teaspoon*
Cayenne pepper	*1/2 teaspoon*	*1/2 teaspoon*
Onions, chopped	*2 each*	*2 each*
Ghee, as needed	*6 ounces*	*170 grams*
Coconut, finely chopped	*4 ounces*	*115 grams*
Gingerroot, grated	*1/2 ounce*	*15 grams*
Green chilies, chopped	*3 each*	*3 each*
Garlic cloves	*5 each*	*5 each*
Shrimp, peeled and deveined	*3 pounds*	*1.3 kilograms*
Fish Stock	*1 pint*	*480 milliliters*
Lemon juice	*2 teaspoons*	*2 teaspoons*
Yogurt	*8 ounces*	*225 grams*
Arrowroot, to bind	*as needed*	*as needed*
Salt, to taste	*1 teaspoon*	*1 teaspoon*
Sugar	*1 teaspoon*	*1 teaspoon*

1. Toast the cloves, cardamon, bay leaves, tumeric, and cayenne. Cool and grind.

2. Sauté onions in ghee until golden brown. Add coconut, ginger, green chilies, spices, and garlic to the ghee and fry gently for 3 minutes.

3. Add the shrimp, stock, and lemon juice, and cook for 5 minutes or until the shrimp is cooked through.

4. Add the yogurt; thicken with arrowroot if necessary. Adjust seasoning to taste with salt and sugar.

Scallops with Crispy Noodles

Yield: 10 servings

To read about rehydrating dried ingredients, refer to page 201 in Chapter 6.

Scallops	*3 1/2 pounds*	*1.6 kilograms*
Coating		
Eggs	*2 each*	*2 each*
Cornstarch	*2 ounces*	*60 grams*
Vegetable oil, as needed	*2 fluid ounces*	*60 milliliters*
Chinese mushrooms, rehydrated and diced	*6 each*	*6 each*
Black fungus, rehydrated	*1 ounce*	*30 grams*
Spanish onion, sliced thin	*1 each*	*1 each*
Snow peas	*10 ounces*	*285 grams*
Carrots, sliced	*2 each*	*2 each*
Baby corn, drained	*4 ounces*	*115 grams*
Straw mushrooms	*4 ounces*	*115 grams*
Salt, to taste	*1/2 teaspoon*	*1/2 teaspoon*
Black pepper, to taste	*1/4 teaspoon*	*1/4 teaspoon*
Red wine	*8 fluid ounces*	*240 milliliters*
Oyster sauce	*4 fluid ounces*	*120 milliliters*
Soy sauce	*2 fluid ounces*	*60 milliliters*
Fish sauce	*2 fluid ounces*	*60 milliliters*
Chinese noodles, fresh	*1 pound*	*450 grams*
Coriander leaves	*1 bunch*	*1 bunch*

1. Remove muscle tabs from scallops. Slice them if they are very large.

2. Combine the ingredients for the coating; mix with the scallops.

3. Heat the oil in a wok, add scallops, stir-fry and remove.

4. Wipe out the wok, add more oil, add vegetables in sequence from firm to soft, and stir-fry until tender. Add red wine, oyster sauce, soy sauce, and fish sauce; mix well.

5. Return scallops to the wok; stir gently to mix ingredients and heat the scallops.

6. Deep-fry the noodles in 350°F (175°C) oil until crispy. Drain.

7. Serve scallops over the noodles and garnish with coriander leaves.

Shrimp in Chili Sauce

Yield: 10 servings

Shrimp	*3 1/2 pounds*	*1.6 kilograms*
Chili sauce		
Gingerroot, minced	*2 ounces*	*60 grams*
Garlic, minced	*2 ounces*	*60 grams*
Scallion, minced	*2 ounces*	*60 grams*
Chili bean paste	*1 ounce*	*30 grams*
Tomato ketchup	*12 ounces*	*285 grams*
Rice vinegar	*2 fluid ounces*	*60 milliliters*
Soy sauce	*2 fluid ounces*	*60 milliliters*
Egg whites, beaten	*2 each*	*2 each*
Cornstarch	*2 ounces*	*60 grams*
Shrimp	*3 1/2 pounds*	*1.6 kilograms*
Oil, as needed	*5 fluid ounces*	*150 milliliters*
Gingerroot, minced	*1 tablepoons*	*1 tablespoons*
Garlic, minced	*1 tablespoons*	*1 tablespoons*
Scallions, shredded	*1 bunch*	*1 bunch*
Baby corn, drained	*8 ounces*	*225 grams*
Straw mushrooms	*8 ounces*	*225 grams*
Snow peas	*1 pound*	*450 grams*
Sliced scallions (optional)	*3 ounces*	*85 grams*
Dry sherry	*2 fluid ounces*	*60 milliliters*
Sugar, to taste	*2 ounces*	*60 grams*
Chicken Stock	*4 fluid ounces*	*120 milliliters*
Cornstarch slurry	*1 tablespoon*	*1 tablespoon*
Sesame oil, to finish	*1 tablespoon*	*1 tablespoon*

To read more about preparing shrimp, see page 249.

1. Peel and devein shrimp and set aside.

2. Combine the ingredients for the sauce and bring to a boil.

3. Combine the egg whites, cornstarch, and 2 ounces (60 milliliters) of oil.

4. Heat the remaining oil in a wok; add ginger, garlic, and scallion; stir-fry until aromatic.

5. Add shrimp, corn, straw mushrooms, and snow peas, stir-fry until shrimp is just cooked.

6. Add the chili sauce, and mix together; add sesame oil and sliced scallions. Check seasonings and serve.

Shrimp Tempura

Yield: 100 pieces

Shrimp, 21 to 25 count, peeled and deveined; score to prevent curling	*5 pounds*	*225 kilograms*
Salt, to taste	*1/2 teaspoon*	*1/2 teaspoon*
Pepper, to taste	*1/4 teaspoon*	*1/4 teaspoon*
Tempura batter		
Cold water	*24 fluid ounces*	*720 milliliters*
Baking powder	*1 3/4 ounces*	*50 grams*
Flour, all-purpose	*24 ounces*	*680 grams*
Sesame oil	*4 fluid ounces*	*120 milliliters*
Tempura dipping sauce		
Water (ice-cold)	*1 pint*	*480 milliliters*
Soy sauce	*8 fluid ounces*	*240 milliliters*
Ginger, minced	*1 tablespoon*	*1 tablespoon*
Shiro-mirin	*2 fluid ounces*	*60 milliliters*
Katsuo dashi	*2 fluid ounces*	*60 milliliters*
Flour or cornstarch, as needed	*3 ounces*	*85 grams*

1. Dry and season shrimp. Heat the oil to 375°F (190°C).

2. To make tempura batter: Combine all ingredients and mix together. Batter should be of medium thickness. Chill until needed.

3. To make sauce: Combine all ingredients, mix together. Let rest while preparing the shrimp.

4. Dredge shrimp in flour or cornstarch. Dip shrimp in batter, deep-fry in hot oil until golden brown; drain on absorbent paper.

5. Serve with dipping sauce.

Tempura is a cooking style brought to the Japanese by Portuguese sailors. The best tempura is made with an ice-cold butter that forms a very "lacy" coating on shrimp, fish, and vegetables.

Serve shrimp tempura as an appetizer, "by the piece," as pub fare, or on a bed of rice as an entrée.

Katsuo dashi is a broth made by simmering dried bonita (tuna) flakes and dried kelp in water.

Squid and Peppers

Yield: 10 servings

Coating mix		
Egg whites, beaten	*2 each*	*2 each*
Cornstarch	*2 ounces*	*60 grams*
Vegetable oil, as needed	*4 fluid ounces*	*120 milliliters*
Squid	*3 pounds*	*1.3 kilograms*
Sauce		
Hoisin sauce	*1 fluid ounce*	*30 milliliters*
Soy sauce	*4 fluid ounces*	*120 milliliters*
Oyster sauce	*1 tablespoon*	*1 tablespoon*
Sugar, to taste	*1 tablespoon*	*1 tablespoon*
Black pepper	*1/4 teaspoon*	*1/4 teaspoon*
Chicken Stock	*12 fluid ounces*	*360 milliliters*
Cornstarch slurry	*1 tablespoon*	*1 tablespoon*
Peppers, assorted colors, rough cut	*2 pounds*	*900 grams*
Gingerroot, minced	*1 tablespoon*	*1 tablespoon*
Garlic, minced	*2 ounces*	*60 grams*
Scallions, shredded	*3 each*	*3 each*

The squid for this dish may be prepared as follows: Separate the body and tentacles. Slit the body, lay it flat and score with crosshatch incisions to make a diamond pattern.

To make a cornstarch slurry, dilute cornstarch with cold water to make a thin paste.

1. Clean, trim, and score the squid.

2. Combine the egg whites, cornstarch, and 2 ounces (60 milliliters) of oil.

3. To make the sauce: Combine all ingredients, bring to a simmer, and thicken to medium consistency with slurry.

4. Heat oil in a wok, add ginger, garlic, and scallion; stir-fry until aromatic. Add squid and stir-fry until barely cooked.

5. Add peppers and stir-fry until tender-crisp and very hot.

6. Add the sauce, mix together, adjust seasonings and serve.

21 Vegetable Side Dishes

Vegetables deserve as much care and attention as any other element on the plate. Remember to prepare all vegetables properly before cooking. Techniques for peeling, rinsing, trimming, and cutting a selection of basic and unique vegetables can be found on pages 183 to 201.

You may wish to adapt some of the recipes here to expand your meatless-menu options. Herein, recipes are grouped as follows:

- *Green Vegetables*
- *White Vegetables*
- *Red and Yellow Vegetables*
- *Braises and Stews*
- *Grilled Vegetables*
- *Mixed Vegetables*
- *Asian Vegetable Dishes*

Steamed vegetables have an increased appeal for those who prefer low-fat and low-calorie foods. Don't neglect seasonings, however.

Peeling broccoli and asparagus stems removes inedible skins and helps ensure even cooking.

Cauliflower, carrots, or peeled asparagus may all be cooked in this manner. Adjust cooking time as necessary.

Suggested sauces include lemon-butter, Mornay, Hollandaise, Herbed Mayonnaise, mayonnaise-mustard combination, and warm vinaigrette.

Steamed Broccoli

Yield: 10 servings

Broccoli, peeled	2 pounds	900 grams
Water	6 fluid ounces	180 milliliters
Salt, to taste	1/2 teaspoon	1/2 teaspoon
Pepper, to taste	1/4 teaspoon	1/4 teaspoon

1. Arrange the broccoli on a steamer rack so that the pieces are not crowded.

2. Bring the water to a full boil in the bottom of the steamer.

3. Add the broccoli to the steamer, replace the lid, and steam the vegetable for 5 to 7 minutes or until tender. Season the broccoli with salt and pepper to taste.

VARIATION

Steamed Green Beans: Clean 2 pounds (900 grams) of green beans. Snap off the end of the bean and remove any tough strings. Steam as above.

Add a small amount of reduced heavy cream in place of the butter.

Add chopped fresh mint just before serving.

For a summer side, cool the peas, toss lightly with sour cream, and add chopped peanuts.

Pan-Steamed Peas

Yield: 10 servings

Peas, fresh, shelled	2 pounds	900 grams
Water, boiling	6 fluid ounces	180 milliliters
Butter	2 ounces	60 grams
Salt, to taste	1/2 teaspoon	1/2 teaspoon
Pepper, to taste	1/4 teaspoon	1/4 teaspoon

1. Place the peas in a shallow sauteuse with 1/4-inch (.5 centimeter) of boiling water. Cover the pan.

2. Pan-steam the peas over high heat for about 2 to 3 minutes, shaking the pan occasionally. Drain away excess water and return pan to the heat.

3. Remove the cover and add the butter, salt, and pepper. Toss the peas to coat them evenly.

VARIATION

Pan-Steamed Asparagus: Trim the asparagus and peel the stem ends. Place the stalks in a pot. Fill the pot up about 1/2 inch (1 centimeter) with boiling water. Pan-steam for about 3 to 4 minutes or until just tender. Do not overcook. Serve immediately with Hollandaise Sauce, melted butter, or lemon-butter.

French-Style Peas (*Petits Pois à la Française*)

Yield: 10 servings

Pearl onions	*2 ounces*	*60 grams*
Butter	*2 ounces*	*60 grams*
Peas, fresh, shelled	*1 1/4 pounds*	*560 grams*
Chicken Stock	*4 fluid ounces*	*120 milliliters*
Salt, to taste	*1/2 teaspoon*	*1/2 teaspoon*
Pepper, to taste	*1/4 teaspoon*	*1/4 teaspoon*
Lettuce, Boston or romaine, shredded	*12 ounces*	*340 grams*
Beurre Manié	*as needed*	*as needed*

1. Smother the pearl onions in the fresh butter without browning them.

2. Add the peas and stock. Season the stock with salt and pepper. Cook the mixture quickly, covered, for a few minutes. Add the lettuce.

3. Add the beurre manié gradually in small pieces until the mixture is thickened. Season to taste with salt and pepper.

VARIATION

Petits Pois à la Fermière: Add 4 ounces (115 grams) of small new carrots with the onions.

The lettuce should be added as close to serving time as possible. You may reduce the amount of lettuce if desired.

A Bouquet Garni of parsley and chervil may be added with the Chicken Stock.

You may want to finish with 2 to 4 ounces (60 to 115 grams) of crisp chopped bacon at the end.

Viennese-Style Green Peas

Yield: 10 servings

Butter, melted	*2 ounces*	*60 grams*
All-purpose flour	*1 ounce*	*30 grams*
White Beef Stock, hot	*12 fluid ounces*	*360 milliliters*
Sugar, to taste	*1/2 teaspoon*	*1/2 teaspoon*
Salt, to taste	*1/2 teaspoon*	*1/2 teaspoon*
Pepper, to taste	*1/2 teaspoon*	*1/2 teaspoon*
Peas, fresh	*1 3/4 pounds*	*750 kilograms*
Parsley, chopped	*1 tablespoon*	*1 tablespoon*

1. Heat the butter. Add the flour and cook it out to form a light roux.

2. Add the hot Beef Stock. Stir the mixture well and simmer it for 10 minutes. Add the sugar, salt, and pepper to taste.

3. Add the peas and bring the mixture to a boil. Stir in the parsley to finish.

Chicken Stock may be used in place of White Beef Stock.

Some chefs prefer to parcook the fresh peas in boiling salted water first.

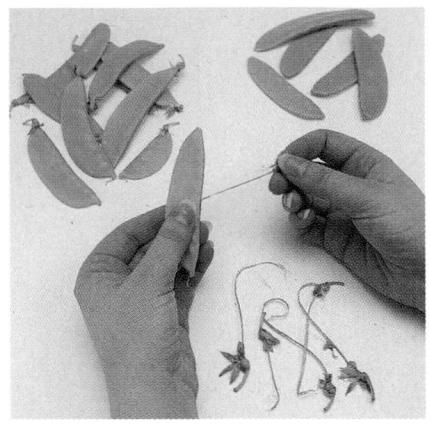

Remove the tough string from snow peas before cooking.

If you prefer, prepare the dish as follows: Sweat the shallots and garlic in the oil; add the gingerroot, snow peas, and squash. Add the chicken stock and stew. Season with chives and pepper.

Gingered Snow Peas and Yellow Squash

Yield: 10 servings

Snow peas	*1 1/4 pounds*	*570 grams*
Yellow squash	*12 ounces*	*340 grams*
Gingerroot, chopped	*2 teaspoons*	*2 teaspoons*
Shallots, chopped	*1 tablespoon*	*1 tablespoon*
Garlic, minced	*1 teaspoon*	*1 teaspoon*
Chicken Stock	*6 fluid ounces*	*180 milliliters*
Chives, fresh, chopped	*2 tablespoons*	*2 tablespoons*
White pepper, to taste	*1/4 teaspoon*	*1/4 teaspoon*

1. Remove the stem end and strings from the snow peas. Rinse them well. Slice off the stem end of the squash. Rinse it well and cut it into a medium dice.

2. Combine the vegetables with the ginger, shallots, garlic, stock, and chives.

3. Steam the vegetables until they are tender, about 2 to 3 minutes.

4. Season to taste with the pepper.

Include green and yellow peppers for additional color.

If desired, drain off most of the oil before proceeding with step 3. The drained oil should be reserved and refrigerated, as it is now infused with shallots and can be used to season other sauces or vinaigrettes.

Asparagus with Roasted Pepper and Shallot Chips

Yield: 10 servings

Asparagus, trimmed and peeled	*2 pounds*	*900 grams*
Olive oil	*2 fluid ounces*	*60 milliliters*
Shallots, peeled and sliced thin	*3 ounces*	*85 grams*
Red peppers, roasted, diced or batonnet	*4 ounces*	*115 grams*
Salt, to taste	*1 teaspoon*	*1 teaspoon*
Pepper, coarse-grind, to taste	*1/2 teaspoon*	*1/2 teaspoon*
Oregano leaves, chopped	*2 teaspoons*	*2 teaspoons*

1. Slice the asparagus on the bias into 2-inch (5-centimeter) pieces. Steam or boil until tender. Drain immediately.

2. Heat the oil in a skillet over medium heat. Add the shallots and sauté until the slices are crisp and browned. Remove with slotted spoon and blot on absorbent toweling.

3. Add the asparagus, red peppers, and salt and pepper to taste to the olive oil and sauté, tossing frequently until heated. Add the oregano and heat another minute.

4. Serve with shallot chips scattered over the top of the asparagus-and-red-pepper mixture.

Italian-Style Spinach

Yield: 10 servings

Bacon, pancetta, or prosciutto, chopped	3 ounces	85 grams
Olive oil	1 fluid ounce	30 milliliters
Onions, fine dice	2 ounces	60 grams
Garlic cloves, minced	2 each	2 each
Spinach, chopped	2 pounds	900 grams
Salt, to taste	1/2 teaspoon	1/2 teaspoon
Nutmeg, ground (optional)	1/4 teaspoon	1/4 teaspoon
Parmesan cheese, grated	2 ounces	60 grams
Black pepper, ground	1/2 teaspoon	1/2 teaspoon

1. Sauté the bacon or ham in the olive oil.

2. Add the onion, garlic, and spinach; sauté the spinach until it is limp.

3. Season the spinach with the salt, nutmeg, Parmesan cheese, and pepper; serve immediately.

This works well with most cooking greens: kale, escarole, swiss chard, turnip, collard and beet greens, broccoli, and rabe.

Spinach Pancakes

Yield: 20 servings

Milk	12 fluid ounces	360 milliliters
Butter, melted	1 ounce	30 grams
Flour	5 ounces	140 grams
Eggs	4 each	4 each
Sugar	1/2 teaspoon	1/2 teaspoon
Spinach, steamed, squeezed dry, and puréed	1 pound	450 grams
Salt, to taste	1 teaspoon	1 teaspoon
Pepper, to taste	1/2 teaspoon	1/2 teaspoon
Nutmeg, ground (optional)	to taste	to taste

1. Combine the milk, butter, flour, eggs, and sugar to form a batter.

2. Add the spinach and season the batter with salt, pepper, and nutmeg to taste.

3. Cook the pancakes in plättar pans or on a griddle until done. Serve them immediately.

Make smaller pancakes for canapés; top with herbed cream cheese and diced roasted red pepper.

This Scandinavian-style pancake is typically served with lingonberry jam as an appetizer. It may also be served as a side dish to accompany roasted or sautéed veal or poultry.

Plättar pans are special cast-iron griddles used to prepare these pancakes.

Zucchini with Chorizo and Tomatoes

Yield: 10 servings

Zucchini	*2 pounds*	*900 grams*
Chorizo, ground	*2 ounces*	*60 grams*
Butter	*1 ounce*	*30 grams*
Tomato Concassé	*4 ounces*	*115 grams*
Salt, to taste	*1/2 teaspoon*	*1/2 teaspoon*
Pepper, to taste	*1/4 teaspoon*	*1/4 teaspoon*

Caramelized onions are a good addition to this dish.

Top individual portions with grated jack cheese mixed with bread crumbs and flash under a salamander until crumbs are golden and cheese is melted.

1. Trim the ends from the zucchini; cut as desired (tourné, batonnet, rounds).

2. Render the chorizo in a sauté pan; pour off most of the fat. Add the whole butter and heat.

3. Add the zucchini and tomatoes and toss them until cooked through.

4. Adjust the seasoning with salt and pepper to taste.

Pan-Fried Zucchini

Yield: 10 servings

Zucchini, trimmed and sliced	*2 pounds*	*900 grams*
Flour, as needed	*2 ounces*	*60 grams*
Beer Batter	*1 pint*	*480 milliliters*
Olive oil	*as needed*	*as needed*
Salt, to taste	*1/2 teaspoon*	*1/2 teaspoon*
Black pepper, to taste	*1/4 teaspoon*	*1/4 teaspoon*

The recipe for Beer Batter can be found on page 666.

To read about pan-frying, see pages 319 to 322. Figure 9-36 (page 332) shows a picture of pan-frying zucchini.

This recipe makes a nice accompaniment to broiled or fried fish. It also makes a nice appetizer. Serve them on their own with tomato coulis dip or a seasoned mayonnaise, or on an appetizer plate with Broccoli and Cheddar Fritters.

Other vegetables can be batter-dipped and fried. Experiment with mushrooms, broccoli florets, and carrots battonnet.

1. Dredge the zucchini in flour. Evenly coat the zucchini slices (or sticks) with the batter and add them to a hot, oiled pan in a single layer. Do not crowd them.

2. Pan-fry the zucchini on the first side for approximately 1 minute, or until golden brown. Turn and complete the cooking on the second side.

3. Remove the zucchini from the hot oil and blot briefly on absorbent paper toweling.

4. Season zucchini slices with salt and pepper.

Green Beans with Walnuts

Yield: 10 servings

Green beans, blanched	*2 1/2 pounds*	*1.25 kilograms*
Chicken Stock, hot	*4 fluid ounces*	*120 milliliters*
Shallots, minced	*2 teaspoons*	*2 teaspoons*
Garlic, minced	*2 teaspoons*	*2 teaspoons*
Walnut oil	*1 fluid ounce*	*30 milliliters*
Walnuts, chopped and toasted	*4 tablespoons*	*4 tablespoons*
Chives, sliced	*2 teaspoons*	*2 teaspoons*

1. Place the green beans in a sauté pan with the hot stock. Top them with the shallots, garlic, and walnut oil.

2. Cover and pan-steam the beans for approximately 3 minutes or until they are tender. Drain. Garnish with toasted walnuts and chives.

Vegetable Stock or water may be used in place of the Chicken Stock.

Haricots verts are small tender green beans. They are available in early summer.

Green Beans with Bacon, Shallots, and Mushrooms

Yield: 10 servings

Green beans	*2 1/2 pounds*	*1.25 kilograms*
Bacon, julienned	*4 ounces*	*115 grams*
Shallots, minced	*1 ounce*	*30 grams*
Mushrooms, sliced	*8 ounces*	*225 grams*
Salt, to taste	*1/2 teaspoon*	*1/2 teaspoon*
Pepper, to taste	*1/4 teaspoon*	*1/4 teaspoon*

1. Blanch, shock, and reserve the green beans.

2. Sauté the bacon until crisp. Remove the bacon and drain on absorbent paper toweling.

3. Sauté the shallots in the bacon fat.

4. Add the mushrooms and sauté them.

5. Add the green beans and cook them to the desired doneness. Season to taste with salt and pepper. Sprinkle them with the reserved bacon.

Blanching is explained on page 328.

Cauliflower Polonaise

Yield: 10 servings

Polonaise is a French term referring to a dish prepared in the Polish style, in this case a vegetable served with a garnish of bread crumbs, parsley, and chopped, hard-boiled eggs.

A Blanc may be used to cook the cauliflower to retain its white color; see page 448.

Cauliflower, cut into florets	2 pounds	900 grams
Water	as needed	as needed
Butter	3 ounces	85 grams
Bread crumbs, fresh	3 ounces	85 grams
Eggs, hard-boiled, chopped	2 each	2 each
Parsley, chopped	2 tablespoons	2 tablespoons
Salt, to taste	1/2 teaspoon	1/2 teaspoon
White pepper, to taste	1/2 teaspoon	1/2 teaspoon

1. Boil or steam the cauliflower until it is tender. If necessary, refresh and reheat at service time.

2. Brown the butter lightly in a sautoir. Add the bread crumbs and cook until golden brown.

3. Remove them from the heat; add the chopped egg and parsley and mix well. Season to taste with salt and pepper.

4. Sprinkle the crumb mixture over individual portions of the heated cauliflower.

VARIATION

Asparagus Polonaise: Substitute 2 pounds (900 grams) of peeled asparagus for the cauliflower. The asparagus should be cooked through but slightly firm. Shock if holding for service.

Glazed Turnips

Yield: 10 servings

This recipe works well with any root vegetable: rutabagas, beets, parsnips, carrots, or salsify.

Turnips, battonnet	2 pounds	900 kilograms
Butter	2 ounces	60 grams
Maple syrup	3 fluid ounces	90 milliliters
Nutmeg, ground	1/4 teaspoon	1/4 teaspoon
Cinnamon, ground	1/4 teaspoon	1/4 teaspoon
Salt, to taste	1 teaspoon	1 teaspoon
Pepper, to taste	1/2 teaspoon	1/2 teaspoon
Parsley, chopped	1 teaspoon	1 teaspoon

1. Boil turnips in salted water until tender. When turnips are done, drain.

2. Melt butter in sauté pan and add maple syrup, nutmeg, cinnamon, salt, and pepper.

3. Add turnips and toss until turnips are coated with glaze and hot. Finish with more butter if desired. Garnish with chopped parsley.

Parsnip and Pear Purée

Yield: 10 servings

Parsnips, boiled until tender	*1 1/2 pounds*	*675 grams*
Bartlett pears, boiled until tender	*3/4 pound*	*340 grams*
Heavy cream, heated	*4 fluid ounces*	*120 milliliters*
Salt	*to taste*	*to taste*
White pepper, ground	*to taste*	*to taste*

1. The parsnips and pears should be very hot. Push them through a fine sieve or food mill.

2. Add the hot heavy cream gradually and blend the mixture to a smooth, light purée. Season the purée with salt and pepper to taste.

Additional optional ingredients include caramelized onions, roasted garlic, and boiled potatoes, to be pushed through the food mill with the parsnips and pears. Butter may be used in place of the heavy cream.

The purée goes well with game and other winter dishes.

Belgian Endive à la Meunière

Yield: 10 servings

Belgian endive	*10 each*	*10 each*
Salt	*1 ounce*	*30 grams*
Sugar	*1 ounce*	*30 grams*
Lemon juice	*1 fluid ounce*	*30 milliliters*
Milk, as needed	*4 fluid ounces*	*120 milliliters*
Flour, as needed	*4 ounces*	*115 grams*
Clarified butter, as needed	*4 ounces*	*115 grams*
Lemon juice	*1 fluid ounce*	*30 milliliters*
Parsley, chopped	*1 tablespoon*	*1 tablespoon*

1. Pare the endive cores with a sharp knife and flatten each head slightly.

2. Parcook the endive in water flavored with salt, sugar, and 1 fluid ounce (30 milliliters) of lemon juice; drain it thoroughly.

3. Dip the endive in milk. Dredge the endive in flour; shake off the excess.

4. Sauté the endive in the clarified butter until it is crisp and brown. Finish in a moderate oven, if necessary. Remove from the pan.

5. Deglaze the pan with 1 fluid ounce (30 milliliters) of lemon juice.

6. Add the parsley and swirl it. Pour the pan liquid over the endive; return the endive to the pan to coat.

Summer Squash "Noodles"

Yield: 10 servings

Cut only the brightly colored exterior of the squash. Use a mandolin.

Use the noodles as a side dish in many recipes calling for pasta, or as a bed for sautéed or grilled items.

Yellow squash, long julienne	*1 pound*	*450 grams*
Zucchini, long julienne	*1 pound*	*450 grams*
Leeks, long julienne	*1 pound*	*450 grams*
Butter, or olive oil, as needed	*3 ounces*	*85 grams*
Salt, to taste	*1/2 teaspoon*	*1/2 teaspoon*
Pepper, to taste	*1/2 teaspoon*	*1/2 teaspoon*
Mixed fresh herbs (tarragon, basil, cilantro, oregano), minced	*2 tablespoons*	*2 tablespoons*

1. Toss the yellow squash, zucchini, and leeks together to mix evenly.

2. Heat the butter in a sauté pan over medium heat. Add the julienned vegetables and cook, tossing frequently, until heated through and tender.

3. Season the vegetables with the salt and pepper; add the chopped herbs.

Boiled Carrots

Yield: 10 servings

Use this as a guide for boiling vegetables. It can serve more as a method than a recipe. Cooking times will vary according to the density of the vegetable.

For more information about simmering and boiling, and blanching and parcooking vegetables, see page 328.

Boiled vegetables may be tossed with compound butter, lemon juice, fresh herbs, soy sauce, or a number of other seasonings, depending on desired results.

Carrots, trimmed and cut into even pieces	*2 pounds*	*900 grams*
Water, boiling, salted	*3 quarts*	*3 liters*

1. Add the carrots to the boiling water. If necessary, return the cover to the pot to allow the water to return to boil as quickly as possible.

2. Boil the carrots for 4 to 7 minutes (depending upon the thickness of the cut). Remove them from the water. Serve at once, seasoned as desired, or drain, shock, and reserve.

VARIATIONS

Boiled Green Vegetable: Peel, trim, and cut according to type. Add vegetables to boiling water. Cook uncovered to keep green color.

Boiled Red and Yellow Vegetables: The lid may be left in place to encourage best development of color.

Boiled White Vegetables: Add an acid (lemon juice or vinegar) or use the Blanc on page 448 for the whitest vegetables.

Glazed Carrots

Yield: 10 servings

Butter	*3 ounces*	*85 grams*
Carrots, oblique, battonnet, or sliced	*2 pounds*	*900 grams*
Sugar (optional), to taste	*1 tablespoon*	*1 tablespoon*
Salt, to taste	*1/2 teaspoon*	*1/2 teaspoon*
White pepper, to taste	*1/4 teaspoon*	*1/4 teaspoon*
Chicken Stock	*12 fluid ounces*	*360 milliliters*

1. Melt the butter and add the carrots.

2. Cover the pan and lightly sweat the carrots.

3. Add the sugar, salt, pepper, and stock.

4. Cook, covered, at low heat until the carrots are almost done.

5. Remove the cover and allow the liquid to reduce to a glaze.

Pecan Carrots

Yield: 10 servings

Carrots, oblique	*2 pounds*	*900 grams*
Pecans, toasted, chopped	*1 ounce*	*30 grams*
Chives, chopped	*2 teaspoons*	*2 teaspoons*
Shallots, small dice	*3/4 ounce*	*20 grams*
Honey	*1 1/2 ounces*	*45 grams*
Water, reserved from blanching carrots	*10 fluid ounces*	*300 milliliters*
Salt, to taste	*1/2 teaspoon*	*1/2 teaspoon*
White pepper, to taste	*1/4 teaspoon*	*1/4 teaspoon*

1. Blanch carrots in a microwave or in boiling water.

2. Drain liquid, reserving 10 fluid ounces (300 milliliters) for glaze. Cool carrots on a sheet tray.

3. Mix the shallots, honey, water, salt, and pepper in a sauce pan. Reduce liquid by half.

4. Add carrots and toss until carrots are cooked, coated with the glaze, and the glaze is reduced to a thick syrup.

5. Add the pecans and chives right before service.

Carrots can be glazed in one of two ways. The classic method calls for carrots to be cooked in a lightly sweetened broth that reduces to a thick syrup. Or, they may be prepared by boiling or steaming, then finishing by tossing with honey until heated through and glazed.

If carrots are cooked before a glaze is formed, remove them with a slotted spoon and reduce the liquid. Return the carrots to the pan to finish the process.

If desired, substitute 1 pound (450 grams) parsnips for half the carrots. Water may be used instead of stock.

Salsify is also known as "oyster plant." Once it is peeled and cut, it should be held in acidulated water, or cooked immediately to prevent discoloration.

The sauce may be cooked in a prepared blanc; see page 448.

The recipe for Cream Sauce may be found on page 536.

Carrots and Salsify with Cream

Yield: 10 servings

Carrots, battonnet	*1 pound*	*450 grams*
Salsify, battonnet	*1 pound*	*450 grams*
Lemon juice	*1 fluid ounce*	*30 milliliters*
Flour	*2 tablespoons*	*2 tablespoons*
Butter	*2 ounces*	*60 grams*
Sugar	*1/2 ounce*	*15 grams*
Cream sauce, as needed	*8 fluid ounces*	*240 milliliters*
Salt, to taste	*1/2 teaspoon*	*1/2 teaspoon*
Pepper, to taste	*1/4 teaspoon*	*1/4 teaspoon*

1. Blanch the carrots by steaming or boiling in water.

2. To blanch salsify, add lemon juice and flour to water to keep the salsify white.

3. Drain and reserve the vegetables.

4. Heat the butter and sugar; add the carrots and salsify and cook them thoroughly until they are glazed.

5. Add the Cream Sauce and bring to a simmer, coating thoroughly.

6. Adjust the seasoning with salt and pepper to taste.

Glazed Beets

Yield: 10 servings

Some chefs prefer to bake the beets in the oven for 1 hour rather than boiling them. The belief is that this intensifies their color and flavor. Be sure to pierce them before baking, as you would potatoes.

Fresh beets, trimmed	*2 pounds*	*900 grams*
Butter	*2 ounces*	*60 grams*
Vinegar or lemon juice	*1 tablespoon*	*1 tablespoon*
Sugar, honey, or maple syrup	*2 fluid ounces*	*60 milliliters*
Salt, to taste	*1/2 teaspoon*	*1/2 teaspoon*
Pepper, to taste	*1/4 teaspoon*	*1/4 teaspoon*

1. Boil the beets in their skins until they are tender.

2. Peel and cut them into allumettes.

3. Melt the butter; add the vinegar, sugar, and beets.

4. Cook the beets over high heat, tossing occasionally until they are glazed.

5. Adjust the seasoning with salt and pepper to taste.

Corn Fritters

Yield: 10 servings (3 fritters per serving)

Corn on the cob, husked	1 dozen	1 dozen
Flour	4 ounces	115 grams
Sugar	2 ounces	60 grams
Salt, to taste	1 teaspoon	1 teaspoon
Pepper, to taste	1/4 teaspoon	1/4 teaspoon
Eggs, beaten	2 each	2 each
Cheddar cheese, grated (optional)	2 ounces	60 grams

1. Cut the kernels from the cobs. Scrape well to release all milk.

2. Blend the dry ingredients. Add the corn, eggs, and cheese. Mix to make a batter.

3. Heat the oil for frying to 365°F (180°C) and drop the batter by spoonfuls into the hot oil.

4. Fry until golden brown on all sides. Blot on toweling and serve while very hot.

You may want to add diced red or green pepper to the batter. For more heat, add diced jalapeños or serranos.

Add chili powder to dry ingredients (1 to 2 teaspoons/5 to 10 grams) if desired.

To soufflé the fritters, separate the eggs and add the yolks to the batter. Beat the whites to a medium soft peak and fold them into the corn batter. Fry as directed.

For more information about preparing corn and milking the cob, refer to Chapter 6, pages 198 and 199.

Creamed Corn

Yield: 10 servings

Corn on the cob, husked	10 each	10 each
Leeks, white, fine dice	6 ounces	170 grams
Heavy cream	1 pint	480 milliliters
Salt, to taste	1/2 teaspoon	1/2 teaspoon
Pepper, to taste	1/2 teaspoon	1/2 teaspoon
Nutmeg, ground, to taste	1/8 teaspoon	1/8 teaspoon
Chervil, chopped	1 tablespoon	1 tablespoon

1. Cut the kernels from the cobs. Scrape well to release all milk. Cook over low heat for about 5 minutes.

2. Combine the leeks and the heavy cream; reduce the cream by half.

3. Season the leeks with the salt, pepper, and nutmeg if desired.

4. Add the corn to the reduced cream and leek mixture; stew the corn until it is tender and liquid has reduced.

5. Add the chopped chervil.

Scraping down the cob releases the flesh and juices from the corn for the richest flavor in your creamed corn.

Although leeks and chervil are not essential to this dish, they do provide additional flavor.

Frozen corn may be used if necessary. In that case, you may want to increase the amount of reduced heavy cream.

VEGETABLE SIDE DISHES

Mexican Corn

Yield: 10 servings

Corn on the cob, husked	10 each	10 each
Green peppers, diced	2 ounces	60 grams
Red peppers, diced	2 ounces	60 grams
Butter	1 ounce	30 grams
Salt, to taste	1/2 teaspoon	1/2 teaspoon
Pepper, to taste	1/4 teaspoon	1/4 teaspoon

1. Steam or boil the corn and cut the kernels from the cob.

2. Sauté the peppers in the butter until tender. Add the corn and cook until hot. Adjust the seasoning with salt and pepper to taste.

To intensify the flavor of the corn, dampen the husk and pan-smoke, roast, or grill it. The peppers may be roasted as well.

Jalapeño or roasted New Mexico chilies may be diced and included. Tomato Concassé also makes a good addition.

Garnish with chopped cilantro if desired.

Baked Acorn Squash with Cranberry-Orange Compote

Yield: 12 servings

Butter, melted	6 ounces	170 grams
Brown sugar	4 ounces	115 grams
Acorn squash, halved, seeded	3 each	3 each
Salt, to taste	1/2 teaspoon	1/2 teaspoon
Pepper, to taste	1/4 teaspoon	1/4 teaspoon
Cranberry-orange compote		
Cranberries	1 pound	450 grams
Orange juice	6 fluid ounces	180 milliliters
Water, as needed	4 fluid ounces	120 milliliters
Sugar, as needed	2 tablespoons	2 tablespoons
Orange zest, blanched	2 ounces	60 grams

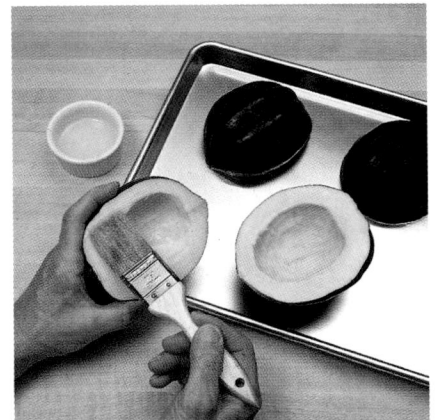

Brush the cut side of the squash lightly with melted-butter glaze, and cook, cut side down, until almost tender.

1. Heat the butter and brown sugar together in a saucepan to make a glaze. Brush it on the squash. Reserve the remainder of the glaze.

2. Bake the squash halves in a moderate oven, cut side down, until they are almost tender. Baste them periodically with the reserved glaze. When almost tender, turn over, prick flesh, and baste with remaining glaze. Finish cooking with cut side up.

3. Combine the cranberries, orange juice, and water to barely cover the berries. Add the sugar to taste. Simmer the berries over medium heat until they are softened and thickened, approximately 10 minutes. Add the orange zest.

4. To serve, cut the squash into wedges; spoon the hot cranberry mixture over the squash.

Red wine may be used to replace some of the water. This will help retain the bright cranberry color.

Use honey or maple syrup to replace brown sugar.

Braised Red Cabbage

Yield: 10 servings

Onions, medium dice	4 ounces	115 grams
Granny Smith apples, diced	8 ounces	225 grams
Vegetable oil, or rendered bacon fat	1 1/2 fluid ounces	45 milliliters
Water	8 fluid ounces	240 milliliters
Red wine	2 fluid ounces	60 milliliters
Red wine vinegar	2 fluid ounces	60 milliliters
Sugar	1 ounce	30 grams
Red currant jelly	2 ounces	60 grams
Cinnamon stick	1 each	1 each
Whole clove	1 each	1 each
Bay leaf	1 each	1 each
Juniper berries	3 each	3 each
Red cabbage, chiffonade	2 pounds	900 grams
Arrowroot	1/2 teaspoon	1/2 teaspoon
Salt, to taste	1/2 teaspoon	1/2 teaspoon
Pepper, to taste	1/2 teaspoon	1/2 teaspoon

Add a little acid (vinegar, wine, or lemon juice) and keep the pot covered as you braise red cabbage to keep it from turning blue or green.

As with choucroute, some chefs prefer to thicken the cabbage with raw grated potatoes rather than arrowroot.

1. Slowly sweat the onions and apples in the oil or bacon fat.

2. Add water, wine, vinegar, sugar, and jelly. Check the flavor; it should be tart and strong.

3. Place the cinnamon stick, clove, bay leaf, and juniper berries in a sachet.

4. Add the cabbage and sachet. Cover the pan and braise the mixture until the apples are tender, checking occasionally to make sure the liquid does not completely evaporate.

5. When the cabbage and apples are cooked; remove the sachet. Mix the arrowroot with cold water or wine. Use this to thicken the cooking liquid slightly if necessary. Adjust the seasoning with salt and pepper to taste.

Braised Lettuce

Yield: 8 servings

Romaine lettuce heads	2 each	2 each
Onions, medium dice	5 ounces	140 grams
Carrots, sliced thin	5 ounces	140 grams
Butter	2 1/2 ounces	70 grams
Brown Veal Stock	10 fluid ounces	300 milliliters
Bacon strips	10 each	10 each
Salt, to taste	1/2 teaspoon	1/2 teaspoon
Pepper, to taste	1/2 teaspoon	1/2 teaspoon

Belgian endive may be substituted for the Romaine. The endive should be prepared individually, one per person, with the bacon wrapped around the outside. There is no need to roll the endive.

Serve one roll per portion on a bed of the cooked onions and carrots, dressed with a bit of the braising liquid.

(Recipe continued on next page)

1. Blanch the lettuce briefly. Shock it in cold water and reserve it.

2. Sweat the onions and carrots in butter, and add the Brown Veal Stock; place the mixture in a baking dish. Simmer 5 minutes.

3. Quarter the romaine lengthwise. Squeeze it to remove any excess water. Remove the cores and roll each quarter "cigar-fashion."

4. Wrap the bacon strips around each roll. Place the rolls in the reserved liquid.

5. Adjust the seasoning with salt and pepper to taste. Braise the lettuce, covered, in a 375°F (175°C) oven until the bacon is completely cooked. Brown the bacon under a salamander or broiler before serving.

Ratatouille

Yield: 10 servings

Use a light tomato purée or tomato juice to replace some or all of the stock.

Add herbs as available or desired; oregano, marjoram, and thyme would all be suitable.

Add a Bouquet Garni or Sachet d' E´pices during cooking time if desired.

Garlic, minced	*1 tablespoon*	*1 tablespoon*
Olive oil	*1 fluid ounce*	*30 milliliters*
Shallots, minced	*1 tablespoon*	*1 tablespoon*
Red onions, small dice	*3 1/2 ounces*	*100 grams*
Tomato paste	*1 ounce*	*30 grams*
Chicken or Vegetable Stock	*12 fluid ounces*	*360 milliliters*
Yellow squash, seeded, small dice	*3 1/2 ounces*	*100 grams*
Zucchini, seeded, small dice	*8 ounces*	*225 grams*
Green peppers, small dice	*3 ounces*	*85 grams*
Eggplant, peeled, medium dice	*6 ounces*	*170 grams*
Mushrooms, quartered or sliced	*12 ounces*	*340 grams*
Tomato Concassé	*6 ounces*	*170 grams*
Salt, to taste	*1/2 teaspoon*	*1/2 teaspoon*
White pepper, to taste	*1/2 teaspoon*	*1/2 teaspoon*
Basil, chopped	*2 tablespoons*	*2 tablespoons*

1. Sauté the garlic in the oil. Add the shallots and sauté until they are soft.

2. Add the red onions and sauté until soft.

3. Add the tomato paste and sauté the mixture briefly.

4. Combine the vegetables and stew covered, until the vegetables are very tender.

5. At service time, season the ratatouille to taste with salt, pepper, and chopped basil.

Stewed Tomatoes Creole

Yield: 10 servings

Onions, small dice	4 ounces	120 grams
Garlic, cloves, minced	2 each	2 each
Green peppers, small dice	2 ounces	60 grams
Red peppers, small dice	2 ounces	60 grams
Vegetable oil	1 fluid ounce	30 milliliters
Zucchini, small dice	6 ounces	170 grams
Mushrooms, small dice	4 ounces	115 grams
Tomatoes, peeled and seeded	1 pound	450 grams
White wine, dry	4 fluid ounces	120 milliliters
Vegetable Stock	8 fluid ounces	240 milliliters
Okra, sliced	1 pound	450 grams
Basil, chopped	1 teaspoon	1 teaspoon
Oregano, chopped	1/2 teaspoon	1/2 teaspoon
Parsley, chopped	1 teaspoon	1 teaspoon
Salt, to taste	1/2 teaspoon	1/2 teaspoon
Pepper, to taste	1/2 teaspoon	1/2 teaspoon

1. Sauté onions, garlic, and peppers in oil until onions are translucent and peppers are tender.

2. Add zucchini and mushrooms; sauté 2 to 3 minutes.

3. Dice the tomatoes; add them to the zucchini mixture with the wine and stock. Bring to a simmer.

4. Add the okra; stew until the ingredients are cooked and the flavor is well developed.

5. Add parsley; season and serve.

Choose the smallest okra pods you can find for this dish.

Place individual or family-size servings of the stew into gratin dishes or timbales. Top with Garlic Croutons and grated Parmesan cheese. Broil to lightly brown in a broiler or under a salamander.

Grilled Ratatouille Provençale

Yield: 10 servings

The classic Ratatouille is a combination of sautéed vegetables (see page 806). This variation grills the vegetables first, adding a new level of flavors.

An excellent side dish for an omelette and fries at brunch or steak and fries (steak frites) at dinner.

This recipe may also be used as a topping for pizza or tossed with pasta. Garnish pizza or pasta with Niçoise olives, Parmesan cheese, and anchovies.

Ratatouille may also be served chilled or at room temperature.

Store any remaining garlic-rosemary oil in the refrigerator. It may be used for seasoning in sautéeing or in vinaigrettes and mayonnaises.

Garlic-rosemary oil		
Garlic, cloves, peeled, cut in half	*25 each*	*25 each*
Olive oil	*1 pint*	*480 milliliters*
Rosemary sprigs	*5 each*	*5 each*
Zucchini, trimmed, sliced	*8 each*	*8 each*
Eggplants, sliced thick	*5 each*	*5 each*
Onions, sliced	*3 each*	*3 each*
Tomato Concassé	*8 ounces*	*225 grams*
Green peppers, roasted, skinned, and seeded, batonnet	*3 each*	*3 each*
Red peppers, roasted, skinned, and seeded, batonnet	*3 each*	*3 each*
Sugar, if necessary	*1 teaspoon*	*1 teaspoon*
Salt, to taste	*1/2 teaspoon*	*1/2 teaspoon*
Pepper, to taste	*1/2 teaspoon*	*1/2 teaspoon*
Balsamic vinegar	*1 fluid ounce*	*30 milliliters*
Basil leaves, chiffonade	*20 each*	*20 each*

1. To make garlic-rosemary oil: Put garlic in a large, shallow pan and add oil to barely cover. Add rosemary sprigs and simmer, partially covered, over very low heat, until garlic is cooked but not falling apart; 15 to 20 minutes.

2. Blanch and shock zucchini. Brush with garlic-rosemary oil and grill to mark, about 3 minutes.

3. Brush eggplant on both sides with oil. Grill, turning, until just charred, about 7 minutes. Chop into medium dice. Repeat this procedure with onion slices.

4. Put garlic and 1 ounce (30 milliliters) of remaining oil in a large, deep saucepan and heat over medium flame. Add grilled vegetables, peppers, and tomatoes; stir gently over medium heat to finish cooking vegetables and blend flavors.

5. Season with sugar, salt, pepper, and balsamic vinegar. Garnish with basil chiffonade.

Grilled Vegetables

Yield: 10 servings

Vegetables, assorted, according to season	*2 1/4 pounds*	*1 kilogram*
Marinade		
Vegetable oil	*1 pint*	*480 milliliters*
Soy sauce	*5 fluid ounces*	*150 milliliters*
Lemon juice	*1 fluid ounce*	*30 milliliters*
Garlic, minced	*1 tablespoon*	*1 tablespoon*
Fennel seeds, whole	*1/2 teaspoon*	*1/2 teaspoon*
Salt, to taste	*1 teaspoon*	*1 teaspoon*
Pepper, to taste	*1 teaspoon*	*1 teaspoon*

Vegetables that grill well include eggplant, zucchini, summer squash, onions, tomatoes, Belgian endive, potatoes, squashes, radicchio, and radishes.

Include in the marinade gingerroot, scallions, chilies, rice wine vinegar, fresh herbs, or any other seasonings you desire.

For other marinade suggestions, see pages 430 to 434.

1. Slice the vegetables into pieces thick enough to withstand the grill's heat. If necessary, parcook or blanch the vegetables prior to grilling them.

2. Combine all the ingredients for the marinade. Coat the vegetables evenly with the marinade. Let any excess drain completely away from the vegetables.

3. Place the vegetables on a hot grill; grill them on both sides (the time will vary depending upon the type of vegetable and thickness of the cut), turning each once to create crosshatch marks, if desired.

4. Complete the cooking on the second side. Brush with the marinade throughout cooking time.

VARIATION

Mediterranean-Style Grilled Vegetables: Select a good variety of vegetables. Cut them into slices about 3/4 inch (1 centimeter), leaving them rather large. Grill as directed, using an infused oil for the marinade, then cut into strips and toss with plumped raisins, toasted pine nuts, and capers. Drizzle with additional olive oil.

Shiitake stems are too tough to include in many preparations, but they can be reserved to use in broths and essences.

Once grilled, the mushrooms can be returned to the marinade, allowed to cool to room temperature and added to salads or other dishes as a garnish.

Serve this as an appetizer, along with goat cheese wrapped in phyllo, a salad of roasted peppers, or other accompaniments.

For information about toasting seeds, see Chapter 6, page 203.

Grilled Shiitake Mushrooms with Soy-Sesame Glaze

Yield: 10 servings

Shiitake mushrooms, stems removed	1 1/2 pounds	680 grams
Soy-sesame glaze		
Soy sauce or tamari	4 fluid ounces	120 milliliters
Water	2 fluid ounces	60 milliliters
Peanut or corn oil	2 fluid ounces	60 milliliters
Tahini paste	2 ounces	60 grams
Sesame oil	1 tablespoon	1 tablespoon
Garlic, minced	1 tablespoon	1 tablespoon
Ginger, minced	2 teaspoons	2 teaspoons
Hot pepper flakes (optional)	1/2 teaspoon	1/2 teaspoon
Scallions, trimmed, left whole	2 bunches	2 bunches
Sesame seeds, toasted	2 tablespoons	2 tablespoons

1. Wipe the mushroom caps with a soft cloth to clean. If desired, slice large caps in half.

2. Blend all ingredients for the glaze in a bowl, add mushrooms and scallions, and marinate 15 to 60 minutes.

3. Remove the mushrooms and scallions from the glaze and allow the excess to drain away.

4. Grill mushrooms and scallions until they are marked on all sides and cooked through.

5. Garnish with sesame seeds and serve at once.

Here the vegetables are finished in butter. Finishing can also be done in a small amount of stock, cream, or sauce.

Vegetables "Jardinière"

Yield: 10 servings

Carrots, battonnet	8 ounces	240 grams
Celery, battonnet	6 ounces	170 grams
White turnips, battonnet	8 ounces	240 grams
Peas, fresh	8 ounces	240 grams
Butter	3 ounces	85 grams
Parsley, chopped	1 tablespoon	1 tablespoon
Salt, to taste	1/2 teaspoon	1/2 teaspoon
Pepper, to taste	1/2 teaspoon	1/2 teaspoon
Sugar, to taste	1/2 teaspoon	1/2 teaspoon

(Recipe continued on facing page)

1. Blanch vegetables separately in boiling salted water, shock, and drain.

2. Reheat vegetables by tossing in butter over medium heat.

3. Add parsley, salt, pepper, and sugar, if desired.

Macédoine of Vegetables

Yield: 10 servings

Mushrooms, quartered	*2 ounces*	*60 grams*
Shallots, minced	*2 tablespoons*	*2 tablespoons*
Butter	*2 ounces*	*60 grams*
Onions, large dice	*2 ounces*	*60 grams*
Celery, large dice	*4 ounces*	*115 grams*
Carrots, large dice, parcooked	*6 ounces*	*170 grams*
White turnips, large dice, parcooked	*6 ounces*	*170 grams*
Rutabaga, large dice, parcooked	*6 ounces*	*170 grams*
Red peppers, large dice	*2 ounces*	*60 grams*
Chives, finely cut	*1 tablespoon*	*1 tablespoon*
Tarragon, chopped	*1 tablespoon*	*1 tablespoon*
Basil, chiffonade	*1 tablespoon*	*1 tablespoon*
Salt, to taste	*1 teaspoon*	*1 teaspoon*
Pepper, to taste	*1/2 teaspoon*	*1/2 teaspoon*

Use any compatible combination of vegetables in this dish. Vary seasonings and herbs as desired.

For more information about parcooking vegetables, refer to chapter 10, page 328.

1. Sauté the mushrooms and shallots in butter until their moisture is reduced.

2. Add the onion and celery and sauté until the onions are translucent.

3. Add the remaining vegetables; sauté until they are heated through and tender.

4. Add the herbs; toss them to mix. Adjust the seasoning with salt and pepper to taste. Serve.

Broccoli in Garlic Sauce

Yield: 10 servings

To make a cornstarch slurry, add cold water to cornstarch and mix well to form a very thin paste. Add the slurry to a boiling liquid a little at a time to avoid overthickening.

Broccoli, peeled, cut into small pieces	2 pounds	900 grams
Garlic sauce		
Garlic, mashed to a paste	1 tablespoon	1 tablespoon
Oil, as needed	1 tablespoon	1 tablespoon
Sherry	2 fluid ounces	60 milliliters
Rice vinegar	2 fluid ounces	60 milliliters
Soy sauce	2 fluid ounces	60 milliliters
Hot bean paste	1 tablespoons	2 tablespoons
Sugar	1 ounces	30 grams
Chicken Stock	1 pint	480 milliliters
Cornstarch slurry	2 fluid ounces	60 milliliters
Peanut oil	2 fluid ounces	60 milliliters
Ginger, minced	1 tablespoon	1 tablespoon
Garlic, minced	2 tablespoon	2 tablespoons
Scallions, chopped	3 each	3 each
Red pepper, julienne or shredded	1/2 pound	115 grams

1. Blanch broccoli in boiling water, shock, and drain (do not overcook).

2. To make the sauce: Sweat the garlic in a little oil. Combine all ingredients, bring to a boil, thicken with cornstarch slurry to medium consistency.

3. To finish the broccoli, heat the oil, add the ginger, garlic, and scallions, stir-fry until aromatic. Add red pepper and broccoli and stir-fry until tender. Add sauce and bring to the simmer. Serve at once.

Garden Treasures

Yield: 10 servings

Broccoli, peeled, cut in medium-size pieces	8 ounces	225 grams
Carrots, medium dice	8 ounces	225 grams
Celery, medium dice	8 ounces	225 grams
Peanut or corn oil	3 fluid ounces	90 milliliters
Ginger, minced	2 teaspoons	2 teaspoons
Garlic, minced	2 teaspoons	2 teaspoons
Scallion, sliced on the bias	4 ounces	115 grams
Zucchini, medium dice	8 ounces	225 grams

(Recipe continued on facing page)

Yellow squash, medium dice	8 ounces	225 grams
Salt, to taste	1 teaspoon	1 teaspoon
White pepper, to taste	1/2 teaspoon	1/2 teaspoon
Sesame oil	1 tablespoon	1 tablespoon

Blanching is explained in Chapter 10, page 328.

1. Blanch broccoli, carrots, and celery in boiling water (do not overcook).

2. Heat oil, add ginger, garlic and scallion, stir-fry.

3. Add broccoli, carrots and celery, stir-fry briefly, then add zucchini and yellow squash, stir-fry until tender.

4. Add salt, pepper, and sesame oil; mix together.

5. Serve while very hot.

Gingered Green Beans and Cabbage

Yield: 10 servings

Green beans	20 ounces	570 grams
Peanut oil	2 fluid ounces	60 milliliters
Ginger, minced	1 ounce	30 grams
Garlic, mashed to a paste	1 tablespoon	1 tablespoon
Lemongrass, minced	1 stalk	1 stalk
Napa cabbage, sliced	20 ounces	570 grams
Salt, to taste	1/2 teaspoon	1/2 teaspoon
Pepper, to taste	1/4 teaspoon	1/4 teaspoon
Hot bean paste	2 teaspoons	2 teaspoons
Sugar, to taste	1 teaspoon	1 teaspoon

The green beans can weep or wrinkle as they are held. To avoid this, prepare the green beans in small batches and do not hold them for extended periods.

1. Blanch the beans in boiling salted water until they are tender-crisp and bright green. Drain well. Rinse to cool if necessary.

2. Heat the oil in a wok, add ginger, garlic, lemongrass, and beans, stir-fry until aromatic.

3. Add cabbage, and stir-fry until the cabbage has just become limp.

4. Add salt, pepper, bean paste, and sugar to taste.

Hot and Spicy Eggplant

Yield: 10 servings

This dish may be served as a meatless entrée. Accompany it with additional sauce and serve with steamed rice and additional vegetables.

Japanese eggplant	2 1/4 pounds	1 kilogram
Sauce		
Hot bean paste	2 teaspoons	2 teaspoons
Rice vinegar	1 fluid ounce	30 milliliters
Sugar	2 teaspoons	2 teaspoons
Soy sauce	2 fluid ounces	60 milliliters
Chicken Stock	1 pint	480 milliliters
Oyster sauce	1 fluid ounce	30 milliliters
Sesame oil	2 teaspoons	2 teaspoons
Cornstarch slurry, as needed	2 teaspoons	2 teaspoons
Oil (as needed to stir-fry)	2 fluid ounces	60 milliliters
Ginger, minced	1 teaspoon	1 teaspoon
Garlic, minced	1 teaspoon	1 teaspoon
Scallion, chopped	1 tablespoon	1 tablespoon
Preserved vegetables, fine dice	2 ounces	60 grams
Green peppers, fine dice	4 ounces	115 grams
Red peppers, fine dice	4 ounces	115 grams
Salt, as needed	1/2 teaspoon	1/2 teaspoon

1. Peel eggplant, cut into 2-inch (5-centimeter) strips, steam for 8 minutes, remove and let it cool.

2. To make the sauce: Combine all ingredients except the cornstarch slurry and bring to a boil.

3. Thicken sauce with slurry, adding just enough to thicken the sauce to a coating consistency.

4. To finish the eggplant, heat the oil in a wok, add ginger, garlic, scallion, and preserved vegetables, stir-fry until aromatic.

5. Add peppers, stir-fry until tender; add eggplant and sauce, stir-fry until well mixed, check seasoning, add sesame oil to taste.

Hot and Spicy Mixed Vegetables

Yield: 10 servings

Carrots, medium dice	*8 ounces*	*225 grams*
Vegetable oil	*1 fluid ounce*	*30 milliliters*
Ginger, minced	*1/2 teaspoon*	*1/2 teaspoon*
Garlic, minced	*1/2 teaspoon*	*1/2 teaspoon*
Scallions, chopped	*1 tablespoon*	*1 tablespoon*
Broccoli, medium dice	*12 ounces*	*340 grams*
Celery, medium dice	*4 ounces*	*15 grams*
Zucchini, medium dice	*2 ounces*	*340 grams*
Yellow squash, medium dice	*8 ounces*	*225 grams*
Asparagus, medium dice	*8 ounces*	*225 grams*
Hot bean paste	*1/2 teaspoon*	*1/2 teaspoon*
Salt	*1/2 teaspoon*	*1/2 teaspoon*
Soy sauce	*1 tablespoon*	*1 tablespoon*
Oyster sauce	*1 tablespoon*	*1 tablespoon*
Sesame oil	*2 teaspoons*	*2 teaspoons*

1. Blanch carrots, shock, and drain.

2. Heat oil, add ginger, garlic and scallions, stir-fry; add vegetables according to firmness, stir-fry until vegetables are done.

3. Add bean paste, salt, soy sauce, oyster sauce, and sesame oil, mix together.

Rainbow Garden

Yield: 10 servings

Celery, shredded	*4 ounces*	*115 grams*
Carrots, shredded	*12 ounces*	*340 grams*
Oil	*2 fluid ounces*	*60 milliliters*
Ginger, minced	*1 teaspoon*	*1 teaspoon*
Garlic, minced	*1 teaspoon*	*1 teaspoon*
Scallions, chopped	*1 tablespoon*	*1 tablespoon*
Zucchini, shredded	*12 ounces*	*340 grams*
Daikon, shredded	*6 ounces*	*170 grams*
Yellow squash, shredded	*6 ounces*	*170 grams*
Light soy sauce	*1 fluid ounce*	*30 milliliters*
Oyster sauce	*1 fluid ounces*	*30 milliliters*

1. Blanch celery and carrots (do not overcook).

2. Heat oil, add ginger, garlic, and scallions, stir-fry; add vegetables and stir-fry until tender, add soy and oyster sauces.

Transfer the coated vegetables immediately into the hot oil. For the best results, keep the batter chilled until right before you use it.

The recipe for Tempura Batter may be found on page 788.

Vegetable Tempura

Yield: 10 servings

Vegetables, assorted, cut into small pieces	*2 1/4 pounds*	*1 kilogram*
Tempura Batter, chilled	*as needed*	*as needed*
Dipping sauce	*20 fluid ounces*	*600 milliliters*

1. Blot the vegetables dry before coating them with batter.

2. Coat the vegetables evenly with the batter. The batter should not be too thick.

3. Deep-fry the vegetables by the swimming method until the batter is golden brown and puffy. Remove from the fryer with a spider and blot them briefly on absorbent toweling.

4. Serve the vegetables with a dipping sauce (honey-mustard or soy sauce, or sesame and ginger, for example).

CHAPTER *22* | *Potato, Grain, and Pasta Dishes*

The recipes in this chapter make excellent side dishes to accompany entrée selections. Some can be adapted to make entrées—some meatless, some with fish, chicken, or meats. Pastas and risottos can be portioned into suitable appetizers or selections on an hors d'oeuvre buffet. The recipes have been grouped as follows:

- *Boiled Potatoes*
- *Baked Potatoes*
- *Potato Casseroles*
- *Panfried and Sauteéd Potatoes*
- *Potato Purées*
- *Deep-Fried Potatoes*
- *Rice—Boiled and Pilafs*
- *Risotto*
- *Cornmeal Dishes*
- *Other Grains*
- *Beans*
- *Pasta*
- *Dumplings*

Steamed New Potatoes with Fines Herbes

Yield: 10 servings

New red potatoes	*2 1/4 pounds*	*1 kilogram*
Butter, melted, hot	*2 ounces*	*60 grams*
Fines Herbes	*2 tablespoons*	*2 tablespoons*
Salt, to taste	*1/2 teaspoon*	*1/2 teaspoon*
Pepper, to taste	*1/4 teaspoon*	*1/4 teaspoon*

Select potatoes that are of a uniform size. Very small potatoes, about the size of a walnut, are very good when prepared this way.

Fines Herbes are on page 427.

1. Scrub the potatoes, but do not peel them.

2. Steam the potatoes over boiling water in a steamer until they are tender (can be pierced easily with a paring knife).

3. Roll the potatoes in the melted butter and herbs. Season them to taste with salt and pepper and serve.

Boiled Parslied Potatoes

Yield: 10 servings

Potatoes, tournéed	*2 1/4 pounds*	*1 kilogram*
Butter	*2 ounces*	*60 grams*
Parsley, chopped	*3 tablespoons*	*3 tablespoons*
Salt, to taste	*1/2 teaspoon*	*1/2 teaspoon*
Pepper, to taste	*1/4 teaspoon*	*1/4 teaspoon*

Hold the potatoes in water to prevent discoloration until it is time to cook them.

1. Place the potatoes in a pot with enough cold water to cover them by about 2 inches (5 centimeters). Gradually bring the water to a simmer over an open burner. Simmer the potatoes until they are easily pierced with the tip of a paring knife.

2. Drain the potatoes. Return them to the pot and let them dry briefly over very low heat until no more steam rises from the potatoes, or spread them out on a sheet pan and dry them in a low oven.

3. Heat the butter in a sauteuse over medium heat. Add the potatoes; roll and toss them to coat evenly with butter; heat them through.

4. Add the parsley, salt, and pepper. Toss the potatoes to coat. Serve them immediately.

VARIATION

Potatoes with Lemon and Thyme: Boil potatoes as directed. Roll in hot butter to finish and season with lemon juice and chopped thyme leaves.

Baked Idaho Potatoes with Fried Onions

Yield: 10 servings

Idaho potatoes	10 each	10 each
Sour cream	10 fluid ounces	300 milliliters
Chives, minced	2 tablespoons	2 tablespoons
Onions, large, sliced thin	1 each	1 each
Salt, to taste	1 teaspoon	1 teaspoon
Flour	2 ounces	60 grams
Cornstarch	2 ounces	60 grams
White pepper, to taste	1/2 teaspoon	1/2 teaspoon

1. Pierce the potatoes with a kitchen fork or knife. Bake in a 425°F (220°C) oven for about 1 hour, or until very tender and cooked through.

2. Blend the sour cream and chives and reserve for service.

3. Separate the onion slices into rings.

4. Combine the flour, cornstarch, salt, and pepper. Add the onion and toss to coat well.

5. Deep-fry the onions in 375°F (190°C) oil until very crisp. Drain on toweling.

6. To serve, pinch or cut open the potato, place a dollop of sour cream with chopped chives on the flesh and top with onions.

Idaho or russet potatoes are a high-starch variety. They become mealy and fluffy after baking.

Some chefs rub potatoes with either oil or coarse salt to develop a crisp skin.

Baked Stuffed Potatoes

Yield: 10 servings

Idaho potatoes	10 each	10 each
Butter, softened	2 ounces	60 grams
Salt, to taste	1/2 teaspoon	1/2 teaspoon
Pepper, to taste	1/4 teaspoon	1/4 teaspoon
Egg yolk	1 each	1 each
Cream or milk, hot, as needed	4 fluid ounces	120 milliliters
Parmesan cheese (optional)	2 ounces	60 grams

1. Bake the potatoes until they are tender as directed above.

2. Remove the tops of the potatoes by slicing them lengthwise. Scoop out the potato pulp.

3. Rice the pulp while very hot and mix with the butter, salt, and pepper. Work in the egg yolk and hot cream or milk.

4. Pipe the potato mixture back into the shells.

5. Sprinkle the potatoes with Parmesan. Return them to the oven until they are heated through and lightly browned on top.

These potatoes may be known as "Pommes au Four," Potatoes Jackson, or Twice-Baked Potatoes.

Add grated cheese (Cheddar, gruyère, Parmesan or fresh goat cheese) to the filling.

Roasted Potatoes with Garlic and Rosemary

Yield: 10 servings

Potatoes that are quite small (quail's egg size) may be left whole. Large potatoes may be cut into wedges or large dice as desired. Cooking time may vary from 45 minutes to one hour.

Potatoes, Red Bliss, medium	2 1/4 pounds	1 kilogram
Olive oil	1 fluid ounce	30 milliliters
Garlic, minced	1 tablespoon	1 tablespoon
Rosemary leaves	1 tablespoon	1 tablespoon
Salt, to taste	1 teaspoon	1 teaspoon
Pepper, to taste	1/2 teaspoon	1/2 teaspoon

1. Scrub the potatoes and dry them thoroughly. Cut if necessary.

2. Combine oil, garlic, rosemary, salt, and pepper in a bowl. Roll the potatoes in this mixture until they are evenly coated.

3. Bake the potatoes on an oiled sheet pan until they are tender (can be easily pierced with a paring knife). Serve while very hot.

Potatoes au Gratin

Yield: 10 servings

Idaho potatoes will release enough starch as they cook to thicken the milk and cream. However, you may prefer to make this dish using a prepared Mornay Sauce (see page 535).

To make Scalloped Potatoes, slice potatoes directly into a baking dish containing the milk and seasonings. Spread into an even layer; bake at 350°F (175°C) for 1 to 1 1/2 hours or until a crust forms.

Idaho potatoes, peeled and sliced 1/8-inch (.25-centimeter) thick	2 1/4 pounds	1 kilogram
Milk, cold	1 pint	480 milliliters
Heavy cream, hot	1 pint	480 milliliters
Salt, to taste	1/2 teaspoon	1/2 teaspoon
Pepper, to taste	1/4 teaspoon	1/4 teaspoon
Nutmeg, ground, to taste	pinch	pinch
Gruyère cheese, grated	5 ounces	140 grams
Parmesan cheese, grated	4 ounces	115 grams
Bread crumbs, fresh	3 ounces	85 grams
Butter	3 ounces	85 grams

1. Add the potatoes to the milk and bring it to a boil. Simmer until the potatoes are parcooked.

2. Add the cream and season the potatoes to taste with the salt, pepper, and nutmeg.

3. Layer the potatoes in a buttered hotel pan, alternating them with the grated cheeses. Finish with cheese on top. Sprinkle with bread crumbs and dot with butter.

4. Bake the gratin in a slow oven (300 to 325°F/150 to 165°C), loosely covered, until the potatoes are cooked, about 30 to 45 minutes. Remove the cover and bake until the cheese is browned and a crust has formed.

Dauphinoise Potatoes

Yield: 10 servings

Milk, scalded and cooled	24 fluid ounces	720 milliliters
Eggs, beaten	2 each	2 each
Salt, to taste	1/2 teaspoon	1/2 teaspoon
Pepper, to taste	1/4 teaspoon	1/4 teaspoon
Nutmeg, ground (optional)	pinch	pinch
Butter, softened	1 ounce	30 grams
Garlic clove, crushed	1 each	1 each
Potatoes, peeled, sliced thin	2 1/4 pounds	1 kilogram
Gruyère cheese, grated	5 ounces	140 grams

1. Combine the milk, eggs, salt, pepper, and nutmeg. Heat the mixture but do not boil it; it should thicken slightly.

2. Butter a hotel pan and rub it with the crushed garlic clove.

3. Layer the potatoes in the hotel pan. Add the milk and the egg mixture. Top it with the grated cheese.

4. Cover and bake the potatoes in a bain-marie at 300°F (150°C) until they are tender, about 1 1/2 hours. Uncover them and let the cheese brown lightly.

Add sliced truffles to the potatoes as they are layered into the pan.

Savoyarde Potatoes

Yield: 10 servings

Chef's potatoes, peeled and sliced thin	2 1/4 pounds	1 kilogram
Butter, softened	1 ounce	30 grams
Garlic clove, crushed	1 each	1 each
White Stock or broth	24 fluid ounces	720 milliliters
Eggs	2 each	2 each
Gruyère cheese, grated	6 ounces	170 grams
Salt, to taste	1/2 teaspoon	1/2 teaspoon
Pepper, to taste	1/4 teaspoon	1/4 teaspoon
Nutmeg, ground (optional)	pinch	pinch

1. Layer the potatoes in a casserole that has been liberally buttered and rubbed with the garlic clove.

2. Bring the stock to a boil. Remove it from the heat and allow to cool slightly. Add the eggs and season the mixture to taste with the salt, pepper, and nutmeg.

3. Pour the stock mixture over the potatoes.

4. Top the potatoes with the Gruyère cheese.

5. Cover the casserole and cook in a slow oven (300°F/150°C) until the potatoes are very tender, about 1 1/2 hours. Remove the cover and continue baking until the crust is golden.

A bain-marie (water bath) is important in these classic potato casseroles. They require very gentle cooking in order to produce a very smooth, creamy texture.

Sweet Potatoes Baked in Cider with Currants and Cinnamon

Sweet potatoes have a higher moisture content than most white potatoes. This means that they may cook a little more quickly than the previous potato casseroles.

For extra sweetness uncover in the last few minutes and sprinkle with brown sugar.

Yield: 10 servings

Sweet potatoes, peeled and sliced thin	*2 1/4 pounds*	*1.1 kilogram*
Butter	*2 ounces*	*60 grams*
Shallots, minced	*1 ounce*	*30 grams*
Apple cider, unpasteurized	*8 fluid ounces*	*240 milliliters*
Currants, plumped	*2 ounces*	*60 grams*
Cinnamon, ground	*1 teaspoon*	*1 teaspoon*
Salt, to taste	*1/2 teaspoon*	*1/2 teaspoon*
Pepper, to taste	*1/4 teaspoon*	*1/4 teaspoon*

1. Shingle the sweet potato slices in a well-buttered casserole or gratin dish. Sprinkle them with the shallots. Add the cider; there should be enough to thoroughly moisten the potatoes.

2. Add the currants and cinnamon. Cover the dish loosely with aluminum foil and bake the potatoes at 325°F (165°C) until they are very tender. Season them with salt and pepper. Serve them immediately.

Hash Brown Potatoes

Potatoes can be diced or shredded.

Homefries are made by cooking raw diced potatoes as directed for hash browns. The skillet should be covered to "steam" them, then removed so they will brown properly.

Yield: 10 servings

Vegetable oil	*as needed*	*as needed*
Potatoes, peeled and cooked, small or medium dice or shredded	*2 1/4 pounds*	*1 kilogram*
Salt, to taste	*1/2 teaspoon*	*1/2 teaspoon*
Pepper, to taste	*1/4 teaspoon*	*1/4 teaspoon*
Parsley, chopped	*2 teaspoons*	*2 teaspoons*

1. Heat the oil in a griswold. Add the potatoes and season them with the salt and pepper.

2. Cook the potatoes until they are heated through, stirring occasionally.

3. Allow the potatoes to brown well on the bottom; turn the entire cake and brown it on the other side. Garnish with parsley and serve.

VARIATIONS

Lyonnaise Potatoes: Sauté 8 ounces (225 grams) of sliced onions before adding the potatoes.

O'Brien Potatoes: Sauté 4 ounces (115 grams) each of red and green peppers before adding the potatoes.

Potatoes Hashed in Cream

Yield: 10 servings

Chef's potatoes (waxy)	*2 1/4 pounds*	*1 kilogram*
Milk or light cream, heated	*24 fluid ounces*	*720 milliliters*
Salt, to taste	*1/2 teaspoon*	*1/2 teaspoon*
Pepper, to taste	*1/4 teaspoon*	*1/4 teaspoon*

1. Parcook the potatoes in boiling, salted water.

2. Drain them well, cool until they can be handled easily, then peel and cut into a small dice.

3. Combine the potatoes and the heated cream in a sautoir. Simmer the potatoes until they are completely cooked and the milk is thickened. Season to taste with salt and pepper.

To make a breakfast menu option from this dish, add ham and peas and top with a poached egg.

Châteaubriand Potatoes

Yield: 10 servings

Chef potatoes	*2 1/4 pounds*	*1 kilogram*
Butter	*2 ounces*	*60 grams*
Parsley, chopped	*1 ounce*	*30 grams*
Glace de Viande	*2 ounces*	*60 grams*
Salt, to taste	*1/2 teaspoon*	*1/2 teaspoon*
Pepper, to taste	*1/4 teaspoon*	*1/4 teaspoon*

1. Tourné the potatoes to the approximate size of olives.

2. Cook them over moderate heat in the butter until they are tender and have a golden exterior.

3. Add the parsley; season to taste.

This is the traditional accompaniment to steaks from the beef tenderloin prepared as Châteaubriand.

Reserve the potato trimmings for soups, chowders, and to use as thickeners in such recipes as choucroute.

Potato Pancakes

Yield: 10 servings

Potato pancakes are often served with braised meats. Serve sour cream or applesauce with them.

The cooking method for potato pancakes is illustrated on page 321.

Potatoes, peeled	*2 1/4 pounds*	*1 kilogram*
Onions, trimmed	*1 pound*	*450 grams*
Lemon juice, to taste	*1 fluid ounce*	*30 milliliters*
Eggs	*2 each*	*2 each*
Salt, to taste	*1/2 teaspoon*	*1/2 teaspoon*
Pepper, to taste	*1/4 teaspoon*	*1/4 teaspoon*
Bread flour	*1 ounce*	*30 grams*
Matzo meal, as needed	*1 ounce*	*30 grams*
Vegetable oil	*4 fluid ounces*	*120 milliliters*

1. Grind or grate the potatoes and onions together; toss them with the lemon juice to prevent discoloration.

2. Place the grated potatoes and onions in a cheesecloth; squeeze out the liquid. Place them in a stainless steel bowl.

3. Add all the remaining ingredients, except the oil.

4. Heat 1/4 inch (.50 centimeter) of the oil in a griswold.

5. Drop the potato batter into the hot oil by level serving spoons. When the pancakes are lightly browned, turn them and brown the other side. Finish them in a 375°F (190°C) oven until they are brown and crisp.

Roësti Potatoes

Yield: 10 servings

Coarsely grate cooked potatoes for this dish.

This is often served with Swiss-Style Shredded Veal (page 579).

Yukon Gold or Yellow Thin potatoes	*2 1/4 pounds*	*1 kilogram*
Clarified butter, as needed	*3 ounces*	*85 grams*
Salt, to taste	*1/2 teaspoon*	*1/2 teaspoon*
Pepper, to taste	*1/4 teaspoon*	*1/4 teaspoon*
Butter, whole	*2 ounces*	*60 grams*

1. Parcook the potatoes until they are slightly underdone. Cool and store them under refrigeration until needed. Peel and coarsely grate the potatoes.

2. Heat a well-seasoned sauté pan and add a small amount of the clarified butter.

3. Place the potatoes in the heated pan with the remaining clarified butter. Season with salt and pepper, and dot the outside edge with whole butter.

4. Cook the potatoes until they are golden brown and form a cake. Turn the entire cake, dot the edge with the whole butter, and cook the other side until golden brown and heated through.

Potatoes Anna

Yield: 10 servings

Potatoes, long yellow	2 1/4 pounds	1 kilogram
Salt, to taste	1/2 teaspoon	1/2 teaspoon
Pepper, to taste	1/4 teaspoon	1/4 teaspoon
Butter, clarified	4 to 8 ounces	115 to 125 grams

1. Peel the potatoes and trim them into uniform cylinders. Cut the cylinders into thin slices.

2. Arrange the potatoes in layers in a buttered sautoir. Season each layer with salt and pepper and sprinkle with clarified butter.

3. Cover the potatoes and begin cooking them on the stove top until the bottoms are browned. Turn the potato cake and brown the other side. Place in a hot oven and cook until tender, about 30 to 35 minutes in all.

4. Drain off the excess butter and turn out the potato cake onto a platter. Slice into portions.

Cook the potatoes on the stove until the bottoms are brown.

Waxy potatoes are best since they hold their shape during cooking. Slice on a mandolin.

Swedish-Style Candied Potatoes

Yield: 10 servings

New red potatoes	2 1/4 pounds	1 kilogram
Sugar	6 ounces	170 grams
Lemon juice, to taste	2 teaspoons	2 teaspoons
Butter	3 ounces	85 grams
Salt, to taste	1/2 teaspoon	1/2 teaspoon
Pepper, to taste	1/4 teaspoon	1/4 teaspoon

1. Peel the potatoes and shape them as desired (tourné, large dice, parisienne).

2. Parcook the potatoes in boiling, salted water. Drain them.

3. Place the potatoes, sugar, and lemon juice in a sauté pan. Cook the potatoes, tossing them gently, from time to time until they are caramelized.

4. Add the butter and salt and pepper to taste.

Glazed Sweet Potatoes

Yield: 10 servings

Sweet potatoes	*2 1/4 pounds*	*1 kilogram*
Fresh pineapple, cut into chunks	*8 ounces*	*225 grams*
Lemon juice, to taste	*2 fluid ounces*	*60 milliliters*
Sugar	*8 ounces*	*225 grams*
Cinnamon, ground	*1 teaspoon*	*1 teaspoon*
Butter	*2 ounces*	*60 grams*
Salt, to taste	*1/2 teaspoon*	*1/2 teaspoon*
Pepper, to taste	*1/2 teaspoon*	*1/2 teaspoon*

1. Bake the sweet potatoes in a moderate oven (350°F/175°C) until tender.

2. Combine all the remaining ingredients in a saucepan and bring to a boil. Simmer the mixture until it is thick.

3. Peel the potatoes and cut them into large chunks. Pour the glaze over them and toss to coat them lightly. Add salt and pepper to taste.

Potato Purée

Yield: 10 servings

For the best flavor and texture, be sure that all the ingredients are very hot when they are combined.

Potatoes, peeled and sliced thin	*2 1/4 pounds*	*1 kilogram*
Milk, heated	*12 fluid ounces*	*360 milliliters*
Butter, melted	*4 ounces*	*115 grams*
Salt, to taste	*1 teaspoon*	*1 teaspoon*
Pepper, to taste	*1/2 teaspoon*	*1/2 teaspoon*

1. Cook the potatoes until they are very tender. Drain and return them to the heat to dry.

2. Purée the potatoes through a food mill while they are still very hot.

3. Add the heated milk and butter and whip until smooth and light. Season with salt and pepper to taste.

VARIATIONS

Buttermilk Whipped Potatoes: Use buttermilk to replace the milk. Add 2 to 3 tablespoons of minced chives with the salt and pepper.

Roasted Garlic Mashed Potatoes: Add 1 to 2 whole heads of roasted garlic to the potatoes when they are being puréed.

Sweet Potato Purée: Substitute sweet potatoes for the white potatoes; use cooking liquid to replace half the milk. Season with cinnamon, nutmeg, and salt and pepper as desired.

Duchesse Potatoes

Yield: 10 servings

Potatoes, peeled and quartered	*2 1/4 pounds*	*1 kilogram*
Egg yolks	*4 each*	*4 each*
Butter, softened	*3 ounces*	*85 grams*
Salt, to taste	*1 teaspoon*	*1 teaspoon*
Pepper, to taste	*1/4 teaspoon*	*1/4 teaspoon*
Nutmeg, ground	*few grains*	*few grains*

1. Cook the potatoes in boiling salted water until they are just tender.

2. Drain and dry the potatoes; keeping them hot, purée them.

3. Mix in the egg yolks; add the butter and seasonings. Blend and use as desired for borders or in other applications.

To read more about preparing potatoes, refer to page 199.

Croquette Potatoes

Yield: 10 servings

Idaho potatoes	*2 pounds*	*900 grams*
Parmesan cheese, grated (optional)	*4 ounces*	*115 grams*
Butter, softened	*2 ounces*	*60 grams*
Egg yolks	*3 each*	*3 each*
Salt, to taste	*1/2 teaspoon*	*1/2 teaspoon*
Pepper, to taste	*1/4 teaspoon*	*1/4 teaspoon*
Flour	*3 ounces*	*85 grams*
Bread crumbs, dry	*4 ounces*	*115 grams*

1. Cook the potatoes until they are very tender. Drain and dry them.

2. Purée the potatoes while they are very hot.

3. Add the cheese, butter, and egg yolks, mixing them well, and season the appareil with salt and pepper.

4. Shape the croquettes as required.

5. Dredge the croquettes in flour and coat with bread crumbs. Deep-fry them in 375°F (190°C) oil until they are golden brown. Serve them immediately.

These are sometimes referred to as Dauphine potatoes.

Add ground nuts to the bread crumbs if desired.

827

Lorette Potatoes

Yield: 10 servings

These potatoes are often rolled into logs, cut to size, and bent to form a crescent shape.

To read about the proper selection and maintenance of oils for deep-frying, read page 323.

The recipe for Pâté à Choux can be found on page 1081.

Potatoes, baking, peeled and quartered	1 pound	450 grams
Butter, softened	2 1/2 ounces	70 grams
Parmesan cheese, grated	2 ounces	60 grams
Eggs, beaten	2 each	2 each
Nutmeg, ground	pinch	pinch
Salt	1/2 teaspoon	1/2 teaspoon
Pepper	1/4 teaspoon	1/4 teaspoon
Pâte à Choux, room temperature	12 ounces	340 grams
Vegetable oil or frying fat	as needed	as needed

1. Cook the potatoes in boiling salted water until they are tender. Drain and dry them; keep them hot; purée.

2. Add the butter, eggs, nutmeg, salt, and pepper to the potatoes and mix well.

3. Mix in the Pâte à Choux.

4. Pipe or roll the mixture into the desired shapes on strips of parchment paper. Lower the potatoes into the deep fryer. Deep-fry the lorettes at 375° F (190°C) until they are golden.

Berny Potatoes

Yield: 10 servings

Croquette Potatoes	2 pounds	900 grams
Black truffles, chopped	2 ounces	60 grams
Egg wash	2 each	2 each
Slivered almonds, ground	2 ounces	60 grams
Bread crumbs, dry	2 ounces	60 grams

1. Mix the Croquette Potatoes with the truffles. Shape into balls.

2. Dip the balls in the egg wash.

3. Combine almonds and bread crumbs. Coat the balls with the almond-bread crumb mixture.

4. Deep-fry the potato balls at 375° F (190°C) until they are golden brown, about 4 to 5 minutes.

Macaire Potatoes

Yield: 10 servings

Idaho potatoes	*2 1/4 pounds*	*1 kilogram*
Butter	*2 ounces*	*60 grams*
Salt, to taste	*1/2 teaspoon*	*1/2 teaspoon*
Pepper, to taste	*1/4 teaspoon*	*1/4 teaspoon*
Clarified butter, as needed	*6 ounces*	*170 grams*

1. Bake the potatoes until they are very tender.

2. Remove the pulp while it is hot; mash the whole butter into the potatoes and mix it in well. Season the mixture with the salt and pepper.

3. Shape the mixture into cakes.

4. Panfry them in the clarified butter until they are golden on both sides and very hot.

French-Fried Potatoes

Yield: 10 servings

Idaho potatoes	*2 1/2 pounds*	*1 kilogram*
Vegetable oil or frying fat	*as needed*	*as needed*
Salt, to taste	*1 teaspoon*	*1 teaspoon*

1. Cut the potatoes into the desired shape, rinse them in cold water, and dry them thoroughly.

2. Add the potatoes in batches to oil heated to 325°F (165°C). Blanch for 2 minutes.

3. Drain well and transfer the potatoes to pans lined with absorbent paper.

4. Finish the potatoes in 375°F (190°C) oven until they are golden brown and cooked through. Drain them well and serve immediately.

French fries can be cut into a variety of shapes from straw or match stick to "pont-neuf" or steak fries.

After grating the potatoes, do not rinse in cold water. The starch on the potatoes is necessary to hold the potato together as a nest.

Almost inevitably, a certain percentage of potatoes will not "soufflé." The higher the starch content, the greater the chance of success. These "eggs" are sometimes served in a potato "nest."

This technique works well with many root vegetables; make an attractive assortment using yucca, yams, rutabagas, lotus roots, and beets.

Potato Nest

Yield: 10 servings

Idaho potatoes, grated	*2 pounds*	*900 grams*

1. Grate the potatoes immediately before preparing the potato nest. Do not rinse them in cold water.

2. Arrange the grated potatoes in the bottom of a basket. Fit a second basket in place on top, to hold potatoes in.

3. Deep-fry the potatoes in 350°F (175°C) oil until they are crisp, brown, and thoroughly cooked. Drain them briefly.

Souffléed Potatoes

Yield: 10 servings

Idaho potatoes	*2 1/4 pounds*	*1 kilogram*
Salt, to taste	*1 teaspoon*	*1 teaspoon*

1. Slice the potatoes into 1/8-inch (.25-centimeter) thick oblongs and dry them thoroughly on absorbent toweling.

2. Heat the oil or fat in a deep-fat fryer or rondeau to 300°F (150°C).

3. Add the potato slices in small batches. Shake the baskets or pot carefully to prevent the potatoes from sticking. When the slices blister, remove and drain them in a single layer on absorbent paper toweling.

4. Heat the oil or fat to 375°F (190°C). Add the blanched potato slices. Fry them until they are puffed and golden. Drain them well and serve immediately.

Sweet Potato Chips

Yield: 10 servings

Sweet potatoes, peeled	*2 1/4 pounds*	*1 kilogram*
Salt, to taste	*1/2 teaspoon*	*1/2 teaspoon*
Pepper, to taste	*1/4 teaspoon*	*1/4 teaspoon*

1. Cut the potatoes very thin, using a mandolin.

2. Blanch them in 325°F (165°C) oil until they are tender.

3. Finish frying the potatoes in oil at 375°F (190°C) until they are very crisp.

4. Drain the sweet potatoes well. Season them with salt and pepper to taste and serve them immediately.

Basic Boiled Rice

Yield: 10 servings

Water	2 quarts	2 liters
Salt, to taste	1/2 teaspoon	1/2 teaspoon
Long-grain white rice	10 ounces	285 grams

1. Bring the water and salt to a rolling boil.

2. Add the rice in a thin stream, stirring it with a fork to prevent the grains from clumping as they are added. When the water returns to a boil, reduce the heat to a simmer.

3. Simmer the rice for approximately 15 minutes, or until the grains are tender. Drain the rice immediately; let steam dry.

This method is sometimes referred to as the "pasta" method. The result is fluffy cooked grain.

To use this recipe to prepare other grains, refer to the table in Appendix II.

Rice Pilaf

Yield: 10 servings

Onion, diced	1 1/2 ounces	45 grams
Butter	1 ounce	30 grams
Long-grain white rice	14 ounces	400 grams
Stock, hot	28 fluid ounces	840 milliliters
Bay leaf	1 each	1 each
Salt, to taste	1/2 teaspoon	1/2 teaspoon
Pepper, to taste	1/4 teaspoon	1/4 teaspoon

1. Sweat the onion in butter.

2. Add the rice and stir it to coat with the butter.

3. Add the hot stock and bay leaf.

4. Bring the liquid to a boil. Cover the pot and transfer it to a moderate oven (350°F/175°C) and cook for 18 to 20 minutes until the liquid is absorbed and the rice is tender.

5. Use a kitchen fork to separate the grains of rice and to release the steam.

An average portion of cooked rice served as a side dish is about 3 ounces (85 grams).

Add sprigs of fresh thyme to the pilaf in step 3.

The pilaf method is explained on pages 342 and 343.

Wild Rice Pilaf

Yield: 10 servings

Onions, diced	*1 ounce*	*30 grams*
Butter	*1/2 ounce*	*15 grams*
Wild rice	*14 ounces*	*400 grams*
Chicken Stock	*2 1/2 pints*	*1.25 liters*
Salt, to taste	*1/2 teaspoon*	*1/2 teaspoon*
Pepper, to taste	*1/4 teaspoon*	*1/4 teaspoon*

1. Sweat the onions in the butter.

2. Add the wild rice and sauté briefly.

3. Add the stock and seasonings. Bring the liquid to a simmer.

4. Cover the pot and finish the pilaf in a 350°F (175°C) oven. Drain off the excess liquid, if necessary. The cooking time is 45 to 50 minutes.

Frequently, wild rice is cooked separately and blended with long-grain white rice in a ratio of either equal parts or 2 parts white rice to 1 part wild rice.

Cilantro Lime Rice

Yield: 10 servings

Vegetable oil	*1 fluid ounce*	*30 milliliters*
Onions, minced	*8 ounces*	*225 grams*
Garlic, minced	*1 tablespoon*	*1 tablespoon*
Long-grain converted rice	*12 ounces*	*340 grams*
Water	*24 fluid ounces*	*720 milliliters*
Salt, to taste	*1/2 teaspoon*	*1/2 teaspoon*
Pepper, to taste	*1/4 teaspoon*	*1/4 teaspoon*
Cilantro, minced	*4 tablespoons*	*4 tablespoons*
Lime juice	*1 fluid ounce*	*30 milliliters*
Lime zest, grated or minced	*2 teaspoons*	*2 teaspoons*

1. Heat oil in medium-size rondeau.

2. Add onions and sweat.

3. Add garlic and cook until aroma is apparent.

4. Add rice and coat with oil; add water and season with salt and pepper to taste.

5. Cook 20 to 25 minutes, with fork stir in cilantro and lime juice and zest.

6. Hold for service.

Adding lime juice or zest to the rice before it is fully cooked will interfere with proper cooking. The grain may never become fully tender. Be sure to add it only after the rice is tender.

Brown Rice with Pecans and Scallions

Yield: 10 servings

Butter	*1 1/2 ounces*	*45 grams*
Onions, minced	*2 ounces*	*60 grams*
Brown rice	*14 ounces*	*400 grams*
Chicken Stock, seasoned, hot	*2 1/2 pints*	*1.25 liters*
Bouquet Garni	*1 each*	*1 each*
Pecans, toasted, chopped	*2 ounces*	*60 grams*
Scallions, sliced	*3 each*	*3 each*
Salt, to taste	*1/2 teaspoon*	*1/2 teaspoon*
Pepper, to taste	*1/4 teaspoon*	*1/4 teaspoon*

1. Sauté onions in butter until translucent.
2. Add rice, and sauté until translucent.
3. Add stock, and Bouquet Garni, and return to a simmer.
4. Cover with a lid and bake in a 350°F (175°C) oven 45 minutes to an hour.
5. Sauté pecans in butter until lightly brown.
6. Fluff rice with a fork and add pecans and scallions. Season to taste.

For an Indian flavor, add 2 to 3 teaspoons of curry powder as the onions sauté. Add plumped raisins and toasted almonds in the last step instead of pecans and scallions.

Basic Risotto

Yield: 10 servings

Onions, diced	*2 ounces*	*60 grams*
Butter	*3 ounces*	*85 grams*
Arborio rice	*14 ounces*	*420 grams*
Chicken Stock, hot	*2 pints*	*1 liter*
Dry white wine	*8 fluid ounces*	*2.25 milliliters*
Parmesan cheese, grated	*3 ounces*	*85 grams*
Salt, to taste	*1/2 teaspoon*	*1/2 teaspoon*
Pepper, to taste	*1/4 teaspoon*	*1/4 teaspoon*

1. Sweat the onions in half of the butter.
2. Add the rice and mix it thoroughly with the butter. Cook it, stirring, until a toasted aroma develops.
3. Add 1/3 of the stock, stirring the rice frequently until the rice has absorbed the stock. Add the remaining stock in 2 more additions, stirring constantly. Add the wine and stir in the same manner. Cook the risotto until the rice is al dente and most of the liquid is absorbed. The texture should be creamy.
4. Add the grated Parmesan cheese and the remaining butter. Season to taste with salt and pepper.

The technique for risotto is illustrated on page 344.

Arborio rice is a short-grain rice that cooks to the ideal "creamy" consistency. Although other grains may be prepared in this manner, the end result will not be exactly the same.

VARIATION

Saffron Risotto: Add 1/2 teaspoon of saffron threads to the onions as they sauté.

Risotto with Escarole and Parmesan

Yield: 10 servings

Serve risotto as a bed for other dishes.

Add any variety of blanched or parcooked vegetables:
- *diced squash or pumpkin*
- *green beans*
- *garden peas*
- *sautéed Tomato Concassé*
- *roasted peppers*

Basic Risotto, prepared with Fish Stock	*1 recipe*	*1 recipe*
Escarole, lightly steamed, chopped	*12 ounces*	*340 grams*
Parsley, minced	*1 1/2 ounces*	*45 grams*
Butter	*2 ounces*	*60 grams*
Parmesan cheese, grated	*4 ounces*	*115 grams*
Salt, to taste	*1/2 teaspoon*	*1/2 teaspoon*
Pepper, to taste	*1/4 teaspoon*	*1/4 teaspoon*

1. Prepare the risotto according to the directions in the basic recipe (page 833) through step 3.

2. Add the escarole with the final addition of stock or wine. Finish cooking.

3. Stir in parsley, Parmesan, and butter. Serve the risotto immediately.

Risotto with Asparagus Tips

Yield: 10 servings

Basic Risotto, prepared with Vegetable Stock	*1 recipe*	*1 recipe*
Asparagus tips, blanched	*6 ounces*	*170 grams*
Parsley, minced	*1 1/2 ounces*	*45 grams*
Butter	*4 ounces*	*115 grams*
Parmesan cheese, grated	*4 ounces*	*115 grams*
Salt, to taste	*1/2 teaspoon*	*1/2 teaspoon*
Pepper, to taste	*1/4 teaspoon*	*1/4 teaspoon*

1. Prepare the risotto according to the directions in the basic recipe (page 833) through step 3.

2. Add the asparagus tips with the final addition of stock or wine. Finish cooking.

3. Stir in the parsley and butter. Finish the risotto with the Parmesan cheese. Season to taste with salt and pepper. Serve it immediately.

Saffron Risotto with Shrimp

Yield: 10 servings

Garlic cloves, minced	2 each	2 each
Onions, minced	4 ounces	115 grams
Butter	5 ounces	140 grams
Stock, seasoned	2 1/2 pints	1.25 liters
Arborio rice	14 ounces	400 grams
Bay leaves	2 each	2 each
Saffron threads, crushed	pinch	pinch
Parsley, chopped	2 tablespoons	2 tablespoons
Parmesan cheese, grated	2 ounces	60 grams
Shrimp, diced and sautéed	10 ounces	285 grams
Salt, to taste	1/2 teaspoon	1/2 teaspoon
Pepper, to taste	1/4 teaspoon	1/4 teaspoon

1. Sauté garlic and onion in 3 ounces (85 grams) butter.

2. Add rice, stir until grains are coated with butter.

3. Add one-third of the stock, stir until rice absorbs liquid.

4. Add bay leaves, saffron, and one-third of stock, continue to stir.

5. Add remaining stock, continue to stir.

6. When all liquid is absorbed, add parsley, Parmesan cheese, remaining butter, and sautéed shrimp.

7. Stir rice only enough to mix ingredients. Season to taste with salt and pepper.

Although this recipe is included with side dishes, it might make a better first course or appetizer selection.

Use a variety of seafood, including mussels, clams, or squid to make a substantial main course offering.

Basic Polenta

Yield: 20 servings

Water	2 1/2 quarts	2.5 liters
Salt	1 tablespoon	1 tablespoon
Yellow cornmeal, coarse	1 pound	450 grams
Butter	2 ounces	60 grams

1. Bring the water to a boil in a heavy pot. Add the salt.

2. Add the cornmeal to the boiling water in a thin stream, stirring constantly.

3. Cook the polenta over moderate heat, stirring constantly for about 35 minutes or until it pulls away from the sides of the pot.

4. Pour the polenta into a lined sheet pan. Cool thoroughly.

5. Cut the polenta into the desired shape. Bake, sauté, pan-fry, or grill to reheat.

The method for preparing Polenta is found on pages 342 to 343.

Polenta may be served directly from the pot as a "soft polenta."

Polenta with Parmesan Cheese

Yield: 20 servings

Shallots, chopped fine	1 ounce	30 grams
Garlic cloves, chopped fine	2 tablespoons	2 tablespoons
Butter	2 ounces	60 grams
Chicken Stock	2 1/2 quarts	2.5 liters
Yellow cornmeal, coarse	1 pound	450 grams
Egg yolks	3 each	3 each
Parmesan cheese, grated	6 to 8 ounces	170 to 225 grams
Salt, to taste	1/2 teaspoon	1/2 teaspoon
Pepper, to taste	1/4 teaspoon	1/4 teaspoon

Chilled and firm polenta may be layered with vegetables, meats, or cheeses, topped with a sauce or cheese and baked as an entrée or appetizer.

1. Sauté the shallots and garlic in the butter until they are translucent.

2. Add the stock and bring to a boil.

3. Add the cornmeal in a stream, stirring constantly until it has been all added. Simmer the mixture for 45 minutes, stirring often; when done, it should pull away from the sides of the pot.

4. Remove the pot from the heat and blend in the egg yolks, Parmesan cheese, and seasonings.

5. Pour the polenta onto a greased sheet pan and refrigerate until very firm.

6. Cut into the desired shapes.

7. Panfry or grill the polenta until golden brown on both sides.

Hush Puppies

Yield: 10 servings

Corn oil, as needed	1 pint	480 milliliters
White cornmeal	5 ounces	140 grams
Flour	20 ounces	60 grams
Baking powder	1 teaspoon	1 teaspoon
Salt, to taste	1 teaspoon	1 teaspoon
Sugar	1 teaspoon	1 teaspoon
Pepper, to taste	1/2 teaspoon	1/2 teaspoon
Cayenne pepper	pinch	pinch
Egg, beaten	1 each	1 each
Milk	4 fluid ounces	120 milliliters
Butter, melted	1 ounce	30 grams
Onion, minced	1 ounce	30 grams
Garlic clove, minced	1 each	1 each

Hush Puppies are a classic accompaniment to fried fish, especially catfish or trout that has been dipped in cornmeal and pan-fried.

(Recipe continued on facing page)

1. In a deep skillet, heat 2 inches (5 centimeters) of oil to 365°F (185°C).

2. Mix cornmeal, flour, baking powder, salt, sugar, and black and cayenne peppers in a mixing bowl.

3. Blend the egg, milk, butter, onion, and garlic.

4. Stir egg mixture into cornmeal to make a stiff batter.

5. Drop heaping teaspoons of batter into hot oil, until skillet is full; do not crowd.

6. When they are golden brown, remove from oil with a slotted spoon and drain on paper towels.

7. Keep warm in oven until ready to serve.

Add whole corn kernels and or diced jalapeño peppers if desired.

Garlic Cheese Grits

Yield: 10 servings

Water, salted to taste	*2 quarts*	*2 liters*
Regular grits	*12 ounces*	*340 grams*
Butter	*6 ounces*	*170 grams*
Cheddar cheese, sharp, grated	*12 ounces*	*340 grams*
Milk	*12 fluid ounces*	*360 milliliters*
Eggs, lightly beaten	*4 each*	*4 each*
Garlic cloves, minced	*2 each*	*2 each*
Worcestershire sauce	*1 teaspoon*	*1 teaspoon*
Tabasco	*1/2 teaspoon*	*1/2 teaspoon*
Cayenne pepper	*pinch*	*pinch*
Salt, to taste	*2 teaspoons*	*2 teaspoons*
Pepper, to taste	*1/4 teaspoon*	*1/4 teaspoon*

To make soufléed grits, separate the eggs. Add the yolks in step 2. Beat the whites to medium peaks and fold into the grits just before pouring into a baking dish.

Prepare in individual timbales or soufflé dishes.

1. Bring the water to a rolling boil. Stir in grits; simmer about 30 minutes or until thick. Remove from heat and stir in butter and 10 ounces (300 grams) of cheese until melted.

2. Combine milk, eggs, garlic, Tabasco, Worcestershire sauce, and cayenne. Add mixture to grits. Add salt and pepper to taste.

3. Pour into buttered dish and top with remaining cheese.

4. Bake in 350°F (175°C) oven until firm, about 1 hour. Let set for 10 minutes before slicing and serving.

Couscous

Yield: 10 servings

Couscous can also be prepared by cooking it directly in simmering water or broth. The recipe for Couscous with Lamb Stew in found on page 776.

The method for preparing Couscous is illustrated on page 330.

Couscous	*1 pound*	*450 grams*
Salt, to taste	*1/2 teaspoon*	*1/2 teaspoon*
Olive oil	*as needed*	*as needed*

1. Soak the couscous for about 5 minutes in enough warm water to cover, then drain it in a colander.

2. Set the colander over a pot of simmering water; cover the pot and let the couscous steam for 3 to 4 minutes. Uncover the pot and stir the couscous with a fork to break up any lumps. (Rinse the couscous at this point if it is not the precooked variety, and continue to steam it for another 5 minutes.)

3. Fluff the couscous with a fork, and season it to taste with salt. Drizzle a small amount of olive oil over the couscous, if desired.

Bulgur with Dried Cherries and Apples

Yield: 10 servings

This may be prepared as a breakfast dish. Use skim milk instead of stock.

Chicken or Vegetable Stock or water	*1 quart*	*1 liter*
Bulgur wheat	*10 ounces*	*285 grams*
Salt	*1/2 teaspoon*	*1/2 teaspoon*
Dried cherries, plumped	*2 ounces*	*60 grams*
Dried apples rings, coarsely chopped	*5 each*	*5 each*

1. Bring the stock or water to a boil.

2. Add the bulgur and stir well. Reduce the heat to low and simmer for about 3 to 4 minutes. Remove the pan from the heat.

3. Fold in the salt, cherries, and apples, using a fork. Cover the pan and allow to rest for about 10 minutes before serving.

Quinoa Pilaf with Red and Yellow Peppers

Yield: 10 servings

Vegetable oil	*1 fluid ounce*	*30 milliliters*
Shallots, minced	*1 ounce*	*30 grams*
Garlic, minced fine	*1 tablespoon*	*1 tablespoon*
Quinoa	*12 ounces*	*340 grams*
Chicken Stock	*1 1/2 pints*	*720 milliliters*
Bay leaf	*1 each*	*1 each*
Thyme, sprig	*1 each*	*1 each*
Red pepper, roasted and diced	*3 ounces*	*85 grams*
Yellow pepper, roasted and diced	*3 ounces*	*85 grams*
Salt, to taste	*1 teaspoon*	*1 teaspoon*
Pepper, to taste	*1/2 teaspoon*	*1/2 teaspoon*

1. Heat oil in a saucepan over medium heat. Add the shallots and garlic, and sauté them for 2 or 3 minutes.

2. Add the quinoa, stock, bay leaf, and thyme. Stir well with a kitchen fork, and bring the stock to a simmer over medium heat. Reduce the heat to low.

3. Cover the pot and simmer the quinoa over low heat (or in a 325°F/160°C oven) for about 15 minutes, or until the quinoa is tender and very fluffy.

4. Remove and discard the bay leaf and thyme sprig. Fluff grain with a fork to break up any clumps, and fold in the roasted peppers.

5. Check the seasoning and add the salt and pepper to taste before serving.

Quinoa (pronounced "KEEN wah") is a relative newcomer to our markets, but it is one of the more ancient grains grown in the New World. When properly cooked, quinoa is a light, fluffy grain with a subtle flavor.

Any leftover quinoa could be combined with diced vegetables such as cucumbers, carrots, celery, avocado, and tomato, and then dressed with a vinaigrette. Serve it chilled as a salad, or as the filling for a pita sandwich garnished with alfalfa and radish sprouts.

Kasha with Spicy Maple Pecans

Yield: 10 servings

Kasha is toasted buckwheat groats. They have a delicious nutty aroma and taste. A classic Russian dish, Kasha varnishka is made by serving cooked kasha with bowtie pasta.

Kasha is first coated with egg whites in order to prevent if from lumping as it cooks. Other grains, such as brown rice or pearl barley could be prepared using this recipe. Simply omit the first step of sautéeing them in the egg whites. The cooking time for white rice is 16 minutes, 35 minutes for brown rice, and 25 minutes for pearl barley.

Serve this dish with roasted chicken or turkey, or broiled bluefish or marlin. Or prepare a vegetarian meal by adding cabbage rolls stuffed with vegetables and simmered in tomato sauce, steamed fresh asparagus or peas, glazed carrots, and pickled beets.

Egg whites, lightly beaten	*2 each*	*2 each*
Kasha (buckwheat groats)	*12 ounces*	*340 grams*
Stock or water	*1 1/2 pints*	*720 milliliters*
Salt, to taste	*1/2 teaspoon*	*1/2 teaspoon*
Butter	*1 ounce*	*30 grams*
Pecans, toasted and chopped	*3 ounces*	*85 grams*
Maple syrup	*2 fluid ounces*	*60 milliliters*
Cayenne pepper, to taste	*1/4 teaspoon*	*1/4 teaspoon*

1. Combine the egg whites and kasha in a saucepan and cook over low heat, stirring constantly, for 2 minutes.

2. Add the stock or water, salt, and butter to the kasha and bring to a boil over high heat. Reduce the heat to low and simmer the kasha, covered, for about 15 minutes.

3. Remove the kasha from the heat and allow the rice to "steam" for about 5 minutes. Remove the lid and fluff the kasha by lifting it gently with two forks to remove any lumps.

4. While the kasha steams, place the pecans, maple syrup, and cayenne in a small skillet. Heat over low heat until the pecans are well coated and the maple syrup has reduced to a very thick consistency.

5. Scatter the spiced pecans over the kasha and serve.

Black Beans

Yield: 10 servings

This recipe may be used to prepare other beans. Refer to the table in Appendix II for the approximate cooking times.

Use a pork broth or ham stock if available (see page 440).

Onion, chopped	*1 each*	*1 each*
Vegetable oil	*1 fluid ounce*	*30 milliliters*
Black beans, soaked overnight in water to cover	*12 ounces*	*340 grams*
Fresh ham hocks	*1 each*	*1 each*
Chicken Stock, as needed to cover	*3 quarts*	*3 liters*
Standard Sachet d'Épices	*1 each*	*1 each*

1. Sweat the onions in oil.

2. Add the beans, ham hock, Chicken Stock to cover, and Sachet d'Épices; simmer the beans until they are done.

3. Remove half of the beans and purée them. Return them to the pot and mix the purée with the whole beans.

Black Beans with Peppers and Chorizo

Yield: 10 servings

Black beans, dried, soaked overnight	*12 ounces*	*340 grams*
Water or stock	*3 quarts*	*3 liters*
Vegetable oil	*2 fluid ounces*	*60 milliliters*
Bacon strips, minced	*2 each*	*2 each*
Onions, diced	*6 ounces*	*170 grams*
Garlic cloves, minced	*2 each*	*2 each*
Chorizo, sliced	*4 ounces*	*115 grams*
Red pepper, diced	*4 ounces*	*115 grams*
Green pepper, diced	*4 ounces*	*115 grams*
Scallions, sliced thin	*1 bunch*	*1 bunch*
Salt, to taste	*1/2 teaspoon*	*1/2 teaspoon*
Pepper, to taste	*1/4 teaspoon*	*1/4 teaspoon*
Basil, chopped	*1/4 teaspoon*	*1/4 teaspoon*
Oregano, chopped	*1 teaspoon*	*1 teaspoon*
Cilantro, chopped	*1 teaspoon*	*1 teaspoon*

Serve this stew as a bed or sauce for grilled fish, game, or pork.

Use as a filling for enchiladas, empañadas, or burritos.

Add a dash of cider vinegar or lime juice for a final seasoning adjustment.

1. Cook the beans in enough water or stock to cover them for about 90 minutes, or until they are tender to the bite. Reserve them in their cooking liquid.

2. Heat the oil and add the bacon. Cook the bacon until it is rendered. Add the onion and garlic, and sauté them until they are lightly browned.

3. Add the chorizo and red and green peppers; sauté them until the peppers are tender.

4. Add the drained, cooked beans and enough cooking liquid to keep them moist (the consistency should be that of a thick stew). Simmer the beans until all the flavors are developed and all the ingredients are heated through (about 45 minutes).

5. Add the scallions, salt, pepper, and fresh herbs to adjust the seasoning.

Refried Beans

Yield: 10 servings

Adding the chili powder and cumin seed to the hot oil in step 2 helps to more fully release their flavor.

To make your own chili powder, refer to page 425.

Pinto beans, soaked overnight	12 ounces	340 grams
Stock, as needed to cover	3 quarts	3 liters
Onions, chopped fine	8 ounces	225 grams
Garlic cloves, minced	3 each	3 each
Cumin seeds, ground	1 teaspoon	1 teaspoon
Chili powder	2 teaspoons	2 teaspoons
Bacon fat or lard	6 ounces	170 grams
Tomato Concassé	3 ounces	225 grams
Salt, to taste	1/2 teaspoon	1/2 teaspoon
Pepper, to taste	1/4 teaspoon	1/4 teaspoon
Monterey Jack cheese, grated	5 ounces	140 grams

1. Cook the beans in the stock until they are very soft.

2. Sauté the onions, garlic, cumin, and chili powder in the bacon fat; add the Tomato Concassé, and cook the mixture for 2 minutes.

3. Add the cooked beans and continue to cook the mixture, mashing the beans with a spoon as they cook.

4. Season the beans to taste with salt and pepper. Top the beans with grated Monterey Jack cheese before serving, and heat them briefly under a salamander or broiler.

Southwest White Bean Stew

Yield: 10 servings

This is a good accompaniment to grilled or smoke-roasted foods. Serve it to replace Refried Beans for a lower-fat alternative.

Navy beans, cooked, drained	28 ounces	800 grams
Vegetable oil	2 teaspoons	2 teaspoons
Sweet peppers, assorted, small dice	4 ounces	115 grams
Jalapeño peppers, seeded and diced	2 ounces	60 grams
Garlic, minced	1 ounce	30 grams
Chicken or Vegetable Stock	1 pint	480 milliliters
Sherry wine vinegar	2 fluid ounces	60 milliliters
Tomato Concassé	4 ounces	115 grams
Cilantro, chopped	2 tablespoons	2 tablespoons

1. Purée about 2 cups of the cooked beans, and combine with whole beans.

2. Heat the oil and add the sweet peppers, jalapeño peppers, and garlic. Sauté until the peppers are tender.

(Recipe continued on facing page)

3. Add the bean mixture and stock. Cook at a very gentle simmer, stirring constantly, until the beans are heated through.

4. Add the vinegar and tomatoes, continue to stew until very hot and the flavors are fully developed.

5. Add the cilantro just before serving.

Braised Lentils with Eggplant and Mushrooms

Yield: 10 servings

Lentils, green or brown	*12 ounces*	*340 grams*
Water or White Beef Stock	*3 quarts*	*3 liters*
Olive oil	*1 fluid ounce*	*30 milliliters*
Garlic cloves, minced	*2 each*	*2 each*
Onion, diced	*6 ounces*	*170 grams*
Cinnamon, ground	*1/2 teaspoon*	*1/2 teaspoon*
Turmeric, ground	*1/2 teaspoon*	*1/2 teaspoon*
Lemon zest	*1/4 teaspoon*	*1/4 teaspoon*
Eggplant, large dice	*2 pounds*	*900 grams*
Mushrooms, sliced or quartered	*4 ounces*	*115 grams*
Salt, to taste	*1/2 teaspoon*	*1/2 teaspoon*
Pepper, to taste	*1/4 teaspoon*	*1/4 teaspoon*
Gratin		
Bread crumbs, fresh	*4 ounces*	*115 grams*
Butter, melted	*2 ounces*	*60 grams*

Add a Sachet d'Épices containing lemon zest, thyme sprigs, and peppercorns as the lentils cook.

1. Cook the lentils in enough water or stock to cover them by 1 inch (2.5 centimeters) until they are tender (about 30 to 40 minutes). Drain the lentils, reserving the cooking liquid.

2. Heat the oil in a rondeau. Add the garlic and onion; cook until lightly brown. Add the cinnamon, turmeric, and lemon zest. Sauté until very aromatic.

3. Add the eggplant, stirring to coat it evenly with oil. Add the mushrooms, spices, and lemon zest. Cook the mixture until the mushrooms begin to release their juices.

4. Add the lentils and enough cooking liquid to moisten them well. Cover the rondeau and place it in a moderate oven (350°F/175°C). Braise the mixture for 30 minutes or until the eggplant is completely tender. Adjust the seasoning to taste with salt and pepper.

5. For the gratin: Combine the bread crumbs with the butter and place on top of the lentils. Return the rondeau to a hot oven until a crust has developed and browned evenly. (This may be done as individual portions in gratin dishes, if desired.)

To use this ragout as a sauce, add white wine (5 fluid ounces/150 milliliters) and Jus de Veau Lié or Demi-Glace (6 fluid ounces/180 milliliters) and simmer to reach a good sauce consistency.

Lentil Ragout

Yield: 10 servings

Slab bacon, finely diced	2 ounces	60 grams
Onions, fine dice	8 ounces	225 grams
Leeks, fine dice	6 ounces	170 grams
Carrots, fine dice	6 ounces	170 grams
Celery, fine dice	5 ounces	140 grams
Garlic, minced	1 tablespoon	1 tablespoon
Tomato paste	3 ounces	85 grams
Sherry wine vinegar	1 fluid ounce	30 milliliters
French lentils	12 ounces	350 grams
Chicken Stock, as needed	3 pints	1.5 liters
Standard Sachet d'Épices, plus		
Caraway seeds	1/4 teaspoon	1/4 teaspoon
Lemon, peel	1 strip	1 strip
Salt, to taste	1 teaspoon	1 teaspoon
White pepper, to taste	1/2 teaspoon	1/2 teaspoon

1. Render bacon; add onion, leeks, carrots, celery, and garlic; sauté.

2. Add tomato paste; sauté for several seconds to concentrate the flavor.

3. Add all lentils, stock and sachet; simmer until lentils are tender (about 30 minutes).

4. Remove sachet and discard. Adjust the seasoning to taste with vinegar, salt, and pepper.

Stewed Garbanzo Beans
with Tomato, Zucchini, and Cilantro

Garbanzo beans are also referred to as chickpeas or ceci.

Yield: 10 servings

Garbanzo beans, dried	12 ounces	340 grams
Water	3 quarts	3 liters
Olive oil	1 fluid ounce	30 milliliters
Garlic clove, minced	1 each	1 each
Zucchini, diced	8 ounces	225 grams
Tomato Concassé	4 ounces	115 grams
Cilantro, chopped	1 ounce	30 grams
Salt, to taste	1/2 teaspoon	1/2 teaspoon
Pepper, to taste	1/4 teaspoon	1/4 teaspoon
Lime juice, fresh	2 teaspoons	2 teaspoons

(Recipe continued on facing page)

1. Presoak the beans by the long or quick method.

2. Cook the beans in plenty of water until they are tender enough to mash, about 2 hours. Reserve them in their broth.

3. Heat the olive oil in a sauteuse. Add the garlic and cook until an aroma is apparent.

4. Add the zucchini and Tomato Concassé. Sauté the vegetables until they are tender and heated through.

5. Add the garbanzo beans to the sauteuse, along with enough bean broth to keep them moist. Stew them until they are heated through.

6. Add cilantro and adjust the seasoning to taste with salt, pepper, and lime juice.

Hoppin' John

Yield: 10 servings

Black-eyed peas	*8 ounces*	*225 grams*
Bacon, large dice	*4 ounces*	*115 grams*
Onions, diced	*4 ounces*	*115 grams*
Garlic cloves, minced	*2 each*	*2 each*
Red pepper flakes, crushed	*1/2 teaspoon*	*1/2 teaspoon*
Long-grain rice	*8 ounces*	*225 grams*
Chicken Stock	*1 quart*	*1 liter*
Bay leaf	*1 each*	*1 each*
Thyme sprig	*1 each*	*1 each*
Salt, to taste	*1/2 teaspoon*	*1/2 teaspoon*
Pepper, to taste	*1/4 teaspoon*	*1/4 teaspoon*

Hoppin' John is one of many dishes that combine beans and grains. Other examples include Moors and Christians (black beans and rice) and New Orleans (red beans and rice).

Black-eyed peas should be sorted and rinsed before cooking, but soaking is not necessary.

1. Simmer the black-eyed peas in enough water to cover them by 2 inches (5 centimeters) until they are just tender. Drain and reserve them.

2. Render the bacon in a pot. Remove the crisped bacon; drain and reserve it. Pour off all but 2 to 3 tablespoons of the bacon fat.

3. Add the onion, pepper, garlic, and red pepper flakes. Sauté them until they are translucent. Add the rice and stir until it is coated.

4. Add the stock and the black-eyed peas; bring the mixture to a simmer. Add the bay leaf, and thyme. Cover the pot and cook the mixture in an oven at 325° F (165°C) until the beans and rice are thoroughly cooked (about 20 minutes).

5. Remove the pot from the oven. Return the bacon to the dish, and season it to taste with the salt and pepper.

The original pastas were made from barley, rye, or spelt flours. Later, when wheat was introduced to Italy, wheat (especially hard wheats) became more common.

Fresh pasta is used to make both flat and filled pastas.

Basic Pasta Dough

Yield: 1 1/2 pounds (680 grams)

Semolina or bread flour	1 pound	450 grams
Eggs	6 each	6 each
Salt	pinch	pinch
Water, as needed	2 fluid ounces	60 milliliters

1. Combine all the ingredients in a large bowl and knead the mixture until it is smooth.

2. Cover the dough and allow to rest for 1 hour before rolling and shaping.

VARIATIONS

Spinach Pasta: Add 6 ounces (170 grams) of puréed raw spinach. Add additional flour as needed for consistency.

Tomato Pasta: Sauté 2 to 3 ounces (60 to 85 grams) of tomato paste to concentrate the flavor. Let it cool and add with the eggs.

Fresh Herb Pasta: Add 2 to 4 tablespoons of finely chopped fresh herbs to basic dough.

Pumpkin, Beet, or Carrot Pasta: Sauté 3 to 4 ounces (85 to 115 grams) of cooked, puréed pumpkin, beet, or carrot until dry. Cool and add with the eggs.

Black Pepper Pasta is used in a recipe on page 848. It would also be good with caramelized leeks and shallots stewed in cream.

Black Pepper Pasta

Yield: 1 1/2 pounds (680 grams)

Basic Pasta Dough	1 recipe	1 recipe
Egg yolk	1 each	1 each
Olive oil	1 teaspoon	1 teaspoon
Water	2 teaspoons	2 teaspoons
Black peppercorns, cracked	2 teaspoons	2 teaspoons

1. Prepare the Basic Pasta Dough as above, adding yolk, oil, and peppercorns.

2. Mix dough and let rest for 1 hour.

3. Roll out into noodles and air-dry for 30 minutes.

VARIATION

Spice Pasta: Add toasted and cracked or ground spices in place of the peppercorns.

Basic Boiled Pasta

Yield: 10 servings

Water	4 quarts	4 liters
Salt, to taste	1 tablespoon	1 tablespoon
Dried pasta	1 pound	450 grams

1. Bring the water and the salt to a rolling boil in a large pot.

2. Add the pasta to the water and stir it well to separate the strands. Let the pasta cook until it is tender but not soft.

3. Drain the pasta at once. Add desired sauce or garnish at this point, according to the specific recipe.

Fresh pastas may cook in less than 3 minutes; dried pastas may take up to 8 minutes or longer, depending upon the size and shape of the noodle.

If the pasta is to be held, plunge it into an ice-water bath to stop the cooking. Drain immediately and drizzle a small amount of vegetable oil over pasta; toss to prevent from sticking together.

The method for cooking, draining, and cooling pasta is illustrated on page 341.

Spaghetti alla Carbonara

Yield: 10 servings

Olive oil	2 fluid ounces	60 milliliters
Pancetta	8 ounces	225 grams
Eggs	3 each	3 each
Milk or half-and-half cream	24 fluid ounces	720 milliliters
Romano cheese, grated	5 ounces	140 grams
Spaghetti, cooked al dente	2 1/2 pounds	1.15 kilograms
Salt, to taste	1/2 teaspoon	1/2 teaspoon
Pepper, to taste	1/4 teaspoon	1/4 teaspoon

1. Heat the olive oil in a sauteuse and add the pancetta. Sauté the pancetta until it is crisp. Remove with a slotted spoon and reserve.

2. Beat the egg yolk, milk, and cheese.

3. Add the hot (or reheated) spaghetti to the olive oil and toss until coated and very hot.

4. Add the milk-egg-cheese mixture to the spaghetti. Cook over gentle heat until the sauce thickens and coats the spaghetti smoothly.

5. Add salt and pepper to taste and serve immediately.

This dish is said to have been popular among G.I.s during World War II. When properly made, the eggs should remain very creamy. It is important to heat them to at least 165°F (73°C) to inactivate any pathogens.

Use fettuccini, linguini, or other flat, long pasta.

Wild Mushroom and Artichokes over Black Pepper Pasta

Yield: 10 servings

Black Pepper Pasta is found on page 846. If you prefer, substitute any good-quality dried pasta.

Black Pepper Pasta	1 1/2 pounds	680 grams
Shallots, minced	1 ounce	30 grams
Butter	1/2 ounce	15 grams
Wild mushrooms, assorted, sliced	6 ounces	140 grams
White wine	2 fluid ounces	60 milliliters
Heavy cream	8 fluid ounces	240 milliliters
Artichoke bottoms, cooked	10 each	10 each
Tomato Concassé	8 ounces	225 grams
Salt, to taste	1/2 teaspoon	1/2 teaspoon
Parsley, chopped	1 tablespoon	1 tablespoon

1. Cook the pasta in boiling salted water until al dente. Drain.
2. Sauté shallots in butter until translucent; add mushrooms; sauté.
3. Add wine; reduce until almost dry. Add heavy cream; reduce until slightly thickened.
4. Add cooked pasta and toss until pasta is hot and fully cooked.
5. Add artichoke bottoms, Tomato Concassé, and reheat; season.
6. Sprinkle with chopped parsley.

Shrimp with Curried Pasta

Yield: 10 servings

To make Curried Pasta, add 2 tablespoons of curry powder to the flour used to prepare the Basic Pasta Dough (page 846). Cut into fettuccini or tagliatelle.

Shellfish Butter is found on page 549.

Shrimp, peeled and deveined	30 ounces	840 grams
Salt, to taste	1/2 teaspoon	1/2 teaspoon
Pepper, to taste	1/4 teaspoon	1/4 teaspoon
Vegetable oil, as needed	2 fluid ounces	60 milliliters
Butter	3 ounces	85 grams
Shallots, minced	1 ounce	30 grams
Brandy	4 fluid ounces	120 milliliters
Fish Fumet	20 ounces	570 grams
Heavy cream, reduced	10 fluid ounces	300 milliliters
Shellfish Butter	5 ounces	140 grams
Scallions, sliced on the bias	3 ounces	85 grams
Curried Pasta, cooked al dente	2 pounds	900 grams

(Recipe continued on facing page)

1. Season the shrimp to taste with salt and pepper.

2. Sauté the seasoned shrimp in the hot oil. Remove them from the pan and pour off the excess oil.

3. Add the whole butter and shallots to the oil; cook the shallots until they are translucent.

4. Add the brandy to deglaze the pan; reduce the liquid.

5. Add the Fish Fumet and heavy cream; let the mixture reduce until it lightly coats the back of a spoon.

6. Finish the sauce with the Shellfish Butter. Return the shrimp to the pan and add the scallions. Adjust the seasoning if necessary.

7. Serve the shrimp on a bed of drained, heated pasta.

To reheat pasta, place the al dente noodles into simmering water. Let the pasta reheat thoroughly, then drain well before dressing or returning to a sauce.

Lasagne di Carnevale Napolitana

Yield: 10 servings

Lasagne noodles (dry)	10 ounces	285 grams
Italian sausage, crumbled	10 ounces	285 grams
Cheese filling		
Ricotta	14 ounces	400 grams
Parmesan cheese, grated	4 ounces	115 grams
Salt, to taste	1/2 teaspoon	1/2 teaspoon
Pepper, to taste	1/4 teaspoon	1/4 teaspoon
Nutmeg, ground (optional)	to taste	to taste
Eggs	3 each	3 each
Parsley, chopped fine	3 tablespoons	3 tablespoons
Meat Sauce	1 quart	1 liter
Mozzarella cheese, sliced thin **or shredded**	10 ounces	285 grams
Parmesan cheese, grated	4 ounces	115 grams

The recipe for Meat Sauce is on page 539.

A meatless vegetable lasagne is included in Chapter 19, page 721.

1. Cook the noodles in boiling salted water until al dente. Drain and rinse with cold water.

2. Sauté the sausage over moderate heat until evenly cooked. Drain on absorbent paper.

3. Combine all the ingredients for the cheese filling and mix well.

4. Spread a thin layer of the Meat Sauce in a large baking dish.

5. Layer the ingredients. Begin with a layer of the lasagne noodles, arranged so that there is an overlap of about 3 inches (7.5 centimeters) at the sides of the pan.

6. Follow the noodles with a layer of the cheese filling (about 1/4-inch/.6 centimeters thick), then a layer of the sausage, a layer of the sauce, a thin layer of the mozzarella cheese, and a sprinkle of the Parmesan.

7. Continue layering the ingredients in this manner until they are used up; finish with a layer of noodles.

(Recipe continued on next page)

8. Fold the overhanging noodles over the top of the lasagne. Cover the lasagne with the remaining meat sauce and top with the remaining Parmesan cheese.

9. Place the lasagne in a preheated 375°F (190°C) oven and bake for 15 minutes.

10. Reduce the heat to 325°F (165°C). Bake the lasagne for another 45 minutes. If the top browns too quickly, cover it lightly with aluminum foil. The top should be a light golden brown.

11. Remove the lasagne from the oven and let it stand for 30 to 45 minutes before serving.

To make cappelletti, as shown here, cut the pasta into squares.

To make Saffron Pasta, make an infusion of one generous pinch of saffron in 4 fluid ounces (120 milliliters). Add to the Basic Pasta Dough (page 847) instead of plain water. Use only enough to make a good pliable dough. Roll the pasta into sheets.

Lobster Tortellini with Ginger-Lime Sauce

Yield: 10 servings

Filling

Lobster meat, chopped fine	*10 ounces*	*285 grams*
Egg whites, lightly beaten	*2 tablespoons*	*2 tablespoons*
Heavy cream	*2 tablespoons*	*2 tablespoons*
Shallots, minced, smothered	*1 teaspoon*	*1 teaspoon*
Garlic, minced, smothered	*1 teaspoon*	*1 teaspoon*
Chives, minced	*1/2 teaspoon*	*1/2 teaspoon*
Saffron Pasta	*1 1/2 pounds*	*680 grams*

Ginger sauce

Shallots, minced	*1 ounce*	*30 grams*
Ginger, minced	*1 tablespoon*	*1 tablespoon*
Lime juice, fresh, to taste	*2 fluid ounces*	*60 milliliters*
Dry white wine	*3 fluid ounces*	*90 milliliters*
Fish Stock or Fumet	*1 pint*	*480 milliliters*
Arrowroot	*2 teaspoons*	*2 teaspoons*
Heavy cream	*4 fluid ounces*	*120 milliliters*
Lime zest	*as needed*	*as needed*

1. For the filling: Purée the lobster meat to a coarse paste in a food processor. Add the egg whites and cream; process the mixture to a fine paste.

2. Add the shallots, garlic, and chives. Pulse the machine on and off a few times to incorporate into the lobster pieces.

(Recipe continued on facing page)

3. Roll out the dough into thin sheets; cut into circles. Place one teaspoon of the lobster filling on each circle. Fold the circles into tortellini. Reserve.

4. Combine the shallots, ginger, lime juice, and wine in a saucepan. Reduce the mixture over medium heat until syrupy.

5. Add the Fish Stock; bring the mixture to a simmer.

6. Dissolve the arrowroot in cold water. Add this mixture to the sauce; simmer the sauce until it is lightly thickened. Add the heavy cream. Simmer the sauce for 2 more minutes and strain.

7. Cook the tortellini in simmering water; drain and reserve.

8. Serve the tortellini in shallow bowls. Ladle the sauce over pasta and serve at once.

Cook filled pastas in simmering, not boiling, water. If possible, try to cook ravioli, agnolotti, tortellini, cappelotti, and other filled pastas just at the time they are to be served.

Chorizo-Filled Pasta with Tomato–Basil Coulis and Fresh Tomato Salsa

Yield: 10 servings

Filling

Pork, lean, diced	*5 ounces*	*140 grams*
Rice, cooked	*2 1/2 ounces*	*70 grams*
Jalapeño peppers, minced, to taste	*1 teaspoon*	*1 teaspoon*
Garlic cloves, minced	*3 each*	*3 each*
Chorizo, chopped	*10 ounces*	*285 grams*
Salt, to taste	*1/2 teaspoon*	*1/2 teaspoon*
Oregano, fresh	*1/2 teaspoon*	*1/2 teaspoon*
Cider vinegar	*1 teaspoon*	*1 teaspoon*
Chili powder	*1/2 teaspoon*	*1/2 teaspoon*
Cayenne, ground	*1/4 teaspoon*	*1/4 teaspoon*
Basic Pasta Dough	*20 ounces*	*570 grams*
Tomato-Basil Coulis	*20 fluid ounces*	*600 milliliters*
Fresh Tomato Salsa	*6 ounces*	*170 grams*

The recipe for Basic Pasta Dough is on page 846. Tomato Coulis is on page 551 (add fresh basil or pesto to taste). Fresh Tomato Salsa is on page 936.

1. Place the pork and rice in a food processor, using the steel blade; blend the mixture until it is smooth.

(Recipe continued on next page)

Shape the pasta as desired into ravioli, tortellini, or agnolotti.

2. Add the remaining ingredients for the filling and pulse the machine on and off until the ingredients are just combined. Remove the filling from the processor and refrigerate it.

3. Roll the pasta into thin sheets. Cut the sheets into sixteen 3-inch (7.5 centimeter) circles. Keep the dough circles covered until they are ready to be filled.

4. Brush the pasta circles lightly with water. Place 1 teaspoon (5 milliliters) of the filling on each pasta circle. Fold the circles in half and crimp the edges with the tines of a fork to seal them.

5. Add the filled pasta circles to boiling water and simmer for approximately 5 minutes.

6. Pool 2 ounces (60 millimeters) of the Tomato-Basil Coulis on each of four heated plates. Place 4 filled pasta circles on the coulis. Garnish with 1 tablespoon of salsa.

Spaetzle Dough

Yield: 10 servings

The methods for preparing spaetzle are explained and illustrated on page 344.

This soft dumpling is frequently used to garnish soups. In that case, it should not be sautéed in butter.

Eggs	*4 each*	*4 each*
Milk	*6 fluid ounces*	*180 milliliters*
Salt, to taste	*1/2 teaspoon*	*1/2 teaspoon*
Pepper, to taste	*1/4 teaspoon*	*1/4 teaspoon*
Nutmeg, ground, (optional)	*to taste*	*to taste*
Flour	*12 ounces*	*340 grams*
Butter	*as needed*	*as needed*

1. Combine the eggs, milk, and seasonings in a large bowl; mix well.

2. Work in the flour by hand.

3. Let the dough rest for 10 minutes.

4. Using a spaetzle machine (or other shaping technique), drop the dough into a large pot of boiling, salted water. Simmer until done.

5. Remove the spaetzle with a spider, shock in cold water; drain well.

6. Sauté the spaetzle in whole butter, season to taste with salt and pepper, and serve.

Spinach and Cheese Spaetzle

Yield: 10 to 12 servings

Eggs	*4 each*	*4 each*
Salt, to taste	*1/2 teaspoon*	*1/2 teaspoon*
Pepper, to taste	*1/4 teaspoon*	*1/4 teaspoon*
Nutmeg, ground, to taste	*pinch*	*pinch*
Sap Sago cheese, grated	*3/4 ounce*	*20 grams*
Spinach, blanched, chopped	*12 ounces*	*340 grams*
Flour	*1 pound*	*450 grams*
Milk	*3 to 4 fluid ounces*	*90 to 120 milliliters*
Butter	*2 ounces*	*60 grams*

1. Combine the eggs, salt, pepper, nutmeg, cheese, and spinach. Mix them well.
2. Work in the flour by hand and adjust the consistency with the milk to form a smooth batter.
3. Using a spaetzle machine (or other shaping technique), drop the dough into a large pot of boiling salted water. Simmer the spaetzle until they are done.
4. Remove the spaetzle with a spider, shock them in cold water, and drain them well.
5. Before serving, sauté the spaetzle in whole butter.

Gnocchi Piedmontese

Yield: 10 servings

Potatoes, peeled	*2 pounds*	*900 grams*
Butter	*1 ounce*	*30 grams*
Egg yolks	*2 each*	*2 each*
Eggs	*2 each*	*2 each*
Semolina flour	*2 to 4 ounces*	*60 to 115 grams*
Salt, to taste	*1/2 teaspoon*	*1/2 teaspoon*
Pepper, to taste	*1/4 teaspoon*	*1/4 teaspoon*
Nutmeg, ground	*pinch*	*pinch*
Butter	*2 ounces*	*60 grams*
Parmesan cheese, grated	*3 ounces*	*85 grams*
Parsley, chopped, as needed	*1 ounce*	*30 grams*

1. Peel and boil the potatoes. Rice them while very hot and add butter, egg yolks, and eggs. Mix well.
2. Incorporate the flour until a stiff dough is formed.
3. Roll out the dough and cut into the desired shapes. Shape over the tines of a fork.
4. Cook in boiling salted water for 5 to 6 minutes.
5. Serve the gnocchi tossed with the butter, cheese, and chopped parsley.

In order to produce the lightest gnocchi, add the least possible amount of flour, just enough to keep it from sticking as you shape it.

This makes a good appetizer or first course selection.

Semolina Gnocchi

Yield: 30 pieces

Milk	2 1/2 quarts	2.5 liters
Butter	4 ounces	115 grams
Salt	1 tablespoon	1 tablespoon
Semolina flour	1 pound	450 grams
Egg yolks, beaten	4 each	4 each
Parmesan cheese, fresh, grated	6 ounces	170 grams

1. Combine the milk, butter, and salt in a pot and bring mixture to a boil.

2. Pour in the semolina flour in a steady stream; stirring constantly to avoid lumps. Return the liquid to a boil.

3. Cook for 20 to 25 minutes or until very thick and stiff.

4. Add the egg yolks and the Parmesan cheese away from the heat.

5. Shape the gnocchi mixture into quenelles or spread it on a sheet pan to a thickness of 1/2 inch (1.25 centimeters). Cool it completely and cut it as desired.

6. Cook in simmering water for about 5 minutes. Serve with a sauce if desired.

Some experts question whether or not eggs should be included in this gnocchi recipe. You may prefer to use 2 whole eggs instead of 4 yolks. Or, you may omit them, adding more milk if necessary for correct consistency.

Chinese Dumplings (Fried or Boiled)

Yield: 20 pieces

Dough

Flour	1 pound	450 grams
Water, hot	8 fluid ounces	240 milliliters

Filling

Pork, ground	12 ounces	340 grams
Chinese cabbage	8 ounces	225 grams
Scallions, chopped	2 ounces	60 grams
Gingerroot, minced	1 teaspoon	1 teaspoon
Soy sauce	1/2 fluid ounce	15 milliliters
Sesame oil, dark	1/2 fluid ounce	15 milliliters
Egg white	1 each	1 each
Salt, to taste	1/2 teaspoon	1/2 teaspoon
White pepper, to taste	1/4 teaspoon	1/4 teaspoon

Serve with the dipping sauce for Shrimp Tempura (page 788) or other dipping sauce.

The technique for shaping and steaming these dumplings is found on page 329.

(Recipe continued on facing page)

1. Mix the flour and water. Let the dough set for 30 minutes. Divide the dough into 1/2-ounce (15-gram) portions and roll out into thin circles for individual dumpling skins.

2. Combine all the filling ingredients. Mix well. Check the consistency and seasoning of the filling by sautéing a small amount.

3. Place 1 tablespoon of filling on each dumpling skin and seal the edges tightly.

4. Cook the dumplings in boiling water until cooked through, about 8 minutes. Or, pan-fry the dumplings on one side only until golden brown and cooked through. Serve them immediately.

Bread Dumplings

Yield: 40 pieces

Onions, fine dice	*8 ounces*	*225 grams*
Butter	*4 ounces*	*115 grams*
Rolls, hard, stale, small dice	*2 pounds*	*900 grams*
Flour	*8 ounces*	*225 grams*
Milk	*1 pint*	*480 milliliters*
Eggs	*10 each*	*10 each*
Parsley, fresh, chopped	*1 ounce*	*30 grams*
Salt, to taste	*1/2 teaspoon*	*1/2 teaspoon*
White pepper, ground	*to taste*	*to taste*
Nutmeg, ground (optional)	*to taste*	*to taste*

Roll the dumpling mixture in cheesecloth or plastic wrap as you would a galantine. Poach in simmering water to an internal temperature of 160°F (70°C). Slice into portions.

1. Sauté the onions in the butter until they are lightly browned; cool.

2. Moisten the rolls with the milk. Let them sit for 30 to 40 minutes.

3. Combine the rolls and milk with the cooled onions, eggs, parsley, salt, pepper, and nutmeg.

4. Stir in the flour.

5. Let the mixture rest for 30 minutes, covered. Add additional egg-and-milk mixture if the bread is very dry.

6. Shape the mixture into 2-inch (5-centimeter) dumplings by hand.

7. Poach the dumplings in boiling salted water for 15 minutes. Hold them in the same water until ready to serve.

Biscuit Dumplings

Yield: 30 pieces

This is the classic accompaniment to chicken stew.

Cake flour	1 pound	450 grams
Baking powder	4 teaspoons	4 teaspoons
Milk	1 pint	480 milliliters
Parsley, chopped (optional)	2 tablespoons	2 tablespoons

1. Sift together all the dry ingredients.

2. Add the milk and mix lightly. Do not overmix. The consistency should be slightly softer than biscuit dough.

3. Drop 1-ounce (30-gram) portions from a spoon about an inch (2.5 centimeters) apart into simmering sauce or stew. Cover the pot; cook the dumplings for 20 to 25 minutes.

CHAPTER 23

Breakfast Recipes

Breakfast is considered by some to be one of the most difficult and thankless meals to master. There are endless varieties of egg preparations alone. The chef must have the skill to quickly meet each early-morning patron's specific request. Although these are considered breakfast items, many of these items may also be served at brunch, lunch, or dinner. Quiche, in particular, is often paired with salad at lunch, or baked in tartelette pans and served as canapés. Muffins, Danish, bagels, and fresh breads prepared on the premises are also excellent breakfast items. Those recipes may be found in Chapter 28. Smoked salmon service information and other crêpe recipes may be found in Chapter 26, and sausages may be found in Chapter 27.

The recipes are arranged as follows:

- Boiled and Poached Eggs
- Fried Eggs and Omelets
- Baked Eggs and Quiches
- Soufflés
- Cereals
- Pancakes and Other Batters
- Breakfast Meats
- Fruits, Beverages, and Butters

Soft-Cooked Eggs

Yield: 10 servings

Eggs	20 each	20 each

1. If the eggs are used directly from the refrigerator, temper them in warm water before cooking them.

2. Place the eggs in boiling water. Time the cooking from the point that the boiling resumes. For coddled eggs in the shell, cook for 2 to 5 minutes. For soft eggs in a glass, cook for 4 minutes. For soft eggs, cook for 5 minutes.

3. Shock the eggs in cold water for 2 to 3 seconds. Serve them warm. Serve the coddled eggs in the shell in an egg stand; peel the soft eggs and arrange them as poached eggs.

Hard-Boiled Eggs

Yield: 10 servings

Hard-boiled eggs can be eaten plain, pickled (page 949), made into egg salad (page 901) or Deviled eggs (page 950). These are also chopped and used as a garnish for numerous items.

Eggs, cold	20 each	20 each

1. Place the eggs in pot. Fill the pot with enough cold water to cover the eggs.

2. Bring the water to a gentle boil and immediately lower the temperature to a simmer. Begin timing the cooking at this point.

3. Cook small eggs for 12 minutes, medium eggs for 13 minutes, large eggs for 14 to 15 minutes, and extra large eggs for 15 minutes.

4. Serve the eggs hot in the shell (2 per portion), or cool them quickly in cool water and peel as soon as possible for cold preparations.

Poached Eggs

Yield: 10 servings

Poached Eggs Mornay: Brush toast with butter, top with the poached eggs, nappé with Mornay Sauce, sprinkle with grated cheese, and gratiné.
Poached Eggs with Mushrooms: Fill tartlets with creamed mushrooms, top with poached eggs, and nappé with Hollandaise.

Eggs	20 each	20 each
Water	as needed	as needed
Distilled white vinegar	as needed	as needed

1. In a large, shallow pot, bring a mixture of water and vinegar (using a ratio of 1 quart [1 liter] of water to 1 tablespoon of vinegar) to 200°F (95°C).

2. Break the eggs into cups one at a time, being careful not to break the yolks.

3. Slide the eggs into the simmering water and simmer them until they are done, 3 to 4 minutes. (Poached eggs should feel soft when touched; if they feel hard, they are overcooked.)

(Recipe continued on facing page)

4. Remove the eggs carefully with a skimmer and drop into ice water to stop the cooking process.

5. Remove the eggs from the cold water and trim any excess white to make them even.

6. For service, reheat the poached eggs in slightly salted, 120 to 140°F (50 to 60°C) water. Remove the eggs with a skimmer, dry, and serve.

Eggs Benedict

Yield: 10 servings

Poached eggs	20 each	20 each
Toasted English muffins, split and buttered	10 each	10 each
Canadian bacon, sliced and heated	10 slices	10 slices
Hollandaise Sauce	1 pint	480 milliliters

1. If eggs have been poached in advance, reheat in 160°F (70°C) water until warmed through. Blot on toweling and shape if necessary.

2. Top English muffin halves with sliced Canadian bacon. Top with eggs.

3. Ladle warm Hollandaise Sauce over eggs.

Fried Eggs

Yield: 10 servings

Eggs	20 each	20 each
Butter, clarified, or oil or bacon fat, rendered, as needed	4 fluid ounces	120 milliliters

1. Break the eggs into a bowl without damaging the yolks.

2. Heat the clarified butter in a pan until it is very hot but not smoking. Slide the eggs into the pan and reduce the heat to medium-low or low.

3. When the egg whites have set, tilt the skillet, allow the fat to collect at the side of the pan, and baste the eggs with the fat as they cook. This is known as "sunny-side up." Or, add a small amount of water and cover the pan to steam the eggs. Or, turn over the eggs near the end of their cooking time and cook them to the desired doneness (20 to 30 seconds more for "over-light," 1 minute more for "overhard").

VARIATION

Huevos Rancheros: Spoon salsa over a crisp fried corn tortilla. Top with 2 poached eggs and grated Monterey Jack cheese. Serve with refried beans on the side or spread directly on the tortilla. Finish with sour cream and chopped cilantro.

Poached Eggs with Chicken Liver Chasseur: Brush toasted English muffins with butter and top with sautéed chicken livers, poached eggs and Sauce Chasseur (page 530).

Poached Eggs Perdue: Brush toasted English muffins with butter and top with a ragoût of chicken, poached eggs, and asparagus tips.

Poached Eggs Massena: Heat fresh artichoke bottoms, fill with Béarnaise Sauce, top with poached eggs, nappé with tomato sauce, and sprinkle with chopped parsley.

Poached Eggs Farmer-Style: Brush toast with butter and top with a peeled tomato slice, boiled ham, creamed mushrooms, and poached eggs.

Poached Egg Parmesan: Slice an eggplant into rounds, bread it using the standard breading procedure, and deep-fry. Top each eggplant slice with ricotta cheese and a peeled tomato slice. Season them with salt and pepper. Heat in a 350°F (175°C) oven for 5 minutes. Place poached eggs on top of the tomatoes. Top with a slice of Provolone cheese and sprinkle with Parmesan. Brown under a broiler.

Poached Egg Chicken Curry: Prepare 4 ounces (115 grams) of roux with curry powder to taste. Add 1 pint (480 milliliters) cream and 1 pint (480 milliliters) apple juice and cook until the mixture is thickened and the starchy flavor is cooked out. Add 1 cup carrot julienne, 1 cup celery julienne, and 2 cups cooked chicken julienne. Top toasted English muffins or croutons with poached eggs and some of the curry mixture. Garnish with Mango Chutney and Banana Fritters.

Scrambled Eggs

Yield: 10 servings

Eggs	20 each	20 each
Salt, to taste	1/2 teaspoon	1/2 teaspoon
Pepper, to taste	1/2 teaspoon	1/2 teaspoon
Butter, as needed	3 ounces	85 grams

Garnish with grated cheese, crumbled bacon, diced ham, leftover meats, fish, or poultry, if desired. (See also the recommended garnishes for poached eggs, pages 858 to 859.)

For buffet service, scrambled eggs may be precooked in small batches. Add heavy cream, milk, or broth; this prevents the egg from stiffening too fast.

1. Break eggs into a bowl. Whip them well and season to taste immediately before cooking.
2. Heat the butter in a pan over low heat. Add the beaten eggs; stir them with a wooden spoon until they are soft and creamy. A bain-marie can be used for an even smoother texture.

VARIATIONS

(all additions are per-portion amounts)

Scrambled Eggs Greek-Style: Slice small eggplants lengthwise into 1/2-inch (1.25-centimeter) slices. Season them with salt and sauté them in oil. Sauté 1 ounce (30 grams) of tomato concassé with garlic to taste; season with salt and pepper. Place the scrambled eggs on top of eggplant slices; top the eggs with the tomato concassé.

Scrambled Eggs Hunter-Style: Sauté 3/4 ounce (20 grams) of diced bacon. Add 2 beaten eggs and 1/2 teaspoon of chopped chives, and scramble. Sauté 1/4 teaspoon of minced shallots and 3 ounces (85 grams) of sliced mushrooms in butter. Season them with salt and place on top of the eggs.

Scrambled Eggs with Bratwurst: Season peeled tomato slices with garlic, salt, and pepper and sauté them in butter on both sides. Top the tomatoes with the scrambled eggs and cooked bratwurst.

Scrambled Eggs Swedish-Style: Heat 1 tablespoon (15 grams) of butter. Add 1 finely crushed juniper berry and 1 ounce (30 grams) of smoked salmon, julienned. Add 2 beaten eggs and 1 teaspoon (750 grams) of chopped chives and scramble. Serve with toast.

Scrambled Eggs Gratiné: Top the scrambled eggs with Mornay Sauce, sprinkle them with grated cheese, and brown them lightly under a broiler.

Plain Rolled Omelet

Yield: 10 servings

Clarified butter may be used. Add the salt and pepper immediately before cooking.

Eggs	30 each	30 each
Salt, to taste	1/2 teaspoon	1/2 teaspoon
Pepper, to taste	1/4 teaspoon	1/4 teaspoon
Butter, as needed	4 ounces	115 grams

1. Beat the eggs well; season with salt and pepper.
2. Heat the butter in an omelet pan over high heat, tilting the pan to coat the entire surface.
3. Pour the egg mixture into the pan and scramble with a fork or wooden

(Recipe continued on facing page)

spoon. Move the pan and utensil at the same time until the egg mixture has coagulated slightly (at this point, add the filling if desired).

4. Let the egg mixture finish cooking without stirring.

5. Tilt the pan and slide a fork or a spoon around the lip of the pan, under the omelet, to be sure it is not sticking. Slide the omelet to the front of the pan and use a fork or a wooden spoon to fold it inside to the center.

6. Turn the pan upside down, rolling the omelet onto the plate seam side down. The finished omelet should be oval-shaped, with little or no color.

VARIATIONS

(all additions are per-portion amounts)

Enchilada Omelet: Fill the omelet with one ounce (30 grams) each diced red, yellow, and green peppers, and jalapeño jack cheese. Serve with guacamole and salsa on the side. Wrap in a flour or corn tortilla or serve tortillas on the side.

Herb Omelet: Sprinkle the omelet with 2 to 3 teaspoons of finely chopped fresh herbs before rolling it.

Tomato Omelet: Fill the omelet with 2 ounces (60 grams) of relatively thick tomato coulis or tomato concassé.

Fruit-Filled Omelet With Cheese: Fill the omelet with 2 tablespoons jelly, chutney, or other fresh fruits. Add 2 tablespoons marscapone or cream cheese blended with sweetened sour cream.

Cheese Omelet: Fill the omelet with 1 ounce (30 grams) of grated or diced cheese, alone or with other items. (Possible combinations include sun-dried tomatoes and goat's milk cheese, Gorgonzola and walnuts, cream cheese and olives, sautéed leeks and Gruyère.)

Omelet Florentine: Fill the omelet with 1 1/2 ounces (45 grams) of blanched spinach leaves sautéed with shallots and seasoned with salt and nutmeg.

Omelet Marcel: Sauté 3 ounces (85 grams) of sliced mushrooms and 1 ounce (30 grams) of sliced ham in butter. Prepare the basic omelet, cut it lengthwise, and fill it with the mushroom-ham mixture. Sprinkle the omelet with chopped chives.

Omelet Opera: Sauté 2 ounces (60 grams) of chicken livers in Madeira Sauce. Prepare the basic omelet, cut it lengthwise, and fill it with the livers. Garnish the omelet with 3 asparagus tips and nappé it with Hollandaise Sauce.

Seafood Omelet: Fill the omelet with 2 to 3 teaspoons of sour cream, crème fraîche, or yogurt with 2 ounces (60 grams) of cooked shrimp, smoked salmon, lobster, or other cooked and/or smoked fish, caviar, or seafood.

Shellfish Omelet: Fill the omelet with 3 or 4 oysters, clams, or mussels, stewed briefly in butter with wine and shallots.

Meat and Cheese Omelet: Fill the omelet with 1 ounce (30 grams) of diced meat such as turkey, goose, salami, or other sausage, and 1 ounce (30 grams) grated cheese. Add sun dried tomatoes, herbs, or other flavorings.

Western Omelet: Fill the omelet with 1 ounce (30 grams) each of diced sautéed ham, red and green peppers, and onions. Add cheese, if desired.

Spanish Omelet: Fill the omelet with 2 ounces (60 grams) tomato concassé or sauce, and 1 ounce (30 grams) each of diced onions and green peppers.

Frittata (Farmer-Style Omelet)

Yield: 10 servings

Frittatas are often cut into small pieces and served hot or cold as tapas.

Two fluid ounces (60 milliliters) of oil or butter may replace the bacon. Or, use sausage instead.

Other cooked vegetables such as peas, diced carrots, and asparagus, may be added, as well as herbs such as oregano, parsley and thyme.

The frittata may be finished in the oven.

Bacon, lean, diced	*12 ounces*	*340 grams*
Onions, minced	*10 ounces*	*285 grams*
Potatoes, cooked and diced	*10 ounces*	*285 grams*
Eggs	*20 each*	*20 each*
Salt, to taste	*1/2 teaspoon*	*1/2 teaspoon*
Pepper, to taste	*1/4 teaspoon*	*1/4 teaspoon*

1. Cook the bacon in a skillet until it is crisp.

2. Add the onions and sauté for 1 minute.

3. Add the potatoes and sauté until they are lightly browned.

4. Meanwhile, beat the eggs with the salt and pepper. Pour them over the ingredients in the skillet and stir gently.

5. Reduce the heat to low, cover the skillet, and cook until the eggs are nearly set.

6. Remove the cover and place the skillet under a broiler to brown the eggs lightly. Cut the frittata into wedges and serve.

Souffléed Omelet

Yield: 10 servings

Souffléed omelets offer an elegant presentation to any brunch menu but it is very important that they be prepared à la minute.

As with rolled omelets, many other ingredients may be incorporated. See the suggestions on pages 860 to 861.

Eggs	*30 each*	*30 each*
Salt, to taste	*1/2 teaspoon*	*1/2 teaspoon*
Pepper, to taste	*1/4 teaspoon*	*1/4 teaspoon*
Cheddar cheese, Vermont yellow, grated	*8 ounces*	*225 grams*
Chives, fresh, minced	*2 tablespoons*	*2 tablespoons*
Butter, clarified, or oil	*as needed*	*as needed*

1. Separate the eggs. Beat the yolks and season them to taste with salt and pepper.

2. Add the grated cheese and chives to the beaten yolks.

3. Beat the egg whites to medium peaks and fold them into the yolks.

4. Pour the batter into a preheated, well-oiled skillet. When the sides and bottom have set, finish the omelet in a hot oven until fully set but not dry. Garnish with additional chives. Serve immediately.

Baked Eggs

Yield: 10 servings

Butter, as needed	2 ounces	60 grams
Filling	1 pound	450 grams
Eggs	20 each	20 each
Salt, to taste	1/2 teaspoon	1/2 teaspoon
Pepper, to taste	1/4 teaspoon	1/4 teaspoon
Butter, as needed	5 ounces	140 grams

1. Warm ramekins; brush insides with butter.

2. Place the filling in the ramekins. Top each with an egg, season with salt and pepper, and top with a small piece of whole butter.

3. Set the ramekins in a prepared bain-marie with boiling water and cover with a lid or vented aluminum foil. Cook in a preheated 350 to 375°F (175 to 190°C) oven until done, about 4 to 5 minutes. The egg whites should be stiff and the yolks should be soft. Serve in the ramekins.

Possible fillings for Baked Eggs include ratatouille, ragoûts, sautéed, diced chicken livers, sautéed mushrooms, and/or other vegetables; Duxelles; hash browns, succotash, and flannel hash; refried beans with salsa, cheeses, tomato concassé, and sautéed spinach with garlic.

Other suggestions can be found with poached-egg garnishes (pages 858 and 859) and omelet fillings (page 861).

Shirred Eggs

Yield: 10 servings

Butter, melted, as needed	2 ounces	60 grams
Eggs	20 each	20 each
Salt, to taste	1/2 teaspoon	1/2 teaspoon
Pepper, to taste	1/4 teaspoon	1/4 teaspoon
Heavy cream, hot	5 fluid ounces	150 milliliters

1. Brush a gratin dish or flameproof ramekins with melted butter.

2. Break the eggs into gratin dish or ramekins; cook them over low to medium heat on stove top for 1 to 2 minutes or until their underside has set.

3. Season the eggs, add the heavy cream and bake the eggs in a 350°F (175°C) oven until they are done (4 to 5 minutes).

Medium to large eggs are the preferred size for breakfast cookery.

Prepared mustard, curry powder, or grated cheese may be added to the cream before pouring it over the eggs. Fillings and garnishes such as those recommended above may also be added. These can be prepared individually or in a larger gratin for buffet service.

Corn and Pepper Pudding

Yield: 10 servings

Onions, fine dice	5 ounces	140 grams
Butter or oil	as needed	as needed
Red pepper, fine julienne	1 each	1 each
Yellow pepper, fine julienne	1 each	1 each
Green pepper, fine julienne	1 each	1 each
Jalapeño peppers, minced (optional)	1/2 each	1/2 each
Milk, half-and-half, or cream	1 pint	480 milliliters
Eggs	4 each	4 each
Corn kernels, fresh or frozen	10 ounces	285 grams
Sugar	1 teaspoon	1 teaspoon
Cumin, ground	1/2 teaspoon	1/2 teaspoon
Oregano, fresh, chopped	1 1/2 teaspoons	1 1/2 teaspoons
Basil, fresh, chopped	1 teaspoon	1 teaspoon
Cilantro, chopped	2 teaspoons	2 teaspoons
Monterey Jack cheese, grated	6 ounces	170 grams
Salt, to taste	1/2 teaspoon	1/2 teaspoon
Pepper, to taste	1/4 teaspoon	1/4 teaspoon

Garnish the surface with extra cheese and flash under a salamander.

The mixture can also be poured into a partially baked pie shell and baked as a quiche.

For a "tamale pie," follow the recipe for Basic Pie Dough, substituting cornmeal or masa harina for half of the flour. Roll out the bottom crust, fill with the pudding, and top with the remaining dough. Dust with cayenne or chili powder. Bake about 45 minutes.

Additional ingredients such as dried tomato concassé, diced green chilies, chili powder, and cooked beans (pinto or black) can be added.

Roast the peppers and corn before adding if desired.

1. Sauté the onion in butter or oil until translucent.

2. Add the julienned peppers and jalapeño peppers. Cover the pan and sweat the peppers until they are tender. Drain off liquid.

3. Whisk together the milk (or half-and-half or cream) and the eggs. Add the pepper mixture, corn, sugar, cumin, herbs, and cheese. Mix them together well and season the mixture to taste with the salt and freshly ground pepper.

4. Butter a casserole or ramekins and pour in the pudding mixture. Bake the mixture in a bain-marie in a preheated 350°F (175°C) oven until a knife blade inserted in the center of the pudding comes out clean, about 45 minutes for a single large pudding (less time is needed for the ramekins).

5. Let the pudding stand for 15 minutes, cut it into wedges or squares, and serve it hot or at room temperature.

Leek and Tomato Quiche

Yield: 1 9-inch tart

Scallions, whites, skinned	*1 bunch*	*1 bunch*
Leeks, white and light green parts, sliced thin	*8 ounces*	*225 grams*
Butter	*2 ounces*	*60 grams*
Tomato Concassé	*10 ounces*	*285 grams*
Salt, to taste	*1/2 teaspoon*	*1/2 teaspoon*
Cayenne, ground	*to taste*	*to taste*
Heavy cream	*12 fluid ounces*	*360 milliliters*
Eggs	*3 each*	*3 each*
Monterey Jack, Gruyère, Cheddar cheeses, grated	*3 1/2 ounces*	*100 grams*
Herbs fresh, minced: tarragon, basil, or other	*2 tablespoons*	*2 tablespoons*
Crust, 9-inch, partially baked	*1 each*	*1 each*

Two recipes for pie crusts may be found on page 1080.

To ensure a crisp bottom crust, sprinkle some grated cheese onto bottom of crust when it comes out of the oven.

1. Sauté the scallions and leeks in butter until they are translucent.

2. Add the Tomato Concassé and sauté it until the liquid evaporates. Season with salt and cayenne pepper.

3. Whisk together the heavy cream and eggs. Stir in the cheese and season it with the herbs and more salt and pepper.

4. Spoon the filling mixture into the crust. Add the custard mixture gradually, stirring with a fork to distribute the filling ingredients evenly.

5. Set the quiche pan on a baking dish and bake it in a 350°F (175°C) oven until a knife blade inserted in the quiche's center comes out clean, about 40 to 45 minutes. Serve the quiche hot or at room temperature.

Quiche Lorraine

Yield: 1 9-inch tart

Slab bacon, lean, chopped	8 ounces	225 grams
Butter or oil	as needed	as needed
Heavy cream or crème fraîche	12 fluid ounces	360 milliliters
Eggs	3 each	3 each
Salt	1/2 teaspoon	1/2 teaspoon
Pepper	1/2 teaspoon	1/2 teaspoon
Gruyère cheese (optional), grated	6 ounces	115 grams
Crust, 9-inch, partially baked	1 each	1 each

1. Sauté the bacon in butter or oil until it is browned. Remove the bacon with a slotted spoon; drain.

2. Whisk together the heavy cream, or crème fraîche, and eggs to make a custard. Season to taste with salt and pepper.

3. Scatter the drained bacon and cheese evenly over the crust. Add the custard mixture gradually, stirring it with a fork to distribute the filling ingredients evenly.

4. Set the quiche pan on a baking dish and bake it in a 350°F (175°C) oven until a knife blade inserted in the quiche's center comes out clean, about 40 to 45 minutes. Serve the quiche hot or at room temperature.

VARIATIONS

Spinach Quiche: Include 12 ounces (340 grams) of spinach, well rinsed, blanched, squeezed dry, and chopped coarsely. Reduce the bacon to 4 ounces (115 grams). Lightly season with nutmeg.

Quiche Provençale: Substitute 12 ounces (340 grams) of reduced ratatouille for the bacon and cheese. Gratinée with cheese at service, if desired.

Vegetable Quiche: Substitute 1 pound (450 grams) of finely diced sautéed vegetables (snow peas, snap peas, green peas, asparagus, zucchini, yellow squash, carrots, etc.) for the bacon and cheese.

Southwestern Quiche: Include 8 ounces (225 grams) of julienned green chilies. Omit the bacon. Use Monterey Jack and Cheddar cheese. Add diced jalapeño peppers, or salsa, if desired. The pie crust recipe may be amended by replacing the flour with a blend of equal parts masa harina and flour.

Quiche may also be baked without a pastry crust as follows: Butter a shallow casserole or baking dish. Sprinkle it with grated Parmesan cheese if desired. Spread the filling ingredients over the casserole bottom. Pour the egg mixture over the flavorings. Bake the quiche in a bain-marie until a knife inserted near its center comes clean.

Quiche may also be baked in prebaked tartlet shells, individual timbale molds, or custard cups (as for quiche without crust, above).

Sautéed onions may be added to the Quiche Lorraine or any of the variations.

Savory Cheese Soufflé

Yield: 10 servings

Butter	2 ounces	60 grams
Flour	2 ounces	60 grams
Milk	1 1/4 quarts	1.2 liters
Egg yolks	15 each	15 each
Butter	as needed	as needed

(Recipe continued on facing page)

Parmesan cheese, grated	*3 ounces*	*85 grams*
Gruyère or Emmentaler		
cheese, grated	*3 ounces*	*85 grams*
Salt, added to taste	*1/2 teaspoon*	*1/2 teaspoon*
Black pepper, ground, to taste	*1/2 teaspoon*	*1/2 teaspoon*
Nutmeg, ground	*to taste*	*to taste*
Egg whites	*10 each*	*10 each*

Soufflés serve many functions as brunch items, side dishes, appetizers, and entrées.

In some instances, cayenne may be used in place of nutmeg.

Fresh, chopped herbs would also be excellent in the soufflé.

1. Prepare a light roux with the butter and flour.

2. Gradually add the milk, whipping out any lumps after each addition. Simmer the mixture for 15 minutes, stirring frequently. Remove the sauce from the heat.

3. Beat the egg yolks in a small bowl. Temper the yolks with hot sauce, and add them to the sauce. Reserve the base in a large bowl. (Soufflé base may be prepared up to this point and refrigerated or frozen for later use.)

4. Butter a 1 quart (1-liter) soufflé dish or 10 individual dishes. Sprinkle the sides and bottom with some Parmesan cheese. Tap the dish(es) on the counter to shake off any excess cheese; reserve the remaining Parmesan.

5. Stir in the Gruyère or Emmentaler cheese, salt, pepper, and nutmeg into the reserved soufflé base.

6. Whip the egg whites to soft peaks. Fold the whites into the base, half at a time.

7. Spoon the soufflé batter into the prepared molds to within 1/2 inch (1.5 centimeters) of the rim. Wipe the rim carefully to remove any batter. Tap the soufflé(s) gently on the counter to settle the batter.

8. Sprinkle the soufflé top(s) with the remaining Parmesan cheese.

9. Place the soufflé(s) in the bottom third of a preheated 425° F (220° C) oven and bake until puffy and a skewer inserted in their centers comes out relatively clean (14 to 18 minutes for individual soufflé(s), 30 to 35 minutes for a single large soufflé).

VARIATIONS

Herbs and Soufflé: Pesto, prepared mustard, tarragon, parsley, chives, chervil, or curry may be added to taste.

Spinach Soufflé: Add 4 ounces (115 grams) of blanched, squeezed, coarsely chopped spinach, 4 ounces (115 grams) of minced, sautéed onions or leeks, and/or 4 ounces (115 grams) of sautéed chopped mushrooms. Kale or watercress may be substituted for the spinach.

Seafood Soufflé: Add 8 ounces (225 grams) of cooked, diced seafood with 1 teaspoon chopped, fresh tarragon; 1 to 2 teaspoons dry sherry, 4 ounces (115 grams) of green peas, and/or 2 tablespoons (10 grams) of chopped sun-dried tomatoes. Omit the nutmeg.

Vegetable Soufflé: Add 4 ounces (115 grams) of reduced vegetable coulis or purée (roasted red peppers, green peas, roasted eggplant, pumpkin or squash, potato, or sweet corn all make good choices. Omit the nutmeg. Season with fresh herbs.).

Cheese Soufflé: Increase the amount of Gruyère to 6 ounces (170 grams) or replace the Gruyère with crumbled goat's milk or blue-veined cheese, Brie, or Camembert.

Cream of Wheat

Yield: 10 servings

Water	3 quarts	3 liters
Salt	1 teaspoon	1 teaspoon
Cream of wheat	7 ounces	200 grams

1. Bring the water to a rolling boil. Add salt.

2. Add the cream of wheat in a stream, stirring to prevent lumping.

3. Continue to cook over low to medium heat until the cereal has become thick and creamy.

Approximate cooking times of some breakfast grains:

Cream of Wheat: 15 to 20 minutes

Farina: 5 to 20 minutes

Grits, quick-cooking: 5 minutes

Grits, regular: 15 to 20 minutes

Oatmeal, rolled: 10 minutes

Buckwheat: 15 minutes

Hominy, whole: 30 minutes

Add dried fruits, chopped, toasted nuts, raisins, and ground spices as desired, or top with granola.

Cereals may be cooked in a mix of milk and water for a creamier texture, or finish with cream.

Serve with a small pitcher of milk or cream and brown sugar or syrup.

Oatmeal with Cinnamon and Dried Fruits

Yield: 10 servings

Water, warm	as needed	as needed
Raisins, seedless, or dried currants	2 ounces	60 grams
Dried apricots, chopped	2 ounces	60 grams
Dates, chopped	2 ounces	60 grams
Water, or a combination of water and milk	1 quart	1 liter
Oatmeal, rolled	6 ounces	170 grams
Ground cinnamon	1 teaspoon	1 teaspoon
Heavy cream, heated (optional)	10 fluid ounces	300 milliliters

1. Add enough warm water to the dried fruits to cover, and let soften while preparing the oatmeal.

2. Bring the salted water, or water and milk to a full boil. Add the oats in a thin stream and reduce the heat to a gentle simmer. Simmer the oatmeal for approximately 10 minutes or until it is tender.

3. Drain the fruits and add them to the oatmeal along with the cinnamon. If desired, top each serving of oatmeal with heated heavy cream.

Hot cereals should be thick and creamy but not heavy or sticky. Constant stirring produces a gummy finished product. Stir the cereal only as often as necessary to prevent scorching.

Granola

Yield: 5 quarts

Rolled oats	2 1/2 pounds	1.15 kilograms
Nuts, any type except peanuts	4 ounces	115 grams
Wheat germ	12 ounces	340 grams
Coconut, unsweetened, shredded	4 ounces	115 grams
Oil	8 fluid ounces	240 milliliters
Honey	12 fluid ounces	360 milliliters
Brown sugar	8 ounces	225 grams
Dried fruits, apricots, cherries, figs, etc.	12 ounces	340 grams
Raisins	5 ounces	140 grams

1. Mix oats, nuts, wheat germ, and coconut together on a sheet pan. Toast in a 325°F (165°C) oven until coconut is browned, stirring often to toast evenly. Put in a large bowl and reserve.
2. Bring oil, honey, and brown sugar to a full rolling boil; stir until all sugar is dissolved.
3. Pour hot syrup mixture over oat mix and stir until well coated.
4. Add dried fruits and mix well.
5. Pack into sheet pans and cool thoroughly.
6. Break up cooled granola and store in an airtight container in the refrigerator.

This granola formula contains nuts and seeds. It is important to carefully measure the amount of granola being served to avoid offering a dish too high in fat and calories.

Some people prefer to bake the granola again after it has been combined with the hot syrup in step 3. Bake it on the sheet pans.

Serve granola with milk, over yogurt, or over ice cream or fresh berries. Additional ingredients include sesame, pumpkin, and sunflower seeds.

"Muesli" Parfait

Yield: 10 to 12 servings

Milk	12 fluid ounces	360 milliliters
Sugar	6 ounces	170 grams
Lemon juice	3 fluid ounces	90 milliliters
Rolled oats	6 ounces	170 grams
Grapes, seedless, halved	1 pound	450 grams
Pears, small dice	4 each	4 each
Apples, small dice	4 each	4 each
Bananas, 1/4 inch dice	3 each	3 each
Heavy cream, whipped to stiff peaks	6 fluid ounces	180 milliliters
Almonds, toasted	4 ounces	115 grams

1. Combine milk, sugar, and lemon juice, add oats and soak 2 hours minimum or overnight.
2. Combine all fruits. Add the soaked oat mixture to fruit and toss to combine.
3. Whip cream and fold into fruit mixture. Serve cold in parfait glasses topped with almonds.

For this mousselike dish, carefully fold in the ingredients to create a beautiful presentation.

You may choose to include some of the granola above or substitute it for the oats.

Other nuts and seasonal fruits may be added. Substitute plain or lemon yogurt for the milk, sugar, and lemon mixture if desired.

Basic Pancakes

Yield: 10 servings

Flour	*24 ounces*	*680 grams*
Salt	*2 teaspoons*	*2 teaspoons*
Sugar	*6 ounces*	*170 grams*
Baking soda	*1 tablespoon*	*1 tablespoon*
Baking powder	*2 tablespoons*	*2 tablespoons*
Milk or buttermilk	*3 pints*	*1.5 liters*
Eggs, lightly beaten	*6 each*	*6 each*
Butter, melted	*3 ounces*	*85 grams*
Vegetable oil	*as needed*	*as needed*

For an extra-rich version, use light cream to replace part of the milk.

Seasonal fruits such as blueberries, raspberries, and parcooked dried apples (dusted with cinnamon) all make excellent additions. Add more sugar if necessary. If using frozen berries, it is not necessary to thaw them first, but you may want to check the consistency before adding all the milk.

Chopped toasted nuts provide additional texture.

Pancakes can be served with sweet Compound Butters found on pages 878.

1. Sift together the flour, salt, sugar, baking soda, and baking powder into a large mixing bowl.

2. In a separate bowl, whisk together the milk, eggs, and some of the melted butter.

3. Add the wet ingredients to the dry. Add the remaining butter. Stir with a wooden spoon to combine. The batter will be slightly lumpy.

4. Brush the griddle or skillet lightly with the oil; heat the oil until it is moderately hot.

5. Drop the batter onto the griddle, using a 2-ounce (60-milliliter) ladle, leaving about 1 inch (2.5 centimeters) of space between the pancakes.

6. Cook the pancakes until the undersides are brown, the edges begin to dry, and bubbles begin to break the surface of the batter, about 3 to 5 minutes.

7. Turn the pancakes and cook them until the second side is brown. Repeat using the remaining batter.

8. Serve the pancakes immediately or keep them warm, uncovered, in a slow oven. Do not hold the pancakes longer than 30 minutes, or they will become tough.

VARIATIONS

Pigs in a Blanket: Make 5-inch (12-centimeter) pancakes and roll each pancake around a precooked link sausage. Serve 2 to 3 on a plate with maple syrup.

Silver Dollar Pancakes: Thin batter with a bit more milk. Make pancakes about 2 to 3 inches (4 to 5 centimeters) in diameter. Serve 6 to 8 on a plate.

Whole-Grain Pancakes: Substitute Buckwheat flour, whole wheat flour, or oatmeal for 3/4 cup of the white flour.

Johnny Cakes: Substitute cornmeal for half of the flour. Add cooked corn kernels if desired.

Cottage Cheese Pancakes: Add 1 1/2 pints drained cottage cheese to the mixture.

Souffléed Pancakes: Separate eggs and add yolks to batter. Whip egg whites to medium peak and fold into batter just before cooking.

Pumpkin or Banana Pancakes

Yield: 30 cakes, 10 servings

Oat bran	*8 ounces*	*225 grams*
Flour	*8 ounces*	*225 grams*
Baking soda	*4 teaspoons*	*4 teaspoons*
Sugar	*2 tablespoons*	*2 tablespoons*
Bananas, mashed, or pumpkin, cooked	*8 ounces*	*225 grams*
Vanilla	*1 teaspoon*	*1 teaspoon*
Yogurt, nonfat	*1 pint*	*480 milliliters*
Vegetable oil	*2 fluid ounces*	*60 milliliters*
Egg whites	*8 each*	*8 each*

1. Combine and mix the dry ingredients.

2. Add fruit, vanilla, yogurt, and oil; mix until just combined. Add wet ingredients to dry, and combine gently. Do not overmix.

3. Prior to service, beat whites to a medium peak and fold into the mixture.

4. Brush the griddle or skillet lightly with the oil; heat the oil until it is moderately hot.

5. Drop the batter onto the griddle, using a 2-ounce (60-milliliter) ladle, leaving about 1 inch (2.5 centimeters) of space between the pancakes.

6. Cook the pancakes until the undersides are brown, the edges begin to dry, and bubbles begin to break the surface of the batter, about 3 to 5 minutes.

7. Turn the pancakes and cook them until the second side is brown. Repeat using the remaining batter.

8. Serve the pancakes immediately or keep them warm, uncovered, in a slow oven. Do not hold the pancakes longer than 30 minutes, or they will become tough.

This is a lower-fat and -calorie pancake than the Basic Pancakes recipe on page 871.

Warm some maple syrup, season lightly with cinnamon and nutmeg, and offer with pumpkin or banana cakes.

This sweet pancake can also be served as a dessert. Form the cooked pancake into a muffin time, heat until crisp, cool, and serve with a large scoop of cinnamon-flavored ice cream, banana slices (grilled if desired) and caramel sauce.

Crêpes

Yield: 20 servings (2 per serving)

Eggs	3 each	3 each
Milk	10 fluid ounces	300 milliliters
Butter, melted	1 ounce	30 grams
Flour	4 ounces	115 grams
Salt	1/2 teaspoon	1/2 teaspoon
Vegetable oil	as needed	as needed

Crêpes can be used for sweet or savory dishes. They may be filled with creamy, meat, and vegetable mixtures such as Cream Sherried Chicken (page 877), Vegetable stews (pages 806 to 808), or with sweet items such as Cinnamon Apples (page 877), fresh berries and whipped cream, or simply buttered with a sweet butter (pages 878 to 879). Refer to Chapter 29 for other dessert ideas.

For savory items, replace part or all of the milk with light beer.

Heavy cream can be substituted for 1/4 cup (60 milliliters) of the milk.

Add either 4 ounces (120 grams) of well-drained, chopped corn kernels or 4 ounces (120 grams) cup finely chopped mild green chilies, pimientos, or scallions to the batter for cornmeal crêpes.

1. Combine all ingredients except the oil in the bowl of a food processor or blender and blend for 30 seconds. Scrape down the sides of the bowl and process another minute, until the batter is very smooth. Or, mix the liquid ingredients with a wire whip. Add the flour and salt and beat until smooth.

2. Adjust the consistency with water or flour; the batter should be the consistency of heavy cream.

3. Let the batter rest, refrigerated, for 30 minutes.

4. Heat a crêpe pan over medium-high heat. Brush it lightly with oil.

5. Ladle about 3 tablespoons of batter in the center of the pan. Tilt the pan to swirl the batter over the surface to the edges.

6. Cook the crêpe until the edges are brown and the underside is golden. Flip and cook 1 minute more. Slide the crêpe onto a plate.

7. Repeat the procedure with the remaining batter. Stack the finished crêpes slightly off-center so they will be easier to separate.

8. To serve the crêpes, fill them, if desired, and roll them or fold them in quarters or in a pocket-fold.

Prepare in a flat pan with a bit of butter. Crepes are often filled and flavored with a variety of ingredients.

VARIATIONS

Whole-Grain Crêpes: Substitute 2 ounces (60 grams) whole-grain flour (wheat, rye, buckwheat) or cornmeal for half of the all-purpose flour.

Herbed Crêpes: Add 3 to 4 tablespoons of finely chopped fresh herbs to the batter.

Wild Rice Crêpes: Add up to 3 ounces (75 grams) of cooked, drained wild rice to the batter.

Spinach Crêpes: Add 1 ounce (30 grams) of cooked, squeezed, and finely chopped spinach leaves, 3 thinly sliced scallions, and a pinch of nutmeg to the batter.

Buttermilk Crêpes: Replace 8 fluid ounces (240 milliliters) of the milk with buttermilk.

Cornmeal Crêpes: Substitute 2 ounces of cornmeal or masa harina for half of the flour. Add crushed corn kernels if desired.

Waffles

Yield: 12 servings

All-purpose or cake flour, sifted	*8 ounces*	*225 grams*
Salt	*1 teaspoon*	*1 teaspoon*
Sugar	*2 ounces*	*60 grams*
Baking powder	*1 1/2 tablespoons*	*1 1/2 tablespoons*
Egg yolks	*4 each*	*4 each*
Milk	*12 fluid ounces*	*360 milliliters*
Butter, melted	*4 ounces*	*115 grams*
Egg whites, room temperature	*4 each*	*4 each*

1. Sift together the flour, salt, sugar, and baking powder in a large mixing bowl.

2. In a separate bowl, beat together the egg yolks, milk, and melted butter.

3. Add the wet ingredients to the dry. Stir with a wooden spoon just to combine. The batter will be slightly lumpy.

4. Preheat the waffle iron. Lightly oil.

5. Whip the egg whites to soft peaks and fold into the batter in two parts.

6. Ladle the batter onto the waffle iron. Close the iron and cook the waffles until they are crisp, golden, and cooked through.

The batter for waffles is simple to make and can be prepared up to one day in advance and held in the refrigerator.

Serve with warmed maple syrup and butter, fresh fruit and whipped cream, or one of the chilled fruit butters on pages 878 and 879.

French Toast

*Yield: 1 1/4 quarts (1.1 liter);
enough for approximately 20 slices of bread*

Milk	*1 quart*	*1 liter*
Eggs	*8 each*	*8 each*
Sugar, as needed	*2 ounces*	*60 grams*
Cinnamon, ground (optional)	*pinch*	*pinch*
Nutmeg, ground (optional)	*pinch*	*pinch*
Salt	*pinch*	*pinch*
Bread, sliced, day-old: wheat, French, challah, or other	*3 pieces*	*3 pieces*

1. Combine the milk, eggs, sugar, cinnamon, nutmeg, and salt and mix them into a smooth batter. Keep this batter refrigerated until needed.

2. Heat a skillet (use a nonstick pan or lubricate the skillet with a small amount of vegetable oil or butter to prevent sticking) over moderate heat.

3. Dip the bread into the batter, coating the slices evenly. Fry the slices on one side until evenly browned; then turn them and brown the other side.

4. Serve the French toast at once.

Dust the French toast with powdered sugar if desired.

Traditional accompaniments are syrup or honey and butter.

Add toasted chopped nuts to the syrup, or substitute a warm fruit compote or a fruit compound butter for the syrup.

A flat top may be used for high volume service.

The amount of bread this will coat will depend on size of slice and freshness of bread. Generally day-old bread works best.

Red Flannel Hash

Yield: 10 servings

An optional cooking method is to combine the ingredients and place them into an oiled hotel pan. The hash can be cooked in a hot oven until it is heated through and a crust has formed on the top. This is a convenient way to prepare hash for buffet service.

A traditional presentation is with toast or English muffins topped with poached or fried eggs.

Butter	*2 ounces*	*60 grams*
Onions, minced	*6 ounces*	*170 grams*
Green peppers, minced	*4 ounces*	*115 grams*
Corned beef, cooked and minced or ground	*1 pound*	*455 grams*
Chef's potatoes, grated, cooked	*8 ounces*	*225 grams*
Beets, grated, cooked, peeled	*8 ounces*	*225 grams*
Scallions, minced	*4 ounces*	*115 grams*
Parsley, fresh, chopped	*1 ounce*	*30 grams*
Thyme leaf, fresh, chopped	*1 tablespoon*	*1 tablespoon*
Salt, to taste	*1/2 teaspoon*	*1/2 teaspoon*
Pepper, to taste	*1/4 teaspoon*	*1/4 teaspoon*
Vegetable oil	*as needed*	*as needed*

1. Heat the butter over medium heat in a sauté pan. Add the onions and peppers; cook until they are translucent and tender. Remove the vegetables from the pan and place them in a large bowl.

2. Combine all the remaining ingredients (except for the vegetable oil) with the cooked onions and peppers and mix until evenly combined.

3. Heat the oil in a griswold over high heat. Add the hash mixture and press it into an even layer in the pan. Turn the heat down; cook the hash until a good crust has formed on the bottom.

4. Turn the hash and cook it until a crust has formed on the second side and the hash is thoroughly heated. Cut the hash into wedges and serve it at once.

Pan-Fried Ham Steak with Red-Eye Gravy

Yield: 10 servings

Ham steaks	3 pounds	1.3 kilograms
Cold water	10 ounces	10 ounces
Brewed coffee, strong	10 ounces	10 ounces
Pepper, to taste	1/2 teaspoon	1/2 teaspoon

1. Place the ham steaks in a cold cast iron skillet, and place over medium heat.

2. Cook the steaks, turning occasionally, until fat is very crisp and the steaks are very hot with a dark glaze—about 12 to 15 minutes.

3. Remove the steaks to warmed plates or a platter.

4. Pour off excess fat from the skillet and return to medium heat. Add cold water to the skillet, stirring and scraping the pan to release and dissolve the drippings.

5. Add the coffee, and reduce the gravy slightly over medium heat. Season to taste with salt and pepper. Pour the gravy over the steaks and serve at once.

Cut steaks into 4- to 5-ounce (115- to 140-gram) portions. When using Smithfield or country-style ham, you may want to blanch the steaks to remove excess salt. Place in a skillet and add enough cold water to cover. Bring to a simmer over low heat, simmer for a few minutes, drain, and pat dry before continuing with recipe. Whole salted hams are often soaked overnight.

The classic accompaniments are Cinnamon Apples, and grits and biscuits.

Creamed Chipped Beef

Yield: 10 servings

Chipped beef, coarse chop	12 ounces	340 grams
Butter	4 ounces	115 grams
Onions, (optional) chopped	5 ounces	140 grams
Flour	2 ounces	60 grams
Milk	1 quart	1 liter
White pepper, to taste	1/4 teaspoon	1/4 teaspoon
Salt, to taste	1/2 teaspoon	1/2 teaspoon
Bread slices, toasted and halved	20 each	20 each

1. Sauté the beef in some the butter until the edges curl. Remove the beef.

2. Add the onions and sweat (optional); add the flour and make a pale roux. Whisk in the milk, stirring constantly so it doesn't lump. Cook until the sauce thickens. Add the beef. Season to taste with salt and pepper.

VARIATION

Sausage Gravy: Replace beef with 12 ounces (340 grams) of ground sausage. Render the fat from the sausage and substitute some of the fat for the butter to make the roux if desired.

After sautéing the beef, remove and add flour to make a pale roux.

You may substitute a prepared Béchamel for the roux and milk if desired.

The chipped beef or air-dried beef may be very salty, so adjust seasoning accordingly.

If you like, add 5 hard boiled chopped eggs to the chipped beef before service.

Creamed Sherried Chicken on Toast Points

Yield: 10 servings

Chicken meat, cooked, light and/or dark, cubed	12 ounces	340 grams
Butter	4 ounces	115 grams
Flour	2 ounces	60 grams
Milk	1 quart	1 liter
Chives, fresh, chopped	1 teaspoon	1 teaspoon
Parsley, fresh, chopped	1 teaspoon	1 teaspoon
Dry sherry	2 fluid ounces	60 milliliters
Green peas, cooked	4 ounces	115 grams
White pepper, to taste	1/4 teaspoon	1/4 teaspoon
Salt, to taste	1/2 teaspoon	1/2 teaspoon
Bread slices, toasted and halved	20 each	20 each

You may substitute a prepared Béchamel for the butter, flour, and milk.

This is a breakfast/brunch-sized portion. For a more substantial entrée, increase the amount of chicken and vegetables.

It makes an especially elegant brunch item when served in a puff pastry shell.

1. Sauté the chicken in some the butter until the meat is warmed. Remove and reserve.

2. Add the flour and make a pale roux. Whisk in the milk, stirring constantly so it doesn't lump. Simmer until the sauce thickens.

3. Return the chicken along with the chives, parsley, sherry, and peas. Simmer just long enough to heat. Season to taste with salt and pepper.

4. Serve over toast points.

VARIATION

Creamed Asparagus on Toast: Prepare as above, substituting 1 pound (450 grams) of asparagus tips for the chicken and peas, or use 8 ounces (225 grams) each of asparagus and chicken.

Cinnamon Apples

Yield: 8 servings

Butter	2 ounces	60 grams
Sugar	1 ounce	30 grams
Granny Smith apples, peeled, cored, and sliced	2 each	2 each
Apple cider	4 fluid ounces	120 milliliters
Cinnamon	1 tablespoon	1 tablespoon

Often called "fried apples" in the south, these apples are usually served at breakfast with sausage or ham and biscuits, or as part of a buffet spread. They may also be served as a dessert with ice cream, cookies, or shortbread.

1. Heat the butter in a sauté pan over low heat; add sugar.

2. Add apples and cook until they are slightly caramelized. Add the cider and reduce to a syrup, about 5 to 10 minutes. Season to taste with cinnamon.

Fresh-Fruit Compote

Yield: 10 servings

Strawberries, hulled and sliced	*6 ounces*	*170 grams*
Blackberries	*6 ounces*	*170 grams*
Blueberries	*6 ounces*	*170 grams*
Raspberries	*6 ounces*	*170 grams*
Strawberry or Raspberry Coulis	*12 ounces*	*340 grams*

1. Gently fold together all ingredients.

2. Keep chilled until service.

The recipe for Fruit Coulis is on page 1073.

You can omit the coulis, and sprinkle the fruit with a little sugar. Allow it to macerate for several hours, or until the sugar is completely dissolved and the juices have begun to release from the fruit.

Serve with pancakes, waffles or crêpes, yogurt or cottage cheese.

Serve as a dessert item over shortbread or ice cream. An appropriate liquor may be added for desserts.

Dried-Fruit Compote

Yield: 10 servings

Dried apricots	*3 ounces*	*85 grams*
Prunes, pitted	*3 ounces*	*85 grams*
Dates, pitted	*2 ounces*	*60 grams*
Dried apples	*2 ounces*	*60 grams*
Dried cherries	*1 ounce*	*30 grams*
Water or apple juice	*12 fluid ounces*	*360 milliliters*
Cinnamon stick	*1 each*	*1 each*
Cloves, whole	*2 each*	*2 each*
Sugar	*1 tablespoon*	*15 grams*
Lemon juice, to taste	*a few drops*	*a few drops*

1. Combine all ingredients except the lemon juice; bring to a simmer.

2. Simmer until liquid is thickened, about 20 minutes. Adjust the seasoning with lemon juice.

3. Reserve warm for service.

This compote can be served on its own, or added to cooked cereals such as oatmeal or bulgar.

Serve chilled with plain or vanilla yogurt.

Replace some of the water or juice with a red wine, if desired.

Add diced fresh apples, with or without the skin, for a flavor and texture contrast.

Strawberry Compound Butter

Yield: 1 pound (450 grams)

Butter, softened	12 ounces	340 grams
Strawberries, puréed	5 ounces	140 grams

Chopped strawberries may be added for texture.

Other berries may be substituted. Raspberries are especially nice.

1. Beat the butter and strawberries together until blended.
2. Roll in parchment paper or pipe into rosettes.
3. Refrigerate or freeze until service.

Orange-Mango Compound Butter

Yield: 1 pound (450 grams)

Butter, softened	12 ounces	340 grams
Orange juice concentrate	2 ounces	60 grams
Mangos, puréed	4 to 6 ounces	115 to 170 grams

The mango may be omitted if not available. Increase the amount of orange juice to taste. Other tropical fruits also blend well with butter. Try papaya or guava. Substitute lemon or lime juice.

1. Beat the butter, orange juice concentrate, and mango purée together until blended.
2. Roll in parchment or pipe into rosettes.
3. Refrigerate or freeze until service.

Maple Syrup-Pecan Butter

Yield: 1 pound (450 grams)

Butter, softened	12 ounces	340 grams
Maple syrup	2 fluid ounces	85 grams
Pecans, toasted	2 ounces	60 grams

Substitute 4 fluid ounces (120 milliliters) of honey for the syrup.

1. Beat the butter, syrup, and nuts together until blended.
2. Roll in parchment or pipe into rosettes.
3. Refrigerate or freeze until service.

Hot Chocolate

Yield: 10 servings

Sugar	*5 ounces*	*140 grams*
Dutch cocoa	*2 ounces*	*60 grams*
Water	*6 fluid ounces*	*180 milliliters*
Milk	*2 quarts*	*2 liters*
Vanilla	*1/4 teaspoon*	*1/4 teaspoon*

1. Combine the sugar and cocoa in a saucepan. Add water and mix to a paste.

2. Stir in milk; bring to a simmer. Add vanilla to taste.

3. Serve in heated cups.

Garnish with whipped cream, chocolate shavings, peppermint sticks, or marshmallows as desired.

Breakfast Shake

Yield: 1 serving

Plain or vanilla yogurt	*8 ounces*	*225 grams*
Honey	*1 teaspoon*	*1 teaspoon*
Melon, cubed	*2 ounces*	*60 grams*
Peaches, peeled and sliced	*2 ounces*	*60 grams*

1. Combine all ingredients in a blender.
2. Purée until extremely smooth.
3. Serve at once.

Other fruits may be used to replace the melon and peaches. Try banana and strawberry, mango and pineapple, or raspberry and apricot.

Frozen yogurt may also be added.

CHAPTER 24 Salads and Salad Dressings

The salad recipes that are included in this chapter range from those appropriate for a first course or side dish to entrées. Almost all can be served as a main course with a few modifications. Although many have suggested dressings or accompaniments, you may always consider other dressings, ingredients, and presentations. Other salad recipes may be found in Chapter 26, Hors d'Oeuvres and Appetizers.

The recipes have been grouped in the following order:

- Green Salads
- Composed Salads
- Vegetable Salads
- Mediterranean Salads
- Meat and Fish Salads
- Potato Salads
- Grain, Pasta, and Bean Salads
- Vinaigrettes
- Mayonnaise and Creamy Dressings

Keep lettuce well chilled until ready for service.

Optional vegetable garnishes: sliced or shredded carrots or radishes; halved, quartered, or sliced tomatoes; raw or blanched green beans; peas, broccoli or cauliflower florets; crumbled, diced, or shredded cheese (goat, Cheddar, Swiss, blue, etc); croutons, roasted pepper strips, sun-dried tomatoes, olives.

A number of vinaigrettes and dressings can be found later in this chapter on pages 906 to 915.

Mixed Green Salad

Yield: 10 servings

Mixed greens: Romaine, bibb, Boston, red leaf, green leaf	30 ounces	840 grams
Vinaigrette or other dressing	10 fluid ounces	300 milliliters

1. Rinse the lettuces thoroughly. Drain well and spin dry. Keep the lettuce well chilled until ready for service.

2. Place the amount of lettuce required (2 to 3 ounces/60 to 85 grams per portion) in a mixing bowl.

3. Add sufficient dressing to lightly coat the leaves. Toss the salad gently to coat evenly.

4. Mound the lettuce on chilled salad plates and garnish as desired with 5 to 10 ounces (150 to 300 grams) of cucumbers, radishes, carrots, tomatoes, and peppers.

Sherried Watercress and Apple Salad

Yield: 10 servings

Sherry vinaigrette		
Vegetable oil	6 fluid ounces	180 milliliters
Sherry wine vinegar	3 fluid ounces	90 milliliters
Brown sugar	1 teaspoon	1 teaspoon
Salt, to taste	1/2 teaspoon	1/2 teaspoon
Pepper, to taste	1/4 teaspoon	1/4 teaspoon
Watercress, rinsed, stems trimmed	5 bunches	5 bunches
Golden Delicious apples, cored, julienne	2 each	2 each
Celery stalks, diced or cut on bias	5 each	5 each
Walnut halves, toasted	2 ounces	60 grams

1. Combine the oil, vinegar, sugar, salt, and pepper in a bowl and whisk until a lightly thickened vinaigrette forms.

2. Add the watercress, apples, and celery; toss until evenly coated with the vinaigrette.

3. Scatter the toasted walnuts over the salad; serve at once.

Spinach-Arugula Salad with Blood Oranges and Goat Cheese

Yield: 10 servings

Spinach leaves, cleaned	*24 ounces*	*680 grams*
Arugula, cleaned	*2 bunches*	*2 bunches*
Frisée	*1 head*	*1 head*
Carrots, sliced thin or julienned	*4 ounces*	*115 grams*
Curry Vinaigrette	*10 fluid ounces*	*285 milliliters*
Blood oranges, cut into segments	*3 each*	*3 each*
Goat cheese logs, sliced 1/2-inch thick	*10 slices*	*10 slices*
Poppy seeds, as needed (optional)	*2 tablespoons*	*2 tablespoons*

Curry Vinaigrette is on page 910.

1. Combine spinach, arugula, and frisée.

2. Toss greens with Curry Vinaigrette until coated.

3. Lift greens onto plate, allowing excess vinaigrette to drain into bowl.

4. Top salad with orange segments and goat cheese. Scatter with poppy seeds.

Mesclun Salad with Apples and Goat Cheese

Yield: 10 servings

Dressing

Safflower oil	*24 fluid ounces*	*720 milliliters*
Rice wine vinegar	*3 fluid ounces*	*90 milliliters*
Granny Smith apples, peeled and minced	*3 ounces*	*85 grams*
Curry powder	*2 tablespoons*	*2 tablespoons*
Shallots, minced	*2 teaspoons*	*2 teaspoons*
Salt, to taste	*1/2 teaspoon*	*1/2 teaspoon*
Pepper, to taste	*1/4 teaspoon*	*1/4 teaspoon*
Mesclun mix, such as frisée, oak leaf, arugula, etc.	*2 1/4 pounds*	*1 kilogram*
Goat cheese logs, sliced	*10 ounces*	*285 grams*
Sesame seeds, toasted	*3 teaspoons*	*3 teaspoons*
Poppy seeds	*2 teaspoons*	*2 teaspoons*
Peppers, roasted, julienne	*6 ounces*	*140 grams*
Almonds, whole or slivered, toasted	*3 ounces*	*85 grams*

Mesclun is a mixture of salad greens. The exact components will vary, both according to the region and the season. If you wish blend mesclun with Romaine and leaf lettuces.

(Recipe continued on next page)

Cut the goat cheese logs into slices so that you will have 3 slices per plate.

Romaine is crisp, tender, and fairly mild in taste. Rinse thoroughly to remove sand.

There are serious health risks posed by preparing this dish with the raw (or even coddled) egg suggested by the traditional recipe. You may either omit the egg (as we have done here) or use a pasteurized egg product.

1. Combine all of the ingredients for the dressing and mix well.

2. Combine the greens with approximately 1 fluid ounce (30 milliliters) of the dressing and toss to coat. Place on a salad plate.

3. Garnish each salad as follows: Dip 1 slice of the goat's cheese in the sesame seeds and 1 slice in the poppy seeds, and leave 1 slice plain. Place on the salad. Add the roasted peppers and toasted almonds.

Caesar Salad

Yield: 2 servings
(for tableside presentation)

Romaine lettuce, cut bite-size pieces	*8 to 10 ounces*	*240 to 285 grams*
Garlic cloves, halved	*2 each*	*2 each*
Anchovy fillets	*2 to 3 each*	*2 to 3 each*
Lemon juice	*1 fluid ounce*	*30 milliliters*
Extra-virgin olive oil	*2 fluid ounces*	*60 milliliters*
Pepper, coarse grind, to taste	*1/2 teaspoon*	*1/2 teaspoon*
Parmesan cheese, grated	*4 ounces*	*225 grams*
Croutons, plain or garlic-flavored	*6 ounces*	*170 grams*

1. Rinse and dry lettuce. Tear into bite-sized pieces and chill.

2. Rub the salad bowl with the garlic and mash it to a paste.

3. Blend the anchovies and gradually incorporate the lemon juice and olive oil to make a dressing.

4. Add the cheese and blend it into the dressing.

5. Add the Romaine and toss until the leaves are evenly coated.

6. Season to taste with pepper. Add croutons and serve.

Spinach, Avocado, and Grapefruit Salad

Yield: 10 servings

Avocados, ripe, sliced	*4 each*	*4 each*
Grapefruit, sectioned	*4 each*	*4 each*
Spinach, cleaned, stemmed	*2 pounds*	*900 grams*
Vinaigrette	*12 fluid ounces*	*360 milliliters*

(Recipe continued on facing page)

1. Toss together the avocados and grapefruit (this will prevent the avocados from browning).

2. Toss the spinach leaves with the grapefruit vinaigrette; use only enough dressing to coat the leaves very lightly.

3. Arrange the spinach on chilled plates. Top with the avocados and grapefruit.

4. Drizzle additional dressing on the avocado mixture.

Grapefruit Vinaigrette: Make the Basic Vinaigrette on page 906 using grapefruit juice to replace the vinegar. Peanut or corn oil is a good choice here, since the oil should have a neutral flavor. Omit the mustard and use brown sugar.

Wilted Spinach Salad with Warm Bacon Vinaigrette

Yield: 10 servings

Warm bacon vinaigrette

Bacon, diced	*8 ounces*	*225 grams*
Shallots, minced	*1 1/2 ounces*	*45 grams*
Garlic cloves, mashed	*2 each*	*2 each*
Brown sugar	*4 ounces*	*115 grams*
Cider vinegar	*3 ounces*	*85 grams*
Vegetable oil	*5 to 6 fluid ounces*	*150 to 180 milliliters*
Salt, to taste	*1 teaspoon*	*1 teaspoon*
Black peppercorns, cracked	*1 teaspoon*	*1 teaspoon*
Spinach, stemmed, torn	*1 1/2 pounds*	*680 grams*
Eggs, hard-boiled, chopped	*5 each*	*5 each*
Mushrooms, sliced	*6 ounces*	*170 grams*
Red onion, sliced into thin rings	*1 each*	*1 each*
Croutons, as needed	*4 ounces*	*225 grams*

Wilted green salads are popular lunch options. Or, serve this as a side dish with a grilled or roasted entrée.

1. To make the vinaigrette: Render the bacon. Remove the diced bacon from the pan and reserve. Add the shallots and garlic to the bacon fat and sweat. Blend in the brown sugar to melt. Whisk in the cider vinegar and then oil. Season to taste with salt and pepper. Bring to a simmer.

2. Add the spinach to the hot dressing; toss until just wilted. Transfer to a plate. Top with eggs, mushrooms, onion rings, croutons, and reserved bacon.

Buffalo-Style Chicken Salad

Yield: 10 servings

Prepare lettuce as directed on pages 194 to 196. Blue Cheese Dressing is on page 914.

*To make **Buffalo-Style Chicken Wings,** broil or deep-fry seasoned chicken wings until cooked through but not browned. Heat the butter, cayenne, lemon juice, and hot sauce, and brush onto the wings. Finish by baking until crisp. Serve with a blue cheese dipping sauce and celery sticks.*

Chicken legs, skinless, boneless	*10 each*	*10 each*
Mixed lettuce greens	*20 ounces*	*570 grams*
Basic Vinaigrette	*6 fluid ounces*	*180 milliliters*
Butter	*3 ounces*	*85 grams*
Cayenne, ground	*3/4 teaspoon*	*3/4 teaspoon*
Lemon juice	*2 tablespoons*	*2 tablespoons*
Parsley, fresh, chopped	*1/2 ounce*	*15 grams*
Frank's Hot Sauce	*1 1/2 tablespoons*	*1 1/2 tablepoons*
Salt, to taste	*1/2 teaspoon*	*1/2 teaspoon*
Celery, stalks, cut allumette	*50 each*	*50 each*
Tomato Concassé	*10 ounces*	*285 grams*
Celery leaves, chopped	*2 ounces*	*60 grams*
Blue Cheese Dressing	*20 fluid ounces*	*600 milliliters*

1. Cut meat from chicken leg into 4 strips. Deep-fry until very crisp, about 6 to 7 minutes.

2. Toss lettuce greens with vinaigrette and arrange on plate.

3. Place deep-fried chicken meat in a bowl and toss with the butter, cayenne pepper, lemon juice, parsley, hot sauce, and salt.

4. Arrange chicken on the salad with the celery sticks and Tomato Concassé. Drizzle with the Blue Cheese Dressing and sprinkle with celery leaves.

Chef Salad

Yield: 10 servings

Serve this salad with a choice of dressings: Vinaigrette, page 906 Catalina, page 910 Blue Cheese, page 914 Ranch-Style, page 913.

Assorted greens	*2 pounds*	*900 grams*
Smoked ham, boneless, sliced	*1 pound*	*455 grams*
Chicken breasts, cooked and sliced	*10 each*	*10 each*
Tomatoes, peeled and quartered	*10 each*	*10 each*
Eggs, hard-boiled and quartered	*10 each*	*10 each*
Cucumber, sliced	*1 each*	*1 each*
Carrots, sliced	*1 each*	*1 each*
Salami, sliced very thin, rolled tightly	*3 each*	*3 each*
Cheddar cheese, julienne	*10 ounces*	*285 grams*
Gruyère cheese, julienne	*10 ounces*	*285 grams*
Chives, chopped	*2 tablespoons*	*2 tablespoons*

(Recipe continued on facing page)

1. Place the greens in a chilled bowl or arrange them on a chilled plate.

2. Arrange the chicken, vegetables, eggs, and cheeses on the lettuce.

3. Top with the chopped chives.

4. Serve dressing on the side or drizzled over the salad.

Cobb Salad

Yield: 10 servings

Vegetable oil	*6 fluid ounces*	*180 milliliters*
Cider vinegar	*2 fluid ounces*	*60 milliliters*
Lemon juice	*1 fluid ounce*	*30 milliliters*
Dijon mustard	*1 ounce*	*30 grams*
Parsley, chopped	*1/2 ounce*	*15 grams*
Romaine lettuce, torn into shreds	*2 pounds*	*900 grams*
Turkey breast, boneless, skinless, cubed	*1 pound*	*455 grams*
Tomatoes, peeled and seeded, large dice	*20 ounces*	*680 grams*
Avocado, peeled and cubed	*2 each*	*2 each*
Celery stalk, sliced on the bias	*2 each*	*2 each*
Scallions, sliced on the bias	*4 each*	*4 each*
Bacon slices, cooked, diced	*5 each*	*5 each*
Blue cheese, crumbled	*10 ounces*	*285 grams*

A classic presentation for this dish would be to arrange the turkey, avocado, tomato, and blue cheese in alternating strips. The ingredients should be cut in uniform, bite-sized chunks.

1. Blend the oil, vinegar, lemon juice, mustard, parsley, salt, and pepper thoroughly in a large mixing bowl.

2. Add the lettuce and toss until combined. Divide the lettuce into bowls or on platters.

3. Arrange the turkey, tomato, avocado, celery, and scallions over the bed of lettuce. Drizzle the dressing still remaining in the mixing bowl over the salad. Top with crumbled blue cheese and bacon. Serve at once.

Taco Salad

Yield: 10 servings

Tortilla shells can be purchased already prepared. To make them, used nested frying baskets and deep-fry flour or corn tortillas at 375°F (190°C) until crisp. Drain and cool before filling.

Ground beef	2 1/2 pounds	1.15 kilograms
Taco Sauce (below)	1 pint	480 grams
Iceberg lettuce, chiffonade	2 pounds	900 grams
Tortilla bowls, fried, corn or flour	10 each	10 each
Black beans, cooked	12 ounces	340 grams
Pinto beans, cooked	12 ounces	340 grams
Tomatoes, diced	10 ounces	285 grams
Red onions, diced	1 each	1 each
Sour cream	5 fluid ounces	150 milliliters
Cheddar or Monterey Jack cheese, shredded	10 ounces	285 grams
Black olives, sliced	20 each	20 each
Fresh Tomato Salsa	20 ounces	680 grams

1. Brown ground beef. Drain well, and combine with Taco Sauce.

2. Lay a bed of lettuce in the bottom of the tortilla bowl. Top with beans, tomatoes, onions, sour cream, cheese, olives and salsa.

Taco Sauce

Yield: 1 pint (480 milliliters)

To make a cornstarch slurry, dilute cornstarch with cold water to make a very thin paste.

Onion, small dice	1 ounce	30 grams
Garlic, cloves, minced	2 each	2 each
Vegetable oil	2 fluid ounces	60 milliliters
Oregano, ground	2 teaspoons	2 teaspoons
Cumin, ground	1 tablespoon	1 tablespoon
Chili powder	1 tablespoon	1 tablespoon
Chicken Stock	8 fluid ounces	240 milliliters
Tomato purée	6 fluid ounces	180 milliliters
Cornstarch slurry	as needed	as needed

1. Sweat onions and garlic in oil.

2. Add spices and cook briefly.

3. Add stock and tomato purée and simmer. Thicken with cornstarch slurry, if needed. Chill well before using in salads.

Lobster Salad with Avocado & Apples

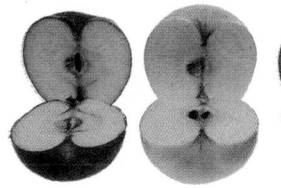

The apple's crisp texture mixes well with the lobster and avocado.

Yield: 10 servings

Vinaigrette

White wine vinegar	*4 fluid ounces*	*120 milliliters*
Peanut oil	*12 fluid ounces*	*360 milliliters*
Crème fraîche	*3 fluid ounces*	*90 milliliters*
Salt, to taste	*1/2 teaspoon*	*1/2 teaspoon*
Pepper, to taste	*1/4 teaspoon*	*1/4 teaspoon*
Sugar, to taste	*1/4 teaspoon*	*1/4 teaspoon*
Apples, peeled	*10 ounces*	*285 grams*
Avocados, peeled	*8 ounces*	*225 grams*
Tomatoes, peeled, small dice	*8 ounces*	*225 grams*
Lemon juice	*3 fluid ounces*	*90 milliliters*
Vegetable oil	*1 fluid ounce*	*30 milliliters*
Salt, to taste	*1/2 teaspoon*	*1/2 teaspoon*
Pepper, to taste	*1/4 teaspoon*	*1/4 teaspoon*
Lobsters, cooked	*10 each*	*10 each*
Mixed baby lettuce greens	*20 ounces*	*570 grams*
Vinaigrette	*1 pint*	*480 milliliters*
Chives, finely sliced	*1 bunch*	*1 bunch*
Chervil, sprigs	*1 bunch*	*1 bunch*

1. Whisk the first set of ingredients together to make the dressing.

2. Cut the apples and avocados into pearl-size balls using a small parisienne scoop.

3. Combine the apples and avocados with the tomato, lemon juice, oil; season with salt and pepper.

4. Leave lobster claws whole, slice tail meat into medallions.

5. Toss baby greens lightly with a small amount of vinaigrette, season with salt and pepper.

6. Use about 3 tablespoons (45 milliliters) of dressing to make a pool on a chilled plate. Place a small pile of lettuce at the top of the plate and arrange the lobster tail slices in a circle on the plate. Set claws at the base of the lettuce.

7. Scatter tomato mixture over lobster and sprinkle with chives and chervil.

The lobsters should weigh 1 to 1 1/2 pounds (450 to 680 grams) each. To read more about working with lobsters, refer to pages 249 and 250.

Goat Cheese in Filo with Roasted Pepper Salad

Yield: 10 servings

There are a number of vinaigrette recipes in this chapter. Refer to pages 906 to 910 for suggestions.

Goat cheese in filo		
Goat cheese log, fresh	10 ounces	285 grams
Fines Herbes, chopped	1/2 ounce	15 grams
Phyllo dough	6 sheets	6 sheets
Butter, melted	4 ounces	115 grams
Red peppers, roasted	8 ounces	225 grams
Yellow peppers, roasted	8 ounces	225 grams
Green peppers, roasted	4 ounces	115 grams
Pearl onions, roasted	20 each	20 each
Olive oil	2 fluid ounces	60 milliliters
Balsamic vinegar	1/2 fluid ounce	15 milliliters
Salt, to taste	1/2 teaspoon	1/2 teaspoon
Pepper, to taste	1/4 teaspoon	1/4 teaspoon
Baby Romaine leaves	as needed	as needed
Basic Vinaigrette	1 pint	480 milliliters

1. Roll cheese in the Fines Herbes.

2. Place one filo sheet on a clean towel and brush with butter. Place another sheet on top and brush with butter. Continue to layer filo sheets with butter until filo is used.

3. Place the goat cheese log on the filo and roll up. Place on an oiled sheet pan, brush with butter, score filo 20 times, and bake at 400°F (205°C) for 15 minutes until golden brown.

4. Combine peppers, onions, oil, vinegar, salt, and pepper.

5. Toss the lettuce greens with vinaigrette and season with salt and pepper.

6. For each plate, arrange the lettuce on one side and make a bed of the pepper salad.

7. Cut the filo log into slices; place slices on each salad.

Coleslaw

Yield: 10 servings

Sour cream	*6 fluid ounces*	*180 milliliters*
Mayonnaise	*2 fluid ounces*	*60 milliliters*
Cider vinegar	*2 fluid ounces*	*60 milliliters*
Dry mustard	*1 tablespoon*	*1 tablespoon*
Sugar	*1 1/2 ounces*	*45 grams*
Celery seed	*2 teaspoons*	*2 teaspoons*
Salt, to taste	*1/2 teaspoon*	*1/2 teaspoon*
Pepper, to taste	*1/4 teaspoon*	*1/4 teaspoon*
Green cabbage, shredded	*1 1/2 pounds*	*680 grams*
Carrots, shredded	*6 ounces*	*170 milliliters*

1. Mix the sour cream, mayonnaise, vinegar, mustard, sugar, and celery seed together in a large bowl until smooth. Add salt and pepper to taste.

2. Add the cabbage and carrots and toss until evenly coated.

Citrus Slaw with Avocado and Red Onion

Yield: 10 servings

Spinach, finely shredded	*1 pound*	*450 grams*
Red cabbage, finely shredded	*6 ounces*	*170 grams*
Savoy cabbage, finely shredded	*6 ounces*	*170 grams*
Red onion, julienne	*4 ounces*	*115 grams*
Grapefruit Vinaigrette, as needed	*1 pint*	*480 milliliters*
Avocado, sliced or diced	*2 each*	*2 each*
Grapefruit, peeled, cut into segments	*2 each*	*2 each*
Black peppercorns, cracked	*1 teaspoon*	*1 teaspoon*

Grapefruit Vinaigrette is on page 884.

An average avocado weighs about 3 to 5 ounces (85 to 140 grams).

1. Toss the spinach, cabbages, and red onion together in a bowl, and add enough of the vinaigrette to coat ingredients.

2. Toss the avocado gently with the remaining vinaigrette to coat.

3. Drain the avocado and arrange it on top of the cabbage mixture; top with the cracked peppercorns.

Corn and Jícama Salad

Yield: 10 servings

Corn kernels, cooked	*1 1/2 pounds*	*680 grams*
Jícama, peeled, small dice	*1 pound*	*450 grams*
Lime juice	*1 fluid ounce*	*30 milliliters*
Cilantro leaves, chopped	*1 teaspoon*	*1 teaspoon*
Cayenne pepper, to taste	*1/8 teaspoon*	*1/8 teaspoon*
Salt, to taste	*1/2 teaspoon*	*1/2 teaspoon*
White pepper, to taste	*1/4 teaspoon*	*1/4 teaspoon*

1. Toss together in small bowl and refrigerate until service.

Add other fresh chilies to this salad: jalapeño, serrano, or Anaheim.

Grill or roast the corn if you prefer.

Carrot and Raisin Salad

Yield: 10 servings

Water	*8 fluid ounces*	*240 milliliters*
Sugar	*1 ounce*	*30 grams*
Salt, to taste	*1/4 teaspoon*	*1/4 teaspoon*
Lemon juice	*1 tablespoon*	*1 tablespoon*
Raisins	*5 ounces*	*140 grams*
Carrots, grated	*1 1/2 pounds*	*680 grams*
Mayonnaise	*3 fluid ounces*	*90 milliliters*
Catalina Dressing	*3 fluid ounces*	*90 milliliters*

Basic Mayonnaise is found on page 911.

1. Combine water with the sugar, salt, and lemon juice and bring to a boil. Pour over the raisins and steep until the raisins are plump. Drain and cool.

2. Mix raisins and carrots with the two dressings. Chill.

Celeriac and Tart Apple Salad

Yield: 10 servings

Celeriac, trimmed, cut into matchsticks	*1 1/2 pounds*	*680 grams*
Dressing		
Mayonnaise	*3 fluid ounces*	*90 milliliters*
Crème fraîche	*3 ounces*	*85 grams*
Dijon mustard	*2 ounces*	*60 grams*
Lemon juice	*1 fluid ounce*	*30 milliliters*
Salt, to taste	*1 teaspoon*	*1 teaspoon*
Pepper, coarse grind, to taste	*1/2 teaspoon*	*1/2 teaspoon*
Blanc, as needed to cover	*1 quart*	*1 liter*
Lemon juice	*as needed*	*as needed*
Granny Smith apples, peeled and diced	*3 each*	*3 each*

1. Combine all ingredients for dressing and blend well.

2. Add celeriac to the blanc as it is cut. When ready to blanch celeriac, rinse well and add to simmering water combined with 1 ounce (30 milliliters) of lemon juice. Parcook approximately 2 minutes; drain and refresh.

3. Toss apples with dressing. Add celeriac and adjust seasonings to taste with salt, pepper, and lemon juice.

If crème fraîche is unavailable, substitute sour cream.

The recipe for Blanc is found on page 448.

Serve this salad to accompany pâtés or terrine or as part of an hors d'oeuvre variées platter.

Jícama and Cucumber Salad

Yield: 10 servings

Jicama, julienned	*1 1/2 pounds*	*680 grams*
Cucumber, peeled, seeded, and sliced	*1 pound*	*450 grams*
Red pepper, julienne	*1 each*	*1 each*
Lime juice	*1 fluid ounce*	*30 milliliters*
Yogurt	*6 fluid ounces*	*170 grams*
Cumin seeds, toasted, ground	*3/4 teaspoon*	*3/4 teaspoon*
Salt, to taste	*1/2 teaspoon*	*1/2 teaspoon*
Pepper, to taste	*1/4 teaspoon*	*1/4 teaspoon*

1. Combine jícama, cucumber, and red pepper in a medium bowl. Toss with the lime juice.

2. Mix yogurt, cumin, salt, and pepper. Pour over jícama mixture. Mix to combine.

3. Chill for 2 hours before serving.

Jícama has a sweet flavor somewhat similar to water chestnuts. Cut away the fibrous outer layer.

Waldorf Salad

Yield: 10 servings

The recipe for Basic Mayonnaise is on page 911.

Serve on Boston or Bibb lettuce.

Apples, peeled, cored, and cubed	*1 1/4 pounds*	*570 grams*
Celery, large dice	*6 ounces*	*170 grams*
Mayonnaise	*3 fluid ounces*	*90 milliliters*
Lettuce leaves	*20 each*	*20 each*
Walnuts, chopped coarsely	*2 ounces*	*60 grams*

1. Combine the apples, celery, and mayonnaise; chill.

2. Serve on a bed of lettuce. Top with walnuts.

Tomato and Mozzarella Salad

Yield: 10 servings

Balsamic Vinaigrette may be found on page 906.

You may prefer to use a plain extra-virgin olive oil or an infused oil (garlic or basil would be appropriate).

Tomatoes, sliced	*1 pound*	*450 grams*
Fresh mozzarella, sliced	*1 pound*	*450 grams*
Basil, fresh, chiffonade	*1 ounce*	*30 grams*
Balsamic Vinaigrette	*10 fluid ounces*	*300 milliliters*
Pepper, ground, to taste	*1/4 teaspoon*	*1/4 teaspoon*

1. Place the tomatoes and mozzarella slices alternately on a plate. Drizzle the vinaigrette over the top. Garnish with the basil and fresh ground pepper.

Panzanella

Yield: 10 servings

The traditional method for preparing this salad calls for the bread cubes to be soaked in cold water for several hours, then squeezed to remove the excess moisture.

Italian or French bread, 2-inch cubes	*8 ounces*	*225 grams*
Tomatoes, large cubes	*1 1/2 pounds*	*680 grams*
Garlic, minced	*2 tablespoons*	*2 tablespoons*
Celery, hearts, cut on a bias	*4 each*	*4 each*
Cucumber, seeded and diced	*8 ounces*	*225 grams*
Red peppers, diced	*6 ounces*	*170 grams*
Yellow peppers, diced	*6 ounces*	*170 grams*
Anchovy fillets, diced	*20 each*	*20 each*
Capers, drained	*2 tablespoons*	*2 tablespoons*
Basil, chopped coarse	*1/4 ounce*	*8 grams*
Basic Vinaigrette	*10 fluid ounces*	*300 milliliters*

1. Combine the bread, tomatoes, garlic, celery, cucumber, peppers, anchovies, capers, and basil. Add the vinaigrette and toss to coat.

Niçoise Salad with Tuna

Yield: 10 servings

Green beans, cooked	*1 pound*	*455 grams*
Red onions, julienne	*2 each*	*2 each*
Red Bliss potatoes, quartered	*2 pounds*	*900 grams*
Capers, chopped	*1 ounce*	*30 grams*
Parsley, chopped	*1 ounce*	*30 grams*
Basic Vinaigrette	*1 pint*	*480 milliliters*
Mixed greens, washed and rinsed	*1 1/2 pounds*	*680 grams*
Tuna fish, canned	*2 pounds*	*900 grams*
Plum tomatoes, peeled and quartered	*5 each*	*5 each*
Eggs, hard-boiled, peeled and quartered	*10 each*	*10 each*
Anchovy fillets	*20 each*	*20 each*
Calamata olives	*40 each*	*40 each*

1. Toss together the green beans, onions, potatoes, capers, and parsley. Add the vinaigrette and toss. Let them marinate for several hours. Drain and reserve excess vinaigrette.

2. Lay the lettuce on a platter. Place the tuna fish in the center. Arrange the bean-and-potato mixture around the tuna. Garnish the plate with the tomatoes, eggs, anchovies, and olives.

Niçoise salads often contain tuna. Contemporary renditions may call for a 3-ounce (85-gram) piece of grilled tuna instead of canned tuna. However, a Niçoise salad without tuna can be prepared, with or without hard-boiled eggs.

Basic Vinaigrette is on page 906.

Greek Salad

Yield: 10 servings

Romaine lettuce	*1 1/2 pounds*	*680 grams*
Tomatoes, cored	*4 each*	*4 each*
Cucumber, sliced or diced	*6 ounces*	*170 grams*
Red onion, sliced into rings	*4 ounces*	*115 grams*
Feta cheese, drained, crumbled	*5 ounces*	*140 grams*
Black olives, pitted	*3 ounces*	*85 grams*
Green olives, pitted	*3 ounces*	*85 grams*
Stuffed Grape Leaves	*10 each*	*10 each*
Lemon Parsley Vinaigrette	*12 fluid ounces*	*360 milliliters*

1. Make a bed of lettuce.

2. Arrange remaining ingredients on lettuce.

3. Drizzle with vinaigrette.

*To make a **Lemon Parsley Vinaigrette**, follow the recipe on page 906 for Basic Vinaigrette. Use lemon juice to replace the vinegar. Add 2 to 3 tablespoons chopped, flat-leaf parsley.*

The recipe for Stuffed Grape Leaves is on page 990.

Cucumber Yogurt Salad

Yield: 10 servings

Add one or more of the following fresh herbs: oregano, thyme, mint, or basil.

Yogurt	1 1/2 pints	720 milliliters
Cucumbers, peeled, seeded, and chopped	5 each	5 each
Scallions, chopped	1 tablespoon	1 tablespoon
Cumin, to taste	1 1/2 teaspoons	1 1/2 teaspoons
Salt, to taste	1/2 teaspoon	1/2 teaspoon
White pepper, to taste	1/4 teaspoon	1/4 teaspoon

1. Combine all ingredients; chill for several hours before serving.

Moroccan Carrot Salad

Yield: 10 servings

The recipe for Curry Vinaigrette may be found on page 910.

This salad may be served at room temperature for the fullest flavor.

Raisins	2 ounces	60 grams
Orange juice	4 fluid ounces	120 milliliters
Carrots, shredded	1 pound	455 grams
Golden Delicious apples, shredded	1 pound	455 grams
Curry Vinaigrette	4 fluid ounces	120 milliliters
Salt, to taste	1/2 teaspoon	1/2 teaspoon
Pepper, to taste	1/4 teaspoon	1/4 teaspoon

1. Combine the raisins and orange juice; let the raisins become plump. Drain the fruit; reserve the juice.

2. Combine the raisins, carrots, and apples.

3. Beat together the reserved orange juice, Curry Vinaigrette, salt, and pepper. Add the dressing to the shredded carrots; combine until all ingredients are thoroughly coated.

Mediterranean Peppers with Lemon Thyme Vinaigrette

Yield: 10 servings

Lemon thyme vinaigrette

Thyme-infused olive oil	*6 fluid ounces*	*180 milliliters*
Lemon juice	*2 fluid ounces*	*60 milliliters*
Thyme, chopped	*1 tablespoon*	*1 tablespoon*
Oregano, chopped	*1 tablespoon*	*1 tablespoon*
Parsley, chopped	*1 tablespoon*	*1 tablespoon*
Shallots, minced	*1 teaspoon*	*1 teaspoon*
Salt, to taste	*1/2 teaspoon*	*1/2 teaspoon*
Pepper, to taste	*1/4 teaspoon*	*1/4 teaspoon*
Red pepper, roasted, cut into strips	*2 each*	*2 each*
Green pepper, roasted, cut into strips	*2 each*	*2 each*
Yellow pepper, roasted, cut into strips	*2 each*	*2 each*
Tomatoes, julienne	*7 ounces*	*200 grams*
Feta cheese, crumbled	*4 ounces*	*115 grams*
Niçoise olives, pitted	*2 ounces*	*60 grams*
Capers	*1 ounce*	*30 grams*
Croutons	*2 ounces*	*60 grams*
Pine nuts, toasted	*2 ounces*	*60 grams*

This vinaigrette would be good on grain salads or to marinate cooked beans.

To make an oil infused with thyme, heat the oil (1 pint/480 milliliters) to 190°F (88°C). Remove it from the heat and add 5 to 6 sprigs of fresh thyme. Steep for several hours. Strain and pour into a clean bottle. Add 2 to 3 fresh sprigs. Let it rest for a week before using.

1. Combine vinaigrette ingredients. Blend well.

2. Add peppers, tomatoes, feta cheese, olives, and capers to vinaigrette; combine evenly.

3. Let marinate 30 to 40 minutes at room temperature or up to 24 hours under refrigeration.

4. Serve topped with pine nuts and croutons.

When mincing parsley, hold the tip of the blade in place with the free hand.

Tabbouleh may be served on a falafel plate (see page 714) or used as a pita sandwich (add sliced cucumbers and alfalfa sprouts).

Tabbouleh Salad

Yield: 10 servings

Bulgur wheat	*1 pound*	*455 grams*
Parsley, chopped fine	*1 1/2 ounces*	*40 grams*
Mint, chopped fine	*1/2 ounce*	*15 grams*
Red onion, chopped fine	*1 each*	*1 each*
Tomato, fine dice	*6 ounces*	*140 grams*
Olive oil	*6 fluid ounces*	*180 milliliters*
Lemon juice, to taste	*1 ounce*	*30 grams*
Salt, to taste	*1/2 teaspoon*	*1/2 teaspoon*
White pepper, to taste	*1/4 teaspoon*	*1/4 teaspoon*

1. Place the bulgur wheat into a large bowl and add lukewarm water to cover. Cover and let stand until all water is absorbed (30 to 45 minutes). Drain off any excess water; the bulgur wheat should be dry.

2. Mix in the remaining ingredients. Season to taste Chill until needed.

Add spice blends (Curry, Chili Powder, Barbeque Spice, or Fines Herbes) to the mayonnaise if desired.

Additional garnish items include toasted walnuts, halved seedless grapes, or chopped red or green onions.

Chicken Salad

Yield: 2 quarts (2 liters)

Chicken meat, cooked, cubed	*4 pounds*	*1.9 kilograms*
Mayonnaise	*16 ounces*	*480 milliliters*
Celery, minced	*1 1/2 pounds*	*680 grams*
Salt, to taste	*1 teaspoon*	*1 teaspoon*
Pepper, to taste	*1/2 teaspoon*	*1/2 teaspoon*
Poultry seasoning	*to taste*	*to taste*

1. Combine all ingredients; mix well and adjust seasoning.

Serve as a sandwich on rye bread with lettuce, tomato, and Swiss cheese.

Ham Salad

Yield: 2 quarts (2 liters)

Smoked ham, fine dice, or ground	*4 pounds*	*1.9 kilograms*
Mayonnaise	*16 ounces*	*480 milliliters*
Sweet relish	*2 to 3 ounces*	*60 to 85 grams*
Prepared mustard	*1 to 2 ounces*	*30 to 60 grams*

1. Mix all ingredients together and adjust seasoning.

Crab or Lobster Salad

Yield: 2 quarts (2 liters)

Crab or lobster meat	*2 1/2 pounds*	*1 kilogram*
Mayonnaise	*16 ounces*	*480 milliliters*
Celery, minced	*12 ounces*	*340 grams*
Lemon juice, to taste	*1 fluid ounce*	*30 milliliters*
Salt, to taste	*1 teaspoon*	*1 teaspoon*
Pepper, to taste	*1/2 teaspoon*	*1/2 teaspoon*
Old Bay Seasoning	*to taste*	*to taste*

1. Add all ingredients together; mix well; adjust seasoning.

All of the salads on this page may be served on a cold salad platter or in sandwiches.

Add the following ingredients to the salads according to desired results:
- *Minced green or red onion*
- *Dill, fennel, or cumin seed*
- *Chopped fresh herbs*
- *Prepared mustards*
- *Diced vegetables (raw, blanched, or grilled)*

Tuna Salad

Yield: 2 quarts (2 liters)

Tuna, canned, drained	*2 1/2 pounds*	*1 kilogram*
Mayonnaise	*10 ounces*	*285 grams*
Celery, chopped fine	*4 ounces*	*115 grams*
Onion, minced	*4 ounces*	*115 grams*
Garlic powder	*to taste*	*to taste*
Worcestershire sauce	*2 teaspoons*	*2 teaspoons*
White pepper, to taste	*1/2 teaspoon*	*1/2 teaspoon*
Salt, to taste	*1/2 teaspoon*	*1/2 teaspoon*
Dry mustard	*1/2 teaspoon*	*1/2 teaspoon*

1. Drain tuna thoroughly; flake and place in large bowl.

2. Add mayonnaise, celery, onion, seasonings, and mustard; mix well.

Use these to stuff cherry tomatoes or profiteroles as an hors d'oeuvre or canapé.

Shrimp Salad

Yield: 2 quarts (2 liters)

Shrimp, peeled and deveined	*2 1/2 pounds*	*1 kilogram*
Mayonnaise	*16 ounces*	*480 milliliters*
Celery, minced	*12 ounces*	*340 grams*
Onion, fine dice	*6 ounces*	*340 grams*
Salt, to taste	*1 teaspoon*	*1 teaspoon*
Pepper, to taste	*1/2 teaspoon*	*1/2 teaspoon*

1. Chop the shrimp coarsely (if using small shrimp, leave whole).

2. Add all ingredients together, mix well, and adjust seasoning.

Seafood Ravigote

Yield: 10 servings

Shallow-poaching is explained in Chapter 10 on pages 332 to 335.

Fines Herbes may be found on page 427.

Shallots, minced	*4 each*	*4 each*
Shrimp, 16 to 20 count, peeled and deveined	*20 each*	*20 each*
Frogs legs, pairs, cut in half	*10 each*	*10 each*
Bay scallops, remove muscle tab	*10 ounces*	*285 grams*
Mussels, scrubbed	*20 each*	*20 each*
White wine	*10 fluid ounces*	*285 milliliters*
Fish Stock	*14 fluid ounces*	*400 milliliters*
Egg yolks	*4 each*	*4 each*
Mustard	*1 tablespoon*	*1 tablespoon*
Lemon juice	*1 tablespoon*	*1 tablespoon*
Vegetable oil	*8 fluid ounces*	*480 milliliters*
Fines Herbes, minced	*1 teaspoon*	*1 teaspoon*
Salt, to taste	*1 teaspoon*	*1 teaspoon*
Pepper, to taste	*1/2 teaspoon*	*1/2 teaspoon*
Boston lettuce	*20 leaves*	*20 leaves*
Tomatoes, peeled, cut into wedges	*20 each*	*20 each*
Lemons wedges	*10 each*	*10 each*
Cucumbers, julienne	*4 ounces*	*115 grams*

1. Combine shallots, shrimp, frog legs, scallops, mussels, wine, and stock; bring to a simmer and poach seafood until cooked through.

2. When seafood is done, remove, and chill; strain poaching liquid.

3. Reduce poaching liquid to 1 1/2 fluid ounces (50 milliliters); place in a stainless steel bowl and cool.

4. Add egg yolks, mustard, and lemon juice to the reduction; mix well.

5. Whisk oil into reduction, starting very slowly in the beginning and increasing the speed as the oil is absorbed to make a mayonnaise.

6. Add herbs, salt and pepper to taste.

7. Remove meat from frog legs; , combine all of the seafood with the mayonnaise.

8. Serve Seafood Ravigote on lettuce leaves; garnish with tomato and lemon wedges and cucumber.

Egg Salad

Yield: 2 quarts (2 liters)

Eggs, hard-boiled, chopped fine	*24 each*	*24 each*
Mayonnaise	*10 ounces*	*300 milliliters*
Celery, minced	*6 ounces*	*170 grams*
Onion, minced	*3 ounces*	*85 grams*
White pepper, to taste	*1/2 teaspoon*	*1/2 teaspoon*
Salt, to taste	*1/2 teaspoon*	*1/2 teaspoon*
Garlic powder, to taste	*1/2 teaspoon*	*1/2 teaspoon*
Dijon mustard, to taste	*1 tablespoon*	*1 tablespoon*

1. Mix all ingredients together. Keep chilled.

Use this salad to make sandwiches. A whole-grain bread with lettuce, tomato, and onion is a lunch menu classic.

Potato Salad

Yield: 10 servings

Red Bliss potatoes	*2 1/4 pounds*	*1 kilogram*
Eggs, hard-boiled, chopped	*4 each*	*4 each*
Onions, diced	*5 ounces*	*140 grams*
Celery, diced	*5 ounces*	*140 grams*
Dijon mustard, to taste	*1 ounce*	*30 grams*
Mayonnaise	*16 ounces*	*480 milliliters*
Worcestershire sauce, to taste	*1/2 teaspoon*	*1/2 teaspoon*
Salt, to taste	*1/2 teaspoon*	*1/2 teaspoon*
Pepper, to taste	*1/4 teaspoon*	*1/4 teaspoon*

1. Place the potatoes in a pot. Cover with cold salted water and bring to a simmer. Cook until the potatoes can be easily pierced. Drain and dry. When they are cool enough to handle, slice or dice.

2. Combine vegetables and eggs in a bowl. Mix the mustard with the mayonnaise and Worcestershire sauce to taste.

3. Gently toss with the potatoes. Adjust seasoning. Chill.

Chopped fresh herbs (parsley, chives, or tarragon) may be added to taste in step 2.

Boil potatoes until tender. Before serving, garnish with parsley or chives.

European-Style Potato Salad

Yield: 10 servings

Potatoes, all-purpose or Yukon Gold	*3 pounds*	*1.35 kilograms*
Onions, fine dice	*5 ounces*	*140 grams*
Red wine vinegar	*3 fluid ounces*	*90 milliliters*
Beef Stock	*8 fluid ounces*	*240 milliliters*
Mild Mustard, prepared	*to taste*	*to taste*
Salt, to taste	*1/2 teaspoon*	*1/2 teaspoon*
Pepper, to taste	*1/4 teaspoon*	*1/4 teaspoon*
Sugar	*to taste*	*to taste*
Vegetable oil	*3 fluid ounces*	*90 milliliters*
Parsley or chives, chopped	*1 tablespoon*	*1 tablespoon*

1. Cook the potatoes until tender in simmering water. Peel and slice the potatoes while they are still very hot.

2. Combine the onions, vinegar, and stock. Bring the mixture to a boil. Add the mustard, salt, pepper, and sugar to taste. Add the oil to the dressing.

3. Immediately pour the dressing over the potatoes.

4. Sprinkle the potato salad with the parsley or chives and serve it at room temperature.

German Potato Salad

Add diced sausage to this salad, or serve it as an accompaniment to grilled or pan-broiled knockwurst (or other sausages).

Yield: 10 servings

Potatoes, all-purpose, or Yukon Gold	*2 1/4 pounds*	*1 kilogram*
Bacon, diced	*4 ounces*	*115 grams*
Onions, diced	*8 ounces*	*225 grams*
White wine vinegar	*4 fluid ounces*	*120 milliliters*
Vegetable oil	*4 fluid ounces*	*120 milliliters*
Salt, to taste	*1/2 teaspoon*	*1/2 teaspoon*
Pepper, to taste	*1/4 teaspoon*	*1/4 teaspoon*
Dijon Mustard	*2 tablespoons*	*2 tablespoons*
Chicken Stock, heated	*16 fluid ounces*	*480 milliliters*
Chives, snipped	*2 ounces*	*60 grams*

1. Cook the potatoes in simmering water until tender. Drain.

2. Sauté the bacon until it is nearly cooked. Add and sweat the onion; then drain off the excess fat.

3. Add the vinegar, oil, salt, pepper, mustard, stock, and chives to the bacon and simmer. Pour the dressing over the hot sliced potatoes. Serve the salad warm.

Curried Rice Salad

Yield: 10 servings

Curry powder	*2 tablespoons*	*2 tablespoons*
Basic Vinaigrette	*6 fluid ounces*	*180 milliliters*
Long-grain rice, cooked	*2 pounds*	*900 grams*
Peas, cooked	*8 ounces*	*225 grams*
Onions, diced	*4 ounces*	*115 grams*
Granny Smith apples, diced	*4 ounces*	*115 grams*
Pumpkin seeds, toasted	*2 ounces*	*60 grams*
Golden raisins, plumped	*2 ounces*	*60 grams*
Salt, to taste	*1/2 teaspoon*	*1/2 teaspoon*
Pepper, to taste	*1/2 teaspoon*	*1/2 teaspoon*

Use a variety of rices in this salad if available.

1. Lightly toast the curry powder in a pan on the stove. Add to the vinaigrette and allow it to steep for several minutes.

2. Mix the rice, peas, onions, apples, pumpkin seeds, and raisins.

3. Add the vinaigrette to the rice and toss lightly. Adding just enough vinaigrette to moisten the rice. Season to taste with salt and pepper.

Macaroni Salad

Yield: 10 servings

Elbow macaroni, cooked, cooled	*2 pounds*	*900 grams*
Celery, chopped	*5 ounces*	*140 grams*
Onions, fine dice	*4 ounces*	*115 grams*
Green pepper, (optional) diced	*4 ounces*	*115 grams*
Red pepper, (optional) diced	*2 ounces*	*60 grams*
Garlic, cloves, mashed	*2 each*	*2 each*
Basic Mayonnaise, as needed	*12 ounces*	*360 milliliters*
Salt, to taste	*1 teaspoon*	*1 teaspoon*
Pepper, to taste	*1/2 teaspoon*	*1/2 teaspoon*

1. Combine all ingredients with just enough mayonnaise or dressing to bind.

2. Season to taste with salt and pepper.

Add shredded cheese (Cheddar, Monterey Jack, or Pepper Monterey Jack) if desired.

Pasta Salad with Pesto Vinaigrette

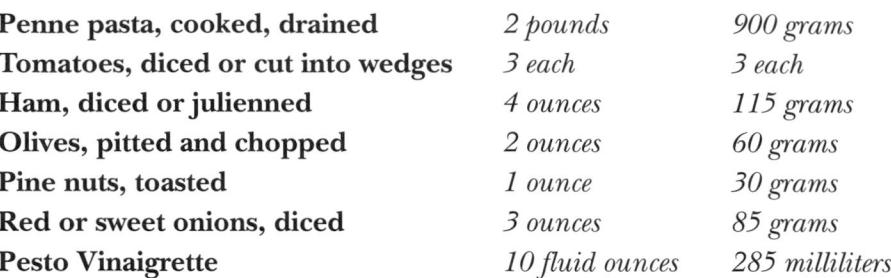

Yield: 10 servings

To make Pesto Vinaigrette, prepare the pesto as directed on page 422. Prepare the Basic Vinaigrette on page 906. Add enough pesto to give the vinaigrette a distinct "pesto" flavor.

Penne pasta, cooked, drained	*2 pounds*	*900 grams*
Tomatoes, diced or cut into wedges	*3 each*	*3 each*
Ham, diced or julienned	*4 ounces*	*115 grams*
Olives, pitted and chopped	*2 ounces*	*60 grams*
Pine nuts, toasted	*1 ounce*	*30 grams*
Red or sweet onions, diced	*3 ounces*	*85 grams*
Pesto Vinaigrette	*10 fluid ounces*	*285 milliliters*

1. Combine all ingredients.
2. Marinate several hours under refrigeration.

Lentil Salad

Yield: 10 servings

Use Roasted Garlic and Mustard Vinaigrette, Curry Vinaigrette, or Lemon Thyme Vinaigrette.

Lentils, cooked and drained	*2 pounds*	*900 grams*
Scallions, chopped	*6 ounces*	*170 grams*
Walnuts, chopped	*6 ounces*	*170 grams*
Vinaigrette, as needed	*6 fluid ounces*	*180 milliliters*
Salt, to taste	*1/2 teaspoon*	*1/2 teaspoon*
Pepper, to taste	*1/4 teaspoon*	*1/4 teaspoon*

1. Mix the lentils, scallions, and walnuts together. Add enough Vinaigrette to coat and season to taste with salt and pepper.

Mixed Bean Salad

Yield: 10 servings

Cooking times for these beans can be found in a table in Appendix II.

Vinaigrette Gourmand is on page 906.

Black beans, cooked, drained	*10 ounces*	*285 grams*
Pinto beans, cooked and drained	*10 ounces*	*285 grams*
Chick peas, cooked and drained	*10 ounces*	*285 grams*
Red lentils, cooked and drained	*5 ounces*	*140 grams*
Red onions, small dice	*6 ounces*	*170 grams*
Celery, chopped	*4 ounces*	*115 grams*
Parsley, chopped	*2 tablespoons*	*2 tablespoons*
Vinaigrette Gourmand	*10 fluid ounces*	*285 milliliters*
Salt, to taste	*1/2 teaspoon*	*1/2 teaspoon*
Pepper, to taste	*1/4 teaspoon*	*1/4 teaspoon*

1. Combine all ingredients. Gently toss with the vinaigrette. Let marinate under refrigeration for 24 hours. Season to taste with salt and pepper.

Warm Black-Eyed Pea Salad

Yield: 10 servings

Olive oil	*8 fluid ounces*	*240 milliliters*
Onions, minced	*4 ounces*	*115 grams*
Garlic, cloves, minced	*1 ounce*	*30 grams*
Lemon zest	*1 teaspoon*	*1 teaspoon*
Black-eyed peas, dried	*12 ounces*	*340 grams*
Chicken Stock	*1 1/2 quarts*	*1 1/2 liters*
Rosemary, sprigs	*2 each*	*2 each*
Thyme, sprigs	*2 each*	*2 each*
Bay leaves	*2 each*	*2 each*
Lemon juice, as needed	*4 fluid ounces*	*120 milliliters*
Basil, fresh, chiffonade	*2 tablespoons*	*2 tablespoons*
Salt, to taste	*1/2 teaspoon*	*1/2 teaspoon*
Pepper, to taste	*1/4 teaspoon*	*1/4 teaspoon*

This salad is a good accompaniment to pan-fried fish. Or, use it to make an entrée with sautéed greens and a rice pilaf, served with Cornbread (page 1027).

1. Heat 1 ounce (30 milliliters) of oil in a pan over high heat. Add the onions and half of the garlic and lemon zest; sauté until tender.

2. Add the peas, stock, rosemary, thyme, and bay leaves; bring to a boil. Reduce the heat and simmer the peas until they are thoroughly tender, about 1 hour. Add water if necessary to keep the peas covered throughout the cooking time.

3. While the black-eyed peas are cooking, combine the remaining oil, garlic, lemon juice, and basil.

4. Drain the peas; remove and discard rosemary, thyme, and bay leaves. Add hot peas to the lemon-basil vinaigrette, and toss gently until evenly coated. Season to taste with salt and pepper

5. Serve warm or at room temperature.

Basic Vinaigrette

Yield: 1 quart

Oil choices include:
- *Corn or vegetable*
- *Peanut*
- *Sesame (light)*
- *Safflower*
- *Extra-virgin olive*
- *Hazelnut*
- *Walnut*
- *Avocado*

Vinegar options include:
- *Wine (white or red)*
- *Herb-infused (tarragon, etc.)*
- *Cider*
- *Balsamic*
- *Citrus juices (lemon, lime, orange, or grapefruit)*

Vegetable oil	24 fluid ounces	720 milliliters
Vinegar	8 fluid ounces	240 milliliters
Salt	to taste	to taste
Pepper	to taste	to taste
Coleman's mustard, dry (optional)	1/2 teaspoon	2.5 milliliters
Herbs, chopped (optional)	2 tablespoons	30 milliliters
Sugar (optional)	1/4 to 1/2 teaspoon	1/4 to 1/2 teaspoon

1. Combine all of the ingredients and whip them until they are thoroughly blended.

2. Taste the vinaigrette and adjust the seasoning with additional salt, pepper, or sugar.

VARIATION

Balsamic Vinaigrette: Use balsamic vinegar (6 fluid ounces/180 milliliters) and increase the oil to 26 fluid ounces (780 milliliters). Extra-virgin olive oil or a nut oil (walnut, hazelnut, or almond) would be a good choice.

Vinaigrette Gourmand

Yield: 1 quart

Vinaigrettes may separate out into their individual components as they sit. Whisk well to recombine the dressing before adding it to a salad.

Vinaigrette		
Lemon juice	4 fluid ounces	120 milliliters
Red wine vinegar	4 fluid ounces	120 milliliters
Extra-virgin olive oil	8 fluid ounces	240 milliliters
Shallots, minced	2 ounces	60 grams
Garlic, minced	1 ounce	30 grams
Stock, thickened	1 pint	480 milliliters
Basil, chopped	1 ounce	30 grams
Sage, chopped	1 ounce	30 grams
Parsley, chopped	1 ounce	30 grams
Red pepper flakes	1 teaspoon	1 teaspoon
Tomato Concassé	10 ounces	285 grams

1. Bring ingredients for the vinaigrette to a boil.

2. Sweat the shallots and garlic in a little stock, add the herbs, pepper flakes, and Tomato Concassé. Stir mixture in to the vinaigrette.

Mustard-Herb Vinaigrette

Yield: 1 quart

Cider vinegar	8 fluid ounces	240 milliliters
Dijon mustard	2 fluid ounces	60 milliliters
Parsley, chopped	2 tablespoons	2 tablespoons
Onion powder	1/2 teaspoon	1/2 teaspoon
Garlic powder	1/8 teaspoon	1/8 teaspoon
Whole white pepper, fresh-ground	1/8 teaspoon	1/8 teaspoon
Sugar, granulated	2 teaspoons	2 teaspoons
Fines Herbes	2 tablespoons	2 tablespoons
Vegetable oil	24 fluid ounces	720 milliliters
Water	as needed	as needed
Salt	1/4 teaspoon	1/4 teaspoon

Be sure to gradually add the olive oil to the ingredients. Mix and serve immediately or store under refrigeration.

1. Combine all of the ingredients except the oil and water.

2. Gradually incorporate the oil in a thin stream. Add the water as needed to adjust the flavor.

3. Adjust the seasoning to taste with the salt and pepper. Serve the vinaigrette immediately or store it under refrigeration.

Your guests may ask for salad dressings on the side. Take the time to instruct your waitstaff about how you would like them to alert your pantry cooks to those special orders. Your patron's requests can be honored.

Peanut Oil and Malt Vinegar Salad Dressing

Yield: 1 quart

Peanut oil	20 fluid ounces	600 milliliters
Malt vinegar	10 fluid ounces	300 milliliters
Dark brown sugar, to taste	2 ounces	60 grams
Tarragon, chopped	2 tablespoons	2 tablespoons
Chives, chopped	2 tablespoons	2 tablespoons
Parsley, chopped	2 tablespoons	2 tablespoons
Garlic, minced	2 teaspoons	2 teaspoons
Salt, to taste	1/2 teaspoon	1/2 teaspoon
Pepper, to taste	1/4 teaspoon	1/4 teaspoon

1. Combine all of the ingredients well with a whip.

2. Let the dressing age for 24 hours before using; recombine the ingredients thoroughly before service.

Roasted Garlic and Mustard Vinaigrette

Yield: approximately 1 to 1 1/2 quarts (1 to 1.5 liters)

To roast garlic, place the entire head in a hot oven (425°F/220°C) and bake it for 20 to 30 minutes. Squeeze the roasted garlic from the papery husks.

Garlic, roasted and puréed	*to taste*	*to taste*
Salt	*to taste*	*to taste*
Dijon mustard	*to taste*	*to taste*
Black pepper, fresh ground	*to taste*	*to taste*
Cider vinegar	*16 fluid ounces*	*1/2 liter*
Vegetable oil	*8 to 16 fluid ounces*	*1/2 to 1 liter*

1. Combine the garlic and salt; work them into a paste.

2. Combine the garlic mixture with the mustard, pepper, and vinegar.

3. Gradually incorporate the oil in a thin stream, mixing thoroughly. Adjust the seasoning as needed.

4. Serve the vinaigrette immediately or store it under refrigeration for later service.

Lemon Garlic Vinaigrette

Yield: 1 quart (1 liter)

This vinaigrette can be used to finish steamed vegetables or as a marinade for grilled vegetables.

Lemon juice	*6 fluid ounces*	*180 milliliters*
Olive oil	*12 fluid ounces*	*360 milliliters*
Salad oil	*12 fluid ounces*	*360 milliliters*
Garlic paste	*1 tablespoon*	*1 tablespoon*
Rosemary, minced	*1 teaspoon*	*1 teaspoon*
Salt, to taste	*1/2 teaspoon*	*1/2 teaspoon*
Pepper, ground, to taste	*1/4 teaspoon*	*1/4 teaspoon*
Sugar, to taste	*2 teaspoons*	*2 teaspoons*

1. Combine all ingredients.

Lime and Olive Oil Vinaigrette

Yield: 1 quart (1 liter)

Extra-virgin olive oil	*20 fluid ounces*	*600 milliliters*
Lime juice	*4 fluid ounces*	*120 milliliters*
Lemon juice	*2 fluid ounces*	*60 milliliters*
White wine vinegar	*2 fluid ounces*	*60 milliliters*
Shallots, minced	*1 1/2 ounces*	*45 grams*
Red peppercorns, cracked	*1 tablespoon*	*1 tablespoon*
Salt, to taste	*1/2 teaspoon*	*1/2 teaspoon*
Chives, chopped	*4 ounces*	*115 grams*

1. Combine all the ingredients. Whisk well to blend.

It is easier to juice lemons and limes if they are at room temperature. Roll them on a work surface to increase their yield.

Georgia Peanut Salad Dressing

Yield: 1 quart (1 liter)

Peanut oil	*10 fluid ounces*	*300 milliliters*
Malt vinegar	*5 fluid ounces*	*150 milliliters*
Peanut butter	*1 ounce*	*30 grams*
Dark brown sugar	*1 ounce*	*30 grams*
Tarragon, chopped	*1 tablespoon*	*1 tablespoon*
Chives, chopped	*1 tablespoon*	*1 tablespoon*
Parsley, chopped	*1 tablespoon*	*1 tablespoon*
Garlic	*1 teaspoon*	*1 teaspoon*
Salt, to taste	*1/2 teaspoon*	*1/2 teaspoon*
Pepper, to taste	*1/4 teaspoon*	*1/4 teaspoon*

1. Combine all of the ingredients.

2. Let the dressing age for 24 hours before using it; recombine the ingredients thoroughly before service.

Add 1/2 to 1 teaspoon of red pepper flakes to this recipe for added heat. Use it to dress cooked chilled spaghetti or linguini, or as a bed for grilled pork or beef.

Curry Vinaigrette

Yield: 1 quart (1 liter)

To use lemongrass, peel away the tough outer layers. Mince the tender interior portion.

Olive oil	*1 1/2 pints*	*720 milliliters*
Curry powder	*3 tablespoons*	*3 tablespoons*
Shallots, minced	*1 ounce*	*30 grams*
Garlic, minced	*1/2 ounce*	*15 grams*
Gingerroot, minced	*1/2 ounce*	*15 grams*
Lemongrass, minced	*1/2 ounce*	*15 grams*
Cider vinegar	*8 fluid ounces*	*240 milliliters*
Lemon juice	*1 1/2 fluid ounces*	*45 milliliters*
Honey, to taste	*1 1/2 fluid ounces*	*45 milliliters*
Salt, to taste	*1 teaspoon*	*1 teaspoon*
Black pepper, coarse-ground	*1/2 teaspoon*	*1/2 teaspoon*

1. Heat 3 ounces (90 milliliters) of oil over low heat. Add curry, shallots, garlic, ginger, and lemongrass. Continue to heat until shallots are translucent. Remove from heat and let cool.

2. Combine flavored oil with the vinegar, lemon juice, and honey. Season with salt and pepper to taste. Blend well.

Catalina Dressing

Yield: 1 quart (1 liter)

To make paprika oil, heat 6 ounces of oil until hot; add 1 ounce (30 grams) of paprika. Remove it from the heat and allow it to steep for 10 to 12 hours before using it in this dressing.

Eggs	*2 each*	*2 each*
Dark brown sugar	*4 ounces*	*115 grams*
Cider vinegar	*4 fluid ounces*	*120 milliliters*
Paprika oil	*4 fluid ounces*	*120 milliliters*
Allspice, ground	*1/8 teaspoon*	*1/8 teaspoon*
White pepper, ground, to taste	*1/4 teaspoon*	*1/4 teaspoon*
Garlic powder	*1/4 teaspoon*	*1/4 teaspoon*
Onion powder	*1/4 teaspoon*	*1/4 teaspoon*
Salt	*1/2 teaspoon*	*1/2 teaspoon*
Dijon mustard	*2 teaspoons*	*2 teaspoons*
Vegetable oil	*12 fluid ounces*	*720 milliliters*

1. Combine all of the ingredients except the vegetable oil; blend well.

2. Gradually incorporate the vegetable oil in a thin stream.

3. Adjust the seasoning if necessary.

Basic Mayonnaise

Yield: 1 quart (1 liter)

Egg yolks	3 each	3 each
White wine vinegar	1 fluid ounce	30 milliliters
Water	1 fluid ounce	30 milliliters
Dry mustard	2 teaspoons	2 teaspoons
Vegetable, olive, or peanut oil, as desired to achieve flavor	24 fluid ounces	720 milliliters
Salt, to taste	1/2 teaspoon	1/2 teaspoon
Pepper, to taste	1/2 teaspoon	1/2 teaspoon
Lemon juice, to taste	1 fluid ounce	30 milliliters

1. Combine the yolks, vinegar, water, and mustard in a bowl. Mix them well with a balloon whip until the mixture is slightly foamy.

2. Gradually add the oil in a thin stream, constantly beating with the whip, until the oil is incorporated and the mayonnaise is thick.

3. Adjust the flavor with salt, pepper, and lemon juice.

4. Refrigerate the mayonnaise immediately. Use as desired.

Green Mayonnaise: Finely chop 4 ounces (115 grams) of spinach. Squeeze it in cheesecloth to extract the juice. Add the juice to the mayonnaise. Add additional chopped fresh herbs to taste.

Herb Mayonnaise: Add 1 to 2 ounces (30 to 60 grams) of Fines Herbes (page 422).

Aïoli (Garlic Mayonnaise)

Yield: 1 quart (1 liter)

Egg yolks	2 each	2 each
Garlic cloves, mashed to a paste	8 each	8 each
White wine vinegar	1 fluid ounce	30 milliliters
Water	1/2 fluid ounce	15 milliliters
Dry mustard	1 teaspoon	1 teaspoon
Vegetable oil	1 pint	480 milliliters
Extra-virgin olive oil	10 fluid ounces	300 milliliters
Salt, to taste	1/2 teaspoon	1/2 teaspoon
Pepper, to taste	1/4 teaspoon	1/4 teaspoon
Lemon juice	2 teaspoons	2 teaspoons

1. Combine the yolks, garlic, vinegar, water, and mustard in a bowl. Mix them together well with a balloon whip until the mixture is slightly foamy.

2. Gradually add the oils in a thin stream, constantly beating them with a whip until they are incorporated and the mayonnaise is thick.

3. Adjust the flavor to taste with the salt, pepper, and lemon juice.

4. Refrigerate the mayonnaise immediately.

*To make a **Rouille,** add puréed roasted red peppers and red pepper flakes to taste.*

Anchovy Caper Mayonnaise

Yield: 1 quart (1 liter)

This is an excellent companion to cold roast beef sandwiches.

Mayonnaise	*1 quart*	*1 liter*
Lemon juice, to taste	*3 fluid ounces*	*90 milliliters*
Dijon mustard	*1 tablespoon*	*1 tablespoon*
Shallots, minced	*4 each*	*4 each*
Parsley, chopped	*1 ounce*	*30 grams*
Nonpareils capers, drained and minced	*1 fluid ounce*	*30 milliliters*
Anchovy fillets, minced	*6 each*	*6 each*
Salt, to taste	*1/2 teaspoon*	*1/2 teaspoon*
Pepper, to taste	*1/4 teaspoon*	*1/4 teaspoon*

1. Combine all the ingredients; mix well.

2. Refrigerate the mayonnaise until service time; stir it to recombine the ingredients.

Caesar-Style Dressing

Yield: 1 quart

This dressing can be adapted to create a signature house Caesar Salad. It is somewhat different than the classic dressing for the salad prepared at tables, but all of the important flavor elements are still there.

Anchovy fillets	*3 ounces*	*85 grams*
Mild mustard	*1/2 ounce*	*15 grams*
Garlic cloves, mashed to a paste	*3 each*	*3 each*
Worcestershire sauce	*1 tablespoon*	*1 tablespoon*
Red wine vinegar	*6 fluid ounces*	*180 milliliters*
Pepper	*1 teaspoon*	*1 teaspoon*
Lemon juice, freshly squeezed	*1 fluid ounce*	*30 milliliters*
Parmesan cheese, freshly grated	*2 ounces*	*60 grams*
Tabasco	*1/2 teaspoon*	*1/2 teaspoon*
Olive oil	*18 fluid ounces*	*540 milliliters*

1. Combine all of the ingredients except the olive oil.

2. Gradually incorporate the oil in a thin stream.

3. Adjust the seasoning as needed. Serve the dressing immediately or refrigerate for later service.

Green Goddess Dressing

Yield: 1 quart (1 liter)

Spinach leaves	*2 ounces*	*60 grams*
Watercress leaves	*2 ounces*	*60 grams*
Parsley leaves, fresh	*1 tablespoon*	*1 tablespoon*
Tarragon leaves, fresh	*1 tablespoon*	*1 tablespoon*
Garlic clove, mashed to a paste	*1 each*	*1 each*
Vegetable oil	*4 fluid ounces*	*120 milliliters*
Mayonnaise	*12 fluid ounces*	*360 milliliters*
Prepared mustard	*1 tablespoon*	*1 tablespoon*
Salt, to taste	*1/2 teaspoon*	*1/2 teaspoon*
Pepper, to taste	*1/2 teaspoon*	*1/2 teaspoon*
Lemon juice, to taste	*1 fluid ounce*	*30 milliliters*

1. Purée the spinach, watercress, parsley, tarragon, and garlic with the oil in a food processor.

2. Combine the purée with the mayonnaise and mustard.

3. Add the salt, pepper, and lemon juice to taste.

4. Refrigerate the dressing immediately.

Ranch-Style Dressing

Yield: 1 quart (1 liter)

Sour cream	*12 ounces*	*360 milliliters*
Mayonnaise	*12 ounces*	*360 milliliters*
Buttermilk	*8 fluid ounces*	*240 milliliters*
Lemon juice	*1 fluid ounce*	*30 milliliters*
Red wine vinegar	*2 fluid ounces*	*60 milliliters*
Garlic cloves, mashed to a paste	*2 each*	*2 each*
Worcestershire sauce	*1 1/2 fluid ounces*	*45 milliliters*
Parsley, chopped	*1 tablespoon*	*1 tablespoon*
Chives, chopped	*1 tablespoon*	*1 tablespoon*
Shallots, chopped	*1 tablespoon*	*1 tablespoon*
Dijon mustard	*1 tablespoon*	*1 tablespoon*
Celery seed	*1 teaspoon*	*1 teaspoon*

This makes a good dip for a crudité platter.

1. Combine all ingredients well.

2. Store under refriegeration until needed.

Creamy Black Pepper Dressing

Yield: 1 quart (1 liter)

Basic Mayonnaise	*1 quart*	*1 liter*
Parmesan cheese, grated, to taste	*3 to 4 ounces*	*85 to 115 grams*
Anchovy paste	*2 ounces*	*60 grams*
Garlic, mashed to paste	*1 ounce*	*30 grams*
Salt, to taste	*1 teaspoon*	*1 teaspoon*
Black peppercorns, coarse-ground	*2 tablespoons*	*2 tablespoons*

1. Combine all ingredients.

2. Mix well and let rest under refrigeration. Adjust seasoning before serving.

Blue Cheese Dressing

Yield: 1 quart (1 liter)

If you prefer a chunky-style dressing, reserve 4 ounces (115 grams) of the cheese and crumble it into the dressing after it has been blended.

Blue cheese, crumbled	*12 ounces*	*340 grams*
Basic Mayonnaise	*1 pint*	*480 milliliters*
Sour cream	*8 ounces*	*240 milliliters*
Buttermilk	*6 fluid ounces*	*180 milliliters*
Milk	*3 fluid ounces*	*90 milliliters*
Lemon juice	*1 tablespoon*	*1 tablespoon*
Worcestershire sauce, to taste	*1 1/2 fluid ounces*	*45 milliliters*
Garlic, mashed to a paste	*1/4 teaspoon*	*1/4 teaspoon*
Salt, to taste	*1/2 teaspoon*	*1/2 teaspoon*
Pepper, to taste	*1/4 teaspoon*	*1/4 teaspoon*

1. Combine all of the ingredients; mix them to a smooth consistency.

2. Adjust the seasoning to taste.

3. Chill the dressing until it is needed.

Cucumber Dressing

Yield: 1 quart (1 liter)

Cucumbers, peeled and seeded	2 each	2 each
Lemon juice	2 fluid ounces	60 milliliters
Sour cream	8 ounces	240 milliliters
Dill, chopped	3 tablespoons	3 tablespoons
Sugar (optional)	1 tablespoon	1 tablespoon
Salt, to taste	1 teaspoon	1 teaspoon
White pepper, to taste	2 teaspoons	2 teaspoons
Tabasco	to taste	to taste

1. Purée the cucumber in a food processor.

2. Add the remaining ingredients and blend them just until they are incorporated.

3. Adjust the seasoning, if necessary.

Rémoulade Sauce

Yield: 1 quart (1 liter)

Mayonnaise	24 ounces	680 milliliters
Capers, drained and chopped	2 ounces	60 grams
Cornichons, chopped	2 ounces	60 grams
Chives, chopped	3 tablespoons	3 tablespoons
Chervil, chopped	3 tablespoons	3 tablespoons
Tarragon, leaves, chopped	3 tablespoons	3 tablespoons
Dijon mustard	1 tablespoon	1 tablespoon
Anchovy paste	1 teaspoon	1 teaspoon
Salt, to taste	1/4 teaspoon	1/4 teaspoon
Black pepper, to taste	1/4 teaspoon	1/4 teaspoon
Worcestershire sauce, to taste	1/2 teaspoon	1/2 teaspoon
Tabasco, to taste	2 to 3 dashes	2 to 3 dashes

This is the traditional sauce served with fried fish and seafood.

1. Combine all of the ingredients. Mix them together well.

2. Hold the sauce under refrigeration.

Tartar Sauce

Yield: approximately 1 quart (1 liter)

Some people prefer this sauce to Rémoulade. It may be served with fried or broiled fish.

Mayonnaise	*1 quart*	*1 liter*
Sweet pickle relish, drained	*1 1/2 cups*	*360 grams*
Capers, drained and chopped	*2 ounces*	*60 grams*
Eggs, hard-boiled and chopped	*2 each*	*2 each*
Salt, to taste	*1/2 teaspoon*	*1/2 teaspoon*
White pepper, to taste	*1/2 teaspoon*	*1/2 teaspoon*
Worcestershire sauce, to taste	*1/2 teaspoon*	*1/2 teaspoon*
Tabasco, to taste	*2 to 3 dashes*	*2 to 3 dashes*

1. Combine all of the ingredients and stir until they are evenly blended.

2. Chill the sauce thoroughly.

C H A P T E R **25** *Sandwiches and Pizzas*

The recipes that follow run the gamut from coffee shop classics to vegetarian pizzas. Along with traditional sandwiches and pizzas, other snack and "street" food from around the world may be found in this chapter. Although specific breads and ingredients are suggested, almost all can be varied to suit your needs. Most can be served as appetizers, entrées, or afternoon or late night snacks. Chapter 19 includes sandwich recipes; tuna salad and similar salad spreads may be found in Chapter 24; other spreads and finger foods may be found in Chapter 26. Many of the recipes in the entrée chapters can also be adapted, as well; consider meatball subs, fried fish fillet sandwiches, and roast turkey clubs.

The recipes are organized as follows:

- *Hot Coffee Shop and Deli Standards*
- *Grilled Hot Sandwiches*
- *Tex-Mex and Caribbean Foods*
- *Pizzas and Savory Breads*
- *Cold Sandwiches*
- *Tea Sandwiches*

Chicken Burgers

Yield: 10 servings

Chicken meat, ground	*2 1/2 pounds*	*1.15 kilograms*
Bread crumbs, fresh	*6 ounces*	*170 grams*
Duxelles, cooked dry, cooled	*1 pound*	*450 grams*
Mixed herbs, chopped: chives, oregano, basil, rosemary	*2 tablespoons*	*2 tablespoons*
Butter, melted, as needed	*4 ounces*	*115 grams*
Salt, to taste	*1 teaspoon*	*1 teaspoon*
White pepper, to taste	*1/2 teaspoon*	*1/2 teaspoon*
Provolone cheese, sliced	*10 ounces*	*285 grams*
Kaiser rolls	*10 each*	*10 each*

The recipe for Duxelles can be found on page 421.

Use other cheeses such as Cheddar or Jack if preferred. Consider a portion size of 1/2 ounce (15 grams).

Ground turkey may be substituted for the chicken.

1. Gently mix chicken, bread crumbs, duxelles, herbs, salt, and pepper.

2. Form into patties.

3. Lightly butter a flat top or griddle. Brown the patties. Finish in a 350°F (175°C) oven.

4. Prior to service, top with provolone cheese and return to oven to melt.

5. Slice roll, leaving bread hinged. Brush with melted butter, then grill.

4. Place chicken on grilled roll, serve open-faced.

Sloppy Joes

Yield: 10 servings

Vegetable oil, as needed	*2 fluid ounces*	*60 milliliters*
Onions, chopped	*8 ounces*	*225 grams*
Celery, chopped fine	*4 ounces*	*115 grams*
Garlic cloves, minced	*2 each*	*2 each*
Ground beef	*3 pounds*	*1.3 kilograms*
Tomato Concassé	*8 ounces*	*225 grams*
Ketchup	*16 ounces*	*480 milliliters*
Beef Stock	*16 fluid ounces*	*480 milliliters*
Worcestershire sauce	*2 tablespoons*	*2 tablespoons*
Dry mustard	*2 teaspoons*	*2 teaspoons*
Cayenne	*1/4 teaspoon*	*1/4 teaspoon*
Salt, to taste	*1/2 teaspoon*	*1/2 teaspoon*
Pepper, to taste	*1/2 teaspoon*	*1/2 teaspoon*
Kaiser rolls	*10 each*	*10 each*

Southwestern-Style Sloppy Joes: *Add 4 ounces (115 grams) chopped, roasted New Mexico chilies, add 1 jalapeño pepper. Substitute tomato sauce for the ketchup. Season with chili powder, cumin, and oregano. Top with beans and cheese. Serve on a roll or a crisp corn tortilla.*

Italian-Style Sloppy Joe: *Substitute Italian sausages for some of the hamburger. Add oregano, green peppers, and mushrooms. Use tomato sauce. Serve on Italian bread and top with Parmesan cheese.*

(Recipe continued on facing page)

1. Heat the oil in a sauce pan. Add the onions and celery; sweat about 5 minutes. Add the garlic and continue to sweat for 2 minutes.

2. Add the ground beef and cook until no longer pink. Drain off excess grease.

3. Stir in the tomato, ketchup, beef stock, Worcestershire sauce, and mustard. Simmer about 30 minutes, stirring occasionally. Check consistency. Season to taste with salt and pepper.

4. Split open the roll and grill. Serve the beef mixture on the grilled roll.

The recipe for Barbecue Sauce may be found on page 552 (or see page 610).

Can also be prepared in this manner: Use a rub (see page 425). Grill, smoke, or braise with stock and onions.
Also good with top or bottom round, or beef trimming.
Serve with coleslaw.

Barbecued Beef Sandwich

Yield: 10 servings

Beef brisket, fresh	*4 pounds*	*1.8 kilograms*
Barbecue Sauce	*20 fluid ounces*	*600 milliliters*
Hoagie or kaiser roll	*10 each*	*10 each*
Butter, melted, as needed	*4 ounces*	*115 grams*

1. Place brisket on rack, roast in 325° (180°C) oven until fork tender, about 5 hours.

2. Cool, trim off excess fat. Slice or shred. Mix with barbecue sauce, reheat in 350° oven or on stove top.

3. Slice roll, leaving bread hinged. Brush with melted butter, then grill.

4. Place barbecued beef on grilled roll, serve open-faced.

Hot Turkey Suprême with Caramelized Onions

Yield: 10 servings

Caramelized onions:		
Onions, sliced thin	*1 pound*	*450 grams*
Whole butter, as needed	*4 ounces*	*115 grams*
Turkey, sliced	*2 1/2 pounds*	*1.15 kilograms*
Sauce Suprême	*1 3/4 pints*	*840 milliliters*
Chicken Stock, heated	*10 fluid ounces*	*30 milliliters*
Bread, slices, lightly toasted	*15 each*	*15 each*
Swiss cheese, sliced thin	*20 slices*	*20 slices*

The recipe for Sauce Suprême may be found on page 534.

1. Sauté onions in clarified butter until caramelized. Reserve.

2. Combine turkey with 8 fluid ounces (240 milliliters) Sauce Suprême and the chicken stock. Cover and warm in oven.

3. Cut bread slices on the diagonal.

4. Shingle three triangles of bread on sheet pan. Top with 1 slice cheese. Spread 4 ounces (115 grams) of sauced turkey over cheese. Spread caramelized onions over turkey. Cover onions with another slice of Swiss cheese.

5. Place in 350°F (175°C) oven until sandwich is heated through and cheese is melted, 5 to 8 minutes.

6. Place sandwich on plate. Nappé with sauce.

Meat Loaf Sandwich with Mushroom Gravy

Yield: 10 servings

The recipe for Brown Sauce may be found on page 552; for Meat Loaf on page 618; and for Potatoes Hashed in Cream, page 823.

This is one of several classic "blue plate" specials found on diner menus throughout the country.

Mushrooms, sliced	1 pound	450 grams
Clarified butter, as needed	2 ounces	60 grams
Brown Sauce	16 fluid ounces	480 milliliters
Salt, to taste	1/2 teaspoon	1/2 teaspoon
Pepper, to taste	1/4 teaspoon	1/4 teaspoon
Pullman bread, slices	10 each	10 each
Meat loaf, warmed	2 1/2 pounds	1.15 kilograms
Potatoes hashed in cream	10 servings	10 servings

1. Sauté the mushrooms in the butter until tender. Add the brown sauce. Season to taste with salt and pepper.

2. Lightly toast the bread. Place the bread on the plate. Place a 4-ounce (115-gram) slice of meat loaf on the bread. Spoon the potatoes beside the meat loaf.

3. Pour the mushroom gravy over the meat loaf and potatoes.

Western Sandwich

Yield: 10 servings

Another classic diner or coffee shop item, this sandwich is often served with ketchup or chili sauce on the side.

Additional seasonings might include oregano, cilantro, tomato concassé, or cheese. May be prepared as scrambled eggs or as a rolled omelet.

Eggs, beaten	10 each	10 each
Milk	8 fluid ounces	240 milliliters
Ham, diced	10 ounces	285 grams
Onion, minced	4 ounces	115 grams
Green peppers, chopped fine	4 ounces	115 grams
Salt, to taste	1 teaspoon	1 teaspoon
Pepper, to taste	1/2 teaspoon	1/2 teaspoon
Butter, as needed	3 ounces	85 grams
Kaiser rolls, warmed	10 each	10 each

1. Mix together the eggs, milk, ham, onion, green peppers, salt and pepper.

2. Melt the butter in a pan. Pour in the egg mixture. Cook until partially firm. Turn over and cook until firm.

3. Serve on the warm Kaiser rolls.

Reuben Sandwich

Yield: 10 servings

Russian dressing

Mayonnaise	*20 fluid ounces*	*600 milliliters*
Chili sauce, prepared	*6 fluid ounces*	*180 milliliters*
Horseradish, prepared	*1 1/2 ounces*	*40 grams*
Onions, minced, blanched	*2 ounces*	*60 grams*
Worcestershire sauce	*1 1/2 teaspoons*	*1 1/2 teaspoons*
Salt, to taste	*1/2 teaspoon*	*1/2 teaspoon*
Pepper, to taste	*1/4 teaspoon*	*1/4 teaspoon*
Rye bread, slices	*20 each*	*20 each*
Swiss cheese, sliced thin	*20 ounces*	*570 grams*
Corned beef brisket, cooked, sliced	*2 pounds*	*900 grams*
Sauerkraut, braised	*20 ounces*	*570 grams*
Butter, room temperature, as needed	*4 ounces*	*115 grams*

1. Mix together the ingredients for the dressing.

2. On one slice of bread, layer the cheese, Russian dressing, a thin layer of corned beef, the sauerkraut, more corned beef, and a second slice of cheese (of which the underside has been spread with Russian dressing). Top with a bread slice.

3. Butter both sides of sandwich. Cook until golden brown. If necessary, finish in oven to melt the cheese and heat through.

Allow approximately five hours at 325°F (160°C) to roast a four-pound beef brisket.

If time allows, prepare the dressing a day in advance.

Although classically served grilled, this sandwich may be served cold.

Three-Cheese Melt

Yield: 10 servings

Bread, slices	*20 each*	*20 each*
Butter, melted, as needed	*4 ounces*	*115 grams*
Pepper Jack cheese, 1 slice each	*10 ounces*	*285 grams*
Colby Cheddar cheese, 2 slices each	*20 ounces*	*570 grams*
Blue cheese, crumbled	*5 ounces*	*140 grams*

1. Brush butter on one side of bread. Top with 1 slice of Colby, 1/2 ounce (15 grams) of crumbled blue cheese, pepper Jack cheese, and another Colby.

2. Cook sandwiches until golden on one side. Turn and grill the other side. If necessary, place in oven and continue cooking until cheese has melted.

Other cheeses which may be substituted include Monterey Jack, Provolone, or Swiss.

You may wish to include other ingredients such as sliced tomatoes, green olives, alfalfa sprouts, or sautéed mushrooms.

Tuna Melt

Yield: 10 servings

The recipe for tuna salad may be found on page 899.

Tuna salad	*2 1/2 pounds*	*1.15 kilograms*
Bread, slices, lightly toasted	*20 each*	*20 each*
Swiss cheese, sliced	*10 ounces*	*285 grams*
Butter, as needed	*4 ounces*	*115 grams*

1. Place 4 ounces (115 grams) of the tuna salad on a slice of bread. Top with cheese and another slice of bread. Lightly butter the sandwich top and bottom. Grill until golden brown.

Grilled Vegetable and Cheese Sandwich

Yield: 10 servings

Slice the eggplant approximately 1/3 inch (1 centimeter) thick.

The peppers may be roasted in advance. The eggplant should be grilled to order. If it is necessary to grill in advance, marinate the eggplant in sherry vinegar to hold.

Grilled onion and zucchini may also be added. A thick roasted tomato purée may be added instead of the tomato slice.

Fresh or smoked mozzarella may replace the other cheeses if desired.

Herb Mayonnaise may be found on page 911. Aïoli (also page 911) may be substituted.

Eggplant, sliced	*10 each*	*10 each*
Vegetable oil, as needed	*2 fluid ounces*	*60 milliliters*
Whole wheat bread slices	*20 each*	*20 each*
Green pepper, roasted, peeled	*4 each*	*4 each*
Red pepper, roasted, peeled	*4 each*	*4 each*
Monterey Jack cheese	*10 ounces*	*285 grams*
Sharp Cheddar cheese	*10 ounces*	*285 grams*
Tomatoes, sliced	*20 each*	*20 each*
Herb Mayonnaise, as needed	*5 ounces*	*140 grams*

1. Brush the eggplant with a little oil to grill. Grill on both sides until cooked, but firm.

2. Toast the bread on a flat top or griddle. Place one slice of the cheese on each toast to melt.

3. On one slice, spread a little herb mayonnaise, add about 1/3 of each of the roasted peppers, a tomato slice, and the grilled eggplant. Top with the other slice of bread.

4. Secure with 4 frilled toothpicks and quarter as you would a club sandwich.

Croque Monsieur

Yield: 10 servings

White bread, pullman, slices	*20 each*	*20 each*
Gruyère cheese, sliced, 10 each	*10 ounces*	*285 grams*
Ham, sliced, 20 each	*15 ounces*	*425 grams*
Dijon Mustard, as needed	*5 ounces*	*140 grams*
Butter, as needed	*4 ounces*	*115 grams*

1. On one slice of bread, place a slice of gruyère and ham. Spread lightly with mustard. Place another slice of ham, spread a bit more mustard and close with the second slice of bread. Butter each side of the sandwich.

2. Lightly butter a flat top or griddle. Cook the sandwich until golden brown. If necessary, place in the oven and continue cooking until cheese has melted.

Croque Madame: Replace the ham with chicken. Use Emmenthaler instead of Gruyère. Grill as directed.

Monte Cristo: Prepare the Croque Monsieur or Madame. Dip in beaten egg and grill as directed.

Chicken and Green Chili Tacos

Yield: 10 servings

Onions, chopped coarse	*6 ounces*	*170 grams*
Vegetable oil, as needed	*2 fluid ounces*	*60 milliliters*
Green chilies, drained, julienne	*6 ounces*	*170 grams*
Jalapeño peppers, fine dice, to taste	*2 teaspoons*	*2 teaspoons*
Garlic clove, minced	*1 each*	*1 each*
Tomato Concassé	*1 1/2 pounds*	*680 grams*
Chicken meat, cooked, chopped coarse or shredded	*2 pounds*	*900 grams*
Dry sherry	*2 fluid ounces*	*60 milliliters*
Salt, to taste	*1/2 teaspoon*	*1/2 teaspoon*
Pepper, to taste	*1/4 teaspoon*	*1/4 teaspoon*
Taco shells, heated	*20 each*	*20 each*
White farmer cheese, grated or crumbled	*10 ounces*	*285 grams*
Iceberg lettuce, shredded	*1 1/2 pounds*	*680 grams*

1. Sauté the onions in a little oil. Add the green chilies, jalapeños, and garlic; cook an additional 2 minutes. Add the Tomato Concassé and chicken meat. Heat through. Add the sherry and reduce. The mixture should be fairly dry. Season to taste with salt and pepper.

2. Place about 3 ounces (85 grams) of the chicken mix in each taco shell. Top with cheese, lettuce, and additional tomatoes, if desired. Serve 2 tacos per portion.

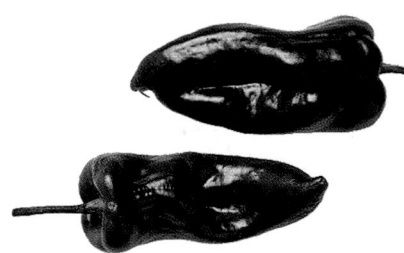

Ranging in its many varieties from mild to fiery hot, the pungency is concentrated in the white tissue attached to the seeds. Handle chilies with care.

Fresh green New Mexico chilies can be used: roast, peel, seed, and julienne.

Fresh goat cheese may be used if farmer cheese is not available.

Adjust the amount of jalapeños according to desired flavor.

Roasted Vegetable Quesadilla
with Red Chili Sauce

Yield: 10 servings

The recipe for Red Chili Sauce is found on page 549.

For a lower-fat version, roll in corn tortillas, and garnish with yogurt on the side. Or use the Chipotle Chili version on page 549.

You may prepare this by using 2 smaller tortillas and preparing the quesadilla sandwich-style. Flip and brown the other side of the quesadilla also. Tortillas should be grilled on a clean, nongreased surface.

Eggplants, roasted, but firm	2 each	2 each
Onions, grilled, roasted or sautéed, chopped	4 ounces	115 grams
Tomatoes, roasted, seeded, and chopped	1 pound	455 grams
Red peppers, roasted, peeled, and chopped	3 each	3 each
Green peppers, roasted, peeled, and chopped	3 each	3 each
Garlic, roasted, mashed to paste	2 each	2 each
Flour tortilla, large	10 each	10 each
Red Chili Sauce	16 fluid ounces	480 milliliters
Monterey Jack cheese	15 ounces	425 grams
Cilantro	2 tablespoons	2 tablespoons
Sour cream	10 ounces	285 grams

1. Scoop out the flesh from the eggplant and chop coarsely. Add the onions, tomatoes, red and green peppers, and garlic. Mix to a textured spread consistency.

2. Place the tortilla on a flat top or in a pan and grill on one side. Flip over, spread a thin layer of Red Chili Sauce and sprinkle the grated cheese to melt. Add the vegetable mixture. When the cheese has melted, add the cilantro. Remove from the heat.

3. Fold, cut into wedges and serve with 1 ounce (30 milliliters) of the sauce and sour cream.

Chicken and Walnut Quesadilla

Yield: 10 servings

Flour tortillas, large	*10 each*	*10 each*
Monterey Jack cheese, grated	*10 ounces*	*285 grams*
Chicken meat, coarsely chopped, cooked, heated	*20 ounces*	*570 grams*
Jalapeño peppers, fine dice, as needed	*2 each*	*2 each*
Walnuts, toasted, chopped	*4 ounces*	*115 grams*
Cilantro, chopped	*2 teaspoons*	*2 teaspoons*
Garnish		
Salsa	*1 pint*	*480 milliliters*
Sour cream	*10 fluid ounces*	*285 milliliters*

1. Place the tortilla on a flat top or in a pan; grill on one side. Flip over and sprinkle the grated cheese to melt. Add the cooked chicken meat, jalapeños, and walnuts. When the cheese has melted, add the cilantro.

2. Fold, cut into wedges and serve with the salsa and sour cream.

The cilantro may be omitted from the quesadilla and added to the garnish.

The recipe for various salsas may be found on page 936.

Goat cheese may be substituted for the Monterey Jack.

For a nonmeat version, replace the chicken with cooked pinto or black beans.

As noted with the preceding recipe, you may prepare this quesadilla using 2 small tortillas rather than 1 large.

Beef Tacos

Yield: 10 servings

Ground beef	*2 1/2 pounds*	*1.15 kilograms*
Taco Sauce	*16 fluid ounces*	*480 milliliters*
Taco shells, heated	*20 each*	*20 each*
Cheddar or Monterey Jack cheese, shredded	*10 ounces*	*285 grams*
Iceberg lettuce, shredded	*2 pounds*	*900 grams*
Tomato Concassée	*2 1/2 pounds*	*680 grams*

1. Brown ground beef. Drain well, combine with taco sauce.

2. Place two ounces of the beef mix in each taco shell. Top with grated cheese, lettuce, and tomatoes.

The recipe for Taco Sauce may be found on page 888.

Adjust the seasonings using the Chili Powder Blend on page 425.

Additional garnishes include chopped cilantro, chopped red onions, and sliced black olives.

This basic taco filling may also be used to fill burritos, enchiladas, or quesadillas. Serve with Red Chili Sauce, page 549.

Media Noche (El Cubano)

Yield: 10 servings

This classic Cuban sandwich has variations found throughout the Spanish Carribean, and parts of the United States.

It is a popular sandwich, customarily eaten after a late night movie, dance, or party; hence the name "midnight."

The Cuban roll is a sweeter version of our hero roll. If neither is available, use Challah, Italian, or French bread.

Hero rolls	10 each	10 each
Mayonnaise, as needed	5 ounces	140 grams
Mustard, as needed	5 ounces	140 grams
Roast pork, cold	1 pound	450 grams
Ham, sliced thin	1 pound	450 grams
Swiss cheese, 10 slices	1 pound	450 grams
Lettuce leaves	20 each	20 each
Tomato slices	30 each	30 each
Pickles, sliced	10 each	10 each
Butter, as needed	6 ounces	170 grams

1. Slice open the roll. Spread with mayonnaise and mustard. Layer the pork, ham, cheese, lettuce, tomato, and sliced pickle.

2. Brush each side of the roll with butter.

3. Lightly butter a sandwich griddle or flat top. Grill the sandwich, flatten top with a spatula, and turn. Cook until both sides are golden brown and cheese has melted. Slice on a diagonal.

Bruschetta with Tapenade, Tomato, and Gorgonzola

Yield: 10 servings

See the facing page for the recipe for Tapenade.

The oil and fresh ground pepper may be presented to the table at service, if desired.

Make smaller bread rounds and serve as a canapé.

Italian bread, sliced on bias	10 slices	10 slices
Olive oil, extra virgin, as needed	2 fluid ounces	60 milliliters
Tapenade	10 ounces	285 grams
Tomato Concassé	1 pound	455 grams
Gorgonzola cheese	10 ounces	285 grams
Black pepper, coarse-ground, to taste		

1. Brush the bread with a little oil. Grill.

2. Spread with the tapenade. Top with tomato. Crumble the gorgonzola on top. Season with freshly ground pepper.

3. Flash under a salamander.

4. Drizzle with oil before serving.

Tapenade

Yield: 1 pound (450 grams)

Niçoise olives, pitted	8 ounces	225 grams
Anchovy fillets, rinsed, dried	4 ounces	115 grams
Capers, rinsed	2 ounces	60 grams
Garlic, minced	1 tablespoon	1 tablespoon
Olive oil, extra virgin, as needed	1 fluid ounce	30 milliliters
Lemon juice, as needed	1 fluid ounce	30 milliliters
Pepper, to taste	1 teaspoon	1 teaspoon

1. In a mortar and pestle or food processor, mash together olives, anchovies, capers, and garlic. Add oil and lemon juice.

2. Adjust seasoning with pepper and additional ingredients as desired.

Tapenade is a classic spread from Provence. It is used as a condiment for fish and meat and as a spread for canapes, pizzas, and bruschetta.

The actual amount of ingredients will depend on desired use.

When using a food processor, be careful not to overprocess. The tapenade should have a somewhat coarse texture.

Grilled Duck Sausage, Roasted Garlic and Peppers on Focaccia

Yield: 10 servings

Duck sausage	2 3/4 pounds	1.25 kilograms
Focaccia, thin	20 pieces	20 pieces
Olive oil, as needed	5 fluid ounces	150 milliliters
Garlic, bulbs, roasted	5 each	5 each
Red peppers, roasted, peeled, julienne	5 each	5 each
Green peppers, roasted, peeled, julienne	5 each	5 each
Onions, roasted, sliced	3 each	3 each
Salt, to taste	1 teaspoon	1 teaspoon
Pepper, to taste	1/2 teaspoon	1/2 teaspoon

1. Grill sausage and slice.

2. Brush the focaccia pieces with olive oil.

3. Spread roasted garlic on focaccia pieces, top with sausage, peppers, and onion. Grind pepper over ingredients and top each with second slice of focaccia.

The recipe for Focaccia may be found on page 1033. To read about roasting garlic, see page 191. The onion may be roasted in the same manner.

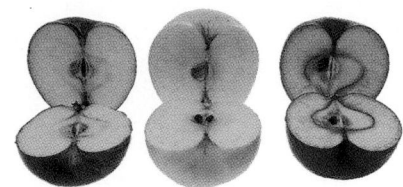

When possible, buy from local product sources for the freshest fruits and vegetables.

The Pizza Dough recipe is on page 1033.

To read about roasting shallots, see page 191.

Apple Cheddar Pizza

Yield: 10 servings

Pizza Dough	*3 1/2 pounds*	*1.6 kilograms*
Assorted apples, thinly sliced, skin on	*1 1/2 pounds*	*680 milliliters*
Mushrooms, sliced, lightly sautéed	*1 1/2 pounds*	*680 milliliters*
Sliced shallots, roasted	*1 pound*	*455 grams*
Aged sharp cheddar cheese, grated	*3/4 pound*	*340 grams*
Rosemary, chopped	*2 teaspoons*	*2 teaspoons*
Thyme, chopped	*2 teaspoons*	*2 teaspoons*
Pecans, walnuts, or butternuts, toasted	*4 ounces*	*115 grams*

1. For pizza dough: Mix honey, water, and yeast until yeast dissolves. Add enough bread flour to make a pancake-batter consistency. Refrigerate overnight. On day of service, let starter sit at room temperature for one hour.

2. Add remaining flours and salt; mix until ingredients are well incorporated. Additional flour may be needed; dough should pull cleanly away from sides of bowl.

3. Knead dough with hands for 5 minutes.

4. Place dough in stainless steel bowl; cover and let rest.

5. When dough has doubled in bulk, punch down; scale to 4 ounces (115 grams).

6. Place on plastic-wrap-lined tray, cover. Refrigerate until needed. Allow one hour for rising.

7. Roll whole-wheat pizza dough into disks. Top with mashed, roasted shallots, mushrooms, and herbs.

8. Lay apple slices on pizza, so there will be two slices on each of four wedges. Top with cheese and nuts.

9. Bake in a 350°F (175°C) oven until done.

Grilled Vegetable Pizza

Yield: 10 servings

Pizza Dough	3 1/2 pounds	1.6 kilograms
Marinade		
Olive oil, extra-virgin	6 fluid ounces	180 milliliters
Balsamic vinegar	2 fluid ounces	60 milliliters
Garlic, minced	1 teaspoon	1 teaspoon
Basil, chopped	2 teaspoons	2 teaspoons
Thyme, chopped	2 teaspoons	2 teaspoons
Oregano, chopped	2 teaspoons	2 teaspoons
Parsley, chopped	2 teaspoons	2 teaspoons
Salt, to taste	1/2 teaspoon	1/2 teaspoon
Pepper, to taste	1/4 teaspoon	1/4 teaspoon
Green peppers, halved	2 each	2 each
Red peppers, halved	2 each	2 each
Onions, thick-sliced	2 each	2 each
Fennel, quartered	1 each	1 each
Yellow squash, sliced	2 each	2 each
Zucchini, sliced	2 each	2 each
Goat cheese, crumbled	20 ounces	570 grams
Parmesan cheese, grated	10 ounces	285 grams

The started dough must be refrigerated overnight. On the day of service, let dough sit at room temperature.

Pizza Dough may be found on page 1033.

Other vegetables that may be grilled include eggplants, radishes, and tomatoes.

To read about grilling vegetables, see pages 300 to 305.

1. For the pizza dough: Mix honey, water, and yeast until yeast dissolves. Add enough bread flour to make a pancake batter consistency. Refrigerate overnight. On day of service, let starter sit at room temperature for one hour.

2. Add remaining flours and salt; mix until ingredients are well incorporated. Additional flour may be needed, dough should pull away cleanly from sides of bowl.

3. Knead dough by hand for five minutes.

4. Place dough in stainless steel bowl; cover and let rest.

5. When dough has doubled in bulk, punch down, measure out 4-ounce (115 gram) portions.

6. Place on a plastic-wrap-covered tray. Refrigerate until needed. Allow one hour for the second rise.

7. Combine olive oil, balsamic vinegar, garlic, herbs, salt, and pepper. Toss vegetables with vinaigrette and grill. Allow to cool.

8. When vegetables are cooled, cut into appropriate sizes.

9. Roll whole-wheat pizza dough into disks. Top with vegetables, goat and Parmesan cheese. Bake in a 350°F (175°C) oven until done.

CIA Club

Yield: 10 servings

For a party, buffet, or reception presentation, select a large round country loaf, split it horizontally and layer the ingredients as described in this recipe, omitting the middle slice of bread. Secure with club frills, arranging as many portions as desired and cut the sandwich into wedges.

Create your own signature club by adding other ingredients: salami, pastrami, avocados, alfalfa sprouts, cheese, or Green Goddess Dressing.

Mayonnaise, as needed	6 fluid ounces	180 milliliters
Bread, slices, lightly toasted	30 each	30 each
Red leaf lettuce leaves	20 each	20 each
Turkey, sliced thin	20 ounces	570 grams
Ham, sliced thin	20 ounces	570 grams
Tomatoes, sliced thin	20 each	20 each
Bacon, cooked, cut in half	30 each	30 each

1. Spread mayonnaise on one slice of toast

2. Layer in this order: lettuce, turkey, ham, toast, more mayonnaise on both sides, more lettuce, tomato, and bacon. Top with toast that has mayonnaise spread on the underside.

3. Secure with a frilled toothpick. Cut into 4 wedges. Garnish with pickles and olives.

"Philly" Hoagie (Italian Combo)

Yield: 10 servings

Prepare the dressing a day in advance to "marry" the flavors.

Hot pickled peppers may be sliced and added to the dressing. Season the dressing with salt and pepper.

Serve with quartered garlic pickle on the side.

Submarine roll	10 each	10 each
Dressing		
Olive oil	6 fluid ounces	180 milliliters
Vinegar	3 fluid ounces	90 milliliters
Oregano, chopped	1 tablespoon	1 tablespoon
Prosciutto	1 1/2 pounds	680 grams
Sweet cappicola, imported, sliced thin	10 ounces	285 grams
Genoa salami, sliced thin	10 ounces	285 grams
Provolone, sliced	20 ounces	570 grams
Iceberg lettuce, shredded	10 ounces	285 grams
Tomato slices	30 each	30 each
Onion slices	30 each	30 each

1. Slice roll open, leaving it hinged. Brush inside of roll with dressing.

2. Arrange prosciutto, cappicola, salami, and provolone on roll. Top with shredded lettuce. Place 3 slices of tomato on top of lettuce. Top with onions and additional dressing.

Roasted Vegetables in Pita
with Roasted Garlic Tahini Dressing

Yield: 10 servings

Eggplant, roasted, but firm	2 each	2 each
Onions, grilled or roasted, chopped	4 ounces	115 grams
Tomatoes, oven-dried, chopped	1 pound	455 grams
Red peppers, roasted, peeled, and chopped	3 each	3 each
Green peppers, roasted, peeled, and chopped	4 each	4 each
Arugula, cleaned, stemmed	1 bunch	1 bunch
Olive oil, as need	4 fluid ounces	120 milliliters
Lemon juice, as needed	4 fluid ounces	120 milliliters
Garlic bulbs, roasted	3 each	3 each
Humus B'Tahini	1 pint	480 milliliters
Pita breads	10 each	10 each

1. Scoop out the flesh from the eggplant and chop coarsely. Add the onion, tomatoes, red and green peppers; toss lightly with the olive oil and 2 fluid ounces (60 milliliters) of lemon juice.

2. Mash the roasted garlic to a paste. Blend it with the tahini to taste.

3. Cut a pita in half. Stuff some of the arugula into the pita. Spoon some of the vegetables into each half. Drizzle the tahini over the open end of each half. Serve 1 ounce (30 milliliters) of tahini on the side.

To read about oven-roasting tomatoes, see page 192.

To read about roasting garlic, see page 191. Onions may be roasted in the same manner.

Watercress is an excellent substitute for arugula.

You may prefer to grill some or all of the vegetables. See pages 300 to 305 to read about grilling.

Roasted Garlic Tahini Dressing

1. Follow the recipe for Humus B' Tahini on page 939. Replace the roasted garlic with that called for in the original recipe.

2. Thin the mixture with the remaining lemon juice and enough water to get a dressing consistency. Season to taste with lemon juice and soy sauce.

Oven-Dried Tomato, Cream Cheese, and Arugula Sandwich

Yield: 10 servings

Tomatoes, oven-dried, peeled, seeded, and chopped	*10 each*	*10 each*
Cream cheese, softened	*1 1/4 pounds*	*570 grams*
Salt, to taste	*1/2 teaspoon*	*1/2 teaspoon*
Pepper, to taste	*1/4 teaspoon*	*1/4 teaspoon*
Basil, chopped	*1/4 ounce*	*8 grams*
Arugula, cleaned, stemmed	*3 bunches*	*3 bunches*
Baguettes, split	*2 each*	*2 each*

To read about oven-roasting (drying) tomatoes, see page 192.

Fresh mozzarella cheese can be used in place of the cream cheese.

1. Chop the oven-dried tomatoes.

2. Mix with cream cheese and season with salt, pepper, and basil.

3. Spread the cream cheese mixture on the baguettes, top with arugula.

4. Place the top of the baguette on the sandwich and cut each baguette into 5 portions.

Cucumber with Herb Cream Cheese Tea Sandwich

Yield: 10 servings

Cream cheese	*10 ounces*	*285 grams*
Herbs, fresh, chopped fine	*2 tablespoons*	*2 tablespoons*
Heavy cream, as needed	*2 fluid ounces*	*60 milliliters*
Bread, thin slices	*20 each*	*20 each*
Cucumbers, sliced thin	*3 each*	*3 each*

Select fresh herbs as available: chives, dill, parsley, and chervil are all good choices.

For larger or older cucumbers, you can cut the bitterness by peeling, slicing, and salting them. Let them rest for 1 hour, then blot them dry or squeeze out the lemon juice.

1. Blend the cream cheese and fresh herbs with a little heavy cream to get a smooth spreading consistency.

2. Spread the cream cheese mixture on the bread slices. Place the cucumber slices on one slice of the bread. Top with the other slice.

3. Cut into quarters, or cut off the crusts and cut into 3 or 4 strips.

Apples with Curry Mayonnaise Tea Sandwich

Yield: 10 servings

Curry powder	1 tablespoon	1 tablespoon
Mayonnaise	5 ounces	140 grams
Granny Smith apples, peeled, sliced thin	5 each	5 each

1. Toast curry powder. Cool. Blend into the mayonnaise.

2. Spread the curry mayonnaise on the bread slices. Place the apple slices on one slice of the bread. Top with the other slice.

Use prepared curry powder or the blend on page 426.

Add plumped currants and toasted chopped nuts. Use bananas or mangos instead of the apples.

You may substitute Curry Vinaigrette (page 910) for the mayonnaise.

Elena Ruz Tea Sandwich

Yield: 10 servings

Brioche or challah bread, sliced	20 slices	20 slices
Cream cheese, as needed	10 ounces	285 grams
Strawberry preserves, as needed	10 ounces	285 grams
Turkey, sliced thin	20 ounces	570 grams
Butter, as needed to grill	4 ounces	115 grams

1. Spread one slice of bread with cream cheese. Spread another with strawberry preserves. Place turkey on the cheese and top with the other slice.

2. Butter both sides of the sandwich and cook on a flat top or griddle until lightly golden.

The Elena Ruz is a Cuban tea sandwich named for a Havana debutante in the 1920s.

Gorgonzola with Pears Tea Sandwich

Yield: 10 servings

Cream cheese	2 ounces	85 grams
Gorgonzola cheese	5 ounces	140 grams
Heavy cream, as needed	2 fluid ounces	60 milliliters
Raisin pumpernickel bread, sliced thin	20 each	20 each
Pears, peeled and sliced	5 each	5 each

1. Blend the cream cheese and gorgonzola with a little heavy cream to get a smooth spreading consistency.

2. Spread the gorgonzola mix on the bread slices. Place the pear slices on one slice of the bread. Top with the other slice of bread.

3. Cut into quarters or strips.

The flavors of pears and gorgonzola blend well together and are a classic combination in many dishes.

Roquefort or a milder blue cheese may be preferred.

Substitute cucumbers for the pears.

933

Tomato with Oregano Sour Cream Tea Sandwich

Yield: 10 servings

Butter may be used instead of sour cream.

Cream cheese	5 ounces	140 grams
Sour cream, as needed	5 fluid ounces	150 milliliters
Oregano, chopped	2 tablespoons	2 tablespoons
Salt	1/2 teaspoon	1/2 teaspoon
Pepper	1/4 teaspoon	1/4 teaspoon
Bread, thin slices	20 each	20 each
Tomato slices	20 to 30 each	20 to 30 each

1. Mix the cream cheese, sour cream, oregano, salt, and pepper.

2. Spread the sour cream on the bread slices. Place the tomato slices on one slice of the bread. Top with the other slice.

3. Cut in quarters or strips. Remove crust if desired.

Watercress with Herb Mayonnaise Tea Sandwich

Yield: 10 servings

As with all of these tea sandwiches, they may be served open-faced or cut in rounds as a canape.

Herb Mayonnaise may be found on page 911.

Whole butter or Maitre d'Hôtel Butter (page 547) may be used in place of the mayonnaise.

Bread, thin slice	20 each	20 each
Herb Mayonnaise, as needed	5 fluid ounces	150 milliliters
Watercress, cleaned, thick stems removed	2 bunches	2 bunches

1. Spread the bread with a little of the herb mayonnaise. Lay the watercress on one slice of the bread. Top with the other slice.

2. Cut the sandwich in quarters or strips. The crusts may be removed if desired.

C H A P T E R 26 | *Hors d'Oeuvres and Appetizers*

Hors d'oeuvres and appetizers are one of the menu categories that most often needs an infusion of fresh ideas. The appeal of small dishes with brilliant flavors and a intriguing presentation is universal. Some guests may look to the first course selections as a way to sample a wide range of dishes without becoming "bogged down" with a larger menu item.

This catering style is enhanced with a special tasting menu, often composed of the chef's selections for the night, and is composed to make the best use of whatever is best from the market.

The recipes in this chapter have been grouped as follows:

- *Dips and Spreads*
- *Marinated Salads and Ceviche*
- *Meat Dishes*
- *Eggs and Cheese*
- *Strudels, Fritters, and Crêpes*
- *Asian*
- *Fish and Seafood*
- *Fruit and Vegetable*

Fresh Tomato Salsa

Yield: 10 servings

Increase the amount of lime juice or tomatoes, as desired.

Tomato Concassé	*8 ounces*	*225 grams*
Jalapeño peppers, seeded, minced	*1/2 ounce*	*15 grams*
Red onion, peeled, minced	*2 ounces*	*60 grams*
Cilantro, fresh, chopped	*3 tablespoons*	*3 tablespoons*
Lime juice	*1 tablespoon*	*1 tablespoon*

1. Combine all ingredients and mix well.

2. Refrigerate for several hours to let flavors combine.

3. Check seasoning before serving.

Black Bean Salsa

Yield: 20 servings

To read about roasting shallots, see page 191.

Green bell peppers, roasted New Mexico peppers, and roasted or smoked corn kernels are also good additions. Diced raw jícama adds a crunchy texture.

Black beans (soaked overnight)	*2 1/4 pounds*	*1 kilogram*
Cilantro, chopped fine	*2 ounces*	*60 grams*
Shallots, roasted whole, chopped fine	*4 each*	*4 each*
Jalapeño peppers, fine dice	*2 each*	*2 each*
Yellow peppers, fine dice	*1 each*	*1 each*
Red peppers, fine dice	*1 each*	*1 each*
Olive oil	*4 fluid ounces*	*120 milliliters*
Lemon juice	*2 fluid ounces*	*60 milliliters*
Cumin, ground	*2 teaspoons*	*2 teaspoons*
Coriander, ground	*2 teaspoons*	*2 teaspoons*
Cayenne, ground, to taste	*1/4 teaspoon*	*1/4 teaspoon*
Pepper, to taste	*1/4 teaspoon*	*1/4 teaspoon*

1. Simmer black beans for about 1 hour, or until just tender.

2. Allow to cool to room temperature, in cooking liquid.

3. Drain the beans and place them in a bowl.

4. Mix all the remaining ingredients, carefully.

5. Cover and marinate in a refrigerator 2 to 3 hours until service.

Guacamole

Yield: 10 servings

Avocados, sliced	*8 ounces*	*225 grams*
Garlic clove, chopped fine	*1 each*	*1 each*
Scallions, chopped fine	*1 ounce*	*30 grams*
Jalapeño peppers, seeded, chopped fine	*1 tablespoon*	*1 tablespoon*
Lemon juice	*1 tablespoon*	*1 tablespoon*

1. Mash avocado to a paste.

2. Add remaining ingredients and blend.

Serve as soon as possible. If this must be held, place plastic wrap directly on surface to prevent discoloration.

Lime juice may be used in place of the lemon juice. For very hot, spicy foods, increase the amount of lime juice. Tomato Concassé may also be added.

Baba Ghannouj (Eggplant and Tahini Dip)

Yield: 10 servings

Eggplant	*3 each*	*3 each*
Lemon juice, to taste	*4 fluid ounces*	*120 milliliters*
Tahini	*8 ounces*	*225 grams*
Parsley, chopped	*3/4 ounce*	*20 grams*
Salt, to taste	*1 teaspoon*	*1 teaspoon*
Olive oil	*2 fluid ounces*	*60 milliliters*

1. Place the eggplants on flat-top stove or in a skillet and char the skin, turning constantly. Place on sheet tray and bake at 400°F (205°C) until eggplant is soft. Remove and cool.

2. Peel the eggplant, remove the seeds under cold water, and purée the pulp.

3. Combine pulp and remaining ingredients in food processor. Purée until smooth. Adjust seasoning.

For additional flavor, add roasted garlic (page 191) and a bit of soy sauce.

Serve as a sauce or a dip with crudité or toasted pita wedges.

If desired, you may grill the eggplant as indicated on page 938.

Moutabel with Belgian Endive

Yield: 30 pieces

Moutabel		
Eggplants, large	*2 each*	*2 each*
Tahini paste, to taste	*1/2 cup*	*120 milliliters*
Garlic cloves, minced	*2 each*	*2 each*
Lemon juice, to taste	*1 lemon*	*1 lemon*
Tabasco	*to taste*	*to taste*
Olive oil, extra virgin	*2 fluid ounces*	*60 milliliters*
Salt, to taste	*1/2 teaspoon*	*1/2 teaspoon*
Pepper, to taste	*1/2 teaspoon*	*1/2 teaspoon*
Belgian endive leaves	*30 each*	*30 each*
Roasted peppers, julienne	*3 each*	*3 each*
Sesame seeds, toasted	*2 tablespoons*	*2 tablespoons*

1. Grill or roast the eggplants until completely soft. Cool.

2. When the eggplants have cooled enough to handle, wash the charred skin off under cold running water. Remove as many of the seeds as possible.

3. Rough-chop the eggplant and add to a food processor. Add the tahini paste, garlic, lemon juice, salt, pepper, and Tabasco. Purée mixture until smooth, scraping the sides down occasionally with a spatula.

4. Add the olive oil in a slow steady stream. Check seasonings and adjust as necessary. The final product should be thick.

5. Soak endive leaves in ice water for 15 minutes. Drain well.

6. Pipe Moutabel onto the endive leaves.

7. Arrange the julienne of peppers on top of the moutabel and sprinkle with the toasted sesame seeds.

Hummus B'Tahini

Yield: 2 3/4 pounds (1.25 kilograms)

Chickpeas, cooked	*2 pounds*	*900 grams*
Garlic cloves, mashed to a paste	*6 each*	*6 each*
Tahini	*10 ounces*	*285 grams*
Salt, to taste	*3 to 4 teaspoons*	*3 to 4 teaspoons*
Lemon juice	*4 to 8 fluid ounces*	*120 to 240 milliliters*

1. Drain the chickpeas.

2. Purée the peas with the garlic, tahini, and water as necessary, for a smooth consistency. Adjust seasoning with salt and lemon juice to taste.

A typical presentation of this dish is to place the hummus in a crock, drizzle it with olive oil, and serve it with grilled or toasted pita bread.

A bit of soy sauce may be added instead of the salt.

Yogurt Tahini Sauce

Yield: 10 servings

Yogurt	*14 ounces*	*400 grams*
Tahini	*6 ounces*	*170 grams*
Olive oil	*1 fluid ounce*	*30 milliliters*
Salt, to taste	*1/2 teaspoon*	*1/2 teaspoon*
White pepper, to taste	*1/4 teaspoon*	*1/4 teaspoon*
Lemon juice, to taste	*1 fluid ounce*	*30 milliliters*

1. Combine all ingredients and blend until smooth. Refrigerate the sauce.

2. Let the sauce rest for 2 to 3 hours to allow the flavors to develop.

This sauce is used to accompany Falafel (page 714). It also makes a good option for a crudité platter.

If available, blend in a few tablespoons of Hummus (above) for additional flavor.

Caponata—Eggplant-Vegetable Salad

Yield: 20 servings

Serve this salad as part of a sampler plate. Or use it as a topping for bruschetta or a filling for a calzone.

If served as a full side dish on a plate, expect about 10 servings.

Eggplant, peeled, battonnet	8 ounces	240 grams
Kosher salt, as needed	4 ounces	115 grams
Virgin olive oil	3 fluid ounces	90 milliliters
Red onion, sliced	4 ounces	115 grams
Yellow pepper, battonnet	4 ounces	115 grams
Red pepper, battonnet	4 ounces	115 grams
Zucchini, green part only, battonnet	8 ounces	225 grams
Garlic, minced	2 ounces	60 grams
Fennel, sliced	4 ounces	115 grams
Jalapeño peppers, minced	2 each	2 each
Sun-dried tomatoes, cut in half	3 ounces	85 grams
Pine nuts, toasted	2 ounces	60 grams
Basil, chopped	1 tablespoon	1 tablespoon
Oregano, chopped	1 tablespoon	1 tablespoon
Parsley, chopped	2 tablespoons	2 tablespoons
Lemon juice, to taste	2 fluid ounces	60 milliliters
Balsamic vinegar, to taste	1 tablespoon	1 tablespoon
Salt, to taste	1/2 teaspoon	1/2 teaspoon
Pepper, to taste	1/4 teaspoon	1/4 teaspoon

1. Place the eggplant in a colander with the salt and toss. Allow to stand for an hour, rinse thoroughly, squeeze out the excess juices from the eggplant.

2. In half the olive oil, sauté the onions, peppers, and zucchini quickly, leaving them still crisp. Remove from the pan and place in a bowl to cool.

3. Add the rest of the olive oil to the same pan and add the garlic, eggplant, and fennel. Cook until the raw flavor of the garlic is gone; add to the bowl.

4. Next add the jalapeños, sun-dried tomatoes, pine nuts, and the herbs; toss. Add the lemon juice, balsamic vinegar, salt, and pepper to taste; chill well.

Celery Root and Roasted Red Pepper Rémoulade

Yield: 10 servings

Red peppers, roasted	*3 each*	*3 each*
Celery root, shredded	*1 pound*	*450 grams*
Mayonnaise, fresh	*8 fluid ounces*	*240 milliliters*
Avocado, diced	*3 each*	*3 each*
Olive oil	*2 tablespoons*	*2 tablespoons*
Lemon juice	*2 fluid ounces*	*60 milliliters*
Salt, to taste	*1/2 teaspoon*	*1/2 teaspoon*
Pepper, to taste	*1/4 teaspoon*	*1/4 teaspoon*

Celery root is also known as celeriac.

1. Cut the red pepper into fine julienne.

2. In a small bowl combine shredded celery root and the red pepper.

3. Add mayonnaise. Place mixture into 10 ramekins. Refrigerate.

4. Peel avocado and dice it just before service.

5. Place avocado strips in a bowl. Cover with olive oil and lemon juice.

6. Season with salt and pepper.

7. Remove ramekins from refrigerator. Invert onto a small plate.

8. Garnish with marinated avocado strips.

"Ceviche" of Artichoke Hearts

Yield: 10 servings

Ceviche is a dish made by marinating raw fish in a mixture of lime juice and seasonings. In this vegetarian version, the classic marinade is used to flavor artichoke bottoms.

Serve in a ring of thinly sliced tomatoes and garnish with Guacamole (page 937) if desired.

Artichoke bottoms, cooked	*10 each*	*10 each*
Lime juice	*3 fluid ounces*	*90 milliliters*
Tomato Concassé	*10 ounces*	*285 grams*
Red onions, sliced in thin rings	*4 ounces*	*115 grams*
Jalapeño peppers, chopped fine	*1/2 ounces*	*15 grams*
Scallions, split, sliced on a bias	*2 ounces*	*60 grams*
Garlic cloves, chopped fine	*2 each*	*2 each*
Olive oil	*2 tablespoons*	*2 tablespoons*
Cilantro, chopped	*1 tablespoon*	*1 tablespoon*

1. Mix the ingredients.

2. Allow to marinate two hours in refrigerator.

3. Adjust the seasoning to taste with salt and pepper. Serve well chilled.

Charred Tuna and Scallop Ceviche

Yield: 15 servings

The fish for ceviche must be extremely fresh and handled with the utmost concern for food safety. Keep the fish as cold as possible and clean and sanitize work surfaces and knives thoroughly before and after use.

Tuna steak	*1 pound*	*450 grams*
Vegetable oil, as needed	*1 fluid ounce*	*30 milliliters*
Bay scallops	*1 pound*	*450 grams*
Lime juice	*1 1/2 fluid ounces*	*45 milliliters*
Tomato Concassé	*4 ounces*	*115 grams*
Red onions, small dice	*1 ounce*	*30 grams*
Salt, to taste	*1/2 teaspoon*	*1/2 teaspoon*
Pepper, to taste	*1/4 teaspoon*	*1/4 teaspoon*

1. Rub tuna steak with oil and sear in a hot, well-seasoned pan (it should resemble a steak cooked black and blue, still raw on the inside).

2. Chill tuna rapidly, cut into pieces the size of the scallops.

3. Clean bay scallops of tough outer muscle.

4. Mix the tuna, scallops, lime juice, tomato, and onion together; marinate at least 12 hours.

5. Place a portion of ceviche on chilled plates.

Ceviche of Snapper

Yield: 10 servings

Red Snapper fillet	*1 1/4 pounds*	*570 grams*
Tomato Concassée	*10 ounces*	*285 grams*
Lemon or lime juice, fresh-squeezed	*6 fluid ounces*	*180 milliliters*
Red onions, sliced in thin rings	*3 ounces*	*85 grams*
Scallions, bias-cut	*2 ounces*	*60 grams*
Olive oil	*2 fluid ounces*	*60 milliliters*
Jalapeño peppers, fine dice or julienne	*1/2 ounce*	*15 grams*
Garlic, mashed to paste	*1 teaspoon*	*1 teaspoon*
Cilantro, fresh, chopped	*4 tablespoons*	*4 tablespoons*
Tomato, slices	*20 each*	*20 each*
Guacamole	*1 recipe*	*1 recipe*

1. Trim the snapper, removing all bones. Cut into strips or dice.

2. Combine all of the ingredients. Marinate the fish for a minimum of 4 hours to a maximum of 12 hours before service.

3. Serve the ceviche with sliced tomatoes and guacamole on chilled plates.

Serve ceviche in a halved avocado or hollowed tomato. Or, place it in Boston lettuce leaf "cups" or a tortilla fried to make a bowl.

The recipe for Guacamole may be found on page 937.

Beef Carpaccio

Yield: 16 servings

The recipe for Caponata is on page 940.

To shave Parmesan cheese, use a swivel-bladed peeler.

Carpaccio may also be served with Aïoli (page 911) or a mustard sauce prepared by adding mustard to taste to the Basic Mayonnaise recipe also found on page 911.

Most restaurants find it easiest to store the carpaccio in the freezer at all times. It is then sliced and plated to order and immediately returned to the freezer. The thin plated slices thaw immediately. And the quality of the tenderloin is maintained.

Beef tenderloin	2 pounds	900 grams
Vegetable oil	2 ounces	60 milliliters
Rosemary, chopped	1 tablespoon	1 tablespoon
Sage, chopped	1 tablespoon	1 tablespoon
Thyme, chopped	1 tablespoon	1 tablespoon
Pepper, cracked	1 tablespoon	1 tablespoon
Balsamic vinegar	1 tablespoon	1 tablespoon
Kosher salt, to taste	1 to 2 teaspoons	1 to 2 teaspoons
Garnish		
Caponata	24 ounces	680 grams
Arugula leaves, washed, drained	2 bunches	2 bunches
Extra-virgin olive oil	2 ounces	60 milliliters
Parmesan cheese, shaved	3 ounces	85 grams
Parsley, chopped	2 tablespoons	2 tablespoons
Black pepper, to taste	1/2 teaspoon	1/2 teaspoon
Capers, rinsed	2 tablespoons	2 tablespoons
Black olives, cured	16 each	16 each
Pepperocini	16 each	16 each

1. Trim the beef of all fat and sinew. Combine the rest of the ingredients and mix.

2. Pull out a layer of plastic wrap and lay the tenderloin on top. Rub the herb mixture onto the tenderloin.

3. Wrap tightly in plastic wrap and freeze for at least 1 hour to facilitate slicing.

4. Slice the carpaccio very thin on an electric slicer. Place the slices of carpaccio in-between plastic wrap. Place a few drops of vegetable oil on top of the plastic. Starting from the center with a spoon, lightly push toward the outside to flatten the meat.

5. Plate the carpaccio on a chilled plate with the caponata and arugula.

6. Drizzle over the meat a few drops of the extra-virgin olive oil, shaved Parmesan cheese, parsley, ground pepper, and capers. Garnish with the olives and pepperocini.

Charred Beef with Garlic Herb Mayonnaise

Yield: 20 servings

Beef tenderloin, chilled	2 1/2 pounds	1 kilogram
Vegetable oil	1 tablespoon	1 tablespoon
Shallots, minced	2 ounces	60 grams
Cider vinegar	3 fluid ounces	90 milliliters
White wine	6 fluid ounces	180 milliliters
Egg yolks	6 each	6 each
Water	1 1/2 fluid ounces	45 milliliters
Olive oil	16 fluid ounces	480 milliliters
Basil, chopped	2 teaspoons	2 teaspoons
Oregano, chopped	2 teaspoons	2 teaspoons
Parsley, chopped	2 teaspoons	2 teaspoons
Chives, chopped	2 teaspoons	2 teaspoons
Garlic, mashed to a paste	2 teaspoons	2 teaspoons
Spinach leaves, puréed	3 ounces	85 grams
Salt, to taste	1/2 teaspoon	1/2 teaspoon
Pepper, to taste	1/4 teaspoon	1/4 teaspoon
Scallions, sliced on bias	4 each	4 each

1. Rub beef tenderloin with oil, sear very brown in a hot pan; chill (beef should still be raw). Chill quickly, wrap tightly, and keep refrigerated until ready to slice.

2. Combine shallots, cider vinegar, and white wine; reduce by half over high heat. Remove from pan to a bowl and let cool to room temperature.

3. Add yolks and water to reduction and blend.

4. Slowly add olive oil to make a mayonnaise, whisking eggs constantly during the addition.

5. Add herbs, garlic, and spinach to the mayonnaise. Season with salt to taste.

6. Slice beef into thin slices.

7. Arrange 2 1-ounce (30-gram) slices on each plate, cover with plastic wrap; using the back of the spoon, spread the beef out on the plate, remove wrap.

8. Sprinkle with black pepper.

9. Garnish with the mayonnaise and scallions.

Chicken Croustade

Yield: 10 servings

Croustades can be baked in advance and then held until you are ready to fill and serve. Store the croustade shells covered in a dry storage area.

Diced shellfish may replace the chicken in the croustade. For a meatless version, add blanched vegetables, such as asparagus tips, or diced artichoke bottoms, and other grated cheeses to replace the ham and chicken.

White or wheat bread	10 slices	10 slices
Vegetable oil, as needed	2 fluid ounces	60 milliliters
Heavy cream	12 fluid ounces	360 milliliters
Chicken meat, small dice	12 ounces	360 grams
Prosciutto ham, small dice	6 ounces	180 grams
Pepper, to taste	1/4 teaspoon	1/4 teaspoon
Egg yolks	2 each	2 each
Parmesan cheese, grated	1 ounce	30 grams
Parsley, chopped	1 tablespoon	1 tablespoon
Basil, chopped	2 tablespoons	2 tablespoons
Parmesan cheese	as needed	as needed

1. Cut out bread with plain round cutter and flatten with a rolling pin.

2. Oil small muffin tins and place the bread rounds inside.

3. Bake in a 325°F (160°C) until golden.

4. Reduce the heavy cream by half and reserve until needed.

5. Sauté the chicken in a little oil until the meat has lost its raw appearance. Add the prosciutto and continue to cook until the prosciutto is heated thoroughly.

6. Add the reduced cream, black pepper, and bring to a simmer.

7. Temper the egg yolks with the hot mixture. Add the egg yolks to the mixture, and bring back to a simmer.

8. Add the cheese, parsley, and basil; adjust the seasonings to taste with salt and pepper.

9. Fill the croustades, sprinkle with a little grated Parmesan cheese and gratinée just before serving.

Chicken Stir Fry with Peanuts

Yield: 10 servings

Peanut oil	*1 1/2 fluid ounces*	*45 milliliters*
Chicken julienne	*8 ounces*	*225 grams*
Onions, sliced	*2 ounces*	*60 grams*
Celery, sliced thin	*2 ounces*	*60 grams*
Red peppers, julienne	*2 ounces*	*60 grams*
Snow peas, cut in half	*2 ounces*	*60 grams*
Shiitake mushrooms, sliced	*2 ounces*	*60 grams*
Water chestnuts, sliced	*2 ounces*	*60 grams*
Chicken Stock	*4 fluid ounces*	*120 milliliters*
Soy sauce	*1 tablespoon*	*1 tablespoon*
Hoisin sauce	*1 teaspoon*	*1 teaspoon*
Garlic, mashed to a paste	*1/2 teaspoon*	*1/2 teaspoon*
Ginger, ground	*1/2 teaspoon*	*1/2 teaspoon*
Arrowroot	*1/2 teaspoon*	*1/2 teaspoon*
Boston lettuce, leaves	*10 each*	*10 each*
Romaine lettuce, leaves	*10 each*	*10 each*
Scallions, sliced thin	*2 each*	*2 each*
Peanuts, dry roasted, chopped	*2 tablespoons*	*2 tablespoons*

This could also be served as an entrée. The recipe will be enough for 2 to 3 entrée-sized portions. Serve with rice or noodles.

Cut the red peppers into 1-inch (2.5-centimeter) strips.

1. Heat a sauté pan or wok; add half the oil.

2. Add chicken and stir-fry lightly; remove, reserve.

3. Add remaining oil and stir-fry onions, celery, peppers, peas, and mush-rooms; add water chestnuts.

4. Mix stock, soy and, hoisin sauces, garlic, ginger, and arrowroot together; add to the vegetable mixture and bring to a boil.

5. Remove vegetable mixture from heat and mix in chicken. Allow to cool slightly.

6. Arrange lettuces on a plate, place portion of warm stir-fry next to lettuce.

7. Garnish stir-fry with scallions and peanuts.

Paper-Wrapped Chicken

Yield: 80 pieces

Select rice paper that is approximately 4-inch by 4-inch (10-centimeters square).

Rice paper must be dipped in room-temperature water to soften before filling and rolling.

Paper-wrapped chicken may be folded into a triangle shape or rolled in the traditional egg roll shape.

Stuffing

Chicken breast meat, cooked and shredded	*3 pounds*	*1.3 kilograms*
Scallions, chopped fine	*1 bunch*	*1 bunch*
Sugar	*1 tablespoon*	*1 tablespoon*
Sherry	*1 fluid ounce*	*30 milliliters*
Soy sauce	*2 fluid ounces*	*60 milliliters*
Sesame oil	*2 ounces*	*60 milliliters*
Salt	*1 teaspoon*	*1 teaspoon*
White pepper	*1 teaspoon*	*1 teaspoon*
Egg, beaten	*1 each*	*1 each*
Rice paper sheets	*80 sheets*	*80 sheets*

1. Combine all ingredients for the stuffing; mix together.

2. Place 1 tablespoon (15 grams) of filling on each phyllo dough sheet; egg-wash edges and roll.

3. Deep-fry in 350°F (175°C) hot fat until golden brown; drain on absorbent paper.

Vitello Tonnato

Yield: 10 servings

Veal roast, boneless, cooked	*1 1/2 pounds*	*680 grams*
Albacore tuna, canned, drained	*6 ounces*	*170 grams*
Anchovy fillets	*4 each*	*4 each*
Onions, fine dice	*1 1/2 ounces*	*40 grams*
Carrots, fine dice	*1 1/2 ounces*	*40 grams*
Dry white wine	*4 fluid ounces*	*120 milliliters*
White wine vinegar	*2 fluid ounces*	*60 milliliters*
Water	*2 fluid ounces*	*60 milliliters*
Olive oil	*3 fluid ounces*	*90 milliliters*
Egg yolks, hard-cooked, sieved	*2 each*	*2 each*
Capers, drained, chopped	*1 tablespoon*	*1 tablespoon*

(Recipe continued on facing page)

1. Slice the veal thinly; divide into servings.

2. Combine the tuna, fillets, onion, carrots, wine, vinegar, and water in a food processor. Process to a relatively smooth paste.

3. Arrange the sliced veal on chilled plates. Coat the veal with the tuna sauce; drizzle with olive oil. Garnish the veal with the egg yolks and capers.

Pickled Eggs

Yield: 10 servings

Eggs, hard-cooked, peeled	*10 each*	*10 each*	
Dry mustard	*2 teaspoons*	*2 teaspoons*	
Cornstarch	*2 teaspoons*	*2 teaspoons*	
White wine vinegar	*1 1/2 pints*	*720 milliliters*	
Sugar	*2 teaspoons*	*2 teaspoons*	
Turmeric, or curry powder, ground	*1 teaspoon*	*1 teaspoon*	

Serve the eggs with pickled beets and thin sliced onions, if desired.

Serve with mayonnaise, rye bread, and assorted greens.

1. Place the eggs in an earthenware or stainless steel mixing bowl. Reserve them.

2. In a small saucepan, dilute the mustard and cornstarch in 1 tablespoon of cold water. Add the vinegar, sugar, and turmeric. Bring the mixture to a boil over medium heat and simmer it gently for 10 minutes.

3. Pour the mixture over the eggs. Cool the eggs and pickling solution to room temperature, and refrigerate overnight.

V A R I A T I O N

Replace 8 fluid ounces (240 milliliters) of the vinegar with beet juice.

The eggs may be separated and the filling mixed in advance, but if they are not to be served immediately, the whites and the yolks should be held separately until as close as possible to service. Garnishes may include chopped parsley, snipped chives, sliced scallion tops, dill sprigs, pimiento strips, chopped olives, caviar, or shredded carrots. Spices may include toasted cumin seeds (ground after toasting), oregano, paprika, cayenne, or crushed red pepper flakes.

Substitute softened butter or compound butter, sour cream, puréed cottage cheese, softened cream cheese, yogurt, or crème fraîche.

Deviled Eggs

Yield: 20 pieces

Eggs, hard-cooked, cooled	*10 each*	*10 each*
Mayonnaise	*6 fluid ounces*	*180 milliliters*
Mustard, prepared	*1 tablespoon*	*1 tablespoon*
Salt, to taste	*1/2 teaspoon*	*1/2 teaspoon*
Pepper, to taste	*1/2 teaspoon*	*1/2 teaspoon*

1. Slice the eggs in half lengthwise. Separate the yolks from the whites. Reserve the whites separately.

2. Rub the yolks through a sieve into a bowl or food processor. Add the mayonnaise, mustard, salt, and pepper. Mix or process the ingredients into a smooth paste.

3. Pipe (using a star tip) or spoon the yolk mixture into the cavities of the egg whites.

VARIATIONS

Deviled Eggs with Tomato: Add Tomato Concassé to the yolk mixture. Add a small amount of fresh or dried herbs (basil, oregano, sage, thyme) and/or 1/2 teaspoon of sautéed minced garlic or shallots to the tomatoes, if desired.

Deviled Eggs with Greens: Add 1 teaspoon per yolk of blanched, puréed spinach, watercress, sorrel, lettuce, or other greens to the yolk mixture.

Deviled Eggs with Vegetables: Add small dice of cooked, raw, and/or marinated vegetables, such as celery, carrot, red onion, peppers, fennel, mushrooms (wild or cultivated), tomato, green beans, peas, corn, and eggplant.

Deviled Eggs with Peppers: Purée roasted sweet bell peppers (red or green), pimientos, and/or hot chilies. Add 2 to 3 fluid ounces (60 to 90 milliliters) of purée (hot chilies to taste) per 6 yolks.

Deviled Eggs with Cheese: Add up to 2 ounces (60 grams) of grated hard or soft cheese. Purée the filling well in a food processor.

Deviled Eggs with Fish or Shellfish: Add approximately 4 ounces (115 grams) of finely diced fish or shellfish (also any vegetables desired; see above) to the yolk mixture. Or, make a paste of fish by puréeing it with butter, mayonnaise, or heavy cream. Use smoked fish (especially small pieces or trimmings), shrimp, fresh-cooked or canned tuna, salmon, crab, or lobster.

Mozzarella Roulade

Yield: 2 1/2 pounds (1 kilogram)

Salt	7 ounces	200 grams
Water	1 gallon	3.75 liters
Mozzarella cheese curd, cut in cubes	2 pounds	900 grams
Basil leaves, very fresh	40 each	40 each
Prosciutto, sliced paper thin	1/2 pound	225 grams

Cut the mozzarella curd into 1-inch (2.5-centimeter) cubes.

1. Add the salt to the water and bring to 180°F (80°C). Divide the cubed cheese curd into two batches and cook each separately.

2. Place the cheese curd in a colander that will fit into the water so that the curd is submerged.

3. While the water is still on the heat, submerge the colander with the cheese curd into the water.

4. With a wooden spoon, work the curd until it becomes a mass and takes on a stringiness. Maintain the water temperature at 180°F (80°C) during this process.

5. Take the cheese out of the water, still in the colander, and knead lightly with the wooden spoon until almost all of the cubes are broken up. Reserve the water for final assembly of the cheese. (The mozzarella cheese will be tough if it is overworked.)

6. Lay out a sheet of plastic wrap; place the hot mozzarella on top. Place another sheet of plastic wrap on top; roll out with a rolling pin to about 1/8 inch (.25 centimeter).

7. While the cheese is still warm, grind the black pepper on the cheese, then lay the basil leaves and prosciutto over in a even layer.

8. Roll into a roulade with plastic wrap and secure the ends tightly with string.

9. Place the roulades back in the hot water for 2 to 3 minutes to lock in the garnish. Remove from the hot water. Re-tie the ends of the roulades to insure that they are tightly rolled. Chill the roulades overnight before slicing.

Mozzarella Roulades Canapés
with Prosciutto and Basil

Yield: 30 canapés

Red, green, and yellow peppers, brunoise	3 ounces	85 grams
Olive oil	2 fluid ounces	60 milliliters
Sherry vinegar	2 fluid ounces	60 milliliters
Pepper, to taste	1/4 teaspoon	1/4 teaspoon
Prosciutto-mozzarella roulades	2 pounds	900 grams
Mascarpone cheese	4 ounces	115 grams
Wheat pullman loaf, sliced lengthwise	2 slices	2 slices
Oregano leaves, to garnish	30 small	30 small

1. Toss the peppers with the vinegar, olive oil, and black pepper. Let them marinate at least a half an hour.

2. Place the sliced Pullman loaves on a sheet pan and brown lightly under the salamander on both sides.

3. Cut circles out of the toasted bread that match the diameter of the prosciutto-mozzarella roulade.

4. Pipe a small dollop of mascarpone cheese on top of the toasted bread.

5. Slice the roulade 3/16-inch thick and place on top of the bread.

6. Drain the diced peppers. Spoon a little of the pepper mixture on one side of each roulade; pipe a small dollop of mascarpone cheese next to it. Place a small leaf of oregano in the mascarpone cheese.

Gorgonzola Custard

Yield: 10 servings

Butter	2 ounces	60 grams
Onions, minced	6 ounces	170 grams
Heavy cream	20 fluid ounces	600 milliliters
Eggs	6 each	6 each
Gorgonzola	5 ounces	140 grams
Salt, to taste	1/2 teaspoon	1/2 teaspoon
Pepper, to taste	1/2 teaspoon	1/2 teaspoon

(Recipe continued on facing page)

1. Sauté the onions in the butter until they are translucent. Cool them.

2. Combine the onions, half-and-half, eggs, and Gorgonzola cheese in a mixing bowl. Season to taste.

3. Spoon the custard into buttered 4-fluid ounce (120-milliliter) ramekins.

4. Bake the custards in a bain-marie in a preheated 350°F (175°C) oven until a knife blade inserted in their centers comes out clean. Serve the custards hot or at room temperature, either unmolded or in ramekins.

Gorgonzola is an Italian blue-veined cheese. Its texture ranges from creamy to crumbly.

Warm Iowa Blue Cheese Mousse

Yield: 30 2-ounce (60-gram) timbales

Maytag blue cheese, room temperature	*9 ounces*	*250 grams*
Cream cheese, room temperature	*6 ounces*	*170 grams*
Pepper, to taste	*1/2 teaspoon*	*1/2 teaspoon*
Eggs	*9 each*	*9 each*
Heavy cream	*1 1/2 pints*	*720 milliliters*
Chives, fresh, sliced	*2 ounces*	*60 grams*
Salt, to taste	*1/2 teaspoon*	*1/2 teaspoon*
Grapes, green, seedless	*40 each*	*40 each*

Maytag blue cheese is one of the first European-style blue cheeses made in this country. Other blue cheeses may be used or the blue cheese may be replaced with other cheeses as desired.

1. Combine two-thirds of the blue cheese (reserve the remainder for the garnish), the cream cheese, and pepper in a food processor until the mixture is very smooth.

2. Add the eggs, three-quarters of the heavy cream, and half of the chives. Pulse the processor on and off until the ingredients are just blended. Place the mixture in buttered 2-ounce (60-milliliter) timbale molds and cover the molds with buttered parchment paper.

3. Bake the mousse in a bain-marie, until a knife inserted near the center comes away clean. Maintain the water's temperature at about 180°F (82°C).

4. Reduce the remaining cream by half and season to taste with the salt and pepper. Add the remaining chives and grapes to the cream immediately before service.

5. Unmold the mousse and coat it with the sauce. Garnish with the reserved blue cheese.

Wild Mushroom Strudel with Goat Cheese and Madeira Sauce

Yield: 10 servings

The recipe for Sauce Madeira is on page 525.

To work with phyllo, allow it to thaw under refrigeration. Place the dough (unfolded) on a plastic-lined sheet pan. Cover the portion of dough you are not working on with additional plastic topped with very lightly dampened cloth.

Shallots, minced	1 1/2 ounces	40 grams
Garlic minced	1/2 ounce	15 grams
Butter	3 ounces	85 grams
Mushrooms, wild, assorted, sliced	20 ounces	570 grams
White wine	3 1/2 fluid ounces	100 milliliters
Goat cheese	4 ounces	115 grams
Parsley, chopped	1 tablespoon	1 tablespoon
Chives, chopped	1 tablespoon	1 tablespoon
Chervil, chopped	1 tablespoon	1 tablespoon
Tarragon, chopped	1 tablespoon	1 tablespoon
Phyllo dough	6 sheets	6 sheets
Sauce Madeira	14 fluid ounces	420 milliliters
Sour cream	2 fluid ounces	60 milliliters
Mushroom caps, sautéed (fluted if desired)	10 each	10 each
Watercress	1 bunch	bunch

1. Sauté shallots and garlic in a little of the butter; add mushrooms and sweat, add wine, reduce until almost dry, remove from heat and cool.

2. Add goat cheese and herbs to mushroom mixture.

3. Layer three sheets of phyllo, spreading melted butter between each sheet.

4. Add half of the goat cheese mixture to the phyllo, roll up and brush once more with butter. Score the top of the strudel and chill. Repeat steps 3 and 4 with remaining phyllo and filling.

5. Bake strudels at 400°F (200°C) until golden brown. Slice and serve with heated sauce and sour cream; garnish with mushroom caps and watercress.

Fennel and Chorizo Strudel

Yield: 10 servings

Butter, melted	5 ounces	140 grams
Shallots, minced	2 each	2 each
Chorizo, sliced thin	10 ounces	280 grams
Fennel, diced	8 ounces	225 grams
Tarragon, minced	2 tablespoons	2 tablespoons
Egg, beaten	1 each	1 each
Bread crumbs, dry	3 ounces	85 grams
Salt, to taste	1/2 teaspoon	1/2 teaspoon
Pepper, to taste	1/2 teaspoon	1/2 teaspoon
Butter, melted	as needed	as needed
Phyllo dough	6 sheets	6 sheets

Some sauces that would be good with this strudel include Mushroom Sauce (page 527) or Fresh Tomato Sauce (page 537).

1. Heat a small amount of the butter in a sauteuse. Add the shallots and sauté them until they are translucent.

2. Add the chorizo and allow some of the fat to render. Add the fennel and cook until it is tender. Process to a coarse paste in a food processor.

3. Add the tarragon leaves, egg, and enough bread crumbs to lightly bind the mixture. Adjust the seasoning to taste.

4. Brush each sheet of phyllo with butter, sprinkle with bread crumbs, and top with another sheet. Repeat the process; when three sheets are stacked, place half of the chorizo-fennel mixture in the center of the dough and roll up the sheets. Brush the top with butter. Repeat with the remaining dough and filling. Score the top on the diagonal to divide the strudels into 10 sections. Chill well.

5. Bake the strudels at 400°F (205°C) until they are browned. Slice and serve two slices per portion.

VARIATION

For an Alsatian-style strudel, substitute garlic sausage for the chorizo and replace the fennel with an equal amount (or more) of chopped cabbage.

Broccoli and Cheddar Fritters

Yield: 10 servings

This recipe also works well with cauliflower.

Flour, sifted	*12 ounces*	*340 grams*
Eggs	*4 each*	*4 each*
Milk	*12 fluid ounces*	*360 milliliters*
Baking powder	*1 1/2 tablespoons*	*1 1/2 tablespoons*
Salt	*1 teaspoon*	*1 teaspoon*
Worcestershire sauce, to taste	*1/2 teaspoon*	*1/2 teaspoon*
Tabasco sauce, to taste	*2 to 3 dashes*	*2 to 3 dashes*
Broccoli, florets, cooked	*1 pound*	*450 grams*
Sharp cheddar	*8 ounces*	*225 grams*

1. Combine the flour, eggs, milk, baking powder, salt, Worcestershire sauce, and Tabasco. Mix into a smooth batter.

2. Fold in the broccoli and cheese. Drop the mixture by spoonfuls into 350°F (175°C) oil. Deep-fry the fritters until they are uniformly brown; turn them, if necessary, during frying.

3. Remove the fritters with a spider and drain briefly on absorbent toweling. Serve immediately.

Rissoles

Yield: 10 servings

The recipe for Pie Crust is found on page 1080. Curry Powder is on page 426.

Egg wash is prepared by beating together 8 eggs with enough cold milk to thin the eggs. About 3 to 4 fluid ounces (90 to 120 milliliters) of milk should be enough.

Onions, minced	*3 ounces*	*85 grams*
Garlic clove, minced	*1 each*	*1 each*
Butter	*1/2 ounce*	*15 grams*
Shrimp, small dice	*8 ounces*	*225 grams*
Salt, to taste	*1/2 teaspoon*	*1/2 teaspoon*
Curry Powder	*1 1/2 teaspoons*	*1 1/2 teaspoons*
Tomato paste	*1 teaspoon*	*1 teaspoon*
Bay leaf	*1 each*	*1 each*
Fish Stock	*3 fluid ounces*	*90 milliliters*
Apples, diced	*1 each*	*1 each*
Pie Crust	*1 1/2 pounds*	*680 grams*
Egg wash	*12 fluid ounces*	*340 milliliters*
Bread crumbs	*as needed*	*as needed*

1. Sauté onions and garlic in butter until golden brown.

2. Add shrimp, salt, curry powder, tomato paste, and bay leaf; sauté briefly.

3. Add stock and apples, cook until slightly thickened, about 3 to 4 minutes. Remove this filling mixture and chill.

(Recipe continued on facing page)

4. Roll out pie crust 1/8-inch (.25-centimeter) thick.

5. Cut into rounds 4 inches (10 centimeters) in diameter.

6. Place stuffing on rounds, fold in half, seal edges with egg wash.

7. Dip stuffed dough in egg wash and roll in bread crumbs.

8. Deep-fry at 375°F (190°C) until golden brown, drain on paper towels; serve at once.

Samosa

Yield: 10 servings

Dough

Flour	*12 ounces*	*340 grams*
Vegetable oil	*1 1/2 fluid ounces*	*45 milliliters*
Salt, to taste	*1/2 teaspoon*	*1/2 teaspoon*
Water, warm	*6 fluid ounces*	*180 milliliters*

Filling mixture

Butter	*1 1/2 ounces*	*40 grams*
Onions, small dice	*8 ounces*	*225 grams*
Gingerroot, minced	*1 tablespoon*	*1 tablespoon*
Garlic, cloves, minced	*2 each*	*2 each*
Serrano chili peppers, minced	*1 each*	*1 each*
Coriander, whole, crushed	*3/4 teaspoon*	*3/4 teaspoon*
Curry powder, to taste	*2 teaspoons*	*2 teaspoons*
Tomato paste	*1 tablespoon*	*1 tablespoon*
Lemon juice	*1 tablespoon*	*1 tablespoon*
Shrimp, chopped fine	*1 pound*	*450 grams*
Fish Stock	*8 fluid ounces*	*240 milliliters*

1. Mix all ingredients for the dough until smooth. Let dough rest for 1 hour in the refrigerator.

2. Roll dough out in pasta machine until very thin; cut into 2-inch by 8-inch (5-centimeter by 20-centimeter) strips.

3. Sauté onion in butter until translucent.

4. Add gingerroot, garlic, pepper, and spices; sauté, until aroma is strong.

5. Add tomato paste, lemon juice, and shrimp; sauté 2 minutes without browning.

6. Add stock, simmer until almost all liquid has evaporated. Remove filling from the pan, let chill completely.

7. Place a small amount of filling on the end of the dough and fold up as you would a flag. Seal the end with egg wash.

8. Deep-fry until golden brown at 375°F (190°C). Drain on absorbent paper and serve while still very hot.

HORS D'OEUVRES AND APPETIZERS

957

Corn Crêpes with Asparagus Tips and Smoked Salmon

Yield: 10 servings

Slice the salmon thinly and drape it over the asparagus.

Use very slender asparagus for the most attractive presentation. When asparagus is not in season, substitute haricots verts.

This makes a good brunch offering.

The recipe for Hollandaise Sauce is on page 540.

You may choose to smoke or roast the corn and roast the peppers for additional flavor.

Corn crêpes		
Corn kernels	8 ounces	225 grams
Flour	4 ounces	115 grams
Eggs	4 each	4 each
Milk	8 fluid ounces	240 milliliters
Vegetable oil	2 teaspoons	2 teaspoons
Salt, to taste	1/2 teaspoon	1/2 teaspoon
Pepper, to taste	1/2 teaspoon	1/2 teaspoon
Corn salad		
Corn kernels, fresh	12 ounces	340 grams
Red peppers, diced	2 ounces	60 grams
Green peppers, diced	2 ounces	60 grams
Vinaigrette	6 fluid ounces	180 milliliters
Cilantro, chopped	2 teaspoons	2 teaspoons
Parsley, chopped	2 teaspoons	2 teaspoons
Smoked salmon slices	10 ounces	285 grams
Asparagus, spears, cooked	20 each	20 each
Hollandaise Sauce, finished with chives	1 pint	480 milliliters

1. Mix all ingredients for the crêpes together to form a batter, adjust consistency with more liquid or flour if necessary.

2. Cook crêpes in a heated and oiled crepe pan. Turn and cook on second side, then remove to a plate. Stack crepes with parchment paper between each one to keep separate.

3. Combine all ingredients for the corn salad and let flavors marry for 1 hour.

4. Fill the crêpe with the salad. Place, seam side down, in a baking dish.

5. Warm the crêpes in the oven for 1 to 2 minutes.

6. Arrange the crêpes, salmon, and asparagus on the plate. Garnish crêpe with Hollandaise Sauce.

Spinach Crêpe with Seafood

Yield: 30 servings

Spinach crêpes

Spinach leaves, puréed	*10 ounces*	*285 grams*
Milk	*1 quart*	*1 liter*
Eggs, beaten	*10 each*	*10 each*
Flour	*10 ounces*	*285 grams*
Salt, to taste	*1 teaspoon*	*1 teaspoon*
Vegetable oil	*2 fluid ounces*	*60 milliliters*

Seafood filling

Butter	*4 ounces*	*115 grams*
Shallots, minced	*1 tablespoon*	*1 tablespoon*
Mushrooms, minced	*5 ounces*	*140 grams*
Shrimp (31/35), diced	*1 pound*	*450 grams*
Lump crabmeat, picked	*10 ounces*	*285 grams*
Bay scallops, diced	*10 ounces*	*285 grams*
Béchamel or Velouté	*1 pint*	*480 milliliters*
Red peppers, peeled, brunoise	*5 ounces*	*140 grams*
Salt, to taste	*1/2 teaspoon*	*1/2 teaspoon*
Pepper, to taste	*1/2 teaspoon*	*1/2 teaspoon*
Old Bay Seasoning	*1/4 teaspoon*	*1/4 teaspoon*
Sauce Mousseline	*20 fluid ounces*	*600 milliliters*

This recipe will produce approximately 30 individual crêpes. Serve 2 or 3 per portion as a brunch or lunch entrée.

The recipe for Béchamel is on page 535; Velouté is on page 531; Sauce Mousseline is on page 543.

1. Mix the spinach purée, milk, and eggs together; add to flour; mix well until smooth. Add more flour if necessary, but batter should be thin.

2. Cook crêpes in a heated oiled 8-inch crepe pan. Add about 2 fluid ounces (60 milliliters) of batter and swirl pan so batter covers entire bottom.

3. When crêpe browns, turn and cook other side, briefly.

4. Stack finished crêpes on a plate, separated with paper. If crêpe is uneven, it can be trimmed.

5. To prepare the filling, sauté the shallots and mushrooms in butter.

6. Add seafood, sauté until cooked.

7. Add béchamel and red pepper, bring to a simmer (reduce if necessary).

8. Season and chill.

9. Stuff and roll crêpes, place on a tray, heat in the oven until filling is hot.

10. Coat crêpes with sauce mousseline and brown lightly under a salamander or broiler.

Sushi

Yield: 160 pieces

Short-grain rice	*2 pounds*	*900 grams*
Dried seaweed	*20 sheets*	*20 sheets*
Rice vinegar	*8 fluid ounces*	*240 milliliters*
Sugar	*3 ounces*	*85 grams*
Salt	*1 teaspoon*	*1 teaspoon*
Pickled ginger, as needed	*1 pound*	*450 grams*
Dipping sauce, as needed	*1 quart*	*1 liter*

There are a number of different fillings you may use: avocado, King crab legs, pickled Daikon, red salmon, Kamaboko, cucumber, Shiitake, carrots, scallions.

Sushi has become associated with another Japanese specialty, sashimi. Slices of very fresh fish, such as yellowfin or red tuna, squid, or mako shark are often served with sushi.

Use the same dipping sauce as for the tempura on page 975.

Or simply serve the sushi with soy sauce and wasabi, allowing the guests to season the soy sauce to their own taste.

1. Wash rice until water is clear; cover rice with water (water should be one inch over rice), cook 30 minutes until tender.
2. Cool rice; add vinegar, sugar, and salt.
3. Place a bamboo sushi mat on work surface and, lay one sheet of seaweed on top of the mat. Cover the seaweed with a layer of rice.
4. Add any fillings you wish (see list on the left).
5. Roll the rice up carefully; use vinegar to seal the seam.
6. Cut each roll into 8 pieces.
7. Serve the sushi with several slices of pickled ginger and dipping sauce.

VARIATION

California Roll: Fill the rice with cooked crabmeat and avocado. Typically rolled into a cone shape.

Shrimp Spring Roll

Yield: 80 pieces

Filling

Oil	*4 ounces*	*120 milliliters*
Gingerroot, minced	*2 tablespoons*	*2 tablespoons*
Scallions, chopped	*14 ounces*	*400 grams*
Shrimp, peeled, deveined, and chopped	*3 pounds*	*1.3 kilograms*
Bamboo shoots, shredded	*10 ounces*	*285 grams*
Black fungus, soaked, roughly cut	*1 1/2 ounces*	*40 grams*
Chinese cabbage, shredded	*3 pounds*	*1.3 kilograms*
Bean sprouts	*2 pounds*	*900 grams*
Mushrooms, thinly sliced	*1 pound*	*450 grams*
Black soy sauce	*4 fluid ounces*	*120 milliliters*
Sesame oil	*2 ounces*	*60 milliliters*
Salt	*1 tablespoon*	*1 tablespoon*
White pepper	*2 teaspoons*	*2 teaspoons*
Cornstarch	*3 ounces*	*85 grams*
Water	*4 fluid ounces*	*120 milliliters*
Spring roll sheets	*80 pieces*	*80 pieces*
Flour	*5 ounces*	*140 grams*

Use 4 pounds (1.8 kilograms) of ground or shredded pork instead of the shrimp, if you prefer.

To make a flour paste to seal the spring rolls, mix flour with enough cold water to reach the consistency of a thin pancake.

Serve with prepared duck sauce or other dipping sauces.

1. To make the filling: heat the oil in a wok. Stir-fry gingerroot and scallions in oil for a few minutes.

2. Add shrimp, bamboo shoots, and black fungus. Stir-fry until shrimp is tender.

3. Add cabbage, bean sprouts, mushrooms, and scallion greens; stir-fry until all vegetables are cooked.

4. Add soy sauce, sesame oil, and seasonings; mix together.

5. Drain away the excess liquid; mix in cornstarch that has been dissolved in water, return this mixture to vegetables; cook until cornstarch has thickened.

6. Remove the filling mixture from the heat, cool thoroughly.

7. Place 1 full tablespoon (15 grams) of filling on each spring roll sheet, brush edges of sheet with flour-water paste, roll, and seal.

8. Deep-fry in 350°F (175°C) hot fat until golden brown, drain on absorbent paper.

VARIATION

Vegetables and seasonings: There can be many variations to the vegetables and seasonings used in spring rolls.

Vietnamese Fried Spring Rolls

Yield: 80 pieces

Nuoc mam *is a Vietnamese fish sauce. If not available, any fish sauce may be substituted.*

Filling

Mushrooms, Chinese, rehydrated	6 each	6 each
Mushrooms, Tree ear, rehydrated	1 tablespoon	1 tablespoon
Water chestnuts, peeled and chopped	4 ounces	115 grams
Crab meat	4 ounces	115 grams
Shrimp, minced	8 ounces	225 grams
Pork butt, ground	1 1/2 pounds	680 grams
Onion, minced	6 ounces	170 grams
Shallots, minced	2 ounces	60 grams
Garlic cloves, minced	1 ounce	30 grams
Nuoc mam	2 tablespoons	2 tablespoons
Dry sherry	2 tablespoons	2 tablespoons
Pepper	1 teaspoon	1 teaspoon
Eggs	3 each	3 each

Wrappers

Sugar	4 ounces	115 grams
Water, warm	1 quart	1 liter
Rice paper, 6 1/2-inch diameter rounds	80 each	80 each
Peanut oil, for frying	as needed	as needed

Dipping sauce

Carrots, small, shredded	1 each	1 each
Daikon, small, shredded	4 ounces	115 grams
Sugar	7 ounces	200 grams
Garlic, minced	2 ounces	60 grams
Red chili peppers, fresh, seeded, minced	8 each	8 each
Lime or lemon juice	8 fluid ounces	240 milliliters
Rice vinegar	16 fluid ounces	480 milliliters
Nuoc mam	16 fluid ounces	480 milliliters
Water	16 fluid ounces	480 milliliters

1. Combine all of the ingredients for the filling; mix together.

2. Combine the sugar and water, place rice paper in water briefly, to soften.

3. Remove rice paper and blot to remove excess water. Place a small amount of filling on each paper, fold and roll.

4. Deep-fry in 350°F (175°C) peanut oil until golden brown. Serve them with the dipping sauce.

(Recipe continued on facing page)

5. For the dipping sauce: Mix the carrot and daikon with one-quarter of the sugar, let stand 15 minutes.

6. Combine garlic, chili pepper, and remaining three-quarters of the sugar; purée in a food processor until smooth.

7. Add lime juice, vinegar, fish sauce, and water; purée until sugar is dissolved; add carrot-and-daikon mixture.

Gyoza

Yield: 80 pieces

Gyoza skin

Flour	*2 pounds*	*900 grams*
Hot water	*20 fluid ounces*	*600 milliliters*

Filling

Ground pork	*2 pounds*	*900 grams*
Shrimp, chopped	*1 pound*	*450 grams*
Cabbage, chopped	*1 pound*	*450 grams*
Gingerroot, minced	*1 tablespoon*	*1 tablespoon*
Scallions	*3 ounces*	*85 grams*
Soy sauce	*2 fluid ounces*	*60 milliliters*
Salt, to taste	*2 teaspoons*	*2 teaspoons*
Pepper, to taste	*1 teaspoon*	*1 teaspoon*
Sesame oil, dark	*2 fluid ounces*	*60 milliliters*
Eggs, beaten	*2 each*	*2 each*
Dry sherry	*1 fluid ounce*	*30 milliliters*

This is a dumpling that can be steamed or made with wonton skins and deep-fried until golden brown.

1. Combine flour and water; mix until a smooth dough is formed, allow to rest for 30 minutes.

2. Cut dough into 1/2-ounce (15-gram) pieces; roll into a 5-inch (13 centimeter) circle.

3. Combine all ingredients for the filling; mix together and adjust seasonings.

4. Place 1 teaspoon of filling on each piece of dough, fold and seal.

5. Place gyoza in the steamer; steam over boiling water for 10 minutes.

Thai Fish Cakes

Yield: 80 pieces

Fish, any lean white variety	4 pounds	1.8 kilograms
Red Curry Paste	2 ounces	60 grams
Fish sauce (nuoc mam)	4 fluid ounces	120 milliliters
Cornstarch	2 ounces	60 grams
Sugar	1 ounce	30 grams
Eggs	4 each	4 each
Lemon zest	4 teaspoons	4 teaspoons
Green beans, sliced	12 ounces	340 grams
Onion, fine chopped	6 ounces	140 grams
Peanut oil	as needed	as needed
Cucumber Relish	1 recipe	1 recipe

1. Purée fish in a food processor until pastelike in consistency.

2. Add remaining ingredients to fish; mix well; refrigerate 30 minutes or until firm.

3. Portion and shape into 1 1/2-ounce (40-gram) patties

4. Fry in oil, browning each side.

5. Serve with cucumber relish (below).

Serve 2 cakes per portion with the Cucumber Relish, as an appetizer.

Make the cakes very small for service on a cocktail reception buffet.

Red Curry Paste is on page 429.

Cucumber Relish

Yield: 3 quarts (3 liters)

Cucumber, peeled and seeded, fine dice	3 each	3 each
Sugar	4 ounces	115 grams
White vinegar	12 fluid ounces	360 milliliters
Salt, to taste	1 tablespoon	1 tablespoon
Red chili pepper flakes, crushed	2 ounces	60 grams
Shallots, fine dice	2 ounces	60 grams
Water, boiling	24 fluid ounces	720 milliliters
Cilantro, chopped	2 ounces	60 grams

1. Combine all ingredients and mix together; marinate until sugar and salt are dissolved.

2. Chill until ready to serve.

Diced red onion may be included in the relish.

Oriental Pearl Balls

Yield: 80 portions (1 1/4 ounces/40 grams each)

Sweet rice	*1 1/2 pounds*	*680 grams*
Ground pork	*3 pounds*	*1.3 kilograms*
Soy sauce	*1 fluid ounce*	*30 milliliters*
Sesame oil, dark	*1 tablespoon*	*1 tablespoon*
Eggs	*3 each*	*3 each*
Water chestnuts, chopped	*6 ounces*	*170 grams*
Dry shrimp, chopped	*1 ounce*	*30 grams*
Scallion, chopped	*2 each*	*2 each*
Ginger, chopped	*1 tablespoon*	*1 tablespoon*
Cornstarch	*1 ounce*	*30 grams*
Salt, to taste	*1 teaspoon*	*1 teaspoon*
White pepper, to taste	*1 teaspoon*	*1 teaspoon*
Chicken Stock	*4 fluid ounces*	*120 milliliters*
Sugar	*1 tablespoon*	*1 tablespoon*
Sherry, dry	*1 fluid ounce*	*30 milliliters*

1. Soak sweet rice in cold water for 60 minutes, drain and spread on a sheet pan.

2. Combine all remaining ingredients, mix together, form into 1-inch (2.25-centimeter) meatballs.

3. Roll meatballs in sweet rice, completely coating all of the outside.

4. Set pearl balls in steamer, steam over high heat for 15 minutes. The filling should reach an internal temperature of 160°F (70°C) and the rice will become translucent and be fully cooked.

Raw Tuna Marinated in Sake
with Shiitake Salad

Yield: 10 servings

Tuna fillet	*20 ounces*	*570 grams*
Sake	*2 tablespoons*	*2 tablespoons*
Shiitake salad		
Shiitake mushrooms, stemmed, julienne	*7 ounces*	*200 grams*
Carrots, julienne	*3 1/2 ounces*	*100 grams*
Red onions, julienne	*3 1/2 ounces*	*100 grams*
Scallions, sliced thin on the bias	*2 ounces*	*60 grams*
Bok choy, chiffonade	*1 3/4 ounces*	*50 grams*
Rice wine vinegar	*4 fluid ounces*	*120 milliliters*
Soy sauce	*1 fluid ounce*	*30 milliliters*
Gingerroot, grated	*1 teaspoon*	*1 teaspoon*
Sesame oil, dark	*1 teaspoon*	*1 teaspoon*
Wasabi sauce		
Sour cream	*5 fluid ounces*	*150 milliliters*
Wasabi powder	*2 teaspoons*	*2 teaspoons*
Soy sauce	*2 teaspoons*	*2 teaspoons*

1. Slice tuna 1/4-inch (.5-centimeter) thick into 1 3/4-ounce (50-gram) pieces. Flatten between two pieces of parchment or plastic wrap until very thin. Marinate in sake.

2. Toss ingredients for shiitake salad together and let marinate for several minutes at room temperature or up to hours under refrigeration.

3. Blend ingredients for sauce. Keep chilled until required.

4. Arrange tuna on plate; place mushroom salad in center of plate. Top with sauce.

Carpaccio of Salmon

Yield: 10 servings

Salmon fillet, raw	*1 1/2 pounds*	*680 grams*
Mushrooms, sliced thin	*20 each*	*20 each*
Pepper, cracked, to taste	*1/2 teaspoon*	*1/2 teaspoon*
Extra-virgin olive oil	*4 fluid ounces*	*120 milliliters*
Green mayonnaise		
Spinach leaves, blanched	*2 1/2 ounces*	*70 grams*
Parsley, chopped	*2 teaspoons*	*2 teaspoons*
Tarragon, chopped	*2 teaspoons*	*2 teaspoons*
Chives, chopped	*2 teaspoons*	*2 teaspoons*
Dill, chopped	*2 teaspoons*	*2 teaspoons*
Basic Mayonnaise	*1 1/4 pints*	*600 milliliters*
Lemon juice	*2 tablespoons*	*2 tablespoons*
Salt, to taste	*1/2 teaspoon*	*1/2 teaspoon*

To prepare the spinach for the green mayonnaise, plunge the cleaned leaves into boiling salted water. Remove them as soon as they are wilted (30 to 60 seconds) and rinse with cold water. Squeeze in cheesecloth to dry, then chop very fine.

The recipe for Basic Mayonnaise may be found on page 911.

1. Slice salmon in very thin pieces, arrange on a plate and cover with plastic wrap.

2. Using a spoon, spread out the salmon to the edge of the plate. Chill well.

3. Purée spinach leaves and herbs in blender.

4. Mix purée with mayonnaise, lemon juice, and salt.

5. Adjust consistency with water if sauce is too thick.

6. Garnish with mushrooms and sprinkle with pepper and oil.

7. Serve green mayonnaise on the side in a sauce boat.

Gravad Lox

Yield: 2 fillets

Use aquavit or vodka to replace the brandy, if desired.

Serve with bagels and cream cheese as a brunch or breakfast offering.

Kosher salt	7 ounces	200 grams
Dark brown sugar	1 pound	450 grams
White peppercorns, cracked	3/4 ounce	20 grams
Dill, freshly chopped	2 bunches	2 bunches
Lemons, juiced	2 each	2 each
Olive oil	1 fluid ounce	30 milliliters
Brandy	3/4 fluid ounce	25 milliliters
Salmon fillets, cleaned	2 each	2 each

1. Combine the salt, sugar, peppercorns, and dill to make the dry cure.

2. Combine the lemon juice, olive oil, and brandy. Brush this mixture on the salmon fillets.

3. Pack the cure evenly on the salmon fillets and wrap them tightly.

4. Place the wrapped fillets in a pan and weight them. Marinate the salmon under refrigeration for 2 to 3 days.

5. Unwrap the salmon and scrape off the cure.

6. Slice the salmon thinly on the bias to serve it.

Smoked Salmon Set-Up

Yield: 15 to 20 servings (buffet service)

Additional garnish items to add to this platter include: sliced and toasted French bread, cornichons, pickled onions, cured olives, and pepperoncini.

For individual plated appetizers, you may wish to drizzle some of the Roasted Garlic and Mustard Vinaigrette (page 908).

Smoked salmon fillet	1 each	1 each
Eggs, hard-boiled, whites and yolks separated and chopped fine	3 each	3 each
Capers, rinsed and drained	3 tablespoons	3 tablespoons
Red onion, minced, rinsed	4 ounces	115 grams

1. Slice salmon on a bias very thin, starting from the tail.

2. Arrange the salmon on a platter and garnish with separate piles of the chopped egg whites and yolks, capers, and onions.

Smoked Salmon Mousse Barquettes

Yield: 10 servings

Fish Velouté	*6 ounces*	*170 grams*
Smoked salmon, diced	*5 ounces*	*140 grams*
Aspic, softened	*1 ounce*	*30 grams*
Pepper, to taste	*1/2 teaspoon*	*1/2 teaspoon*
Heavy cream, whipped	*4 fluid ounces*	*120 milliliters*
Barquettes, prebaked, made from Pâte Brissée	*10 each*	*10 each*

1. Combine the velouté and smoked salmon in a food processor. Process the ingredients to a smooth consistency.

2. Add the aspic while the processor is running, incorporating it into the salmon mixture. Adjust the seasoning to taste.

3. Remove the salmon mixture from the processor and fold in the whipped cream. Pipe the mixture into the barquettes and chill to a firm mousse.

Make the Velouté following the recipe on page 531, using Fish Stock. Use enough roux for a fairly thick consistency.

Pâté Brissée is on page 1080. Roll and cut it to fit barquette molds, or other shapes, as desired.

Salmon with a Yogurt Gratin

Yield: 10 servings

Salmon fillets	*10 each*	*10 each*
Salt, to taste	*1/2 teaspoon*	*1/2 teaspoon*
Black pepper, ground, to taste	*1/2 teaspoon*	*1/2 teaspoon*
Dill, fresh, chopped	*4 tablespoons*	*4 tablespoons*
Fish Stock, hot	*6 fluid ounces*	*180 milliliters*
Yogurt, plain	*12 fluid ounces*	*360 milliliters*
Egg yolks, lightly beaten	*2 each*	*2 each*
Heavy cream, whipped	*6 fluid ounces*	*180 milliliters*

1. Cut the salmon into 3-ounce (85-gram) portions and pound thin. Season with the salt, pepper, and dill.

2. Combine the hot stock with the yogurt to temper the yogurt.

3. Fold the egg yolks into the whipped heavy cream. Fold the yogurt mixture into the cream mixture to make a glaçage.

4. At service, place the salmon on an ovenproof plate and coat it with the glaçage. Bake in 450°F (230°C) oven until the salmon is barely cooked through, 3 to 4 minutes. Glaze it under a salamander or broiler, if desired.

Poached Scallops Mornay

Yield: 10 servings

Instructions for Fish Stock may be found on page 443. The Mornay Sauce recipe is on page 535.

Sea scallops	*10 each*	*10 each*
Salt, to taste	*1/2 teaspoon*	*1/2 teaspoon*
Pepper, to taste	*1/4 teaspoon*	*1/4 teaspoon*
Butter, softened	*1 ounce*	*30 grams*
Shallots, minced	*2 teaspoons*	*2 teaspoons*
Fish Stock or water	*1 pint*	*480 milliliters*
Dry white wine	*10 fluid ounces*	*300 milliliters*
Mornay Sauce	*1 1/2 pints*	*720 milliliters*
Parmesan cheese, grated	*6 ounces*	*170 grams*

1. Remove the muscle tabs from the scallops. Season with salt and pepper.

2. Butter a shallow pan and sprinkle it with shallots. Place scallops in the pan and add the stock and wine.

3. Bring the liquid to a simmer over direct heat and cover with parchment paper. Poach the scallops in a 350°F (175°C) oven until done.

4. Remove the scallops; cover with paper to keep them warm.

5. Strain poaching liquid into a sauce pot; reduce to one-quarter of its original volume; add Mornay Sauce, reduce until sauce is the correct consistency. Place the scallops in a gratin.

6. Coat scallops with sauce; sprinkle with Parmesan. Broil or brown under a salamander. Serve at once.

Cold Poached Scallops with Tarragon Vinaigrette

Yield: 10 servings

Bay scallops	*20 ounces*	*570 grams*
Dry white wine	*1 pint*	*480 milliliters*
Fish Stock	*1 pint*	*480 milliliters*
Shallots, minced	*1 1/2 ounces*	*45 grams*
Tarragon vinaigrette		
Arrowroot, as needed	*1 to 2 teaspoons*	*1 to 2 teaspoons*
Tarragon vinegar	*4 fluid ounces*	*120 milliliters*
Extra virgin olive oil	*4 fluid ounces*	*120 milliliters*
Tarragon, chopped	*2 teaspoons*	*2 teaspoons*
Salt, to taste	*1/2 teaspoon*	*1/2 teaspoon*
Peppercorns, cracked	*1/4 teaspoon*	*1/4 teaspoon*
Asparagus, blanched	*20 pieces*	*20 pieces*
Tomato Concassé	*5 ounces*	*140 grams*

(Recipe continued on facing page)

1. Shallow-poach the scallops in wine, stock, and shallots. Keep them warm while finishing the vinaigrette.

2. Reduce the cooking liquid by half; reserve 4 fluid ounces (120 milliliters) for vinaigrette.

3. Bring reserved cooking liquid to a simmer. Dilute the arrowroot in cold water and add as needed to thicken very lightly.

4. Add vinegar, oil, tarragon, and pepper to the vinaigrette.

5. Add the asparagus and tomatoes to the vinaigrette to reheat them.

6. Serve scallops with the warm vinaigrette, asparagus, and tomatoes.

Scallop Mousseline Timbales

Yield: 10 servings

Bay scallops, fresh, cleaned	*1 pound*	*450 grams*
Butter, diced, chilled	*3 ounces*	*85 grams*
Egg whites	*3 each*	*3 each*
Salt, to taste	*1/2 teaspoon*	*1/2 teaspoon*
Black pepper, ground, to taste	*1/2 teaspoon*	*1/2 teaspoon*
Nutmeg, ground	*a few grains*	*a few grains*
Heavy cream, cold	*12 fluid ounces*	*360 milliliters*
Fresh herbs, as available		
or desired	*1 ounce*	*30 grams*

To read more about preparing mousselines, refer to Chapter 11, page 361.

Garnish the mousseline with diced shellfish: shrimp, scallops, lobster, or prawns. A good ratio is 4 ounces (115 grams) of garnish in this recipe.

1. Purée the scallops, butter, egg whites, salt, pepper, and nutmeg in a food processor just until a smooth paste forms.

2. Remove the paste from the bowl to a chilled bowl. Place it over an ice bath.

3. Incorporate the heavy cream and herbs, taking care not to overmix.

4. Place the mixture in buttered timbales; cover with buttered parchment. Bake the timbales in a water bath until an internal temperature of 130 to 135°F (55 to 57°C) is reached. Remove them from the water bath.

Scallop Timbale Sampler
with Saffron-Cream Sauce

Yield: 10 servings

The Scallop Mousseline recipe may be found on page 971; Fines Herbes is on page 427; Fish Fumet is on page 443.

Garnish with asparagus tips and morels, if desired.

Saffron cream

Fish fumet	*8 fluid ounces*	*240 milliliters*
White wine	*8 fluid ounces*	*240 milliliters*
Shallots	*1/2 ounce*	*15 grams*
Heavy cream, reduced	*8 fluid ounces*	*240 milliliters*
Saffron, crushed	*1 teaspoon*	*1 teaspoon*
Scallop Mousseline	*1 recipe*	*1 recipe*
Fines Herbes, chopped	*1 tablespoon*	*1 tablespoon*
Tomato, flesh only, fine dice	*2 ounces*	*60 grams*
Shrimp, cooked, fine dice	*2 ounces*	*60 grams*

1. To make the saffron cream: Combine the fumet, wine, and shallots; reduce the mixture by half. Bring the heavy cream and saffron to a simmer; reduce by half. Combine both reductions; simmer until thick enough to coat a spoon. Let the mixture cool.

2. Divide the basic mousseline mixture into three equal parts. Add the fines herbes to one portion; add the tomato and shrimp to the second; add 2 tablespoons (30 milliliters) of saffron cream to the third.

3. Layer each flavor of scallop mousseline in ten small timbales.

4. Cover the timbales with buttered parchment and bake them in a water bath until a skewer inserted near the center of a serving comes out clean.

5. To serve, heat the remaining saffron cream and pool it on heated plates. Unmold one of each type of mousseline onto each plate.

Broiled Shrimp with Garlic
and Aromatics

Yield: 10 servings

Bread crumbs, dry	*8 ounces*	*225 grams*
Garlic cloves, minced	*10 each*	*10 each*
Parsley, chopped	*1 teaspoon*	*1 teaspoon*
Oregano, chopped	*1 teaspoon*	*1 teaspoon*
Butter, melted	*12 ounces*	*340 grams*
Salt, to taste	*1/2 teaspoon*	*1/2 teaspoon*
Pepper, to taste	*1/4 teaspoon*	*1/4 teaspoon*
Shrimp, 31/35 count, frozen, tail intact and butterflied	*30 each*	*30 each*

(Recipe continued on facing page)

1. Combine the bread crumbs, garlic, parsley, oregano, and three-quarters of the butter. Adjust the seasoning to taste with the salt and pepper.

2. Arrange the shrimp on gratin dishes (3 per portion) and brush with the remaining butter.

3. Place 1 to 2 teaspoons each of the bread crumb mixture on the shrimp and broil under a salamander until very hot and cooked through. Serve at once.

Cajun-Style Barbecued Shrimp

Yield: 10 servings

Shrimp, peeled and deveined	*40 each*	*40 each*
Onions, minced	*6 ounces*	*170 grams*
Garlic cloves, mashed to a paste	*3 each*	*3 each*
Butter	*1 1/2 ounces*	*40 grams*
Beer	*6 fluid ounces*	*180 milliliters*
Shellfish Stock	*1 1/2 pints*	*720 milliliters*
Pepper, coarse-grind	*2 teaspoons*	*2 teaspoons*
Rosemary leaves, chopped	*1 tablespoon*	*1 tablespoon*
Thyme leaves, chopped	*1 tablespoon*	*1 tablespoon*
Oregano leaves, chopped	*1 tablespoon*	*1 tablespoon*
Lemon juice, to taste	*1 tablespoon*	*1 tablespoon*
Worcestershire sauce, to taste	*1 tablespoon*	*1 tablespoon*
Butter, cut into chips	*6 ounces*	*170 grams*
Yellow peppers, small dice, blanched	*3 ounces*	*85 grams*
Green peppers, small dice, blanched	*3 ounces*	*85 grams*
Red peppers, small dice, blanched	*3 ounces*	*85 grams*
Salt, to taste	*1/2 teaspoon*	*1/2 teaspoon*
Long-grain white rice, cooked	*20 ounces*	*570 grams*

Fresh thyme adds a special flavor to this sauce.

1. Peel and devein shrimp; (make stock from shells if possible).

2. Sauté onions and garlic in butter until translucent.

3. Sprinkle onions and garlic in bottom of a shallow pan suitable for poaching.

4. Arrange shrimp in pan; add beer and stock. Scatter with pepper.

5. Bring to simmer, cover with a piece of parchment paper, poach in a 360°F (180°C) oven for 4 to 6 minutes.

6. When done remove shrimp, cover, keep warm.

7. Add rosemary, thyme, oregano, lemon juice, and Worcestershire sauce to poaching liquid, reduce until slightly syrupy, remove from heat.

8. Add butter chip by chip, swirling the pan so the butter blends in. Stir in peppers. Adjust seasoning to taste with salt and pepper.

9. Serve sauce over shrimp accompanied by a small timbale of rice.

Coconut Macadamia Shrimp with Ginger Soy Sauce

Yield: 10 portions

Shrimp (16/20)	*20 each*	*20 each*
Marinade		
Hoisin sauce	*2 fluid ounces*	*60 milliliters*
Dry sherry	*2 fluid ounces*	*60 milliliters*
Rice wine vinegar	*2 fluid ounces*	*60 milliliters*
Soy sauce	*1 fluid ounce*	*30 milliliters*
Garlic, cloves, mashed to a paste	*2 each*	*2 each*
Batter		
Flour	*6 ounces*	*170 grams*
Macadamia nuts, ground	*4 ounces*	*115 grams*
Baking soda	*2 1/2 teaspoons*	*2 1/2 teaspoons*
Coconut milk	*10 fluid ounces*	*300 milliliters*
Eggs, beaten	*3 each*	*3 each*
Flour, for dredging	*2 ounces*	*60 grams*
Coconuts, fresh, grated	*4 ounces*	*115 grams*
Sauce		
Ginger, ground	*1/2 ounce*	*15 grams*
Garlic cloves, mashed to a paste	*2 each*	*2 each*
Dry sherry	*5 fluid ounces*	*150 milliliters*
Fish or Chicken Stock	*10 fluid ounces*	*300 milliliters*
Soy sauce	*3 fluid ounces*	*90 milliliters*
Arrowroot	*1 tablespoon*	*1 tablespoon*
Scallions, sliced on the bias	*5 each*	*5 each*
Black sesame seeds	*1 ounce*	*30 grams*

1. Peel and devein shrimp, leaving tail on. Butterfly them.

2. Mix together the ingredients for the marinade. Add the shrimp, toss to coat evenly, and marinate for 1 hour; drain away excess marinade.

3. Combine all ingredients for the batter while the shrimp marinates. Keep chilled until required.

4. Dredge shrimp in flour, dip in batter up to tail. Dredge shrimp in coconut, press lightly to flatten shrimp and allow coconut to adhere.

5. Refrigerate 1 hour to allow breading to set.

6. Combine all ingredients for the sauce, except the arrowroot, and bring to a simmer. Add the diluted arrowroot, simmer until thickened, and reserve.

7. Deep-fry the shrimp 350°F (175°C) until golden brown and shrimp are cooked; drain briefly on paper towels.

8. Ladle some sauce on each plate; arrange shrimp on sauce, garnish with scallions and sesame seeds.

Fish Tempura with Dipping Sauce

Yield: 10 servings

Flounder fillets	*2 1/4 pounds*	*1 kilogram*
Salt, to taste	*1/2 teaspoon*	*1/2 teaspoon*
Pepper, to taste	*to taste*	*to taste*
Tempura batter		
Water, cold	*8 fluid ounces*	*240 milliliters*
Flour	*5 ounces*	*140 grams*
Cornstarch	*2 ounces*	*60 grams*
Sesame oil	*2 tablespoons*	*2 tablespoons*
Egg yolk, fresh	*1 each*	*1 each*
Dipping sauce		
Daikon, minced	*4 fluid ounces*	*120 milliliters*
Water, cold	*4 fluid ounces*	*120 milliliters*
Shiro mirin	*1 tablespoon*	*1 tablespoon*
Katsuo dashi	*1 tablespoon*	*1 tablespoon*
Wasabi powder	*1 teaspoon*	*1 teaspoon*

1. Trim the flounder and cut into strips (goujonettes). Season with salt and pepper.

2. Season the fish with the salt and pepper; pat dry with absorbent toweling.

3. Mix the ingredients for the tempura batter, making sure that the mixture stays very cold.

4. Mix all of the ingredients for the dipping sauce and chill the mixture until it is needed for service.

5. Heat the oil in the fryer to 350°F (175°C). Dip each fish finger into the batter and drop it carefully into the hot oil. Deep-fry the fish until golden brown and puffy. Turn if necessary for even color.

6. Remove the fish from the oil with a spider and drain them briefly on absorbent toweling. Serve them at once with the dipping sauce.

Use shrimp or chicken in this recipe, if you prefer.

Information about filleting fish and cutting it into goujonettes can be found on pages 246 and 248.

Katsuo dashi is a broth prepared by simmering dried bonita flakes in water. It is available prepared commercially.

Stuffed Shrimp

Yield: 50 pieces

Shrimp (16/20)	*50 each*	*50 each*
Butter, melted	*2 ounces*	*60 grams*
Bread crumbs, fresh	*4 ounces*	*115 grams*
Stuffing		
Butter	*3 ounces*	*85 grams*
Onions, minced	*2 ounces*	*60 grams*
Scallions, minced	*2 each*	*2 each*
Flour	*2 ounces*	*60 grams*
White wine	*5 fluid ounces*	*150 milliliters*
Crabmeat, picked	*14 ounces*	*400 grams*
Heavy cream	*6 fluid ounces*	*180 milliliters*
Salt, to taste	*1/2 teaspoon*	*1/2 teaspoon*
Pepper, to taste	*1/4 teaspoon*	*1/4 teaspoon*
Lemon juice, to taste	*2 teaspoons*	*2 teaspoons*

1. Peel the shrimp, leaving the tail on. Remove the vein and butterfly.

2. To make stuffing: Sauté onions and scallions in butter.

3. Add flour and cook 2 to 3 minutes.

4. Add wine, crabmeat, and heavy cream; bring to a boil, stirring constantly.

5. Cook 5 minutes, season to taste with salt, pepper, and lemon juice. Stuffing should be very thick or simmer longer to thicken; chill.

6. Stuff shrimps and sprinkle with buttered bread crumbs.

7. Bake in 420°F (215°C) oven until hot and browned.

Moules Marinière

Yield: 10 servings

Mussels, scrubbed and debearded	*80 each*	*80 each*
Dry white wine	*12 fluid ounces*	*360 milliliters*
Shallots, minced	*4 ounces*	*115 grams*
Bay leaf	*1 each*	*1 each*
Black peppercorns, cracked	*1/2 teaspoon*	*1/2 teaspoon*
Thyme sprig	*1 each*	*1 each*
Garlic cloves, minced	*6 each*	*6 each*
Butter, softened	*6 ounces*	*170 grams*
Parsley, chopped	*1 tablespoon*	*1 tablespoon*
Chives, chopped	*1 tablespoon*	*1 tablespoon*

Refer to pages 252 to 253 for more information about working with mussels.

1. Scrub and debeard mussels; discard any that remain open.

2. Combine the wine, shallots, bay leaf, peppercorns, thyme, and garlic. Bring to a simmer.

3. Add the mussels; cover the pot, and steam until the shells open.

4. Remove the mussels and keep warm while finishing the sauce.

5. Strain the steaming liquid, whisk in the butter, add parsley and chives and season to taste with salt and pepper.

6. Serve the sauce ladled over the mussels; serve eight mussels per order.

Mussels and Clams with Saffron and Tomatoes

Yield: 10 servings

Shallots, minced	*6 each*	*6 each*
Garlic cloves, minced	*2 each*	*2 each*
Saffron threads, crushed	*1/4 teaspoon*	*1/4 teaspoon*
Butter	*2 ounces*	*60 grams*
White wine	*8 fluid ounces*	*240 milliliters*
Fish Stock	*20 fluid ounces*	*600 milliliters*
Mussels, washed, scrubbed and debearded	*30 each*	*30 each*
Little Neck clams	*30 each*	*30 each*
Tomato Concassé	*12 ounces*	*340 grams*
Parsley, chopped	*1 tablespoon*	*1 tablespoon*
Lemon juice	*1 tablespoon*	*1 tablespoon*
White bread slices	*10 slices*	*10 slices*
Parmesan cheese, grated	*6 ounces*	*170 grams*
Butter	*3 ounces*	*85 grams*
Seafood seasoning	*1/2 teaspoon*	*1/2 teaspoon*
Scallions, sliced	*1 each*	*1 each*
Pepper, to taste	*1/2 teaspoon*	*1/2 teaspoon*

1. Sauté shallots, garlic, and saffron in butter until shallots are translucent.

2. Add wine and fish stock; bring to a simmer.

3. Add mussels, clams, and Tomato Concassé, cover; steam until the shells open.

4. When the shells open, remove the top shell from each and discard.

5. Arrange mussels and clams in a soup plate.

6. Reduce cooking liquid by one-third its original volume, add parsley, lemon juice, and seasonings.

7. Pour cooking liquid over mussels and clams.

8. Toast bread, remove crusts, cut each slice into four triangles.

9. Mix butter, Parmesan cheese, and seafood seasoning; spread mixture on bread; heat in oven until cheese melts.

10. Garnish with scallions and black pepper.

Oysters Diamond Jim Brandy

Yield: 10 servings

Oysters, fresh	*50 each*	*50 each*
Tomato Concassé	*4 ounces*	*115 grams*
Butter	*2 ounces*	*60 grams*
Shallots, minced	*2 ounces*	*60 grams*
Crème fraîche, as needed	*20 ounces*	*60 grams*
Pernod, to taste	*dash*	*dash*
Royal Glaçage	*1 1/4 pounds*	*570 grams*
Salt, to taste	*1/2 teaspoon*	*1/2 teaspoon*
Pepper, to taste	*1/2 teaspoon*	*1/2 teaspoon*

1. Rinse and shuck the oysters, to order. Reserve the oyster liquor to flavor the Royal Glaçage.

2. Heat the Tomato Concassé and butter; add the shallots and sauté until they are tender and the liquid is reduced. Add a small amount of crème fraîche to bind the mixture. Add the Pernod, salt, and pepper to taste.

3. Place 1/2 teaspoon (2.5 grams) of the tomato mixture in the deep half of the oyster shell. Top with an oyster and coat each with the flavored royal glaçage.

4. Brown the oysters under a broiler. The oysters' edges should be lightly curled.

Oysters Gratinée

Yield: 10 servings

The recipe for Demi-Glace is found on page 522.

Shucking oysters is demonstrated in Figure 6-111 on page 252.

Oysters, on the half shell	30 each	30 each
White wine	5 fluid ounces	150 milliliters
Fish Stock	5 fluid ounces	150 milliliters
Shallots, minced	2 each	2 each
Mushrooms, minced	4 ounces	115 grams
Demi-Glace	1 pint	480 milliliters
Tomato purée	2 fluid ounces	60 milliliters
Salt, to taste	1/2 teaspoon	1/2 teaspoon
Pepper, to taste	1/2 teaspoon	1/2 teaspoon
Bread crumbs, fresh	6 ounces	170 grams
Butter, melted	2 ounces	60 grams

1. Remove oysters from their shells (save shells), place in a buttered pan, add wine and fish stock.

2. Shallow-poach oysters until their edges curl, remove and place back in the shells.

3. Strain poaching liquid, add shallots and mushrooms, reduce by half.

4. Add demi-glace and tomato purée; reduce until sauce consistency.

5. Add parsley and season.

6. Blend the bread crumbs with the melted butter.

7. Return the oyster to the shell. Coat the oysters with the sauce, sprinkle with bread crumbs, and bake oysters at 425°F (220°C) until hot and brown.

Fresh Artichoke Bottoms with Oysters in Warm Champagne Vinaigrette

Yield: 10 servings

Oysters, shucked, liquor reserved	20 ounces	600 grams
Dry white wine	6 fluid ounces	180 milliliters
Pepper, to taste	1/2 teaspoon	1/2 teaspoon
Shallots, minced	1 tablespoon	1 tablespoon
Olive oil	2 fluid ounces	60 milliliters
Champagne vinegar	2 fluid ounces	60 milliliters
Tomatoes, julienne	5 ounces	140 grams
Chives, chopped	2 tablespoons	2 tablespoons
Artichoke bottoms, sliced thinly	20 ounces	600 grams

(Recipe continued on facing page)

1. Poach oysters in white wine, pepper, and shallots.

2. Add olive oil and vinegar to the poaching liquid.

3. Add tomatoes and chives and bring to a simmer.

4. To serve, slice artichoke bottom and fan out on a serving plate. Arrange oysters on top. Drizzle with the poaching liquid and garnish.

Clams Casino

Yield: 10 servings

Casino butter		
Bacon, diced	*4 ounces*	*115 grams*
Onions, minced	*4 ounces*	*115 grams*
Green peppers, minced	*3 ounces*	*85 grams*
Red peppers, minced	*3 ounces*	*85 grams*
Salt, to taste	*1/2 teaspoon*	*1/2 teaspoon*
Pepper, to taste	*1/2 teaspoon*	*1/2 teaspoon*
Worcestershire sauce, to taste	*1/2 teaspoon*	*1/2 teaspoon*
Butter, softened	*1 pound*	*450 grams*
Clams, Little Neck, Cherrystone, or Top Necks	*5 dozen*	*5 dozen*
Bacon, slices, blanched, quartered	*5 each*	*5 each*

1. Prepare the casino butter: Render the diced bacon until it is crisp. Add the onions and peppers; sauté until they are tender. Remove from the heat and allow them to cool.

2. Combine the onion and pepper mixture with the salt, pepper, Worcestershire sauce, and butter. Blend all ingredients until they are evenly mixed.

3. Roll into a log, chill well, and slice once firm. Open the clams to order and loosen the meat from the shells. Top each clam with a slice of butter and a piece of blanched bacon. Broil the clams until the bacon is crisp; serve them immediately.

The Casino Butter may be prepared in advance and frozen for later use. For more information about preparing compound butters, refer to page 295.

The technique for opening clams is demonsrated on page 253.

Clam Fritters

Yield: 10 servings

The proper selection and care of frying oils may be found on page 323.

The recipes for Tartar and Rémoulade Sauces may be found on pages 915 and 916.

Other shellfish or flaky firm fish may be prepared in this manner also.

Flour	7 ounces	200 grams
Baking powder	1 tablespoon	1 tablespoon
Salt	1/4 teaspoon	1/4 teaspoon
White pepper	1/4 teaspoon	1/4 teaspoon
Clams, chopped, juices reserved	10 ounces	285 grams
Reserved clam juice	6 fluid ounces	180 milliliters
Milk	4 fluid ounces	120 milliliters
Tartar Sauce or Rémoulade Sauce	1 pint	480 milliliters

1. Combine all the dry ingredients.

2. Combine all the wet ingredients, including the chopped clams.

3. Combine the wet and dry ingredients.

4. Drop the mixture by spoonfuls into 375°F (190°C) oil.

5. Fry the fritters until they are golden brown. Serve them with Tartar Sauce, Rémoulade Sauce, other mayonnaise-based sauces, or cocktail sauce.

Deviled Crab Cakes

Yield: 10 servings

Butter	*4 ounces*	*115 grams*
Onions, minced	*1 ounce*	*30 grams*
Celery, minced	*1 ounce*	*30 grams*
Red peppers, minced	*1 1/2 ounces*	*40 grams*
Flour	*3 1/2 ounces*	*100 grams*
Fish Stock	*10 fluid ounces*	*300 milliliters*
Crabmeat, cleaned	*1 1/2 pounds*	*680 grams*
Old Bay Seasoning	*1/4 teaspoon*	*1/4 teaspoon*
Salt, to taste	*1/2 teaspoon*	*1/2 teaspoon*
Cayenne, to taste	*1/4 teaspoon*	*1/4 teaspoon*
Parsley, chopped	*1 tablespoon*	*1 tablespoon*
Flour for dredging	*2 ounces*	*60 grams*
Egg wash	*6 fluid ounces*	*180 milliliters*
Bread crumbs for coating, as needed	*6 ounces*	*170 grams*

Deviled crab may also be presented as follows: clean out the carapace (body) of the crab. Remove legs, stuff the crab with the filling, and bake; then gratinée to brown deboned fish.

This recipe may be used for crab stuffing; omit the breading. Stuff the mixture into pan-dressed, clean, sterilized crab shells or scallop shells. These are available commercially.

1. Sauté onion, celery, and pepper in butter.

2. Add flour and cook 2 to 3 minutes.

3. Incorporate fish stock and crabmeat; bring to a simmer, stirring constantly.

4. Cook 5 minutes, add seasonings; chill.

5. Shape into ten cakes, dredge in flour.

6. Dip cakes in egg wash, then dredge in bread crumbs.

7. Deep-fry at 350°F (175°C) until golden brown; drain on absorbent toweling.

Marinated Mackerel in White Wine

Yield: 10 servings

Sauce Rémoulade (page 915) would make a good accompaniment to this fish.

Mackerel, drawn, head removed	*1 1/2 pounds*	*680 grams*
Marinade		
White wine	*1 pint*	*480 milliliters*
Carrots, sliced thin	*1 ounce*	*30 grams*
Onions, sliced thin	*2 ounces*	*60 grams*
Salt, to taste	*1/2 teaspoon*	*1/2 teaspoon*
Thyme, sprig	*1 each*	*1 each*
Bay leaves	*4 each*	*4 each*
Pepper, to taste	*1/4 teaspoon*	*1/4 teaspoon*
Parsley stems	*3 to 4 each*	*3 to 4 each*

1. Trim the fish, rinse it to remove all traces of blood. Drain it well.

2. Combine all of the ingredients for the marinade. Bring it to a boil and simmer it, covered, for 45 minutes.

3. Place the mackerel in a poaching vessel. Pour the hot marinade over the fish; poach it slowly (170°F/75°C) for 8 to 10 minutes. Remove the pan from the heat; cool it in the poaching liquid. Chill it well.

4. Serve the fish chilled.

Melon and Prosciutto

Yield: 10 servings

Cantelope, ripe, sliced thin	*30 slices*	*30 slices*
Prosciutto, sliced thin	*10 ounces*	*285 grams*
Limes, wedges	*10 pieces*	*10 pieces*

1. Chill the melon until ready to serve. Place it on chilled plates.

2. Drape the prosciutto over the melon and serve each with a lime wedge.

Serve melon and prosciutto with figs, when they are in season. Be sure the fruit is perfectly ripe.

Dates Stuffed with Boursin Cheese

Yield: 18 to 20 pieces

Fresh dates	*1 pound*	*450 gram*
Boursin cheese	*6 ounces*	*170 grams*
Cream cheese	*6 ounces*	*170 grams*
Pistachios, chopped	*4 ounces*	*115 grams*

1. Split the dates lengthwise and remove the pit. Line the dates in the same direction on a half-sheet pan lined with parchment paper.

2. Mix the cheeses until well blended and soft.

3. Place the pistachios in a chinoise and dip in boiling water 10 to 20 seconds; drain on paper towels. Peel them while still hot. Split them in half following the natural seam of the nut.

4. Place the cheese mixture in a pastry bag with a plain tip.

5. Pipe the cheese mixture into the cavity of the date.

6. Garnish with pistachios and refrigerate uncovered. Make sure all the pistachio garnishes are facing the same direction.

7. When the cheese has set (about an hour), cover with plastic wrap to store.

Split dates lengthwise and remove the pit.

Boursin cheese is available with black peppercorns or with herbs and garlic. The peppercorn version is preferable here.

New Potatoes with Snails and Brie

Yield: approximately 60 pieces

Basil leaves	*4 ounces*	*115 grams*
Garlic cloves, minced	*2 each*	*2 each*
Pine nuts, toasted	*1 ounce*	*30 grams*
Parmesan cheese, grated	*1 ounce*	*30 grams*
Extra-virgin olive oil	*2 ounces*	*60 milliliters*
Water	*24 fluid ounces*	*720 milliliters*
White wine	*8 fluid ounces*	*240 milliliters*
Mirepoix	*8 ounces*	*240 grams*
Bay leaves	*4 each*	*4 each*
Thyme sprigs	*2 each*	*2 each*
Pepper, cracked	*1 tablespoon*	*1 tablespoon*
Salt	*2 teaspoons*	*2 teaspoons*
"B" size red or new potatoes	*4 pounds*	*2 kilograms*
Snails, rinsed well in a colander	*60 each*	*60 each*
Olive oil	*2 tablespoons*	*2 tablespoons*
Brie, slices	*1 1/2 pounds*	*680 grams*

The recipe for Mirepoix is on page 420.

A prepared Pesto (page 422) may be used in place of the basil, garlic, pine nuts, cheese, and oil.

(Recipe continued on next page)

1. Make a basil purée: Purée the basil, garlic, nuts, and cheese.

2. Slowly add the olive oil. Refrigerate until needed.

3. Combine the water, wine, mirepoix, bay leaves, thyme, pepper, and salt; simmer 5 minutes. Add the rinsed snails, simmer 5 minutes. Cool and store the snails in the liquid.

4. Cut the potatoes in half lengthwise and square off the bottom. Scoop out a hole in the center of the potato.

5. Blanch the potatoes in salted boiling water until they are three-quarters done.

6. Deep-fry the potatoes until golden; drain on paper towels, keep warm.

7. Sauté snails in olive oil. Add the basil sauce, away from heat; mix well.

8. Place a snail in each of the potatoes with a little of the basil sauce. Top with a piece of Brie and melt in a 425°F (220°C) oven.

Caviar in New Potatoes with Dilled Crème Fraîche

Yield: 40 pieces

Potatoes, "A" Red Bliss	*20 each*	*20 each*
Butter, softened	*2 ounces*	*60 grams*
Salt, to taste	*1/2 teaspoon*	*1/2 teaspoon*
Pepper, to taste	*1/4 teaspoon*	*1/4 teaspoon*
Crème fraîche	*5 fluid ounces*	*150 milliliters*
Dill, chopped	*1 ounce*	*30 grams*
Caviar	*3 1/2 ounces*	*100 grams*
Chives, sliced	*2 ounces*	*60 grams*

Select potatoes that are no more than 1 inch (2.5 centimeters) in diameter for the best results.

As a first course, serve 4 pieces per portion.

1. Bake the potatoes until they are very soft; split them in half. Scoop out the flesh and work the butter into it.

2. Return the mashed potatoes to their shells. Combine the crème fraîche and the dill; top the potatoes with it. Place a portion of the caviar on each potato half.

3. Sprinkle the potatoes with fresh chives and serve warm.

VARIATION

Three Caviars on Game Chips with Crème Fraîche: Make game chips by slicing Idaho potatoes very thin. Deep-fry 6 slices per portion. Top each slice with a dollop of crème fraîche and place three different caviars on top of the crème fraîche. Garnish the potatoes with chopped chives or chopped dill.

Black Bean Cakes

Yield: 10 servings

Black beans, soaked overnight	*14 ounces*	*400 grams*
Vegetable Stock, to cook beans	*28 fluid ounces*	*840 milliliters*
Garlic, minced	*1 tablespoon*	*1 tablespoon*
Onions, minced	*3 ounces*	*85 grams*
Jalapeño peppers, minced	*1 each*	*1 each*
Chili powder	*3/4 teaspoon*	*3/4 teaspoon*
Cumin, ground	*3/4 teaspoon*	*3/4 teaspoon*
Cardamom, ground	*3/4 teaspoon*	*3/4 teaspoon*
Cilantro, chopped	*1 teaspoon*	*1 teaspoon*
Salt	*1/2 teaspoon*	*1/2 teaspoon*
Lime juice	*1 teaspoon*	*1 teaspoon*
Egg white, beaten	*1 each*	*1 each*
Cornmeal, for dusting	*4 ounces*	*115 grams*
Clarified butter	*1 1/2 ounces*	*40 grams*
Garnish		
Yogurt, drained	*1 1/2 ounces*	*40 grams*
Sour cream	*1 1/2 fluid ounces*	*45 milliliters*
Fresh Tomato Salsa	*8 ounces*	*225 grams*

Soaking beans (long and quick soaking methods) is described on page 202.

Fresh Tomato Salsa is on page 936.

To drain yogurt, place it in a cheesecloth-lined colander. Place it in a bowl. Let it drain for 12 to 24 hours.

Diced red and green peppers, blanched corn, rice, and other cooked beans may be incorporated into these cakes.

1. Cook presoaked black beans in vegetable stock until tender, let stock reduce at the end of cooking.

2. Purée two-thirds of the beans, recombine the purée with the whole beans.

3. Sauté, the onion, garlic, and pepper in oil, add herbs and spices, and sauté until aromatic. Let this mixture cool. Add to bean mixture and blend.

4. Add lime juice and egg white, form into patties.

5. Dust patties in cornmeal; sauté in clarified butter.

6. Mix the sour cream and yogurt together. Serve with salsa as garnish.

Santa Fe-Style Black Bean Cakes with Sautéed Crab and Corn

Yield: 10 servings

The recipe for Fresh Tomato Salsa may be found on page 936.

Black beans, soaked overnight	12 ounces	340 grams
Ham hock, smoked	1 each	1 each
Bouquet garni		
Black peppercorns	8 each	8 each
Rosemary sprig	1 each	1 each
Thyme sprig	1 each	1 each
Parsley stems	4 each	4 each
Garlic cloves, whole	5 each	5 each
Onions, minced	4 ounces	115 grams
Chicken Stock, as needed	3 quarts	3 liters
Eggs, beaten	2 each	2 each
Cake flour	1 ounce	30 grams
Salt, to taste	1/2 teaspoon	1/2 teaspoon
Pepper, to taste	1/2 teaspoon	1/2 teaspoon
Crabmeat, picked	10 ounces	285 grams
Corn kernels	10 ounces	285 grams
Clarified butter, or olive oil	4 fluid ounces	120 grams
Cilantro, chopped	3 tablespoons	3 tablespoons
Fresh Tomato Salsa	1 pound	450 grams

1. Simmer the beans, ham hock, bouquet garni, and onions, in enough chicken stock to cover by about 3 inches (7.5 centimeters). Simmer for 1 1/2 hours, or until the beans are tender. Drain off the liquid and discard the bouquet garni.

2. Purée the beans to a chunky paste. Stir in the eggs and flour. Adjust the seasoning with salt and pepper. Form the mixture into cakes.

3. Sauté the crabmeat and corn in the clarified butter until they are hot. Adjust the seasoning and add the chopped cilantro. Keep warm.

4. Sauté the bean cakes in butter or oil until they are heated through. Serve the cakes on a pool of salsa and top them with the crabmeat-and-corn mixture.

Stuffed Mushrooms with a Gratin Forcemeat

Yield: 10 servings

Mushrooms, large	*40 each*	*40 each*
Clarified butter	*2 ounces*	*60 grams*
Shallots, minced	*1 each*	*1 each*
Garlic clove, minced	*1 each*	*1 each*
Ruby port	*1 fluid ounce*	*30 milliliters*
Chicken livers	*8 ounces*	*225 grams*
Salt, to taste	*1/2 teaspoon*	*1/2 teaspoon*
Pepper, to taste	*1/2 teaspoon*	*1/2 teaspoon*
Rosemary, leaves, chopped	*2 teaspoons*	*2 teaspoons*
Parsley, chopped	*1 tablespoon*	*1 tablespoon*

1. Wipe the mushrooms clean; remove the stems. Chop the stems coarsely. Reserve each cap separately.

2. Heat the butter and sauté the shallots and garlic until they are translucent. Deglaze the pan with the wine. Add the chopped mushroom stems and sauté until they are dry.

3. Sauté the chicken livers in the pan (add more clarified butter, if necessary) until they are seared on all sides. Purée the livers in a food processor. Push them through a sieve, if desired. Add the salt, pepper, and rosemary.

4. Pipe the mixture into the mushroom caps. Heat 4 caps per portion in a hot oven (425°F/220°C) at the time the mushrooms are ordered. Sprinkle them with additional wine and chopped parsley.

Select large mushroom caps if these are to be served as a plated appetizer. For cocktail receptions, look for mushroom caps of a size that could conveniently be eaten as a single mouthful.

Stuffed Grape Leaves

Yield: 10 servings

These are a common component in Greek salads, falafel plates, and Mediterranean-style sampler plates.

Garlic, chopped	*1 ounce*	*30 grams*
Onion, fine dice	*12 ounces*	*340 grams*
Olive oil	*4 fluid ounces*	*120 milliliters*
Rice, uncooked	*12 ounces*	*340 grams*
Tomato Concassé	*1 1/2 pounds*	*680 grams*
Salt, to taste	*1/2 teaspoon*	*1/2 teaspoon*
Pepper, to taste	*1/4 teaspoon*	*1/4 teaspoon*
Parsley, chopped	*1 ounce*	*30 grams*
Pine nuts (optional), roasted	*1 ounce*	*30 grams*
Grape leaves, rinsed	*50 each*	*50 each*
Vegetable Stock, to cover	*1 quart*	*1 liter*
Lemon juice	*3 fluid ounces*	*90 milliliters*

1. Sweat garlic and onion in oil until tender and translucent.

2. Add uncooked rice, stir to coat with oil.

3. Add tomato, salt, and pepper. Combine and heat through.

4. Remove from pan, mix in parsley and pine nuts. Cool and reserve.

5. Place grape leaves in saucepan with water to cover. Bring to a boil, blanch until softened.

6. Spread each leaf open on a flat surface. Place 1 tablespoon (15 grams) of rice mixture in the center of each leaf, then roll like an egg roll.

7. Place a rack on the bottom of a braising vessel. (This will prevent the stuffed grape leaves from sticking.) Place the rolls, side-by-side but un-crowded, on top of the rack.

8. Cover with stock or water and lemon juice. Use a weighted plate to keep them submerged, and under pressure. Braise on stove top for 1 hour. Cool overnight. Serve chilled.

Broccoli Flan

Yield: 10 servings

Broccoli, cooked, puréed	*1 pound*	*450 grams*
Eggs, beaten	*4 each*	*4 each*
Heavy cream	*3 fluid ounces*	*90 milliliters*
Cream cheese, softened	*4 ounces*	*115 grams*
Salt, to taste	*1/2 teaspoon*	*1/2 teaspoon*
Pepper, to taste	*1/4 teaspoon*	*1/4 teaspoon*

1. Combine all of the ingredients until they are smooth. Do not overmix them.

2. Place the mixture in ten buttered timbales; put into a pan and cover with buttered parchment.

3. Bake in a water bath until a skewer inserted near the center of timbale comes out clean.

4. Remove and keep warm. Unmold and serve. The broccoli flan may be served with a variety of sauces.

Red Pepper Mousse

Yield: 10 servings

Vegetable oil	*1 fluid ounce*	*30 milliliters*
Onions, small dice	*3 ounces*	*85 grams*
Garlic cloves, finely minced	*2 each*	*2 each*
Red peppers, small dice	*4 each*	*4 each*
Salt, to taste	*1/2 teaspoon*	*1/2 teaspoon*
Pepper, to taste	*1/4 teaspoon*	*1/4 teaspoon*
Chicken Stock	*10 fluid ounces*	*300 milliliters*
Saffron, ground	*pinch*	*pinch*
Tomato paste	*1 ounce*	*30 grams*
Gelatin	*4 teaspoons*	*4 teaspoons*
Cold water, stock, or dry white wine	*3 fluid ounces*	*90 milliliters*
Heavy cream, whipped to medium peaks	*8 fluid ounces*	*240 milliliters*

(Recipe continued on next page)

1. Heat the oil. Add the onions and garlic; sauté until they are lightly browned.

2. Add the red peppers, salt, pepper, chicken stock, saffron, and tomato paste. Simmer the mixture until all the ingredients are tender and the liquid is reduced.

3. Bloom the gelatin in cold water, stock, or dry white wine. Dissolve over simmering water.

4. Purée the red pepper mixture in a blender. Add the dissolved gelatin while the mixture is still hot and blend to combine all the ingredients thoroughly. Strain the mixture through a tamis, if desired.

5. Cool the red pepper mixture over an ice bath until it mounds when dropped from a spoon.

6. Fold the whipped cream into the pepper mixture, and place it in oiled molds. Chill. Unmold the mousse just before serving.

VARIATIONS

Broccoli Mousse: Replace the red peppers with 6 to 8 ounces (170 to 225 grams) of chopped broccoli.

Carrot Mousse: Replace the red peppers with 6 to 8 ounces (170 to 225 grams) of chopped carrots.

C H A P T E R *27* *Sausages, Pâtés, and Terrines*

The recipes included are found as breakfast items, appetizers, hors d'oeuvres, and buffet and reception standards. Others may be served as entrées and some are used as fillings or stuffing for foods such as chicken breasts or pasta. Before preparing these recipes, you may wish to review the techniques, described in the text on pages 353 to 374. There are also recipes within the entrée recipe chapters and Chapter 26 which require forcemeats. With experience, you can make variations and substitutions as desired. Once you are familiar with the technique, you will be able to create dishes to suit your needs.

The chapter is organized as follows:

- *Basic Forcemeats*
- *Basic Preparations*
- *Sausages*
- *Pâtés*
- *Terrines*
- *Galantines*
- *Roulades*
- *Specialty Items*

Pâté de Campagne

Yield: approximately 3 pounds (1.36 kilograms)

An average moold will hold 3 pounds (1.3 kilograms) and yield 24 slices.

Pork butt, diced	2 1/2 pounds	1.15 kilograms
Pork liver, cleaned and diced	1/2 pound	230 grams
Onion, chopped fine	4 ounces	115 grams
Garlic, cloves, minced	2 each	2 each
Parsley sprigs, chopped fine	5 each	5 each
Flour	2 1/2 ounces	70 grams
Eggs	2 each	2 each
Salt	3/4 ounce	20 grams
White pepper	1/2 teaspoon	1/2 teaspoon
Pâté spice	pinch	pinch
Brandy	1 fluid ounce	30 milliliters
Heavy cream	4 fluid ounces	120 milliliters
Fatback, sliced thin	as needed	as needed

1. Grind 1 pound (450 grams) of the pork butt with the pork liver, onion, garlic, and parsley through the medium and then fine die of a grinder.

2. Grind the remainder of the pork butt through a coarse die. Combine the fine- and coarse-ground meats in a large bowl. Working over an ice bath, stir in the remainder of the ingredients, except the fatback, until they are just blended. Make a test quenelle to check for seasoning and consistency.

3. Use the fatback to line a pâté mold. Bake in a water bath at 325°F (160°C) to an internal temperature of 150°F (65°C).

German-Style Bratwurst (5/4/3 Forcemeat)

Yield: approximately 5 1/4 pounds (2.5 kilograms)

Also called Emulsion forcemeat, this is commonly used for sausage.

Make a test quenelle to check for seasoning and consistency before stuffing the forcemeat into the casing.

Pork butt (approximately 25 percent fat), diced	5 pounds	2.25 kilograms
Bratwurst seasoning (below)	2 ounces	55 grams
Ice, shaved	8 ounces	225 grams
Hog or sheep casing, rinsed well	as needed	as needed
Seasoning mix [for 25 pounds (11.35 kilograms) of meat]		
Salt	8 ounces	910 grams
White pepper, ground	1 1/2 ounces	170 grams
Celery seed, ground	1/2 tablespoon	1/2 tablespoon
Mace, ground	3/4 teaspoon	3/4 teaspoon
Sage, rubbed	1/4 ounce	30 grams

(Recipe continued on facing page)

1. Season the meat with the spices. Mix well. Grind the meat, using a fine die.

2. Place the ground meat in a mixer or food processor. Add shaved ice and mix at low speed. Process the meat until the ice is incorporated, about 1 minute.

3. Increase the speed slightly and mix another minute. The meat should feel tacky; temperature should be around 40°F (4°C).

4. Stuff the mixture into the prepared hog or sheep casing. Tie the casing at 4-inch (10 centimeter) intervals with fine twine.

5. Poach the sausages in 170°F (75°C) water for about 30 minutes to an internal temperature of 155°F (68°C). Chill them in ice and water.

Use for frankfurters, bratwursts, knockwursts, and weisswurst.

Chicken Liver Gratin-Style Forcemeat

Yield: approximately 2 pounds (900 grams)

Vegetable oil	*1 fluid ounce*	*30 milliliters*
Chicken livers, cleaned	*10 ounces*	*285 grams*
Onions, minced	*4 ounces*	*115 grams*
Shallots, minced	*2 ounces*	*60 grams*
Bay leaf	*1 each*	*1 each*
Thyme leaves, dried	*1 teaspoon*	*1 teaspoon*
Salt, to taste	*2 teaspoons*	*2 teaspoons*
Pepper, to taste	*1/4 teaspoon*	*1/4 teaspoon*
Lean pork, cubed	*10 ounces*	*285 grams*
Pork fat, cubed	*10 ounces*	*285 grams*
Eggs	*2 each*	*2 each*
Curing salt (optional)	*1/4 teaspoon*	*1/4 teaspoon*

1. Heat a small amount of oil in a sauté pan. Add the livers, onions, shallots, bay leaf, thyme leaves, salt, and pepper. Cook the livers over low heat until they are done, but do not allow them to take on any color.

2. Refrigerate the liver mixture to chill it thoroughly.

3. Grind the liver mixture, lean pork, and pork fat through a coarse die, then again through a medium or fine die.

4. Place the ground meats in the chilled bowl of a food processor. Process them with the eggs and curing salt until a smooth paste is formed.

5. Make a test quenelle to check the forcemeat for consistency and seasoning. Make any necessary adjustments. Keep the forcemeat chilled until it is ready to use for various charcuterie and garde-manger items.

A number of herbs and spices may be used to vary the flavor of this forcemeat, according to the discretion of the chef or the needs of a specific recipe.

This may be used to prepare pâtés, and terrines, and as a stuffing for poultry.

Chicken Mousseline Forcemeat

Yield: approximately 1 3/4 pounds (750 grams)

Chicken breast, boneless, cubed	1 pound	450 grams
Egg	1 each	1 each
Heavy cream, chilled	10 fluid ounces	285 milliliters
Salt, to taste	2 teaspoons	2 teaspoons
White pepper, to taste	1/4 teaspoon	1/4 teaspoon
Fresh herbs, chopped (dill, parsley, tarragon, etc., as desired or available)	2 tablespoons	2 tablespoons

1. Grind the chicken through the fine die of a grinder and place it in the chilled bowl of a food processor.

2. Process the chicken with the egg until it is a smooth paste, but do not allow it to exceed 40°F (4°C).

3. Add the heavy cream, salt, pepper, and fresh herbs. Pulse the machine on and off just until the ingredients are blended.

4. Make a test quenelle by poaching it in simmering water or stock to test for consistency and seasoning. Make any necessary adjustments. Keep the forcemeat chilled until ready to use for quenelles, stuffing, or other charcuterie and garde-manger items.

This recipe can be prepared in the bowl of a standard food processor. It may be scaled up according to need.

Substitute fish or shellfish for the chicken to make a fish mousseline.

Pâté Dough

Yield: 2 pounds (900 grams)

Bread flour, sifted	20 ounces	580 grams
Powdered milk (optional)	1 3/4 ounces	35 grams
Baking powder	1/4 ounce	7 grams
Salt	1/2 ounce	15 grams
Shortening	3 1/2 ounces	100 grams
Butter	2 1/2 ounces	70 grams
Milk or water	8 to 10 fluid ounces	225 to 285 milliliters
Eggs	2 each	2 each
Lemon juice or vinegar	1/2 fluid ounce	15 milliliters

1. Combine the flour, powdered milk, baking powder, and salt in a food processor. Mix the ingredients well until the mixture resembles a coarse meal.

2. Transfer the mixture to a mixer bowl. Incorporate the shortening, butter, milk, eggs, and lemon juice or vinegar with a dough hook. If the dough seems too dry, add up to 1 fluid ounce (30 milliliters) of additional water.

3. Let the dough rest for 1 hour before rolling it out.

The flavor of this dough can be varied by adding ground spices and herbs, lemon zest, or grated cheese. Rye or whole wheat flour or cornmeal may be used to replace up to one-third of the bread flour for a different flavor, texture, and appearance.

This will yield enough dough for one pâté en croûte.

Pâté Spice

Yield: 14 3/4 ounces (425 grams)

Whole white peppercorns	*1 1/2 ounces*	*45 grams*
Coriander, ground	*3 ounces*	*85 grams*
Thyme	*1 3/4 ounces*	*50 grams*
Basil	*1 3/4 ounces*	*50 grams*
Cloves	*3 ounces*	*85 grams*
Nutmeg	*1 1/2 ounces*	*45 grams*
Bay leaf	*1/2 ounce*	*15 grams*
Mace	*3/4 ounce*	*20 grams*

Combine all of the ingredients and grind them, using a mortar or blender.

If desired, you may add dried mushrooms (cèpes, bolétes, chanterelles, or porcini) to this mixture. One ounce (30 grams) should be adequate.

Aspic Gelée

Yield: 1 gallon (3.75 liters)

Clarification		
Onion brûlé	*1 each*	*1 each*
Mirepoix	*1 pound*	*450 grams*
Ground beef	*3 pounds*	*1.35 kilograms*
Egg whites, beaten	*10 each*	*10 each*
Tomato Concassé	*12 ounces*	*340 grams*
Stock	*1 gallon*	*3.75 liters*
Standard Sachet d'Épices	*1 each*	*1 each*
Kosher salt	*1 teaspoon*	*1 teaspoon*
Gelatin powder	*4 ounces*	*115 grams*

1. Mix the ingredients for the clarification and blend with stock. Mix well.

2. Bring the mixture to a slow simmer, stirring frequently until raft forms.

3. Add the Sachet d'Épices and simmer for 45 minutes or until the appropriate flavor and clarity are achieved. Baste raft occasionally.

4. Strain the consommé; adjust the seasoning with salt and white pepper to taste.

5. Soften the gelatin in cold water, then melt over simmering water. Add to the cooled clarified stock. Refrigerate until needed. Warm as necessary for use.

Use an appropriate stock, depending upon the intended use. For example, prepare a lobster stock and use ground fish for the clarification if the aspic is to be used to coat a seafood item.

The classic method for preparing an Aspic Gelée calls for a very strong and extremely gelatinous stock to be made by adding veal shank and calves' feet to a standard stock as it simmers. The high percentage of cartilage in the shank and feet will act in the same way as powdered gelatin does.

Andouille Sausage

Yield: 7 1/2 pounds (3.4 kilograms)

Be sure that the ingredients and equipment remain cool (below 40°F/4°C) throughout preparation.

Pork butt, boned and cubed	6 1/4 pounds	2.8 kilograms
Cayenne, ground	2 1/2 tablespoons	2 1/2 tablespoons
Salt	2 1/4 ounce	80 grams
Curing salt (T.C.M.)	1/4 ounce	7 grams
Thyme, ground	3/4 teaspoon	3/4 teaspoon
Mace, ground	1 teaspoon	1 teaspoon
Cloves, ground	1/4 teaspoon	1/4 teaspoon
Allspice, ground	1 teaspoon	1 teaspoon
Marjoram	2 teaspoons	2 teaspoons
Onions, chopped	1 1/4 pounds	570 kilograms
Garlic, minced	1 1/4 ounces	40 grams
Sheep casing, rinsed	as needed	as needed

1. Spread the meat over a sheet pan.

2. Combine the spices in a bowl; then sprinkle them over the meat. Incorporate well.

3. Grind the meat, onions, and garlic using a fine die.

4. Make a test quenelle to check for seasoning and consistency.

5. Stuff the meat into the sheep casing. Tie or twist it off at 8-inch (20 centimeter) intervals.

6. Cold-smoke the sausages for 12 to 14 hours.

7. Cook them using the desired method.

Breakfast-Style Sausage

Yield: 6 pounds (2.75 kilograms)

Pork butt, diced	5 pounds	225 kilograms
Jowl fat, diced, frozen	1 pound	450 grams
Salt, to taste	2 tablespoons	2 tablespoons
Bell's Poultry Seasoning	pinch	pinch
Dextrose	3/4 ounce	20 grams
Gingerroot, ground	pinch	pinch
Water, cold	1 pint	480 milliliters
Sheep casing, rinsed	as needed	as needed

(Recipe continued on facing page)

1. Spread the meat and fat over a sheet pan.

2. Mix the spices in a bowl, then sprinkle them over the meat and fat. Incorporate well.

3. Grind the meat and fat, using first a coarse, then a medium or a fine die.

4. Mix the meat in a mixer fitted with a paddle attachment for approximately 60 seconds. Add the cold water while mixing.

5. Make a test patty, panfry it, and taste it to check the seasoning consistency, which should be adjusted as necessary.

6. Stuff the mixture into the sheep casing.

7. Twist off the casing at approximately 4 1/2-inch (12 centimeter) intervals.

8. Cook the sausages, using the desired method (panfry, bake, etc.).

Italian Festival Sausage

Yield: 7 pounds (3.15 kilograms)

Pork butt, cubed, 75% lean	5 pounds	2.25 kilograms
Salt	1 1/2 ounces	40 grams
Dextrose	1/2 ounce	15 grams
Pepper, coarse grind	1/2 ounce	15 grams
Paprika	1 tablespoon	1 tablespoon
Fennel seeds, whole	3/1 ounce	30 grams
Parmesan cheese, grated	8 ounces	225 grams
Provolone cheese, grated	1 pound	450 grams
Parsley, chopped	1/2 ounce	15 grams
Red wine, very cold	8 fluid ounces	240 milliliters

1. Spread the meat in a even layer on a sheet pan.

2. Mix the spices in a bowl and blend them with the meat.

3. Grind the meat and spices through a medium plate, then mix in a mixer with the cheeses, parsley, and wine at low speed for 1 minute. Mix at medium speed for another minute, or until tacky.

4. Make a test patty, and adjust seasonings or consistency if necessary.

5. Stuff into sheep casings, and cut into links of the desired length.

Chicken and Herb Sausage

Yield: 12 pounds (5.5 kilograms)

Cut the chicken and pork into 1 inch (2.5 centimeter) dice.

Keep all ingredients and equipment well-chilled throughout preparation.

You will need about 1 tablespoon of salt to adequately season every 4 pounds (900 grams) of a forcemeat.

Salt	*3 ounces*	*85 grams*
Chicken, diced	*5 pounds*	*2.25 kilograms*
Pork, diced	*5 pounds*	*2.25 kilograms*
Jowl fat, diced	*1 1/2 pounds*	*680 grams*
Eggs	*7 each*	*7 each*
Milk, ice cold	*18 fluid ounces*	*540 milliliters*
Gingerroot, ground	*1/2 teaspoon*	*1/2 teaspoon*
Mace, ground	*1/4 teaspoon*	*1/4 teaspoon*
Cardamom, ground	*1/4 teaspoon*	*1/4 teaspoon*
White pepper, ground	*1/4 teaspoon*	*1/4 teaspoon*
Coriander, ground	*1/4 teaspoon*	*1/4 teaspoon*
Chives, snipped	*1/2 bunch*	*1/2 bunch*
Parsley, chopped	*1/2 ounce*	*15 grams*
Lemon, zested and grated	*1/2 ounce*	*1/2 gram*
Casing, hog or beef middle, rinsed	*as needed*	*as needed*

1. Sprinkle the salt over the chicken and pork; toss to coat evenly.

2. Grind the meat, using a medium die. Chill thoroughly in the freezer, but do not allow it to freeze solid.

3. Grind the jowl fat separately, using a medium die. Refrigerate.

4. When the meat is very cold (about 38°F/3°C), place it in a vertical chopping machine.

5. Run the machine for approximately 30 seconds.

6. Mix the eggs and milk. Incorporate them into the meat mixture.

7. Incorporate the fat.

8. Add the spices, herbs, and lemon zest.

9. Make a test quenelle to check for seasoning and consistency.

10. Use the forcemeat to fill the casings. Twist or tie the filled casings into links.

11. Poach the sausages to an internal temperature of 160°F (70°C).

Duck Sausage

Yield: 10 pounds (4.5 kilograms)

Shallots, chopped fine	*8 ounces*	*225 grams*
Butter	*1 ounce*	*30 grams*
Garlic, minced	*1 ounce*	*30 grams*
Red wine	*1 1/2 pints*	*720 milliliters*
Duck, diced, cold	*6 pounds*	*2.7 kilograms*
Fatback, cold	*3 pounds*	*1.35 kilograms*
Thyme, chopped	*1 teaspoon*	*1 teaspoon*
Sage, chopped	*2 tablespoons*	*2 tablespoons*
Parsley, chopped	*4 tablespoons*	*4 tablespoons*
Pepper, coarse-ground	*1 tablespoon*	*1 tablespoon*
Curing salt	*3/8 ounces*	*10 grams*
Salt	*2 ounces*	*60 grams*
Dextrose	*3/4 ounce*	*20 grams*
Sheep casing, rinsed	*as needed*	*as needed*

The meat from duck legs will produce a flavorful, moist sausage. To see the procedure for boning poultry legs, refer to Figure 6-92 on page 242.

1. Sauté the shallots in the butter.

2. Add the garlic and red wine; reduce it to sec.

3. Grind the duck meat and fatback using a fine die.

4. Combine the meat, fat, shallot-garlic mixture, and spices; mix them together thoroughly.

5. Make a test quenelle to check for seasoning and consistency.

6. Stuff the mixture into the sheep casing. Twist or tie it off at 4-to-5-inch (10- to 12-centimeter) intervals.

7. Smoke the sausages lightly.

8. Poach the sausages to an internal temperature of 160°F (70°C).

Spicy French-Style Apple Sausage

Yield: 6 pounds (2.75 kilograms)

Pork butt, chilled, diced	5 pounds	2.25 kilograms
Salt	1 tablespoon	1 tablespoon
Pepper	2 teaspoons	2 teaspoons
Gingerroot, ground	1 teaspoon	1 teaspoon
Allspice, ground	1 teaspoon	1 teaspoon
Cloves, ground	1 teaspoon	1 teaspoon
Apples, 1/8-inch dice	8 ounces	240 grams
Chablis, or other white wine	4 fluid ounces	120 milliliters
Sheep casing, rinsed	as needed	as needed

1. Spread the meat over a sheet pan.

2. Mix the spices in a bowl, then sprinkle them over the meat. Incorporate them well.

3. Grind the meat, using first a coarse, then medium, then fine die.

4. Add the apples to the meat mixture and combine them in a mixer fitted with a paddle attachment until the mixture is well blended. Add the wine while mixing.

5. Make a test patty, panfry it, and taste it to check the seasoning and consistency, adjust as necessary.

6. Stuff the mixture into the sheep casing.

7. Twist off the casing at approximately 4-inch (10-centimeter) intervals.

8. Cook the sausages using the desired method.

Greek Sausage—Loukanika

Yield: 8 pounds (3.6 kilograms)

The caul fat suggested here is optional. You may wish to mold the sausage onto skewers and grill or broil them instead of pan-frying patties.

Pork (approximately 40 percent fat), diced	6 pounds	2.7 kilograms
Salt	2 tablespoons	2 tablespoons
Black pepper, ground	2 teaspoons	2 teaspoons
Cayenne, ground	1/2 teaspoon	1/2 teaspoon
Oregano, chopped	2 teaspoons	2 teaspoons
Thyme, chopped	1 teaspoon	1 teaspoon
Allspice, ground	1/2 teaspoon	1/2 teaspoon
Parsley, chopped	2 ounces	60 grams
Water, very cold	6 fluid ounces	180 milliliters
Onions, chopped fine	12 ounces	340 grams
Bay leaves	2 each	2 each
Caul fat	1 1/2 pounds	680 grams

(Recipe continued on facing page)

1. Spread the meat over a sheet pan.

2. Mix the spices in a bowl, then sprinkle them over the meat. Incorporate them well.

3. Grind the meat, using a fine die.

4. Mix in a mixer fitted with a paddle attachment for approximately 60 seconds. Add the water while mixing.

5. Make a test patty and panfry it to check the seasoning.

6. Shape the meat into patties. Wrap the patties in caul fat.

7. Panfry, broil, or bake the patties until they are done.

Italian-Style Sausage

Yield: 11 pounds (5 kilograms)

Pork (approximately 25 percent fat, 75 percent lean), diced	*10 pounds*	*4.5 kilograms*
Pepper, coarse-ground	*1 ounce*	*30 grams*
Salt	*3 tablespoons*	*3 tablespoons*
Sweet Hungarian paprika	*1/4 ounce*	*7 grams*
Fennel seed	*1 1/2 ounces*	*40 grams*
Dextrose	*1 ounce*	*30 grams*
Cold water	*1 pint*	*480 milliliters*
Hog casing, rinsed	*as needed*	*as needed*

Use a fine die to grind the meat.

1. Combine the diced meat, spices, and dextrose on a sheet pan. Toss to coat evenly.

2. Grind the meat, using a coarse, then medium, then fine die.

3. Mix the meat, using a mixer fitted with a paddle attachment for 30 seconds on slow speed. Add the water while mixing.

4. Mix the meat for 30 seconds more on fast speed.

5. Make a test quenelle or patty to check for seasoning and consistency.

6. Stuff the mixture into the hog casing.

7. Tie the casing at 4 1/2-inch (12 centimeter) intervals.

8. Cook the sausages using the desired method.

VARIATION

Hot Italian Sausage: Add the following spices: ground coriander (1/2 ounce/15 grams), Spanish and Hungarian paprikas (3/4 ounce/20 grams each), crushed red pepper flakes (1 3/4 ounces/75 grams) and 2 teaspoons cayenne.

Fresh Chorizo

Yield: 12 pounds (5.5 kilograms)

To make a variation on this chorizo recipe, add minced scallions (6 to 8 ounces/170 to 225 grams) during step 1.

Make a test quenelle to check for consistency and seasoning.

Spanish chorizo is usually stuffed in casings. Mexican chorizo is often left in bulk.

To make a smoked sausage, place sausage on lined sheet trays and refrigerate uncovered overnight. Then cold-smoke for 12 to 14 hours. If not smoking, curing salt is optional.

Pork, ground fine	2 pounds	900 grams
Pork, lean, ground coarse	6 pounds	2.7 kilograms
Jowl fat, ground fine	4 pounds	1.8 kilograms
Curing salt (T.C.M.)	1/2 ounce	15 grams
Onion powder	1/2 teaspoon	1/2 teaspoon
Cumin, ground	3 tablespoons	3 tablespoons
Spanish paprika	3/4 ounce	20 grams
Dextrose	2/3 ounce	18 grams
Cayenne, ground	2 1/2 tablespoons	2 1/2 tablespoons
Garlic powder	2 teaspoons	2 teaspoons
Red peppers, crushed	1 teaspoon	1 teaspoon
Vinegar	2 1/2 fluid ounces	75 milliliters
Nonfat dried milk	3 ounces	85 grams
Cold water	6 fluid ounces	180 milliliters
Hog or sheep casing, rinsed	as needed	as needed

1. Combine all of the ingredients except the water and casing. Mix them together in a mixer fitted with a paddle attachment. Add the water while mixing.

2. Stuff the mixture into the casing. Twist or tie off the casing at 3- to 4-inch (8- to 10-centimeter) intervals.

3. Cook the sausages using the desired method.

Seafood Sausage

Yield: 4 pounds (1.8 kilograms)

Bread, unsliced, white, with crust, diced	2 1/2 ounces	70 grams
Egg whites	5 each	5 each
Heavy cream	1 pint	480 milliliters
Sole fillets or pike, cubed and chilled	1 1/2 pounds	680 grams
Ice, crushed	as needed	as needed
Salt	1 tablespoon	1 tablespoon
Sweet Hungarian paprika	1/2 teaspoon	1/2 teaspoon
Coriander, ground	1/2 teaspoon	1/2 teaspoon
Cayenne, ground	pinch	pinch
Garnish		
Bay scallops	8 ounces	225 grams
Shrimp, count, deveined and diced	8 ounces	225 grams

(Recipe continued on facing page)

King crab meat or lobster tail, diced	8 ounces	225 grams
Pistachios or truffles	2 ounces	60 grams
Parsley or chervil, chopped	1 tablespoon	1 tablespoon
Pork casing, rinsed	as needed	as needed

Roll this forcemeat into a roulade in plastic wrap. Poach at 160°F (70°C) to an internal temperature of 150°F (65°C). When the sausage is cool, wrap it in phyllo or brioche and bake until the dough is browned. Slice and serve as a hot appetizer.

1. Combine the bread, egg whites, and 4 fluid ounces (120 milliliters) of the heavy cream. Chill the mixture.

2. Place the fish in a food processor with a 1/4 cup (60 grams) of ice and purée it.

3. Add the bread-and-cream mixture to the fish and mix them well.

4. Add the salt and spices.

5. Gradually incorporate the rest of the heavy cream.

6. Poach a test quenelle to check the seasoning and binding.

7. Fold in the garnish ingredients and stuff the mixture into the pork casing. Tie off the casing into links with twine at 4- to 5-inch (10- to 13-centimeter) intervals.

8. Blanch the sausages in 170°F (75°C) water to an internal temperature of 150°F (65°C). Shock them in ice and refrigerate.

9. Cook the sausages, using the desired method (poach, sauté, grill, etc.).

Smoked Venison Sausage

Yield: 5 pounds (2.25 kilograms)

Venison, diced	3 1/2 pounds	1.6 kilograms
Fatback, or jowl fat, diced	1 1/2 pounds	680 kilograms
White pepper, ground	1 tablespoon	1 tablespoon
Ginger, ground	1 1/2 teaspoon	1 1/2 teaspoon
Nutmeg, ground	1 1/2 teaspoon	1 1/2 teaspoon
Curing salt	1/4 teaspoon	1/4 teaspoon
Sugar	2 teaspoons	2 teaspoons
Sage	1/2 teaspoon	1/2 teaspoon
Salt	4 teaspoons	4 teaspoons
Cold water	8 fluid ounces	240 milliliters
Sheep casing, rinsed	as needed	as needed

1. Spread the meat and fatbacks over a sheet pan.

2. Sprinkle the spices over the top. Incorporate them well.

3. Grind the meat, using, first a coarse, then medium, then a fine die.

4. Mix the meat with a mixer fitted with a paddle attachment for approximately 60 seconds. Add the water while mixing.

5. Poach a test quenelle to check seasoning and consistency.

6. Stuff the meat into the sheep casing. Tie the casing at 4 1/2-inch (12-centimeter) intervals.

7. Cold-smoke the sausages to the desired golden color.

8. Cook the sausages, using the desired method.

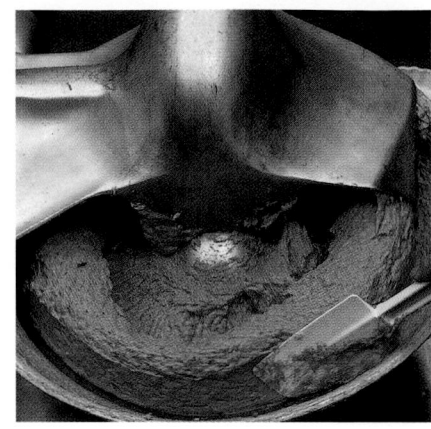

This recipe will make 1 pâté, yielding about 24 slices.

Use this forcemeat as desired for a variety of charcuterie and garde-manger items. Keep it well chilled at all times.

Pâté spice is on page 997, or refer to other spice blends on pages 425 to 428.

See page 365 for an illustration of filling a mold for Pâté de Campagne.

Pheasant Pâté

Yield: 2 pounds (900 grams)

Pheasant, legs, meat only, diced	*10 ounces*	*285 grams*
Pork, lean, diced	*10 ounces*	*285 grams*
Pork, fat, diced	*10 ounces*	*285 grams*
Eggs	*2 each*	*2 each*
Shallots, minced, sweated, cooled	*2 ounces*	*60 grams*
Salt	*3/4 ounce*	*20 grams*
White pepper, ground	*1/4 ounce*	*7 grams*
Pâté Spice, or other spice blend	*pinch*	*pinch*
Curing salt (optional)	*1/4 teaspoon*	*1/4 teaspoon*
Fatback, sliced thin, as needed	*4 ounces*	*115 grams*

1. Grind the pheasant meat, pork, and pork fat through the coarse die of a grinder, then again through a finer die.

2. Place the ground meats and fat in the chilled bowl of a food processor and add all of the remaining ingredients. Process the forcemeat until it is smooth and well emulsified.

3. Place in a lined terrine mold and bake at 350°F (175°C) in a water bath to an internal temperature of 150°F (65°C). Cool, weight overnight and slice for service.

VARIATIONS

Rabbit forcemeat: Replace the pheasant meat with lean, diced rabbit meat. If desired, reserve the loin meat and cut it into dice or julienne for a garnish. Marinate the loin meat in a small amount of brandy. Garnish the forcemeat with chopped nuts, mushrooms, or sweated vegetables for additional color and flavor, as desired.

Venison forcemeat: Replace the pheasant meat with lean, diced venison. Use lean meat from the loin as a garnish, as described for rabbit forcemeat, above.

Duck Pâté en Croute

Yield: 2 pounds (900 grams)

*To make the **Brine,** combine 1 pint (480 milliliters) water with 1 ounce (30 grams) salt, 1 teaspoon curing salt (T.C.M.), 2 teaspoons pickling spice and 1 garlic clove. Bring to a boil; strain and cool.*

Forcemeat

Duck, 4 1/2 pounds	*1 each*	*1 each*
Brine	*1 pint*	*480 milliliters*
Pork fat, cubed	*7 ounces*	*200 grams*
Orange zest, grated	*2 tablespoons*	*2 tablespoons*
Sage, chopped	*1 tablespoon*	*1 tablespoon*
Tarragon, chopped	*2 tablespoons*	*2 tablespoons*
Juniper berries, crushed	*6 each*	*6 each*

(Recipe continued on facing page)

Curing Salt (T.C.M.)	1/2 teaspoon	1/2 teaspoon
Shallots, minced	1 ounce	30 grams
Garlic, cloves, minced	2 each	2 each
Oil, as needed	2 fluid ounces	60 milliliters
Red port	2 fluid ounces	60 milliliters
Madeira	2 fluid ounces	60 milliliters
Orange, juice only	1 each	1 each
Glace de Volaille, or Viande	1 ounce	30 grams
Duck livers, cleaned	4 ounces	120 grams
Bacon fat	1 ounce	30 grams
Egg	1 each	1 each
Apricots, quartered	1 ounce	30 grams
Dried cherries, soaked in Triple Sec	1 ounce	30 grams
Pistachio nuts, peeled	2 ounces	60 grams
Triple Sec, as needed	3 ounces	85 grams
Basic Pâté Dough, rolled thin, covered, chilled	1 recipe	1 recipe
Ham, thin sliced, for lining dough	4 ounces	115 grams
Gelatin, powdered (optional)	1/2 teaspoon	1/2 teaspoon
Egg albumen (optional)	1/2 teaspoon	1/2 teaspoon
Aspic gelée, as needed	6 ounces	170 grams

Serve 2 2-ounce (60-gram) slices per portion for an appetizer.

Chicken livers may be used if duck liver is not available.

Curing salt is added in a ratio of 4 ounces per 100 pounds (115 grams per 45.5 kilograms).

A basic recipe for pâté dough is on page 996. Aspic Gelée is on page 997 (use Game Bird Stock and ground duck meat in the clarification if possible).

1. Bone duck, clean leg and thigh meat; cube.

2. Trim breasts, submerge in brine, cure for 4 hours.

3. Combine cubed leg meat, pork fat, and seasonings; marinate refrigerated for 1 hour.

4. Sauté shallots and garlic in oil, add wines and orange juice, reduce by half, add glace, cool and add to marinating meat.

5. Sauté chicken livers in hot bacon fat, drain on paper towels, cool.

6. Grind marinated meat once through a course die and again through a medium die; purée in food processor; add egg, process until smooth.

7. Fold in cooked livers, drained apricots, cherries, peeled pistachio nuts, and 2 ounces (60 grams) of reserved Triple Sec.

8. Oil the pâté pan, line it with dough; line dough with thin sliced ham.

9. Place half of the forcemeat in the mold.

10. Drain duck breasts, rinse, pat dry, sprinkle with gelatin powder and egg albumen, and set on top of forcemeat.

11. Fill mold with remaining forcemeat.

12. Fold over dough, paint with egg wash, add top and bake to an internal temperature of 150°F (65°C).

13. Fill with aspic when pâté has cooled between 90 to 100°F (30 to 35°C).

Marinating the meat and fat before grinding.

The procedure for lining a pâté mold with dough is described on pages 366 to 368.

Grind the quail leg and thigh meat, the pork butt and pork fat together using the progressive grinding techniques explained on page 357.

The brine on page 1006 can be used to cure the quail breasts. See pages 305 and 306 to read more about smoke-roasting.

The recipe for Aspic Gelée is on page 997.

Quail Pâté en Croute

Yield: 1 pâté

Tomato cilantro pâté dough		
Basic pâté dough	*1 recipe*	*1 recipe*
Coriander, ground	*2 teaspoons*	*2 teaspoons*
Cumin, ground	*2 teaspoons*	*2 teaspoons*
Tomato paste	*1 1/2 ounces*	*45 grams*
Cilantro, fresh, chopped	*2 tablespoons*	*2 tablespoons*
Garlic, cloves, minced	*2 each*	*2 each*
Shallots, minced	*2 teaspoons*	*2 teaspoons*
Oil, as needed	*1 fluid ounce*	*30 milliliters*
Tequila	*3 ounces*	*90 grams*
Quail leg/thigh meat, ground	*10 ounces*	*300 grams*
Pork butt, ground	*6 ounces*	*180 grams*
Pork fat, ground	*6 ounces*	*180 grams*
Salt	*2 teaspoons*	*2 teaspoons*
Curing salt (T.C.M.)	*1/2 teaspoon*	*1/2 teaspoon*
Pepper, ground	*1/2 teaspoon*	*1/2 teaspoon*
Thyme, chopped	*1 teaspoon*	*1 teaspoon*
Oregano, chopped	*1/2 teaspoon*	*1/2 teaspoon*
Scallions, minced	*3 each*	*3 each*
Garnish		
Jalapeño Monterey Jack cheese, medium dice	*4 ounces*	*120 grams*
Chorizo or tasso, medium dice	*4 ounces*	*120 grams*
Sun-dried tomatoes, medium dice	*8 each*	*8 each*
Quail breasts, boned, brined, and smoke-roasted	*16 each*	*16 each*
Ham, sliced thin, for lining dough	*as needed*	*as needed*
Egg wash, as needed	*3 ounces*	*85 grams*
Aspic Gelée, as needed	*6 ounces*	*170 grams*

1. Prepare pâté dough as directed on page 996 with the addition of the coriander, cumin, tomato paste and cilantro.
2. Sweat garlic and shallots in oil, add tequila, reduce by three-quarters; cool.
3. Place the ground meats and pork, fat, salt, curing salt, herbs, and scallions in the bowl of a food processor; pulse until smooth.
4. Fold garnish into forcemeat, working over ice. Trim smoked quail breasts; add trim to forcemeat.
5. Line a prepared hinge mold with dough; line dough with sliced ham.
6. Evenly spread one-third of the forcemeat on the bottom of the mold; place 8 quail breasts on top, add one-third more forcemeat and the remaining 8 quail breasts.
7. Spread the remaining one-third of the forcemeat on top, fold the ham and dough over, and bake to an internal temperature of 165°F (75°C).
8. When the pâté has cooled to 110°F (43°C), fill it with Aspic Gelée.

Salmon Pâté en Croute

Yield: 1 pâté

Saffron pâté dough

Water	5 fluid ounces	150 milliliters
Saffron	large pinch	large pinch
Pâté dough	1 recipe	1 recipe
Dill, chopped	2 tablespoons	2 tablespoons
Chives, finely cut	2 tablespoons	2 tablespoons

Forcemeat

Shrimp, peeled, deveined, diced	12 ounces	360 grams
Salmon, diced	12 ounces	360 grams
Salt, to taste	2 teaspoons	2 teaspoons
Egg whites	2 each	2 each
Heavy cream	16 fluid ounces	480 milliliters
Old Bay Seafood Seasoning	1 tablespoon	1 tablespoon
Nutmeg, to taste	a few grains	a few grains
Tabasco, to taste	2 to 3 drops	2 to 3 drops
Chives, minced	2 tablespoons	2 tablespoons
Basil, chopped	1 tablespoon	1 tablespoon

Garnish

Shrimp, cut in thirds	5 ounces	140 grams
Crayfish tails, cleaned	6 ounces	170 grams
Gelatin (optional)	1/2 teaspoon	1/2 teaspoon
Egg albumen (optional)	1/2 teaspoon	1/2 teaspoon
Truffle, small dice	1 each	1 each
Salmon strips, 1-by-1-by-12 inches	6 ounces	170 grams

Brush the dough with egg wash after the dough has dried slightly to avoid "checkering."

When pâté cools to 110°F (43°C), fill with aspic, infused with cinnamon, basil, and mint.

Make a test quenelle from the forcemeat to check seasoning and consistency according to the technique described on pages 363 and 364.

Make an Aspic Gelée using salmon broth. See page 997.

1. For pâté dough: Bring water to a boil, add saffron, cover, and remove from heat. Steep for 10 minutes.

2. Replace 5 fluid ounces (150 milliliters) plain water from original recipe with saffron water. Add the herbs to the dough. Prepare as directed on page 996.

3. For forcemeat: Place diced shrimp, salmon, and salt in a food processor, pulse until smooth, add the egg whites, pulse until incorporated.

4. Add cream slowly, pulsing until incorporated.

5. Pass the forcemeat through a fine tamis into a bowl set over an ice bath; fold in Old Bay, nutmeg, Tabasco and herbs.

6. Toss the garnish (shrimp and crawfish tails) in gelatin and egg albumin; fold into the forcemeat along with the truffle.

7. Oil hinged pâté pan, line with dough, fill halfway with forcemeat.

8. Place a salmon strip down the center, cover with the remaining forcemeat, finish the pâté in the normal manner.

9. Bake at 325°F (165°C) until internal temperature of 140°F (60°C).

Turkey Pâté en Croute

Yield: 1 pâté

The recipe for Pâté Dough is on page 996.

The turkey leg, pork butt, and pork fat should be ground together working from a coarse grinding plate to a fine one, as described on page 357.

The recipe for Aspic Gelée is on page 997.

Sweet potato dough		
Pâté Dough	*1 recipe*	*1 recipe*
Sweet potato purée	*5 ounces*	*140 grams*
Cinnamon, ground	*1/2 teaspoon*	*1/2 teaspoon*
Cardamom, ground	*1/2 teaspoon*	*1/2 teaspoon*
Mace, ground	*1/2 teaspoon*	*1/2 teaspoon*
Shallots, minced	*1 ounce*	*30 grams*
Garlic, cloves, minced	*2 each*	*2 each*
Oil	*1 fluid ounce*	*30 milliliters*
Brandy	*3 fluid ounces*	*90 milliliters*
Turkey leg/thigh meat, cleaned, ground	*12 ounces*	*360 grams*
Pork butt, ground	*6 ounces*	*180 grams*
Pork fat, ground	*6 ounces*	*180 grams*
Salt, to taste	*2 teaspoons*	*2 teaspoons*
Curing salt (T.C.M.)	*1/2 teaspoon*	*1/2 teaspoon*
Juniper berries, crushed	*6 each*	*6 each*
Dijon mustard	*1 ounce*	*30 grams*
Dill, chopped	*2 tablespoons*	*2 tablespoons*
Sage, chopped	*2 tablespoons*	*2 tablespoons*
Nutmeg, ground, to taste	*1/2 teaspoon*	*1/2 teaspoon*
Pepper, to taste	*1/2 teaspoon*	*1/2 teaspoon*
Glace de Viande or Volaille, melted	*1 ounce*	*30 grams*
Garnish		
Apricots, dried	*2 ounces*	*60 grams*
Cherries, dried	*2 ounces*	*60 grams*
Currants, dried	*1 ounce*	*30 grams*
Triple Sec	*4 ounces*	*115 grams*
Turkey breast 1-inch-by-1-inch strip 8 to 10 inches long	*8 ounces*	*225 grams*
Ham, sliced, for lining dough	*4 ounces*	*115 grams*
Egg wash	*1 each*	*1 each*
Aspic Gelée, as needed	*6 ounces*	*170 grams*

1. For sweet potato dough: Substitute sweet potato purée for water in the dough recipe.

2. For forcemeat: Sweat shallots and garlic in oil, deglaze with brandy, cool.

3. Combine shallot mixture with ground meats, salts, herbs, mustard, pepper, and Glace de Viande; marinate 1 hour.

4. Place forcemeat ingredients in food processor; pulse until smooth. Make a test quenelle to check consistency and seasoning.

5. Fold all garnish into the forcemeat by hand over an ice bath except turkey strip.

6. Line a greased hinge mold with dough and sliced ham.

(Recipe continued on facing page)

7. Fill mold halfway, position turkey strip in center of forcemeat.

8. Cover turkey with remaining forcemeat, fold over ham and dough; finish as for pâté en croute (see pages 366 to 368). Brush the dough with egg wash and cut chimneys once dough is set.

9. Remove the pâté when the internal temperature reaches 165°F (73°C). Fill with Aspic Gelée once it cools.

Tuscany-Style Pâté en Croute

Yield: 1 pâté

Forcemeat

Pheasants	*2 each*	*2 each*
Pork butt, diced	*6 ounces*	*180 grams*
Pork fat, diced	*6 ounces*	*180 grams*
Salt, to taste	*1 teaspoon*	*1 teaspoon*
Garlic, cloves, minced	*3 each*	*3 each*
Shallots, minced	*1 ounce*	*30 grams*
Oil, as needed	*1 tablespoon*	*1 tablespoon*
Curing salt (T.C.M.)	*1/2 teaspoon*	*1/2 teaspoon*
Basil, chopped	*1 tablespoon*	*1 tablespoon*
Parsley, chopped	*1 tablespoon*	*1 tablespoon*
Oregano, chopped	*1 tablespoon*	*1 tablespoon*
Pepper, ground	*1 teaspoon*	*1 teaspoon*
Egg	*1 each*	*1 each*

Garnish

Sun-dried tomatoes, medium dice	*2 ounces*	*60 grams*
Pine nuts, toasted	*1 ounce*	*30 grams*
Fennel seeds	*1 tablespoon*	*1 tablespoon*
Jalapeño peppers, minced	*2 each*	*2 each*
Beef tongue, medium dice	*6 ounces*	*180 grams*
Pâté Dough, plain	*1 recipe*	*1 recipe*
Ham, sliced thin	*4 ounces*	*115 grams*
Egg wash, as needed	*3 fluid ounces*	*90 milliliters*

The recipe for Pâté Dough is on page 996.

For a different presentation, make the cap piece for the pâté from caramel-colored and plain dough as follows:

Roll caramel-colored and remaining plain pâté dough through a pasta machine until dough is approximately 1/8-inch (.25 centimeter) thick; cut 20 strips of each color 1/4-inch (.5 centimeter) wide by 18 inches (95 centimeters) long.

Weave the two colors of dough together. Roll lightly with a rolling pin cut out to the size of the mold, paint with egg wash; and finish pâté.

1. Debone pheasants. Cube leg meat (you should have about 20 ounces/570 grams); trim breasts and reserve separately.

2. Grind the leg meat, pork butt and pork fat together through a coarse, then medium die.

3. Combine with the ground pheasant, salts, herbs, pepper, and egg; pulse in a food processor until smooth.

4. Fold all garnish ingredients except pheasant breasts, into forcemeat by hand over an ice bath.

5. Line greased pâté en croute mold with plain pâté dough; line dough with sliced ham.

6. Fill mold halfway with forcemeat, arrange pheasant breasts in center, cover with remaining forcemeat.

7. Fold ham and dough over forcemeat.

8. Bake until done.

9. When the pâté has cooked to 110°F (43°C), fill it with Aspic Gelée.

Country Terrine

Yield: 1 terrine

Brandy	2 fluid ounces	60 milliliters
Bay leaves, crushed	6 each	6 each
Sage, chopped	1 tablespoon	1 tablespoon
Thyme, chopped	1 tablespoon	1 tablespoon
Savory, chopped	1 tablespoon	1 tablespoon
Salt, to taste	2 teaspoons	2 teaspoons
Pepper, to taste	1/2 teaspoon	1/2 teaspoon
Dijon mustard	1 ounce	30 grams
Garlic, cloves, minced, sweated	5 each	5 each
Chicken livers, cleaned and seared	3 ounces	90 grams
Sugar	1 tablespoon	1 tablespoon
Curing salt (T.C.M.)	1/2 teaspoon	1/2 teaspoon
Chicken meat, cubed	12 ounces	340 grams
Pork meat, lean, cubed	6 ounces	170 grams
Fatback, cubed	6 ounces	170 grams
White bread, crusts removed	2 ounces	60 grams
Milk	2 fluid ounces	60 milliliters
Egg	1 each	1 each
Tabasco, to taste	2 to 3 drops	2 to 3 drops
Ham, medium dice	6 ounces	170 grams
Pistachio nuts, whole, peeled	4 ounces	115 grams
Truffle, small dice	1 each	1 each
Sliced bacon	3/4 pound	340 grams

1. Combine the brandy and bay leaves. Bring to a boil and let steep until cool. Strain.

2. Add the strained brandy, the sage, thyme, savory, salt, pepper, Dijon mustard, the sweated garlic, seared chicken livers, sugar, and the curing salt to the cubed meat and fat.

3. Grind the meat through the large die of the grinder, reserve half of the ground mixture for the garnish. Grind the remainder through the medium die.

4. Soak the bread in the milk and then squeeze out the excess. Add the medium-ground meat and egg to the soaked white bread; purée in a food processor.

5. Combine all ingredients (except the bacon) by hand over an ice bath; make a test quenelle.

6. Line a terrine mold with plastic wrap, then with sliced bacon. Fill terrine, bake in a 160°F (70°C) water bath to an internal temperature of 150°F (65°C).

7. Let cool to 110°F (43°C) and press overnight with a 2-pound weight.

Keep all ingredients and equipment very cool throughout each stage of grinding and processing.

The procedure for making a test quenelle is explained on page 363.

Once a terrine is cooled and weighted overnight, you may wish to fill the mold with Aspic Gelée.

Country-Style Duck Terrine

Yield: 4 pounds (1.8 kilograms)

Duck breast, large dice	*1/2 pound*	*225 grams*
Salt, to taste	*4 1/2 teaspoons*	*4 1/2 teaspoons*
Pepper, to taste	*1 teaspoon*	*1 teaspoon*
Curing salt (T.C.M.)	*1/2 teaspoon*	*1/2 teaspoon*
Brandy	*3 fluid ounces*	*90 milliliters*
Onions, diced	*4 ounces*	*115 grams*
Garlic, cloves, chopped	*2 each*	*2 each*
Butter	*1 ounce*	*30 grams*
Tarragon, chopped	*4 teaspoons*	*4 teaspoons*
Basil, chopped	*4 teaspoons*	*4 teaspoons*
Fatback, cubed	*12 ounces*	*340 grams*
Pork, cubed	*8 ounces*	*225 grams*
Duck leg, cubed	*1 pound*	*450 grams*
Duck livers or foie gras	*8 ounces*	*225 grams*
Egg	*1 each*	*1 each*
Parsley, chopped	*2 ounces*	*60 grams*
Pistachios, chopped coarse	*4 ounces*	*115 grams*

1. Season the duck breast with 1/2 teaspoon of the salt, a pinch of pepper, and curing salt; marinate it in the brandy and reserve.

2. Sauté the onion and garlic in the butter until translucent. Cool the mixture.

3. Add the onion mixture to the tarragon, basil and fatback, then freeze the mixture until the fatback is very cold and slightly firmed.

4. Combine the fatback mixture with the pork, duck leg meat, livers, remaining salt, curing salt, and pepper. Grind the mixture, using a coarse, then medium die.

5. Combine one-third of the meat mixture with the egg in a food processor. Process to a smooth consistency.

6. Poach a test quenelle to check the seasoning and binding.

7. Fold the parsley, pistachios, and marinated duck breast meat into the mixture.

8. Pack into a terrine mold that has been coated with sliced fatback or lined with plastic wrap.

9. Place the terrine in a 170°F (75°C) bain-marie. Bake in a 250°F (121°C) oven to an internal temperature of 160°F (70°C).

VARIATIONS

Rabbit Terrine: Add 5 mashed and minced juniper berries to the herb mixture. Substitute rabbit leg for the duck. Substitute gin for the brandy. Substitute a rabbit loin and 1 tablespoon (7 grams) of butcher's pepper for the garnish of diced duck breast.

(Recipe continued on next page)

Artichoke Terrine: Double the herb mixture. Substitute chicken livers for the duck. Add an inlay of 10 cooked artichokes. Substitute artichokes in a 1/2-inch (1-centimeter) dice for the duck-breast garnish.

Venison Terrine: Add 5 mashed and minced juniper berries and the blanched zest of 2 oranges to the herb mixture. Substitute venison trim for the duck leg. Substitute chestnuts for pistachios. Substitute venison loin for duck-breast garnish. Add 8 ounces (225 grams) of chopped dried fruits.

Roasted Eggplant and Pepper Terrine

Yield: 1 terrine

The recipe for a Basic Vinaigrette may be found on page 906; Vegetable Stock is on page 445.

To dissolve gelatin, first mix it with cold water and allow the gelatin to soften. Then dissolve it, either over a warm water bath or in a microwave on the lowest power setting.

If you wish, incorporate other cooked vegetables, such as sliced artichoke bottoms, blanched green beans, okra, or baby corn to add color, texture, and flavor to this dish.

Serve with a small salad of mixed wild greens tossed with a Roasted Garlic Vinaigrette.

Eggplant	*3 pounds*	*1.3 kilograms*
Vinaigrette	*6 fluid ounces*	*180 milliliters*
Red peppers, roasted, peeled, and seeded	*2 pounds*	*900 grams*
Gelatin, powdered	*2 ounces*	*60 grams*
Tomato juice or Vegetable Stock	*1 quart*	*1 liter*
Salt, to taste	*2 teaspoons*	*2 teaspoons*
Pepper, to taste	*1 teaspoon*	*1 teaspoon*
Oregano, chopped	*1 teaspoon*	*1 teaspoon*
Thyme, chopped	*1 teaspoon*	*1 teaspoon*
Basil, chopped	*1 teaspoon*	*1 teaspoon*

1. Cut the eggplant into sheets, using a mandolin. Marinate in the vinaigrette for 30 minutes. Remove from the vinaigrette, grill on both sides until tender, and let cool.

2. Line a terrine mold with plastic wrap.

3. Select the most attractive slices of eggplant to layer the terrine, overlapping the slices as necessary to fully line the mold.

4. Lay in alternating layers of eggplant and red pepper.

5. Blend the dissolved gelatin with the tomato juice or vegetable broth. Season generously with salt, pepper, and fresh herbs. Pour this over the terrine.

6. Place the covered terrine in a waterbath and bake in a 325°F (165°C) oven to an internal temperature of 140°F (60°C). The temperature of the waterbath should remain below 160°F (70°C) throughout cooking time.

7. Remove the terrine and allow it to cool. Cover the terrine with a press plate and chill overnight.

Potato, Trout, and Leek Terrine

Yield: 1 terrine

Yellow potatoes, large	*2 pounds*	*900 grams*
Horse carrots, peeled	*1 pound*	*450 grams*
Leeks, cleaned	*1 bunch*	*1 bunch*
Gelatin	*2 ounces*	*60 grams*
Chicken consommé	*1 quart*	*1 liter*
Kosher salt, to taste	*1 tablespoon*	*1 tablespoon*
Sherry	*1/3 cup*	*80 milliliters*
Basil, sprigs, bruised	*2 each*	*2 each*
Marjoram, sprigs, bruised	*2 each*	*2 each*
Trout, fillets, skinned	*4 each*	*4 each*
White pepper, to taste	*1/2 teaspoon*	*1/2 teaspoon*

Yukon Gold or Yellow Finn potatoes work well in this recipe. They are able to hold their shape during cooking and slicing.

1. Peel the potatoes, slice 1/4-inch (.5 centimeter) thick and cook until tender in salted water. Remove from the water and lay out on lined sheet pans to air-dry under refrigeration.

2. Peel carrots, slice 1/8-inch (.25-centimeter) thick, lengthwise; blanch in salted water. Shock; drain on paper towels.

3. Remove 3 inches (8 centimeters) from the top of the leeks and remove the root end. Rinse well. Split in half and blanch in boiling water about 30 seconds. Shock and press out excess moisture. Drain on paper towels.

4. Line a terrine mold with plastic wrap.

5. Bloom the gelatin in the consommé, and heat until the gelatin is dissolved (110 to 140°F/43 to 60°C). Season the aspic with salt; add the dry sherry and herbs.

6. Lightly flatten the trout fillets. Season with salt and ground white pepper.

7. Line the mold with a layer of leeks, potatoes, and then carrots.

8. Place one trout fillet on the vegetables. Use fillet trimmings to make one even layer.

9. Pour in enough aspic to cover the trout fillet. Repeat two times; finish with vegetables.

10. Cover and place the terrine in a 140°F (60°C) water bath. Bake until an internal temperature of 135°F (58°C).

11. Let cool to 110°F (43°C) and press overnight with a weight.

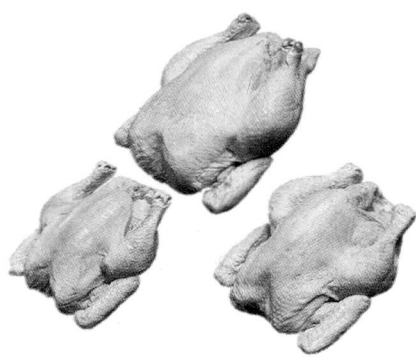

Once the chicken is boned, keep the skin intact.

Pâté Spice is on page 997; Chicken Stock is on page 442.

The method for preparing a Galatine is explained on pages 370 and 371. The photographs in Figure 11-18 show how to roll and wrap a galatine.

Chicken Galantine

Yield: 5 1/2 pounds (3 kilograms)

Panada		
Eggs	*2 each*	*2 each*
Brandy	*3 tablespoons*	*45 milliliters*
Pâté Spice	*1 teaspoon*	*1 teaspoon*
Flour	*3 ounces*	*85 grams*
Salt, to taste	*1 tablespoon*	*1 tablespoon*
White pepper, to taste	*1/2 teaspoon*	*1/2 teaspoon*
Heavy cream	*8 fluid ounces*	*240 milliliters*
Chicken, boned, wing tips removed,		
skin removed intact, 3 pounds	*1 each*	*1 each*
Pork butt, 1-inch cubes, chilled,		
as needed	*2 pounds*	*900 grams*
Madeira	*6 fluid ounces*	*180 milliliters*
Ham, or cooked tongue,		
1/4-inch cubes	*4 ounces*	*120 grams*
Black truffles, chopped fine	*2 tablespoons*	*2 tablespoons*
Pistachios, blanched, peeled, and		
chopped coarse	*4 ounces*	*120 grams*
Chicken Stock	*as needed*	*as needed*

1. Prepare the panada: Mix the eggs with brandy, spice, flour, salt, and pepper.

2. Bring the heavy cream to a boil. Remove it from the heat.

3. Temper the egg mixture with the hot cream. Return the tempered egg mixture to the heat and cook it until it is thickened. Chill thoroughly.

4. Weigh the leg and thigh meat from the chicken. Add an equal amount of pork butt, or enough for approximately 4 pounds (2.15 kilograms) of meat. Grind the chicken leg and thigh meat and pork twice, using a coarse then a fine die. Chill.

5. Cut the chicken breast meat into 1/2- to 3/4-inch (1 centimeter) cubes. Season it to taste. Marinate the meat in the Madeira under refrigeration.

6. Drain the chicken breast; add the Madeira and panada to the ground meat mixture. Blend well.

7. Fold the ham, truffles, and pistachios into the forcemeat by hand, working over an ice bath. Mix well.

8. Gently fold in the reserved chicken breast over ice.

9. Roll the galantine securely in the reserved skin and cheesecloth.

10. Poach the galantine, in enough simmering stock to cover it, to an internal temperature of 160°F (70°C).

11. Cool the galantine in the stock in a hotel pan. Refrigerate it overnight. Remove the galantine from the stock and wrap it in new cheesecloth to firm its texture. Chill overnight. To serve the galantine, unwrap and slice it.

Roulade of Foie Gras

Yield: 2 pounds (900 grams)

Livers (A or B grade)	*1 3/4 pounds*	*800 grams*
Salt	*1 tablespoon*	*1 tablespoon*
Sugar	*1 teaspoon*	*1 teaspoon*
White pepper, ground	*1 teaspoon*	*1 teaspoon*
Ruby port	*2 fluid ounces*	*60 milliliters*
Armagnac	*2 fluid ounces*	*60 milliliters*

1. Soak the livers in cold water for 1 hour.

2. Add warm water to soften the livers.

3. Separate the lobes and carefully split them, removing all the veins.

4. Place the livers in a bowl and add the salt, sugar, pepper, port and Armagnac. Marinate for 12 hours under refrigeration. Turn after 6 hours.

5. Bring the livers to room temperature; pour off the marinade.

6. Roll the livers in plastic wrap into a 2-inch (5 centimeter)–diameter galantine. Roll the galantine in cheesecloth if desired and tie it.

7. Bring a pot of water to160°F (70°C). Add the galantine.

8. Poach the galantine for 20 minutes.

9. Place the entire poaching pan in an ice bath and cool.

10. Let the galantine rest, refrigerated, for 24 hours before slicing.

Chicken Roulade

Yield: 1 roulade (25 servings)

Chicken breasts	25 ounces	700 grams
Gelatin (powdered)	1 1/2 teaspoons	1 1/2 teaspoons
Forcemeat		
Chicken, ground	9 ounces	255 grams
Egg whites	2 each	2 each
Heavy cream	3 1/2 fluid ounces	100 milliliters
Shallots, minced	1 teaspoon	1 teaspoon
Garlic, minced	1/2 teaspoon	1/2 teaspoon
Thyme, chopped	1/2 teaspoon	1/2 teaspoon
Basil, chopped	1/2 teaspoon	1/2 teaspoon
Chervil, chopped	1/2 teaspoon	1/2 teaspoon
Garnish for forcemeat		
Red peppers, roasted, small-dice	4 ounces	115 grams
Yellow peppers, roasted, small-dice	4 ounces	115 grams
Green peppers, roasted, small-dice	4 ounces	115 grams

1. Flatten chicken breasts with a meat mallet; sprinkle with gelatin and keep chilled.

2. To make the forcemeat: Purée the ground chicken in a food processor, add egg whites; mix in.

3. Slowly add cream; pulse in.

4. Add shallots, garlic, thyme, basil, and chervil; mix in.

5. Fold the garnish into the forcemeat by hand over an ice bath.

6. Spread forcemeat on top of chicken breasts, roll up in jelly-roll fashion, wrap in plastic wrap.

7. Poach in a 165°F (74°C) water bath to an internal temperature of 140°F (60°C); chill.

8. Slice the roulade into 1 1/2-ounce (45-gram) slices.

SAUSAGES, PÂTÉS, AND TERRINES

1018

Terrine of Foie Gras

Yield: 1 terrine

Foie gras, grade "A"	*2 pounds*	*900 grams*
Salt	*1 ounce*	*30 grams*
White pepper, ground	*1 teaspoon*	*1 teaspoon*
Sauterne or Armagnac	*1 1/2 fluid ounces*	*45 milliliters*

1. Drain the livers on absorbent toweling and pat dry.

2. Combine the liver with the salt, pepper, and Sauterne or Armagnac. Toss gently to coat evenly.

3. Let the livers marinate in the refrigerator overnight.

4. Remove the foie gras from the refrigerator and return to room temperature for 1 hour.

5. Preheat the oven to 250°F (120°C).

6. Line a heat proof mold (ceramic, enameled cast iron, earthenware, etc.) with plastic wrap. Leave enough excess wrap to fold over the top of the terrine.

7. Fit a large foie gras lobe into the terrine, smooth side down, and flatten well to eliminate any air pockets. Fill in the mold with the remaining smaller pieces, pressing out the air pockets. Top the terrine with another large lobe, smooth side up.

8. Fold the plastic wrap over the foie gras and secure. If the mold has a tight-fitting lid, it should be put in place.

9. Place the mold in a hot water bath (set it on a folded towel to stabilize the terrine mold) and keep the temperature of the water at 160 to 165°F (70 to 73°C) for about 1 hour, or to an internal temperature of 130°F (55°C).

10. Transfer the terrine to a cold water bath and let it cool there for 10 minutes. Remove the terrine.

11. Cover the terrine with a press plate or a piece of cardboard cut to fit. Pour off most of the fat, and reserve it for other use. Lightly weight the lid and refrigerate the terrine for 2 to 3 days.

12. Unmold the lid, and rewrap the terrine in fresh plastic wrap and aluminum foil. Allow the flavor to develop under refrigeration for another 2 days before slicing and serving.

A traditional presentation of this dish in Gascony would be to place the porcelain terrine on the table. A bowl of hot water and a serving spoon would be provided so that the guests could scoop out portions of the foie gras themselves. A basket of sliced and grilled bread is available as well.

A more formal presentation would be to slice the foie gras and serve it on a plate surrounded with toasted brioche and a small salad dressed with a Walnut Oil Vinaigrette.

Use two spoons to shape mousseline forcemeat into quenelles.

Prepare the mousseline on page 996, substituting a lean white fish such as flounder or halibut for the chicken.

Beurre Manié is a mixture of equal parts of softened butter and flour mixed together. It is used to thicken liquids.

Fish Quenelles on a Bed of Spinach

Yield: 10 servings

Butter	*1 ounce*	*30 grams*
Mousseline Forcemeat	*1 1/4 pounds*	*570 grams*
Shallots, minced	*2 each*	*2 each*
Fish Stock	*12 fluid ounces*	*360 milliliters*
White wine	*8 fluid ounces*	*240 milliliters*
Beurre Manié	*2 ounces*	*60 grams*
Heavy cream	*4 fluid ounces*	*120 milliliters*
Spinach, reduced and cooked	*12 ounces*	*340 grams*
Parmesan cheese, grated	*2 ounces*	*60 grams*

1. Butter a shallow pan, sprinkle with shallots.

2. Shape Mousseline Forcemeat into quenelles with two spoons; arrange close together in the pan.

3. Add stock and wine, bring to a simmer; poach quenelles on top of the stove.

4. When quenelles are done, remove, place on a bed of cooked spinach, cover and keep warm.

5. Reduce poaching liquid by half and thicken with Beurre Manié.

6. Add heavy cream, return to a simmer and season.

7. Pour sauce over quenelles, sprinkle with Parmesan cheese, gratiné under the broiler.

Cold Beef Daube

Yield: 18 to 20 servings

Oxtail, cut into 4 pieces	*1 each*	*1 each*
Beef tongue	*1 each*	*1 each*
Pig's head, or short ribs, 5 pounds	*1/2 each*	*1/2 each*
Beef Stock	*2 gallons*	*7.5 liters*
Standard Sachet d'Épices	*1 each*	*1 each*
Leeks, tops	*1 pound*	*450 grams*
Mirepoix	*1 pound*	*450 grams*
Juniper berries, cracked	*10 each*	*10 each*
Garlic heads	*4 each*	*4 each*
Bay leaves	*3 each*	*3 each*
Thyme, sprigs	*4 each*	*4 each*
Mushroom stems	*6 ounces*	*170 grams*
Whole black peppercorns	*12 each*	*12 each*
Parsley stems	*16 each*	*16 each*
Parsley, chopped	*2 ounces*	*60 grams*
Shallots, chopped	*2 ounces*	*60 grams*
Chives, chopped	*2 ounces*	*60 grams*

1. Combine all of the ingredients; simmer them for 2 hours. Remove the tongue and continue to simmer for 2 more hours.

2. Remove all of the meats and reserve them.

3. Strain the stock to 1/2 gallon (2 liters) and return it to the heat. Reduce it. Adjust the seasonings to taste; strain the stock.

4. Julienne the tongue. Dice the meat from the oxtail and pig's head.

5. Return all the meat to the stock. Bring the liquid to a boil.

6. Pour the daube into mold lined with plastic wrap.

7. Refrigerate for 24 hours before slicing the daube.

Duck Rillettes

Yield: 5 pounds (2.25 kilograms)

Serve the rillettes with toasted bread or crackers as a canapé, or use this mixture to fill profiteroles.

Rillettes can be stored under refrigeration for several weeks as long as the fat seal is sufficient to prevent air from coming in contact with the meat.

Duck leg meat, boned, and diced	5 pound	2.25 kilograms
Chicken Stock	3 quarts	3 liters
Mirepoix, large dice	1 pound	450 grams
Standard Sachet d'Épices, plus	1 each	1 each
Peppercorns	12 each	12 each
Bay leaves	3 each	3 each
Garlic cloves, bruised	4 each	4 each
Cloves, whole	4 each	4 each
Duck fat, as needed	1 pound	450 grams

1. Place the duck meat, stock, Mirepoix and sachet in a pot.

2. Bring to a simmer over low heat and cook slowly until the meat is extremely tender, about 2 to 2 1/2 hours.

3. Strain out the duck meat and transfer to a mixing bowl. Let the meat cool slightly.

4. Remove and discard the sachet, carrot, and celery from the stock. Reserve both the stock and the fat on the stock.

5. Mix the duck meat with the paddle attachment until the meat breaks up into pieces. Add enough of the reserved stock and fat from the stock to produce a spreadable consistency.

6. Pack this mixture into crocks or timbales. Pour enough melted duck fat over the duck to coat and seal. Cover and refrigerate until ready to serve or to use in other preparations.

VARIATIONS

Pork Rillettes: Substitute 5 pounds of fatty pork cut into cubes to replace the duck.

Smoked Chicken Rillettes: Substitute 3 pounds (1.35 kilograms) of cured, cold-smoked chicken leg meat and 2 pounds (900 grams) of pork butt for the duck.

Trout Savarin

Yield: about 12 to 14 servings

Forcemeat

Butter	*1 tablespoon*	*1 tablespoon*
Shallots, minced	*1 ounce*	*30 grams*
Vermouth	*4 fluid ounces*	*120 milliliters*
Trout, fillets, flattened slightly	*4 each*	*4 each*
Shrimp, peeled, deveined	*6 ounces*	*170 grams*
Salt, to taste	*2 teaspoons*	*2 teaspoons*
Egg whites	*2 each*	*2 each*
Heavy cream	*8 ounces*	*225 grams*
Nutmeg, to taste	*a few grains*	*a few grains*
Tabasco, to taste	*2 to 3 drops*	*2 to 3 drops*

Garnish

Shrimp, diced	*5 ounces*	*140 grams*
Gelatin (optional)	*as needed*	*as needed*
Egg albumen (optional)	*as needed*	*as needed*
Chives, minced	*1 tablespoon*	*1 teaspoon*
Dill, chopped	*1 tablespoon*	*1 tablespoon*
Tarragon	*2 teaspoons*	*2 teaspoons*
Nori seaweed	*1 sheet*	*1 sheet*

Use plastic wrap to line the mold and to cover before baking.

1. To make the forcemeat, sweat shallots in butter; add vermouth; reduce by three-quarters; cool.

2. Combine 6 ounces (170 grams) of trout, shrimp, vermouth reduction, and salt in a food processor and pulse until smooth.

3. Add egg whites, pulse in, add the cream slowly, pulsing to incorporate. Stir in seasonings by hand.

4. Pass forcemeat through a fine tamis.

5. Toss diced shrimp with a little gelatin and egg albumen; fold into forcemeat.

6. Fold herbs into forcemeat. Make a test quenelle to check the seasoning and consistency.

7. Line a tunnel mold with plastic wrap.

8. Lay the trout fillets in the mold, skin side in, and top trout with Nori seaweed; fill with forcemeat.

9. Cover top with plastic wrap, bake in a 160°F (70°C) water bath to an internal temperature of 140°F (60°C).

10. Cool to 90°F (32°C), and press overnight with a (2-pound) weight.

11. Unmold terrine and slice as desired.

CHAPTER 28 *Breads*

Filling your bread basket with an array of muffins, rolls, and breads is a good way to make your restaurant different from your competitors. The selection in this chapter includes such favorites as blueberry and corn muffins, Irish soda bread, popovers, and zucchini bread. These "quick" breads are prepared with chemical leaveners.

There is also an appealing array of yeast-raised breads. You will find a dill-flavored bread, one studded with sunflower seeds, and a peasant-style loaf with pecans. Bagels, challah, and cinnamon buns are also included here.

Basic Muffins

Yield: 6 dozen

Sugar	*1 pound, 5 ounces*	*600 grams*
Butter	*12 ounces*	*340 grams*
Shortening (emulsified)	*5 ounces*	*140 grams*
Salt	*3/4 ounce*	*25 grams*
Eggs	*1 pound, 2 ounces*	*500 grams*
Bread flour	*2 1/2 pounds*	*1.15 kilograms*
Baking powder	*2 ounces*	*60 grams*
Milk	*2 pounds*	*900 grams*

1. Cream together the sugar, butter, shortening, and salt for 2 minutes.

2. Gradually add the eggs, scraping sides of bowl occasionally and, when incorporated, mix on speed 2 (if using a 3-speed mixer) for 2 minutes. (You will need to increase mixing speed if using a 4-speed mixer.)

3. Add the remaining ingredients on low speed for 1 minute, scrape bowl, and then mix on speed 2 for 2 more minutes.

4. Scale 2 ounces (60 grams) of batter for each 1 dozen muffins if using a regular-size cupcake pan or 3 ounces (85 grams) for a muffin pan.

5. Bake at 425°F (220°C) for 11 to 13 minutes if using a cupcake pan and 16 to 18 minutes if using a muffin pan or until golden brown on top and firm to the touch.

The batter can be made up and stored in a tightly sealed container for up to 48 hours. Batters with acidic ingredients cannot be prepared in advance. You can scale into muffin pans and freeze. If you do bake off directly from the freezer, adjust baking time by 10 minutes. Some chefs recommend thawing them first.

Raisins and nuts or seeds may be added for variety.

Blueberry Muffins

Yield: 4 dozen

Confectioners' sugar	*1 pound*	*450 grams*
Shortening	*8 ounces*	*225 grams*
Butter	*8 ounces*	*225 grams*
Salt	*1/2 ounce*	*15 grams*
Eggs	*1 pound*	*450 grams*
Milk	*1 pound*	*450 grams*
Bran	*8 ounces*	*225 grams*
Baking powder	*1 ounce*	*30 grams*
Cake flour	*1 3/4 pounds*	*800 grams*
Blueberries	*1 pound, 6 ounces*	*625 grams*

(Recipe continued on facing page)

1. Cream together the sugar, shortening, butter, and salt.

2. Gradually add the eggs, scraping sides of bowl occasionally.

3. Gradually add some of the milk.

4. Sift together the flour and the baking powder (two times), mixing in until smooth. Alternate dry ingredients with milk.

5. Gently fold in the blueberries.

6. Scale 1 pound, 14 ounces (850 grams) of batter for each 1 dozen muffins and divide evenly into prepared muffin cups.

7. Bake at 425°F (220°C) for 20 minutes or until light brown on top.

Baking muffins and biscuits at a higher temperature will give a quicker, higher rise, without drying out the product.

This recipe may be used to make any type of fruit or nut muffin by substituting the desired ingredients for the blueberries.

Corn Muffins

Yield: 3 dozen

Sugar	1 pound	450 grams
Shortening	8 ounces	225 grams
Salt	1/2 ounce	15 grams
Eggs	8 ounces	225 grams
Milk	1 1/2 pounds	680 grams
Cornmeal	1 pound	450 grams
Pastry flour	1 1/2 pounds	680 grams
Baking powder	1 1/2 ounces	40 grams

For a savory muffin, add cheddar cheese, diced jalapeño or New Mexico green chilies and/or whole corn kernels. Reduce the sugar by 20 to 30% if desired.

1. Cream together the sugar, shortening, and salt.

2. Gradually add the eggs, scraping sides of bowl occasionally.

3. Gradually add the milk and then the cornmeal, mixing until incorporated.

4. Sift together the flour and the baking powder (two times) and add to the mixture, mixing in until smooth.

5. Scale 2 pounds (900 grams) of batter for each 1 dozen muffins and divide evenly into prepared muffin cups.

6. Bake at 425°F (220°C) for 20 minutes or until light brown on top.

VARIATION

Cornbread: Prepare batter as directed above, and scale into small loaf pans (for individual loaves) or small cast iron skillets or pans.

Bran Muffins

Yield: 4 dozen

Add approximately one pound of nuts, or chopped fresh or dry fruit.

Sugar	1 pound	450 grams
Shortening	8 ounces	225 grams
Salt	1/2 ounce	15 grams
Eggs	1 pound	450 grams
Milk	1 pound	450 grams
Bran	8 ounces	225 grams
Bread flour	1 1/2 pounds	680 grams
Baking powder	1 1/2 ounces	40 grams
Honey	4 ounces	115 grams
Molasses	4 ounces	115 grams

1. Cream together the sugar, shortening, and salt.

2. Gradually add the eggs, scraping sides of bowl occasionally.

3. Gradually add the milk and then the bran, mixing until incorporated.

4. Sift together the flour and the baking powder (two times) and add to the mixture, mixing in until smooth.

5. Add in the honey and molasses.

6. Scale 2 pounds (900 grams) of batter for each 1 dozen muffins and divide evenly into prepared muffin cups.

7. Bake at 400°F (205°C) for 20 minutes or until light brown on top.

Date Nut Bread

Yield: 10 loaves (1 pound, 14 ounces/850 grams each)

Dates	4 1/2 pounds	2 kilograms
Nuts	1 pound	450 grams
Water	2 1/4 quarts	2.25 liters
Baking soda	1 3/4 ounces	50 grams
Brown sugar	2 1/2 pounds	1.15 kilograms
Shortening	1 pound, 2 ounces	500 grams
Salt	1 ounce	30 grams
Eggs	1 pound, 2 ounces	500 grams
Pastry flour	5 pounds	2.25 kilograms
Baking powder	2 ounces	60 grams

(Recipe continued on facing page)

1. Soak dates and nuts in water overnight.

2. Combine baking soda, brown sugar, shortening, and salt; cream together for 10 minutes.

3. Add eggs slowly, scraping bowl down often.

4. Mix the flour and baking powder together and add to batter until combined.

5. Add soaked dates and nuts, and water; mix only until blended.

6. Scale 1 pound, 14 ounces (850 grams) into prepared loaf pans; bake in a 350°F (175°C) oven for 45 to 60 minutes or until done on top.

Pumpkin Bread

Yield: 10 loaves (1 pound, 14 ounces/850 grams)

Raisins	*2 pounds, 4 ounces*	*1 kilogram*
Water	*1 3/4 pounds*	*800 grams*
Pumpkin, cooked	*3 pounds, 5 ounces*	*1.5 kilograms*
Sugar	*4 1/2 pounds*	*2 kilograms*
Eggs	*1 1/2 pounds*	*680 grams*
Baking soda	*3/4 ounce*	*40 grams*
Salt	*1 ounce*	*30 grams*
Cloves, ground	*1/4 ounce*	*7 grams*
Nutmeg, ground	*1/4 ounce*	*7 grams*
Cinnamon, ground	*1/4 ounce*	*7 grams*
Oil	*1 1/2 pounds*	*680 grams*
Bread flour	*3 pounds*	*1.3 kilograms*
Pastry flour	*8 ounces*	*225 grams*
Baking powder	*1 1/4 ounces*	*40 grams*

Use canned pumpkin or cool fresh pumpkin by cutting in quarters, removing seeds and pulp, then steaming (or parboiling, then baking). Remove the flesh and purée.

Toasted reserved pumpkin seeds or nuts may be added to the batter.

1. Soak raisins in water overnight.

2. Combine pumpkin, sugar, eggs, baking soda, salt, and spices; mix together, using a paddle, for 8 minutes.

3. Gradually add oil, scraping bowl often.

4. Add flours and baking powder, mix to incorporate, then add raisins and water.

5. Scale 1 pound, 14 ounces (850 grams) into prepared loaf pans.

6. Bake in a 350°F (175°C) oven for 45 minutes to 1 hour, until bread is firm to the touch and has no beads of moisture.

Fresh zucchini makes a delicious bread. In preparation, remove all seeds and grate.

Muffins may also be made from this batter.

Zucchini Bread

Yield: 9 loaves (1 pound, 14 ounces/850 grams)

Zucchini, large	*5 pounds*	*2.25 kilograms*
Sugar	*4 1/2 pounds*	*2 kilograms*
Eggs	*1 1/2 pounds*	*680 grams*
Baking powder	*1 1/4 ounces*	*38 grams*
Baking soda	*3/4 ounce*	*115 grams*
Salt	*1 ounce*	*30 grams*
Cloves, ground	*1/4 ounce*	*115 grams*
Cinnamon, ground	*1/4 ounce*	*8 grams*
Oil	*1 1/2 pounds*	*680 grams*
Bread flour	*3 pounds*	*1.3 kilograms*
Pastry flour	*8 ounces*	*225 grams*
Pecans	*1 pound*	*455 grams*

1. Trim zucchini, split, remove seeds, and grate.

2. Combine all ingredients and zucchini and mix with a whip for 5 minutes on high speed, scraping bowl often.

3. Scale 1 pound, 14 ounces (400 grams) into prepared loaf pans.

4. Bake in a 350°F (175°C) oven for 45 minutes to 1 hour.

Banana Nut Bread

Yield: 13 loaves (1 pound, 12 ounces/800 grams)

Cake flour	*3 pounds*	*1.3 kilograms*
Shortening (emulsified)	*2 1/2 pounds*	*1.15 kilograms*
Orange zest	*1/2 ounce*	*15 grams*
Sugar	*5 pounds*	*2.25 kilograms*
Cake flour	*2 pounds*	*900 grams*
Salt	*2 1/2 ounces*	*70 grams*
Baking powder	*3 1/4 ounces*	*95 grams*
Bananas, ripe	*5 pounds*	*2.25 kilograms*
Honey	*1 1/4 pounds*	*570 grams*
Eggs	*3 pounds*	*1.3 kilograms*
Pecans or walnuts, chopped	*1 pound*	*450 grams*
Vanilla	*1 1/2 ounces*	*40 grams*

(Recipe continued on facing page)

1. Combine cake flour, shortening, and orange zest, in 20-quart bowl with paddle; mix on second speed for 2 minutes, then add sugar.

2. Sift together the remaining flour, salt, and baking powder; add to bowl along with the bananas and honey, mix on first speed for 3 minutes; scraping bowl often.

3. Gradually add eggs on first speed and when all the eggs have been incorporated, mix for 5 minutes on second speed.

4. Add nuts and vanilla.

5. Scale 1 pound, 12 ounces (340 grams) of batter into prepared loaf pans and bake at 350°F (175°C) for 45 to 60 minutes or until done.

Irish Soda Bread

Yield: 10 servings (1 pound/450 grams)

Cake flour	5 pounds	2.25 kilograms
Baking powder	5 ounces	140 grams
Sugar	12 ounces	340 grams
Salt	1/2 ounce	15 grams
Shortening	11 ounces	315 grams
Raisins	8 ounces	225 grams
Caraway seeds (optional)	1 1/4 ounces	35 grams
Milk	2 3/4 pints	1.3 liters

1. Sift dry ingredients.

2. Work in shortening gently.

3. Add raisins and caraway (if desired).

4. With paddle on low speed, blend in milk to make a shaggy mass.

5. Knead 20 seconds on a floured surface.

6. Divide into 1 pound (450 grams) round loaves. Put on sheet pan.

7. Dust top with flour; with dough knife, press a cross into top of loaf. Do not cut completely through.

8. Bake at 400 to 425°F (205 to 220°C) for 30 minutes, until browned and cooked through.

To read about the straight dough mixing method, see pages 386 to 387.

If desired, make 4 dozen large (4 ounce/115 gram) biscuits, or about 10 dozen 1 1/2 ounce (40 gram) mini biscuits.

For **Flaky Biscuits,** sift the dry ingredients, working fat by hand as with a pie dough, blend in eggs and buttermilk just until blended. Bake at 450°F (225°C) for about 15 minutes.

Biscuits

Yield: 5 dozen (3 ounces/85 gram)

Bread flour	*3 pounds*	*1.3 kilograms*
Pastry flour	*3 pounds*	*1.3 kilograms*
Salt	*1 1/2 ounces*	*40 grams*
Baking powder	*8 ounces*	*225 grams*
Sugar	*12 ounces*	*340 grams*
Butter	*1 pound*	*450 grams*
Whole eggs	*8 each*	*8 each*

(place eggs in a 2-quart measure, add enough buttermilk to fill to top)

Buttermilk	*as needed*	*as needed*

1. Use straight dough-mixing method for 4 minutes; use speed two.
2. Roll dough to 1/2-inch thickness; let relax. Cut with round cutter.
3. Place biscuits on a sheet pan.
4. Brush with egg wash and bake at 425°F (220°C) for 20 to 22 minutes or until golden brown.

VARIATION

Scones: Add 1 1/2 pounds (680 grams) of plumped currants to above recipe.

Popovers

Yield: 2 dozen

Butter, as needed	*8 ounces*	*225 grams*
Eggs	*6 each*	*6 each*
Milk	*1 pint*	*480 milliliters*
Butter, melted	*3 ounces*	*90 milliliters*
All-purpose flour, sifted	*8 ounces*	*225 grams*
Salt	*1 teaspoon*	*1 teaspoon*

1. Generously butter 4 ounce (115 gram) ramekins. Place on a sheet pan. Place the pan in a preheated 425°F (220°C) oven.
2. Whisk together the eggs, milk, and melted butter. Beat them until the mixture is frothy.
3. Combine the flour and salt in a separate bowl. Beat in the liquid gradually. Continue to beat the mixture until it is smooth and well blended.
4. Spoon the batter into prepared ramekins. They should be about three-quarters full. Place on a sheet pan. Return to oven; reduce the heat to 375°F (190°C) and bake the popovers, undisturbed, for 50 minutes.
5. Remove the popovers from the oven. For moister popovers, remove them from the ramekins and serve immediately. For crisp popovers, slit the side of each popover to allow the steam to escape, then return them to the oven until the tops are firm, crisp and brown, about 10 minutes.

Pain de Campagne

Yield: approximately 3 pounds (1.3 kilograms) dough

Cornmeal	*as needed*	*as needed*
Water	*18 fluid ounces*	*500 milliliters*
Compressed yeast	*1/2 ounce*	*15 grams*
Extra virgin olive oil	*2 fluid ounces*	*60 milliliters*
Hard wheat flour (10 to 11% protein)	*1 3/4 pounds*	*850 grams*
Salt	*1/2 ounce*	*15 grams*

1. Line baking sheets with parchment. Scatter with cornmeal.
2. Combine the water, yeast, and oil until dissoved.
3. Add the flour and salt. Mix the dough until smooth and elastic.
4. Cover the bowl and allow the dough to ferment for 75 minutes.
5. Punch down and scale as desired. Round off dough.
6. Set dough on prepared sheet pan and proof for 1 hour.
7. Press the dough down to flatten; shape as desired.
8. Panproof an additional 30 minutes.
9. Bake in at 425°F (220°C) for approximately 30 minutes.

VARIATIONS

Hard Rolls: Use dough press to scale dough, or cut 1 1/2 ounces (45 grams) pcr hard roll. Round off and do an initial panproofing of 1 hour. Flatten each ball of dough into a rectangle and roll up to shape into hard roll, pressing seams closed. Panproof for 1 hour after shaping. Score, panproof another 30 minutes, and bake at 450°F (230°C) for 20 minutes.

Baguettes: Scale dough at 14 ounces (400 grams) per baguette. After initial panproof, flatten and stretch dough into a long rectangle. Roll into a baguette, pressing seams closed. Panproof for 1 hour after shaping. Score baguettes in several places with a diagonal slash. Panproof another 30 minutes, and bake at 450°F (230°C) for 30 minutes.

Pizza Dough: Scale at 10 ounces (285 grams) per pizza. Flatten after initial panproof, stretching and shaping into a disc. Panproof another 30 minutes before adding toppings. Bake at 450°F (230°C) for 25 to 30 minutes in a pizza oven or directly on the hearth. (For appetizer or individual pizzas, scale dough at 6 ounces/170 grams per pizza.)

Foccacia: Scale the dough at 10 ounces (285 grams) per foccacia. Brush with additional oil and top as desired with one or more of the following: chopped onions, chopped olives, rosemary or other herbs. To shape foccacia, press balls of dough flat, and stretch slightly. Baking time is approximately 30 minutes at 450°F (230°C).

Ciabatta: Increase the water to 22 fluid ounces (660 milliliters). Omit the olive oil. Shape the dough into rectangles rather than rounds. Panproof time for step 6 is increased to 90 minutes. Bake at 450°F (230°C) (with steam, if possible) for 30 minutes.

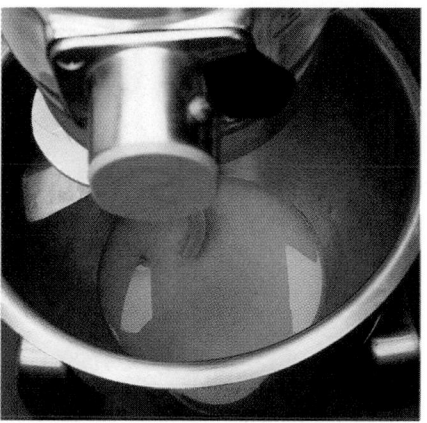

Be sure to add the ingredients in the sequence given in the instructions.

The recipe makes about 5 loaves (10 ounces/285 grams per loaf), or 2 1/2 dozen rolls (1 1/2 ounces/15 grams per roll).

Read pages 380 to 386 for more information about preparing yeast-raised breads.

Sourdough Starter

Yield: approximately 6 pounds (2.75 kilograms)

Hard wheat flour	*4 pounds*	*1.8 kilograms*
Water (at 70°F/21°C)	*2 1/4 pounds*	*1 kilogram*

1. Blend the flour and water just until combined.
2. Place in a food-grade plastic bucket or stainless steel bowl. Cover tightly with plastic wrap and allow to ferment at room temperature for 24 to 48 hours.
3. After sourdough has properly fermented, it is ready for use.

VARIATION

Rye Sourdough Starter: Replace the hard wheat flour with rye flour.

Sourdough French Bread: Use 8 ounces (225 grams) of sourdough starter in the formula for Pain de Campagne on page 1033 in this Chapter. Reduce the yeast to 1/4 ounce (7.5 grams). Fermentation time may increase up to 1 hour, depending upon the consistency of the starter. Shape and bake as directed for Pain de Campagne.

To keep the starter alive, add enough water and flour to replace the amount used, maintaining the same level of starter.

If the sourdough is not used frequently, it is essential to refeed every 6 to 12 hours, or 4 to 6 times after the initial fermentation.

The consistency of the starter can be varied to suit personal tastes. Use a very loose or slack starter for a faster fermentation. A stiff starter produces a slower fermentation.

Sourdough starters are highly acidic. When working with them be sure to protect your hands by wearing plastic gloves or preparing the dough in a mixer with a dough hook.

Pumpernickel Bread and Rolls

Yield: approximately 12 pounds (5.5 kilograms)

Yeast	*6 ounces*	*170 grams*
Caramel color	*as needed*	*as needed*
Pumpernickel flour	*2 pounds*	*900 grams*
First clear flour	*2 pounds*	*900 grams*
High-gluten flour	*2 pounds*	*900 grams*
Salt	*2 1/2 ounces*	*70 grams*
Caraway seeds	*1 1/2 ounces*	*40 grams*
Oil	*1 1/2 fluid ounces*	*45 milliliters*
Sour rye flour	*2 1/2 ounces*	*70 grams*
Water, medium temperature	*4 pounds*	*1.8 kilograms*
Raisins	*1 pound*	*450 grams*

1. Dissolve yeast in water; add caramel color.
2. Use the rest of the ingredients following the straight dough-mixing method for 7 minutes, at medium speed.
3. Proof until double in bulk; then scale 3 pounds (1.3 kilograms) for presses (to make rolls).
4. Line sheet pan with parchment paper and cornmeal.
5. Water-wash and bake at 400 to 425°F (200 to 225°C).

Multigrain Bread

Yield: about 12 pounds (5.5 kilograms) dough

Cornmeal	*4 ounces*	*115 grams*
Clear flour	*5 pounds*	*2.5 kilograms*
Bran	*8 ounces*	*225 grams*
Oatmeal	*8 ounces*	*225 grams*
Cracked wheat	*8 ounces*	*225 grams*
Wheat flour	*4 ounces*	*115 grams*
Molasses	*1 ounce*	*30 grams*
Sugar	*10 ounces*	*285 grams*
Shortening	*6 ounces*	*170 grams*
Milk powder	*6 ounces*	*170 grams*
Salt	*2 ounces*	*60 grams*
Yeast	*6 ounces*	*170 grams*
Water	*4 1/2 pounds*	*2 kilograms*

Scale pieces at 2 pounds (900 grams) for small loaves; 3 pounds (1.3 kilograms) for large loaves or Pullman loaves; 3 pounds (1.3 kilograms) is also one "press" if you are using a dough divider for rolls. One press makes 3 dozen rolls.

1. Line baking sheets with parchment. Scatter with cornmeal.
2. Combine the cornmeal, clear flour, bran, oatmeal, cracked wheat, and wheat flour.
3. Add the remaining ingredients. Mix the dough until smooth and elastic.
4. Cover the bowl and allow the dough to ferment for 75 minutes.
5. Punch down and scale as desired. Round off dough.
6. Set dough on prepared sheet pan and proof for 1 hour.
7. Press the dough down to flatten, shape as desired.
8. Pan proof an additional 30 minutes.
9. Bake in at 425°F (°220°C) for approximately 30 minutes.

Peasant Pecan Loaf

Yield: about 10 pounds (4.5 kilograms)

Use the same method for mixing, proofing, scaling, and shaping dough as for Pain de Campagne, page 1033.

Whole wheat flour	*4 1/2 pounds*	*2 kilograms*
Oatmeal	*8 ounces*	*225 grams*
Honey	*4 3/4 ounces*	*130 grams*
Water	*3 pounds*	*1.3 kilograms*
Yeast	*4 ounces*	*115 grams*
Salt	*1 1/4 ounces*	*35 grams*
Dry milk	*3 ounces*	*85 grams*
Butter	*4 3/4 ounces*	*130 grams*
Pecans (medium pieces)	*1 pound*	*450 grams*
Raisins	*1 pound*	*450 grams*

1. Follow the straight dough-mixing method, adding pecans and raisins just before dough is finished mixing.

2. Bake in pans or shape into loaves.

3. Bake at 375 to 390°F (175 to 200°C).

Fresh dill brings a wonderful flavor to this bread.

The straight dough mixing method is as follows: Combine all of the "wet" ingredients first and blend until smooth. Add the dry ingredients, mixing to form a dough, then kneading until smooth and elastic.

Cottage Dill Bread

Yield: about 12 1/2 pounds (6 kilograms)

Cottage cheese	*3 pounds*	*1.3 kilograms*
Sugar	*4 1/2 ounces*	*125 grams*
Onions, minced	*1 1/2 ounces*	*40 grams*
Butter, soft	*3 ounces*	*85 grams*
Salt	*1 ounce*	*30 grams*
Dill, chopped	*1 ounce*	*30 grams*
Baking soda	*1 ounce*	*30 grams*
Eggs	*6 ounces*	*170 grams*
Horseradish	*pinch*	*pinch*
Yeast	*5 ounces*	*140 grams*
Water	*12 ounces*	*340 grams*
Bread flour	*5 1/4 pounds*	*2.4 kilograms*

1. Follow the straight dough-mixing method

2. Scaling instructions: 3 pounds (1.3 kilograms) per press for loaves and rolls of specific size.

3. After baking, brush with butter and sprinkle with a pinch of salt.

Raisin Bread

Yield: 16 to 17 loaves (18 ounces = 500 grams each)

Yeast	*8 ounces*	*225 grams*
Milk	*2 quarts*	*2 liters*
Eggs	*8 ounces*	*225 grams*
Sugar	*14 1/2 ounces*	*410 grams*
Bread flour	*6 1/2 pounds*	*2.9 kilograms*
Cinnamon	*1/2 ounce*	*15 grams*
Salt	*2 1/2 ounces*	*70 grams*
Shortening	*1 1/4 pounds*	*570 grams*
Raisins	*5 1/2 pounds*	*2.5 kilograms*

1. Place the milk and the yeast in a bowl and stir to dissolve.

2. Add all the other ingredients, mixing on low speed until the flour is incorporated.

3. Mix for 10 to 12 minutes on second speed or until the dough is developed. Turn into an oiled bowl to keep the dough from forming a skin; place in a warm area to rise.

4. When dough has doubled in size, punch down and scale into 18-ounce (500-gram) pieces. Bench rest for 15 to 20 minutes, then shape into a loaf.

5. Give a final proof then bake in a 380°F (193°C) oven for 35 minutes or until done.

Sunflower Seed Bread

Yield: 1 dozen loaves (18 ounces = 500 grams);
12 dozen rolls (1 1/2 ounces = 45 grams)

Yeast	*2 ounces*	*60 grams*
Water	*2 quarts*	*2 liters*
Milk powder	*6 ounces*	*170 grams*
Honey	*4 ounces*	*115 grams*
Eggs	*4 ounces*	*115 grams*
Sugar	*3 ounces*	*85 grams*
Bread flour	*6 1/2 pounds*	*2.9 kilograms*
Bran flour	*12 ounces*	*340 grams*
Salt	*2 ounces*	*60 grams*
Shortening	*6 ounces*	*170 grams*
Sunflower seeds	*12 ounces*	*340 grams*
Topping		
Sunflower seeds	*as needed*	*as needed*
Egg wash	*as needed*	*as needed*

(Recipe continued on next page)

1. Place water, milk powder, and yeast in a bowl and stir to dissolve.

2. Add all the other ingredients mixing on low speed until the flour is incorporated.

3. Mix for 10 to 12 minutes on second speed or until the dough is developed. Cover and place in a warm area to rise.

4. When dough has doubled in size, punch down and scale at 1 1/2 ounces (45 grams) each for rolls; 18 ounces (500 grams) for loaves.

5. Bench rest for 15 to 20 minutes, then shape.

6. Final proof then bake in a 400°F (205°C) oven for 25 minutes for rolls and 40 minutes for loaves or until done.

Bagels

Yield: 9 dozen bagels (2 1/2 ounces = 75 grams)

Yeast	*1 ounce*	*30 grams*
Water	*6 pounds*	*2.75 kilograms*
Sugar	*6 1/2 ounces*	*185 grams*
Malt syrup	*1 ounce*	*30 grams*
High-gluten flour	*12 1/2 pounds*	*5.75 kilograms*
Salt	*4 ounces*	*115 grams*

1. In 40-quart (40-liter) bowl, dissolve yeast in water, add sugar and malt, add flour, sprinkle salt over top and mix to incorporate.

2. Mix on second speed for 9 minutes, using a dough hook.

3. Let proof for 60 to 75 minutes.

4. Roll dough 7/8-inch (2.5 centimeters) thick, cut out with doughnut cutter; reroll dough scraps 1 time only.

5. Place on parchment-covered sheet pan that has been sprinkled with cornmeal.

6. Proof until dough has three-quarters proofed (75 percent increase in volume).

7. Place the bagels into pot of boiling water that has been mixed with malt syrup (4 tablespoons malt syrup to 10 quarts (9.5 liters) water). Make sure bagels have been turned over so that both sides have been dipped. Start upside down for 10 seconds, turn over for 10 seconds, remove with a skimmer and place on a sheet pan.

8. Bake at 450°F (230°C) for 25 minutes until brown. Do not use steam when baking.

VARIATION

Poppy seeds, sesame seeds, chopped onions, garlic powder, etc. may be used to flavor the bagels. Place bagel face down onto seeds or other toppings before baking and return to sheet pan right side up. If using salt, sprinkle.

Challah Bread

Yield: 3 loaves

Water	*1 quart*	*1 liter*
Yeast	*4 ounces*	*115 grams*
Vegetable oil	*8 fluid ounces*	*240 milliliters*
Egg yolks	*1 pound*	*450 grams*
Sugar	*8 ounces*	*225 grams*
Salt	*1 1/2 ounces*	*40 grams*
High-gluten flour	*5 1/4 pounds*	*2.4 kilograms*

Eggwash is made by blending beaten eggs with milk or water. For 8 fluid ounces (120 milliliters), you will need 4 eggs and 2 ounces (60 grams) of liquid.

1. Place the water and yeast in a bowl and dissolve.
2. Add all the other ingredients, mixing on low speed until the flour is incorporated.
3. Mix for 10 to 12 minutes on second speed, or until dough is properly developed. Place dough in oiled bowl; turn over (this keeps the dough from forming a skin). Place in a warm area to rise.
4. When dough has doubled in size, punch down and scale accordingly.
5. Divide dough into three pieces, each 3 pounds (1.3 kilograms); cut again into 6 pieces to make 1 loaf.
6. Roll dough into strips 8-inches long, thinner on the ends and thicker in the middle.
7. Braid the bread; place on pan, brush with egg wash, and proof again.
8. Bake in a 380°F (193°C) oven for 20 to 30 minutes or until golden brown.

Cinnamon Buns

Yield: 5 dozen

Sweet dough	*4 pounds*	*1.8 kilograms*
Egg wash	*8 fluid ounces*	*120 milliliters*
Butter, melted, as needed	*4 fluid ounces*	*115 milliliters*
Raisins, plumped	*1 1/2 pounds*	*680 grams*
Cinnamon sugar, as needed	*6 ounces*	*170 grams*
Apricot glaze, melted as needed	*6 ounces*	*170 grams*
Fondant, melted, as needed	*4 ounces*	*115 grams*

Blend cinnamon into sugar to taste for cinnamon sugar.

1. Roll dough into a rectangle, brush edge lengthwise with egg wash and brush remaining dough with butter.
2. Sprinkle dough with raisins and cinnamon sugar, being careful not to cover egg-washed area.

(Recipe continued on next page)

3. Roll dough up like a roulade, sealing with egg-washed edge.

4. Cut into 1 1/2-ounce (45-gram) slices; brush tops with egg wash.

5. Place on a 6 by 10-inch (15 by 25 centimeter) sheet pan, egg-washed side up; proof until double in size.

6. Bake in a 380 to 400°F (193 to 200°C) oven until golden brown on all sides; remove and brush immediately with apricot glaze.

7. Drizzle with fondant.

Sweet Dough

Yield: about 11 1/2 pounds (5.2 kilograms) dough

Water	2 quarts	2 liters
Yeast	6 ounces	170 grams
Eggs	1 pound	450 grams
Malt syrup	1 1/2 ounces	45 grams
Milk powder	4 ounces	115 grams
Pastry flour	1 pound	450 grams
Bread flour	4 1/2 pounds	2 kilograms
Salt	3/4 ounce	20 grams
Sugar	8 ounces	225 grams
Seasoning: ground cardamon, nutmeg or lemon zest	1/2 ounce	15 grams
Butter, softened	1 pound	450 grams
Egg wash, as needed	8 fluid ounces	240 milliliters

1. Combine the water and yeast in a bowl. Stir to dissolve.

2. Add the eggs and malt and blend.

3. Add the remaining ingredients (except the egg wash) and mix on low speed until the flour is incorporated.

4. Increase the speed and mix for 8 minutes, or until the dough is fully developed (elastic, smooth, and supple).

5. Spread the dough in an even layer on a parchment-lined sheet pan and refrigerate for 30 minutes.

6. Scale the dough at 10 ounces (285 grams) for a coffee cake, or into 3 pound (1.3 kilogram) sections to cut into rolls. (Scale individual rolls at anywhere between 1 1/2 to 3 ounces (45 to 85 grams) depending upon intended result).

7. Place the shaped dough into prepared pans.

8. Brush the coffee cakes or rolls with egg wash and allow to proof once more.

9. Bake at 380°F (195°C) for about 20 minutes, or until golden brown.

10. Let rolls or coffee cakes cool slightly, then glaze or decorate as desired.

Stollen

Yield: 27 loaves (1 1/2 pounds/680 grams each)

Fruit mixture

Meyers rum	*8 fluid ounces*	*240 milliliters*
Raisins, light	*2 1/2 pounds*	*1.15 kilograms*
Raisins, dark	*2 1/2 pounds*	*1.15 kilograms*
Candied fruit, fine dice	*11 ounces*	*315 grams*
Almonds, chopped	*6 ounces*	*170 grams*

Base dough

Bread flour	*4 pounds*	*1.8 kilograms*
Cake flour	*2 pounds*	*900 grams*
Yeast	*7 ounces*	*200 grams*
Lukewarm milk (85°F/33°C)	*2 1/4 pints*	*1.15 liters*
Sugar	*10 ounces*	*285 grams*
Butter, unsalted, soft	*2 pounds*	*900 grams*
Cardamom, ground	*1/4 ounce*	*8 grams*
Nutmeg, grated or ground	*1/4 ounce*	*8 grams*
Salt	*3/4 ounce*	*20 grams*
Butter, melted	*2 pounds*	*900 grams*
Vanilla sugar	*2 pounds*	*900 grams*

1. Prepare the night before: Soak fruit in rum, storing at room temperature.

2. To make dough: Dissolve yeast in the milk.

3. Add remaining dough ingredients, mix together on first speed until incorporated. Switch to second speed and mix for 8 minutes.

4. Proof dough until doubled in size, then return to mixer and slowly add fruit and nuts on first speed until blended in.

5. Scale into 27 loaves (1 1/2 pounds/680 grams each); shape, water wash, and proof until risen two-thirds larger.

6. Bake in a 380°F (193°C) oven for 45 minutes until golden brown; remove from oven and butter wash and roll in vanilla sugar.

VARIATION

Marzipan Stollen: Stollen can be filled with marzipan before being folded over and sealed.

*To make **Vanilla Sugar**, split a vanilla bean in half and bury it in 2 pounds (900 grams) of sugar. Use granulated or powdered sugar as desired. Powdered sugar is typically used for stollen.*

Stollen is a German yeast-raised bread usually made for the winter holidays.

Danish

Yield: about 12 pounds (5.5 kilograms)

Various fillings and toppings may be found in Chapter 30 on pages 1096 to 1104.

The straight dough mixing method may be found on pages 380 to 385.

This recipe can also be used for coffee cake.

Scale coffee cakes at 10 ounces (285 grams) each. Individual danishes are scaled from 1 1/2 to 3 ounces (45 to 85 grams).

Yeast	8 ounces	225 grams
Milk	2 pounds	900 grams
Sugar	10 ounces	285 grams
Salt	1 1/2 ounces	40 grams
Butter	8 ounces	225 grams
Egg yolks	1 pound	450 grams
Pastry flour	1 1/2 pounds	680 grams
Bread flour	3 pounds	1.3 kilograms
Cardamom, mace or nutmeg, ground	1/4 ounce	8 grams
Butter	3 pounds	1.3 kilograms

1. Dissolve yeast in milk directly in the mixing bowl. Use the straight dough-mixing method, mixing for 8 minutes.

2. Roll butter between two pieces of bread floured-parchment paper, filling two-thirds of the length of the paper.

3. Place dough on a bread-floured sheet pan; refrigerate for 30 minutes.

4. Remove dough and roll out to the size of a sheet pan (approximately 1/2-inch thick).

5. Place the rolled butter (butter and dough should be 65°F/(18°C) on two-thirds of the dough; fold in thirds to layer in butter; seal.

6. Turn the dough 90 degrees, roll out; make a 3-fold.

7. Refrigerate 30 minutes, roll out again and do a second 3-fold.

8. Refrigerate 30 minutes, roll out again and do the last 3-fold.

9. Cut into segments to make up danish. Bake at 375 to 400°F (190 to 205°C).

Croissants

Yield: 9 dozen

Milk	3 pints, 3ounces	1.5 liters
Yeast	5 ounces	140 grams
Salt	1 1/2 ounces	40 grams
Sugar	4 1/2 ounces	125 grams
Butter, soft	8 ounces	225 grams
Bread flour	5 1/4 pounds	2.4 kilograms
Roll in		
Butter, unsalted	3 pounds, 12 ounces	1.7 kilograms
Bread flour	4 ounces	115 grams

(Recipe continued on facing page)

1. Combine first set of ingredients and mix for only 2 1/2 minutes at medium speed.

2. Place dough in a rectangular shape on table and let rest while mixing roll-in butter.

3. Combine the roll-in butter and flour, using a paddle on "pulse" first speed until butter is chopped up; then switch to second speed only until butter is smooth and firm with no lumps. Roll the butter in flour to two-thirds the size of the dough.

4. Roll rectangular dough to the size of a sheet pan and place the rolled butter on the dough so that two-thirds of the dough is covered.

5. Lock butter into the dough by way of a 3-fold (the dough will have 5 layers, 3 of dough, 2 of butter), seal the ends and sides, and turn 90 degrees.

6. Roll out immediately to a rectangle twice the size of a sheet pan, brush off extra flour, give a 3-fold, turn 90 degrees, roll to fit the sheet pan, cover, and rest in the refrigerator for 20 to 30 minutes.

7. Repeat step 6 two more times. Brush the dough with melted shortening (not too warm) to seal the sides and top of dough.

8. Mark the dough with three indentations to indicate the number of 3-folds that have been done, wrap in plastic and refrigerate overnight.

9. On the next day, roll out the dough, cut to fit croissant-cutter width and roll-up to make crescents. Egg wash, proof, egg wash again before baking, and bake at 380°F (193°C) for 28 minutes, or until medium golden brown.

Dough has to be made up 1 day in advance and allowed to rest overnight in the refrigerator.

Dough can be frozen for up to 3 weeks, beyond that the yeast loses its potency. Frozen dough should be taken out of the freezer and placed in the refrigerator to thaw 1 day before using.

Pan Filling for Sticky Buns

Yield: 17 pounds (8.15 kilograms)

Granulated sugar	*5 pounds*	*2.25 kilograms*
Brown sugar	*5 pounds*	*2.25 kilograms*
Butter or primex	*5 pounds*	*2.25 kilograms*
Salt	*1 ounce*	*30 grams*
Honey	*1 pound*	*450 grams*
Orange or apricot jam	*1 pound*	*450 grams*
Water	*if needed*	*if needed*

1. Cream all ingredients together until light and fluffy.

2. Add water if a softer mix is desired.

3. If a darker color is desired use dark brown sugar or decrease granulated sugar and increase brown sugar.

This is a multi-functional pan dressing for sticky buns, upside-down cakes, or cinnamon nut bread.

Use this pan filling with Sweet Dough to make Sticky Buns (see page 1039).

Toasted nuts and/or raisins or currants may be added.

Holland Dutch Topping

Yield: 3 pounds (1.3 kilograms)

Replace the shortening with butter (all or part) for a richer flavor.

To vary the consistency, use more or less water. The less you use, the more flaky the finished topping.

Use with sweet dough (page 1039) to prepare coffee cakes.

Yeast	*1 1/2 ounces*	*40 grams*
Water, warm	*1 1/2 to 2 pints*	*.75 to 1 liter*
Rice flour	*14 ounces*	*400 grams*
Sugar	*1 ounce*	*30 grams*
Shortening	*1 1/2 ounces*	*40 grams*
Salt	*1/2 ounce*	*15 grams*

1. Dissolve yeast in warm water.

2. Add to dry ingredients.

3. Allow to rise one time and apply to rolls or bread.

C H A P T E R 29 *Kitchen Desserts*

Kitchen desserts are those that can easily be prepared without a separate bakery or pastry shop on the premises. Many classic desserts, such as soufflés or crêpes are among the offerings found here.

Even if you can purchase prepared tortes and cakes, you may turn to this chapter in order to find a number of sauce recipes that you may use to customize the desserts you are serving your guests.

The recipes have been grouped as follows:

- *Puddings*
- *Creams and Custards*
- *Soufflés and Other Egg Desserts*
- *Crêpes*
- *Frozen Desserts*
- *Fruits*
- *Dessert Sauces*

Rice Pudding with Fresh Raspberries

Yield: 15 servings

The recipe for Raspberry Sauce may be found on page 1072.

Rice	*6 ounces*	*170 grams*
Milk	*54 fluid ounces*	*1.6 liters*
Golden raisins	*8 ounces*	*225 grams*
Nutmeg, ground	*1/4 teaspoon*	*1/4 teaspoon*
Cinnamon, ground	*1/4 teaspoon*	*1/4 teaspoon*
Salt	*1/4 teaspoon*	*1/4 teaspoon*
Sugar	*6 ounces*	*170 grams*
Egg yolks	*3 each*	*3 each*
Vanilla extract	*1/2 ounce*	*15 grams*
Raspberries, fresh	*1 pound, 7 ounces*	*650 grams*
Raspberry Sauce	*17 fluid ounces*	*520 milliliters*

1. Combine rice, milk, nutmeg, cinnamon, salt, and half the sugar; simmer, covered, until rice is cooked and milk is absorbed.

2. Blend the yolks with the remaining sugar. Temper and add to the rice. Bring up to a bare simmer. Remove from the heat.

3. Combine raisins and vanilla.

4. Serve on plates with raspberries and Raspberry Sauce.

Warm Chocolate Pudding

Yield: 18 servings

This is also known as "pudding soufflé." The texture, though lighter than other puddings, isn't quite as light as a classic soufflé. However, it will hold up better for service.

Any pudding not used up can be glazed with Ganache (page 1075).

Butter	*6 ounces*	*170 grams*
Powdered sugar	*3 ounces*	*85 grams*
Egg yolks	*6 each*	*6 each*
White bread, no crusts	*3 ounces*	*85 grams*
Milk	*2 fluid ounces*	*60 milliliters*
Chocolate, semisweet, melted	*4 ounces*	*115 grams*
Bread crumbs	*4 ounces*	*115 grams*
Hazelnuts, ground, toasted	*4 ounces*	*115 grams*
Vanilla extract	*1 tablespoon*	*1 tablespoon*
Egg whites	*10 each*	*10 each*
Sugar	*4 ounces*	*115 grams*

(Recipe continued on facing page)

1. Combine the butter and sugar; cream until light; slowly mix in egg yolks.

2. Soak bread in milk; squeeze out excess milk.

3. Add squeezed bread, chocolate, bread crumbs, nuts, and vanilla; mix together.

4. Combine egg whites and sugar, whip until medium-stiff meringue, fold into chocolate mixture.

5. Fill buttered ramekins three-quarters full, bake in a water bath in a 350°F (175°C) oven, until set or about 45 minutes.

6. Unmold and serve hot with chocolate or vanilla sauce.

Chocolate Pudding

Yield: 50 servings (3 to 4 ounces/85 to 115 grams each)

Milk	*9 quarts*	*8.5 liters*
Sugar	*2 1/4 pounds*	*1 kilogram*
Vanilla bean (optional)	*1 each*	*1 each*
Salt	*pinch*	*pinch*
Cornstarch	*13 1/2 ounces*	*385 grams*
Cocoa powder	*13 1/2 ounces*	*385 grams*
Eggs	*1 pound, 13 ounces*	*820 grams*
Butter	*9 ounces*	*255 grams*

Use 1 tablespoon of good quality-vanilla extract instead of the vanilla bean if you prefer. Add it with the butter in step 4.

If you use a vanilla bean, remove it from the milk, rinse it, pat dry, and use it to scent sugar.

1. Combine milk, 8 ounces (225 grams) of the sugar, and salt; bring to a boil.

2. Split the vanilla bean (if used) and add to the hot milk . Allow to steep 15 minutes off the heat.

3. Sift sugar, cornstarch, and cocoa powder together, mix in the eggs.

4. Add some of the hot milk to the egg mixture to temper it. Mix well, return egg mixture to remaining hot milk.

5. Bring to a second boil, remove from the heat, stir in butter.

6. Pour into prepared molds. Chill thoroughly.

Petits Pots du Crème

Yield: 8 servings

Serve with a dollop of unsweetened whipped cream and shaved chocolate or top with a chocolate-covered coffee bean.

Sugar	*6 ounces*	*170 grams*
Milk, warm	*12 fluid ounces*	*360 milliliters*
Heavy cream, warm	*12 fluid ounces*	*360 milliliters*
Egg yolks, beaten	*1 1/2 ounces*	*40 grams*
Eggs, beaten	*4 1/2 ounces*	*125 grams*
Sugar	*2 ounces*	*60 grams*
Chocolate, semisweet, melted	*3 ounces*	*85 grams*
Vanilla	*1/4 ounce*	*8 grams*

1. Caramelize 4 ounces (115 grams) of the sugar until dark amber.

2. Add milk and cream, bring to a boil, stirring so that caramel dissolves.

3. Combine the remaining sugar with the eggs and egg yolks, temper into hot milk mixture.

4. Add chocolate and vanilla, strain.

5. Fill ramekins four-fifths full, bake in hot water bath in a 325°F (165°C) oven 20 minutes or until just barely set, and the mixture still appears fairly loose.

6. Remove from the water bath when taken from the oven, cool slightly and refrigerate until service.

Chocolate Mousse in Tuiles

Yield: 10 servings

The recipe for Tuiles may be found on page 1093.

Chocolate, semisweet	*10 ounces*	*285 grams*
Butter	*1 1/2 ounces*	*40 grams*
Egg yolks, pasteurized	*5 each*	*5 each*
Sugar	*2 ounces*	*60 grams*
Egg whites, pasteurized	*5 each*	*5 each*
Dark rum or vanilla, to taste	*1 fluid ounce*	*30 milliliters*
Heavy cream, whipped	*8 fluid ounces*	*240 milliliters*
Tuiles	*20 each*	*20 each*

(Recipe continued on facing page)

1. Combine chocolate and butter; melt over a water bath.

2. Whip egg yolks and half the sugar to full volume.

3. Whip egg whites and the remaining sugar to full volume.

4. Fold egg whites into egg yolks.

5. Fold butter–chocolate mixture into egg–sugar mixture.

6. Add rum or vanilla and fold in whipped cream.

7. Scoop or pipe into tuiles at time of service. Serve 2 tuiles per serving.

Lemon Mousse

Yield: 12 servings

Oil, as needed	*2 to 3 fluid ounces*	*60 to 90 milliliters*
Powdered sugar	*2 to 3 ounces*	*60 to 85 grams*
Coconut, chopped fine, toasted	*4 ounces*	*as needed*
Milk	*10 fluid ounces*	*300 milliliters*
Sugar	*10 ounces*	*285 grams*
Egg yolks (pasteurized)	*3 1/2 ounces*	*100 grams*
Cornstarch	*1 ounce*	*30 grams*
Lemon juice	*4 1/2 fluid ounces*	*135 milliliters*
Lemon zest, blanched	*1 ounce*	*30 grams*
Egg whites (pasteurized)	*10 ounces*	*285 grams*

Food-grade P.V.C. molds work best for this dessert. Or, pipe it directly into glasses.

To read about preparing meringues, refer to page 220.

A small amount of bloomed and dissolved gelatin may be added to the mousse for greater stability.

1. For preparing molds: Lightly oil molds, dust with powdered sugar, and place on parchment-lined sheet pan. Fill bottoms with an even layer of coconut.

2. Combine milk with half of the sugar. Make a liaison with yolks, cornstarch, and remaining sugar.

3. Temper the liaison and add to milk mixture. Bring to a boil and add lemon juice and zest.

4. Prepare a soft meringue with egg whites and remaining sugar. Fold into above mixture and immediately pipe out into prepared molds.

5. Refrigerate or freeze until needed.

Bread and Butter Pudding

Yield: 15 servings

Custard

Milk	*1 quart*	*1 liter*
Eggs, beaten	*6 each*	*6 each*
Egg yolks, beaten	*3 each*	*6 each*
Sugar	*6 ounces*	*170 grams*
Vanilla extract	*1 teaspoon*	*1 teaspoon*

Bread

Bread, leftover	*1 1/2 pounds*	*680 grams*
Butter, melted	*3 ounces*	*85 grams*
Raisins	*4 ounces*	*115 grams*

1. To make the custard: Combine all ingredients and mix well.

2. To prepare the bread: Cut in cubes, drizzle with butter, and toast in the oven.

3. Combine custard, bread, and raisins; fill buttered custard cups.

4. Bake in a water bath in a 325°F (165°C) oven for 45 minutes or until custard is set.

Savarin Syrup

Yield: 1 1/2 pints (720 milliliters)

Orange juice	*4 fluid ounces*	*120 milliliters*
Water	*12 fluid ounces*	*360 milliliters*
Sugar	*8 ounces*	*225 grams*
Cinnamon stick	*1 each*	*1 each*
Vanilla extract	*1/2 teaspoon*	*1/2 teaspoon*
Rum	*to taste*	*to taste*

1. Combine all ingredients except rum, bring to a boil, and simmer 5 minutes.

2. Cool, add rum.

Savarin with Fresh Fruit

Yield: 10 servings

Yeast, fresh	*1/2 ounce*	*15 grams*
Milk	*6 fluid ounces*	*180 milliliters*
Bread flour	*12 ounces*	*340 grams*
Eggs	*5 each*	*5 each*
Egg yolks	*3 each*	*3 each*
Sugar	*1 tablespoon*	*1 tablespoon*
Salt	*1/2 teaspoon*	*1/2 teaspoon*
Butter, softened and whipped	*8 ounces*	*225 grams*
Orange zest, blanched	*1/2 ounce*	*15 grams*
Savarin Syrup	*as needed*	*as needed*
Fresh fruit	*as needed*	*as needed*

The recipe for Savarin Syrup may be found on page 1050.

1. Dissolve yeast in the milk.

2. Add enough flour to make a very loose dough.

3. Add the remaining flour on top of the dough. Allow it to ferment until there are visible cracks in the flour's surface.

4. Add the eggs, egg yolks, sugar, salt, and orange zest. Mix the dough on medium speed for 10 minutes.

5. Add the butter. Mix on high speed for 8 minutes.

6. Cover dough, ferment 35 minutes in a warm place; punch down to expel excess carbon dioxide.

7. Pipe dough into molds, filling only halfway full.

8. Proof until doubled in size; bake in a 400°F (205°C) oven until golden brown, cool.

9. Soak in Savarin Syrup, drain, arrange on a plate, and garnish with fresh fruit.

Zabaglione

Yield: 5 to 6 servings

Marsala	*8 fluid ounces*	*240 milliliters*
Sugar	*7 ounces*	*200 grams*
Egg yolks	*10 each*	*10 each*

1. Combine all ingredients, whisk together.
2. Whisk mixture over a simmering water bath until thickened and foamy, incorporating as much as possible.
3. Serve while still warm in a tall glass or other container.

Be sure to bring the eggs up to a temperature of 165°F (73°C) in order to kill any harmful bacteria.

Serve with fresh fruit and lady fingers.

This Zabaglione is similar to a Sabayon Sauce.

Crème Caramel

Yield: 14 servings (4 ounces/115 grams each)

Caramel		
Sugar	*8 ounces*	*225 grams*
Lemon juice, fresh	*few drops*	*few drops*
Water	*3 fluid ounces*	*90 milliliters*
Custard		
Milk	*1 quart*	*1 liter*
Vanilla bean	*1 each*	*1 each*
Eggs, beaten	*6 each*	*6 each*
Egg yolks	*4 each*	*4 each*
Sugar	*8 ounces*	*225 grams*

1. Butter the sides of ramekins.
2. Combine the sugar and lemon juice for the caramel and cook to a rich brown; carefully divide among the bottoms of ramekins.

(Recipe continued on facing page)

This dessert is also referred to as Flan.

The dissolved caramel that appears when turning out the custards is actually the sauce for this dessert.

Crème Caramel and Crème Brûlée may also be prepared in larger casseroles. The presentation is less dramatic but sometimes more practical for buffets or "family-style" seating.

3. Bring milk and 4 ounces (115 grams) of sugar to a boil; remove from heat. (If using a vanilla bean steep it in the hot milk mixture.)

4. Combine the egg yolks and the remaining sugar; stir well to combine.

5. Temper together the eggs with hot milk. Do not return to the heat. Add vanilla flavoring now if using extract instead of a bean.

6. Divide the custard mixture among the ramekins.

7. Place the cups in a bain-marie; bake at an oven temperature of 325°F (165°C).

8. Bake for approximately 35 minutes or until the custard has set.

9. Refrigerate overnight before turning out and serving.

Crème Brûlée

Yield: 12 portions

Heavy cream	*1 1/4 quarts*	*1.2 liters*
Vanilla bean, split	*1/2 each*	*1/2 each*
Sugar	*8 ounces*	*225 grams*
Egg yolks, beaten	*10 ounces*	*285 grams*

1. Combine the heavy cream, vanilla bean, and half the sugar; bring to a boil.

2. Combine the egg yolks, eggs, and remaining sugar.

3. Temper egg–sugar mixture into hot heavy cream; cook until thick enough to coat the back of a spoon; strain through a fine sieve.

4. Fill ramekins seven-eighths full, place in a water bath.

5. Bake in a 325°F (165°C) oven until just barely set, approximately 45 minutes; remove from water bath when cool. Wipe bottom of ramekins and refrigerate overnight.

6. Cover the surface of each custard lightly with sugar; set ramekins in a hotel pan, and surround with ice.

7. Caramelize sugar under the broiler. Serve at once.

The ice bath keeps the custard from becoming reheated as you create the glaze.

Use a hand-held butane torch to caramelize the sugar if you prefer.

Tiramisù

Yield: 8 to 10 servings

Tiramisù means "pick me up" and is believed by some to have originated in Venice. Tiramisù can be decorated with chocolate shavings.

Meyers rum, Tia Maria, and/or Kahlua, although untraditional, may be added to the Espresso Syrup.

Espresso syrup		
Sugar	*2 ounces*	*60 grams*
Water	*2 fluid ounces*	*60 milliliters*
Espresso, brewed, hot	*6 fluid ounces*	*180 milliliters*
Brandy	*2 fluid ounces*	*60 milliliters*
Filling		
Egg yolks	*2 1/2 ounces*	*70 grams*
Sugar	*3 ounces*	*85 grams*
Marsala, sweet	*3 fluid ounces*	*90 milliliters*
Mascarpone, softened	*8 ounces*	*225 grams*
Whipped cream	*8 ounces*	*225 grams*
Finishing		
Lady fingers	*3 dozen*	*3 dozen*
Whipped cream, sweetened	*8 ounces*	*225 grams*
Cinnamon, powdered	*1 tablespoon*	*1 tablespoon*
Cocoa powder	*1 tablespoon*	*1 tablespoon*
Powdered sugar	*1 tablespoon*	*1 tablespoon*

1. For syrup: Combine sugar, water, coffee, and brandy. Cool.

2. For filling: Combine the yolks, sugar, and Marsala; beat in a stainless steel bowl over a water bath (140°F/60°C) until thickened.

3. Remove yolk mixture from the heat, and beat in a mixer on second speed until cold.

4. Fold in smooth mascarpone and whipped cream.

5. Brush lady fingers liberally with syrup. Place in alternating layers in a pan with the filling and refrigerate overnight.

6. To finish: Spread the sweetened whipped cream over the top.

7. Combine the cinnamon, cocoa powder, and sugar; sprinkle over the top.

English Trifle

Yield: 6 servings

Currant jelly	*1 1/2 ounces*	*40 grams*
Vanilla Sauce	*12 fluid ounces*	*360 milliliters*
Sherry or rum	*1 1/4 fluid ounces*	*37.5 milliliters*
Marinated fruits	*6 ounces*	*170 grams*
Sponge cake, soaked, cubed	*3 ounces*	*85 grams*
Whipped cream, for decoration	*6 ounces*	*170 grams*
Chocolate decoration	*6 pieces*	*6 pieces*

Select seasonal fruits and poach them if necessary. Combine them with simple syrup and rum or sherry. Marinate several hours. Drain before adding to trifle.

The recipe for Vanilla Sauce may be found on page 1070.

1. Place currant jelly in the bottom each 4-ounce (120-gram) glass.

2. Alternate layers of sponge cake brushed with sherry, fruit, and Vanilla Sauce.

3. Top with Vanilla Sauce.

4. Before serving, pipe with a rosette of whipped cream on top and decorate with chocolate decoration.

Hot Dessert Soufflé

Yield: 40 servings

Milk	*1 quart*	*1 liter*
Vanilla bean, split lengthwise	*1 each*	*1 each*
Egg yolks	*8 ounces*	*225 grams*
Sugar	*1 pound*	*455 grams*
All-purpose flour	*6 ounces*	*170 grams*
Arrowroot	*2 tablespoons*	*2 tablespoons*

When beating egg whites by hand, place a folded towel under the bowl to prevent slipping.

1. To make the base: Bring the milk to a boil, with vanilla bean and allow to steep for 15 minutes off the heat.

2. Combine egg yolks and sugar, whip until light; sift flour and arrowroot together and add to egg mixture.

3. Temper egg–yolk mixture with some of the hot milk, stir constantly, add back to the remaining milk.

4. Bring to a boil, stirring constantly, whip until cool.

For one Soufflé

Base from above (3 tablespoons)	*1 1/2 ounces*	*40 grams*
Egg whites, whipped to stiff peaks	*2 each*	*2 each*
Flavorings	*to taste*	*to taste*

Flavorings to add to this soufflé (per portion) include fresh fruits (1 ounce/30 grams), cordials like Kahlua, Tia Maria, Grand Marnier, Amaretto (1 tablespoon), ground toasted nuts (hazelnut, almond, macadamia, 1 tablespoon), and melted chocolate (1 ounce/30 grams).

1. Add flavorings to base.

2. Stir one-third of the egg whites into base.

3. Fold in remaining egg whites.

4. Fill prepared molds three-quarters full and bake at 400°F (200°C) for 20 minutes.

Salzburger Nockerl

Yield: 3 servings 4 1/2 ounces (130 grams) each

Egg whites	*6 each*	*6 each*
Sugar	*1 3/4 ounces*	*50 grams*
Vanilla extract, to taste	*1/2 teaspoon*	*1/2 teaspoon*
Egg yolks	*6 each*	*6 each*
Bread flour	*1 1/4 ounces*	*40 grams*
Butter	*1 ounce*	*30 grams*

1. Combine egg whites, sugar, and vanilla; whip to a medium-stiff peak by hand.

2. Beat the egg yolks until smooth. Add to the whites with a folding motion.

3. Sift flour on top and fold in.

4. Portion into a buttered chafing dish and bake in a 550°F (290°C) oven for 5 to 6 minutes or until the peaks are well browned.

Oeufs à la Neige

Yield: 16 servings

The recipe for Vanilla Sauce is on page 1070. Caramel Sauce is on page 1076.

Egg whites	*8 each*	*8 each*
Sugar	*10 ounces*	*285 grams*
Vanilla extract	*1 teaspoon*	*1 teaspoon*
Milk	*1 quart*	*1 liter*
Caramel Sauce	*8 ounces*	*225 grams*

1. Combine egg whites and 7 ounces (200 grams) of the sugar; whip until medium-stiff peaks are formed, fold in vanilla.

2. Heat milk and remaining sugar to a boil; reduce heat to 160 to 170°F (70 to 75°C).

3. Shape meringue into quenelles and place on parchment paper.

4. Lower meringues into poaching liquid, remove paper.

5. Poach 2 minutes on each side, remove, drain, chill.

6. Strain poaching liquid, and make into Vanilla Sauce; flavor with rum.

7. Pool sauce on plate, arrange meringues on top, and drizzle with hot caramel.

Basic Dessert Crêpes

Yield: 20 to 30 crêpes

Eggs	8 ounces	225 grams
Confectioner's sugar	2 ounces	60 grams
Milk	8 fluid ounces	240 milliliters
Bread flour, sifted	8 ounces	225 grams
Heavy cream	1 pint	480 milliliters
Oil	1 tablespoon	1 tablespoon
Vanilla	1/2 teaspoon	1/2 teaspoon
Salt	1/4 teaspoon	1/4 teaspoon
Kirschwasser (optional)	1 tablespoon	1 tablespoon

1. Combine eggs and sugar; whip for 10 minutes on third speed.

2. On first speed, add milk and mix in.

3. Add flour and mix until smooth.

4. Add remaining ingredients; make a smooth batter.

5. Add a small amount of batter to a preheated buttered crêpe pan, swirling pan to coat bottom with batter.

6. Cook over medium heat; when set, turn over and finish on the other side.

7. Fill as desired.

The crêpes can be prepared in advance. Place parchment squares between crêpes to keep them separate. Refrigerate until needed if desired.

Crêpes Suzette

Yield: 6 servings

Sugar	1 1/2 ounces	40 grams
Butter, cubed	6 ounces	170 grams
Orange zest	1 1/2 ounces	40 grams
Orange juice	12 fluid ounces	360 milliliters
Basic Dessert Crêpes	18 each	18 each
Grand Marnier	3 fluid ounces	90 milliliters
Brandy or cognac	3 fluid ounces	90 milliliters

1. Preheat a sauteuse on direct heat.

2. Sprinkle sugar evenly across the bottom of the pan.

3. As the sugar begins to caramelize, add butter, gently shaking the pan. Add butter to the outside edges of the pan (this allows the butter to evenly temper and blend with the sugar).

4. Add orange zest; shake pan gently to thoroughly blend all the ingredients and create a light-orange caramel color.

This is often done tableside for 2 to 4 guests.

Crêpes Suzette were named in honor of a woman in the court of King Edward VIII. Some believe Escoffier first prepared them. Others believe that the dessert was invented by the king's chef.

(Recipe continued on next page)

5. Pour the orange juice on the outside edges of the pan slowly, allowing it to temper and blend with the sugar.

6. Shake pan gently, incorporating all the ingredients and allowing the sauce to thicken.

7. Add the crêpes to the sauce, and flip over. Fold into quarters and move to the edge of the pan.

8. Repeat process with remaining crêpes (move quickly so sauce does not become too thick).

9. Remove pan from the heat, add Grand Marnier, but do not flame. Return to heat.

10. Slide pan back and forth over the heat; allow pan to get hot.

11. Add brandy, tip pan slightly to flame, and then shake pan until flame dies.

12. Plate 3 crêpes per portion; shingle one over the other and nappé with sauce.

Crêpes Normandy

Yield: 6 servings

Apples	3 each	3 each
Brown sugar	6 ounces	170 grams
Butter, cubed	6 ounces	170 grams
Apple juice, or cider	9 fluid ounces	270 milliliters
Calvados	3 fluid ounces	90 milliliters
Basic Dessert Crêpes	12 each	12 each
Heavy cream, whipped	9 fluid ounces	270 milliliters

1. Peel and slice apples.

2. Place a sauteuse over direct heat to warm.

3. Sprinkle brown sugar evenly across the bottom of the pan, allowing the spoon to touch the bottom (this may cause the sugar to crystallize).

4. As the sugar begins to caramelize, add butter, and gently shake the pan. Add the apple juice.

5. Add the remaining butter to the outside edges of the pan; this allows the butter to evenly temper and blend with the sugar.

6. Add apples to pan, coat with sauce, and turn once.

7. Shake pan gently to thoroughly blend all the ingredients as sauce starts to thicken (move quickly so sauce does not become too thick).

8. Sandwich crêpe between fork and spoon. Placing crêpe into sauce, flip over and place several slices of apples in the crêpe; fold in half and move to the edge of the pan.

(Recipe continued on facing page)

9. Repeat process with remaining crêpes (move quickly so sauce does not become too thick).

10. Slide pan back and forth over front edge of the heat; allow pan to get hot.

11. Remove pan, add Calvados, tip pan slightly, flame Calvados, and shake pan until flame dies.

12. Plate two crêpes per portion, nappé with sauce, and spoon a dollop of whipped cream over each crêpe.

Basic Parfait

Yield: 20 servings

Egg yolks	*15 ounces*	*425 grams*
Sugar	*8 ounces*	*225 grams*
Heavy cream, whipped	*1 quart*	*1 liter*
Flavoring: fruit purée, hazelnut paste	*10 ounces*	*285 grams*
Hippen leaves	*20 each*	*20 each*

1. Combine egg yolks and sugar, warm over a water bath, and whip until thickened.

2. Fold in whipped cream and flavoring.

3. Fill molds, freeze, and dip in hot water to unmold if desired.

4. Set on a plate, garnish edge with whipped cream rosettes, and decorate top with a hippen leaf.

VARIATION

Layered Parfaits: Layer different flavors in molds.

Use any of a variety of molds to create a signature frozen parfait dessert. The presence of whipped cream will prevent the parfait from freezing solid.

Oranges come in three different varieties: thin-skinned, thick-skinned, and bitter.

Soufflé Glacé

Yield: 16 servings

Egg yolks	*15 each*	*15 each*
Sugar	*14 ounces*	*400 grams*
Egg whites	*5 each*	*5 each*
Heavy cream	*1 quart*	*1 liter*
Grand Marnier	*4 fluid ounces*	*120 milliliters*

1. Using parchment paper or aluminum foil, make a 1-inch collar around 4-ounce (120-milliliter) soufflé molds.

2. Whip egg yolks with half of the sugar, and whip egg whites with the remaining half of the sugar.

3. Whip heavy cream.

4. Fold egg whites into egg yolks.

5. Fold whipped cream into egg mixture; fold in Grand Marnier.

6. Fill soufflé molds to top of collar; freeze.

7. When frozen, remove collar, and decorate as desired; serve.

VARIATION

Frozen Orange Soufflé: Cut 8 oranges in half; remove the pulp and trim the bottoms so the orange sits flat. Make collars for the oranges. Garnish each portion with orange segments, chocolate ornaments, whipped cream, and mint leaves.

French Ice Cream

Yield: approximately 1 gallon (3.75 liters)

Milk	*1 1/2 quarts*	*1.5 liters*
Heavy cream	*1 1/2 pints*	*720 milliliters*
Sugar	*1 pound*	*450 grams*
Corn syrup	*1 pound*	*450 grams*
Eggs	*20 each*	*20 each*

1. Boil together the milk, heavy cream, 8 ounces (225 grams) of the sugar, and the corn syrup.

2. Make a liaison of the eggs and the remaining sugar, mixing well, then temper it with one-third of the boiling milk.

3. Bring the liquid back to a boil and cook until the mixture coats the back of a spoon.

4. Strain and cool over ice. Ripen overnight in the refrigerator.

5. Process in ice cream freezer. Freezing times may vary according to the equipment being used.

VARIATION

Chocolate Ice Cream: Add 4 ounces (120 grams) of sweet chocolate and 4 ounces (120 grams) of bitter chocolate to the base recipe for chocolate flavor.

Caramel Ice Cream: Caramelize 8 ounces (225 grams) of sugar. Add the boiled milk and corn syrup to the pan to dissolve the caramel. Proceed with the recipe from step 2.

Coffee Ice Cream: Add powdered instant coffee (to taste) to the hot milk in step 1.

This ice cream may also be known as Frozen Custard. The egg yolks give it a rich golden hue.

Ripening (step 4) allows flavors to fully develop and ensures a good texture.

Gélato

Yield: 24–30 servings, approximately 2 quarts (2 liters)

Milk	*1 quart*	*1 liter*
Eggs	*6 to 8 each*	*6 to 8 each*
Sugar	*8 ounces*	*225 grams*
Flavorings	*to taste*	*to taste*

1. Bring milk and half of the sugar to a boil.

2. Mix rest of sugar with the eggs.

3. Add milk mixture to the egg mixture and cook to the stage of nappé.

4. Flavor to taste.

5. Cool and freeze.

Gélato is an Italian ice milk. Flavor as you would ice cream.

Freezing times vary according to type of equipment being used.

Vanilla Ice Cream

Yield: approximately 3 quarts (3 liters)

Use pumpkin purée and cinnamon, nutmeg and allspice; krokant, praline, or fudge pieces folded in after freezing; concentrated fruit purée or other flavoring folded in to give a ripple effect.

Milk	2 pints	480 milliliters
Heavy cream	2 pints	480 milliliters
Vanilla bean, split lengthwise	1 each	1 each
Sugar	8 ounces	225 grams
Egg yolks	8 each	8 each

1. Heat milk and cream with vanilla bean; allow to steep, remove bean, scrape out seeds and add back to milk if desired.

2. Combine sugar and egg yolks; temper and add back to milk–cream mixture.

3. Cook mixture, stirring constantly, until nappé (mixture coats the back of spoon); strain and cool immediately.

4. Add desired flavoring, (see Variations, below), and freeze in the usual manner; add garnish just before ice cream is finished.

5. Store, carefully wrapped, in the freezer.

VARIATIONS

Chocolate Chocolate Chip: Add semisweet chocolate to the milk–cream mixture when heating. Garnish chocolate by folding in, after freezing, 1 or 2 of the following: chocolate chips, toasted nuts, rich chocolate cake, crumbled brownies, or ganache.

Flavored with different liquors: Flavor with any of these: Bailey's Irish Cream, Frangelico, Kahlúa, Crème de Menthe.

Fruit: Add fruit purée to base and fold in diced fruit after freezing the ice cream. Garnish fruit with chopped nuts, plain or toasted, spices, etc.

Lemon Sorbet

Yield: approximately 3 quarts (3 liters)

The classic test to see if the syrup for a sorbet is properly sweetened is this: Float a well-washed raw whole egg in the syrup (step 2). If the exposed surface area of the egg is about the size of a nickel, the syrup is good. If a greater area is exposed, it is too sweet; add water. If the egg is submerged or sinks, add sugar.

Water	1 3/4 quarts	1.7 liters
Sugar	18 ounces	500 grams
Lemon juice, strained	8 ounces	225 grams
Egg white, whipped	1 each	1 each

1. Combine water and sugar, until sugar is totally dissolved.

2. Add lemon juice; cool to room temperature and check flavor and density.

3. Add egg white to syrup base, blending well.

4. Freeze in an ice cream freezer according to manufacturer's directions.

(Recipe continued on facing page)

VARIATIONS

Wine Sorbet: Replace some of the water with white wine.

Orange Sorbet: Replace the lemon juice with orange juice.

Fruit Sorbet: Replace the lemon juice with fruit purée, and replace the water with the liquid the fruit may have been poached in (apple, pear, other firm fruits).

Raspberry Granità

Yield: 15 to 20 servings

Sugar	6 ounces	170 grams
Raspberry purée, strained	1 pint	450 milliliters
Lemon juice	1 teaspoon	1 teaspoon
Water	1 pint	480 milliliters

1. Combine all ingredients; stir together. Pour into a shallow pan.

2. Place in freezer, stir mixture every 15 to 30 minutes. Or, scrape the mixture once frozen to loosen "grains."

3. Serve with fresh fruit and champagne.

Serve in a champagne flute or coupe with a splash of champagne.

Garnish with fresh or poached fruit, mint leaves, and a drizzle of a cordial such as Framboise or Midori.

Serve a sampler of 2 or more flavors.

Sour Cherry Granità

Yield: 12 to 15 servings

White wine	4 fluid ounces	120 milliliters
Honey	2 ounces	60 grams
Sugar	2 ounces	60 grams
Cherries, fresh, pitted, puréed	1 pound	450 grams

1. Combine all ingredients, stir together. Pour into a shallow pan.

2. Place in freezer, stir mixture every 15 to 30 minutes. Or, allow it to freeze solidly, then use a kitchen spoon to scrape the surface, creating "grains."

Green Tea Granità

Yield: 15 to 20 servings

Sugar	*6 ounces*	*170 grams*
Lemon juice	*2 tablespoons*	*2 tablespoons*
Water	*1 3/4 pounds*	*800 grams*
Green tea bags	*4 only*	*4 only*

1. Combine sugar and water, bring to a boil and add tea bags and steep.

2. Strain tea and add lemon to taste. Pour into a shallow pan.

3. Freeze and stir mixture every 15 to 30 minutes. Or, scrape with a kitchen spoon once frozen to create "grains."

Rum Mango Granità

Yield: 16 to 18 servings

Mango, puréed	*8 fluid ounces*	*240 milliliters*
Sugar	*4 ounces*	*115 grams*
Dark rum	*3 tablespoons*	*45 milliliters*
Lemon juice	*3 tablespoons*	*45 milliliters*
Water	*1 pound, 6 ounces*	*625 grams*

1. Combine all ingredients, and stir together. Pour into a shallow pan.

2. Place in freezer and stir mixture every 15 to 30 minutes. Or, scrape with a kitchen spoon once frozen to create "grains."

Mangos are lush and flavorful. Be sure they are fully ripened for this recipe.

Watermelon Granità

Yield: 18 to 20 servings

Watermelon, puréed	*2 1/2 pounds*	*1.15 kilograms*
Sugar	*2 1/2 ounces*	*70 grams*
Lemon juice	*to taste*	*to taste*

1. Combine all ingredients, stir together. Pour into a shallow pan.

2. Place in freezer, stir mixture every 15 to 30 minutes. Or, scrape with a kitchen spoon once frozen to create "grains."

VARIATION

Use other melons—casaba, cranshaw, honeydew, or cantaloupe, for instance. Be sure they are fully ripe, sweet, and juicy.

Fresh Ginger Granità

Yield: 16 to 18 servings

Ginger, fresh	2 ounces	60 grams
Water	8 fluid ounces	240 milliliters
Sugar	4 ounces	115 grams
Water	1 1/2 pounds	680 grams
Lemon juice	4 teaspoons	4 teaspoons

1. Purée ginger with water, add sugar and second amount of water, and heat to 180°F (80°C).

2. Strain, add lemon to taste.

3. Freeze, and stir every 15 to 30 minutes. Or, scrape with a kitchen spoon once frozen to create "grains."

Poached Apples

Yield: 12 servings

Apples, peeled, cut in half, core	6 each	6 each
Poaching Liquid	1 1/2 quarts	1.4 liters
Filling		
Almond paste	6 ounces	170 grams
Sugar	4 ounces	115 grams
Filberts, toasted, ground	4 ounces	115 grams
Nougat	1 ounce	30 grams
Simple syrup	as needed	as needed
Garnish		
Fruit Coulis	1 1/2 pints	720 milliliters
Chocolate ornaments	12 each	12 each
Cookies	12 each	12 each

A basic poaching liquid for fruit may be found on page 1066.

Cookie recipes are on pages 1085 to 1095.

Fruit Coulis is on page 1073.

Nougat is made by heating sugar and lemon juice, as for caramel. Once browned, add sliced almonds. Cool on a marble slab. Pulverize before using in a food processor.

1. Poach apples in poaching liquid until tender; cool.

2. Combine all ingredients for the filling, mix together, and adjust consistency with simple syrup.

3. Cut out apple with circular cutter, and stuff with filling.

4. Pour Fruit Coulis on a plate.

5. Set apple on Fruit Coulis.

6. Garnish apple with chocolate stencil and a cookie.

For Nougat, see page 1065.

Poached Pears

Yield: 12 servings

Pears, peeled, trimmed, and cored	*6 each*	*6 each*
Poaching liquid	*1 1/2 quarts*	*1.5 liters*
Filling		
Almond paste	*6 ounces*	*170 grams*
Sugar	*4 ounces*	*115 grams*
Hazelnuts, toasted, ground	*4 ounces*	*115 grams*
Nougat	*1 ounce*	*30 grams*

1. Poach pears; cool.

2. For filling: Combine all ingredients, mix together, and adjust consistency with poaching liquid as necessary.

3. Cut out each pear with circular cutter; stuff with filling.

4. Serve with a sauce or garnish as desired.

Basic Poaching Liquid for Fruit

Yield: 1 quart (1 liter)

Water	*1 quart*	*1 liter*
Sugar, use for tart fruit	*8 ounces*	*225 grams*
Cinnamon stick (optional)	*1 each*	*1 each*
Cloves (optional)	*2 each*	*2 each*

1. Combine ingredients for poaching liquid, bring to a simmer.

2. Use to poach fresh or dried fruits.

VARIATIONS

Wine: Use red or white wine to replace half of the water.

Fruit: Add fruit purée or juices to the poaching liquid.

Spices: Vary the spices. Add mace, ginger, cardomom, allspice, nutmeg, or star anise.

Saffron: Add saffron for yellow color.

Glazed Pineapple Madagascar

Yield: 8 servings

Pineapple rings, cored, skinned	*8 each*	*8 each*
Green peppercorns, crushed	*1 1/2 tablespoons*	*23 grams*
Sugar	*2 1/2 ounces*	*70 grams*
Orange juice	*12 fluid ounces*	*360 milliliters*
Honey	*1 1/2 teaspoons*	*2.5 milliliters*
Light rum	*4 fluid ounces*	*120 milliliters*
St. Andrew's Glace	*as needed*	*as needed*

1. Rub pineapple slices with green peppercorns and sprinkle one side with sugar.

2. Heat a sauté pan to very hot, add pineapple rings, sugar side down, and allow to caramelize.

3. Turn pineapple; add orange juice, honey, and rum.

4. When pineapple is done, remove and place on dessert plate.

5. Reduce sauce to syrup consistency, and pour over pineapple.

Serve the pineapples with Vanilla Ice Cream, Gélato, or Raspberry Granità. Recipes may be found in this chapter.

Strawberries with Green Peppercorns

Yield: 2 servings

Strawberries	*6 to 8 each*	*6 to 8 each*
Sugar	*1 1/2 ounces*	*40 grams*
Butter, cubed	*3 ounces*	*85 grams*
Orange juice	*3/4 fluid ounce*	*20 milliliters*
Green peppercorns, drained	*1/2 ounce*	*15 grams*
Fraise de Boise	*1 fluid ounce*	*30 milliliters*
Brandy or cognac	*1 fluid ounce*	*30 milliliters*
Vanilla Ice Cream	*2 portions*	*2 portions*

1. Slice strawberries.

2. Heat sauté pan.

3. Sprinkle sugar evenly across the bottom of the sauté pan without allowing the spoon to touch the bottom. (This may cause the sugar to crystallize.)

4. As the sugar begins to caramelize, add butter, and gently shake the pan.

5. Add the remaining butter to the outside edges of the pan; this allows the butter to evenly temper and blend with the sugar.

6. Pour the orange juice on the outside edges of the pan slowly, allowing it to temper and blend with the sugar.

7. Add green peppercorns, mashing lightly with the back of the spoon so

This recipe is adapted for tableside cooking. To prepare larger batches in the kitchen, use the method for Pineapple Madagascar (above).

(Recipe continued on next page)

Fraise de Boise is a strawberry liqueur. Use other fruit-flavored liqueurs or cordials if you prefer.

they do not explode.

8. Add Fraise de Boise; do not flame.

9. Gently shake pan to incorporate all ingredients; sauce starts to thicken. (Move quickly so sauce does not become too thick.)

10. Add strawberries, gently shaking the pan to incorporate all ingredients.

11. Slide pan back and forth over the front edge of the flame, allowing pan to get hot.

12. Remove pan, add brandy, tip pan slightly, flame brandy, and shake pan until flame dies.

13. Spoon finished mixture over ice cream, nappé with sauce and serve at once.

Gratin of Fresh Fruits

Yield: 8 servings

Fresh fruit, seasonal, sliced or attractively cut	*8 portions*	*8 portions*
Sabayon sauce	*1 1/4 pounds*	*570 grams*
Egg yolks	*6 each*	*6 each*
Sugar	*6 ounces*	*170 grams*
White wine	*4 fluid ounces*	*120 milliliters*
Heavy cream, whipped	*6 fluid ounces*	*180 milliliters*

A good-sized serving of fruit is about 1/2 to 3/4 cup of sliced fruits or berries. In the winter, use poached apples or pears and add a tablespoon of plumped dried fruits.

Serve the gratin or the tartlette with ice cream, sorbet, or granità if desired.

1. Arrange fruit on ovenproof plate in an attractive fashion.

2. To prepare sauce: Combine egg yolks, sugar, and wine.

3. Whip egg yolk mixture over a water bath approximately 180°F (80°C), until light and foamy.

4. Remove from heat, allow to cool slightly, fold in whipped cream.

5. Coat the fruit with sauce; brown under broiler; serve immediately.

Individual Warm Fruit Tartlettes

Yield: 10 servings

Fresh fruit, poached, cleaned, sliced	*1 1/2 pounds*	*680 grams*
Puff Pastry	*1 1/4 pounds*	*570 grams*
Cookie crumbs	*3 1/2 ounces*	*100 grams*
Cinnamon sugar	*2 tablespoons*	*2 tablespoons*
Apricot jam, melted and strained	*3 ounces*	*85 grams*
Almonds, sliced and toasted	*2 ounces*	*60 grams*

(Recipe continued on facing page)

1. Roll the dough thin, line greased tartlette molds, and trim edges.

2. Sprinkle cookie crumbs on top of dough.

3. Arrange fruit in tartlettes and sprinkle with cinnamon sugar.

4. Bake in a 350°F (175°C) oven about 30 minutes or until fruit and dough are cooked.

5. Cool slightly, brush with apricot jam, and garnish with sliced almonds.

Fruit Fritter Batter

Yield: about 1 1/2 pints (720 milliliters)

Eggs	*2 each*	*2 each*
Sugar	*1 ounce*	*30 grams*
White wine	*6 fluid ounces*	*180 milliliters*
Apple juice	*6 fluid ounces*	*180 milliliters*
Salt	*pinch*	*pinch*
Lemon rind, blanched, chopped	*1/2 teaspoon*	*1/2 teaspoon*
Orange rind, blanched, chopped	*1/2 teaspoon*	*1/2 teaspoon*
All-purpose flour, sifted	*12 ounces*	*340 grams*

1. Combine eggs and sugar, and whip lightly.

2. Add wine, apple juice, salt, and rinds.

3. Add flour; blend until smooth.

4. To use, dip fruit in batter; deep-fry at 350°F (175°C) until golden brown and drain on absorbent paper.

5. Serve with fruit sauce or whipped cream as desired.

VARIATION

Strawberry Fritters: Dip hulled strawberries into heated and strained strawbery preserves, roll in chopped almonds or toasted coconut, then dip in batter. Fry as directed above.

Vanilla Sauce

Yield: 3 pints (1.5 liters)

This sauce is also known as Custard Sauce *and* Sauce Anglaise. *It can be made over a water bath for more control of the heat source.*

Add good-quality vanilla extract to the sauce in step 3 if you do not wish to use a vanilla bean. One tablespoon will flavor this recipe adequately.

Milk	*1 pint*	*480 milliliters*
Heavy cream	*1 pint*	*480 milliliters*
Vanilla bean	*1 each*	*1 each*
Sugar	*4 ounces*	*115 grams*
Egg yolks	*9 ounces*	*255 grams*
Sugar	*4 ounces*	*115 grams*

1. Heat milk, heavy cream, vanilla bean, and half of the sugar until it boils. Remove the vanilla bean and reserve for other uses.

2. Combine egg yolks and the rest of sugar, then temper with part of the boiling milk while stirring constantly.

3. Pour liaison into the remaining milk and return to the heat.

4. Stirring constantly, cook slowly to stage of nappé or 180°F (80°C).

5. Remove immediately from stove and strain through a chinois, directly into a bain-marie in an ice bath.

Wild Turkey Sauce

Yield: 20 fluid ounces (600 milliliters)

Substitute different flavored liquors for the Wild Turkey.

Serve this sauce with cobblers, fritters, or other baked or fried desserts.

Egg yolks	*6 each*	*6 each*
Sugar	*6 ounces*	*170 grams*
Wild Turkey	*3 fluid ounces*	*90 milliliters*
Heavy cream	*12 fluid ounces*	*360 milliliters*

1. Combine egg yolks and sugar in a stainless steel bowl.

2. Place bowl over a water bath and beat yolks until pale yellow and thickened (you should be able to see the bottom of the bowl when you draw a whip through the mixture).

3. Remove bowl from water bath, add Wild Turkey liquor and stir in.

4. Chill this mixture until very cold.

5. Whip the cream until it is thickened and mounds slightly when dropped from a spoon.

Lemon Curd

Yield: 24 ounces (680 grams)

Sugar	10 ounces	285 grams
Eggs	7 ounces	200 grams
Lemon juice	2 fluid ounces	60 milliliters
Butter, diced	5 ounces	140 grams
Lemon, peeled, grated	1/2 each	1/2 each

1. Whisk together the sugar, eggs, and lemon juice and peel over boiling water until mixture is thick and has reached 165°F (70°C). Do not boil.

2. Add the butter a few pieces at a time.

VARIATIONS

Lemon Mousse: Fold in enough beaten egg whites and whipped cream to make a mousselike consistency. Pipe into molds and refrigerate.

Orange Curd: Substitute orange juice and orange zest for the lemon.

Lime Curd: Substitute lime juice and lime zest for the lemon.

The butter amount can be increased if a firmer consistency is desired.

This mixture can be used for a number of preparations, such as lemon tartlettes, or fillings for cakes and French pastries.

Serve with spicy cakes as a filling or sauce.

Serve with biscuits or breakfast breads as a spread.

This sauce preparation takes approximately 20 minutes.

If a thicker sauce is desired, reduce to desired degree or thicken slightly with arrowroot.

To purée fresh berries, place them in a blender or food processor. A fine sieve can be used to strain out seeds if desired.

Strawberry Sauce

Yield: 2 1/4 pounds (1 kilogram)

Strawberries, halved	*3 pounds*	*1.3 kilograms*
Sugar	*4 ounces*	*115 grams*
Orange juice	*2 fluid ounces*	*60 milliliters*
Orange zest	*1 teaspoon*	*1 teaspoon*
Lemon zest	*1 teaspoon*	*1 teaspoon*
Grand Marnier	*2 fluid ounces*	*60 milliliters*

1. Combine the strawberries, sugar, orange juice, and zest; bring to a boil.
2. Simmer for 2 minutes; purée the sauce, then strain.
3. Add Grand Marnier.
4. Reserve in refrigerator until needed.

Raspberry Sauce

Yield: 12 ounces (340 grams)

Sugar	*2 3/4 ounces*	*80 grams*
Burgundy wine	*3 fluid ounces*	*90 milliliters*
Raspberry purée (fresh)	*7 fluid ounces*	*210 milliliters*

1. Combine all ingredients, simmer 3 minutes and strain.
2. Let cool; use 1 to 1 1/2 ounces (15 grams) per serving.

Raisin Sauce

Yield: 10 fluid ounces (300 milliliters)

Apple cider or juice	*8 fluid ounces*	*240 milliliters*
Brown sugar	*1 ounce*	*30 grams*
Apple brandy	*1 fluid ounce*	*30 milliliters*
Cinnamon, ground	*1/4 teaspoon*	*1/4 teaspoon*
Nutmeg, ground	*a few grains*	*a few grains*
Vanilla bean	*1/2 each*	*1/2 each*
Raisins or currants, plumped	*1 ounce*	*30 grams*
Arrowroot (optional)	*1 teaspoon*	*1 teaspoon*

(Recipe continued on facing page)

1. Combine all ingredients except raisins, bring to a boil, and simmer 1 minute.

2. Thicken to desired consistency with arrowroot. (This is an optional step as sauce may already be thick enough).

3. Stir in raisins and cool; refrigerate until needed.

4. Portion size varies according to application.

Melba Sauce

Yield: 1 pint (480 milliliters)

Raspberry purée	*14 fluid ounces*	*420 milliliters*
Sugar	*1 ounce*	*30 grams*
Chambord	*2 fluid ounces*	*60 milliliters*

1. Combine raspberry purée and sugar, bring to a boil.

2. Add Chambord to taste. Cool thoroughly.

This sauce is prepared to accompany Peach Melba, a dessert compound of poached peaches served with vanilla ice cream and this sauce.

Fruit Coulis

Yield: 1 quart (1 liter)

Fruit	*1 pound*	*450 grams*
Sugar, to taste, depending upon type of fruit	*1 pound*	*450 grams*
Lemons, juiced	*2 each*	*2 each*
Cornstarch, per quart of liquid	*1 ounce*	*30 grams*

1. Mix fruit and sugar together, and bring to a boil; purée if needed, then strain.

2. Reduce on stove to desired consistency; add lemon juice.

3. Thicken with cornstarch if needed.

Sabayon Sauce

Yield: 1 quart (1 liter)

Egg yolks	*9 ounces*	*255 grams*
Sugar	*9 ounces*	*255 grams*
White wine	*6 fluid ounces*	*180 milliliters*
Heavy cream, whipped	*12 fluid ounces*	*360 milliliters*

1. Combine egg yolks, sugar, and white wine.

2. Whip this mixture over a simmering water bath until approximately 180°F (80°C), remove from heat, transfer to mixer bowl, and whip until cool.

3. Fold in whipped cream by hand once mixture is cool.

You will need about 12 yolks to equal 9 ounces (225 grams).

Add a small amount of gelatin (1/4 ounce/7 grams) to stabilize the sauce if desired.

Nuss Sauce

Yield: approximately 1 quart (1 liter)

The recipe for Vanilla Sauce is on page 1070.

Frangelica is a hazelnut-flavored liqueur.

Vanilla Sauce	*1 quart*	*1 liter*
Hazelnuts, toasted, chopped fine	*4 ounces*	*115 grams*
Chocolate, chopped	*1 ounce*	*30 grams*
Frangelica	*1 fluid ounce*	*30 milliliters*

1. Make Vanilla Sauce; cool over ice.
2. Add hazelnuts, chocolate, and Frangelica to sauce.
3. Refrigerate until needed.
4. Portion size varies according to the intended use.

Hard Sauce

Yield: 1 pint (480 milliliters)

Hard Sauce is used to accompany steamed puddings. A rosette is placed on each portion. The pudding's heat melts the sauce.

Butter	*8 ounces*	*225 grams*
Powdered sugar or honey	*4 ounces*	*115 grams*
Dark rum	*3 fluid ounces*	*90 milliliters*
Lemon juice	*10 drops*	*10 drops*

1. Cream butter and sugar lightly.
2. Slowly add liquids. Chill if necessary.
3. Pipe rosettes onto parchment paper and chill.

Cinnamon Sauce

Yield: 2 1/2 pints (1.25 liters)

Sugar	*6 ounces*	*170 grams*
Apple juice	*12 fluid ounces*	*340 milliliters*
Water	*12 fluid ounces*	*360 milliliters*
Orange juice	*4 fluid ounces*	*120 milliliters*
Cinnamon, ground	*1 ounce*	*30 grams*
Lemon juice	*2 fluid ounces*	*60 milliliters*
Clear gel	*1 1/4 ounces*	*38 grams*
White rum	*2 fluid ounces*	*60 milliliters*
Butter	*1/2 ounce*	*15 grams*

(Recipe continued on facing page)

1. Combine the sugar, 8 ounces (225 grams) of apple juice, water, orange juice, cinnamon, and lemon juice; bring to a boil.

2. Combine the remaining apple juice and clear gel, add to above liquid and return to a strong second boil; remove from heat.

3. Add rum and butter, cool and reserve.

4. Portion size varies according to application.

Chocolate Sauce

Yield: 31 plates, 1-ounce (30-gram) portions
20 plates, 1 1/2-ounces (45-gram) portions

Heavy cream	*1 pint*	*480 milliliters*
Honey	*2 ounces*	*60 grams*
Vanilla	*to taste*	*to taste*
Chocolate, melted	*13 ounces*	*370 grams*

1. Combine heavy cream and honey, bring to a boil, remove from heat.

2. Add vanilla and chocolate, let cool.

Alternative preparation: Mix 1 quart (1 liter) Vanilla Sauce with 12 ounces (340 grams) of semisweet chocolate; add chocolate when sauce is hot. Let cool and serve.

Under most conditions, chocolate should not be refrigerated, since this could cause moisture to condense on the surface.

Chocolate Ganache

Yield: 25 ounces (700 grams)

Sugar	*2 ounces*	*60 grams*
Heavy cream	*1 quart*	*1 liter*
Butter	*2 ounces*	*60 grams*
Chocolate, semisweet, chopped	*2 pounds*	*900 grams*
Liqueur (optional)	*2 fluid ounces*	*60 milliliters*

1. Combine sugar, cream, and butter; heat to a boil, and remove from heat.

2. Add chocolate, stir until chocolate is melted. Cool. When cool, add liquor.

Vary the flavor by using different types of chocolate, semisweet and bitter combinations, white chocolate, and liquors.

VARIATIONS

Truffles: Let the Ganache cool. Scoop out 1/4 ounce (7 grams) of Ganache and roll. Coat by rolling in cocoa powder or dipping in chocolate.

Chocolate Glaze: Warm the Ganache and use it to glaze cakes and small pastries.

Soft Ganache: Increase the cream to 40 fluid ounces (1.5 liters). Decrease chocolate by 4 ounces (115 grams).

Chocolate Fudge Sauce

Yield: 1 1/4 quarts (1.2 liters)

Chocolate, bitter	*8 ounces*	*225 grams*
Butter	*3 ounces*	*85 grams*
Water	*12 fluid ounces*	*360 milliliters*
Sugar	*10 1/2 ounces*	*300 grams*
Corn syrup	*7 fluid ounces*	*210 milliliters*
Liquor	*1 fluid ounce*	*30 milliliters*

1. Combine chocolate and butter; melt slowly.
2. Add water and stir in.
3. Add sugar and corn syrup. Stir in.
4. Bring to a simmer; cook for 8 to 10 minutes.
5. Cool slightly; add liquor. Serve warm.

Caramel Sauce

Yield: 1 1/2 quarts (1.5 liters)

Sugar	*8 ounces*	*225 grams*
Water	*2 fluid ounces*	*60 milliliters*
Milk or heavy cream	*1 quart*	*1 liter*
Egg yolks	*6 ounces*	*170 grams*

1. Melt sugar until it is a caramel color and add the water; stir until smooth and caramel sugar is melted.
2. Add milk and eggs; cook until the sauce coats the back of a spoon. Serve warm.

Cinnamon Rum Syrup

Yield: 2 quarts (2 liters)

Orange juice	*1 pint*	*480 milliliters*
Water	*3 pints*	*1.4 liters*
Sugar	*3 pints*	*1.4 liters*
Cinnamon sticks	*1 to 4 each*	*1 to 4 each*
Vanilla extract	*1 teaspoon*	*1 teaspoon*
White rum	*to taste*	*to taste*

1. Combine all ingredients except rum; bring to a boil, simmer 5 minutes, and remove cinnamon sticks.

2. Add rum away from the heat.

3. Let cool.

4. Date and label then refrigerate for future use.

Simple Syrup

Yield: 1 quart (1 liter)

Water	*1 quart*	*1 liter*
Sugar	*8 ounces*	*225 grams*
Lemons, juiced	*3 each*	*3 each*
Oranges, juiced	*3 each*	*3 each*

1. Bring water and sugar to a boil.

2. Cool.

3. Flavor with lemon and orange juices and refrigerate until needed.

To make coffee flavored syrup, add prepared coffee syrup or diluted powdered instant coffee, or espresso to taste.

C H A P T E R 30 : *Cakes and Pastries*

Elaborate pastries and cakes are often thought of as a serious challenge. They tend to involve the preparation of more than one component, as when you may be called upon to prepare a cookie base, a genoise, a bavarian filling, and a buttercream or frosting.

The recipes in this chapter have been grouped as follows:

- *Pastry Doughs*
- *Cookies*
- *Fillings*
- *Meringues*
- *Frostings and Buttercreams*
- *Basic Cakes*
- *Cheesecakes*
- *Layer Cakes and Tortes*
- *Candies*

It is important to use pastry flour and to work the dough as little as possible.

This is sometimes called a 3-2-1 dough, because it's made from 3 parts flour, 2 parts shortening, and 1 part water.

One pound (450 grams) of butter can be changed to 8 ounces (225 grams) of butter and 8 ounces (225 grams) of shortening if desired.

Pie Crust Dough

Yield: 5, 2-crust pies

Butter or shortening	2 pounds	900 grams
Pastry flour	3 pounds	1.3 kilograms
Salt	1 ounce	30 grams
Cold water	1 pound	450 grams

1. Break shortening into flour to form large nuggets the size of walnuts.
2. Dissolve salt in liquid.
3. Add cold liquid to flour and shortening and mix just enough to form a dough.
4. Use 1 ounce (30 grams) of dough for each inch of pie pan size.
5. Bake at 425°F (220°C) for 35 minutes, or until done if you need a pre-baked pie shell.
6. For unbaked shell follow step 4 and fill with amount recipe calls for.

Pâte Brisée

Yield: 3 1/2 pounds (1.7 kilograms)

Butter	1 pound	450 grams
Sugar	1/4 ounce	8 grams
Eggs	2 each	2 each
Water	8 fluid ounces	240 milliliters
Salt	1/4 ounce	8 grams
Pastry flour	2 pounds	900 grams

1. Cream butter and sugar together.
2. Add eggs, water, and salt. Mix until blended in.
3. Add flour; mix until incorporated. Do not overmix.
4. Chill until ready to use.

Pâte à Choux

Yield: 5 pounds (2.25 kilograms)

Water	*1 pound*	*450 grams*
Milk	*1 pound*	*450 grams*
Butter, cut in pieces	*8 ounces*	*225 grams*
Shortening, cut in pieces	*8 ounces*	*225 grams*
Salt	*1/4 ounce*	*8 grams*
Sugar	*1/4 ounce*	*8 grams*
Bread flour	*1 1/2 pounds*	*680 grams*
Eggs, adjust consistency	*1 pint*	*480 milliliters*

1. Combine liquid, butter and shortening, salt, and sugar. Bring to a rolling boil.

2. Add flour all at once, stirring constantly, until mixture forms a ball and pulls away from the sides of the pan.

3. Place mixture into a mixing bowl on second speed for 2 minutes to cool slightly.

4. Slowly add eggs in three to four additions, mixing well between each addition to form a medium-stiff paste.

5. Fill a pastry bag and pipe out as needed for what you are making.

6. Bake at 380 to 400°F (190 to 200°C) for 10 minutes until the structure has attained a little color, then reduce temperature to 250°F (120°C) until the moisture has evaporated, approximately 30 minutes.

VARIATION

French Crullers: If making French Crullers, use 2 ounces (60 milliliters) of the eggs to keep the batter thicker.

As with many basic formulas, the types of ingredients (butter, or shortening, etc.) used in pâte à choux can be varied depending on its intended use. Be aware, however, that these changes will provide different results, such as the quick browning that is caused when milk is used rather than water.

Short Dough for Crust

This dough is also known as pâté sucre. *It is commonly used for tarts.*

Yield: 6 pounds (2.75 kilograms)

Butter	2 pounds	900 grams
Shortening	1 pound	450 grams
Granulated sugar	1 pound	450 grams
Eggs	6 ounces	170 grams
Vanilla	1/2 ounce	15 milliliters
Cake flour	2 pounds	900 grams
Bread flour	1 pound	450 grams
Baking powder	1/2 ounce	15 grams
Salt	1/2 ounce	15 grams

1. Cream the butter, shortening, and sugar in 12-quart (20-liter) mixer with paddle on first speed, 8 to 10 minutes.
2. Slowly blend in eggs and vanilla in three additions.
3. Sift dry ingredients together once only.
4. Blend in dry ingredients just enough to incorporate and make a smooth dough.
5. Chill dough until firm enough to roll out. Dough can be made in advance and stores well in a refrigerator.
6. Prebake either partially, at 350 to 375°F (175 to 190°C) for 15 to 20 minutes until firm but no color, or fully bake depending on need.

Almond Dough

Use 1 ounce (30 grams) per inch of pan size covered; use 20-quart (20-liter) mixer and paddle.

Yield: 5 pounds (2.25 kilograms)

Sugar	1 1/4 pounds	570 grams
Butter	1 1/4 pounds	570 grams
Almonds, crushed fine	1 1/4 pounds	570 grams
Eggs	4 ounces	115 grams
Pastry flour	1 1/2 pounds	680 grams
Baking powder	1/2 ounce	15 grams

1. Cream sugar and butter together.
2. Add almonds and blend.
3. Add eggs gradually, mixing to incorporate.
4. Sift together flour and baking powder; add to dough.
5. Chill until ready for use.
6. Bake at 360°F (180°C) for 20 minutes or until light golden brown.

1082

Linzer Dough

Yield: 4, 10-inch tortes or 275 small cookies

Butter	1 1/2 pounds	680 grams
Sugar	18 ounces	510 grams
Eggs	4 1/2 ounces	125 grams
Vanilla	1/2 teaspoon	1/2 teaspoon
Cake flour	30 ounces	850 grams
Cinnamon, ground	1/2 ounce	15 grams
Cake crumbs, fine	4 ounces	115 grams
Baking powder	1/2 ounce	15 grams
Hazelnuts, ground, toasted	12 ounces	340 grams

1. Combine butter and sugar; cream together.

2. Add eggs and vanilla; mix together.

3. Sift flour, cinnamon, and baking powder together; add to creamed mixture and incorporate.

4. Add hazelnuts and cake crumbs and blend in.

5. Chill dough.

6. Roll out on floured board and cut in desired shape.

7. Bake at 350°F (175°C) for 15 to 20 minutes or until light golden brown.

Linzer Torte: *To make tarts, use dough to line a tart pan, fill with raspberry jam, and top with additional dough shaped into a lattice top.*

Linzer Cookies: *Roll out dough and cut into cookie rounds. Brush with egg wash on rims. Fill center with a little raspberry jam; top with a ring of dough.*

Butter Puff Pastry Dough

Yield: 12 pounds (5.5 kilograms)

Cake flour	1 pound	450 grams
Bread flour	4 pounds	1.8 kilograms
Butter	8 ounces	225 grams
Water	2 1/2 pounds	1.15 kilograms
Salt	1/4 ounce	8 grams
Butter	4 1/2 pounds	2 kilograms

1. Sift cake and bread flours together.

2. Rub the butter into four-fifths of the flour.

3. Add water and salt, and knead into a smooth dough. Allow to relax in the refrigerator.

4. Combine butter with the remaining one-fifth flour, knead until smooth, and roll into an 18-by-18-inch square; cool slightly; do not allow it to become brittle and cold.

5. Roll dough into a rectangle the same width as the butter mix but one-third longer.

(Recipe continued on next page)

6. Place butter on two-thirds of the dough, leaving one-third exposed.

7. Fold the exposed third of the dough over the middle butter-covered third of dough and fold the remaining third of fat-covered dough over the exposed dough. This will produce a three-fold. Roll to original size, seal edges, and turn 90 degrees.

8. Rest dough 20 to 30 minutes between folding and rolling.

9. Roll, book-fold, and turn dough four times, resting between each rolling.

Blitz Puff Pastry

Blitz Puff Pastry is explained on page 397. See Figures 12-19 and 12-20 for an illustration of the dough as it is mixed and rolled.

Yield: 10 pounds (2.25 kilograms)

Bread flour	*2 pounds*	*900 grams*
Pastry flour	*2 pounds*	*900 grams*
Butter, diced	*4 pounds*	*1.8 kilograms*
Salt	*1 ounce*	*30 grams*
Water	*1 quart*	*1 liter*

1. Combine the flours in a large bowl.

2. Cut the butter into the flour very lightly. The pieces of butter should be quite large.

3. Combine the salt and the water and stir until dissolved.

4. Add the water to the dough and mix just when it catches.

5. Refrigerate the dough briefly if necessary, then roll it out into a rectangle.

6. Make three 4-folds, rolling out and refrigerating the dough between each fold.

7. Cut and shape the dough as desired.

Regular Cookie Dough

Yield: 6 pounds (2.75 kilograms)

Sugar	*1 pound*	*455 grams*
Butter	*2 pounds*	*900 grams*
Eggs	*6 ounces*	*170 grams*
Flavor	*1/2 ounce*	*40 grams*
Cake flour	*3 pounds*	*1.3 kilograms*

1. Combine sugar and butter. Cream together.

2. Add eggs and flavoring. Cream together.

3. Add flour and mix just long enough to combine; do not overmix.

4. Chill.

5. Bake at 385°F (195°C). (Baking time depends on the product you are making.)

Add various extracts or citrus zests to achieve the desired flavor.

1-2-3 doughs such as these are composed of 1 part sugar, 2 parts butter, and 3 parts flour. This ratio produces a delicate cookie with a good texture. Using confectioner's sugar in the special formula produces a dough that does not spread as it bakes.

Special Cookie Dough

Yield: 7 pounds (3.15 kilograms)

Confectioners' sugar	*18 ounces*	*500 grams*
Butter	*2 1/2 pounds*	*1.15 kilograms*
Egg whites	*4 ounces*	*115 grams*
Flavor	*to taste*	*to taste*
Cake flour	*3 pounds*	*1.3 kilograms*

1. Combine sugar and butter. Cream together.

2. Add eggs and flavoring. Cream together.

3. Add flour; mix just long enough to combine, do not overmix.

4. Chill.

5. Bake at 385°F (195°C). Baking time depends on the product you are making.

VARIATIONS

Chocolate Cookie Dough: Replace 8 to 10 ounces of the flour with cocoa powder.

Checkerboard Cookies: Make battonet pieces of alternating plain and chocolate doughs and stack in layers. Slice vertically to produce a checkerboard pattern.

Shortbread

Yield: 2 pounds (900 grams)

Chopped nuts or candied or dried fruit may be used.

Butter	12 ounces	340 grams
Sugar	11 ounces	315 grams
Egg yolks	2 each	2 each
Amaretto	2 tablespoons	2 tablespoons
Orange zest	2 teaspoons	2 teaspoons
Cake flour	2 teaspoons	2 teaspoons
Bread flour	8 ounces	225 grams
Salt	1/4 teaspoon	1/4 teaspoon
Egg whites, beaten	1 each	1 each
Almonds, sliced	2 ounces	60 grams

1. Cream butter and sugar (reserving 1 ounce/30 grams) until light.

2. Slowly add egg yolks and scrape down the bowl.

3. Add liquor and orange zest.

4. Add flours and salt.

5. Roll dough between two sheets of parchment paper to the size of a half-sheet pan.

6. Brush top with egg white and sprinkle with sliced blanched almonds and remaining sugar.

7. Bake in a 325°F (160°C) oven for 15 minutes or until golden brown.

8. Cut into portions while slightly warm.

Spritz Cookies

Yield: 30 dozen cookies

Sugar	*2 1/4 pounds*	*1 kilogram*
Butter	*2 1/4 pounds*	*1 kilogram*
Vanilla	*1/4 ounce*	*8 milliliters*
Lemon extract	*1/4 ounce*	*8 milliliters*
Salt	*1 ounce*	*30 grams*
Butter or shortening	*26 ounces*	*735 grams*
Eggs	*9 ounces*	*255 grams*
Milk	*9 fluid ounces*	*270 milliliters*
Pastry flour	*3 3/4 pounds*	*1.7 kilograms*
Bread flour	*1 1/4 pounds*	*570 grams*
Milk powder	*3 ounces*	*85 grams*

1. Cream together sugar, butter, vanilla, lemon, salt, and shortening.

2. Add eggs gradually.

3. Add milk.

4. Sift together pastry and bread flours, and milk powder.

5. Fold flour mixture into butter, mix just until incorporated. Do not over-mix.

6. Pipe out cookies into desired shapes on parchment-lined sheet pans.

7. Bake in a 380°F (190°C) oven for 14 minutes or until light brown on edges.

A round cookie can be garnished with cherries or nuts, added before baking.

Round cookies may be coated with fondant added after baking.

Sandwich two cookies together with jam and dip in tempered chocolate.

Chocolate Chip

Yield: 10 dozen cookies

Instead of using chips, coarsely chop semi-sweet, milk, or white chocolate.

Use walnuts, hazelnuts, or macadamia nuts instead of pecans.

Sugar	*1 1/2 pounds*	*680 grams*
Brown sugar	*1 1/2 pounds*	*680 grams*
Butter	*1 pound*	*450 grams*
Butter or shortening	*1 pound*	*450 grams*
Salt	*1/2 ounce*	*15 grams*
Baking soda	*1 ounce*	*30 grams*
Eggs	*1 1/2 pounds*	*680 grams*
Pastry flour	*3 pounds*	*1.3 kilograms*
Chocolate chips	*4 pounds*	*1.8 kilograms*
Pecans, chopped	*12 ounces*	*340 grams*

1. Combine sugars, butter, shortening, salt, and baking soda; cream together.

2. Add eggs slowly.

3. Add pastry flour. Mix until just combined; do not overmix. Add chocolate chips and nuts, mix just enough to combine.

4. Portion onto parchment-lined sheet pans by drop method or using a portion scoop, 1 1/2 ounces (45 grams) each cookie.

5. Bake in a 350°F (175°C) oven for 15 to 17 minutes or until golden brown on edges.

Pfeffernusse

Yield: 18 dozen cookies

Pferffernusse *is German for "pepper nut." These cookies are traditionally prepared at Christmas-time. Versions of this cookie can be found throughout Europe.*

Honey	*21 ounces*	*600 grams*
Sugar	*14 ounces*	*400 grams*
Water	*5 1/4 fluid ounces*	*158 milliliters*
Eggs	*3 1/2 ounces*	*100 grams*
Brown sugar, light	*1 3/4 ounces*	*50 grams*
Baking soda	*1 ounce*	*30 grams*
Milk	*2 fluid ounces*	*60 milliliters*
Bread flour	*2 3/4 pounds*	*1.25 kilograms*
Rye flour	*8 ounces*	*225 grams*
Allspice, ground	*1 ounce*	*30 grams*
Cinnamon, ground	*1/3 ounce*	*10 grams*
Currants	*8 ounces*	*225 grams*

(Recipe continued on facing page)

1. Heat honey, sugar, and water to 180°F (80°C) or until sugar is dissolved and cool to approximately 100°F (35°C).

2. Combine eggs and brown sugar.

3. Dissolve the baking soda in the milk.

4. Sift the dry ingredients and make a well.

5. Add the honey mixture, egg mixture, milk, and the currants.

6. Dust table with flour; roll dough until it is 1/2 inch (1 centimeter) thick.

7. Cut dough with 1 1/4-inch-diameter (3-centimeter) round cutter.

8. Place on parchment paper and bake in a 425°F (220°C) oven for 15 minutes or until medium golden brown.

Coconut Macaroons

Yield: 15 dozen cookies

Egg whites	*1 pound*	*450 grams*
Sugar	*2 pounds*	*900 grams*
Corn syrup	*4 ounces*	*115 grams*
Coconut, fine, unsweetened	*2 1/2 pounds*	*1.15 kilograms*
Lemon, zest and juice	*1/ 2 each*	*1/2 each*
Cake flour	*2 ounces*	*60 grams*
Vanilla	*1 tablespoon*	*15 milliliters*

Cookies may be garnished with candied fruit before baking.

Bottoms may be dipped in chocolate after they are baked and cooled.

1. Combine egg whites, corn syrup and sugar in a bowl; heat to 110°F (43°C) over a water bath.

2. Add coconut, lemon zest, juice, flour, and vanilla; mix in. Reheat to 125°F (50°C).

3. Using a pastry bag or ice cream scoop (size #100), portion, while still hot, onto a parchment-lined pan. Allow to dry for 1 1/2 hours. Bake in a 375°F (190°C) oven for 30 minutes or until golden brown on edges.

Lemon Cookies

Yield: 5 dozen cookies

Butter	*12 1/2 ounces*	*355 grams*
Powdered sugar	*10 1/2 ounces*	*300 grams*
Egg yolks	*12 ounces*	*340 grams*
Lemons zested	*1 1/2 each*	*1 1/2 each*
Flour, pastry	*16 1/2 ounces*	*470 grams*

1. Cream together butter and sugar. Add egg yolks and lemon zest.

2. Add pastry flour; mix just long enough to combine ingredients. Do not overmix.

3. Pipe out round cookies 1 inch in diameter; bake at 400°F (205°C) for 8 to 10 minutes or until lightly brown.

Dixie Butterscotch Icebox Cookies

Yield: 17 1/2 dozen cookies

Icebox cookies can be refrigerated for several days or frozen for 2 months. They can be sliced and baked daily for the best quality.

Hazelnuts are also known as filberts.

Brown sugar	*26 ounces*	*735 grams*
Sugar	*1 1/2 pounds*	*680 grams*
Shortening, all-purpose	*2 pounds*	*900 grams*
Salt	*1/2 ounce*	*15 grams*
Eggs	*12 ounces*	*340 grams*
Baking soda	*3/4 ounce*	*20 grams*
Cream of tartar	*1/2 ounce*	*15 grams*
Cinnamon	*1/8 ounce*	*4 grams*
Pastry flour	*3 1/2 pounds*	*1.6 kilograms*
Hazelnuts, chopped	*18 ounces*	*500 grams*

1. With a paddle, cream the sugars, shortening, and salt together until light and fluffy.

2. Add eggs slowly to emulsify, scraping bowl down often.

3. Add baking soda, cream of tartar, cinnamon, and flour, mixing to blend in.

4. Add nuts and stir just to incorporate so that mixture does not break down.

5. Scale dough into 1 1/2-pound (680-gram) pieces; and shape into a logs.

6. Cut each log into 30 pieces and place on parchment-lined sheet pan.

7. Bake for 15 minutes at 380°F (190°C) or until lightly brown.

Crumiri Cookies

Yield: 9 dozen cookies

Butter	*1 3/4 pounds*	*800 grams*
Salt	*1/4 ounce*	*8 grams*
Sugar	*1 1/4 pounds*	*570 grams*
Eggs	*1 pound*	*450 grams*
Cornmeal	*1 pound*	*450 grams*
Pastry flour	*1 pound*	*450 grams*
Bread flour	*1 pound*	*450 grams*

1. Cream the butter, salt, and sugar until light and fluffy.

2. Add eggs gradually, scraping down sides of bowl after each addition.

3. Add cornmeal; mix only until incorporated.

4. Sift dry ingredients; add to batter.

5. Bake in a 375°F (190°C) oven for 15 minutes or until done.

Hermit Cookies

Yield: 7 1/2 dozen cookies

Sugar	*1 1/2 pounds*	*680 grams*
Shortening	*8 ounces*	*225 grams*
Butter	*4 ounces*	*115 grams*
Molasses	*6 ounces*	*170 grams*
Salt	*3/8 ounce*	*12 grams*
Allspice, ground	*1/4 ounce*	*8 grams*
Cinnamon, ground	*1/4 ounce*	*8 grams*
Eggs	*6 ounces*	*170 grams*
Water	*5 fluid ounces*	*150 milliliters*
Cake flour	*2 1/2 pounds*	*1.15 kilograms*
Baking soda	*3/4 ounce*	*20 grams*
Raisins	*1 pound*	*455 grams*

1. Cream together the sugar, shortening, butter, molasses, salt, and spices.

2. Gradually add the eggs.

3. Gradually add the water.

4. Sift together the cake flour and baking soda; add to the mixture, and mix until smooth.

5. Add raisins.

6. Scale into 12-ounce (340-gram) units and roll into a circular tube 1 1/2 inches (4 centimeters) in diameter.

7. Bake for 18 to 20 minutes at 360 to 375°F (180 to 190°C).

Cake Brownie

Yield: 1 sheet pan

These two formulas will produce brownies with distinctly different textures.

Make brownie sundaes by topping a brownie with ice cream and fudge sauce.

Use the corners and edges (diced) as a garnish for ice cream.

Sugar	2 pounds	900 grams
Butter	2 pounds	900 grams
Baking powder	4 ounces	115 grams
Salt	4 ounces	115 grams
Corn syrup	1 pound	450 grams
Eggs	2 pounds	900 grams
Baking soda	3/4 ounce	20 grams
Bread flour	2 pounds	900 grams
Cocoa powder	8 ounces	225 grams
Water	27 fluid ounces	810 milliliters
Pecans	1 pound	450 grams

1. Cream together sugar, butter, baking powder, salt, and glucose.

2. Add eggs slowly and mix until incorporated.

3. Sift together dry ingredients.

4. Add dry ingredients alternately with water.

5. Add pecans.

6. Pour into sheet pans, bake 375°F (190°C) for 35 minutes or until done. Cut to the desired size.

Fudge Brownie

Yield: 1 sheet pan

Bitter chocolate	1 1/2 pounds	680 grams
Butter	2 1/4 pounds	1 kilogram
Eggs	30 ounces	850 grams
Sugar	4 1/2 pounds	2 kilograms
Vanilla	1 fluid ounce	30 milliliters
Cake flour	1 1/2 pounds	680 grams
Pecans or walnuts	18 ounces	510 grams

1. Melt chocolate and butter carefully over a water bath; do not exceed 110°F (43°C).

2. Combine eggs, sugar, and vanilla; beat until lemon-colored.

3. Add chocolate and butter to egg mixture, tempering the eggs first.

4. Gently fold in flour.

5. Fold in 1 pound (450 grams) of nuts, pour into sheet pan. Sprinkle remaining nuts on top.

6. Bake at 350°F (175°C) for 40 minutes until done or until brownie is firm to touch on top.

Tuiles

Yield: 6 1/2 dozen cookies

Powdered sugar, sifted	*9 ounces*	*255 grams*
Bread flour, sifted	*6 ounces*	*170 grams*
Almonds, toasted and crushed	*10 ounces*	*285 grams*
Egg whites	*4 ounces*	*115 grams*
Eggs	*6 ounces*	*170 grams*
Vanilla	*1/2 teaspoon*	*1/2 teaspoon*
Butter, melted	*3 ounces*	*85 grams*

To see the procedure for preparing Tuiles illustrated, turn to page 409.

Grated orange or lemon zest can be used for flavor.

1. Combine sugar, flour, and almonds together.

2. Add egg whites, eggs, flavoring, and melted butter; scrape down the bowl well.

3. Spoon 1/2 ounce (15 grams) for each cookie onto a flat sheet pan that has been buttered and floured.

4. Flatten with fork (to prevent fork sticking to dough, dip into water each time.)

5. Bake at 380°F (190°C) for 8 minutes or until pale brown at the edges.

6. Immediately remove from sheet pan and place bottom up into a trough-shaped mold.

7. Store in airtight container.

Florentines

Yield: 3 dozen cookies

If baked on a flat sheet pan, halfway during the baking you will have to push the mixture back into shape with a 3-inch ring.

Butter	7 ounces	200 grams
Sugar	4 ounces	115 grams
Honey	5 ounces	140 grams
Milk	5 fluid ounces	150 milliliters
Almonds, slivered	4 ounces	115 grams
Almonds, sliced	4 ounces	115 grams
Candied fruit, small dice	8 ounces	225 grams
Glazed cherries, halved	18 whole	18 whole
Chocolate, tempered for finishing	as needed	as needed

1. Combine butter, sugar, honey, and milk; boil until 245°F (120°C).

2. Add almonds and candied fruit; stir in.

3. Portion into bun pans using a round scoop to approximately 3-inch (7.5-centimeter) diameter, place a candied cherry half in the center of each.

4. Bake in a 360°F (180°C) oven for 12 to 15 minutes or until a light golden brown.

5. When cool, cover bottoms with chocolate and mark with a cake comb in a wave pattern, Florentine style.

VARIATIONS

Nutcrackers: Use 8 ounces (225 grams) whole toasted hazelnuts instead of almonds.

Candied Fruit: Use 12 ounces (340 grams) candied fruit mixed with 3 ounces (85 grams) almonds.

Hazelnut Florentine

Yield: 6, 10-inch (25 centimeter) circles

If the hazelnut Florentine is left whole the cake should be left in the refrigerator overnight for the Florentine to soften.

Heavy cream	7 fluid ounces	210 milliliters
Sugar	8 ounces	225 grams
Butter	2 ounces	60 grams
Hazelnuts, toasted and ground	12 ounces	340 grams
Cake flour	1/2 ounce	15 grams

1. Combine heavy cream, sugar, and butter; bring to a boil.

2. Add 5 ounces (140 grams) of hazelnuts and flour; bring to second boil.

3. Add remaining hazelnuts, and remove from heat.

4. Spread out on parchment paper in thin 10-inch (25-centimeter) circles.

5. Bake in a 350°F (175°C) oven, cool slightly, cut into 16 equal wedges.

Ladyfingers

Yield: 12 1/2 dozen cookies

Sugar	10 ounces	285 grams
Cornstarch	10 ounces	285 grams
Egg whites	10 each	10 each
Egg yolks	10 each	10 each
Cake flour, sifted	10 ounces	285 grams

1. Warm the egg yolks and half of the sugar over simmering water. Remove from the heat.

2. Beat the egg yolks until very thick and creamy.

3. Beat the egg whites with the remaining sugar to medium peaks and fold into the yolks.

4. Fold the cornstarch and flour into the paper.

5. Pipe out into finger shapes on parchment-lined sheet pans.

6. Dust with powdered sugar.

7. Bake at 375°F (195°C) for 15 minutes.

For chocolate ladyfingers, remove 2 ounces (60 grams) of cake flour and substitute 2 ounces (60 grams) of cocoa powder.

Biscotti al'Anice

Yield: 4 dozen

Butter	5 ounces	140 grams
Sugar	4 ounces	115 grams
Eggs	2 each	2 each
Anise extract	2 teaspoons	2 teaspoons
Salt	1/2 teaspoon	1/2 teaspoon
Flour	6 ounces	170 grams
Baking powder	1/2 teaspoon	1/2 teaspoon

1. Cream the butter and sugar until very light.

2. Combine eggs, anise extract, and salt; scrape down the bowl as necesary.

3. Combine flour, and baking powder; sift and fold in one-third at a time.

4. Pipe mixture onto parchment paper in a 1 1/2-inch-wide strip the length of the pan.

5. Bake in a 350°F (165°C) oven for 15 to 20 minutes or until well risen and golden brown; remove, cool.

6. Slice into 1/2-inch slices, lay them on their sides on a sheet pan, return to the oven and bake another 10 minutes, or until lightly colored.

Biscotti means "twice-baked." It is the second baking that produces the desired texture.

Fold in up to 6 ounces (170 grams) of walnuts that have been toasted and coarsely chopped.

In the first step, remember to use only half the sugar. Bring the mixture to a boil.

Pastry Cream

Yield: 3 pounds (1.3 kilograms)

Milk	*1 quart*	*1 liter*
Sugar	*8 ounces*	*225 grams*
Butter	*3 ounces*	*85 grams*
Cornstarch	*3 ounces*	*85 grams*
Eggs	*6 to 8 each*	*6 to 8 each*
Flavorings, as required	*as needed*	*as needed*

1. Combine milk with half of the sugar and the butter, bring to a boil.

2. Combine remaining sugar with cornstarch, add eggs and mix until smooth.

3. Temper egg mixture, add to milk, return to a boil.

4. Remove from heat, add butter and flavorings.

5. Pour into a hotel pan, cover and refrigerate. Use as needed.

Vanilla Bavarian Cream

You may add a wide variety of flavorings to this cream: espresso, nut extracts, chopped nuts, fruit purées, lemon curd, and cordials and liqueurs.

This recipe makes enough to fill 2, 10-inch (25-centimeter) cakes.

Yield: 4 1/2 pounds (2 kilograms)

Vanilla Sauce	*1 quart*	*1 liter*
Gelatin	*1 ounce*	*30 grams*
Water	*8 fluid ounces*	*240 milliliters*
Flavorings	*to taste*	*to taste*
Heavy cream	*1 quart*	*1 liter*

1. Prepare the Vanilla Sauce.

2. Soften the gelatin in the water.

3. Add the softened gelatin to the warm Vanilla Sauce.

4. Stir until the gelatin is completely melted. Cool the mixture over an ice bath to about 70°F (21°C).

5. Whip the cream to medium peaks.

6. Fold the whipped cream into the Vanilla Sauce.

7. Use as desired to fill cakes or mold and chill.

Wine Cream

Yield: 2, 10-inch (25-centimeter) tortes or 40 servings

Gelatin	1 ounce	30 grams
Water	8 fluid ounces	240 milliliters
Sweet white wine	1 quart	1 liter
Sugar	10 ounces	285 grams
Egg yolks	1 pound	450 grams
Heavy cream	1 quart	1 liter

1. Soften the gelatin in water and reserve.

2. Combine wine, sugar, and egg yolks. Whip over a double-boiler until the stage of nappé or approximately 180°F (80°C), being sure to whip constantly.

3. Transfer mixture to machine and whip to maximum volume.

4. Blend the gelatin mixture into the sabayon; cool over an ice bath to approximately 65 to 70°F (18 to 21°C); remove from ice.

5. Fold in whipped cream and pour into prepared pans.

To make a torte, place a layer of plain or flavored sponge cake in a ring mold. Add a layer of wine cream, another layer of cake, wine cream, and end with a third layer of sponge. Glaze and decorate as desired.

Apple Pie

Yield: 5, 10-inch (25-centimeter) pies

Apples, fresh	7 1/2 pounds	3.3 kilograms
Water	1 1/2 quarts	480 milliliters
Sugar	12 ounces	340 grams
Cinnamon, ground	1/2 ounce	15 grams
Nutmeg, ground	1/4 ounce	8 grams
Lemon	1/4 teaspoon	1 milliliter
Water	8 ounces	225 grams
Cornstarch	4 3/4 ounces	135 grams
Sugar	2 ounces	60 grams
Pie Crust Dough	as needed	as needed

1. Prepare 10-inch (25-centimeter) shells and put aside.

2. Bring water, all but 2 ounces (60 grams) of sugar, spices, and lemon to a boil in a stainless steel pot.

3. Combine water, cornstarch, and remaining sugar; mix together.

4. Add cornstarch mixture to boiling liquid, stirring constantly; bring to a second boil.

5. Remove from heat, gently fold in fruit, scale 2 pounds (900 grams) in each shell, add top or lattice crust; bake for 40 to 50 minutes in a 375°F (190°C) degree oven until done.

Pumpkin Pie

Yield: 9, 10-inch (25-centimeter) pies

Allowing the filling to rest overnight (step 3) lets the flavors fully develop.

The recipe for Pie Crust Dough is on page 1080.

Granulated sugar	*1 pound*	*450 grams*
Light brown sugar	*1 pound*	*450 grams*
Salt	*1 ounce*	*30 grams*
Cinnamon, ground	*1 ounce*	*30 grams*
Ginger, ground	*1/4 ounce*	*7 grams*
Nutmeg, ground	*1/4 ounce*	*7 grams*
Bread flour	*4 ounces*	*115 grams*
Corn syrup	*1 1/2 pounds*	*680 grams*
Pumpkin (solid pack)	*7 pounds*	*3.15 kilograms*
Milk	*8 pounds*	*3.6 kilograms*
Eggs, beaten	*1 quart*	*1 liter*
Pie crust, single, unbaked	*10 each*	*10 each*

1. Mix the sugars, salt, and spices.

2. Stir in the flour.

3. Add the syrup, pumpkin and milk. Let rest overnight.

4. Blend in eggs.

5. Roll out pie dough and fit into pans.

6. Scale filling at approximately 2 pounds (900 grams) per pie.

7. Bake at 400°F (205°C) for about 45 minutes, or until filling is set but still soft.

Pecan Pie

Yield: 6, 10-inch (25-centimeter) pies

Pie Crust Dough	1 recipe	1 recipe
Sugar	6 ounces	170 grams
Bread flour	6 ounces	170 grams
Corn syrup	9 pounds	4 kilograms
Eggs	3 pounds	1.3 kilograms
Vanilla	1 1/2 fluid ounces	45 milliliters
Salt	1 1/2 ounces	40 grams
Butter, melted	10 ounces	285 grams
Pecans	36 ounces	950 grams

1. Prepare unbaked fluted shells (single crust) and set aside.

2. Combine sugar and flour, then add the corn syrup.

3. Add eggs, vanilla, and salt; mix until incorporated.

4. Stir in melted butter.

5. Divide pecans evenly among the pies.

6. Portion 8 ounces (115 grams) of filling for each pie; pour on top of pecans and bake for 40 minutes at 400°F (200°C) until filling sets and crust browns.

The recipe for Pie Crust Dough (page 1080) will make enough dough for 5 double-crusted or 10 single-crusted pies.

Toast the pecans in advance for more flavor, or top each pie with a circle of whole pecans which will toast while the pie is baking.

Lemon Meringue Pie

Yield: 4, 10-inch pies

Water	2 quarts	2 liters
Sugar	2 pounds	900 grams
Salt	1/2 ounce	15 grams
Lemon juice	10 fluid ounces	300 milliliters
Lemon rind	2 ounces	60 grams
Cornstarch	6 ounces	170 grams
Egg yolks	8 ounces	225 grams
Butter	4 ounces	115 grams
Meringue topping		
Egg whites	1 pint	480 milliliters
Sugar	2 pounds	900 grams

1. Combine 3 pints (1.4 liters) of water, 1 pound (450 grams) of sugar, the salt, lemon juice, and rind; bring to a boil.

2. Combine 1 pound (450 grams) of sugar and cornstarch, mix together.

3. Combine egg yolks and 1 pint (480 milliliters) of water, add to sugar–cornstarch mixture, mix until blended and reserve.

Use slightly less than half the pie dough from the recipe on page 1080 to make the shells. Bake blind and cool.

Make sure that the meringue covers the top of the pie, touching the crust so that weeping and shrinking will not occur.

(Recipe continued on next page)

4. When the lemon juice–water comes to a boil, temper into cornstarch–egg-yolk mixture, put back on the heat and return to boil; remove from heat immediately.

5. Stir in butter, scale 26 ounces (735 grams) into prebaked pie shells and let cool.

6. For meringue topping: In a clean bowl, whip egg whites, gradually adding sugar and whip to a stiff peak.

7. Using a pastry bag with a #8 or #9 plain tip or a pallet knife, divide topping between 4 pies and swirl into a nice pattern. Dust with powdered sugar and brown off in a 425°F (215°C) oven.

Cherry Pie

Yield: 15, 10-inch (25-centimeter) pies

Use a number 30 can of cherries (or substitute frozen cherries, thawed and drained).

If filling is not sweet enough, more sugar can be added.

Cherries, frozen, thawed, juice reserved	*10 1/2 pounds*	*4.75 kilograms*
Sugar	*3 pounds*	*1.3 kilograms*
Salt	*1/2 ounce*	*15 grams*
Cherry juice	*1 1/2 pounds*	*680 grams*
Clear gel	*1 pound*	*450 grams*
Lemons juiced	*3 each*	*3 each*

1. Prepare unbaked fluted shells and set aside.

2. Combine nine pounds (4 kilograms) of cherry juice, the sugar, and salt and bring to a boil.

3. Dissolve clear gel in the remaining cherry juice; slowly add to boiling mixture.

4. Bring cherry mixture back up to a boil and cook for 5 minutes until mixture becomes clear, remove from heat.

5. Using a wooden spoon, gently fold in well-drained cherries and lemon juice; cool.

6. Scale 2 pounds (900 grams) of filling for pie, add a top or lattice crust and bake for 1 hour at 400 to 425°F (205 to 220°C) until done and crust browns.

Pithiviers
SOURCE: high

Pithiviers

Yield: 1, 10-inch (25-centimeter) cake

Butter	8 ounces	225 grams
Sugar	8 ounces	225 grams
Almonds, ground	8 ounces	225 grams
Eggs	4 each	4 each
Vanilla or rum	to taste	to taste
Puff Pastry	2 pounds	900 grams

1. Make the almond filling: Cream butter, beat in sugar then almonds.

2. Add eggs one at a time, beating after each addition to prevent separation and refrigerate while rolling out the dough.

3. Roll out the puff dough to make two 10-inch (25-centimeter) circles. Egg wash the rim of one circle.

4. Pipe or spread the almond filling in the center of the first circle. Top with the second circle of Puff Pastry. Seal gently.

5. Cut scalloped edges. Use a sharp knife to cut a pattern in the top of the cake. Brush lightly with eggwash.

6. Chill the cake for 20 to 30 minutes before baking.

7. Bake at 425°F (220°C) for 20 minutes. Dust with confectioners sugar if desired, then bake another 10 minutes.

Mix 2 pints (960 milliliters) of Pithiviers with 1 pint (480 milliliters) of Pastry Cream to make a lighter filling.

Pithiviers is a small town near Orléans in France. This pastry originated there.

The traditional way to decorate this cake is to lightly score curved lines, radiating from the center, over the surface of the top layer.

Frangipan

Yield: 5 sheet pans

Almond paste	*50 ounces*	*1.9 kilograms*
Sugar	*50 ounces*	*1.9 kilograms*
Butter	*50 ounces*	*1.9 kilograms*
Eggs, room temperature	*35 each*	*35 each*
Cake flour	*1 1/2 pounds*	*680 grams*

1. Cream almond paste and sugar with half the butter to a fine crumb.

2. Add remaining butter and cream until light and smooth.

3. Slowly add eggs, scraping bowl occasionaly.

4. Add sifted cake flour all at once and mix just until incorporated.

Hazelnut Filling

Yield: 2 3/4 pounds (1.25 kilograms)

After filling has been refrigerated, it firms up. Let it sit at room temperature before using.

Add 1 part egg white to 1 part water to make the filling spreadable.

Almond paste	*6 ounces*	*170 grams*
Sugar	*6 ounces*	*170 grams*
Shortening, emulsified	*6 ounces*	*170 grams*
Hazelnuts, slightly toasted, ground fine	*18 ounces*	*500 grams*
Cinnamon, ground	*1 teaspoon*	*1 teaspoon*
Egg whites	*4 ounces*	*115 grams*
Water	*4 fluid ounces*	*120 milliliters*

1. Break almond paste in pieces and mix with sugar, using a paddle.

2. Add shortening and mix until smooth.

3. Add hazelnuts and cinnamon alternately with egg whites and water. Mix to a spreadable consistency. Use as a filling for various pastries.

Apple Filling for Strudel

Yield: 30 servings

Granny Smith apples, peeled, cored, and sliced thin	5 pounds	2.25 kilograms
Raisins	4 ounces	115 grams
Cinnamon sugar	1 1/2 ounces	40 grams
Bread crumbs, dry	6 ounces	170 grams
Strudel or phyllo dough	8 sheets	8 sheets
Butter, melted	3 1/2 ounces	100 grams
Vanilla Sauce	3 pints	1.5 liters

The recipe for Vanilla Sauce is on page 1070.

1. Combine apples, raisins, and cinnamon sugar.

2. Combine bread crumbs with butter.

3. Sprinkle bread crumbs on between sheets of dough to make stacks of 4. Place apples on top of crumbs.

4. Roll up dough and place on sheet pan, brush with butter, and dock to allow steam to escape.

5. Bake in a 425°F (220°C) oven for 30 minutes or until crisp.

6. When halfway baked, brush again with melted butter.

7. Serve hot with Vanilla Sauce.

Baker's Cheese Filling

Yield: 4 1/2 pounds (2 kilograms)

Baker's cheese	2 1/2 pounds	1.15 kilograms
Sugar	8 ounces	225 grams
Shortening, butter, or half-and-half	8 ounces	225 grams
Cornstarch	4 ounces	115 grams
Salt	1/2 ounce	15 grams
Eggs	8 ounces	225 grams
Vanilla, to taste	1/4 ounce	8 milliliters
Milk, varies	4 fluid ounces	120 milliliters

Scale at 5 ounces (140 grams) to fill a coffee cake or 1 3/4 ounces (50 grams) for individual Danish. The recipe for Danish is on page 1042.

1. Combine all ingredients except milk and mix together until smooth.

2. Add milk gradually to avoid making lumps; amount added depends on moisture content of cheese.

3. Cover, label, date, and refrigerate until ready to use.

Cream Cheese Filling

Yield: 5 pounds (2.25 kilograms)

Cream cheese, softened	*3 pounds*	*1.3 kilograms*
Sugar	*1 pound*	*450 grams*
Cornstarch	*4 ounces*	*115 grams*
Eggs	*4 ounces*	*115 grams*
Butter, salted, melted	*8 ounces*	*225 grams*
Vanilla	*to taste*	*to taste*

1. Blend the cream cheese and sugar. Cream until light.
2. Add remaining ingredients and blend until smooth.

V A R I A T I O N

Add plumped golden raisins or currants if desired.

Meringue Topping for Pies

Yield: 4 1/2 pounds (2 kilograms)

This meringue may also be referred to as "common" meringue.

Egg whites	*1 1/2 pounds*	*680 grams*
Sugar	*3 pounds*	*1.3 kilograms*

1. Place egg whites in a clean, grease-free bowl.
2. Whip, gradually adding sugar.
3. Whip until medium-stiff peak.
4. Cover top of pies, dust with powdered sugar.
5. Brown pies in a 425°F (220°C) oven.

Regular Meringue

Yield: 3 pounds (1.35 kilograms)

Egg whites	*1 pound*	*450 grams*
Sugar	*2 pounds*	*900 grams*

1. Place the egg whites in a bowl of appropriate size and composition.
2. Beat the egg whites to a frothy stage.
3. Add the sugar and continue beating until soft peaks form.
4. For a hard meringue, continue whipping until hard peaks form.

Italian Meringue

Yield: 3 1/2 pounds (1.8 kilograms)

Sugar	*2 pounds*	*900 grams*
Water	*8 fluid ounces*	*240 milliliters*
Egg whites	*1 pound*	*450 grams*

1. Combine the sugar and water in a sauce pan over moderate heat and bring the mixture to 238°F (114°C).

2. Place the egg whites in a bowl of appropriate size and composition; beat them to the soft-peak stage.

3. Add the sugar to the egg whites in a thick, steady stream while continuing to whip until the desired consistency is reached.

This meringue is prepared as the first step of an Italian buttercream.

Swiss Meringue

Yield: 3 pounds (1.35 kilograms)

Egg whites	*1 pound*	*450 grams*
Sugar	*2 pounds*	*900 grams*

1. Place the egg whites and sugar in a bowl of appropriate size and composition

2. Beat the egg whites and sugar together, holding the bowl over a bain-marie until the mixture reaches 100 to 110°F (35 to 45°C).

3. Beat the egg whites and sugar together to the soft- or the stiff-peak stage as desired.

To read more about meringues, refer to page 220.

Meringue Shells

Yield: 1 1/2 pounds (680 grams)

Sugar	*1 pound*	*450 grams*
Egg whites	*8 ounces*	*225 grams*
Cream of tartar	*1/2 teaspoon*	*2.5 grams*

1. Combine the sugar, egg whites, and cream of tartar in a 12-quart (12-liter) bowl.

2. Beat the mixture over a water bath until it reaches 110°F (40°C).

3. Whip the heated mixture on third speed until it begins to recede from the sides of the bowl.

4. Using a clean grease-free piping bag and a plain tip, pipe out on a parchment-covered sheet into desired shape.

5. Dry in a 175°F (80°C) oven to 4 hours.

6. Store away from moisture.

Meringue shells are used to present ice creams, sherberts, fresh fruits, or poached fruits.

1105

Devil's Fudge Icing

Yield: 6 pounds (2.75 kilograms)

Do not add the hot water all at once in step 2. Reserve some to thin slightly, if necessary, as you make the icing.

Cocoa	8 ounces	225 grams
Butter	4 ounces	115 grams
Shortening, emulsified	4 ounces	115 grams
Corn syrup	12 fluid ounces	360 milliliters
Salt	1/2 ounce	15 grams
Vanilla	1 fluid ounce	30 milliliters
Water, hot	8 fluid ounces	240 milliliters
Confectioners' sugar	2 1/2 pounds	1.15 kilograms

1. Cream the cocoa, butter, shortening, corn syrup, salt, and vanilla together.

2. Add the hot water and mix well.

3. Add sugar and mix until smooth.

4. Store at room temperature in a sealed container.

Cream Cheese Icing

Yield: 6 pounds (2.75 kilograms)

This is a good icing for carrot cakes or spice cakes.

Cream cheese	2 pounds	900 grams
Pastry Cream	4 pounds	1.8 kilograms
Flavoring	as needed	as needed

1. Cream the cheese until smooth soft and free from lumps.

2. Mix with the pastry cream until blended.

3. Use for filling and icing; refrigerate as needed.

French Buttercream

Yield : 7 1/4 pounds (3.25 kilograms)

Egg yolks	16 each	16 each
Whole eggs	8 each	8 each
Sugar	2 pounds 4 ounces	1 kilogram
Water	8 fluid ounces	240 milliliters
Butter, at room temperature	3 pounds	1.3 kilograms

(Recipe continued on facing page)

1. Combine yolks, eggs, sugar, and water; warm in a double-boiler to 110°F (45°C).

2. Mix until light and fluffy.

3. Cream butter until lightened and beat into egg mixture until well incorporated.

4. Flavor as desired.

German Buttercream

Yield: 2 1/4 pounds (1 kilogram)

Butter	*1 pound*	*450 grams*
Pastry cream	*1 pound*	*450 grams*
Powdered sugar	*4 ounces*	*115 grams*

The procedure for making buttercreams is explained on pages 404 and 405.

1. Cream the butter and sugar in a mixing bowl.

2. Gradually add the pastry cream and blend together.

Italian Buttercream

Yield: about 6 pounds (2.75 kilograms)

Sugar	*22 ounces*	*625 grams*
Water	*7 fluid ounces*	*210 milliliters*
Egg whites	*1 pound*	*450 grams*
Butter	*4 pounds*	*1.8 kilograms*
Flavoring	*as needed*	*as needed*

See figure 12-29 for an illustration of making an Italian buttercream.

1. Combine 12 ounces (340 grams) of the sugar and the water in a heavy sauce pan and cook to 240°F (115°C).

2. Place the egg whites in a mixing bowl and beat to medium-stiff peaks with the remaining 10 ounces (285 grams) of sugar.

3. In a slow steady stream add boiling sugar to whipped whites.

4. Continue to whip until mixture has cooled to room temperature.

5. Whip in butter by adding in small quantities.

6. Flavor as desired.

Swiss Buttercream

Yield: 6 pounds (2.75 kilograms)

Use shortening in warmer climates; otherwise use all butter.

Egg whites	*1 pound*	*450 grams*
Sugar	*3 pounds*	*1.3 kilograms*
Butter, cubed	*3 pounds*	*1.3 kilograms*
Emulsified shortening	*6 ounces*	*170 grams*

1. Place the egg whites in a 20-quart (20-liter) bowl over a double-boiler, heat to 110°F (45°C).

2. Whip to soft peaks.

3. Gradually add butter and whip back to soft peaks.

VARIATIONS

Add the following to taste to flavor buttercreams:

- Melted and cooled chocolate
- Cordials and liqueurs
- Concentrated fruit purées
- Essences and extracts
- Dissolved powdered instant coffee
- Lemon Curd (especially for a filling)

Sponge Roulade

Yield: 1 sheet pan

Egg yolks	*8 ounces*	*225 grams*
Sugar	*5 ounces*	*60 grams*
Egg whites	*8 ounces*	*225 grams*
Cake flour, sifted	*6 ounces*	*170 grams*

(Recipe continued on facing page)

1. Whip egg yolks and 2 ounces (60 grams) of sugar.

2. Whip egg whites and 3 ounces (95 grams) of sugar to a medium peak.

3. Fold beaten egg whites into beaten yolks.

4. Sift cake flour twice and fold in.

5. Spread carefully on parchment paper-lined sheet pans.

6. Bake in a 425°F (220°C) oven for 10 to 15 minutes or until done.

7. Immediately after baking, move the sponge onto a cold sheet pan. Keep from drying out.

VARIATION

Chocolate Roulade: Substitute the following for cake flour:

Cake flour	*4 1/2 ounces*	*125 grams*
Cocoa powder	*1 1/2 ounces*	*40 grams*

Vanilla Sponge

Yield: 5, 10-inch (25-centimeter)
or 8, 8-inch (20-centimeter) cakes

Eggs	*3/4 pounds*	*1.7 kilograms*
Sugar	*30 ounces*	*850 grams*
Cake flour	*22 ounces*	*625 grams*
Cornstarch	*8 ounces*	*225 grams*
Butter, melted	*10 ounces*	*285 grams*
Vanilla extract	*1/2 ounce*	*15 grams*

1. Combine egg and sugar in a mixing bowl; heat to 110°F (45°C) over a double-boiler.

2. Sift flour and cornstarch together twice.

3. Whip eggs until foam is three times original volume and starts to recede from the sides of the bowl.

4. Fold in flour–cornstarch mix; fold in butter and vanilla.

5. Bake in a 375°F (190°C) oven for 30 minutes or until top is firm to touch.

To make a Bûche Noël, fill the roulade with a chocolate-flavored buttercream and roll up into a log. Frost with chocolate buttercream made to look like a log and decorate with meringue mushrooms.

Chocolate Sponge

Yield: 5, 10-inch (25-centimeter)
or 8, 8-inch (20-centimeter) cakes

Ratios in these recipes equal 2 parts eggs,
1 part sugar, 1 part flour.

Eggs	*3 3/4 pounds*	*1.64 kilograms*
Sugar	*30 ounces*	*850 grams*
Cake flour	*9 ounces*	*700 grams*
Cocoa powder	*5 ounces*	*140 grams*
Baking soda	*1/2 teaspoon*	*1/2 teaspoon*
Butter, melted	*5 ounces*	*140 grams*

1. Combine egg and sugar in a mixing bowl, heat to 110°F (45°C) over a double-boiler.

2. Sift flour, cornstarch, cocoa powder, and baking soda together two to four times.

3. Whip eggs until foam is three times original volume and starts to recede from the sides of the bowl.

4. Fold in flour, cornstarch, cocoa powder, and baking soda; fold in butter.

5. Divide into five 10-inch cake pans that have been greased on the sides and lined with parchment paper circles on the bottom.

6. Bake in a 375°F (190°C) oven for 30 minutes or until golden brown.

VARIATION

Chocolate Nut Sponge: Add 20 percent of the flour weight in finely ground nuts and reduce the flour weight by 10 percent.

Pound Cake

Yield: 2 cakes

Butter	*1 1/4 pounds*	*1.9 kilograms*
Sugar	*1 1/2 pounds*	*680 grams*
Lemon rind, grated	*1 ounce*	*30 grams*
Salt	*1/4 ounce*	*115 grams*
Cake flour	*1 3/4 pounds*	*800 grams*
Baking powder	*3/4 ounce*	*115 grams*
Eggs	*2 pounds*	*900 grams*

(Recipe continued on facing page)

1. Cream together butter, sugar, lemon rind, and salt.

2. Sift together cake flour, cornstarch, and baking powder.

3. Add eggs alternately in three stages with flour on low speed.

4. Fill into greased pans with a paper on the bottom.

5. Scaling instructions: 1 3/4 pounds of batter (800 grams) per loaf pan; bake at 340°F (170°C).

High-Ratio Cake, White

Yield: 15, 10-inch (25-centimeter) cakes

Sugar	7 pounds	3.15 kilograms
Butter	22 ounces	625 grams
Salt	3 ounces	85 grams
Shortening, emulsified	22 ounces	625 grams
Cake flour	6 pounds	2.75 kilograms
Baking powder	6 ounces	170 grams
Eggs	1 pint	480 mililiters
Milk	2 quarts	2 liters
Vanilla	1 fluid ounce	30 milliliters
Egg whites	1 1/2 quarts	1.5 liters

Scale 3 pounds (1.3 kilograms) for a half sheet cake; fill 3/4 full for cupcakes; use 24 ounces (680 grams) for each 10-inch (25-centimeter) pan.

1. Add the sugar, butter, salt, shortening, cake flour, and baking powder with 1 quart (1 liter) of milk.

2. Mix 4 minutes on medium speed, scraping bowl frequently.

3. Add egg whites and eggs, remaining milk, and vanilla to batter in three stages within 6 minutes.

4. Grease sides and paper bottom of pans.

5. Scale off batter into pans.

6. Bake at 360°F (180°C) for 20 minutes or until cake springs back when touched lightly in center.

VARIATION

Yellow High Ratio Cake: Substitute egg whites with whole eggs.

Fudge Cake

Yield: 8, 10-inch (25 centimeter) cakes

Cake flour	*2 1/2 pounds*	*1.15 kilograms*
Shortening, emulsified	*22 ounces*	*625 grams*
Sugar	*3 pounds*	*1.3 kilograms*
Baking powder	*2 ounces*	*60 grams*
Salt	*1 1/4 ounces*	*45 grams*
Baking soda	*3/4 ounce*	*20 grams*
Cocoa powder	*9 ounces*	*255 grams*
Milk	*2 1/4 pints*	*1.25 liters*
Corn syrup	*8 fluid ounces*	*240 milliliters*
Eggs	*30 ounces*	*850 grams*
Vanilla	*1 fluid ounce*	*30 milliliters*

1. Combine 2 pounds (900 grams) of flour and the shortening; mix together on medium speed for 5 minutes.

2. Add the sugar, the rest of the flour, the baking powder, salt, baking soda, cocoa, 20 fluid ounces (600 milliliters) of milk, and corn syrup to the mixer and continue mixing for another 5 minutes.

3. Add eggs slowly and mix another 3 minutes.

4. Add remaining milk and vanilla in three stages and mix for 2 more minutes.

5. Grease sides and the paper bottom of the pans.

6. Scale off 24 ounces (680 grams) of batter into each pan. (Scale 3 pounds (1.3 kilograms) for a half sheet cake; fill 3/4 full for cupcakes.)

7. Bake at 180°C for 20 minutes or until cake springs back when touched lightly in center.

Angel Food Cake

Yield: 5, 8-inch (20-centimeter) cakes

Egg whites	*2 pounds*	*900 grams*
Vanilla	*1/2 fluid ounce*	*15 milliliters*
Sugar	*2 pounds*	*450 grams*
Cream of tartar	*1/4 ounce*	*8 grams*
Salt	*1/4 ounce*	*8 grams*
Cake flour	*13 ounces*	*370 grams*

(Recipe continued on facing page)

1. Combine egg whites and vanilla and beat for 5 minutes.

2. Combine 1 pound (450 grams) of sugar, cream of tartar, and salt; add gradually to egg whites and beat until mixture forms a wet peak.

3. Sift rest of sugar and flour together and carefully fold into whites.

4. Scale 15 ounces (420 grams) into ungreased 8-inch (20-centimeter) tube pans.

5. Bake at 350°F (175°C) for 35 to 40 minutes or until cake bounces back on top when touched by a finger.

6. When done turn pans over on a rack; allow cakes to cool before removing from pans.

Devil's Fudge Cake

Yield: 6, 10-inch (25-centimeter) cakes

Cake flour	*2 pounds*	*900 grams*
Cocoa	*8 ounces*	*225 grams*
Sugar	*3 1/2 pounds*	*1.6 kilograms*
Salt	*1 1/2 ounces*	*40 grams*
Baking powder	*1 1/2 ounces*	*40 grams*
Cinnamon	*1/8 ounce*	*4 grams*
Baking soda	*1/2 ounce*	*15 grams*
Shortening, emulsified	*1 pound*	*450 grams*
Skim milk	*2 1/2 pounds*	*1 kilogram*
Eggs	*1 1/2 pounds*	*680 grams*

Fill and frost this cake with the Devil's Fudge Icing on page 1106.

1. Combine the flour, cocoa, sugar, salt, baking powder, cinnamon, and baking soda. Sift together and transfer to a mixing bowl.

2. Add the shortening and half of the milk. Mix 4 minutes at medium speed, scraping the bowl frequently.

3. Blend the eggs with the remaining milk and add to the batter in 3 stages, mixing a total of 6 minutes.

4. Scale the batter into prepared baking pans (29 ounces/540 grams for a 10-inch/25-centimeter pan).

5. Bake at 360°F (180°C) for 20 minutes.

Carrot Cake

Yield: 6, 10-inch (25-centimeter) cakes

For more information about preparing pans, refer to page 379.

The classic frosting for this cake is a Cream Cheese Icing, found on page 1106. Or, simply dust the cake with powdered sugar.

Add up to 1 pound (450 grams) of crushed pineapple in step 3 if you wish.

Butter	2 pounds	900 grams
Granulated sugar	2 pounds	900 grams
Brown sugar	2 pounds	900 grams
Eggs	1 3/4 pounds	780 grams
Carrots, grated	4 pounds	1.8 kilograms
Raisins	1 1/4 pounds	720 grams
Lemon juice	4 fluid ounces	120 milliliters
Orange juice	4 fluid ounces	120 milliliters
Lemon zest	2 ounces	60 grams
Orange zest	2 ounces	60 grams
All-purpose flour	3 3/4 pounds	1.7 kilograms
Baking powder	1 1/4 ounces	40 grams
Baking soda	1 ounce	40 grams
Salt	1 ounce	30 grams
Cinnamon, ground	1 ounce	30 grams
Walnuts, chopped	1 1/4 pounds	570 grams

1. Cream butter with both sugars until fluffy.

2. Add eggs slowly, scraping bowl down carefully after each addition.

3. Add carrots, raisins, juices, and zests, mixing until incorporated.

4. Sift together the flour, baking powder, baking soda, salt, and spices; then add the walnuts and blend in.

5. Add the dry ingredients to the batter, mixing well.

6. Portion in prepared pans and bake at 325°F (160°C) for 50 to 60 minutes or until done.

7. Remove from pan when cool.

Roman Apple Cake

Yield: 1 sheet pan or 6, 8-inch (20 centimeter) cakes

Butter	*12 ounces*	*340 grams*
Sugar	*2 1/2 pounds*	*1.15 kilograms*
Salt	*1/2 ounces*	*15 grams*
Mace, ground	*1/2 teaspoon*	*1/2 teaspoon*
Cinnamon, ground	*1/2 teaspoon*	*1/2 teaspoon*
Eggs	*8 ounces*	*225 grams*
Milk	*1 pint*	*480 milliliters*
Baking soda	*1 ounce*	*30 grams*
Cake flour	*42 ounces*	*1.9 kilograms*
Baking powder	*1 ounce*	*30 grams*
Apples, chopped	*3 pounds*	*1.3 kilograms*

Rome apples are a good choice for this cake. Other suitable apples include Cortland, Winesap, or York.

1. Cream together the butter, sugar, and spices.

2. Add eggs slowly, scraping the bowl occasionally.

3. Alternately add dry ingredients and liquids in several additions.

4. Add chopped apples.

5. Spread onto a prepared sheet pan or scale 14 ounces (400 grams) for 8-inch (20-centimeter) layers.

6. Bake 350°F (175°C) for 30 minutes or until firm to touch and cake pulls away from sides of pan. (Timing depends on size of pan being used.)

Gugelhopf (Yeast-Raised)

Yield: 3, 10-inch (25-centimeter) cakes

This sweet, yeast-raised cake is typically served with afternoon coffee or tea.

If a gugelhopf mold is unavailable, use a tube pan.

Milk	20 fluid ounces	540 milliliters
Yeast	1 3/4 ounces	50 grams
Bread flour	1 1/2 pounds	680 grams
High-gluten flour	3 pounds	1.3 kilograms
Salt	1 ounce	30 grams
Malt	1/2 ounce	15 grams
Sugar	10 ounces	285 grams
Whole eggs, room temperature	10 ounces	285 grams
Vanilla bean seeds	2 each	2 each
Lemon zest	1 ounce	30 grams
Orange zest	1 ounce	30 grams
Candied orange peel	3 1/2 ounces	100 grams
Rum raisins	1 pound	450 grams
Butter, soft	10 ounces	285 grams
Almonds, sliced	4 ounces	115 grams

1. Prepare a sponge with the first three ingredients; ferment approximately 1 1/2 hours.

2. Combine the sponge with the remaining ingredients (except for the raisins and orange peel). Make into a smooth, developed dough. Let rise in a warm place for 45 minutes.

3. Blend raisins and orange peel into dough by hand until well incorporated.

4. Scale out, round up and bench proof for 15 minutes. Reround, push a rolling pin into the center of the dough and place in greased and almond-coated gugelhopf pans.

5. Proof until dough is almost up to the rim, wash with water and bake in a 400°F (200°C) oven until done, about 45 minutes.

6. Cool slightly and unmold onto wire racks.

7. Dust with powdered sugar before serving.

Kugelhopf

Yield: 2, 10-inch (25-centimeter) cakes

Raisins, dark	*8 ounces*	*225 grams*
Raisins, light	*8 ounces*	*225 grams*
Butter, unsalted	*8 ounces*	*225 grams*
Sugar	*6 1/2 ounces*	*190 milliliters*
Salt	*1/4 ounce*	*8 grams*
Eggs	*6 each*	*6 each*
Bread flour	*8 ounces*	*225 grams*
Cake flour	*8 ounces*	*225 grams*
Baking powder	*1/2 ounce*	*15 grams*
Walnuts	*8 ounces*	*225 grams*
Lemon zest	*2 teaspoons*	*2 teaspoons*
Rum	*8 ounces*	*225 grams*
Almonds, sliced	*3 ounces*	*85 grams*

Unlike the previous recipe, this cake is made by the creaming method. It is best when freshly made.

This is also often served at breakfast or for an afternoon tea. Almonds and currants may be substituted for the walnuts and raisins.

1. Soak raisins in warm water overnight. Drain them before preparing the cake.

2. Cream butter, sugar, and salt until light and smooth.

3. Add eggs gradually. Scrape the bowl as necessary for an evenly blended batter.

4. Add sifted flours and baking powder.

5. Fold in walnuts, drained raisins, and lemon zest by hand.

6. Place in greased and almond-coated gugelhopf pan.

7. Bake at 345°F (175°C) for 45 minutes or until the cake springs back when pressed lightly.

CIA Christmas Fruitcake

Yield: 20, 3-pound (1.3-kilogram) cakes

Garnish the tops of the fruitcakes with whole blanched almonds, glacé cherries, or other nuts and dried friuts as desired prior to baking.

Your yield will vary depending upon the size pan you are using.

Fruit mixture

Raisins, light	7 1/2 pounds	3.4 kilograms
Raisins, dark	7 1/2 pounds	3.4 kilograms
Diced fruit	15 pounds	6.8 kilograms
Glacé cherries	2 1/2 pounds	1.15 kilograms
Honey	2 1/2 pounds	1.15 kilograms
Sherry, dry	4 pounds	1.8 kilograms
Sugar	4 pounds	1.8 kilograms
Shortening	5 pounds	2.25 kilograms
Eggs, enriched	5 pounds	2.25 kilograms
Bread flour	5 pounds	2.25 kilograms
Salt	1/2 ounce	15 grams
Ginger, ground	1/2 ounce	15 grams
Cloves, ground	1/2 ounce	15 grams
Cinnamon, ground	1/2 ounce	15 grams
Walnuts	5 pounds	2.25 kilograms

1. For fruit mixture: Soak all fruit with honey and sherry together overnight.

2. Combine sugar and shortening; mix for 4 minutes on first speed.

3. On first speed, slowly add eggs; when one-third of eggs are left, add half the flour with the remaining eggs and mix for 10 minutes.

4. Add salt and spices to remaining flour and add to batter; mix in until smooth.

5. By hand, add the fruit mixture and the nuts to the cake batter mixing well to incorporate.

6. Scale 3 pounds (1.3 kilograms) per container, baking at 275°F (135°C) until done or about 2 1/2 hours.

Cheesecake

Yield: 2, 10-inch cakes

Cornstarch	*4 ounces*	*115 grams*
Sugar	*1 1/2 pounds*	*680 grams*
Cream cheese	*5 pounds*	*2.25 kilograms*
Eggs	*1 pound*	*450 grams*
Egg yolks	*2 ounces*	*60 grams*
Vanilla extract	*1 fluid ounce*	*30 milliliters*
Lemon, zest, grated	*1 each*	*1 each*
Heavy cream	*10 fluid ounces*	*300 milliliters*
Crust, prepared	*as needed*	*as needed*

1. Premix the cornstarch with the sugar; using a paddle, cream together the sugar and the cream cheese.

2. Combine eggs, egg yolks, vanilla, and lemon zest; add gradually, one-quarter at a time, to the cream-cheese mixture, making sure to scrape sides, bottom of the bowl, and the paddle after each addition.

3. Add heavy cream and mix to incorporate.

4. Fill cake pans that have been lined with parchment paper circles and a pre-baked 1/2-inch-thick layer of sponge or another type of crust.

5. Using a water bath, bake at 300°F (150°C) for about 60 to 90 minutes or until the center is slightly set.

6. Chill. Unmold the next day.

VARIATIONS

Marble Cheesecake: Add cocoa powder or melted chocolate to a small amount of batter; using a small parchment bag, pipe into cheesecake and swirl in.

For graham cracker crust: Use 5 pounds (2.25 kilograms) crushed graham crackers, 1 pound (450 grams) sugar, 1 pound (450 grams) melted butter, and 4 ounces (115 grams) egg whites. Mix together, press into form and pre-bake at 350 to 375°F (175 to 190°C) for 5 to 7 minutes until set. Use 8 ounces (225 grams) per 10-inch pan.

You may use a prebaked Pâté Sucré (page 1082), Shortbread (page 1086), or a layer of Sponge Cake (page 1108) as desired. Whatever crust you select, be sure it is fully baked before adding the cream cheese filling.

This cake can be made without cornstarch by adding 5 more eggs.

Sicilian Cheesecake

Yield: 12 servings

This cake has a coarser texture than the preceding recipe.

You may wish to use a blender rather than a food processor to make the ricotta as smooth as possible.

Adding the sugar syrup to the yolks should raise their temperature to a safe level. If you prefer you may wish to use pasturized eggs.

Candied fruit	1 1/2 ounces	40 grams
Maraschino liqueur	2 fluid ounces	60 milliliters
Apricot purée	8 ounces	225 grams
Sponge cake	1, 10-inch	1, 25-centimeter
Sugar	5 1/2 ounces	155 grams
Lemon juice, fresh	1 fluid ounce	30 milliliters
Water	3 fluid ounces	90 milliliters
Cream of tartar	pinch	pinch
Eggs, separated	3 each	3 each
Cinnamon, ground	1 teaspoon	5 grams
Lemon zest	1 teaspoon	1 teaspoon
Ricotta, puréed	1 3/4 pounds	800 grams
Heavy cream, whipped	6 fluid ounces	180 milliliters
Chocolate, bitter, coarse-grated	3 1/2 ounces	100 grams
Hazelnuts, chopped fine	2 ounces	60 grams

1. Combine candied fruit and liqueur, marinate for 30 minutes.

2. To make the torte: Spread half of the apricot purée in the bottom of a spring-form pan.

3. Lay a 1/2-inch slice of sponge cake on top of purée.

4. To make filling: Boil 4 ounces (120 grams) of the sugar with the water and cream of tartar, boil until 230°F (110°C), pour slowly in a thin stream, into the egg yolks while beating constantly.

5. Add cinnamon, zest, and ricotta; mix in.

6. Whip egg whites with the remaining sugar; fold into ricotta mixture; fold in whipped cream, chocolate, hazelnuts, and candied fruit.

7. Pour over sponge cake, top with second layer of sponge cake.

8. Spread remaining apricot purée over top, wrap in plastic wrap and freeze.

9. Before serving, place cake in refrigerator to soften.

Chiffon Cheesecake

Yield: 2, 10-inch (25-centimeter) cakes

Bakers' cheese	*2 1/2 pounds*	*1.15 kilograms*
Vegetable oil, vegetable shortening, or margarine	*11 fluid ounces*	*330 milliliters*
Egg whites	*25 ounces*	*700 grams*
Water, hot, as needed	*1/2 to 1 pound*	*225 to 450 grams*
Sugar	*1 pound*	*450 grams*
Milk powder	*4 ounces*	*115 grams*
Bread flour	*4 ounces*	*115 grams*
Cornstarch	*2 1/2 ounces*	*70 grams*
Vanilla extract	*1 fluid ounce*	*30 milliliters*
Lemon extract	*1 teaspoon*	*1 teaspoon*
Egg whites	*1 pound*	*450 grams*

If you prefer, use a pasteurized egg product to replace the egg whites.

The water should be at or near 180°F (82°C) in step 2.

1. Combine cheese, oil, and 9 ounces (255 grams) of egg whites; mix until smooth.

2. Add hot water in three parts, mixing until smooth (add only enough water to get cake-batter consistency).

3. Add vanilla and lemon extracts.

4. Make a meringue from the remaining egg whites and sugar and fold into cheese mixture.

5. Bake in a pan with your choice of cookie bottom, in a water bath, in a 350°F (175°C) oven for 60 minutes or until done.

Sacher Torte Layers

Yield: 2, 10–inch (25-centimeter) cakes

To make a Sacher Torte, spread apricot or raspberry jam on one layer. Top with a second layer. Spread a thin layer of jam over the top and sides of the cake and allow it to firm briefly. Warm Chocolate Ganache (page 1075) and spread or pour to make a smooth glaze on the cake. Decorate the top by piping an "S" or the word "Sacher" on each portion.

Butter	*14 ounces*	*400 grams*
Confectioner's sugar	*10 ounces*	*285 grams*
Egg yolks	*10 1/2 ounces*	*300 grams*
Eggs	*7 ounces*	*200 grams*
Chocolate, melted	*1 pound*	*450 grams*
Egg whites	*14 ounces*	*400 grams*
Sugar	*4 ounces*	*115 grams*
Bread flour	*5 ounces*	*140 grams*
Almonds, toasted, ground	*14 ounces*	*400 grams*

1. Cream butter and powdered sugar; add eggs and yolks slowly.

2. Add chocolate all at once and blend.

3. Beat the egg whites with the remaining sugar to medium peaks. Fold this into the batter.

4. Fold in flour and almonds. Pour into prepared pans.

5. Bake in a 325°F (165°C) oven for 45 minutes or until a cake tester comes out clean.

Rum Torte Cake

Yield: 12, 8-inch (20-centimeter) tube cakes

Shortening, part butter	*2 pounds*	*900 grams*
Sugar	*3 1/2 pounds*	*1.6 kilograms*
Salt	*1 ounce*	*30 grams*
Orange, zested	*1 each*	*1 each*
Lemon, zested	*1 each*	*1 each*
Egg yolks	*22 ounces*	*625 grams*
Eggs	*22 ounces*	*625 grams*
Cake flour	*3 pounds*	*1.3 kilograms*
Baking powder	*1 1/2 ounces*	*40 grams*
Milk	*1 1/2 pounds*	*680 grams*
Rum Syrup		
Sugar	*3 pounds*	*1.3 kilograms*
Glucose	*1 pound*	*450 grams*
Water	*26 fluid ounces*	*780 milliliters*
Cream of tartar	*1/4 ounce*	*8 grams*
Rum liquor	*3 fluid ounces*	*90 milliliters*

(Recipe continued on facing page)

1. Combine shortening, sugar, salt, and zests; cream until light.

2. Add egg yolks and eggs slowly, cream until light.

3. Sift flour and baking powder together.

4. Alternately add milk and flour and mix until smooth.

5. Fill prepared tube pans with 1 pound (450 grams) of mix; bake in a 360°F (180°C) oven for 26 minutes or until done; invert pans after baking.

6. Dip cooled cake in rum syrup, drain on screens and dust with powdered sugar.

7. Combine all ingredients for the syrup except the rum; bring just to a boil; cool. Add rum.

Joconde Cake Layer

Yield: 6, 10-inch (25-centimeter) layers

Eggs	*10 ounces*	*285 grams*
Sugar	*8 ounces*	*230 grams*
Egg whites	*4 1/2 ounces*	*125 grams*
Almond flour	*8 ounces*	*225 grams*
Pastry flour	*2 ounces*	*60 grams*
Butter, melted	*2 ounces*	*60 grams*

1. Combine eggs and 6 ounces (170 grams) of sugar; whip until the mixture is very light and has doubled or tripled in volume.

2. Combine egg whites and the remaining sugar and whip until a medium-stiff meringue forms.

3. Fold meringue into egg mixture.

4. Fold in almond flour and pastry flour.

5. Fold in butter.

6. Divide mix between 6 prepared 10-inch (25-centimeter) cake pans.

7. Bake in a 425°F (220°C) oven for 15 minutes.

To make an Opera Torte, prepare and cool Jocondes. Make a simple syrup flavored with coffee (page 1077), soft and hard Ganache (page 1075), and a coffee-flavored buttercream (page 1106). Brush Joconde layers with simple syrup and assemble as follows: cake layer, soft ganache, cake, buttercream, and a third cake layer. Spread buttercream over top and sides of torte and glaze with hard ganache.

Hazelnut Torte Cake Layers

Yield: 5, 10-inch (25-centimeter) layers

To make a Hazelnut Torte, spread a chocolate-flavored buttercream between 3 cake layers, as well as on the top and sides of the cake. Garnish with a Hazelnut Florentine (page 1094). If desired, pipe a rosette of buttercream on each slice and lay a triangle of the Florentine onto the slice.

Egg yolks	*30 each*	*30 each*
Confectioners' sugar	*9 ounces*	*255 grams*
Egg whites	*30 each*	*30 each*
Sugar	*9 ounces*	*255 grams*
Hazelnuts, ground	*11 ounces*	*315 grams*
Cake flour	*11 ounces*	*315 grams*
Bread flour	*4 ounces*	*115 grams*
Vanilla extract	*1/2 fluid ounce*	*15 milliliters*
Lemon extract	*1 teaspoon*	*1 teaspoon*
Cinnamon, ground	*1/2 ounce*	*7 grams*

1. Whip egg yolks and Confectioners' sugar to full volume.

2. Combine egg whites and sugar; whip to a medium-stiff meringue.

3. Fold meringue into egg yolk mixture, fold in hazelnuts, flours, and flavorings.

4. Bake in a 375°F (190°C) oven for 30 minutes.

Havana Torte Cake

Yield: 8, 10-inch (25-centimeter) cakes

Batter 1

Butter	*30 ounces*	*850 grams*
Sugar	*30 ounces*	*850 grams*
Almond paste	*26 ounces*	*735 grams*
Eggs	*38 ounces*	*1.1 kilograms*
Hazelnuts, ground and toasted	*34 ounces*	*960 grams*
Bread flour	*34 ounces*	*515 grams*

Batter 2

Egg whites	*3 1/2 pounds*	*1.6 kilograms*
Sugar	*50 ounces*	*2 kilograms*
Hazelnuts, ground and toasted	*46 ounces*	*1.3 kilograms*
Cocoa powder, sifted	*11 ounces*	*315 grams*
Cinnamon, ground	*1 ounce*	*30 grams*

(Recipe continued on facing page)

1. For the first batter, cream butter, sugar, and almond paste together; add eggs slowly, scraping bowl frequently.

2. Sift together hazelnuts and flour, add to above.

3. For the second batter, make a meringue from egg whites and sugar and fold into hazelnuts, cocoa, and cinnamon.

4. Put half of the second batter into a prepared pan, all of the first batter, then the remainer of the second batter.

5. Bake cake at 350°F (175°C) for 50 minutes. Cool on a rack.

Ice with a thin layer of buttercream to smooth surfaces, coat with hard ganache, mark and decorate as desired.

Dobos Torte Cake Batter

Yield: 14 circles for 2, 10-inch (25-centimeter) cakes

Egg yolks	*1 1/4 pounds*	*570 grams*
Sugar	*1 pound*	*450 grams*
Vanilla extract	*2 teaspoons*	*2 teaspoons*
Egg whites	*1 3/4 pounds*	*800 grams*
Cake flour, sifted	*1 pound*	*450 grams*
Butter, melted	*5 ounces*	*140 grams*

To make a Dobos Torte, sandwich seven layers with chocolate buttercream (or mocha-flavored). If you wish, spread a thin layer of caramel on the seventh layer and cut into 16 wedges. Set them on an angle on the torte as a decoration.

1. Whip egg yolks, half the sugar, and the vanilla on high speed, as for foaming method.

2. Combine egg whites and rest of the sugar, whip until a medium-stiff meringue forms.

3. Fold in the yolks and whites together.

4. Fold the cake flour into the batter.

5. Fold the cooled butter into the batter.

6. Spread the batter onto fourteen 10-inch (25-centimeter) circles on parchment paper.

7. Bake in a 450°F (230°C) oven for 5 minutes or until lightly browned.

Apple Cream Cheese Torte

Yield: 24 servings or 2 tortes

Other fruit may be used in this torte: pears, peaches, nectarines, or plums.

Crust

Butter	*12 ounces*	*340 grams*
Sugar	*6 ounces*	*170 grams*
Vanilla	*1 teaspoon*	*1 teaspoon*
All-purpose flour	*18 ounces*	*500 grams*

Filling

Cream cheese, softened	*1 1/2 pounds*	*680 grams*
Sugar	*4 ounces*	*115 grams*
Eggs	*2 each*	*2 each*
Vanilla	*2 teaspoons*	*2 teaspoons*

Topping

Apples, peeled and cored	*1 3/4 pounds*	*800 grams*
Sugar	*1/2 cup*	*120 mililiters*
Cinnamon, ground	*2 teaspoons*	*2 teaspoons*
Nutmeg, grated	*1/2 teaspoon*	*1/2 teaspoon*
Almonds, sliced	*3/4 cup*	*180 mililiters*

1. To make crust: Cream butter and sugar, add vanilla and flour, and mix together.

2. Divide mixture and pat out onto the bottom and 1 inch (2.25 centimeters) up the sides of a 10-inch (25-centimeter) cake pan.

3. To make filling: Combine all ingredients, spread over the crusts.

4. To make the topping: Cut the apples into thick wedges. Combine apples, sugar, cinnamon, and nutmeg.

5. Arrange apple mixture neatly on top of cream cheese mixture; sprinkle with almonds.

6. Bake in a 450°F (230°C) oven for 10 minutes, reduce temperature to 400°F (200°C) and bake 25 minutes longer.

7. Cool completely. Serve with whipped cream if desired.

Pecan Diamonds

Yield: 1 full sheet pan (about 200 bite-sized diamonds)

Shortbread dough	2 1/2 pounds	1.15 kilograms
Butter	2 pounds	900 grams
Brown sugar, light	2 pounds	900 grams
Sugar, granulated	8 ounces	225 grams
Honey	1 1/2 pounds	680 grams
Heavy cream	8 ounces	225 grams
Pecans chopped	4 pounds	1.8 kilograms

1. Roll out the dough (1/8-inch/1-centimeter thick) and fit it into a ungreased sheet pan.

2. Bake the dough until it is firm but has no color. Allow it to cool completely before filling.

3. To prepare the filling, combine the butter, sugars, and honey. Heat this mixture until it melts. Bring to a boil, and boil for 3 minutes without stirring.

4. Add the nuts to the mixture, then add the heavy cream. Stir until blended and remove from the heat.

5. Pour the mixture evenly into the prepared crust.

6. Bake at 350°F (175°C) for 25 to 30 minutes, or until the top of the filling is evenly foamy and the crust is browned.

7. Allow the pecan diamonds to cool thoroughly before cutting, usually 1 day.

Use any nuts you prefer to replace the pecans: hazelnuts, almonds, walnuts, cashews, or macadamias.

These cookies store well at room temperature. For more extended storage, wrap them very tightly and refrigerate or freeze.

These may be served as a "friandise" at the end of the meal, presented with the check instead of a mint.

CAKES AND PASTRIES

1127

CAKES AND PASTRIES

Chocolate-Coated Almonds, Dragee Method

Yield: approximately 220 pieces

The nuts should not be toasted prior to preparing this confection, as they will roast as the sugar caramelizes and coats them in step 3.

Sugar	5 ounces	140 grams
Water	1 1/2 fluid ounces	45 milliliters
Almonds, blanched, whole	1 pound	450 grams
Butter	1 tablespoon	1 tablespoon
Dark chocolate, tempered	12 ounces	340 grams
Cocoa powder	2 tablespoons	2 tablespoons

1. Combine the sugar and water and cool to 230°F (110°C), the "long thread" stage.

2. Remove from the heat and add the nuts. Stir until the sugar crystallizes. Add the butter.

3. Return the pot to the heat and stir constantly until the sugar remelts and caramelizes onto the nuts.

4. Pour the nuts out onto a marble slab and immediately break them into separate pieces. Allow the nuts to cool on the slab, then freeze for 3 minutes.

5. Add the chocolate to the nuts in three separate stages.

6. During the last stage, add the cocoa powder. Let the nuts set, then shake off any excess cocoa.

APPENDIX *1* Seasonal Availability of Produce

Fruit or Vegetable	Jan.	Feb.	Mar.	Apr.	May	June	July	Aug.	Sept.	Oct.	Nov.	Dec.
Apples	☆								☆	☆	☆	☆
Apricots					○	●	●	○				
Artichokes			○	○	○	○						
Arugula	○	○	○	○	○☆	○☆	○☆	○☆	○☆	○	○	○
Asparagus			○	○★	○★	○☆						
Avocados	○	○	○	○	○	○	○	○				○
Beans, shell			○☆	○☆	○☆	○☆	○☆	○☆	○☆			
Beans, snap						○☆	○☆	○☆	○☆	○☆		
Beets, gold							○	○	○	○☆	○☆	○☆
Beets, red							●	●	●	○☆	○☆	○☆
Berries						○	○	○	○	○		
Blood oranges	○	○	○									
Bok choy									☆	☆		
Boysenberries						☆	☆	☆				
Broccoli						○☆	○☆	○☆	○☆	○☆	○☆	○☆
Broccoli rabe	○	○	○	○			☆	☆	☆	☆	☆	○☆
Brussels sprouts	○	○	○							○☆	○☆	○
Bulb fennel	○	○	○	○	○				☆		○	○
Cabbages	○	○	○	○	○	○	○	○	○	○	○	○
Cantaloupes						○	○☆	○☆	○☆	○		
Carrots	○	○	○	○	○	○	○	○	○	○	○	○
Cauliflower						○	○	○	○	○		
Celeriac	○	○	○	○	○	○	○	○	○	○	○	○
Chard	○	○	○	○	○☆	○☆	○☆	○☆	○☆	○☆	○	○
Chayote	●	●									●	●
Cherries						☆	☆					
Chinese cabbage										○	○	
Collards								○☆	○☆	○☆	○☆	
Corn					☆	★	★	★	☆			
Cucumbers	○	○	○	○	●	●★	●★	○	○	○	○	○
Eggplant, baby				○	○	○☆	○☆	○☆	○☆	○		
Eggplant, white						○☆	○☆	○☆				
Endive									○	○	○	○
Escarole	○	○	○	○	○☆	☆	☆	☆	☆	○☆	○	○
Fiddlehead ferns		☆	☆	☆	☆							
Figs							○	○	○	○		
Frisée	○	○	○	○	○	○	○	○	○	○	○☆	○☆
Gooseberries								☆				
Gourds									☆	☆	☆	☆
Grapes						○	○	○	○	○	○	○
Herbs			○	○☆	○☆	○☆	○☆	○☆	○☆	○	○	
Jicama	○	○	○	○	○	○	○	○	○	○	○	○
Kale								☆	☆	☆	☆	
Kiwi	○	○	○			○	○	○	○	○	○	○
Kohlrabi						●☆	●★	○☆				
Kumquats	○	○	○									
Leeks										○	○	○

California: ○   Local ☆
California, Peak: ●   Local, Peak ★

Standard items such as potatoes and onions are generally available year-round and are not included in this chart.

(continued on facing page)

Fruit or Vegetable	Jan.	Feb.	Mar.	Apr.	May	June	July	Aug.	Sept.	Oct.	Nov.	Dec.
Leeks, baby						○	○	○	○	○	○	○
Lettuce, baby			○	○	○	○	○	○	○	○	○	
Lettuce, bibb	○	○	○	○	○	○☆	○☆	○☆	○	○	○	○
Lettuce, iceberg	○	○	○	○	○	○	○	○	○	○	○	○
Lettuce, leaf	○	○	○	○	○	○	○	○	○	○	○	○
Mache	○	○	○☆	○★	○★	○☆	○☆	○☆	○	○	○	○
Mangoes	○	○	○	○	○	○	○	○				
Mustard greens							○☆	○☆	○☆			
Nectarines						○	●	●	○			
Okra							○	○	○	○		
Papayas	○	●	●	●	○	○	○	○	○	○	○	○
Parsnips				○	○	○	○	○☆	○☆	○☆	○	○
Peaches							☆	★	☆			
Pears	○☆							★	★	★	○☆	○☆
Peas, green	○	○	○	○	○	○	○					
Peas, snow	○	○	○	○	○	○	○					
Peppers, green bell						○	○☆	○☆	○☆	○	○	○
Peppers, red bell								○☆	○☆	○☆		
Pineapples	○	○	●	●	●	●	●	○			○	○
Plums						☆	★	☆				
Potatoes, baby red					○	○☆	○☆	○☆	○☆	○		
Radicchio	○	○	○	○		☆	☆	☆	☆	○☆	○	○
Raspberries						☆	☆	☆	☆	☆		
Romaine	○	○	○	○★	○★	○☆	○☆	○☆	○	○	○	○
Rutabagas									☆	☆	☆	☆
Salsify	○	○	○	○						○	○	○
Scallions								☆	☆			
Spinach	○	○	○	○	○★	○★	○☆	○☆	○	○	○	○
Squash, acorn									☆	☆	☆	☆
Squash, baby						○☆	○☆	○☆	○☆	○☆		
Squash, butternut									☆	☆	☆	☆
Squash, cheese									☆	☆	☆	☆
Squash, crookneck							○☆	○☆	○☆	○☆		
Squash, dumpling									☆	☆	☆	☆
Squash, golden									☆	☆	☆	☆
Squash, patty pan							○☆	○☆	○☆	○☆		
Squash, spaghetti									☆	☆	☆	☆
Squash, zucchini				○	○	○	○☆	○☆	○☆	○☆	○	
Strawberries						☆	☆	☆	☆	☆		
Sunchokes	○	○	○	○	○						○	○
Tangerines	○	○	○									
Tomatoes						○☆	○☆	○☆	○☆	○☆	○☆	
Tomatoes, cherry							○☆	○☆	○☆	○☆	○☆	
Turnips	○	○	○	○	○	○	○	○	○☆	○☆	○☆	○
Watercress	○	○	●	●	○	○	○	○	○	○	○	○
Watermelons						○	○	○	○	☆		

California: ○   Local ☆
California, Peak: ●   Local, Peak ★

Standard items such as potatoes and onions are generally available year-round and are not included in this chart.

APPENDIX 2 *Tables*

Foodbourne Illnesses   *1134*

First-Aid Supplies   *1136*

Cooking Ratios and Times
    for Selected Grains   *1136*

Approximate Soaking and Cooking Times
    for Selected Dried Legumes   *1137*

FOODBORNE ILLNESSES

Disease and (Incubation Period*)	Symptoms	Cause	Food Involved	Preventative Measures
Botulism (12–36 hours)	Sore throat, vomiting, blurred vision, cramps, diarrhea, difficulty breathing, central nervous system damaged (possible paralysis). Fatality rate up to 70%.	*Clostridium notulinum:* anaerobic bacteria that form spores with high resistance to heat. Found in animal intestines, water, and soil.	Refrigerated, low-acid foods or improperly canned foods, such as spinach, tuna, green beans, beets, fermented foods, and smoked products. Rare in commercially canned foods.	Toxin is sensitive to heat, so maintain a high temperature while canning food and boil 20 minutes before serving. Do not use food in swollen cans or home-canned food for commercial use.
Staphylococcus (2–4 hours)	Vomiting, nausea, diarrhea, cramps.	*Staphylcoccus aureus:* facultative bacteria found in the nose, throat, and in skin infections of humans.	Foods that are high in protein, moist, handled much, and left in the danger zone. Milk, egg custards, turkey stuffing, chicken/ tuna/potato salads, gravies, reheated food.	Store foods below 40°F (4°C) and reheat thoroughly to 165°F (74°C). People with infected cuts, burns, or respiratory illnesses should not handle food. Keep food out of the danger zone.
Ergotism (varies)	Hallucinations, convulsions, gangrene of extremities.	Ergot: a mold that grows on wheat and rye.	Wheat and rye.	Do not use moldy wheat and rye
Chemical Poisoning (minutes to hours)	Varied	Pesticides on fruits and vegetables, cyanide in silver polish, zinc inside tin cans, copper pans.		Wash fruits and vegetables before using; discard polish with cyanide; wash utensils after polishing; store pesticides away from food; avoid cooking and storing foods in cans since zinc is leached out of tin by acidic foods and is poisonous; don't allow food to touch unlined copper.
Plant and Animal Poisoning (varies—often rapid)	Varies.	Aklaloids; organic acids.		Avoid poisons: Identify wild mushrooms. Don't ingest rhubarb leaves, too much nutmeg, green-skinned potatoes, fava leaves, raw soybeans, blowfish, moray eel, or shark liver.
Salmonellosis (6–48 hours)	Headache, diarrhea, cramps, fever. Can be fatal or lead to arthritis, meningitis, and typhoid.	*Salmonella:* aerobic bacillus that lives and grows in the intestines of humans, animals, birds, and insects.	Egg, poultry, shellfish, meat, soup, sauces, gravies, milk products, warmed-over food.	Reheat leftovers to an internal temperature of 165°F (74°C). Since *Salmonella* can be killed by high temperatures, cook to proper temperatures. Eliminate rodents and flies, wash hands after using bathroom, avoid cross-contamination.

*Incubation period is the time between infection and onset of symtoms.

FOODBORNE ILLNESSES *(continued)*

Disease and (Incubation Period*)	Symptoms	Cause	Food Involved	Preventative Measures
Shigellosis (12–48 hours)	Diarrhea, cramps, fever, dehydration.	*Shigella sonnei* and other species found in feces of infected humans, food, and water.	Beans, contaminated milk, tuna/turkey/ macaroni salads, apple cider, and mixed, moist foods.	Safe water sources, strict control of insects and rodents, good personal hygiene.
Bacillus cereus (8–16 hours)	Cramps, diarrhea, nausea, vomiting.	*Bacillus cereus:* anaerobic bacteria that produce spores and are found in soil and any food.	Cereal products, cornstarch, rice, custards, sauces, meat loaf.	Spores are able to survive heating, so reheat to 165°F (74°C) and keep foods out of the danger zone.
Streptococcus (1–4 days)	Nausea, vomiting, diarrhea	Various species of *streptococcus* bacteria which are facultative anaerobes. Some are transmitted by animals and workers contaminated with feces, others from the nose and throat of infected humans.	Milk, pudding, ice cream, eggs, meat pie, egg/potato salads, poultry.	Cook food thoroughly and chill rapidly. Strict personal hygiene. Use pasteurized dairy products.
Trichinosis (4–28 days)	Fever, diarrhea, sweating, muscle pain, vomiting, skin lesions.	*Trichinella spiralis:* a spiral worm that lives in the intestines where it matures and lays eggs and later invades muscle tissue. Transmitted by infected swine and rats.	Improperly cooked pork allows larvae to live.	Cook pork to 150°F (65°C). Avoid recontamination of raw meats. If frying, cook to 170°F (75°C).
Infectious Hepatitis (10–50 days)	Jaundice, fever, cramps, nausea, lethargy.	Hepatitis virus A: grows in feces of infected humans and human carriers. Transmitted by water and from person to person, and infects the liver.	Shellfish from polluted water, milk, whipped cream, cold cuts, potato salad.	Cook clams, and shellfish, etc., thoroughly to a temperature exceeding 150°F (65°C). Heat-treat and disinfect suspected water and milk. Enforce strict personal hygiene.
Perfringens (9–15 hours)	Diarrhea, nausea, cramps, possible fever, vomiting (rare).	*Clostridium perfringens:* spore-forming anaerobic bacteria that can withstand most cooking temperatures and are found in soil, dust, and the intestinal tract of animals.	Reheated meats, raw meat, raw vegetables, soups, gravies, stews.	Cool meat that is to be eaten later quickly and reheat to 165°F (74°C). Avoid cross-contamination of raw meat and cooked meat. The only way to kill spores is to pressure cook at 15 lb. steam pressure to reach 250°F (120°C).

*Incubation period is the time between infection and onset of symtoms.

FIRST-AID SUPPLIES

Adhesive strips in assorted sizes
Bandage compresses
Sterile gauze dressings, individually wrapped
Rolled gauze bandage
First-aid adhesive tape
Cotton swabs (for applying antiseptic or removing particles from eye)
Tourniquet
Tongue depressors (for small splints)
Scissors
Tweezers

Needle (for removing splinters)
Rubbing alcohol (for sterilizing instruments)
Mild antiseptic (for wounds)
Antibiotic cream
Syrup of ipecac (to induce vomiting)
Petroleum jelly
Aspirin or acetaminophen
Emergency numbers (post numbers for ambulance, fire, hospital, poison center, near phone)

COOKING RATIOS AND TIMES FOR SELECTED GRAINS

Type	*Ratio of Grain to Liquid (Cups)*	*Approximate Yield (Cups)**	*Cooking Time*
Barley, pearled	1:2	4	35 to 45 minutes
Barley groats	1:2 1/2	4	50 minutes to 1 hour
Buckwheat groats (Kasha)	1:1 1/2 to 2	2	12 to 20 minutes
Couscous**	——	1 1/2 to 2	20 to 25 minutes
Hominy, whole***	1:2 1/2	3	2 1/2 to 3 hours
Hominy grits	1:4	3	25 minutes
Millet	1:2	3	30 to 35 minutes
Oat groats	1:2	2	45 minutes to 1 hour
Polenta	1:3 to 3 1/2	3	35 to 45 minutes
Rice, Arborio (risotta)	1:3	3	20 to 30 minutes
Rice, basmati	1:1 1/2	3	25 minutes
Rice, converted	1:1 3/4	4	25 to 30 minutes
Rice, long-grain, brown	1:3	4	40 minutes
Rice, long-grain, white	1:1 1/2 to 1 3/4	3	18 to 20 minutes
Rice, short-grain, brown	1:2 1/2	4	35 to 40 minutes
Rice, short-grain, white	1:1 to 1 1/2	3	20 to 30 minutes
Rice, wild	1:3	4	30 to 45 minutes
Rice, wild, pecan	1:1 3/4	4	20 minutes
Wheat berries	1:3	2	1 hour
Wheat, bulgur, soaked†	1:4	2	2 hours
Wheat, bulgur, pilaf†	1:2 1/2	2	15 to 20 minutes
Wheat, cracked	1:2	3	20 minutes

*From 1 cup of uncooked grain.
**Grain should be soaked briefly in tepid water and then drained before it is steamed.
***Grain should be soaked overnight in cold water and then drained before it is cooked.
†Grain may be cooked by covering it with boiling water and soaking it for 2 hours or cooking it by the pilaf method.

APPROXIMATE SOAKING AND COOKING TIMES
FOR SELECTED DRIED LEGUMES

Type	Soaking Time	Cooking Time
Adzuki beans	4 hours	1 hour
Black beans	4 hours	1 1/2 hours
Black-eyed peas*	——	1 hour
Chickpeas	4 hours	2 to 2 1/2 hours
Fava beans	12 hours	3 hours
Great Northern beans	4 hours	1 hour
Kidney beans (red or white)	4 hours	1 hour
Lentils*	——	30 to 40 minutes
Lima beans	4 hours	1 to 1 1/2 hours
Mung beans	4 hours	1 hour
Navy beans	4 hours	2 hours
Peas, split*	——	30 minutes
Peas, whole	4 hours	40 minutes
Pigeon peas*	——	30 minutes
Pink peas	4 hours	1 hour
Pinto beans	4 hours	1 to 1 1/2 hours
Soybeans	12 hours	3 to 3 1/2 hours

* Soaking is not necessary.

A P P E N D I X 3 *Weights and Measures Conversions*

WEIGHT MEASURES CONVERSIONS*

U.S.	Metric (rounded)
1/4 ounce	8 grams
1/2 ounce	15 grams
1 ounce	30 grams
4 ounces	115 grams
8 ounces (1/2 pound)	225 grams
16 ounces (1 pound)	450 grams
32 ounces (2 pounds)	900 grams
40 ounces (2 1/4 pounds)	1 kilogram

*Values have been rounded.

VOLUME MEASURES CONVERSIONS*

U.S.	Metric (rounded)
1 teaspoon	5 milliliters
1 tablespoon	15 milliliters
1 fluid ounce (2 tablespoons)	30 milliliters
2 fluid ounces (1/4 cup)	60 milliliters
8 fluid ounces (1 cup)	240 milliliters
16 fluid ounces (1 pint)	480 milliliters
32 fluid ounces (1 quart)	950 milliliters (.95 liter)
128 fluid ounces (1 gallon)	3.75 liters

*Values have been rounded.

TEMPERATURE CONVERSIONS*

Degrees Fahrenheit (°F)	Degrees Celcius (C°)
32°	0°
40°	4°
140°	60°
150°	65°
160°	70°
170°	75°
212°	100°
275°	135°
300°	150°
325°	165°
350°	175°
375°	190°
400°	205°
425°	220°
450°	230°
475°	245°
500°	260°

*Values have been rounded.

INFORMATION/HINTS AND TIPS FOR CALCULATIONS

1 gallon = 4 quarts = 8 pints = 16 cups (8 fluid ounces) = 128 fluid ounces.

1 fifth bottle = approximately 1 1/2 pints or exactly 25.6 fluid ounces.

1 measuring cup holds 8 fluid ounces (A coffee cup generally holds 6 fluid ounces).

1 egg white = 2 fluid ounces (average).

1 lemon = 1 to 1 1/4 fluid ounces of juice.

1 orange = 3 to 3 1/2 fluid ounces of juice.

To convert ounces and pounds to grams: multiply ounces X 28.35; multiply pounds X 453.59.

To convert Fahrenheit to Celcius: subtract 32 from °F X 5 ÷ 9 = °C.

To round to the next closest whole number, round up if final decimal is 5 or greater; round down if less than 5.

WEIGHTS AND MEASURES EQUIVALENCIES

Dash	less than 1/8 teaspoon
3 teaspoons	1 tablespoon (1/2 fluid ounce)
2 tablespoons	1/8 cup (1 fluid ounce)
4 tablespoons	1/4 cup (2 fluid ounces)
5 1/3 tablespoons	1/3 cup (2 2/3 fluid ounces)
8 tablespoons	1/2 cup (4 fluid ounces)
10 2/3 tablespoons	2/3 cup (5 1/3 fluid ounces)
12 tablespoons	3/4 cup (6 fluid ounces)
14 tablespoons	7/8 cup (7 fluid ounces)
16 tablespoons	1 cup
1 gill	1/2 cup
1 cup	8 fluid ounces (240 milliliters)
2 cups	1 pint (480 milliliters)
2 pints	1 quart (approximately 1 liter)
4 quarts	1 gallon (3.75 liters)
8 quarts	1 peck (8.8 liters)
4 pecks	1 bushel (35 liters)
1 ounce	28.35 grams (rounded to 30)
16 ounces	1 pound (453.59 grams rounded to 450)
1 kilogram	2.2 pounds

Glossary

A

Abalone: A mollusc with a single shell and a large, edible adductor muscle similar to that of scallops.

Aboyeur (Fr.): Expediter or announcer; a station in the brigade system. The aboyeur accepts orders from the dining room, relays them to the appropriate stations of the kitchen, and checks each plate before it leaves the kitchen.

Acid: A substance having a sour or sharp flavor. Most foods are somewhat acidic. Foods generally referred to as "acids" include citrus juice, vinegar, and wine. A substance's degree of acidity is measured on the pH scale; acids have a pH of less than 7.

Adulterated food: Food that has been contaminated to the point that it is considered unfit for human consumption.

Aerobic bacteria: Bacteria that require the presence of oxygen to function.

Aïoli (Fr.): Garlic mayonnaise. (Also, in Italian, *allioli;* in Spanish, *aliolio.*)

Albumen: The major protein in egg whites.

Al dente (It.): To the tooth; to cook an item, such as pasta or vegetables, until it is tender but still firm, not soft.

Alkali: A substance that tests at higher than 7 on the pH scale. Alkalis are sometimes described as having a slightly soapy flavor. Olives and baking soda are some of the few alkaline foods.

Allumette: Vegetables, potatoes, or other items cut into pieces the size and shape of matchsticks, 1/8 inch x 1/8 inch x 1 to 2 inches is the standard.

Amino acid: The basic molecular component of proteins, one of the essential dietary components.

Anaerobic bacteria: Bacteria that do not require oxygen to function.

Angel food cake: A type of sponge cake made with egg whites that are beaten until stiff.

AP/As Purchased weight: The weight of an item before trimming or other preparation (as opposed to edible portion weight or EP).

Appareil: A prepared mixture of ingredients used alone or as an ingredient in another preparation.

Appetizer: Light foods served before a meal. These may be hot or cold, plated or served as finger food.

Aquaculture: The cultivation or farm-raising of fish or shellfish.

Aromatics: Plant ingredients, such as herbs and spices, used to enhance the flavor and fragrance of food.

Arrowroot: A powdered starch made from a tropical root. Used primarily as a thickener. Remains clear when cooked.

Aspic: A clear jelly made from stock (or occasionally from fruit or vegetable juices); may be thickened with gelatin. Used to coat foods or cubed and used as a garnish.

B

Bacteria: Microscopic organisms. Some have beneficial properties, others can cause food-borne illnesses when contaminated foods are ingested.

Bain-marie: A water bath used to cook foods gently by surrounding the cooking vessel with simmering water. Also, a set of nesting pots with single, long handles used as a double boiler. Also, steam table inserts.

Bake blind: To partially or completely bake an unfilled pastry crust.

Baking powder: A chemical leavener made with an acidic ingredient and an alkaline one; most commonly these are sodium bicarbonate (baking soda) and cream of tartar. When exposed to liquid, it produces carbon dioxide gas, which leavens doughs and batters. *Double-acting baking powder* contains ingredients that produce two leavening reactions, one upon exposure to liquid, the second when heated.

Baking soda: Sodium bicarbonate, a leavening agent that may be used in combination with an acidic ingredient such as sour milk or as a component of baking powder.

Barbecue: A cooking method involving grilling food over a wood or charcoal fire. Usually some sort of rub, marinade, or sauce is brushed on the item before or during cooking.

Bard: To cover an item with slabs or strips of fat, such as bacon or fatback, to baste it during roasting. The fat is usually tied on with butcher's twine.

Barquette: A boat-shaped tart or tartlet, which may have a sweet or savory filling.

Baste: To moisten food during cooking with pan drippings, sauce, or other liquid. Basting prevents food from drying out.

Baton/Batonnet (Fr.): Items cut into pieces somewhat larger than allumette or julienne; 1/4 inch x 1/4 inch x 2 to 2 1/2 inches is the standard. Translated to English as "stick" or "small stick."

Batter: A mixture of flour and liquid, with the inclusion of other ingredients as needed. Batters vary in thickness but are generally semiliquid and thinner than doughs. Used in such preparations as cakes, quick breads, pancakes, and crepes.

Bavarian cream/Bavaroise: A type of custard made from heavy cream and eggs; it is sweetened, flavored, and stabilized with gelatin.

Béarnaise: A classic emulsion sauce similar to hollandaise made with egg yolks; a reduction of white wine, shallots, and tarragon; and butter-finished with tarragon and chervil.

Béchamel: A white sauce made of milk thickened with a light roux and flavored with onion. It is one of the *Grand sauces*.

Bench proof: In yeast dough production, the rising stage that occurs after the dough is panned and just before baking.

Beurre blanc (Fr.): "White butter." A classic emulsified sauce made with a reduction of white wine and shallots thickened with whole butter and possibly finished with fresh herbs or other seasonings.

Beurre manié (Fr.): "Kneaded butter." A mixture of equal parts by weight of whole butter and flour, used to thicken gravies and sauces.

Beurre noir (Fr.): "Black butter." Butter that has been cooked to a very dark brown or nearly black; a sauce made with browned butter, vinegar, chopped parsley, and capers. It is usually served with fish.

Beurre noisette (Fr.): "Hazelnut butter" or "brown butter." Whole butter that has been heated until browned.

Binder: An ingredient or appareil used to thicken a sauce or hold together another mixture of ingredients.

Bisque: A soup based on crustaceans or a vegetable purée. It is classically thickened with rice and usually finished with cream.

Bivalve: A mollusc with two hinged shells. Examples are clams and oysters.

Blanch: To cook an item briefly in boiling water or hot fat before finishing or storing it.

Blanquette: A white stew, usually of veal but sometimes of chicken or lamb. It is served after the sauce has been thickened with a liaison.

Bloom: To soften gelatin in warm liquid before use.

Boil: A cooking method in which items are immersed in liquid at or above the boiling point (212°F/100°C).

Bolster: A collar or shank at the point on a knife where the blade meets the handle.

Boning knife: A thin-bladed knife used for separating raw meat from the bone; its blade is usually about 6 inches long and may be flexible or rigid.

Botulism: A food-borne illness caused by toxins produced by the anaerobic bacterium *Clostridium botulinum*.

Boucher (Fr.): Butcher.

Bouillabaisse (Fr.): A hearty fish and shellfish stew flavored with saffron. A traditional specialty of Marseilles, France.

Bouillon (Fr.): Broth.

Boulanger (Fr.): Baker, specifically of breads and other nonsweetened doughs.

Bouquet garni: A small bundle of herbs tied with string. It is used to flavor stocks, braises, and other preparations. Usually contains bay leaf, parsley, thyme, and possibly other *Aromatics*.

Braise: A cooking method in which the main item, usually meat, is seared in fat, then simmered in stock or another liquid in a covered vessel.

Bran: The outer layer of a cereal grain and the part highest in fiber.

Brazier/Brasier: A pan, designed specifically for braising, that usually has two handles and a tight-fitting lid. Often is round but may be square or rectangular.

Brigade system: The kitchen organization system instituted by Auguste Escoffier. Each position has a station and well-defined responsibilities.

Brine: A salt, water, and seasonings solution used to preserve foods.

Brioche: A rich yeast dough traditionally baked in a fluted pan with a distinctive topknot of dough.

Brisket: A cut of beef from the lower forequarter, best suited for long-cooking preparations like braising. Corned beef is cured beef brisket.

Broil: A cooking method in which items are cooked by a radiant heat source placed above the food, usually in a broiler or *salamander*.

Broth: A flavorful, aromatic liquid made by simmering water or stock with meat, vegetables, and/or spices and herbs.

Brown stock: An amber liquid produced by simmering browned bones and meat (usually veal or beef) with vegetables and aromatics (including caramelized mirepoix).

Brunoise (Fr.): Small dice; 1/8-inch cube is the standard. For a brunoise cut, items are first cut in julienne, then cut crosswise. For a fine brunoise, 1/16-inch square, cut items first in fine julienne.

Butcher: A chef or purveyor who is responsible for butchering meats, poultry, and occasionally fish. In the brigade system, the butcher may also be responsible for breading meat and fish items and other *mise en place* operations involving meat.

Buttercream: A mixture of butter, sugar, and eggs or custard; it is used to garnish cakes and pastries.

Butterfly: To cut an item (usually meat or seafood) and open out the edges like a book or the wings of a butterfly.

Buttermilk: A dairy beverage liquid with a slightly sour flavor similar to that of yogurt. Traditionally, the liquid by-product of butter churning, now usually made by culturing skim milk.

C

Calorie: A unit used to measure food energy. It is the amount of energy needed to raise the temperature of 1 gram of water by 1°C.

Canapé: An hors d'oeuvre consisting of a small piece of bread or toast, often cut in a decorative shape, garnished with a savory spread or topping.

Capon: A castrated male chicken, slaughtered at under 8 months of age and weighing 5 to 8 pounds (2.3 to 3.6 kilograms). Very tender, it is usually roasted or poêléed.

Caramelization: The process of browning sugar in the presence of heat. The temperature range in which sugar caramelizes is approximately 320 to 360°F (160 to 182°C).

Carbohydrate: One of the basic nutrients used by the body as a source of energy; types include simple (sugars) and complex (starches and fibers).

Carry-over cooking: Heat retained in cooked foods that allows them to continue cooking even after removal from the cooking medium. Especially important to roasted foods.

Casing: A synthetic or natural membrane (usually pig or sheep intestines) used to enclose sausage *forcemeat.*

Casserole/en casserole (Fr.): A lidded cooking vessel that is used in the oven; usually round with two handles. Also, foods cooked in a casserole.

Cassoulet (Fr.): A stew of white beans baked with pork or other meats, duck or goose confit, and seasonings.

Caul fat: A fatty membrane from a pig or sheep intestine that resembles fine netting; used to *bard* roasts and *pâtés* and to encase sausage *forcemeat.*

Cellulose: A complex *carbohydrate;* it is the main structural component of plant cells.

Cephalopod: "Head-footed"; marine creatures whose tentacles and arms are attached directly to their heads; includes squid and octopus.

Chafing dish: A metal dish with a heating unit (flame or electric) used to keep foods warm and to cook foods at tableside or during buffet service.

Champagne: A sparkling white wine produced in the Champagne region of France; the term is sometimes incorrectly applied to other sparkling wines.

Charcuterie (Fr.): The preparation of pork and other meat items, such as hams, *terrines,* sausages, *pâtés,* and other *forcemeats.*

Charcutière (Fr.): In the style of the butcher's wife. Items (usually grilled meat) are served with sauce Robert and finished with a julienne of *gherkins.*

Chasseur (Fr.): Hunter's style. A mushroom–tomato sauce made with a white wine reduction and demi-glace, and finished with butter and parsley.

Cheesecloth: A light, fine mesh gauze used for straining liquids and making sachets.

Chef de partie (Fr.): Station chefs. In the brigade system, these are the line-cook positions, such as saucier, grillardin, etc.

Chef de rang (Fr.): Front waiter. A *demi-chef de rang* is a back waiter or busboy.

Chef de salle (Fr.): Head waiter.

Chef de service (Fr.): Director of service.

Chef de vin (Fr.): Wine steward.

Chef's potato: All-purpose potato.

Chef's knife: An all-purpose knife used for chopping, slicing, and mincing; its blade is usually between 8 and 14 inches long.

Chemical leavener: An ingredient (such as *baking soda* or *baking powder*) whose chemical action is used to produce carbon dioxide gas to leaven baked goods.

Chiffonade: Leafy vegetables or herbs cut into fine shreds; often used as a garnish.

Chili/Chile: The fruit of certain types of capsicum peppers (not related to black pepper), used fresh, dried, or smoked as a seasoning. Chilies come in many types (for example, jalapeño, chipotle, poblano) and varying degrees of spiciness.

Chili powder: Dried, ground or crushed chilies, often with other ground spices and herbs.

Chine: Backbone. A cut of meat that includes the backbone; in butchering, to separate the backbone and ribs to facilitate carving.

Chinoise: A conical sieve used for straining and puréeing foods.

Cholesterol: A sterol found exclusively in animal products such as meat, eggs, and cheese.

Chop: To cut into pieces of roughly the same size. Also, a small cut of meat including part of the rib.

Choron: Sauce béarnaise finished with tomato purée.

Choucroute (Fr.): Sauerkraut. *Choucroute garni* is sauerkraut garnished with various meats.

Chowder: A thick soup that may be made from a variety of ingredients but usually contains potatoes.

Cioppino: A fish stew usually made with white wine and tomatoes, believed to have originated in San Francisco.

Clarification: The process of removing solid impurities from a liquid (such as butter or stock). Also, a mixture of ground meat, egg whites, mirepoix, tomato purée, herbs, and spices used to clarify broth for consommé.

Clarified butter: Butter from which the milk solids and water have been removed, leaving pure butterfat. Has a higher smoking point than whole butter but less butter flavor.

Coagulation: The curdling, stiffening, or clumping of protein strands usually due to the application of heat or acid.

Coarse chop: To cut into pieces of roughly the same size; used for items such as mirepoix, where appearance is not important.

Cocoa: The pods of the cacao tree, processed to remove the cocoa butter and ground into powder. Used as a flavoring.

Cocotte (Fr.): Casserole. A cooking dish with a tight-fitting lid for braising or stewing. Also, a small ramekin used for cooking eggs. (*En cocotte* is often interchangeable with *en casserole*).

Cod, salt: Cod fish that has been salted, possibly smoked, and dried to preserve it.

Coddled eggs: Eggs cooked in simmering water, in their shells or in ramekins or coddlers, until set.

Colander: A perforated bowl, with or without a base or legs, used to strain foods.

Combination method: A cooking method that involves the application of both moist and dry heat to the main item (for example, braising or stewing).

Commis (Fr.): Apprentice. A cook who works under a chef de partie to learn the station and its responsibilities. *A commis de rang* is a back waiter or busboy.

Communard (Fr.): The kitchen position responsible for preparing staff or "family" meals.

Complex carbohydrate: A large molecule made up of long chains of sugar molecules. In food, these molecules are found in starches and fiber.

Compote: A dish of fruit—fresh or dried—cooked in syrup flavored with spices or liqueur.

Compound butter: Whole butter combined with herbs or other seasonings and usually used to sauce grilled or broiled items or vegetables.

Concassée/concasser (Fr.): To pound or chop coarsely. Usually refers to tomatoes that have been peeled, seeded, and chopped.

Condiment: An aromatic mixture, such as pickles, chutney, and some sauces and relishes, that accompanies food (usually kept on the table throughout service).

Conduction: A method of heat transfer in which heat is transmitted through another substance. In cooking, when heat is transmitted to food through a pot or pan, oven walls, or racks.

Confiserie/Confiseur (Fr.): Confectionery/confectioner. A *pâtissier* specializing in, and responsible for, the production of candies and related items, such as *petits fours*.

Confit: Meat (usually goose, duck, or pork) cooked and preserved in its own fat.

Consommé: Broth that has been clarified using a mixture of ground meat, egg whites, and other ingredients that trap impurities.

Convection: A method of heat transfer in which heat is transmitted through the circulation of air or water.

Convection oven: An oven that employs convection currents by forcing hot air through fans so it circulates around food, cooking it quickly and evenly.

Coquilles Saint-Jacques (Fr.): Scallops. Also, a dish of broiled scallops with any of several garnishes.

Coral: Lobster roe, which is red or coral-colored when cooked.

Corned beef: Beef brisket preserved with salt and spices. The term "corned" refers to the chunks of salt spread over the brisket during the corning process.

Cornichon (Fr.): A small, sour, pickled cucumber; gherkin.

Cornstarch: A fine, white powder milled from dried corn; used primarily as a thickener for sauce and occasionally as an ingredient in batters.

Coulibiac (Fr.): A preparation of fish (usually salmon), kasha or rice visiga, onion, mushrooms, and herbs, baked in a pastry crust. (Also Russian, *kulibyaka.*)

Coulis: A thick purée, usually of vegetables but possibly of fruit. (Traditionally meat, fish, or shellfish purée; meat jus; or certain thick soups.)

Country-style: A forcemeat that is coarse in texture, usually made from pork, pork fat, liver, and various garnishes.

Court bouillon (Fr.): "Short broth." An aromatic vegetable broth that usually includes an acidic ingredient, such as wine or vinegar; most commonly used for poaching fish.

Couscous: Pellets of semolina usually cooked by steaming, traditionally in a couscoussière. Also, the stew with which this grain is traditionally served.

Couscoussière: A set of nesting pots similar to a steamer used to cook couscous.

Couverture: Fine, semisweet chocolate used for coating and decorating. Its high cocoa butter content gives it a glossy appearance after tempering.

Cream: The fatty component of milk; available with various fat contents. Also, a mixing method for batter cakes.

Cream soup: Traditionally a soup based on a béchamel sauce. Loosely, any soup finished with cream, a cream variant such as sour cream, or a liaison; these soups are usually based on béchamel or velouté.

Cream puff: A pastry made with pâte à choux, filled with *crème pâtissière,* and usually glazed.

Crème anglaise (Fr.): Custard sauce or vanilla sauce; "English cream."

Crème brulée (Fr.): Custard topped with sugar and caramelized under the broiler before service.

Crème fraîche (Fr.): Heavy cream cultured to give it a thick consistency and a slightly tangy flavor; used in hot preparations since it is less likely to curdle when heated than sour cream or yogurt.

Crème patisserie (Fr.): "Pastry cream." Custard made with eggs, flour or other starches, milk, sugar, and flavorings, used to fill and garnish pastries or as the base for puddings, pies, soufflés, and creams.

Crêpe: A thin pancake made with egg batter; used in sweet and savory preparations.

Croissant: A pastry consisting of a yeast dough with a butter roll-in, traditionally rolled in a crescent shape.

Cross-contamination: The transference of disease-causing elements from one source to another through physical contact.

Croûte, en (Fr.): Encased in a bread or pastry crust.

Croûton (Fr.): A bread or pastry garnish, usually toasted or sautéed until crisp.

Crumb: A term used to describe the texture of baked goods; for example, an item can be said to have a fine or coarse crumb.

Crustacean: A class of hard-shelled arthropods, primarily aquatic, which includes edible species such as lobster, crab, shrimp, and crayfish.

Cuisson (Fr.): Poaching liquid, including stock, fumet, court bouillon, or other liquid, which may be reduced and used as a base for the poached item's sauce.

Cure: To preserve a food by salting, smoking, and/or drying.

Curing salt: A mixture of 94 percent table salt (sodium chloride) and 6 percent sodium nitrite used to preserve meats. (Also known as tinted curing mixture, or T.C.M.—a food coloring is added as an identifier.)

Curry: A mixture of spices used primarily in Indian cuisine; may include turmeric, coriander, cumin, cayenne or other chilies, cardamom, cinnamon, clove, fennel, fenugreek, ginger, and garlic. Also, a dish seasoned with curry or curry paste.

Custard: A mixture of milk, beaten egg, and possibly other ingredients, such as sweet or savory flavorings, which is cooked with gentle heat, often in a bain-marie or double-boiler.

D

Danger zone: The temperature range from 45 to 140°F (7 to 60°C), the most favorable condition for rapid growth of many pathogens.

Danish pastry: A pastry consisting of rich yeast dough with a butter roll-in, possibly filled with nuts, fruit, or other ingredients and iced. This pastry originated in Denmark.

Daube: A meat stew braised in red wine, traditionally in a daubière, a specialized casserole with a tight-fitting lid and indentations to hold hot coals.

Deck oven: A variant of the conventional oven, in which the heat source is located underneath the deck or floor of the oven and the food is placed directly on the deck instead of on a rack.

Deep-fry: A cooking method in which foods are cooked by immersion in hot fat; deep-fried foods are often coated with bread crumbs or batter before being cooked.

Deglaze/Déglacer: To use a liquid, such as wine, water, or stock, to dissolve food particles and/or caramelized drippings left in a pan after roasting or sautéing.

Degrease/Dégraisser: To skim the fat off the surface of a liquid, such as a stock or sauce.

Demi-glace (Fr.): "Half-glaze." A mixture of equal proportions of brown stock and brown sauce that has been reduced by half. One of the grand sauces.

Dépouillage (Fr.): To skim the surface of a cooking liquid, such as a stock or sauce. This action is simplified by placing the pot off-center on the burner and skimming impurities as they collect at one side of the pot.

Deviled: Meat, poultry, or other food seasoned with mustard, vinegar, and possibly other seasonings; coated with bread crumbs; and grilled.

Dice: To cut ingredients into small cubes (1/4 inch for small, 1/3 inch for medium, 3/4 inch for large).

Direct heat: A method of heat transfer in which heat waves radiate from a source (for example, an open burner or grill) and travel directly to the item being heated with no conductor between heat source and food. Examples are grilling, broiling, and toasting.

Dock: To cut the top of dough before baking to allow it to expand; a decorative and useful element for breads and pastry doughs.

Drawn: A whole fish that has been scaled and gutted but still has its head, fins, and tail.

Dredge: To coat food with a dry ingredient such as flour or bread crumbs.

Dressed: Prepared for cooking; a dressed fish is gutted and scaled, and its head, tail, and fins are removed (same as pan-dressed). Dressed poultry is plucked, drawn, singed, trimmed, and trussed. Also, coated with dressing, as in a salad.

Drum sieve: A sieve consisting of a screen stretched across a shallow cylinder of wood or aluminum (see also *tamis*).

Dry cure: A combination of salts and spices used usually before smoking to process meats and forcemeats.

Dry sauté: To sauté without fat, usually using a nonstick pan.

Dumpling: Any of a number of small soft dough or batter items, which are steamed, poached, fried, or simmered (possibly on top of a stew); may be filled or plain.

Durum: A species of hard wheat primarily milled into semolina flour for use in pastas.

Dutch oven: A kettle, usually of cast iron, used for stewing and braising on the stove top or in the oven.

Dutch process: A method for treating cocoa powder with an alkali to reduce its acidity.

Duxelles: An appareil of finely chopped mushrooms and shallots sautéed gently in butter.

E

Egg wash: A mixture of beaten eggs (whole eggs, yolks, or whites) and a liquid, usually milk or water, used to coat baked goods to give them a sheen.

Emincer (Fr.): To cut an item, usually meat, into very thin slices.

Emulsion: A mixture of two or more liquids, one of which is a fat or oil and the other of which is water-based, so that tiny globules of one are suspended in the other. This may involve the use of stabilizers, such as egg or mustard. Emulsions may be temporary, permanent, or semipermanent.

Endosperm: The inside portion of a grain, usually the largest portion, composed primarily of starch and protein.

Entremetier (Fr.): Vegetable chef/station. The position responsible for hot appetizers and often soups, vegetables, starches, and pastas; may also be responsible for egg dishes.

EP/Edible Portion: The weight of an item after trimming and preparation (as opposed to the as purchased weight or AP).

Escalope (Fr.): Same as scallop; a small boneless piece of meat or fish of uniform thickness.

Espagnole sauce (Fr.): "Spanish sauce." Brown sauce made with brown stock, caramelized mirepoix and tomato purée, and seasonings.

Essence: A concentrated flavoring extracted from an item, usually by infusion or distillation; includes items like vanilla and other extracts, concentrated stocks, and fumets.

Estouffade (Fr.): Stew. Also, a type of brown stock based on pork knuckle and veal and beef bones that is often used in braises.

Etouffé (Fr.): "Smothered." A cooking method similar to braising in which items are cooked with little or no added liquid in a pan with a tight-fitting lid. (Also étuver, à l'étuvée; a Cajun stew.)

Extrusion/Extruding machine: A machine used to shape pasta. The dough is pushed out through perforated plates rather than being rolled.

F

Fabrication: The butchering, cutting, and trimming of meat, poultry, fish, and game.

Facultative bacteria: Bacteria that can survive both with and without oxygen.

Farce (Fr.): Forcemeat or stuffing; *farci* means stuffed.

Farina (It.): Flour or fine meal of wheat.

Fat: One of the basic nutrients used by the body to provide energy. Fats also provide flavor in food and give a feeling of fullness.

Fatback: Pork fat from the back of the pig, used primarily for barding; clear fat.

Fermentation: The breakdown of carbohydrates into carbon dioxide gas and alcohol, usually through the action of yeast on sugar.

Fiber/Dietary fiber: The structural component of plants that is necessary to the human diet. Sometimes referred to as roughage.

FIFO/First In, First Out: A fundamental storage principle based on stock rotation. Products are stored and used so the oldest product is always used first.

Filé: A thickener made from ground, dried, sassafras leaves; used primarily in gumbos.

Fillet/Filet: A boneless cut of meat, fish, or poultry.

Filleting knife: A flexible-bladed knife used for filleting fish; similar in size and shape to a boning knife.

Fines herbes: A mixture of herbs, usually parsley, chervil, tarragon, and chives.

Fish poacher: A long, narrow pot with straight sides and possibly a perforated rack, used for poaching whole fish.

Flat fish: A fish skeletal type characterized by its flat body and both eyes on one side of its head (for example, sole, plaice, and halibut).

Flat-top: A thick plate of cast iron or steel set over the heat source on a range; diffuses heat, making it more even than an open burner.

Fond (Fr.): Stock; base or foundation.

Fondant: An icing made with sugar, water, and glucose; used primarily for pastry and confectionery.

Foodborne illness: An illness in humans caused by the consumption of an adulterated food product. In order for a foodborne illness to be considered official, it must involve two or more people who have eaten the same food and it must be confirmed by health officials.

Food mill: A type of strainer with a crank-operated, curved blade. It is used to purée soft foods.

Food processor: A machine with interchangeable blades and disks and a removable bowl and lid separate from the motor housing. It can be used for a variety of tasks, including chopping, grinding, puréeing, emulsifying, kneading, slicing, shredding, and cutting julienne, by using appropriate attachments.

Forcemeat: A mixture of chopped or ground meat and other ingredients used for pâtés, sausages, and other preparations. See *Farce*.

Formula: A recipe; measurements for each ingredient may be given as percentages of the weight for the main ingredient.

Fortified wine: Wine to which a spirit, usually brandy, has been added (for example, port or marsala).

Free-range: Livestock that is raised unconfined (by current definition, a minimum pen size of 3 feet x 3 feet).

French knife: See *Chef's knife*.

Fricassée (Fr.): A stew, of poultry or other white meat, with a white sauce.

Fritter: Sweet or savory foods coated or mixed into batter and deep-fried (also in French, *beignet*).

Friturier (Fr.): Fry chef/station. The position responsible for all fried foods; it may be combined with the rôtisseur position.

Fumet (Fr.): A type of stock in which the main flavoring ingredient is allowed to smother with wine and aromatics; fish fumet is the most common type.

G

Galantine: Boned meat (usually poultry) that is stuffed, rolled, poached, and served cold, usually in aspic.

Game chips: Potatoes sliced into thin circles and deep-fried.

Ganache: A filling or glaze made of heavy cream, chocolate, and/or other flavorings. Used for Truffles.

Garbure (Fr.): A thick vegetable soup usually containing beans, cabbage, and/or potatoes.

Garde-manger (Fr.): Pantry chef/station. The position responsible for cold food preparations, including salads, cold appetizers, pâtés, etc.

Garni (Fr.): Garnished.

Garnish: An edible decoration or accompaniment to a dish.

Gelatin: A protein-based substance found in animal bones and connective tissue. When dissolved in hot liquid and then cooled, it can be used as a thickener and stabilizer.

Gelatinization: A phase in the process of thickening a liquid with starch in which starch molecules swell to form a network that traps water molecules.

Génoise (Fr.): A sponge cake made with whole eggs, used for petits fours, layer cakes, and other desserts.

Germ: The embryo of a cereal grain, which is usually separated from the endosperm during milling because it contains oils that accelerate the spoilage of flours and meals.

Gherkin: A small pickled cucumber; a *cornichon* in French.

Giblets: Organs and other trim from poultry, including the liver, heart, gizzard, and neck.

Glace (Fr.): Reduced stock; ice cream; icing.

Glacé (Fr.): Glazed or iced.

Glaze: To give an item a shiny surface by brushing it with sauce, aspic, icing, or another appareil. For meat, to coat with sauce and then brown in an oven or salamander.

Gluten: An elastic protein formed when hard wheat flour is moistened and agitated. Gluten gives yeast doughs their characteristic elasticity.

Goujonette (Fr.): Fish fillet cut in strips and usually breaded or batter-coated and then deep-fried.

Grand sauce: One of several basic sauces that are used in the preparation of many other small sauces. The grand sauces are: demi-glace, velouté, béchamel, hollandaise, and tomato. (Also called mother sauce.)

Gratiné (Fr.): Browned in an oven or under a salamander *(au gratin, gratin de)*. *Gratin* can also refer to a forcemeat in which some portion of the dominant meat is sautéed and cooled before grinding.

Griddle: A heavy metal surface, which may be either fitted with handles, built into a stove, or heated by its own gas or electric element. Cooking is done directly on the griddle.

Grill: A cooking technique in which foods are cooked by a radiant heat source placed below the food. Also, the piece of equipment on which grilling is done. Grills may be fueled by gas, electricity, charcoal, or wood.

Grill pan: A skillet with ridges that is used to simulate grilling on the stove top.

Grillardin (Fr.): Grill chef/station. The position responsible for all grilled foods; may be combined with rôtisseur.

Griswold: A pot, similar to a rondeau, made of cast iron; may have a single short handle rather than the usual loop handles.

Guinea hen/fowl: A bird related to the pheasant. It is slaughtered at about 6 months of age and weighs 3/4 to 1 1/2 (350 to 700 grams). Its tender meat is suitable to most techniques.

Gumbo: A Creole soup/stew thickened with filé or okra.

Gumbo filé powder: See *Filé*.

H

Haricot (Fr.): "Bean." *Haricots verts* are green beans.

Hash: Chopped, cooked meat, usually with potatoes and/or other vegetables, which is seasoned, bound with a sauce, and sautéed. Also, to chop.

Heimlich maneuver: First aid for choking; the application of sudden, upward pressure on the upper abdomen to force a foreign object from the windpipe.

Hilum: The scar on the side of a bean where it was attached to the pod.

Hollandaise: A classic emulsion sauce made with a vinegar reduction, egg yolks, and melted butter flavored with lemon juice. It is one of the grand sauces.

Hollow-ground: A type of knife blade made by fusing two sheets of metal and beveling or fluting the edge.

Hominy: Corn that has been milled or treated with a lye solution to remove the bran and germ.

Homogenization: A process used to prevent the milkfat from separating out of milk products. The liquid is forced through an ultrafine mesh at high pressure, which breaks up fat globules, dispersing them evenly throughout the liquid.

Hors d'oeuvre (Fr.): "Outside the work." An appetizer.

Hotel pan: A rectangular, metal pan, in any of a number of standard sizes, with a lip that allows it to rest in a storage shelf or steam table.

Hydrogenation: The process in which hydrogen atoms are added to an unsaturated fat molecule, making it partially or completely saturated (hence, solid) at room temperature.

Hydroponics: A technique that involves growing vegetables in nutrient-enriched water, rather than in soil.

Hygiene: Conditions and practices followed to maintain health, including sanitation and personal cleanliness.

I

Infection: Contamination by a disease-causing agent, such as bacteria, consumed via foods.

Infusion: Steeping an aromatic or other item in liquid to extract its flavor. Also, the liquid resulting from this process.

Instant-reading thermometer: A thermometer used to measure the internal temperature of foods. The stem is inserted into the food, producing an instant temperature read out.

Intoxication: Poisoning. A state of being tainted with toxins, particularly those produced by microorganisms that have infected food.

J

Julienne: Vegetables, potatoes, or other items cut into thin strips; 1/8-inch square x 1 to 2 inches is standard. Fine julienne is 1/16-inch square.

Jus (Fr.): Juice. *Jus de viande* is meat gravy. Meat served au jus is served with its own juice or *jus lié*.

Jus lié (Fr.): Meat juice thickened lightly with arrowroot or cornstarch.

K

Kasha (Russ.): Buckwheat groats that have been hulled and crushed; usually prepared by boiling.

Kosher: Prepared in accordance with Jewish dietary laws.

Kosher salt: Pure, refined rock salt used for pickling because it does not contain magnesium carbonate. It thus does not cloud brine solutions. Also used to kosher items. (Also known as coarse salt or pickling salt.)

L

Lard: Rendered pork fat used for pastry and frying.

Lardon (Fr.): A strip of fat used for larding; may be seasoned. (Also, lardoon.)

Leavener: Any ingredient or process that produces air bubbles and causes the rising of baked goods. (See chemical and mechanical leaveners, yeast, baking soda, baking powder.)

Legume: The seeds of certain plants, including beans and peas, which are eaten for their earthy flavors and high nutritional value. Also, the French word for vegetable.

Liaison: A mixture of egg yolks and cream used to thicken and enrich sauces. (Also loosely applied to any appareil used as a thickener.)

Liqueur: A spirit flavored with fruit, spices, nuts, herbs, and/or seeds and usually sweetened.

Littleneck: Small, hard-shell clams often eaten raw on the half shell.

Littleneck (Pacific): A Pacific-coast clam, usually steamed. (Also-known as manila clam.)

Low-fat milk: Milk containing less than 2 percent fat.

Lox: Salt-cured salmon. (Gravad lox or gravlax).

Lyonnaise (Fr.): Lyons-style; with onions and usually butter, white wine, vinegar, and demi-glace.

M

Macaroni (It.): Pasta; often used to refer to elbow-shaped pasta.

Madère (Fr.): A sauce made with demi-glace flavored with Madeira.

Madeira: A Portuguese fortified wine that is treated with heat as it ages, giving it a distinctive flavor and brownish color.

Mahimahi: A firm-fleshed Atlantic and Pacific fish with a light, delicate flavor, suitable to all cooking methods. (Also called dolphin fish or dorado.)

Maître d'hôtel (Fr.): Dining room manager or food and beverage manager, informally called maître d'. This position oversees the dining room or "front of the house" staff. Also, a compound butter flavored with chopped parsley and lemon juice.

Mandoline: A slicing device of stainless steel with carbon steel blades. The blades may be adjusted to cut items into various cuts and thicknesses.

Marbling: The intramuscular fat found in meat that makes the meat tender and juicy.

Marinade: An appareil used in cooking to flavor and moisten foods; may be liquid or dry. Liquid marinades are usually based on an acidic ingredient, such as wine or vinegar; dry marinades are usually salt-based.

Marmite: See *Stockpot.*

Marzipan: A paste of ground almonds, sugar, and egg whites that is used to fill and decorate pastries.

Matelote (Fr.): A fish stew traditionally made with eel.

Matignon (Fr.): An edible mirepoix that is often used in poêléed dishes and is usually served with the finished dish. Typically, matignon includes two parts carrot, one part celery, one part leek, one part onion, one part mushroom (optional), and one part ham or bacon.

Mayonnaise: A cold emulsion sauce made of oil, egg yolks, vinegar, mustard, and seasonings.

Mechanical leavener: Air incorporated into a batter to act as a leavener. Usually, eggs or cream are whipped into a foam, then are folded into the batter.

Medallion (Fr.): A small, round scallop of meat.

Meringue (Fr.): Egg whites beaten until they are stiff, with added sugar or sugar syrup, used as a topping or shaped and baked until stiff. Three types are regular or common, Italian, and Swiss.

Mesophilic: A term used to describe bacteria that thrive within the middle-range temperatures between 60 to 100°F (16 to 43°C).

Metabolism: The sum of chemical processes in living cells by which energy is provided and new material is assimilated.

Meunière, à la: "In the style of the miller's wife." A cooking technique for items dressed with lemon and served with beurre noisettes.

Microwave: A method of heat transfer in which electromagnetic waves (similar to radio waves) generated by a device called a magnetron penetrate food and cause the water molecules in it to oscillate. This rapid molecular motion generates heat, which cooks the food.

Mie (Fr.): The soft part of bread (not the crust); *mie de pain* is fresh white bread crumbs.

Millet: A small, round, glutenless grain that is boiled or ground into flour.

Milling: The process by which grain is ground into flour or meal.

Mince: To chop into very small pieces.

Mirepoix: A combination of chopped aromatic vegetables—usually two parts onion, one part carrot, and one part celery—used to flavor stocks, soups, braises, and stews.

Mise en place (Fr.): "Put in place." The preparation and assembly of ingredients, pans, utensils, and plates or serving pieces needed for a particular dish or service period.

Mode, à la (Fr.): "In the style of" (usually followed by a descriptive phrase). Boeuf à la mode is braised beef; pie à la mode is served with ice cream.

Molasses: The dark-brown, sweet syrup that is a by-product of sugar cane refining.

Mollusk: Any of a number of invertebrate animals with soft, unsegmented bodies usually enclosed in a hard shell; included are clams, oysters, and snails.

Monosodium glutamate (MSG): A flavor-enhancer without a distinct flavor of its own; used primarily in Chinese, processed foods, and prepared seasoning blends. It may cause allergic reactions in some people.

Monounsaturated fat: A fat with one available bonding site not filled with a hydrogen atom. Food sources include avocados, olives, and nuts.

Monté au beurre (Fr.): "To lift with butter." A technique used to enrich sauces, thicken them slightly, and give them a glossy appearance by whisking in whole butter.

Mother sauce: See *Grand sauce.*

Mousse (Fr.): A dish made with beaten egg whites and/or whipped cream folded into a flavored base appareil; may be sweet or savory.

Mousseline (Fr.): A mousse; a sauce made by folding whipped cream into hollandaise; or a very light forcemeat based on white meat or seafood lightened with cream and eggs.

N

Napoléon: A pastry made of layered puff pastry rectangles filled with pastry cream and glazed with fondant.

Napper/Nappé (Fr.): To coat with sauce; thickened.

Nature (Fr.): "Ungarnished; plain." *Pommes natures* are boiled potatoes.

Navarin (Fr.): A stew, traditionally of lamb or mutton, with potatoes, onions, and possibly other vegetables.

New potato: A small, waxy potato that is usually prepared by boiling or steaming and is often eaten with its skin.

Noisette (Fr.): Hazelnut. Also, a small portion of meat cut from the rib. *Pommes noisette* are tournéed potatoes browned in butter. *Beurre noisette* is browned butter.

Nonbony fish: Fish whose skeletons are made of cartilage rather than hard bone (for example, shark, skate). (Also called cartilaginous fish.)

Nouvelle cuisine (Fr.): "New cooking." A culinary movement emphasizing freshness and lightness of ingredients, classical preparations, and innovative combinations and presentation.

Nutrition: The processes by which an organism takes in and uses food.

O

Oblique/Roll cut: A knife cut used primarily with long, cylindrical vegetables such as carrots. The item is cut on a diagonal, rolled 180 degrees, then cut on the same diagonal, producing a piece with two angled edges.

Oeuf (Fr.): Egg.

Offal: Variety meats, including organs (brains, heart, kidneys, lights (or lungs), sweetbreads, tripe, tongue), head meat, tail, and feet.

Offset spatula: A hand tool with a wide, bent blade set in a short handle, used to turn or lift foods from grills, broilers, or griddles.

Oignon brûlé (Fr.): "Burnt onion." A peeled, halved onion seared on a flat-top or in a skillet and used to enhance the color of stock and consommé.

Oignon piqué (Fr.): "Pricked onion." A whole, peeled onion to which a bay leaf is attached, using a whole clove as a tack. It is classically used to flavor béchamel sauce and some soups.

Omelet: Beaten egg that is cooked in butter in a specialized pan or skillet and then rolled or folded into an oval. Omelets may be filled with a variety of ingredients before or after rolling.

Organic leavener: Yeast. A living organism operates by fermenting sugar to produce carbon dioxide gas, causing the batter to rise.

Organ meat: Meat from an organ, rather than the muscle tissue of an animal.

Oven spring: The rapid initial rise of yeast doughs when placed in a hot oven. Heat accelerates the growth of the yeast, which produces more carbon dioxide gas and also causes this gas to expand.

P

Paella: A Spanish dish of rice cooked with onion, tomato, garlic, saffron, vegetables, and various meats, including chicken, chorizo, and/or shellfish.

Paella pan: A specialized pan for cooking paella; it is wide and shallow and usually has two loop handles.

Paillarde (Fr.): A scallop of meat pounded until thin; usually grilled.

Palette knife: A flexible, round-tipped knife used to turn pancakes and grilled foods and to spread fillings and glazes; may have a serrated edge. (Also called a metal spatula.)

Panada: An appareil based on starch (such as flour or crumbs), moistened with a liquid, that is used as a binder.

Panbroil: A cooking method similar to dry sautéing that simulates broiling by cooking an item in a hot pan with little or no fat.

Pan-dressed: See *Dressed.*

Panfry: A cooking method in which items are cooked in deep fat in a skillet over medium heat; this generally involves more fat than sautéing or stir-frying but less than deep-frying.

Pan gravy: A sauce made by deglazing pan drippings from a roast and combining them with a roux or other starch and additional stock.

Papillote, en (Fr.): A moist-heat cooking method similar to steaming, in which items are enclosed in parchment and cooked in the oven.

Parchment: Heat-resistant paper used in cooking for such preparations as lining baking pans, cooking items *en papillote,* and covering items during shallow poaching. Also used to make cones for decorating.

Parcook: To partially cook an item before storing or finishing by another method; may be the same as blanching.

Paring knife: A short knife used for paring and trimming fruits and vegetables; its blade is usually 2 to 4 inches long.

Parisienne scoop: A small tool used for scooping balls out of vegetable or fruit. (Also called a melon baller.)

Parstock: The amount of stock (food and other supplies) necessary to cover operating needs between deliveries.

Pasta (It.): Noodles made from a dough of flour (often semolina), water and/or eggs. This dough is kneaded, rolled, and cut or extruded, then cooked by boiling.

Pasteurization: A process in which milk products are heated to kill microorganisms that could contaminate the milk.

Pastry bag: A bag—usually made of plastic, canvas, or nylon—that can be fitted with plain or decorative tips and used to pipe out icings and puréed foods.

Pâte (Fr.): Noodles or pasta; dough or batter.

Pâte à choux: Cream puff paste, made by boiling a mixture of water, butter, and flour, then beating in whole eggs.

Pâte brisée: Short pastry for pie crusts.

Pâte feuilletée: Puff pastry.

Pâte sucrée: Sweet short pastry.

Pâté (Fr.): A rich forcemeat of meat, game, poultry, seafood, and/or vegetables, baked in pastry or in a mold or dish.

Pâté en croûte: Pâté baked in a pastry crust.

Pâté de campagne: Country-style pâté, with a coarse texture.

Pathogen: A disease-causing microorganism.

Pâtissier (Fr.): Pastry chef/station. This station is responsible for baked items, pastries, and desserts. This is often a separate area of the kitchen.

Paupiette: A fillet or scallop of fish or meat that is rolled up around a stuffing and poached or braised.

Paysanne/Fermier cut: A knife cut in which ingredients are cut into flat, square pieces, 1/2 inch by 1/2 inch by 1/8 inch is standard.

Pesto (It.): A thick, puréed mixture of an herb, traditionally basil, and olive oil used as a sauce for pasta and other foods and as a garnish for soup. Pesto may also contain grated cheese, nuts or seeds, and other seasonings.

pH scale: A scale with values from 0 to 14 representing degree of acidity. A measurement of 7 is neutral, 0 is most acidic and 14 is most alkaline. Chemically, pH measures the concentration/activity of the element hydrogen.

Phyllo dough: Pastry made with very thin sheets of a flour-and-water dough layered with butter and/or crumbs; similar to strudel. Used for sweet and savory dishes. (Also called filo.)

Pickling spice: A mixture of herbs and spices used to season pickles, often includes dill weed and/or seeds, coriander seeds, cinnamon stick, peppercorns, bay leaves, and others.

Pilaf: A technique for cooking grains in which the grain is sautéed briefly in butter, then simmered in stock or water with various seasonings. (Also called pilau, pilaw, pullao, pilav.)

Pincé (Fr.): To caramelize an item by sautéing; usually refers to a tomato product.

Poach: A method in which items are cooked gently in simmering liquid.

Poêlé: A method in which items are cooked in their own juices (usually with the addition of a matignon, other aromatics, and melted butter) in a covered pot, usually in the oven. (Also called butter roasting).

Poissonier (Fr.): Fish chef/station. The position responsible for fish items and their sauces; may be combined with the saucier position.

Polyunsaturated fat: A fat with more than one available bonding site not filled with a hydrogen atom. Food sources include corn, cottonseed, safflower, soy, and sunflower oils.

Port: A fortified dessert wine. Vintage port is high-quality, unblended wine aged in the bottle for at least 12 years; ruby port may be blended and is aged in wood for a short time; white port is made with white grapes.

Prawn: A crustacean that closely resembles shrimp; often used as a general term for large shrimp.

Pressure steamer: A machine that steams food by heating water under pressure in a sealed compartment, allowing the steam to reach higher-than-boiling temperature (212°F/100°C). The food is placed in a sealed chamber that cannot be opened until the pressure has released and the steam properly vented from the chamber.

Primal cuts: The portions produced by the initial cutting of an animal carcass. Cuts are determined standards that may vary from country to country and animal type to type. Primal cuts are further broken down into smaller, more manageable cuts, sometimes called fabricated cuts.

Proof: To allow yeast dough to rise. A proof box is a sealed cabinet that allows control over both temperature and humidity.

Protein: One of the basic nutrients needed by the body to maintain life, build and repair tissues, form enzymes and hormones, and perform other essential functions. Protein can be obtained from animal and vegetable sources. One gram of protein equals 4 calories.

Pulse: The edible seed of a leguminous plant, such as a bean, lentil, or pea. (Often referred to simply as legume.)

Purée: To process food (by mashing, straining, or chopping it very fine) in order to make it a smooth paste. Also, a product produced using this technique.

Q

Quahog: A hard-shell clam larger than 3 inches in diameter, usually used for chowder or fritters. (Also called a quahaug.)

Quenelle (Fr.): A light, poached dumpling based on a forcemeat (usually chicken, veal, seafood, or game) bound with eggs that is shaped in an oval by using two spoons; oval shape.

Quick bread: Bread made with chemical leaveners, which work more quickly than yeast. (Also called a batter bread.)

R

Radiant heat: See *Direct heat.*

Raft: A mixture of ingredients used to clarify consommé (see *Clarification*). The term refers to the fact that the ingredients rise to the surface and form a floating mass.

Ragoût (Fr.): Stew.

Ramekin: A small, ovenproof dish, usually ceramic. (Also in French, *ramequin.*)

Reach-in refrigerator: A refrigeration unit, or set of units, with pass-through doors. They are often used in the pantry area for storage of salads, cold hors d'oeuvres, and other frequently used items.

Recommended Dietary Allowance (RDA): A standard recommendation by the USDA of the amounts of certain nutrients that should be included in the diet in order to prevent deficiencies.

Reduce: To decrease the volume of a liquid by simmering or boiling; used to provide a thicker consistency and/or concentrated flavors.

Reduction: The product that results when a liquid is reduced.

Refresh: To plunge an item into, or run under, cold water after blanching to prevent further cooking.

Remouillage (Fr.): "Rewetting." A stock made from bones that have already been used for stock; it is weaker than a first-quality stock and is often reduced to make glaze or added in lieu of water when making new stock.

Render: To heat foods (e.g. bacon and suet) in order to clarify the fat for use in sautéing or pan-frying.

Ring-top: A flat-top with removable plates that can be opened to varying degrees to expose more or less direct heat.

Risotto: Rice that is sautéed briefly in butter with onions and possibly other aromatics, then combined with stock, which is added in several additions and stirred constantly, producing a creamy texture with grains that are still *al dente;* short-grain or Arborio.

Roast: A dry heat cooking method in which items are cooked in an oven or on a spit over a fire.

Roe: Fish or shellfish eggs.

Roll-in: Butter or a butter-based mixture that is placed between layers of pastry dough, then rolled and folded repeatedly to form numerous layers. When the dough is baked, the layers remain discrete, producing a very flaky, rich pastry.

Rondeau: A shallow, wide, straight-sided pot with two loop handles.

Rondelle: A knife cut that produces flat, round or oval pieces; used on cylindrical vegetables or items trimmed into cylinders before cutting.

Rôti (Fr.): Roasted.

Rôtisseur (Fr.): Roast chef/station. The position responsible for all roasted foods and related sauces.

Roulade (Fr.): A slice of meat or fish rolled around a stuffing; also, filled and rolled sponge cake.

Round: A cut of beef from the hind quarter that includes the top and bottom round, eye, and top sirloin. It is lean and usually braised or roasted. Also, in baking, to shape pieces of yeast dough into balls to ensure even rising and a smooth crust.

Round fish: A classification of fish based on skeletal type, characterized by a rounded body and eyes on opposite sides of its head.

Roux (Fr.): An appareil containing equal parts of flour and fat (usually butter) used to thicken liquids. Roux is cooked to varying degrees (white, pale/blond, or brown), depending on its intended use.

Royale (Fr.): A consommé garnish made of unsweetened custard cut into decorative shapes.

S

Sabayon (Fr.): Wine custard. Sweetened egg yolks flavored with marsala or other wine or liqueur, beaten in a double-boiler until frothy. Contemporary sabayon might substitute a citrus juice or other acid for the wine. (The Italian name is *zabaglione*.)

Sachet d'épices (Fr.): "Bag of spices." Aromatic ingredients, encased in cheesecloth, that are used to flavor stocks and other liquids. A standard sachet contains parsley stems, cracked peppercorns, dried thyme, and a bay leaf.

Salamander: A small broiler usually positioned above a stove, often used to gratinée or reheat food. See *Broil*.

Salé (Fr.): Salted or pickled.

Saltpeter: Potassium nitrate. Used to preserve meat (a type of *Curing salt*).

Sanitation: The preparation and distribution of food in a clean environment by healthy food workers.

Sanitize: The killing of pathogenic organisms by chemicals and/or moist heat.

Saturated fat: A fat whose available bonding sites are entirely filled with hydrogen atoms. These tend to be solid at room temperature and are primarily of animal origin. (Coconut and palm oil are vegetable sources of saturated fat.) Food sources include butter, meat, cheese, chocolate, and eggs.

Saucier (Fr.): Sauté chef/station. The *chef de partie* responsible for all sautéed items and their sauces.

Sauté: A cooking method in which items are cooked quickly in a small amount of fat in a pan on the range top. (*See Sauteuse, Sautoir.*)

Sauteuse: A shallow skillet with sloping sides and a single, long handle. Used for sautéing and referred to generically as a sauté pan.

Sautoir: A shallow skillet with straight sides and a single, long handle. Used for sautéing and referred to generically as a sauté pan.

Savory: Not sweet. Also, the name of a course (savoury) served after dessert and before port in traditional British meals. Also, a family of herbs (including summer and winter savory).

Scald: To heat a liquid, usually milk or cream, to just below the boiling point. May also refer to blanching fruits and vegetables.

Scale/Scaling: To measure ingredients by weighing; to divide dough or batter into portions by weight.

Scallop: A bivalve whose adductor muscle (the muscle that keeps its shells closed) and roe are eaten. Also, a thin slice of meat. See *Escalope*.

Score: To cut the surface of an item at regular intervals to allow it to cook evenly.

Scrapple: A boiled mixture of pork trimmings, buckwheat, and cornmeal.

Sear: To brown the surface of food in fat over high heat before finishing by another method (for example, braising) in order to add flavor.

Sea salt: Salt produced by evaporating sea water. Available refined or unrefined, crystallized, or ground. (Also *sel gris*, French for "gray salt.")

Semolina: The coarsely milled hard wheat endosperm used for gnocchi, some pasta, and couscous.

Shallow-poach: A method in which items are cooked gently in a shallow pan of simmering liquid. The liquid is often reduced and used as the basis of a sauce.

Shelf life: The amount of time in storage that a product can maintain quality.

Shellfish: Various types of marine life consumed as food including univalves, bivalves, cephalopods, and crustaceans.

Shirred egg: An egg cooked with butter (and often cream) in a ramekin.

Sieve: A container made of a perforated material, such as wire mesh, used to drain, rice, or purée foods; also the act of processing food through a sieve.

Silverskin: The tough, connective tissue that surrounds certain muscles; also elastin.

Simmer: To maintain the temperature of a liquid just below boiling. Also, a cooking method in which items are cooked in a simmering liquid.

Simple carbohydrate: Any of a number of small carbohydrate molecules (mono- and disaccharides), including fructose, lactose, maltose, and sucrose.

Single-stage technique: A cooking technique involving only one cooking method—for example boiling or sautéing—as opposed to more than one method, as in braising.

Skim: To remove impurities from the surface of a liquid, such as a stock or soup, during cooking.

Skim milk: Milk from which all but 0.5 percent of the milkfat has been removed.

Slurry: Starch dispersed in cold liquid to prevent it from forming lumps when added to hot liquid as a thickener.

Small sauce: A sauce that is a derivative of any of the grand sauces.

Smoke-roasting: A method for roasting foods in which items are placed on a rack in a pan containing wood chips that smolder, emitting smoke, when the pan is placed on the range top or in the oven.

Smoking: Any of several methods for preserving and flavoring foods by exposing them to smoke. Methods include cold-smoking (in which smoked items are not fully cooked), hot-smoking (in which the items are cooked), and smoke-roasting.

Smoking point: The temperature at which a fat begins to break when heated.

Smother: To cook in a covered pan with little liquid over low heat.

Sodium: An alkaline metal element necessary in small quantities for human nutrition; one of the components of most salts used in cooking.

Sommelier (Fr.): Wine steward or waiter.

Sorbet (Fr.): A frozen dessert made with fruit juice or another flavoring, a sweetener (usually sugar), and beaten egg whites, which prevent the formation of large ice crystals. Sherbet is the closest English equivalent, and it contains milk.

Soufflé (Fr.): "Puffed." A preparation made with a sauce base (usually béchamel for savory soufflés or pastry cream for sweet ones), whipped egg whites, and flavorings. The egg whites cause the soufflé to puff during cooking. Also deep-fried potatoes.

Sourdough: Yeast dough leavened with a fermented starter instead of, or in addition to, fresh yeast. Some starters are kept alive by "feeding" with additional flour and water.

Sous chef (Fr.): Under-chef. The chef who is second in command in a kitchen; usually responsible for scheduling, filling in for the chef, and assisting the *chefs de partie* as necessary.

Spa cooking: A cooking style that focuses on producing high-quality, well-presented dishes that are nutritionally sound, low in calories, fats, sodium, and cholesterol.

Spider: A long-handled skimmer used to remove items from hot liquid or fat and to skim the surface of liquids.

Spit-roast: To roast an item on a large skewer or spit over, or in front of, an open flame or other radiant heat source.

Sponge: A thick yeast batter that is allowed to ferment and develop a light, spongy consistency and is then combined with other ingredients to form a yeast dough.

Sponge cake: A sweet-batter product that is leavened with a beaten egg foam. (Also called a *génoise.*)

Spring-form pan: A round, straight-sided pan whose sides are formed by a hoop that can be unclamped and detached from its base which facilitates the removal of the product.

Squab: A domesticated pigeon that has not yet begun to fly. It is slaughtered 3 to 4 weeks old, weighing under 1 pound (450 grams). Its light, tender meat is suitable for sautéing, roasting, and grilling.

Stabilizer: An ingredient (usually a protein or plant product) that is added to an emulsion to prevent it from separating (for example, egg yolks, cream, and mustard). Also, an ingredient, such as gelatin that is used in various desserts to prevent them from separating (for example, Bavarian creams).

Standard breading procedure: The procedure in which items are dredged in flour, dipped in beaten egg, then coated with crumbs before being panfried or deep-fried.

Staphylococcus aureus: A type of facultative bacteria that can cause food-borne illness. It is particularly dangerous because it produces toxins that cannot be destroyed by heat.

Steam-jacketed kettle: A kettle with double-layered walls, between which steam circulates, providing even heat for cooking stocks, soups, and sauces. These kettles may be insulated, spigoted, and/or tilting. (The latter are also called trunnion kettles.)

Steamer: A set of stacked pots with perforations in the bottom of each pot. They fit over a larger pot that is filled with boiling or simmering water. Also, a perforated insert made of metal or bamboo that can be inserted in a pot and used to steam foods.

Steaming: A cooking method in which items are cooked

in a vapor bath created by boiling water or other liquids.

Steel: A tool used to hone knife blades. It is usually made of steel but may be ceramic, glass, or diamond-impregnated metal.

Stew: A cooking method nearly identical to braising but generally involving smaller pieces of meat and, hence, a shorter cooking time. Stewed items also may be blanched, rather than seared, to give the finished product a pale color. Also, a dish prepared by using the stewing method.

Stir-fry: A cooking method similar to sautéing in which items are cooked over very high heat, using little fat. Usually this is done in a wok and the food is kept moving constantly.

Stock: A flavorful liquid prepared by simmering meat, poultry, seafood, and/or vegetables in water with aromatics until their flavor is extracted. It is used as a base for soups, sauces, and other preparations.

Stockpot: A large, straight-sided pot that is taller than it is wide. Used for making stocks and soups. Some have spigots. Also called a marmite.

Stone-ground: Meal or flour milled between grindstones; this method retains more nutrients than some other grinding methods.

Straight: A forcemeat combining pork and pork fat with another meat in equal parts that is made by grinding the mixture together.

Straight mix method: The dough mixing method in which all ingredients are combined at once by hand or machine.

Suprême (Fr.): The breast fillet and wing of chicken or other poultry. Sauce suprême is chicken velouté enriched with cream.

Sweat: To cook an item, usually vegetables, in a covered pan in a small amount of fat until it softens and releases moisture.

Sweetbreads: The thymus glands of young animals, usually calves, but possibly lambs or pigs. Usually sold in pairs of lobes.

Swiss: To pound meat, usually beef, with flour and seasonings; this breaks up the muscle fibers, tenderizing the meat.

Syrup: A liquid sweetener (maple or corn); sugar that is dissolved in liquid, usually water, with possibly the addition of flavoring such as spices or citrus zest.

T

Table d'hôte (Fr.): A fixed-price menu with a single price for an entire meal based on entrée selection.

Table salt: Refined, granulated rock salt. May be fortified with iodine and treated with magnesium carbonate to prevent clumping.

Tamis: See *Drum sieve.*

Tang: The continuation of the knife blade into its handle. A full tang extends through the entire handle. A partial tang only runs through part of the knife. A rattail tang is thinner than the blade's spine and is encased in the handle and is not visible at the top or bottom edge.

Taper-ground: A type of knife blade forged out of a single sheet of metal, then ground so it tapers smoothly to the cutting edge. Taper-ground knives are generally the most desirable.

Tart: A pie without a top crust; may be sweet or savory.

Tartlet: A small, single-serving tart.

T.C.M./Tinted curing mixture: See *Curing salt.*

Temper: To heat gently and gradually. May refer to the process of incorporating hot liquid into a liaison to gradually raise its temperature. May also refer to the proper method for melting chocolate or fondant.

Tempura: (Jap.): Seafood and/or vegetables that are coated with light batter and deep-fried.

Tenderloin: A cut of meat, usually beef or pork, from the hind quarter.

Terrine: A loaf of forcemeat, similar to a pâté, but cooked in a covered mold in a bain-marie. Also, the mold used to cook such items, usually an oval shape made of ceramic.

Thermophilic: Heat-loving. A term used to describe bacteria that can thrive within the temperature range from 110 to 171°F (43 to 77°C).

Tilting kettle. A large, relatively shallow, tilting pot used for braising, stewing, and, occasionally, steaming; also known as tilt skillet or brazier.

Timbale: A small pail-shaped mold used to shape rice, custards, mousselines, and other items. Also, a preparation made in such a mold.

Tomalley: Lobster liver, which is olive-green in color.

Total utilization: The principle advocating the use of as much of a product as possible in order to reduce waste and increase profits.

Tournant (Fr.): Roundsman or swing cook. A kitchen staff member who works as needed throughout the kitchen.

Tourner/Tourné: To cut items, usually vegetables, into barrel, olive, or football shapes.

Tourné knife: A small knife, similar to a paring knife, with a curved blade used to cut tournéed items. Also known as a bird's beak knife.

Toxin: A naturally occurring poison, particularly those produced by the metabolic activity of living organisms, such as bacteria.

Trash fish: Fish that have traditionally been considered unusable. (Also called "junk fish" or underutilized fish.)

Trichinella spiralis: A spiral-shaped parasitic worm that invades the intestines and muscle tissue; transmitted primarily through infected pork that has not been cooked sufficiently.

Tripe: The edible stomach lining of a cow or other ruminant. Honeycomb tripe comes from the second stomach and has a honeycomb-like texture.

Truss: To tie up meat or poultry with string before cooking it in order to give it a compact shape for more even cooking and better appearance.

Tuber: The fleshy root, stem, or rhizome of a plant that is able to grow into a new plant. Some, such as potatoes, are eaten as vegetables.

Tunneling: A fault in baked batter products caused by overmixing; the finished product is riddled with large holes or tunnels.

U

Univalve: A single-shelled mollusc, such as abalone and sea urchin.

Unsaturated fat: A fat with at least one available bonding site not filled with a hydrogen atom. These may be monounsaturated or polyunsaturated. They tend to be liquid at room temperature and are primarily of vegetable origin.

Utility knife: A smaller, lighter version of the chef's knife; its blade is usually between 5 and 7 inches long.

V

Variety meat: Meat from a part of an animal other than the muscle; for example, organs. Also, *offal*.

Velouté: A sauce of white stock (chicken, veal, seafood) thickened with white roux; one of the grand sauces. Also, a cream soup made with a velouté sauce base and flavorings (usually puréed) that is usually finished with a liaison.

Venison: Meat from large game animals; often used to refer specifically to deer meat.

Vertical chopping machine (VCM): A machine, similar to a blender, that has rotating blades used to grind, whip, emulsify, or blend foods.

Vinaigrette (Fr.): A cold sauce of oil and vinegar, usually with various flavorings; it is a temporary emulsion sauce. (The standard proportion is three parts oil to one part vinegar.)

Virus: A type of pathogenic microorganism that can be transmitted in food. Viruses cause such illnesses as measles, chicken pox, infectious hepatitis, and colds.

Vitamins: Any of various nutritionally essential organic substances that do not provide energy (noncaloric) but usually act as regulators in metabolic processes.

W

Waffle: A crisp, pancakelike batter product that is cooked in a specialized iron that gives the finished product a textured pattern, usually a grid. Also a special vegetable cut which produces a grid or basket-weave pattern.

Walk-in refrigerator: A refrigeration unit large enough to walk into. It is occasionally large enough to maintain zones of varying temperature and humidity to store a variety of foods properly. Some have reach-in doors as well. Some are large enough to accommodate rolling carts as well as many shelves of goods.

Whip: To beat an item, such as cream or egg whites, to incorporate air. Also, a special tool for whipping made of looped wire attached to a handle.

White chocolate: Cocoabutter flavored with sugar and milk solids. It does not contain any cocoa solids, so it does not have the characteristic brown color of regular chocolate.

White mirepoix: Mirepoix that does not include carrots and may include chopped mushrooms or mushroom trimmings. It is used for pale or white sauces and stocks.

White stock: A light-colored stock made with bones that have not been browned.

Whole-wheat flour: Flour milled from the whole grain, including the bran and germ. Graham flour is a whole-wheat flour named after Sylvester Graham, a 19th-century American dietary reformer.

Wok (Chin.): A round-bottomed pan, usually made of rolled steel, that is used for nearly all cooking methods.

Y

Yam: A large tuber that grows in tropical and subtropical climates; it has starchy, pale-yellow flesh and is often confused with the sweet potato.

Yeast: Microscopic fungus whose metabolic processes are responsible for fermentation. It is used for leavening bread and in cheese-, beer-, and wine-making.

Yogurt: Milk cultured with bacteria to give it a slightly thick consistency and sour flavor.

Z

Zabaglione: See *Sabayon*.

Zest: The thin, brightly colored outer part of citrus rind. It contains volatile oils, making it ideal for use as a flavoring.

Recommended Reading List

FOOD HISTORY

American Food: The Gastronomic Story. Evan Jones. Overlook Press, 1992.

Consuming Passions, The Anthropology of Eating. Peter Farb and George Armelagos. Houghton Mifflin, 1980.

De Honesta Voluptate, 5 volumes. Platine (Bartolomeo de Sacehi di Padena). Mallinkrodt Chemical Works, 1967.

The Diepnosophists (Banquet of the Learned), 3 volumes. Athenaeus. Translated by C.D. Yonge. Henry G. Bohn, 1854.

Eating in America, A History. Waverley Root and Richard de Rochemont. Ecco Press, 1995.

Fabulous Feasts: Medieval Cookery and Ceremony. Madeleine Pelner Cosman. Braziller, 1976.

Food and Drink Through the Ages, 2500 B.C. to 1937 A.D. Barbara Feret. Maggs Bros. Ltd. 1937.

Food History. Reay Tannahill. Crown Publishers, Inc., 1988.

Gastronomy: The Anthropology of Food and Food Habits. Margaret Arnoh, ed. Mouton Pub. (Aldine), 1979.

Kitchen and Table: A Bedside History of Eating in the Western World. Colin Clair. Abelard-Schuman, 1965.

Much Depends on Dinner. Margaret Visser. MacMillan, 1988.

Our Sustainable Table. Robert Clark, ed. North Point Press, 1990.

The Pantropheon: or, A History of Food and Its Preparation in Ancient Times. Alexis Soyer. Paddington Press, 1977.

The Rituals of Dinner. Margaret Visser. Grove Press, 1986.

The Roman Cookery of Apicius. Translated and adapted by John Edwards. Hartly & Marks, 1984.

The Travels of Marco Polo. Marta Bellonci. Translated by Teresa Waugh. Facts on File, 1984.

Why We Eat What We Eat. Raymond Sokolov. Simon & Schuster, 1993.

Women Chefs. Jim Burns and Betty Ann Brown. Aris Books, 1987.

SANITATION AND SAFETY

Applied Foodservice Sanitation, 4th ed. Educational Foundation of the National Restaurant Association Staff. Educ. Staff, 1993.

Basic Food Sanitation. The Culinary Institute of America. Hyde Park, New York: 1986.

HACCP: Reference Book. Educational Foundation of the National Restaurant Association Staff. Educ. Staff, 1993.

NUTRITION AND NUTRITIONAL COOKING

Choices for a Healthy Heart. Joseph C. Piscatella. Workman Publishing, 1987.

Food and Culture in America: A Nutrition Handbook. Pamela Goyan Kittler and Kathryn P. Sucher. Van Nostrand Reinhold, 1989.

Handbook of the Nutritional Value of Foods: in Common Units. U.S. Department of Agriculture. Dover Publications, 1986.

Jane Brody's Good Food Book: Living the High Carbohydrate Way. Jane Brody. W. W. Norton, 1985.

The Living Heart Diet. DeBakey, Gotto, Jr., Scott, and Foreyt. Simon & Schuster, 1986.

Nutrition: Concepts and Controversies, 5th ed. Hamilton, Whitney, and Sizer. West Publishing Co., 1991.

Techniques of Healthy Cooking. The Culinary Institute of America, Mary Donovan, ed. Van Nostrand Reinhold, 1993.

EQUIPMENT

Food Equipment Facts: A Handbook for the Foodservice Industry, 2nd ed. Carl Scriven and James Stevens. New York: Van Nostrand Reinhold, 1989.

Professional Chef's Knife Book. The Culinary Institute of America. Van Nostrand Reinhold, 1978.

The Williams-Sonoma Cookbook and Guide to Kitchenware. Chuck Williams. Random House, 1986.

GENERAL PRODUCT IDENTIFICATION

The Cook's Ingredients. Adrian Bailey, ed. Reader's Digest Association, 1990.

Tastings: The Best from Ketchup to Caviar. Jenifer Harvey Lang. Crown Publishers, Inc., 1986.

The Von Welanetz Guide to Ethnic Ingredients. Diana and Paul Von Welanetz. Warner, 1987.

MEATS, POULTRY, AND GAME

The Meat Buyers Guide. National Association of Meat Purveyors. National Assoc. of Meat Purveyors, 1992.

The Meat We Eat, 13th ed. John R. Romans, et al. Interstate Printers & Publishing, 1994.

FISH AND SHELLFISH

The Complete Cookbook of American Fish and Shellfish, 2nd ed. John F. Nicolas. Van Nostrand Reinhold, 1990.

The Encyclopedia of Fish Cookery. A. J. McClane. H. Holt, & Co., 1977.

McClane's Fish Buyer's Guide. A. J. McClane. Henry Holt & Co., 1990.

FRUITS AND VEGETABLES

The Blue Goose Buying Guide. Blue Goose, Inc., 1990.

The Foodservice Guide to Fresh Produce. Produce Marketing Association, 1987.

Jane Grigson's Fruit Book. Jane Grigson. Atheneum, 1982.

Jane Grigson's Vegetable Book. Jane Grigson. Penguin Books, 1980.

Rodale's Illustrated Encyclopedia of Herbs. Rodale Press Staff and William H. Hylton, ed. Rodale Press, 1987.

Uncommon Fruits and Vegetables: A Commonsense Guide from Arugula to Yucca: An Encyclopedic Cookbook of America's New Produce. Elizabeth Schneider. HarperCollins, 1990.

DAIRY AND CHEESES

Cheese: A Guide to the World of Cheese and Cheese-Making. Bruno Battistotti. Facts on File, 1984.

Cheese Buyer's Handbook. Daniel O'Keefe. McGraw-Hill, 1978.

Cheeses of the World. U.S. Department of Agriculture. Dover Publications, 1972.

The World of Cheese. Evan Jones. Alfred A. Knopf, 1978.

NONPERISHABLE GOODS

The Book of Coffee and Tea. Joel, David, and Karl Schapira. St. Martin's Press, 1982.

The Complete Book of Spices: A Practical Guide to Spices & Aromatic Seeds. Jill Norman. Viking Studio Books, 1991.

Spices, Salt and Aromatics. Elizabeth David. Penguin Books, 1970.

PREPARATIONS AND RECIPES

The Art of Making Sausages, Pâtés, and other Charcuterie. (orig. title: *Charcuterie and French Pork Cookery*). Jane Grigson. Alfred A. Knopf, 1976.

Pasta Classica: The Art of Italian Pasta Cooking. Julia Della Croce. Chronicle Books, 1987.

Pâtés and Terrines. Frederich W. Elhart. Hearst Books, 1984.

The Professional Chef's® Art of Garde Manger, 5th ed. Frederic H. Sonnenschmidt and John Nicholas. Van Nostrand Reinhold, 1993.

Sauces. James Peterson. Van Nostrand Reinhold, 1991.

Soups for the Professional Chef. Terence Janericco. Van Nostrand Reinhold, 1993.

GENERAL/CLASSIC COOKING

The Chef's Compendium of Professional Recipes, 3rd ed. John Fuller, Edward Renold, and David Faskett. Butterworth-Heinemann, 1992.

Classical Cooking the Modern Way, 2nd ed. Eugen Pauli. Van Nostrand Reinhold, 1989.

The Complete Guide to the Art of Modern Cooking. Auguste Escoffier. Van Nostrand Reinhold, 1990.

The Cook Book. Terence and Caroline Conran. Crown Publishers, Inc., 1980.

Cooking for the Professional Chef, rev. ed. Kenneth C. Wolfe. 2nd ed. Delmar Publishing, 1982.

Couleurs, Parfums et Saveurs de Ma Cuisine. Jacques Maximin. Editions Robert Laffont, 1984.

Culinary Olympics Cookbook. American Culinary Federation and Ferdinand E. Metz. Chet Holden, ed. Cahners Publishing Company and *Restaurants & Institutions* Magazine, 1983.

Dining in France. Christian Millau. Stewart, Tabori & Chang, 1986.

Escoffier: The Complete Guide to the Art of Modern Cookery. Auguste Escoffier. Van Nostrand Reinhold, 1995.

Escoffier Cook Book. Auguste Escoffier. Crown, 1941.

The Grand Masters of French Cuisine. Selected and adapted by Celine Vence and Robert Courtine. G.P. Putnam & Sons, 1978.

Great Chefs of France. Anthony Blake. Harry N. Abrams, 1978.

Introductory Foods, 10th ed. Marion Bennion. Macmillan, 1994

Jacques Pepin's The Art of Cooking. Jacques Pepin. Alfred A. Knopf, 1992.

James Beard's Theory and Practice of Good Cooking. James Beard. Random House, 1990.

La Technique. Jacques Pepin. Simon & Schuster, 1989.

Le Répertoire de la Cuisine. Louis Saulnier. Barron, 1976.

Ma Gastronomie. Ferdinand Point. Lyceum, 1974.

Paul Bocuse's French Cooking. Paul Bocuse. Translated by Colette Rossant. Pantheon, 1987.

The Physiology of Taste. Jean Anthelme Brillat-Savarin. Translated by Anne Dreyton. Penguin Books, 1994.

The Saucier's Apprentice: A Modern Guide to Classic French Sauces for the Home. Raymond A. Sokolov. Alfred A. Knopf, 1976.

AMERICAN COOKING/RECIPES

An American Bounty. The Culinary Institute of America. Mary Donovan, ed. Rizzoli International Publishing, 1995.

American Cooking. James Shenton, et al. Time-Life Books, 1971.

Chez Panisse Cooking. Paul Bertolli. Random House, 1994.

City Cuisine. Susan Feniger and Mary Sue Milliken. William Morrow, 1989.

Epicurean Delight: The Life and Times of James Beard. Evan Jones. Alfred A. Knopf, 1990.

I Hear America Cooking. Betty Fussel. Viking, 1986.

Jasper White's Cooking from New England: More Than Three Hundred Traditional & Contemporary. . . . Jasper White. HarperCollins, 1993.

Jeremiah Tower's New American Classics. Jeremiah Tower. Harper & Row, 1986.

The Mansion on Turtle Creek Cookbook. Dean Fearing. Grove-Atlantic, 1987.

The New York Times Cook Book. Craig Claiborne. Harper-Collins, 1990.

The Trellis Cookbook. Marcel Desaulniers. Simon & Schuster Trade, 1992.

INTERNATIONAL COOKING/RECIPES

The Art of South American Cooking. Felipe Rojas-Lombardi. HarperCollins, 1991.

The Art of Turkish Cooking. Neset Eren. Hippocrene Books, 1993.

Authentic Chinese Cuisine, 9 volumes, various authors. Shufunotomo, 1984.

The Belgian Cookbook. Enid Gordon. MacDonald, 1983.

The Belgian Cookbook. Nika Hazelton. Atheneum, 1970.

The Book of Latin American Cooking. Elizabeth Lambert Ortiz. Ecco Press, 1994.

A Book of Mediterranean Food. Elizabeth David. Penguin Books, 1986.

A Book of Middle Eastern Food. Claudia Roden. Alfred A. Knopf, 1974.

Classical and Contemporary Italian Cooking for Professionals. Bruno Ellmer. Van Nostrand Reinhold, 1990.

Classic Indian Cooking. Julie Sahni. William Morrow, 1980.

Classic Scandinavian Cooking. Nika Hazelton. Scribner and Sons, 1987.

The Classic Italian Cookbook. Marcella Hazan. Alfred A. Knopf, 1976.

The Complete Indian Cookbook. Michael Pandya. Larousse, 1980.

The Cooking of Eastern Mediterranean. Paula Wolfert. HarperCollins, 1994.

The Cooking of The South-West of France: A Collection of Traditional & New Recipes from France's Magnificent Rustic Cuisine. Paula Wolfert. HarperCollins, 1988.

Couscous and Other Good Food from Morocco. Paula Wolfert. HarperCollins, 1987.

Croatian Cuisine. Ruzica Kapetanovic and Alojzije Kapetanovic. Associated Pub., 1992.

The Cuisine of Hungary. George Lang. Atheneum, 1971.

The Cuisines of Mexico. Diana Kennedy. HarperCollins, 1989.

The Czechoslovak Cookbook. Joza Brizova, et al. Crown, 1965.

Egyptian Cuisine. Nagwa E. Khalil. Worldwide Graphics, 1980.

The Encyclopedia of Asian Food and Cooking. Jacki Passmore. Hearst, 1991.

The Food and Cooking of Russia. Lesley Chamberlain. Knopf, 1982.

Food from My Heart. Zarela Martinéz. Macmillan, 1992.

The Food of France. Waverly Root. Random House, 1977.

The Foods and Wines of Spain. Penelope Casas. Knopf, 1982.

The Foods of Vietnam. Nicole Routhier. Stewart, Tabori & Chang, 1989.

Foods of the World. Richard Williams, ed. Time-Life Books, 1971.

French Provincial Cooking. Elizabeth David. Penguin Books, 1986.

French Regional Cooking. Jean Ferniot. Random House, 1991.

The German Cookbook. Mimi Sheraton. Random House, 1965.

Giuliano Bugialli's Classic Techniques of Italian Cooking. Simon & Schuster, 1982.

Gourmet's Old Vienna Cookbook. Langseth Christensen. Gourmet Books, 1982.

The Great Scandinavian Cookbook. Karin Fredrikson, ed., translated by J. Ellison. Crown, 1967.

Greek Food. Rena Salamon. Fontana, 1983.

In a Persian Kitchen. Maideh Mazda. C. Tuttle Co., 1960.

Italian Food. Elizabeth David. Penguin Books, 1986.

Japanese Cooking. Shizuo Tsuji. Kodansha, 1980.

The Joy of Japanese Cooking. Kuwako Takahashi. C. E. Tuttle, 1992.

Lebanese Cooking. Madelain Farrah. International Spec. Books, 1985.

Madhur Jaffrey's Far Eastern Cookery. Madhur Jaffrey. HarperCollins, 1989.

The Mediterranean Diet. Nancy Harmon Jenkins. Bantam, 1994.

Mexico: The Beautiful Cookbook. Susanna Palazuelos and Marilyn Tausand. Collins Publishers, 1991.

The Modern Art of Chinese Cooking. Barbara Tropp. Morrow, 1982.

Modern Thai Cooking. M. L. Kritakara. Duang Kamol, 1977.

Musings of a Chinese Gourmet. F. T. Cheng. Hutchinson, 1954.

Paula Wolfert's World of Food. Paula Wolfert. HarperCollins, 1994.

Pierre Franey's Cooking in France. Pierre Franey and Richard Flaste. Alfred A. Knopf, 1994.

The Polish Cookbook. Z. Czerny. Vanous, 1982.

Roger Vergé's Cuisine of the South of France. Roger Vergé, translated by Roberta Smoler. Morrow, 1980.

Roger Vergé's Vegetables in the French Style. Roger Vergé. Artisan, 1994.

Simple Cuisine. Jean-Georges Vongerichten. Prentice Hall, 1990.

The Taste of France: A Dictionary of French Food & Wine. Fay Sherman and Klaus Boehm. Houghton-Mifflin, 1982.

A Taste of Japan. Jenny Ridgewell. Thomson Learning, 1993.

A Taste of Mexico. Patricia Quintana, Stewart Tabori & Chang, 1993.

A Taste of Morocco. Robert Carrier. C. N. Potter, 1987.

Traditional Korean Cooking. Chin-hwa Noh. Hollym International, 1985.

BAKING AND PASTRY

The Baker's Manual, 4th ed. Joseph Amendola. Van Nostrand Reinhold, 1993.

Flatbreads and Flavors. Jeffrey Alford and Naomi Duguid. William Morrow, 1995.

Great Dessert Book. Christian Teubner and Sybil Schonfeldt. Hearst, 1983.

The New International Confectioner, 5th ed. Wilfred J. France. Virtue, 1987.

Nick Malgieri's Perfect Pastry. Nick Malgieri. Macmillan. 1989.

Practical Baking, 5th ed. William J. Sultan. Van Nostrand Reinhold, 1990.

The Professional Pastry Chef, 3rd ed. B. Friberg. Van Nostrand Reinhold, 1996.

Swiss Confectionery, 2nd ed. Richemont Craft School. Bakers and Confectioners Craft School Richemont, 1986.

Understanding Baking, 2nd ed. Joseph Amendola and Donald E. Lundberg. Van Nostrand Reinhold, 1992.

CHEMISTRY OF COOKING

The Experimental Study of Food, 2nd ed. Campbell Penfield Griswold. Houghton-Mifflin, 1970.

Food Science, 3rd ed. Helen Charley. MacMillan, 1994.

On Food and Cooking: The Science and Lore of the Kitchen. Harold McGee. MacMillan, 1988.

WINES/SPIRITS

Exploring Wine: The Culinary Institute of America's Complete Guide to Wines of the World. Steven Kolpan, Brian H. Smith, Michael A. Weiss, and The Culinary Institute of America. Van Nostrand Reinhold, 1996.

Hugh Johnson's Modern Encyclopedia of Wine. Hugh Johnson. Simon & Schuster, 1991.

Larousse Encyclopedia of Wine. Christopher Foulkes, ed. Larousse, 1994.

Windows on the World Complete Wine Course. Kevin Zraly. Dell, 1995.

DICTIONARY/ENCYCLOPEDIA

Books for Cooks: A Bibliography of Cookery. Marguerite Patten. R.R. Bowker, 1975.

The Chef's Companion: A Concise Dictionary of Culinary Terms. Elizabeth Riely. Van Nostrand Reinhold, 1986.

A Concise Encyclopedia of Gastronomy. André Louis Simon. Overlook Press, 1983.

Culture and Cuisine: A Journey Through the History of Food. Jean François Revel. Translated by Helen R. Lane. Da Capo Press, 1984.

The Dictionary of American Food and Drink. John F. Mariani. Morrow, 1994.

Food. André Simon. Burke Publishing Co., Ltd., 1949.

Food: An Informal Dictionary. Waverly Root. Simon & Schuster, 1980.

Food Lover's Companian. Sharon Herbst. Barron, 1990.

Gastronomy. Jay Jacobs. Newsweek Books, 1975.

The Gastronomy of France. Raymond Oliver, translated by Claud Durrell. Wine & Food Society with World Publishing Co., 1967.

Gastronomy of Italy. Anna Del Conte. Prentice-Hall, 1987.

Herings Dictionary of Classical and Modern Cookery. Walter Bickel. Virtue, 1981. Distributed by Van Nostrand Reinhold.

Knight's Foodservice Dictionary. John B. Knight and Charles A. Salter, eds. Van Nostrand Reinhold, 1987.

Larousse Gastronomique (American edition). Jenifer Harvey Lang, ed. Crown Publishers, Inc., 1988.

The Master Dictionary of Food and Wine. Joyce Rubash. Van Nostrand Reinhold, 1990.

The New York Times Food Encyclopedia. Craig Claiborne. Times Books, 1985.

The World Encyclopedia of Food. Patrick L. Coyle. Facts on File, 1982.

BUSINESS AND MANAGEMENT

Becoming a Chef: with Recipes and Reflections from America's Leading Chefs. Andrew Dornenburg and Karen Page. Van Nostrand Reinhold, 1995.

Food and Beverage Cost Control. Donald Bell. McCutchen Publishing Corp., 1984.

Food and Wine Online: A Professional's Guide to Network Services. Gary Holleman. Van Nostrand Reinhold, 1995.

Foodservice Organizations. Marion Spears. Macmillan, 1994.

Math Principles for Foodservice Occupations. Robert G. Haines. Delmar Publishing, 1988.

Math Workbook for Foodservice and Lodging. Hattie Crawford and Milton McDowell. Van Nostrand Reinhold, 1988.

Menu Mystique. Norman Odya Krohn. Jonathan David Publishing, 1983.

Principles of Food, Beverage, and Labor Cost Controls. Paul Dittmer. Van Nostrand Reinhold, 1993.

Professional Table Service. Sylvia Meyer, translated by Heinz Holtmann. Van Nostrand Reinhold, 1993.

Recipes into Type. Joan Whitman and Dolores Simon. HarperCollins, 1993.

The Successful Business Plan, 2nd ed. Rhonda Abrams. Oasis Press, 1993.

What Every Supervisor Should Know. Lester Bittle and John Newstrom. McGraw, 1992.

JOURNALS AND PUBLICATIONS

American Brewer

Art Culinaire

The Art of Eating

Bakery Production & Marketing

Beer: The Magazine

Beverage World

Bon Appétit

Bewer's Digest

Caterer and Hotelkeeper

Chef

Chef's Institutional

Chocolate News

Chocolatier

Cooking for Profit

Culinary Trends

Food and Wine

Food Arts

Food for Thought

Food Management

Foodservice and Hospitality

Foodservice Director

Fresh Cut

The Friends of Wine

Gastronome

Gourmet

Hospitality Management

Hospitality World

Hotel and Motel Management

Hotels and Restaurants International

Journal of Gastronomy

Market Watch—Wine, Spirits & Beer

Modern Baking

Nation's Restaurant News

Nutrition Action Healthletter

Pizza Today

Prepared Foods

Progressive Grocer

Restaurant Business

Restaurant Hospitality

Restaurants and Institutions

Restaurant USA

Saveur

Wine Advocate

Wine and Spirits

The Wine Spectator

Food Associations

American Culinary Federation
P. O. Box 3466
St. Augustine, FL 32085
(904) 824–4468

American Hotel and Motel Association
1201 New York Avenue NW
Suite 600
Washington, DC 20005-3931
(202) 289–3100

American Institute of Wine and Food
1550 Bryant St.
Suite 700
San Francisco, CA 94103
(415) 255–3000

Chefs in America Foundation
3407 Toledo Street
Coral Gables, FL 33134
(305) 448–9279

**Council on Hotel/Restaurant and
Institutional Education**
1200 17th Street NW
Washington, DC 20036
(202) 331–5990

**International Association of
Women Chefs and Restaurateurs**
110 Sutter Street
Suite 305
San Francisco, CA 94104
(415) 362–7336

International Association of Culinary Professionals
304 West Liberty
Suite 201
Louisville, KY 40202
(502) 581–9786

The James Beard Foundation
167 West 12th Street
New York, NY 10011
(212) 675–4984

National Ice Carving Association
P.O. Box 3593
Oak Brook, IL 60522-3593
(708) 323–6696

National Restaurant Association
1200 17th Street, NW
Washington, DC 20036
(202) 331–5900

Oldways Preservation and Exchange Trust
45 Milk Street
Boston, MA 02109
(617) 695–9102

Roundtable for Women in Foodservice
3022 West Eastwood
Chicago, IL 60625
(800) 898–2849

Share Our Strength (SOS)
1511 K Street, NW
Suite 94
Washington, DC 20005
(202) 393–2925

Index

A

Abalone, 118
Aboyeur, 25
Acorn squash, baked, with cranberry-
    orange compote, 804
Actual cost pricing, 22
Administrative responsibilities, 17
Adobo, 431
À la carte restaurants, 5
À l'anglaise coating, 303
Alcohol, in the workplace, 46
Al dente stage, 330
Allumette cut, 187
Almond dough, 1082
Almonds, chocolate-coated, 1128
Ambiance, 29
American cook books, 1164
American cuisine, 5
American Culinary Federation (ACF),
    24
American Heart Association (AHA)
    dietary standards, 48, 50
Americans with Disabilities Act (ADA),
    45
Amino acids, essential, 56
Anchovy, 113
Anchovy caper mayonnaise, 912
Anchovy pesto, 742
Angel food cakes, 390, 391, 1112-1113
Anne of Austria, 5
Anti-oxidants, 59
Appareils, 183, 203
    folding foams into, 223
Appetizers, 936-992
Apple cake, Roman, 1115
Apple cheddar pizza, 928
Apple cider soup, 484
Apple cream cheese torte, 1126
Apple pie, 1097
Apples, 122-124
    advance preparation of, 203
    cinnamon, 876

poached, 1065
varieties of, 124
Apple sausage, spicy French-style, 1002
Apple soup, chilled, 488
Apple strudel, filling for, 1103
Apple with curry mayonnaise sandwich,
    933
Apprenticeship programs, 12
Apricots, 129
Aromatic combinations, 208-212
    for braised foods, 350
Arrowroot, 177, 378
Artichoke heart ceviche, 942
Artichokes:
    advance preparation of, 201-202
    with oysters and champagne vinai-
        grette, 980-981
Artichoke soufflé, 710
    in red pepper shells, 710
Artichoke spinach ricotta pie, 711
Artichoke terrine, 1014
Arugula pesto, 422
Asparagus:
    advance preparation of, 202-203
    creamed, on toast, 876
    pan-steamed, 792
    polonaise, 798
    with roasted pepper and shallot
        chips, 794
Asparagus soup, cream of, 466-469
Aspic gelée, 358, 997
As purchased (AP) cost, 20
Au sec reduction, 225, 294
Avocados, 132

B

Baba Ghannouj, 937
Baccala, 114
Back waiter, 25-16
Bacon cream sauce, 616
Bacterial growth, stages of, 37

Bagels, 1038
Baguettes, 1033
Bain-Marie technique, 75, 226
Baking, 375-414
    creams, bavarians, and mousses for, 400-404
    ingredients in, 376-378
    of pie and pastry dough, 391-396
    of quick breads, cakes, and batters, 386-391
    of roll-in doughs, 396-400
    techniques for, 307-312, 378-380
    of yeast-raised breads, 380-386
Baking blind, 394
Baking pans, selecting and preparing, 379-380
Baking powder, 175
Baking recipe books, 1165
Balsamic vinaigrette, 906
Balsamic vinegar sauce, 672
Banana nut bread, 1030-1031
Banana pancakes, 871
Barbecued beef sandwich, 919
Barbecued shrimp, 973
Barbecued sirloin steak, 562
Barbecued spareribs, 771
Barbecue marinade, 430
Barbecue sauce, 552
    mango/bourbon, 553
    North Carolina style, 610
Barbecue spice mix, 425
Barbecuing, 302-307
Barding technique, 309
Barley soup:
    with beef, 504
    with corned beef, 505
Barquettes, smoked salmon mousse, 969
Basil compound butter, 547
Basil sauce, 695
    cream, 725
Bass, 113-114
    golden, 117
    poached, with clams, bacon, and peppers, 701
    poached, with watercress sauce, 703
    striped, 113-114
Batonnet cut, 187
Batters:
    for biscuits, scones, and soda bread, 391
    creaming method for, 387-389
    foaming method for mixing, 390-391
    fruit fritter, 1069
    for quick breads and cakes, 386-391
    straight mixing method for, 386-387
    two-stage mixing method for, 389-390
Bavarian cream:
    for pastries and cakes, 400-404
    vanilla, 1096
Bean and cheese croutons, 435
Bean and cornmeal loaf, with salsa, 730
Bean cakes, 987

with sautéed crab and corn, 988
Beans. *See also* Green beans
    black, 840, 841
    dried, 162, 163
    garbanzo, 844-845
    Hoppin' John, 845
    in purée soups, 269
    quick-soak method for, 341
    refried, 842
    soaking, 203-204
    varieties of, 141
Bean salad, 904
Bean salsa, 936
    black, 714
Beans and rice:
    Mexican-style, 729
    Puerto Rican style, 729
Bean soup:
    black, 477
    senate, 479
    white, 478
Bean stew, 758
    white, 842-843
Béarnaise reduction, 541-542
Béarnaise sauce, 541, 693
Béchamel, 287-289
    ratios for, 285
Béchamel sauce, 535
Beef:
    barbecued sirloin, 562
    blackened, with corn-and-pepper sauce, 564-565
    Bourguignonne, 566
    braised short ribs, 569
    brisket of, 92
    broiled sirloin with chili butter, 561
    charred, with garlic herb mayonnaise, 945
    chili con carne, 573
    chuck, 87
    corned, with cabbage, 574-575
    creamed chipped, 875
    estouffade of, 572
    flank and skirt steaks, 91-92
    loin of, 90, 91
    London broil, 565
    miscellaneous cuts of, 92-93
    poached tenderloin, with peppercorn sabayon, 575
    prime rib au jus, 557
    with red onions and peanuts, 768-769
    rib of, 87, 90
    roast strip loin, 559
    rouladen in Burgundy sauce, 571
    round, 91
    shank of, 91
    sirloin strip steak with sauce *marchand de vin,* 562
    skewered, 769
    with spicy peanut sauce, 770
    standing rib roast of, 558-559
    strip steak Provençale, 563
    stroganoff, 556

stuffed flank steak, 568-569
    Swiss steak, 570
    tenderloin, with red chili sauce, 557
    tenderloin with blue cheese herb crust, 560
    tenderloin with garlic glaze, 564
    tenderloin with scallion butter, 561
    top round, *au jus,* 558
    tournedos à la Niçoise, 556
    Wellington, 560
    Yankee pot roast, 567
Beef broth, 451
Beef carpaccio, 944
Beef chart, 88-89
Beef consommé, 454
Beef daube, cold, 1021
Beef enchiladas, 766
Beef goulash, 735
Beef primals, 87-92
Beef sandwich, 919
Beef stew, 572
    à la Bourguignonne, 566
Beef stock, 439
Beef tacos, 925
Beef tenderloin with spicy tomato sauce, 734
Beef teriyaki, 768
Beet fennel ginger soup, 489
Beet pasta, 846
Beets, glazed, 802
Belgian endive, 799
Bell peppers, 140-141
Berries, 124-125
Beta-carotene, 59
Beurre blanc, 336
    lemon, 545, 663, 691
    tarragon, 546
Beurre blanc sauce, 295-296
Beurre manié, 206, 423
Beverages, 174-175
Binders, for forcemeat, 358
Biological contamination, 35
Biscotti al'Anice, 1095
Biscuit dumplings, 856
Biscuits, 1032
    batter for, 391
Bisques, 271-273
    lobster, 485
    oyster, 486-487
    pumpkin, 486
    shrimp, 484
Bistros, 16
Bivalves, 113, 119-120
Black bean and cornmeal loaf, with salsa, 730
Black bean cakes, 987
    with sautéed crab and corn, 988
Black beans, 840
    with peppers and chorizo, 841
Black bean salsa, 714, 936
Black bean sauce, 638
Black bean soup, 477
Blackening mixture, 565

Black-eyed pea salad, 905
Black pepper pasta, 846
　　wild mushrooms and artichokes over, 848
Blanc, 448
Blanching technique, 326, 330
Blanquette, 347
Blender, immersion, 271
Blitz puff pastry, 397
Bloomed gelatin, 378
Blueberry muffins, 1026
Blue cheese dressing, 914
Blue cheese herb crust, 560
Blue cheese mousse, 953
Blue cheeses, 155, 156
Bluefish, 114
　　with Creole mustard sauce, 668
　　smoked-roasted, with leek compote and horseradish sauce, 684
Bocuse, Paul, 5
Boiling, 340-343
　　special methods of, 343-346
Bone marrow, removing, 237
Bones:
　　blanching for stocks, 216-217
　　browning, 217
Boning knife, 70
Bordelaise sauce, 529
Borscht, 503
Botulism, 33-34
Boucher, 25
Bouillabaisse, 115, 347
Bouillon, 214-215
　　court, 215
Boulanger, 25
Bouquet garni, 209, 424, 988
Boursin cheese, dates stuffed with, 985
Braising technique, 348-352
Bran muffins, 1028
Bratwurst, German-style, 994-995
Bread, 1026-1044
　　banana nut, 1030-1031
　　challah, 1039
　　cottage dill, 1036
　　Danish, 1042
　　date nut, 1028-1029
　　docking, 384-385
　　Irish soda, 1031
　　multigrain, 1035
　　pain de campagne, 1033
　　peasant pecan loaf, 1036
　　pumpernickel, 1034
　　pumpkin, 1029
　　raisin, 1037
　　sourdough, 1034
　　stollen, 1041
　　sunflower seed, 1037-1038
　　sweet dough, 1040
　　yeast-raised, 380-386
　　zucchini, 1030
Bread and butter pudding, 1050
Bread crumbs, making, 204
Bread dumplings, 855

Breading, 321
　　procedure for, 322-324
Bread panadas, 358
Breakfast recipes, 858-879
Breakfast sausage, 998-999
Breakfast shakes, 879
"Brigade system," 24
Brillat-Savarin, Jean-Anthelme, 2, 5
Brioche, 380
　　dough for, 752
Broccoli:
　　in garlic sauce, 812
　　steamed, 792
Broccoli and cheddar fritters, 956
Broccoli flan, 991
Broccoli mousse, 992
Broccoli rabe, 725
Broccoli soup, cream of, 466
Broilers, 80
Broiling, 302-307
Broth, 214-215
　　beef, 451
　　double chicken, 450
　　lamb, 452
　　as sauces, 299
　　Scotch, 513
　　selecting ingredients for, 260
　　smoked turkey, 453
　　techniques for making, 260-262
Brownies:
　　cake, 1092
　　fudge, 1092
Brown sauce, 277-278
Brown stock, 214
Bruschetta, tapenade, tomato, and gorgonzola, 926
Budnersuppe, 504
Buffalo, Indian grilled, 615
Buffalo chopper, 78
Bulgur wheat, with dried cherries and apples, 838
Buns:
　　cinnamon, 1039-1040
　　sticky, 1043
Burgers:
　　chicken, 918
　　vegetable, 716
Burgundy sauce, 571
Busboys, 25-16
Business, literature about, 1166
Business Chef, The (Miner), 22
Butcher, 25
Butter, 150-151. *See also* Compound butters
　　casino, 981
　　chili, 546
　　clarifying, 220-221
　　Maître d'Hôtel, 547
　　maple syrup-pecan, 878
　　pecan-lime, 673
Buttercream, 404
　　French, 1106-1107
　　German, 1107

　　Italian, 1107
　　Swiss, 1108
Butter emulsion sauces, 292
Butterflying technique, 229-235, 234
　　for shrimp, 251
Buttermilk, 151-152
Buttermilk crâpes, 872
Butter puff pastry dough, 1083
Butter roasting, 313-316
Butterscotch icebox cookies, 1090
Butterscotch sauce, 406

C

Cabbage, 132-134
　　red, 805
　　stuffed, 761
Cabbage roll, stuffed, on lentil ragout, 727
Caesar salad, 884
Cajun cooking, 121
Cake brownies, 1092
Cakes, 1108-1128
　　angel food, 390, 391
　　coffee, 1040
　　creams, bavarians, and mousses for, 400-404
　　decorating, 411-414
　　frangipan, 1102
　　"high-ratio," 389, 1111
　　joconde, 1123
　　pithiviers, 1101
　　preparing batter for, 386-391
Calamari, 255
　　deep-fried, 665
California rolls, 960
Calories, 53-54
Canapés, mozzarella roulade, 952
Candies, 407-410
Canned food, 177-179
Canneloni, with Swiss chard and walnuts, 720
Can sizes, 178
Capon, poêlé of, with tomatoes and artichokes, 630
Caponata, 940, 944
Captain, 25
Caramel ice cream, 1061
Caramelization, 376
Caramel sauce, 406, 1076
Carbohydrates, 54-55
Careers, foodservice, 15-17
Carême, Marie-Antoine, 5
Carrot and raisin salad, 892
Carrot cake, 1114
Carrot mousse, 992
Carrot pasta, 846
Carrots:
　　boiled, 800
　　glazed, 801
　　pecan, 801
　　with salsify and cream, 802
Carrot salad, Moroccan, 896

Carryout foodservices, 16
Carryover cooking, 311
Carte, 5
Carving, 312-313
Casino butter, 981
Cassoulet, 758-759
Catering, 16
Catfish, 114
  with crab and cornbread crumbs,
    705
Cauliflower, polonaise, 798
Cauliflower soup, cream of, 467
Caviar, 122
  on game chips with crème fraîche,
    986
  in new potatoes with dilled crème
    fraîche, 986
Celeriac and apple salad, 893
Celery root and red pepper rémoulade,
  941
Celery soup, cream of, 466-469
Cephalopods, 113, 121-122
  preparing, 255
Cereals, boiling, 344-346
Ceviche, 118
  artichoke heart, 942
  charred tuna and scallop, 942
  of snapper, 943
Challah bread, 380, 1039
Champagne vinaigrette, 980-981
Champignon, 73-74
Charcuterie, 353-373
  background of, 354-356
  cured and smoked items, 371-372
  cured salmon, 372-373
  daube, 373
  forcemeats, 356-363
  galantines, 370-371
  pâté de champagne, 364-365
  pâté en croûte, 366-368
  quenelles, 363-364
  sausages, 369-370
  specialties of, 363-373
  terrines, 368-369
Chasseur sauce, 530
Châteaubriand sauce, 531
Cheddar cheese rusks, 436
Cheddar cheese sauce, 536
Cheddar cheese soup, 470
Cheese, 152-155
  blue-veined, 155, 156
  deviled eggs with, 950
  fresh, 152, 153
  grating, 154-155
  hard, 154, 155
  literature about, 1163
  semi-soft, 154
  soft, 153-154
Cheesecake, 1119
  chiffon, 1121
  Sicilian, 1120
Cheesecloth, 74
Cheese croutons, 435
Cheese melt sandwich, 921

Cheese omelet, 861
Cheese pastry filling, 1103
Cheese sauce, 536
Cheese soufflé, 866-867
Cheese soup, 470
Chef de cuisine, 24
Chef's knife, 70
Chefs. *See also* Professional chefs
  contemporary, 5-6
  education for, 12-14
  managerial responsibilities of, 17-30
  media attention for, 6-7
  networking with, 14
  pantry, 25
  pastry, 25
  types of, 24-25
Chef salad, 886-887
Chefs de partie, 25
Chemical contamination, 34-35
Chemistry of cooking, books about,
  1165
Cherries, 125
Cherry granità, 1063
Cherry pie, 1100
Chestnuts, advance preparation of, 199
Chestnut stuffing, 652
Chicken, 104. *See also* Chicken breast
  aromatic, 778-779
  blanquette, 587
  broiled Tex Mex, 639
  with cashews, 781
  chicken-fried, 628
  creamed sherried, on toast points,
    876
  cumin-lime grilled, 632
  in curry sauce, 779
  Eugene, 646
  fricassée, 640
  grilled, with basil and mozzarella,
    636
  grilled, with black bean sauce, 638
  grilled paillards of, with tarragon
    butter, 636
  hot sesame, 782
  miso, 783
  pan smoked, with apples and pepper-
    corns, 631
  paper-wrapped, 948
  poached, Florentine, 643
  Provençal, 622
  roast, with pan gravy, 629
  roast, with lemon grass, 784
  roast, with walnut sauce, 749
  Southern fried, 628
  Tandoori-style, 778
  teriyaki, 780
  with vegetables, 642-643
Chicken and herb sausage, 1000
Chicken and shrimp gumbo, 495
Chicken and spinach enchiladas, 766
Chicken breast:
  Asian-style broiled, 638-639
  Chardonnay, 624
  with eggplant, 627

  grilled, with fennel, 637
  with ham and sherry, 748
  with mushroom and ham stuffing,
    626
  with olives, capers, and herbs, 622
  with oyster stuffing and garlic sauce,
    635
  poached, with tarragon sauce, 644
  preparing, 242-243
  smoked, with barbecue sauce, 632
  with tarragon sauce, 625
  with tomato coulis, 627
Chicken broth, 450
Chicken burgers, 918
Chicken cacciatore, 751
Chicken consommé, 456
Chicken croustade, 946
Chicken enchiladas, 766
Chicken entrées, 622-646
Chicken fajitas, grilled, 636
Chicken galantine, 1016
Chicken legs:
  with duxelles, 633
  hunter-style, 641
Chicken liver gratin-style forcemeat,
  995
Chicken marsala, 577
Chicken mole, 765
Chicken mousseline forcemeat, 996
Chicken mulligatawny soup, 510
Chicken noodle soup, 450
Chicken pot pie, 642
Chicken quesadilla, 925
Chicken rillettes, smoked, 1022
Chicken roulade, 1018
Chicken salad, 898
  Buffalo-style, 886
Chicken sandwich, grilled, 636
Chicken soup, 516
  cream of, 468
  egg drop, 517
Chicken stir fry, 947
Chicken stock, 442
  Asian-style, 442
Chicken suprêmes:
  with fines herbes sauce, 623
  Maréchal, 627
Chicken tacos, 923
Chicken wings, Buffalo-style, 886
Chiffonade cut, 187
Chiffon cakes, 390, 391
Chile soup, 499
Chili:
  Big Jim's, 574
  con carne, 573
  vegetarian, 731
Chili butter, 546, 561, 593
Chili enchiladas, 766
Chili peppers, 140, 141
  advance preparation of, 194-196
  toasting, 203
Chili powder, 425
Chili sauce, 787
  green, 550

red, 549, 924
Chinois, 74
Chipped beef, creamed, 875
Chocolate, 173-174, 176
    tempering for coating, 408-409
Chocolate chip cookies, 1088
Chocolate chocolate chip ice cream, 1062
Chocolate-coated almonds, 1128
Chocolate cookie dough, 1085
Chocolate fudge sauce, 1076
Chocolate ganache, 1075
Chocolate glaze, 1075
Chocolate ice cream, 1061
Chocolate ladyfingers, 1095
Chocolate mousse, 1048-1049
Chocolate pudding, 1046-1047
Chocolate roulade, 1109
Chocolate sauce, 405, 1075
Chocolate sponge cake, 1110
Cholesterol, 57-59
Chopping, course, 187
Chops, cutting, 229, 234
Chorizo, 1004
Choron sauce, 542
Choucroute garni, 760
Chowders, 273, 491-494
Chutney:
    mango, 774
    pineapple, 676
Ciabatta, 1033
Cilantro lime butter, 547
Cilantro pesto, 422
Cinnamon apples, 876
Cinnamon buns, 1039-1040
Cinnamon rum syrup, 1077
Cinnamon sauce, 1074-1075
Cioppino, 115, 685
Citrus fruits, 125-127
    advance preparation of, 198-199
Citrus marinade, 432
Clam chowder:
    Manhattan-style, 492
    New England, 491
Clam fritters, 982
Clams, 119
    casino, 981
    cleaning and opening, 253
    with mussels, saffron, and tomatoes, 978
Classic cook books, 1163-1164
Cleaning:
    defined, 43
    of knives, 67
    standards for, 41-44
Cleavers, 70
Club sandwich, 930
Coating chocolate, 408-409
Cobb salad, 887
Coconut macadamia shrimp, 974
Coconut macaroons, 1089
Cod, 114
    potato-roasted, 679
Coffee, 174-175

Coffee cake, 1040
Coffee ice cream, 1061
Colander, 74
Cold smoking, 372
Coleslaw, 891
Collard greens and hambone soup, 496
Combi stoves, 80
Commis, 25
Communard, 25
Communication, value of, 27
Complementary proteins, 56
Complex carbohydrates, 55
Compotes, 298, 299
    fruit, 877
    leek, 684
Compound butters, 297-298, 547-549
    orange-mango, 878
    strawberry, 878
Computers, as kitchen tools, 23-24
Conch, 118
Condiments, 162-164
Confections, 407-410
Confiseur, 25
Confit, red onion, 599
Consommé:
    beef, 454
    chicken, 456
    fish, 455
    game hen, 458
    mushroom, 457
    smoked turkey with fennel ravioli, 459-460
    techniques for making, 262-265
Consultant positions, 16
Contamination, types of, 34-35
Convection oven, 79-80
Convection steamer, 79
Cook books, 1163-1165
Cookie dough, 1085
Cookies, 407-409
    butterscotch icebox, 1090
    checkerboard, 1085
    chocolate, 1085
    chocolate chip, 1088
    crumiri, 1091
    Florentines, 1094
    hazelnut Florentines, 1094
    hermit, 1091
    lemon, 1090
    macaroons, 1089
    pecan diamond, 1127
    spritz, 1087
    tuiles, 1093
Cooking. *See also* Dry-heat cooking; Moist-heat cooking; Nutrition; Nutritional cooking
    carryover, 311
    combination methods of, 346-352
    healthy, 47-48, 63
    historical figures in, 5
    historical perspective on, 2-4
    professional, 181-182
    submersion methods of, 338-346
Cooking dictionaries, 1166

Cooking encyclopedias, 1166
Cooking publications, 1167
Cooking schools, 16
Cooking seminars, 13
Cooking techniques, basic, 220-227
Cooking terms, glossary of, 1142-1159
Cooling, safe, 38-39
Coquilles St. Jacques, 120
    au gratin, 694
Cordials, 167-171
Corn:
    advance preparation of, 200-201
    creamed, 803
    Mexican, 804
Corn and jicama salad, 892
Corn-and-pepper pudding, 864
Corn-and-pepper sauce, 564
Cornbread, 1027
Corn chowder, 493
Corn crêpes, 958
Corned beef, 92, 574-575
Corned beef and barley soup, 505
Corn fritters, 803
Cornish game hen, 105
    breast of, 634
    poached, with star anise, 645
    roast, with garlic sauce, 750-751
Cornmeal crêpes, 872
Corn muffins, 1027
Corn soup, Amish-style, 462
Cornstarch, 177, 378
Cost control, 19-20
Costs:
    of errors, 22-23
    of food, 20-21
Cottage cheese pancakes, 870
Coulis, 291-292
    fruit, 1073
    red pepper, 550-551, 677, 713
    sun-dried tomato, 683
    tomato, 551
    tomato-basil, 670
Country-style forcemeat, 357, 360
Country-style pâté, 364-365
Court bouillon, 215
    vinegar, 446
    wine, 446
Couscous, 728, 838
    with lamb stew, 776-777
Crab, 120
    preparing, 253
Crab cakes, deviled, 983
Crab salad, 899
Crab soup, 497
Cranberry-orange compote, 804
Cranberry-peppercorn sauce, 651
Crayfish, 120-121
    preparing, 253
Cream, 149, 150. *See also* Bavarian cream; Buttercream; Pastry cream
    for pastries and cakes, 400-404
    whipping, 223
    wine, 1097
Cream cheese icing, 1106

Cream cheese pastry filling, 1104
Cream cheese torte, apple, 1126
Creaming method, for mixing batters, 386, 387-389
Cream of wheat, 868
Cream sauce, 536
    bacon, 616
    basil, 725
    pepper, 674
Cream soups, 267-269, 466-469, 472
Crème brûlée, 1053
Crème caramel, 1052-1053
Crème fraîche, 151
    dilled, 986
    liaison, 423
Crêpe pans, 75
Crêpes, 872
    corn, 958
    dessert, 1057
    Normandy, 1058-1059
    souffléed, 710
    spinach, mushroom, and red pepper coulis, 713
    spinach and seafood, 959
    Suzette, 1057-1058
Croissants, 1042-1043
    dough for, 396-400
Croque Monsieur sandwich, 923
Croquettes, risotto, 724
Croustade, chicken, 946
Croutons, 435
    bean and cheese, 435
    goat cheese, 436
    making, 205
    rye bread, 436
Crullers, 1081
Crust. *See also* Pie crust
    graham cracker, 1119
    short dough for, 1082
    smoked-salmon-and-horseradish, 682
Crustaceans, 113, 120-121
Cryovac packing, 84
Cucumber-dill sauce, 683
Cucumber relish, 964
Cucumbers, 134-136
Cucumber salad dressing, 915
Cucumber sandwich, 932
Cucumber yogurt salad, 896
Cuisine bourgeoisie, 3
Cuisson, 75, 276, 335
Culinary Historians of New York, 24
Culinary influence, spread of, 2
Cultured milk products, 151-152
Cumin-lime marinade, 431
Curds:
    citrus, 1071
    fruit, 406
Cured meat, 371-372
Cured salmon, 372-373
Curried mussels, 692
    Thai, 692
Curried pasta, 848-849
Curried rice salad, 903

Curry:
    India prawn, 785
    vegetable, 723
Curry paste, red, 429
Curry powder, 426
Curry sauce, 779
Curry vegetable turnovers, 718
Curry vinaigrette, 896, 910
Custard:
    gorgonzola, 952-953
    roasted garlic, 458
Customer base, defining, 28
Cutlets:
    cutting and pounding, 227
    veal, 585
Cutting:
    basic knife cuts, 184-189
    special and decorative knife cuts, 189-191
    surfaces for, 68
Cuttlefish, 121

D

Daily operations, reviewing, 26
Dairy products, 148-155
    literature about, 1163
Danish bread, 1042
Danish doughs, 396-400
Date nut bread, 1028-1029
Dates, stuffed with Boursin cheese, 985
Daube, 349, 373
    cold beef, 1021
Deck ovens, 80
Decorateur, 25
Decorating:
    of cakes and pastries, 411-414
    of tortes, 413-414
Deep-frying, 324-327
de la Varenne, Pierre François, 5
de Medici, Caterina, 5
Demi-glace, 278-280, 980, 522
    preparing derivatives of, 280-282
Desserts, 1046-1077. *See also* Cakes; Pastries
    cookies, candies, and confections, 407-410
    crêpes, 1057-1059
    frozen, 406-407
    fruit, 1067-1069
    granitàs, 1063-1065
    ice cream, 1061-1062
    mousse, 1048-1049
    poached fruit, 1065-1066
    puddings, 1046-1047, 1050
    sauces and glazes for, 404-406, 1070-1077
    soufflés, 1055, 1060
Dessert soufflés, 403, 1055
Deviled eggs, 950
Devil's fudge cake, 1113
Diagonal cut, 189

Diamond cut, 188-189
Dicing, 187-188
    of onions, 191
Diet:
    carbohydrate and fiber requirements for, 55
    protein requirements for, 56
    traditional, 51-52
    vitamin requirements for, 60
Dietary guidelines, 48-51
Dietary supplements, 52-53
Dill bread, 1036
Dilled crème fraîche, 986
Dill sauce, 532
Dining room brigade system, 25-26
Disease, foodborne, 33-34
Docked breads, 384-385
Dolphin, 114
"Dominant meat," 359
Doneness:
    for moist-heat cooking, 330-331
    for submersion cooking, 338-339
Double-basket deep-frying, 326-327
Double-boiler, 75
Double broth, 262
Double panning, 394
Dough. *See also* Phyllo dough
    almond, 1082
    brioche, 752
    cookie, 1085
    Linzer, 1083
    pasta, 846
    pâté, 358
    pie and pastry, 391-396, 1080
    pizza, 1033
    puff pastry, 1083
    roll-in, 396-400
    shaping, 383-385, 383-385
    short, for crust, 1082
    spaetzle, 852
    sweet potato, 1010
    yeast, 380-383
Dover sole, 117
Dried fruits, 203
    compote of, 877
Dried vegetables, 203
Drugs, in the workplace, 46
Drum sieve, 73-74
Dry curing, 371
Dry goods, 158
Dry-heat cooking, 301-327
    grilling, broiling, and barbecuing, 302-307
Dry ingredients, sifting, 378-379
Dry marinades, 212
Dry roux, 207
Dry sauté technique, 579
Duck, 105-106
    wild, 106
Duck breast, marinated grilled, 650
Duck confit, 758
Duckling:
    roast, with plum sauce, 649

roast, with red pears, ginger, and green peppercorns, 648
roast, with sauce bigarade, 647
Duck pâté, 1006-1007
Duck rillettes, 1022
Duck sausage, 1001
grilled sandwich of, 927
Duck terrine, country-style, 1013
Dumplings:
biscuit, 856
bread, 855
Chinese, 854-855
Duxelles, 212
dry, 421
Duxelles sauce, 421

E

E. coli bacteria, 32
Eating Well, 17
Edible portion (EP) cost, 20
Education:
chefs', 12-14
continuing, 12-14
Eel, 114
skinning, 257
Egg drop soup, chicken, 517
Eggplant, 136-138
advance preparation of, 199-200
hot and spicy, 814
with tahini dip, 937
Eggplant and pepper terrine, 1014
Eggplant parmesan, 724
Eggplant ravioli, 722
Eggplant-vegetable salad, 940
Eggs, 156-158
baked, 863
Benedict, 859
deviled, 950
fried, 859
hard-boiled, 858
pickled, 949
poached, 858-859
scrambled, 319, 860
separating, 221
shirred, 863
soft-cooked, 858
thickening with, 378
Egg salad, 901
Egg whites, 157
whipping, 221-223
Egg yolks, 157
El Cubano sandwich, 926
Elena Ruz sandwich, 933
Émincé, preparing, 228
Empty calories, 53-54
Emulsion forcemeat, 357, 362-363
Enchiladas:
beef, 766
chicken, 766
chili, 766
Endive, Belgian, 799
English trifle dessert, 1055

En papillote cooking, 115, 116, 334
Entrées. *See also* International entrées
fish, 658-707
meat, 556-619
poultry, 622-655
vegetarian, 710-732
Entremetier, 25
Environmentalism, 13-14
Equipment, 65-81
hand tools, 71-72
knives, 66-71
large, 77-79
literature about, 1162
pots, pans, and molds, 74-77
refrigeration, 80-81
small, 72-74
stoves, ovens, and ranges, 79-80
Erwtensoep, 507
Escalope, 96
Escargots, 119
Escarole-feta turnovers, 718
Escoffier, Georges Auguste, 5, 42, 213
Espresso syrup, 1054
Essences, 215, 299
wild mushroom, 447
Estouffade, 215, 349, 438
Étouffé, 121
oyster, 612-613
Executive dining rooms, 16
Executive responsibilities, 17
Extracts, 166-167

F

Factor method pricing, 22
Falafel, 714
Fanning cut, 190-191
Fats, 57-59, 167
for deep-frying, 325
rendering and clarifying, 220-221
smoking points of, 168
Fat-soluble vitamins, 59
Fearing, Dean, 5
Fennel and chorizo strudel, 955
Fennel ravioli, 459
Fermented milk products, 151-152
Fermière cut, 188
Fiber, 55
FIFO (first in, first out) storage system, 37
Filé gumbo powder, 177
Filleting, of fish, 245
Filleting knife, 70
Filling. *See also* Pastry filling; Stuffing
lasagna, 849
saffron, 704
for pies and tarts, 394
for sticky buns, 1043
Fines herbes, 427
Fines herbes sauce, 526, 623
Finnan haddie, 114
Fire safety, 45
First-aid supplies, 1136

Fish, 106-118. *See also* Shellfish
cutting steaks from, 248-251
deviled eggs with, 950
dry cure for, 427
filleting, 246-248
hot and sour, 784-785
literature about, 1163
marinade for, 431
market forms of, 109, 111-112
nonbony, 113
pan-dressed, 245, 245
scaling, trimming, and gutting, 245
Fish cakes, Thai, 964
Fish chowder, 494
Fish consommé, 455
Asian, 455
Fish entrées, 658-707
Fisherman's platter, 662
Fish fabrication techniques, 244-251
Fish fumet, 443
Fish poacher, 77
Fish quenelles, 1020
Fish soup, Bergen, 501
Fish station, 25
Fish stock, 216, 444
Fish tempura, 975
Fish velouté, 969
Five spice, Chinese, 426
Flan, broccoli, 991
Flank steak, 568-569
braised stuffed, 763
stuffed, 568-569
Flat fish, 113, 117-118, 248
Flat-top range, 79
Flavorings, 166-167, 170
baking, 378
combinations of, 208-212
Florentine dishes, 3
Flounder, 117-118
à la Orly, 666
deep-fried, with rémoulade sauce, 665
filleting, 249
stuffed with crab and lemon beurre blanc, 662-663
Flour, 158-162
thickening with, 378
Flour panadas, 358
Fluting technique, 190
Foam:
folding into an *appareil,* 223
whipping ingredients to make, 221-223
Foaming method, for mixing batters, 386, 390-391
Foccacia, 1033
Foie gras, 106
roulade of, 1017
terrine of, 1019
Fond, 75, 276
Fondant, 405
preparing candies from, 410
Fondue, tomato, 676

Food:
    costs of, 20-21
    hazardous, 35-36
    prepared, canned, and frozen, 177-179
    reheating, 39
    "resting," 311
    safe cooling of, 38-39
    safe handling of, 13, 32-41
    storing, 37-38
    technology and, 3-4
    thawing, 39-40
Food and Drug Administration (FDA), 32, 34
Food associations, 1170
Foodborne illness:
    reducing the risk of, 34-40
    table of, 1134-1135
Food chopper, 78
Food Guide Pyramid, 48, 49
Food history, literature about, 1162
Food mill, 73
Food photography, 16-17
Food preparation, literature about, 1163-1165
Food processor, 78
Foodservice:
    alternative careers in, 16-17
    career paths in, 15-17
    carryout, 16
Foodservice establishments, types of, 15-16
Foodservice industry:
    growth in, 6
    trends in, 12
Foodservice Organizations (Spears), 22
Foodservice professionals, 9-10. *See also* Professional chefs
Food slicer, 78
Food writers, 16
Forcemeats, 356-363
    basic types of, 356-357
    chicken liver gratin-style, 995
    chicken mousseline, 996
    country-style, 360
    emulsion (5/4/3), 362-363, 994-995
    gratin, 360-361, 989
    for leg of lamb, 746
    mousseline, 361-362
    preparation guidelines for, 357-358
    straight, 358-360
Forgione, Larry, 5
Forks, kitchen, 72
Fork tenderness, 338
Frangipan cake, 1102
French bread, sourdough, 1034
French crullers, 1081
Frenching technique, 229, 233
French knife, 70
French toast, 873
Fricassée, 347
Fried eggs, 859
Fried spring rolls, 962-963
Frittata, 862

Fritters:
    broccoli and cheddar, 956
    clam, 982
    corn, 803
    fruit, 1069
    strawberry, 1069
Friturier, 25
Frogs' legs, 122
Front waiter, 25
Frozen desserts, 406-407
Frozen foods, 177-179
Fruitarians, 52
Fruitcake, 1118
Fruit compote, 877
Fruit coulis, 1073
Fruit curds, 406
Fruit fritters, 1069
Fruit gratin, 1068
Fruit ice cream, 1062
Fruits, 122-131. *See also* Citrus fruits
    dried, 171, 173, 203
    general information about, 123
    literature about, 1163
    peeling, 186-187
    poaching liquid for, 1066
    tropical, 126, 127-129
Fruit sauces, 406
Fruit sorbet, 1063
Fruit tartlettes, 1068-1069
Frying:
    deep, 324-327
    pan, 321-324
    stir, 320-321
Fry station, 25
Fudge brownies, 1092
Fudge cake, 1112
    devil's, 1113
Fudge icing, 1106
Fudge sauce, chocolate, 1076
Fumet, 215, 299
    fish, 443

G

Galantines, 370-371
Game, 103
    literature about, 1162-1163
    marinade for, 432, 433
    rosemary and gin marinade for, 434
    teriyaki marinade for, 434
Game birds, 103
    wild, 106
Game bird stock, 442-443
Game hen consommé, 458
Game hens, 105
Game stock, 437
Ganache, 405
    chocolate, 1075
    soft, 1075
Garam masala, 428
Garbanzo beans, stewed, with tomato, zucchini, and cilantro, 844-845
Garbure, 273
Garde-manger, 25, 353-373

    specialties of, 363-373
Garlic:
    advance preparation of, 192-193
    roasting, 908
Garlic and mustard vinaigrette, 908
Garlic custard, 458
Garlic glaze, 564, 615
Garlic mayonnaise, 911
Garlic sauce, 635, 812
Garlic Tahini dressing, 931
Garnishes, soup, 274
Gaufrette cuts, 191
Gazpacho, 273, 490
Geese, 105-106
Gefilte fish, 115
Gelatin, 177
    thickening with, 207-208, 378
Gélato, 407, 1061
Ginger granità, 1065
Ginger sauce, 850
    soy, 974
Glaçage, royal, 544
Glace de gibier, 438
Glace de poisson, 438
Glace de viande, 438
Glace de volaille, 438
Glacier, 25
Glazes:
    chocolate, 1075
    dessert, 404-406
Glove law, 13
Gnocchi:
    Piedmontese, 853
    semolina, 854
Goat cheese croutons, 436
Goat cheese in filo salad, 890
Gorgonzola custard, 952-953
Gorgonzola turnovers, with roasted pepper, 718
Gorgonzola with pears sandwich, 933
Goujonette, 248
Goulash, 347
    beef, 735
    pork, 609
Goulash soup, 506-507
Graham cracker crust, 1119
Grain dishes, 831-845
Grains, 158-162
    cooking ratios and times for, 1136
Grand cuisine, 4-5
Grand sauces, 276-277
Granité, 407
Granità:
    ginger, 1065
    green tea, 1064
    raspberry, 1063
    rum mango, 1064
    sour cherry, 1063
    watermelon, 1064
Granola, 869
Grapefruits, 127
Grapefruit vinaigrette, 885, 891
Grape leaves, stuffed, 990
Grapes, 129

varieties of, 127
GRAS (generally recognized as safe) standards, 35
Gratin dish, 77
Gratin forcemeat, 357, 360-361, 989
Gravad lox (gravlax), 116, 354, 372, 968
Gravy:
 country-style, 628
 cream, 628
 pan, 629
 preparing, 312
 red-eye, 875
 sausage, 875
Greek sausage, 1002-1003
Green beans:
 with bacon, shallots, and mushrooms, 797
 gingered, with cabbage, 813
 steamed, 792
 with walnuts, 797
Green mayonnaise, 967
Greens:
 advance preparation of, 196-198
 cooking, 134
 deviled eggs with, 950
Green tea granità, 1064
Green vegetables, boiled, 800
Gremolata, 741
Griddles, 75-77, 80
Grilling, 302-307
 of poultry, 241
 of vegetables, 809
Grills, 80
Grinding:
 progressive, 357
 equipment for, 78-79
Grits:
 garlic cheese, 837
 souffléed, 837
Grouper fish, 114
Guacamole, 655, 937
Guerard, Michel, 5
Gugelhopf, 1116
Guiding hand, 184
Gumbos, 273
 chicken and shrimp, 495
Gyoza, 963

H

Haddock, 114
Halibut, 118
 pan-fried, with puttanesca sauce, 661
 poached, with saffron sauce, 697
Ham, 98, 99
Ham and mushroom stuffing, 626
Ham bone and collard greens soup, 496
Ham salad, 898
Ham steak, pan fried, with red-eye gravy, 875
Hand tools, 71-72
Hard-boiled eggs, 858-859
Hard rolls, 1033

Hard sauce, 1074
Hash:
 red flannel, 874
 roast beef, 619
Haute cuisine, 3
Hazard Analysis Critical Control Point (HACCP) system, 33, 40-41
Hazardous foods, 35-36
Hazelnut filling, 1102
Hazelnut Florentine cookies, 1094
Hazelnut torte cake, 1124
Head waiter, 25
Heart, beef, 92
Herb croutons, 435
Herb crêpes, 872
Herbes de Provence, 427
Herb mayonnaise, 911
Herb omelet, 861
Herb pasta, 846
Herb pastes, 212
Herbs, 145-148
 advance preparation of, 198
 dried, 164-165
Herb soufflé, 867
High-density lipoproteins (HDLs), 57
"High-ratio" cakes, 389, 1111
Hoagie sandwich, 930
Hollandaise sauce, 292-295, 540
Holstein schnitzel, 739
Hors d'oeuvres, 936-992
Horseradish sauce, 532, 684
Hot and sour sauce, 784-785
Hot and sour soup, 518
Hot and spicy sauce, 814
Hot chocolate, 879
Hotel pans, 77
Hotels, dining facilities in, 16
Hot smoking, 372
Huevos rancheros, 859
Human resource management, 24-26
Hummus b'tahini, 939
Hunan sauce, 776
Hush puppies, 836-837

I

Ice cream, 150, 407
 caramel, 1061
 chocolate, 1061
 chocolate chocolate chip, 1062
 coffee, 1061
 French, 1061
 fruit, 1062
 liquor-flavored, 1062
 vanilla, 1062
Icing:
 cream cheese, 1106
 devil's fudge, 1106
Illnesses, foodborne, 1134-1135
Immersion blender, 271
Information management, 23-24
International cook books, 1164-1165
International entrées, 734-789
Inventory, 20

Irish stew, 747
Italian meringue, 223, 1105
Italian sausage, 999, 1003
 hot, 1003

J

Jambalaya, 121
Jardinière cut, 189
Jicama and cucumber salad, 893
John Dory fish, 114-115
Johnny cakes, 870
Journals, cooking, 1167
Judgment, importance of, 15
Julienne cut, 187
Jus, preparing, 312
Jus d'agneau, 441
Jus de gibier, 437
Jus de pork, 440
Jus de veau, 437
Jus de veau lié, 523
Jus de Volaille, 750-751
Jus lié, 282-284, 312
 pork, 605

K

Kasha, with spicy maple pecans, 840
Kettles, 79
Kidneys, 236
Kitchen brigade system, 24-25
Kitchen fork, 72
Kitchen safety, 42-46
Knife cuts:
 basic, 185-189
 decorative, 189-191
Knife skills, 184-191
Knives, 66-71
 holding, 184
 sharpening, 70-71
 types of, 69-70
Kugelhopf, 1117

L

Lacto/ovo-vegetarians, 52
La Cuisine Classique, 4
La Cuisine de France, 295
Ladyfingers, 1095
Lamb, 100-103
 blanquette, 587
 braised shanks of, 597
 carving, 312-313
 chops, with Arizona chili butter, 593
 chops, with artichokes, 595
 émincé, with green peppercorns, 589
 grilled chops, with garlic, 594
 grilled chops, with mint sauce, 592-593
 Italian grilled, 774
 marinade for, 432
 noisettes Judic, 590
 rack of, 229, 233

Lamb *(continued)*:
    roast leg, boulangère, 590
    roast leg, with mint sauce, 592
    roast rack, Persille, 591
    shanks, Printanière, 597
    spicy Hunan, 776
    stuffed leg of, 746
Lamb broth, 452
Lamb entrées, 589-597
Lamb patties, Pakistani-style, 775
Lamb stew, 596
    with couscous, 776-777
Lamb stock, 440-441
Larding, 309
Larousse Gastronomique, 297
Lasagna:
    di Carnevale Napolitana, 849-850
    filling for, 849
    vegetable, 721
Lattice pie tops, 395
Leafy greens, advance preparation of,
    196-198
Lean dough, 380
Leaveners, 175-177, 376-378
Leek and tomato quiche, 865
Leek compote, 684
Leeks, advance preparation of, 193
Le Guide Culinaire (Escoffier), 5, 213
Legumes:
    dried, 162, 163
    soaking and cooking times for, 1137
Lemon beurre blanc, 545, 663, 691
Lemon cookies, 1090
Lemon curd, 1071
Lemon vinaigrette:
    garlic, 908
    parsley, 895
    thyme, 897
Lemongrass, 910
Lemon meringue pie, 1099-1100
Lemon mousse, 1049, 1071
Lemon sorbet, 1062-1063
Lentil ragout, 727, 844
Lentils, 162, 163
    braised, with eggplant and mush-
        rooms, 843
Lentil salad, 904
Lentil soup, 480
    French, 481
Lettuce, 137, 138
    braised, 805-806
Lettuce soup, cream of, 466-469
Le Vrai Cuisinier François (de la
    Varenne), 5
Liaison, 207, 423
Lime and olive oil vinaigrette, 909
Lime curd, 1071
Line cooks, 25
Linzer dough, 1083
Liqueurs, 167-171
Liquor-flavored ice cream, 1062
Littleneck clams, 119
Liver, 236
    beef, 92

calf's, with bacon cream sauce, 616
Lobster, 121
    broiled, with drawn butter, 706
    broiled stuffed, 669
    preparing, 251-253
Lobster bisque, 485
Lobster salad, 889, 899
Lobster sauce, 535
Lobster tortellini, with ginger-lime
        sauce, 850-851
London broil, 565
Lotte, 115
Loukanika, 1002-1003
Low-density lipoproteins (LDLs), 57
Lox, gravad, 968
Lozenge cut, 188-189

M

Macaroni and cheese, 726
Macaroni salad, 903
Mackerel, 115
    broiled, with pimiento butter, 669
    grilled, with tomato fondue, 676
    marinated in white wine, 984
Madeira sauce, 525, 617, 738, 954
Magazines, industry, 17
Mahi mahi, 114
    with pineapple chutney, 676-677
Maître d'hôtel, 25
Management, 17-30
    of human resources, 24-26
    of information, 23-24
    legal responsibilities of, 26
    literature about, 1166
    of physical assets, 18-19
    of time, 26-27
Mandoline, 78-79
Mango/bourbon barbecue sauce, 553
Mango chutney, 774, 659
Manilla clams, 119
Maple syrup-pecan butter, 878
Marchand de vin sauce, 527, 562
Marinades, 211-212
    Asian-style, 430
    barbecue, 430
    citrus, 432
    cumin-lime, 431
    fish, 431
    lamb and game, 432
    meat, 430
    red wine game, 433
    rosemary and gin, 434
    for sauerbraten, 735
    teriyaki, 434
Marinara sauce, 538
Marketing, 27-30
Marketing tools, 28-29
Marmite, 75
Marrow, removing, 237
Marsala sauce, 525, 615
Marzipan stollen, 1041
Mashing, of garlic and shallots, 192-193

Matelotes, 114, 206, 257, 347
Matignon, 209, 313, 314, 420
Mayonnaise, 911
    anchovy caper, 912
    garlic, 911
    green, 693, 967
    herb, 911
Meal, 158-162
Measuring:
    in baking, 378
    equipment for, 72-73
Meat. *See also* Forcemeats; Poultry;
        Variety meats
    beef, 86-93
    boning, 234, 235
    breading, 322-324
    butterflying, 229-235, 234
    carving, 312-313
    curing and smoking, 371-372
    game, 103
    identifying and purchasing, 84-103
    inspection and grading of, 84-85
    kosher, 86
    literature about, 1162-1163
    marinade for, 430
    market forms of, 86
    poêléing, 313-316
    pork, 96-100
    rabbit, 103
    seasoning mix for roasting, 428
    storing, 84
    veal, 93-96
Meatballs, Indian, 618
Meat entrées, 556-619
Meat fabrication techniques, 227-237.
        See also Poultry fabrication
Meat grinder, 78
Meat loaf, 618-619
    Asian, 619
    Italian, 619
Meat loaf sandwich, 920
Meat sauce, 539
Meat slicer, 78
Meat stock, 216
Medallions, shaping, 229, 230
Media, 6-7
    effective use of, 24
Media Noche sandwich, 926
*Mediterranean Diets in Health and Disease,
        The* (Braun), 32
Mediterranean Food Pyramid, 48, 49
Melba sauce, 1073
Melon, 129
    with prosciutto, 984
    varieties of, 128
Melon baller, 72
Menu:
    developing, 16, 62-63
    as a marketing tool, 28-29
Menudo, 508
Menu pricing, 21-22
Meringue, 222-223, 395, 1104
    Italian, 1105
    Swiss, 1105

Meringue shells, 1105
Mesclun salad, 883-884
Middle class, cooking style of, 3
Mie de pain, 204
Milk, 149-150
Milk products, fermented and cultured, 151-152
Mille feuille, mushroom, 719
Mincing, 187
Minerals, 59-60
Minestrone, 273, 463
    Genovese, 509
    seafood, 514
Mint sauce, 592
Mirepoix, 140, 209, 310, 985
    browning bones and, 217
    recipe for, 420
Mise en place, 183
    advance vegetable preparation, 191-203
    appareils for, 203-208
    aromatic and flavoring combinations, 208-212
    basic cooking techniques, 220-227
    fish and shellfish fabrication, 244-257
    knife skills, 184-191
    meat fabrication techniques, 227-237
    poultry fabrication, 237-243
    stocks, broths, and court bouillons, 213-219
Mise en place recipes, 420-448
Miso sauce, 783
Mixing bowls, 73
Mixing methods, for batters, 386-391
Moist-heat cooking, 329-352
    steaming, 330-338
    submersion techniques, 338-346
Moisture, pathogens and, 36
Molds, 74-77
    baking, 379-380
    for tarts, 394
Mole:
    chicken, 765
    pork and beef tamales with, 762
Molluscs, preparing, 253-254
Monkfish, 115
    roasted, with Niçoise olives and Pernod sauce, 681
Monounsaturated fats, 57
Monte Cristo sandwich, 923
Mornay sauce, 535, 970
Mother sauces, 276-277
Moules marinière, 977
Mousse:
    broccoli, 992
    carrot, 992
    chocolate, 1048-1049
    frozen, 407
    Iowa blue cheese, 953
    lemon, 1049, 1071
    for pastries and cakes, 400-404
    red pepper, 991-992
Mousseline, 357

Mousseline forcemeat, 357, 361-362
Mousseline sauce, 543, 693, 959
Moutabel, with Belgian endive, 938
Mozzarella roulade, 951
    canapés of, 952
Muesli parfait, 869
Muffins:
    basic, 1026
    blueberry, 1026-1027
    bran, 1028
    corn, 1027
Mulligatawny soup, 510
Multigrain bread, 1035
Mushroom and ham stuffing, 626
Mushroom consommé, 457
Mushroom essence, 447
Mushroom *jus,* 524
Mushroom mille feuille, 719
Mushroom ragout, 719
Mushrooms, 138-140. *See also* Shiitake mushrooms
    advance preparation of, 196
    beef consommé with, 454
    stuffed with gratin forcemeat, 989
Mushroom sauce, 527
Mushroom sausage, 588
Mushroom soup, 471
Mushroom strudel, with goat cheese, 954
Mussels, 119-120
    with clams, saffron, and tomatoes, 978
    cleaning and debearding, 254
    curried, 692
    marinière, 692, 977
Mustard-herb vinaigrette, 907
Mustard sauce, 614-615
    Creole, 542-543, 668
    tarragon green peppercorn, 545
Mutton, 100-103
Mutual supplementation, 56

N

Nappé condition, 279
National Association of Catering Executives (NACE), 24
National Restaurant Association (NRA), 24
Navarin, 347
Nectarines, 129
Networking, 14
New England boiled dinner, 576
New England shore dinner, 706-707
New potatoes:
    caviar in, with dilled crème fraîche, 986
    with snails and Brie, 985-986
    steamed, with fines herbes, 818
Niçoise salads, 895
Nonperishable goods, 158-179
    literature about, 1163
Noodles, dried, 162, 164
Nouvelle cuisine, 5

Nuss sauce, 1074
"Nutraceuticals," 52-53
Nutrients, types of, 53-61
Nutrition, 4, 47-63
    continuing education in, 13
    dietary recommendations for, 48-51
    literature about, 1162
    purchasing for, 63
Nutritional cooking
    guidelines for, 61-62
    practice of, 62-63
Nuts, 171, 172
    toasting, 205

O

Oatmeal, with cinnamon and dried fruits, 868
Oblique cut, 189
Occupational Health and Safety Administration (OSHA), 44
Octopus, 121-122
    cleaning, 255, 256
Oeufs à la neige dessert, 1056
Oignon brûlé, 210-211
Oignon piqué, 210-211
Oils, 57-59, 162, 167, 168
    for deep-frying, 325
Omelets:
    cheese, 861
    enchilada, 861
    farmer-style, 862
    Florentine, 861
    fruit filled, with cheese, 861
    herb, 861
    Marcel, 861
    meat and cheese, 861
    opera, 861
    plain rolled, 860-861
    preparing, 319
    seafood, 861
    shellfish, 861
    souffléed, 862
    Spanish, 861
    tomato, 861
    Western, 861
Omelet pans, 75
Onions, 139, 140
    advance preparation of, 191
    studded and burnt, 210-211
Onion soup, gratiné, 464
Open-burner range, 79
Operating costs, reducing, 14
Operations review, 26
Orange curd, 1071
Orange-mango compound butter, 878
Orange roughy, en papillote with shrimp and scallions, 690
Oranges, 127
Orange sorbet, 1063
Orange soufflé, frozen, 1060
Organic beef, 87
Organic foods, 13
Organic poultry, 103-104

Organ meats, 92-93, 96
Ossobuco alla Milanese, 741
Oven cooking, pots and pans for, 77
Ovens, 79-80
  for baking, 380
Overportioning, 22-23
Ovo-vegetarians, 52
Oxtails, 92
  braised, 616-617
Oxtail soup, 460
  à l'Anglaise, 511
Oyster bisque, 486-487
Oyster étouffé, 612-613
Oysters, 120
  with artichoke and champagne vinai-
      grette, 980-981
  cleaning and opening, 253
  Diamond Jim Brandy, 979
  gratinée, 980
Oyster stuffing, 635

P

Pacific littleneck clams, 119
Paella, 757
Paillards, 96
  preparing, 228
Pain de campagne, 1033
Palette knife, 72
Palois sauce, 544
Panadas, 358, 1016
Pan-broiling, 302-303
Pancakes, 870
  cottage cheese, 870
  Johnny cakes, 870
  pumpkin or banana, 871
  silver dollar, 870
  souffléed, 870
  spinach, 795
  whole grain, 870
Pan-frying, 321-324
Pan gravy, 312
Pan-proofing, 384
Pans, 74-77
  baking, 379-380
  specialty, 77
Pan-steaming, 337-338
Pantry chef, 25
Paprika oil, 910
Parchment cones, 411-412
Parchment liners, cutting, 226-227
Par-cooking, 330
Parfaits, 1059
  "Muesli," 869
Paring knife, 70
Parisienne scoop, 72
Parmesan croutons, 435
Parsnip and pear purée, 799
Parstock, 19
Pasta, 846-856
  black pepper, 846, 848
  boiling, 343-344, 847
  chorizo-filled, with tomato-basil
      coulis and tomato salsa, 851-852

curried, 848-849
dried, 162, 164
herb, 846
pomodoro, 726
primavera, 725
pumpkin, beet, or carrot, 846
saffron, 850
spice, 846
spinach, 846
tomato, 846
whole wheat, with broccoli rabe, 725
Pasta dough, 846
Pasta filling:
  chorizo, 851
  lobster, 850
Pasta salad, 904
Pastries, 1080-1108. *See also* Cookies
  creams, bavarians, and mousses for,
      400-404
  decorating, 411-414
Pastry bags, 72, 412-413
Pastry chef, 25
Pastry cook books, 1165
Pastry cream, 401-403, 1096
Pastry dough, 391-396, 1083. *See also*
      Puff pastry dough
Pastry filling, 399, 1102-1104
  baker's cheese, 1103
  cream cheese, 1104
  hazelnut, 1102
  strudel, 1103
Pâté:
  à choux, 208, 358, 399-400, 1081
  brissée, 969, 1080
  de campagne, 364-365, 994
  duck, en croute, 1006-1007
  en croute, 366-368
  pheasant, 1006
  quail, en croute, 1008
  salmon, en croute, 1009
  sucrée, 392
  turkey, en croute, 1010-1011
  Tuscany-style, en croute, 1011
Pâté dough, 358, 996
  saffron, 1009
  tomato cilantro, 1008
Pâté mold, 77
Pâté spice, 997
Pathogens, 36-37
Pâtissier, 25
Paupiette, 248
Paysanne cut, 188
Peaches, 129
Peanut sauce, spicy, 770
Peanut soup, 498
Pearl balls, 965
Pears, 129-131
  poached, 1066
Peas, 162, 163. *See also* Snow peas
  advance preparation of, 202
  bonne femme, 206
  French-style, 793
  pan-steamed, 792
  varieties of, 141

Viennese-style, 793
Pea soup, 476, 507
Pecan bread, 1036
Pecan diamond cookies, 1127
Pecan-herb loaf, with tomato-tahini
    sauté, 715
Pecan-lime butter, 673
Pecan pie, 1099
Peelers, 72
Peeling:
  of garlic and shallots, 192-193
  of onions, 191
  techniques for, 185
Pepper, 165-166, 169, 208
Peppercorn sabayon, green, 575
Pepper cream sauce, 674
Pepper crust, 559
Pepper pot soup, 498-499
Peppers:
  advance preparation of, 194-196
  bell, 140-141
  chili, 140, 141
  deviled eggs with, 950
Pepper salad, roasted, 675
Perch, 115
  Bordelaise-style, 700
Perigeaux sauce, 526
Permit fish, 115
Pernod sauce, 681
Persillade, 212, 422
Pesco-vegetarians, 52
Pesto, 212, 422
  anchovy, 742
Pesto vinaigrette, 904
Petits fours, 407-408
Petits pois à la Fermière, 793
Petits pots du crème dessert, 1048
Pfeffernusse, 1088-1089
pH, pathogens and, 36
Pheasant, 106
  roast, with cranberry-peppercorn
      sauce, 651
Pheasant pâté, 1006
Phyllo dough, 391, 396-400
  handling method for, 399
Physical contamination, 35
Physiology of Taste, The (Brillat-Savarin),
    5
Phytochemicals, 59
Pickled eggs, 949
Pie:
  apple, 1097
  cherry, 1100
  fillings for, 394
  lemon meringue, 1099-1100
  pecan, 1099
  preparing, 393-396
  pumpkin, 1098
  toppings for, 394-395, 1104-1105
Pie crust, 391-396, 1080
Pie plates, lining, 394
Pigs in a blanket, 870
Pike fish, 115

Pilaf:
  boiling, 344
  quinoa, 839
  rice, 831, 832
Pimiento butter, 548, 669
Pinçage process, 272, 278
Pincé process, 284
Pineapple chutney, 676
Pineapple Madagascar dessert, 1067
Piquant sauce, 528
Pistou, 212
Pizza:
  apple cheddar, 928
  grilled vegetable, 929
Pizza dough, 1033
Plums, 130, 131
Plum sauce, 649
Plum soup, chilled, 487
Poached eggs, 858-859
Poaching, 339-340
  shallow, 334-337
Poaching liquid, for fruit, 1066
Pod vegetables, 141-142
Poêléing, 313-316
Poêlé poussins, 630
Point, Fernand, 5
Poissonier, 25
Polenta, 835
  boiling, 344-346
  with parmesan cheese, 836
Polyunsaturated fats, 57
Pommes dauphines, 208
Pommes frites cut, 187
Pommes pont neuf cut, 187
Pompano fish, 115
Popovers, 1032
Pork, 96-100. *See also* Pork chops; Pork
    loin
  barbecued, North Carolina-style, 610
  cutlet, sauce charcutière, 598
  cutlets, with mushrooms and crab-
    meat, 602
  medallions, with eggplant, 744
  medallions, with red onion confit,
    599
  in orange and lemon sauce, 764
  pan-fried breaded cutlets of, 602-603
  pan-fried chop, Forestière, 603
  roast, with *jus lié,* 605
  sautéed medallions, with fruit, 601
  scalopine, with herb sauce, 599
  scalopine marsala, 577
  stir-fried, 773
  tenderloin, with apples and caraway,
    600
  tenderloin, with honey and thyme,
    606-607
Pork chart, 97
Pork chops:
  broiled, 607
  broiled, with sesame ginger butter,
    608
  baked stuffed, 604
  with fennel, 743

  grilled with spicy sauce, 742
Pork entrées, 598-610
Pork goulash, 609
Pork loin:
  roasted Genoa style, 745
  stuffed with apples and prunes, 606
  trimming and cutting, 234, 235
Pork primals, 97-100
Pork rillettes, 1022
Pork stew, with chestnuts, 772
Pork stock, 440
Portion control, 21, 63
Port wine sauce, 654
Potager, 25
Potato, trout, and leek terrine, 1015
Potato dishes, 818-830
Potatoes, 142, 818-830. *See also* New
    potatoes; Sweet potatoes
  advance preparation of, 201
  Anna, 825
  au gratin, 820
  baked Idaho with fried onions, 819
  baked stuffed, 819
  Berny, 828
  boiled parslied, 818
  buttermilk whipped, 826
  Châteaubriand, 823
  croquette, 827
  dauphinoise, 821
  duchesse, 827
  french-fried, 829
  hash brown, 822
  hashed in cream, 823
  with lemon and thyme, 818
  Lorette, 828
  Lyonnaise, 822
  Macaire, 829
  O'Brien, 822
  puréed, 826
  roasted garlic mashed, 826
  roasted with garlic and rosemary, 820
  Roësti, 824
  savoyarde, 821
  scalloped, 820
  souffléed, 830
  Swedish-style candied, 825
  varieties of, 143
Potato kale soup, 512
Potato nest, 830
Potato pancakes, 824
Potato salad, 901
  European-style, 902
  German, 902
Pot au feu, 265
Pot roast, 349
  Yankee, 567
Pots, 74-77
  specialty, 77
Poultry, 103-106. *See also* Chicken;
    Turkey
  carving, 313
  literature about, 1162-1163
  seasoning mix for roasting, 428
Poultry entrées, 622-655

Poultry fabrication, 237-243
Poultry leg, boning, 243
Pound cake, 1110-1111
Poussin, 104
Prawn curry, India, 785
Prepared foods, 177-179
Presentation. *See* Serving
Pressure steamer, 79
Pricing, 29
  menu, 21-22
Primal meat cuts, 86
Prime cost pricing, 22
Prime rib, roast, 557
Printanière cut, 189
Produce, seasonal availability of, 1130-
    1131
Product identification, literature about,
    1162
Professional chefs, 11-30
  attributes of, 14-15
  career paths for, 15-17
  craftsmanship among, 12-14
Professional image, 14
Professional networking, 14
Professional organizations, 24
Progressive grinding, 357
Prosciutto, with melon, 984
Protein, 55-56
  pathogens and, 36
Pudding:
  bread and butter, 1050
  chocolate, 1046-1047
  corn and pepper, 864
  rice, 1046
Puffer fish, 115
Puff pastry, blitz, 397, 1084
Puff pastry dough, 396-400, 1083
Pumpernickel bread, 1034
Pumpernickel rolls, 1034
Pumpkin bisque, 486
Pumpkin bread, 1029
Pumpkin pancakes, 871
Pumpkin pasta, 846
Pumpkin pie, 1098
Purchase inventory, 20
Purchasing, 19-20
  of dairy products and eggs, 148-149
  of fish, 107-108
  of meat, 84-103
  of nonperishable goods, 158
  nutritional, 63
Puréeing equipment, 78-79
Purée soups, 269-271
Puttanesca sauce, 661

Q

Quail, 106
Quail pâté, 1008
Quatre épices, 428
Quenelles, 363-364
  chicken consommé with, 456
  de brochet, 115

Quenelles *(continued):*
    fish, 1020
    fish consommé with, 455
Quesadilla:
    chicken and walnut, 925
    roasted vegetable, 924
Quiche:
    leek and tomato, 865
    Lorraine, 866
    Provençal, 866
    Southwestern, 866
    Spanish, 866
    vegetable, 866
Quick bread, preparing batter for, 386-391
Quinoa pilaf, with peppers, 839

R

Rabbit, 103
    with oyster étouffé, 612-613
    poêlé of, with prunes, 630
    preparing, 243-244
    skewered, with sausage and prosciutto, 614
    stewed, with prunes, 611
Rabbit stew, liquarian, 613
Rabbit terrine, 1013
Rack of lamb, frenching, 229, 233
Ragout, 347
    lentil, 727
    mushroom, 719
Raisin bread, 1037
Raisin sauce, 1072-1073
Ranges, 79-80
Ranhofer, Charles, 5
Raspberry granità, 1063
Raspberry sauce, 1072
Ratatouille, 664, 806
    grilled Provençal, 808
Ravioli:
    eggplant, 722
    fennel, 459
Ray, preparing, 116
Reach-in refrigerator, 81
Recipe books, 1163-1165
Recipes:
    developing, 62-63
    as tools, 21
Recycling issues, 13-14
Red cabbage, braised, 805
Red onion confit, 599
Red pepper coulis, 550-551, 677, 713
Red pepper mousse, 991-992
Red snapper, poached, Veracruz, 702
Reduction, 224-225
    Béarnaise, 541-542
    standard, 429
Red vegetables, boiled, 800
Refined sugars, 55
Refried beans, 842
Refrigeration, types of, 81
Refrigeration equipment, 80-81
Regulations:

food safety, 13
    for organic products, 13
Reheating, 39
    of sauces, 299
    of soups, 274
Relish, 299
    cucumber, 964
Remouillage, 213, 214, 441
Rémoulade, celery root and roasted red pepper, 941
Rémoulade sauce, 665, 915
Research and development kitchens, 17
Responsibility, importance of, 15
Restaurant business, trends in, 6-7
Restaurant design, 29
Restaurant Operator's Manual, The (Reich), 22
Restaurants:
    evolution and history of, 4-6
    need for chefs in, 16
    types of, 15-16
Reuben sandwich, 921
Rhubarb, 130, 131
Rib roast:
    carving, 312
    standing, 558-559
Ribs, short, 569
Rice. *See also* Risotto
    boiled, 831
    brown, with pecans and scallions, 833
    cilantro lime, 832
    pilaf, 831, 832
Rice and beans:
    Mexican-style, 729
    Puerto Rican style, 729
Rice crêpes, 872
Rice pudding, with raspberries, 1046
Ricers, 74
Rice salad, curried, 903
Rice soup, 475
Rich dough, 380
Rillettes, 1022
Ring-top range, 79
"Rising star" chefs, 5-6
Risotto, 833
    with asparagus tips, 834
    boiling, 346
    with escarole and parmesan, 834
    saffron, 833
    saffron, with shrimp, 835
Risotto croquettes, cheese-filled, with tomato sauce, 724
Rissoles, 956-957
Roast beef hash, 619
Roasted food, gravy for, 312
Roasting:
    of eggplant, 200
    of garlic and shallots, 193
    of peppers, 195-196
    of poultry, 238-239
    techniques for, 307-312
    of tomatoes, 194
Roasting pans, 77
Roasts, tying, 229, 231, 232

Roast station, 25
Rock Cornish game hen, 105
Roll cut, 189
Roll-in doughs, 396-400
Rolls:
    docking, 384-385
    hard, 1033
    pumpernickel, 1034
    sweet dough, 1040
Rondeau, 75
Rondelle cut, 189
Root vegetables, 142-144
Rosemary and gin marinade, 434
Rosemary ginger butter, 547
Rôtisseur, 25
Rouille, 911
Roulade:
    chicken, 1018
    chocolate, 1109
    of foie gras, 1017
    mozzarella, 951
    spinach, with mushrooms and sour cream, 716-717
    sponge, 1108-1109
Round fish, 113-117, 248
Roundsman, 25
Roux, 206-207
    basic, 423
    uncooked, 206
Royalty, cooking styles of, 3
Rubs, 212
Rum mango granità, 1064
Rum torte cake, 1122-1123
Rusks, cheddar cheese, 436
Rye bread croutons, 436
Rye sourdough starter, 1034

S

Sabayon, 406
Sabayon sauce, 1068, 1073
Sacher torte, 1122
Sachet d'épices, 210, 424
Safe handling procedures, 13
Safety, 31-46. *See also* Kitchen safety
    in handling knives, 67-68
    literature about, 1162
Saffron-cream sauce, 972
Saffron filling, 704
Saffron pasta, 850
Saffron poaching liquid, 1066
Saffron pâté dough, 1009
Saffron sauce, 679, 697
Salad dressing, 906-916. *See also* Vinaigrette
    blue cheese, 914
    Caesar-style, 912
    Catalina, 910
    creamy black pepper, 914
    cucumber, 915
    Georgia peanut, 909
    Green goddess, 913
    peanut oil and malt vinegar, 907
    ranch-style, 913

Salads, 882-905
  bean, 904
  black-eyed pea, 905
  Buffalo-style chicken, 886
  Caesar, 884
  carrot and raisin, 892
  celeriac and apple, 893
  chef, 886-887
  chicken, 898
  citrus slaw with avocado and red onion, 891
  cobb, 887
  coleslaw, 891
  corn and jicama, 892
  crab or lobster, 899
  cucumber yogurt, 896
  curried rice, 903
  egg, 901
  eggplant-vegetable, 940
  European-style potato, 902
  German potato, 902
  goat cheese in filo with roasted pepper, 890
  Greek, 895
  ham, 898
  jicama and cucumber, 893
  lentil, 904
  lobster, with avocado and apples, 889
  macaroni, 903
  Mediterranean pepper, 897
  mesclun with apples and goat cheese, 883-884
  mixed green, 882
  Moroccan carrot, 896
  Niçoise with tuna, 895
  panzanella, 894
  pasta, 904
  potato, 901
  seafood ravigote, 900
  sherried watercress and apple, 882
  shiitake, 966
  shrimp, 899
  spinach, avocado, and grapefruit, 884-885
  spinach-arugula with blood oranges and goat cheese, 883
  tabbouleh, 898
  taco, 888
  tomato and mozzarella, 894
  tuna, 899
  Waldorf, 894
  wilted spinach with bacon vinaigrette, 885
Salamanders, 80
Sales positions, 16
Salmon, 115-116
  baked in phyllo with saffron sauce, 678-679
  in brioche, 752
  broiled steaks of, 668
  carpaccio of, 967
  cold poached, with green mayonnaise, 693
  with cucumbers en papillote, 691

  cured, 372-373
  filleting, 247
  fillet of, with smoked-salmon-and-horseradish crust, 682
  grilled, with roasted pepper salad, 675
  noisettes of, with cucumber-dill sauce, 683
  poached, with asparagus and basil sauce, 695
  poached, with Béarnaise sauce, 693
  poached, with mousseline sauce, 693
  smoked, 968
  smoked fillet of, with tomato coulis, 683
  with yogurt gratin, 969
Salmonellosis, 33
Salmon mousse barquettes, 969
Salmon pâté, 1009
Salmon soup, 506
Salsa, 298
  black bean, 714, 936
  cruda, 671
  fresh, 730
  fresh tomato, 936
  tomato, 988
Salt, 165-166, 169, 208
  curing, 359
  seasoning with, 62
Salzburger nockerl dessert, 1056
Samosa, 957
Sandwiches, 918-934. *See also* Tacos
  apples with curry mayonnaise, 933
  barbecued beef, 919
  bruschetta, 926
  CIA club, 930
  croque monsieur, 923
  cucumber with herb cream cheese, 932
  Elena Ruz tea, 933
  gorgonzola with pears, 933
  grilled duck sausage, 927
  grilled vegetable and cheese, 922
  hoagie, 930
  hot turkey, 919
  meat loaf, 920
  media noche, 926
  Monte Cristo, 923
  reuben, 921
  roasted vegetable, 931
  sloppy Joe, 918-919
  tapenade, 927
  three-cheese melt, 921
  tomato, cream cheese, and arugula, 932
  tomato with oregano sour cream, 934
  tuna melt, 922
  watercress with herb mayonnaise, 934
  western, 920
Sanitation, literature about, 1162
Sanitizing, defined, 43
San Pedro fish, 114-115
Saturated fats, 57

Sauce Espagnole, 277-278
Saucepans, 75
Saucepots, 75
Sauce recipes, 522-553
Sauces, 275-300
  Albuféra, 533
  balsamic vinegar, 672
  basil, 695
  Béarnaise, 541, 693
  Béchamel, 535
  bigarade, 647
  Bordelaise, 529
  brown, 522
  caramel, 1076
  caramel/butterscotch, 406
  charcutière, 598
  Chasseur, 530
  Châteaubriand, 531
  chili, 787
  Chipotle, 549
  chocolate, 405, 1075
  chocolate fudge, 1076
  Choron, 542
  cinnamon, 1074-1075
  contemporary, 277
  from cooking liquids, 337
  cranberry-peppercorn, 651
  creams, bavarians, and mousses as, 400-404
  Creole mustard, 668
  cucumber-dill, 683
  demi-glace, 522
  dessert, 404-406
  for dipping tempura, 975
  duxelles, 421
  fines herbes, 526, 623
  fruit, 406
  garlic, 635, 812
  ginger, 850
  ginger soy, 974
  grand sauces, 276-277
  hard, 1074
  Hollandaise, 540
  horseradish, 684
  hot and sour, 784-785
  hot and spicy, 814
  Hunan, 776
  jus de veau lié, 523
  Madeira, 525, 617, 954
  Maltaise, 540
  marchand de vin, 527, 562
  marinara, 538
  Marsala, 525, 615
  melba, 1073
  miscellaneous, 298-299
  miso, 783
  Mornay, 535, 970
  mousseline, 543, 693, 959
  Nantua, 533
  nuss, 1074
  palois, 544
  pepper cream, 674
  Perigeaux, 526
  Pernod, 681

Sauces *(continued):*
  piquant, 528
  plum, 649
  port wine, 654
  puttanesca, 661
  raisin, 1072-1073
  raspberry, 1072
  rémoulade, 915
  Robert, 276, 528-529
  sabayon, 1068, 1073
  saffron, 679, 697
  saffron-cream, 972
  for sautéed food, 318-319
  serving, 299-300
  Spanish, 702
  strawberry, 1072
  suprême, 276, 534
  taco, 888
  tarragon, 625, 644
  tartar, 916
  techniques for, 277-298
  tempura, 788
  teriyaki, 768, 780
  tomato-tahini, 715
  vanilla, 400-401, 1070
  velouté, 267, 531
  vin blanc, 295, 696
  wasabi, 966
  watercress, 703
  Wild Turkey, 1070
  Zingara, 584
Sauerbraten, 735-736
Sausage, 369-370
  Andouille, 998
  breakfast-style, 998-999
  chicken and herb, 1000
  chorizo, 1004
  duck, 1001
  Greek, 1002-1003
  Italian, 1003
  Italian festival, 999
  mushroom, 588
  seafood, 1004-1005
  smoked venison, 1005
  spicy French-style apple, 1002
Sausage gravy, 875
Sausage sandwich, duck, 927
Sauteuse, 75, 295
Sautéing, 316-319
Savoir, 75
Savarin, with fresh fruit, 1051
Savarin syrup, 1050
Saveur, 17
Scales, 73
Scaling, 378
Scallion butter, 548, 561
Scallop and tuna ceviche, 942
Scalloped potatoes, 820
Scallop mousseline timbales, 971
Scallops, 120
  cold poached, 970-971
  with crispy noodles, 786
  Mornay, 970
  with saffron rice, asparagus, and

  tomato sauce, 659
  stir-fry, 660
Scallop timbale sampler, 972
Scaloppine, 96
  marsala, 577
  pork, 599
  veal, 583, 584, 740
Schmaltz, 104
Science, relationship to food, 3-4
Scones, batter for, 391
Scrambled eggs, 319, 860
  with bratwurst, 860
  gratiné, 860
  Greek style, 860
  hunter style, 860
  Swedish style, 860
Scungilli, 255
Sea bass:
  black, with ratatouille, 664
  poached, with clams, bacon, and
    peppers, 701
  with vegetables, 755
Seafood. *See also* Fish; Shellfish
  fish consommé with, 455
  Newburg, 686
  poached, in tomato broth with fen-
    nel, 707
Seafood minestrone, 514
Seafood omelet, 861
Seafood platter, broiled, 678
Seafood salad, ravigote, 900
Seafood sausage, 1004-1005
Seafood soufflé, 867
Searing, 310
Seasonings, 166-167, 170
  for roasted meats, 428
  of soups, 274
Sea urchin, cleaning, 255, 257
Seeds, 171, 172
  toasting, 205
Seed vegetables, 141-142
Seizing, defined, 315
Semi-vegetarians, 52
Service:
  commitment to, 14-15
  importance of, 29-30
Service temperature, holding food at,
  39
Serving:
  of sauces, 299-300
  of soups, 273-274
Sesame chicken, hot, 782
Sesame ginger butter, 608
Shad, 116
Shakes, breakfast, 879
Shallots, advance preparation of, 192-
  193
Shallow-poaching, 334-337
Shark, 116
  broiled, with scallions and tomato-
    basil coulis, 670
Sharpening stones, 71
Sheet pans, 77
Shellfish, 118-122

  categories of, 113
  deviled eggs with, 950
  fabrication techniques for, 251-257
  literature about, 1163
  storing, 109
Shellfish butter, 549
Shellfish omelet, 861
Shellfish soup, 754
Shellfish stock, 444
Shells, meringue, 1105
Sherbets, 407
Sherry vinaigrette, 882
Shiitake mushrooms, grilled with soy-
  sesame glaze, 810
Shiitake salad, 966
Shoot vegetables, 144
Shortbread, 1086
Shortenings, 162
  for baking, 376
Shredding, 187
Shrimp, 121
  broiled, with garlic and aromatics,
    972-973
  Cajun-style barbecued, 973
  in chili sauce, 787
  coconut macadamia, 974
  Creole, 688
  with curried pasta, 848-849
  deep-fried breaded, 667
  jambalaya, 687
  popcorn, 667
  preparing, 251
  stuffed, 976
  tempura, 788
Shrimp and chicken gumbo, 495
Shrimp bisque, 485
Shrimp salad, 899
Shrimp sauce, 534-535
Shrimp spring rolls, 961
Side dishes, vegetable, 792-816
Sieves, 73-74
Sifting, of dry ingredients, 378-379
Simmering, 340-343
Simple carbohydrates, 55
Simple syrup, 1077
Sinclair, Gordon, 42
Skate, preparing, 116
"Skewer" test, 311
Skirt steak, cleaning, 229, 233
Slicing equipment, 78-79
Slicing knife, 70
Sloppy Joes, 918-919
Slow cookers, 80
Slurries, 205-206
Small sauces, 277
Smoked meat, 371-372
Smoke-roasting, 307
Smokers, 80
Smoking, safety and, 45-46
Snails, 119
  with new potatoes and Brie, 985-986
Snapper, 116
  ceviche of, 943
  en papillote, 689

Snipe, 106
Snow peas:
    advance preparation of, 202
    gingered with yellow squash, 794
Soda breads, 1031
    batter for, 391
Sofrito, 421
Sole:
    broiled lemon, on leeks, 671
    deep-fried, Anglaise, 667-668
    Dover, 117, 248, 250
    with mango chutney and grilled
        bananas, 659
    poached, vin blanc, 696
    Véronique, 698
Sorbet, 407, 1062-1063
Soufflé:
    artichoke, 710
    cheese, 866-867
    dessert, 403
    frozen, 407, 1060
    glacé, 1060
    herb, 867
    hot dessert, 1055
    seafood, 867
    spinach, 867
    vegetable, 867
Soufflé dish, 77
Souffléed crêpes, 710
Soup recipes, 450-519
Soups, 259-274, 450-519. *See also*
        Bisques; Chowders; Cream soups;
        Gumbos
    basic techniques for, 260-273
    Billi Bi, 502
    broths, 260-262
    chilled, 487-488, 490
    clear vegetable, 265-267
    cock-a-leekie, 504-505
    cold, 273
    consommés, 262-265, 454-460
    goulash, 506-507
    guidelines for serving, 273-274
    mulligatawny, 510
    pepper pot, 498-499
    potage au pistou, 464-465
    potage garbure, 465
    potage purée Crecy, 482
    purée, 269-271
    shellfish, 754
    special, 273
Soup station, 25
Sour cream, 151
Sour cream liaison, 423
Sourdough French bread, 1034
Sourdough starters, 377, 1034
Sous chef, 24-25
Soy sauce, ginger, 974
Soy-sesame glaze, 810
Spaetzle:
    boiling, 344
    spinach and cheese, 853
Spaetzle dough, 852
Spaghetti alla Carbonara, 847

Spanish sauce, 702
Spareribs:
    Chinese-style barbecued, 771
    pork, 99
Spatulas, 72
Spice mix, barbecue, 425
Spice pasta, 846
Spice poaching liquid, 1066
Spice rub, 561
Spices:
    blends of, 208-209
    dried, 164-165, 169
Spinach, Italian-style, 795
Spinach and tomato pesto, 422
Spinach artichoke ricotta pie, 711
Spinach crêpes, 713, 872
    seafood, 959
Spinach pancakes, 795
Spinach pasta, 846
Spinach rolls, stuffed, 712
Spinach roulades, with mushrooms and
        sour cream, 716-717
Spinach salad:
    with arugula, 883
    with avocado and grapefruit, 884-885
    wilted, with bacon vinaigrette, 885
Spinach soufflé, 867
Spirits, books about, 1165-1166
Spit-roasting, 307
Split pea soup, 476, 507
Sponge cake, 1108-1110
Sponge mixing method, 381-383
Sponge roulade, 1108-1109
Spring rolls:
    shrimp, 961
    Vietnamese fried, 962-963
Squash, 135, 136. *See also* Acorn squash;
        Summer squash
Squash soup, 474
    apple cider, 484
Squid, 122
    cleaning, 255, 256
    deep-fried, 665
    and peppers, 789
    stuffed, 753
Stalk vegetables, 144
Starches, 159-160
Station chefs, 25
Steak. *See also* Strip steak
    chicken-fried, 628
    cutting, 229
    fish, 248-251
    flank, 568-569
    sirloin, 561, 562
    skirt, 229
    Swiss, 570
Steamers, 77, 79
Steaming, 330-338
Steam-jacketed kettle, 79
Steels, 71
Stew:
    bean, 758, 842-843
    beef, 566, 572
    Casablanca, over couscous, 728

chile, 499
    Irish, 747
    lamb, 596, 776-777
    meat, 758
    pork, 772
    rabbit, 613
Stewing, 346-348
Sticky buns, pan filling for, 1043
Stir-frying, 316, 320-321
    chicken, 947
    pork, 773
Stock, 213-219, 420-448
    beef, 439
    chicken, 442
    fish, 444
    game, 437
    game bird, 442-443
    lamb, 440-441
    meat and fish, 216
    pork, 440
    preparing, 216-219
    ratios for, 215-216
    shellfish, 444
    turkey, 442
    veal, 437, 439
    vegetable, 445
Stockpots, 75
Stollen, 1041
Storage:
    of dairy products and eggs, 148-149
    of fish, 108-109
    of herbs, 148
    of knives, 68
    of meat, 84
    of nonperishable goods, 158
    of shellfish, 109
    of yeast breads, 385-386
Storage areas, managing, 20
Storage containers, 73
Stoves, 79-80
Stove top cooking, pots and pans for,
        75
Straight forcemeat, 357
Straight mixing method, for batters,
        386-387
Strainers, 73-74
Straining, 225
Strawberries, with green peppercorns,
        1067-1068
Strawberry compound butter, 878
Strawberry fritters, 1069
Strawberry sauce, 1072
Strengtheners, baking, 376
Strip loin, roast, 559
Strip steak:
    broiled, 562
    Provençale, 563
Strudel:
    Alsatian-style, 955
    apple filling for, 1103
    fennel and chorizo, 955
    vegetable, 717
    wild mushroom with goat cheese,
        954

Stuffed cabbage, 761
Stuffing:
  chestnut, 652
  for cornish hens, 750-751
  mushroom and ham, 626
  oyster, 635
  pork loin, 745
  for scalopine, 740
  for swordfish, 756
  wonton, 519
Submersion cooking techniques, 338-346
Subprimal meat cuts, 86
Sugars, 171, 174
  caramelization of, 376
  refined, 55
Sugar snap peas, 202
Summer squash, 136
Summer squash "noodles," 800
Sunflower seed bread, 1037-1038
Suprêmes:
  chicken, 623, 627
  preparing, 243
  turkey, 653
Sushi, 960
Sweetbreads, 235-236
Sweeteners, 171, 174
  baking, 376
Sweet peppers, advance preparation of, 194-196
Sweet potato chips, 830
Sweet potato dough, 1010
Sweet potatoes, 142
  baked with cider, currants, and cinnamon, 822
  glazed, 826
  puréed, 826
Sweet potato soup, 483
Swissing technique, 349
Swiss meringue, 223
Swiss steak, 570
Swivel peeler, 195
Swordfish, 116
  grilled, with pepper cream sauce, 674
  with red pepper coulis, 677
  stuffed, 756
Syrup, 171, 174, 405-406. *See also* Simple syrup
  cinnamon rum, 1077
  espresso, 1054
  savarin, 1050

T

Tabbouleh salad, 898
Table d'hôte, 4
Tacos:
  beef, 925
  chicken and green chili, 923
Taco salad, 888
Taco sauce, 888
Tahini dip, 937
Tahini dressing, roasted garlic, 931
Tahini sauce, yogurt, 939
"Takeout cuisine," 6

Tamales:
  beef and pork, 762
  vegetarian, 732
Tamis, 73-74
Tapenade sandwich, 927
Tarragon beurre blanc, 546
Tarragon butter, 636
Tarragon sauce, 526, 615, 625, 644
  mustard, 545
Tarragon vinaigrette, 970
Tartar sauce, 916
Tartlettes, fruit, 1068-1069
Tart molds, lining, 394
Tarts:
  fillings for, 394
  preparing, 393-396
  toppings for, 394-395
Tautog, preparing, 116
Tea, 174-175
Teaching positions, 16
Technology, relationship to food, 3-4
Temperature:
  conversions for, 1140
  pathogens and, 37
Tempering process, 224
Tempura:
  fish, 975
  shrimp, 788
  vegetable, 816
Tempura dipping sauce, 975
Tenderloin:
  beef, 557, 560, 561, 564, 575
  pork, 600, 606-607
  trimming, 228, 230
Teriyaki beef, 768
Teriyaki chicken, 780
Teriyaki marinade, 434
Teriyaki sauce, 768, 780
Terrines, 368-369
  artichoke, 1014
  country, 1012
  country-style duck, 1013
  of foie gras, 1019
  potato, trout, and leek, 1015
  rabbit, 1013
  roasted eggplant and pepper, 1014
  venison, 1014
Terrine mold, 77
Thawing, 39-40
Thermometers, 73
Thickeners, 177, 205-208
  baking, 378
  for forcemeat, 358
Tilapia, 117
  with capers and tomatoes, 699
Tilefish, 117
Tilting kettle, 79
Timbale mold, 77
Timbales:
  scallop mousseline, 971
  scallop, with saffron-cream sauce, 972
Time management, 26-27
Tinted curing mix (TCM), 359
Tiramisù, 1054

Toasting, of nuts and seeds, 205
Tofu, grilled marinated, with black bean salsa, 714
Tomato and mozzarella salad, 894
Tomato and spinach pesto, 422
Tomato-basil coulis, 670
Tomato cilantro pâté dough, 1008
Tomato concassé, 193-194
Tomato coulis, 551
  sun-dried, 683
Tomatoes, 144-145
  advance preparation of, 193-194
  deviled eggs with, 950
  stewed, 807
Tomato fondue, 676
Tomato omelet, 861
Tomato oregano butter, 547
Tomato pasta, 846
Tomato salsa, 936, 988
Tomato sandwich:
  with cream cheese and arugula, 932
  with oregano sour cream, 934
Tomato sauce, 289-291, 537, 538-539
Tomato soup, cream of, 469
Tomato-tahini sauce, 715
Tongue, 236-237
  beef, 92
  beef, Madeira sauce, 617
Tools
  hand, 71-72
  maintaining, 27
  sharpening, 70-71
Toppings:
  Holland Dutch, 1044
  for pies, 1104-1105
  for pies and tarts, 394-395
Top round roast, 558
Toque blanche, 15, 42
Torte cake:
  dobos, 11251125
  Havana, 1124-1125
  hazelnut, 1124
  rum, 1122-1123
Tortes:
  apple cream cheese, 1126
  assembling and decorating, 413-414
  opera, 1123
  sacher, 1122
Tortellini, lobster, with ginger-lime sauce, 850-851
Tournant, 25
Tourné cut, 189
Tourné knife, 70
Tower, Jeremiah, 5
Toxic poisoning, 34
Trace minerals, 60
Traditional diets, 51-52
Training:
  chef, 12-14
  importance of, 26-27
Tranche, 248
Trichinosis, 33
Trigger fish, 117
Tripe, beef, 93
Tripe soup, 508

Troisgros, Jean, 5
Tropical fruits, 126, 127-129
Trout, 117
  Amandine, 658-659
  baked lemon-stuffed, 680
  pan-fried with bacon, 663
  with saffron filling, 704
  sauté meunière, 658
  savarin, 1023
Truffles, 1075
Truite au bleu, 117
Trussing technique, 238-239
Tubers, 142-144
Tuiles, 1093
Tuna, 117
  broiled, with salsa cruda, 671
  grilled, with pecan-lime butter, 673
  grilled, with roasted peppers and balsamic vinegar sauce, 672
  raw, marinated, 966
Tuna and scallop ceviche, 942
Tuna melt sandwich, 922
Tuna salad, 899
Turbot, 118
  poached, with lemon beurre blanc, 691
Turkey, 105
  cutlet of, 655
  pan-smoked, with port wine sauce, 654
  roast, with chestnut stuffing, 652
Turkey broth, 453
Turkey consommé, with fennel ravioli, 459-460
Turkey pâté, 1010-1011
Turkey sandwich, with caramelized onions, 919
Turkey stock, 442
Turkey suprême, roast, with pan gravy, 653
Turnips, glazed, 798
Turnovers:
  escarole-feta, 718
  gorgonzola, with roasted pepper, 718
  vegetable curry, 718
Two-stage method, for mixing batters, 386, 389-390

U

Uniform, professional, 15, 42-43
United States Department of Agriculture (USDA), 85
  Food Guide Pyramid of, 48, 49
Univalves, 113, 118-119
USRDA (United States Recommended Daily Allowance), 59
Utility knife, 70

V

Vanilla Bavarian cream, 1096
Vanilla ice cream, 1062
Vanilla sauce, 400-401, 1070

Vanilla sponge cake, 1109
Variety meats, 235-237
Vatapa, 767
Veal, 93-96, 577-588
  blanquette, 587
  boning, 235
  braised breast, with mushroom sausage, 588-589
  breaded cutlet Gruyère, 585
  Cordon Bleu, 581
  fricassée of, 586
  medallions, with red pepper sauce, 582
  piccata, 738
  saltimboca, 737
  sautéed, with crabmeat and asparagus, 578
  sautéed, with mushrooms and marsala sauce, 580
  scaloppine marsala, 577
  scaloppine Shaker Village, 583
  scaloppine, stuffed, 740
  scaloppine, with tomato sauce, 583
  scaloppine, with sauce Zingara, 584
  shoulder Poêlé, 585-586
  Swiss-style shredded, 579
Veal primals, 94-96
Veal stock, 437, 439
Vegans, 52
Vegetable and cheese sandwich, grilled, 922
Vegetable bisque, 271
Vegetable broths, 261
Vegetable burger, 716
Vegetable curry, 723
Vegetable curry turnovers, 718
Vegetable cuts, 185
Vegetable lasagna, 721
Vegetable pizza, grilled, 929
Vegetable quesadilla, 924
Vegetable quiche, 866
Vegetables:
  advance preparation of, 191-203
  boiled, 800
  deviled eggs with, 950
  dried, 171, 173, 203
  garden treasures, 812-813
  general information about, 131-132
  grilled, 809
  hot and spicy, 815
  jardinière, 810-811
  literature about, 1163
  Macédoine of, 811
  Mediterranean-style grilled, 809
  peeling, 186-187
  pod and seed, 141-142
  rainbow garden, 815
  steamed, 792
  sweating, 278
  tempura, 816
  turning, 189
Vegetable sandwich, roasted, 931
Vegetable shortening, 162
Vegetable side dishes, 792-816
Vegetable soufflé, 867

Vegetable soups, 461
  clear, 265-267
Vegetable station, 25
Vegetable stock, 445
Vegetable strudel, 717
Vegetarian chili, 731
Vegetarian entrées, 710-732
Vegetarianism, 14, 52
Vegetarian Pyramid, 50
Vegetarian soup:
  split pea, 476
  sweet potato, 483
Vegetarian tamales, 732
Velouté, 285-287, 969
  derivatives of, 284
Velouté sauce, 531
Velouté soups, 267-269
  Dieppoise, 515
Venison, 103
  with garlic glaze, 615
  with marsala sauce, 615
  roast, with mustard sauce, 614-615
  with tarragon sauce, 615
Venison sausage, smoked, 1005
Venison terrine, 1014
Vergé, Roger, 5
Vertical chopping machine (VCM), 78
Vichyssoise, 273
Vinaigrette, 298
  bacon, 885
  balsamic, 906
  basic, 906
  champagne, 980-981
  curry, 896, 910
  gourmand, 906
  grapefruit, 885, 891
  lemon garlic, 908
  lemon parsley, 895
  lemon thyme, 897
  lime and olive oil, 909
  mustard-herb, 907
  pesto, 904
  roasted garlic and mustard, 908
  sherry, 882
  tarragon, 970
Vin blanc sauce, 296-297, 696
Vinegar court bouillon, 446
Vinegars, 162-164, 168
Vitamins, 59
  dietary requirements for, 60
Vitello tonnato, 948-949
Volume measures, conversions for, 1140

W

Waffle cut, 191
Waffles, 873
Waldorf salad, 894
Walk-in refrigerators, 80-81
Walnut sauce, 749
Ware washing, 43-44
Wasabi sauce, 966
Water, as a nutrient, 60-61
Water-bath technique, 226

Watercress sandwich, with herb mayonnaise, 934
Watercress sauce, 703
Watercress soup, 473
Watermelon granità, 1064
Waters, Alice, 5
Water-soluble vitamins, 59
Weakfish, 117
Weights and measures, conversions for, 1140
Western sandwich, 920
Wet curing, 371
Wheat, cream of, 868
Whipped cream, 223
Whipping, to make a foam, 221-223
Whips, 72
White *mirepoix*, 209, 420
White stock, 213-214
White vegetables, boiled, 800
Wiener schnitzel, 739
Wine court bouillon, 446

Wine cream, 1097
Wine marinade, 431, 433
Wine poaching liquid, 1066
Wines, 167-171
    adding to sauces, 281
    books about, 1165-1166
Wine sauce, port, 654
Wine slurry, 205
Wine sorbet, 1063
Wine steward, 25
Winter squash, 135, 136
Wonton soup, 519
Wonton stuffing, 519
Woodcock, 106
Work environment, orderly, 27
Workplace, drugs and alcohol in, 46

Y

Yams, 142
Yeast, 175

proofing, 377
Yeast breads, 380-386
    baking, 385
    cooling and storing, 385-386
Yeast dough:
    mixing, 380-383
    shaping, 383-385
Yellow vegetables, boiled, 800
Yogurt, 151
Yogurt gratin, 969
Yogurt tahini sauce, 939

Z

Zabaglione, 406, 1052
Zesting, 198-199
Zucchini:
    with chorizo and tomatoes, 796
    pan-fried, 796
Zucchini bread, 1030
Zwiebel rostbraten, 736

Photo credits:
page xxvi   The Image Bank/Mercury Archives
page 8   Will Faller
page 49, Figure 3-2   The Oldways Preservation & Exchange Trust